The Freud–Klein Controversies 1941–45

Just after Freud's death in 1939 the British Psycho-Analytical Society was the setting for a fierce debate. Controversy erupted over the validity and status of the ideas introduced into psychoanalysis by Melanie Klein; to what extent did her ideas deviate from Freud's basic propositions and what should be done about it? Although the central disagreements were about theory and technical practice, power in the psychoanalytic society and its future organization were also at stake, along with central questions about the diffusion and transmission of the discipline. To debate the controversies the Society held a series of scientific discussions, its Training Committee investigated the parameters of valid technique, and its officers considered the democratic structure of its organization.

For this book the editors have had access to previously closed archive material and it is presented here for the first time with the minimum of censorship. This collection of papers, précis of discussions, minutes, resolutions, and relevant aspects of the personal correspondence between the participants, provides the first definitive record of controversies which were to be repeated in different forms in psychoanalytic societies all over the world. It will be of great interest to all those concerned with the development of psychoanalysis and with understanding the process of scientific discovery in any field. Throughout the book the editors have included a series of commentaries and notes designed to provide a context for the documents, as well as brief biographical information about the major participants.

The New Library of Psychoanalysis was launched in 1987 in association with the Institute of Psycho-Analysis, London. Its purpose is to facilitate a greater and more widespread appreciation of what psychoanalysis is really about and to provide a forum for increasing mutual understanding between psychoanalysts and those working in other disciplines such as history, linguistics, literature, medicine, philosophy, psychology, and the social sciences. It is intended that the titles selected for publication in the series should deepen and develop psychoanalytic thinking and technique, contribute to psychoanalysis from outside, or contribute to other disciplines from a psychoanalytical perspective.

The Institute, together with the British Psycho-Analytical Society, runs a low-fee psychoanalytic clinic, organizes lectures and scientific events concerned with psychoanalysis, publishes the *International Journal of Psycho-Analysis* and the *International Review of Psycho-Analysis*, and runs the only training course in the UK in psychoanalysis leading to membership of the International Psychoanalytical Association – the body which preserves internationally agreed standards of training, of professional entry, and of professional ethics and practice for psychoanalysis as initiated and developed by Sigmund Freud. Distinguished members of the Institute have included Wilfred Bion, Anna Freud, Ernest Jones, Melanie Klein, John Rickman, and Donald Winnicott.

Volumes 1–11 in the series have been prepared under the general editorship of David Tuckett, with Ronald Britton and Eglé Laufer as associate editors. Subsequent volumes are under the general editorship of Elizabeth Bott Spillius, with Christopher Bollas, Juliet Mitchell-Rossdale and Rosine Jozef Perelberg as associate editors.

NEW LIBRARY OF PSYCHOANALYSIS
11
General editor: David Tuckett

The Freud–Klein Controversies 1941–45

Edited by

PEARL KING

and

RICCARDO STEINER

TAVISTOCK/ROUTLEDGE
LONDON AND NEW YORK

First published 1991
by Routledge
11 New Fetter Lane, London EC4P 4EE

Simultaneously published in the USA and Canada
by Routledge
a division of Routledge, Chapman and Hall, Inc.
29 West 35th Street, New York, NY 10001

Reprinted in paperback in 1992

Typeset by Hope Services (Abingdon)
Printed and bound in Great Britain by Mackays of Chatham PLC, Kent

British Library Cataloguing in Publication Data

The Freud–Klein controversies 1941–45 – (New library of
psychoanalysis; 11)
1. Great Britain. Psychoanalysis, history
I. King, Pearl, *1918–* II. Steiner, Riccardo, *1939–*
III. Series
150.19'5'0941

Library of Congress Cataloging in Publication Data

The Freud–Klein controversies 1941–45 /
edited by Pearl King and Riccardo Steiner.
p. cm. – (New library of psychoanalysis; 11)
Papers, précis of discussion, minutes, and personal correspondence
of various members of the British Psycho-Analytical Society
Includes bibliographical references
1. British Psycho-Analytical Society – History. 2. Freud, Anna,
1895– . 3. Klein, Melanie. I. King, Pearl, 1918– .
II. Steiner, Riccardo. III. British Psycho-Analytical Society.
IV. Series.
BF11.F74 1991
150.19'52'06041 – dc20   89–39366
CIP

ISBN 0–415–08274–9

Contents

Contents

Contents

'If we do not learn from history we shall be doomed to repeat it.'

George Santayana

To the Members, Associate Members and Students
of the British Psycho-Analytical Society

Biographical notes[1] on the main participants in the Freud–Klein Controversies in the British Psycho-Analytical Society, 1941–45

PEARL KING

1 Dr Michael Balint (1896–1970)   Michael Balint worked with Ferenczi in Budapest, becoming a member of that Society in 1926. In 1938 he moved to England and became a member of the British Society in 1939. Jones, who found him difficult to work with, arranged for him to settle in Manchester, where he started training candidates for the British Society. He only attended the first two Scientific Discussions, but was an active participant in the final Business meetings reported in Section 5. After Sylvia Payne became President in 1944 she invited him to come to London, where he played a leading role in the Society's training and scientific activities, finally becoming its President from 1968 to 1970. He was a lively and independent thinker, interested in the cross-fertilization of psycho-analytic ideas with other disciplines, particularly through the use of group techniques, which he developed when he joined the staff of the Tavistock Clinic in 1948.

2 Dr John Bowlby (1907–   )   John Bowlby qualified as an Associate Member in 1937 and as a Member in 1939. Although he trained with Joan Riviere and at the beginning of these controversies was regarded as a supporter of Melanie Klein, he gradually established a more independent position, and 'became alienated by what he saw as the intolerance of the Kleinians' (JB).[2] He was an Army psychiatrist during the war, but in 1943 he was posted in Hampstead, and could then attend meetings regularly. He attended the later Extraordinary Business meetings and the last five special Scientific Discussions. With William Gillespie he supported the setting up of the Medical and Child Welfare Committees in 1943 (Section 2, Chapter 8), which finally demonstrated to Glover that he was unlikely to be elected the next President when Jones retired. In 1944 John Bowlby was elected as Training Secretary, in spite of the fact that he was not a training analyst, and to the disapproval of Klein and Riviere. He was instrumental with Sylvia Payne in drawing up the training regulations which incorporated the training requirements of the Viennese alongside those of the British Society, and was Secretary of the Ad Hoc Committee on Training which worked out the details of the training agreement. He went on to make important contributions to various committees, becoming Chairman of the Board and Council, before moving to his seminal research on the effects of mother/child separation at the Tavistock Clinic.

3 Dr Marjorie Brierley (1893–1984)   Marjorie Brierley qualified as an Associate Member in 1927 and as a Member in 1930. She served on many committees, including the Board and Council, and the Training Committee. She resigned from the Training Committee when the Viennese arrived in order that Anna Freud could serve on it. JB described her as 'small and slight, with an extremely lined face'. 'She spoke in a small hesitant voice. Her mind was acute, however, and she probably had a better grasp of scientific principles than anyone else' (JB). She played an active role both in the first series of Business meetings reported in Section 1 and in the Scientific Discussions reported in Section 2, and she was a member of the committee of three that organized the ten Scientific Discussions on Controversial Issues. Although she trained with Edward Glover and was regarded as his protégée, she was able to maintain an independent position during the discussions, always urging the need for a scientific evaluation of the differences between Klein and her opponents. She was upset when Glover retired from the Society and she took little part in its activities after that. When her husband (who had previously been married to her friend Susan Isaacs) retired as Professor of Botany at Reading University, they went to live in the Lake District, which JB describes as 'a loss to the Society' for 'as an open minded, well-informed and tolerant member she played a useful part' in debate.

4 Mrs Dorothy Burlingham (1891–1979)   Dorothy Burlingham was an American, who trained with Theodor Reik and Sigmund Freud in Vienna, becoming a member of the Vienna Society. There she started a small nursery school (initially for her children) with Erik Erikson and Peter Blos as the teachers. Anna Freud was consultant and this was the beginning of their close collaboration together. They instituted the first seminars in child analysis. She became an active member of the Vienna Society. After the Anschluss she joined the Freud family in London, becoming a Member of the British Society in 1938 and a training analyst in 1940. She accompanied Anna Freud to all the Extraordinary Business Meetings in 1942, and the first six special Scientific Discussions, to which she made one written contribution. When Anna Freud withdrew from the Training Committee, she stopped attending these meetings. With Anna Freud she organized the Hampstead War Nurseries, and later helped to start the Hampstead Child Therapy Clinic in 1951, specializing in work with blind children.

5 Dr S. H. Foulkes (1898–1976)   Siegmund H. Foulkes moved from Frankfurt to Vienna where he trained with Helena Deutsch and became a member of the Vienna Society in 1930, after which he returned to Frankfurt and joined the Berlin Society. In May 1933 after Hitler took over Germany, Ernest Jones invited him to come to London. He obtained British medical qualifications in 1936, becoming a Member of the British Society in 1937. He was out of London for most of the controversial discussions, but attended two Business Meetings and sent in two contributions for the Scientific Discussions. He was a training analyst for the 'B' group and a supporter of the Viennese point of view. He served on various committees and became the founder of the Group Analytic Society.

6 Miss Anna Freud (1895–1982)   Anna Freud trained as a teacher, worked with her father, attended meetings of the Vienna Society, becoming a Member of it in 1922 after reading a paper on 'Beating Phantasies and Day-dreams'. She became Librarian and assisted Freud in his writings. She gave lectures to teachers with Willi Hoffer and started a clinical seminar on child psychoanalysis among her peer group, which included Dorothy Burlingham, Eva Rosenfeld, Peter Blos, and Erik Erikson. She was a training analyst in 1925, and in 1926 she became Secretary of the International Psychoanalytical Association and also of the Vienna Training Institute. Her lectures on 'The Technique of Analysis of Children' were discussed in the British Society in 1927 (Section 1, Chapter 1). In 1937, with Edith Jackson and Josephine Stross, she started the Jackson Clinic for poor children under two years old, but in 1938 the Nazis closed it down.

After the Anschluss in 1938, when Hitler marched into Austria, Anna Freud moved to London with her family and many colleagues, and became 'nurse' to her seriously ill father, Sigmund Freud. She was immediately elected a Member and a training analyst of the British Society (Section 1, Chapter 1). She attended all the Business Meetings during 1942 that led up to the Special Scientific Discussion Meetings which were arranged to assess the contributions of Melanie Klein. In the Scientific Discussions which followed, while her comments were courteous and to the point, she left it to Glover, Friedlander, and the Hoffers to do most of the arguing. As she said to Barbara Lantos, 'We are here as guests of this country and we were not brought here to create trouble.' When Glover resigned from the Training Committee, she also withdrew from that committee (Section 5, Chapter 6), and was less active in the British Society, until approached by Sylvia Payne to explore the conditions under which she and her Viennese colleagues could again participate in psychoanalytic training with the Society. Anna Freud was a member of the Ad Hoc Committee on Training which was set up to work out the details of the two parallel courses of training, Course 'A' and Course 'B'. In 1947 she was elected to the Board and Council where her contributions were important in relation to the new translation of Freud's writings. Later in that year she started the Hampstead Child Therapy Training Course, and in 1951 the Hampstead Child Therapy Clinic (now the Anna Freud Clinic) was founded. She continued her work for the IPA, being elected a Vice-President of the IPA for many years, and finally becoming its Honorary President in 1973.

7 *Dr Kate Friedlander* (1895–1949)   Kate Friedlander trained as a psychoanalyst at the Berlin Institute, and read her membership paper in March 1933, shortly before Hitler took over Germany. She was one of the analysts whom Jones invited to London, together with Paula Heimann, and was elected an Associate Member later in 1933. She obtained British medical qualifications in 1936, becoming a Member of the British Society in 1938. She worked closely with Anna Freud, often representing her interests in the Society. She was present at all the Business Meetings (Section1) and the first series of discussions of scientific issues during which she made five written contributions. When Glover resigned from the Society, she withdrew from the rest of the Special Scientific Discussions, but continued to attend the remaining business meetings. Later she took part in the training scheme under the new arrangements with Anna Freud. She helped to start the Hampstead Child Therapy Training

Course which could provide trained staff for the West Sussex Child Guidance Unit that she had pioneered. She was particularly interested in the treatment of juvenile delinquents. Her early death in 1949 was a severe loss to the British Society.

8 *Dr William H. Gillespie* (1905–   )   In 1930 William Gillespie started his analytic training in Vienna with Hitschmann, but moved to London to complete it. There he worked with Ella Sharpe, Sylvia Payne, and James Strachey. He was elected an Associate Member in 1937 and a Member in 1940. He attended most of the Business Meetings reported in this book, being responsible with John Bowlby for proposing the formation of a Medical Committee in 1943. He also came to many of the Special Scientific Meetings and took part in the later free discussions. His reputation as a fair and independent thinker led to his election to many official positions and committees in the Society and Institute. He was elected as its President in 1950 and again in 1970. His contributions to the stability of the British Society could be compared to that of his friend and colleague, Sylvia Payne. He served on the Executive Council of the International Psychoanalytical Association for many years, being elected its President from 1957 to 1961, during which time he drafted its revised Statutes and Bye-Laws.

9 *Dr Edward Glover* (1888–1972)   Edward Glover went to Berlin with his brother James to be analysed by Karl Abraham in 1920. He became an Associate Member in 1921 and a Member in 1922. His brother James was close to Jones, and when he died in 1926 Edward took over many of his offices. Originally a supporter of Klein, he became more critical of her, later joining her daughter Melitta Schmideberg in her criticism of her mother. He was a good administrator, he helped Jones in his negotiations with the British Medical Association (Section 1, Chapter 1), and Jones made him his deputy for many tasks. By 1940 he was on all the main committees of the Society and Institute. He attended the first five Extraordinary Business Meetings which Jones himself chaired, but he took the chair at the first seven of the Special Scientific Meetings, to which he made six written contributions. He was Chairman of the Training Committee until his resignation from the Society in January 1944. After that he took no further part in activities of the Society, joining the Swiss Psychoanalytic Society and playing a leading role in the Institute for the Scientific Treatment of Delinquency (ISTD).

10 Dr Paula Heimann (1899–1982)   Paula Heimann trained at the Berlin Institute, where she was analysed by Theodor Reik. She became an Associate Member of the Berlin Society in 1932. When the Nazis took over Germany in 1933, Jones invited her to come to London, as her life was in danger. She was elected an Associate Member of the British Society later in 1933. Jones insisted that she obtain British medical qualifications, and this she did in 1937. During this period she went into analysis with Melanie Klein. She was elected a Member in 1939. She became a loyal supporter of Melanie Klein, and one of the presenters of her point of view during the Scientific Controversies. She attended all the Business Meetings and all the ten Special Scientific Meetings held to discuss the differences, at two of which she presented the main papers for discussion (Section 2, Chapter 9, Section 4, Chapter 1). Following these controversies she became a training analyst in 1944, and went on to play an important role in the Society, working on many committees and becoming Joint Training Secretary with Hedwig Hoffer in 1954. (This was the first time that a Kleinian and a supporter of Anna Freud had held such an important position.) Initially, she represented the Kleinians, but later she became an 'Independent' following her growing disagreement with the Kleinian point of view.

11 Mrs Hedwig Hoffer (1888–1961)   Hedwig Hoffer was born in south Germany, but moved to Vienna when she married Willi Hoffer. She was analysed by Anna Freud, and did her analytic training in the Vienna Society where she became a member and later a training analyst. She moved to London in 1938 with the Freuds and was given membership and training analyst status in the British Society. She was present at all the first seven Scientific Discussions, making three written contributions. She also attended all the Business Meetings reported in Section 1. She subsequently made important contributions to the training activities of the Society, becoming Joint Training Secretary with Paula Heimann, which demonstrated that a Kleinian and a member of the 'B' group could work together successfully.

12 Dr Willi Hoffer (1897–1967)   Willi Hoffer obtained a Ph.D. in psychology in Vienna in 1922, and only later in 1929 did he get his MD. He was particularly concerned, as was Anna Freud, with helping deprived children and educators. He trained as a psychoanalyst, and was analysed by Herman Nunberg from 1921 to 1922, becoming a member of the Viennese Society. He soon became a training analyst. He worked closely with Anna Freud in Vienna, then moved to London with her, acting as her male protector, professional medical 'cover' and supporter in the British Society. He was elected a member of the British Society in 1938 and recognized as a training analyst. He attended seven of the Business Meetings, and was the only Viennese member to come to discuss the Final Report of the Training Committee in March 1944. He came to all the first seven Special Scientific Discussions, withdrawing from them with Anna Freud after she had resigned from the Training Committee. After the reconciliation, he represented with Anna Freud the Viennese on the Ad Hoc Committee of Training which negotiated the revised training scheme that included two parallel training courses. He was elected a member of the Training Committee in 1948, Editor of the *International Journal of Psycho-Analysis* in 1949, Vice-President of the International Psychoanalytical Association in 1951, and finally he was elected President of the British Society in 1959. By then all three groups valued his contributions to psychoanalysis and to the life of the Society.

13 Mrs Susan Isaacs (1885–1948)   Susan Isaacs lectured in psychology and logic. She was elected an Associate Member in 1921 and a Member in 1923. She was first analysed by Flugel and later in 1927 by Joan Riviere. She was the Principal of the Malting House School, Cambridge, from 1924 to 1927 where she did her pioneering research in child development – the first applied research in child development in Britain to be done by a psychoanalyst. In 1933 she was appointed as the head of the new Department of Child Development in the Institute of Education, London University, where she was working during these controversies. Her background of research work in this area was particularly important during the Special Scientific Discussions. She worked closely with Melanie Klein during the Discussions reported in this book, as is evident in their correspondence. She attended all except one of the Extraordinary Business Meetings, and the first six of the Scientific Discussions, until she became ill. In 1944 she was elected to the Board and Council and the Training Committee, serving on the Ad Hoc Committee on Training along with Melanie Klein. Her early death in 1948 was a severe loss to the British Society.

14 Dr Ernest Jones (1879–1958)   Ernest Jones was the founder of the British Psycho-Analytical Society and its President from 1919 to 1944, during which time he was active on all the main committees of the Society. (For details of his life see Section 1, Chapter 1.) In

1926 he had invited Melanie Klein to come to London, and during the 1920s and early 1930s he was regarded as a supporter of her work and many of her ideas. But as Riccardo Steiner has shown (Section 2, Chapter 1). Melanie Klein felt 'let down' because Jones had brought the Freuds to London. When the controversies finally erupted (Section 1, Chapter 1) with the demand for the Extra-ordinary Business Meetings, Jones himself chaired all those reported in Section 1, with remarkable fairness and patience, leaving Glover to chair the first series of Special Scientific Discussions organized by the committee elected to do so. He did not attend any of them, but he did make one written contribution. He continued to hold the reins as President all through this period, until he resigned in 1944 and Sylvia Payne took over (King 1979).

15 Mrs Melanie Klein (1882–1960)   Melanie Klein was elected a member of the Hungarian Society in 1919, after a period in analysis with Sandor Ferenczi. She then moved to the Berlin Society where she worked with Karl Abraham, becoming a member of the Berlin Society. (For details of her life, see Section 1, Chapter 1; King 1983; Grosskurth 1986.) She became a member of the British Society in 1927, and of the Training Committee in 1929. She contributed to the training and scientific activities of the Society from then onwards. She attended all the Business Meetings called to discuss how to deal with the controversies that were taking place in the Society (not all arising from opposition to her work), and all the Special Meetings arranged to discuss the scientific disagreements with her work. She was a member of the Ad Hoc Committee on Training set up to work out the details of the two parallel courses of training, Course 'A' and Course 'B' (Section 5, Chapter 6).

16 Dr Barbara Lantos (188?–1962)   Barbara Lantos qualified as a psychoanalyst with Sandor Ferenczi, and was a member of the Hungarian Society. She moved to London in 1935, at the suggestion of Kate Friedlander. She became an active supporter of Anna Freud, attending all the controversial Business Meetings and the first series of the Special Scientific Meetings. She made two written contributions to these discussions, and withdrew from them when Anna Freud did. She was officially considered a member of the 'B group' and joined the Training Committee in 1953 as one of its representatives. Later, when she was elected Scientific Secretary of the Society, she was able to maintain a more independent position.

17 Miss Barbara Low (1877–1955)   After obtaining a degree at University College, London, Barbara Low trained as a teacher. She was introduced to psychoanalysis by her brother-in-law David Eder, a psychoanalytic pioneer, and she was a founder member of the British Psycho-Analytical Society. Until the arrival of Melanie Klein, Barbara Low and David Eder were the only Jewish members in the Society. She went to Berlin to have analysis with Hanns Sachs, as did Sylvia Payne and Ella Sharpe. Following this, she actively urged the setting up of a psychoanalytic clinic along the lines of the Berlin 'Poliklinic'. She was extremely active in the Society's affairs, always taking a lead in debate. She was always interested in education, and her public lectures appealed to a wide circle of educators. She was Librarian and served on the Public Lectures Committee. When confronted with the new Kleinian ideas, she adhered firmly to the older concepts, and was consequently a supporter of Glover and Anna Freud during the Controversial Discussions. She was one of the four members who signed the proposal calling for these Extraordinary Business Meetings, all of which she attended. She put forward important resolutions for discussion. She made one written contribution to the Special Scientific Discussions, but withdrew from them after Glover resigned.

18 Dr Sylvia M. Payne (1880–1976)   Sylvia Payne was awarded the CBE for her work with war casualties during the 1914–18 War. She then came to psychoanalysis from general practice. She went to Berlin to have analysis with Hanns Sachs, and later she had analysis with James Glover. She qualified as an Associate Member in 1922 and was elected a Member in 1924. She commuted from Eastbourne where her husband, who was a local doctor, sent her patients. She was thus independent of Jones or Glover for referrals. She held many important offices in the Society and was a trusted administrator and colleague.

She was Honorary Secretary of the Society and Institute for fifteen years, before being elected President in 1944, following the Controversies in the Society. She came to all except the first two Extraordinary Business Meetings and was responsible for arranging for a stenographer to take verbatim minutes at these meetings. She attended all the Special Scientific Discussions, chairing the last three, and she contributed four written contributions. As President she was largely responsible for the success of the negotiations with Anna Freud in 1946, which resulted in a revised training scheme that offered two parallel training courses (Section 5, Chapter 6), chairing the Ad Hoc Committee on Training which worked out the details. She believed that psychoanalysis flourished in an atmosphere of scientific controversy, and although a 'moderate', she always valued contributions from colleagues from different theoretical orientations. It is largely due to her that there is only one psychoanalytical society in Britain today. 'She performed an invaluable service to the Society during these years and I have the highest admiration for her as an honest, courageous, clear-sighted woman' (JB). She was elected President for a second time in 1954.

19 Dr John Rickman (1891–1951)   After working for a Quaker War Victims Relief Unit in Russia in 1916, John Rickman went to Vienna at the suggestion of Rivers (an anthropologist and Associate Member of the British Society), to be analysed by Freud. He became an Associate Member in 1920 and a Member in 1922. He played a key role in the early administration of the Society and Institute, in its publications activities and its link with allied professions, being editor of the *British Journal of Medical Psychology* for many years. Later he became interested in Melanie Klein's work, with whom he had more analysis prior to the Second World War. She had therefore included him in her group during the Controversies, although he took little part in them after the first two Business Meetings, owing to his interest in the work he was then doing as an army psychiatrist (King 1989a). Rickman was involved in the last three Business Meetings (Section 5, Chapters 1, 2, and 3) when Glover's public attack on Army psychiatrists was discussed. He returned to take an active part in the reconciliation with Anna Freud, becoming President of the Society in 1948, after Sylvia Payne's term of office expired, for by then he was considered part of the 'Middle group', not a Kleinian. His early death in 1951 was a great loss to the Society, which sadly missed his capacity to make links with colleagues in other disciplines.

20 Mrs Joan Riviere (1883–1962)   Joan Riviere came to psychoanalysis from a literary and artistic background, after studying the German language in Germany. She went into analysis with Ernest Jones in 1915 and became a founder member of the British Psycho-Analytical Society in 1919, and then went to Freud for more analysis. In 1920 she started translating Freud's writings into English for publication in the new *International Journal of Psycho-Analysis* and she became its Translation Editor. With Jones and Alix and James Strachey, she worked on the Glossary Committee which decided how to translate Freud's technical terms into English.

From 1921 onwards she took an active part in training activities, collaborating with Melanie Klein and presenting her views on early infantile development to the Viennese Society in 1935 as part of the series of exchange lectures (Section 1, Chapter 1). She took an active part in the Extraordinary Business Meetings, dealing with Melitta Schmideberg's attack on Melanie Klein. She attended all of these discussions and all of the Specific Scientific Meetings arranged to discuss Klein's work. During this period she was obviously a great help to Klein, though from the correspondence, she was never as important to her as Susan Isaacs became. Later, she told John Bowlby that 'she felt that she had no place in the circle of disciples that came to surround Mrs Klein'.

21 *Dr Melitta Schmideberg* (1904–83)   Melitta Schmideberg was the only daughter of Melanie Klein. She trained as a psychoanalyst at the Berlin Institute, where she met and married her husband Walter Schmideberg, also a psychoanalyst and a friend of Freud. After her mother moved to London, she also came to London, joining the British Society as an Associate Member in 1932. She was elected a Member the next year. She wrote many papers and eventually became a training analyst. At first she shared and appreciated her mother's point of view, but following the death of her elder brother in 1934, she became increasingly critical of both her work and her behaviour. She went into analysis with Edward Glover, who was himself becoming increasingly critical of Klein's contributions. As time went on the atmosphere in Scientific Meetings became more unpleasant as Melitta increased her criticism, which was supported by Glover. Many of those present felt that Jones was unable to control Melitta. From her letters it is clear that Melanie Klein felt that her daugher was ill, and her compassion for her made her often unable to defend herself. With the advent of colleagues from Vienna the theoretical differences became more obvious, together with the fear that the essentials of psychoanalysis were in danger. However, Resolution G which she put forward and discussed at the second Extraordinary Business Meeting (Section 1, Chapter 3) was concerned with the effect of Kleinian proselytizing on the conduct of the affairs of the Society, rather than concern about theoretical issues. She was one of the four Members who signed the proposal calling for these Extraordinary Business Meetings. She attended most of these meetings, only missing the one when Glover's letter of resignation was read. However, she came to only one of the Special Scientific Discussions, though she made two written contributions. Following the resignation of Glover, she went

to America where she developed her interest in the treatment of delinquents arising from her work at the Institute for the Scientific Treatment of Delinquency. She resigned from the British Society in 1962.

22 Mr Walter Schmideberg (1890–1954)   Walter Schmideberg came from an aristocratic Austrian family. While he was a captain in the Austro-Hungarian Army, he met Max Eitingon,[3] an Army psychiatrist, who introduced him to Freud, who put him in touch with Ferenczi in Budapest. When he returned to Vienna he was invited to attend the small group of Viennese analysts, which became the Vienna Psychoanalytical Society. He had 'control' analysis with Freud for a time. In 1921 he moved to Berlin, where he became a member of that Society, and helped Eitingon to organize the first Psychoanalytical 'Poliklinic', and the Berlin Congress of the International Psychoanalytical Association in 1922. It was here that he met Melitta Klein, then a medical student, and married her. After she had completed her medical and psychoanalytical training, they moved to London in 1932, where they were both made Associate Members, himself becoming a Member in 1935. Although his association with Freud had helped him to be open to new ideas, he felt that some of Klein's formulations were difficult to justify without losing certain important 'classical' concepts. Hence his insistence in Resolution 'H', that 'deviation from the fundamental principles of Freudian psychoanalysis' be identified and those supporting the deviation be excluded from training activities, or speaking on behalf of the Society. He came to all the Business Meetings held in 1942, but did not come to any of the Special Scientific Discussions, or take much part in the Society after Glover had resigned.

23 Dr W. C. M. Scott (1903–   )   Clifford Scott came to London from Canada in 1931 to be trained in psychoanalysis. He was Melanie Klein's first candidate to qualify as a psychoanalyst, which he did in 1933, having worked with Ernest Jones and Ella Sharpe. He was elected a Member in 1935. He worked as a psychiatrist while he did his training in child analysis, which he had specifically come to London to do. During the war, he worked in the Emergency Medical Service (EMS) and was posted out of London, so he was only able to come to the first of the Special Scientific Discussions and sent in one written contribution. He was, however, able to attend the AGM in 1943 to take part in the discussions of the proposal for a Medical Committee and the Business Meeting when Glover resigned. Melanie Klein in a letter to her group spoke appreciatively of his intervention. After the war Scott held many important posts in the Society, where he was generally regarded as an 'Independent', and thus trusted enough to be elected as its President in 1953; the next year he decided to return to Canada to start a Psychoanalytical Society there, of which he became its first President.

24 *Miss Ella Freeman Sharpe* (1875–1947)   Ella Sharpe started her professional career as an English mistress and co-head of a Pupil Teachers' Training Centre. She was a keen student of Shakespeare and became interested in psychoanalysis. In 1917 she came to the Medico-Psychological Clinic, London, to study psychoanalysis, later going to Berlin for analysis with Hanns Sachs in 1920, who shared her interest in art and literature. On her return to London she was elected an Associate Member of the Society, becoming a Member in 1923. She was soon involved in teaching. Her lectures on technique were published in 1930 in the *International Journal of Psycho-Analysis* (vols 11 and 12) and later in book form. JB writes: 'Her clinical seminars were excellent . . . she was a good teacher and took trouble preparing them.' She was elected to the Training Committee and to the Board and Council a number of times, being a Director of the Institute when war broke out. She favoured the status quo, 'but as an independent eager to heal breaches she was actively supportive' (JB). She played an active part in all the Extraordinary Business Meetings, and she attended all the Scientific Discussions, making four written contributions. Of particular importance was her contribution to the debates in the Training Committee on 'valid technique' and her comments on supervision.

25 *Dr Adrian Stephen* (1883–1948)   Adrian Stephen came from an erudite and cultured background, which he shared with his two sisters, Virginia Woolf and Vanessa Bell. His father, Sir Leslie Stephen, whose friends included Henry James, George Meredith, and Byrne Jones, edited the *Dictionary of National Biography*. Adrian himself was one of the younger members of the Bloomsbury set. In 1907 he was called to the Bar, Lincoln's Inn. After spending the war as a conscientious objector, working on a farm with his wife, Karin, they both applied to train as psychoanalysts. They both went into analysis with James Glover. After Glover died, Adrian went to Ella Sharpe for analysis. Jones made him take a medical degree, which he obtained in 1925. He became an Associate Member in 1927 and a Member in 1930. In the years before the war he was a member of the Board and Council from 1932 to 1937, after which 'he became

increasingly restive under the perpetual domination of the Society by Ernest Jones and Edward Glover' (JB). When he joined the Army, he became even more restive about the Society, being one of the four members who signed the proposal calling for these Extraordinary Business Meetings, and attending most of them. He took a leading role in the activities of the Medical Committee and in the campaign for changes in the constitution to introduce a limitation in the tenure of office. He attended four of the first series of Scientific Meetings (to which he made three written contributions) and was elected as Scientific Secretary of the Society after Glover's resignation, and thus he became a member of the Board and Council. He was elected to the Training Committee, and in 1946 he became Editor of the *International Journal of Psycho-Analysis* for one year. He was devoted to the Society, and sadly he died in 1948 just as he was at last in a position to serve it.

26 *Dr Karin Stephen* (1889–1953)   Karin Stephen, Adrian's wife, obtained a double first in the Moral Sciences Tripos at Cambridge, becoming a Fellow of Newnham College. She was a pupil of Bertrand Russell, to whom she was related by marriage. She was elected to membership of the Aristotelian Society in 1912, publishing a book on Bergson, *The Misuse of Mind: A Study of Bergson's attack on Intellectualism*. In 1914 she married Adrian Stephen, and their lives ran in parallel. After the war they both applied to be trained as psychoanalysts, but Jones made them take a medical degree first. They went into analysis with James Glover. After he died she went into analysis with Sylvia Payne, and after qualifying in medicine, she became an Associate Member in 1927, getting her membership in 1931. When she was at Cambridge she started becoming deaf, a handicap which increased with age. She was skilled in presenting psychoanalysis to non–analysts, and published a book on it for medical students. She was active on the Public Lectures Committee, and often clashed with Jones who was concerned lest members gave a wrong picture of psychoanalysis. She was never made a training analyst (perhaps because of her deafness), and her critical feelings about the Society's training come out in her contributions to the Extraordinary Business Meetings, most of which she attended, being one of the four members who originally proposed these meetings. She was not so much interested in the scientific differences, but like her husband very concerned to promote freedom of speech and democracy in the Society.

27 *Mr James Strachey* (1887–1967)   James Strachey came from a distinguished and cultured background. At school he became friendly with Rupert Brooke, the poet. Later he joined his brother Lytton

Strachey at Cambridge and was drawn into his literary circles, eventually being elected a member of the 'Apostles'. His fascination with the intellectual company there led to his obtaining only a pass degree in law. In the First World War, James became a conscientious objector and worked for a Quaker organization. While at Cambridge he had become interested in psychoanalysis, and when he and Alix Strachey wanted to train, they were told to get a medical degree first. After six weeks they gave it up, and James wrote to Freud who took him on for analysis. Eventually Freud was analysing both of them. It was not long before Freud was also getting them to translate his papers into English. When they returned to London, they were elected as Associate Members in 1922, becoming Members of the Society the next year. Analysis with Freud carried more weight than a medical degree. James and Alix joined the Glossary Committee with Jones and Joan Riviere, and in 1922 they started translating Freud's Case Histories. Strachey was made a training analyst, and undertook many supervisions (or controls) of candidates. In 1932 and 1933 he gave the lectures on technique to candidates. In 1939, when Jones retired, he was appointed Editor of the *International Journal of Psycho-Analysis*, and he was made an ex-officio member of the Board and Council, and of the Publications Committee when it was reinstated in 1946. He was elected to the Training Committee in 1939 where he played a leading role all through these Controversies. He was very intolerant of the arguments and mounting criticisms in the Society, as is shown by his letter to Glover dated 23 April 1940 (Section 1, Chapter 1). He only attended the Fifth Extraordinary Business Meeting and the Business Meeting of the one called to discuss the Final Report of the Training Committee on 8 March 1944. Nor did he come to any of the Special Discussions to Consider Scientific Differences, in spite of having being elected a member of the committee to organize them. However, his contribution to the vital discussions that took place at the Training Committee, and his balanced statement of the limits of their task played a vital part in keeping the Society to the 'middle way'. After the war, in 1948, the Freud Memorial Fund Committee[4] asked Strachey to undertake the translation of the 'Memorial edition' of Freud's works, and he started on his important contribution to psychoanalysis, the translation of Freud's writings and their publication in what became known as the Standard Edition.

28 Dr D. W. Winnicott (1896–1971)   Donald Winnicott trained as a paediatrician and, in 1923, he was appointed as physician-in-charge of the Paddington Green Children's Hospital, London. He also went into analysis at that time with James Strachey, but was not accepted as a candidate until 1927. He worked with Ella Sharpe and Nina Searl and qualified in adult psychoanalysis in 1934. He qualified as a child analyst in 1935, having worked with Nina Searl, Melanie Klein, and Melitta Schmideberg as his 'controls', and was elected a Member in 1936. After this he went into analysis with Joan Riviere. He was thus considered to be a 'Kleinian' by the time these discussions took place. With his years of experience as a paediatrician, he was an important addition to Melanie Klein's group, and she named him as one of five Kleinian training analysts, and according to the records circulated in July 1942 (Section 1, Chapter 7) he had supervised four child training cases. With Melanie Klein he proposed Resolution 'K', and he conscientiously attended all the Extraordinary Business Meetings and only missed one of the Special Scientific Meetings, taking an active part in the free discussions. But Winnicott was an individualist, and from a letter to Susan Isaacs (dated 13 June 1942) Klein had problems with him because he did not give her his contributions early enough for her or the group to vet them, and he had made a number of 'blunders'. In 1944 he was elected to the Board and Council, and in 1951, he became Training Secretary. By this time he was no longer referred to as 'Kleinian', but was considered to be 'Independent' or 'Middle group' for training purposes, although he hated to be labelled by anyone. After this, his prestige in the Society grew and he was elected President from 1956 to 1959 and again from 1965 to 1968. However, he never lost his appreciation of Melanie Klein's earlier contributions, even though she became increasingly critical of his work.

Notes

1 I am grateful to Sonu Shamdasani, Assistant in the Archives of the British Society, for collecting the basic information concerning the dates and offices held by those included in these biographical notes. I am also grateful to Jill Duncan for collecting obituaries and other information on the participants for me.
2 I am indebted to John Bowlby for some background notes that he wrote for me on his memories of some of the participants in these discussions. Where I have actually quoted from his notes I have indicated this by inserting (JB) by the quoted passages.
3 Max Eitingon became the President of the Berlin Institute, and later of the IPA. After the Nazis came to power in Germany, he went to Palestine, now Israel.

4 Hogarth Press had informed the Board that it would cost £20,000 to produce 2,000 sets of the 'complete' works of Freud. Hence the need for a fund-raising committee. Anna Freud was appointed consultant to the committee.

Preface and acknowledgements

In this book we have brought together minutes, documents and relevant correspondence, which cover the reports of the actual discussions that took place in the British Psycho-Analytical Society between 1941 and 1945. We have not attempted to evaluate or comment on them, except where it has been necessary to add information in order to explain or clarify the primary data. It is our hope that by making this material available in this form, we will stimulate interest and further research into the development of the history of psychoanalytic ideas and of the social institutions within which they are nurtured and transmitted.

We are, therefore, grateful to the Council of the British Psycho-Analytical Society and the Board of the Institute of Psycho-Analysis for permission to publish the minutes and other documents contained in this book, which are now part of their archives. We are also grateful for permission to draw extensively from the archives of the British Psycho-Analytical Society. We would also like to thank the Chairman of the Melanie Klein Trust for permission to use their archives, which are now deposited at the Wellcome Foundation, London, but we are sad that we were not able to get comparable access to Anna Freud's archival material now deposited in the USA, although the Anna Freud Centre, the Freud Museum and Mark Paterson of Freud Copyrights gave us what help they could in this matter, as well as encouragement to continue with this project.

It is appropriate that we also express our gratitude to the family of Ernest Jones, and his son Mervyn Jones, who, over the years has given material from his father's papers to the archives of the British Society, and on which the Editors have been able to draw.

We would like to thank the Hogarth Press and the Institute of Psycho-Analysis for permission to include alongside the quotations from earlier translations of Freud's writings, used by the participants in these discussions, the Standard Edition translation of the quotations. We acknowledge permission from Macmillan, London, to quote a part of one letter published in 'Anna Freud' by Young-Bruehl. We are grateful for the support of the Publications Committee and for the help of David Tuckett, who as the past Editor of the New Library of Psychoanalysis, negotiated the decision to publish this material, and has continued in that role.

We would also like to thank the following: Margaret Parker, who typed all the minutes and other documents included in this book, meticulously checking them after they were scanned, but who sadly died before the manuscript was completed; Norman Cohen, who scanned all these documents for use on our computer, and helped us with the task of computerizing the entire manuscript; Laura Schwenk who helped by typing the draft notes and references for Sections 2 and 4, and Norma Miller who helped with checking and proof-reading Section 3 and the references.

Our particular thanks, however, go to Jill Duncan, Executive Officer to the Archives and the Library at the Institute of Psycho-Analysis, for putting together, checking and proof-reading all the references and the index, and above all for acting as the anchor person at the Institute, always ready to help us in many practical ways.

The Editors are grateful to Peter Rudnytsky for discovering the text of Melanie Klein's reply to the Draft Report of the Training Committee, which was missing from the Minutes of the Training Committee (p. 668) and which is included in this paperback edition as an Appendix (p. 932).

They would like to express their thanks to Clifford Yorke who used his wide knowledge of the issues discussed in the Scientific Discussions and his experience in proofreading to check through the hardback edition for errors. They are also grateful to Anne Hayman for pointing out a number of errors.

Pearl King and Riccardo Steiner

Introduction

PEARL KING

'Unless psychoanalysis is regarded as a closed system, incapable of extension, correction or development, its practitioners are bound to be confronted with new observations, which cannot always be satisfactorily accounted for with the help of existing psychoanalytic theories, and new hypotheses will be put forward to account for them' (King 1981). This poses the question, How are they to be assessed and when should they be added to the general body of psychoanalytic knowledge and passed on to students?

During the years 1940 to 1946 the members of the British Psycho-Analytical Society were faced with this very question in relation to the findings of Mrs Melanie Klein and the theories she had developed from her findings and research. Was her work a continuation of psychoanalysis, the main lines of which had been first formulated by Sigmund Freud, or were her contributions based on such different assumptions that she could be considered as diverging from Freud's basic hypotheses enough for it to be said that she was founding another school of psychoanalysis, rather as Carl Jung had earlier?

Psychoanalysts are not alone in having to face and come to terms with the problem of how to incorporate new findings and theories into their understanding of their main body of knowledge. In any branch of learning, be it in the fields, for example, of science, medicine, sociology, literature, and even history, this problem will have to occur if that branch of knowledge is to develop and if research and scholarship is to be encouraged. Riccardo Steiner has discussed some of the difficulties in his paper on the 'Controversial Discussions' in which he places these psychoanalytic controversies

1

within the framework of the more general study of the history of scientific 'revolution' (Steiner 1985).

Any study of the development of scientific, philosophical, or political ideas will give ample evidence of the bitter arguments that not uncommonly occur over different points of view and conflicting explanations of observed phenomena, over the relevance of new discoveries and the pain of giving up entrenched positions, and with regard to the implications of accepting new ideas. Again, not uncommonly every new idea can be felt as or assumed to be an attempted take-over of the profession, even as one which would destroy past knowledge and undermine accepted assumptions. The process of reform and resistance is irretrievably tied to the rise and fall of personal fortune, wider ideological issues, and deep psychological factors at the base of different character types.

It is hardly surprising that attempts to resolve fundamental controversies in any profession have often led to bitter interpersonal feuds, the collecting or banding together of adherents against opponents, and certainly to much unhappiness of those individuals affected by these issues, while the process of sifting out, integrating, or discarding the new ideas or discoveries proceeded. What actually happened during such discussions has not to my knowledge been carefully reported, so that it has not been possible to study the process of how such professional dilemmas were resolved, what methods were used, what the pitfalls were, and, hopefully, thereby to learn from a study of them how to understand better the psychological and social pressures which were at work and which can result in either a malignant or a beneficial outcome of the situation.

One might ask why there is so much unhappiness and even nastiness when professional and intellectual people are faced with issues which may involve changing or adjusting their previously held opinions or points of view? It must be partly because, to individuals whose skill and self-esteem is closely linked to their intellectual achievements, any attack or criticism of the assumptions on which they base their work may be felt as a personal attack on themselves as people. In the case of psychoanalysts, this is even more apparent, as they have to draw on their whole psyche at a deep level to do their work well and creatively. In this context their theory and the concepts which they use become very important as a means of ordering and giving meaning to the phenomena which they deal with, heavily invested as it is with emotions, and with irrational and unconscious assumptions.

In this book we have put together a collection of verbatim

2

minutes, reports, and other material, drawn mainly from the records and Archives of the British Psycho-Analytical Society. When it was decided to hold these discussions of controversial issues, Sylvia Payne, the Honorary Business Secretary of the Society, brought in a stenographer to record the discussions, which could then be available to those who were not able to be present, owing to their involvement in the war. The material that we have collected from these sources illustrate poignantly the problems and issues outlined above, and is intended mainly to offer a resource to those interested in pursuing a fuller understanding of scientific and institutional change.

The detailed discussions and the events included in this material cover a period of only four years during the Second World War. We are offering a slice cut out of the history of the British Psycho-Analytical Society and put under a microscope. Fifty years later, the reader has the opportunity to empathize with the various speakers and try to understand and evaluate the issues and divergences that were being discussed, many of which are as relevant to psychoanalysts today as they were then. In order to try to give an impression of the way events and arguments unfolded, we decided to arrange the material, as far as possible, in its chronological order, so that the reader can imaginatively be in the situation with the participants, as psychoanalysts are during their work with their patients. An analyst and his or her patient do not know what the outcome will be, as was the case with the key participants in these events.

Over the course of the various events the reader will meet the main protagonists and come to know them through their contributions and sometimes their correspondence. No attempt has been made to edit out angry, upsetting, or prejudiced comments. As already mentioned, the cut and thrust of debate could be very personal and very emotional, as in other scientific controversies of this kind. But we think the reader will come to see that the discussions as a whole constitute a fascinating and, in the end, profoundly thorough and impressive exploration of the issues. Some details are given about the major participants in the short biographies before this Introduction. It may also be helpful for the reader to be aware that, for scientific purposes, the main argument was between Edward Glover, Melitta and Walter Schmideberg, Willi and Hedwig Hoffer, Barbara Low, Dorothy Burlingham, Barbara Lantos, and Kate Friedlander, who, along with Anna Freud, opposed the new ideas of Melanie Klein, whose main supporters were Susan Isaacs, Joan Riviere, Paula Heimann, Donald Winnicott, and John Rickman. In the middle were the participants who were not committed to either point of view but who wanted some compromise to be reached which would maintain the possibility of continuing dialogue and who searched for the common ground. Among these were Ernest Jones, Sylvia Payne, Ella Sharpe, Marjorie Brierley, William Gillespie, John Bowlby, James Strachey, Michael Balint, and Adrian and Karin Stephen.

One obstacle to achieving a completely developmental approach was that, after the initial meetings that took place during 1942, some of the attempts to resolve the divergences or to change the organization overlapped with one another because they took place in different forums. In what follows, so as to achieve as near a chronological approach as possible, the various phases of these controversies have been divided into five sections. However, wherever necessary, extracts or quoted material are inserted in order to fill in gaps in the sequence of events.

Section 1 starts with a chapter on the background and development of the Freud–Klein controversies in the British Psycho-Analytical Society, by Pearl King, and then continues with the verbatim minutes of five Extraordinary Business Meetings. The meetings were initially called at the request of four members, but many others members sent in resolutions for discussion. These took place between February and June 1942. Section 1 also includes information relevant to the issues raised at those meetings, and a discussion on how to organize the discussion of the scientific differences.

A commentary by Riccardo Steiner introduces Section 2, which includes the first five discussions of scientific differences, around the paper by Susan Isaacs on 'The Nature and Function of Phantasy', which took place between January and May 1943. A paper by Paula Heimann on 'Some Aspects of the Role of Introjection and Projection in Early Development' was not discussed until October and November, even though Paula Heimann's paper was circulated in June 1943. In July an important discussion of Society policy took place with regard to the future of the professional relations and activities of the Society, and decisions were made which, with hindsight, can be seen to have had an important effect on the future course of these controversies. The verbatim minutes of this meeting are included as Chapter 8 in this section.

Section 3 contains papers and memoranda devoted to an exploration of the effect of the scientific divergences on the training of candidates and on the choice of training analysts. This covered a period from September 1943 to March 1944. While the information included in this section was confidential to the members of the Training Committee (with the exception of the final report to

4

Members), the tenor of the discussions and the conclusions some of the Members seemed to be reaching certainly had an effect on the behaviour of some members of the Committee, and must have been picked up by others. In particular, these discussions influenced the attendance and subject matter of the scientific discussions in Section 4.

Section 4 contains the remaining three discussions of scientific differences covering the period from February to May 1944. The eighth Scientific Meeting discussed the paper by Susan Isaacs and Paula Heimann on 'Regression'. Glover, Hoffer, and Friedlander had circulated comments in December, but they did not come to the meeting to discuss the paper. The ninth and tenth meetings discussed a paper by Melanie Klein on 'The Emotional Life and Ego-Development of the Infant with Special Reference to the Depressive Position'. The atmosphere in these discussions was different from that in Section 2, as they were not attended by supporters of Glover or Anna Freud. The Kleinian contributions were therefore mainly being discussed by the original members of the British Society.

Section 5 includes three Extraordinary Business Meetings dealing with Glover's resignation, with complaints from members about attacks that Glover had made on Army psychiatrists (whom he must have partly blamed for his defeat in the elections for the Medical Committee), and the reports and recommendations from the various committees set up to deal with the training and constitutional issues discussed in the first section of the book. The last two chapters describe the re-arrangement of the training programme of the Institute to accommodate Anna Freud and her colleagues, and the 'Gentlemen's agreement' to ensure fair representation of different points of view on the main committees of the Society and the Institute. Finally, an attempt is made to discuss the influences of these controversies on the later development of the British Psycho-Analytical Society.

The evolution of controversies in the British Psycho-Analytical Society

Background and development of the Freud–Klein Controversies in the British Psycho-Analytical Society

PEARL KING

This chapter will cover the background and history of the British Psycho-Analytical Society and the gradual development of controversy, up to the time when there was a demand to hold meetings to discuss the general disquiet and resentments of members. I aim to emphasize the immediate context out of which the various controversies 'exploded' and were no longer tolerated. At this point they were felt to endanger the future of the British Psycho-Analytical Society and of psychoanalysis in Britain itself. Overtly, controversy was mainly couched in terms of scientific differences of opinion about what was considered to be accepted psychoanalytical theory and technique, as formulated by Freud, and what view of it should be taught to students of psychoanalysis or included in public lectures by analysts representing the Society. Inevitably, these issues also masked deeper ones to do with who should decide these questions, and therefore, which individuals and groups held power in the Society.

The development of psychoanalysis in Britain

The history of psychoanalysis in Great Britain is closely linked with Ernest Jones, the creator of the British Psycho-Analytical Society. He qualified in medicine with several gold medals in 1900, and was working extremely hard building the foundations of what promised to be a very successful conventional career as a consultant physician and neurologist, when he began to become interested in problems of psychopathology. It was at this point that he was introduced to

Freud's work, through his brother-in-law, Wilfred Trotter. Trotter had seen Mitchell Clarke's review of *Studies in Hysteria* (Breuer and Freud, S. 1895) in *Brain*, a neurological journal, in 1898. When he brought it to the attention of Ernest Jones, both men became so intrigued with Freud's ideas that they decided to learn German. Able to read other papers by Freud in the original German, Jones put into practice what he had read, using the new therapy on his first psychoanalytic patient from 1905 to 1906.[1] Soon after, Jones began to make the first of what was to be a lifetime of international contacts.

In 1907 he met Jung in Amsterdam and was then invited to the Burghölzi Hospital in Switzerland, where Jung worked. The following year he took an active part in the First International Psycho-Analytical Congress, held in Salzburg. There he read a paper on 'Rationalization in Everyday Life', introducing a new concept and giving a new meaning to the word (Jones 1923). More importantly, it was here that he met Freud for the first time and thus began a personal and scientific association that was to last until Freud's death in 1939 in England.

However, in London Jones was finding the lot of the pioneer in psychoanalysis no less beset with trouble than Freud had done in Vienna. Medical colleagues in London were as suspicious of mentioning sexual matters with patients as they were in Vienna. His difficulties were no doubt an important reason for his accepting in 1908 the post of Director of the Psychiatric Clinic and later that of Associate Professor of Psychiatry in Toronto, where he remained until 1913. During this period he made numerous visits to Europe which culminated in a period of personal analysis with Ferenczi, one of Freud's close associates. He was also extremely active in promoting the spread of psychoanalytic knowledge in Canada and the United States, where he helped to found the American Psycho-Analytic Association (APA) in 1911. The first book on psychoanalysis to be published in English was the first edition of his 'Papers on Psycho-Analysis' (Jones 1912).

When he returned to England, in 1913, Ernest Jones formed the London Psycho-Analytical Society. In it he collected a number of people interested in psychoanalysis, but only four of whom were practitioners of it. He soon found himself involved in endless discussions, which paralleled those between Freud and Jung, on the validity of certain theoretical propositions, such as infantile sexuality and its role in the aetiology of neurosis. Eventually, he so despaired of this group ever becoming a satisfactory base for the growth of psychoanalysis in England that he, together with some of its members, dissolved it, and founded on 20 February 1919 the British Psycho-Analytical Society. Even then, Jones was faced with the question, Who were appropriate people to be members of a psychoanalytical Society and what basic psychoanalytic theories should they hold?

On this occasion it was agreed that caution should be exercised in the selection of new members to ensure that they were genuinely interested in psychoanalysis. It became the seventh society to be affiliated to the International Psychoanalytical Association (IPA). The Society decided to form a library and to take steps to translate psychoanalytic writings into English. Joan Riviere and James and Alix Strachey worked with Jones on these tasks, and together they formed the Glossary Committee to work out how best to translate Freud's concepts from German into English. In 1920 the *International Journal of Psycho-Analysis* was founded. It was the first psychoanalytic journal in the English language.

Meanwhile, steps were being taken to establish a setting within which the new British Society could function and develop. The Institute of Psycho-Analysis was set up as a company in British law in 1924, largely through the initiative and energy of John Rickman, in order to deal with financial and other matters concerning book publication, and especially to facilitate the publication of books in the International Psycho-Analytical Library series, with the Hogarth Press, which in 1924 thus became joint publishers with the Institute.

In 1926, thanks to a very generous gift from Mr Prynce Hopkins, an American benefactor, it proved possible to establish a clinic for the benefit of 'needy patients'. Premises were obtained at 96 Gloucester Place, and this house continued as the headquarters of the British Psycho-Analytical Society, the Institute, and the London Clinic of Psycho-Analysis until 1950, when the Institute moved to its present headquarters at Mansfield House, New Cavendish Street, London. The achievements of the Clinic were made possible by the co-operation of the individual Members and Associate Members. For the next thirty years, it was a mutually agreed and unwritten obligation of members of the Society that each would give one session a day freely to the Clinic or else perform some equivalent service. Later, a limit was placed on this obligation and it was reduced to 1,000 hours and included cases seen by students in their training. During the first fifty years of its existence approximately 3,080 patients had been psychoanalysed free or for a small fee, under the auspices of the London Clinic of Psycho-Analysis.

The professional recognition of psychoanalysis

By 1926, under the guidance of Ernest Jones, the British Society, as we know it today, had emerged. But this growth had not been without its difficulties. Medically qualified psychoanalysts were uncertain where they stood when they referred patients to their lay colleagues, as it was possible that they could be accused by the General Medical Council of malpractice, and unofficial enquiries had not proved consoling on this matter. In addition to this anxiety, attacks on psychoanalysis in the press had continued, and they culminated in a letter to *The Times* by the Chairman of the National Council for Mental Hygiene, a lay body, stating that they were setting up a committee to investigate psychoanalysis. Jones and Rickman arranged for protests to be made to the appropriate medical bodies, complaining that a lay organization was not the appropriate body to investigate the activities of members of the medical profession.

Accordingly, the British Medical Association agreed to set up its own committee to investigate psychoanalysis, consisting of twenty eminent physicians, and Jones was invited to be a member of it. Some of its members attended all twenty-eight meetings. Ernest Jones attended twenty-four of these meetings, and he, with Edward Glover's help, worked hard to prepare evidence and comment on criticism, and so on. After twenty-eight meetings, the Committee recommended in 1929 that the claims of 'Freud and his followers to the use and definition of the term [psychoanalysis] are just and must be respected'. It defined psychoanalysis as 'the technique devised by Freud, who first used the term, and the theory which he has built upon his work' (BMA Report 1928). This was the first time that an official national body of the medical profession had recognized psychoanalysis as a serious branch of science, an independent one, on which they were not competent to pass judgement. Further, they recognized the distinction between psychoanalysts and 'pseudo'-analysts, as well as the qualifications established by membership of the International Psychoanalytical Association.

Jones's achievements in this committee, in which he was greatly assisted by Glover, made psychoanalysts into a recognized professional group and the Institute of Psycho-Analysis, as the only body competent to train psychoanalysts, therefore their relevant professional association for training purposes, under the auspices of the International Training Commission of the International Psychoanalytical Association. In this way psychoanalysts could legitimate and differentiate themselves from other psychotherapeutic practitioners. In effect, they had had their claims to specialist status accepted. Jones, in fact, had enabled psychoanalysis to be treated in much the same way as any other specialism in medicine, and for the time being had achieved for it exactly the same status and rights to self-government that members of other professions, such as anaesthetists, were achieving at that time (Stevens 1966: 30–51).[2]

The minutes and other papers from this BMA Committee are very illuminating in the light of the disagreements that emerged later in the Society, particularly those between Klein and Glover. On 22 November 1928 Glover attended a meeting as an expert witness, and while there, along with Jones, was subjected to considerable criticism and attack. Among other criticisms, doubt was expressed both about dubious professional practices and standards, and the presence among psychoanalysts of 'non-medical men' (they did not even mention the women!). Jones and Glover defended themselves by being adamant that it was a condition of the British Psycho-Analytical Society that, 'although membership is open to both medical and nonmedical persons . . . those who wish to practise without a medical qualification give an undertaking that they will not engage in independent practice. This means that they leave all problems of diagnosis to medical practitioners and take no patients except those recommended to them by a medical practitioner, with whom they then remain in consultant contact' (Proceedings of the BMA Committee on Psychoanalysis). This requirement was confirmed at a meeting of the British Psycho-Analytical Society on 1 June 1927.

Jones thus gained for psychoanalysis in Britain medical recognition of its differentiation from other forms of psychotherapy. This was the first time an official national body of the medical profession from any country had recognized the distinction between 'psychoanalysts' and 'pseudo-analysts', as well as the qualifications established by membership of the International Psychoanalytical Association.

A Special Meeting of the British Society was arranged at the time of the Oxford Congress in July 1929, so that the Society could express its appreciation of Jones's work, and they were joined by twenty-five guests, among whom were Dr Eitingon from Berlin, the President of the IPA; Fraulein Anna Freud from Vienna, Secretary of the IPA; Dr and Mrs Ferenczi from Hungary; Dr Brill from New York; and Dr Hanns Sachs from Berlin. Edward Glover (a Director of the Institute and Assistant Medical Director of the London Clinic of Psycho-Analysis) presented Jones, on behalf of the

Society, with a Presidential chair, a gold pencil, and a gold cigar cutter, suitably inscribed. Mrs Jones received a special box of chocolates! This was also the second time that Anna Freud had visited Britain.

Psychoanalysis in Britain during the 1920s

Let us pause for a moment to consider what professional life was like for psychoanalysts after the First World War. There was no organized training, but it had been agreed in 1918 at the Budapest Congress that all potential analysts should have some personal experience of psychoanalysis. Consequently, European and American analysts travelled to Vienna, Berlin, and Budapest to have some personal analysis for shorter or longer periods (6–18 months). During the 1920s several members of the British Society went to Vienna for analysis with Freud; these included John Rickman, Joan Riviere, and James and Alix Strachey. Sylvia Payne, Barbara Low, and Ella Sharpe went to Berlin for analysis with Hanns Sachs, while James and Edward Glover, and later Alix Strachey, went to Abraham, who had also been analysing Melanie Klein. In Budapest, Ferenczi had already analysed Ernest Jones and Melanie Klein, and in the 1920s he also analysed John Rickman, David Eder, and Margery Franklin.

In 1925 there were fifty-four Members and Associate Members of the Society, and they came from a number of professional disciplines. Among the members were psychiatrists, specialists in neurology, general practitioners, teachers, university lecturers (in psychology, English, logic, and anthropology), university graduates and those with no university degrees, whom one could call 'Gentlemen (or Gentlewomen) Scholars'. Initially, Jones tried to persuade non-medically trained applicants to take a medical degree. He failed with Alix and James Strachey, who gave it up after six weeks and went to Vienna to be analysed by Freud. Such an analysis was a sure passport to membership of the British Society!

From this information it must be apparent that the group of analysts, who were among the core of the emerging British Psycho-Analytical Society, had their personal experience of analysis in Vienna, Berlin, and Budapest, and that the approach to psychoanalysis current in these three Societies would help to form the soil from which the British approach to psychoanalysis developed. As a group of professional colleagues they were probably not very different from the members of the Vienna Society

14

(Leupold-Lowenthal 1980). There was one difference, however, which was that, while the majority of the members of the Vienna Society had grown up with a Jewish background, at that period only two members of the British Society, Barbara Low and David Eder, were Jewish, and the rest came from Scottish, English, or Welsh Christian backgrounds, with a strong bias towards agnosticism and humanism. The implications of these different backgrounds must, however, have played some part in the later controversies.

These early psychoanalysts were fascinated and excited with the possibility of applying psychoanalytic ideas and understanding to the various problems and social issues that they were concerned with, either as citizens or in their professional capacity. The papers read at Scientific Meetings at this time covered a wide selection of topics, applying Freud's ideas to child development, education, anthropology, child guidance, politics, history, literature and art, as well as to the treatment of neurotic and psychotic patients.

In addition to the task of translating and applying the contributions of Freud and his continental colleagues to their work with patients, they were developing their own psychoanalytic interests. These interests included the role of anxiety, hostility, and aggression, the theory of symbolism, character problems, the origin and structure of the superego, problems of psychoanalytic technique, a psychoanalytic theory of psychoses, and the psychoanalysis of children.

The selection and training of psychoanalysts

The problems leading to the disbanding of the London Psycho-Analytic Society, which I have just mentioned, were not unique. Even at that time the question as to who should be recognized as a psychoanalyst was an issue for the IPA.[3] At the Budapest Congress of the IPA in 1918 Nunberg had proposed that in future every analyst should be analysed, and at the Hague Congress (1920) it was agreed to investigate the possibility of granting a Diploma and formulating the conditions of membership of Branch Societies. Questionnaires were sent out to all Branch Societies for their views.

Some years later in 1925 at the Bad Homburg Congress of the IPA in Germany, the first conference of delegates from Branch Societies took place. It was called to discuss the whole problem of psychoanalytical training and the plan to form an international training organization 'in order that there might be a uniform system

15

of psychoanalytical instruction in different countries' (Eitingon 1925).

Eitingon's opening speech is an historical gem (Eitingon 1928), in which he formulated what are still the main principles underlying our current approach to training; that is, Institutional responsibility for selection, training, and qualification of candidates, personal analysis, supervised analysis of patients, and theoretical courses. At the Business Meeting which followed, it was agreed that each Branch Society should elect a Training Committee of not more than seven members, and that the Training Committees of the Branch Societies should combine to form an International Training Board. Accordingly, in March 1926 the British Society elected its first Training Committee, consisting of E. Jones, J. Glover, J. Rickman, J. C. Flugel, and D. Bryan, and they drew up draft suggestions for the selection and training of candidates for submission to the International Training Board.

By the first meeting of the International Training Commission at Innsbruck in 1927, Eitingon reported that training in the three large Societies (Berlin, London, and Vienna) was being carried out along similar lines, and that the special conditions of each country had not mitigated 'against the requirements arising out of the internal Structures of our scientific theory and our practical work'. He said that a training begun in London could be continued in Vienna and finished in Berlin, as they were working on such similar lines!

However, while there was much similarity between their attitudes to the procedures and principles of training adopted by the three Societies, there were certain differences of emphasis or theoretical concern in the sphere of psychoanalytical theory, which emanated originally from the particular interests of Ernest Jones from 1910 onwards. In his early contributions, he emphasized the importance of pre-genital and innate determinants over and above the influence of external or environmental stress, and their vital role in determining beliefs and perceptions of reality. Of particular importance was the role he ascribed to hate and aggression, and the influence of fear in relation to anxiety. However, Jones had not put these ideas forward as controversial issues, but as a consolidation of Freud's early formulations (King 1979).

As noted previously, the question of the importance of medical qualifications for the practice of psychoanalysis was discussed at length in the British Society. After careful consideration of all the issues involved and the analysis of questionnaires that had been sent to all members, the British Society agreed in 1927 that lay candidates should be 'urged to obtain medical qualifications but that they should not be excluded on the sole ground of their not obtaining them'. As part of the new psychoanalytic profession by organized medicine, non-medical psychoanalysts, however, had to agree to medical colleagues interviewing their patients and taking medical responsibility for them prior to the commencement of their treatment. Internationally there was also discussion, with Societies taking different positions. Most of the European Societies supported Freud's point of view on this question and were in favour of training lay as well as medically trained practitioners, in contrast to the point of view adopted by the analysts from the USA, who wanted psychoanalysis to be a sub-speciality of medicine and would accept only medically trained candidates.

Meanwhile, in Britain the training of candidates had become organized and the Training Committee more effectively in control of it. Courses of lectures on psychoanalytic theory were given by Edward Glover and on technique by Ella Sharpe, which were published in the *International Journal of Psycho-Analysis*. Between 1932 and 1933 Edward Glover conducted an investigation into the technique of psychoanalysis, as practised by members of the British Society at that time, but it was not published until 1940. It gives a valuable insight into the approaches to analytic practice and how problems were viewed during the 1930s, but it also shows that certain theoretical divergences were becoming apparent, that had a bearing on the technique of analysis and therefore on what should be taught to candidates as psychoanalysis (King 1981).

The development of interest in child analysis and the growing influence of Melanie Klein

In 1909 Freud (Freud, S. 1909) published his 'Analysis of a Phobia in a Five-Year-Old Boy', the famous case of 'Little Hans'. In the case of this boy the observations and handling were carried out by the boy's father, a medical colleague. By 1925 two outstanding pioneers of child analysis had emerged, Anna Freud in Vienna and Melanie Klein in Berlin. As will become clear later, they had, however, approached the conceptual and technical problems of child analysis in divergent ways.

Who was Melanie Klein, and how did she come to have such an impact on the psychoanalytical movement on a worldwide canvas? She was born in Vienna in 1882, the youngest of four children of a Viennese medical practitioner, and it seems clear that the atmosphere she grew up in encouraged her intellectual development, which was

17

also greatly helped by her favourite sister and brother, both of whom sadly died prematurely. Their illness, together with her father's profession, must have contributed to Melanie Klein's wish to study medicine, and when that was not possible, to become interested in therapy. She was married to Arthur Klein in 1903. Her husband was an industrial chemist and his work necessitated travelling around, living in small towns. She missed the intellectual stimulation of Vienna and she was not happy. When in 1910 her husband found work in Budapest, she then found the intellectual stimulation she had felt deprived of, and here she first discovered Freud's writings. New worlds opened up to her; she sought analysis with Sandor Ferenczi and he encouraged her to start analysing children. She read her first paper to the Hungarian Society in 1919 on 'The Development of a Child' (Klein 1921), and was elected a Member of that Society. She left Budapest shortly after her husband went to work in Sweden, and in 1921 she moved to Berlin where Karl Abraham, whom she had met at the Hague Congress, was working. He had encouraged her attempts to analyse children, and she established a practice in Berlin with adults and children. In 1924 she persuaded Abraham to take her on as a patient and came to feel that Abraham was her sponsor and to a certain extent her protector in the Berlin Society.

From early on, James and Alix Strachey, who had come across Melanie Klein's work in Berlin,[4] were impressed by her work, and when in 1925 she offered to give a series of six lectures on child psychoanalysis to members of the British Society, the Council agreed with enthusiasm that Jones should invite her to do so. Nina Searl and Sylvia Payne had already given papers in 1924 on the technique of child psychoanalysis to the British Society, and this was an area of growing interest to British members. Melanie Klein found that her scientific interests and approach to clinical work were in accord with those of many members of the British Society, some of whom she had met previously in Berlin. When Karl Abraham died suddenly in December 1925, Melanie Klein was bereft of his support. She was encouraged to settle in London in 1926 (where she was to work until her death in 1960), and to leave the Berlin Society, where the approach of Anna Freud to the treatment of children was more acceptable than was her approach.

There were two main reasons why her approach to her clinical work was not acceptable in the Berlin Society. The first one was that she was attempting to treat children's play as if it were the equivalent of an adult patient's free associations. The second was that she was not afraid to interpret the negative material and aggressive impulses of adult patients as and when they appeared, without the customary

nurturing of the positive affects of the patient, without which it was
widely held in the Berlin Society that psychoanalysis could not
proceed. Through her work with children she had been able to
observe the intense anxiety that aggressive thoughts and actions
aroused in patients and which she found had to be verbalized for
work to continue.

But it was not only mutual interest in the development of child
analysis that led Melanie Klein to choose the British Psycho-
Analytical Society as the potentially fertile soil into which she could
put down her roots and continue her researches. Some of the points
of view and theoretical formulations put forward by Ernest Jones,
which were generally accepted in the British Society, were parallel to
some of those held by Melanie Klein. Among these were the
importance of pre-genital and innate determinants over and above
the influence of external and environmental stress, and their vital role
in determining beliefs and perceptions of reality; the role of hate and
aggression and their relation to morbid anxiety and guilt; and the
early development of female sexuality (Jones 1935). Those familiar
with the work of Melanie Klein will be aware that these were all
clinical topics and areas of theoretical concern which she later
developed in her contributions.

Melanie Klein attended her first meeting as a guest of the British
Society in October 1926, and in November she made her first
contribution, entitled 'Notes on the Psycho-analysis of a Child Aged
Five Years' (Klein 1926), in which she linked up phantasies with the
child's experience of weaning and toilet training. In February 1927,
still as a visitor, she gave another short communication on 'The
Importance of Words in Early Analyses' (Klein 1927), that being the
term first used instead of 'child analysis'. After this paper Melanie
Klein appears as a Member of the British Society, although I can find
no record of her actual election.

In May 1927, Barbara Low read an abstract of Anna Freud's
Introduction to the Technique of the Analysis of Children (Freud, A.
1927), published in German.[5] Anna Freud held that it was important
to foster a positive response from the child, to help it to trust and
depend on the analyst. She did not believe that it was possible for a
transference to develop, as it did with adults, as the affects of the
child were still tied to their parents, and their real relationships
would interfere with the development of a transference neurosis,
which was an essential curative factor in the treatment of adult
neurotics. Her approach was therefore more explanatory and
educative than interpretative, as she did not feel that the play of
children could be equated to the free association of adults, which was

19

one of the basic assumptions of Klein. Nor did she agree with the 'prophylactic' analyses of children, which was an important point in Melanie Klein's approach. She was primarily concerned with how to help ill children.

Melanie Klein opened the discussion on Barbara Low's summary of Anna Freud's book with a detailed criticism of it, and the other discussants (J. Riviere, M. N. Searl, E. F. Sharpe, E. Glover, and E. Jones) were mostly in agreement with her criticism. The contributions to this discussion were later published in the *International Journal of Psycho-Analysis* (*IJPA*) (Klein 1927, vol. 8: 339–91),[6] much to the disapproval of Freud himself. These criticisms of Freud's daughter, however justified, did not lay a friendly basis for future collaboration. Following these discussions Melanie Klein must have felt her approach supported enough to develop her ideas further. In February 1928, she presented her paper on 'Early Stages of the Oedipus Conflict' (Klein 1928), which she had read to the International Psycho-Analytical Congress at Innsbruck the previous year and which tackled one of the key issues which had been raised in the previous discussions.

From 1929 onwards, the British Society increasingly flourished. The agreement with the BMA had strengthened their professional standing and identity and they were still excited by psychoanalysis and the discoveries that they were enabled to make with the help of Freud's work and ideas. Melanie Klein's contributions were looked on as further explorations of Freud's discoveries, rather than as new or alien ideas incompatible with psychoanalysis.

Indeed, in May 1929 Melanie Klein was recognized as a training analyst and she started work with her first candidate. In October she was elected a member of the Training Committee, a position which she held for many years. Meanwhile she continued to make regular contributions to the scientific life of the Society, giving her paper on 'The Importance of Symbol-Formation in the Development of the Ego' (Klein 1930) early in the next year. In this way, by the end of 1934 Melanie Klein had contributed eleven papers or short communications to the British Society. At this time, many analysts used her ideas if they were felt to be helpful. Moreover, failure to use them did not create animosity, nor was it taken as evidence of disloyalty to her, as was the case later when she felt more under attack.

Meanwhile, in 1933 the Nazis had seized power in Germany and Jewish analysts had to escape. The British Society welcomed several from Berlin, including Paula Heimann, Heinz Foulkes, and Kate Friedlander. Later Eva Rosenfeld and Hans Thorner also moved to

London. But, as might be expected, they brought with them some of the ambivalence previously shown to Melanie Klein's ideas in Berlin, some supporting and others disagreeing with them. Nevertheless, these years could be called the honeymoon period in the relationship between Melanie Klein and the British Society.

There was, however, another growing source of opposition to her contributions. When Melanie Klein came to London she left her daughter Melitta behind in Berlin where she was doing her medical and analytical training. While there she met and married Walter Schmideberg, a member of the Berlin Society. In 1930 they both moved to London, and Melitta was elected a Member in 1933. She was awarded the Clinical Essay Prize for 1933 by the Institute of Psycho-Analysis for her paper entitled 'The Play-Analysis of a Three-Year-Old Girl' (Schmideberg 1934). She contributed twenty-four other papers and communications to the scientific life of the Society between the years 1930 and 1942. However, as time went on she found herself increasingly disagreeing with her mother's point of view, and gradually she became her arch opponent, challenging her ideas and attacking her in Scientific Meetings. She was sometimes supported by Barbara Low, but in 1935 she was also joined by Edward Glover, with whom she was in analysis. He had originally supported Melanie Klein's work with children, but when in 1935 she read her paper entitled 'A Contribution to the Psychogenesis of Manic-Depressive States' (Klein 1935), he felt that she had gone too far. She had dared to venture into the realm of the psychiatrist and to explore psychotic states and mechanisms in adults. It was in this paper that Melanie Klein first formulated her concept of the depressive position, together with her concept of part and whole objects, describing the development of the object relations of the child, and spelling out the intrapsychic concomitants of the process as it affected the child's inner world and internal objects. She also distinguished between paranoid and depressive anxiety. Her critics particularly objected to her use of phantasy, her interpretation of Freud's concept of the death instinct, the early dating of the development of the superego, and the concept of internal objects with its deceptive overtone and its tendency to reification rather than conceptualization. Melanie Klein read this paper in January, and it was not until October that the Society had a full discussion of it, opened by Ernest Jones. Not everyone was antagonistic to this development of Melanie Klein's ideas, and several analysts, including John Rickman (Rickman 1937), Donald Winnicott (Winnicott 1935), and Ella Sharpe (Sharpe 1935), read important papers using the conceptual tools her paper had formulated.

21

Two areas of controversy, with hindsight, can be seen to be emerging at this point. One was that because she often formulated her ideas in descriptive rather than conceptual terms her theories were easy to apply to a quick understanding of a patient's material and could easily be shared with colleagues without the hard work that would have been involved in conceptualizing them in terms of the metapsychology of classical theory. In Marjorie Brierley's words (Brierley 1949a), 'Generalizations tended to be expressed in perceptual rather than conceptual terms' and the language of phantasy was mixed with abstract terminology. The other area of controversy was that her critics felt that Melanie Klein was putting forward a view of early development and the genesis of psychic functioning with consequences for the technique of therapy which they did not feel were consistent with psychoanalysis as they knew it.

The exchange lectures between London and Vienna

Meanwhile it was becoming increasingly clear that there were a number of important differences in both theory and technique between members of the British and Viennese Societies. Jones summarized these differences as being about the early development of sexuality, especially in the female, the genesis of the superego and its relation to the Oedipus complex, the concept of the death instinct, and the technique of child analysis (Jones 1935).

In 1934 Ernest Jones was again elected President of the IPA, and he had become concerned at the divergencies that seemed to be growing up between London and Vienna on a number of topics, partly, though not entirely, influenced by the contributions of Melanie Klein in the British Society. He (Jones 1936) felt that these divergencies arose in part from the growing lack of personal contact between the analysts in Vienna and in London, and the fact that 'nowadays far more Psychoanalysis is learnt from the spoken word than through the written word'. He complained that as the habit of reading had declined, so 'the habit of writing had taken on a more narcissistic bent'. He then commented that 'the new work and ideas in London have not yet, in our opinion, been adequately considered in Vienna' (ibid.).

In order to deal with this problem of the divergence of points of view, Jones and Federn, Vice-President of the Vienna Society, arranged a series of exchange lectures during 1935/6, in the hope that these differences might be mutually understood, if not resolved. Jones himself gave the first paper on 'Early Female Sexuality', and he

22

described these divergencies as follows: 'the early development of sexuality, especially in the female, the genesis of the superego and its relation to the Oedipus complex, the technique of child analysis and the concept of the death instinct' (Jones 1935). He strongly disagreed with the phallo-centric view of female development and the underestimation of the role of the mother in the development of the child. He quoted Freud as saying, 'Everything connected with this first mother attachment has in analysis seemed to me so elusive, lost in a past so dim and shadowy, so hard to resuscitate that it seemed as if it had undergone some special inexorable repression' (ibid.). Jones pointed out that there was a need for more work on the earliest years of a girl's attachment to her mother, and that this was what Melanie Klein and other British child analysts were exploring. He went on to say that 'differences of opinion in respect to the later stages of development are mainly, and perhaps altogether, due to different assumptions concerning the earlier stage' (ibid.). In concluding this paper Jones wrote, 'I think the Viennese would reproach us with estimating the early phantasy life too highly at the expense of external reality, and we should answer that there is no danger of any analysts neglecting external reality, whereas it is always possible for them to under-estimate Freud's doctrine of the importance of psychical reality' (ibid.).

The first return paper was given by Robert Wälder (Vienna) on 'Problems of Ego Psychology',[7] and he not only gave it to a Scientific Meeting, but also a small group was arranged to discuss the differences with him in more detail. The next paper was given by Joan Riviere (London) on 'The Genesis of Psychical Conflict in Early Infancy'. In this paper (Riviere 1936) she attempts to formulate the earliest psychical developmental processes in the child, the oral-sadistic impulses and their attendant anxieties, and the fundamental defence mechanisms against them employed by the ego, with reference to the defensive functions of projection and introjection. She hoped that a study of the factors operating in the first two years of life would throw light on 'ego-development and the genetic origin of the superego, together with the relation of these to infantile sexuality and libido development'. This paper is interesting not only for the point of view that was presented, but also for its bibliography, which included a wide cross-section of members of the British Society, who were in accord with various aspects of the approach that Joan Riviere was discussing. The return paper was again given by Robert Wälder on 'The Problem of the Genesis of Psychical Conflict in Early Infancy' (Wälder 1937), in which he carefully discusses the points raised in Joan Riviere's paper.

It is doubtful how much clarification or mutual understanding was achieved during these 'Exchange Lectures', as they were called. More serious matters claimed the attention of psychoanalysts, which were a greater threat to psychoanalysis than such divergencies. These were connected with anti-Semitism in Germany, and the possible threat to Austria and therefore to the Vienna Society.

The Nazi persecution and the German invasion of Austria

On the Continent the dark clouds of Fascism and anti-Semitism were growing. In 1938 the Nazis occupied Vienna, and the life and liberty of Freud and his family and of his colleagues were in very serious danger. In this emergency analysts in many parts of the world, but perhaps especially in England and America, immediately came to the rescue. Much of the responsibility was taken by Ernest Jones supported by the British Society and the Home Office of the British government. Jones at once went to Vienna and, with the help of Princess Marie Bonaparte and the American Ambassador in Paris, he negotiated successfully with the Nazis for Freud, his family, and colleagues to be allowed to leave Austria. The Freuds arrived in London on 6 June 1938.

The British Society at this time welcomed and gave its membership to many members of the Vienna Society. Some of them subsequently went on to the United States, but a large number settled permanently in England to the great enrichment of psychoanalysis in London. These latter included not only Sigmund Freud himself, but also his daughter Anna Freud and other leading members of the Vienna Society. Melanie Klein, however, was not too happy about Jones's action in bringing the Freuds to England. As Steiner has described in Section 2, Chapter 1, she anticipated difficulties immediately.

When describing the achievements of Jones later, on the occasion of the centenary of his birth, Anna Freud wrote:

He persuaded the Home Secretary to issue permits not only for my father and his nearest family, but also to his personal doctors, to the family help, and beyond this to a number of his psychoanalytic co-workers, the Bibrings, the Kris and the Hoffers: altogether a list of some eighteen adults and six children. I had, if possible, even more admiration for another task which he undertook. It cannot have been easy to persuade the British Society to open their doors to an influx of members from Vienna, i.e. to colleagues who

24

held different scientific views from their own and who could only be expected to disrupt peace and internal unity. I never knew how he did it; I was careful not to ask too much. In any case, it happened. Not only did the British Society accord the incomers immediate membership and, where appropriate, training analyst status, they also assured their financial security by arranging a scheme whereby their private patients could be treated under the auspices of the British Society and Clinic. I have never ceased to be grateful to the British Society for their attitude at this crucial moment and the memory of it influenced many of my later actions.

(Freud, A. 1979:286)

However, as Anna Freud had pointed out, the acceptance of these Viennese colleagues also meant that differences between the Viennese and some British analysts had now to be contained within the British Society, and the question would soon arise as to what kind of psychoanalytic theory and technique was to be taught to our students.

The potential difficulties intensified as Klein's original contributions multiplied. In October 1938 she read her paper 'Mourning and its Relation to Manic-depressive States' (Klein 1940), in which she expanded her concept of the depressive position, the destruction of good internal objects when the child's hatred and sadism are active, and the process of reparation through the operation of love and the libido, which she linked with process of mourning. As Melanie Klein spelled out her contributions in greater detail, they began to be perceived by some as an alternative to the formulations of classical psychoanalysis, although she maintained, I think correctly, that she was well grounded in Freud's contributions, which in a number of cases she felt that she had extended and developed. Furthermore, her theory of early development and the genesis of psychic functioning seemed to have consequences for the technique of analysis which some members did not feel were consistent with psychoanalysis as they knew it. Up to this time there had been a widespread acceptance in the British Society of the view that Melanie Klein had made most important and valuable contributions to child analysis and that these had extensive implications in the wider field of general theory and technique. It became obvious, however, that this view was not shared by most of the Viennese colleagues. One result of this was the consolidation of the forces supporting Melanie Klein and the emergence of what later came to be known as the 'Kleinian group', with the uncommitted members forming the main part of the British Society or the 'Middle group'.

The possibility of war with Nazi Germany

The last eighteen months before war was declared had been a very busy time for Jones and many members of the British Society, as they were engaged in trying to evacuate as many psychoanalysts as possible from Austria following Hitler's invasion of that unhappy country (Steiner, R. 1988). At a Special Meeting held on 30 March 1938, to consider 'the problem of settling our Psycho-Analytical colleagues from Vienna (and elsewhere) in this country', it was decided to circulate all members to try to discover where it might be possible for the refugees to settle and to get work. They then agreed to form a Hospitality Committee to meet and to give immediate help to Austrian colleagues who were able to enter the country. Thus an attempt was made to mobilize the whole Society to assist in this matter.

Because it was clear to most analysts by then that Hitler had to be opposed by force, their concern during this period seems to have been directed towards discovering how they could contribute as individual psychoanalysts, and help to deal with panic and mental breakdowns arising from air raids. Three symposia were held in the Society during this time, one on 'Psychoanalytic Aspects of the War Crisis' and two on 'Mental Casualties in Wartime'. At one of these meetings Dr Mira from Spain spoke of his experiences during the Spanish Civil War in Barcelona.

Although the officers of the Society were too preoccupied to be concerned with relations to other professional groups, it was left to individuals such as John Rickman to try to point out to medical colleagues and others what we were up against. He had already been to Vienna to assist in the rescue of Austrian colleagues and had seen at first hand what it was like to be invaded by the Nazis, so he spoke with authority.

He worked with members of the Medical Peace Campaign and the Quaker Medical Society with regard to their medical responsibilities during a time of risk of war. He organized other meetings and discussions with professional colleagues from different disciplines, who met together in the Medical Section of the British Psychological Society to discuss the psychological problems of war. While other members of the Society gave occasional lectures on relevant topics, it was Rickman who was invited by the Editor of the *Lancet*, a prestigious medical journal, to write their leading articles whenever there was an important political crisis, and his articles were often quoted in leading newspapers. He

26

therefore had considerable influence on contemporary medical and lay opinion.[8]

Some members of the British Society were angry because of the aloof and arrogant attitude of some of their officers – mainly, I think, Jones and Glover – in relation to their handling of the Society's relationships with other professional groups. They had been particularly arrogant in their dealings with the Tavistock Clinic, a psychotherapy clinic formed in 1920, and which followed mainly Freudian theories and technique, but which also included those who were influenced by Jung. A candidate who was working there when applying for training was told to leave it, if he was accepted for psychoanalytic training. I assume that they were afraid of diluting the pure gold of psychoanalysis! In 1938, W. R. Bion, who was in analysis with John Rickman, was the first accepted applicant for training to refuse to fit in with this requirement, and he continued to work at the Tavistock.

In criticizing this approach later, Adrian Stephen (brother of Virginia Woolf, the novelist) complained of the secrecy with which the affairs of the Society had been conducted, and how little or nothing had been done to involve members of the Society in the war effort. He said:

> Compare this with the achievements of the Tavistock Clinic: . . . the entire organisation of Army Psychiatry is in their hands, and if two or three Psycho-Analysts have been given Commissions and can take some share in the war effort and in any scientific work that is done, no thanks at all are due to their connection with this Society. . . . The men who manage the Tavistock clinic may have no profound grasp of psycho-pathology, but they can teach us something in the way of practical psychology . . . in the tactful handling of negotiations.
>
> (Stephen 1941)

Some of the contributions of members during the Extraordinary Business Meetings recounted in this book vividly describe many reasons for this attitude to the officers of the Society.

The outbreak of war
and its effects on the British Society and Institute

After Hitler had invaded Poland and refused to withdraw his forces, Britain, along with their Allies, declared war on Germany on 3 September 1939. It was a sombre moment, but it was also a relief to

27

many, as it was important to stop the spread of National Socialism and to oppose the increasing aggression of the Nazis and the German Army. The longer it was put off, the more time there would be for Germany to re-arm.

On 23 September 1939 Sigmund Freud died, after a long and painful illness, and as both Sylvia Payne and Balint pointed out several times in these discussions, it meant that an important father figure had been lost, and the siblings were left to disagree among themselves. The Society paid tribute to his memory on 4 October 1939 and discussed the question of a permanent memorial to him. Among other projects suggested, the possibility of producing a biography or a complete English edition of Freud's collected works were mentioned. A Sub-committee consisting of Anna Freud, Jones, Payne, Rickman, Riviere, and Strachey was set up to consider the matter further.

When war was declared many medical psychoanalysts joined the Emergency Medical Service (EMS), which was set up to deal with casualties arising from the war emergency, with air-raid casualties, and with members of the Forces who needed medical care in Britain. Part of the Maudsley Hospital moved up to Mill Hill, and became part of the EMS dealing with psychiatric casualties in the north-west areas of London. William Gillespie and Clifford Scott worked there, and so did a number of other psychoanalysts and post-war candidates. Some of those who joined the EMS were not immediately involved, and could go on working at their peace-time jobs until hostilities increased. Others moved on to join the Army as the psychiatric services became more organized. Nevertheless, in spite of the number of members who joined up, many of them still managed to attend the Extraordinary Business Meetings reported in this section of the book (King 1989a).

The London Clinic of Psycho-Analysis agreed to organize a Temporary Psychological Aid Centre on three afternoons a week for the purpose of providing advisory consultations and short emergency treatments, in addition to the psychoanalytical routine of offering full psychoanalysis to patients. This facility was offered in collaboration with the official scheme for the organization of mental casualties in the London area during wartime.

Among the analysts who left London after the outbreak of hostilities in September 1939 were Melanie Klein, Susan Isaacs, and Joan Riviere. Scientific Meetings continued, however, and were well attended, although the original members of the British Society were often outnumbered by their colleagues from European Societies, who were unable to leave London because as enemy aliens they could not move freely about the country. The meetings continued to be held on the first and third Wednesdays of each month, as they had been held in Vienna, and I am sure that the opportunity to be in a majority at such meetings was an important stabilizing experience for those who were refugees from Europe. As Melanie Klein did not return to London until October 1941, and as most of her close associates had also been absent during that period, the Wednesday Scientific Meetings must have felt like a fortnightly reunion of the ex-Viennese Members of the Society, and their attendance at them must have been an important supportive experience for them.

Soon after war was declared Anna Freud and Dorothy Burlingham, with the help of analytic colleagues and other workers from Vienna, opened the Hampstead War Nurseries. They had some houses in London and later opened one in the country, away from the bombing. They continued with this project until the end of hostilities, reporting their work to the Society from time to time. Reports of this work are referred to at various points in the later discussions.

Donald and Clare Winnicott worked on problems of caring for difficult and disturbed children who had to be evacuated. They designed and set up hostels for them, each run by a 'Mother' and a 'Father' figure, and they made arrangements for counselling the staff. Susan Isaacs took part in 'The Cambridge Evacuation Survey: A Wartime Study in Social Welfare and Education', which she edited and published in 1941. Melanie Klein, Donald Winnicott, and John Rickman were associated with an advisory group that assisted in this research. Glover and Winnicott took part in a nationwide survey of civilian mental health called the 'Neurosis Survey', between the years 1939 and 1943, and we have the results they submitted to the Ministry of Health in our Archives. The whole survey was later published.

These and other activities were carried on by members alongside the discussions and meetings, the minutes and records of which are contained in the following chapters of this book. Sylvia Payne wrote of this period:

Before the British Society had time to assimilate and unite with their colleagues who came from Vienna, it was faced with a scattering of its own members owing to the attack on London. I do not think that we realised the full significance of this until members began to return to London in the Summer of 1941. The evacuation of members meant not only the breaking up of private practices which caused economic anxiety, but the complete cessation of personal contacts, which tended to increase the significance of personal and scientific differences of outlook which were already in existence.

(Payne 1942)

The intensification of tensions
in the British Psycho-Analytical Society

On 12 September 1939, nine days after war had been declared, an Emergency Meeting of the Directors of the Board of the Institute of Psycho-Analysis was called by telegram. The members of the Board were Ernest Jones (Chairman), Edward Glover (Deputy), John Rickman (Secretary), David Matthew (Treasurer), Sylvia Payne, Ella Sharpe, Marjorie Brierley, and Edward Bibring. Six members attended this Emergency Meeting.

At this period the Board of the Institute of Psycho-Analysis was the legal body responsible for the administration of the building, for finance, for the London Clinic of Psycho-Analysis, for the Library and its safety, for all publications, and for the staff they employed. The Institute was also responsible for organizing the training of candidates, while the Training Committee dealt with the selection of students and their progress, under the auspices of the International Training Commission. The Board normally reported back to the members of the Institute only at Annual General Meetings (when the Board was elected by 'block vote'), and in their Annual Report.

The British Psycho-Analytical Society and its Council, however, were responsible for scientific activities, for the election of Members and Associate Members of the Society, for the election of its Council and of a Training Committee, which had to report its activities to the International Training Commission, and it was the Society, not the Institute, that was affiliated to the International Psychoanalytical Association. Thus, the members of the Society elected the Training Committee at their AGMs, but the Training Committee was responsible to the Board for certain of its activities. Thus there was an anomaly which was not understood by many members in these following discussions, but which was one source of their trouble. The relation between the Institute and the Society was obviously one that needed re-thinking and clarification. The officers who ran the Institute activities were appointed by the Board and not elected, and I think that this must have been behind the continuous pressure for more democracy that was one of the themes in the resolutions and discussions recorded in the following chapters.

The Board made a number of decisions to deal with the adaptation of the Institute to wartime conditions, the removal of the James Glover Library to safety, arrangements for fire-watching, and the blackout, as well as their normal functions of administering the Institute, the Clinic, and the Society. Those members of the Board who could manage to had met six times between September 1939 and 23 October 1940, before they realized that they needed to have an authorized Emergency Committee to run the affairs of the Institute *and* Society. During this period, the Council did not meet officially at all, and most members would not have known what was being done on their behalf. Some members of the Board were beginning to feel pressure for greater democracy and were unhappy with the current rules and procedures.

At their previous meeting in May, David Matthew and John Rickman had proposed that two Members of the Board shoud retire annually and not be entitled to be re-elected for two years and that no Member should hold the same office in the Society or Institute for more than three consecutive years. A worried but useful discussion took place. They were, however, unanimously agreed that the practice of the Board putting up 'block nominations' should cease, and that Members should be encouraged to send in nominations, whether or not they had been Board Members.[9] At the next meeting, on 23 October 1940, it was agreed to appoint an Emergency Committee to carry out immediate administrative duties.

The Committee to consist of two Directors who are in London every week. These two Directors shall have authority to settle all immediate administrative matters. No Director shall have the authority to settle matters affecting the Institute as a whole except in a critical situation needing immediate decision. When the policy of the Board is involved a third Director shall be consulted.

It was then agreed that an Extraordinary Meeting of the Institute should be held on the occasion of the next Scientific Meeting of the Society, on 6 November 1940, so that this minute could be communicated to members. Dr Edward Glover and Dr Payne were appointed to this Committee and at the request of Dr Jones, Dr Glover had been appointed Deputy Chairman of the Board.

While it was obviously appropriate and not illegal for the Board to take control of affairs in this way, it did mean that power was in the hands of a few people, even though they had to be re-appointed every year. This situation led to mounting resentment, as analysts who had experienced authority in the Services became increasingly unwilling to accept the authority of officers who had not been elected for several years, and who held multiple offices, and by the rules of the Society (and of the Institute) there was no limitation in the length of time they could hold office.

These events and arrangements have been reported in some detail in order to clarify the situation for the reader, but it should be borne in mind that most of the members who took part in the subsequent Extraordinary Business Meetings were not aware of matters discussed by the Board of the Institute, whose transactions were confidential, so that complaints made during subsequent Business Meetings that Members were not sufficiently involved were obviously correct.

I referred earlier to the movement out of London of many British psychoanalysts. By the end of 1941, some of them, including Melanie Klein, returned to London. This was after the fall of France and the evacuation of the British Army from Dunkirk and during the Battle of Britain fought by the Royal Air Force. At this time there were only four of Melanie Klein's associates, besides herself, who were recognized as training analysts: namely, Susan Isaacs, Joan Riviere, D. W. Winnicott, and John Rickman. When Melanie Klein and her associates were again able to attend more regularly, discussions became more acrimonious, and consequently, as the atmosphere in Scientific Meetings became increasingly unpleasant, members became concerned about what was happening to the Society.

Strachey, who was then Editor of the *International Journal of Psycho-Analysis* and Secretary of the Training Committee, was becoming impatient with the wrangling over scientific differences,[10] and he seldom came to Society meetings. His attitude, however, was vividly expressed in the following letter which he wrote to Edward Glover, Chairman of the Training Committee, on 23 April 1940:

Dear Glover,

I'm celebrating the arrival of spring in bed with a some sort of feverish cold – so I'm afraid there's no chance of my getting to London for the Training Committee tomorrow. I should rather like you to know (for your personal information) that – if it comes to a show-down – I'm very strongly in favour of compromise at all costs. The trouble seems to me to be with extremism, on both sides. My own view is that Mrs K. has made some highly important contributions to PA, but that it's absurd to make out (a) that they cover the whole subject or (b) that their validity is axiomatic. On the other hand I think it's equally ludicrous for Miss F. to maintain that PA is a Game Reserve belonging to the F. family and that Mrs K's ideas are totally subversive.

These attitudes on both sides are of course purely religious and the very antithesis of science. They are also (on both sides) infused by, I believe, a desire to dominate the situation and in particular the future – which is why both sides lay so much stress on the training of candidates; actually, of course, it's a megalomaniac mirage to suppose that you can control the opinions of people you analyse beyond a very limited point. But in any case it ought naturally to be the aim of a training analysis to put the trainee into a position to arrive at his own decisions upon moot points – not to stuff him with your own private dogmas.

In fact I feel like Mercutio about it. Why should these wretched fascists and (bloody foreigners) communists invade our peaceful compromising island? – But I see I'm more feverish than I'd thought. Anyhow, I feel that any suggestion of a 'split' in the society ought to be condemned and resisted to the utmost.

Yours sincerely,
James Strachey
(Archives of the British Psycho-Analytical Society)

The disagreements with Kleinian theories were not the only source of friction. Feelings were running strong for and against the need for a revision of the constitution in favour of limiting tenure of offices and the possibility of holding multiple offices in the Society. That is: Who was to have power in the Society and how was that power to be used? But was it fair to change the rules of the Society during wartime when many Members could not participate in the discussions and voting? As I mentioned earlier, certain Members of the Society had long been critical of the behaviour of both Jones and Glover in their handling of the public relations of the Society. On 5 November 1941 the Society discussed a paper by Barbara Low on 'The Psycho-Analytic Society and the Public' (Low 1941).[11] The topics raised caused so much interest that discussion of the paper went on for three Scientific Meetings, and became very heated. Sylvia Payne was particularly upset by what was happening and wrote to Melanie Klein on 20 November 1941 about it (Section 2, Chapter 1: p. 260). At these meetings the Members must have brought up all their complaints about how the Society was run, its poor relations with other professional bodies, as well as their disquiet over the scientific differences and what was to be regarded as approved psychoanalytic theory. During the third discussion on

17 December 1941, Rickman[12] lost his temper, attacking the officers of the Society for their rudeness to the public and their lack of capacity to respond to the needs of the wider community.

Following these Scientific Meetings, four members (Barbara Low, Melitta Schmideberg, and Adrian and Karin Stephen) demanded that the Council call an Extraordinary Business Meeting to discuss the state of affairs in the Society. This meeting was fixed for 25 February 1942, and Members were asked to send in any other resolutions on topics which they wanted discussed by 5 February 1942. The Council received sixteen resolutions dealing with different aspects of Members' disquiet (see Chapter 2).

Many of the resolutions embodied anxiety concerning the discrepancy between Melanie Klein's approach to psychoanalysis and what they referred to as 'Freudian psychoanalysis', and the consequent anxiety that students and the public should be exposed to her theories which they felt were in many ways alien to their understanding of psychoanalysis. Other resolutions were concerned with the appointment of officers and training analysts, and the anxiety lest the control of the Society should fall into the hands of one side or the other. It was feared by some that Glover, who had become deputy to Jones (who had been President since 1919), was expecting to take his place for a similar period of time, and then he would be in a more powerful position to oppose the Kleinians. Others were unhappy about the proselytizing which they felt the Kleinians were engaged in through their supervisions, private seminars, and re-analysis of analysts. They felt that those in re-analysis with a Kleinian would not be capable of the necessary independence of mind which should be shown by office-holders and training analysts.

These resolutions made it clear to Melanie Klein and her colleagues that some Members of the Society would like to remove her from it, or at least to prevent her work from being taught to candidates. She decided that her group would have to take these attacks seriously, and she wrote to Joan Riviere asking her to organize the contributions of her colleagues. Joan Riviere replied:

I think I can do what you suggest, that is, if people will consent to be 'organised'. There is a difficulty that two people are my patients, which you must remember. Also I suppose Rickman might resent my being asked to take a lead. In any case I suggest *you* write to Dr Rickman and ask him to put his contribution on paper as fully as possible and send it on (to me), so that we can consider it along with other people's. And will you write to my two patients?[13]

34

Melanie Klein then wrote to members of her group.

3rd January 1942

Dear ———

In order to save time I am sending this letter to those of our group with whom I have had no opportunity to talk on the following matter. After the last meeting, I came to the conclusion that if we are to have any success in whatever we undertake against such a skilful person as Glover, we should organise our efforts – all the more as the time at our disposal at the General Meeting will necessarily be restricted. I asked Mrs Riviere whether she would undertake to co-ordinate our contributions by suggesting, if necessary, alterations, in order to avoid overlapping and unnecessary repetitions. She agreed to do so. (I think it would be best if it were not known by outsiders that she is doing this.) If you intend to say anything at the General Meeting, would you agree to the pooling of our resources in this way? If so, would you please put down your intended contribution as fully as possible, and also as soon as possible, and send it to Mrs Riviere.[14]

The Council met to consider these resolutions, and the Chairman, Ernest Jones, classified them under four different headings, in order to simplify the discussion of them. The next seven chapters cover the accounts of the discussion of these resolutions, and other issues that arose from consideration of the original resolutions. Chapter 7 contains information referred to during the discussions, together with extracts from the AGM at which members decided what practical action to take in order to deal with the issues and anxieties discussed during the previous five meetings, while Chapter 8 covers the discussions as to how to explore the scientific differences.

Notes

1 In fact, Freud's psychoanalytical writings were first reported in Britain in 1883 by F. W. H. Myers at a general meeting of the Society for Psychical Research, which was later published in its proceedings. That was the first time that Freud's psychoanalytical ideas were available in English, and it is interesting to note that it was while attending meetings of this society that both Joan Riviere and James Strachey came across psychoanalysis. It seems to have been a society concerned with exploring the unknown, and as such was a good stepping-stone to psychoanalysis. Indeed, Freud himself eventually became an honorary member.

2 I am indebted to David Tuckett for drawing my attention to the parallel moves that were taking place with other medical specialities – for example, anaesthetics.

3 This was the international body of psychoanalysts responsible initially for organizing scientific congresses, but later it developed an important role in relation to regulating and monitoring the training of candidates in the different component societies that were affiliated to it.

4 Klein's influence on Alix Strachey is vividly recorded in the correspondence between her and James Strachey published in *Bloomsbury/Freud – The Letters of James and Alix Strachey 1924 to 1925*, edited by P. Meisel and W. Kendrick, London: Chatto & Windus, 1987.

5 In this book Anna Freud describes her approach to 'children's analysis' and her technique, and she formulates the theoretical basis for the point of view that she adopts. In the course of doing so, she compares her approach to that of Melanie Klein. From this book it is clear that Anna Freud had carefully considered Klein's contributions, and she did not always disagree with them.

6 Freud expressed his disapproval to Jones for publishing the contributions to this discussion in the *IJPA* as a 'Symposium on Child Analysis' in his correspondence with him. He interpreted it as an attack on his daughter, Anna.

7 Unfortunately, it has not been possible to discover a copy of this paper or a reference to it.

8 From remarks quoted by Steiner from Jones's correspondence with Klein (p. 229), Jones either did not know about Rickman's activities or disapproved of them.

9 Eventually, some years later, it was agreed that those members elected by the Society to the *Council*, should be elected *en bloc* as the *Board*, at the AGM of the Institute of Psycho-Analysis.

10 In fact, a careful study of those who attended the ten Discussions of Scientific Controversies revealed that he only took part in one of them, even though he was elected as a member of the committee of three charged with organizing them. The main part of this work was done by Marjorie Brierley, and the meetings were chaired initially by Glover and later by Sylvia Payne.

11 I have never been able to trace this paper, but its contents are summarized by Barbara Low during the later discussions.

12 Rickman apologized for his behaviour during the Extraordinary Business Meeting on 25 Feb. 1942 (p. 43).

13 Melanie Klein Archives. The Wellcome Institute, London.

14 Ibid.

2

Resolutions and the First Extraordinary Business Meeting

An EXTRAORDINARY MEETING called by four Members (Miss Barbara Low, Mrs Melitta Schmideberg, Drs Adrian and Karin Stephen) will be held on Wednesday, February 25th, 1942, at 1.30 p.m., 96 Gloucester Place, London, W.1.

Agenda

1. The following resolutions have been received from Members for discussion at the meeting. They are placed on the agenda in alphabetical order of the proposers' names.

Resolution A – Dr Dennis Carroll

(1) That the status quo be preserved until absent Members are able to resume their contact with the Society.
(2) That, if changes are considered desirable at the present time by the meeting on February 25th, a decision should not be taken about them until there has been a preliminary discussion of the scientific aims and methods of the Society, and that such discussions should be so arranged that the absent members could communicate their views by post.

Resolution B – Dr Kate Friedlander

That no alteration in the constitution be made until Members at present on war service, etc., are able to take free part again in Society discussions and to co-operate in Society activities.

Resolution C – Miss I. P. Grant Duff

(1) That no alteration be made in the constitution of the British Psycho-Analytical Society until such time as the war emergency conditions have passed, or until such time as all Members are, once more, able to take an active part in the affairs of the Society.

I have the following reasons for this resolution:

(a) Many of our Members are absent and therefore unable to take part in the discussions or in the voting. This makes it impossible to know whether any suggested change is the wish of the majority of our Members or only of a small clique.

(b) The alteration suggested on the meeting on December 17th, 1941, is bad in itself for it replaces elasticity with rigidity. It seems saner at any given time to be able to keep or change officers as we see fit than to be bound by law to change them whether it is desirable or not.

(c) That Members of this Society have a right to demand a certain standard of manners in their meetings, but the promoters of a change in our constitution behaved in a manner so impolite as to be an insult to all their fellow Members. I hold therefore that we refuse any change in our constitution to show our detestation of such behaviour. I think this protest to be important, for such behaviour is not only a wrong done to all the Members of the Society but injures the science for which we stand. This would not be so in a rational world but human beings are not rational.

For these reasons I urge that there be no change in our constitution until the war emergency has passed or until such time as all our Members are once more able to take an active part in the affairs of the Society.

(2) I move further that as agreed at the beginning of the war we retain our present office bearers until the war emergency has passed or until such time as all our Members are once more able to take an active part in the affairs of the Society, for whereas many of our Members have, for one reason or another, left London, our present office bearers, blitz or no blitz, have been in London to carry on the work of the Society and we can be certain of their remaining at the post to look after our affairs, whatever may occur.

Resolution D – Proposed by Mrs Susan Isaacs, seconded by Mrs Riviere

That in order to carry out more effectively the purpose of the International Psychoanalytical Association as set out in Statute 3, and

in particular 'the mutual support of the members in all endeavours to acquire and disseminate innate psychoanalytical knowledge', the following alterations and additions to the rules of the British Psycho-Analytical Association are desirable:
(a) Rule to be added:

'The activities of the Society shall be the general responsibility of the body of Members as a whole and the Council and officers of the Society shall be answerable to the whole membership for any decision or action taken by them.'

(b) Alteration in Rule 5:

Subject to the provisos contained in (a) above the affairs of the Society shall be conducted by a Council consisting of the President, the four honorary secretaries (Scientific, Training, Business, and External Affairs), Honorary Treasurer, and three other Members who shall be elected annually in July. Except in the case of the Treasurer, no person shall hold office for more than two years or be eligible for election to that or any other office for a period of two years after his term of office expires; and no person shall hold more than one office at a time.

Resolution E – Miss Barbara Low

(1) That *prior to* a discussion of the creation of a sub-committee (or of any other body) for the reconstruction or revision of the constitution and administration of the Society and Institute, the Society shall discuss the question of sectional differences in the views of Members and how such differences affect the basic purpose of the Psycho-Analytic Institute and Society, which is (according to Rule 2) to further and apply Freud's scientific theories.
(2) Failing the acceptance of this resolution, that a Sub-Committee be created to put forward proposals for reconstruction in the following directions:
(a) In reference to tenure of office for officers and members of the Council, Training Committee, and of any other existing Committee, or of any Committee which may in the future be created.
(b) In reference to training and control analysts and the uniformity of theory conveyed by them.
(c) In reference to the relations and activities to be developed by the Institute and Society on the one hand and the public on the other

(e.g., in the spheres of publicity work, press work, public lectures and study groups, admittance to Society meetings, etc.).

Resolution F – Proposed by Dr John Rickman, seconded by Dr Paula Heimann

That a reconsideration of the policy of the Society in its relation to other scientific bodies and to the public generally having become desirable a committee and secretary for co-ordination of external affairs be appointed.

Resolution G – Dr Melitta Schmideberg

(1) That prior to any consideration of resolutions dealing with the constitution of the Society
(a) it be discussed whether or not it interferes with the necessary independence of mind of the office bearers and training analysts to be themselves in the process of undergoing analysis and control analysis.
(b) Whether or not existing methods of training, official and unofficial, create undue dependence and intimidation, further the formation of cliques, and so lead to a tendentious use of administrative or training posts in the Society.
(2) That a formal protest be recorded against the unparliamentary methods of discussion employed by certain Members in the meeting on December 17th, 1941, and the Chairman be requested to make use of his powers.

Resolution H – Mr Walter Schmideberg

That before any resolutions dealing with the administration and activities of the Society are considered,
(a) It be reaffirmed that the aim of the Society is to further Freudian psychoanalysis,
(b) The meeting discuss the method of dealing with deviation from the fundamental principles of Freudian psychoanalysis.
(c) It be laid down that the teaching of candidates and the instruction of the lay public under the auspices of the Institute be in accordance with the principles of Freudian psychoanalysis; that Members giving public lectures in an official or unofficial capacity should make it

40

clear that issues on which the Psycho-Analytic Society has not reached a conclusion are controversial issues and not part of the accepted theory of Freudian psychoanalysis.

(d) That those responsible for publications under the auspices of the Institute or Society should reject manuscripts the content of which is in any important respect counter to the principles of Freudian psychoanalysis, and see that in case of controversial views being expressed in any publication this fact is made clear to the reader by the author, editor, or both.

Resolution J – Dr Adrian Stephen

That it is desirable that the rules of the Society be so altered that the continual re-election to office (other than the office of Honorary Treasurer) is rendered impossible.

Resolution K – Proposed by Dr D. W. Winnicott, seconded by Mrs Melanie Klein

That this Society should reaffirm its aims as set forth in Statute 3 of International Psychoanalytical Association.

VOTES ON THESE RESOLUTIONS can be sent by post to arrive on the day of the Extraordinary Meeting, and appropriate ballot sheets are enclosed. Members attending the meeting must bring their ballot sheets with them as duplicates cannot be supplied owing to paper shortage.

2. Election to Associate Membership of Miss Elizabeth Schwarz

(signed) SYLVIA M. PAYNE
Acting Business Secretary

Resolutions classified by the Chairman

A *Resolution arising out of minutes*
   Protest about behaviour. M.S. (G.D.)

B *Resolution to leave rules unaltered until*
 I Normal activity can be resumed. D.C., G.D., K.F.

II. After discussion of
    1. Scientific aims and methods.   D.C.
    2. Scientific differences.   B.L.
    3. Presentation of 'Freudian psychoanalysis'.   W.S.
    4. Aims of Society.   D.W.W.
    5. Analysis of office bearers and training analysts.   M.S.
    6. Certain alleged effects of training methods.   M.S.

C   *Resolution to institute Committee to explore questions of:*
    1. Tenure of office.
    2. Training differences
    3. Public affairs.   B.L.

D   *Resolutions proposing immediate changes in rules*
    1. Tenure of office.   S.I., A.S.
    2. External Committee and Secretary.   J.R.
    3. External Secretary on Council.   S.I.
    4. Responsibility.   S.I.

Minutes of Extraordinary Meeting
on [Wednesday] February 25th, 1942, at 1.30 p.m.
at 96 Gloucester Place, London, W.1.

Dr Jones was in the Chair and 29 members were present (Dr Glover, Dr Rickman, Miss Sharpe, Dr Isaacs, Mrs Klein, Drs Heimann, Gillespie, Wilson, Steiner, Weiss, M. and W. Schmideberg, A. and K. Stephen, Miss Low, Mrs Burlingham, Miss Freud, Drs Herford, Friedlander, Franklin, Haas, Winnicott, Lantos, Thorner, Dr W. and Mrs Hoffer, Mrs Ruben).

One guest was present (Dr Macdonald).

DR JONES opened the meeting and said that he wished first to determine the status of this meeting.[1] It was called by the Business Secretary an Extraordinary Meeting but this was not his opinion at all. It should rank as a Business Meeting, because it differs from such only inasmuch as it was not called by the Council spontaneously but by request of some members. The Chairman also refers to the rules and states that an alteration had been made in the rules which was not included in the duplicated copies of the rules as sent to the Members. The question whether this is an Extraordinary Meeting or a Business Meeting also involves the question whether this meeting has power to alter rules.

DR ADRIAN STEPHEN stated that this was notified to the members as an Extraordinary Meeting. He would have behaved differently had he thought that it was a Business Meeting. Members would have brought forward different proposals. (After some discussion) Dr Stephen suggests that it would be quite impossible to discuss the whole lot of proposals and that the discussion should be confined to those proposed by the conveners of the meeting.[2]

DR JONES summed up that the meeting was convened as an Extraordinary Meeting. Has it the powers of a Business Meeting or has it not? My ruling is it has the powers.

DR M. SCHMIDEBERG: At the annual general meeting there is never any time for this.

MISS LOW: If this meeting has the power to alter the rules, could we agree to discuss alterations but leave it for a later time.

DR ADRIAN STEPHEN: Some of the resolutions have no relation at all with the matters in question. I suppose Rule 22 does say that a meeting of this kind does not permit alteration of rules.

DR JONES then summed up the discussion asking the members to decide whether this meeting was a Scientific or a Business Meeting, i.e., an Extraordinary Meeting or an Extraordinary Business Meeting. Votes were taken and it was decided that it was to be considered an Extraordinary Business Meeting.

DR RICKMAN: Before we proceed I wish to make a statement. It is obvious that at the last meeting I lost my temper.[3] I was angry. I do not apologize for my anger to which I have a right, to which everybody has a right. But I do apologize for the words I used, to the Directors and to the members of the Society.

The Chairman then communicated to the members that Drs Payne and Brierley apologized for not being able to be present owing to illness and that Miss Sheehan-Dare could not be present owing to having broken her arm.

The minutes of the last Annual General Meeting were read by Dr Glover and passed.

DR JONES then stated that of the twenty or so resolutions sent in some are identical or at least overlap, some are ambiguous and need further definition, that he had therefore taken the liberty of grouping them and would pass copies to the members. It would be wasteful to pass the resolutions in their alphabetical order.

DR ADRIAN STEPHEN: We could only hold an Extraordinary Meeting under Rule 14d. Dr S. proposed then that the four members who convened the meeting should state the special business for which the meeting was required and stated that he had no desire to shut out other contributors at other times. In fact he was in favour of some of the other resolutions, but they should be discussed at some other time.

DR JONES: That seems sense, I agree to that. Of course, everyone has a right to speak on this topic and to send resolutions. The question is, have any resolutions been sent in that are not on the matter in question?

DR ADRIAN STEPHEN: The great difference is that none of the proposals made by the conveners propose change of rules. I have proposed 'that it is desirable that the Rules of the Society be so altered that the continual re-election to office . . . is rendered impossible'. This resolution is simply stating the opinion of the majority of the members present.

MISS LOW: I have made no suggestion for alteration of rules. I suggested 'that a Sub-Committee be created to put forward proposals for reconstruction' and 'to discuss the question of alteration of rules'. The last thing in the world of which I thought would be immediate change of rules.

DR KARIN STEPHEN stated that she did not send in any resolution because she had not received the notice asking members to do so.[4] She strongly seconded the idea that the meeting should confine themselves to the points raised by Miss Low, Adrian Stephen, and Melitta Schmideberg.

DR JONES put the question whether any one had sent in a resolution not bearing on the subject.

DR ADRIAN STEPHEN: For instance Resolution H (Walter Schmideberg). It is about what is and what is not Freudian psychoanalysis. This is hardly covered by the promoters' subject.

DR JONES: In his opinion (W. Schmideberg's) this ought to be discussed prior to any discussion on other matters.

DR ADRIAN STEPHEN: Cannot agree to this. As well one could propose to discuss the distance of the earth from the sun.

DR MELITTA SCHMIDEBERG suggested saving time by starting the discussion at once.

MISS LOW: One last word. This meeting comes out of the previous discussions and my statement at the first meeting, I feel it would be more sensible if the promoters could say their say first and then the others. We shan't finish today anyhow and we would like to hear everybody's opinion. Therefore I suggest that the promoters should make their statements first and then everybody in his turn.

44

This was agreed upon. The Chairman thereupon called on Miss Low to make her statement.

MISS LOW: I ask for two things. Not to attempt to conclude any discussion today or to vote. Absent people will not have a chance of knowing what is going on or of speaking their opinion. We ought to defer any voting until we finish our discussion. It might be one month or two months, but there is no point in a hasty voting. I just want to say that when I first spoke, I brought forward only one of the resolutions, a narrower one, about the relations of the Psycho-Analytic Society to the public, I thought then and said that these were very dependent on the inner situation of the Society. I now say, though I do not want in any way anyone to think that I want to withdraw my previous statement, I now want to say why I have put in the first part of my resolution 'that prior to . . . the Society shall discuss the question of sectional differences'. I am a great believer that machinery can do a lot. If we had a much more democratic machinery so that we could employ all the powers of all the members it would be a fruitful state of affairs.

It is obvious that there are some vital scientific differences which do affect what the Society is out to do. When I referred to Rule II of the International Statutes, that our aim is to promote Freud's theories, one member said to me 'I entirely disagree'. That set me thinking very much. Of course we cannot reach complete scientific unanimity, but can we not have a minimum sort of basis on which we could unite: what can we give the public, how to train our candidates, etc. I give the example of the Fabian Society, which includes various parties on a minimum programme as, for instance, nationalization of land and capital. We want to find out: can we agree on this minimum amount? I believe from what happened at Dr Brierley's paper[5] at the last meeting that there is a great desire for this unity [Brierley 1942: 107–112]. It should be possible to translate the different opinions into a common language. This seems to me a profound matter and therefore I should wish this to be considered first.

DR SCHMIDEBERG, asked by the Chairman to make her preliminary statement, says that she does not wish to do so now.

MISS LOW: (Paper) [This is not what she said, she produced it next day. S.M.P.] Some members present may remember that when I made the first statement on November 5th from which the subsequent discussions followed during November and December, I chose the title 'The Psycho-Analytical Society and the Public', but I pointed out even then that our unsatisfactory relation to the public was an outcome, to a large extent, of our unsatisfactory internal relationships. I urged the creation of a better constitution which would help to remedy some of our internal difficulties and thus enable us to present a more united front to the outside world.

Much water has run under the bridges since first I raised the problem, and the ensuing discussions have revealed most convincingly great differences in scientific views and very strange personal emotions which make co-operative work of the utmost difficulty. Therefore I have added to my original resolution on the Agenda, which deals with a 'Reconstruction Committee' for our constitution and general mechanism, another resolution dealing with the question of the scientific outlook of the members.[6] As I propose to deal with both these resolutions in detail when it is my turn to speak to the agenda, I want now only to make a few general points. Although I have put down first, as a priority resolution, the one dealing with scientific differences in outlook, I should not wish it to be assumed that I minimize in any way my original resolution in reference to a reconstructed resolution. Indeed, I now feel that the most necessary thing is that two sub-committees should be created, working side by side, to hammer out with patience and effort, on the one hand the best constitution we can evolve, on the other, some common theory for scientific work to which all members can subscribe.

What is it we need to aim at, to begin with the last-mentioned task? First, surely, to keep steadily in mind that this Society and Institute, as laid down in our statutes, exists to investigate, apply, and spread the truths of psychoanalysis. This does not imply a slavish or static attitude, a blind clinging to every statement found in Freud's own writings, a hostility to new developments arising from his work. No one in the world would be more opposed to such an attitude than Freud himself: every great man is worthy of, and deserves, intelligent followers, to say the least.

But there must be a common basis from which all members start, and to which they refer for test-values and there must not be introduced ideas in opposition to this basic theory, which yet continue to call themselves part of the psychoanalytic theory. We must aim at an approach to a scientific attitude, which I take to mean as much objectivity as possible, trust in each other's integrity, in scientific work, and a willingness to listen to new ideas. We might take as our motto the maxim of that great scientist who said: 'Accept rarely; listen and investigate endlessly.'

Turning to my second resolution, dealing with a re-constructed constitution, I should like to point out now only in what ways our present machinery is greatly inadequate. We have a constitution

46

which deprives the mass of the members of any opportunity to make use of their powers and gifts in the Society, which is run by a small group in respect to most of its affairs. The Council and other Committees consist of the same officers year after year,[7] so that fresh ideas get no hearing, and the true function of the Council is not carried out, namely the suggesting of ideas and plans to lay before the members for discussion. Instead of that, the Council repeatedly makes decisions and effects plans over the heads of the members, which leads to feelings of frustration and resentment, and these create cliques and rivalries. A truly democratic constitution, affording to each member good scope for his other abilities, would do much to remove and prevent the painful personal emotions which have been violently displayed during our recent discussions. Psychoanalysts are still pioneers in a relatively hostile or indifferent world. If we care genuinely to spread its truths, surely we shall be willing to close our own ranks, to sink some of our personal differences and prejudices and so earn the confidence of the public.

DR KARIN STEPHEN: (Paper) Without urging the hasty passing of resolutions at the present moment, especially while our members are scattered owing to the war, I should like to speak briefly on two points.

(1) On the reasons why I feel our present system of re-electing the same people to office over and over again is unsatisfactory,

(2) On the need for a careful investigation into our system of training in analysis. I think it is clear to all of us that our Society is in an unhealthy condition and has been for years. This, I believe, is in part due to the practice of re-electing the same officers year after year so that although a change in this could not, by itself, be expected to put everything right, it is a change which we shall need to make.

The objection to the practice is that it concentrates too much power in the hands of one or two people, and excludes the rest of the members from participating in the Society's affairs. This is bad both for the officers and for the members themselves and perhaps the worst feature is that it produces an atmosphere which stifles independent thought, not only over practical but also over scientific matters.

I cannot agree with Miss Grant Duff's objection that the proposed change would be undesirable because it would substitute a rigid for an elastic system of election. It is the experience of every organization that, unless the rules definitely preclude members from standing for re-election, there is an almost inevitable tendency for the same people to be elected over and over again. The elasticity is only in theory, in practice there is the most complete rigidity. This

47

certainly has been our experience, and the result has been the establishment, in practice, of permanent officials. Permanent officeholders easily become autocratic and tend more and more to find it a nuisance to consult the members on what they do in the name of the Society, so that gradually members lose contact with the Society's affairs and have no means of knowing or controlling what is done in their name.

There is also another grave objection: intimidation. This is exercised, wittingly or unwittingly, in various ways. Those who become entrenched in power are apt to grow contemptuous of and condescending to the rest of the members and this always arouses resentment. Resentment leads either to intimidation or else to non-cooperation. In the end it usually results in open revolt, with ill-will on both sides. Our Society has suffered for years under the first phase, intimidation and non-cooperation; we are now witnessing the second phase, open revolt and ill-will, which requires courage, independence and a free exchange of ideas. Both are fatal to creative work. By redistributing and reducing the concentration of power the proposed changes might end the existing causes of friction and create a better atmosphere for real scientific work. But resentment in a state of helplessness has not been the only reason for intimidation; there have also been more practical reasons for it: I mean economic dependence, which is another bad effect of the concentration of power in one or two hands. The inevitable result of this is that those who wield the power come to be regarded by the public as the sole official representatives of the Society and therefore have in their hands the distribution of the vast majority of the cases who apply for psychoanalytic treatment. Members who depend on having cases passed on to them cannot afford to make themselves unpopular with those on whom their livelihood depends, either by criticism or even by vigorous independent thinking.

The proposal to change our habits of re-electing members to office seems to be a practical way of beginning to remedy this humiliating and crippling state of affairs, which undoubtedly exists at present. By distributing power it should have good effects in reducing intimidation, and by enabling many members to take a share in the management of the Society's affairs and know what they are and how they are conducted, it should do something to revive their interest and to prevent the public from identifying psychoanalysis with one or two figure-heads. It should also make it possible for members who have ability to exercise this ability, and it might do something to draw them together into a more united body of co-workers.

I am not overlooking the obvious fact that disagreements both personal and scientific exist among us, but I have some hope that, in a franker and more healthy atmosphere, members may come to see the advisability of fighting out their personal quarrels in private, and that scientific divergences of opinion, perseveringly thrashed out among us, may lead rather to an advance in our understanding of our subject than to rifts and the opposition of hostile camps. I deplore the tendency to blind orthodoxy expressed in some of the resolutions, and I think no one would have deplored them more than Freud himself. Our concern is with the understanding of the complicated problems of human nature itself, in health and in disease, on which Freud was the first to throw any real light, but our object should be to follow him not in blind faith, but in his own devotion to the truth, the whole truth, and nothing but the truth.

It would be foolish to pretend that our Society is at present doing much valuable work in this pursuit of truth, but I still hope that, if we can rid ourselves of intimidation, we may yet contribute usefully to science.

The reform of our constitution, though necessary some time or other, will not alone, however, put us on our feet. We are, I think, suffering from other evils which are more difficult to remedy but which must be tackled if we are to function properly. One of these is touched on in Dr Schmideberg's resolution dealing with our present training arrangements.

It is unsatisfactory in the extreme that so many members should be in the patient–analyst relation with one another over periods of years and years. Straightforward adult equality relations, such as should hold between fellow scientists, are hardly possible in these circumstances, and if it is true, as was stated at one of our previous meetings, that members and candidates who are being analysed cannot always be sure that their analysts will respect their confidence, the position is even more impossible still, and it suggests that the choice of training analysts has not been a happy one.

It is not easy to see how this bad state of affairs is to be remedied, but the really appalling and ever increasing length of our training analyses suggests that there is something wrong with our present system of training, and this means that there is something wrong with our way of conducting analysis, or else with the selection of candidates or possibly with both these. Training analyses go on interminably. Why is this? Are training analysts finding that their methods are not producing the results they aim at? The views of members on how analysis really achieves its aims, when it does do this, are seldom heard. I do not believe that we have devoted a meeting to this question since James Strachey [Strachey 1934] a very long time ago now, read his paper on 'Mutative Interpretation' which, interesting though it may have been, can hardly be taken as entirely conclusive. Why is this vital question not discussed oftener? Do we really not know what we are doing?

There is, to my mind, no doubt whatever that analysis is capable of being used efficiently as a therapeutic instrument, given the right sort of analyst and the right sort of cases, but I have grave doubts whether the methods employed and passed on in training by our Society are entirely on the right lines; I have heard it said by some of our members that psychoanalysis may not be a good therapeutic method, but that its practice is justified by its value as a method of research. I do not know how many there are who hold this view, but it must put them in an intolerably false position if they go on accepting patients for treatment, since patients do not come to be investigated for research purposes but to be treated for and relieved of illness. Moreover, if this view is true, what about a training analysis whose whole object is to produce the modifications in the candidate's personality which are essential to fit him to be an analyst himself?

I do not know to what extent the Training Committee is satisfied with the way in which training is working out: I know that some are uneasy about it. We insist at present on candidates undergoing these long training analyses and claim that by this means their personalities can be so modified as to fit them to become good analysts in the majority of cases. The first thing we need is a perfectly frank pooling of our knowledge and experience to find out if this claim is substantiated in fact. I doubt whether, as things stand at present, anyone is in a position to say definitely whether it is or not.

I believe personally that, given the right sort of analyst, and the right sort of analysand, analysis can sometimes bring about changes in the personality which are extremely beneficial, but I do not know in what percent of cases this actually happens, nor can I pretend to be able to make more than a guess as to the exact way it happens, when it does happen, and still less to say exactly why it fails, when it does fail, nor which cases will succeed and which will fail, nor even to be at all sure of the extent of the success or failure until some considerable time after the end of the analysis. Perhaps others are clearer in their understanding of these things, perhaps many are equally in the dark. I think it is essential that the whole question should be gone into in order that we may decide how much we may justly claim, especially as regards this vital matter of training.

We are in no way to blame if we cannot do all that we should like to do, but we should be seriously to blame if we permitted any bluff or self-deception or shirking of the issue, since this would stand in the way of further advances in our knowledge and skill and mislead us over this central problem of how best to select and train the candidates who will join us in our work and carry it on in the future.

I do not agree with Dr Schmideberg that we should postpone dealing with the simpler problem of reforming our methods of election in order first to tackle these other more difficult questions, but I do suggest that we should devote a meeting or several meetings if necessary, at some future date, to a thorough discussion of the whole problem of training.

I also consider the third point raised by Miss Low dealing with the conduct of our external affairs to be important and to need thorough investigation by all our members, but others have taken this matter up and I will not go into it further myself now.

I should like now to support Miss Low's proposal to form groups to discuss the three questions of (1) change in our methods of electing our officers, (2) the problem of training, (3) the conduct of our external affairs.

I should suggest that at this meeting we do not elect committees but ask one person to be secretary to each of these three groups and invite all members who are interested to send in their views to the appropriate secretary. Also that all those who wish should be able to contribute to the costs, to have copies of these letters setting forth other people's views duplicated and circulated to them. In this way all members, including those who cannot attend meetings, will be able to exchange views and thrash out these problems, so that later, when the time is ripe, a fully considered decision on them can be taken by the whole society.

DR ADRIAN STEPHEN: I proposed that we should consider the desirability of making alterations in our rules on November 17th.[8] I might have based my proposals then on purely academic, theoretical, general grounds, because I think it is generally recognized that if office bearers go on year after year it becomes impossible to get a change, and the Society becomes run in a routine way and people become uninterested in the business because they don't understand it. As a matter of fact, I thought that if I did urge the change on general considerations I might get the answer, 'This is all very well, but all this doesn't apply to our Society – it is just abstract'. I therefore brought forward some quite definite instances of the way in which our affairs have suffered from our habit of re-electing the same officers. The greater part of my statements have not been met at all, and those that have been met have – well – hardly been met. As they have not been met I suppose one may take it that the charge

51

goes by default; that is, my remarks must be accepted as being true, and if they are true I think it necessarily follows that we are in a very deplorable state and some change in our constitution is desirable.

Several members have objected to my proposal,[9] saying that alterations in our constitution won't make any difference: really important is the scientific side of the work. This, I think, is confusion of thought. The Society exists for scientific work. The whole object of our constitution is to enable scientific work to be done as well as possible. Improvements of the constitution are therefore being brought forward in order to improve the conditions for scientific work. You can't divide the constitution from the scientific work as if they were in water-tight compartments. Of course, changes in the constitution won't, by themselves, do everything. Such changes are not irrelevant to our scientific work and are necessary if it is to prosper. Alterations of the constitution therefore should be considered as being of scientific importance.

DR SYLVIA PAYNE:[10] (Statement read by Miss Sharpe) I must apologize for being ill at this moment and I have asked Miss Sharpe to read this small contribution. The Society is faced with a crisis the result of which may affect the progress of the development of psychoanalysis for many years. I would therefore ask members not to be precipitate in making judgements and to remember that at the moment owing to the world crisis we are more liable to be biased by personal considerations than in peacetime.

I mean by this that I think that the intensity, not the origin, of the present crisis in the Society is partly dependent on the fear of economic insecurity brought about by the disintegration of members' private work and the fear of not being able to re-establish the work on which their livelihood depends.

I should call this a precipitating factor, not a first cause, and I think it concerns the attack on the constitution rather that what is much more serious, namely the feeling that incompatible opinions are held by certain groups of members.

It is important, however, because when economic fear is added to difference of scientific outlook all tolerance is liable to disappear and the struggle becomes principally one for power.

How can we avoid this menace? We can relieve the anxiety of some members by adopting certain safeguards in connection with our constitution, to ensure that the same members do not hold office too long. We can study the problem of our public relations.

The Society can be regarded as having passed through the first phase of its development which has been brought to a close by the semi-retirement of our first President who was a pioneer of

52

psychoanalysis in England, and who by his ability and determination founded the Society in days when psychoanalysis was looked at with disgust and suspicion. The end of this period also coincides with the death of Professor Freud,[11] the discoverer of psychoanalysis. Perhaps therefore it is not strange that a conflict should arise.

The important side of the crisis is that which arises from differences in opinion. I feel sure that we all hold the view that if progress is to continue, and if research is to be carried out in a scientific community, differences of opinion must be tolerated, and even welcomed. Freedom to have and to express different ideas is surely one of the alleged aims of democracy and is what we are now fighting for in the world war. It is said to be characteristic of the British that they do not regard those who hold different views as necessarily evil and dangerous. There are, however, basic principles which are common to all parties in a democracy and these are a safeguard against the exploitation of freedom by individuals. In a scientific society there must be basic scientific conceptions to form a foundation on which the work can be built up.

How often do the opponents of direct psychological research point out to us the difficulty of being objective in our work? It is true and I believe that we should all of us take care not to forget it.

Another fact which makes it extraordinarily hard sometimes to judge the scientific value of psychological work is that the scientific value cannot be estimated only by the therapeutic result. If we are honest we will recognize that great psychological changes have in the past been produced in the minds of individuals by other individuals who succeed by one means or another in inculcating a faith, belief, love of a God image or idea into the mind, and it does not matter whether the image or idea is scientifically valid or not as long as it is believed.

The basic conceptions of psychoanalysis were laid down by Professor Freud, and this Society and Institute were founded on them.

It might be said, Why should we limit our basic principles to those laid down by Freud? My answer to this is that we have in the past done so publicly and voluntarily, both by adherence to the International Psychoanalytical Association and by acclaiming our intention to the Committee set up by the British Medical Association,[12] who passed the resolution that only those analysts adhering to the conceptions of Freud had the right to call themselves psycho-analysts.

The basic conceptions of psychoanalysis are:

1 the concept of a dynamic psychology,

2 the existence of the unconscious,
3 the theory of instincts and of repression,
4 infantile sexuality,
5 the dynamic of the transference.

In my view all work which really recognizes and is built upon these conceptions has a right to be called psychoanalysis.

If we accept the concept of a dynamic psychology we cannot claim to explain the problems of all types of mental conflict by the insight into any one particular phase of psychological development.

If this is true, which I believe it is, I cannot see why people with a true scientific outlook should not work in the same society on different aspects of mental functioning, some relating to the most primitive phases of mental development, and others on more differentiated parts of the mind, conscious and unconscious. We know so little at present about the nature of cure. We are not able to sort out cases properly, and send the right case to the right person. We ought to be able to do so as everyone does not require the same approach to regain mental health.

The recent work on the unconscious oral aspect of psychological development initiated by Mrs Klein is of great value and is the road by which we should gain deeper knowledge into the earliest phases of ego development and into psychotic illness. When new work is added to old, especially when it includes therapy, there is often a tendency to think that past knowledge has been superseded, and it takes time for new knowledge to be put into relation to old. I think we are at the moment struggling with a problem of this kind. In my view the new work could and ought to be brought into a balanced relation with the old and if it is not it will be owing to undue claims and emotional factors in all of us. The work done by analysts working on what I will call classical lines stands for that which Freud himself practised and thought. It has given good results in the hands of good analysts, and it is obvious that work will be continued and extended on the same lines which have not been exhaustively studied or used. Considering the relatively small amount of work which has been done by psychoanalysts, it is surely premature to make big generalizations and attempt to exclude work which is in progress whether it concerns the earlier or later phases of ego development provided the basic fundamental conceptions are not lost sight of.

There are of course many controversial ideas which should be openly discussed without personal animosity. If no one is ever willing to cede an idea or modify a point of view I cannot see anything for the future but a blind striving for leadership.

54

I would suggest that in the next few months before the Annual Meeting is held that we make a scientific effort to find out first how much there is in common rather than search for differences. This investigation should include a discussion on technique, with special reference to the possibility in certain circumstances of direct interpretation, whether of unconscious phantasy or transference, taking over the character of a suggestion rather than of an analytical communication.

MISS SHARPE: (Remarks after reading Dr Payne's paper) I welcome Dr Payne's suggestion that before the next Annual General Meeting we should have scientific discussions – my own desire especially being that this Society should discuss its policy concerning the body of teaching that the Society considers essential.

Our training course has, as you know, been seriously and grievously interrupted during these war years and our students, those who remained in London, have had a thin fare.

But I think I can gather something of profit from this very fact, something that may be helpful in deliberations such as I suggest. My control work at least has been uninterrupted during the war years and I have had an opportunity of watching what tendencies arise when students are not having the advantages that lectures and discussions give of an all round presentation of p.a. science.

For the purposes of the seminars on 'Dream Analysis' I am now taking, I made a survey some weeks ago of my control work over the last three years – to find out how I could help the students most – what did they need? – what had been vital omissions, or errors in dealing with patients? due to this lack of an all-round presentation of p.a. When I made these notes for my own guidance I had no idea in my mind of communicating them to anyone else. But I think you might find them useful. I can put them in such a form as to safeguard individuals. My notes will reveal my own point of view concerning certain essentials of our training. The whole future of p.a. lies with our students. Nothing is as important as this part of our work.

I can give you accurate reports of these 'tendencies', as I call them, straws showing the drift of the currents, but that formulation of our policy concerning the essentials of our teaching should be accomplished by the pooling of all the wisdom and scientific integrity and far-sightedness that this Society possesses.

DR BRIERLEY: (Statement read by Dr Jones) The rules as they stand require the annual election of officers. It is therefore already open to the Society to change their officers every year or to prevent re-election for any number of years if a majority of members so desire. Members should exercise their powers of voting, their right to discuss, suggest and criticize to the full in the spirit of Statute III, favour any amount of discussion in preparation for peace conditions etc. that may be desired but do not regard this as a suitable time to make constitutional changes, because (a) all members cannot take part, (b) at any time before the end of the war emergencies may arise.

Wiser to leave conduct of affairs to the three people – Dr Glover, Dr Payne, Dr Macdonald, who have remained on the spot and given ample proof of their willingness and their ability to carry on under the most trying conditions.

DR JONES: It seems after what we have just heard that the themes of interest appear to centre on to two main matters and it is therefore open for you now to discuss these matters:

(1) whether the members consider it desirable to make certain changes in our constitution,
(2) whether it is desirable to have a thorough discussion of what some people call our scientific aims and methods, others scientific differences, others the aims of the Society, etc.

I think Dr Payne has summed them up when she speaks of considering in discussion how much common ground there is. Several resolutions centre on this. So we have two themes related to each other, as some members think that alteration of rules will help the scientific issue. I think we must have the opinion of the Society on this point, whether you prefer to discuss the change of rules first, or whether you prefer first of all to discuss the scientific issue.

MRS ISAACS: Most people consider that the rules exist for the purposes of furthering our scientific aims, so that I would urge that the views of those who hold that scientific difficulties could be settled before the rules are altered should not be heard.

Thereupon the Chairman asks Mrs Isaacs to make her statement.

DR SUSAN ISAACS. (Contribution; Paper) I wish to propose the following resolution: That in order to carry out more effectively the purpose of the IPA as set out in Statute III, and in particular 'the mutual support of the members in all endeavours to acquire and disseminate psychoanalytical knowledge', the following alterations and additions to the Rules of the BPA are desirable:
(a) Rule to be added:
'The activities of the Society shall be the general responsibility of the body of members as a whole, and the Council and Officers of the Society shall be answerable to the whole membership for any decision or action taken by them.'
(b) Alteration in Rule 5:

56

'Subject to the provisos contained in (a) above, the affairs of the Society shall be conducted by a Council consisting of the President, the four Honorary Secretaries (Scientific, Training, Business, and External Affairs), Honorary Treasurer and three other members, who shall be elected annually in July. Except in the case of the Treasurer, no person shall hold office for more than two years or be eligible for election to that or any other office for a period of two years after his term of office expires; and no person shall hold more than one office at a time.'

(I wish to say, before beginning, that the number of Honorary Secretaries – whether three or four – is not a special point of this particular resolution. This question is being raised under Resolution F. It makes no difference to the points I wish to submit.)

Let me remind you of Statute III: 'The aim of the Association is the cultivation and furtherance of the psychoanalytical branch of science founded by Freud, both as pure psychology and in its application to medicine and the mental sciences; further, the mutual support of the members in all endeavours to acquire and disseminate psychoanalytical knowledge.'

Thanks to Miss Low and others, some of the difficulties in the work of this Society in recent years have now been brought into the open.

We all know that in every scientific society questions of prestige or personal loyalty are apt to arise. The scientific aim is always clear; the degree to which it is attained always partial and relative.

It is particularly the tragedy of the Society that what Freud called 'the constitutional incapacity of men for scientific research' in the field of human psychology has shown itself so often amongst us, the psychoanalysts, as well.

But analysts could at least be expected to know that to achieve the aim of scientific disinterestedness depends upon certain conditions. Merely to assert our aim won't of itself carry us there. To exhort each other to put aside personal issues won't necessarily make this happen. Nor is it enough to label our own views 'scientific detachment'. Moreover, intellectual honesty is not represented by sitting on the fence, or passive 'waiting and seeing', at every stage of controversy.

A more active effort towards our goal of co-operating in scientific work is greatly needed.

No doubt many causes have contributed to bring about the present state of affairs. The difficulties which have arisen in the conduct of scientific matters (papers, discussions, and publications, etc.) are in part determined by our failures and mistakes in the conduct of the

Society as a whole. As has been fully brought out in the discussions, scientific collaboration cannot be free and effective if those taking part are suffering from acute personal emotions, some at least of which are bound up with dissatisfactions regarding the conduct of practical affairs in the Society.

But there are certain special difficulties inherent in the nature of our work, and it is my view that these inherent difficulties require that we should give far closer attention to the machinery of the Society, as creating the conditions for our scientific work, than has been realized.

First of all, there are those difficulties arising from the very special course of the transferences and counter-transferences among analysts and analysands in our members. We know that these transferences are more intense and troublesome, far harder to allow for in our judgements, than the influence of relationships such as teacher and pupil among other scientific workers. In other words, peculiarly strong ambivalent personal feelings are active in our company, quite inevitably; and I would point out that this in itself demands and justifies the most careful possible scrutiny of our formal relationships, the rules and regulations for the conduct of our practical and scientific business, in order to leave as little opportunity as possible for these feelings to affect our conduct.

Again, from the very nature of our training and our work, we are far more immediately aware of the existence of unconscious feelings and purposes, of the whole network of underlying personal responses, expressed in the form and manner of our contributions and discussions, than other scientific workers are. In other words, we see unconscious impulses at work in each other much more quickly than non-analysts would do. This is true of all of us, and quite mutual. The ordinary social mechanisms of denial, isolation, displacement, etc., do not function automatically between us. How could we expect them to do so? We are people who have learnt to recognize these things.

Now we all agree that we have no right to turn deliberately to interpretations of unconscious motive in our colleagues, as a weapon of controversy. There is no need to point out that it is a weapon with two edges. But it is no less incumbent upon us as analysts to recognize that in fact we cannot help being more readily affected by our mutual awareness of unconscious motives, than, say, physicists and chemists are. Our scientific honesty as analysts requires us to acknowledge that this is apt to occur. We do not attain scientific detachment or disinterestedness by denying these facts. We have to learn to reckon with and allow for this influence in ourselves and

58

others, to be aware of it as a part of our total relationships to our colleagues, whilst exercising a self-denying ordinance with regard to its deliberate use.

But I must add that the fact that we may not analyse each other aloud does not mean that we give up the right to measure the actual behaviour of ourselves and our colleagues, when taking part in controversy, by the ordinary human standards of decency, fairness, and honesty.

Another source of difficulty in our work, which I believe to be profoundly important, may seem at first sight paradoxical. It is that we in this Society do in fact impose upon ourselves implicitly a higher standard of controversy and scientific discussion than many other, perhaps than most other societies. Just because we are more alive to the pull of the unconscious, because we claim to understand and in some measure are able to understand the distorting influence of unconscious attitudes, because we cannot hoodwink ourselves quite so easily as those whose work is not concerned with human motives, we are more deeply distressed by bias and unscrupulousness when we become aware of these in ourselves and our colleagues. We very often do not know what to do about it, but we feel it.

Our very sensitivity to the hidden sources of bias thus leads us to be intolerant of our errors and to adopt a perfectionist standard of controversy which contributes quite as much to hamper discussions, as do the loyalties and rivalries which lead to fear of differing from important people, and so on.

We feel we ought to be better in these respects because we see how much we fail; and this paradoxical but familiar fact tends to make us worse.

Doubtless there are other inherent sources of difficulty in our work. Since we cannot altogether get rid of these influences, can we not at least find ways of limiting and controlling them?

Let me come to practical proposals:

If our aim, the justification of our existence as a society, be the cultivation and furtherance of psychoanalytic science, and the mutual support of members in all endeavours to acquire and disseminate psychoanalytic knowledge, then it seems clear that our rules and constitution, the framework of our collaboration, should be such as to give the maximum safeguard against personal feelings, whether these spring from the relationships of analyst and analysand, control analyst and pupil, or from ordinary attractions and rivalries.

One of the first essentials here is surely to recognize that the officers and council of the Society are to be regarded as the servants of the Society, not its rulers. The present wording of Rule 5, 'That the management of the Society shall be in the hands of', seems to me entirely contrary to the aim of Statute III, 'the mutual support of members'. I suggest this wording should be altered to 'The affairs shall be conducted by'.

But there is need for an explicit recognition of the responsibility of members as a whole, since only in this way can every member feel that he is expected to take an active interest in the affairs of the Society, whether these are the relation of psychoanalytic science to other sciences and the public, or to internal matters affecting the conduct of scientific discussions, the training of future analysts – and other points which so closely affect the preservation and furtherance of the essentials of psychoanalytic science founded by Freud.

It is quite useless to expect scientific freedom of thought and expression, a sense of active collaboration for these ends, among the younger or less prominent members, unless they feel they have a responsible part in the ordinary conduct of affairs. And the future of our science obviously depends upon the ability of the younger members to take over practical and scientific responsibility.

For these reasons, I wish to propose the additional rule (a), and to say that this statement that the Council and officers shall be answerable is not meant to be a pious expression merely, or a bare principle, but to be implemented in specific ways – such as regular and frequent business meetings, full agendas, the circularization of Council's reports and of members' comments, making correspondence with outside bodies known to members, etc., so that every member can be kept fully informed as to actions and decisions taken.

To pass on to the suggested alterations in Rule 5: like all learned societies, we need some continuity in our officers and committees, so as to ensure stability in our policies and plans. But there must also be change, if there is to be life. The due balance of change and permanence can only be ensured by retiring some officers and some members of Council every year.

Theoretically we have the right to do this now. But we also know that this privilege has not in fact been exercised in recent years and for the reasons already discussed. Unless there is a rule which makes all officers and members of Council ineligible for re-election after a specified period, the way is open for personal feelings to operate. Not to re-elect them is felt by all to be a personal challenge, a matter of loyalty and hostility, and so on.

Only by some such time limit can we reduce the force of these personal influences. The temporary loss of the services of specially gifted members would be offset by the greater feeling of responsibility, and of ease in personal relationships, among the members as a whole. This would foster an atmosphere more conducive to the free interchange of knowledge and experience, to the mutual support of members.

Obviously, not all officers should change at the same time. Especially in the beginning of the new plan, care would have to be exercised not to bring about too large a change at any one moment. But such details could easily be dealt with, if the broad principle were established.

For the same reasons, there should not be any multiplication of offices. If any one person holds more than one office, then his power and prestige, explicit or implicit, become again too great – once more stimulating instead of allaying all those personal feelings already spoken of, which are so unfavourable to our scientific relationships.

Especially, I suggest that if our scientific work is to be unhampered, the office of Scientific Secretary should not be held by anyone who also wields other constitutional powers.

What I wish to urge is that by the means suggested in this resolution, and in other ways which could be devised, it is essential that we modify our rules so that they shall give the greatest possible support to every member against the difficulties and inhibitions arising from personal relationships, and shall encourage responsibility and initiative, both in practical and scientific affairs.

I would associate myself with Dr Karin Stephen's answer to Miss Grant Duff's statement about elasticity and rigidity of rules. Change would in fact bring about greater elasticity rather than rigidity.

DR M. SCHMIDEBERG: The main issue of Drs Carroll and Friedlander and Miss Grant Duff is that it is not fair towards the absent Members to decide upon alterations of rules in their absence. I think this should be discussed first.

MRS JOAN RIVIERE: (To second Resolution D) (Paper read by Dr Gillespie) The resolution I second proposes an alteration in Rule 5 of the Society, and other measures to the same end. Rule 5 is a very general statement, allowing the utmost scope to the officials, and it clearly signifies an autocratic constitution of the Society as an active body. In our rules, no responsibility is laid upon the ordinary members of the Society, except the one of paying their subscriptions; members have no duty or obligation to do anything for psychoanalysis. The officers and Council alone are to conduct the affairs of the Society. I submit that it is questionable whether an autocratic organization is conducive to our aims.

Obviously, no one should lay down the law in science – every worker has a right to put forward his results and a right to be heard. Creative and original work will come from individuals, but the testing of it must ensue from the sum of the work of many upon it, before its validity can be finally established. This rule, which leaves the management of our work and the promotion of our scientific aim in the hands of a few persons, is a handicap to that aim in several ways. It offers no scope to the rank and file of the Society to undertake some of the responsibility for cultivating and furthering psychoanalytical science, or giving each other mutual support, which are our aims.

I believe that the majority of the rank and file of members in the Society feel that the officials, the 'elect', behave as if they and they only owned the talisman of psychoanalytic truth, and as if that ownership presupposed that they could control and dictate, both to the outside world and to the non-elect in the Society, what is and what is not to be done with and done by this magic talisman. Now this is undoubtedly a subjective attitude on the part of the rank and file, but it has some elements of actual truth.

One feature of the autocratic system has been the rarity of Business Meetings and the failure to inform members and hear their views on matters which the Executive have to deal with. I second Mrs Isaacs' proposals in this respect most heartily. By this means we should ensure greater participation by ordinary members in our activities. I particularly recommend that more of the matters to be discussed should be put on the notices of the Business Meetings, so that members' interest should be stimulated and they should attend; and also that they should be informed by post subsequently of decisions taken. Reports published in the Journal only come out at long intervals even in peacetime, and are never at all informative about business conducted.

Then there are details which could be improved – such as that the book of our rules is not regularly sent out to each member, as it should be when they are altered or newly printed, or to new members when admitted, Another detail – but a highly significant one – is that the usual machinery for a secret ballot has not often been provided at this Society. In far broader issues, too, one sees a sort of myth at work to the effect that normal psychological impulses and emotions don't operate in our Society. I don't think it is surprising that people can't vote against an existing officer when they have to do so in full view of three or four other members.

Business cannot be conducted properly by ignoring emotional relations and pretending they don't exist; they have to be grappled with, though not stifled, and efforts made to regulate them, so that their energy can find an outlet usefully in the work. All work springs from emotional relations, and no scientific contribution will be worth much, and is only intolerably dull, if it shows no personal interest, no individual enthusiasm for the views it puts forward.

As regards our other aim, I would mention that when members do give each other mutual support, such as sharing and pooling observations and conclusions in a certain line of investigation, or confirming or supporting each other's views in Society meetings, they are frowned upon and even regarded as unscientific for doing so. Among recent emotional attitudes in the Society, we have seen the opinion that a member brands himself as outside the pale if he announces that he has reached a certain conclusion in his work or can confirm another person's views – as if the tentative standpoint of science were incompatible with any conclusions – it does seem to be to some people – or as if one lost one's right to change one's mind later on. In fact, any sort of confidence in one's work seems to be regarded with suspicion and dislike. I suggest we should recognize more clearly what as psychoanalysts we ought to understand without any difficulty – that emotional factors are not in themselves bad in scientific work (in fact no work can exist without them), but that some emotions are more helpful than others to productive work. Distinction should be made between useful and useless impulses. Enthusiasm does not require to be withered with scorn and contempt; but all emotions should be kept well in check and not allowed to go beyond what is reasonable in their expression.

I believe that most present causes of difficulty in the Society arose fundamentally from the autocratic system, and that a democratic constitution, which implies that all share in the responsibility for the work being done, would effect great improvements. In general the members have tended far too much to accept and subscribe to their position of very limited activity; but one must remember that enforced inactivity breeds apathy.

. If we had a better organization for the co-operation of all members, I think that we should feel that the officers are executive agents of the membership themselves, in the duty and responsibility we all actually have of cultivating and furthering the science of psychoanalysis, founded by Freud.

MRS M. SCHMIDEBERG: (Paper) We all agree of course with many of the things Dr Isaacs said, with the need for intellectual honesty, with the drawbacks of emotional bias, etc., etc. But let us turn back to the practical issue. Much has been said and probably will be said both for and against the changes proposed. What intrigues me, however, is why there should be such an urgency about them. Why can we not wait with the discussion of them till the war is over? I was impressed to see that three resolutions were put forward by such different members as Drs Carroll and Friedlander and Miss Grant Duff, all on the same subject. This indicates, if indeed proof was needed, that it is a matter of common sense and ordinary decency not to make alterations in the constitution whilst our members are away on war service.

Our members fall into three groups. The first is away on war service. Our obligation towards them is evident.

The second group consists of those who remained in London since the war and during the Blitz. It would certainly be bad form to sing our own praises, but it is a fact that, had it not been for us, the Clinic would have closed down and the meetings would have been suspended. We may not all go as far as Dr Jones who in June 1940 expressed the opinion that we were under the obligation to set an example to the population in moments of crisis as we know so much more about the unconscious, but it is safe to state that had all analysts left London, had the Clinic closed down whilst other psychotherapists went on with their work, that would have reflected badly on psychoanalysis. True there have been moves among analysts in this direction. At the outbreak of war Drs Rickman and Matthew wanted us to close the Clinic, during the Blitz Dr Jones very earnestly appealed to us to stop meetings, pointing out what a serious loss to psychoanalysis it would be if we were all killed at once.

DR JONES interrupts stating that he never did such a thing.

MRS SCHMIDEBERG replies that Dr Jones even suggested that no more than six members should meet at any one time.

DR JONES states again that he did not make such a suggestion.

Fortunately however, we survived. I believe there were other attempts as well to discourage our activities.

The third group consists of those members who for one reason or another were away from London. Some of these have since returned. It is a strange coincidence that almost all promoters of the change are recruited from this group. Dr Winnicott and Miss Low are the only ones whom I have seen at meetings last year. Now, why should these members have such an urge to alter the constitution immediately? It is possible, of course, that this sudden bout of energy is due to the good rest they enjoyed in the country. It is conceivable, however, that there are other reasons. The possibility cannot be excluded that there may be some connection between these attempts and the previous ones of trying to induce us to stop with our activities.

Another point strikes me: Dr Isaacs, seconded by Mrs Riviere, put forward the proposal that the number of the Honorary Secretaries be increased, that the tenure of office be limited to two years (with the exception of the Treasurer), and that no person should hold more than one office at a time. No one has ever held more than one office at a time.

DR JONES: Yes, this has never been the case.

DR M. SCHMIDEBERG: I understand that Mrs Isaacs means that members should not at the same time be on the Council and on the Training Committee.

DR JONES: This has nothing to do with the Society.[13]

MRS SCHMIDEBERG asks Dr Isaacs thereupon what her proposal actually meant then.

MRS ISAACS' reply, if any, could not be understood.

MRS M. SCHMIDEBERG, asked by the Chairman to go on with her paper, declares that she would interrupt it and go on after this question has been cleared.

DR JONES, summing up, states that there are four different situations:

(a) those members who think that changes of the constitution are desirable,
(b) those members who think they are undesirable owing to the absence of many members.

(MISS LOW, interrupting with the question 'What changes?'
   DR JONES, replying 'Any changes')

(c) those who think that preliminary discussion should be held first, either altogether or by a special committee.

MRS ISAACS says these things are all related, but we must decide here in a practical sense.

MRS ISAACS: They ought to go side by side. Discussion of changes of rules and the scientific discussion may go on for ever. We should first decide which rules are most favourable for the scientific aims of the Society. I wish to add that all members who were called out of London during the war are immensely grateful to those who carried on here and that this is not affected by the discussion going on about scientific aims. It is not possible for all members even in peacetime to attend all meetings. When the Emergency Council was agreed upon many members were not present either.[14] Are we really not to discuss any frame which would be more favourable to the achievement of our scientific aims until the end of the war? The changes proposed are in the interests of our scientific work. How many members are really unable to come to an important Business

Meeting? The war may last many more years and also then all may not be demobilized for some time further.

DR ADRIAN STEPHEN: How many members are really unable to get leave to attend a meeting?

DR M. SCHMIDEBERG mentions a number of twenty-two.

DR JONES: Many members are here today who have not attended Scientific Meetings since the war broke out.

(Then a rather confused discussion follows on the importance of members being present or absent from meetings.)

MISS LOW: Since nobody is in favour of change of rules this afternoon what should prevent us from setting up a body to consider the question, send out circulars, etc., so that after a certain time we could come to a conclusion?

DR JONES: To avoid matters being discussed by small groups.

MISS LOW: I do not mean a Committee in the ordinary way, but something wider to which all members who are interested, present and absent, can contribute. Could we not have both for the questions of scientific aims and of alteration of rules a convener who should ask everybody to send in their views. If you should think one convener is not enough, two or three helpers could be appointed. It is necessary to encourage members to send in their views. This would not be so restricted as a Committee.

DR JONES: The problem is how to get the junior members to share the activities and responsibility. I think these subjects should better be discussed at meetings of the Society.

MISS LOW: As long as absent members are communicated.

DR KARIN STEPHEN: My proposal was to ask someone to be a sort of letterbox to whom everybody could communicate their views. These views could then be duplicated and circulated to all who want to see them and are willing to subscribe to the costs. By this means we shall succeed in getting a widely spread discussion.

DR ISAACS: This letterbox will not take the place of full discussion (Dr Jones interposes 'Or full responsibility') or the exchange of views and contact at meetings.

DR JONES suggests: Could not the problem of scientific aims be kept for discussion at the Scientific Meetings?

DR M. SCHMIDEBERG: We do not want all the Associate Members and candidates present at those discussions.

DR GLOVER: Whatever arrangements we made about the letter-box, one should have to have preliminary statements of the issues before the preliminary discussions. Take the example of today.

Occasional visitors may not quite get what it is all about and what issues are involved.

DR RICKMAN: We must have more Business Meetings and officers must report what is going on, what congresses are being held, etc. These Business Meetings would then not be merely a discussing machine but would also enable us to know what is going on. We must separate discussion of proposals and the thrashing out of our differences.

DR M. SCHMIDEBERG: We first want to find out the feeling of the Society about the resolutions.

DR GLOVER: So far we have had discussion on the question of alteration of rules and the scientific aims. Certain views overlap on the relation of scientific discussion and administration of the Society. The discussion has been so far one-sided. From my own part I feel it essential to bring out what is the practical relationship between the scientific aims and the business administration of the Society. How does this relationship work out? This has not been dealt with at all today. It would be sidetracking this issue to consider it purely as a scientific matter.

DR ISAACS: It is very important to discuss the scientific differences before any attempt is made to alteration of rules.

DR GLOVER: That still does not meet my point that you must consider the relationship of scientific aims to every detail of organization of the Society – for instance lectures, the training of candidates and so on. There is a great variety of issues, they belong to a third, intermediary category and thorough ventilation should be given to it. The subjects of discussion are therefore (1) scientific aims, (2) business, (3) the use made of business administration for scientific aims.

DR FRANKLIN: Couldn't we have the business meetings in the evening again? (Shouts of agreement from various members)

The Chairman takes a vote by show of hands and states that most members could manage to be present in the evening.

DR JONES tries to get Dr Isaacs' opinion clear. A good many members, specially the conveners of this meeting, said that they did not want a change of the constitution to be made immediately. Does anybody support Dr Isaacs in her view to carry out a change of rules now?

DR ISAACS points out that she would like to have her resolution put forward before the others.

DR JONES: Do we agree that we should have another Business Meeting to discuss specifically these administrative changes?

General shouts of 'No' to be heard.

MRS ISAACS: I am not pressing for an immediate change of rules but only after further discussion.

MISS LOW: I think that we should discuss those resolutions that have never been discussed at all, namely Friedlander's, Carroll's, Grant Duff's, Low's, Walter Schmideberg's, Melitta Schmideberg's, Rickman's.

The Chairman states that the next step is to have another business meeting to discuss these resolutions not yet discussed. This is agreed upon.

MISS LOW suggests to discuss them as grouped by Dr Jones, but thinks that Dr Jones now suggests a different procedure.

MR W. SCHMIDEBERG: Quite so. (To Dr Jones) What was your paper for, then?

DR GLOVER: Both Mrs Isaacs and Mrs Riviere made an artificial and really idealistic contrast between the scientific aspect of the subject, discussion of which might go on endlessly, and the business side which they think could be considered separately and soon. Although they agree that the two are in theory related, Mrs Isaacs believes that preliminary changes of the constitution would improve the scientific atmosphere. There is a certain priority of logic. Dr Jones has ordered the resolutions in a certain order. If Mrs Isaacs suggests that hers should be discussed first, I think it should be discussed last.

DR GILLESPIE: If B1 were passed would this eliminate the rest of the resolutions?

DR GLOVER: If B1 were passed this would eliminate D, but not the rest of B or C.

DR ADRIAN STEPHEN: It would eliminate Dr Isaacs' resolution. I do not agree with my resolution being put under D.

DR JONES: Could we get a step further by considering B1 now?

DR WINNICOTT: Some members have left this meeting already and it would be difficult to vote now if they are not present. (These were Dr Wilson, Mrs Ruben.)

DR JONES: Members do not wish to go further today?

DR KARIN STEPHEN: Is it decided to have the letter-box system?

DR ADRIAN STEPHEN: It would eliminate Dr Isaacs' resolution. I do agree to my proposals being put under D.

DR JONES: Could we get a step further by considering B1 now?

DR JONES: It is really a question of contributions. (Dr K. Stephen: 'Yes, I suggested this.') How many members would like to have it?

Only four members indicated their wish for this. No contra vote was taken.

MISS SHARPE: I think perhaps we might end by something I am sure you will all agree upon.

At the end of the discussion Miss Sharpe wanted to propose a vote.

MISS SHARPE: I wish to propose a very grateful vote of thanks to the Emergency Committee (truly the servants of this Society) that has carried on the administration of the Institute and Society during the last two-and-a-half critical years, Dr Payne, Dr Glover, Dr Macdonald.

The Institute has remained open throughout these years, enabling p.a. treatment to go on without interruption, and enabling some members to keep together what they had of private practice. Consultations have gone on as usual, patients were allocated for treatment or sent elsewhere if we could not deal with them. 'The finances have been kept up to date by Dr Macdonald, who has also supervised library affairs.[15] The fabric of the building has needed attention, fire watching was an urgent and difficult problem.

Training Committees have taken place as usual and those students who remained in London have at least been advised concerning their reading and 'control' work has been continuous with students who could carry it on. And always Miss Freud has been ready and willing to take yet another seminar filling up the gap left by members who could not be in London. Moral support, if any were necessary, has always been forthcoming for our faithful workers, Mrs Neurath and Mr Palmer.

My memories of this Institute in the war will be of arrival in the morning from the country, desolate streets, the Institute open, Mrs Neurath[16] perhaps having spent the previous night fire-watching. During my time in the building, any day after a heavy bombing night, I heard the voice of at least one member of the Emergency Committee, and very often all three would come in sometime during the day. And Walter Schmideberg's cheerful voice would greet one as one went back to the comparative safety of the country for the night.

These are the people who have kept the work of the Institute going for two-and-a-half years, and if heavy bombing returns this Society knows upon whom it can depend.

I propose a vote of grateful thanks to Dr Payne, Dr Glover, and Dr Macdonald.

DR GLOVER: I should like to say a word. I assure you that from the first moment it has been a feeling of pleasure to keep the place going. I am sorry that Dr Payne has to be absent, but am sure she would agree with me. (Dr G. then gives warm appreciation to Dr Macdonald who has given up much valuable time for an almost thankless task.)

DR JONES, after consulting the opinion of the members present, states that the next Business Meeting to continue the discussion will be held on Wednesday, March 11th, at 8 p.m. It is decided to ask those members who sent in resolutions but cannot be present to send in statements.

Notes

1 This meeting was called at lunchtime to avoid evening bombing.
2 Miss Barbara Low, Dr Melitta Schmideberg, Drs Adrian and Karin Stephen.
3 This was at the previous Scientific Meeting, 17 Dec. 1941, during the third discussion of Barbara Low's paper on 'The Psychoanalytic Society and the Public', the paper having been previously discussed at Scientific Meetings held on 5 and 19 Nov. 1941.
4 Four members had called for this Extraordinary Meeting, but following that request, a notice had been circulated asking members to send in resolutions for discussion at that meeting.
5 Dr Brierley's paper, read on 18 Feb. 1942, was entitled 'Some Notes on a Concept of Internal Objects'.
6 See Resolution E (p. 39).
7 This complaint goes back to well before the War Emergency Committee was elected.
8 He should have said 19 Nov.
9 See Resolution J (p. 41).
10 Sylvia Payne was Honorary Secretary of the Society and a member of the Emergency War Committee.
11 Professor Freud died on 23 Sept. 1939.
12 In 1927–8.
13 At this time the training of candidates, the London Clinic, publications, and the business administration of the organization were carried out under the auspices of the Institute of Psycho-Analysis, a legally registered body. To the Members, however, they would be more aware of the fact that the Training Committee, which was elected by the Society, was chaired by Edward Glover.

He was also the Scientific Secretary, Director of the Clinic, and deputy to Ernest Jones, as President, so that he chaired Scientific

Meetings whenever Jones was absent, as he had been doing since the beginning of hostilities. Jones was guilty of a sleight of hand, as he must have known that this was what was worrying the Members.

14 This was agreed at a Business Meeting of the Society on 6 Nov. 1940 when Glover was in the chair and only 15 members were present. From the beginning of the war most of the important decisions had been made by the Board of the Institute of Psycho-Analysis, whose members were as follows: E. Jones, Chairman; E. Glover, Deputy Chairman; David Matthews, Treasurer; Edward Bibring; Marjorie Brierley; Sylvia Payne; John Rickman; and Ella Sharpe. Most important decisions that affected Members had been made up to this time at the meetings of the Board of the Institute, and where appropriate, Business Meetings of the Society were called to communicate to Members the decisions of the Board. No wonder members felt shut out of the task of running and caring for the Society!

15 Dr R. A. Macdonald, as Acting Librarian, informed the Board Meeting held on 6 Dec. 1939, that he had arranged for the Glover Library to be moved to the house of Lady O'Brian, Crabtree Cottage, Bordon, Hants, and that he would bring books to members as they were needed. The replaceable books in the Ernest Jones Library would, he hoped, be housed in the Nottingham University Library, while the irreplaceable books might go to a Buckinghamshire village. The Board thanked him for his efforts to safeguard the library.

16 Mrs Neurath was appointed full-time secretary on 4 Oct. 1939 at a salary of £4.0s.0d. per week. She played an important stabilizing role in the Institute, not only caring for the place but also helping to maintain communication among members, and in particular she must have facilitated the distribution of the minutes in this publication.

3

The Second
Extraordinary Business Meeting

Minutes of Extraordinary Business Meeting
held on March 11th, 1942

Dr Jones was in the Chair and 25 members were present (Dr Glover, Mrs Klein, Dr Rickman, Mrs Riviere, Mrs Isaacs, Dr M. Schmideberg, Dr Wilson, Dr Friedlander, Dr W. Hoffer, Dr Weiss, Dr Herford, Miss Freud, Mrs Burlingham, Miss Low, Mrs H. Hoffer, Dr Lantos, Mrs Ruben, Dr Franklin, Mr W. Schmideberg, Dr Winnicott, Miss Sharpe, Dr Gillespie, Dr Thorner, Dr Heimann).

One guest was present (Dr R. A. Macdonald).

DR JONES opened the meeting and said that reading the minutes of the last Extraordinary Meeting in full would take too long. The Chairman asked the members to hand in their statements before the end of the meeting. Dr Payne was unable to abstract the minutes yet and the Chairman asked the members for permission to postpone reading of the minutes until the next meeting. This was agreed.

DR JONES: I take it that our programme is to go in a systematic way through the various resolutions sent in. The obvious way is to take them in groups and I think that my classification is a fair one. One Member had asked not to exclude the affairs of the Institute from the discussion.[1] There is of course no intention to exclude anything, but there is no resolution bringing them in. We cannot ramble vaguely, but we all hope we shall find some suitable place to raise them.

MISS B. LOW: The question of training is raised in my resolution to institute committees.

DR JONES, pointing out that this resolution will be discussed in its due order: The resolution classified under B1² proposed by Drs Carroll and Friedlander and Miss Grant Duff, proposes to leave alterations of rules until the end of the war. To leave the rules unaltered means to leave the affairs in the hands of the Emergency Committee. The question will come up again at the next annual meeting. Shall we throw that open to discussion?

DR GLOVER mentions that two statements to this point had been sent in, one by Miss Grant Duff and another by Drs Carroll and Stengel. Proposed to read them to the meeting. Agreed.

MISS I. F. GRANT DUFF: (Paper, read by the Chairman) It seems unwise to alter our rules now when so many of our members are obliged to be away and therefore cannot pull their weight in the discussions of the changes to be made. It may be argued that they can vote from a distance but this is not the same thing as taking part in the discussion. It may further be argued that they can write their views, but, (a) the written word does not carry the same weight as the spoken word; (b) absent Members cannot answer to new points as they arise, nor, if anything they have written is not quite clear, can they elucidate their point, therefore Members who are present would have an unfair advantage over Members who are absent. Discussion would also lack in fulness. Besides this, many absent Members are exceedingly busy and may not have time to write their views at length. Also in one case a Member is known not to have received the agenda sent to him, so he cannot possibly have expressed his views. (c) Under present circumstances therefore it is impossible to know whether any changes suggested represent the views of a majority in the Society or only of a minority.

The alteration suggested that officers of the Society should only hold their office for a certain length of time, and also not be eligible for re-election until a set time is passed after his term of office has elapsed is a bad law for it replaces elasticity with rigidity. It seems saner that at each election Members should be able to decide whom they wish to have as their officers. Why, for instance, should the Members be obliged to change their officers at some future date because some Members wished for a change in 1942? This is not rational. By the present rule Members can keep or change their officers as they see fit.

DR D. CARROLL AND DR E. STENGEL: (Paper, read by the Chairman) Being unable to attend the meeting on 11.3.42 we wish to bring the following arguments to the meeting:

While appreciating the various proposals put forward for increasing and improving the usefulness and efficiency of the Society we feel that it is highly undesirable to carry out fundamental changes at the present time. Moreover we feel that such resolutions as H (a) and K are surely not necessary, and we have every confidence that no Member of the Society needs to reaffirm his loyalty and scientific adherence to Freudian psychoanalysis and to the avowed aims of our Society.

We realize that in a rapidly changing world the position of psychoanalysis may alter in its relation to human society, but we have the fullest confidence that those at present responsible for the guidance of the Society may be entrusted to the fullest extent to make the adaptations that may become necessary and, what is more, to avoid such alterations as would be likely, in any sense, to imperil our Society's position and integrity.

Having been unable to take part in the discussions preceding the present meeting we would like to say that we fully appreciate the desire for psychoanalytic unity that has prompted the resolutions put forward, but, being able – through geographical necessity – to take a detached view of the position as a whole, we do believe that the effect of some of the resolutions could only be to weaken the Society by increasing and exaggerating some of the differences of opinion that have been manifest for some time.

We cannot see any real disadvantage in maintaining the status quo, and would point out that there would be nothing in such a decision to shut the door on progress or on advantageous watch or liaison with other bodies.

We hope that the discussions at the meeting will result in a clearing of the atmosphere and in the establishment of a greater mutual confidence in each other – after all the resolutions as a whole speak loudly of lack of confidence in each other among ourselves and we would appeal to the Society, as two of many absent Members, to find a way to re-establish this mutual trust, without which the work of the Society must suffer.

Please read this at the meeting.

DR K. FRIEDLANDER. (Paper) Since Miss Low has given her first communication[3] the various discussions in the Society have shown that our difficulty in our approach to the public has as its basis the difficulties in the Society itself. It has, I think, also become clear that our scientific activities are severely hampered by this undercurrent of hostility between the various groups in the Society. The atmosphere in the Society is not such as to stimulate free discussion and free scientific work, and there is no doubt about it that we have for years

74

past neglected urgent scientific problems. The reason for this is that the attitude which promotes scientific work, the attitude of benevolent friendliness, has been lacking, not only in some of the officials but also in Members of the Society. There was no common effort to overcome difficulties, but rather was there the attempt to get the groups further and further apart.

So it will be clear that I agree with those Members who want to have the atmosphere in the Society changed. I differ with some of them as to the best method with which this change can be brought about. Because in my opinion the only way in which a fundamental difference in time, probably only in a long time, will take place is by proper scientific work and by trying to put the work before personal considerations. That is to say I think that the only way in which this Society has a chance of continuing its existence as a scientific body is on the basis of the proposals of Dr Brierley's communication.

The discontent in the Society seems to be universal and as it happens often in such situations, any change is welcome. Everybody is only too willing to blame those in authority for what has gone wrong and to believe that a change in that quarter will miraculously save the situation. I don't know whether members have thoroughly considered what that would mean: at the next election all the present officials would have to resign and new ones to be elected. First of all I am very doubtful whether enough people would be available now to fill the posts; secondly, in a difficult wartime situation like the present it would be most unwise to have only Members handling our affairs who are new to the job, because I think to be an official is a great responsibility which entails a lot of time, effort and experience. So that I see only two possibilities for these proposals having been made at all. One, that Members have not thought it out properly and in wanting the Society to be changed jump at any such chance without thinking about the result, or the second possibility that it is again another move with some ulterior and personal motive behind it, a situation which we have learned to detest so much in recent years.

It is certainly striking that the proposals for an immediate change in the constitution come from Members who have not attended the Society regularly since the outbreak of war and who will be unable to do so in the near future. They have also not been aware of the fact that attempts have been made to better the situation, as a result of which we have had the past discussions. That is to say, these various discussions were the result of an already changing atmosphere.

For a fundamental change to occur in our Society not our constitution has to be changed but an active attempt has to be made

75

by everybody to come back to science. Only those Members present at every meeting are able to do that, and are able to judge the situation as it is at any given moment. It is not correct.to believe that the situation in the Society has been caused by the attitude of the officials. As I mentioned before it has been caused by the attitude of Members as well. Both officials as well as Members will have to readjust their attitude, and there is no reason to believe that the officials will be less able to do so than the Members. I also repudiate the idea that we as Members can do nothing to influence the behaviour of our officials, that we are simply a herd which is dependent on the attitude of somebody in authority.

As long as our situation is as precarious as it is now a change in the constitution will not alter anything in the Society to the better, but the upheaval can only cause further change and lead to a split in the Society. We have at first to make the attempt to become a scientific body again and then we can decide whether we want any constitutional change. Let us for once try to face the real problems and not shift them on to an unimportant side issue. We ourselves have to change the atmosphere in the Society into one which promotes scientific work. What we want from our Chairman and officials is to further that aim, and not until we are convinced that they will not support us in the matter is there any justification to put the blame on them. As long as every Member is given a right to speak and their contributions are taken up impartially by the Chairman, as long as discussions are not cut short before they have properly begun, I do not see who should hinder us to create the atmosphere we ourselves want.

MISS B. LOW: (To a point of order) Dr Friedlander says that the proposals for change in the constitution come from Members who have not attended meetings since the outbreak of the war. I made the first proposals and have attended every meeting. If Dr Friedlander wants to substantiate her statement she must give names.

DR JONES: Perhaps Dr Friedlander meant those proposals which definitely propose immediate change of rules while you propose a Reconstruction Committee.

MRS ISAACS: The statement does not apply to Mrs Riviere, and Dr Winnicott either.

DR JONES: Dr Winnicott did not propose any change of rules.

MISS B. LOW: It might meet the case if Dr Friedlander would change the wording of her statement and put in names.

Dr Friedlander agreed to this.

DR ISAACS: This is just one of the personal points which, as many

Members pointed out, ought not to be raised in our discussions. The proposals should be considered on their own merits and not in relation to the Members making them.

DR JONES: Dr Friedlander says she thinks the most important point is to re-establish a scientific atmosphere and that no change of rules should be made now. Dr Isaacs last time thought that both matters were connected with each other and that the scientific atmosphere could not be improved unless the rules were changed first.

DR ISAACS: I would put it a little differently. A change of rules would aim at producing a change in certain attitudes of Members, which would lead to a better scientific atmosphere. No one wants to sweep away all the officials at one go. I was thinking of a transitional state to secure sufficient continuity.

DR JONES: I don't think we have really quite got to that yet.

DR RICKMAN: The phrase used by Dr Friedlander, 'change of constitution', sounds a very big thing. Resolution D(a) does not propose any change, it is an addition to the rules.

DR MELITTA SCHMIDEBERG: An addition with the character of alteration.

DR JONES: We are discussing whether we want to change any rules.

DR RICKMAN: We only want to change some rules, not the constitution. 'Constitution' is an affect-loaded word.

DR MELITTA SCHMIDEBERG: Dr Isaacs should be asked to substantiate the urgency of her proposal. Why should changes be made now when most members are absent?

DR JONES: That is very just. It should be discussed whether now is an urgent or suitable time, even if people do think changes necessary.

DR MELITTA SCHMIDEBERG: If members like Drs Carroll and Stengel feel that advantage is being taken of their absence, even if they are wrong in that their feelings should be considered.

MISS ANNA FREUD: I see a much more important point why this is not a suitable time for changes. If we alter the rules before settling the scientific differences it seems that we take neither the rules nor the difficulties very earnestly. If we follow Dr Brierley's suggestions we must keep our minds open for all sorts of results, even that there might be views in our Society which are incompatible. It seems a wrong time to alter the rules before we know all that. It is like renovating the house before we know who wants to live in it. Also the renovation of our training system would perhaps depend on these results. I think we should decide all this after the discussion of the scientific differences and not before.

DR JONES: At our last meeting it seemed that practically everybody except Mrs Isaacs did not want to rush at any practical administrative decision but thought first to thrash things out. This seems wise to me. May I suggest that we pass by the first letter of the classification of resolutions, and come to grips with the others now.

DR GLOVER: I find myself in a dilemma about speaking to the resolutions on no change. I feel it might be regarded as not quite proper to express an opinion – for two reasons: (a) it might be thought that, as office bearer of some years' standing, I have an axe to grind; (b) whether the expression were democratic or autocratic, it might be regarded by some Members as yet another attempt at intimidation. On the other hand I feel that I have a perfect right, indeed an obvious duty, to speak on the scientific aims of the Society and the way in which these can be stultified by any group which decides to use the Administrative, Training, or other Committee of the Society in order to advance sectional interests.

If it were the case that the passing of no change resolutions would preclude discussion of the real issue – viz. the existence of power politics – or that it would preclude discussion of the means by which play of power politics can be scotched or preferably stamped out, I would quite definitely oppose no change resolutions. The fact is, however, the only thing that would be excluded by the passing of a no change resolution would be the making of immediate changes in the constitution; and as the resolutions on aims and on the possible formation of committees open up the political issues at stake I prefer to postpone my own contribution until these resolutions are dealt with.

DR JONES: It seems to me that if we were to pass no change resolutions at this point it would exclude all other resolutions.

DR GLOVER: No, only D,[4] not B and C.

MISS LOW pointed out that, for instance, her own resolution did not propose immediate change, only indirectly.

DR JONES: Yes, indirectly.

MISS LOW: I think it was agreed last time to go on with B.

DR WINNICOTT: Miss Freud's excellent point yet stultifies matters. What should happen if the war goes on for ten years?

DR JONES: This is what I suggest: not to discard B, but to hold it in suspense for the time being.

MRS RIVIERE communicates that both Drs A. and K. Stephen asked her to put before the meeting their contributions, parts of which refer specifically to 'no change'.

The Chairman asks Mrs Riviere to read the papers.

DR KARIN STEPHEN: (Paper, to Resolution D1,[5] read by Mrs J. Riviere) We have before us proposals to change our methods of election and other proposals not to make any changes in our constitution under war conditions. I should like to suggest that we agree to take no final action until we hold a last Business Meeting before the Annual General Meeting in July when the elections will take place, but that in the meanwhile, we think and talk the whole question out thoroughly, both here, at meetings, and also among ourselves. Personal discussion is best of all, but I think exchange of ideas by way of the letter-box I suggested last time might be useful as well, to supplement this, because it is so difficult at present for many of us to meet frequently, or even to meet at all. If the trouble which this would involve is felt to be an obstacle I would willingly undertake as much of it as the Society wishes.

We need also to find out whether it is true that Members who are absent from London on war service would really not be able to come up to attend the final Business Meeting, after the preliminary exchanges of views which could be carried on by post, in order to have their say and hear what others have to say and then vote. Much has been said about the unfairness of making important changes in their absence but we have still to discover whether this is a valid objection. A number of the absent Members are themselves most anxious for the changes to be made (this point was emphasized by Dr Schmideberg) and I believe we shall find that, if the absent Members are given due notice and really want to be present, there will be very few who cannot arrange their leave, or get special emergency leave, to attend important meetings.

If this is the case I think it would be a very great mistake to postpone the proposed change beyond this summer. By allowing things to go on as they have been doing for the whole period of the war, we run a grave danger by missing opportunities for preparing for the peace,[6] and if we do not prepare for it our Society will find itself in a very bad position because others will not neglect to make their preparations and psychoanalysis will be left out of the reconstruction as it was left out of the war-planning [King 1989a].

I believe this change is urgently necessary, partly for the practical reasons I have just given, but also for other reasons, equally vital. They are needed, I am sure, for our own sakes in order to do away with the unsatisfactory atmosphere inside the Society, to help us to throw off the frustration which has reduced us to apathy and disunity. If we are to do good scientific work we must get rid of this stifling atmosphere. We have lived under it so long that it will not be easy to turn over a new leaf, but I agree with Mrs Isaacs that more democratic machinery, though by itself it cannot liberate us, will do something to enable us to help ourselves, and without it I am afraid we shall end in disaster, perhaps even quite soon. Our President pointed out last time that the difficulty has always been that Members were so unwilling to express their views, to take initiative and responsibility, and so on. We all know that this was a justified criticism, but what he seems not to have realized was the reason for this curious state of affairs, which has lain in the attitude of our executive officials themselves towards the rest of us. It is the state of affairs which almost inevitably must arise whenever officials remain too long in office and so come to regard themselves as the rulers rather than as the servants of the organization which they represent, a point already stressed by Mrs Riviere.

If we can secure new officials who really do regard their duties as executive we may find ourselves capable of instructing them, but this healthy state of affairs can only be reached by changing our present methods of election, and this would, after all, not be any very extraordinary or revolutionary proceeding but merely one which would bring them in line with the practice adopted by all other scientific organizations.

DR ADRIAN STEPHEN: (Paper, to Resolution D1, read by Mrs Riviere) Resolutions of four different kinds were brought before the Society at its last meeting. I propose to deal with each in turn. There were resolutions concerning purely scientific matters which, though they are of great interest and importance, were completely irrelevant to the purpose for which the meeting was called. About these I shall say nothing more than that they should have been immediately ruled out of order on this particular occasion, though, of course, they should have been discussed when a suitable time could be found.

There were resolutions proposing immediate changes in the Society's rules. About these I shall only say that though I consider certain changes desirable, I do not think that they should be carried through without careful formulation and a much fuller opportunity for discussion than the Society has yet been granted. In saying this I do not forget that proposals for change have been on the agenda for perhaps a couple of meetings but that by no means implies that the Society has had sufficient opportunity to discuss them.

There were resolutions also the object of which was to prevent us undertaking any changes in our constitution so long as the war lasts no matter how long a period that may be and no matter how pressing the need for change. With regard to this set of resolutions there is more to be said. When a resolution of this kind was passed at the beginning of the war there might have been much in its favour.[7] London was expecting to be blitzed and later was blitzed and it seemed as if it would go on being blitzed at frequent intervals till the end of the war. Members were leaving London and it seemed as if more and more would leave and as though it might hardly be possible for the Society to carry on at all. It seemed perhaps best for the Society to go into 'cold storage'.

The conditions are now changed. Members have been returning to London. London has not been blitzed for about nine months and in the last three months the centre of gravity of fighting has moved elsewhere. It is now possible for the Society to look forward – not to a normal existence, but to a far more normal existence than was possible at that time.

I know indeed that it is stated that according to our official records over twenty Members are still away. That is probably true. On the other hand it must be considered that absence from London does not necessarily imply inability to attend meetings. At the last few meetings which I have been able to attend a good proportion of the Members present have come up from the country for the purpose of attending and there can be no doubt whatever that almost every Member could come to meetings several times a year if he so desired. The plea that any large number of Members are kept away owing to war work – owing to their patriotic duties – though it is no doubt inspired by the kindest and most honourable feelings – is, when looked into carefully, completely devoid of foundation.

Even if the Blitz had not stopped, however, and even if far fewer Members were able to attend meetings than is actually the case, it still seems that the condition of the Society is so serious that we cannot afford to turn a blind eye to it till the time – in the possibly far distant future – when we return to peaceful conditions.

DR JONES: There is apparently no wish to press this point now until we come to some decision, perhaps in May or June, in regard to change of rules.

I think we can now pass to B2.[8] The first four resolutions have many points in common although the wording is different. What is the most profitable way of coming to grips with the essential thing, namely the problem of scientific differences? Is it better to have a series of short papers bringing out clearly the different points of view, or to have a general free discussion without preparation? I should be glad of suggestions.

MR WALTER SCHMIDEBERG: It would be best to go on in the order of the resolutions and hear the papers.

DR JONES: Yes, but, as I say, these four resolutions have many things in common.

MR WALTER SCHMIDEBERG: We may see whether they have something in common or not. Words may deceive.

DR JONES: We heard Dr Carroll's contribution. Then comes Miss Low's proposal. I think that was either with or without a sub-committee.

MISS LOW: I should like to say first that I think some of the discussions have been entirely unnecessary, because I never said anything about immediate changes, I asked to discuss changes. I entirely agree with Miss Freud. Changes cannot be settled until we really find out what are, or if there are, genuine scientific differences. This is important. Do some of these differences mean scientific differences or do they mean the exploitation of personal power? I hold that genuine scientific differences could and should be discussed scientifically. We want to leave out everything else. I want to put this first. This, I think, does not in the least prevent discussion of the other points. The only way to get at the scientific differences is what I propose: to create a sub-committee which is to try and hammer out what scientific differences we can find – this will take months – to try and put as clearly and as fundamentally as possible before a meeting of the Society the results of its labour. (For continuation see paper.)

MISS B. LOW: (Paper) (Statement of my Resolution on Agenda B2 of Business Meeting, February 11th, 1942, which is as follows:

That a Sub-Committee be formed to discuss the question of scientific differences in the views of members ... (See original Agenda paper, Resolution E.)

Those of you who were present at our last Business Meeting on February 25th may remember that I pointed out then the addition I had made on the Agenda. I had added to my original resolution (which asked for a Reconstruction Sub-committee to discuss changes in the constitution and machinery of our Society and Institute), a second asking for a sub-committee to discuss the scientific differences existing among our Members. I said then, and I want to repeat and emphasize the point, that I did not in any way withdraw or modify my demand for a Reconstruction Committee to consider changes in our constitution and machinery. I held, and I hold, most strongly the view that our constitution is undemocratic, and our Society dominated by one small set of permanent officials, with the result that decisions are made over the heads of the Members, who are constantly in the dark as to the what, how, and why of the arrangements made by the Council and other committees, which do not necessarily represent the wishes of the majority. Such policy has produced most disadvantageous consequences to the Society as a whole and to individual Members. In spite of the urgent need of reconstruction, I now feel that it is essential to put a still more urgent need forward, probably giving it first claim.

The discussions which have taken place since our first meeting and the present one have revealed the devastating extent of the animosities, rivalries, and unresolved conflicts among Members, often masquerading as differences in scientific views. It seems, therefore, that our first job is to try and sift the extent of our genuine scientific differences, and with this end in view I propose the formation of a sub-committee to do the necessary sifting works. I suggest a sub-committee of six people – two to represent each of the main sections in our Society – two for that which stands in closest relation to Freud's basic ideas, two for that which supports most closely Mrs Klein's views, and two for what I call the 'Middle' Party. These six, with a chairman, should meet systematically and continuously and try to hammer out a working minimum basis for unity, a basis which will adhere to Freud's fundamental theories, leaving freedom to develop or modify these according to the genuine findings of the research worker. No one in his senses, I imagine, asks for a slavish following of everything that Freud has written, but no one can claim the title of psychoanalyst if he is espousing and putting into action theories which are in opposition to Freud's findings. The sub-committee, I suggest, must be willing to face patiently laborious investigation: to meet varying points of view with tolerance, and to sacrifice time and energy to the job. I suggest, therefore, that it would be desirable that those people who are sufficiently interested to make this sacrifice should offer their services, and from the list of those persons, the Society should elect the sub-committee. Probably only those who live in London, or can conveniently come to London whenever needed, will be suitable for the work. It must be clearly understood that the proposed sub-committee will make no decisions of any kind, but will merely place its findings before the Society when any clarification of ideas has been reached. No one need fear the creation of another small autocratic body, seeking to impose its views – of whatever colour – on the majority. I hope my proposal will be discussed, and suggestions and criticism be brought to bear upon it. I believe – and I think many Members also believe – that such a Committee may prove a starting point for a new approach to many controversial matters, and for a better relationship between Members.

MISS LOW (cont.): I don't know whether I might be allowed to say something to what Miss Freud has said. I am very much in agreement with her, but I don't think there should be those rather sweeping statements like 'Members are so ready to put the blame on the officers'. I say we ought to blame ourselves, but in the Society there has really been a most craven attitude. A lot of it is the fault of the officers. People in official positions are more responsible for right conduct than Members. This is all I want to say about the scientific differences now.

DR JONES: This matter of a committee is a proposal which we should discuss. I think we might go on, however. It is Mr W. Schmideberg's turn now.

MR WALTER SCHMIDEBERG: (Paper) Mr Chairman, Ladies and Gentlemen, In putting forward the resolution 'that it be re-affirmed that the aim of the Society is to further Freudian psychoanalysis' I believe I am acting in the spirit of my teacher, Professor Sigmund Freud.

There are not many analysts who learned psychoanalysis from Freud himself. I consider myself fortunate that I have been one of these. The resolution means exactly what it says: 'To further Freudian psychoanalysis', and not as Dr Jones was good enough to put in a somewhat flattering way: 'presentation of Freudian psychoanalysis', because to present Freudian psychoanalysis in this Society would be like bringing coal to Newcastle – at least I hope so. Alternately it may, as Dr Adrian Stephen pointed out at the last Business Meeting, take years, and even then might not be successful. To quote an appropriate sentence from Freud's *History of the Psychoanalytic Movement*: having drawn attention to the fact that some analysts, even after years of experience, behave like patients, he says 'that total rejection of all analytic knowledge may ensue whenever a strong resistance arises at any deep level' [Freud, S. 1914b: 336; SE 14: 48]. To return to my resolution: 'To further Freudian psychoanalysis'. When I was a boy – and that is already a long time ago – I was greatly amazed when our teacher of physics walked about in the classroom in goloshes and with his bent finger drew sparks from our noses. I am still equally impressed when I turn on the wireless to listen to the programme of some faraway country. Both these performances are based on the same phenomenon, electricity. I once wrote: 'Edison said that the electrical discoveries he made would not be worked out fully for another hundred years. Equally the psychological discoveries of Freud will require as long to come to their full development.' I remember how Freud exhorted us in a meeting some twenty years ago – I do not think any of those present today took part in it, as the Viennese Society then comprised only eight or ten members – that we had to learn to think for ourselves and to further the development of psychoanalysis through our own discoveries. Believe me, Freud was neither intolerant nor dogmatic. He was free from any rigidity. I made control analysis with him as early as 1919, in fact I believe I was the first to suggest what since has been termed 'control analysis'. The analysis of the patient which I carried out under Freud took place at the house of the patient, she facing me and knitting. You would look in vain for the description of such a technique in the Collected Papers. I could easily adduce many further examples of elasticity. The divergency between the living personality and the oral teaching of Freud and that of the rigid printed rules is a tremendous one. Professor Freud was a man who warmly welcomed every progress and innovation in the realm of psychoanalysis. Hence I have been rather surprised to find that some of his pupils try to limit psychoanalysis to what can be found in the Collected Papers. Listening to the papers of some colleagues and their description as to how they succeeded to elicit associations from the patient in the strict isolation of the classical situation, I am reminded of my old teacher who walked about in the classroom in goloshes and with his bent fingers drew sparks from our noses. There is a tremendous development implying many important discoveries, from the Leyden jar to the giant generator. We have not achieved the latter in psychoanalysis, and I fear that we will never get as far if we remain fixed to the former. The need for further development and progress is of paramount importance for psychoanalysis, as for all other sciences. I welcome warmly every new discovery or idea, but 'inspiration' must be duly checked by scientific criticism. So much as to 'further'.

As you know, the Statute III reads as follows: 'The aim of the Psycho-Analytical Association is the cultivation and furtherance of the psycho-analytic branch of science, founded by Freud.' In the twenty years that have passed since this was written, psychoanalysis has been popularized to such a degree that almost anything can be claimed – and in fact has been claimed – to be psychoanalysis, or derived from psychoanalysis. All modern psychotherapy has, in some way or other, been deeply influenced by Freud. I remember the following story which we were told here shortly before the outbreak of war. When in California a beauty queen was elected it was stated that the selection has been made strictly according to scientific principles, based on Freud's views on sex appeal. You will admit we must draw the line somewhere.

When I first came to this country some ten years ago, this Society was very much under the influence of Mrs Melanie Klein. She has greatly stimulated discussion and research. Much attention was paid to introjection and projection mechanisms, to sadism and pre-genital phantasies. True, I met many old friends, ideas of Freud, Ferenczi,

Abraham, and others under new names. Even 'Boehm's hidden penis' (that is how we used to call the phantasy of the father's penis hidden in the mother) was found – *Honi soit qui mal y pense* – in Mrs Klein's luggage. Will anybody please, who comes across it, return it to its rightful owner, Dr Felix Boehm, Berlin, Tiergartenstrasse 10? It is one of his few precious possessions. Some of you may remember that I paid particular attention to the pre-genital phantasies and the introjection and projection mechanisms in the case history of an agoraphobic schizophrenic, which I read in London and in Vienna. Altogether there was then a happy atmosphere in this Society, and I daresay we thought a lot of ourselves, and of our advanced views and good technique. But, as Heraclitus said 2,500 years ago: 'No man descends in the same stream twice.' Have not things changed since? Since about 1934 or 1936 a certain group was beginning to take on more and more the qualities of a religious sect. The 'good mother' and the 'internal objects' began to replace – or to overshadow – the Oedipus complex, and the creed of the 'deep unconscious love' coincided with increasing aggression and intolerance against non-believers. Papers became more and more confused as the years went by. I listened to them in silence and some of them made me think that the accusation of our enemies that it is impossible to distinguish between the phantasies of the patients and of those of the analyst contained more than a grain of truth. Reality seemed to disappear or to become distorted. Everything was internalized and still more internalized. I sometimes thought I was following Alice through the looking-glass and even seemed to hear the voice of the Mad Hatter. Karl Abraham has made an analysis of Couéism. I hope somebody will undertake to analyse Kleinism. I myself do not feel called upon to do so, yet it would be so easy.

Only recently we heard a paper which was based on the complete reversal of the analytic situation. The analyst associated freely, only very occasionally interrupted by a monotonous 'yes' or 'no' of the patient. In the discussion the analyst was congratulated upon this achievement. We must draw the line somewhere.

The following passage by Freud aptly describes the situation: 'it is so unintelligible, obscure, and confused that it is difficult to take up any standpoint in regard to it. Wherever one lays hold of anything, one must be prepared to hear that one has misunderstood it, and it is impossible to know how to arrive at the correct understanding of it. *It is put forward too in a peculiarly vacillating manner, one moment as quite a minor deviation, which does not justify the fuss that has been made about it, and the next as a new message of salvation, which is to begin a new epoch in psychoanalysis,* in fact reveal a new aspect of the universe for everything else. When one thinks of the disagreement displayed in the various public and private expressions of these views, one is bound to ask oneself how much of this is due to the own lack of alertness and how much to lack of sincerity' [Freud, S. 1914b: 350; SE 14: 60].

This, Ladies and Gentlemen, is how Freud characterized the teaching of Jung thirty years ago – and not as you might perhaps think, Kleinism today.

Unpleasant as these matters are, we must ventilate them and make a serious attempt to arrive at some solution, before our prestige gets damaged still further. This should not prove impossible, provided there is sufficient goodwill on all sides. I do not think I can finish better than with a sentence Freud wrote to a friend twenty-five years ago: 'Once I am no longer with you, you must stand fast together.'

DR D. W. WINNICOTT: (Paper) In my contribution to the recent discussion on the Society and its internal and external problems, I expressed the conviction that the one thing that should integrate the various elements that comprise our Society was the scientific aim in our work. I said, further, that no way of achieving unity other than this one could be acceptable to me; in fact, I implied that the present chaotic state would be healthier than order resulting from any agency other than pursuing a scientific aim. This seemed to me to be clear, and yet from talking the matter over with Members since that discussion, I find that there is room for further elucidation of my meaning.

What is this scientific aim? The scientific aim is to find out more and more of the truth. I was going to say, to seek fearlessly, but the question of fear and fearlessness must be left out of the definition. We as analysts should know better than most that some fear of truth is inevitable. Playing the scientist can be quite a good game, but being a scientist is hard. For those in the front line of scientific research there must be hardship and danger as well as infinite gratification. Psychoanalysis is still a piece of front line research, in spite of the already considerable applicability of its discoveries.

This search for truth is a cycle of three phases: piecemeal objective observation; construction and testing of theory based on observed facts; and imaginative reaching out in front of accredited theory towards the invention of new instruments of precision, these opening up new fields for objective observation. Freud contributed brilliantly at each of the three points in the cycle. There are, of course, several alternatives to the purely scientific aim. Shall I take three? One which has a wide appeal is the therapeutic. Some psychoanalysts may wish to adopt as their main target therapeutic success. Therapeutics, we should all agree, is perfectly good as a day's work, but we should not allow ourselves to be diverted from our scientific aim by the urge to cure, that is, if we are to follow the example of Freud.

Our patients will not suffer if treatment remains for us as it always was to Freud – one of the secondary aims of psychoanalysis. If we are not afraid to fail to cure, our decks are cleared for scientific work, and incidentally we are then better therapists than we should have been had we been too much concerned about failure to cure.

Another alternative to the scientific aim has to do with personal ambition. Ambition and prestige cannot be brushed aside as insignificant or improper. It is most important for a man's full development that he should attain some sort of position among his colleagues while he is young. And it is natural that a doctor should want to be recognized as a success in his own line by doctors, and a psychiatrist by psychiatrists, and so on.

But, while as individuals we are entitled to get what prestige we can from being analysts, as a Society we must not let ambition lead us. We must just work on, and continue working, as Freud did, even when our discoveries make us unwelcome in the non-analytic world.

We must not expect anything out of our labours except to get further, and it is this forging ahead that offers true gratification. For us there is no resting-place inside psychoanalysis, the science we are serving.

I need not enlarge on the way in which Freud's life illustrated professional self-reliance, self-discipline in regard to the wish to be esteemed in early manhood, and absolute absence of compromise with public opinion, as opposed to scientific criticism.

But more important and more difficult to describe without being misunderstood is the third alternative to the purely scientific aim. Freud's work is alive, and we are all guided by it, but we have it in our power to stifle the spirit of it by clinging to the latter, and by losing sight of the fact that to continue his work is to continue to reach out into the unknown in order to gain more knowledge and understanding. It would be possible so to stress the importance of the study of Freud's actual discoveries and theories that (perhaps without its being realized) this study, and the application of what we learn by this study, would become our sole aim. Some speakers in our recent discussions seem to interpret the aim of the Psycho-Analytic Society in just this very sense – a sense which I am convinced was not intended by those who framed Statute III of the Rules of the International Psychoanalytical Association.

To illustrate this I need only compare the wording of Miss Low's resolution with that of the Statute. Miss Low says that the basic purpose of the Institute and Society is 'to further and apply Freud's scientific theories'. Freud himself could modify his views and alter or widen his conceptions.

Freud would not have wished us to limit our search for truth, and I have no doubt that the reason why psychoanalysis meant so much to him was because it provided a method by which he and those coming after him can go on indefinitely using, to discover more and more about the problems of human feeling.

What I want to emphasize is the great difference that I see between following a scientific aim and on the other hand restricting our work to the study and application of psychoanalytic theory in the form in which it had crystallized out at any one point in its history. It may be said that all this is obvious, and I do believe that I am putting into words a general feeling, but even if the point be obvious, I do not think anyone will mind its being emphasized and developed.

If our Society is to survive in health it must be constantly on the alert against whatever gives scientific research a second place. On a background so prepared we must each of us work to contribute in one or more of the three ways which I have already described:

1 Objective observation of facts;
2 Construction and testing of theory based on observed facts; and
3 Imaginative reaching out in front of accredited theory towards the invention of new apparatus, and the perception of new fields for objective observation.

Because I feel so deeply the importance of all this for our Society, I ask you to take this opportunity of reaffirming our aim as that stated in Rule 3 of the International Association:

The aim of the Association is the cultivation and furtherance of the psychoanalytical branch of science founded by Freud, both as pure psychology and in its applications to medicine and the mental sciences: further, the mutual support of the members in all endeavours to acquire and disseminate psychoanalytical knowledge.[9]

DR JONES: The phrasing of the object of our Society strictly describes our work as a branch of science which was founded by Freud. It should be distinguished from medicine and other branches of science. It should not be regarded as primarily psychotherapy, but as an instrument of psychological research.

MRS KLEIN wishes to second Dr Winnicott's resolution.

MRS KLEIN (to second Dr Winnicott's resolution): I wish to

Klein

support Dr Winnicott's resolution that we should reaffirm the scientific aim of the International Psychoanalytical Association and direct our interest and endeavours towards an unrestricted search for progress in our scientific work. This no doubt is what we all aim to achieve, but it is necessary to remind ourselves that this purpose can be disturbed and deflected in various ways. If our clinical work has led us to new hypotheses and we are afraid that these may contradict accepted theory, or are disturbed by the immediate difficulty of fitting a discovery into our store of knowledge, we inhibit at the source the progress of our work.

It has already been pointed out by some speakers that in developing our science we are guided by the spirit of Freud's writing and not bound by the letter of it. In no way can we act more in the spirit of Freud's work than by refusing to allow progress to be checked by timidity in facing problems and difficulties which are not capable of immediate solution. How did Freud himself progress in his work? I have always been deeply impressed with Freud's capacity to face his discovery that some of his patients' stories about early seductions were untrue. Were then all the conclusions he had drawn from these reports false – had he been altogether on the wrong track?

He says in his autobiography [Freud, S. 1925b: 61; SE 20:7]: 'My confidence in my technique and its results suffered a severe blow'. It was some time before he could pull himself together and find the explanation of this discrepancy. I have sometimes pondered about what would have happened had he yielded to his discouragement at this juncture, and I have thought that psychoanalysis could never have developed if he had not been able to revise his views. As it happened it was at this particular point that Freud discovered one of the greatest truths about the human mind, namely the existence of psychic reality: a discovery which became one of the pillars upon which psychoanalysis rests. It was part of Freud's greatness as a man and as a scientist that he was not prevented by failures and difficulties from persisting in a line of thought which he felt would prove to be right in the end. More than once Freud found himself confronted with the problem that a new piece of work did not altogether tally with, or that it even contradicted, his earlier findings; and it seemed as if one of his greatest discoveries might burst the frame which encompassed the work hitherto developed. The sequence of books which was inaugurated by his *Beyond the Pleasure Principle* [Freud,S. 1920; SE 18:3] revolutionized psychoanalysis and seemed to shake its foundations. At the time of its publication, one of Freud's early collaborators, Dr Eitingon, said to me: 'This is putting dynamite to the house; but', he added, 'Freud knows what he does.'

To what extent these new findings had influenced theory is shown in *Inhibitions, Symptoms and Anxiety*, in which Freud newly assessed and re-defined some fundamental conceptions, for instance regarding the origin of anxiety. By then it had become clear that the great discoveries of those years were not so much a revolution as an evolution, and that they had initiated the second epoch in the development of psychoanalysis. In *Inhibitions, Symptoms and Anxiety* Freud brought together the harvest of the years from 1920 onwards. Some fundamental problems, formerly unresolved, had now found a solution, but here and there we find in his writings relevant hints thrown out, full of possibilities to be followed up, indications which he himself, however, did not pursue any further. For instance, he put the question: 'when does separation from an object produce anxiety, when does it produce mourning and when does it produce, it may be, only pain?' and replies to it as follows: 'Let us say at once that there is no prospect of answering these questions at present. We must content ourselves with drawing certain distinctions and adumbrating certain possibilities' [Freud, S. 1926; SE 20:69]. Thus we see that Freud did not draw all the possible conclusions from the unbounded wealth of his new discoveries. Even the new concepts which he had worked out in more detail are not always brought in line with some of his earlier statements. Though he revised and readjusted some older concepts, he did not by any means do this on every point of theory. Clearly this was and is still a task to be carried out by those who follow him. What else could Freud himself have meant in those sentences, such as the one I quoted earlier, but that he left the answer to certain questions for the future? We are in the midst of the second epoch in the history of psychoanalysis and many questions which in the beginning of this epoch were unanswerable are now nearer to solution.

Considering that psychoanalysis is still a young science and in its developmental stages, we should not be surprised that inferences from Freud's work must differ according to which particular aspect of his discoveries is taken up and pursued further. Whether we lean more strongly towards some of his earlier findings which, though he went beyond them he never altogether discarded, or whether, on the other hand, we lay the emphasis on his later conclusions starting with *Beyond the Pleasure Principle* – this is bound to have a bearing on the differences in our conclusions. The necessity for greater co-operation in our Society as a means of furthering our scientific aims has been voiced by some speakers. Dr Jones, who has done so much for this Society and for psychoanalysis in general, has always been aware of this necessity. He was alive to the importance of bringing about a better understanding between the Viennese group and ourselves, and watching with concern the widening gap between the standpoints of the two groups, suggested in 1934 exchange lectures, himself giving the first of them in Vienna [Jones 1935].[10] This was a promising beginning, and it is regrettable that in the years during which our Viennese colleagues have been in our midst little progress has been made towards clarifying the issues.

That this necessity is felt more generally among our Members was shown at a recent meeting, when Dr Brierley read a paper calling for co-operation among us in order to elucidate outstanding problems. This appeal evoked a strong response, and appreciation of the constructive spirit of the paper was expressed from various sides, as well as the demand that arrangements should be made for detailed discussions on lines more fruitful than hitherto. This would be one of the ways in which we could carry out in spirit the scientific aim of the Psycho-Analytical Association, which Dr Winnicott's resolution urges us to keep in mind.

DR MELITTA SCHMIDEBERG: (Paper) The one point on which all four speakers and probably all Members who have not spoken agreed is the paramount importance of settling or at least of clarifying the scientific differences. It has been said that it is the task of the Scientific Meetings to hammer out scientific differences. This is, no doubt, how it should be. But the fact is that we have not succeeded in the last seven years, in spite of numerous attempts on our part to achieve that the issues at stake should be discussed in a scientific manner. I want to go into the reasons why this has proved impossible and – 'pour faire une omelette il faut casser des oeufs'.

In the somewhat strained atmosphere of the last meeting there was one relieving piece of humour, Mrs Riviere's statement that the reason why we are dissatisfied with the conditions of the Society is because as analysts we set ourselves such high standards. Amusing as this remark is, unfortunately the reverse is true, namely that the behaviour and attitude of the Society fall below the lowest possible standards of professional courtesy and scientific discipline. I may add that I am not particularly spoiled, as I studied medicine in Berlin, a city not exactly reputed for its gentle manners. Certainly the level of the Analytic Society is poor according to British standards. A pleasant contrast is provided by the ISTD,[11] with its co-operative spirit and courtesy. Though one might have expected some friction owing to the fact that the physicians belong to all schools of psychotherapy, the reverse is the case.

Mrs Isaacs and Mrs Riviere pleaded that analysts were entitled to such human emotions as enthusiasm or bad temper. Who of us would deny this truth? What we demand is not that analysts should be devoid of human reactions and emotions, but that they should control them, according to scientific tradition and discipline.

Regrettable, as no doubt bad manners are, there are worse things. The two most serious aspects of the present situation are, that it should have become necessary for a Member of the British Psycho-Analytical Society to put forward a resolution asking to reaffirm that the purpose of the Society is to further Freudian psychoanalysis and, second, that the greater part of the Members feel browbeaten or badly treated by a comparatively small clique.

What brought about the present deplorable and untenable situation in the Society? In attempting a brief historical survey I cannot refrain from mentioning some rather personal details. Once more: 'Pour faire une omelette il faut casser des oeufs'.

Some fifteen years ago, before the arrival of Mrs Klein, the Society was, I am told, friendly but dull. When I first attended meetings in 1929–30, I was favourably impressed by the friendly spirit of co-operation and the eagerness to work out problems. I did not realize then that this friendly atmosphere was largely conditioned by a mechanism only too familiar to analysts by the existing contrast with other Societies, in particular the divergencies with Anna Freud, then in Vienna, nor did I know then that it did not embrace the whole of the Society. Some members, e.g. Dr Bryan and Professor Flugel, have been pushed in the background. All of us have paid ample tribute to Mrs Klein's stimulating effect and her valuable scientific contributions. But it is time to pay some attention to the other side of the picture.

I am not familiar with all the details of the Chadwick affair, but I remember the concerted attacks on her when she read a paper. I have been told that she was put forward several times for election as a full Member by the Board but was every time blackballed by the Kleinian clique. Since then she ceased to attend meetings. About 1932 started the crusade against Miss Searl. To give only one example of the methods employed: when she gave lectures for candidates Kleinian training analysts and full Members attended them in order to attack her concertedly in the subsequent discussion in front of the candidates. This induced the Training Committee to lay down the rule that Members should not attend lectures for candidates. In the meetings no occasion was omitted to make a joint attack on her.

After the crusade against Miss Searl[12] was brought to a successful conclusion, the methods worked out were employed against others. I have no wish to mention my personal experiences, such as a

Member in a leading position and official capacity trying seriously to diagnose me as a paranoiac and to persuade my husband that we should leave this country because I had dared to protest against certain intrigues and organized attacks. It is sufficient to say that the knowledge that my opponents can say nothing against me that they have not already said and do nothing to wreck my reputation and practice that they have not already attempted, gives me an enviable sense of security and freedom in discussions.

But it would be claiming too much honour to pretend that I have been the only victim. Drs Franklin and Yates avoided coming to the Society for years, though the former works regularly at the ISTD. Miss Grant Duff, Miss Low, Dr Friedlander have been cold-shouldered. Drs Carroll and Matte could not open their mouths without being attacked. When Dr Karin Stephen read a paper Dr Glover had to denounce the heresy-hunting in the subsequent discussion. When Drs Bowlby and Middlemore brought original contributions they were unfairly attacked. In the last ten years I heard Dr A. Stephen take part in scientific discussions only two to three times, Mrs A. Strachey not once. Mr Strachey has been patronized or attacked in indirect ways, disparaging remarks were systematically spread about Dr Brierley and Miss Sharpe; serious attempts were made to wreck Dr Glover's reputation. I do not wish to enumerate all the Members who were badly treated nor do I need to remind you of the treatment meted out to the Viennese. By the way, Mrs Klein regretted that the Viennese did not take more part in the activities of the Society; I think Miss Freud will be able to explain why! To sum up: it is sufficient to say that every Member who was not 120 per cent Kleinian has been attacked systematically, directly or indirectly.

In the last meeting one or two members took exception to dogmatism. I think the Kleinians would be well advised not to start a discussion on this topic, but if they wish they can have it of course. In addition, other methods were worked out: when unpopular persons spoke, by smiles and glances the impression was conveyed that the speaker was an utter idiot; when one of theirs spoke a suitable background of admiration was created. Then there were the whispering campaigns. It is interesting to compare what used to be said about Drs Rickman, Winnicott, and Matthew before they became Kleinians with what was later on said when they did.

I want to stress that I have no wish to identify myself with all the various Members who had been attacked some time or other. For instance I did not agree with Miss Searl's theoretical views nor did I ever have a particular liking for her personally. In fact I remember a time when I used to be reproached for not admiring her sufficiently. But it is impossible not to object to the methods employed against her. On her own admission she had ceased to be a Freudian when she left the Society. But if the same measure were fairly applied then some other members ought not to be here today. No doubt some of the criticism voiced by the Kleinians was justified. They may be right in claiming that some of the Members they attacked were embittered or unbalanced, or muddleheaded or not very good analysts. But to what conclusion would we arrive if we scrutinized their ranks from this point of view? No society can exist without a reasonable measure of tolerance. Analysts who believe themselves to be tolerant are in practice less so than any group of people I know, with the possible exception of the Nazis. Some persons have the gift to bring out the best in others. Certain Members seem to have the aptitude to bring out the worst.

So many Members are puzzled by the fact that these Kleinian methods have been tolerated over a great number of years, and wonder why it is that they could have been so effective. No doubt the Kleinians have an admirably organized co-operation and had the power to make or wreck many a Member's practice and reputation. They derived much glamour from Mrs Klein's earlier work and claimed credit for all work ever done concerning the pre-genital phases, projection and introjection phenomena, notwithstanding the fact that much of this was actually the merit of Freud, Abraham, Ferenczi and others. Still the main factor on which the Kleinians base their influence are the control analyses and analyses. They went to surprising lengths to secure analysands and pupils. Some of the facts are such that they cannot be divulged in a meeting, but I will give two examples. A candidate was in analysis with a non-Kleinian analyst with good therapeutic results. Though the latter fact was generally admitted, a Member in a leading position approached him in a friendly talk and suggested that he should change over to a 'deep analyst', preferably of course to Mrs Klein. No doubt quite by chance, he mentioned to the candidate at this occasion that he intended to send him two two-guinea cases. Again, it must have been a coincidence that several other Kleinian analysts also made him various promises, all in the same week. By a still stranger coincidence none of these materialized when he decided not to change his analyst.

Another candidate took objection to the behaviour of his analyst over a certain matter, and wanted to change to another one. His analyst, a leading Kleinian, used every conceivable method of emotional appeal to dissuade him: she pointed out that he would wreck his career and that there was the danger of him committing suicide as other analysts were probably unable to analyse his depressive position. Nevertheless he clung to his decision. Then suddenly another Kleinian analyst asked him to come and see her. I do not know how she had learned about the matter, but she expressed her concern about it to him, and eventually wept over his intention to leave his analyst. This decided him and he stayed. I have for obvious reasons given no names, but if anybody wishes I can of course substantiate the instances quoted and give further details. These two cases have by no means been the only ones. I wish to state that no case has come to my notice where a non-Kleinian analyst behaved in such a manner.

Now why do the Kleinians go to such lengths to hold or to procure analysands? Because they hope to turn analysands into converts. We have heard, more than once, Members get up and declare with shining face their faith and conversion, in a manner reminiscent of the Salvation Army. The excessive positive transference they show, the oversensitiveness with which they react to the slightest criticism of Mrs Klein, and the corresponding hostility towards non-Kleinian analysts is striking. I admit, it may happen occasionally that a patient of mine speaks well of me. But if I found that all my patients were expressing themselves in glowing terms about me, were unduly sensitive on my behalf, and displaced all the negative transference on my colleagues, I would, most certainly, begin to doubt my technique.

The system of analysis and control analysis has become a key factor in the Kleinian game of power politics. Its role is reminiscent to that confession used to play in the Catholic church. It yields power and information. The latter can be then used for political purposes. Suppose a training analyst, Dr B., is in analysis with Mrs A.; then the latter will learn not only about Dr B., but also about B.'s analysand Dr C., and possibly C.'s patient D., and will be in the position to influence indirectly the lives and actions of all these. There is one more factor: the Kleinians seem to have developed particular methods to induce their patients to displace the negative transference onto other, non-Kleinian, analysts. Whether such manipulation of the transference is desirable from the therapeutic point of view may be doubted but it has certainly proved useful in the game of analytic power-politics.

Control analysis too has acquired a special flavour. In most cases a Kleinian control analysis proved to be only a forerunner of a Kleinian analysis, as the control analyst as a rule succeeded in convincing his pupil that his former analysis was insufficient. Such a conviction can

96

be conveyed the more easily, as legitimate hopes can be held out that a Kleinian analysis is likely to further his career and practice. Such tactics were employed even with candidates who were still in analysis with others. Gullible non-Kleinian training analysts learned by bitter experience that to send their candidates to a Kleinian control analyst was asking for trouble. Kleinian control analysts seemed adept at upsetting the mental balance and self-confidence of candidates. In this they were ably supported by the Kleinian candidates who tried their hardest to convince each of their colleagues of the unsatisfactoriness of his work and analysis. Having eventually succeeded in upsetting the balance of a non-Kleinian candidate, it was of course easy to suggest to him his need for a real 'deep analysis'.

The need of many analysts, some in leading position, for further analysis, is, unfortunately, often only too obvious. But proof is lacking that analysts are so much more balanced even after they have been analysed for some five to ten years, or even more. Proof exists, however, that existing methods of training have produced disastrous consequences. I read of the fight of the democracies against fascism originally described as the fight to preserve the bad against the worse. Well, there are occasions where we must fight in order to preserve the bad. Few things have created so much unhappiness and disaster as the striving for perfection with its accompanying intolerance and fanaticism. We must learn to accept ourselves and others as they are. The urge to undergo control analysis and analysis in analysts who have been practising for years seems to spring largely from fear of responsibility. We must learn to stand on our own feet. Members who are afraid of responsibility are in my opinion unsuited to hold a position of authority.

It seems that these methods employed by the Kleinians have become less effective since we have begun to discuss them openly. Hence they were forced to attempt new strategies. This is in my opinion their main motive for wishing to alter the constitution, or, as Dr Rickman prefers to call it, for adding new rules. Last year's meetings were reasonably satisfactory and the discussion was in accordance with scientific standards – it deteriorated again this autumn, since the Kleinians favoured us with their appearance – and it seems that it is more this they object to than the reverse.

Let me state briefly our main objections to the Kleinians. It is not the difference of opinion. Everybody is entitled to his opinion, and to free expression of it, within the accepted limits of scientific tradition. What we object to is first, that the Kleinians try to force their opinion on us, and to browbeat us by subtle, and by not so subtle, methods into accepting it. Mrs Riviere said in the last meeting that it cannot be left to the office bearers to decide what is and what is not psychoanalysis. They do not possess the magic talisman. Surely, this is a reversal of facts. None of the office bearers ever tried to dictate to us on scientific matters. It is the Kleinians who consistently for a number of years attempted to do so; it was they who tried to declare what was psychoanalysis, what unconscious contents we ought to have found in the analysis of our patients, what Freud would have said, or would have liked, and even what he was supposed to have said – without bothering to find out whether he actually did say so.

Second, we object to being held responsible for the Kleinian views. They have no right to claim openly or by implication that their views are representative or that they are an improvement on the existing theory (implying that the non-acceptance of their views reflects badly on the other analysts as being due to intellectual backwardness or emotional bias). It is for them to substantiate the correctness and value of their views, not for us to disprove it.

The Kleinians shelter behind ambiguity and vagueness. Anybody who attempts to disentangle their views is sure to be told that he misunderstood them. They are satisfied with hurling this accusation at their critics, and *make no attempts* to provide lucid explanations and equivocal statements that are not so prone to be misunderstood. They seem afraid of committing themselves or of taking the responsibility for the views expressed. They again and again put forward opinions which they take back or modify almost in the same breath. They lack the most elementary scientific discipline. In a manner somewhat reminiscent of Dr Goebbels they try to impress us by repeating time after time the same slogans, by putting forward exaggerated claims and dogmatic statements, by accusing their opponents and intimidating the hesitants, by a constant play on emotions of every sort, instead of presenting and substantiating their theories according to scientific standards.

Their reluctance to accept responsibility for their actions is striking. Nor can we ever be quite sure whether they will claim credit on behalf of their adherents or disown them; we do not know that when they put forward a resolution whether it means what it says or if they take it back, whether it has been withdrawn. At the last but one meeting the meeting decided to have all speeches minuted and sent to absent members. Later on several members objected on the ground that their speech had been impromptu. This is surely strange. How much importance can we attach to the speech of a Member, impromptu or not, if we do not know whether he will

98

be ready to take the responsibility for it a few days or even a few hours later? It is paradox that so many of those who seem so anxious to be in positions of authority should be so afraid of taking responsibility.

The ensuing situation is hardest for the candidates. It is all very well to say that the candidates should get an all round training, and be familiarized with every sort of research. This is obviously how it should be. But what is it like in practice? They are torn between two extreme views, each presented with dogmatic intolerance, and have only the choice of becoming dogmatically narrow-minded themselves, or of being utterly confused. It does not help matters that some of the training analysts show no sympathy for the impossible situation in which the candidates find themselves, but exploit the situation – in the manner I described above – and take out on the candidate what is meant for the analyst.

DR JONES: Dr Schmideberg has really admirably illustrated the difficulty of discussing these matters without personal attacks. The problem is now how to turn it into more profitable work.

MRS KLEIN: One word. Mr Schmideberg suggested that I claimed Boehm's discoveries (and Freud's, Abraham's, Ferenczi's) as mine. If he will look into my book he will find Boehm's name mentioned aside from the others.

DR JONES: We are only at the beginning of the discussion. It is now ten past ten, but we have still time to discuss Miss Low's practical proposal. I take it is your wish to have more Business Meetings. I shall welcome suggestions about dates.

After some discussion on the time point it is agreed to continue this meeting until 10.30 p.m.

DR JONES: Would you mind if we interrupt our discussion? We should have attended to the election of Miss Elisabeth Schwarz to Associate Membership.

By vote of hands taken as passed.

DR JONES: Miss Low made very practical suggestions. I should like to hear more about getting to grips with our problems.

MISS ANNA FREUD: I want to say something to Miss Low's and Mr Walter Schmideberg's proposals.

I understand Miss Low's wish for a sub-committee to discuss scientific differences. I would much prefer, however, not to call it a 'committee', but a 'seminar' or a 'study group'. We tried to urge all Members in the last meetings to take active part in the scientific discussions. Is it wiser to restrict the circle of Members taking part in the discussion now? We know it is a matter of individual ability to express one's opinion in a discussion. Dr Brierley made it clear that she preferred to read a written paper. This would exclude one important person of the Middle group from the sub-committee proposed. This is my only reason against narrowing down the discussion.

I welcome most of what Walter Schmideberg brought forward. But he brings two matters into line which are not of the same order. The one is that a certain limitation or control should be brought into training matters. He proposes unified training policies or if necessary two training policies. Then he expresses the same wish in regard to publication matters. There he goes too far in placing censorship on papers. This would be the worst kind of orthodox attitude. I resented it very much in the past, not when this Society criticized my little book on the psychoanalysis of children, but I resented it when the Society refused to have it printed in England [Freud, A. 1927]. What is the use of criticism, when a Member is not allowed to publish his views? In Vienna we published Mrs Klein's book as a matter of course. We always held the view that publication of all views is necessary. For instance we published Rank's *Trauma of Birth* [Rank 1934] about which we had great doubts. I believe Mr Schmideberg will agree if he thinks it over.

DR JONES: Walter Schmideberg referred to things written in an 'unofficial capacity'.

MR WALTER SCHMIDEBERG: I meant certainly no censorship, but if a book or paper showed a definite diversion from Freud's psychoanalysis, that we should publish them but add, 'this is their view and not the agreed view of the psychoanalytic Society' because we are responsible to a greater body than our Society, namely the International Association.

DR JONES: Certainly.

DR MELITTA SCHMIDEBERG: Also to the public. We don't want to be made responsible for opinions we don't hold.

DR JONES: To come back to the practical proposals we heard. Miss Low did not mean so much the committee to discuss, but to clarify the points and to present them to the Society.

MISS LOW: Things get so confused in a discussion. If we could present after some months certain points we could get on much better.

DR JONES: I rather agree with Miss Low that a smaller number could get nearer to clarifying the problems, a very large group would go on discussing them. Two or three people could work it out and then present it to the Society.

MRS BURLINGHAM: When discussing things it happens that new points come out.

DR JONES: I don't call it a discussion committee, but one preparing to present problems for discussion.

DR FRANKLIN proposes discussions at full meetings, but some members to have the function to sift what had been said and report to the next meeting.

DR JONES: We tried having two or three papers and by that to state the points.

DR FRANKLIN: This is not the same.

DR MELITTA SCHMIDEBERG: The Scientific Secretary could always arrange the questions to be discussed in the Society meetings.

DR GLOVER: The special point of view I have would probably touch on points reserved for later discussion. I apologize beforehand to the Chairman if I am out of order in appearing to stray from the immediate topic of scientific aims. In discussing this question of scientific aims, we may miss a more important point. Also although I appreciate the Chairman's view on creative and destructive contributions it gives rise to some difficulty, because if I am to establish my own pet theme I may have to make use of material which might appear to be purely critical and destructive. Incidentally some confusion has arisen owing to references in various quarters to good, enthusiastic emotions and bad or destructive emotions.

I have read carefully all the contributions made to all the meetings and my immediate practical remarks were stimulated first by Dr Winnicott at the first meeting and by Mrs Isaacs and Riviere at the last meeting and again by Winnicott tonight. Dr Winnicott had expressed many admirable sentiments on scientific aims etc. or scientific procedure, and naturally no one from any side is going to take exception to these. But this is not the main issue.

I should like to make it clear at the outset that in my opinion the central issues before the Society are these: first, whether or not there exists in the Society any section or group which seeks to use the machinery of the Society to increase its own influence, or to limit the free exercise of scientific opinion on the part of other Members or again to exercise some form or other of pressure on Members holding different or opposing views; second, whether this section attempts to secure influence through the various committees of the Society (mark the term 'committees', not 'the executives'), and third, whether it develops a private organization outside the Society for the purpose of influencing affairs inside the Society.

It is my considered opinion that there is such a section and that until the existing machinery of the Society is permitted to function, as it was originally intended it should, it is impossible to secure a proper atmosphere in which real scientific issues can be discussed. Let me make my view perfectly clear. I have said before and repeat now that the issues are not just (a) how to deal with legitimate scientific differences or deviations, or (b) whether the constitution can be improved or not. The issue is: whether *so long as this struggle for factional power goes on* it is possible to discuss usefully *either* scientific differences *or* the working of the constitution. *I think it is not possible:* I think that *under the existing conditions* the belief that changes in the constitution can produce a change of heart or head is purely magical. No change for the better can take place, no possibility of free scientific discussion can exist until this ultimately non-scientific issue of power is brought into the open. As I said at the last meeting, we must have a preliminary political discussion before we have a preliminary scientific discussion. Those who listened carefully to the contributions of Mrs Isaacs and Mrs Riviere to our last discussion would observe that no reference was made to this central problem. True, both Mrs Isaacs and Mrs Riviere took the view that scientific issues were interrelated with Society administration. They believed that changes in the constitution should antedate in order to improve scientific discussion and they made no bones (or at any rate Mrs Riviere made no bones) about the view that the autocratic and intimidating attitude of executives was the real dragon to be dealt with. Indeed one could not help forming the impression that they believed or that Mrs Riviere believed there existed in the Society a band of much misunderstood devotees of science struggling against the oppression of emotionally prejudiced and wrong-headed executives, that scientific truth was on their side: in a word that the hour had struck for the champions of the oppressed to make their appearance. I should like now to make clear my reasons for thinking that this view, however sincerely held, is the opposite of the facts.

When I first joined the Society in the early twenties I regarded my Associate and later my Full Membership as a privilege. And it was one. This remained so until about 1930–4. With a few exceptions those Members who originally attended the meetings had in common a keen and enthusiastic interest in psychoanalysis: they were keen to learn it and they were keen to develop it. However shy and timid they were at meetings, they had in common a good scientific attitude. It would almost seem that in those early days there was some reality in the rosy picture painted by Mrs Isaacs at the last meeting when she spoke of 'we analysts seeing our unconscious impulses much more quickly than other mortals', that we have a higher standard of controversy and discussion and so on.

102

(Incidentally Mrs Riviere was more cautious – she avoided this pitfall, but both were agreed in implying that the 'bad' emotions were those of obstinate, autocratic, omnipotent-minded people who treated the good emotions of the enthusiastic scientists with unjustifiable suspicion. Though no doubt those accused of harbouring bad emotions might plaintively urge that scientific criteria are better than either good or bad emotions.)

To return: the young Society however untrained was a good Society. The earliest sign of tendentiousness occurred when, as its membership slowly increased, the new systems came into operation – the private cabal and the block vote. By the Salzburg Congress (1925) it was already clear to me that a good deal of gossip and rather disgruntled criticism of some Members by others took place outside meetings but as it was mostly to the effect that so and so wasn't a good analyst, negative transference, I disregarded it as a perfectionist defence covering lack of creative capacity on the part of the critic or critics. The first caballing outside the Society was a very tentative and abortive affair run on the pattern of the famous BMG campaign in Parliament (BMG = Balfour Must Go). Only in this case it was a JMG campaign, which was stillborn because any one with any sense in his head could see that Dr Jones was the only possible leader of the Society. It consisted in arranging beforehand to pool black balls so that candidates for Associate or Full Membership who were disapproved of could be excluded. Apropos of the recent charges against the executive of autocratic intimidation and contempt, it is necessary to emphasize here two points: (a) the block voting was arranged in private; (b) it was openly repudiated by the Council, which introduced a resolution raising the number of black balls necessary from 1–4 to 1–3. This resolution was defeated because, although it had a plain majority, it needed a two-thirds majority. Now why did the block-voting system gradually lose its effect, as it did after some years? The answer is partly that there was a gradual increase in the numbers of those who refused to use it. But mainly because it was no longer necessary. The focus of power in the Society moved from the Business Meetings to the Training Committee.[13] And there it still lies. Make no mistake about this. Whatever may be said for or against the Council is relatively unimportant compared with what can and must be said about the struggle to control training of candidates. Now the Training Committee didn't really get into full swing until after the Oxford Congress (1929) and at first it seemed . . .

DR JONES: These appear to me to be matters which will arise at a later stage and possibly you would wish to contribute in more detail then.

DR GLOVER: Yes, I will willingly drop at this point, but I should like to end where I began. I do want to emphasize this point. To my mind the main issue is this question: Is it possible for any group in the Society to influence Members, Associates, or candidates by the use of the machinery of committees? By sticking to the discussion of scientific aims first, there is a risk to pass over that greater issue.

I admired the spirit of Dr Winnicott's speech, but that at the moment is not the point.

DR JONES: When Dr Glover refers to the two friends of Mrs Klein who complained about dictators, there are certainly other members not belonging to her group complaining about the same.

DR GLOVER: Quite true, but these two stressed particularly the relations of scientific and business matters.

DR ISAACS: Owing to private circumstances I could not attend all these meetings. I came up on December 17th to the third. Miss Low then made a claim for democracy, after that Mrs Schmideberg drew a lurid picture, then appealed to the members to come to some conclusion. I had for many years my views. It seems a desirable thing to raise the problem now. I think that these phrases Dr Glover has used are not really quite just to the spirit of my own and Mrs Riviere's contributions. All the Members are responsible, but the leadership has in some way not been as wise and far-seeing as they should be. So one had to address oneself to that problem. It is a problem of the leadership and mostly of the relation between leadership and constitution. The present contributions asking for more democratic rules were stimulated by the pictures of the undesirable state in the Society.

DR MELITTA SCHMIDEBERG: There is some element of truth in the statement 'all the members are responsible'. But it has been said in order not to make certain statements too pointed. The argument reminds me of the Nazi propaganda current in America before America entered the war, that all nations at war were responsible for it. There is some difference between the position of Holland and Germany.

Mrs Klein stresses the fact that she mentioned all the names of analysts whose views she put forward in her book. We have heard that the spirit of co-operation should enter into our discussions. But we have heard here accusations of some people who have not this spirit.

MR WALTER SCHMIDEBERG: Mrs Klein is quite right that in her books she referred to all the names she mentioned. But so many don't know it, and it was put forward by the Kleinians as her invention. It can be said that Mrs Klein should beware of her friends, with her enemies she will be able to deal herself.

The next Business Meeting was fixed for Wednesday, April 15th, at 8.15 p.m.

Notes

1 These Extraordinary Business Meetings were, of course, held under the auspices of the British Psycho-Analytical Society, which was the scientific body which ran the scientific activities of the Society, which was affiliated to the International Psychoanalytical Association and from which members drew their professional recognition as psychoanalysts. The Board of the Institute of Psycho-Analysis, however, was responsible for training activities, for appointing the Editor of the Journal, the Director of the London Clinic of Psycho-analysis, and for administering the finance, the Library, and 96 Gloucester Place, where it was housed. Only Full Members were, at this time, permitted to be Members of the Institute, and be elected to the Board, which only reported back to its members at the AGM of the Institute. Jones had been trying, at the last meeting, to keep those matters which were the responsibility of the Institute out of the discussion.

2 Resolution to leave rules unaltered until normal activity can be resumed.

3 This was the paper that Miss Low read to the Society on 5 Nov. 1941 on 'The Psychoanalytic Society and the Public'.

4 D refers to resolutions proposing immediate changes in the rules.

5 D1 refers to limitations in the tenure of office.

6 See report of the AGM of the Society held in July 1943.

7 See the description of the administrative measures taken by the Board of the Institute at the beginning of hostilities, (p. 30) in King's introductory comments.

8 B2 or original resolution E was the discussion of scientific differences – B.L.

9 This quotation is taken from the Statutes of the International Psychoanalytical Association which was in use at that time.

10 Jones gave the first paper of these exchange lectures in 1935. See p. 22 of the Introduction.

11 Institute for the Scientific Treatment of Delinquency.

12 According to an entry in the minutes of the Training Committee of 11 May 1936, she asked for an interview with Jones regarding her position as a training analyst. In November 1937 she resigned from the Society, and at the Business Meeting on 1 Dec. 1937, she gave three reasons for this

action: (1) She thought that the Society was not developing along the best lines to advance the knowledge of the truth as first represented by Freud. (2) She considered that an analyst should be able to convey to the patient that psychoanalysis did not represent the highest ideals, in other words that there was room for the expression of a religious ideal; (3) that she was in touch with a group interested in spiritual healing and wished to be able to send suitable cases for treatment. . . . Jones expressed the regret of the Society that Miss Searl should feel obliged to take this action, and said that the Society wished him to convey best wishes for her future work, and assure her that the valuable work that she had done for psychoanalysis would not be forgotten.

13 At this time both the Training Committee and the Council were elected at the AGM of the Society, but while the Council reported back to members at Business Meetings, the Training Committee worked under the auspices of the Institute of Psycho-Analysis. Until the outbreak of hostilities, the President, Ernest Jones, chaired both bodies, which were often felt as remote from Members.

4

The Third
Extraordinary Business Meeting

**Minutes of Business Meeting
held Wednesday, April 15th, 1942, at 8.15 p.m.**

Dr Jones was in the Chair and 27 members were present (Glover, Payne, Adrian and Karin Stephen, Melitta and Walter Schmideberg, Low, H. Hoffer, Burlingham, A. Freud, Herford, Lantos, Friedlander, Franklin, Ruben, Winnicott, Brierley, Sharpe, Yates, Haas, Gillespie, Isaacs, Riviere, Klein, Wilson, Steiner, Heimann) and Dr Macdonald.

THE CHAIRMAN stated that last time the minutes were left over and suggested to do the same this time as reading the minutes would take very much time.

DR PAYNE: That would take the whole evening.
It was decided not to read the minutes.

DR JONES made then preliminary remarks to bring the meeting back to the situation.

A considerable number of Members in various speeches so far, Dr Schmideberg's very pointedly, have pointed out that the essential aim we are striving for is to get the possibility of discussing the scientific work and the scientific differences in an objective fashion. We know that this matter is by no means easy though it should be interesting. We know, being human beings, there will be impulses of resistance to be coped with, but we are psychoanalysts. In my view this problem of scientific differences or, rather, the scientific differences are in themselves not really so important as some Members consider. The much more grave and important matters are

107

the personal differences and animosities which lie beyond. At the last meeting Dr Glover and Dr Schmideberg both emphatically endorsed the view which I don't endorse. They brought before the meeting something of the nature of these personal differences in the attack Dr Schmideberg made on a large number of members.[1] Some of her accusations were of a general character, and these must be proved or disproved. On the other hand she also made a number of specific criticisms of analysts. That is the thing that is holding up the work of the Society, both in the amount of time taken at Scientific Meetings and in regard to the emotional factors brought into topics of scientific interest that should be discussed in an objective way. We can no longer avoid the situation. It is a challenge to the Society.

There has been of late criticism of officers and committees of the Society, partly about things done on behalf of the Society – they were very exaggerated – and partly about things that were not done or should have been done. The Society has however voiced the wish to take over into its own hands more of the running of the Society and in particular of its affairs. In front of any question of external relations, etc., we must get in order our own affairs. Therefore the question now arises: it is now up to the Society, which has clamoured for responsibility more than hitherto, to see whether it is capable of dealing with this challenge which is vital to its existence. To go on as we have done for the last four to five years is impossible. The question is whether the Society can rise to the situation and deal with this critical situation or not.

Dr Payne who unfortunately had to miss some of these meetings – and we missed her help (cheers) – had no opportunity of speaking and I think it will be right to ask her if she would like to open this discussion.

DR PAYNE: (Paper) Although I have not been able to be present at the last two meetings I have studied complete records carefully and I think I have kept in touch with the ideas and feelings which have been expressed.

I feel confident that if the votes of all Members were recorded there would be a majority in favour of making a genuine attempt to overcome our differences by studying the scientific aspect of the problems, and at the same time taking steps to ensure that our constitution is carried out in a more democratic manner than it has been in the past.

It appears, however, that all Members do not accept this point of view, and at the last meeting an attack was launched by a few Members, apparently with the object of forcing the resignations of another group, at least I cannot imagine that anyone would make

108

accusations of such a grave character against individual Members except with this object. In other words there are forces in the Society working for rupture and disintegration or at the best a continuation of strife. I should like to say something about the development, as it seems to me to be symptomatic of a tendency to regression in the collective unit of the Society.

In the first place, speaking as a Member, I wish to record a protest against the method used in carrying out the attack. It has always been my personal opinion that at Business Meetings we must guard against the danger of reproducing the completely uncensored atmosphere of the psychoanalytical session. The purpose of the uncensored analytical hour is to produce a situation favourable for the abreaction of personal emotions, etc. We do not want such an atmosphere here: personal emotions must be subjected to scientific interests and the needs of the Society as a whole. There must be a measure of renunciation of self-gratification and adequate control. Of course criticism of administration and of Members must be allowed, but there are rules of social behaviour which operate for the protection of all citizens whether bad or good, and the equivalent of these are essential in any society.

At the last meeting accusations of what in law would be called mal-praxis were made against Mrs Klein and her immediate supporters. Names of members were used freely without their consent. The charges were grave and in my opinion such charges cannot be made without the liability of libel actions being incurred. No Member has the right to accuse another Member of such practices in semi-public unless he or she has thoroughly investigated the evidence on which the charges are made, and separated idle gossip, indiscreet passing comment, and conjectures from real evidence. The evidence should contain

1 proof that the words were spoken, in what circumstances and to whom,
2 signed statements by witnesses,
3 the consent and evidence of the person alleged to have been injured.

Charges thus substantiated should be made in writing and placed before a Business Meeting or a committee appointed by a Business Meeting. Accusations made wildly and indiscriminately react mainly against the accuser, and it is doubtful that Members should be asked to refute in public charges delivered in this fashion. In England such behaviour does not incriminate the named parties, although it will hurt and the accusations may be believed by people who are uninformed or liable always to believe the worst of others.

The second point which I should like to bring forward concerns the tension and anxiety in the Society which led to the present situation. The declared justification for the attack to which I have referred is the alleged belief that members of the group have been guilty of striving for power for power's sake under the cloak of scientific differences. A resort to power politics is a regression both in the masses and in the individual and immediately mobilizes activities of a pre-genital character. I believe the actual accusation to be untrue. It is obvious that members sharing the same views will strive to be represented on administrative bodies in a society and have a right to do so. It is obvious also that individuals will rightly or wrongly criticize others who oppose them or are rivals, but there is a wide gap between behaviour determined by individual character traits and an organized conspiracy to gain power by a group of members. It is the latter which the said group is accused of. I could if it was expedient bring forward evidence to expose the foolishness of some of the accusations, and it seems to be necessary to do so, if only to prevent a recurrence of this asocial behaviour. I would much rather concentrate on constructive efforts to utilize all the potentialities which we have in the Society. The conflict is extraordinarily like that which is taking place in many countries and I feel sure that it is in some way a tiny reverberation of the massive conflict which pervades the world. Surely as first line psychologists we can tolerate insight into our collective problem without falling to bits and disintegrating the unit.

We have in our Society people of widely different gifts and temperaments and psychoanalysis has not made them more alike. I believe that we have failed to make use of the abilities of some Members because we tend to want them to conform too much to a pattern. On the one hand, we have Members with gifts and interests specially suited for the intensive study of the psychoses. On the other, we have Members with unique gifts for studying the application of psychoanalytical truths to the problems of education. We have also people who can work to organize other specialized branches of psychoanalysis connected with training. We need to recognize that there is a place for all these branches of our science, and then we might be able to free ourselves from the immediate fear of personal extinction which precedes the adoption of power politics, and work to enable the Society to make a contribution to post-war reconstruction.

MISS SHARPE: (Paper) In the interests of a code of professional

110

conduct which all of us think not only desirable but imperative if the Society is ever to lift itself out of the present morass, I am sure Dr Schmideberg will be the first to understand why I refer to her speech at the last Business Meeting. I heard my name had been mentioned and I asked to read the report. I found I had been cited as one to whom some wrong had been done by a group within the Society.

My first plea, in the interests of a professional code, is that my consent should have been obtained before my name was used in making a charge like this. I have no wish to cry peace where there is no peace, nor to hinder the exposure of anything inimicable to the Society where proof can be given, though I think there should be established a professional procedure for dealing with charges brought against Members.

If I have preferred to be a non-conductor of the uncomplimentary things I have heard have been said, I claim respect for my own individuality which any psychoanalyst should be able to give. But I must speak the truth as I know it from personal experience when a charge is brought against others on my behalf. I have no personal knowledge of any attempt to injure me or my practice from inside my consulting room, no patient or candidate has ever uttered a word of anything said or done by others to undermine confidence in my work. My practice has suffered precisely nothing through these unhappy dissensions, personal and scientific.

The other thing, for the sake of truth, I wish to comment upon, is Dr Schmideberg's reference to Dr Middlemore, of whom I knew more than anyone. I cannot allow the impression to remain that she felt any lack of appreciation of her work from the Society. She had unceasing encouragement from those whose opinion matters to her personally and scientifically. Dr Glover and Dr Payne were unfailing practical friends to her personally and to her work. Dr Rickman and Dr Winnicott were full of zest over the points she discussed with them, literary and scientific. She maintained good relationships with both Mrs Klein and Dr Isaacs. I alone know what certain interviews with Dr Jones meant to her and this gives me an opportunity of telling him. There emerged in those interviews the pattern of the truly scientific attitude, unprejudiced by personal self-interestedness – the older scientist sensitively aware of the peculiarly individual calibre of the younger one. He evoked, stimulated, suspended his judgement, and above all exercised no domination, following her observations and never deflecting them to any predilections of his own. So one would have every serious student treated by those who have authority of place and prestige no matter what the angle of investigation may be.

No, Dr Middlemore had none but the warmest feelings for the Society and especially for those whose names I have mentioned – and they and all of you will be glad to know that even in these unpropitious days her book is in its second printing [Middlemore 1941]. From reviews of it and especially from letters received one has a good hope that a stone is well and truly laid in the foundation of the prophylactic work of applied psychoanalysis, which Dr Middlemore not only hoped but believed her book would accomplish, and alongside her foundation stone one rejoices that Miss Freud's work will surely weld others.

DR JONES: I am sure I am voicing the feeling of most Members in expressing gratification at the news of the publication of Dr Middlemore's book.

MRS RIVIERE: (Paper) Mr President, at the last Business Meeting certain personal accusations were made by three speakers: Mr and Mrs Schmideberg and Dr Glover, against Mrs Klein and her collaborators. These accusations were of such a character that the further business of the Society cannot proceed until something has been said about them. It will not be possible for either practical or scientific work to be carried on in any Society where such accusations can be made unless protests are raised, as has already been done, by fair-minded members.

As I said in my recent remarks, seconding a resolution at the first of these meetings, in the work of a Society, personal feelings, however necessary and valuable they may be, must be kept in check and under social discipline. I shall therefore not express to the Society the feelings of indignation that were roused by the calculated and premeditated attacks on Mrs Klein's personality and behaviour in scientific matters, by these three speakers at the last meeting. These attacks were gross in character and false and unfounded in content. But one fact stands out so plainly and unequivocally that there can now be no denying or overlooking it. And I believe that if the Society as a whole, or at any rate those members who form the majority, who have the interests of our scientific work genuinely at heart, appreciate this fact and face it squarely, it might be possible to improve the wretched plight this Society has got into.

The fact I refer to is this: that almost nothing can now be discussed in the Society impersonally and on its merits – almost never can anything be put forward now without personalities being introduced by one of these Members, either as veiled hints or quite openly, which at once completely eclipse the topic under discussion and usurp the whole stage: personal motives, personal feelings, and personal criticisms take its place. To many of us whose work and

112

scientific views have met with constant attacks and misrepresent-ations from the same quarter over a period of years, these open personal accusations have come as no surprise. We have had to recognize that much of the so-called scientific criticism of our work expressed by these Members was based on the personal ill-feeling and animosity which at the last few meetings has come unmistakably into the open. Many Members who have recognized this personal hostility behind the ostensibly scientific criticisms of Mrs Klein's work have shown for years that they resent this introduction of personalities and personal attacks into the forum of a Scientific Meeting and that they are tired of its continual repetitions and reverberations. People cease to attend meetings when this kind of thing is almost all they get to hear. In the last few months there has been quite a considerable manifestation in the Society of a strong wish to promote co-operation in scientific work, to avoid disputes, and to meet other sections half-way. Notably we had Dr Brierley's conciliatory paper urging us to mutual tolerance; and lately Miss Freud's interesting report was followed by a genuinely appreciative and co-operative discussion; and proposals for seminars received instant response and agreement. Efforts to clear the air were made in the Business Meetings by Dr Payne, Dr Winnicott, and Dr Friedlander, urging us to attend to our scientific interests and not allow personal factors to interfere with them; and Mrs Isaacs gave an illuminating explanation of the source of our special difficulties, and the exceptional need there is in our Society for specially strong controlling measures to counteract these personal factors inevitable in our situation. So from many different angles among the membership, efforts have been made with promise of success to bring more peace and co-operation to the fore. Nevertheless, Dr Glover brushed all this aside and even claimed that his personal accusations were a more important issue than the scientific one. It was therefore quite unmistakable, and all Members who desire the Society to be conducted peaceably and scientifically cannot fail to recognize, that when Mr and Mrs Schmideberg and Dr Glover brought forward their contribution of personalities last time, they could only have had one object. Instead of encouraging and promoting these efforts at co-operation in our work, they were striving – and I say this unequivocally, as Dr Payne has said – to *stir up and increase* hostile personal feelings, and stimulate and prolong prejudice, rancour and feuds. Their speeches were not momentary outbursts of uncontrolled feelings; they were lengthy and deliberate and formed part of a settled and premeditated policy.

The personalities are directed only against a small group. In Dr

Glover's and Dr Schmideberg's recent contributions quite manifest and open personal attacks and insinuations against the character and the mentality of particular members have come into the foreground: as, for instance, in Dr Glover's recent paper on intuition,[2] with its offensive aspersions on the character and quality of Mrs Klein's motives and methods in her work. Mrs Isaacs and I brought forward in this Business Meeting an entirely legitimate and genuine proposal to alter a rule, which actually embraced a demand, first made by Miss Low at the beginning of this discussion, and supported both on the spot and subsequently by several other Members (among them three or more who are *absent*). Dr Glover in *his* speech then alluded more than once to me and Mrs Isaacs as the *only Members* who wished to change the Society's rules; and this misrepresentation of the facts was corrected by the President. Along with this went his open accusations against us of being inspired by personal and self-interested motives – in plain words, of suggesting a change of officers simply because we wanted to be officers ourselves. Actually, our papers to this resolution made it clear enough that what we were proposing was that offices and responsibilities should be *more widely* distributed and shared among the membership as a *whole*; we were proposing an arrangement that could not give anyone 'power' for more than two years and could not by any possibility give either of us or any Member considerable power for a long and indefinite period, such as Dr Glover has actually had. This malicious suggestion of his shows, as did his remarks on intuition, that no point of view sponsored by one of Mrs Klein's adherents will be discussed *on its merits*, but that some Members will reduce the matter at once to the level of personalities and try to destroy the proposition and attack the proposer. Dr Glover's attempt to rouse personal feeling against us, and his willingness to misrepresent facts in order to do so, was evident.

Something must be said about the specific charges made by the three speakers at the last meeting. As regards Dr Schmideberg's fantastic statement that 'the greater part of the Members feel browbeaten or pushed out by a small clique', one need say little. There can have been few who did not hear her with much regret and regard her remarks as both scandalous and ludicrous: for instance it is manifestly absurd to suggest that the position of such Members as Dr Bryan, Professor Flugel, Dr Adrian Stephen, Mrs Strachey, or Dr Franklin has been in any way adversely affected by Mrs Klein, or that they have been the object of any personal feeling on the part of Mrs Klein or her co-workers.

As regards Miss Chadwick, many members who in no way

belong to Mrs Klein's group agree that they were in full accord with the majority voting of the Society in the matter. In reference to Miss Searl, again many members who in no way belong to Mrs Klein's group approved her decision to resign. I would remind you that in her final speech to the Society, Miss Searl made friendly references to Mrs Klein; and she used these words, which I think should be borne in mind by us now: namely, 'that the Society had not made the best use it might have done either of Freud's work or of Mrs Klein's'; and at this last meeting she attended she expressed a wish both to Mrs Klein and to myself to go on meeting us. Miss Searl's own work was criticized by many Members, and by no means only by 'Kleinians', in a correct scientific manner. If doing this is to be called a crusade, we should have to cease our discussions and disband the Society. The same applies to criticisms made of Dr Matte's work, and that of other Members, whether young or old. As for Dr Bowlby's paper, it had a very good reception and only one point was questioned. Dr Middlemore's paper had an almost enthusiastic reception, and met with unanimous interest and appreciation, as many members will testify. Dr Yates was very grateful for Mrs Klein's help and most certainly did not feel her influence any deterrent in her work; she has been on most friendly terms with Mrs Klein since she took up other work. Dr Karin Stephen does not agree that she felt herself browbeaten; Mrs Strachey is anxious to deny that there is any truth whatever in the suggestion that she was browbeaten or pushed out; if Mr Strachey has been patronized, I am sure *he* is not aware of it. All such suggestions are ludicrous.

As for disparaging remarks having been made about some Members' capacity as analysts, it must be remembered that every worker in any field is subject to the judgement of his fellow workers as to his capacity. That is a fate we are all liable to in the nature of things, and one which has advantages as well as disadvantages. But though opinions must and will exist, the Society is not here to consider these personal matters.

Another charge made both by Mr and Mrs Schmideberg against Mrs Klein was that of giving out as her own, scientific observations and theories put forward by other workers and associated with their names. Mrs Klein herself answered the latter charge on the spot by saying that she had, on many occasions, acknowledged her indebtedness or the similarity of her findings to Freud, to Abraham and to Ferenczi (and indeed, one might add, to Dr Schmideberg herself, on every occasion) in her writings, and to Boehm specifically in her book, *The Psychoanalysis of Children* [Klein 1932]. You will all remember the terms of Mr Schmideberg's references to this matter.

And you will remember that after Mrs Klein had replied, Mr Schmideberg tried to slip out of the difficulty by saying it was not so much she herself but her adherents who had stolen Boehm's point. How inconsistent this was with his remarks about her bringing it over in her luggage, you could see plainly; for the truth of the matter was evidently of no importance. (It is not irrelevant to mention also that a week after this meeting one Member cast *doubt* on Mrs Klein's word, by asking her seriously, and even heatedly, why Mrs Klein in her reply had not *then and there given the page* in her book where the reference occurred. This incident shows the state of mind of acute prejudice and distrust which can be stirred up by these false accusations against other Members.) Mrs Klein's word can be proved to be reliable, as any Member could find for himself, by looking in the index of her book. The facts are that her acknowledgements to Boehm can be found in five separate and distinct passages in *The Psychoanalysis of Children* [Klein 1932] on p.103, p. 189, p. 327, p. 333, and pp. 348 and 349. Four of these references deal with Boehm's views about the hidden penis and in them Mrs Klein quotes papers by him, either in footnotes or in the text of the book. Two or three of them are longish footnotes, which also *discuss* his contribution. The last two pages, 348 and 349, consist of nearly two full pages in the text of the book, discussing Boehm's views and papers relating to homosexuality, which are closely linked with the other topic. This whole charge of deliberate plagiarism of a scientific observation is therefore entirely unwarranted and false. Moreover, it will also occur to many Members that the whole question of plagiarism in scientific work is out of place, provided references are made; observations and data are published in scientific work for the *express purpose* of furthering the work everyone is doing.

I have gone into this point in some detail because it is an explicit charge, and it is a simple matter to quote the facts and lay them before you in no uncertain light. Mr Schmideberg's accusation was a complete fabrication and the only conclusion that can be drawn is that he intended a deliberate misrepresentation. Such distortions constitute a serious threat to the possibility of future work in the Society and thus to the future of psychoanalysis. There is no doubt that the constant introduction of such injurious personalities in Society meetings has discouraged many Members with scientific interests and led them to feel it almost useless to bring up problems for discussion here.

This brings me to the much less explicit charge, expressed mainly by Dr Glover and made also by Dr Schmideberg, that Mrs Klein and her group use political means to influence and convert as many people as they can to her scientific views – the charge of what they call 'power politics' or the struggle for power. This charge is so vague and so unsupported by evidence that on the face of it it seems to be an invention of the minds of those who believe it. Even if some Members are so unscrupulous and so little interested in scientific matters as to put their personal ambition before any other consideration, it is difficult to see what scope or opportunity a Member in Mrs Klein's position could have to carry out this aim effectively. Moreover, it is a *commonplace* in the world of science that every scientific worker seeks to convince others of the truth of his conclusions and to teach others so as to enable them to make observations similar to his own. It would never be questioned that any worker was justified in endeavouring to find support and recognition for what he is putting forward, and assistance in developing it further. This being undeniable, there cannot be any objection in a free country to Members finding support wherever they can – the only objection could arise in the emotions of Members who hold different views – but in scientific work those emotions are by definition excluded as subjective.

At one time Dr Glover often expressed himself publicly in strong terms about the value of Mrs Klein's contribution to science. In his review of her book [Glover, E. 1933: 199] he says, 'I have no hesitation in stating that in two main respects her book is of fundamental importance for the future of psychoanalysis.' He then says that, on the one hand, her observations of children are unique and also that her conclusions are bound to influence theory and practice for some time to come. Later he says, 'I have again no hesitation in saying the book constitutes a landmark in analytic literature worthy to rank with some of Freud's own classical contributions.' Since about 1935, however, he has changed his mind, which he is entitled to do; but he has made no considered statement to the Society of his reasons for so doing. Whatever his own views, he is not entitled to resent or to interfere with others who have retained, or adopted, or developed views he formerly held himself. They are as free as he to hold what opinion they choose. Nor are Dr Glover and Dr Schmideberg entitled to take any exception to the fact that some leading members of the Society occasionally support Mrs Klein's work in public and speak of it in terms as eulogistic as Dr Glover himself once did; nor can they take exception to the fact that several qualified analysts as well as Associates find her work so helpful and productive scientifically that they have desired analysis themselves with her.

There will always be plenty of people who do not care to

investigate those particular problems on which Mrs Klein's work has thrown new light. Dr Glover himself said in the 'Symposium on Therapeutic Results' at the Marienbad Congress in 1936: 'This implies a certain *need for specialization* in analytic work, a state of affairs which seems in any case inevitable' [Glover, E. 1937:128]. Those who are not interested in these particular problems can continue work on their own lines; but they cannot protest if her work meets with recognition and encouragement.

As for Dr Schmideberg's charge that attempts have been made to influence candidates to change their analysts or not to change them, the probability is that such incidents as she referred to would look very different if the facts about them were fully and fairly stated. In any case I do not think the degree of veracity of Dr Schmideberg's other statements entitle her to much credence in her representation of such occurrences.

The same thing applies to Dr Glover's attempts to be sinister by talking about such things as private cabals and block votes. There is nothing criminal about the facts, if there is about the terms he uses. Members of a society who agree on any point, whether scientific or political, do get together and discuss their work and their difficulties, whether external or internal, and always will do so. They are giving each other mutual support. There is not the slightest evidence or justification for Dr Glover's imputation that they get together in order in some mysterious and entirely unspecified way to attack or undermine the position or the rights of other members. Even if they wished to do so, it would not be practicable in a free society. The Members Mrs Klein's group are supposed to influence by their scheming for power are free people, and can perfectly well resist her, if they choose. One must point out that since such charges are *incapable of proof*, they can only be made with the *object* of stirring up ill-feeling and damaging Mrs Klein, and with her, her work in which, it has to be remembered, many Members outside her 'clique' find a great deal of value.

The conclusion is plain. This is not how matters should be conducted in any Society. Members must discuss scientific or practical topics *impersonally* and *on their merits*, and not bring forward or insinuate their private opinions of other Members' character and motives to the Society. Misrepresentations and unsupported charges against the motives, the character or the mentality of any of us simply obstruct the scientific work of the Society. Conduct and behaviour can be challenged at a suitable time and place, and in a suitable way, but only if capable of proof; people's motives and their strivings – for power, for instance – just like their appearance or mannerisms, are not matters for discussion here. Such topics are *out of order*. Both the Members and the President could help, and help each other, to keep the meetings to the discussion of the impersonal scientific or practical matters by which we can further psychoanalysis, and not allow these personalities to be forced on us. All the Members who wish to carry out the Society's aim and do genuine scientific work must firmly resist such attempts to stir up prejudice, hostility, and feuds.

It only remains for me to say, on behalf of Mrs Klein and her collaborators, that we greatly hope the efforts at conciliation that have been made lately will continue and bear good fruit, and that we may all soon find ourselves engaged with good will and co-operation in some profitable scientific discussion again.

MISS LOW: I think we have been listening to a most extraordinary statement from Mrs Riviere, because she does nothing but charge other persons in her speech. The interpretation she puts on Dr Glover's speech at the last meeting can only be said to be misinterpretation. Her attacks on Mrs Schmideberg and on Dr Glover are only apparently attacks against them, as she charges . . . (end of the sentence not clearly heard). They are not all fabrications. I think too that we must get rid of personal animosities. But is this the way?

One experience I had with one of Mrs Riviere's co-operators after I had said at the last meeting that I want before all a discussion of our differences. I do not deny for one moment my desire to have the constitution of the Society changed. A Member came to me after the last meeting and said, 'Where are your democratic views now? You have thrown them over.' This is a distortion. I had merely said that I would like first to deal with the other question that had been brought up. Dr Glover had said he wanted to discuss the whole problem of whether power politics was having a hand in the Society – and we are told that this is scandalous! We have a perfect right to say so. I do not like the personal attack Mr and Mrs Schmideberg made. It is unwise to put forward grave charges unless one gives facts.

I should like to make one reference to what Miss Sharpe said. I greatly respect Miss Sharpe, but there is one thing I think she has not quite seen. It is not the same to speak as an individual than as a Member of the Society. It is not enough to say, 'I have never had any personal experience in regard to the charges made'. It is a fact that in the Society charges have been made. It is not true that in this Society there are no people who have never felt browbeaten. I am not the person to be browbeaten, but there are enough people who would say that my work is no good and who would send me no patients.

Mrs Riviere has no patients to send to other Members, but I say frankly, if she had she would send them to her own friends. That is a natural thing. You can see, I think, how that can affect the whole working of the Society when one set in the Society says we will keep our people to ourselves.

I think it is so easy to sidetrack the real matters by the kind of arguments Miss Sharpe brought. We want the people like Miss Sharpe to take a prominent place as a Member of the Society and not as an individualist. We shan't get any further this way. What is the good of Mrs Riviere rebutting Dr Schmideberg's and Dr Glover's charges, and then she starts herself making charges? I think we should form a group to hammer out the scientific differences.

We have been listening to a statement from Mrs Riviere which fills me (and I hope all other listeners) with amazement. With much moral indignation Mrs Riviere arraigns Dr Glover, Dr Walter and Dr Melitta Schmideberg, for what she terms are gross charges, made up of insult and misstatement, against certain of their fellow Members. Yet in almost every sentence she speaks, she herself makes use of misstatements, gross misinterpretation, and of very obvious personal animus. May I remind Mrs Riviere that (to use a vulgarism), 'What is sauce for the goose is sauce for the gander', and you do not get rid of charges merely by calling them lies. Moreover, it is unwise to put forward grave charges unless one is able and willing to give all the necessary proof. They object to the method of personal attack, whether made by the Drs Schmideberg or by Mrs Riviere and her friends, and will repudiate baseless charges from whatever source they come. And this leads me on to a very important aspect of our present situation, namely, that the Society as a whole must make itself responsible for what happens in the Society. It is on this point that I want to differ from Miss Sharpe in the implications of what she has just said. She has, of course, complete right to say that she will only speak and judge from her personal experience in dealing with unproven charges, but as a member of committees I hold that it is an obligation to sift any charges brought, to discover all she can for herself, and to protest against any attacks dictated merely by personal animus, from whatever source. Otherwise, the influence of a respected personality can be used to further quite destructive ends. I hope, for instance, that she and many other Members will strongly protest against Mrs Riviere's charge against Dr Glover, namely, that it was 'scandalous' for him to demand a discussion on the grave problem of the pursuit of power politics, which in his opinion was dictating the policy of the Society. Dr Glover's proposed enquiry is wholly legitimate and should be supported by every sincere well-wisher of the Society.

It must be clear now to all that special charges can only be dealt with by a small committee, made up of persons as impartial as can be got, and the findings should be presented to the whole Society. For the rest, let us form a representative group here and now to hammer out our scientific differences, and to draw up, if possible, some minimum basis of agreement, which the Society shall finally judge. Only thus, I hold, can the present impasse be resolved.

DR JONES: A matter of procedure comes in here. We can go on with criticism, accusations, and charges probably at a very great length. I have to raise a question of principle. Mrs Riviere answered a number of accusations that had been made and she made criticisms of her own. The question is: if a member feels compelled to bring a charge against another or a group affecting their professional standard, in which form should it be made, before what body, and how should it be dealt with? This is exactly what's wrong with the Society, in one word, that we have no procedure for that kind of thing and therefore it is brought in a discussion of the Society. We must settle that, where, to whom to bring it, and who should be the arbiter.

DR M. SCHMIDEBERG: Obviously it should come up before Business Meetings.

DR JONES: Yes, that is one way, or the Business Meeting can decide for a body to deal with it, or a permanent body can be set up.

DR K. STEPHEN: Charges ought to be made in writing.

DR JONES: Yes, they are usually made in writing. But this is very little use if no action is taken about it.

DR A. STEPHEN suggests a committee to deal with such charges, either an *ad hoc* committee or a permanent one which should report to the Society on the evidence.

DR JONES: It would not be easy for us to agree on the appointment of such a committee.

DR A. STEPHEN agrees to this.

DR K. STEPHEN: I should suggest to have some outside and unbiased person or group of persons.

MISS FREUD: Surely no unanalysed person?

DR A. STEPHEN: Such a person must have a technical knowledge of psychoanalysis.

DR JONES: At any rate you see there are several proposals on the spur of the moment. I insist that this matter must be dealt with now.

DR ISAACS: I agree with Dr Payne that charges must be made in

121

detail. Mrs Riviere gave the detailed answer to the charges made. It must be a matter of evidence and not just of some charges.

DR WILSON: I would suggest that the written material should be sent to the President and that he should then communicate something of the subject matter to the Society so that the committee elected should be equally balanced. The President should point out if the matter is unfairly balanced.

DR JONES: That is prejudging. We must not only decide on the procedure but also on the subsequent procedure.

DR PAYNE: Could the evidence submitted in writing first be presented to an outside person to decide, from the legal point of view, whether the evidence is sufficient for the charge to be dealt with at all? Then it would come before a Business Meeting.

DR JONES: We must have some tribunal and also authority to take consequences.

DR ISAACS: What would the consequences be?

DR PAYNE: They might be expelled from the Society.

DR M. SCHMIDEBERG: If we wanted to go to law we would go to law. We may, however, bring forward matters which would not be sufficient from a legal point of view, but still enough so for us.

DR ISAACS: I am in favour of outsiders.

DR JONES agrees with Dr M. Schmideberg that it is not a matter of legal ways.

DR K. STEPHEN: But that outsider would not be a judge.

MRS RIVIERE: But he ought to have a trained legal mind.

DR ISAACS: Have we not a rule for expressing the strongest disapproval for a Member's actions?

DR JONES: It has never been put into force and never would be without severe investigation. I wonder whether the Society is capable of even selecting a body, say two, three or four people – what would you like?

DR K. STEPHEN: Are there any precedents for that?

DR JONES: Some years ago we had to deal with a charge of plagiarism. I took it up and pressed for substantiation before a committee. Three members spent three months investigating.[3] They came to the unanimous opinion adverse to the accuser. She then said, I don't care a scrap about their findings, the members of the committee are all biased.

DR M. SCHMIDEBERG: As I was the Member myself, I want to say that the conditions were not kept. I never saw the answers to my charges.

DR K. STEPHEN: Any precedents in other societies?

DR JONES: I cannot quote straight off. If a member of a hospital staff behaved that way he would certainly be interviewed by a special committee and the finding would have to be accepted by the person or he would have to resign.

DR GLOVER quotes an example.

I think I can recall another precedent in this Society. I had occasion once to take exception to unprofessional remarks made about me by a colleague. I took a serious view of it and asked the President to deal with it. I did not of course make any official fuss but said I would be quite content if he took up the matter with the Member in question and tell her that the practice must be stopped. As he did this I was content to leave it.

DR M. SCHMIDEBERG: Obviously the whole thing brings back the fundamental issue that the Society cannot even agree on a committee.

DR PAYNE: The majority could decide.

DR K. STEPHEN thinks it might create bad feelings if a minority were overruled.

DR A. STEPHEN: As I am a professional lawyer myself I am in favour of having a chairman (an outsider) with two assessors, one appointed by the accusee and the other by the accuser, and advisers to inform the chairman about special matters, like in an Admiralty Court.

DR JONES: This is a very serious attempt at fairness and should be considered.

DR HAAS: For example, a lawyer presiding and analysts as assessors.

DR JONES: I remember an example in New York. A medical man as umpire would probably create a friendly atmosphere. Some respected medical man.

DR A. STEPHEN (referring to Dr Haas): This is the same proposal as mine in a different form.

DR M. SCHMIDEBERG: Would such a man be ready to go to all the trouble without being paid?

DR PAYNE: The Society cannot afford to pay somebody.

DR JONES: It appears that there is no Member who could be trusted to be unbiased.

DR M. SCHMIDEBERG: If I trust one Member the others would not trust him.

DR JONES: I can think of Miss Freud. Who could make other suggestions?

MRS RIVIERE: The committee should be able to make known their findings.

DR FRANKLIN: I should like to propose four names: Dr Jones, Miss Anna Freud, Miss Sharpe, Dr Brierley.

DR JONES: And Dr Payne.

DR M. SCHMIDEBERG: I would not trust any committee unless an outsider is on it.

DR PAYNE: Could it be some Member of the Society who never comes to a meeting?

DR K. STEPHEN: Dr Culpin.[4]

DR PAYNE: Yes, Culpin.

MISS A. FREUD: It occurs to me that if we choose somebody whom we respect he will not respect us anymore afterwards.

DR WILSON: Dr Culpin resigned from the Society.

DR BRIERLEY: If the Society holds the detailed evidence we might be able to see whether the matter is worth going further. The matter is a private quarrel which better would not go outside the Society.

DR M. SCHMIDEBERG: I am glad that Dr Jones said that it is a question of the existence of the Society and I think it is more important than the esteem of a person.

DR A. STEPHEN: There is not much point in keeping his esteem by hiding.

DR FRANKLIN says she is in favour of Dr Culpin.

DR GLOVER: What bearing will this procedure have on the discussion of our rota of resolutions here? It might be then impossible to fruitfully pursue the discussion of the resolutions. Earlier it was pointed out that the business organization of the Society would interfere with the scientific activities. I took the other view that, while I am glad to hear about scientific difficulties, I should like to investigate the influence of the business organization on the scientific work. If now all charges were immediately referred to a committee, all these Business Meetings would have to stop until this committee would sit.

DR K. STEPHEN: We should have a strict definition of what is a charge.

MRS RIVIERE: I cannot follow. Surely only the personal charges would be investigated. Why can we not continue our discussion of other scientific matters?

DR JONES: Are you referring to scientific matters in Business or Scientific Meetings?

MRS RIVIERE: In Business Meetings.

DR WILSON: Let us go on with our discussion and then see what remains.

MR W. SCHMIDEBERG agrees with Dr K. Stephen to state what is a charge. Some Members are very touchy.

DR JONES: This will be decided by the general feeling of the Society.

MR W. SCHMIDEBERG agrees with Dr Wilson to go on with the discussion and to decide that at the end, if we ever reach an end.

MISS LOW: If the matter is to come before a committee, you will want a lot of details. That will take very long.

DR JONES: Selection of two or three details can be made.

MISS LOW: Why not go on with the discussion?

DR JONES: We can do that.

DR PAYNE: There should be a ruling that accusations should not be thrown about.

DR M. SCHMIDEBERG: But what is a charge?

DR JONES: This could be decided by the Society. But in the day-to-day work I don't think we could interrupt a speech at every sentence to decide whether or not it contained a charge. Perhaps it could be left to the Chairman to say, 'You'd better leave this out'.

MISS LOW: That's what we have been asking of the Chairman all the time.

DR JONES: I did not want to be autocratic.

DR PAYNE: We shall ask Dr Jones to do that in future meetings. (Loud applause)

DR JONES: I shall not be present if the meetings are to be held in the evening.

It seems we are getting on. How far is this general agreement? The question is at the moment of inviting Dr Culpin, as a universally respected man without knowledge of the dealings of the Society, but friendly, to act as umpire with two assessors.

DR M. SCHMIDEBERG: I would not like to commit myself to Dr Culpin, I don't know him. First let us agree what should be the function of the Chairman.

DR JONES: I agree very much with that.

DR A. STEPHEN: Could we vote about Culpin?

DR GLOVER: Another suggestion was made to go on with the discussion. Is this discussion to stop?

DR M. SCHMIDEBERG: The things brought up before the committee would be similar to the discussion at the Business Meetings.

DR GLOVER: The training question comes further down the list of resolutions. Dr Jones, when I spoke at the last meeting, rightly pointed out that there would be further opportunity to speak about this. It might well be that, in discussing training, points may be raised which would be considered charges.

DR JONES: I think that the proposal that the Chairman be entrusted to decide, should refer more to Scientific Meetings. When it comes to Business Meetings it is part of our business. If anyone today or next time brings a charge I should certainly allow it.

DR K. STEPHEN suggests that such a charge should be left for later.

DR JONES: So far most people are in favour of continuing the meetings. What do you think, Dr Glover?

DR GLOVER: I only put the question of the influence of such a committee on the discussion of resolutions.

DR A. STEPHEN: It has no influence at all, as little as a judge would have.

DR JONES: I shall now put to the vote a suggestion which has been brought forward, that a committee be formed consisting of Dr Culpin plus one person for the Member bringing the charge and one against the charge.

DR M. SCHMIDEBERG: What would be the procedure?

DR A. STEPHEN: You bring a charge in detail, the other person replies to it, and you would either appear yourself or be represented by somebody else.

DR M. SCHMIDEBERG: It is vital that both parties have access to all the procedure.

MISS A. FREUD: I cannot really believe that this or any other Society declares itself incapable of deciding anything among themselves. I have the feeling very many people are of the same opinion. If we would be allowed to hear the evidence we might be able to decide. If we once have law courts about any matter, we shall have to have them in other matters and this peace court will end in dissolving the Society. If we should be able to solve our personal problems and those of our patients I cannot see why we should not be able to solve the Society's problems.

MISS LOW agrees with Miss Freud that it is a fantastic idea to take an outsider. Of course the outside world will know about it. As an alternative; let the details be put before the Society.

DR JONES: The whole Society?

MISS LOW: Of course the Society must have all the information. And as Miss Freud says, we must be able to deal with it.

DR JONES: Will the Society give the necessary time?

MISS LOW: Surely the Society will be willing.

DR A. STEPHEN: Miss Low underrates the amount of time necessary.

DR JONES is of the same opinion.

DR WILSON: Could the findings of the committee be put before the Society?

DR JONES: Yes.

MISS LOW: Let us drop Dr Culpin and have a chairman from the Society.

DR JONES: To be agreed by a majority vote? ('Yes!') And if Members refuse to submit to a majority vote?

MISS LOW: Then we must do without those Members.

DR A. STEPHEN: Can we appoint such a committee without altering our rules?

DR JONES: A Business Meeting can appoint any committee.

DR FRANKLIN: Would it be more agreeable if the names I mentioned would not be judges, but collect and sift the material and put it before the Society and then we have a series of meetings to pass judgement?

DR JONES: To shorten the detail work. Let us think of that.

DR GILLESPIE agrees to this suggestion and wonders whether that would meet Dr M. Schmideberg's objection.

DR WILSON suggests to get also the opinion of absent Members.

DR PAYNE: We cannot do that.

DR M. SCHMIDEBERG: I prefer Dr Culpin.

MR W. SCHMIDEBERG: I want to propose the following ruling. If a Member makes a charge he or she should give the details immediately. That would be the simplest way without a committee.

DR M. SCHMIDEBERG: In fifteen minutes I could not give the details but I offered in my speech to substantiate everything I said.

DR GLOVER: It seems to me profoundly wrong to submit to any committee things which ought to be discussed in Business Meetings.

DR PAYNE: The substantiation should be in writing.

DR JONES: We have now three suggestions:

1 Dr Culpin with two assessors.
2 Miss Freud's to bring at least one of the charges before the Business Meeting and judge what it leads to.
3 To elect a committee from the Society.

(Tea)

DR K. STEPHEN: We must have somebody who is not emotionally involved.

DR WILSON agrees.

DR PAYNE: We must have evidence.

MR W. SCHMIDEBÉRG: Dr Culpin will not understand enough of it.

DR JONES: I think that there are a few people who would not be emotionally concerned. Other Members think that all are.

I shall repeat the three proposals:

1 Dr Culpin as chairman of a committee.

2 Internal body of the most impartial Members to be found to sift and present the evidence to the Society.

3 The Society should hear the evidence as it comes along.

DR GLOVER: Who settles what goes before the Committee?

DR JONES: That's quite easy, namely the person who considers himself accused puts it to the Society and vote decides.

DR WINNICOTT: I am appalled by the situation. I cannot believe that we have to spend all that time on such matters, especially in wartime, I don't like any of these suggestions. Every chance should be given to those who have made the accusations, Dr M. Schmideberg in particular, to withdraw what they have said. Could Dr Culpin be invited to make a preliminary investigation and to give his opinion as to whether we should go further in the matter? We all know him as a very fair-minded man.

DR M. SCHMIDEBERG: I have no intention of withdrawing what I said.

DR JONES: We have to decide these proposals by voting.

MRS RIVIERE: What happens if Dr Culpin decides that we should not go into it?

DR WINNICOTT: The Society can decide to accept it or not.

DR JONES does not consider that Dr Winnicott's suggestion alters much.

DR WILSON: Would it be quite impossible for Dr Jones to be President in the chair?

DR M. SCHMIDEBERG: I would not agree to him.

DR WINNICOTT: If someone says that the President would be incapable of making an objective observation, it seems to me extraordinary if no Member gets up and makes a comment.

MISS LOW: If alterations in the constitution were made I think some of these things and charges could be avoided. If the constitution would prevent the concentration of power we should perhaps not have one or the other Chairman.

DR PAYNE: Which charge do you mean?

MISS LOW: That a person has been able to grab patients, to collect candidates, and more or less imply that certain analysts were not good analysts.

DR PAYNE: How can you prevent that?

MISS LOW: You can make it very difficult. If you had two-thirds of the Training Committee changed every two years, it would give them less power.

DR PAYNE: A myth has grown up about the power of the Training Committee.

128

MISS SHARPE: Is this a definite charge?

MISS LOW: It is not. But if a body exists year after year – I am not suggesting any personal strategy, but they can make their plans. If always the same people hold seminars, that will create a tradition. Every Society has such a ruling to prevent that.

DR JONES refers to people on a hospital staff.

MISS SHARPE: I want to point out that I think that all members of the Training Committee are agreed that there should be more frequent changes. Miss Low must remember –

DR JONES: I am sorry to have to interrupt. To go on would be trailing a red herring.

DR FRIEDLANDER: I want to make a proposal. The charges made were of two kinds: (a) personal charges accusing other people of unprofessional behaviour; (b) Dr Glover started to say something, but I did not hear any personal charge from him but an introduction that there is something wrong in the way that certain committees are formed.

I agree to investigate charges of unprofessional behaviour. That can be done in a committee of the Society. I am against outside people, There are certain rulings. The other points should be brought before the Business Meeting. We ought to know all about it to be able to judge.

DR JONES: The whole discussion is about the first kind of charges.

DR FRIEDLANDER: Mrs Riviere talked about Mrs and Mr Schmideberg and Dr Glover making charges. We should first sift the charges and then decide what to do.

DR JONES: If we decide a procedure, we then can select the charges.

MRS RIVIERE: Dr Friedlander suggests that the whole Society should undertake the whole investigation.

DR JONES: No.

DR FRIEDLANDER explains again her proposal. The second point is what we all ought to know.

DR GLOVER: There is a third category, the scientific –

DR ISAACS wants to hear Dr Payne's opening speech, because in the beginning she thought the charges were all of the same order.

DR BRIERLEY: Dr Friedlander wants the Society to assess how much is private enmities and how much is a serious practical issue that affects the Society. We want to know what the grating is in the machine.

DR M. SCHMIDEBERG: I am not sure whether Dr Brierley means –

DR BRIERLEY: I mean to leave any personal charges until we

129

know what the scientific difficulties are that are hampering our work.

DR JONES: Let people decide what they think the most outrageous and what the vital charges are.

DR A. STEPHEN: Charges should be investigated whether the accused people want it or not, like a public crime, as they affect the whole Society.

DR M. SCHMIDEBERG: I want to have the charges investigated if necessary tonight. My veracity has been challenged and other insulting things have been said.

DR JONES: It has been said that your statements are ludicrous and you have cause to ask for these charges to be investigated.

MRS KLEIN: My opinion is that the gravest charge is that Dr Glover prepared the ground to make the accusation, that there is a section, which of course can only be referred to Klein and her co-workers, which struggles for power; and Mrs Schmideberg made it too. That is more important than the scientific issue.

DR FRIEDLANDER: I only know what I heard last time. I cannot see why Dr Glover should not first make his charges and then we can decide.

DR BRIERLEY: That is just the point.

DR A. STEPHEN: The gravest charge is made by Mrs Riviere against Dr Glover.

DR PAYNE: Shall I read out this bit of Dr Glover's speech?

DR GLOVER: To a point of order. Is it decided that my speech is to be read? Then I claim the right to make my complete speech.

DR HEIMANN: Some members feel that Dr Glover has raised the question of power politics, and Dr Friedlander says that this charge has not been made.

DR FRIEDLANDER: Dr Glover says he cannot go on because the question of the Training Committee is not on the Agenda yet. It seems that there is going to be an investigation into what Dr Glover was going to say.

DR JONES: To take such a general matter as power politics will take a long time to thrash it out. Take an easier and more concrete one.

MRS RIVIERE: It is too late now, we want an opportunity to decide which charge to take.

DR JONES: Dr Friedlander wants to know the kind of charge before deciding the procedure.

MRS RIVIERE: Do others feel the same?

DR HAAS: The charge against Dr Glover should be considered before any charge against another member, because he is an office bearer.

MRS RIVIERE: Dr Jones seems to let slide the question of a tribunal.

DR JONES: I am trying to get at it. Dr Friedlander's objection has to be listened to.

DR M. SCHMIDEBERG: Let us decide on the committee and go on discussing, sifting the charges and then decide which charges to submit.

DR JONES: We come back to the three proposals:

1 Dr Culpin,
2 A committee of impartial Members to sift and present evidence,
3 The evidence brought before Business Meetings and decided.

I am putting to the vote:

1 Those in favour of inviting Dr Culpin with two assessors chosen by both sides to submit their findings to the Society – 9 members in favour; 3 definitely against – majority.
2 A committee of the most impartial Members of the Society, elected by the majority of the Society – Those in favour: 2 members; those against – majority.
3 Discussion of the evidence at Business Meetings – those in favour – majority.

The question of holding future meetings in the evening or afternoon was then discussed. It was decided that the next Scientific Meeting should be held at 8.15 p.m., the next Business Meeting to be held on Wednesday, May 13th, at 8.15 p.m. It was further decided that Members not present should be notified of the time of the next Scientific Meeting.

Notes

1 On 15 April 1942, after this meeting, Klein wrote to her group about how to deal with the attacks made by Melitta Schmideberg, on herself and others. She wrote:

> The fact that in the years until Dr S. turned against me *her* criticism was dreaded in the Society can easily be mentioned, because people will remember that very well . . . Dr Yates, before reading her first paper, begged her for clemency during the discussion. . . . one can certainly refer to the sharpness of her criticism of younger members and of people in general, up to the time when she turned against me. Another of her victims was Anna Freud at the Congress in Lucerne in the

131

summer, 1934, and I am sure that Anna Freud remembers this paper very well.

(Klein Archives)

2 On 4 Feb. 1942, Glover read a paper to the Society on 'Intuition and Interpretation'; I cannot trace if it was published in this form.
3 Some papers relating to this investigation into charges of plagiarism are in the Archives of the British Psycho-Analytical Society.
4 Dr Millais Culpin was a respected research psychiatrist whose field of interest was in industrial psychology and the effect on people of their working conditions.

5

The Fourth
Extraordinary Business Meeting

**Minutes of Business Meeting
held on Wednesday, May 13th, 1942, at 8.15 p.m.**

Dr Jones was in the Chair and 25 members were present (Glover, Payne, W. Hoffer, H. Hoffer, M. Schmideberg, W. Schmideberg, Weiss, Anna Freud, Burlingham, Low, Haas, Ruben, Friedlander, Lantos, Herford, Brierley, Sharpe, Franklin, Wilson, Klein, Riviere, Isaacs, Winnicott, Heimann, Steiner).

DR JONES thanks for the appreciation shown to him on the occasion of his election to fellowship of the Royal College of Physicians. Psychoanalysis has changed its form more or less during the last ten years.

DR JONES, the Chairman, then proceeded to the question of reading the minutes of the last Business Meeting, stating that they were rather lengthy as were the ones before which were not read through. The Chairman suggests that Dr Payne might summarize them to save time.

DR PAYNE summarized the minutes of the last meeting (April 15th, 1942).

DR GLOVER informed the Members of letters received by Miss Sheehan-Dare and Dr Foulkes from Exeter and the damage they suffered, also Dr Foulkes' request to members to lend him any sets or spare numbers of the Journal, *Zeitschrift* and *Imago*.

THE CHAIRMAN then outlined the present situation. In the meeting before last you will remember that Dr Glover and Dr Schmideberg read papers discussing the question of the activities of

133

what they call a clique in the Society. In the course of that Dr Schmideberg made the very remarkable statement that the majority of Members felt themselves ill-treated by that clique. At the opening of the next meeting three members came to me and said that they wished to bring forward evidence to rebut this thing – which they did. Dr Schmideberg, one gathers, is prepared to substantiate what she said. I pointed out that the Society had never had any reason hitherto to devise any machinery for dealing with such problems, fortunately.

This seemed to be our next move: how would the Society prepare to meet a situation in which a great number of Members is accused of browbeating or badly treating others and other Members say that this is quite untrue? The question is how to investigate such charges. I made the point that you could not get any judicial elucidation of the truth by a large body involved in the discussion of the situation. Nevertheless the Society after two or three hours' discussion decided that that was the only way they were prepared to set about the matter. They did not decide, however, which point they wish to investigate. You have at the moment therefore a very clear issue before you, there are only two choices.

We have not so far come to the point which you now have to decide, whether on the one hand to pass by these matters and to proceed to other topics, which means that no objections are raised to such statements being made, or, on the other hand, to deal with that statement itself, discuss it, investigate, ascertain whether it is true or false, come to a conclusion and express an opinion about it.

MISS LOW: I do not understand why you are talking about one statement. If we decide to make an investigation of statements, then it is statements.

DR JONES: The reason why we state that point is that this was the point we had reached and which gave rise on one hand to the protests, on the other hand to the question of a machinery of investigation. We can concentrate on this matter or pass on to other matters. We will hear the different opinions.

MISS LOW: I don't think the issue has been put correctly. If we are going to decide what to speak about or not, or to vote, we must state it correctly. Various statements have been made and we must refer to all of them. Mrs Riviere's statement to my mind includes many statements which want investigation. Otherwise it might mean that her statement is going to be passed over.

DR JONES: It was on the same topic, an answer to it.

MR SCHMIDEBERG: The logical conclusion of the last meeting was that the whole investigation should be put before the Society. This should be done now.

134

MISS SHARPE: I want to make a correction of the report of what I said. I made a very careful discrimination. I said then that no report of a disparaging nature had reached me via my consulting room. Things have been reported to me, disagreeable and disparaging remarks have been reported to me by Members. I said that I have chosen to be a non-conductor of such matters.

DR M. SCHMIDEBERG: The last meeting voted on the investigation. Dr Stephen said that it is not the matter of a Member but of the whole Society if charges are made. Dr Jones said we cannot go on with the discussion if Members can be attacked like that. It was also decided as Mrs Riviere was asked whether she wants to press a charge against me, I 'said that I want it to be investigated and Dr Jones said I have the right to insist on it.

DR GLOVER: If I remember right, Mrs Riviere was pressed if she wanted to make a charge against Dr Schmideberg. She said she wanted to proceed with the charges against myself.

DR ISAACS: She said this when the President asked her which charge against Mrs Klein and her adherents, made by the speakers on March 11th, she would select as the first to be investigated.

MRS RIVIERE: I did not ask for an enquiry, nor have I suggested it at any time or in any way.

DR HAAS: I was under the impression that Mrs Riviere made charges and I thought these charges should be investigated. I thought that the most important charge was that against Dr Glover as he is an officer of the Society.

DR M. SCHMIDEBERG: Does any Member want charges not to be investigated? If so, what was the purpose of the discussion at the last meeting?

MR W. SCHMIDEBERG: I said if somebody makes charges it is only fair to substantiate them. Then the whole question came up whether to ask Dr Culpin, etc.

DR BRIERLEY: I feel certain that every Member in this room would be glad to clear up the whole matter. We gathered from Mrs Riviere's speech that she felt Dr Glover had made charges, although he could not finish his contribution. We should like to hear what Dr Glover has to say.

DR GLOVER: (Paper) Of the twenty training analysts in Britain eighteen are situated in London, where virtually all the training work in this country is carried out. By reason of their position and function these eighteen training analysts can make or mar the future of psychoanalysis in –

DR JONES: I am quite sure Dr Glover has a great deal to say and will, of course, have every opportunity to say it. I don't know how

135

far he is going to embark on the matter of the Training Committee and how far you wish to go into it now. I have been trying to keep things to a point and to deal with them as thoroughly as possible. It may be impossible to deal with any matter without touching upon the others.

DR GLOVER: On various occasions resolutions which came at the end of the Agenda were discussed first. I base my appeal on the fact that certain charges have been made against me and that I want a free hand in dealing with them. (Going on with his paper)

(Paper) By reason of their position and function these eighteen training analysts can make or mar the future of psychoanalysis in Britain. Eight at least of these eighteen can in my opinion be regarded as the backbone of the Klein party.

DR JONES: I have been asked specially to attend to the question of courtesy. 'Klein party' is not a courteous phrase to use.

DR GLOVER apologizes for using the word 'Klein party' and proposes to call it 'Mrs Klein and her adherents'.

MRS RIVIERE asks for names to be given.

DR GLOVER: I appeal to the President that I may continue. I am perfectly willing to lay papers on the table. (Goes on with paper)

(Paper) Eight at least of these eighteen can in my opinion be regarded as adherents to the views of Mrs Klein: indeed if we include one other who strongly supports her views the number would be raised to nine. However, let us call it eight. By way of contrast three of the eighteen training analysts are Viennese Freudians. At least five, possibly six (and I really don't mind if you call it seven), are in my opinion English Freudians (or, as they have sometimes been labelled, Middle groupers).

Now the number of active members normally residing in and around London is forty-five. (I exclude here those who have recently gone abroad or have ceased to take any interest or part in the Society.) Of these forty-five, it can in my opinion be said with reasonable accuracy that twelve (possibly thirteen) are either out-and-out adherents of Mrs Klein's views or so near as to make no difference. There are in my opinion twenty-three English Freudians and seven Vienna Freudians to which I think may fairly be added two from the Berlin group, making a total of nine. Thus we see that of twelve, possibly thirteen adherents of Mrs Klein eight, possibly nine, hold key positions of authority as training analysts – a percentage ratio of at least 61 per cent, possibly 60 per cent. The corresponding ratio in the case of English Freudians or Middle groupers is at least 22 per cent, possibly 26 per cent, but you can call it 30 per cent if you like. In the case of the Vienna (plus Berlin) group 33 per cent.

In addition to this it should be remembered that two of the three Viennese had already acquired training status in Vienna: the point being that they were not selected by our Committee – merely taken over. Five of the six English Freudian training analysts were elected before the Klein controversy began. In the six years up to 1940 every training analyst appointed (five in all) was an adherent of Mrs Klein. True, one non-Kleinian was appointed in 1940 and one Viennese Freudian in 1941. But it should be recalled that after 1938 the Training Committee had a different balance of forces. Dr Jones resigned, Mr Strachey, Miss Freud, and Mrs Bibring were added and I was appointed Chairman.

I trust the bearing of these facts on the present crisis in the Psycho-Analytical Society is clear, but in case it is not, I will repeat now what I said in the introductory part of an unfinished speech given at a Business Meeting two months ago.[1]

My main contention then was that discussion of scientific aims and differences existing within the Society is only a pious exercise unless it is *preceded* by discussion of the following crucial issues, viz. (1) whether partisan groups of Members exist in a state of active organization and (2) whether they seek to exploit official committees within the Society in order to secure power, and by 'power' I mean in particular the power to establish their professional views and methods, whether these views and methods have been accepted by the Society or not. My next point was that although in the early days of the Society there was a good deal of backstairs activity it was mostly in the form of *unorganized* criticism, mostly gossip. The first definite sign of organization was manifested in the development of the block vote – a system whereby nominations for Associate or Full Membership could be successfully blackballed by concerted action. Finally I pointed out that this block vote system fell into disuse, not simply because, with the gradual increase in Society membership it was not so easy to blackball effectively but because, with the formation of the Training Committee, the real power of the Society no longer resided in the Council or in the Annual Business Meeting. It passed from the Council to the Training Committee. I have held all along and repeat again that the idea of the Council as an autocratic body governing the destinies of psychoanalysis has for the past fourteen years been a myth. The Council is, like any other Council, a pedestrian body, regulating the business administration of the Society. *The destinies of psychoanalysis in this country lie in the hands of the Training Committee.*

Now the statistics I have put before you tonight are open to anyone to check.[2] No breach of confidence regarding the activities of the Training Committee is involved by stating them here and now. And so I trust you will not regard these statements as 'misrepresentations', 'gross in character', or 'false and unfounded in content', or 'dominated by personal ill feeling', 'hostility', or 'animosity'. I hope you will not regard them as 'personal accusations' or as 'veiled hints' or as 'offensive aspersions' or as 'unscrupulous inventions'. Lastly I hope you will not regard them as a proof of any 'deliberate striving' on my part 'to stir up and increase personal feeling and stimulate and prolong personal rancour and feud'. Those of you who were present at the last Business Meeting will no doubt remember some of these phrases. I have selected them from a number of epithets used by Mrs Riviere when with half-pained and wholly solemn deliberation she made a number of charges against me.[3] It is both interesting and important to consider what actually happened at that last Business Meeting. A visitor from the planet Mars would, I think, have formed the impression that the troubles of the Society had the same origin as certain poltergeist phenomena, that is to say that they were due to the reprehensible conduct of a few naughty, ill-disposed, and, scientifically speaking, biased individuals ˙ who had wantonly attacked, by various scurrilous means, the scientific work of a serious and rather long-suffering group. He might even have sympathized with Mrs Isaacs when she re-affirmed the old pedagogic view which runs that naughty children should be expelled from school if they don't behave. She referred specifically to Rule 20 of our constitution.[4]

In my opinion the real danger of the proceedings of the last Business Meeting lay in the fact that they might have drawn a red herring across the real trail. They might have distracted attention from what is in my opinion the crucial question; namely, *what procedures apart from the scientific discussion of evidence, can be and are used in this Society to propagate controversial views.* I am not much concerned tonight with the fact that Mrs Riviere made a series of what are usually called 'attacks' on me personally. I think she made a psychological blunder by behaving in this way and Miss Low was in the right when she pointed out in effect that people who take a highminded line about real or imaginary offensiveness should not themselves behave offensively. I don't think personal attacks matter very much to the person at whom they are directed. What really matters now is the accuracy of Mrs Riviere's statements.

Having throughout these Business Meetings listened to quite a number of little homilies on the nature of science I was curious to discover what degree of scientific objectivity Mrs Riviere could maintain in the field of polemic. But it was soon obvious, to me at any rate, that her partisan enthusiasm had outrun her scientific discretion. Mrs Riviere failed because, to put it colloquially but I hope not too offensively, the herring was just a little too red.

The confusion that might have arisen in the minds of Members not well versed in the internal history of the Society was not caused by Mrs Riviere. On the same evening two Members whose repute stands deservedly high in the Society – I refer to Dr Payne and Miss Sharpe – made speeches which might have conveyed the impression that they supported Mrs Riviere's thesis in its entirety. Mrs Riviere herself was evidently under this impression. She specifically referred to both speeches in support of her own attack. This source of confusion must be cleared up tonight.

Now it may interest you to know that since the last meeting I have been approached by several prominent Members of the Society asking me to ignore Mrs Riviere's attack however justified I might be in replying. Despite these appeals, there are four considerations which compel me to make a brief reply: (a) when pressed by the Chairman, Mrs Riviere flatly stated that the charges she had made against me should be referred to a tribunal;[5] (b) the Society took the healthy course of insisting that any such charges should be investigated – not by a small Committee working *in camera* but in the full publicity of a Business Meeting; (c) I could not maintain my self-respect if I stood by in silence when any attempt is made to find scapegoats for the sins of groups or for that part for the sins of the Society as a whole including its office bearers of whom I am one (I refer of course to Mrs Riviere's attack on the Schmidebergs). And (d) by allowing attention to be *focused* on charges of scientific misconduct made against *individuals*, attention might be *distracted* from the more serious problem of the scientific methods adopted by groups.

My reply to Mrs Riviere then takes the simple form of examining the accuracy of any specific charges she made, however trivial they may appear. I dislike spending time on personalities as much as you do but we must know where Mrs Riviere stands in this respect. For instance: she said that in a recent paper of mine on intuition I made 'offensive aspersions on the character and quality of Mrs Klein's motives and methods in her work'. I made no such aspersions; and propose to submit the paper for publication in the *International Journal of Psycho-Analysis*. To take a more trivial instance, Mrs Riviere made the following statement: 'Dr Glover in *his* speech then alluded more than once to me and Mrs Isaacs as the *only Members* who wished to change the Society's rules and this misrepresentation of the facts was corrected by the President'. Now the original of my curtailed speech was handed to Mrs Neurath *during* the meeting. Any

Member who cares can read it. It contains no such statement. Dr Jones' remark is also on record. It corrected no such misrepresentation. Mrs Riviere continued: 'Along with this went his open accusations of being inspired by personal and self-interested motives – in plain words, of suggesting a change of office simply because we wanted to be officers ourselves'. Now, curiously enough, the only point in my speech to which this could possibly refer was where I insisted that it was important to find out whether groups could exert influence on the development of scientific opinion through committees of this Society – a perfectly legitimate question, by the way. Moreover, I added the following clause (here are my exact words): 'Mark the word "committees", *not* the "executives" '. I think possibly Mrs Riviere must have got me mixed up with Dr Payne. The only specific mention of self-interest I have heard during these discussions was made by Dr Payne on February 25th when she wrote that 'the intensity of the crisis is partly dependent on fear of economic insecurity'.

Again Mrs Riviere in order to contest my statements about the block vote stated that Miss Chadwick was rejected by a majority vote of the Society. On the contrary, Miss Chadwick on each occasion was supported not only by the Council but by a large majority of the Members. She was rejected by a small but compact minority using the block vote. This is borne out by the fact that following this series of rejections of Miss Chadwick and others the Council proposed a resolution intended to curtail the power of blackballing.

Now I am perfectly aware that these points may appear trifling to you; I mention them merely that you may judge for yourselves of the objective value of Mrs Riviere's speech: I don't propose to spend any more time on personalities. But here are some interesting sidelights. Mrs Riviere said my reference to 'power politics' was vague and 'seems to be an invention'. As to being an invention, I quote now from Dr Payne's statement of February 25th. Dr Payne wrote: 'The fear of economic insecurity is important, however, because when economic fear is added to difference of scientific outlook all tolerance is likely to disappear and the struggle becomes principally one for power.' Actually I am not interested in this aspect of power politics. I am however concerned with any form of power the object of which is to influence scientific opinion without recourse to demonstration or discussion.

Perhaps the most interesting of Mrs Riviere's arguments was her quotation of certain laudatory references of mine in a review of Mrs Klein's book. She went on: 'Since about 1935 however he has changed his mind which he is entitled to do: but as he has made no considered statement to the Society of his reasons for so doing, whatever his own views he is not entitled to resent or interfere with others' etc., etc., etc. [Glover,E. 1933:199]. A stranger reading this might imagine that Mrs Klein had not produced any views since she first published her book in 1932. Actually my main scientific differences with Mrs Klein date from the time she began to postulate *central* depressive positions and manic defences: and Mrs Riviere must have forgotten that I commenced my public criticism after the Lucerne Congress. (My considered Review was called 'Some Aspects of Psycho-analytical Research', read in October 1934.) I omit here numerous public references and criticisms both spoken and written I have made since that date not only in London but at the Paris weekend conference.

Then I note that Mrs Riviere makes great play with Dr Brierley's 'conciliatory paper' etc., etc., stating that I brush all this tolerance aside. It may interest her to know that Dr Brierley's paper [Brierley 1942],[6] the views contained in which I have been familiar with for many years, was given when it was at *my* express request although Dr Brierley would have welcomed more time to prepare it and said so in her introduction.

But I think that is about enough. Let me end by quoting one more sentence Mrs Riviere said: 'It is a *commonplace* in the world of science that every scientific worker seeks to convince others of the truth of his conclusions and to teach others *so as to enable them to make observations similar to his own*' (my italics). I could not myself have stated my criticism of the policy followed by Mrs Klein and her adherents more devastatingly or more convincingly.

Now as to Dr Payne's speech.[7] No one who knows Dr Payne will question her transparent sincerity, her desire for peace, or her genuine indignation at anything she conceives to be underhand. But I think that on this occasion her patent desire to avoid a split in the Society led her to make some rather hasty judgements. This is certainly not her customary policy. On the contrary, on February 25th she wrote, 'I would therefore ask Members not to be precipitate in making judgements'. On the issue of power politics I have already quoted her and would only add this comment. When Dr Payne gives her opinion that it is untrue to say that the Klein group 'have been guilty of striving for power for power's sake', she is pushing an open door. No one to my knowledge has said so, unless of course Dr Payne herself when she referred to the factor of economic insecurity and that was not specifically directed to the Klein group. I must however confess that I would have been a little more impressed by her protest against methods and emotional atmosphere if she had made this protest, not just when Dr Schmideberg criticized the Klein group but when Mrs Klein on earlier occasions attacked Dr Schmideberg in a personal manner. And incidentally may I say that I do not think family affairs are the business of the Society: I would myself prefer that any reference to them were ruled out of order from whatever quarter it came. But if some Members insist on drawing conclusions from this line of argument, all I can say is that it takes two to make a quarrel, familial or extra-familial.

Now as to the attacks on the Schmidebergs: I think you will agree that both of these Members are fully capable of making their own reply. But I am also certain that you will demand they have fair play, that you would not countenance anything remotely resembling a concerted personal attack on them or, alternatively, that if any such attempt were made it would not succeed in distracting your attention from the main issues, viz. (a) whether the statements they made have any ground, (b) whether, if they have any ground, their use is justified by any light they may throw on the present crisis in the Society. I have read with care the passages in the speeches, to which exception was taken at the last meeting by three Members. And it seems to me that before we consider the question of approval or disapproval of these passages we should first of all decide what degree of honesty or frankness we are prepared to endure in order to improve the scientific function of the Society. I am sure you would disapprove of tactlessness for tactlessness' sake, but I am equally sure you would not approve of any glossing over facts just for the sake of appearances. So, for goodness sake don't let's have any excess of high moral indignation, any saintly martyrdoms, or any impeccable self-righteousness. Everyone here knows that the standard of professional and scientific discretion in psychological societies is lower than that of natural science societies or ordinary medical societies. I have often heard our President complain bitterly of the lack of professional standards in this Society, but I must admit that he had in mind chiefly the behaviour of some lay analysts. You may perhaps remember his public strictures on this subject and the circular, signed also by myself, that he sent to all practising lay Members.

Now I don't pretend to have personal knowledge of all the seventeen or so specific incidents to which Dr Schmideberg referred: and bearing in mind a point made earlier by Dr Jones, I am perfectly ready to agree that the adherents of Mrs Klein should not be turned into scapegoats. But I am bound to say that in at any rate half the instances quoted, I have first-hand proof that her statements are *not*

142

groundless. And I am by no means the only Member of the executive or of the Society who is in this position. But let me confine myself to the three points to which I have a right to refer on this occasion: after hearing the speech given by Miss Sharpe at the last meeting some of you may have been inclined to believe that Dr Schmideberg was mistaken in the facts in question and that therefore the whole of her criticisms were also likely to be misplaced. Now no one of us would deny that Miss Sharpe is transparently honest. I have personally no doubt of her desire for a peaceful solution of our difficulties and I respect the motive which led her to say that she had 'no personal knowledge' from 'inside her consulting room' of 'anything said or done to undermine confidence in her work'. But she did agree both implicitly and explicitly that she had heard of the uncomplimentary things said about her outside her consulting room.[8] Again about her references to Dr Middlemore, whilst I do not question the accuracy of Miss Sharpe's memory, I think she painted in retrospect a picture of Dr Middlemore's relations with various members of the Society which must have seemed a little rosy to some. I knew from personal contact with Dr Middlemore that from the very first paper she gave when still a candidate she had few illusions as to the criticisms to which she was subject or from which direction they came.

Secondly; as to Dr Schmideberg's reference to myself, I need only give you one relevant instance. I had reported to me verbatim by an eye surgeon friend of mine in the provinces exactly what had been said about me and from what source it came. I reported the incident to the President, asking him to make a suitable protest and so I regard the case as closed.

As I say, we must decide first of all what degree of courage and frankness it is expedient to maintain by Members in supporting professional traditions. For myself I am perfectly prepared to admit that I have been unduly timid and diplomatic in the past, always hoping that the atmosphere would improve, and I believe that in their heart of hearts there are many other executives and committee members who feel the same about their past lack of firmness in this respect.

Already I feel conscience stricken about the length of time I have been compelled to devote to rebutting accusations. I can only plead in extenuation that it is none of my choosing. I have been driven after many years of silence to speak my mind. And so coming to my last point, I would remind you that at the last meeting Dr Friedlander said I had been attacked not so much for what I had said but for what it was anticipated I would say. This was a sound observation, and I feel entitled now to ask that you should listen to the unread portion of the

143

speech I prepared two months ago. I will then leave you to judge for yourselves.

I have already recapitulated my introduction: here is the actual remainder word for word. The last sentence of my historical survey began:

'The focus of power in the Society moved from the Business Meeting to the Training Committee. And there it still lies. Make no mistake about this, whatever may be said for or against the Council is relatively unimportant compared with what can and must be said about the struggle to control training of candidates.'

Here I go on:

'Now training committees subject to the sanction of the International Training Commission[9] have very considerable autonomy of function. The committee selects candidates, prepares the curriculum, does all the teaching, appoints all the teachers (the training analysts, the control analysts, the seminar leaders, the lecturers) and does all the examining. In other words *it controls absolutely and without appeal entrance to the Society*. The Society can reject Training Committee nominees but it cannot (nor can any Member) train other nominees except through the Training Committee.'

DR JONES: No others than candidates? The Society has never given up its power of nominating candidates.

DR GLOVER: Strictly speaking that is true as far as non-practising analysts are concerned such as anthropologists, etc., but as far as practising analysts are concerned, no others than persons who have passed the training can become a Member of the Society. The Training Committee controls absolutely and without appeal the entrance into the Society. The Training Committee can make or mar candidates – it can make but not mar training analysts[10] – it can make or mar the Society, and in the long run it can make or mar psychoanalysis in this country. Small wonder then the block vote and membership of the Council faded into insignificance or that elections for the Training Committee were more keenly contested and canvassed than the Council elections ever were.

Now on paper at any rate the Training Committee would appear to be a body imbued with a proper regard for scientific aims. And actually when it started work it did sincerely devote itself to these aims. Naturally its work was full of flaws. There was much that could have been criticized, in particular the growing tendency of partisans to praise their own candidates and explicitly or implicitly to

144

criticize the candidates of other training analysts. But this might have been passed over as a harmless manifestation of the counter-transference of the training analysts concerned. Even so at one time the Training Committee made a serious effort to cope with part of this difficulty by refusing to accept any reports on candidates that were not personally sponsored by the training analyst, the control analyst, or the seminar leaders, i.e. by excluding hearsay reports which tended to reflect either gossip or prejudice or both. After a time, however, it became apparent that the difficulty was not just one of counter-transference. Existence of differences in point of view, differences about the content and internal regulation of analysis, differences between classical Freudian views and so-called new or deep analysis (representing what was about that time called inaccurately the English School) began to percolate into the teaching system. And from that time on it would be fair to say that partisan influences were at work. Two trends of opinion made their appearance, one that students should be taught only accepted Freudian principles, and the other that there was no objection to teaching students material which was not only in my opinion, but in the opinion of many Members of the Society, controversial. For a time this cleavage was glossed over by all concerned and naturally there was never an openly avowed aim of gaining adherents or making converts, but the mere fact that a struggle of this sort was going on behind the scenes threatened the future integrity of the Society. I think it is obvious that if you set out to gain adherents through the training organization, it is not really very important whether the Society discusses scientific issues or not. Because in the long run the Society will come to consist of 'adherents' only.

Now I would like to specify explicitly what I regard as the most important practices which are subject to abuse. I use the term 'abuse' in its scientific sense, i.e. a method which does not conform to (bypasses) the accepted procedures of science. There are: (1) the advancement of candidates because of pre-existing allegiances or because of an earlier private therapeutic analysis; (2) the criticism, particularly in control analyses, direct or implicit of candidates who do not hold those allegiances; (3) the canvassing for adherents, for example persuading even already licensed candidates that it would be well for them to undertake a 'deeper' analysis; (4) (*and this I would like to say is the really vital point) the teaching to candidates as accepted psychoanalytical theory and practice material or method which is still controversial and regarding which the Society itself has not come to any conclusion*; (5) the election and advancement of lecturers, seminar holders, control analysts, and training analysts on the strength of

145

their allegiances and not simply on their scientific and teaching capacities; (6) a *private* discussion as to the placing and advancement of candidates and training analysts, i.e. the making of provisional training arrangements to be put subsequently before an official meeting of the committee, when, as is only natural, they are likely to be passed.

You must realize of course that a specific list of this sort sounds much more obvious than it appears when the committee is in actual session, also that for the purposes of this paper I am concerned only with abuses – not with legitimate scientific difficulties and problems such as the length of training analyses. But already there are two important indications of the bad effect of this training situation. The one with which you are most familiar is of course the absence of real scientific discussion at meetings of the Society. The old block vote of the Business Meeting has for some years become the block expression of partisan opinion at Society meetings. But a more serious state of affairs is to be observed amongst candidates. And here I must make a confession. I have all along been one of those who held that candidates are not or should not be sucking infants – that they should be able to stand up to differences of opinion and method existing amongst their teachers and that they should learn to form their own opinions on controversial matters. Experience has taught me, however, that this is too much to expect from any but the most superior candidates; but even well-balanced candidates are unfavourably affected by the situation. From recent experiences of taking seminars I should say that our present candidates are in a welter of confusion, bafflement, and bewilderment. Nor is it possible for the candidate to escape – for his transferences once established will handcuff him securely to his analytical father or mother. When the committee is allocating candidates to training analysts I sometimes am tempted to write a new version of the old Gilbert and Sullivan snatch: 'Every little boy or girl, born in this world alive, is either a little Liberal or else a little Conservative'.

This is the consequence of what in effect is a propaganda system of training. Ask any candidate and he will tell you more about schisms in the Society than many a Member of the Society. So we might as well be frank. It is now an open secret that the Training Committee has for some time been at a deadlock on this issue. It was already almost at a deadlock before the war, when two leaders, Anna Freud and Melanie Klein, were openly agreed that it was impossible for candidates sponsored by one group to be taught or controlled by training analysts drawn from the other. I personally am now inclined to agree with them. It seemed to me just before the war that if no

146

agreement could be reached, a split in training methods must follow. Discussion along these lines was just coming to a head when, owing to the Blitz and to the departure from London of many training and control analysts, a strange peace descended on the committee. But I know this was only temporary, and as the Klein representatives were absent I felt it proper to propose that no changes should be made until such time as discussions could be again representative. I felt that this was the proper course, indeed the only course, that would be fair to absent members. But if and when these discussions are resumed (this, I would remind you, was written two months ago) and if or when a deadlock is again reached (and this, I think, is certain unless everyone agrees to stop proselytizing), I would feel it my duty to report this fact to the Council and through the Council to the Society.

Two last comments – the question may be asked, why was this state of affairs not reported earlier. Well, firstly, as I have said, many of these influences are and have been for many years intangible – secondly, anyone who has done committee work knows perfectly well that it is important to try as patiently as possible to reduce internal oppositions and clashes in a committee without coming to open rupture or reporting failure; and thirdly, as I have indicated, but for the war the deadlock would no doubt have already been reported to the Society.

The second comment is perhaps more important. It is perfectly clear from previous discussions that quite a different interpretation can be offered of the situation I have described. It can be said and no doubt will be said that what I have called the partisan group are really the scientists and that their legitimate and laudable efforts are merely obstructed by reactionary-minded people who cannot recognize scientific progress when they see it. (This, by the way, was an accurate prophecy.) I must leave you to judge as to this. There is certainly nothing to be gained by doubting the sincerity or intensity of purpose of those who hold these views. But that is not a proof of the validity of the methods. In any case, what is sauce for the goose is sauce for the gander – neither is there any point in questioning the sincerity of those who regard the present situation as an abuse of scientific traditions. Those appeals to sincerity cancel out. So does all the talk of good or bad emotions, of constructive and destructive criticisms, of democratic and autocratic government. What finally matters is that we should purge the Society of propagandist techniques and return to scientific methods of exposition, discussion and teaching.

That marks the end of the speech I prepared but did not give two months ago.[11] It only remains to add that the issue is a grave one and that it cannot be avoided by artificial compromises. Make converts and adherents of the public if you want, or if you enjoy it. But don't make converts or adherents of people who, whether they are good or bad scientists, by nature, are our only available investigators. Frankly I am coming to believe that the principals, the leaders in these controversies, will never agree. They can only hope to convert each other – a forlorn hope, I think. The only people who will ever compromise as the result of discussion are those who are already compromised in their minds. That may be an unduly pessimistic view, but it is at any rate a view that should be considered on its merits before embarking on ambitious or misleading projects of '*scientific reconciliation*'.

DR M. SCHMIDEBERG: May I make my statement briefly? It is not long and has a bearing on some of Dr Glover's points.

(Paper) As Dr Glover dealt with a number of points raised I will try to be brief. Mrs Riviere claims that I made the 'phantastic statement' 'that the greater part of the Members feel browbeaten or pushed out by a small clique'. I said no such thing. Nor did I say as she implied that Dr Karin Stephen was 'browbeaten' or that Mrs Strachey was browbeaten or 'pushed out'. Before Mrs Riviere challenges the veracity of others she should go to some trouble to find out the truth. (By the way, Dr Jones misquoted me when he alleged that I said the greater part of the Members feel browbeaten by a comparatively small clique.)

DR JONES interrupted to state that Mrs Schmideberg had used these words and that they were in the minutes.

MRS SCHMIDEBERG replies that in her copy of her speech this was not contained.

DR JONES looks up the copy of the minutes and points out to Dr Schmideberg that the words used are in her speech. It was stated that Mrs Schmideberg had referred to another part of her paper than that in which she had mentioned the word 'browbeaten'.

DR M. SCHMIDEBERG: (Paper continued) Before Mrs Riviere challenges the veracity of others she should go to some trouble to find out the truth. When she alludes to e.g. Dr Bryan, or Professor Flugel, does she give their version of the situation, or her own? Is she sure that the remarkable statement concerning Dr Yates' relation to Mrs Klein expresses Dr Yates' view? She wisely refrains from commenting on my remarks concerning Miss Grant Duff, Miss Low, Dr Friedlander, Drs Brierley, Franklin, Carroll, and Glover or on the Viennese. I want to remind you only of one detail. Some years ago Miss Low stated that Members were intimidated and Dr Carroll said that whilst he had no difficulties in speaking outside the Society he did not like to speak in the Society. I am surprised that there should be any need to prove this point. The general unsatisfactoriness of the situation has been recently stressed by Miss Low, Drs Stephen, Wilson, and others. Mrs Isaacs felt it was so bad that we could not wait with the reorganization of the Society till the war was over.

Now Mrs Riviere seems to give the impression that everything is all right, or at least rapidly improving were it not for three wicked members, namely Dr Glover, my husband, and myself. She seems to base her optimism largely on the following: 'Notably we had Dr Brierley's conciliatory paper urging us to mutual tolerance; and lately Miss Freud's interesting report was followed by a genuinely appreciative and co-operative discussion.' It is somewhat pathetic that the fact that two good papers were followed by a normal discussion should be regarded as such a remarkable event. During the Blitz winter all discussions were correct and friendly. The only remarkable thing about the discussion of Miss Freud's paper[12] was that the Kleinians abstained from attacking it.

When she says that Dr Bowlby's paper had a very good reception and only one point was challenged, surely Mrs Riviere must have forgotten that at the Business Meeting when Dr Bowlby's name was put forward for election as Member, Dr Rickman, seconded by Dr Winnicott and somewhat less obviously Mrs Riviere, raised the question whether Associates should be elected on the strength of such papers.[13] This question was definitely answered by Miss Sharpe, Mr Strachey, Dr Glover, and myself, though probably not in the sense Dr Rickman expected. I remember that a few days before Dr Bowlby's paper driving home from Miss Freud's seminar I said to one of the Viennese – it was either Dr Hoffer or Dr Bibring – 'Next Wednesday you are going to get a sidelight on the London Society. You probably cannot appreciate Bowlby's courage for taking the line he is going to take. You will see how he will be attacked and he must be defended.' Mrs Riviere claims the right to express criticism in discussions, in particular in respect to Dr Matte.[14] I would be the last to deny this right, but it seems that a double measure is being applied. If some six Members make a concerted attack on a beginner, then that is a legitimate discussion. If a non-Kleinian tries to clarify a certain point or only asks for a definition, then this is personal hostility and a disturbance of scientific work. As to Dr Matte, he has been, as you probably know, Professor of Physiology at the University of Santiago, before he became an analyst. At present he holds a teaching position at the

Duke University, North Carolina. Whilst in London he worked at the Maudsley Hospital. He has as much, if not more, knowledge of academic tradition as most Members. I suggest that Mrs Riviere enquires from him whether in his opinion the discussions and the atmosphere in this Society were in accordance with academic standards. I am sure he will give her a detailed answer.

To come to the next point: I hope Mr Schmideberg will forgive me if I take up a point that largely concerns him as well – the issue whether Boehm has been given due credit by Mrs Klein. It seems that Mrs Riviere chose this as a test case. She correctly looked up in the index of Mrs Klein's book that Boehm's name is mentioned on pp. 103, 189, 327, 333, and 348. She omitted however to read the introduction to this book [Klein 1932]. May I read two passages from it?

> My thanks are next due to Dr Edward Glover for the warm and unfailing interest he has shown in my work, and the way in which he has assisted me by his sympathetic criticism. He has been of special service in pointing out the respects in which my conclusions agree with the already existing and accepted theories of Psycho-Analysis.
>
> (Melanie Klein: *The Psycho-Analysis of Children*, 1932, Preface, p. 12)

and

> Last but not least, let me very heartily thank my daughter, Dr Melitta Schmideberg, for the devoted and valuable help which she has given me in the preparation of this book.   (Same as above)

I may add that this help consisted partly in making the bibliography, index, and the necessary references. Dr Glover went through the whole manuscript independently and made detailed notes as to which authors should be quoted. At Mrs Klein's request I then went to see Dr Glover and compared his notes with mine. I hope that owing to our concerted efforts the references of Mrs Klein's book are now reasonably accurate. The same cannot be said about her papers. In the one on 'Symbol-formation' (Klein 1930), on 'Early Stages of the Oedipus Complex' (Klein 1928), 'Intellectual Inhibition' (Klein 1931), in her 'Notes on a Case described by Dr Bryan' (1928 [unpublished]), on 'Person Play of Children' (Klein 1929 [unpublished]), 'Psychogenesis of Manic-depressive States' (Klein 1935), and on 'Mourning' (Klein 1940) – seven papers altogether – all dealing with phantasies concerning the father's penis in the mother's womb, Boehm is not mentioned. Nor does his name appear in the book on upbringing by five psycho-analysts (Rickman 1936), when the same subject is discussed. In the detailed bibliography Dr Jones attached to his papers on the 'Phallic Phase' (Jones 1933) and on 'Female Sexuality' (Jones 1935) Dr Jones gives all credit for these views to Mrs Klein and does not mention Boehm. The same applies to two papers by Dr Brierley, one by Dr Payne (1936), one by Dr Stephen (1934), several by Miss Searl, Mrs Riviere, and others. Boehm's theory is unfamiliar to most English analysts. I remember that Mr Schmideberg asked me with surprise when he first attended meetings here, why no credit was given to Boehm? Were this contribution of Boehm's common knowledge, surely Mrs Riviere would not have to make an effort trying to prove it.

There are some who think that Mrs Riviere attaches undue importance to such a trivial matter. I do not agree. To give adequate credit to others, to bring a new theory into line with the existing one, is a touchstone of scientific attitude.

What is the record of the Kleinians in this respect? Dr Foulkes after having conscientiously discussed the voluminous literature concerning introjection and allied topics comes to the following conclusion: 'My review may have disappointed some of you who perhaps hold an exaggerated opinion of the originality of the points specially stressed in this country. But on the other hand I have, I think, been able to show, far from sidetracking the work done on this subject by British analysts, that it has on the contrary sprung from our noblest traditions: Ferenczi, Freud, Abraham' (Foulkes 1937). Dr Brierley states that the examination of the literature (she seems to allude to papers by Dr Foulkes and me) makes it quite plain that 'Mrs Klein is no more responsible for the introduction of the concepts of introjection and projection mechanisms than she is for the concepts of oral and anal sadism'. Surely Dr Brierley would not have stressed this fact, if the contrary impression had not prevailed in some quarters.

Mrs Klein stated at the last but one Scientific Meeting that she had pointed out how the work of mourning takes place, and added that in her opinion traumatic shocks are being dealt with in a similar manner. In so doing she forgot that the first point has been described by Freud in 'Mourning and Melancholia' [Freud, S. 1917d: 152–70; SE 14:243–58], the second one in *Beyond the Pleasure Principle* [Freud, S. 1920; SE 18:3].

DR JONES: This has nothing to do with the present subject.

DR M. SCHMIDEBERG: Yes, it has, as Mrs Riviere objected to the statements concerning plagiarism. Dr Glover was interrupted five times and when other people speak nobody interrupts them.

151

DR PAYNE: The present situation demonstrates the impossibility of investigating charges at a Business Meeting. It seemed to me after the last meeting that I should have collected the documents, charges, etc. and compiled them to present them to this meeting. This would have made a lot of preliminary work necessary and it was absolutely impossible to do it.

DR M. SCHMIDEBERG: But we do object to this preliminary work.

DR PAYNE: It is necessary to trust some people in a Society, otherwise it might stop altogether.

DR GLOVER: I quite understand Dr Payne's point of view. The question of trust and mistrust has openly been discussed by the Society and should not be applied to Dr Schmideberg only. Dr Payne is speaking as if it applied only to Dr Schmideberg's case.

DR PAYNE: I am merely speaking about the practical issue.

DR JONES: Does the Society wish to go on in this rambling fashion? (To Dr M. Schmideberg) I quite see you want to substantiate what you said.

DR M. SCHMIDEBERG: The meeting agreed that I should substantiate my charges.

DR JONES: You are taking too many charges at once.

DR PAYNE: Statements do not substantiate a point.

DR JONES: Take only one point at a time. Your statement is too long.

DR M. SCHMIDEBERG: I am answering Mrs Riviere's charges.

DR JONES: If you wish to go on with that we will go on with it, but with only one point at a time.

DR M. SCHMIDEBERG: I am only taking one point, that is the reliability of Mrs Klein's quotations.

MISS ANNA FREUD: We agreed to take one point.

DR M. SCHMIDEBERG: Take the Boehm issue.

MISS LOW: Would Mrs Schmideberg take three or four points?

DR JONES agrees.

DR GLOVER: The whole of this meeting has been dealing with charges in general. I took up much time in so doing. But all of these arise out of Mrs Riviere's paper. Mrs Schmideberg does a similar thing on her own behalf. I cannot see why this should be objected to and that she should have to limit herself.

DR JONES: So you want everybody to make a statement and then the others to make counter-statements and so on.

DR LANTOS: We were able to follow Dr Glover's speech. I am not able to follow Dr Schmideberg's speech, because it is too quick and too much.

DR WILSON: Perhaps she could say it on another occasion.

152

DR JONES: I have not had the opportunity of voicing my opinion on Dr Glover's speech, but I do think that he raised the central issue. All this, however, seems to be counter-charges. If we do not take one thing at a time, it will be a complete muddle. Either we take one point at a time or we take Dr Glover's more fundamental attitude and see what it amounts to.

DR BRIERLEY: Let us stick to the central topic for the time being.

DR JONES: Yes, let us stick to the central topic for the time being and then if the Society wishes we can go into all these other questions.

DR WILSON: Can we not give Dr Schmideberg an opportunity to make her statement as a whole at another meeting?

DR JONES: Not more than at this meeting. We can give her this opportunity now. I must keep to the Society's wishes.

DR M. SCHMIDEBERG: Will Dr Jones apply the same policy to all the other speakers?

DR JONES: I said also that Dr Glover raised the most essential issue. May I briefly summarize. We are all agreed that people who hold certain scientific views are usually interested in the propagandist attitude of getting them accepted by colleagues. That is the normal interest in every Society. The point of issue in this Society is: Is it possible to define what is the legitimate method of spreading these views to others and what is an illegitimate method? Dr Glover is definitely of the opinion that Mrs Klein and her colleagues have used methods to spread their scientific views and he maintains that they use methods that are illegitimate and derogatory to science and interfere with the necessary freedom of opinion and discussion which is so essential to the progress of scientific thought. There are certainly legitimate and illegitimate methods and one can use either. Let me quote an analogy, a Chemical society for instance. It is quite conceivable that a professor may bribe a pupil to put forward a view promising him a high position. As I said, there are legitimate methods and there are illegitimate methods. To define the border is not so easy. What evidence is there that this border has been trespassed? Dr Glover has brought instances for five definite points. It seems that we shall have to investigate this.

ANNA FREUD: I quite misunderstood then the decision of the Society to discuss this part of Dr Glover's speech. I thought it meant to leave the subject of accusations and come to facts. What impressed me in Dr Glover's speech was that it stressed the situation in the Training Committee without stressing accusations.

I really think that if all members of the Training Committee used the most legitimate methods in dealing with the matters now in

153

question, we should still be at the same deadlock. If there are two controversial views in a society it is not possible to compromise. If we let ourselves be sidetracked in our own minds to investigate the methods used we will arrive nowhere. Nowhere in the world people use only legitimate methods. If someone is convinced of his views he will use all methods available. What is interesting is that the question in itself cannot be solved and this is what we should discuss.

DR JONES: Mrs Klein's problem is an ultimate problem. The question is whether this is a short cut or whether to investigate first the emotional factor which impedes discussion would be better. It is a great difficulty to combine controversial views in teaching bodies. When good feeling exists there is infinitely more chance in dealing with this great difficulty than when dealing with these grave charges. My object is not to sidetrack but to go the shortest way to the subject.

DR WILSON: I hate controversy, I like to feel I am friendly with all sections of the Society. I cannot judge as I do not know what happened outside the Society. I had the honour to be analysed by Dr Jones, for some time by Dr Edward Glover's brother, and by Mrs Klein. I do feel that in the course of my analysis by Mrs Klein I over and over again had brought up to me what a clever woman she was. Ever again she has said, that is not my work, that is Abraham's work, etc.

DR JONES: We should keep to the point Miss Freud has raised. Shall we keep to the question of teaching in the Society or first make an attempt to face the emotional difficulties that exist?

ANNA FREUD: I thought if we got clear about it that the best behaviour won't change anything, we might feel less strongly about the question of behaviour.

DR GLOVER: The students are taught controversial material and are hopeless and helpless.

MISS SHARPE: May I put it from another point of view? (Paper) The training problem that the Society has to solve can be put in a few words. The solution of it would remove many other difficulties which beset us. The situation is this:

The British Psycho-Analytical Society offers to students a training in psychoanalysis. Students expect that when they have successfully completed the course prescribed for them they will then be recognized as qualified psychoanalysts and Members of the Society – exactly in the same way as they would be recognized in any profession after passing successfully a prescribed curriculum. The Society is in a false position towards students until it offers this security to them when they take up their training.

Such security can only be given by a unified policy concerning curriculum, a unified Training Committee, and a Society that will honour its own training.

We accept students who come to us in all good faith and who know nothing of the schisms within the body. Sooner or later they find out that there are not only marked scientific divergencies, but divergencies of technique in psychoanalytic practice. Finally they find that even when they have completed their course, they are not accepted whole-heartedly by the whole Society as adequately analysed and adequately trained, not even by all members of the very Training Committee responsible for their training.

It is a phantastic situation such as no student would find in any other serious teaching institute.

However the problem is solved, however long and difficult the task is, there is surely only one satisfactory outcome as far as the future of our students is concerned. The curriculum must be approved by the whole Society, there must be a Training Committee who will loyally co-operate and abide by the wishes of the whole Society. Every student who follows through the course successfully must be recognized as a qualified practitioner. And I hope a professional code of conduct will be formulated, including this article: that it shall be considered a breach of professional conduct, if by direct or indirect methods, the status of members trained by this Society is injured or prejudiced, such breach of conduct to be communicated in writing to the appointed authorities.

MR W. SCHMIDEBERG: In a little speech I wrote out I said almost the same as Miss Freud – and we are not conspirators.

(Paper) Listening to the various contributions to this discussion, I am struck by the fact that so many of the speakers concentrate on side issues and personal factors at such length. There is the danger of losing sight of the real issue, namely the fate of Freudian analysis in this country. Nor do some Members realize that the question is not whether a split should or should not take place, but to acknowledge the fact that it has already taken place years ago.

In my resolution of March 11th, 1942, I expressed the hope that with some good will on both sides it might still prove possible to come to an understanding. I ended then with a quotation of Freud in which he exhorted us 'to stand fast together'.

Should we eventually arrive at the decision that we can no longer work together fruitfully, we should at least part without personal ill feelings.

DR JONES: Mrs Isaacs, you have not spoken at all yet.

MRS ISAACS: I don't think I have anything to say in this matter at all.

DR JONES: About Miss Freud's point.

MRS ISAACS: We have decided to discuss that.

DR JONES: The question at issue is whether to follow Miss Freud's suggestion to consider the best way in a situation which has arisen, or to deal with Dr Glover's paper about methods of propaganda.

DR GLOVER: I don't think the issue is just that.

MRS ISAACS: I really do want to know what we are discussing. If we should take up Miss Freud's point of view, with which I sympathize, I agree that it will want a great deal of work. But I cannot see that I can say much more at this point. If we had gone back to the discussion of resolutions it would be more to the good.

DR M. SCHMIDEBERG: Could Miss Freud state what she means?

MISS LOW: Is it really conceivable that with the feeling we have and the charges and counter-charges that were made, are we likely to be able to look at each other's views? I do think that to begin with this is sidetracking. In a state of emotion in which most of us are.

ANNA FREUD: I did not mean that we should suddenly drop all these points and go into the scientific question. What I mean is: to review the practical consequences for the training of candidates is inevitable even if all people concerned behave well. Let me show it by an example and take Miss Evans' paper to illustrate this.[15] If Miss Evans' name should be brought before the Society for election as a Member we shall have one of these deadlocks in the Society, and with the best intentions on each side we shall either have to harm a candidate who did her best to conform with her training, or we shall have to go against our own scientific principles. On the one hand Miss Evans has followed the training she got. She has given a paper, approved by many members of the Society, which raised in the other half of the Society the feeling that it would not be desirable for the Society that she works on these lines. This is one example, and many of this kind could be found. These examples should be discussed.

DR JONES agrees.

DR PAYNE: Miss Evans was analysed by Miss Searl and Miss Sheehan-Dare.

DR JONES: We need not go further into the particular case. But how, Miss Freud, would you propose to discuss this situation?

MR W. SCHMIDEBERG: It was myself who first brought up this point without mentioning names. I said then that we must draw a

156

line somewhere. That this cannot be regarded any longer as analysis is obvious. (Dr M. Schmideberg: 'As Freudian analysis.') So I will have to read my first resolution again for us to come to an understanding.

DR JONES: This is impossible without thrashing out the scientific points.

DR GLOVER: There are other instances. But let us take a hypothetical case. Someone applies for training. The committee is to consider to whom to allocate him for his training analysis. The members of the committee know that if he is sent to one or other of a group, he will become an adherent to this group. This is a grave responsibility. If all analytical training were equal, it would not matter who analyses a candidate, but as it is for the candidate it is a life or death matter.

DR M. SCHMIDEBERG: We have to face this most important question.

DR JONES: A similar question arises in other spheres, for instance in medicine where some teachers take some extreme views, as Lister did at a time when he was not yet recognized. A candidate taught by him goes up for examinations, is examined by strangers, they hear these views. This happens from time to time. This situation is dealt with in medicine by tolerance.

DR GLOVER: Everyone knows that medical students deal with this in a much simpler way. They buy for 5s. a book giving the various views of the various examiners and serve them up to the examiners; in other words, they lie to them. But no difficulty arises.

DR HERFORD: What is analysis? It is an effort to see clearly and not to accept theories. I was analysed by different analysts and never had difficulties in the theory. That is the important thing. The question is to help the patient to see himself clearly.

DR WILSON: Each trainee should be analysed by two analysts. (Shouts from members 'No') I should suggest tossing pennies.

DR FRANKLIN: Some of us know surely that the different points of view are not different in every item of analysis. How far are candidates told if a theory is controversial? Or methods.

MISS SHARPE: During the course of the last three or four years I had three candidates to analyse. I can say with regard to those three that one of them because of his own phantasies will probably become a great exponent of the introjected object theory; he has said himself in the analysis, 'I believe that that is the focus of further development'. I have two others who will not go on these lines at all because of their individual . . . I should feel happier, if we are going to talk about schools, if out of the Kleinian school would come a proportion of people whose main interest were not centred on this special point. I don't see individualities developing.

DR FRIEDLANDER: As Miss Evans' paper has been mentioned, would it be possible to establish the differences, to find out why one part of the Society thinks this is analysis and another thinks it is not?

DR JONES: Do you mean to do this in a Business Meeting or rather in a Scientific Meeting?

DR WINNICOTT: I feel that a word should be said here. I was in touch with Miss Evans about her case. On first contact with analysis by Mrs Klein and one of her colleagues Miss Evans wrote a paper about this case in which she did misjustice to the theory. This paper was not read by me or any of Mrs Klein's adherents. It would seem to me that it would be a very wrong thing to take this paper as a test case. It was a naughty paper.

Dr Glover did say in his paper that at a certain stage he found that he disagreed with Mrs Klein's theory. It does come down to what Miss Freud said.

MR W. SCHMIDEBERG: I have a priority claim on this test paper, which Dr Winnicott now disowns. Dr Winnicott contradicts himself. In the discussion (and in my resolution I said that many analysts praised this paper) he among others congratulated Miss Evans on her paper.

DR WINNICOTT: Miss Evans' work with this case was delicate work with delicate material and I appreciated Miss Evans' work. It was the paper which was naughty.

ANNA FREUD: Many of us would not have taken that paper seriously at all because Miss Evans had only started work, if Dr Winnicott and other members had not actually congratulated her and so gave the impression of not only agreeing but considering it an exceptionally good piece of work.

DR JONES: I don't see the relevance of that.

MISS LOW: (Miss L.'s statement) Miss Freud's remark is relevant. Miss Freud cannot accept this paper; it does not seem to be analysis. If Dr Winnicott says not the paper but the ideas were good, this does not alter anything. It seems that it is not a scientific thing at all we have to deal with here, the emotional question must come first. And as now such a lot of emotion is bound up with the discussions that have taken place I cannot see how the scientific question can be started on before we get our emotions clear. I do not see myself sitting down with Mrs Riviere at a table and discussing scientific matters, because I feel so outraged at the attacks on other Members of this Society for whom I have respect. I may be a very bad exception in the Society, but I could not dispassionately begin to discuss scientific matters until the emotions are cleared.

DR FRIEDLANDER: I want to stick to my point. What we see is that at the meeting when Miss Evans gave her paper a great number of Members congratulated her on it because she was a member of a group, although her paper was not taken seriously, otherwise nobody would have congratulated her. If it is necessary to congratulate her simply because she belongs to a group things are not all right. Otherwise why does Dr Winnicott now say something quite different?

DR JONES: The point you make is that people were congratulating her in a hypocritical way.

DR FRIEDLANDER: That paper was brought up because it was such a typical example of what is not analysis, and Members congratulated her.

DR JONES: Why should they not?

DR W. HOFFER: If it is a naughty paper!

DR WINNICOTT: Miss Evans took this case to prove the theories about internalized objects. I congratulated her on the work she had done on that case under great difficulties.

DR M. SCHMIDEBERG: We want to know whether Dr Winnicott, Dr Heimann, Mrs Riviere, and Mrs Klein agree with the main points in Miss Evans' paper.

MR W. SCHMIDEBERG: Miss Evans gave in about twenty drawings the proof of the correctness of Mrs Klein's views about introjected objects. The patient said occasionally 'Yes' or 'No'. On that Miss Evans was congratulated by various members. Others thought that this was making fun of psychoanalysis. I asked Miss Evans whether the case was not a schizophrenic who are sometimes apt to make fun of the analyst.

MRS RIVIERE: Would it help to emphasize that there is a difference between Miss Evans' paper and her control analysis? I do not know her paper and was not present at that meeting. We heard that Dr Winnicott, her control analyst, thought her work with this case was good. I understand she wrote her paper entirely independently without her control analyst or analyst knowing of it. It was a misleading paper. Dr Winnicott who is the only person to know says it was a bad exposition.

MR W. SCHMIDEBERG: I think Miss Evans said she did read the paper for those who understand.

MRS RIVIERE: She did this in a foolish way, stirring up misunderstanding.

DR JONES: Evidently.

159

MR W. SCHMIDEBERG: We have no means of studying whether her case work was good.

MR W. SCHMIDEBERG: May I refer to a remark of Miss Anna Freud, where the success in this case was. The patient went from bad to worse and became a prostitute.

DR WINNICOTT: This is not so. It was impossible to deduce from her paper that any good work had been done at all.

MISS LOW: She was really thanked by certain people –

DR JONES: By whom? (Somebody shouts, 'Mrs Klein'.)

MRS KLEIN: I said I don't know about the method of investigating the patient's associations, but I did stress the fact that it was a case of a patient who said 'No' to the transference and to interpretation, and was treated by Miss Evans. I mentioned that there is something in the material of drawings which is of value. My impression was that she spoke against herself when she gave the paper. I said to Miss Freud that it was an entirely unrepresentative paper and case. I disagree with the whole presentation, with her conclusions, and, most of all, with presenting it to a Society in our situation.

DR M. SCHMIDEBERG interrupts, referring to Dr Matte.

MRS KLEIN: This is not a paper that can be a basis for a discussion.

ANNA FREUD: I can only say I am sorry that I ever mentioned Miss Evans' case. I promise never to raise a point any more. Don't take this as an accusation, but it is most unsatisfactory.

DR W. HOFFER: We had the same withdrawing from a position of the group of Mrs Klein as now in Miss Evans' case in scientific discussion with Dr Winnicott and Mrs Rosenfeld before. It means that as soon as we come to a special point the opposite partner turns round and withdraws his point of view. I think it is of no use to enter into discussion at all because the basis of the discussion lacks scientific control and consideration. The partners on the other side should at first try to clear up their own views and then join a scientific society.

DR M. SCHMIDEBERG: I agree with Dr Hoffer's statement about the withdrawal of statements.

ANNA FREUD: It would have caused the greatest relief in that meeting if Mrs Klein or any one of her followers would have criticized the method used in the case. We all showed that we had no intention to criticize Miss Evans but were shocked by the method used. Then would have been the time to clarify the matter. But that impression was not given by anybody of Mrs Klein's group.

DR PAYNE: One of the difficulties is certainly that everybody goes on the defensive when objected to. I think this is because of the emotional factor. The point of issue here of scientific technique may be expressed by the term of direct interpretation. ('No' from Members)

ANNA FREUD: It was the pure symbolic interpretation which shocked the others and the lack of interpretation of resistance. It would be a good test case to discuss methods.

DR WILSON: Would it be possible to have the differences tabulated in order to know what is the difference between Freudian analysis and Mrs Klein's views?

DR JONES: This would be extraordinarily hard to define.

DR WILSON: I never heard it defined.

ANNA FREUD: No one could have found any trace of analysis in that paper. (To Dr Jones) Do you remember I wrote to you after that meeting about the paper and to Dr Payne also?

DR BRIERLEY: *(These were not Dr Brierley's actual words but they express more exactly what she intended to say than the shorthand notes because the reporter found it so difficult to hear.)* It's obvious that our scientific and practical problems are urgent, e.g., the training dilemma Dr Glover pointed out again tonight. We cannot dispose of the 'feud' adequately by penalizing any one person. Its effects are too widespread and reactions unfavourable to full public health come from many quarters. The Society should limit its inquest to the deleterious public effects and try to agree as quickly as possible on some way of preventing their continued operation.

DR GLOVER: I appreciate Dr Brierley's point of view but I still object to the emotional factor being exclusively related to the Klein–Schmideberg reactions.

DR BRIERLEY: We must get a proper atmosphere.

DR JONES: If you want to be really helpful you must make this more specific. What you say is a generality.

DR BRIERLEY: I quite agree. If we decide I could make a statement.

DR JONES: I am concerned with the future.

DR BRIERLEY: The shorter the inquest the better.

DR M. SCHMIDEBERG: I wish any member would put forward suggestions how the tension can be diminished. If not, I cannot see what we can do but discuss Anna Freud's point.

DR JONES: I wonder whether the persons concerned would admit to be willing to play a more subsidiary part in the discussions for some time to give some chance to the Society as a whole. It is my place to check these emotional reactions. You have an instance just now when you see that one cannot discuss.

MR W. SCHMIDEBERG: I have no objection to discussing the scientific issue. Would it not be possible that I and someone of the

161

other group in a Scientific Meeting discuss one point which is not clear? For instance, the introjected objects. I remember that Miss Low asked in two consecutive sessions if Mrs Klein could state what introjected objects are.

MISS LOW: Yes, and Mrs Klein's answer was that she had stated it in her book. If she genuinely wanted to enlighten me she would have tried to give a definition. Other members have made that request besides me. It is necessary to find out where exactly we do differ. I have tried to discuss it several times. On one occasion Dr Winnicott answered me, 'I seek scientific truth'. That is a complete withdrawal from any genuine discussion. We all seek, or think we seek, scientific truth, but what particular scientific truth is concerned is the matter at issue.

May I come back to my suggestion of a committee for . . . investigation of the scientific differences. Every section of opinion should send representatives. Could we not stop the present fruitless discussion and elect such a committee and try to get down in black and white what our differences are?

DR LANTOS: As many people spoke who have emotions, may I speak for the people who have not emotions and are ready to settle down to discussions and are not interested in the question of accusations. It is hard to find out where the limit is between legitimate and illegitimate methods. I think, and perhaps others too, that people who are interested in the accusative side of the matter should find each other and discuss it. But we cannot follow that way of discussion. We don't see the use of it for the future. The past is the past. We have to think about what shall be done. If emotions are higher in some people than in others, perhaps we can wait until it calms down. It was not a general emotional outbreak about Miss Evans' paper, it was genuine surprise. From the meeting I had the impression that Miss Evans' case was regarded as a good case and her paper as a good paper by Mrs Klein and her followers. I had this impression for they behaved like that. If the reason was kindness, the kindness was unkind to Miss Evans. Our impression was that the others were satisfied with her paper. We were so surprised tonight when we heard what Dr Winnicott and Mrs Klein said. Perhaps we were a bit emotional to see that such surprises are possible.

DR ISAACS: I was not here at the meeting in question and have not read Miss Evans' paper. I would myself agree that criticisms should be made of every paper, independent of personal consideration.

DR PAYNE referred to the fact that Miss Evans had analysis with Miss Searl and Miss Sheehan-Dare. She has been working as a Candidate for a very long time. She has worked against great difficulties, internal and external and financial. She had very bad luck as a patient of Miss Searl's. Then she went to Miss Sheehan-Dare and this analyst left London after just about a year. Miss Evans was left in the air again. I understand that after being in the air for a long time and still struggling, she had the chance of analysis with Mrs Klein. When she wrote that paper it seems to me she was carried away. Dr Winnicott and Mrs Klein had been more charitable in their words at the meeting than they were in their minds. Mrs Klein specified her comments tonight and they did not sound to me entirely favourable. When the word 'unkind' was used it was not used against you. (To Miss Freud)

MR W. SCHMIDEBERG: Should we have at the next Business Meeting the vote on all the resolutions put forward?

MISS LOW: We have not been through them all yet.

DR M. SCHMIDEBERG: In July we shall have the elections. We must settle the question whether the status quo is to go on for another year or whether we shall have elections.

DR PAYNE: There are elections every year.

DR M. SCHMIDEBERG: There were three resolutions about the status quo and I suggest that these be voted upon at the next meeting.

THE CHAIRMAN: Then sound the opinion of members as to date and time of the next meeting.

It was decided to have the *next Scientific Meeting on June 3rd at 1.45 p.m.*, Dr Winnicott giving a paper, the *next Business Meeting on June 10th at 8.15 p.m.*

Editorial comment

After this meeting, Klein wrote to Susan Isaacs on 22 May 1942:

> I had supper with Dr Payne before the meeting, and discussed with her the next steps to take. She definitely intends to make a statement in reply to Glover's statement, in which she will give the numbers and refute some of his false assertions. . . . My impression, however, was that she is tired, exhausted, and very hopeless about the whole situation. . . . I think her mood has changed, not only because as time goes on one gets more tired, but also because the last Business Meeting seemed to her so catastrophic as regards the situation with the Viennese. I think that she was very bucked by my previous wish to co-operate with the Viennese, and had set her hopes on a possible compromise or co-operation with them. She seems very doubtful about that now. . . . I think that we must

face the fact that the situation in the Society is incurable. .... I confess to being tired and disheartened, and to having only one wish – and that is not having anything more to do with all these matters. I am now aware that it is necessary for us to remain members, and I think that we should stick to this point of view. There seems little or no prospect of their voting us out from the Society; but I think we shall have to resort to withdrawing our interest from meetings, etc.

(Archives of the British Psycho-Analytical Society)

On 21 May 1942, Marjorie Brierley had sent the following letter to Melanie Klein, which of course she had not received when she wrote the above letter. It became known as the 'Armistice letter', as Brierley advocated the idea that the Society should pass an 'Armistice Resolution', at the next meeting [see p. 174].

May 21st, 1942

Dear Mrs Klein,

Thank you for your letter.[16] I meant to have replied to it sooner; the delay has been due to further thinking over and over our crisis. I had no sort of objection to the study group itself nor had it occurred to me that the Society should be asked to choose the members. I just think that as a matter of policy in abnormal conditions, it would have been a good plan to notify the Society of your intentions. I am genuinely sorry to hear that for the moment (I hope only for the moment) the scheme has fallen through.

I am thinking of asking Dr Jones if I may read a short statement at the next business meeting because I am sure my efforts last time did not convey my real meaning.

It seems to me imperative for the Society to secure a temporary armistice in which scientific inquiry can proceed. At least the point of deciding whether or not irreconcilable differences of theory and practice do exist. If the Society splits now, it will fragment from emotional tension. If it splits after investigation (and, as you know, I do not regard this as inevitable) it would then divide on honest grounds of proved incompatibility.

It is about what seems to me to be the most necessary conditions for a workable armistice and their maintenance during a truce period that I want to make myself clear. If an adequate measure of agreement can be reached about these I should like to suggest that the Society pass a self-denying ordinance in respect of all current charges and counter-charges, personal attacks, vendettas, party politics and so forth. It should require ALL members to refrain from over-stepping the bounds of legitimate criticism in discussion. At the same time it should strongly affirm their right to complete freedom of speech within the limits of common courtesy. In the first instance, it would be the duty of the Chairman to see these conditions were observed but in the event of any member or members feeling outraged by a ruling from the Chair, the whole meeting could act as referee, then and there, the ruling of the meeting being final. Whatever other practical steps we took, it would have to be generally understood that it must be the common responsibility of members to preserve any agreed armistice conditions.

I cannot agree that merely restraining Dr Schmideberg whilst neglecting all other less obvious sources of trouble is an adequate way out. It does seem to me a simple fact, that, up to now, your own attitude and that of your friends, towards your work, has been felt by many members to be a difficulty in the way of getting to grips with the work itself. This statement does not impugn either your work or yourself and is definitely not made with hostile intent. The intent is to make clear what I believe to be a very real source of difficulty and a disadvantage all round. My own relations with you and your friends have always been amicable and I hope they may remain so, but this has not prevented my feeling profoundly uneasy about this matter of attitude to work, and this uneasiness has certainly not been confined to me.

Various labels have been attached to this subtle something in attitude from time to time. They might be summed up in the phrase 'inadequately scientific'. This, however, is no reason against accepting your express wish to be scientific now and in the future. It's rather the best reason for accepting it and doing everything to help you keep to it. Susan Isaacs is particularly well equipped to help here. Up to the present, conditions seem to have made her rather too anxious to support your work, rather than to explain it. What is most urgently needed now is not support but the fullest possible exposition.

Yours sincerely,
Marjorie Brierley

Notes

1 [Original footnote] This speech incidently was cut short at the introduction on the suggestion of the Chairman, his ground being that references to the training position should be considered later.

2 The statistics were checked by Sylvia Payne after the meeting (see p. 167).

3 Glover is referring to Mrs Riviere's paper on 15 April 1942.

4 I think that this rule referred to expulsion from the Society.

5 [Original footnote] Just before this paper was read Mrs Riviere pointed out a possible misunderstanding, stating that what she wanted investigated was not her charges against others but the charges made by others against Mrs Klein. This does not alter my view that I should reply to her counter-charges.

6 Paper read on 18 Feb. 1942: 'Some Notes on a Concept of Internal Objects'.

7 Speech read at the meeting on 15 April 1942.

8 [Original footnote] Miss Sharpe herself made this point before this paper was read, so I need not go further.

9 The International Training Commission was set up in 1925 to monitor the training activities of all the component societies of the IPA. A summary of reports on each candidate had to be kept in a special book, which was periodically submitted to the Commission by each training committee. In 1938 at the Paris Congress, the Americans objected to being supervised by an outside body, especially one which supported the training of lay analysts, and withdrew any co-operation with the IPA in this matter. The British Society continued to fill up this book until 1944, when Glover, who was also Secretary of the IPA, resigned from the Society.

10 [Original footnote] Added since writing the original speech two months before.

11 Glover was stopped by Jones from completing the paper that he had been giving at the meeting on 11 March 1942 because it dealt with training matters.

12 At the Scientific Meeting on 18 March 1942, Anna Freud had read 'Excerpts from an Annual Report on Work in a War-time Nursery'.

13 The title of John Bowlby's membership paper was 'The Environmental Factor in the Development of Neurosis and Neurotic Children'. It was read on 3 May 1939, and he was elected a Member of the Society at the AGM in July 1939, together with Paula Heimann and Ronald Fairbairn.

14 Dr Matte is now better known as Dr Matte-Blanco, and has since made important contributions to psychoanalysis.

15 On 21 Jan. 1942 Miss Gwen Evans read a paper titled 'The Analysis of a Child's Drawings'. As described later by Dr Payne, when she wrote this paper she had recently gone into analysis with Mrs Klein.

16 Klein had written to Brierley asking her if she would take part in a study group she was thinking of starting.

6

The Fifth
Extraordinary Business Meeting

Minutes of Business Meeting
held on Wednesday, June 10th, 1942, 8.15 p.m.

Dr Jones was in the Chair and 31 members were present (Glover, Payne, A. and K. Stephen, Weiss, M. Schmideberg, J. Strachey, Wilson, A. Strachey, B. Low, Bowlby, Winnicott, Klein, Riviere, Isaacs, Heimann, Anna Freud, W. Schmideberg, Burlingham, Lantos, Haas, Ruben Friedlander, E. & W. Hoffer, Sharpe, Brierley, Franklin, Gillespie, Herford) and 1 guest (Dr Macdonald).

THE CHAIRMAN raises the question whether the minutes should be read, which considering their length would take up much time. It is decided to proceed with the Agenda. Dr Glover wants to make a statement.

DR GLOVER: I asked the President's permission to make a statement.

Some time after the last meeting Dr Payne wrote to me in her function as Training Secretary that she had been asked by Mrs Klein (*Dr Payne*: And several other members) to communicate with me on a statistical issue contained in my speech made at the last meeting, the suggestion being that I might have been guilty of ambiguity, or that the figures might give rise to false impressions.

For example she raised the question as to whether Dr Wilson and Miss Sheehan-Dare should have been counted as adherents of Mrs Klein. I realize that this puts Dr Payne in a rather difficult position and while I do not agree with the view that my figures can give rise to misapprehension, I think it only fair to all parties to make clear

167

tonight that this view is held. Should the Society either tonight or at some future time desire to go into these matters, I shall be perfectly ready to substantiate my point of view.

MRS KLEIN asked the Chairman's permission also to make a statement. On enquiry into its subject it appeared to be on the same subject and the Chairman expressed the opinion that it would not be a good time to go further into the matter at present.

DR JONES: In other words: there has been a suspicion on both sides. If the Society wishes to go into it we can do so. I have felt myself it would be desirable to proceed further with the original Agenda and the resolutions that were sent in. We have not dealt exhaustively with any single one really, but you must decide yourself in what way to continue the discussion. My proposal is to go on with the resolutions which have not been discussed yet.

W. SCHMIDEBERG: Did we not come to the conclusion at the last meeting, that we should proceed with voting first about the status quo?

DR M. SCHMIDEBERG: We must achieve a decision before the Annual General Meeting whether there shall be elections or not, and should therefore vote on that point before discussing other points.

DR JONES: That has not been discussed yet even.

DR M. SCHMIDEBERG: The first three meetings were devoted to this discussion. We must know before the next meeting whether we shall have to elect officers or not.

DR JONES: That is no news to me. We can deal tonight with the resolutions. We have considered so far one side of them, those which are in favour of the status quo. We have, however, not yet considered Miss Low's proposal of a committee, nor Dr Rickman's resolution.

DR M. SCHMIDEBERG: We have not considered the resolutions on the Training Committee which come first.

MISS LOW: Can we not first vote on the status quo, which means the resolutions proposed by Drs Carroll and Friedlander and Miss Grant Duff? If these were accepted we should not need annual elections.

DR JONES AND DR PAYNE are of the opinion that 'status quo' refers to annual election of officers without restrictions as to tenure of office, but not to the Emergency Commission.

MISS LOW: The body now ruling is an emergency body. If we keep this the body will be left as it is.

DR PAYNE: Owing to the fact that absent members sent in their voting papers a considerable time ago, we kept those ballot papers in a box under seal. They are now unidentifiable and are now no good.

We shall have to write to absent members again and give them a chance of voting on those resolutions we are going to vote on.

DR GLOVER: I do not agree. None of the absent members has seen the minutes so have no reason to change their minds.

DR PAYNE: There are members who want to alter their previous votes. I am one myself and Dr Brierley is another.

DR BRIERLEY states that her ballot paper was identified so that she could alter it.

DR BOWLBY is of the opinion that there is too short notice for such a ballot.

DR PAYNE: Members were given notice in the Agenda of this Business Meeting that there will be voting.

DR JONES: There has been very strong feeling on important issues like a change of the constitution. Members who had little opportunity of attending the Business Meetings should have opportunity of sending in their votes by post.

MRS RIVIERE: The decision would only be postponed by about a week.

DR A. STEPHEN: As one of the proposers I would like to have the discussion postponed for a bit but I do object to it being voted upon without being discussed.

DR M. SCHMIDEBERG: I have to repeat that the result of the voting will affect the question of elections.

DR A. STEPHEN: It will not. It is inviting the Society to express their opinion whether a change in the constitution is desirable or not.

It would have the effect that perhaps a committee would be elected to make suggestions. I have no intention to rush any change through. It should only be made after full and fair discussion and it would not be right to vote without a full and fair discussion.

DR M. SCHMIDEBERG refers to Mrs Grant Duff's resolution.

DR JONES: In the matter of elections in July, what is the idea going to be about the Emergency Commission? Because, whether the Society is run by an Emergency Commission or by an ordinary staff of officers, in both cases they must be elected.

DR M. SCHMIDEBERG: There is a great difference, whether we have to elect twenty-one Members or agree to keep the Emergency Committee.

W. SCHMIDEBERG: If the Blitz starts again all the Members will leave London again and only the Emergency Commission will stay.

DR K. STEPHEN: We could consider whether we want an Emergency Commission.

DR M. SCHMIDEBERG: We must vote on it.

169

MRS RIVIERE: We can vote today, but the absent members can send in their votes by post. Is there any objection to that?

DR FRANKLIN: Have the absent members had abstracts of the discussions?

DR PAYNE: It was quite impossible for the executive to send abstracts unless we get more people to do the typing, etc.

DR BOWLBY: If it were decided to vote today this would not meet Dr A. Stephen's proposal to have a discussion before voting.

DR A. STEPHEN: If the Society would rather not, I am perfectly willing to postpone it.

DR JONES: Let us go back to the original Agenda. Dr Carroll in his resolution speaks about the status quo. Did he mean by this the Emergency Commission? (Dr Payne confirms this.) Then it goes together with Miss Grant Duff's.

DR ISAACS: The question of the Emergency Commission is quite distinct from the question of our rules.

DR JONES: We are discussing now which of these resolutions it is most practical to take first.

MISS LOW: Would it not be possible to discuss anything that is really relevant to the question of change of our constitution or maintaining the Emergency Commission? My resolutions are not relevant to this at all, so they could be postponed.

DR JONES: There are complaints that resolutions have not been discussed sufficiently. Is there amongst them a resolution on the Emergency Commission?

DR PAYNE points out that Miss Grant Duff means it in her resolution.

DR FRIEDLANDER: At the beginning of the war it was decided to have no election of officers but to institute an Emergency Commission to deal with the business of the Society, and this is to what Miss Grant Duff refers.

DR JONES: What if the office bearers should say that they are no longer able to do their duties?

MISS LOW: Then we should only have to elect substitutes for those.

W. SCHMIDEBERG: It seems to me essential that if the war should come here again we should not be left without officers.

DR GLOVER: A decision to maintain the status quo can only bind the Society for a year.

DR LANTOS: In a way there is another war on. After we have discussed so many questions and emotions, the question is whether it is the right thing to make elections, whether we would not prefer to have elections when these acute emotions have boiled down and we

170

have had scientific discussions. Why a certain amount of members are against elections, is not for the going on of a state without elections [*sic*], but we don't feel we want to have elections now after all those discussions we had, with all these emotions for and against single members. I feel not very inclined unless I am forced to take part in elections, I should prefer rather to think about what can be done for the Society in the scientific way and after that think about office bearers. I don't think that the office bearers are so bad that we must elect new ones immediately.

DR WILSON: I second this very strongly. I do not feel in an emotional time like this it is desirable to have elections.

DR A. STEPHEN: My own resolution does not affect the elections at all, as far as I see. All I want is to consider whether it would not be a good thing to change some of our rules in the future. The effect of my resolution would be that the Members appointed consider the matter, make recommendations, which we could then vote on, etc. It has nothing to do with the question of elections.

DR HAAS: Rule 3 of the Statutes says, 'Nominations for officers and Council, resolutions, etc., shall be sent in to the Secretary not later than one month before the date of the Annual Meeting.' We must therefore consider today whether we want elections at the Annual Meeting or not. (Shouts of 'Quite true'.)

DR JONES: Would someone be willing to voice the proposal to the effect that the Emergency Committee should be formed or that the present one should continue?

MISS LOW: I should be quite glad to propose that no elections should be held and the present office bearers continue in their offices until such time as we think more suitable for elections. Could one add that if desirable more Members can be called upon by the Emergency Council?

DR K. STEPHEN: I think that more Members should take part in the business administration now than when the Emergency Commission was elected.

DR M. SCHMIDEBERG: Dr Karin Stephen is very optimistic about there not being war situations in London any more.

DR ISAACS: I suppose this would take the place of several of the original resolutions. (Dr Jones: Yes.) Would absent members be allowed to voice their opinion too?

MISS ANNA FREUD: We should ask the office bearers what is their opinion about it. If anybody is asked under the present conditions to undertake duties they should have a word in it.

DR LANTOS: We add that we ask them very much.

DR GLOVER: If any member of the Emergency Committee wants

to resign he could do it now and thc Society be given opportunity to replace him. Miss Grant Duff and Dr Carroll in their resolutions ask for the status quo to be retained. I think their consent to that should be secured. We had asked the Members to vote on the resolutions and many have done it, and so far only two members wish to alter their votes. Those who have voted might feel strongly if their votes were abolished. Their case has been strengthened and not weakened in the meantime.

MISS ANNA FREUD: Might we ask Dr Payne, who had most of the work, how many Members she thinks should be added to the Emergency Committee?

DR PAYNE: I cannot carry on two things, be Business and Training Secretary at the same time. When I took it on, there was nothing carried on in London, and the Business Secretary's work was not much. Activities have increased in the meantime a good deal. It would be a good thing to elect a Business Secretary and Treasurer in one person. It would also give thfs Member a good opportunity to get into matters. Dr Rickman is really elected Business Secretary and I have only been doing his work. In 1940 he asked me to take it on altogether.

DR M. SCHMIDEBERG: We want to express our thanks to Dr Payne and also to Dr Macdonald who did a great deal of work.

DR JONES: I wonder how this is going to work. We shall then have an Emergency Council and officials.

DR FRANKLIN: Can we not say that no elections be held except to fill vacancies?

DR JONES: That opens the whole question again.

DR BRIERLEY: The Emergency Council consists of Dr Glover and Dr Payne. All Dr Payne wants is someone to take over the business side. Cannot the Emergency Council co-opt a Member for that purpose? (Shouts: 'Yes.')

DR KARIN STEPHEN: I don't quite see the point of the Emergency Council co-opting. The Members could say themselves whom they want to be added to the Emergency Council. Members should take part in the elections.

DR JONES: That would run counter to the point made to avoid elections.

DR LANTOS: The Emergency Council could co-opt and the result will be presented to the Members.

MISS ANNA FREUD: We cannot have it both ways. We have the right to have elections and have a big list of nominations. But if we forego that right I don't think it would be sensible to have small elections instead. It would be elections again in the emotional

172

atmosphere. I am sure the Emergency Council would find means to contact the Members.

DR JONES: This seems to me the formulation that can be drawn from all the suggestions and if you agree we shall vote on it.

'That the present Emergency Committee be continued for a year, with permission for them to co-opt one or more Members if necessary, and that no elections be held this year.'

Vote no.1

Members vote secretly by writing Yes or No on slips of paper on ballot No. 1 – Dr Jones's formulation.

(Dr Payne collects the votes in a box.)

DR JONES: Now I take it it will be in order to consider the proposals of changing the constitution. There are several proposals to this effect. Perhaps somebody might be willing to formulate them in a simple manner. The issue is whether Members want to change the constitution or not.

DR BRIERLEY: We are so anxious that further discussion should be held in a better atmosphere. Would it be possible to move a proposal that an armistice[1] be concluded before continuing our business?

DR JONES: We have voted on the Emergency Council, but not on the constitution.

MISS LOW: Could we have Dr Brierley's statement before we go on?

DR JONES: Do you think it would be relevant now?

DR PAYNE: I think so.

MRS KLEIN: May I, if there is any statement being made, make one also which I had no occasion to make previously?

DR JONES: I really should like to know what it is about, whether it is relevant to the topic we are discussing.

MRS RIVIERE: It concerns something arising out of the minutes which has already been dealt with by Dr Glover, and Dr Payne made some investigation into the subject. Mrs Klein thought it would come under the discussion of the resolutions. (*Dr Jones:* We will come to that.) As it is answering Dr Glover's accusations we thought we had better get it over before any armistice suggestion is considered.[2]

DR JONES: If it was arising out of the minutes, you should have made your statement before.

173

DR PAYNE: As concerns the statistics I propose to call the Training Committee to investigate and then to send a statement to all members.[3]

DR JONES: Dr Payne withdrew her statement because Dr Glover was ready to make his about it being a controversial subject and we agreed that further discussion should be postponed until further investigations have been made.

MRS RIVIERE: Mrs Klein was the person most concerned.

DR JONES: We plunge again into a heated controversy if we take this up.

DR K. STEPHEN: Could we get over it by saying that the armistice would not prevent going into the subject?

DR JONES: Certainly the training question is important enough to be discussed.[4]

DR BRIERLEY: (Statement) These meetings have made at least two things clear. (1) We must find out whether the differences in theory and practice amongst us are, or are not, so fundamental as to make it impossible for us to remain one Society. This is essentially a scientific problem, and we must insist on a scientific solution. (2) There is no reasonable hope of solving this problem unless we secure a period of public truce.

Members are now aware of the tensions and circumstances that have brought about the present crisis. These meetings have convinced many Members that no useful purpose will be served by prolonging our communal inquest on these adverse conditions. In view of our state of emergency, Dr Payne, Miss Sharpe, Miss Low, and myself agreed that I should move a definite armistice resolution. At the last meeting Miss Low asked, 'Could we not stop the present fruitless discussion . . . and try to get down in black and white what our differences are?'

We therefore suggest:

(1) *That the Society immediately pass a self-denying ordinance in respect of all current charges and counter-charges, and all activities directed against individual Members or groups of Members.*
(2) *That the Society require all Members to refrain from personal attack or innuendo in discussion, but also, strongly affirm the right of all Members to complete freedom of speech within the limits of common courtesy.*

In the first instance, it would be the duty of the Chairman to ensure that these, or any other agreed armistice conditions, were observed. But it is vital that Members should accept the safeguarding of public peace and public freedom as their individual and collective

174

responsibility. Thus, in the event of any Member or Members feeling outraged by a ruling from the Chair, we would suggest that the meeting act as Referee, then and there, and that the decision of the meeting be final.

In our conduct of business under truce conditions, we would appeal to all Members (including ourselves) to aim, not merely at an armed truce, but at a real lowering of tension, a generous peace without reprisals. (General expressions of approval)

DR M. SCHMIDEBERG: How far would that interfere or not with the discussion of resolutions which have not yet been discussed?

DR BRIERLEY: The resolutions would be discussed under these strict conditions and Members who infringe upon them would be called to order.

DR PAYNE: I should like to second that proposal.

DR JONES: It is plain there is no hope for useful co-operation unless we do act under these terms. How shall those who wish to act so confirm this wish by voting on this resolution?

DR M. SCHMIDEBERG: I have no objection, but how can one get it more precise what this resolution means?

DR JONES: Shall we vote by ballot?

It was decided to vote by show of hands and the resolutions was accepted unanimously.

DR JONES: I hope from my heart that this will be acted upon with the best of intentions. To proceed now with our discussion; let us see how far we have come. Now as to change of our constitution there are several resolutions bearing on that. Shall we discuss them further or vote on them? (Shout: Vote on.)

After discussion it was decided that the Members present at the meeting vote by ballot slips now, notwithstanding their having done so before. A discussion followed on the question whether the resolutions to retain the status quo refer to the Emergency Council and officers or to the constitution.

DR A. STEPHEN: I think that the first resolution of Dr Carroll is ambiguous.

DR PAYNE: He sent a letter which is in the minutes.

MRS RIVIERE: I submit that the resolution which has already been voted on today covers the resolutions of Dr Carroll and Miss Grant Duff.

DR M. SCHMIDEBERG: Let us vote on the resolutions as they were sent in.

DR JONES: All right.

MRS RIVIERE objects and there followed a discussion on the order of resolutions to be voted upon.

DR ISAACS: Would it be possible for Members to send in their voting sheets instead of voting here and now?

DR KARIN STEPHEN: We would then have more time for discussion now.

DR JONES: There is still the suggested ambiguity about Dr Carroll's resolution.

DR PAYNE reads out of the minutes of the business meeting on 11 March 1942, the resolution and letter of Drs Carroll and Stengel.

DR JONES: Let us first settle the question whether to vote on every single resolution or to vote on group of resolutions.

Vote no. 2

Vote by show of hands shows a majority in favour of grouping the resolutions.

DR A. STEPHEN: There are two points I want to make quite clear to start with.

(1) My resolution is not a proposal for immediate alteration of rules. If it were passed it would merely mean the expression of a general opinion that a change should take place as to the method of electing our officers. The natural consequence of this resolution to be passed would not be an immediate change, but the election of a committee to consider it for the future.

(2) However much some of us would like to do so, it is impossible to put the Society and the Institute into cold storage for the duration.

DR A. STEPHEN: (Paper) There are two points that I want to make clear to start with. The first is that my resolution is not a proposal for the immediate alteration of our rules. I know some Members have regarded it as such, but in fact its carrying would merely amount to the expression of an opinion of a general, of a *very* general, character, that it was desirable to make certain changes in our methods of election. The natural consequence would probably be the appointment of a committee, preferably one elected by the whole Society, and this committee would be instructed to draw up definite proposals. Members could, if they chose, communicate their views to the committee itself; but in any case, when it presented its findings, they would have the opportunity both of criticizing its proposals and of voting on them.

Mine is no attempt to rush through a sudden change without the co-operation and consent of Members as a whole; but it is an attempt to deal as soon as may be with an evil that has already nearly killed the Society and may very well kill it altogether before many years have passed.

Next I want to say that however much some of us would like to do so it is as a matter of fact impossible to put our Society and Institute into cold storage. We cannot just freeze them and bring them to life again unchanged when the war is over. They are living organisms and they will either die outright or they will go on living and developing in one way or another, good or bad, and that whether we like it or not. The question before us is whether we shall take charge of our own future or whether we shall just allow ourselves to drift – to remain stationary is impossible.

Next, as to my reasons for believing in the necessity for a periodic change of officers. However much some members may disagree with me on many points, I believe that I can count on everyone's support for two fundamental propositions. The first is that it is the main object of the Society to discover the truth. The *Institute* has other objects, of course, such as the treatment of patients and the training of candidates, but I am speaking at this moment of the *Society*. Certainly the rules of the Society and the statutes of the International Association define certain broad limits to subject-matter of our investigations; we are to investigate the same class of phenomena as was investigated by our founder, Freud, but, having regard to that limitation of subject-matter, our aim is to discover the truth whatever the truth may turn out to be. If this is not our main object then we are not what we so definitely and so often claim to be – a scientific body.

My second proposition is this, that the most important condition for the discovery of the truth is freedom of discussion. In using the phrase 'freedom of discussion', of course, I have not in mind a situation where the ordinary rules of debate with regard to relevance and with regard to order generally are neglected; these rules are, indeed, valuable aids to free discussion: but I *do* have in mind a situation where as little pressure as possible, other than the pressure of scientific evidence and of logical argument, is brought to bear on Members to prevent their holding and expressing any opinion they like, so long as they obey the ordinary rules of debate. In particular I have in mind a situation where no economic or moral pressure is allowed to interfere with Members' freedom.

If these two propositions are granted – first as to our object being the search for truth, and second as to the importance of free discussion – then I think I can show not only that my own proposals with regard to change in our rules ought to be passed; but that all those other proposals which suggest that there must *first* be a discussion of our scientific differences ought to be rejected.

The argument that I want to place before the Society can easily be put into a nut-shell. If we are to discuss our scientific differences it is surely wisest to establish the best possible conditions for our discussions. These conditions do not now exist, and one main object of the suggested changes in our rules is to create them. It is surely best, therefore, to create the necessary conditions first and to hold the discussions afterwards rather than to take our business the opposite way round.

That is my argument in a nut-shell, but, of course, its validity entirely depends on my being able to show that the best possible conditions for free discussion do not now exist and that it is possible to create better conditions. If I can show this the rest of my argument logically follows and I do not think there is much difficulty in showing it.

If we look back at the history of the Society and Institute we shall see that we have been in the habit of allowing our official positions to be occupied year after year by the same men. Not only this, we have only allowed, and are at present allowing, three or four official positions to be held simultaneously by one man who has constantly been reappointed to hold these positions. We have allowed, that is to say, all the power of the Society and Institute, all the prestige which they derive, after all, primarily from Freud and from no one else, to become, as it were, the private property of one or two men. One or two men have in consequence done to represent the Society and Institute not only inside it but outside it and have collected into their own hands all the professional patronage which naturally comes to men in such positions. Do not let me be misunderstood. I have no wish to say that men who hold our official positions would not have acquired a large measure of power quite independently of the positions which we have allowed them to occupy. This is, indeed, obviously true in the case of our President, who, after all, had an established position before the Society came into existence and has done scientific work of real importance. But even he must owe something to the fact that for about thirty years he alone has been thought fit to be our President and to hold other positions also, and in the case of all other Members besides our President my argument is of far greater cogency. My argument is this, that by allowing the prestige and the professional patronage of the Society and Institute to be permanently concentrated in the hands of a few men we have given these few men the power, should they wish to exercise it, to make or to break a large proportion of our Members. I am not even alleging that these one or two men have actually made or broken anyone – about that there can be differences of opinion and that allegation it would be difficult to prove – but what I do say is that they have had the power to make or to break many of our Members and that this power, whether actually exercised or not, is disastrous to freedom of speech.

Possibly, remembering what our President said last February, some Members will think that I am wrong in saying that the same men have held three or four posts simultaneously, but that is not so. Our President was, I have no doubt, perfectly right in what he said, which was that no Member had ever held simultaneously more than one office in the Society.

I am sure that in saying this he was referring only to the offices which are mentioned in the Society's rules, the offices of President, Hon. Secretary and Hon. Treasurer. No one has ever been both President and Secretary or Secretary and Treasurer simultaneously – that is perfectly true. But there is nothing to prevent anyone being President both of the Society and of that other body which is so closely allied to it, the Institute, and so holding two offices simultaneously even if they are not technically both offices of the Society. Further, what is very much more important, there is nothing to prevent anyone holding such posts as President or Secretary of the Society and President of the Training Committee and Director of the Clinic and other posts too. And it cannot be denied that such posts are held simultaneously and year after year by the same man.[5]

A reconstruction of the Society's rules would have to involve not merely the offices mentioned in them but those other posts which, though they are not described in our rules as offices at all, are often far more important than those which are so described. It would have to involve also the whole relation of the Society to the Institute.

If it be asked why we should reconsider the rules of election relating to these posts I will answer that it is simply for this reason, if for no other, that so long as year after year these posts or, at any rate, the most important of them are automatically assigned, whether by formal election or by co-option or by other means, to one or two men – so long as that happens we shall fail to establish the conditions in which freedom of discussion can flourish or, perhaps, even exist at all. It is impossible to believe that Members whose professional reputation, whose livelihood even, perhaps, depends on the good opinion of one or two powerful men can feel quite free to hold and to express views of which one or other of these men is likely to disapprove. It is not, of course, true of all or of nearly all our Members that they are absolutely dependent on our officials, but it is true of many of them, especially, I think of some of the lay Members and of some of the younger medical Members and of Members who have not yet had time to establish themselves in this country, and it is true enough in general to make the atmosphere of our Society one in which freedom of discussion can hardly be said to exist at all.

Nor does the concentration of power in the hands of a few men stifle free discussion by economic force alone. We analysts, if we deserve the title of analysts at all, should surely know enough of ourselves to know, not that we are different from other men, but that we are very, very like them, and that we are certainly not *less* subject than they are to the influence of what is called 'transference' emotion. And who is in a stronger position to exercise the power conferred on them by our transferences than men who are elected year after year without question to rule over us almost as it by Divine Right? It is not merely to weaken the economic power of our officers but to weaken their transference power also that I believe a periodic change is necessary, but of this transference relation between the Members and their officers it is surely unnecessary to say more.

Let me, to end up with, make it quite clear that I do not say, and I do not believe, that changes in our rules are by themselves enough to produce scientific work, nor do I say that they would bring about immediately that alteration in the atmosphere which is necessary for such work. We cannot hope for that: but I do say that to suggest discussing our scientific differences before we create the conditions necessary for any scientific discussion at all is to turn a blind eye to the facts, and I do say that, while our rules remain as they are, scientific discussion is, if not foredoomed to failure, at any rate severely and unnecessarily handicapped, and those rules therefore should be thoroughly overhauled.

DR JONES: Dr Stephen very forcibly put forward the view that our proceeding with discussion next year takes a pessimistic tinge. Let us hope that he takes a too gloomy view on that.

MISS LOW: I want to say that I really do feel very much in support of Dr Adrian Stephen. Whether you agree with every point, I do not think that matters. One cannot be in the Society a long time without knowing that his general point of view is certainly correct.

Members have voting papers, but again and again they are not independently used owing to the powerful influence which Dr Stephen has already touched upon. I think that had we been more independent-minded we should have altered the Society's constitution long ago. But we all have a share in the responsibility for the present state of affairs and I don't want to free myself from blame. Our emotions cannot be done away with. There will always be

180

transference of various kinds. By altering some of our rules it could be made possible to minimize the emotional factors which rule all of us. It is specially important that the constitution factor shall not depend upon the transference situation between analysts so that a member is obliged to feel his means of livelihood depends on the way in which he casts his vote. The keeping of power and offices in the hands of the few who in their turn make the appointments, breeds disappointment and resentment. I think, for instance, that it is a queer situation that Members who have only recently entered the Society are taking lectures and seminars and some of us of long-standing position in the Society and of wide and varied experience are not allowed any opportunity to share in the work. I can take myself as an illustration. I take myself since I have the right to speak of myself and not of others without their permission.

I think we have agreed to drop the past and therefore it would be better for Dr Stephen to turn to future possible developments. It is with the future in view that I wish to re-affirm the necessity of getting to work at once on a discussion of scientific differences and unities, and on this point I must disagree with Dr Stephen that it would be useless to attempt this without first rehearsing all past problems. Let us form forthwith a body for such discussion by which means we may hope for some agreement in our ranks and a less gloomy prospect for the future of the Society than the one Dr Stephen forebodes.

DR M. SCHMIDEBERG: I very much dislike to disagree with Dr Adrian Stephen. He says that certain of the rules of the Society and the statutes of the International Association define certain broad limits to subject-matter of our investigations: we are to investigate the same class of phenomena as was investigated by our founder, Freud, but, having regard to that limitation of subject-matter, our aim is to discover the truth whatever the truth may turn out to be. That would imply that we investigate – Some members wish to discuss the alteration of rules as to tenure of office, others wish to discuss the relation of the Institute to Freudian doctrine.

DR A. STEPHEN: I only meant that the object of the Society is to investigate psychoanalytic material and find out the truth about it.

MISS ANNA FREUD: It seems to me essential that before we vote on the resolution originally proposed by Dr Friedlander and then formulated by Dr Jones, we make some addition. This is 'at the present moment'. Otherwise it would mean that our constitution is excellent as it is. We only mean that this present moment is not a good one to vote on a change in the constitution, as proposed by Dr Stephen.

DR JONES: He says it was urgent because it means freedom of discussion.

MISS ANNA FREUD: He only wants it discussed.

DR ADRIAN STEPHEN: I wanted that this question should be brought up to discussion. The method of change should be a matter of discussion. If we once express an opinion that such a change is desirable, then the committee could discuss how to do it.

DR JONES: There is not much to discuss.

DR A. STEPHEN: There is very much to discuss about it.

DR KARIN STEPHEN: (Paper) Personal charges have unfortunately taken up the time of recent Business Meetings but now at last we have got back to the resolutions, and we must *not* allow partisan feeling to obscure the real issues.

So much violent emotion has been stirred up that there is a real danger that, when it comes to voting on the resolutions, Members may be tempted to vote for their own party, to defeat the other side, rather than use their judgement and consider the proposals on their own merits, and then vote for what they believe will be best, in the long run, for psychoanalysis.

Among other resolutions we have before us a proposal to limit tenure of office, and it has been suggested that this proposal has an 'ulterior motive': that it is being put forward by a 'clique' among our Members whose object is to capture power over the Society.

DR JONES: You say that there is a charge of a personal nature that a clique put forward this proposal to achieve their own ends. Do you mean that?

DR K. STEPHEN: I thought somebody put it forward.

DR JONES: Not to my knowledge.

DR BOWLBY: Dr Stephen is not making the charge, she is denying it.

DR JONES: She is implying it.

DR K. STEPHEN: (cont. paper) That would certainly be undesirable, just as it would be equally undesirable for those who have already held office for many years and exercised the powers which this position has conferred on them, to attempt to cling to office and retain power. If any Members entertain such ulterior motives, we shall be well advised to prevent them succeeding in their plans and I believe the best way to do this is to *remove the bone of contention* by voting in favour of altering our methods of election in such a way as to make it impossible in future for any individual or group to capture power over the Society or to retain power for more than a limited period.

If you will allow me, I should like to put before you my reasons for considering that the present arrangement is unsatisfactory, reasons which led me to consider that it was doing serious damage both to ourselves personally and to our scientific work, long before I became aware of the present dissensions.

My objection was that it was allowing too much power to be concentrated in the hands of one or two individuals over whose actions the rest of the members had lost control and whom they now could not stand up to.

It is true that, nominally, our constitution has always been democratic, since every year we go through the form of re-electing our officers, but their re-election has long been a foregone conclusion, so that, in fact, they always have been re-elected and their power, in consequence, has become little short of a dictatorship.

They were able, if they liked, to take decisions in the Society's name without consulting or even informing anyone, and they have frequently done so, and even when they have chosen to go through the form of explaining what they proposed to do and inviting discussion they have been in a position to exercise powerful pressure on the decisions reached, and this they have also frequently done. In fact, whether they wished to or not, they could hardly have avoided doing so.

Consider, after all, how much power they had to advance or hinder the careers and future prospects of the rest of the Members. As the only recognized representatives of the Society, year in year out, they were bound to become the obvious people to be consulted by those of the general public who wanted to be analysed or by doctors who wished to refer patients to the Society for analysis and therefore they had in their hands the distribution of all these cases. In this and many other ways too they were in a position to see to it that Members and Associates who were on good terms with them got on, and those who were on bad terms with them did not. Such a situation almost inevitably gave undue weight to their personal likes and dislikes. Moreover it was they who interviewed and selected new candidates: ex officio they permanently occupied controlling positions on the Council, the Board, and the Training Committee and at all the Society's meetings, presiding, and arranging the Agenda; their influence in every sphere was overwhelming, and so it came about, one way and another, that although, in theory, everyone was perfectly at liberty to disagree with them, or criticize their actions, or bring forward new proposals, many simply could not afford to do it, and even for those who were economically independent of their good will it was by no means easy to take any line which would be unpopular with them. It took considerable moral courage, more indeed than most of us possessed, especially as anyone who did succeed in doing it was most unlikely to find much support from the rest of the Members, some of whom did not care to risk incurring displeasure by defending an unpopular cause, while others were too diffident, or too shocked to raise their voices.

Other factors besides purely economic ones, of course, played a considerable part in this passive acceptance: people in power are either excessively admired or excessively disliked, and both attitudes interfere equally with independence, which flourishes best on a footing of equality. Even in purely scientific matters the same sort of considerations were bound to weigh. Here too many Members, I know, found it difficult to express opinions which were frowned on by those in power. Few of us are practised speakers and many found themselves literally tongue-tied when faced with the prospect of being either snubbed, or patronized, or tripped up, or cold-shouldered, or branded as 'unorthodox', and left unsupported by fellow Members.

All this has had a deteriorating effect on our Society which has been plainly visible to all of us. It is not good for human beings to wield unchecked power: they become dictatorial and arrogant and there is too much temptation for them to favour supporters and penalize opponents or rivals. And it is humiliating for those who allow themselves to be ruled in this way: either they become subservient, or they become aggressive, or they become depressed and apathetic.

In such an atmosphere initiative and independent thought cannot be expected to flourish, and in fact, in our Society, they have *not* flourished. Considering the amount we already know and the possibilities which exist for the further development of psychoanalysis, the poverty of our achievements is extraordinary. Our discussions are timid and dull, or else acrimonious, and seldom lead anywhere. Our affairs have not prospered, in spite of the prestige of Freud's discoveries, the Psycho-Analytic Society counts for remarkably little in the eyes of the world.

And, worst of all, perhaps, we ourselves have missed the stimulus and incentive to do the best we are capable of which we should have got, and shall I hope now get before very long, which comes from working together to advance the thing we all care about so deeply and sincerely, the work of psychoanalysis itself.

This picture I have drawn of the condition to which our Society has been reduced is not a flattering one, but I am afraid it is fairly true, true of myself just as much as of any of the rest of us. I am not

184

drawing it in order to blame anyone. It is the sort of thing that happens to people when they set up the wrong kind of organization: it happens to the rulers and to the ruled. Other people have suffered in the same way from the same sort of mistakes, and we analysts do not seem to be much better than the rest of humanity, though I hope we are no worse than they are.

But certainly it is not a satisfactory or a creditable state of affairs and we must consider how to put an end to it as quickly as possible. If it is a fact that much of the trouble comes from allowing our Society to become something which is too much like a dictatorship, then the remedy is to exchange this for something more democratic.

The view has been put forward that changing our methods of election can do no good and we have a number of resolutions beginning, 'prior to discussing the question of changing our constitution we must first' either thrash out our scientific differences, or reaffirm our belief in Freud, and so on. This is an attitude with which I cannot agree and I think it rests on the mistake which we must take special care to avoid, the mistake of allowing the question of changing our methods of election to become confused with the struggles over securing power or of opposed scientific schools of thought who want to use this power to support their side.

It may be that some Members feel that if we start making the proposed changes there might be a danger of the other side getting into office and that this must be prevented because they would be able to use their power to make their views prevail in the Society. So they may feel that it is necessary for someone who supports their own views to remain in power so that these may prevail instead. Obviously, however, this is hardly the way to secure the free, impartial atmosphere we need for healthy co-operation and scientific progress. As far as impartiality goes, it would be no better for the side which has power at present to retain that power than it would be for it to be turned out in order that power might be captured by the other side.

So it is no use saying that the best thing to do is to call a halt and leave things as they are and get on with our scientific discussion.

What is fundamentally wrong is that holding executive office in our Society should mean capturing or holding on to power for anyone, whichever side he may happen to be on. Under our present system holding office has, unfortunately, come to mean this, and I do not see how we are to avoid the disruption of power struggles to which this mistake has given rise except by limiting the tenure of office so as to leave as little power as possible attached to it to tempt anyone either to capture it or to hang on to it. This really would put an end to power struggling for good and dispose of 'ulterior motives' and so remove at least one serious cause of friction.

When the question of who is to capture power to make his scientific views prevail has been disposed of by arranging matters so that neither side can do this,[6] the atmosphere will probably cool down, but until this has been done I do not see how there can be any genuine armistice, though there is nothing I should welcome more. Following the military analogy, however, one can sincerely hope for a fair plebiscite under an armistice till all armies of occupation have withdrawn to the frontiers. This is why it seems to me that 'prior to' trying to discuss our scientific differences we ought first to get rid of the temptation offered by power, by limiting tenure of office. Even when this has been accomplished I do not imagine that our differences will be easy to settle and it might certainly then be helpful to call an armistice from personal abuse, but that is another matter. I realize the special difficulties of wartime. If we can devise some temporary measure for ensuring impartiality and fair hearing for all parties, it might be possible to put off taking any final decisions till later on, but merely leaving things as they are, on account of the war situation, means, in fact, leaving one party in possession of the field, which is no real solution at all. The ideal solution would be to entrust the conduct of the Society's affairs at the present time to executive officers who were not interested parties, or, failing that, to ones who did not possess any great power to influence other Members and so to re-inforce one side and intimidate the other. Even with the best will in the world our existing officers could not conceivably be regarded as fulfilling these conditions, and indeed no one could fulfil them who retained office permanently. While the present arrangements exist, there will always be Members who will be seriously handicapped in putting forward their views both on scientific questions and on the conduct of the Society, and there will always be quarrelling and ill feeling.

It may be argued that Members ought not to allow themselves to be intimidated by their officers, even as things are, and ought not to need external changes to fortify their courage. Possibly so: but it is not easy, and we have not succeeded in doing it heretofore and now we are in a bad way, and why, after all, should we continue to put ourselves in a position which has proved too difficult for us when there is such an easy and obvious way out? We are perfectly well able to improve the whole position and introduce a new atmosphere which we shall find it much easier to cope with, if we want to do this, simply by changing the machinery of our elections so that, instead of having permanent officials re-elected to office year after year, we can split up power among a succession of different officials who, during their limited term of office, would hold themselves responsible to the rest of the Members and would not be in a position to exert undue influence over them, even if they should wish to do so.

Then, at least, we really should be in a position to attack our scientific differences with some hope of success.

Such a proposal is, after all, nothing very revolutionary or unheard of. On the contrary we are, I believe, almost unique among scientific bodies in being without these democratic safeguards.

If there are good reasons why, in our special case, such safeguards are undesirable, let us hear them: if there are no such reasons, then surely we had better make the change.

MISS ANNA FREUD: We are in a different position from other scientific bodies, because we are doing our own training. If we had no training institute attached to our Society it would be very much easier.

MR JAMES STRACHEY: I very much disagree with what Dr Stephen said. He is creating a melodramatic situation. What are the two parties that struggle for power? They are in fact represented among the officers. So I do not see the point at all.

As regards the practical situation, we may prefer to elect particular people. They wish to prevent us from doing so by a mechanical rule.

DR ISAACS: The issue is whether we have now a democratic constitution. The fact that the great majority of scientific bodies do have a limit to tenure of office shows that it is commonsense and I don't think that there is any evidence that we can discard the general practice among scientific societies. I was myself very sorry that Dr Karin Stephen expressed her views so much in terms of parties. It is beside the main issue. I would like to emphasize again what I said at earlier meetings, that if one has not a rule limiting tenure of office then every election becomes an immensely personal matter and transference comes in. This can be minimized.

I would like to support Dr Adrian Stephen in what he said about the effect of limitation of responsibility and overemphasis, overvaluation of individuals in the Society upon freedom of speech. I believe that that holds true quite apart from the economic motive. The particular economic conditions do demand that we should give very special attention to the framework of our rules. In the light of that aim the rules exist to further our aims.

DR M. SCHMIDEBERG: Dr Stephen and Mrs Isaacs suggest that no Member should hold office for longer than two years nor hold two official positions at the same time. I have made a rough

187

calculation and find that it would require something like seventy-eight members to comply with this request.

DR A. STEPHEN: I have never said anything like that. With regard to Mr Strachey's remarks: since he disputes the question of economic power – and this is the only power I meant – there is a significant instance. Two years ago I made a speech about the question of lay Members. Nobody objected then. But when I went out of the door a Member came up to me, and said, 'Oh, if I only had two thousand a year I should have spoken every word like you.' That shows the economic power.

DR M. SCHMIDEBERG: Could Dr Adrian Stephen specify what he means by alteration of rules?

DR A. STEPHEN: The re-election of the same persons every year leads to a narrowing of the freedom of discussion. Therefore I think we should alter the rules to prevent re-election. Details should be worked out in a committee.

DR ISAACS: The word 'office bearer' does not refer to a member of a committee. In a small Society like ours this could not be applied. It means the members of the Council. I agree with Dr Adrian Stephen that the details should be worked out later.

DR BOWLBY: I suppose that by supporting these resolutions nobody is committed to anything. If they are carried it will then be for the Members to think of the detailed way in which they think the improvement should be made. If no way could be found no change would be made.

There is a personal point I feel strongly about. Psychoanalysis is established in the community far more than Members in this room do appreciate. I speak here as one who has been away for two years in the Army. I can say I feel very strongly that the Army not only welcomes our work, it reads Freud's books and is very interested in the matter. I have myself been canvassing for more psychoanalysis for the Army and have found sympathy. The Society has been insulated. There is far more demand for psychoanalysis than is appreciated.[7] Psychoanalysis has arrived at a time when a change may take place from the time when the Society was concentrated in a few hands.

DR JONES: We are possibly too ambitious but we have been very dissatisfied with our status, so it is gratifying to hear it from the other side.

DR HAAS: I have information that there is a very strong feeling against psychoanalysis.

DR MACDONALD: I find the same as Dr Bowlby, there is very much interest in psychoanalysis.

DR JONES: So far all speeches about this resolution have been in favour.

DR A. STEPHEN: I do not think Mr. Strachey was in favour of it.

DR JONES agrees.

DR M. SCHMIDEBERG: I think that those who are against it have said so much before that they don't think it necessary to say any more.

DR JONES: Mr Strachey thinks that a change should not be brought about soon. On the other hand the arguments brought are convincing that the change is urgent. We must settle what we mean.

DR A. STEPHEN: It is necessary to decide whether we want a change, but it will take time to discuss the particulars. This is a delicate matter.

DR JONES: So it will take an hour.

DR K. STEPHEN: It will take much more.

DR JONES: There is an Annual General Meeting next month. A committee could be appointed tonight to discuss the matter and present the conclusions to the Annual General Meeting.

MISS LOW: There are the absent members who ought to be asked too.

MISS ANNA FREUD: Is it not a reason against the urgency of the matter that we have now temporary officers who are limited to the period of emergency?

DR JONES: I am, for instance, not a member of the Emergency Committee. This dreadful danger of tyranny that hangs over the Society seems to make it very urgent.

MRS RIVIERE: Could we not say that in the opinion of this meeting it is desirable that changes in the rules governing the tenure of office should be considered forthwith.

DR LANTOS: We cannot vote on a question like that.

MISS LOW: Could we not have a sub-committee?

DR MACDONALD: I think that a tabulation of resolutions would clear the air whether there shall be a change of the constitution or not. Let us split the thing into two halves, formulate the idea first and have it on the minutes.

DR M. SCHMIDEBERG: We have five resolutions on the Agenda and we ought to vote.

DR FRIEDLANDER: I want to draw your attention to the fact that at the beginning of the meeting we found it would not be desirable to change our officers. If the new vote decides that a change is to be made what shall we do?

DR JONES: We should have one year's time to work it out.

DR PAYNE: Not if we are going to have Business Meetings all the winter.

DR BOWLBY: I would suggest to appoint a sub-committee to consider the question.

MRS RIVIERE: I would support this proposal.

DR GLOVER: It seems to me that we are going round in a circle. Some speeches were in favour and one or two against a change in the rules. We had all these arguments before. The resolution makes the assumption that the actual trouble in the Society is the tenure of office. It seems not fair to those who have said that they don't think that a change is desirable at the present time.

DR K. STEPHEN: The same Members say that no change is desirable at all. (Shouts: Nobody)

DR ISAACS: If a favourable vote were taken tonight, the time of the change could be decided later on a report of the sub-committee. I am not one of those who suggested, as Dr Glover says, that the tenure of office is the sole reason for the trouble in the Society. It is one of the reasons.

DR A. STEPHEN: Nor do I say it is the sole reason.

DR JONES: To take up Dr Bowlby's suggestion we might perhaps formulate it like this: 'That a committee be appointed to investigate the question of tenure of office and the multiplicity of offices'.

DR M. SCHMIDEBERG: I suggest that we vote on the resolutions put forward by Dr Carroll, Dr Friedlander, and Miss Grant Duff, and separately on those of Dr Isaacs, Dr Stephen, and Dr Bowlby. It seems to be unfair to absent members to change their resolutions.

DR JONES: The meeting has decided to group the resolutions to simplify voting. I propose therefore that voting should take place on the following resolution:

'That a committee should be appointed to investigate the questions of tenure of office and the holding of multiple official positions'

Ballot no. 2 by secret ballot

Dr Payne collected the ballot slips in a box.

Vote no. 3

DR JONES: Now there is resolution F[8] left for us to deal with, proposed by Dr Rickman.

DR ISAACS: I suggest to postpone it.

DR JONES: Or to withdraw it for the time being. (Consent from members.)

DR JONES: Have we worked through them all now?

MISS LOW: The resolutions concerning training questions have not been voted upon.

It was agreed that these resolutions should be withdrawn for the time being.

It was further decided that the Members absent from this meeting should be asked to vote by ballot slips on the two resolutions voted upon by this meeting and that their former voting papers should be cancelled. After receipt of the ballot slips from absent Members the votes will be counted and the result communicated to all Members.[9]

It was further decided that no more Scientific Meetings should be held before the Annual General Meeting and that the Annual General Meeting will probably be held on July 15th[10] provided that the Auditors finish the balance sheets in time.

Notes

1 Letter from Brierley to Klein re. passing an 'armistice' resolution (see p. 164).

2 See memorandum by Mrs Klein in answer to allegations by Glover against her and her colleagues (p. 196).

3 Later Sylvia Payne compiled and circulated a list of training analysts, showing how many candidates and controls or supervisions they were each responsible for. See chart on pp. 193–5.

4 At the AGM, held on 29 July 1942, the question of training was again discussed.

5 See earlier discussions of the division of responsibility between the Society and the Institute of Psycho-Analysis, which was later clarified, and a 'gentleman's agreement' made that the Board be composed of those Members elected on to the Council of the Society.

6 The 'gentleman's agreement' which was worked out in 1946 between Sylvia Payne, Anna Freud, and Melanie Klein, did achieve a relative balance of power in the Society for many years.

7 This experience is described in more detail in 'Activities of British Psychoanalysts during the Second World War and Influence of their Interdisciplinary Collaboration on the Development of Psychoanalysis in Great Britain', by Pearl King (King 1989a: 15–33).

8 Resolution F concerns the appointment of a committee and secretary for external affairs, proposed by Rickman and Heimann.

9 On 19 June 1942, Sylvia Payne, as Hon. Business Secretary, circulated the results of the two resolutions:

Resolution 1: 34 in favour, 13 against; majority in favour = 21 for the continuation of the Emergency Committee for a year (see p. 173).

Resolution 2: 25 in favour, 22 against; majority in favour = 3 for the setting up of a committee to investigate tenure of office, etc. (p. 190).

10 The AGM was held on 29 July 1942.

7

Additional background information

Editorial comments

Following certain allegations by Glover at the meeting on May 13th, 1942, against the Kleinians, concerning the number of candidates and controls (supervisions) who were being trained by Mrs Klein and her group, Sylvia Payne and the Training Committee agreed to work out the correct figures for the number of candidates that each training analyst in the Society, was or had been analysing, and how many controls (supervisions) they were or had been undertaking. These figures were worked out and circulated round the Members of the Society.

Statistics of training from 1927 to 1942 (June 30)
(for the information of Members)

		Candidates	Controls	Seminars	Lectures
Dr Jones	2	1 qualified 1 resigned	10	7 single	3 courses 1 single
Dr Glover	4	2 qualified 1 in training 1 America	6	6 courses of theor. sem. monthly 4 single	3 courses
Dr Payne	9	1 advised to resign after 3 weeks 1 qualified 3 in training 1 transferred 2 training suspended by war 1 resigned	9	4 single pract. 1 course	2 courses
Miss Sheehan-Dare	2	1 transferred 1 qualified	5 adult 1 child	2 courses (child)	

		Candidates	Controls	Seminars	Lectures
Miss Sharpe	12	2 resigned 1 transferred 1 suspended (war) 5 qualified 3 in training	15	5 single pract. 3 courses pract.	3 courses
Mrs Klein	4	1 resigned 1 returned to America 1 qualified 1 suspended (war)	3 adult 6 child	3 single 1 course adult pract. 4 courses child	4 courses
Mrs Riviere	4	1 transferred 1 resigned (Amer.) 2 qualified	6	3 single 1 course	1 course
Mr Strachey	6	3 qualified 3 resigned	6	5 courses 1 single	2 courses
Dr Rickman	7	4 resigned 1 suspended (war) 1 transferred 1 qualified	6	1 single 1 course pract.	2 courses
Miss Searl	3	1 resigned 2 transferred	5 child	5 single 1 course pract.	2 courses
Dr Brierley	3	1 qualified 1 suspended (war) 1 in training	3	3 years theor.	3 courses
Dr Wilson el. 1937	1	1 suspended (war)	2	–	–
Dr M. Schmideberg	1	1 in training	3 adult 3 child	1 course 1938 (child)	1 course
Mrs Isaacs	1	1 transferred (war)	2 child (child)	1 course 1938	3 courses
Dr Winnicott			4 child	1 course (child)	
Miss Freud	4	1 resigned 1 suspended (war) 2 in training	4 adult 1 child	4 courses	–
Dr G. Bibring	2	2 transferred	4	2 courses	–
Dr E. Bibring	2	2 transferred	3	1 course	–

		Candidates	Controls	Seminars	Lectures
Dr W. Hoffer	3	1 in training 1 suspended (war) 1 qualified	3	–	–
Mr E. Kris	1	transferred	1	–	1 course
Mrs D. Burlingham	2	1 transferred 1 in training	3	–	–

July 1942

S. M. PAYNE
Hon. Training Secretary

Editorial comments

During the Business Meetings on 11 March and 13 May 1942, Edward Glover made certain accusations against Melanie Klein and her colleagues. She was initially hesitant about replying to them, but eventually she made up her mind to do so. She went to the Business Meeting on 10 June 1942, ready to make a statement to refute his accusations, but Jones refused to let her speak, on the grounds that 'it would not be a good time to go further into the matter at present'. She tried to do so later and was put off by Jones, and then the 'armistice resolution' was passed and she was made to feel that by making her statement, refuting Glover's accusations, she would be going against the spirit of it.

After the meeting she found that Glover was still circulating his accusations. In a letter to Joan Riviere, on 23 June 1942, she wrote:

Dear Joan,
I send you a copy of a letter from Dr Brierley which I received this morning. I gather she assumes that I shall not reply anything to Dr Glover's speech and that it will be sufficient to reconsider the numbers. I think it will be necessary to say a word or two that though we do wish for the truce and are very willing to keep to it, first of all we must be able to reply to accusations which remained unanswered. Dr Glover has still circularized his accusations after the meeting, and even after the truce had been suggested. We can hardly be expected to start the truce without having first replied to the charges made against us, charges which have been publicized even after the truce had been suggested. . . .

(Klein Archives)

Melanie Klein therefore decided to send a copy of her statement to all members with the following covering letter:

Dear ———
At the Business Meeting on June 10, I intended to refer to certain facts in answer to particular statements made by Dr Glover at previous meetings, but the opportunity was not forthcoming, and the meeting went on to Dr Brierley's suggestion of a 'truce' and other matters.

I greatly welcomed this expression of opinion in the Society in favour of discontinuing all charges, personal attacks and innuendoes. It is my wish to observe and maintain the spirit of the armistice resolution, indeed in reviewing the events of the past few years I cannot find much evidence of warfare on the part of myself and my collaborators. This truce would, however, be a farce if it were merely superimposed on error or omission of fact, and I regard it as a duty to put before the membership in the following memorandum the facts in reference to sufficiently grave issues.

Yours sincerely, Melanie Klein.

Memorandum relating to some proceedings in the Society on and before
May 13, 1942
(Melanie Klein)

At the Business Meetings of the British Psycho-Analytical Society on March 11 and May 13 last, Dr Glover introduced into the discussion on the resolutions statements of his own concerning the conduct and activities of myself and of other members interested in or agreeing with my scientific views. His speeches have been heard by a large number of Members and read by others; in fairness to my own work and that of my colleagues, it is therefore necessary for me to have an opportunity to point out the inaccuracies in his statements. I was prepared to make a reply at the meeting of June 10, but the discussion was rapidly taken up on other matters and I had not the opportunity. I made it clear subsequently at the meeting that the matter could not be allowed to drop without any reply from me; and since the Business Meetings are terminated, I am now circulating the facts as seen from my standpoint.

The following extracts are taken from the copies of Dr Glover's speeches handed to the Secretary for the Minutes.

196

March 11, 1942
(1) The central issues before the Society are:
First: whether there is any section or group that seeks to use the machinery of the Society to increase its own influence, or to limit the free exercise of scientific opinion, or to exercise pressure on Members holding different or opposing views.
Second: whether this section attempts to secure influence through the various Committees of the Society (Committees, *not* executives).
Third: whether it develops a private organization outside the Society for the purpose of influencing affairs inside the Society.

It is my considered opinion that there is such a section and that until the existing machinery of the Society is permitted to function as it was originally intended it should, it is impossible to secure a proper atmosphere in which real scientific issues can be discussed. I have said before and repeat now that the issues are *not* just how to deal with legitimate scientific differences or deviations, or whether the constitution can be improved or not. The issue is: whether *so long as this struggle for factional power goes on* it is possible to discuss usefully *either* scientific differences *or* the working of the constitution. . . the focus of power in the Society moved from the Business Meetings to the Training Committee. And there it still lies. Whatever may be said for or against the Council is relatively unimportant compared with what can and must be said about the struggle to control training of candidates.

May 13, 1942
(2) Of the 20 training analysts in Britain 18 are situated in London, where virtually all the training work in this country is carried out. By reason of their position and function these 18 training analysts can make or mar the future of psychoanálysis in Britain. Eight at least of these 18 can in my opinion be regarded as adherents to the views of Mrs Klein: (Mrs Riviere asks for names to be given) indeed if we include one other who strongly supports her views the number would be raised to 9. However, let us call it 8. By way of contrast 3 of the 18 training analysts are Viennese Freudians. At least 5, possibly 6 (and I really don't mind if you call it 7) are in my opinion English Freudians (or, as they have sometimes been labelled, 'Middle groupers').

Now the number of active members normally residing in and around London is 45. (I exclude here those who have recently gone abroad or have ceased to take any interest or part in the Society.) Of these 45, it can in my opinion be said with reasonable accuracy that 12 (possibly 13) are either out and out adherents of Mrs Klein's views or so near as to make no difference. There are in my opinion 23 English Freudians and 7 Vienna Freudians to which I think may fairly be added 2 from the Berlin group, making a total of 9. Thus we see that of 12, possibly 13 adherents of Mrs Klein 8, possibly 9 hold key positions of authority as training analysts – a percentage ratio of at least 61%, possibly 69%. The corresponding ratio in the case of English Freudians or Middle groups is at least 22%, possibly 26%, but you can call it 30% if you like; in the case of Vienna (plus Berlin) group 33%.

In addition to this it should be remembered that two of three Viennese had already acquired training status in Vienna: the point being that they were not selected by our Committee – merely taken over. Five of the 6 English Freudian training analysts were elected before the Klein controversy began. In the 6 years up to 1940 every training analyst appointed (5 in all) was an adherent of Mrs Klein. True, one non-Kleinian was appointed in 1940 and one Viennese Freudian in 1941. But it should be recalled that after 1938 the Training Committee had a different balance of forces. Dr Jones resigned, Mr Strachey, Miss Freud, and Mrs Bibring were added and I was appointed Chairman.

(3) . . . the crucial issues are (a) whether partisan groups of members exist in a state of active organization and (b) whether they seek to exploit official committees within the Society in order to secure power and by power I mean in particular the power to establish their professional views and methods, whether these views and methods have been accepted by the Society or not. . . .
The crucial question is *what procedures apart from the scientific discussion of evidence, can be and are used in this Society to propagate controversial views.* . . partisan influences were at work. Two trends of opinion made their appearance, one that students should be taught only accepted Freudian principles, and the other that there was no objection to teaching students material which was not only in my opinion, but in the opinion of many members of the Society, controversial.

(4) Now I would like to specify explicitly what I regard as the most important practices which are subject to abuse. I use the term 'abuse' in its scientific sense, i.e. a method which does not conform (bypasses) the accepted procedures of science. There are (a) the advancement of candidates because of pre-existing allegiances or because of earlier private therapeutic analysis, (b) the criticism, particularly in control analyses, direct or implicit of candidates who do not hold these allegiances, (c) the canvassing for adherents, for example persuading even already licensed candidates that it would be well for them to undertake a 'deeper'

analysis, (d) *(and this I would like to say is the really vital point) the teaching to candidates as accepted psychoanalytical theory and practice material or method which is still controversial and regarding which the Society itself has not come to any conclusion,* (e) the election and advancement of lecturers, seminar holders, control analysts and training analysts on the strength of their allegiances and not simply on their scientific and teaching capacities, (f) a *private* discussion as to the placing and advancement of candidates and training analysts, i.e. the making of provisional training arrangements to be put subsequently before an official meeting of the Committee, when, as is only natural, they are likely to be passed. (Italics throughout are in the original.)

The above are the extracts from Dr Glover's speeches to which I wish to refer. Not only has Dr Glover given no evidence for these charges, but he also ignores that I was in no position to conduct 'a struggle for factional power to control the training of candidates' or to carry out any of the activities he describes. In Extract 4 above, point (d) clearly refers to me and my collaborators. By implication, and in view of the connection between this and the preceding paragraph, it is also suggested that we are guilty of the other five 'practices which are subject to abuse'. Though he did not mention our names at the meeting of March 11, no one doubted that he referred to me and my collaborators, the more particularly since his speech followed and strongly supported Mr and Mrs Schmideberg's grave accusations against us. In her speech of April 15, Mrs Riviere was therefore fully justified in refuting not only Mr and Mrs Schmideberg's statements but Dr Glover's unfounded accusations. It was therefore not correct, as Dr Glover suggested in May, that he had been 'attacked' on April 15 by Mrs Riviere not for what he had said on March 11 but for what it was anticipated he would say; moreover, to call a refutation of untrue charges an attack is clearly reversing the facts. I am now asking Members to consider in the light of the following information the truth or untruth of my having had undue influence over candidates and training.

First, Dr Glover states that eight or nine of the training analysts in the Society are my 'adherents'. He gave no names. I feel quite sure that Dr Rickman, Mrs Riviere, Mrs Isaacs, and Dr Winnicott would agree that they accept my methods and technique, and the substantial part of my views; that is, with myself, *five analysts*. Of these five, Dr Winnicott became a training analyst only in 1940, that is to say at a time when a change in the composition of the Training Committee had already occurred. As Dr Glover puts it 'after 1938 the Training

Committee had a different balance of forces. Dr Jones resigned, Mr Strachey, Miss Freud, and Mrs Bibring were added and I was appointed Chairman.' Dr Winnicott's appointment as a training analyst in 1940 could therefore not have been the result of my using undue and improper influence in this respect.

Now as to the sixth and seventh training analysts who are my 'adherents': whether Dr Wilson and Miss Sheehan-Dare could be called 'out-and-out supporters' of my work (to use Dr Glover's phrase) is for *them* to say. Such a question cannot rightly be assumed off-hand. I have much appreciated their co-operation (as well as the co-operation of all these members) in many different ways over a long period, but I could not tell and have never tried to find out whether anyone is an 'out-and-out supporter' of mine. As regards the eighth training analyst, I presume Dr Glover counts Dr Scott, who however is not a training analyst; he takes child analysis controls. I cannot tell at all who the potential ninth may be, because there are several leading members who have shown much appreci- ation of my work and gratitude for the help it gave them, and I am at a loss to know which it could be. In any case it cannot be stated with certainty that more than five, or at the outside seven, out of eighteen training analysts are fully associated with my work and that includes myself.

Again, Dr Glover states that only twelve or possibly thirteen ordinary Full Members are 'out-and-out supporters' of my views, but he ignores the fact that there are a number of Members who, without being 'out-and-out supporters', would say that they value my work highly and approve of the part I play in the training work of the candidates – actually, without them and their votes I should not have had my position on the Training Committee. I should count altogether *at least* twenty-two Members (and two or three Associates) who make use of my work – not a bad proportion out of Dr Glover's total of forty-five. Moreover, I strongly deprecate – and so do other Members – Dr Glover's attempts to pigeonhole all the Members of the Society into one group or another. It is arbitrary and distorts the facts to attempt artificially to relegate all members into groups. The worst point, however, in his classification is that by dividing the Society artificially into the 'Viennese Freudians', the 'English Freudians', and the 'adherents to the views of Mrs Klein' Dr Glover insinuates that my work and my collaborators' is not securely rooted in the principles of psychoanalysis founded by Freud. Here he begs a question. The Society recently decided to discuss and clarify differences of opinion which have arisen first and foremost between the Viennese Society and the British Society, though there exist also some differences of opinion between British Members. In this way Dr Glover prejudices the outcome of those scientific discussions. Moreover, he is not justified in stating his personal standpoint as if it were the opinion of the majority of the British Society, since it is most unlikely that many English Members besides himself take such a view.

We must not lose sight of the fact that before the advent of the Viennese colleagues the number of Members making use of my work, to a greater or lesser extent, were in a strong majority, and that even since the Viennese and other Continental members have joined this Society, those who set a value on my contribution and approve the part I play in our work number all but half, if not half, the active membership. This being so, I do not consider five or even eight out of eighteen a markedly high proportion of training analysts.

Now as regards actual influence – what Dr Glover considers to be my struggles for power over candidates. In reference to his opinion (Extract 3) that 'a partisan group exists in the Society in a state of active organization to secure power to propagate controversial views': the answer to this is 'No'. No such organization exists or existed with that or any other object among me and my collaborators. No evidence could be produced in support of this statement. Let me remind you that Dr Glover has been Secretary of the Training Committee for ten years, and in the last three years its President. He and Dr Jones have throughout that period seen the candidates and formed their opinion of them before they were discussed at the Committee – certainly an important function. I have never been in a position to admit or to refuse a candidate who applies for training, except as one voice among the seven or eight members of the Training Committee. Dr Glover has not only had a great deal of influence through participating in the first selection of candidates, but has had more opportunity to apportion candidates to particular training analysts than any other Member, by virtue of being Secretary, and as a result of the very long intervals between Training Committee meetings. In these long periods of three months or more, the Secretary often carries out business without calling the Committee, or by consulting one or two other Members only. This applies especially to apportioning candidates for controls. In any case the facts are as follows: and these figures have been supplied from the minutes of the Training Committee.

Since 1927 – that is, fifteen years – the number of candidates in training has been fifty-nine. In that time the number accepted by me for training analysis has been four. In this same period Mrs Riviere took four candidates. Dr Rickman had seven allotted him, of whom three were found unsuitable and suspended. Mrs Isaacs was appointed a training analyst in 1936 and has had one candidate; another was allotted but the war intervened. If Miss Sheehan-Dare and Dr Wilson are included, then it should be said that Miss Sheehan-Dare, who became a training analyst in 1937, had two candidates, and Dr Wilson one.

To compare these figures with those of other training analysts: the minutes show that Miss Sharpe has had eleven candidates in training since 1927. Dr Payne has had eight; Mr Strachey six, Dr Glover four, Dr Brierley and Miss Searl each had three in that period; Dr Jones had two. There were fifty-nine candidates allotted for training in the fifteen years; I and my collaborators had seventeen of them, or twenty at the outside.

To consider now the direct accusation made under Dr Glover's point (d) (Extract 4). It is not correct that I or my collaborators taught to candidates 'as accepted psychoanalytic theory and practice material or method which is still controversial . . .' for when my contributions to theory and practice were presented to students in the period up to 1934 they had already been accepted and approved by the bulk of the British Society. That does not mean that they had been fully accepted by every individual Member, but that they had been recognized by those who had been elected for training. In our theoretical and practical seminars, lectures, and training in general, full due was given by the training staff to my work, and it was represented to students as an important addition to psychoanalytic theory according to the views held in the British Society, though it was of course pointed out to them that Continental Societies had different views about it. One glance at the English psychoanalytic literature from about 1927 or 1928 onwards confirms this. It was for good reasons that the Continental Psycho-Analytical Societies never questioned the fact that the English School through most of its representative members was identified with my work. For instance, the lectures which were inaugurated by the paper Dr Jones read to the Vienna Society in 1935 were explicitly called 'Exchange Lectures'. They dealt with my contributions and those of some other English Members. These papers had essential points of view in common with my work, and all of them were considered highly controversial in Vienna. When Dr Wälder gave the Viennese Exchange Lecture in London in 1937 he did this under the assumption (which was never contradicted) that this discussion was being conducted between the Members of the British Society who had accepted my views and considered them an important addition to psychoanalytical theory on the one hand, and the other the Viennese Society which largely rejected them.

Dr Glover himself had for a number of years before the 'Klein controversy', as he calls it, began, represented my contribution as part of accepted psychoanalytic theory. For instance, in April and May 1934, in a course of lectures on neurosis which he gave to candidates, Dr Glover devoted one of the six evenings exclusively to my work, in particular to the connection which it had established between psychosis and neurosis. He described my contributions as a landmark in the development of psychoanalysis and stated that he was sure that they would influence the theory and practice of psychoanalysis for some time to come. He took pains to point out how my work developed out of Freud's and Abraham's findings and extended and amplified them. He left no doubt whatever about the high esteem in which he held my work and the prominent place it had in his view in psychoanalytic theory. There may be some members who heard and still remember this course of lectures. That this was his considered view can be seen in print in his review of my book [*International Journal of Psycho-Analysis*, Glover, E. 1933]. I had therefore no reason to think of my work, as far as the British Society was concerned, as controversial at this time and no restriction whatever was put on me in this direction so far as I taught it. Nevertheless anybody who carefully reads my book *The Psycho-Analysis of Children* can see for himself that I made it clear at many points where my own findings add to the body of psychoanalysis and diverge from the theory that had been so far arrived at; and this was also my attitude at any time when teaching students.

In the summer of 1934 I read to the Congress at Lucerne my paper 'A Contribution to the Psychogenesis of Manic-Depressive States', which as Dr Glover stated in his speech of May 13 was for him the parting of the ways. He said that his disagreement with me arose over those concepts – but he has never made it clear whether this disagreement implies that he has also changed the views he held about my work before that time or to what extent he has changed these earlier views. When I introduced my new concepts in 1934, I was well aware that they were controversial and from this time, whenever I referred to them in my teaching capacity, I made it clear that they were still very much under discussion and open to argument. I used the same caution in my publications. In his preface to the book *Love, Hate and Reparation*, written jointly by Joan Riviere and myself, Dr Rickman said: 'The work on which this book is based largely derives from Mrs Klein's researches into the early development of the emotional and mental life of the child. It is proper to say

203

that these researches and the conclusions drawn from them are still undergoing the tests of criticism and further application' [Riviere 1937].

It is also interesting to examine how many courses of lectures, etc. I and my collaborators have had. This examination shows that in the fifteen years between 1927 and 1942 I had four adult control analyses and six children control analyses, and I gave three courses of lectures. Dr Jones, Dr Glover and Miss Sharpe have also given three courses of lectures and Dr Payne two. Dr Rickman gave two and Mrs Riviere one. In my courses of lectures on technique I made it amply clear that my concepts of the depressive position and manic defences are still considered as controversial and that I personally am responsible for them. It is a striking fact that if I had wished to smuggle in this knowledge under a false flag, as it were, I was so little concerned about having more controls and giving more lectures and seminars. This shows that if I had wished to do so I was, to say the least, very unsuccessful in my strivings for power. Actually I was so much engrossed in those years in working out this new work and testing it in all its aspects and clarifying it for myself before I proceeded to further publications – one of them being my paper on 'Mourning' [Klein 1940] – that I was little concerned with teaching it in that period, and still less with making converts and gaining adherents.

I would ask you to compare the foregoing facts and statements with Dr Glover's pronouncement that candidates were 'taught as accepted psychoanalytic theory and practice material or method which is still controversial and regarding which the Society itself has not come to any conclusion'.

Finally, I should like to say that as long as this Society has any claim to be called a scientific Society there must be disagreement, and what Dr Glover calls controversy, between the Members; though it need not be embittered by personal animus. A scientific Society is a group of people who are seeking to discover new truth, not a group who are resting content at any stage in the search for knowledge and are satisfied with that.

Melanie Klein
23rd July 1942 (Archives of the British Psycho-Analytical Society)

Following the receipt of this memorandum Melanie Klein received a number of letters. Karin Stephen wrote on 28 July 1942:

Dear Mrs Klein
Adrian and I were much interested in your statement which we entirely agree with. Really Glover is behaving like a lunatic, but

fortunately people are really, I think, becoming shocked at his lack of straightforwardness and recognize how dangerous it would be to let him stay in power. So, although it must be maddening for you, it is probably a good thing in the long run that he has made these wild accusations! . . .

(Klein Archives)

And Ernest Jones, who had previously stopped her reading her statement at the last Business Meeting, also wrote to Melanie Klein, on 26 July 1942:

Dear Mrs Klein,
I have read your memorandum with great interest and, as you know, am in a position to be able personally to corroborate every word of it. I am sure most of the Society is heartily sick of the wrangling, which only three or four members enjoy. I hope and expect that the Annual Meeting will go off without any of these indulgences. I feel convinced that if the Society shows a firm front it would be well possible to prevent a few members from holding up our scientific progress which after all is much more interesting.
      With kindest personal regards,
        Yours sincerely,
        Ernest Jones
        (Melanie Klein Archives: The Wellcome Foundation, London)

Editorial comments

Various important decisions were made at this Annual General Meeting, concerning the problems that were discussed at the previous five Extraordinary Business Meetings. No verbatim minutes were kept and the following extracts from the minutes relate to these decisions.

Extracts from the Annual General Meeting of the British Psycho-Analytical Society was held on Wednesday, July 29th, 1942 at 8 pm., at 96 Gloucester Place, London W.1.

The President, Dr Jones, was in the Chair.
Members present: Drs Jones, Glover, Payne, Miss Anna Freud, Mrs Burlingham, Drs M. Schmideberg, W. Hoffer, Friedlander, Lantos, A. Stephen, K. Stephen, Mr W. Schmideberg, Dr Herford, Miss

Low, Dr Weiss, Mrs H. Hoffer, Ruben, Dr Haas, Miss Sharpe, Drs Franklin, Macdonald, Miss Sheehan-Dare, Drs Brierley, Yates, Balint, Mrs Klein, Isaacs, Riviere, Dr Heimann, Mr Strachey, Drs Winnicott and Wilson.

(DECISIONS WITH REGARD TO A COMMITTEE TO CONSIDER
CONSTITUTIONAL ISSUES)

10 *Constitution of committee 'to investigate the question of tenure of office and the holding of multiple official positions'*

Miss Low spoke of the constitution of this committee and suggested that it should consist of 9 members. Other members suggested 7 and 5. Votes were taken and it was decided by a majority that the committee should consist of 5 members. Several names on the nomination list were withdrawn but then nominated at the meeting. The final list was voted on by secret ballot. It was decided to obtain the votes of absent members and the result of the election would therefore not be available until these had been received.[1]

(DECISIONS WITH REGARD TO THE INFLUENCE OF THE PRESENT
DIVERGENCES ON THE TRAINING SITUATION)

11 Miss Low announced that she wished to discuss resolution E(1) and also an interim resolution which was introduced by her, Dr M. Schmideberg and Mr W. Schmideberg, combining their resolutions E(ii), H(c) and G(a,E)[2] to the effect that 'the training committee discuss the effect of the present divergences on the training situation, consider the bearing of Dr Glover's and Mrs Klein's statements and any other point touching on the subject made during the recent discussions, and report back to the Business Meeting. Members should have the opportunity of discussing the findings and of resuming the discussion of the original resolutions.'

A general discussion then took place on these two resolutions.
(1) With regard to the interim resolution, Dr Glover stated that the Training Committee were already tackling the problem referred to and had settled to holding a meeting for this purpose in September. Miss Anna Freud said that the Training Committee must have time and that the success or failure might be influenced if they were to come to conclusions by a certain date. Dr Balint suggested that a report should be asked for by a certain date. The resolution was put

to the meeting and carried unanimously and no time limit was thought advisable.

(2) With regard to E(1), Dr Brierley read a statement on a memorandum which she had drawn up in connection with a plan for the study of scientific differences and distributed to the members.[3] *It was decided to allot one Scientific Meeting a month to the discussion of scientific differences.* Mrs Riviere proposed that a small committee of three should be formed to organize the programme for these meetings. Dr Glover suggested that a first Scientific Meeting in October should be introductory to the session and the second should be devoted to theoretical discussion according to a settled plan.

It was finally proposed that the Committee should consist of Drs Glover and Brierley and Mr James Strachey. This was put to the meeting and passed.

12 Miss Low suggested that the question of the Society's public relations should be added to the task of the Committee 'to investigate, etc.'. Dr Friedlander suggested that the Society should wait until it had settled its internal differences before tackling the problem of external relations, and the meeting supported this point of view.

(b) Hon. Business Secretary's Report, 1941–2

The year 1941–2 has been one of unusual experiences for the Society. World events and the death of Professor Freud have combined with developments in the International Psychoanalytical Association to bring about internal disturbances and a tendency to separate into groups in the two main Psycho-Analytical Societies, which survived the worldwide political revolutions, namely the British and the American.

Before the British Society had had time to assimilate and unite with their colleagues from Vienna, it was faced with a scattering of its own Members owing to the attack on London. I do not think that we realized the full significance of this until Members began to return to London in the summer of 1941. The evacuation of Members meant not only the breaking of private practices which caused economic anxiety, but the complete cessation of personal contacts, which tended to increase the significance of personal and scientific differences of outlook which were already in existence. Unfortunately the Society was entering a transitional stage in its development caused partly by the approaching retirement of the first

President and partly by a need for expansion and development if it was to continue to exist. . . .

Arising out of three consecutive Scientific Meetings on the question of the Society's relation to the public, a series of Business Meetings were held, on February 25th, 1942 (29 Members present), March 11th (25 Members present), April 15th (27 Members present), May 13th (25 Members present) and June 10th (31 Members present).

At the meeting on June 10th, the following resolutions were voted upon and accepted:

  (i) That the present Emergency Committee be continued for a year, with permission to co-opt one or more Members if necessary, and that no elections be held this year.

 (ii) (a) That the Society immediately pass a self-denying ordinance in respect of all current charges and counter-charges, and all activities directed against Members or groups of Members.

     (b) That the Society require all Members to refrain from personal attacks or innuendoes in discussion, but also strongly affirm the right of all Members to complete freedom of speech within the limits of common courtesy.

(iii) That a committee be appointed to investigate the questions of tenure of office and the holding of multiple official positions.

The first and third resolutions were voted by secret ballot, absent Members sending their votes by post. The second decision was taken by a show of hands.

signed:
S. M. Payne

Editorial comment

On 22 May 1942, Marjorie Brierley wrote to Miss Low a letter which sums up many of the issues raised so far, and it is particularly relevant with regard to the planning of the Scientific Discussions that are reported in the next chapter:

Dear Miss Low,

The idea of holding Society meetings instead of setting up a large sub-committee to thrash out our scientific problems seems to me to have a good deal in its favour. It would avoid many of the drawbacks of a sub-committee but would not preclude the setting up of committees for special purposes if, at any time, they appeared to be needed. It is essential that enquiry should get underway in one form or another and I am prepared to support the 'meetings' (unless there seem good reasons for changing my mind). I would suggest that we do not hold extra meetings but that we devote alternate ordinary meetings to systematic discussion of controversial issues. But the problem cannot be narrowed down to a nutshell of single statements by Melanie Klein and Anna Freud; it's much too big. It would need a good deal of preliminary programme organization to ensure that the most vital issues were covered in the course of the year. This could be done through the usual channels, unless otherwise decided at the Annual Meeting. For instance, Members could be asked to state what, in their opinion, are key issues when they send in offers of papers for forthcoming sessions. We might even ask them to give papers bearing on our current problems if they are in a position to do so.

I do not agree with the present form and phrasing of the Resolution and cannot sign it for the following reasons:

(1)   It is far too belligerent and not in accord with the spirit of the Armistice resolution. The last thing we can profit by is a series of prize-fights or ordeals by combat. What we need most is to arrive at a clearer understanding of each other's points of view. If we can get people to explain themselves, without fear or favour, we shall obtain the data required to arrive at some assessment of our scientific position. We shall never get this by issuing challenges to a series of duels *à outrance* but only by encouraging people to elaborate their opinions freely in an atmosphere of friendly toleration. It will take a great deal of co-operative effort to arrive at sound conclusions, not a number of tournaments.

(2)   I dislike the usage of 'Freudian' as distinct from the more general term 'psychoanalytic' theory and practice. Psychoanalysis is not a creed but a science, and the work of Freud is not a final revelation of absolute truth but a system of hypotheses designed to explain as accurately as possible the working of the human mind as inferred by him from clinical and other psychological data. Freud continuously modified and expanded his hypotheses, his theory evolving parallel with his growth in knowledge. If psychoanalysis is to survive, this process of development must continue. A living science is evolutionary and democratic, not static and authoritarian. Apart from such questions of general principle, the use of the adjective 'Freudian' narrows too straitly the immediate problem. It is not a question only of finding out whether irreconcilable differences between Anna Freud and Melanie Klein

209

but rather, whether we can ALL continue to co-exist as members of one Society and, particularly, whether that Society can re-establish its right to be considered a genuinely scientific society.

(3) It is the training dilemma which makes the question of differences so much more important than they would be in any ordinary society. As a result of enquiry, the Society may find itself in a position to give some ruling re. scope and methods of training that will be neither too elastic nor too rigid. We shall not solve our difficulties by trying to turn out standardized trainees but by aiming at increasing the number of analysts capable of thinking for themselves and adapting their training lessons both to problems of theory and to the needs of their patients.

(4) Penalization threats are surely unnecessary if agreement can be reached as to training conditions. I have never been able to see why any individual analyst speaking in public should be regarded as representing the Society, unless specially authorized to do so. Members of other societies always speak as private individuals unless appointed as delegates to conferences, etc.

I have gone into this at some length but I feel it is so important that any enquiry should begin under favourable conditions, and I do not feel the present wording of your resolution will create a propitious atmosphere.

In haste,

Yours very sincerely,

Marjorie Brierley

Notes

1 The result of the postal ballot was circulated to members on 7 Sept. 1942. The following members were elected: Anna Freud, Edward Glover, Barbara Low, Sylvia Payne, and Adrian Stephen.
2 See shortened version of the resolutions in Section 1, Chapter 2.
3 Brierley's plan is attached to the Agenda for the meeting to discuss how to organize the scientific discussions (Section 1, Chapter 8).

8

The organization of the Scientific Discussions

British Psycho-Analytical Society
Circular Note

At the Annual Meeting, held on July 29th, 1942, it was decided to allot one Scientific Meeting a month to the discussion of scientific differences and a Committee of three Members – Dr Glover, Dr Brierley, and Mr James Strachey – was formed to organize the programmes of these meetings. I enclose a copy of a memorandum, drawn up by Dr Brierley, for your information and shall be glad to receive from you any suggestions you might wish to make with regard to subjects, range, order, or procedure. These should be sent as soon as possible.

The first Scientific Meeting devoted to this discussion will be held in October 1942.

> Yours sincerely,
> EDWARD GLOVER
> Chairman of Committee   July 31st, 1942

Memorandum, drawn up by Dr Brierley

Reference

Agenda 29 July 1942. Item 9(a) – Scientific differences Resolution E(1) – Miss Low

A Possible (?) Programme for Special Scientific Meetings of the Society

The questions to be answered

Is a theory of mental development expressed mainly in terms of the vicissitudes of infantile object-relationship compatible or incompatible, in principle or in detail, with theory in terms of instinct vicissitude? Are such theories antithetic or complementary? How far do current differences in theory imply radical alterations in technique?

The aim of the programme

To cover the most vital issues in a more or less logical sequence, but to concentrate each meeting within a manageable and fairly narrowly defined field.

First desideratum

To arrive at a clear statement, understood and accepted by all Members, of precise points of difference, agreement, ambiguity, or uncertainty, existing at the present time; and to set these out before the Society in strictly definable terms. Such a statement could be signed by all participants, and accepted by a majority vote of the Society as an accurate statement. One way of arriving at such a statement would be as follows:

Procedure

Meetings during the first term devoted to simple and concise explanations and re-statements of views on the development of the psyche from infancy to the close of the Oedipus phase – roughly the first five years.

These meetings would conveniently fall into three groups:-

(1) The mental life of the suckling and the weaning period – 6–9 months.
(2) Mental life from *c.* 6 months – two or two-and-a-half years.
(3) Mental life from *c.* two-and-a-half – five years of age.

212

Second desideratum

Having achieved a clear statement of views, and possibly established certain differences, the Society should then follow up both the theoretical and the practical implications of such differences, paying special attention to all relevant evidence.

Procedure

Meetings during the second and third terms to be devoted to the pursuit and evaluation of these implications, i.e., to the assessment of our scientific position. The theoretical and practical implications are here stated in sequence but could be taken concurrently if this seemed more desirable. The risk of the latter alternative would be that both would be less fully discussed and might be confused. The theoretical implications fall into two categories: (1) general, concerning the structure and functions of mind (pure psychology), and (2) specific, concerning the etiology of mental disorder and the conditions of mental health (medical psychology). Such a division involves a certain amount of repetition, but this should help clarification and diminish risk of oversight.

At least one term, i.e, the second term, could be fully occupied in considering theoretical implications, e.g., as follows:

(A) GENERAL

(1) Ego development, age differentiation, and superego formation.
(2) Mental mechanisms, their relative importance, onset of operation, etc.
(3) Anxiety.
(4) The role of phantasy and of environment in infantile life.
(5) Stages, phases, or positions in infantile development. Progression and regression. Instinct modification.

These lead naturally on to:

(B) ETIOLOGY. THE PSYCHO–NEUROSIS AND PSYCHOSES SERIATIM

(1) Hysteria.
(2) Obsessional neuroses.

213

(3) Paranoia.
(4) Manic depression and melancholia.
(5) Schizophrenia.
(6) Conditions of mental health.

The third term could be spent enquiring into the modifications of technique following on differences in theoretical approach. They are also general and specific.

(A) GENERAL

(1) The aim or goal of analysis.
(2) Type, indications for, and criteria of, interpretation.
(3) Transference.

(B) SPECIFIC

(1) Technique of child analysis.
(2) Handling of specific disorders, e.g., manic depression.

A further statement embodying the results of this comparative study would answer the question of compatibility between object and instinct theory, and would provide a cross-section of present-day theory and practice which could serve as a basis for (1) solution of the training problem, and (2) tentative research programme for the immediate future.

Scientific Discussion at the Meeting held on October 21st, 1942

A meeting of Members and Associate Members was held on Wednesday, October 21st, 1942, at 8 p.m., at 96 Gloucester Place, London, W.1.

Dr Glover was in the Chair and 31 Members and Associates were present (Drs Glover, Payne, K. Stephen, M. Schmideberg, Weiss, Friedlander, W. Schmideberg, Anna Freud, Burlingham, H. & W. Hoffer, Ruben, Frank, Lantos, Franklin, Herford, Low, Sharpe, Brierley, Ries, Taylor, Winnicott, Rosenberg, Evans, Debenham, Heimann, Isaacs, Klein, Balint, Rosenfeld, Gillespie).

214

Three guests were present: Dr Usher, Mrs Neurath, Dr Schlossberg.

Five candidate guests were present: Mrs Meynell, Miss Hedy Schwarz, Mrs Mannheim, Mrs Milner, Mr Hollitscher.

1   DR PAYNE read the minutes of the last meeting which were passed.
Arising out of the minutes the Chairman reported that one or two Members desired to continue the discussion on shock treatment, begun at the last meeting. He suggested that a symposium might be arranged during the next term.
2   DR GLOVER also announced that £50 had been collected for Dr Stoddart's presentation and asked the meeting whether members would prefer the presentation to be made on a special occasion or at a Scientific Meeting. It was left to the Executive to make suitable arrangements.
3   DR GLOVER opened the meeting by referring to the report drawn up by the Committee elected to arrange the Scientific Discussions of theoretical differences of opinion,[1] and spoke of the recommendations of the Committee as merely a basis for discussion at the present meeting. He stated that the first topic for discussion chosen was the role of introjection and projection of objects in the early years of development. Dr Isaacs had been asked to give the first paper and she could not deliver it until December. He divided the report into three main heads. (1) The aims of the series – (2) selection of topics – (3) procedure, and suggested that it might be desirable to start with a more general discussion.

DR K. STEPHEN asked why time should be limited. Dr Glover replied that the idea was that a year should be devoted to discussions and that a number of decisions such as the question of election of officers depended on the issue of these discussions.

The question of the number of meetings was raised and it was pointed out that one scientific meeting a month had been allocated to discussions.

MISS LOW asked whether the Committee felt that the validity of the different views comes before everything else.

DR GLOVER stated the memorandum circulated represented what the Committee could agree upon. He went on to say that as a private Member he wished to give his views on the particular issues, and asked Dr Payne to take the chair while he read a statement. He stated that his views on (a) the aims, (b) forms, (c) procedure to be adopted had been influenced by (a) experience of previous scientific discussions, (b) on where the onus of proof lies in any scientific controversy.

The onus of proof lies on those who advance new theories. Those who support new views should make it clear in what respects they consider their views have either amplified accepted Freudian teaching or call for a modification of it. He went on to state that while onus of proof lies on all persons advancing new views, the present controversies centre round those put forward by Melanie Klein. He held this opinion because other people's original contributions had not been criticized in the recent controversy, and moreover do not bear widely on the development of psychoanalysis. Nor has it been suggested that Anna Freud or any of her colleagues now Members of our Society have aroused acute controversy by advancing heterodox views. He thought that the opening papers should be given by Mrs Klein or one of her supporters.

As regards the technique of investigation, he thought the following questions should be raised in each instance:

(a) what is the evidence on which the view is based?
(b) is the view valid?
(c) if not yet proven, is it nevertheless a plausible assumption?
(d) if valid, is that validity general or does the view in question apply only in certain types of case?
(e) is it incompatible with accepted Freudian teaching? if so which parts of Freudian teaching?
(f) if it does contradict Freudian teaching which part does it contradict and what is the more accurate view?
(g) does the new view by overemphasis or shift of emphasis or in some other way in effect contradict Freudian teaching?

He went on to say that the bearing of these views on the formulation of topics is very definite:

(1) that it would be better if each issue were so stated that it is perfectly clear on whom the onus of proof lies,
(2) that issues should not be in too general terms,
(3) that in some instances the evidence on which the theory is based should be presented,
(4) that the influence of the writings of other workers should be made clear,
(5) that when principal speakers do not include historical references another member might be asked to give a brief résumé of the literature on the subject.
(6) On some occasions one person only should be invited to speak, summarize, and answer questions.

216

After reading this paper Dr Glover resumed the chair. He invited a general discussion.

MISS FREUD thanked Dr Glover for his amplification and stated that she wished it had been sent round instead of the Committee's report. She thought the latter was too general, and avoided a clear definition of the controversy.

DR GLOVER said that his remarks did not constitute an amplification of the report but were his personal views.

MRS KLEIN said that this was important. She wondered if the Committee as a whole agreed with Miss Freud's statement. Her views in the past had received considerable support from Members who had the confidence of the Society. It was possible that her work might deviate but not be necessarily incompatible with Freud's views. Did all the Members agree with Miss Freud and Dr Glover that interest should be concentrated on the one point?

MISS FREUD said that the question of compatibility did not enter in. The two theories could not co-exist. If two points of view do not coincide the first is to find out which is more accurate.

DR PAYNE expressed regret that the discussion should have opened in such an extremely controversial form. It was not well to put forward a viewpoint which is tantamount to coming to a conclusion before discussion had taken place.

DR SCHMIDEBERG said the discussion was not of value of Mrs Klein's views, but who's views shall we discuss?

MISS FREUD said that it was not an attack to formulate differences clearly.

DR PAYNE replied that we had not yet determined where the differences lie.

DR ISAACS said that she had come to the meeting full of hope. She thought the temper was going to be dispassionate, and that views would be stated and evidence produced. It seemed as if Dr Glover's speech had attempted to queer the pitch. The truth was not necessarily something everybody agrees upon. The object was to attempt to get at the truth and not to measure one against the other. It was an extremely difficult problem which would require all available intelligence and honesty. It should not begin by measuring one theory against another.

DR LANTOS said she thought the main problem was a question of teaching and how a more unified theory could be presented. It was obvious that the views which are standing against each other are the so-called Freudian views and Mrs Klein's views. Even if it is true that her views were supported by a large number.

DR GLOVER reminded the meeting that the Training Committee

had been asked to discuss the training question and report to the Society.[2]

DR HEIMANN said she was glad that Dr Glover spoke for himself and not for the Committee.

MISS LOW suggested that Dr Brierley should be asked whether Dr Glover's views represented those of the Committee.

DR BRIERLEY said that the Committee had asked Dr Glover not to make his statement because they did not consider it opportune.

MISS ANNA FREUD asked whether it spoilt an atmosphere to state existing differences. It was said that Dr Glover and she had brought something into the light which did not exist before. It had been discussed for a year. It was known in all psychoanalytical Societies that Mrs Klein's views are known as those of the English School and that they were different from views taught in other psychoanalytical Societies. Exchange Lectures were started between Vienna and London years ago to state these differences.[3] This was a matter that concerned the psychoanalytical movement as such.

MRS KLEIN stated that she reminded the Society of the pride with which they identified themselves with her theories. The matter is oversimplified by singling out her work and contrasting it with Freud's teaching. There were no differences before the Viennese came over. These particular views were put forward as any other scientific problem, and not made an essential issue.

DR SCHMIDEBERG said the differences did not start with the arrival of the Viennese Members. There was a ruling in 1936 after Mrs Riviere had gone to Vienna to the effect that the views should not be called representative of the English group and that no more Exchange Lectures should be given.

MRS KLEIN asked where this had been recorded.

DR SCHMIDEBERG: It should be in the minutes.[4]

DR FRIEDLANDER said that the adherents of Mrs Klein's views would appear in the discussion. She thought the knowledge of the divergent views was widespread. She had heard it from a consultant in 1933.

DR BALINT said he was disappointed. The only point of importance was whether a view was valid or not. Scientific theories cannot be decided by vote. It was not advisable to discuss theories under someone's name.

DR ISAACS said she agreed with what Dr Glover said about the onus of proof. It might turn out that a number of people accepted certain parts of a theory and rejected others. She could not agree to making the issues personal. She agreed with what Dr Balint said.

218

MRS KLEIN said she did not know what Dr Glover meant when he spoke of the early development of the superego.

DR GLOVER said he was again speaking as a Member. He mentioned the topic to illustrate the danger of stating issues in too general terms. If there was a controversy about an issue, the controversial point should be singled out.

DR ISAACS agreed. She said she had been singled out to speak on a certain topic, and realized how many points would have to be kept in mind. The role of introjection and projection was an enormous topic, especially if it included a historical survey. It was too big for one paper. She suggested her paper should be on the place of phantasy in relation to the mechanisms of introjection and projection.

DR GLOVER suggested that this point came under the heading of topics.

MISS LOW spoke of the peculiar view of avoiding names, and said Members made a mistake when they said that scientific theories were not labelled with names. She mentioned the Darwinian theory – New Darwinians – Einstein's theory – Smuts' Holism theory and others. The founder of psychoanalysis was Freud. She protested against what she called shuffling.

DR GLOVER spoke of the self-denying ordinance governing the expression of opinions.

MISS LOW said Dr Glover's statement has been misconstrued.

DR K. STEPHEN said she thought it would be best to pick out any subject most likely to be in dispute, and to state divergences.

DR WINNICOTT said that the Society was divided as to whether we are pursuing a truly scientific aim. It is important to relate theories etc. to the work of Freud but it cannot necessarily be done right away. This was, however, distinct from the search for truth. The non-scientific aim was clearly illustrated by Miss Low's remarks on Darwinism. Scientists are not interested in Darwinism which was actually a brake on biological science. It was to be hoped that we shall not have to go through a phase corresponding to Darwinism in relation to Freud, who himself would have hated such a thing.

DR SCHMIDEBERG said it was not the first time that controversial views had been discussed, that discussions had been unsatisfactory because they were unsystematic and there was a reluctance to work out divergences. Scientists and particularly analysts should not be affected by conflicts. Divergences mean something is not fully understood. We should not suppress but study them, with special attention to terminology. We are bound to arrive at false conclusions if our terms are not properly defined. The following aims should be adopted: (a) not to confuse likeness with identity, (b) not to assume that sequence in time is equivalent to cause and effect, (c) to pay more attention to the criteria of interpretation and deductions employed, (d) to assess plausibility and therapeutic success. In Dr Schmideberg's opinion such differences are largely responsible for the divergences of the conclusions arrived at. It was important to distinguish between ideal criteria stated in principle and those applied in practice. She stated that there is a natural inclination to assume that in the case of a divergence the truth lies somewhere in the middle. A wish for compromise solution was in accordance with good democratic traditions. She then compared scientific methods with those politics. Science eliminates the human element and depends on evidence, logic, and reason. Intellectual sincerity and courage, a clear mind and freedom from undue sensitivity are the virtues of the scientist.

DR GLOVER stated that no one had objected to the 'Aims' stated in the Committee's report. Differences that arise are more specific. Some Members hold strongly that the focus of controversy should be precisely stated not avoiding linking it with names of persons holding the views. Others think that this would create a bad atmosphere. He did not gather that any new project was suggested by them. Dr K. Stephen had suggested that the onus should be on Members to deal with controversial points. The Committee could be requested to bring this point clearly to all contributors and to discuss the points with every lecturer. Speakers cannot be dictated to but the Society can judge whether controversial issues are avoided. Is this compromise acceptable to the meeting?

DR PAYNE suggested Members should send in the points they regarded as controversial.

DR GLOVER said that this had been asked for without result.

DR ROSENBERG said it was difficult to state something which is called 'accepted Freudian teaching'. There are subjects where it is uncertain which are really accepted views.

DR GLOVER said he should have thought that one could gather what accepted Freudian theory was by reading the literature.

DR ROSENBERG said that all Freud's theory changed considerably during his life. For example, his change of view about the importance of early sexual experiences.

DR GLOVER said this point should be cleared up by historical survey.

DR BRIERLEY said that there is no such phrase as 'accepted Freudian teaching' in the Committee's statement.

DR ISAACS said the more the discussion proceeds the more it seemed clear that the topics will require to be circumscribed.

DR GLOVER said it was doubtful whether more than one could be dealt with at one meeting.

DR BALINT suggested that a list of papers should be given on which the views are based.

DR FRANKLIN suggested that papers should be circulated before the discussions.

MISS FREUD asked if Mrs Isaacs could state where the controversy lay in the subject of phantasy.

DR ISAACS referred as an example to the recent paper of Dr Brierley about internal objects.

MISS FREUD thought Dr Brierley concentrated on general definitions and not on controversial points.

DR K. STEPHEN said that people who read papers will know from discussions of the Society how Members' views differ on the subject of 'accepted Freudian theory'.

DR GLOVER said the views of individuals or groups must stand up against the body of scientific teaching as a whole.

MISS FREUD asked if the opinion was limited to this Society or to psychoanalytic literature on the whole.

DR PAYNE said to psychoanalytic literature as a whole.

MISS FREUD said it sounded as if it would simply be an exchange of opinions between Members of this Society.

DR GLOVER said that there had got to be a 'least common measure' of all views.

DR SCHMIDEBERG said Freud's views as he expressed them in the Collected Papers.

DR FRIEDLANDER said all Members should read the important papers relative to the subject. The speaker should give his point of view and the controversial point of view.

DR GLOVER did not agree that it would be difficult for any speaker to put in three or four sentences whether his view conforms to, differs from, or amplifies basic principles.

DR SCHMIDEBERG suggested that Members could be advised about the important literature connected with the topic.

DR BRIERLEY suggested that Dr Isaacs should give a paper on phantasy.

DR ISAACS said for instance, the question of the dating of phantasies, when they occur.

DR GLOVER suggested that the Committee should draw up a list of papers to be read by Members in preparation for discussion.[5]

This was agreed to by Members.

It was agreed to leave it to the Committee to decide which of the following measures should be adopted –

(1) that 3 principal speakers be invited to prepare paper of 20 minutes' length on any given subject,
(2) that 2 principal speakers be invited to prepare papers of 30 minutes' length,
(3) that one speaker be invited to prepare a paper of 45 minutes' length.

With regard to the suggestion that all contributions should be circulated to all Members before the meeting, Dr Payne pointed out that it was impossible for this to be done in the office as eighty copies would be required. Ten copies could be typed in one process and could be distributed in turn from the office. Full circulation would entail the work being done outside, and special financial provision would have to be made.

Members voted for a circulation of scientific papers before discussions.

With regard to finance, Dr Balint suggested that every member who wanted a copy of the papers should send £1 to the Secretary to cover the cost of duplicating papers and discussions. This was agreed to by Members.

In answer to a question whether the Institute could contribute to the cost of duplicating, Dr Payne said that it would do so if necessary.

DR ISAACS suggested that circulated papers should be taken as read so as to leave time for discussion.

DR GLOVER said the speakers should be allowed to make certain points, and so 'speak to' the paper circulated. Probably twenty minutes would be enough time for this.

It was agreed to give speakers at first 5 minutes in the discussion with the right to participate again if time permitted.

DR GLOVER said that often the gist of a matter comes up in discussion only; he therefore favoured a record of the discussion being kept by shorthand notes and by Members handing in the text or précis of their contributions. Contributions handed in to be what was said and not what might have been said.

It was decided by the meeting that a summary of the discussions should be distributed.

DR WINNICOTT suggested the publication of the whole matter in the Journal.

Re topics for discussion:

DR GLOVER said that it was impossible to arrange for the first topic in November. Two meetings could be held in December and the second meeting devoted to discussion. It was decided to have Dr Isaacs' paper at a meeting to be held on December 9th and if necessary to have a second discussion on December 16th.

The question of the topic of the next meeting was discussed.

MISS FREUD said that papers on projection and introjection should logically follow Dr Isaacs' paper on the role of phantasies.

It was decided that the second topic should be on projection and introjection and the Committee should decide on the speaker.

Full minutes of the discussion at this meeting are kept by the Secretary in a separate file.[6]

(signed)

Edward Glover

Notes

1 At the AGM held on 29 July 1942, a small committee of three members were elected to arrange and supervise the discussion of scientific differences in the Society: they were Dr E. Glover, Dr M. Brierley, and Mr James Strachey.

2 At the last AGM on 29 July 1942, it was decided to ask the Training Committee to discuss and to report back to the Society on the effect of the present divergences on the training situation.

3 These took place between 1935 and 1936. See King's introduction (p. 22).

4 See minutes of a Business Meeting held on 20 April 1937: 'Dr Schmideberg asked whether the Member chosen to give an Exchange Lecture was held to represent the Society as a whole or not, and was the lecturer chosen officially by the Council or not. Dr Jones replied that the Exchange Lectures that had been given up to the present time were arranged by him and Dr Federn with the aim of presenting views which had been put forward by Mrs Klein and English Members working in co-operation with her, because the Viennese Society wanted to learn more about these views.' After discussion it was agreed 'that the term "Exchange Lectures" be not used'.

5 I have not yet discovered such a list. I suspect that it was never produced, as it would be a difficult task given the current atmosphere in the Society.
6 These have not yet been found.

Addendum to Section One

The various problems contained in the sixteen resolutions that were discussed over the course of the five Extraordinary Business Meetings reported in Section 1, covered many topics, concerns and suggested changes. But was it fair or democratic to discuss proposals to change the rules of the Society, while so many people were away from London because of their war-work and who could not therefore participate in these discussions and decisions? After discussing these issues, in a setting that might be described as an 'Open Forum' (i.e. in Extraordinary Business Meetings), the Members eventually decided at the AGM on 29 July 1942, to institute three different ways of exploring and perhaps dealing with the causes of concern in the Society.

1. They agreed to set up a committee of five Members 'to investigate the question of tenure of office and the holding of multiple official positions'. This committee was elected by secret ballot and a postal vote of those who were not present. Anna Freud, Edward Glover, Barbara Low, Sylvia Payne and Adrian Stephen were elected.
2. The Training Committee were asked not only to 'discuss the effects of the present divergences on the training situation', but also to 'consider the bearing of Dr Glover's and Mrs Klein's statements and any other point touching on the subject made during the recent discussions', and to 'report back to the Business Meeting' (see Section 3).
3. It was agreed that one scientific meeting a month should be devoted to the discussion of scientific divergences, to be monitored by a small committee, consisting of Edward Glover, Marjorie Brierley and James Strachey. James Strachey was not present at the meeting which elected him to this committee and he took no part in it or in the discussions of scientific divergences.

Jones, as the President, had chaired all the discussions at the Business Meetings and many of the other Scientific meetings, which had continued to take place in spite of bombing and war conditions. The meetings to discuss Scientific divergences (reported in Section 2) were, however, chaired by Glover, as he was chairman of this monitoring committee, which was responsible for circulating the written contributions of Members and for agreeing any changes in the procedures suggested by Members. I have been informed by some Members who were present at these meetings that Glover did much to alienate himself from the more moderate Members of the Society by his partisan chairing of these meetings.

Pearl King

First Series of Scientific Discussions on Controversial Issues

—————————— 1 ——————————

Background to the
Scientific Controversies

RICCARDO STEINER

Introduction

It is not possible nor is it necessary in this introduction to the discussion of scientific controversies for me to give a summary of the scientific disagreements, as they are clearly stated by the participants in the chapters that follow, although I do, of course, discuss them later. The points of view expressed by the participants in these and other discussions reported in this book have not matured in isolation from those of other colleagues, but have evolved out of a network of relationships and shared experiences, supportive or undermining as the case may be.

In order to obtain a deeper understanding of the differences and cross-currents influencing the feelings, fears, assumptions, prejudices, and points of view expressed by the main participants not only during the discussions of scientific differences, but also during the Business and other Meetings that are reported in this book, I have quoted some of the considerable correspondence that exists in various archives. In particular I have selected correspondence between Melanie Klein and her colleagues and the leading members of the British Society, such as Ernest Jones, Sylvia Payne, Barbara Low, Marjorie Brierley, Edward Glover, and Anna Freud. (It is regretted that only limited material from Anna Freud's archives have been available to the editors.)

As a result of this approach it is hoped that I will have been able to communicate the emotional and interpersonal context accompanying these controversies so that the reader will be able to empathize with those taking part in these discussions as human beings, as well as evaluating their own opinion of the correctness or incorrectness of the points of view expressed by the participants.

The threat to Melanie Klein's work

Dear Dr Jones,

At last I am sitting down to reply to your letter. You need not have feared to touch on my feelings, I am sure you overrate very much their strength in connection with my work and with Psychoanalysis in general if in narrating to me these matters you had to remind yourself of my sense of fair play. . . . What you say about your situation in Vienna, i.e. what you described to me in your letter as the first matter, is very easy for me to understand and sympathize with. At the time I resented Anna settling here with a large and representative part of the Vienna group and thought that you had too little considered the disturbance to our work and also that you confronted us with a *fait accompli* (this point you have explained). Some of those Viennese who since went to USA (which of course one could not foresee) have very soon volunteered the information to me and others that they had every possibility to go to America and would have done so, had you not invited and encouraged them to come to England. As regards Freud as I said, I can fully understand your attitude and I also am very glad to think that Freud had a happy year in England in spite of the difficulties which Anna's presence gives rise to here.

However as I said before I understand and even at the time in spite of some misgivings understood the difficulty of the choice you had to make and it is not this matter in itself which would have moved me to reproach you for harm done to Psychoanalysis. . . . The harm from this side [Klein means the presence of Anna Freud and the Viennese] is part of the general situation of deterioration which is due to what you describe as the second matter.

Those are the first paragraphs of a draft of a letter written by Melanie Klein to Ernest Jones probably in the late spring of 1941[1] in response to a letter written to her by E. Jones, on 14 April 1941[2] where he tried to explain to her the reasons why he had in the end to choose London to rescue Freud and his family, although he was quite aware of the anxieties and problems that this could create for Melanie Klein, for her work, and also for the British Psycho-Analytical Society. In his letter Jones clearly explained to Klein his difficult position and the tragedy of the Viennese caught in a struggle 'for life and death and desperate to leave Vienna by hook and by crook'. He also expressed his satisfaction for having rescued Freud 'my best personal friend as well as a great man to whom we all owe so much'.

> Freud [added Jones], apart from his pain spent one of the happiest years of his life in London with all his family and servants gathered round him, including even brother, nephew and grandchildren, and all his own children except one were there. The Viennese members behaved pretty well on the whole. At present they have nearly all left for America, the Bibrings being the last to go, except for old Dr Steiner who came to England independently of my will and who is now also arranging to leave. There remain in England only the Hoffers, whom I regard as very decent people and Anna Freud.

In order to appease Klein, Jones at one moment stated[6] 'she [Anna] is certainly a tough and indigestible morsel. She has probably gone as far in analysis as she can and has no pioneering originality. Much worse than that, however, can be said of a good many of our members, and she undoubtedly has many valuable qualities.'

> At this point in his letter Jones mentioned what he called 'the second matter', to which Klein refers in her letter too. Jones tried to explain to Melanie his views and his version of the problems which had arisen in the British Psycho-Analytical Society owing to the odd changes in Glover's behaviour 'in connection with the change in Melitta' (Klein's daughter, who at that time was in analysis with Glover). See Grosskurth (1986), King (1983), and Segal (1979).
> Jones went on, saying that Glover could have been 'the only available successor to myself as President of the Society. Even today he is the only male medical analyst who can appear before a non-analytical audience without arousing sharp criticism or even ridicule. . . . It is the general opinion that [Melitta's] influence was the more powerful of the two.'
> Concerning Glover's offices as Director of the Clinic and Chairman of the Training Committee when Jones had resigned and semi-retired to the country, he felt that on the whole those decisions were not really wrong. It was natural that Glover had to succeed him at the Clinic; if the Training Committee had appointed him as its Chairman, 'It would have been quixotically futile for me', continued Jones, 'to attempt to displace him unaided.' There was not a suitable alternative, because Jones, disagreeing with Klein, did not think that Rickman was such an alternative: 'with all his admirable and

attractive qualities he has always had grave failings of a particular kind that make him an impossible administrator or a man of affairs . . .' 'To put the whole matter', concluded Jones, 'there are many things I should arrange otherwise were I God, but I do not happen to be. When the last war broke out Freud wrote to me that he refused to take on his shoulders the foolishness of the world and I think this was a wise remark.' Jones knew that Klein would disagree with what he said, because she was, if not at war, certainly more *pars in causa* than him in what he called the second matter. One has only to try to follow what she says to become aware of the intensity of her feelings, which seem to express themselves also through all the erasures she made and the fact that she re-wrote part of the draft several times, slightly changing her statements every time. However, it is quite clear that she felt that the problems created by Glover and her daughter Melitta were quite devastating for her work for the British Psycho-Analytical Society and for psychoanalysis in general. She writes:

> I appreciate some of the points you mention about the background regarding Glover and the whole situation. Whether or not Melitta's influence over him was the more powerful of the two, undoubtedly it is he who is the much more dangerous of the two because owing to his skill, better tactics and various other circumstances he is successful in his consistent endeavours not only to harm the new work in which I have a share but to bring about a regression in Psychoanalysis which goes far beyond the time when this work started.

Klein acknowledged that Jones had been put in a difficult position. Yet at this point she openly stated:

> But I hold that if from May 1935 onwards when this campaign openly started and the work at the meetings began to deteriorate had you consistently and wholeheartedly discouraged and checked these personal attacks and regressive tendencies (thinly veiled by scientific verbiage) you would have had the majority of the members on your side and the whole situation would have developed differently. It is true the Society is weak and without initiative and many individual members seem to lack more than average in discrimination and strength of character – all the more they would have needed a strong lead from you. I have in former years seen the same Society flourish and develop under your leadership and more than anywhere else the torch was carried among us.

But there were even more general and serious difficulties which, according to Klein, could have been overcome had Jones adopted another policy:

> Had you introduced or at least been willing to support a policy that offices should change hands from time to time, many members would have been only too pleased to support this (or to suggest this) at a General Meeting. The reason recently you gave me against such a policy did not convince me for it would have been much more important since you clearly recognized the harmful influence of Glover, to prevent him from fortifying himself in offices and from getting still others which he more and more turned into key positions, using them for furthering his purposes to the detriment of the work and for discrediting Psychoanalysis in the public eye. In your view Glover was your only available successor and this made things more difficult.

'Wouldn't it at least have been better to hint at Payne as a possible President?' Klein added. The following paragraphs of Klein's letter are a full and, at times, moving defence of Rickman and his qualities which she had learned to know since he had gone into analysis with her. Then the letter suddenly becomes even more emotional and personal. And in spite of the difficulties of following Klein's thoughts, due to the fragmented way in which her thoughts have been preserved, it is worthwhile quoting a few other paragraphs because they allow us to catch the human, creative side of her personality facing those difficult moments, which expresses itself with great vividness and sincerity.

> Speaking of my part in this struggle there is something with which I feel much concerned. I should have produced much more since 1935 when I published my first paper referring to my work on depression. I need not tell you that the attacks particularly directed on this part of my work (whereby people for various reasons arbitrarily choose to make a division between these findings and the one which preceded them) did not in any way diminish my conviction about its truth and value, but they increased my difficulty in presenting it.

Klein goes back more than once to her difficulties, yet, at one moment, she also mentions the great creative experience which led to those new discoveries whose acceptance was so difficult:

> My greatest experience in this was *Beyond the Pleasure Principle* and the *Ego and the Id* and *what* an experience it was. In a smaller way I saw in my own work repeatedly a new light appear and things

altered by it. Particularly was this so when I began to understand it in connection with aggression, reparation and the part it plays in the structure of personality and in human life. From there heads a straight road to the insight into depression which so much occupied my mind ever since. . . . I began to understand the origins and contents of depression and of the immense range of human feelings, of the strength of love and hate, sorrow and hope and with it the realization of a very rich inner world. . . . But it is an overwhelmingly difficult task to describe this knowledge to others who cannot see it. I think these findings could not have been unworthy to have been made even by Freud and he would have had the greatness, the strength, the powers to present them to the world. I don't want you to misunderstand me. I am not *afraid* of fighting against anybody, but I *really don't like* fighting. *What I wish* to do is to let quietly others participate in something I know to be true, important, and helpful, to let them share in it and to teach them if they are willing to learn. I have actually much changed in this respect. I am not any more keen to convince others and to debate. The loss of my son, the grief about my daughter have much contributed to this change. . . . The fact that my daughter is one of my main opponents has a bearing on this wish not to fight. . . . That the former friendly and inspiring co-operation of this group as a whole has changed into the contrary is not only disconcerting, it has taught me much about the difficulties of conveying this work to others so that they may hold on and use it.

Yet in praising Jones for having defended her work in standing up against Freud in 1927 and on other occasions Klein's views about the future of psychoanalysis in Britain were quite gloomy unless some radical change were to take place:

The fact that I have observed here is that people have actually in recent years given up much of my former work, including of course other people's work, even their own, but don't seem to recognize that they regressed. How often did you point out that analysts are like fishes and there is a strong tendency to get away from the depths. In my own observations this tendency was a very frequent one among analysts on the Continent after Freud had introduced the Superego. It was too much for most of them to assimilate and develop it. . . . And I think many of them did not even do so. My work on depression also proves too much even for some of those who accepted my work about internal objects and even about persecutory fears. The situation of disruption which

232

arose in our Society of course favours regression in the work proper but I feel sure that my concept of depression is for many people too painful and too difficult to accept and has therefore the effect of making them regress to former and safer 'positions'.

Nevertheless she did not despair:

I often thought about the prophetic words you uttered when in spring 1927 you showed me a letter of Freud, a reply to your asking him about his objections to my conception of the Superego. You told me then it would take me a long time, 15 years, until I would have brought this home to analysts in general. (It is interesting, by the way, that when I quoted your words to Glover some years later, when the concept of the internal objects had further developed, he said with sincere conviction, 'You will never be able to do so; it goes too much to roots'.) I am still far, as we know, from having achieved this aim . . . in a sense further away than I was years ago and with new and perhaps still greater difficulties ahead of me. Mind you I am not despairing and if I have 15 or twenty more years left to live and to work I should be able to accomplish my task. But I realize how difficult it is and what powers of presentation I would need to give evidence for the truth and importance of these findings . . . .

Klein's draft of her letter and Jones's statements contained in his own letter to Klein quoted above are a very important and interesting starting-point for those wanting to understand the complexity and the intricacy of the documents which are presented in this section of the book, and which refer to the ten Scientific Meetings and Discussions held by the British Psycho-Analytical Society in 1943–4. Following a similar title given to them by Glover in 1944,[3] nearly twenty years after the meetings, in 1967 J. Sandler collected the papers concerning eight of those ten Scientific Meetings[4] and circulated them privately in two special numbers of the *Scientific Bulletin of the British Psycho-Analytical Society*. They were called 'Controversial Discussions', and under this title they gradually became known to the community of British psychoanalysts.

The correspondence between Klein and Jones is nevertheless not the only reference point. Those who try to apply to psychoanalysis and to all its historical vicissitudes the instruments of historical research know very well the importance of an exhaustive documentation based on all the existing sources, in this case the source related to all the major protagonists of the debate. The use of all the available sources is a sort of elementary precaution, in order to overcome first of all the inevitable partiality of the viewpoint of those who are trying to write about psychoanalytic history. Although they try to be as objective as possible, they are nevertheless, in one way or another, participants and observers, and conditioned by their personal cultural and historical context.

To that one has to add the specificity of the field of research. It is impossible to try to write historically about psychoanalysis without taking into account the fact that the object of the research, the unconscious and its derivatives and the way it has been theorized and studied by various schools at different moments in time and space, is a factor which is present in the protagonists and in the vicissitudes of psychoanalytic history, and therefore cannot avoid being mentioned more than in other fields of historical research; nevertheless, unconscious factors can influence those who are trying to write this kind of history too. The danger of unconscious partisanships due to the fact that the historian belongs to a particular psychoanalytic school therefore has to be considered too. Although that seems to be similar to the difficulties present in other fields of historical research, one has only to think of the debate on historical interpretation between liberal, radical, Marxist or right-wing historians, for instance. In regard to psychoanalysis and its history the specificity I mention above constitutes a particular problem.

In this case, unfortunately, given the impossibility of access to the sources and the personal documents of many of the protagonists of those scientific debates, it has been impossible to make use of all the documents. It has been impossible to consult among others the papers of Anna Freud which probably also contain very valuable information. Those are problems and shortcomings that the reader has to remember. However, according to what it has been possible to consult, together with Klein's and Jones's statements, the letter written by James Strachey to Edward Glover a few months before the correspondence I have already quoted, should be mentioned too. The reader can find James Strachey's letter to Glover in Section 1, Chapter 1.[5] And together with James Strachey's statements, one should also remember at least some passages of a letter written by Jones to Anna Freud on 21 January 1942[6] during one of the most difficult moments of the life of the British Psycho-Analytical Society when all Members were discussing, in between other problems, the tenure of offices of the officers of the Society, an issue which had been at the centre of Klein's complaints to Jones.

Jones tried to calm Anna Freud's worries:

You are quite wrong in saying that I attach no value to your judgement, and of course I should not have asked for it if that was so. It is true that I consider Mrs Klein has made important contributions. How many of them are actually new is another matter, for I think one would find broad indications of them in earlier psychoanalytical writings. To determine this would be a piece of research well worth while. She undoubtedly magnifies the newness of them, but it is undeniable in my opinion, that she has forcibly brought to our attention the great importance of such mechanisms as introjection and projections and has, I think, demonstrated the existence of these and other mechanisms at an earlier age than was generally thought possible. That is how I should sum the matter up. On the other hand she has neither a scientific nor an orderly mind and her presentations are lamentable. She is also in many ways neurotic and has a tendency, which she is trying to check, to become 'verrant' (too rigidly attached). I would not be surprised further, that the danger would exist in such a person to distort the objective reality by emphasizing certain aspects at the expense of others. Some of us consider, for example, that she shows this in respect to the Oedipus complex and of the part played by the father. These are, however, all matters that will work themselves out in the course of time, the more easily if we concentrate on the scientific problems in place of the personal ones.

This letter continues with an appeal to Anna for co-operation, reminding her of their communal work in the past and 'because of our supreme devotion to the spirit of union as opposed to dis-union, in our psychoanalytical organization. I cannot believe, Anna, that I could appeal to you in vain on this fundamental issue.'

It is interesting that at one moment, Jones, in writing to Anna, seems to have taken at least partially on board Klein's complaints:

I am very dissatisfied with the present unproductive activities of the Society, for which I hold Dr Glover partly, though by no means wholly, to blame. By nature I believe in aristocratic leadership, but I think there are occasions and I wonder if this is not one, where it is more successful to exert that leadership indirectly instead of covertly. Thus I am inclined to the solution of reducing the responsibilities of officials,[7] making their policies or decisions more a matter of business meetings, and having the officials re-elected annually. In this way the voice of those with most weight would come to expression in the general meetings without their having to be hampered by anti-parental complexes.

In Section 1 of this book is reproduced Marjorie Brierley's letter to Melanie Klein on 21 May 1942 during the most difficult and dramatic period preceding the Scientific Meetings and the discussions on how to come to a truce and the hopes of organizing the discussions on a scientific basis. To this letter I think one should add at least part of the letter Marjorie Brierley wrote to Barbara Low on 22 May 1942,[8] which has been used by King in Section 1, Chapter 7: pp. 208–10. Low, one of the oldest members of the first generation of British psycho-analysts, was very keen in supporting Anna Freud at that time. All those documents – and one could continue, quoting, for instance, from the correspondence of Sylvia Payne or Susan Isaacs – do not exhaust the various and intricate aspects and motivations of those events.

Nevertheless, the reader can have at least some ideas which illuminate not only the institutional and scientific context in which, starting with 27 January 1943, those Scientific Discussions took place, but even the enormous weight and importance of the more or less conscious motivations and personal vicissitudes of some of the most important protagonists in determining the particular charac-teristics of the discussions. The same can be said concerning the very important papers on the training and their scientific implications for the life and development of psychoanalysis in England. On one side, as the various voices coming from the letters I quoted show us, it is necessary to link all those documents to the administrative and cultural life of the British Psycho-Analytical Society, starting with the thirties if one does not want to go back even earlier. Jones's autocratic or aristocratic (to use his words) and at the same time open-minded way of ruling the Society and his administrative capacities, together with those belonging to the first generation of the pioneers of British psychoanalysis, were fundamental both for good and ill, even on this occasion. The reader has to refer to the Introduction to this book, Section 1, Chapter 1, and Section 5, Chapter 6 by Pearl King, for this and the way the impinging serious crisis was avoided in the British Psycho-Analytical Society.

What I would like to stress is only that even the Scientific Discussions do not show just the official aspects of the life of the British Psycho-Analytical Society, which regularly held symposia and Scientific Discussions. The Scientific Meetings contained in the documents I am referring to took place in an exceptionally difficult moment of the life of the Society. The actual presentations of the papers and the discussions took place during the worst period of the Second World War in England and on the Continent. The evacuation of the British analysts from London during 1940–1, the way in which the continental analysts managed to stay together in London, and the various activities of the British Society during this period, have been clearly described by King in Section 1, Chapter 1.

Yet some details concerning the everyday life of the Society have been preserved on purpose even in the Scientific Discussions papers, so that the reader can have a sense of the way the British Psycho-Analytical Society continued to function even during those very difficult times. The reader has also to refer to King's brief history of the administrative, educational, and scientific activities and the internal difficulties of the British Psycho-Analytical Society, before the arrival of the refugees from the Continent resulting from Nazi persecution (King 1989a; Steiner 1989).

From all the correspondence I quoted, nevertheless, it is quite clear that the arrival of Sigmund and Anna Freud in England in 1938 together with the fact that Anna started working in London and taking part with her Berlin and the Viennese colleagues, in the scientific, educational, and administrative life of the Society, as well as the death of Freud seemed to increase dramatically the tensions, creating a nearly impossible situation. This was due to the possibility of an alliance between Anna, her friends, and Edward Glover and Melitta, as actually happened. That was what Melanie Klein feared most.[9] It is at this point that the history of those scientific divergences overlaps with the more or less personal unconscious aspects of this whole event. Consider, for instance, the very deep personal relationship which linked Anna Freud to her father for more than twenty years, professionally speaking, reinforced by a training analysis carried out by him on his daughter; or the painful and delicate situation between Melitta and her mother. It is not absolutely certain whether she had been analysed too as were her two brothers, by Melanie Klein in Berlin (Grosskurth 1986), as was rather common between analysts and their relatives during those years. Yet the daughter's tremendously powerful ambivalence and her personal recriminations towards her mother cannot be ignored as well as Klein's reactions towards her, as the letter I have quoted clearly shows. It is when one considers all those factors that the history of the events leading to the Scientific Discussions touches upon its most delicate and difficult point. One cannot ignore all those personal ramifications. Remember the statements present in the letter written by Klein to Jones I referred to several times. At one moment, with great lucidity, Klein refers to the difficulties her colleagues had in accepting the theoretical and also the personal aspects of her discoveries about the depressive position.[10] One could object that Klein's views could be considered arbitrary, because it is always questionable to use other people's objections to one's own views and to psychoanalyse their objections to explain difficulties in accepting precisely those views. That can lead to a vicious circle.

Yet looking at Klein's personal and professional career one cannot deny that with the courage and the conviction of real innovators like Freud in Vienna, she had confronted herself and gradually involved her colleagues in a self-scrutiny which involved not only neurotic but also psychotic anxieties. Yet the difficulties she encountered were related not only to herself and to her colleagues. The arrival of Freud in England and his death in those particular circumstances constituted a dramatic verification of the validity of her clinical and theoretical discoveries. Freud's death involved the whole psychoanalytic movement, suddenly deprived of the living presence and creative work of its founder; yet his death was particularly difficult to bear and mourn for Anna and her Continental colleagues. They were compelled to the working through of the mourning and the depression due to a multiple loss; that of the father and friend but also of their countries which they forcibly had to leave, compelled to an exile in England, a condition which, *per se*, always implies problems of acculturalization and an attempt to preserve often in a defensive way at least for a while one's own personal and professional identity which is felt to be threatened by the new environment (Steiner 1989).[11] From this came the necessity of an identification with the lost object, which had the characteristics of a sort of exclusive and extremely idealized possession of Freud's truth and work which has to be understood in the context of those circumstances, although not exclusively so (Young Bruehl 1988).

It is impossible to ignore that all those factors could also play a part in a debate which had to be considered as purely scientific and had been prepared to avoid personal issue taking a predominant part in the life and the disagreements of the Society. According to Anna Freud's biographers, upon arriving in England Sigmund Freud suggested that efforts should be made to avoid disturbances or conflicts in the British Psycho-Analytical Society. Later on, Anna claimed that as a sign of gratitude for what Ernest Jones had done to save her family from the Nazis, she always tried not to damage the British Society. But the situation must have been quite painful for her and her colleagues during those years, with the terrible news coming from the Continent and the inevitable 'Heimweh' of their close community in Vienna during the thirties and the comprehensible feeling of 'bei uns war es besser' (we did it better in Vienna).

If, then, on the one hand in her own way Anna Freud was claiming a sort of interpretative monopoly of her father's work, if one looks at Klein's statements, she was clearly asserting that she was, if not the most legitimate, certainly the most creative of his followers.[12] Two daughters fighting for their father's love and possession, one could perhaps say. Curiously enough, coming from the same city, although from rather different families, they both shared a similar destiny of having been unwanted by their fathers at birth (Grosskurth 1986; Young Bruehl 1988).

Furthermore there is no doubt that at the moment in which Klein was stressing the fundamental role of the female figure of the mother in the life of the child, she was also looking for a male figure who could protect her at a personal and scientific level. Didn't she reproach Jones for having abandoned her to the mercy of Glover? Didn't she stress at one moment that Freud himself could have made her own discoveries, stressing at the same time the difficulties for a woman in a still male-dominated culture to put forward her revolutionary views and to be accepted? One of the main criticisms of Glover had been that he felt very doubtful that a woman not having a degree in medicine could actually clarify problems connected with psychosis.

If one wants to look at the whole event from this viewpoint (even if one neglects the various ways in which the participants, friends, and supporters had to act, such as these women – Melanie Klein, Susan Isaacs, Paula Heimann, and also Joan Riviere – who closed themselves like a phalanx at one moment),[13] it would be too easy to magnify the personal aspects of those vicissitudes and to try all sorts of wild interpretations. *Mutatis mutandis*, and of course bearing in mind the differences, sometimes one is tempted to recall the shadows of some of the great myths which generated ancient Greek culture and tragedy and were used by Freud: Oedipus, Electra, Antigone, Narcissus, Medea, Iphigenia, Myrrha. There is no doubt, furthermore, on considering the cultural and historical context in which those difficulties arose, that one could refer to or think of some illustrious episodes of past history. After all, it had been Anna Freud who described in a letter to Ernest Jones the emigration of the Jewish analysts due to the Nazi persecution, calling it a new kind of diaspora and mentioning the fact that the Jews had to leave Palestine after the destruction of the Temple of Jerusalem. Her father also said something similar to Richard Sterba (Steiner 1989). But beside the Temple of Jerusalem and the school at Jabneh to be refounded in London, if one looks at the minutes of all those meetings and pays due attention even to the connotative aspects of the language used by all the participants and at expressions like 'orthodoxy', 'innovation', 'expulsion', and so on, one could find other historical precedents too.

I am not thinking only of the great myths concerning those who tried to violate established forbidden boundaries of knowledge. If one studies the subtle capacity of containing and facilitating the discussions used by the British psychoanalysts, [one should remember some of the statements of Marjorie Brierley to Barbara Low and not only to Melanie Klein, or of Sylvia Payne and the only apparent aloof role, which was played by James Strachey[14]] one could be reminded of the fundamental and very often structural role and function of the chorus in ancient Greek tragedy, or, doubtless, one could recall a particular tradition of thought, which had found in the notion of tolerance, in the possibility of coexistence of various churches and ideologies, the most characteristic and often glorious moments of British history when expressed at its best.

It is as if those debates revealed that inside the psychoanalytical vicissitudes and difficulties there is a reason and a history at work, composed of various levels. On one hand, there is the reason which bases itself on human rational achievements through time. Freud and his immediate followers, making use of it, managed to make sense of the complex ramifications of the myths, widening the possibility for the understanding of them for men of our century and locating their origins in the unconscious. On the other hand, there is the more mysterious but ever-present force of the myths revealing itself in episodes of the past, but also reincarnating itself in those who are trying to understand their unconscious origins, both at a personal and at a theoretical level.

The singularity of this event and its possible relationships to so many famous antecedents linked to different and temporal contexts having been indicated, the risk is then, through all sorts of wild interpretations, of reducing it to the personal, unconscious, and more or less mythical motivations of their protagonists. The reader therefore, bearing in mind the complexity of those vicissitudes, should also try to understand those documents considering their cultural context. It is possible to notice, if one takes into account the more or less explicit references to certain founders of British culture in the papers of Susan Isaacs, Paula Heimann, and Melanie Klein, the names of Locke, and Darwin especially particularly regarding his views about primitive emotions. The names of the great academic psychologists like Hazlitt, William James, Lewis, Shirley, Spearman, Stout, and even Jaensch are mentioned too, together with the pioneering work of Middlemore on the interaction between baby and mother in a book which had just been published, *The Nursing Couple*.[15] Is it only by chance that, in one of his interventions, the then still young Donald Winnicott, who was very close to Melanie Klein, used Middlemore's example of the nursing couple to state that there was no such separate entity as the mother and the baby, but that one had to consider the couple as such? Later it would become one of the leitmotifs of his work.

It is more difficult to focus on the cultural references of Anna Freud and her supporters apart from Glover, although it is quite clear that they were all very empirically oriented and were referring to what they had already studied during the twenties in Vienna, together with S. Bernfeld, A. Aichhorn, and others, or had observed in the nursery that Anna and her friends had opened in Vienna for a short period in the mid-1930s (Young Bruehl 1988)[16] and also to their fresh observations coming from the Child War Nurseries opened in Hampstead and later on transferred outside London during the worst period of the war. Yet Anna, her colleagues, and Glover were acting rather as judges, or to use T. Kuhn's illuminating definition about science and its revolutionary transformations, they felt themselves to be the representatives of the dogmatism of a mature science, if one can use the definition 'science' for psychoanalysis (Steiner 1985), in contrast with Klein's new clinical and theoretical views which they found scientifically unsound and unprovable or not testable, using their own ways of observation and conceptualization. Their mature science was based beside what I already mentioned and their particular relationship with Freud on Anna's already classical book, *The Ego and the Mechanisms of Defence*.

One has only to remember Glover's statements and questions at the opening of the meeting on how to organize the discussion of scientific divergences:

what is the evidence on which the view is based?
is the view valid?
if not yet proven, is it nevertheless a plausible assumption?
if valid, is that validity general or does the view in question apply only in certain types of case?
is it incompatible with accepted Freudian teaching?
if it does contradict Freudian teaching, which part does it contradict and what is the more accurate view?
does the new view by overemphasis or shift of emphasis or in some other way in effect contradict Freudian teaching? (Section 1, Chapter 8.)

Chronologically the papers and the discussions cover more or less one year and a half. But starting in February 1943, parallel to the Scientific Discussions, the papers concerning training and the repercussions that scientific disagreements could have on candidates and the future type of training offered by the Society were being circulated to the members of the Training Committee, though not to anyone else. While they were confidential to the members of the Committee, those members themselves were key speakers in the Scientific Discussions. It is important to remember this because there is a sort of complementarity between the papers given at the Scientific Discussions and those concerned with training and technique. The memoranda discussed in the Training Committee have been collected together in Section 3 of this book, and my comments on them under Editorial Comments (2).

Behind many of the scientific divergences was concern with the implications that the various and controversial theoretical views might have on the actual treatment of patients and candidates. As already mentioned in the Introduction to this book, the Scientific Discussions have been split into two sections, because the nature of the contributions changed after the resignation of Glover following his disagreement with the contents of the Draft Report of the Training Committee in November 1943 and the withdrawal of Anna Freud and her colleagues from the discussions after Anna Freud's resignation from the Training Committee. As the reader will notice the discussants of the paper by Susan Isaacs and Paula Heimann on 'regression' were only drawn from the Members of the original British Society.

Pearl King has also clearly dealt with problems concerning the preparation of the Scientific Discussions (which, interestingly enough, culminated with the very dense and intriguing meetings on how to organize the discussions and with the issues concerning the training – I discuss this further at the end of Section 3). In this chapter I shall concentrate on the Scientific Discussions.

To try to summarize the content of all the papers and the discussion which follow would be out of place. I think, nevertheless, that it is worth indicating a series of themes which seem to run through all those discussions and comments. The choice is, of course, based on my own judgement, and the reader should feel free to follow his own if necessary.

The notion of unconscious phantasy (spelled with a 'ph' to differentiate it from the conscious 'fantasy') is probably the major theoretical theme of all the Scientific Discussions. When translating Freud from German into English during the twenties it had already been necessary to adopt a term, which would distinguish the unconscious character of 'phantasy', which Freud used relatively rarely, from its conscious aspects.[17] Susan Isaacs discussed the notion of 'unconscious phantasy' in her first and most important paper, 'The Nature and Function of Phantasy', read on 27 January 1943.

242

Following Klein (and later on I will try to show how the whole strategy of the discussions was organized by Klein and her closest friends), Isaacs stated that unconscious phantasies permeate the whole psychic life of the human being from birth on. 'The primary content of all mental processes are unconscious phantasies. Such phantasies are the basis of all unconscious and conscious thought processes', Isaacs stated at the beginning of her paper (see p. 272). Those unconscious phantasies which are the psychic representatives of the life and the death instincts imply a very primitive and rudimentary relation with an external object and the presence of an internal one, starting with the extremely distorted projections and introjections of the baby; the breast and the mother's body are the first so-called objects, to which the baby relates in phantasy and in reality. Klein had interpreted in the most radical way Freud's notions of inborn symbolism, both philogenetically and ontogenetically during the thirties but also before, under the influence of her teachers Ferenczi and Abraham. In Isaacs' paper the reader can find the blending of British empiricism and evolutionism, to which I referred before, with the most daring hypothesis and convictions of Melanie Klein. It is interesting and important, for instance, to note Isaacs', but also later on Heimann's, insistence on the most primitive layers of psychical life, represented by the unconscious phantasies which at the beginning, for instance, are non verbal and non visual representations of the object or of the internal world but are based on bodily experiences. The most primitive unconscious phantasies, according to Susan Isaacs, are: implicit meaning, meaning latent in impulses, affects, and sensations; highly emotionally charged yet they are the basis of an although partial, object relationship. It is in this way that the first 'good' and 'bad' objects have to be understood and related to the breasts and the body of the mother. It is also important to remember that in her paper Isaacs refers to the unconscious phantasies as the primary content of the unconscious mental life, sometimes as the mental representatives and corollary of the life and death instincts. In other passages Isaacs focuses on the hallucinatory wish-fulfilment described by Freud and considers it as unconscious phantasy based on primary introjection. Sometimes the term 'unconscious phantasy' is used to describe early defences as well as wish-fulfilment (Hayman 1989). Anna Freud and her colleagues could not accept the notion of unconscious phantasy for what concerns the first month of the life of the baby.

Its implications: the existence in the baby of a rudimentary ego and system of defences, which precedes repression, developing Freud's suggestions contained in *Inhibitions, Symptoms and Anxiety* (Freud, S.

1926) and based on omnipotence, denial, idealization, splitting, the projection and introjection of persecutory, but also libidinal phantasies and experiences, which give rise to a primitive persecutory superego but also to an emotionally positive relationship to the external mother, the presence of a rudimentary sense of the reality principle, together with the still prevailing pleasure principle from the beginning of life – all this at that time sounded extremely obscure and 'unheimlich' (uncanny) to the Viennese and their supporters. They mainly referred to Freud's paper of 1911, 'Formulations Regarding the Two Principles of Mental Functioning', where he stated that unconscious phantasy could only exist after repression had established itself as the main defensive mechanism in the psychic apparatus of the child. In her reply to Susan Isaacs' paper, Anna Freud, supported by others, including Dorothy Burlingham and the Hoffers, clearly stated that it was possible to speak of a proper psychic life in the baby only several months after his birth. This primitive psychic life, according to Anna Freud and her followers, nevertheless, *could only be inferred from, not found in*, the clinical material as their opponents were stating. According to Anna Freud, there was a preponderance of needs for satisfying the pleasure principle more than a psychic activity where destructive phantasies took such a part, as Isaacs and, of course, Melanie Klein seemed at least to state: 'During the first months of his life "the baby" is . . . exclusively concerned with his own well being. The mother is important so far as she serves or disturbs this well being. She is an instrument of satisfaction or denial, and as such of extreme importance in the child's narcissistic scheme of things'.

Primary narcissism and auto-erotic phase were fundamental for Anna Freud during the first months of life of the baby. From the statements of the Viennese and Berlinese psychoanalysts one gets the impression that they achieved a sort of empirical evidence that primary narcissism and autoerotism could be clearly observed, during the first *six months* of the life of the baby. Klein and her followers considered this a distortion of Freud's views on those issues. Anna Freud also tackled one of the most important theoretical points of disagreement, the existence and the clinical validity of the death instinct for what concerned the phantasy life of the baby during the first months of life.

The early phantasies most frequently described in Kleinian theory are violently aggressive phantasies. This seems logical to the analysts who are convinced of the preponderance of the death instinct at the beginning of life. The existence of these phantasies is

widely questioned by those to whom the libidinal impulses seem
of overwhelming importance for this time of life. . . . The
underlying difference of opinion does not refer directly to
phantasy activity but, partly to dating as before, and partly to a
divergence of views about instinct theory.

The notion of 'unconscious phantasy' therefore started to dominate all the Scientific Discussions with the shadow of its implications
and became a sort of ideal keyword to differentiate and to antagonize
the various theoretical convictions and hypotheses and their application at a clinical level. For Klein's supporters it became synonymous
with new discoveries. The more the term was analysed, the more it
was enriched with new meanings. For the others it seemed to mean
something not unlike belief in a new and hazily defined mysticism.
Some of the latter group even claimed that the way in which Melanie
Klein and her followers were using the term was scientifically and
psychoanalytically unsound; to the point where they saw it as
something to be exorcised by the expulsion of the entire group led by
Klein.

In this context, one of the most severe and sharp criticisms of
Isaacs' and Klein's notion of unconscious phantasy came from
Glover's reply to Isaacs' paper dated 27 January 1943 (Section 2,
Chapter 3: pp. 325–7). After having pointed out that, according to
him, Isaacs had quoted Freud out of context to support her views,
Glover stated that Isaacs' main concern was 'to build up a new
metapsychology . . . if Isaacs was right then Freud was wrong' added
Glover 'for the two are incompatible in a number of respects'. According to Glover, Isaacs was wrong because 'she disregards, neglects or
misunderstands precisely those parts of Freud's metapsychology
which eliminate the very confusion into which she persistently falls.
In particular she is addicted to a sort of psychic anthropomorphism,
which most of Mrs. Klein's adherents exhibit, namely of confusing
concepts of the psychic apparatus with psychic mechanisms in active
operation in the child's mind, or, again, of confusing both psychic
concepts and functioning mechanisms with one of the psychic
derivatives of instinctual stress, namely phantasy'.

The reader will find in the various criticisms and in the replies of S.
Isaacs herself all the necessary material to understand the way in
which the discussion around her paper developed. Isaacs' paper and
reply and all the other papers, previously discussed by letter or
personally by Melanie Klein, Paula Heimann and Joan Riviere, were
followed by Klein to the smallest detail. The documents at our
disposal show Klein's accuracy, and she monitored even Isaacs'

replies with all sorts of suggestions and interventions, telling her what she thought she should say or not say, in order to find the best tactic to defend and clarify her ideas. This method can be rather questionable sometimes. Yet some of the letters between Klein and her friends as well as official documents[18] do show us the dramatic pressures and circumstances in which all this had to be organized. Compelled to form a sort of fighting working group, when the accusations coming from various sources became too intolerable, Klein, Isaacs, and Heimann, with Joan Riviere acting as a sort of external shield, organized their interventions, their readings of Freud and how to quote him, together also with the non-analytical literature and direct observations, in order to counteract the accusations of their opponents and to demonstrate their contradictions – concerning, for instance, the phantasy life of the baby during the first months of life.

On 27 June 1942 Melanie Klein wrote the following letter[19] to her friends, which will give the reader a clear idea of the strategy that Klein and her group adopted in preparation for the Scientific Discussion meetings:

Dear———

I am sorry that at our last meeting there was no time for a very important point on the agenda, and that is our preparations for the Scientific Discussions which will start and some points of general policy in these matters. We have agreed on one point, and that is that none of us will announce a paper before the general lines of it have been agreed among us. I should like to add that when a particular paper is ready to be read at least two or three of us should see it beforehand.

I want to suggest further that we actually make up our mind to read papers in the near future. Dr Heimann and Mrs Isaacs already have some plans which seem most promising. The general idea we should keep in mind is that we avoid in our papers side issues of a controversial nature. It seems to me that what we might feel to be a side issue might be fruitful to discuss if it has much in common with the general point of view in the Society; but actually controversial points, I think, should be taken up only on fundamental and essential points. Otherwise we dissipate our strength and waste our energy. It seems to me that the same policy might be useful for the general attitude we might take up in discussions. It does not seem worth while taking up people on points which are not, from our point of view, worth while. We are now regarded, at least for the moment, as people who are liable to be quarrelsome. This fiction could I think be disproved, as far as proofs will be accepted, through our attitude. This has in fact been more or less our policy in recent years – apart from occasional lapses, which I think we should avoid. It seems to me that it is of no particular value for us to prove that the others are lacking in knowledge, or go wrong in this or that point, but to show that we have something to convey to them which at least some of them can accept. What counts, I think, is to re-establish our position in the Society in respect to the actual value of our work, and that can only be done patiently by giving them at a time no more than they can digest, and also present it in a way which makes this possible for them. Though this may be a waste of time in some ways, I think it is none if we keep in mind that this work will not be acceptable to a wider circle if we are not able to take up studiously the links with former work, and are not presenting it from this point of view. Therefore, I find it necessary both for the discussions in the Society and with Anna Freud and for our own sake, to refresh our memory on every word Freud has ever written. This would be the sure foundation from which our discussions can start, and then we might even be able among other things to meet the 'Viennese Freudians' on their own ground.

Another precondition for our discussions seems to me that we refresh our memory also on our own work. I myself often cannot account for what I have written in my book and for other papers by myself and some of you, and this puts us at a disadvantage. I hope that in the autumn I shall take a child analysis seminar, and I think it would be advisable for such seminars to remember what has already been worked out about technique so far, so that we might know where we have to add. This brings me to another point which I think advisable in our attitude at discussions and seminars.

The contribution which this work has made to theory is only partly formulated, and partly it is still in the making; it is much more complicated, partly for these reasons, to give chapter and verse on every point than it is as far as Freud only is concerned (though of course even there, there are many points, as we know, which are quite open to argument and are quite unequivocal. They have only become unequivocal in the rigid, watered-down and over-simplified way they are presented by the Anna Freudians). It seems to me therefore that to get clarity about the points which have already been worked out fully, either in print or among us, is an essential thing – that is why I suggest that we should refresh our memories about our own literature. If we are asked about points which we are not quite sure about, or which have not yet been sufficiently clarified among us, I think it will be best for any of us to state this. Such points can then be taken up among us and clarified. This will imply of course also that we meet more often. Now that the Business Meetings have stopped I think we should meet fortnightly, and we could draw up a programme for the most urgent things we want to do. Obviously one of our aims will be to discuss new points which have come up in any of us, and so to ensure progress in our work. Questions of technique, and the help we can gain in this way from each other, are I think another essential point on this programme.

Unfortunately only the observations concerning the paper and the replies of Susan Isaacs to the various criticisms to her paper, written by Klein, have been extensively preserved. They show not only the clinical capacity of Klein but also her theoretical and tactical skill. Put in the dock, Klein seemed to suddenly find the energy and the capacity of her best moments, to fight and to defend her ideas, although she acted mainly behind the scenes, probably due to her wish not to be confronted with Melitta and Glover for most of the time.

Unfortunately because of limited space, it is impossible to quote here all the notes written by Klein. Yet I think it is very interesting to mention at least some passages from her comments on two of the five Scientific Meetings, dedicated to a discussion of Isaacs' paper. Klein's statements touch upon fundamental issues and at the same time they can give us an idea of the historical situation in which those discussions took place. As in similar cases and in other fields of research or human relationships, statements made at a certain point in time do not correspond to later developments and viewpoints on the same subject. Yet they are important exactly for this reason. Klein, for instance, was against being labelled 'Kleinian' at that time. Profoundly hurt and worried by the label 'Kleinian' given to her views by Glover and Anna Freud during the first Scientific Meetings and the Business Meetings, which implied that she was a heretic and opposed to 'Freudian psychoanalysis', Klein was also against the splitting of the Society in groups proposed by Glover. She wrote to Susan Isaacs on 9 April 1943, referring to Isaacs' reply to the criticisms of Anna Freud and the Viennese, in these terms:

At this point it is quite clear that we have to draw attention to certain methods and to expose them. It will of course depend on the way in which you express this (fortunately this is not too great a difficulty for you) but it has to be made quite clear that such methods and tricks cannot be allowed to pass. First of all there are the Freudians and Kleinians; I think a reference to the fact that it is regrettable that Dr Glover in his position as chairman in these discussions should have used these expressions first, might be advantageous (you will remember that during the Business Meeting Dr Jones called him to order for using these expressions and that Glover stopped doing so at the time). Now in putting in a strong protest against A. F. use of these terms I think it would be well to say that her expression 'psychoanalysis as I understand it' is fully adequate to the position and that that is really what she should have kept to throughout. These discussions have amongst other purposes to clarify on what strength different schools of thought claim the right to represent Freud's views. This does not of course exclude that on certain points, speaking of ourselves, we are only too willing to show where divergences from Freud lie, but on fundamental points we claim that what we are representing is psychoanalysis as we understand it.

I think that also this other point made by Klein is of interest, because it shows how at one moment Klein decided to cut through the alliance that had been formed by Glover with Anna Freud, which Klein felt had become extremely dangerous. Here we find Klein getting indignant with Anna Freud too, for what she felt was a denial coming from Anna, and also from Glover, of the validity of her discoveries, while partially accepting them, without acknowledging the sources.

At a certain moment Klein states that they needed to denounce

the trick way of accepting certain things tacitly from me while disputing them partly or on certain grounds. It is not a question of priority only to show this up; I think it is quite essential for the whole success of our discussions to show how much really has been and is being accepted which has already become part of psychoanalysis in the full sense of the word. . . . Not with one word has A. Freud ever acknowledged that she accepted anything from us not even those much disputed phantasies about the attack on mother's body etc. . . . which have now been accepted for a later stage. This ungenerous or rather dishonest attitude has become very clear in the way she evaded your question (put twice to her) about grief; I am convinced now without any doubt that we are faced here with conscious and deliberate dishonesty and that this must not be allowed to pass. . . . It is also I think necessary as yourself already suggested, to draw attention to the fact that Dr Glover seemed to be extremely sincere and frank when he stated his request about former mistakes and seemed to clarify the position in this open and candid way but is actually quite ambiguous. . . . What he is actually doing by this is that he takes up a position which allows him at any convenient moment to say that he has modified his views (as he has made quite clear) while at the same time he keeps any views of mine and of my findings which suit him.

She finally stated in her comments on the last prepared answer which Susan Isaacs had submitted to her for the meeting of 17 May 1943:

There is one point about which Mrs Riviere and Dr Heimann and I agree strongly. It is connected with your reply to Anna's formulation about which I spoke just now. [Klein is referring to what she thought was a contradiction in Anna Freud's statements about narcissism.] One gets the impression that you are keen, for one thing, to agree with her and Friedlander; and together with this, a tendency to understate the importance of the differences. I have told you already that I think it is very wise to point out wherever there is an approximation of view, and all you did in this respect, including those agreements which they do not admit, is very much to the point. But do not let us give in at any point, where we do not quite agree.

Whatever opinion one can have of the validity of Klein's viewpoints, I think it would be difficult not to acknowledge at least her clarity and courage. Unfortunately, as I already pointed out, it is impossible to compare her statements with what might be found perhaps in the personal papers of her major opponent, Anna Freud.

The reader will find many echoes of Klein's notes and statements in Isaacs' replies. It is interesting nevertheless to note that Klein's comments and observations do reveal another side of the whole story. If Klein (as it is clear from what I quoted) felt the need to reject any compromise from the viewpoint of the theory, it is also true that, carried by the wave of the tensions and the debate, she more than once can be observed re-thinking her theories and sometimes even moderating Isaacs' enthusiasms or excessive, one-sided interpretation of her views. The reader will notice that despite the acrimony of the theoretical controversies Isaacs', Heimann's, and also Klein's statements are left open to further comments or improvements. There were obviously tactical reasons for that. Klein was against a polarization of the conflict based on 'you are with me, or you are against me'. She was looking for her own space, not forgetting to stress her dependence on Freud and without forgetting her debt or some of the critical observations, coming from her British colleagues, without whose help she would not have survived. That led her to stress her views and dissent without pushing the situation to a catastrophic solution. Yet sometimes one has the impression that the debate itself stimulated her creatively and one could catch her at work and working over what she had formulated.

I am particularly thinking of what Klein observes, when, in the notes Susan Isaacs had sent her, she noticed for instance that Isaacs had insisted too much on the baby's cannibalism during the first oral phase of sucking and in his first oral desires. Here Klein's doubts and her wish to leave problems open and her need to work them over again are quite clear, and her observations do show her mind at work as if she had nearly forgotten what the whole debate could imply for her and for the survival of her views (Melanie Klein to Susan Isaacs, 9 April 1943):

I find that the cannibalistic element enters too strongly into the concept of the earliest oral desires as you put it. If you look up my book *The Psychoanalysis of Children* (p. 180), you will see that I still accept the oral sucking stage as less sadistic than the oral biting one. That means that though I would not any longer believe and do not in my book either, that there is such a thing as a pre-ambivalent stage, which I only take as a theoretical concept, though I don't believe in a pre-ambivalent stage and I am convinced of the death instinct and the destructive instincts therefore working from the beginning, it is still true in my mind that the 1st relation to the breast, the sucking one, is less destructive than the oral desires which set in a few months later, with the teething or rather the precursor of teething. You will agree with me that we do find in our material ground for the sucking relation to the breast, as the 'good' one, and perhaps is the possibility in the mind to modify the oral sadistic introjection of the object and to keep the internal object, or the object in the process of introjection, relatively safe due to the fact that at the beginning there is an oral sucking relation to the breast? We are confronted here with an extremely difficult problem about which I would wish still to go very carefully. I have been puzzling and puzzling again recently over the contradiction that the death instinct must contribute to the infant's hostile attitude toward

251

stimuli and all the negative phenomena towards the external world which he exhibits in the early days.

Perhaps the best way to conclude this brief excursion into Klein's notes and the strategy adopted by her and firmly suggested to her friends, is to quote the passages which again touch upon a fundamental problem (often misunderstood or misinterpreted): the way Klein thought about 'unconscious phantasies' (Melanie Klein to Susan Isaacs, 14 May 1943):

> I am now coming to a very important point, which has been on my mind ever since our first discussions about your paper. That refers to the end of your paper which I received yesterday. . . . You will remember our discussion in Dr Heimann's flat about your reply, and that I felt I could not agree to the concept of unconscious phantasy being as it were, everything to begin with on the mental side. I have felt ever since you wrote your paper, and I am of course fully responsible for your formulation, having shared it and agreed with it, I have felt uncertain about its going too far.

In discussing Isaacs' ideas about 'adaptation to reality starting at the very beginning and being expressed by the baby's taking the breast or the food', Klein added, 'But if this is true we would have no right to say, that this derives from the UCS phantasy, but only that it goes along with it' (Melanie Klein to Susan Isaacs, 14 May 1943).

If all this can give the reader an idea of the central role played by Isaacs' paper and the various interventions and therefore of the attention with which everything concerning the debate was prepared and discussed in the trenches, so to say, it should not be difficult to realize that even Paula Heimann's paper, 'Some Aspects of the Role of Introjection and Projection in Early Development' and the combined Isaacs–Heimann third contribution on regression could not be understood without referring to the notion of unconscious phantasy.

The same notion was underpinning another of the general themes of the debate. Klein's and Isaacs' conviction of the existence of an early object relationship based on very primitive phantasies was criticized, besides Anna Freud and her followers, by Marjorie Brierley, although in a less severe way. One has only to think of the intervention of Marjorie Brierley, Ella Sharpe, and Sylvia Payne on Klein's way of observing and then theorizing, which they found not always scientifically grounded in various ways. Marjorie Brierley's comments were particularly sharp in this matter. Yet the notion of unconscious phantasy brought with itself a necessary corollory, which constituted one of the greatest theoretical points of Paula Heimann's paper, 'Some Aspects of the Role of Introjection and Projection in Early Development', circulated on 23 June 1943, but not discussed until 20 October 1943 and would also be developed by Melanie Klein in her paper, 'The Emotional Life and Ego-Development of the Infant with Special Reference to the Depressive Position', circulated and discussed on 1 March 1944.

I am referring to the impossibility from a Kleinian viewpoint of maintaining the existence of a phase of proper primary narcissism and auto-erotism in the baby during the first months of life. Paula Heimann, working on the concept of early projection and introjection, made it quite clear that she and her friends were claiming that primary narcissism did not exist and she particularly described narcissism as secondary and as a result of a withdrawal or fugue into an idealized internal object. The Kleinians underlined Freud's contradictory statements about primary narcissism and considered them a limiting concept in his own thinking about narcissism.

The notion of unconscious phantasy therefore became the theoretical rampart, the scientific paradigm, around which the Kleinians organized their defence and the weapon they used to lead their attacks. It is worthwhile noticing that, although Jones was wrong to my mind in stressing that Anna Freud had already given her best before coming to England, there is no doubt that in referring herself to Freud and his work Anna could authoritatively identify herself with the whole of his work although selecting from it what she felt was more suitable to her views and to the situation. The same cannot be said for what concerns Melanie Klein. To her views on the early development of the baby, she had still to add the concept of projective identification, even if her insistence on the complexity of the communication between mother and baby, already present during the first days of life, which we find in her paper make us foresee it. Furthermore, she would later on add her observations on the schizo-paranoid phase which is strictly linked to projective identification and her views on envy. This was to give a different and more negative colour to the way she and her followers would look at narcissism, which, in her paper written in 1944, seems still mainly based on what later H. A. Rosenfeld (1987) was to call 'libidinal narcissism', to differentiate it from the destructive type. Yet Klein was adamant in stressing the defensive aspects of secondary narcissism and of the withdrawal into an idealized internal object, underlying the presence of destructive impulses and the wish of avoiding them, through narcissistic defences. See for instance her interesting remarks on the meaning of the 'status quo ante' in her discussion with Ella Sharpe on this intriguing subject (Section 4, Chapter 6: p. 836).

Yet already in those years Klein had come to very precise, even if still fluid views about the precocious genesis and phantasmatic nature of the primitive superego and on the nature of the sense of guilt, and above all on the fundamental role played by what she called the 'depressive position' in the development of the child. Compelled by Glover's criticisms and also by the uncertainty of many of her British colleagues – for instance, Sylvia Payne – she decided to clarify what she meant by 'depressive position', linking her thinking to that of Freud but at the same time vindicating her right 'to draw new theoretical conclusions which present themselves from our clinical experiences', to use her own words (Klein 1944).

Klein put the depressive position at the centre of her paper, 'The Emotional Life and Ego-Development of the Infant with Special Reference to the Depressive Position'. In spite of the uncertainties that her way of thinking could arouse, she managed to achieve what she wanted, linking her paper to those of Susan Isaacs and Paula Heimann, especially for the way the early splittings, projections, and introjections during the paranoid position were transformed in the depressive position and the so-called partial 'good' and 'bad' objects were better integrated in the 'whole' object of the depressive position, and the emergence of the Oedipus complex, in its less primitive form. Particularly interesting are her statements about depressive guilt and her insistence on the gradual predominance of the libidinal impulses in the baby during the depressive position and their integration with the destructive ones. This integration concerns both the internal and the external objects, mother and father. Klein will further develop this view which brought her to a balanced picture of the child's development. I have already mentioned her views about primary narcissism. Particularly interesting are also her observations about the importance of the depressive position in fostering genuine symbol formation and symbolic activity and the meaning that all that has for the intellectual development of the child.

It is my conviction that some values of the depressive position found an echo in Klein's opponents. After all, under the suggestions of Klein, Isaacs had already stressed in her replies that some ideas, especially those concerning grief[20] in the baby, had been already accepted although in an indirect way by Anna Freud. And there is no doubt that Klein's views were not combated strongly during the discussions arising from her paper by her British colleagues. After all through the battles which had raged in British history, they knew the fascination but also the dangerous nonsense of Manichaean extremism and the need to achieve a constructive compromise within the limitations allowed by the circumstances.

Yet beside the themes dominant in the content of the various papers and discussions, one has to focus on the most general implications behind these. Apart from their disagreements on the data coming from the observation and analysis of children and adult patients and the way these data could be interpreted in order to formulate plausible hypotheses about psychic development, the various contendents focused their debate on the way Freud's work could be interpreted. This was undoubtedly one of the most interesting aspects of the whole debate. To discuss the way to relate to Freud's text (and sometimes in the case of the British even the translation played a part in shifting the interpretation in one way or another) meant to face the problem of the relationship between the past, the present, and the future in psychoanalytical research. How should the work of Freud be considered? Was he going to block or further new research? At least in the German original the thought-provoking richness of Freud's style of writing is commensurate with a constant broadmindedness. Was it therefore legitimate, taking into consideration the theoretical shiftings in Freud's work, to try to develop some of their implications? Or, considering some of Freud's more problematic and sometimes even contradictory statements, to try to go further in the exploration of areas of human development, for instance, the first object relationship of the baby? Those who objected to Melanie Klein referred to a particular way of 'reading' Freud's text, which left out his most problematic and speculative aspects.

I think it is symptomatic, if one looks at the various discussions of the main papers presented by the Kleinians, that the Viennese insisting on the preponderance of the pleasure principle during the first months of life of the baby and the enormous weight given to the principle of need satisfaction and frustration, focused more on biological than on emotional or cognitive aspects of the life of the baby. They practically ignored the papers and books of Freud's late period. Only once, for instance, did Anna Freud mention the theory of the death instinct. Also they rarely used Freud's very important, short paper 'On Negation' (Freud, S. 1925a), a real small masterpiece, on which the Kleinians based many of their claims that Freud could support their views. From this emerged those long discussions on Freud's text, and the context in which quotations

255

from his work should be made and interpreted. Each of the parties fighting each other tried to demonstrate that it was either impossible or possible to find in Freud what they were claiming. If one looks, for instance, at the problem of the pleasure principle and the presence or absence of the reality principle in the earliest days of the life of the baby, it is fascinating to examine how, for example, *The Interpretation of Dreams* (Freud, S. 1900) was read and quoted by Susan Isaacs and her opponents.

On one hand, therefore, there were those who, claiming their special relationship with Freud, considered themselves the trustees of a knowledge which had to be interpreted and transmitted according to particular rules. These rules had to be followed to avoid misrepresentation of Freud and what the Viennese felt, together with Glover, was an over simplification of Freud's thinking done by Melanie Klein and her followers. The violation of those rules, the interpretations of the texts which did not correspond to the way they understood them, seemed to imply a loss of professional identity, that of 'psychoanalyst', quite apart from the personal anxieties roused by Melanie Klein's views about psychotic anxieties present in everyone. Yet to my mind, both the professional and personal identity and the fear related to their damage or their loss were related.

On the other hand, one had to remember – without, of course, magnifying the importance or the diversity or excessively idealizing it – there was that particular indigenous culture in which psychoanalysis had developed in England, to which I have already referred. In starting to translate Freud during the twenties the representatives of this culture, Ernest Jones, Joan Riviere, the Stracheys, and John Rickman, in one way or in another had already 'interpreted Freud and adapted it to their particular national characteristics, in spite of the professional and personal links the British psychoanalysts had with the Viennese. Although he was not keen on abstract speculations, Jones, in founding the International Psychoanalytic Library, helped to translate one of the most speculative books of Freud, *Beyond the Pleasure Principle*.

Due to Klein's stress on constitutional factors in regard to both libidinal and destructive impulses, her views had found a favourable environment in those of the British who had followed a biological line of interest in psychoanalysis, although her enormous stress on the internal life of the child and the adult was accepted too. Jones – like Strachey, for instance – never accepted the theory of the death instinct, but he always stressed the fundamental importance of the internal world in psychoanalysis (King 1979). There is no doubt that the clinical way in which Klein had started using the theory of the death instinct, linking it to primitive paranoid anxieties and discarding the more general non-empirical views of Freud about it, also reflected the way she was influenced by British empiricism. Yet Klein and her friends felt the right to use the whole of Freud and obviously interpreted him sometimes in their own way. One must remember that, after all, Klein started her career as a psychoanalyst influenced by Ferenczi and then by Abraham, the two major interpreters of Freud's work of the first generation of his pupils.

What was therefore at stake was a clash concerning the notion of tradition and innovation, based on the way one could read and interpret the same text and the way they are creatively related one to the other. Furthermore in many of the statements of the various discussants what was at stake was the value of general epistemological principles like: direct observations, interpretation, inference or hypotheses and their limits when applied to psychoanalysis. These discussions and the problems related to them, although both the Freudians and the Kleinians did not refer directly to highly sophisticated epistemological sources (if one excepts perhaps Brierley and Glover), had a long tradition in other fields of research. They had been a typical battle horse in the philosophical and scientific discussions on the Continent, in England, and in America since the beginning of our century. An example of this is the development of the importance of 'assumed hypotheses' and inference in physics and in all the epistemological discussions stimulated by its developments during the first thirty years of our century. Assumed hypotheses and inference became particularly important for what concerns atomic and subatomic models in physics, where direct observational data are not always available. It is worth quoting at this point what, for instance, Willi Hoffer said recommending sticking to 'Freud's elaborated categories':

Advance in science is based on the freedom of every worker in the field to follow up his own thoughts. The presentation of his findings and the checking of his particular experience with that of his fellow workers, establishes in the long run the validity of his recent findings. There need be no haste for such a conclusive test, but it is an ill service to science to readjust former accepted theories, in order to make them apply to later ones.

And Susan Isaacs replied:

I cannot avoid the impression that some of the contributions to this discussion imply that Freud's work and his conclusions are never to be developed any further and that no-one is to formulate

257

theories which he himself had not yet framed or fully developed. But nothing could be more un-Freudian than such an attitude, which would certainly have horrified him.

Outline of Section 2

Chapters 3 to 7 in this section are concerned with the discussion of the paper by Susan Isaacs entitled 'The Nature and Function of Phantasy'. Members were asked to send in written comments, initially, on her paper, but later on the contributions given or read at previous meetings, which were circulated to all Members, after each meeting. These meetings took place once a month and the ones included in this section were chaired by Edward Glover. When Glover wanted to intervene or make a contribution, he asked another Member to take the chair.

Chapter 8 is of a different order. It is a report of the AGM at which a proposal was put forward by William Gillespie and John Bowlby and eventually passed, to form a Medical Committee to consider the suggestions being put forward by various public bodies for the post-war organization of the medical profession and to consider the position of the Institute and its Members. It is important to remember that this discussion took place, not only two years before the war had been won but also within the context of these Scientific Controversies. Another proposal was also put forward to form a Child Welfare Committee to explore post-war plans for the part that the Institute could play in the organization of child welfare services. Anna Freud did not think 'this was the time to form either a committee or section whilst the scientific differences were still unsettled'. Barbara Low 'suggested that new developments might heal old wounds'. Glover must have realized from the change of mood during the discussion and the consequent voting, that he was unlikely to be elected the next President when Jones retired, and in his final letter, read at the Eighth Extraordinary Business Meeting on 3 March 1944 (see Section 5, Chapter 3), he says that he made up his mind to resign following this meeting. This change of mood was reported by Melanie Klein to Dr Matthew in a letter, and I quote part of it to illustrate that this meeting was felt to be a turning point in the controversies:

Dear Dr Matthew,
Just a note to let you know about the meeting, because I am sure you will be interested to hear how it went off. It showed a very

different situation in the Society from that which existed a year ago. The resolution put forward by Gillespie and seconded by Bowlby was very strong, firm and impressive. It not only proved that there is a great need for the Society to be more in touch with medical bodies and to represent analysis at its best with them, but it was a clear expression of what Glover (and Jones in the past) have missed on this line. It was also a clear expression of disapproval of the autocratic methods of Glover, who has not consulted anybody else and seems to do what he likes about these things. Scott, too, made a very good impression by asking for a special point about which the Ministry of Health had been enquiring from various bodies. He expressed a wish that the answer, which was provided only by Glover, should be read out, and here again disapproval was expressed that other people had not been asked to co-operate. But apart from this special though very important point, the whole tenor of the meeting and the attitude of the members showed quite clearly that there had been dissatisfaction with the way in which Glover had conducted those discussions, and there was universal demand that the committee of investigation into the tenure of office should proceed more quickly, in spite of the fact that there has been no decision about the result of the discussions. Bowlby said that it might help the discussions very much if there was a change in the constitution. All that was done without particular emotions, and coming as it did from a different side, impressed, I think, the whole meeting as well as Glover himself.

He was rather subdued and did not react, at least not at the time, with any aggression to those statements. It would also be very difficult for him to do so, because as things stand it would really mean his being in opposition to the majority of the members.

I really think that our discussions so far have very much improved my position and that of my collaborators, and that it has been very fruitful, particularly since some valuable papers have been produced.

Melanie Klein

Notes

1 Draft of letter by Melanie Klein not dated but probably written in the autumn of 1941 (Melanie Klein Archives, the Wellcome Institute, London). The letter is hand-written, sometimes in ink and sometimes in pencil. Sometimes due to Klein's erasures, corrections, corrections of

the corrections, and so on, it is very difficult to read. I had not done a
proper philologic transcription with all the erasures, but I have chosen
the final version. In some cases, especially where she mentions the way
Freud's work helped her better to understand reparation and depression,
I had to reconstruct what seemed to me the most intelligible version
joining together her statements. I hope future scholars interested in
Klein's thinking will be able to publish the whole letter with all the
corrections. Parts of this letter have also been quoted by Grosskurth
(1986).

2 Ernest Jones to Melanie Klein, letter dated 6 April 1941 (Melanie Klein
Archives, the Wellcome Institute, London).

3 E. Glover to S. Payne dated 24 Jan. 1944 (Archives of the British
Psycho-Analytical Society). Glover's actual words are: 'The Controversial series of Discussions'.

4 Paula Heimann objected and the Council refused to allow any more to
be published.

5 James Strachey to Edward Glover. Letter dated 23 April 1940 (Archives
of the British Psycho-Analytical Society).

6 Ernest Jones to Anna Freud. Letter dated 21 Jan. 1942 (Archives of the
British Psycho-Analytical Society).

7 Anna Freud is referring to some of the resolutions discussed in Section 1
of this book.

8 Marjorie Brierley to Barbara Low. Letter dated 22 May 1942 (Melanie
Klein Archives, the Wellcome Institute, London). (This letter is
reproduced in full in Section 1, Chapter 7).

9 Melanie Klein to Sylvia Payne. Letter dated 31 May 1942. At one
moment in referring to Glover, Klein states:

> I am quite sure and have very good grounds to think so that he has for
> many years planned either gradually to crush my work and myself
> completely, or to discredit my work to such a degree that he can get
> me out of the Society. From the moment the Viennese came, they
> were welcome to him as allies in this case.

10 See, for instance, Sylvia Payne to Melanie Klein. Letter dated 20 Nov. 1941:

> Dear Melanie, Problems connected with the Society seem rather
> desperate. I feel that the best thing that I can do is to get a deeper and
> more *complete* understanding of your work in connection with the
> depressed position (*sic*). I have already a considerable insight into it
> but I am aware of limitations and I believe I should help the Society
> most (quite apart from personal considerations) by being more certain
> about things. Is Dr Heimann going to have her research circle? I
> should like to join it if I am admissible. I could attend on a Monday or

Wednesday evening and would suggest 8 o'clock because of the necessity to get transport home early in the blackout. What can be arranged? Yours, Sylvia Payne.

(Melanie Klein Archives, the Wellcome Institute, London)

11 Riccardo Steiner (1989): 'It is a new kind of diaspora', *International Review of Psycho-Analysis*, 16 (1).
12 See the unpublished fragment of a letter sent to Jones probably in 1941, according to Grosskurth (1986), quoted on p. 469:

> The Viennese group under Anna's leadership has in fact considerably withdrawn from Freud's and Abraham's most important points. . . . You yourself remarked in your letter on the great danger to every analyst and for analysis in general which comes from the tendency to get away from the depths and to regress. This danger is nowhere greater than when the superego and the deeper layers of the unconscious are concerned. This is my reason for saying in my letter to you that if the regressive tendencies in our Society prevail psychoanalysis in its essence might go under. These hostile regressive tendencies, though they are particularly directed against my work, in fact also attack much of what Freud himself found and stated between 1920 and 1926. *It is tragic that his daughter, who thinks that she must defend him against me, does not realize that I am serving him better than she.*

13 See, for instance, the letter from Joan Riviere to Melanie Klein, 24 Dec. 1941:

> I think I can do what you suggest, that is if people will consent to be 'organized'. . . . Can you get in touch with Dr Payne. . . . *Do not let her know* that I am 'organizing' our views. You might not forget that I do not much wish to become a scapegoat again and incur further hostility from Jones and Glover as the one who makes a stand in opposition to them. . . . Who do you suggest should I write to besides Heimann? Do you think Money Kyrle or Matthew would wish to speak?

See also the letter from Melanie Klein to members of her group, dated 3 Jan. 1942:

> Dear ———
> In order to save time I am sending this letter to those of our group with whom I had no opportunity to talk on the following matter. After the last meeting, I came to the conclusion that if we are to have any success in whatever we undertake against such a skilful person as Glover, we should organize our efforts all the more as the time at our

disposal at the General Meeting will necessarily be restricted. I asked Mrs Rivierc whether she would undertake to co-ordinate our contributions.

Both letters can be found in Melanie Klein's Archives, the Wellcome Institute, London. From the documents I have been able to study those are the first signs of the creation of the fighting group which would meet or consult regularly to prepare the papers for the Scientific Discussions later on.

14 Even though he had been appointed to the committee to organize the Scientific Discussions together with Glover and Brierley, he did not attend any of them. He did, however, orchestrate the discussions on the Training Committee.

15 M. Middlemore, *The Nursing Couple* (Hamish Hamilton, London, 1941). It is interesting to note that the book's Introduction was written by Edward Glover, and in it he actually stressed that the fixation point for schizophrenia had to be found in the first eight months of life and that 'within a week or so of birth, infants manifest in a primitive form all the various types of response which form the basis of adult characterology' (p. vi) – something that Melanie Klein would have approved of.

16 I am referring only to the documents concerning this book. Anna Freud and her colleagues had all the experiences coming from the Jackson nursery which however lasted only one year and had been planned to help and also study the behaviour of children under two years of age as well as all the experience accumulated with A. Aichhorn and S. Berfeld and others in observing and treating young children in Vienna during the late twenties and in the thirties (see E. Young Bruehl, quoted on pp. 95, 230). The founding of the Hampstead War Nursery obviously had great importance. It is interesting to note that Susan Isaacs in referring to an interview she had with E. Sharpe in order to find out what her position was concerning the increasing tensions between Anna Freud and Melanie Klein, reported to Melanie Klein that Sharpe 'was very indignant with me when I referred to A.F.'s having learnt much from the children in her War Nurseries. She spoke of her having had nurseries already in Vienna. But she listened when I pointed out what I meant and told her of my discussions with A.F. about two-year-olds when she first came to England' (Confidential Notes and comments on talk with E.S., 6 July 1942, Melanie Klein Archives, the Wellcome Institute, London). One could nevertheless add that everybody, even Susan Isaacs, was learning a lot from their experiences with evacuated children.

17 At least this is more or less what Susan Isaacs states in her paper.

262

Yet in the SE 'phantasy' is sometimes used to indicate day-dreams too.

18 See, for instance, Melanie Klein to Sylvia Payne, letter dated 31 May 1942:

> As it is at present I have been pressed into an extraordinary position in which I can be accused in every way, without being able either to justify myself (because this stirs ill feelings in the Society!) or to be protected sufficiently by the officials. I don't wish to be melodramatic (because fortunately in some way it seems to me all so stupid, futile, contemptible that I cannot take it as it possibly deserves) but I and my friends are now treated like outlaws in the Society; I think you overrate the value of considering people's susceptibilities, and underrate the importance of the truth being stated in this flagrant case.
> (Melanie Klein Archives, the Wellcome Institute, London)

19 See Melanie Klein Archives, the Wellcome Institute, London.
20 Melanie Klein Archives quoted. Letter dated May 1943.

Paper by Susan Isaacs on
'The Nature and Function of Phantasy'

**Series of Scientific Discussions on Controversial Issues
existing within the Society
First Scientific Meeting: January 27th 1943**

*British Psycho-Analytical Society
96 Gloucester Place,
London, W.1.*

NOTICE
RE MEETING OF JANUARY 27TH, 1943

A number of Members have raised the question of discussion at this meeting. They point out that the Resolution limiting discussion to periods of 5 minutes was passed on the understanding that papers to be discussed would not exceed 45 minutes' duration, and suggest that since Mrs Isaacs' paper is more than twice that length it would not be possible to discuss it adequately on a 5-minute rule. In view of the fact that Members are supposed to prepare their contributions beforehand and hand them over for record at the meeting, the committee thinks it desirable to modify this rule at this particular meeting. Prepared contributions to this discussion can therefore extend beyond 5 minutes but should be kept as short as possible and should not in any case exceed 10 minutes in duration. Unprepared contributions to the discussion should, however, remain subject to the 5-minute limit.

EDWARD GLOVER
Scientific Secretary

January 13th, 1943

'The Nature and Function of Phantasy'
by Susan Isaacs

(N.B. The paper will be *taken as read* at the meeting.)

Concerning these discussions

I wish to start by making clear my own position with regard to these special discussions.

(a) I fully accept the AIMS of the series as these were formulated in the Report of the Programme Committee. (Please see.) In particular, that our deliberations should aim at an assessment of (i) the *validity* of the differing views: (ii) the nature and degree of any *incompatibility* of views: and (iii) the *importance* of any given views or divergences of views.

(b) The groups of topics put forward by the Programme Committee are evidence enough of the complexity and comprehensiveness of the problem requiring to be considered. These cannot be dealt with in large lumps, but need step by step disentangling, if our aim be to arrive at the truth, not merely to apply labels.

We cannot start at the *end-state* of divergence, but need to consider the point of theory (or fact) where they take their rise. If we start at the latest development of divergent theories, we shall still be forced to go back over the road which has led them apart, if we are to see which path deviated from the straight course of attested evidence. And we shall require to look at the relationship between the two developments at each point of their passage. (I do not *necessarily* mean their historical paths, but rather their logical and evidential course.)

(c) I suggest that the spirit of our inquiries should be that of Freud's own when he wrote, for instance in the Preface to the *New Introductory Lectures*:

> this time again it has been my guiding purpose to make no sacrifice in favour of apparent simplicity, completeness and finality, not to

265

hide any problems and not to deny the existence of gaps and uncertainties. In no other field of scientific work would it be necessary to insist upon the modesty of one's claims. In every other subject this is taken for granted; the public expect nothing else. No reader of a work upon astronomy would feel disappointed and contemptuous of that science if he were shown the point at which our knowledge of the universe melts into obscurity. Only in psychology is it otherwise; here the constitutional incapacity of men for scientific research comes into full view. It looks as though people did not expect from psychology progress in knowledge, but some other kind of satisfaction; every unsolved problem, every acknowledged uncertainty is turned into a ground of complaint against it. Anyone who loves the science of the mind must accept these hardships as well.[1]

[Freud, S. 1916–17: XI; SE 22:6]

(d) In setting out on these special discussions, much of the ground which *ex hypothesi* we shall be covering has been the subject of intensive research by a number of people over a long period of years. It would be impossible to summarize for a limited series of discussions either the whole of the relevant views or of the evidence on which they are based. With regard to the 'English school' in particular, the evidence has been constantly provided in published papers and books. Furthermore, the relations between the new developments in theory and that of earlier investigators (Freud himself, Abraham, Ferenzci and many others) has often been stated at the time when the fresh views and new facts were brought forward. One has only to turn to Melanie Klein's book *The Psychoanalysis of Children*, for example, to see the way in which each new point has been orientated to Freud's own work, step by step and page by page. And so with other authors.

Nevertheless, it is certainly desirable that more work should be done in this direction, bringing out more clearly the various links between the views of earlier and later investigators. Above all, it is necessary to show the way in which many of Freud's own most pregnant hints as to further problems for research, not fully explored by Freud himself nor followed up by all analysts, have been taken up and made use of by Melanie Klein and those who during the last 15–16 years have been identified as the 'English school'.

During the last few years, the need for this sort of exposition had become increasingly clear to some of us and those working in close collaboration with Melanie Klein had for some time been planning to prepare co-operatively a more detailed account of the points in which our views of early mental life carry forward directly the conclusions of earlier writers and where they deviate from these, or alter their emphasis.

Whilst in the main, therefore, nothing new is being essayed in these special papers and discussions, and they are essentially summarizing and recapitulatory in function, yet they do provide us with an opportunity to bring more fully into focus the relationships between earlier and later theories.

The attempt to summarize and recapitulate a long series of researches, moreover, usually leads one not only to clarify obscure points and amplify what perhaps has been stated in too condensed a form but often also to see fresh angles of approach and new light upon particular problems; it is to be hoped that this will happen with these papers and discussions.

The subject of this paper

The Programme Committee asked me to open the first discussion on 'The role of introjection and projection of objects in the early years of development'.

When I started to prepare a statement of my views upon this topic, I found at once that it was far too large a field for a single paper. I also came to the conclusion that we should begin by considering the nature of phantasy in general, when it develops, and its relation to feeling, impulse, and external reality. I therefore asked the meeting on October 21st to agree to my taking up first this question of the nature and function of phantasy.

Some parts of what I have to say may receive general agreement. Certain of the views here presented, or their further implications, are in accordance with the opinions expressed by a number of English analysts in former years. They might now be challenged by some of these analysts, and certainly will be questioned by other people, either wholly or in part. These sections may be rejected either

(a) because some analysts disagree with the whole concept of early phantasy;

or

(b) because they do not accept the notion that early phantasies have the most profound influence upon every aspect of early mental development and that it is possible to discover in detail the mode and extent of the operation of these phantasies in the mind of the infant and young child.

267

If I succeed in stating the issues clearly enough, and bringing out the sort of evidence which is available to help us clarify them, we may then be able to get to grips with the various points of divergence.

'If we cannot see things clearly, we still at least see clearly what the obscurities are.' [Freud, S. 1926: 83; SE 230:123]

The term 'phantasy'

A large part of this paper will be concerned with *defining* 'phantasy'. That is to say, with describing the series of facts which the use of the term 'phantasy' helps us to identify, to organize and to relate to other significant series of facts.

In attempting to define the terms one is going to employ, one is bound to start from the various contents which it already possesses and to accept these where they are consistent with each other. Where there are inconsistent usages, or some connotations which would be conveniently expressed by some other term, one must necessarily reject such references, for the purpose of sharpening the outline of the particular usages which in the end seem to be the most significant. Or, again, one must be ready to extend the reference of a term if inspection of the facts requires this.

The reference of the word 'phantasy' in the development of psychoanalytic thought has been gradually extended. And when the meaning of such a word does get widened, whether deliberately or without noticing, it is usually for a good reason – because the facts, and the theoretical formulations they necessitate, require it. It is *the relationships between the facts* which need to be looked at more closely and clarified in our thought.

Sometimes (in line with everyday language) the use of the term has referred only to *conscious* 'fantasies', of the nature of day-dreams. But Freud's discoveries soon led him to recognize the existence of unconscious phantasies. This reference of the word is indispensable. (The English translators of Freud adopted a special spelling of the word 'phantasy' with the *ph*, in order to differentiate the psychoanalytical significance of the term, i.e., predominantly or entirely unconscious phantasies, from the popular word 'fantasy', meaning conscious day-dreams, fictions, and so on. The psychoanalytical term 'phantasy' essentially connotes *unconscious* mental content, which may seldom or never become conscious.)

This reference of the word has assumed a growing significance, particularly in consequence of the work of Melanie Klein, on the early stages of development.

Again, the word 'phantasy' is often used in contrast with 'reality', the latter word being taken as identical with 'external' or 'material' or 'objective' facts. But when external reality is called 'objective' reality, there is an assumption which denies to psychical reality its own objectivity as a mental fact. Some analysts tend to contrast 'phantasy' with 'reality' in such a way as to undervalue the dynamic importance of phantasy. A related usage is to think of 'phantasy' as something 'merely' or 'only' imagined, as something unreal, in contrast with what is actual, what happens *to* one. Both these attitudes have the significance of underrating the psychical reality and meaning of mental processes as such.

But Freud showed us that this notion of 'merely' or 'only' imagined was not the first consideration, for the purpose of the psychologist.

When and under what conditions 'psychic reality' is in harmony with external reality is one special part of the total problem of understanding mental life as a whole. A very important part indeed; but, still, 'only' one part.

Psychical reality

Of all the fundamental debts which we owe to Freud's genius, none more clearly marks the new epoch of understanding which he initiated than this discovery of *psychical reality*.

Freud taught us that the inner world of the mind has a continuous reality of its own, with its own laws and characteristics, different from those of the external world. In order to understand the dream and the dreamer, his psychological history, his neurotic symptoms, or his normal interests and character, we have to give up that prejudice in favour of external reality, that undervaluation of internal reality, which is the attitude of the ego in ordinary civilized life today. 'A return from the over-estimation of the property of consciousness is the indispensable preliminary to any genuine insight into the course of psychic events.' [Freud, S. 1900: 562; SE 5:612][2]

Or, again:

It takes him [the patient] a long time to understand the proposal that phantasy and reality are to be treated alike and that it is to begin with of no account whether the childhood experiences under consideration belong to the one class or the other. And yet this is obviously the only correct attitude towards these products of his mind. In contrast to material reality, these phantasies possess *psychical* reality, and we gradually come to understand that *in the world of neurosis psychical reality is the determining factor.*

[Freud, S. 1916–17: 308–9; SE 15: 308][3]

Or again:

There is a most surprising characteristic of unconscious (repressed) process to which every investigator accustoms himself only by exercising great self-control. It results from their entire disregard of the reality-test; thought-reality is placed on an equality with external actuality, wishes with fulfilment and occurrence. . . . [Ed. Just as happens without more ado under the supremacy of the old pleasure principle.]

Hence also the difficulty of distinguishing *unconscious phantasies* from memories which have become unconscious. One must, however, never allow oneself to be misled into applying to the repressed creations of the mind the standards of reality; this might result in undervaluing the importance of phantasies in symptom-formation on the ground that they are not actualities; or in deriving a neurotic sense of guilt from another source because there is no proof of actual committal of any crime.

[Freud, S. 1911a: 20; SE 12: 225][4]

A further point which needs to be brought in here, having in mind my general thesis, is that unconscious phantasy is fully active in the normal, no less than in the neurotic mind. It seems sometimes to be assumed that only in the 'neurotic' is psychical reality (i.e., unconscious phantasy) of paramount importance, and that with 'normal' people its significance is reduced to vanishing point, but, once more, Freud is explicit upon this matter.

He says,

Amongst the derivatives of the unconscious instinctual impulses there are some which unite in themselves opposite features. On the one hand, they are highly organized, exempt from self-contradictoriness, have made use of every acquisition of the system Cs, and would hardly be distinguished in our ordinary judgement from the formations of that system. On the other hand, they are unconscious and are incapable of becoming conscious. Thus they belong according to their qualities to the system Pcs, but in actual fact to the Ucs. Of such a nature are the *phantasy-formations* of normal persons as well as of neurotics, which we have recognized

270

as preliminary phases in the formation both of dreams and of symptoms, and which, in spite of their high degree of organization, remain repressed and therefore cannot become conscious.

[Freud, S. 1915b: 123: SE 14:190–1][5]

In an earlier passage in the same paper, Freud emphasizes the enduring significance of the unconscious mind for normal life.

It would certainly be wrong to imagine that the Ucs remains at rest while the work of the mind is performed by the Pcs, that the Ucs is something finished with, a vestigial organ, a residuum from the process of evolution; wrong also to assume that communication between the two systems is confined to the act of repression, the Pcs casting everything which disturbs it into the abyss of the Ucs. On the contrary, the Ucs is living and capable of development and maintains a number of other relations to the Pcs, among them that of co-operation. To sum up, we must say that the Ucs is continued into its so-called derivatives, is accessible to the influence of life, perpetually acts upon the Pcs, and even is, on its part, capable of influence by the latter system.

[Freud, S. 1915b: 122; SE 14:190][6]

Phantasy as psychic content

Now as the work of psychoanalysis has gone on, and in particular the analysis of young children, and our knowledge of early mental life has developed, the relationship which we have come to discern between the earliest archaic mental processes and the later more specialized types of mental functioning commonly called 'phantasies' have led many of us to extend the connotation of the term 'phantasy' in the sense which I am now going to develop. It is the facts which have compelled this extension.

I shall endeavour to show, in the course of this paper, that certain mental phenomena which have been described, but not in reference to the term 'phantasy', do in fact imply the activity of unconscious phantasies. By correlating these phenomena with the unconscious phantasies with which they are bound up, their true relationships to other mental processes can better be understood, and their function and full importance in the mental life be appreciated.

Part of the evidence which I am bringing forward for my views consists in showing the relationships between facts, some of which are in themselves familiar but have been dealt with in a relatively isolated way. I wish to state here my opinion that the primary

271

content of all mental processes are unconscious phantasies. Such phantasies are the basis of all unconscious and conscious thought processes.

It might perhaps turn out that some word other than 'phantasy' would be more useful, if only because of our inveterate prejudice in favour of the mode of operation of external reality, on the one hand, and of conscious mental processes on the other, both of which lead us constantly to denigrate phantasy. Psychoanalysts are far from showing themselves free from this tendency to backslide.

Yet, as again Freud tells us, 'In proportion as we try to win our way to a metapsychological view of mental life, we must learn to emancipate ourselves from our sense of the importance of that symptom which consists in "being conscious".' [Freud, S. 1915b: 125; SE 14: 193][7]

If any other word can be found *which will perform the function* of articulating the proper relationship between the facts requiring to be brought together in our thought, then let us use it. But so far I have not found one which organizes the facts with the same degree of clarity and significance.

In particular, the value of the word 'phantasy' is that it emphasizes the *psychic character* of the processes we are concerned with. A suggestive way in which this fact is sometimes stated is that the special character of mental as comparerd with physical processes is that they have *meaning*. Physical processes are said to have existence, but not *meaning*. A neutral term such as 'process', handy in many ways, or 'energy' required for certain purposes, does not express this essential and distinguishing quality of *meaning*. That is why we have constantly to say '*mental* process', 'mental energy'.

The word 'phantasy' serves to remind us always of this distinctive character of meaning in the mental life.

Abstract concepts and concrete meaning

At this point, some interesting comments made by Dr Brierley in her recent paper 'Some Observations on the Concept "Internal Object" '[8] need to be considered. A discussion of them will help to clarify my own position with regard both to the use of the term 'phantasy' and the relation of the function of phantasy to later developed types of mental process.

Dr Brierley writes:

The impression has been growing on me that one of the major difficulties in coming to grips with Mrs Klein's view is that her generalizations do tend to be expressed in perceptual rather than in conceptual terms. . . . We cannot observe the mental process directly, we can only infer it from the phantasy. In other words we can perceive the phantasy in word or deed, but we cannot perceive the process; we can only conceive it, and it is natural to conceive it as analogous to bodily processes. There is no doubt that such analogies are useful. They do help to bridge the gap between everyday concrete thinking and abstract thinking. . . . But there is a risk of confusing the mental process with the physical act. . . . It is imperative for scientific purposes to distinguish the conceptual from the perceptual mode of thought. The non-sensible nature of mind and mental process renders it obligatory to discuss them in abstract terms. This does not mean that a mental process inaccessible to sensory perception is not as real as a directly observable phenomenon, it means that we cannot describe it in terms of perception. . . . In the expression 'whole good object' Mrs Klein uses the word 'whole' to distinguish a personal object from an organ or part-object. But she also uses the term 'whole' in the sense of undamaged or intact to distinguish it from the object which a child in a certain phase of anxiety feels to be in pieces. But whilst one can think of a mother as being actually dismembered, one cannot conceive of a mental object being literally shattered – one cannot take a hammer to a mental object. . . . If the object is consistently thought of as a mental object, an organization within the ego, this stumbling block is removed. It is possible to think of a mental object system not indeed in terms of wholes or bits and pieces, but in terms of integration or disintegration.

Now this way of stating our problem raises a number of fundamental questions regarding scientific explanation in general, some of which would take us too far afield from our present purpose. I shall confine myself to the psychological problem.

Fortunately, we can draw upon the work of the academic psychologists to elucidate this point (e.g., Ward 1933, James 1910, Stout 1927, Spearman 1923). Their position regarding the relationship of perceptual to conceptual thought has long been made clear, and has been substantiated and elaborated by all recent experimental work.

In the first place, *all* words stand for concepts. We cannot talk without using concepts, even when we describe things such as tables and chairs, or breasts and bodies. The *word* 'breast' or the words 'whole object' are just as conceptual as the words 'introjection' or 'identification'. They are concepts derived from a different level of experience, it is true; but they are concepts.

(N.B. In this sentence, and in what follows, I am using the word 'experience' in accordance with general psychology to refer to *psychic experience as such*, not in the narrower meaning of experience of external happenings in particular.)

Secondly, the mind and mental process, thinking itself, *are not in themselves abstract. As experience*, as we experience them, they are immediate. Thinking is experienced as much as perceiving is. Experience has different modes, e.g., sensation, perception, feeling, and thinking. We cannot describe thinking in terms of feeling or of perceiving; nor perceiving in terms of thinking or feeling. Thinking is a unique mode of experience, an experience of the relations between things or attributes of things perceived. We do not perceive thinking, but we do experience it.

Thirdly, when we *talk about* thinking, we use concepts; but so we do when we *talk about* perceiving. Thinking as an experience is distinct from talking about thinking just as perceiving is different from talking about this process. The concepts we use in talking about perceiving or thinking are alike the result of focusing in attention certain elements in the total content of experience. Even a sensation or a perception is from one point of view partly abstract, since each is attended to by abstracting certain aspects of experience from the total, by means of certain criteria, e.g., in perception, the criteria are certain relationships of space and time and external reference, in thought, other sorts of relationship.

Now in the infant, experience and mental process must be primarily, perhaps at first entirely, affective and sensorial. Then full perceptual experience gradually develops as relationships of time and space and external reference become possible, owing to the development of the sensory organs and of movement. Much later, conceptual experience dawns, with the rise of memory images as material of experience, and as relationships other than those given in the here and now of what is perceived can be focused in experience.

At another point Dr Brierley says: 'phantasy is a sort of ticker-tape that records happenings on the mental stock exchange. But the tape machine writes a perceptual sign language that needs to be decoded into conceptual terms if the mental happenings themselves are to be accurately described.'

Now in this image the true relationship of thought and phantasy is reversed. It is not correct to put it that when the infant feels he is incorporating his mother's breast or some other good thing, he is dramatizing or picturing what is 'really' an abstract process or introjecting. At the first level of experience, introjection *is* felt to be incorporation. (See my quotation from Freud below.) At a some-

274

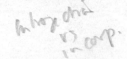

what later level, it is imagined to be, incorporation. Later still, it is felt to be getting something into the mind – that is to say, into the ego, that part of the self as experienced which remembers and imagines and has emotions, as contrasted with that part which moves and touches and gets hot or cold, etc. Far later still, it may be described by the experiencer, in his thinking moments, as 'the process of introjection'.

But if there is any question of codes and decoding, it is surely the abstract term which has to be decoded into concrete experience, perceptions and images, as these are lived. (In her recent paper 'Psycho-physical Problems Revealed in Language: An Examination of Metaphor', Ella Sharpe points out that 'Psychoanalytical research . . . endorsed the views of those who . . . maintain that the displacement is from physical to psychical and not "vice versa".' She quotes Grindon, who says, 'No word is metaphysical without its first having been physical.' And Locke, 'We have no ideas at all, but what originally came either from sensible objects without, or what we felt within ourselves.' [Sharpe, E. 1940: 201] And in her paper goes on to show the derivation or metaphor – without which the intellectual life of man would be impossible – from bodily experiences.)

In the unconscious mind, where everything remains concrete, sensorial, or imaginal, introjection is always experienced as incorporation – although not, of course, always by the mouth. As we know, seeing and hearing, as well as other functions, have an oral value, by displacements as if it were an epi-phenomenon. But we can surely here be at one with the academic psychologists, in recognizing that it is in fact the operative, the dynamic reality of mental process, on the particular level of experience with which we are concerned – the infant's early life, or the unconscious mind of the adult.

Dr Brierley says: 'One cannot take a hammer to a mental object' (see above). *But*

(a) The child feels (later, imagines) that he *does* take a (felt or imagined) hammer to his (felt or imagined) mother. Mrs Klein does not say that object is whole or in bits, as seen by an observer. She does say it is so for the child. She is speaking of what the child is experiencing, on the level of wish and phantasied action and its phantasied intentions and results. And

(b) (this is the important point) – *when the child feels he has dismembered his mother, his mental life is split and disintegrated* – he shows the most acute anxiety, he is confused and behaves chaotically, he cannot see or hear or control what he does and says, and so on. It is not that, *first*, his mental life becomes disintegrated and he *then* interprets this as having dismembered his mother; it is *because he wants to* dismember his mother, intends to, tries to and in imagination does so, that he feels his own ego to be split and disintegrated, and shows in his behaviour that 'mental disintegration' which we can describe and label and talk about.

We, for our purpose of comparing one mind with another and making generalizations, can see what happens to the child, the way he behaves, and can describe it as 'mental disintegration'. But the child experiences it as 'my-mother-inside-me-is-in-bits'.

(I am, of course, not here discussing as such the question of the various causes which contribute to the condition of disintegration of the ego, nor overlooking the point that the integration of the ego is a matter of development; and that the child may want to 'dismember' his mother before his ego has become integrated. I am merely taking Dr Brierley's example, and discussing the causal relationship between the process of 'disintegration' as we *describe* it in abstract terms, and one of the concrete situations which are *experienced* by the child when such a term can be applied to him.)

As Fuchs[9] and Brierley and Melanie Klein herself have often reminded us, it was, first Freud and then Abraham who discovered and demonstrated that we feel and experience, more or less unconsciously, the existence of 'objects' as well as wishes and feelings in our inner world. Many other workers have contributed to our knowledge of their nature and function. Klein's special work has been to show us in more detail than anyone else, and with more vividness and immediacy of understanding, what a person experiences in regard to his inner objects, what they mean to him and how they affect his development.

Phantasies as the specific content of unconscious mental processes

So far I have mainly reminded readers, largely in Freud's own words, of certain well-established (but often forgotten) fundamental truths; the significance of psychical reality and in especial of its unconscious components; the living character of the unconscious and its continual and omnipresent influence upon the conscious mind, both in normal and in neurotic people. And I have emphasized my view that the child *experiences* his psychic reality in terms of his phantasy life.

I now wish to develop more fully my opinion that unconscious phantasies are the primary content of all mental processes. As Freud has said, all mental processes originate in the Ucs, and only under

276

certain conditions become conscious: 'everything conscious has a preliminary unconscious stage' [Freud, S. 1900: 562; SE 5: 612].[10] They arise either directly from instinctual needs, or in response to external stimuli.

'We suppose that it [the id] is somewhere in direct contact with somatic processes, and takes over from them instinctual needs and gives them mental expression.' [Freud, S. 1933a: 98; SE 22:73][11]

I believe that this 'mental expression' is unconscious phantasy. Phantasy is the mental corollary, the psychic representative of instinct. And there is no impulse, no instinctual urge, which is not experienced as (unconscious) phantasy.

Freud refers to 'the mental expression of instinctual needs'. In my view, this means not only *libidinal* desires, but destructive impulses and anxieties also. Moreover, phantasy soon becomes a means of defence against anxieties, a means of inhibiting and controlling instinctual urges, and expression of reparative wishes.

Phantasy expresses the specific content of the urge (or the feeling, e.g., hate, anxiety, fear, love, or sorrow) which is dominating to the child's mind at the moment, e.g., when he feels desires towards his mother, he experiences these as 'I want to suck the nipple, to stroke her face, to eat her up, to keep her inside me, to bite the breast, to tear her to bits, to drown and burn her, to throw her out of me' and so on and so forth.

When he feels anxiety, stirred up by an aggressive wish, he feels, 'I shall be bitten or cut up by my mother'. When he feels loss and grief, he experiences (as Freud taught us), 'My mother has gone forever'. He may feel, 'I want to bring her back', and try to overcome his sense of loss and grief by the phantasy 'I shall bring her back by stroking my genital', when he masturbates. When he wants to restore his mother, he feels 'I want to make her better, to feed her, to put the bits together again' and so on.

(Needless to say, I am not suggesting that these phantasies are experienced in *words*. This point will be fully discussed later on.)

Moreover, as Freud showed ('thought-reality is placed on an equality with external actuality, wishes with fulfilment and occurrence'), he not only feels 'I want to' but actually '*I am doing*' this and that action towards his mother. This is the omnipotent character of early mental processes, when the wish is felt as the deed. And the degree of differentiation between wish and deed is partly determined by the intensity of the desire or emotion, partly by the stage of development reached at the time.

Now Freud has specially emphasized the relation between phantasy and wish-fulfilment. But our experience has shown us that

277

such phantasies as those just now instanced serve various other purposes as well as wish-fulfilment, e.g., denial, reassurance, reparation, omnipotent control, etc. That is to say, phantasies are already at the service of the primary defence mechanisms.

It is, of course, true that in a wider sense all these mechanisms which aim at diminishing instinctual tension, anxiety, and guilt also serve the aim of wish-fulfilment. But it proves helpful to discriminate the specific modes of these different mechanisms and their particular aims.

Every impulse, every feeling, every mode of defence is expressed and experienced in such a specific phantasy, which gives it mental life and shows its specific direction and purpose.

Now I know very well that Freud himself did not say that the 'mental expression' of instinctual urges is the same thing as phantasy. But in my view he came very near to this when he postulated the infant's satisfaction of his wishes in a *hallucinatory* form.

You remember how he was led (by his study of unconscious processes in the minds of adults) to assume that, in the beginning of mental life, 'whatever was thought of (desired) was simply imagined in a hallucinatory form, as still happens with our dream-thoughts every night. This is an attempt at satisfaction by hallucination.' [Freud, S. 1911a: 114; SE 12: 219][12]

Freud does not say that the infant has unconscious phantasies. But the capacity to hallucinate is, in my view, either identical with phantasy or the pre-condition for it.

What does the infant hallucinate? We may assume, first, the nipple, then the breast, and later, his mother, the whole person. And what is he going to do with the hallucinated nipple? As we can see from his behaviour (sucking movements, sucking his own lip or a little later his fingers, and so on), hallucination does not stop at the mere picture, but carries him on to what he is, in detail, going to do with the desired object which he imagines (has unconscious phantasies) that he has obtained. We know already that it is the oral impulse which is at work, and which conjures up the hallucinated nipple. And the intensity of such a wish and the hate of frustration, will stir up a still stronger desire, viz: to take the whole breast into himself and keep it there, as a source of satisfaction. Thus we must assume that the introjection of the breast is bound up with the earliest forms of the phantasy life.

But let us again consider what Freud himself has to say about this. He goes on: 'In so far as it is auto-erotic, the ego has no need of the outside world, but . . . it cannot but for a time perceive instinctual stimuli as painful. Under the sway of the pleasure principle, there

278

now takes place a further development. The objects presenting themselves, in so far as they are sources of pleasure, are absorbed by the ego into itself, "introjected" (according to an expression coined by Ferenczi): while, on the other hand, the ego thrusts forth upon the external world whatever within itself gives rise to pain (v.infra: the mechanism of projection).' [Freud, S. 1915a: 78, 80; SE 14: 135–6, 138–9)[13]

Towards the end of the same paper, Freud adds: 'Love originates in the capacity of the ego to satisfy some of its instincts auto-erotically through the obtaining of "organ-pleasure". It is primarily narcissistic, is then transferred to those objects which have been incorporated in the ego, now much extended, and expresses the motor striving of the ego after these objects as sources of pleasure. . . . The preliminary stages of love reveal themselves as temporary sexual aims, while the sexual instincts are passing through their complicated development. First among these we recognize the phase of incorporating or devouring, a type of love which is compatible with abolition of any separate existence on the part of the object.' [ibid. pp. 80–1]

I am quite aware that Freud, in describing the primary introjection, nowhere calls it an unconscious phantasy. But, as I have already explained, it is to my mind impossible to see how the process of introjection can otherwise be conceived than as operating through phantasy. I therefore hold that we are entitled to claim Freud's concept of primary introjection as a support for our assumption of the activity of Ucs phantasy in the earliest phase of life.

Moreover, it seems to me that we can best understand in terms of early phantasy many of the facts of the infant's behaviour to which Freud himself has drawn our attention. For example:

the situation of the infant when he is presented with a stranger instead of his mother. He will exhibit the anxiety which we have attributed to the danger of loss of object. But his anxiety is undoubtedly more complicated than this and merits a more thorough discussion. That he does have anxiety there can be no doubt; but the expression of his face and his reaction of crying indicate that he is feeling pain as well. He cannot as yet distinguish between temporary absence and permanent loss. As soon as he misses his mother he behaves as if he were never going to see her again; and repeated consolatory experiences to the contrary are necessary before he learns that her disappearance is usually followed by her re-appearance.

[Freud, S. 1926: 167; SE 20: 169][14]

Again, 'In consequence of the infant's misunderstanding of the facts the situation of missing his mother is not a danger-situation but a traumatic one.' [Freud, S. 1926: 168; SE 20: 170][15]

Now, by 'pain' Freud obviously does not mean bodily, but *mental* pain. 'He behaves as if', to my mind, is the same thing as saying he has a phantasy that he will never see his mother again. And his 'misunderstanding of the situation' is precisely that 'subjective interpretation' of his perception of her absence which we have seen constitutes phantasy.

Again, when speaking of oral frustrations, Freud says:

It looks far more as if the desire of the child for its first form of nourishment is altogether insatiable, and as if it never got over the pain of losing the mother's breast. It is probable, too, that the fear of poisoning is connected with weaning. Poison is the nourishment that makes one ill. Perhaps, moreover, the child traces his early illnesses back to this frustration.

[Freud, S. 1933a: 157; SE 22: 122][16]

How is it possible for the child to trace back his early illnesses to this frustration unless at the time of the frustration he experienced it *in his mind* and later on remembered it (in some sense)? At the time when he experiences it, this experience amounts to phantasy. Not only so: Freud says 'the fear of poisoning is connected with weaning'. Here we have that phantasy of mother's milk as poison (because of frustration and projected hate) to which Melanie Klein first drew our attention.

Here is another passage in which Freud seems to refer to the child's phantasies, although he does not actully use this word in describing them.

It is a remarkable fact that even when the difference between the children's ages is only eleven months, the older one is nevertheless able to take in the state of affairs. But it is not only the milk that the child grudges the undesired interloper and rival, but all the other evidences of motherly care. It feels that it has been *dethroned, robbed* and has its rights invaded, and so it directs a feeling of jealous hatred against its little brother or sister, and develops resentment against its faithless mother, which often finds expression in a change for the worse in its behaviour. It begins to be 'naughty', irritable, intractable, and unlearns the control which it has acquired over its excretions. (My [Isaacs'] italics)

[Freud, S. 1933a: 157–8; SE 22: 123][17]

Freud says: 'The child feels it has been dethroned, robbed', etc. I suggest that this is the same thing as saying the child 'has a phantasy that he has been . . .' etc. It is true that this phantasy has been evoked by an external fact, but this fact is exaggerated in the child's mind, and its meaning is derived from his own impulses. And we see the effect of such phantasies in the behaviour which Freud described – the signs of anxiety, the need to defy persecutors, and so on, as we are accustomed to trace them out in the analysis of young children.

Once again:

> The very surprising sexual activity of the little girl in relation to her mother manifests itself in chronological succession in oral, sadistic and finally even phallic impulses directed upon her. It is difficult to give a detailed account of these, because often they are dim impulses which it was impossible for the child to grasp psychically at the time and which were only interpreted later, and express themselves in analysis in forms that are certainly not the original ones. We find aggressive oral and sadistic wishes in a form forced on them by early regression, i.e. *in the dread of being killed by the mother* – a dread which on its side justifies the death-wish against her, if this enters consciousness.
>
> [Freud, S. 1932: 291–2; SE 21:237][18]

Now what does Freud mean by 'dim impulses which it was impossible for the child to grasp psychically at the time and which were only interpreted later'? This can only be the same thing as Melanie Klein describes. She also says that many of the child's early phantasies never become conscious, are never put into words.

Freud speaks of the child's 'dread of being killed by the mother' – here we have the phantasy of the 'bad', vengeful mother whose image is, as we can readily confirm by analysis of the transference in every patient, created not only by the *repression* of the original impulse, but also by its projection.

Phantasy and sensory experience

But even this first 'hallucination', the first unconscious phantasy wish-fulfilment, must make use of *sensation*. Some pleasurable sensation (organ-pleasure) there must be, very early, if the baby is to survive at all. Changes of contact and temperature, the inrush of sound and light stimulation etc., are manifestly felt as painful. (I shall set forth some of the evidence for this later on.) The inner stimuli of hunger and desire for contact with the mother's body are painful, too. But sensations of warmth, the desired contact, satisfaction in sucking, freedom from outer stimulus, etc., etc., soon bring actual experience of pleasurable sensation. The infant takes pleasurable sensation into itself, and expels the painful ones into the 'not-me'.

In her paper 'The Genesis of Psychical Conflict in Earliest Infancy' Joan Riviere wrote:

> from the very beginning there exists a core and foundation in experience for objectivity . . . an experience of bodily pleasure or pain, even a neutral perception, if intense enough, is presumably registered as such and must infallibly have a reality that nothing can alter or destroy. (Such infallibly and objectively true experiences would form the foundation of the later psychical institution of reality-testing). . . . I wish especially to point out, therefore, that from the very beginning of life, on Freud's own hypothesis, the psyche responds to the reality of its experience by interpreting them – or, rather, by *misinterpreting* them – in a subjective manner that increases its pleasure and preserves it from pain. This act of *a subjective interpretation of experience*, which it carries out by means of the processes of introjection and projection, is called by Freud hallucination; and it forms the basis of what we mean by phantasy-life. The phantasy-life of the individual is thus the form in which his real internal and external sensations and perceptions are interpreted and represented to himself in his mind under the influence of the pleasure-pain principle. . . . I would draw your attention to the conclusion that phantasy-life is never 'pure phantasy'. It consists of true perceptions and of false interpretations; all phantasies are thus *mixtures* of external and internal reality.
>
> [Riviere, J. 1936:399]

External perceptions, thus, begin to influence mental processes at a certain point (actually at birth, but they are not then appreciated as such); but, apart from the secondary pre-conscious and conscious adaptations later developed, the psyche deals with external stimuli, as with the instinctual ones, under the dominance of the pleasure-principle.

One essential aspect of the earliest development of phantasy was expounded by Melanie Klein in her papers 'The Psychological Principles of Infant Analysis' [Klein, M. 1927] and 'The Importance of Symbol-Formation in the Development of the Ego' [Klein, M. 1930]. She took up Ferenczi's view that (primary) identification, which is the fore-runner of symbolism, 'arises out of the baby's endeavour to re-discover in every object his own organs and their functioning', and Jones's view that the pleasure-principle makes it possible for two separate objects to be equated because of an affective bond of interest. And she showed, by means of illuminating clinical material, how the primary symbolic function of external objects enables phantasy to be elaborated by the ego, allows sublimations to develop in play and manipulation, and builds a bridge from the inner world to interest in the outer world and knowledge of physical objects and events.

The pleasurable interest in his body, his discoveries and experiments in this direction, are clearly shown in the play of an infant of 3–4 months. In this play he manifests this process of symbol-formation, bound up with those phantasies which we discover in the unconscious mind of young children during their analysis.

Klein has further shown, in her analytic work with children of two years and over, how the child's play exemplifies the dream mechanisms – symbolization, condensation, dramatization, displacement, and the rest. We know that the dream shows these mechanisms to be fundamental processes – the 'primary process' – of the mental life, underlying all our relational thinking and apprehension of external reality. And they must operate in the child's play more freely and fully in the earlier than in the later ages. To an older child, too, a box may symbolize his mother, but it has many practical uses for him in external life as well. For the tiny infant who first discovers the pleasures of dropping things into boxes and tipping them out again and so on and so forth, the symbolic meaning must far outweigh the 'reality' value, which must at first be quite marginal in significance.

Phantasies and words

On the view I am here presenting, then, phantasies are, in their simple beginnings, *implicit meaning*, meaning latent in impulse, affect, and sensation. They are the content of the archaic mental processes by means of which the primary libidinal wishes and aggressive impulses (and, later on, reparative wishes) are experienced and ordered in the psyche.

In the paper quoted above, Mrs Riviere said: 'When we speak of "phantasies" in babies or small children we do not imply an elaborate *mise-en-scène* or coherent dramatizations in them, nor of course to begin with plastic or verbal representations. We surmise that the *child feels as if* it were carrying out the desired action, and that this affective

283

feeling is accompanied by a corresponding physical excitation in certain organs e.g. mouth or musculature.' [Riviere, J. 1936: 399]

Later on (as we shall see) phantasy resides in plastic images – visual, auditory, kinaesthetic, touch, taste, smell, etc. And, since the child understands many words at the end of his first year, his phantasy life by that time certainly makes use of verbal images as well.

But words are by no means an essential scaffolding for phantasy. We know from our own dreams, from drawing, painting and sculpture, what a world of implicit meaning can reside in a shape, a colour, a line, a movement, a mass. We know from our own ready and intuitive response to other people's facial expression, tone of voice, gesture, etc., how much implicit meaning is expressed in these things, with never a word uttered, or in spite of words uttered.

Freud, indeed, makes it perfectly clear that, in his view, words belong to the Pcs only, and *not* to the realm of unconscious phantasy.

It strikes us all at once that now we know what is the difference between a conscious and an unconscious idea. The two are not, as we supposed, different records of the same content situate in different parts of the mind, not yet different functional states of cathexis in the same part; but the conscious idea comprises the concrete idea plus the verbal idea corresponding to it, whilst the unconscious idea is that of the thing alone. The system Ucs contains the thing-cathexes of the objects, the first and true object-cathexes; the system Pcs originates in a hyper-cathexis of this concrete idea by linking up of it with the verbal ideas of the words corresponding to it. It is such hyper-cathexes, we may suppose, that bring about higher organization in the mind and make it possible for the primary process to be succeeded by the secondary process which dominates Pcs.

[Freud, S. 1915b: 133–4; SE 14:202][19]

Dr Brierley, doubtless, had this view of Freud's in mind when she wrote:

It has to be emphasized that all presentation systems are ego-object systems, however rudimentary, and all have an origin in sensory experience, however distorted this may become in phantasy elaboration. Many such systems may come into existence which never become integrated with the definitive ego, and in this sense, Melanie Klein is right in maintaining that some phantasies revealed in analysis have never been conscious, i.e., in the sense that they have never been accessible to the definitive ego or self-consciousness.

[Brierley, M. 1937: 265]

Genetic continuity in development

At this point, it would be useful for us to consider a fundamental fact of general development, one which we shall see illustrated in some detail at a later point, namely, the fact of *genetic continuity*.

Whether in posture, locomotor and manipulative skill, in perception, language, or early logic, any given phase can be shown to have developed out of preceding phases in an ascertainable and intelligible way, alike in general outline and in specific detail.

This does not mean that development proceeds at an even pace throughout. There are definite crises in growth, integrations which from their nature bring radical changes in experience and further achievement. Learning to walk is one of these. But dramatic though it be in the changes it introduces into the child's world, actual walking is but the end phase of a long prepared and activated series of co-ordinations. Learning to talk is another such crisis; but again, one prepared for, foreshadowed and exercised in every detail before it is achieved.

So much is this so in the field of language that the definition of talking is purely a matter of convention. Commonly it is taken to mean the use of two words, an arbitrary standard useful for purposes of comparison, but not intended to blur the continuous course of development. Speech development begins, as has often been shown, with the sounds made by the infant when hungry or feeding in the first weeks of life; and on the other hand, the changes occurring after the mastery of the first word are as continuous and as varied and complete as those occurring before this moment. This fact of genetic continuity has been shown to hold for the most diverse aspects of growth, at every period until maturity is reached.

Probably no psychoanalyst would doubt the fact of genetic continuity, but this fact is not a mere abstract principle. It is a concrete instrument of knowledge, enabling us to trace threads of development backwards and forwards, and to decipher the beginnings of processes which are familiar to us in their later forms.

One aspect of this general fact of genetic continuity having a special bearing upon our present problems is seen in the field of speech, namely, the fact that *comprehension of words long antedates their use*.

285

The actual length of time during which the child shows that he understands much that is said to him, or spoken in his presence, yet has not come to the point of using any words himself, varies much from child to child. In some highly intelligent children, the interval between comprehension and use of words may be as much as one year. But it is always there. There is a general time lag of use behind comprehension, throughout childhood.

One important field in which this operates is that of logical relations. Experimental studies have shown that the child can understand and act upon certain logical relations (such as identity, exception, generalization, etc.) long before he can express those relations in words. And he can understand them in simple concrete terms before he can appreciate more abstract terms. E.g. he can act upon the words 'all but' when he cannot yet understand the word 'except'; but he can comprehend and act upon 'except' before he can use the word himself.

Let me take some examples from the second year of life, to illustrate this continuous genetic development, particularly with regard to the transition from pre-verbal to verbal experience.

Examples of the way in which non-verbal thinking merges into verbal forms have been given to us by the studies of speech development by M. H. Lewis [1936]. I will quote a few instances from his material. First, with regard to rudimentary *references to absent objects*: At 1 year, 1 month and 5 days, the boy is playing with a toy on the floor. He has not played with his ball all day. It is lying in the corner of the room, in shadow. His mother says, 'Baby, where is ballie?' The child turns round and crawls towards it, but halts on the way at another plaything. His mother repeats the question, and he then resumes his journey, seizes the ball, and looks back at his mother.

At 1,4,17: the boy at breakfast time spontaneously turns towards the cupboard where his breakfast honey is kept, and says, 'ha' – his word for honey.

At 1,5,22: he goes to his father, who is sitting down, seizes the lapels of his coat and tries to push them apart, saying 'tick, tick'.

At 1,6,9: he crawls over to the bureau, reaches up to the drawer where chocolate is kept, and says, 'goga, goga', his word for chocolate.

And at 1,6,13, when he is offered a banana, he waves it away, saying 'goga, goga', i.e., chocolate.

And here are clear references to the future:

At 1,6,3, about bath-time, the boy climbs upstairs, the mother following him. At the landing she asks him: 'Where are you going?' He makes straight for the bathroom, saying: 'ba, ba', i.e. bath.

286

Again at 1,9,9; the boy is in his mother's bedroom early one morning. He goes to the door and rattles its handle, saying: 'tea, tea', and then 'Eileen', the name of the maid. His mother asks him 'What will Eileen bring you?' The boy says 'tea'. She adds, 'what else?' and he replies, 'biki' – i.e. 'biscuits'.

And finally regarding the growth of *reference to the past*:

At 1,8,22: the following conversation takes place between the boy and his mother: the mother says, 'Where's Da gone?' The first reply is a repetition of the fact of absence, 'go', i.e. 'gone'. The mother says, 'Where?' The boy replies 'da', i.e. 'Daddy'. But when the mother says, 'Yes, but where?' he replies: 'kul', i.e. 'school'. And at 1,11,9, when the mother is speaking to a visitor in the boy's presence, but not to the boy himself, and is trying to remember the name of some people who had been at the house one month earlier, and whom the boy had then seen, she says, 'What was the name of those people?' the boy then breaks into the conversation by saying, 'Bertie, gogi', i.e. 'Bertie, doggie' – the name of one of the visitors, who had also had a dog with them.

(I would draw special attention to this incident, as again confirming: (a) the great extent to which comprehension of words outruns their use; (b) a child's interest in adult's talk and in their relationships and doings; and (c) the complexity of his grasp of temporal and of social situations, and the clarity and relevance of his memory all at less than two years.)

Such instances of non-verbal and rudimentary verbal logic could be multiplied *ad infinitum* from the observation of the behaviour of children in the second year. They suggest: how complex and integrated the child's perception of his world has already become, how clearly he can show us his mental processes even before he can put them into words, if we have the patience to watch and record his behaviour, and how continuous are the processes by which pre-verbal practical logic develops into verbal understanding.

This general fact of genetic continuity has a specific bearing upon the question of whether the child's phantasy life is active at the time when the relevant impulses dominate his behaviour and his experience, or only become so in retrospect, when later on he can put his experience into words. That is to say, it bears upon the question of *regression*, which I shall discuss directly at a later point.

The facts of general development to which I have just drawn your attention support fully the view that phantasies do not depend for *their existence and activity* upon the child's power to express them in words. If, at two years, such intellectual functions as reference to absent objects, to past and future events and even logical relations,

287

can be seen at work in action well before they can be put into words, then we have no ground for refusing to allow that the child's earliest experiences of feeling and sensation are accompanied by implicit phantasies.

As we have seen, the earliest rudimentary phantasy is bound up with sensory experience; it is an affective interpretation of bodily sensations, an expression of libidinal and aggressive impulses, operating under the pleasure-pain principle. Later on, phantasy is inherent in sights and sounds, in touch and manipulation and perception of objects, as well as in gestures and vocal expression. At this stage, it is still *implicit* phantasy.

Still later, 'free' images, not 'tied' to actual perception, begin to develop, and phantasy thus becomes explicit. Much later still some of it may sometimes be expressed in words.

We cannot be sure when the first 'free' images are experienced, although it seems probable that they develop along with recognition of external reality and anticipation of changes in external reality. The first signs of surprise (about 5 months of age) suggests the presence of 'free' images, i.e., explicit phantasy. Anticipatory movements, signs of awareness of strange people and strange places, etc., before this age, indicate implicit phantasy.

In the second half of the first year, as we shall see later, there is plenty of evidence for non-verbal phantasy of an explicit kind; and even verbal phantasy may be richer than we have been willing to realize, since the child understands many words – the phonetic as well as the intonational form – by the end of the first year, although he himself uses only two (on the average). In the second year, many phantasies are explicitly acted out in gesture and make-believe play (see below); and quite a number are expressed in words.

Other authors

Before passing on to consider those authors who have taken a different view, I shall quote briefly from some authors of the 'English school', who have shown their agreement with this view of the activity and significance of early phantasies.

(a) Edward Glover has brought out the significance of actual sensory experience in the building up of phantasy. 'There are certain painful ego experiences which indicate the existence of a painful "not me" – a pin through the diaper, a hard crumb in the mouth, a hot-water bottle against the ribs. When such stimuli are removed, the pain stops. So the "not-me" is gradually reinforced by experience of stimuli which can, as it were, be discarded. But certain "me" stimuli resemble the pins and crumbs of the "not-me". Some colic pains can be eased by the expulsion of wind. So here again we have a source of confusion between the "me" and "not-me". And here, too, we watch the birth of that great primitive mechanism of projection. If only more enduring colics could be suddenly converted into painful "not-me's" like crumbs, and violently expelled. At the same time the experiences of mouth, hand and stomach are responsible for building up another psychic tendency, which we dimly try to appreciate by the use of the term "introjection". If only the pleasure-producing nipple could be imprisoned in the mouth, the stealing warmth retained in the stomach.'

Glover adds: 'the introjections and projections that influence reality sense are not simply sensory, but more complicated psychic experiences. The most painful, persistent and unmasterable stimuli are the psychic stimuli of frustrated instinct.' [Glover, E. 1932: 13–14]

(b) Merrell Middlemore, in her account of her remarkable studies of the feeding responses of infants in the first days of life (*The Nursing Couple*, 1941), emphasizes the contribution to phantasy both of inner instinctual stimuli and of sensory experience. (It will be noted that she defines 'fantasy' in a somewhat narrower sense than I am adopting; she equates it with what I would call 'explicit phantasy'.) She writes: 'In connection with these different habits of sucking, rudimentary psychic processes arise. In every case these express something of the child's tension of hunger and his struggle for food – something, also, of his pleasure in feeding. But psychic processes connected with feeding develop differently if the baby enjoys the breast, or only after ardent sucking; things are different again if he leaves the breast unsatisfied and wretched.'

Again: 'As the months pass the rudimentary psychic processes are organised to fantasy, which can be defined as an expression in ideas of these same bodily efforts, pains and pleasures of feeding. As the child begins to comprehend his mother as a person, his fantasies are centred in her. Fantasies which express his struggle for food are concerned with biting her breast and draining it of milk, or with hurting the whole mother and swallowing or destroying her; in fantasies which emerge when the child feels hungry, away from the breast, it is the mother who starves him and leaves him alone; in fantasies which, as it were, account for the pains of colic, it is the mother, again, who gives him the bad milk that hurts him, or who attacks him somehow from inside to punish him for biting her and taking her milk. These are examples from the wide range of fantasies concerned with the disturbances and misfortunes of breast feeding. Happy experiences of being suckled give rise to as varied a body of fantasies. In these ideas are developed of a bountiful mother who has stores of food and gives it generously; or the child makes gifts to her in return for the food, or they feed one another and share their pleasures.' [Middlemore, M. 1941: 113–14]

And, 'It will be appreciated that fantasies of an attack on the breast . . . are derived, in the first instance, from the baby's feelings while in the tension of hunger; but this is not always discharged in exciting biting or strong sucking. Thus irritably inert babies must be credited with hunger tension – perhaps with high tension such as might give rise to specially aggressive fantasies – but their "attack" on the breast is by no means vigorous.' [Ibid., p. 189]

With regard to one particular child, Middlemore says: 'What was clear was that the baby was unwilling to suck, while difficulties which began at the breast continued steadily through all kinds of feeding from bottle, spoon and cup. Until she came for treatment she had never put a spoonful of food into her own mouth. The point is that although she had never sucked the breast properly, still less "attacked" it, she entertained very fierce fantasies of biting. What was their physical foundation, unless it was the feelings which disturbed her during hunger?' [Ibid., 190]

(c) Melitta Schmideberg, in her account of 'The Play Analysis of a Three-Year-Old Girl', states that

Her conversion symptoms and anxiety were determined largely by her anxiety of the incorporated object. She felt that the dangerous object inside her was in opposition to her ego. By a strong libidinization and an increase of the synthetic function, the contrast between the incorporated object and the ego became less forcible and she identified herself with the object inside her (with the mouse or the dangerous father). . . .

And the following passage makes a clear reference to the question of when these operative phantasies were at work:

In examining the structure of this case I assume that the determinants for the symptoms I found at three years had been continuously at work from the time the symptoms first occurred. This is not susceptible of proof. But the same assumption was made by Freud when he used the factors revealed in the analysis of adults to explain symptoms which had occurred in childhood. The possibility that the conflicts discovered in the analysis of the three-year-old child were already producing symptoms in the infant a few weeks or months old might be regarded as a probability, provided further analytic studies of young children and behaviouristic observations of young infants should indicate similar conclusions.

[Schmideberg, M. 1934: 257–8]

Authors of divergent views

(a) *Robert Wälder* In his paper on 'The Problem of the Genesis of Psychical Conflict in Earliest Infancy' (Wälder, R. 1937) Wälder stated clearly and forcibly the views of a number of analysts whose conclusions differ on many points from those outlined in this paper.

In his footnote (p. 406), Wälder says: 'The following paper embodies the conclusions of many discussions which have taken place on these problems amongst members of the Vienna Psycho-Analytical Society. For some of these conclusions I alone am responsible; in other cases I have made use of ideas contributed by others.'

I can, therefore, conveniently take his view as representative of those of a considerable number of people.

Wälder refers, first, to the work of Klein, Ernest Jones, Riviere, Glover, Strachey, Rickman and others, and says, 'A large number of other writings testifies to the fruitfulness of the views in question and their applicability in various fields'. He then gives a clear and useful summary of the common elements in the work of these authors, which largely agrees with what I have here put forward, although it touches upon other important points as well – some of which will certainly come up in later discussions in this series.

(In one point, it should be said, his statement of these views is definitely incorrect, being more a judgement of his own about the views than an unbiased account of their nature; namely, his account of the relation between phantasy and reality. I cannot, however, enter into this point here, but I should like to do so on some future occasion.)

Wälder then expounds the views representative of those analysts with whom he is in agreement, and which differ from those of the 'English school'. I must content myself with such quotations as bear especially closely upon the main thesis of this paper.

Pp. 411–12 In the first place, with regard to direct observation we may say that we have far more data at our disposal when the child is somewhat older. When we observe a three-year-old child, we can

291

examine not only his behaviour but also what he says. Moreover, the behaviour of a three-year-old child is highly complex and consists not merely of expressional movements indicating instinctual impulses and the like, but of very complicated activities. In the case of children in the first year verbal communication is entirely lacking. We can only observe their behaviour and this is confined to a very small number of manifestations, of the nature of expressional movement or – and this not directly after birth but somewhat later – declarations and demands. There are no more complicated activities. So when we study the first year, we can only directly observe the child's behaviour, and his modes of behaviour are very limited. One would be inclined to suppose that from the observation of behaviour we can infer only relatively few and simple psychic processes in the infantile organism and that other, more complicated processes either do not occur or, if they do occur, do not betray themselves in behaviour and cannot be detected, at any rate by this kind of observation. I think it is, to say the least, an open question if the possibility exists of deducing with any sufficient degree of probability a large number of complicated psychic processes from the. behaviour of young infants. . . .

Pp. 428–9 All the phantasies (e.g., oral phantasies directed to the mother's body) which have been described as belonging to this early period have been abundantly proved to occur at a later age, in children of about three years old. I believe that we shall obtain evidence that they occur even during the course of the third year. Their existence is not in question, only their occurrence so early in life.

P. 429 Similarly the phantasies belonging to the third year may have their antecedents in processes which occur at the very beginning of life and be woven of this early material, combined with the experiences subsequently acquired during the development of the instincts and the ego, and as a result of external happenings. But I see no grounds which compel us to conclude that the phantasies themselves belong to those early periods.

Finally, Wälder summarizes his conclusions (which we may assume are shared by others), and from this summary I shall quote as follows:

Melanie Klein and her colleagues have described a number of phantasies (in particular, oral phantasies) which we meet with in the analyses of adults and of older children. In doing so they have followed out a line of thought which has always been included in the sphere of analysis and which was embodied especially in

Abraham's writings. We welcome the addition to our knowledge which this line of investigation promises. And we would express our gratitude to Melanie Klein for her promptitude in grasping and working out one of the difficult notions outlined by Freud in *The Ego and the Id*, which has now become the common property of analysis – the fact, namely, that the aggression of the superego is not merely acquired from the object but represents also the subject's own aggressiveness turned in upon himself.

But what follows gives us pause. We hesitate to believe that the *Wälder* phantasies of mankind follow a predestined course and are merely rendered more or less intense by the action of reality, being always to some extent operative; that violent manifestations of aggressiveness during the first year of life are universal; that in infancy there are mechanisms at work resembling those of psychosis, so that psychotic disease in later life can be explained as the effect of modes of reaction which are part of normal development; that the phantasies in question date from a very early period (we should be inclined to place them later, in the third or fourth year of life, though we should admit that they are determined by fixations in the first two years); in fact, we doubt whether we have sufficient clues to enable us to infer the experiences of earliest infancy with that degree of certainty which we commonly look for or whether we can claim any degree of scientific accuracy for detailed conclusion about them. Finally, we cannot but feel that an excursion has been made into the shadowy past, while much that could be more satisfactorily proved and that is indispensable for analysis has been left unregarded.

Anyone who is interested in the elucidation of these problems is bound to test all the points here enumerated upon the largest possible body of material. The constant reiteration of assertion and counter-assertion, based on alleged individual experience, is not likely to be very fruitful.

(Ibid., pp. 472–3)

I wish to draw your attention to the fact that in these passages Wälder agrees with Melanie Klein's views as to the activity and importance of aggressive wishes and phantasies of attack upon the mother's body (and other allied urges and phantasies) in children of three years and over, as well as in adults. But it will be remembered that not so very long ago the existence of such phantasies were, first, unheard of, and then strongly challenged.

The change of position doubtless came about through more careful observation (both direct and in analysis) of the behaviour of young children indicative of such phantasies. We may, then, consider it possible that a still closer and more sustained study of the behaviour of younger children and infants may in its turn lead those who do not now recognize the early activity of early phantasies to accept the evidence in their favour. The open mind which Wälder expresses in the paragraph last quoted from his summary is welcome and encouraging.

(b) *Anna Freud*   Since Wälder's opinions as stated in his paper are the outcome of discussions in the Vienna Society, we may presume that they are in the main shared by Anna Freud; and her own earlier writings would support this view. In some of her more recent writing, however, she expresses views about the development of the child in his first three years which are by no means so far from some of Melanie Klein's conclusions.

In her recent (1942) report on 'Young Children in Wartime', she takes up a position which impresses the reader as very different from Wälder's. In her vivid account of the child *in his second year*, she depicts the varied emotional and intellectual relationship of the child with his mother, remarking, 'Observers seldom appreciate the depth and seriousness of this grief of a small child' who has been separated from his mother; and she explicitly refers to 'the mother–image in the child's mind' (p. 183).

She says, moreover, 'Failure to recognize the mother occurs when something has happened to the image of the mother in the child's mind, i.e., to its inner relationship to her. The mother has disappointed the child and left his longing for her unsatisfied; so he turns against her with resentment and rejects the memory of her person from his consciousness' (p. 185).

Even with regard to the *first year*, Anna Freud brings out that in the second half of the year the child's relationship to his mother is a psychological and social one, and emphasizes that the disturbances of eating and sleeping, etc., which appear in babies of this age who are separated from their mothers are not simply due to bodily discomfort, but definitely to an interruption of psychological contact: '. . . the mother is already appreciated and missed for her own sake'.

Reading these passages, one is impressed with the degree of significance which Anna Freud now gives to some of those experiences and mental processes which led Melanie Klein to formulate her concept of early depression.

Anna Freud speaks of 'the depth and seriousness of this grief of a small child' and refers to the 'mother–image in his mind'.

Now I feel that this description of the 'mother-image in the child's mind' and of 'its inner relationship to her' comes very close to Klein's postulate that the child *introjects* his mother. Melanie Klein holds, further, that the fear of loss or danger to the internalized mother-figure is an essential part of such feelings of grief which the child has when his mother leaves him.

Anna Freud also speaks of the child's resentment against his mother when she leaves him, which leads him to reject her image from his mind. This, too, is an agreement with Melanie Klein's concept, since one element in the 'depressive position' as described by her is the infant's turning against his mother (internally as well as externally) because of his hate, aroused by frustrations. This hate causes him to feel that he has lost the image of the 'good' internal mother; it also disturbs his relation to his actual mother. Anna Freud, too, says: 'Failure to recognize his mother occurs when something has happened to the image of the mother in his mind.'

Melanie Klein's concept of the 'depressive position' contains many other aspects as well; but those now mentioned are an important part of it.

Klein also holds that this situation (essentially the 'depressive position') arises first at the time when the infant suffers frustrations at the breast, and particularly in the experience of weaning. She also considers that such states of feeling as those described here by Anna Freud are also bound up with the earlier omnipotent destructive wishes and with guilt, i.e., with the early superego.

Furthermore, we could not believe that 'deep and serious grief' could exist without *phantasies* concerning the loss of the mother and her longed-for return. But, indeed, Anna Freud (to my mind) *implies* phantasies when she speaks of the 'mother-image in the child's mind'.

In her book *The Ego and the Mechanisms of Defence* (1936), Anna Freud wrote (p. 57): 'According to the theory of the English school of analysis, introjection and projection, which in our view should be assigned to the period after the ego has been differentiated from the outside world, are the very processes by which the structure of the ego is developed.'

She adds, 'the chronology of psychic processes is still one of the most obscure fields of analytical theory. . . . It will probably be best to abandon the attempt so to classify them' (i.e. in time).

Thus, in spite of the very definite line she took in the first of these paragraphs, Anna Freud seemed (in the last sentence quoted) to keep her mind open about this question. And judging by the passages quoted from her recent Report, her views now seem to be, at least on

295

some points, more in agreement with those of Melanie Klein and her co-workers.

Regression

One important question now remains to be briefly discussed, viz: that of *regression*.

In the view I am here presenting, an essential feature of early development is the activity and intensity of early unconscious phantasies, and their far-reaching and *uninterrupted* influence upon further progressive mental development.

At many points of my argument, I have been able to quote Freud in support of particular details. On this matter, my point of view appears to deviate from him, as well as from that of Abraham. Both Freud and Abraham, and many other analysts, hold that early instinctual drives (and the phantasies associated with them) exert their influence upon later developments chiefly by regression.

Now it seems to me that this postulate might have been formulated differently if the picture of early mental life had not had to be mainly inferred or reconstructed, as it was, from the study of adults and older children in analysis. The new and first-hand material gained from the analysis (and the more detailed observation of the behaviour) of young children was bound to lead to a revision of this postulate.

On the basis of her experience with very young children, Klein developed the view that not only are the phantasies expressing instinctual urges active from the very beginning, but they exert their power *continuously throughout development*. Moreover, defence mechanisms begin to operate quite early, and feelings of guilt and grief soon begin to influence the child's mind in an enduring way.

This does not by any means overlook the *fact* of regression nor exclude its influence. But it does change the emphasis placed upon it. It alters our view of the relationship between the process of regression and the early developmental trends.

On this view, regression certainly appears less important; but there is more to the difference than this. The greater emphasis laid upon the early phantasy life, with its accompanying urges and feelings (anxieties, guilt, etc.), includes the recognition that a variety of defence mechanisms are at work. A new light is thrown upon the process of regression itself, since we now know so much more about those stages of development to which regression takes place, and the defence mechanisms which are then called once more into play and reinforced in the service of regression.

I wish now to remind you that Freud's own statements bearing on this question were not always unequivocal. Certain passages in his writings suggest that his mind was perhaps open, and at times even moved in a direction which, if followed through, might have led him to look differently at the relation between earlier and later developmental processes. On these problems as on so many others, his fertile genius threw out inspiring suggestions which he left it to other people to take up and make use of.

In his paper on 'Instincts and Their Vicissitudes' (1915), after speaking of the earliest phase of love as 'the phase of incorporating and devouring', Freud remarks: 'This admixture of hate in love is to be traced in part to those preliminary stages of love *which have not been wholly outgrown.*' (Isaacs' italics) [Freud, S. 1915a: 82; SE 14:139][20]

And in his 'Female Sexuality' (1932) he writes:

Some authors are inclined to disparage the importance of the child's first, most primal libidinal impulses, laying stress rather on later developmental processes, so that – putting this view in its most extreme form – all that the former can be said to do is to indicate certain directions, while the energy with which these directions are pursued is drawn from later regressions and reaction formations. . . . Certain as it is that the libidinal tendencies are reinforced later by regression and reaction-formation and difficult as it is to estimate the relative strength of the various confluent libidinal components, I still think that we must not overlook the fact that *those first impulses have an intensity of their own which is greater than anything that comes later and may indeed be said to be incommensurable with any other force.* (Isaacs' italics)
[Freud, S. 1932:296–7; SE 21:242–3][21]

This emphatic statement of Freud's that 'the first, most primal libidinal impulses' have an intensity greater than anything that comes later and 'incommensurable with any other', and do *not* draw their energy mainly from later 'regression', is a conclusion the importance of which cannot be over-estimated. And, in my view, if the primal impulses have this immediate and overwhelming importance, so also has their psychic content, i.e., the phantasies in which they are experienced and expressed.

I realize that there is much more to be said on this question of regression, which I have only touched upon. It required much fuller discussion, and is sure to come up again and again in our deliberations.

The sorts of evidence available

The evidence upon which the main thesis is advanced in this paper is of four main sorts:

1 Considerations regarding the *relationships between established facts and theories*. When considered fully, these relationships, in my view, require the postulates I have put forward, and by means of these postulates become better integrated and more fully understood.
2 'Behaviouristic' data, i.e., non-analytic observations of the infant by all the means of the modern science of child development.
3 'Clinical' evidence, gained from the actual analysis (by strictly analytic methods) of young children, particularly of the ages two to three years.
4 Confirmatory experience in the analysis of adults, by the various analysts who have for some time made use in their work of the various facts and hypotheses regarding early development, first formulated in the analysis of young children. (See, for instance, papers by Brierley, Glover, Heimann, Isaacs, Jones, Payne, Rickman, Searl, Schmideberg, Scott, Sharpe, Sheehan-Dare, Winnicott etc.)

The 'behaviouristic' and the clinical evidence require to be brought into close relation with each other, regarding every aspect of our problem. Not only does the analytic material illuminate all the details of the observational data – it also suggests the directions in which new observations require to be made. (See, e.g., the observational studies of young infants by Merrell Middlemore, already quoted.)

The external behaviour of the infant or the child of 12–24 months not only gives us much insight into his inner life; it also acts as an essential check upon our analytic inferences. When analytic experience leads us to reconstruct an internal situation or a particular relation to external reality, in the infant and young child, the behaviouristic data (including the ascertainable facts as to perception, memory, make-believe play, vocalizations, practical and verbal logic, etc.) can say whether or not such a reconstruction is possible or likely, at the given age.

The great advance in our knowledge of such details in recent years has given us a far better test and measure of the likelihood of our analytic inferences than was available in the early days of analysis. As we know, Freud arrived at most of his critical theories from the analysis of adults. The fact that the major structures of psychoanalytical theory are confirmed and elaborated by observations of infants and young children should not lead us to overlook the rectification of certain detail of theory, e.g. concerning regression, which our greater knowledge, both of the conscious and of the unconscious minds, of young children, may now call for.

It is also necessary to add that those who have not had the actual experience of analysing (by strictly analytic procedures) children of two to three years of age are not in a favourable position for estimating either the behaviouristic or the analytic evidence. The age of the child has to be emphasized in this connection. The changes occurring in the child's ways of dealing with anxiety are quite considerable between two and three years of age. The younger child gives us far more intimate analytic understanding of what he has felt and experienced during the first two years than the three-year-old can allow us.

It is not possible for me to offer case material evidence in this paper, from the analysis of young children. Nor is it necessary. I may and shall assume that my readers have some familiarity with the many papers which have been published by Melanie Klein and her co-workers.

I shall conclude by making a brief survey of some of the 'behaviouristic' data, illustrating certain of those major trends of development which bear upon my thesis.

(In what follows, I shall include much of the material presented to the Society in two previous papers, not yet published: 'Anxiety in the First Year of Life' (1934), and 'The Nature of the Evidence Concerning Mental Life in the Earliest Years' (Isaacs 1938).)[22]

Facts of general development

We need to know something of (a) the infant's affective relationships, and the changes occurring in these with successive ages; (b) the growth of perception, memory, and imagination; and (c) the development of play.

I shall refer to these aspects of development during the periods

1 Birth to five or six months,
2 Five–six months to 12–14 months,
3 The second year.

BIRTH TO FIVE OR SIX MONTHS

Even with regard to these first few months Wälder greatly underestimates the amount and reliability of our knowledge, and the actual complexity of the infant's responses – and of the *changes occurring in those responses* as he grows from one to five months. The changes and directions of change are at least as significant as the details of behaviour at any given time.

Since Wälder wrote, it may be noted, Merrell Middlemore's observations on the new-born and young infant have been published in *The Nursing Couple* (1941). Her studies show (a) how much more varied and complex even the earliest responses appear to be when studied in close detail by a discerning eye; and (b) how intimately the child's experiences (such as the way he is handled and suckled) influence the succeeding phases of feeling and later phantasy.

Affective responses and object-relationships

At first negative expressional signs considerably outweigh the positive ones. Negative expressional movements and sounds are to be noticed on the very first day, where as positive expressional movements and sounds do not appear until the second month, *except in the taking of food*. Signs of joy and content appear very early in the feeding situation. Apart from this situation, however, almost every external stimulus of more than a minimal intensity, and in particular auditory stimuli, tend to call out negative expressional signs up to the second month. Sounds of a slight intensity remain unobserved during the first and second months, and if they are of more than a minimal intensity they evoke clear signs of anxiety. Even simple stimuli of contact with the body do not at first call out positive reactions. Most of the necessary manipulations of the child's body excite either direct displeasure or else are suffered without any recognizable movements of expression. From the third month onwards such experiences as stroking, blowing on the child and tickling call out a positive response and produce an expression of comforts. From about the fourth month onwards the child laughs when he is touched.

In the first four months all causes of crying arise directly from bodily hurts and needs. The following stimuli in particular call out signs of anxiety: pain, strong sensory stimulation, abrupt changes of posture, uncomfortable posture, fatigue, and hunger. These causes operate from birth up to about five months. After this period, however, other causes begin to appear, for example, the failure of an intended movement on the child's own part, the loss or removal of playthings, the disappearance of the mother or her refusal to play with the child, and jealousy.

That is to say, from this time the infant has much more ability to express his active wishes in varied and specific forms, and these are more clearly directed towards his mother as a person.

Moreover, the positive expressional movements, such as glowing eyes, lifted corners of the mouth, gentle stretching of the body, stretching of the arms towards an object, facial expression of joyful surprise, and positive vocalizations such as crowing, shouting, bubbling, dribbling, and laughter, show a marked increase after three months. At about five months they begin to show some predominance, and at a year they far outweigh the negative reactions and expressional movements. Not only is it true that from the fifth month onwards, crying at the disappearance of a plaything is noticed. It is also recorded that expressional movements of surprise, and of joy and pleasure, are to be seen in a five-month-old child when a plaything, which had been hanging over his crib and is removed from his view, is again placed within his glance, or if the adult who passed by the child again approaches him.

The fourth and fifth months are thus very significant in that they show a marked increase in positive activities as well as a definite growth of the social causes of pain and pleasure. (Closely connected with these changes are certain aspects of development in skill, e.g., (a) the infant first begins to keep his eyes open to any extent when feeding, at about two months; and (b) first becomes able to grasp objects in a directed way at three months of age; (c) experimental activity first begins to appear during the second month, and from the fifth month onwards increases very rapidly in variety and continually, developing gradually into definite play; (d) the growth of continuous directed and experimental activities, as compared with single reactions and random impulsive movements, also appears very marked between the third and the sixth months. (See Bühler 1930, Bernfeld 1929, Lewis 1936, Shirley 1933.)

Shirley too reports that the 'irritability' of infants, by which she means all the various types of negative response including screaming, crying, and fussing, was considerably greater during the first two months than after this age. Infants differ a good deal in the degree of irritability which they show when being handled, but high irritability is characteristic of more babies during the early weeks than at later ages. And with all the infants studied, there was a considerable diminution in this irritability after the end of the second month (Shirley 1933). These facts conform with Bühler's view that

301

stimuli of contact, handling, etc., are not the pleasurable experiences to the infant during the first two or three months, but that they become very much less disagreeable and even pleasurable after this period (Bühler 1930).[23]

The main conclusions to be drawn from these objective studies would seem to be: (1) That in the first two months of life the waking infant reacts with anxiety to the majority of the stimuli that impinge upon him, this becoming progressively less true as he approaches his third month, and thereafter. (2) That the degree to which this is true is partly a function of the individual child. It is true of all, but more true of some than others. Shirley puts this difference down to inborn factors. It may be a function of the inborn strength of aggressive tendencies relatively to the available libido. On the other hand, there is evidence to show that from the very first few hours environmental factors begin to act. Real events occurring within the first few days may in fact have a great deal to do with these apparent temperamental differences. (See Middlemore 1941.)

It would seem, however, with every infant, that we have to give far more experimental weight to the felt hostility of the external world over a considerable period in early development, than we had realized. The occasions on which the child, in his waking moments (apart from feeding and dozing), finds the world disagreeable seem to be far more general and 'normal' than we had allowed. The painful 'not-me's' are not merely accidental and occasional pins and crumbs. In the first two months there appear to be normally more painful 'not-me's' of every sort, than of pleasant experiences which can be built up into the primitive pleasure ego.

It is these sensations and feelings which form the basis of his persecutory fears, his phantasies of being attacked by a 'bad' mother. His own rage and destructive wishes, projected on to his mother, serve to increase his fears of being attacked by her. And every frustration, every failure on her part to remove any source of pain as well as to feed and comfort him, reinforces his picture of her as a 'bad' mother. As we know from later analysis, he identifies the mother who does *not* remove a source of pain with the pain itself, just as he identifies the mother who does feed him and remove painful stimuli, making him comfortable and happy, with his own pleasure and happiness. In well-cared-for and normal babies, the phantasy of the 'good' mother is soon built up on the basis of his experience of the satisfying breast and comforting body. And this picture of the 'good' mother becomes more and more secure as the child's own capacity for active pleasure increases – as well as his perception of his actual mother as she ministers to him.

302

How does it come about that the infant's degree of 'irritability' in the face of outer stimulation lessens? It seems that Bernfeld's view that what happens is a *libidinization* of the various stimuli is probably correct (Bernfeld 1929).

This libidinization comes first of all with stimuli of lesser intensity, and only much later, if at all, to very loud sounds, sudden bright lights, abrupt changes of posture, etc.

Bernfeld's general view is that the key to development in the earliest period is the overcoming of anxiety (objective anxiety, he thinks) and the increase of pleasure in positive activities. 'Discharge movements', movements whose function it is to discharge painful psychic tension, change slowly into pleasurable activities, and it is the anterior end of the body which is first of all 'emancipated from the fright reaction', as he puts it. This comes about by roughly 3 months, so that we now have positive pleasure in seeing and hearing, apart from intense stimuli, and in directed activities bringing these sensory delights.

In the first weeks, *the only situation in which there is this active seeking and satisfaction is the child's reaction to the breast.*

It seems probable (as further data to be quoted shortly will confirm) that the various outer stimuli of lesser intensity, which gradually enter the field of pleasurable attention, do so *in so far as they get taken up into the nucleus of oral satisfaction.*

The first seen object which becomes a source of pleasure to the child is the round breast, and the selective regard for the face which begins as early as two to four weeks is probably strongly stimulated by, even if not entirely derived from, the sight of the breast. There must be a strong encouragement to displacement from the breast to the face in view of the fact that the breast is mostly covered away from the child, whilst the face is always visible. Once, however, the transition has been made from looking at the breast to looking at the face, it is certain that the face must gain a significance of its own through its mobility, its emotional intent, and its association with the satisfying manipulations of the infant by the mother.

Thereafter, the child's own co-ordinations of hand and eye and head and posture, and his slowly differentiated observations of other people, can proceed apace – in the first instance, to the extent to which they serve or are connected with the primary oral satisfaction.

Shirley reports,

The first active social response noted in the babies, which appeared early in the first month, was that of soberly watching an adult's face. Following an adult's movements with the eyes came a little

303

later, and at the end of the first month the babies began to be comforted by the presence and ministrations of an adult. Whereas in the hospital period they had cried at being lifted from the crib, they now (at one month) were quieted by being picked up and held.

Apparently the sound of the mother's voice also had a soothing effect. But these reactions on the part of the babies were passive as contrasted with the reactions of watching and looking, in which they took the initiative.

Watching and following with the eyes developed into smiling in the second month, and soon the babies were expressing their joy in the society of adults and children by cooing, by animated waving and kicking, and by laughing aloud. At three months the babies were recognizing father and mother and other persons who assisted in their daily care, and in the fourth month some of them showed that they were aware of strangers by soberly staring instead of smiling or by signs of timidity or distress.

[Shirley 1933:28]

Watching persons was the babies' greatest distraction during the first three months, and exploratory looking around absorbed their best attention during the early period of sitting on an adult's lap. . . . From birth to the age of six months exploration of the visual environment consisted largely of these reactions of watching persons and looking around.

Furthermore, the earliest signs of affection are those of patting the breast while nursing and of cuddling down contentedly on the mother's shoulder. These movements of patting and cuddling must themselves aid development in co-ordination. The wish of the infant to touch and manipulate the persons of adults is at least equally strong with their experimental interest in physical objects.

In these observations as to the infant's active concern with his mother's body – both loving and aggressive – we have full confirmation of Melanie Klein's hypothesis as to his early wishes and phantasies towards his mother. We see the first dawn of the epistomophilic impulse, as well as of the wish to control and master, and we have clear hints of the way in which, by means of his *play*, the child libidinizes his aggressive wishes and anxieties.

Perception and memory

In discussing affective responses and object-relationships, much has already been said about the infant's perception of objects and early signs of memory. Let us now bring some of these together:

1st month	The baby watches faces.
2nd month	Turns his head or holds it attentively in response to a speaking voice.
3 months	Recognizes mother, father, nurse.
	Shows that he recognizes a changed situation by frowns, attentive gazing, or other slight signs of anxiety.
	Recognizes signs of preparation for feeding and opens mouth expectantly.
4 months	Responds with voice when played with, making playful sounds.
	Reaches out to feel things when on mother's lap.
	Looks fixedly at any small object on table near him.
	Distinguishes between familiars and strangers. (Between the 20th and 40th weeks, frowns or stares or whimpers at stranger, or turns head away), or if fails to accomplish some aim of his own, e.g. sitting up.
5 months	Shows distress when mother goes away.
	Eyes and hands work together in exploring objects near him.
	Plays actively with rattle, reaches out for objects held near him.
	Will watch the movements of a person who moves about, looking up and down at whole body.
	Shows eagerness or annoyance by vocal changes.
	Responds with expressive sounds to those who talk to him.
	Shows joyful movements of surprise and pleasure if a plaything which has been removed is put again within sight, or if mother goes away and returns towards him.
6 months	Bangs a spoon or pats table in way.
	Reaches for any object on sight.
	Frowns or smiles in response to angry or friendly looks.
	Utters several clearly defined syllables.
	Expresses pleasure at seeing familiar persons by voice.

In general, the details of these achievements show that, from this time, not only can the child sit up, co-ordinate hand and eye, face the world, reach and examine objects he is interested in, watch all the movement of grown-ups, distinguish between strangers and familiars

305

and different facial expressions, expresses his feelings vocally, but he is now a person capable of responding in feeling and activity to other people as persons. He is an active agent, with definite aims and activities, capable of feeling disappointment and failure, as well as sadness and joyful surprise. He not merely responds to what other people say and do, but actively seeks their attention and wants pleasurable stimulation from them.

Play. Experimentative play is noted first in the second month. It appears first at the breast.

Towards the end of the second month, the infant ceases to feed steadily on, and changes his attitude. He will drop the nipple and gaze at his mother's face with a smile or a laugh. If she looks at him, he may bury his face in her breast and gurgle. And from ten weeks onwards, he will drop the nipple, suddenly, fling back his head and arch his back, and chatter and coo and gurgle. A week later, he may begin to put up a hand and touch or caress the breast or garments, whilst gazing at his mother. From this age, a slight sound or movement from another person nearby may cause the infant to stop suckling and look around and play. This early play at the breast may prove a hindrance to the suckling. It persists until about the 16th week, when it tends to lessen, at a time when manipulative play with physical objects (rattle, ring, etc. – and his own fingers) is rapidly developing, at times other than feeding.

Furthermore, in Lewis's important study of infant speech, he made full phonetic records of all the utterances of the child up to the full mastery of speech, noting the emotional setting and the actual situation in which each utterance was made. He has shown how the infant's first babbling impulses take origin in the sounds expressive of his feelings in the feeding situation, both those indicating satisfaction and comfort, and those expressing frustration and anger. By spontaneously re-uttering these sounds together, in the repetitive chains of babbling and lalling (from 3 months onwards), the infant turns them into a source of pleasure, masters aggression and anxiety, and creates the first rudimentary art-form (Lewis 1936).

In both the manipulative and the linguistic play of the first half-year, thus, we see at work the mastering of anxiety and aggression by libidinization, by the spreading out of pleasure from the oral nucleus of primary satisfaction.

Moreover, we can discern the first phases of symbol-formation, to the importance of which in the development of the ego Melanie Klein has drawn our attention. In the play of the infant with his own fingers and toes and limbs and mouth, from at least the third month onwards, we see his pleasure and interest in his own body. This pleasure and interest are gradually extended, during the middle part of the year, to experimentative play with objects, which at first, and for some time, are enjoyed mainly as symbols for bodily parts and satisfaction. Later on, as we know, they develop an interest in their own right as parts of external reality. It is in the play of the middle months of this year that we can see most clearly at work the first transition from intense pleasure in his own body to interest in external objects as such.

SIX TO TWELVE MONTHS

Each successive month brings rapid development in perception, skill, memory, and imagination.

At 7 months the infant will actively seek by cooing, etc., to make any grown-up standing near look at him. He will look about searchingly for any toy accidentally lost.

At 8 months he will exercise some effort to take a toy away from a grown-up, and will play a hide and seek game with a handkerchief, watching with interest for the re-appearance of a hidden face, and greeting it with a smile or chuckles. He will show joyful surprise at the return of a familiar adult after the absence of one or more days.

At 9 months, he will pull the garment of any grown-up standing near, to get his attention; and will uncover a toy hidden under a cloth. He may show clear signs of jealousy if a grown-up approaches another child. And may tease another child by offering a toy and removing it again several times.

At 12 months, he is capable of remembering the contents of a box after one minute's interval, showing surprise if the box be now empty and feeling round for the missing object. He will open boxes and use a string to pull an object towards himself. He can reach for a toy hidden behind a screen. He will now deliberately repeat any movement of his own which the grown-ups have laughed at, in order to make them laugh again.

As regards speech, from 7 or 8 months on, the child is beginning to comprehend, not only the intonational but also the phonetic form of many words. His own use of words commonly begins with Dada and Mama or their equivalent, on the average at 9 months; but in this period he also attempts to communicate with others and to exchange feelings and interest by means of an expressive gibberish which often reproduces the tone and melody and manner of adult conversation in the most surprising way. He can use two words besides 'dada' and 'mama', at 12 months.

In many ways, he shows that he has become intensely aware of the disappearance or loss of loved persons, as well as of favourite playthings. And there must be also noted the occasional presence of night-terrors, fear of being left alone, habits such as thumb-sucking, masturbation, hair-pulling, head- and body-rolling and knocking, face scratching, and other habits.

Play. The typical play of children in this second half of the first year includes a great variety of manipulative movements. These can be characterized in three groups:

1 Manipulation of the mother's person: Pulling her hair (which Shirley says is as typical of the 6-months baby as play with his own toes); then, during the next two months, 'random hair-pulling gives way to exploration of the parents' features. The baby pokes his fingers into eyes and nostrils, tries to pry open closed lips and eyelids, fingers, teeth and snatches off spectacles' (Shirley 1933:57).

2 Play with objects: Putting one thing inside another, e.g., poking the finger into the hole of a bead, digging nails into soap, putting finger or hand into a can, dropping a brick into a cup and tipping it out, putting pegs into holes, one brick on top of another, peering through holes in objects, playing hide and seek and peek-a-boo games.

3 All manner of reaching and pulling and pushing, letting things go and grasping them again, pounding, tearing, throwing, opening boxes and drawers. These could be characterized as movements which give him power over external objects.

The details of the child's development in this second half-year, his behaviour to other persons and to objects in his play, together with the level of integration in perception, memory, and expectation appear to justify the view that he now has explicit phantasies, and that these phantasies are already more than mere feeling and sensation. (See the discussion of phantasy above.) The element of feeling must still far outweigh any ideation; his own actual movements and sensations must still dominate the mental picture. But from six months onwards, it seems more than likely that the child is beginning to make use of memory images and expectations of every kind. By the time he can look for lost or hidden objects and persons and can show surprise and disappointment, whether at external happenings or his own failures, it seems probable that images of memory and of anticipation are becoming definite. These can now serve as the vehicle of 'meaning', at the behest of desire and fear. Now, not merely perceived shapes and sounds and movements and contacts, but also remembered and imagined ones, can express wishes and dreads, can represent actions and the results of actions, can take over and elaborate in a primitive way the implicit assumptions of mere feeling.

Moreover, the degree of integration in his perception and memory of persons makes it probable that he is now becoming alive to his own conflict of feelings; he is becoming in some degree aware of love and hate, dependence, desire, and fear, surging in him simultaneously towards one and the same person. Each further month of development naturally makes this hypothesis more trustworthy. But it seems possible to discern the beginnings of this awareness of conflict already at 5 months, when the child first shows his hostility to strange people, and an intense attachment to his loved ones. We cannot prove, but it seems probable that, in the frowns and stony looks which he now gives to strangers, he is already splitting his ambivalence towards his mother and displacing his hostility on to the strangers.

Melanie Klein's views as to the early phantasy life of the infant, and concept of the 'depressive position' take full account of all these facts. The concept of the depressive position was based upon these facts, as she came to understand them through her work in the analysis of children of two to three years of age.

You remember Freud's observations on the play of the boy of 18 months.[24] To my mind, Freud showed his greatness no less in thus teaching us to look at the child's play than in his discovery of infantile sexuality. He showed us, for the first time, how to understand what the child does in his play at an age when he has no words, but only expressive sounds and gestures. He taught us that if we pay attention to the context of an instance of play, the context of his general behaviour and his feelings towards people even at this age, we can learn much of its meaning to the child, and discover the mechanisms (I would say, also the phantasies) at work.

With regard to the details of the child's play in the first year, if we consider it in its context and use the insight gained from the analysis of two-year-olds, it seems possible to discern much of its implicit meaning. For example, it seems likely that, because of his dependence and desire, his love and his hate, the child wishes to control the comings and goings of the grown-ups and their behaviour towards him. And he wishes to control his own feelings, so as not to lose the grown-ups and their love. When he can control persons directly, by his cries, his touch and movements, he does so. When he cannot do so, he vents his wishes and works out his phantasies with parts of his own body and with his playthings. He separates and hides things, knocks things down and bangs and breaks and destroys, he gets pleasure from sucking and handling and reaching and mastering, at his own sweet will. He puts together again things which have been separated, finds what has been lost. In the symbolic language of his play, he restores the nipple to his mouth, brings back the lost mother, sends her away again at his own bidding, attacks and hurts her when she angers him, proves that she cannot deprive him of pleasure. He separates her from father and puts them together again as we have come to understand through early analysis. But to understand in detail what any infant is doing in his play, we need to watch his feelings and his relations with actual people – in fact, the whole *context* of his play.

THE SECOND YEAR OF LIFE

I do not need to go into any detail as regards the child's development in this year. I shall presently consider some actual examples of play in this period.

In general, the material at our disposal for the study of the inner psychic life is very rich and varied. It can be summarized as follows:

(a) overt actions towards particular persons;

(b) gestures, tones, facial expressions, etc.;

(c) the psychological context in which both action and signs of feeling occur, such as previous behaviour and the responses of other people, the presence or absence of this or that person;

(d) the child's play in this or that context, and in its relations to his direct behaviour to other people and his previous experiences;

(e) emotional expressions of pleasure, desire, anger, anxiety, specific fears, grief, depression, etc.;

(f) his speech, and progress or lack of progress throughout the year. Above all, the expressions of anxiety in a particular context and before or after particular actions, and the inhibition of normal responses, offer an index to the presence and to the nature of phantasy. Finally, all these phenomena should be considered not only with regard to particular details, but also with regard to general trends, and the rate and direction of change.

A word with regard to speech: the average vocabulary is two words at one year, and any number of words from 40 to more than 1,200 with a wide variety of phrases and sentences, at two years. The average two-year-old will comment on pictures shown to him, will listen to stories and rhythmic phrases, will join in simple dramatic games, and will talk about his experiences so far as his limited vocabulary and sentence structure allow.

As regards the child in this, the second year, then, we can definitely say that objective studies show the child's perception, rudimentary logic, memory, anticipations, etc., together with the earliest instances of his make-believe play, to be such as to make entirely plausible the view that he has definite and explicit phantasies, highly elaborated and active. And a detailed examination of all the evidence, together with what we have learned from analytic work with children in the succeeding year and later, enables us to infer much of their character with a high degree of certainty.

But we do not have to depend only upon general considerations. We can gather direct evidence from children that a particular phantasy may dominate the child's mind long before it can be put into words.

Examples of Play

Here is one striking example. A little girl of one year 6 months saw a shoe of her mother's from which the sole had come loose and was flapping about. The child was horrified and screamed with terror. For about a week she would shrink away and scream if she saw her mother wearing any shoes at all, other than a familiar pair of soft bedroom slippers. The offending pair was not worn again for several months. The child gradually forgot about her terror and let her mother wear any sort of shoes. At two years and 11 months (15 months later), she suddenly said in a frightened voice to her mother, 'Where are Mummy's broken shoes?' Her mother hastily said, fearing another screaming attack, that she had sent them away. The child then commented, 'They might have eaten me right up!'

The flapping shoe was thus seen by the child as a mouth, and reacted to as such, at 1 year and 8 months, even though the fear could not be named. Here, then, we have clear evidence that a phantasy can be felt and felt as real, long before it can be expressed in words. And does it not seem likely that in seeing her mother's shoe as a threatening biting mouth, the child was expressing her fear of a phantastic vengeful mother, who would bite her up in retaliation for her own biting impulses.

Or consider the following play in a girl of 16 months, one who talks very little. She has a favourite game, which she plays with father and mother. She picks small imaginary bits off a brown embossed leather screen in the dining-room, carries those bits carefully across the room in her finger and thumb, and puts them into the mouth of father and mother alternately. Could the child tell us any more plainly in words that she wants to feed her father and mother as they had fed her? But we can link two further facts. Of all possible objects in the room, various in colour and shape, she chooses this one, the brown screen

311

with small raised lumps on it – to feed her parents with. Is it not likely that this is connected with the fact that the child was found several times during the previous few months (between 12 and 18 months) to have defecated in her cot, smeared herself and put the faeces into her mouth? Is she not, in giving imaginary bits of the brown screen to her parents, trying to overcome the anxieties which her smearing and eating of faeces – and the reproaches of her parents – had aroused in her? Trying to prove that faeces were good and that her parents could eat them too?

Here is another example from a little girl of the same age. From the time, at about one year, when this child was put on to solid food (she had been breast-fed to 6–7 months and then had a bottle), she refused to take her food at all, and screamed in protest unless she was allowed to have on her tray two or three spoons, which she could hand to her mother between the spoonfuls of food which she took. She thus alternated taking food herself with the giving of imaginary food to her mother, and showed by her screams and inability to eat if not allowed to do this, how important it was to her.

Now when this child was some months younger, she had been faced with her first serious loss. When she was 7 months old and on the bottle, her very devoted mother left her for the first time. She went away for the day, leaving her bottle feeds prepared and in the charge of a friend whom the infant knew well and appeared to trust. However, when the child found the mother was not there to feed her, she cried and screamed and obstinately refused to take her bottle. She starved herself all day, missing two feeds. Nor would she accept the food from her mother immediately after her return, but still turned away and determinedly refused the food. Not for three hours was she enough reassured and comforted by her mother's return to accept the food.

From what we know of the refusal of food in older children, it seems likely that the child's resentment and anger at her mother's absence had poisoned the food which had been left for her to take, and even when her mother returned, still distorted her perception of her. (Note the passage from Freud on this theme, quoted above.)

In her later play with the spoons, therefore, it seems likely that the child was overcoming the anxieties connected with her grief and anger at this earlier loss. Just as the boy described by Freud in *Beyond the Pleasure Principle* overcame his dread of loss and his pain and resentment and dependence by his repetitive play with the cotton reel.

My next example may also remind you of the play of the boy described by Freud:

A boy of 16–18 months had a favourite game of shooing imaginary ducks into the corner of the room, driving them from one corner to

312

another. He showed that they were ducks by saying 'Quack quack', although his language was ill-developed and he said nothing else in this game. His facial expression and absorbed manner showed how vividly he saw the ducks, and he could not have behaved more dramatically had they been present. At the time the child was subject to night terrors, and often wakened screaming in the night. Not until he was just over two years, months after this imaginary play with the ducks, could he put the content of his nightmare into words. Then he said, 'White rabbit biting my toes.'

But from the time this boy had been weaned at 7 months, he had turned against milk altogether, obstinately refusing to touch it – and he did not do so for years afterwards. Now you will note that the 'rabbit' which bit his toes in his nightmare was white. It is hard to resist the conclusions (a) that the 'white rabbit' represented (in part, at least) his mother's breast, which he feared would bite him as he had bitten it (in wish or fact) when it frustrated him. (One is reminded of the boy described by Dr Ernest Jones who said of his mother's nipple when she was feeding a younger child, 'That's what you bit me with'.) And (b) that the dread of the biting breast had been the main content of his nightmares in the early part of his second year. And (c) that in his imaginary play with the ducks (also white creatures, and having large prominent mouths), he was trying to overcome his fear of the biting retaliatory breast.

Summary and list of references[25]

1 The *concept of phantasy* has been gradually widened in psychoanalytical thought. It now requires further expansion and clarification, if it is to integrate all the relevant facts.

2 On the views here developed:

(a) Phantasies are mainly *unconscious*, the primary content of unconscious mental processes.

(b) Phantasy is *psychic reality*, the mental representative and corollary of instinctual urges, which cannot operate in the mind without phantasy.

(c) Freud's postulated *'hallucinatory wish-fulfilment'* and his *'primary introjection'* are the basis of the phantasy life.

(d) Phantasy is the *subjective interpretation of experience*.

(e) Phantasies early become elaborated into *defences*, as well as wish-fulfilments.

(f) Phantasies express the *specific content* and show the specific direction and purpose of an urge or a feeling or a defence.

313

(g) Phantasies exert an *uninterrupted and omnipresent* influence throughout life, both in normal and neurotic people.

(h) Individual and age differences lie in the *mode of elaboration* and expression of the phantasies.

3 The related evidence is of four sorts:

A Considerations regarding the *relationships between established facts and theories.*

B *Observational studies* of the behaviour and development of the infant and young child.

C Clinical studies (case material) from the analysis of young children.

D Confirmatory evidence from the analysis of adults.

4 In my argument *under 'A'* I emphasized Freud's view of the unconscious as psychic reality being one important aspect of phantasy as I conceive it. I adduced his view that the Ucs is 'living and capable of development', and operates in normal as well as neurotic people; and his opinion that words belong to the Pcs only, whilst Ucs phantasy is independent of words. I considered Freud's postulates of 'hallucinatory wish-fulfilment' and 'primary introjection' and showed how many of his comments upon examples of the behaviour of the infant and young child appear to *imply* phantasies.

I then referred to the divergent views of analysts represented and summarized by Wälder, and I discussed recent statements about the young child by Anna Freud which, in my view, approximate to Melanie Klein's position in certain respects. I referred to the changes in our view of *regression* which greater understanding of the early defence mechanisms brings about, and quoted relevant passages from Freud.

Finally, *under 'B'*, I adduced some of the relevant facts of behaviour in the first two years, the details of which support and exemplify these conclusions, and I emphasized the fact of *genetic continuity* in development.

[Editor's note: This paper was taken 'as read' for the first Special Scientific Discussion of Controversial Issues, held on January 27th 1943, and Susan Isaacs opened the discussion of her paper as follows.]

Discussion held on January 27th, 1943

Commentary by Mrs S. Isaacs

Preliminary to discussion of her paper.

I do not propose to take up all the time allowed to me, but wish to make some corrections, and to add to and amplify certain parts of my paper.

314

More general points

1 It will have been noted that in this paper I have not attempted to deal either (a) with the phenomenon of repression; or (b) with conscious fantasy, and its links with Ucs phantasy. These links require to be made in detail, both in considering theory and in carrying out our practical work. But they fell outside the immediate scope of this paper.

2 I am dissatisfied with two of the passages in which I discuss Dr Brierley's views.

[First], concerning the 'academic psychologists' [see pp. 273–5]; this passage is far too condensed, certain important steps in the argument being elided. The academic psychologists do not, of course, say all that I seem to be attributing to them. They do bring out the genetic relationship between sensorial, perceptual experience and abstract thinking, between practical and verbal logic.

Spearman, for instance, has shown us that the essential act of cognition lies in the 'seeing' or educing either of relations or of their correlates, upon the basis of the direct apprehension of experience. The recognition of the relations of shapes and sizes and qualities and intensities in perception, and the adjustment of movement to a situation in practical skill, involve these 'neogenetic principles', no less than mathematical reasoning, the creation or appreciation of a symphony, or the framing and verification of a theory. Spearman says: 'Not a cognitive operation can be performed, from the loftiest flight of genius down to the prattle in the nursery, but that it resolves itself wholly into these principles with their ensuing processes. And all this is no less true of the so-called "practical" doings, which common opinion naïvely supposes to constitute some separate domain.'

Spearman has also reminded us how often there is a continual transition from mere perception to 'what deserves to be called thought', as for instance when, in trying to solve a maze test, 'a person is faced with lines, turns, gaps, blind alleys and the like, that present unlimitedly entangled relations for him to unravel. He may perhaps tell you he is looking how to get in; but he is almost as likely to say he is thinking how to do so' (Spearman 1923:353).

Now *we*, the psychoanalysts, take the further step from this position, and recognize the genetic continuity between the earliest feeling-relationships of the infant and his later thought-processes, between those phantasies which never become expressed in words and thus conscious or suffer repression, and those which do receive conscious and verbal elaboration. There are many important

315

differences between the beginnings and the end-states; but the common elements and the continuity of development are as significant as these differences, for the full understanding of mental life.

Again, I am discontented with the last paragraph on pages [275–6] which is also far too condensed, too cut-and-dried. The child may behave in a chaotic way and feel that his mental life is split and disintegrated, because he believes he *has* dismembered his mother. He may also behave in this way as a defence against knowing his hate of his mother and his wish to dismember her, to warn her and save *her* from his destructive impulses, or to save *himself* from unbearable feelings of sorrow and grief.

3 With regard to the problem of *regression*: I have only touched upon these issues, which need much fuller and more detailed treatment. I wish to correct my statement that the phenomena of regression can now be looked upon as 'less important'; on consideration, I do not regard that as true. But this is in any case not the point. What happens is that with our greater knowledge of early mental life, regression is seen to act *differently*, in specific ways which can be ascertained both in general and with each particular patient.

I should like to amplify what I have said about this topic, and go into the whole matter, in a further paper in this series of discussions – if that proved acceptable to members.

4 Finally, I wish to add some comments to what I have said in my paper about Anna Freud's views as these are represented in the recent Report by her and Mrs Burlingham. (I apologize to Mrs Burlingham for not having quoted her name in my paper.)

I do not rely only upon the particular passages quoted from the Report, when I suggest that Anna Freud's position seems to have changed from that expressed in her earlier writings, but rather upon the general impression which the whole Report makes upon the reader. This report should be read by everyone interested, and attention should be paid to what is said about the infant in the first six months of life, as well as other passages regarding the second six months. When sending round the *errata* for my paper, I took the opportunity of adding a further quotation from the Report, which in my view is significant for the present issue: 'and of "its inner relationship to her" '.

What I feel is that if a disinterested and intelligent reader, who knew nothing of the controversies within our Society, were to peruse both Melanie Klein's book and recent papers, and this Report by Anna Freud and Mrs Burlingham, it would never occur to such a reader that there were or could be such deep and *radical* differences of underlying

316

theory and view of the child's inner life and development, as is being claimed. I should be extremely interested to hear from Anna Freud whether she does feel that there still are such deep and radical differences, and how these are reconciled with her views in the Report.

Notes

1   This time once again it has been my chief aim to make no sacrifice to an appearance of being simple, complete or rounded-off, not to disguise problems and not to deny the existence of gaps and uncertainties. In no other field of scientific work would it be necessary to boast of such modest intentions. They are universally regarded as self-evident; the public expects nothing else. No reader of an account of astronomy will feel disappointed and contemptuous of the science if he is shown the frontiers at which our knowledge of the Universe melts into haziness. Only in psychology is it otherwise. There mankind's constitutional unfitness for scientific research comes fully into the open. What people seem to demand of psychology is not progress in knowledge, but satisfactions of some other sort; every unsolved problem, every admitted uncertainty is made into a reproach against it. Whoever cares for the science of mental life, must accept these injustices along with it.
[SE 22:6]

2 'It is essential to abandon the over-valuation of the property of being conscious before it becomes possible to form any correct view of the origin of what is mental.' [SE 5:612]

3   It will be a long time before we can take in our proposal that we should equate phantasy and reality and not bother to begin with whether the childhood experiences under examination are the one or the other. Yet this is clearly the only correct attitude to adopt towards these mental productions. The phantasies possess psychical as contrasted with material reality and we gradually learn to understand that in the world of the neuroses it is the psychical reality which is the decisive kind.
[SE 15:308]

4   The strangest *characteristic of unconscious (repressed) processes*, to which no investigator can become accustomed without the exercise of great self-discipline, is due to their *entire disregard of reality testing: they equate reality of thought with external actuality*, and wishes with their fulfilment – with the event – just as happens automatically under the dominance of the pleasure principle. *Hence also the difficulty of distinguishing* unconscious phantasies from memories *which have become unconscious*. But one must never allow oneself to be misled into applying the

317

standards of reality to repressed physical structures, and on that account, perhaps, into under-valuing the importance of phantasies in the formation of symptoms on the ground that they are not actualities, or into tracing a neurotic sense of guilt back to some other source because there is no evidence that any actual crime has been committed.

[SE 12:225]

5   Among the derivatives of the Ucs instinctual impulses, of the sort we have described, there are some which unite in themselves characters of an opposite kind. On the one hand, they are highly organized, free from self-contradiction, have made use of every acquisition of the system Cs, and would hardly be distinguished in our judgement from the formations of that system. On the other hand they are unconscious and are incapable of becoming conscious. Thus qualitatively they belong to the system Pcs, but factually to the Ucs. Their origin is what decides their fate. We may compare them with individuals of mixed race who, taken all round, resemble white men, but who betray their coloured descent by some striking feature or other, and on that account are excluded from society and enjoy none of the privileges of white people. Of such a nature are those phantasies of normal people as well as of neurotics which we have recognized as preliminary stages in the formation both of dreams and of symptoms and which, in spite of their degree of organization, remain repressed and therefore cannot become conscious.   [SE 14:190–1]

6   It would nevertheless be wrong to imagine that the Ucs remains at rest while the whole work of the mind is performed by the Pcs – that the Ucs is something finished with, a vestigial organ, a residuum from the process of development. It is wrong also to suppose that communication between the two systems is confined to the act of repression, with the Pcs casting everything that seems disturbing to it into the abyss of the Ucs. On the contrary, the Ucs is alive and capable of development and maintains a number of other relations with the Pcs, amongst them that of co-operation. In brief, it must be said that the Ucs is continued into what are known as derivatives, that it is accessible to the impressions of life, that it constantly influences the Pcs, and is even, for its part, subjected to influences from the Pcs.   [SE 14:190]

7 'The more we seek to win our way to a metapsychological view of mental life, the more we must learn to emancipate ourselves from the importance of the symptom of "being conscious".' (SE 14:193)

8 The paper Isaacs was referring to was later rewritten, and constitutes the substantial part of the third chapter – 'Problems connected with the work of Melanie Klein' – of Brierley's book *Trends in Psycho-Analysis*, The Hogarth Press and the Institute of Psycho-Analysis, London, 1951, pp. 57–89.

9 Isaacs is probably referring to S. H. Fuchs' paper 'On Introjections' in the *International Journal of Psycho-Analysis*, 18 (1937): 269–93. For Brierley and Klein, the references can be found in many papers of their collected works.

10 '*Everything conscious has an unconscious preliminary stage.*' [SE 5:612]

11 'We picture it as being open at its end to somatic influences, and as there taking up into itself instinctual needs which find their psychical expression in it.' [SE 22:73]

12 'Whatever was thought of (wished for) was simply presented in a hallucinatory manner, just as still happens to-day with our dream-thoughts every night. It was only the non-occurrence of the expected satisfaction, the disappointment experienced, that led to the abandonment of this attempt at satisfaction by means of hallucination.' [SE 12:219]

13　In so far as the ego is auto-erotic, it has no need of the external world, but, in consequence of experiences undergone by the instincts of self-preservation, it acquires objects from the world, and, in spite of everything, it cannot avoid feeling internal stimuli for a time as unpleasurable. Under the dominance of the pleasure principle a further development now takes place in the ego. In so far as the objects which are presented to it are sources of pleasure, it takes them into itself, 'introjects' them (to use Ferenczi's (1909) term); and, on the other hand, it expels whatever within itself becomes a cause of unpleasure. . . . Love is derived from the capacity of the ego to satisfy some of its instinctual impulses auto-erotically by obtaining organ-pleasure. It is originally narcissistic, then passes over on to objects, which have been incorporated into the extended ego, and expresses the motor efforts of the ego towards these objects as sources of pleasure.

Preliminary stages of love emerge as provisional sexual aims while the sexual instincts are passing through their complicated development. As the first of these aims we recognize the phase of incorporating or devouring – a type of love which is consistent with abolishing the object's separate existence. 　[SE 14:135–6, 138–9]

14　The situation of the infant when it is presented with a stranger instead of its mother. It will exhibit the anxiety which we have attributed to the danger of loss of object. But its anxiety is undoubtedly more complicated than this and merits a more thorough discussion. That it does have anxiety there can be no doubt; but the expression of its face and its reaction of crying indicate that it is feeling pain as well. Certain things seem to be joined together in it which will later on be separated out. It cannot as yet distinguish between temporary absence and permanent loss. As soon as it loses sight of its mother it behaves as if it were never going to see her again; and repeated consoling experiences to the contrary are necessary before it learns that her disappearance is usually followed by her re-appearance. [SE 20:169]

15 'In consequence of the infant's misunderstanding of the facts, the situation of the missing mother is not a danger-situation but a traumatic one.' [SE 20:170]

16 It seems, rather, that the child's avidity for its earliest nourishment is altogether insatiable, that it never gets over the pain of losing its mother's breast. . . . The fear of being poisoned is also probably connected with the withdrawal of the breast. Poison is nourishment that makes one ill. Perhaps children trace back their early illnesses too to this frustration. [SE 20:170]

17 It is a remarkable fact that a child, even with an age difference of only 11 months, is not too young to take notice of what is happening. But what the child grudges the unwanted intruder and rival is not only the suckling but all the other signs of maternal care. It feels that it has been dethroned, despoiled, prejudiced in its rights; it casts a jealous hatred upon the new baby and develops a grievance against the faithless mother which often finds expression in a disagreeable change in its behaviour. It becomes 'naughty', perhaps, irritable and disobedient and goes back on the advances it has made towards controlling its excretions. [SE 22:123]

18 The very surprising sexual activity of little girls in relation to their mother is manifested chronologically in oral, sadistic, and finally even in phallic trends directed towards her. It is difficult to give a detailed account of these because they are often obscure instinctual impulses which it was impossible for the child to grasp psychically at the time of their occurrence, which were therefore only interpreted by her later, and which then appear in the analysis in forms of expression that were certainly not the original ones. Sometimes we come across them as transferences on to the later, father-object, where they do not belong and where they seriously interfere with our understanding of the situation. We find the little girl's aggressive oral and sadistic wishes in a form forced on them by early repression, as a fear of being killed by the mother – a fear which, in turn, justifies her death-wish against her mother, if that becomes conscious. [SE 21:237]

19 We now seem to know all at once what the difference is between a conscious and an unconscious presentation. . . . The two are not, as we supposed, different registrations of the same content in different psychical localities, nor yet different functional states of cathexis in the same locality; but the conscious presentation comprises the presentation of the thing plus the presentation of the word belonging to it, while the unconscious presentation is the presentation of the thing alone. The system Ucs contains the thing-cathexes of the object, the

first and true object-cathexes; the system Pcs comes about by this thing-presentation being hypercathected through being linked with the word-presentations corresponding to it. It is these hypercathexes, we may suppose, that bring about a higher psychical organization and make it possible for the primary process to be succeeded by the secondary process which is dominant in the Pcs. [SE 14:202]

20 'The hate which is admixed with the love is in part derived from the preliminary stages of loving which have not been wholly surmounted.' [SE 14:139]

21 Some writers are inclined to reduce the importance of the child's first and most original libidinal impulses in favour of later developmental processes, so that – to put this view in its most extreme form – the only role left to the former is merely to indicate certain paths, while the (psychical) intensities which flow along those paths are supplied by later regressions and reaction-formations. This does not tally with my impression. Certain as is the occurrence of later reinforcements through regression and reaction-formation, and difficult as it is to estimate the relative strength of the confluent libidinal components, I nevertheless think that we should not overlook the fact that the first libidinal impulses have an intensity of their own which is superior to any that come later and which may indeed be termed incommensurable. [SE 21:242–3]

22 The papers were never published as such. But many of their themes can be found in Isaacs' book *Childhood and After*, London: Routledge & Kegan Paul, 1948.

23 It should be noted that Bühler's observations were made with children entering an institution. Her data certainly show an underestimation of positive feelings in the second and third months. The *direction* of change is confirmed by other observers, but the *degree* to which negative feelings predominate is exaggerated.

24 Isaacs is referring to the famous example concerning the 'o-o-o-oh' and 'da' play of the child described in chapter II of Freud's *Beyond the Pleasure Principle* (SE 18:15).

25 These references are included in the main bibliography.

3

First
Discussion of Scientific Controversies

**Discussion held on January 27th, 1943, on Mrs Susan Isaacs'
paper 'The Nature and Function of Phantasy'**

DR JONES (Paper, read in Dr Jones's absence by Dr Glover): Mrs
Isaacs has evidently first sought for a basis of agreed conclusions
from which to explore later the more difficult matters of divergences, and, although no doubt scope may always be found for
controversy, particularly when the further implications of her
statements are considered, she has in my opinion succeeded
admirably in establishing as nearly a non-controversial basis for her
purpose as possible. The stress she lays in her first few pages on the
apprehension of psychical reality, and the debt we here owe to
Freud, is quite fundamental. I would say that the hall-mark of
psychoanalysts is their feeling for unconscious psychical reality, and I
agree with her remark that even among psychoanalysts this feeling is
often not so highly developed as it might be – despite vocal assertions
to the contrary. What distinguishes other people is their use of the
words 'only' or 'merely', as doctors so commonly do when referring
to neurosis, the imagination, etc.

Her main thesis is the extension of the terms of reference attaching
to the word 'phantasy'. The cry may be raised that she has changed
the meaning of a familiar word, but I do not think so. I am reminded
of a similar situation years ago with the word 'sexuality'. The critics
complained that Freud was changing the meaning of this word, and
Freud himself once or twice seemed to assent to this way of putting
it, but I always protested that he made no change in the meaning of
the word itself; what he did was to extend the conception and, by

322

giving it a fuller content, to make it more comprehensive. This process would seem to be inevitable in psychoanalytical work, since many conceptions, e.g., that of conscience, which were previously known only in their conscious sense, must be widened when we add to this their unconscious significance. Mrs Isaacs' procedure is therefore fully justified in the light of psychoanalytical development. I agree with her further that merely to change the word or invent a new one, as the critics urged Freud to do in the case of the word 'sexual', would not make matters different. Such a dubious procedure might smack of evasion, since what matters is whether the processes we all understand under the word 'phantasy' do really occur in the form she maintains or not; if this essential point is settled, the name is of no consequence.

Coming now to the content of the work, we may summarize Mrs Isaacs' main thesis in the statement (a) that no instinctual urge can operate in the mind without phantasy, (b) that by 'phantasy' we indicate a meaningful interpretation of what is being experienced, and (c) that phantasy arises only from somatic excitation, whether this be external (e.g. sensory stimulation), internal (e.g. instinctual needs) or, more usually, both. Her quotation from Freud ('the mental expression of instinctual needs') is illuminating on this last point. I should, however, differ somewhat from Mrs Isaacs' formulation where she distinguishes wish-fulfilment from defence phantasies, but perhaps she would be willing to re-formulate her statement. Although the distinction is convenient for various didactic purposes, I should have thought it not valid in theory, since the defence phantasies, even denials, must be equally with the others' fulfilments of wishes and also derived from instinctual needs. Otherwise I have nothing to add to her thesis, with which I am in complete agreement.

So far all this would seem, as Mrs Isaacs has shown by numerous examples, to be in full accord with Freud's essential teaching, even though he often uses the phrase 'hallucinatory wish-fulfilment' where we are nowadays more accustomed to speak of phantasy; I can see no real difference between the two phrases. Behind it, however, lies a difference of opinion which becomes manifest with the word 'regression'. It is not at first sight easy to discern the nature of the trouble over this quarrel-provoking word. I have always regarded the matter as simply one of a reciprocally complemental series. If, for example, we compare a phantasy or reaction after puberty with a corresponding one between the ages of, say, three and five, then we may surely say that either may reinforce the other. The continued unconscious operation of the earlier one may strengthen the later one, while contrariwise an emotional event at the later age may through regression reanimate and reinvest an earlier attitude. What proportion of the final cathexis is derived from the earlier and what from the later source has nothing to do with a prior theory, but is to be determined by investigation of each particular case. On the whole experience definitely confirms Freud's emphatic statement, quoted by Mrs Isaacs, that the earlier impulses have an intensity greater than anything that comes later and incommensurable with any other. To the pre-Freudian world the situation of course appeared otherwise, since they knew nothing about the existence of the earlier impulses which Freud revealed. The reason why the matter is to us a commonplace is just because we are familiar with the existence of these earlier ones, and it is this fact that gives the clue to the nature of the present difficulty. For myself I cannot make sense of the whole conception of regression except in so far as we have reason to think that there is something to which the regression takes place. A regression backwards into the blue has no meaning for me. Thus when Wälder talks of extraordinary cannibalistic phantasies being familiar at the age of three or four, but ascribes them to regression, this conveys nothing at all to me if it does not mean a reanimating of corresponding oral phantasies at the age of, say, six months; why a child of four should suddenly be seized for the first time with the desire to eat breasts passes my comprehension. The presence of such phantasies in older subjects had long ago led me to deduce the actual existence of them in young infants, and this inference has in my opinion been amply confirmed by the analysis of them carried out by Mrs Klein and others as well as by the observational data to which Mrs Isaacs has often drawn our attention. In saying this I am naturally not prejudging the numerous obscure problems concerning the precise nature and variety of such phantasies, their relative importance, nor the fitting-in of them into our theoretical scheme: there will be much to say about all such matters once their existence is granted.

In short, both the widening of the conception of phantasy and the dispute about regression lead one to the central problem of whether phantasy does or does not occur in the first year of life. Clearly no a priori arguments, such as Wälder uses, can settle the question. It is a matter, as elsewhere in science, of inference from the data. I would suggest that the most profitable form the discussion can take would be to concentrate on two or three examples, either analytical or observational, and compare alternative explanations of them with the aim of ascertaining which of these most closely and comprehensively covers the facts.

DR GLOVER: The arguments of Mrs Isaacs' paper are based on three assumptions all of which are, in my opinion, unsound.

First of all she suggests that the issue we are about to discuss is between two *developments* of Freudian teaching, in other words that the issue does *not* lie between Mrs Klein's views and the accepted teachings of Freud. Secondly, the endeavours to prove that the views of Freud himself and of many Freudians who have at different times questioned the validity of Kleinian hypotheses really go to support Mrs Klein's theories. Thirdly, she believes that Mrs Klein's views are based on facts and on theories necessary to explain facts, hence that they are in any case right.

As to the first points, I have already read a short paper supporting my view that the present issue lies between Mrs Klein's teachings and the body of accepted Freudian teaching. As to the second, I maintain that Mrs Isaacs' method of quotation from Freud and other writers does not conform to scientific requirements, in particular that the quotations are given without the necessary context which in many cases would show that they do not support Mrs Isaacs' contentions. As to the third assumption, viz., the validity of Mrs Klein's theories and interpretations, this, I maintain, is just what we are here to discuss. To discuss it effectively we must decide how much of Mrs Isaacs' argument is based on facts and how much on her own (that is to say Mrs Klein's) favoured interpretations of unconscious content. Moreover Mrs Isaacs believes that no analyst who has not analysed children of 2–3 years by strictly analytical procedures (by which, I take it, she means the special interpretative technique employed by Mrs Klein and her followers) is in a favourable position to estimate the behaviouristic and analytical evidence, implying that most members of this Society have no very good claim to speak with authority on the early developments of mind. If this be true there is little point in continuing the present series of discussions.

Examining her paper in greater detail it becomes clear that Mrs Isaacs' main concern is to build up a new metapsychology – one that will support her own theory of phantasy. Apparently she is ready to adopt the circular argument that this new set of theories is a proof of the validity of the interpretations on which the theories are based. Anyhow if Mrs Isaacs' new metapsychology is right, then Freud's metapsychology must be wrong, for the two are incompatible in a number of respects.

In my opinion Mrs Isaacs has failed in her attempt to build a new metapsychology. She has failed because she disregards, neglects or misunderstands precisely those parts of Freud's metapsychology which eliminate the very confusions into which she persistently falls. In particular she is addicted to a sort of psychic anthropomorphism, which most of Mrs Klein's adherents exhibit, namely of confusing concepts of the psychic apparatus with psychic mechanisms in active operation in the child's mind, or, again, of confusing both psychic concepts and functioning mechanisms with one of the psychic derivatives of instinctual stress, namely phantasy.

In place of Freud's orderly series of concepts, e.g. of a psychic apparatus dealing with instinctual excitation, controlling the approaches to motility and possessing a sensory receiver, of the organization of psychic systems on the basis of memory traces, the interaction between instinct derivatives (viz. affect and representations), sensory experiences, and presentations, speech and motility, of the origin of 'thing' and verbal cathexes, the building up of object imagos, the operation of the pleasure principle, the development of the reality principle from reality proving, the development of phantasy and reality thinking respectively, their relation to wish-fulfilment and reality proving, primacies of instinct, ego differentiations, fixations, and regressions. In place of these fruitful concepts Mrs Isaacs offers us an array of postulates some of which seem to be regarded by Mrs Isaacs as if they were axiomatic, some of which are simply interpretations – of the 'primary content of all mental processes', i.e., early phantasies that are the basis of all unconscious and conscious thought (a formulation which on some occasions means little more than that phantasies will be phantasies), or introjections 'felt', of unconscious phantasies experienced as mental disintegration, of the 'specific content of feeling', of the infant's taking feeling into or expelling it from itself, of the activity and intensity of early phantasies and their *uninterrupted influence* on development. And so on. I am tempted to single out one fundamental confusion: viz. where Mrs Isaacs, evidently over-looking Freud's concept of the regressive invasion of the sensory end of the psychic apparatus by blocked instinct excitations, regards the capacity to hallucinate as either identical with phantasy or the pre-condition for it (using the term 'phantasy' in her meaning, of course). Quite apart from the fact that one should not confuse hypothetical origins or even larval forms with organized (unconscious) phantasy proper (for, condensation apart, it is of the nature of phantasy that it consists of a relation between a subject, aim, and object of an instinct), this neglect of the significance of reality factors in the laying down of memory traces of sensory experience may accord for a common confusion apparent in Mrs Klein and her adherents' theories. They seem to confuse the relations

326

of psychic reality to phantasy and to reality proving respectively. The regression in oral hallucinatory gratification, e.g. activates the memory traces of the actual experiences at the sensory end of the apparatus. And reality proving is after all concerned with the relation of gratification or frustration of instincts to the external objects of these instincts, not with snapshots of the Himalaya Mountains.

But on this occasion I must content myself with pointing out a few of the Freudian concepts that have fallen by the wayside, e.g., the biological progression of an instinct series, the early formation of object images (the object image seems to have disappeared from this paper), fixation points, regression, the possibility of permanent withdrawal of cathexes from pre-Oedipal fixation systems and, last but not least, the theoretical and clinical significance of the Oedipus complex. For it must be clear that by her postulation of (1) a specific primary content of unconscious phantasy in the first years and (2) of their uninterrupted dynamic influence on later development and by what she calls 'change of emphasis' placed on regression, Mrs Isaacs has not only abandoned Freud's concepts of instinct development but committed herself to a sort of *primary enclave* in the Freudian Ucs. True, she does not describe the boundaries of this enclave as Freud described the repression barrier but it follows inevitably from her presentation that the relations of Freud's dynamic Ucs to the preconscious are no longer valid – for Mrs Isaacs – and that by her reasoning there exists a new dynamic Ucs system within the old dynamic Ucs of Freud.

I hope to return to this subject at greater length in a subsequent contribution but in the meantime it is only fair to Mrs Klein to add that Mrs Isaacs' metapsychology neither proves nor disproves the validity of Mrs Klein's interpretations. This is a central issue which remains to be discussed but it has not been discussed in Mrs Isaacs' paper. Should, however, Mrs Isaacs' metapsychology be accepted by Mrs Klein then I maintain that the compatibility of her ideas with accepted Freudian theory cannot be maintained. It is not possible to have it both ways.

MISS ANNA FREUD: To me a welcome aspect of Mrs Isaacs' paper is that it effectively narrows down our discussion to the subject of mental functioning in the first year of life. Some added clearness about divergence of opinion concerning this phase may save much fruitless argument concerning later stages of development.

Before entering into the subject matter itself, I must take general exception to two implications in the paper before us. The first is the following: On page [265], paragraph (c), Mrs Isaacs quotes from the

Preface to the 'New Introductory Lectures' in a way which suggests that the objections raised in this Society against Mrs Klein's views might be of the same unscientific nature as the arguments commonly used by outside critics against psychoanalysis. It seems to me important to nail down this point in the beginning. If, rightly or wrongly, we are unable to believe in the scientific nature of each other's arguments, we should have been wise not to enter at all into this series of discussions.

My second objection refers to the passage on Psychic Reality, pages [269] and [270]. Mrs Isaacs who, as agreed, gives prominence only to controversial points, would not have devoted so much space to this subject if she had not meant to show that controversy exists about 'the living character of the unconscious'. She gives the impression that only Mrs Klein's theories do full justice to the operative effect of the unconscious as demonstrated by Freud whereas we others have 'an inveterate prejudice in favour of the modes of external reality . . . and of conscious mental processes' and need to be reminded 'that unconscious phantasy is fully active in the normal no less than in the neurotic mind' [Isaacs p. 270]. I wish to emphasize that this is not a controversial point. Divergence of opinion does not exist between us about the operative effect of unconscious content but about the nature of such content.

As regards the aims of the series, as set out on page [216], (a), I cannot see that the conditions of the discussion provide any opportunities for establishing either the validity or the importance of any given views. I therefore concentrate on the point of com-patibility or incompatibility or, to put it in different words, I shall try to show, more clearly than has been done in the paper before us, what consequences the acceptance of Mrs Klein's views has for the theory of psychoanalysis as a whole. To me it seems one of the most bewildering points about these new theories that existing analytic conceptions are explicitly retained and at the same time implicitly denied by the new formulations.

Mrs Isaacs' paper offers a variety of possibilities for substantiating this criticism. To enumerate some of them:

(i) The new use of the term 'phantasy' – apart from other objections against it – does not simply add to and extend the reference which it already possesses. It also narrows it down from use for conscious as well as unconscious processes to use for the unconscious only and thereby alters our conception of conscious phantasy by widening the gulf between it and its unconscious basis and counterpart.

328

(ii) With the suggested new use of the term 'phantasy' early mental processes are grouped together under a common connotation irrespective of whether they are instinct derivatives or not. Hallucinatory expression is equally ascribed to all these processes, again irrespective of whether they are instinct derivatives or not. The singular nature of all instinctual processes in contrast to others as stressed in the libido theory is thereby obscured.

(iii) Phantasy as the imaginal corollary of instinct takes the place of the sensorial corollary (pleasure-pain) which, in Freud's view, was the main mental accompaniment of instinctual urges, their satisfaction or frustration. Not that in Mrs Isaacs' presentation these sensorial accompaniments play no part. But emphasis is shifted from the sensorial to the imaginal experience. When followed up, this cannot fail to influence the theories concerning the pleasure principle as the sole governing principle within the unconscious.

(iv) The nature of the unconscious phantasies described as existent in the first year of life completely alters the conception of unconscious life as such (see later).

(v) As concerns the new theory of regression Mrs Isaacs herself speaks of divergence of opinion. But I think that she underestimates the far-reaching consequences of her point of view, when followed to its logical end, for the theory of the neuroses. It shifts all emphasis from the later stages of development to the earliest ones, gives secondary importance only to the level on which the breakdown of the personality occurs, puts the concept of fixation-points out of action and, incidentally, gives rise to nearly all the existing differences of the technique of psychoanalytic treatment. This, of course, needs and, I hope, will find further elucidation.

Owing to the shortness of time I cannot, as I should wish, elaborate all these points, I shall leave them to others and concentrate on one of them only as a prototype and example. I choose the paragraph *Phantasy as the specific content of unconscious mental processes* – point (iv) of my above enumeration.

Under this heading Mrs Isaacs presents a picture of unconscious life which differs in rather important respects from our conception of the unconscious. This difference is not stated explicitly and in detail; quite on the contrary, a number of quotations from the 'Interpretation of Dreams', the 'Formulations regarding the two Principles of Mental Functioning', and other papers on metapsychology suggest that there are no essential differences. On page [276] for instance, Mrs Isaacs discusses, as a concept with which she fully agrees, the 'primary process' of mental life underlying, as she puts it, 'all our rational thinking' [Isaacs, p. 276]. But on closer view the 'primary process' as seen by Mrs Isaacs is not identical with our view of it. We hold that the primary process of mental functioning possesses various characteristics. There is in the unconscious mind governed by it no integration of impulses, no testing of reality, no negation, no conception of time; there is independent existence of all urges; disregard of mutual contradiction; there is displacement and condensation and the hallucinatory form of wish-fulfilment; gain of pleasure is the governing principle.

Of these characteristics Mrs Isaacs implicitly rejects as many as she retains. She, as we know, retains the concept of hallucinatory wish-fulfilment which becomes the basis of 'phantasy'. She also retains and specially stresses the entire disregard of the reality-test in the unconscious which is irrevocably bound up with hallucinatory wish-fulfilment. Displacement and condensation are implied in the descriptions of phantasy and also specially mentioned.

But whereas this important side of unconscious life remains common property of both theories, other qualities which in ours are indispensable complements, are changed in hers. There is, in Mrs Isaacs' description of the unconscious, no free and independent flow of instinctual urges. The integration of an 'early pleasure ego' occurs so soon that it is practically in existence from the beginning of life. Impulses enter into *conflict* with each other: the baby cannot feel rage against its mother without feeling its love for her threatened and, consequently, either heightened or diminished. Its *ambivalent* feelings cannot exist side by side but have to be projected outward in part. Feelings of guilt begin to influence the infant's mind in an enduring way. *Negation* exists, as shown for instance on page [302] (the mother who does *not* remove the pain). There even seems to be a sense of time, as indicated on page [280] in 'the phantasy of the mother's permanent absence' as opposed to our idea that no difference exists for the child between temporary and permanent, which is a very different matter.

It is not easy to see how the early pleasure ego can assume the functions of a central personality within the unconscious, but only the existence of such an active centre could account for the presence of the so-called early defence. Unconscious life, according to this paper, thus combines qualities of the primary with important characteristics of the secondary process.

These considerations lead to one of two alternative solutions:

(1) either the new theory, due to the assumption of earlier integration, finds no room for the primary process of functioning in the first year of life. This would cut out the identity of functioning at this stage with functioning in dreams and leave us at a loss where to look for the kind of uncorrelated mental life to which dream-function regresses;

(2) or the whole theoretical conception of the primary process is altered so as to include integration with its consequences. This again leaves dream-life unaccounted for.

As stated before, this is only one of several examples of incompatibility of theory with which I feel confronted in this discussion.

DR M. BRIERLEY: Mrs Isaacs' paper raises so many vital issues that I found it very difficult to choose a point or two for brief discussion. But I should like to begin with the definition of phantasy, though this calls for a paper in itself, because I do find the proposed expansion of the definition something of a stumbling-block.

The wholesale equation of subjective interpretation, meaning, and psychic content with phantasy seems to me to go beyond what is required by the facts. Not that I do not appreciate the cogency of Mrs Isaacs' arguments. For instance, I accept the principle of genetic continuity in mental life, our old friend the law of psychological determinism in modern dress. I can see that the expansion of the term 'phantasy' does simplify and clarify the relationship of later unconscious phantasy to archaic mental experience, but I am not sure it does not over-simplify at the cost of obscuring the genetic relationship of reality thinking to these same primitive experiences, and doing less than justice to the formative influences of the environment. This does not mean that I think pre-verbal phantasy improbable; on general grounds it would appear probable. I have not the experience necessary to check upon the direct evidence but have found nothing in work with adults that would rule it out. Indeed I can conceive that there may be philogenetic determinants at work in the baby's mind that would play a similar role to unconscious phantasy in the adult. But if we expand the concept phantasy to cover all primitive subjective experience, we must also extend it forwards and regard all adult thinking, not merely as developed from and continually influenced by, more primitive modes of thinking, but as itself a variety of phantasy. This would obscure a distinction that it is important to maintain. As thinking, it seems more useful to confine the term to one mode of mental activity, whether or not infantile mental activity may be more akin to what in the adult we call 'phantasy-thinking' than to adult reality-thinking.

It is quite true that western thought is prejudiced in favour of external reality. Oriental thought shows the opposite prejudice, that external reality is illusion. We must try to steer clear of both these extremes. The word 'phantasy' itself embodies the western prejudice against psychological reality but its proposed expansion nevertheless tends to tilt the balance to the oriental side. Hence, I should prefer a more neutral word, freer from implicit pre-judgement of the proper relationship between the facts.

Mrs Isaacs has indicated at least one better word without realizing it. She emphasizes that the distinguishing feature of psychological reality is that it has meaning. Thus, she says on page [272], 'The word "phantasy" serves to remind us always of this distinctive character of meaning in the mental life'. On page [282] she quotes a passage from Mrs Riviere saying first that 'From the very beginning there exists a core and foundation in experience for objectivity. . . .' And a little later 'That phantasy life is never pure phantasy'. But 'All phantasies are thus mixtures of external and internal reality'. Then why not use the word 'meaning' itself and say that the infant's experience has some meaning for it from the beginning derived from both internal and external reality sources? Meaning, however primitive, or however differentiated, is a synthesis of internal and external factors. It would then be possible to go forward without prejudice and consider the evidence as to the nature of infantile meaning.

There may be a better word than 'meaning'. All I can stress here is that meaning has the advantage over phantasy of not pre-judging the internal–external reality issue but puts the baby into a reciprocal relationship with its environment from the start. It assumes, what seems to me to fit the facts best, a common origin in primitive mental processes for both phantastic and realistic thinking. I am sure there is no such thing as 'pure phantasy' and equally sure there is no such thing as 'pure reality thinking'. But I am strongly of opinion that, if the infant's first hallucination is to be regarded as its first phantasy, it should also rank as its first memory.

The passages Mrs Isaacs quoted from my paper have been a good deal altered in the version now in the press because I was not at all satisfied with them myself. I am not an epiphenomenalist, but I am satisfied that it is very important to keep the description of experience as lived distinct from the description, inferred from experience, of the objective conditioning of experience. Thus, a mental event, as experience, has meaning and this meaning dictates behaviour. Objectively we think of the event as a mental process, initiating other processes. What is subjectively experienced as incorporation we infer to be objectively a mental process of introjection.

332

The ticker-tape must be a very bad metaphor because Mrs Isaacs read into it something quite different from my intended meaning. I was not concerned with the genetic relations of concepts, the fact that strictly speaking all words are concepts, or that thinking is an immediate experience of the thinker. I was concerned only with the satisfactory formulation of theory and the difference between theory and experience. The distinction between perceptual and conceptual modes of thinking remains valid. Theory is still, as Freud said, 'genuinely a question of hypotheses; that is to say, of the introduction of the right abstract-ideas' (Freud, S. 1933:107; SE 22:81).[1]

The right ideas are not easy to come by. Abstract thinking is a difficult and precarious activity. It is continually moulded, directed, and otherwise influenced by unconscious phantasies and preconceptions. Archaic habits of thought intrude at every turn. Nevertheless it is the only instrument we have for penetrating beyond the experience of living to the laws governing experience and so to its more adequate control. All theoretical formulations run the risk of degenerating into restatements of archaic beliefs. As the example of Jung shows, there is a narrow margin of safety between creating a new mythology and making a valid contribution to knowledge. Keeping one's footing is a matter of trial and error. But human narcissism is always looking for a habitation and has been chivvied out of one place after another. We must be very careful indeed that we do not allow it to find a last refuge in psychological reality or in the omnipotence of phantasy.

DR S. M. PAYNE: Mrs Isaacs' paper is a valuable contribution to the subject of the theory of phantasy and I should like to congratulate her on the way in which she has dealt with different aspects of the problems which arise both in connection with theories initiated by Freud and with subsequent developments arising out of Melanie Klein's work.

The purpose of these meetings is to give opportunity for free discussion of differences of opinion on these problems and it is obvious that we should concentrate our attention mainly on doubts, disagreements, and uncertainties. At the same time it strengthens the position of a critic if points of agreement are clearly stated also.

In the first place I should like to say that I cannot see any reason for denying the presence of some form of primitive phantasy from the beginning of extra-uterine mental life. In fact to deny the presence of phantasy before words are used seems to me to overlook the evidence which is manifested by the most familiar of all psychogenic

333

symptoms, the study of which led to Freud's first discoveries. I mean of course hysterical conversion symptoms. I will remind you that both Freud and Ferenczi suggested that in producing a conversion symptom the hysteric made use of archaic methods to express psychical phenomena. Before the use of words is possible, feelings, emotions, and ideas must be expressed partly in physical reactions of all kinds.

There may well be differences of opinion as to the content of a phantasy which is not expressed in words and there will be differences of opinion as to the time at which certain phantasies most commonly occur. These differences can only be resolved as the result of carefully recorded analytical work.

There is another theme arising out of Melanie Klein's work on early phantasies which seems to me of great value and at the same time introduces complexities which need careful study. This is the bearing these phantasies have on primitive object relationships. The recognition of primitive object relationships in the narcissistic phases and relationship between these object relationships and the object relationships of the genital phases necessitates considerable readjustment of the way in which we regard narcissistic states and auto-erotism.

At the same time there seems to be a tendency to minimize the dynamic significance of object relationship in the genital sense, and the importance of disturbances arising in this phase.

There are two points in Mrs Isaacs' paper which I should like to question:

The first is her claim that phantasy is the *primary content* of all mental processes. I do not think that phantasy, using the word in the usual sense, occurs until there has been a psychic experience which involves the reception of a stimulus and a psycho-physical response. What seems to me to be of paramount importance is to define the significance of primary unconscious phantasy, because it appears as if Mrs Isaacs regards the phantasies occurring at this time to be of a different dynamic significance from unconscious phantasies which we meet with later.

In accordance with the theory of instincts and the libido theory we are accustomed to regard phantasy as a means of working over instinct, and we have held the opinion that phantasies become fixated in certain phases for constitutional or traumatic reasons. Every disturbance which produces a fixation is a situation in which both the constitutional and the environmental factor must be taken into account. It would rather appear as if Mrs Isaacs regarded the group of phantasies to which she refers as always 'fixated'.

334

We all know that memory traces remain of all psychic experiences of any significance but we do not regard unconscious phantasy unless fixated as necessarily cathected and dynamic *as such* throughout life. It seems to me to be against the accepted dynamics of mental functioning to assume that a certain group of unconscious phantasies is permanently cathected as such unless the patient is suffering from a manifest or incipient psychosis. It would be an absurdity to imply the latter to the world as a whole. Further we know that unconscious phantasy has derivatives and substitutes in later phases, and the cathexes of these derivatives have a relation to their predecessors economically. A characteristic of early phantasy life is rapid change and variation, just as a child's mood changes rapidly in a few moments from sorrow to pleasure. There is of course repetition alternately with change. Movement and change are the hallmarks of development and growth of mind and body. This is one reason why the conception of fixation of libido is acceptable as a likely accompaniment of interference with development.

It seems to me that the concepts of fixation and regression are bound up with the dynamics of phantasy.

Another aspect of the problem is the part played by repression in maintaining the dynamic significance of an unconscious phantasy. We regard the repressed phantasy as one which will maintain its influence on the whole of mental life and the fixated phantasy is also typically the repressed phantasy. Mrs Isaacs does not make clear the part played by repression in the maintenance of these primary phantasies.

If a particular group of primary phantasies can be proved to be operative *as such* in every one throughout life I should be inclined to regard the phenomenon in the way that Freud regards symbolism; he says, 'analytic experience convinces us that particular psychic contents, such as symbolism, have no other source than that of hereditary transmission, and research in various fields of folk-psychology seems to justify the assumption that in archaic inherit-ance,there are other, no less specialized, deposits from primitive human development' (Freud, S. 1937:304; SE 23:240–1).[2] If this were so the effect of psychoanalytic interpretation would be limited.

I wish to make it clear that I am not denying that the earliest phases of psychological development influence future development and that difficulties arising in them are likely to influence the whole course of development. What I disagree with is a tendency to regard a particular group of phantasies as pathognomic of mental conflict. It can be said, of course, that Freud regarded the Oedipus complex in this way, but this is not true in the same sense. He regarded the

335

resolution of the Oedipus complex as the most important psychological event in the attainment of mental health because it implied a
successful development to genital· maturity, but he recognized the
fact that developmental difficulties could arise before the Oedipus
conflict was fully developed.

MRS D. BURLINGHAM: I should like to take the opportunity to
say a few words about Mrs Isaacs' remarks regarding the 'Report
about Young Children in Wartime', since I was and am in active
co-operation with the work described in it. Mrs Isaacs quotes two
passages to suggest that the descriptions given come very close to
Mrs Klein's postulates. My opinion is that this is not the case. To me
the apparent conformity refers to the facts under observation, which
we both recognize as being of extreme importance, but not to the
theories behind their interpretation.

To discuss it in detail in two examples.

Example 1: Mrs Isaacs quotes that we talk of 'the child's
relationship to his mother' [p. 294] as a psychological and social one
in the second half of the first year. We emphasize this aspect of it not
because it is already a full object relationship but in contrast to the
relationship which had existed in the first months of life, at that time
purely based on the gratification of bodily needs. In the first period
when the baby has the urge for the satisfaction of its bodily wishes, a
routine undertaken by anyone could fulfil this need. In the second
period to satisfy the child it requires the mother as well and not only
the mother but the mother in a certain mood. The child is then
sensitive to an atmosphere and reacts to this with pleasure or
displeasure. This is the new psychological factor which we were
referring to. It remains an open question whether when deprived of
this atmosphere the child really already calls forth the picture of the
mother or rather the vague sensation of longed-for pleasure and
comfort which we circumscribe by the word 'atmosphere'. I realize
that the probable difference between our and Mrs Isaacs' interpretation lies in the predominance of sensorial over imaginal experience,
i.e. we interpret purely on the basis of the pleasure principle.

And now *example 2*, concerning 'the mother image in the child's
mind in the second year of life'. In talking of the 'mother-image in
the child's mind' we actually mean the memory image. The child at
this age is well able to retain a memory of the mother when she is
absent. This memory image is accompanied by memories of past
gratifications and is therefore pleasurable in itself. When the mother
has ceased to be the person who satisfied the child's needs or when
the child has gone through a period of painful longing, the memory

image, since it is now accompanied by memories of pain and frustration, loses its pleasurable aspect and calls forth pain. This is what we mean when we say that something has happened to the mother image in the child's mind. It would be more correct to say to its sensorial accompaniment. It is only natural for a child to turn away from and not towards such an image when it reappears in reality, that is when the mother returns. The difference between this interpretation and that of Mrs Isaacs is the whole of the difference between the theoretical concept of a memory-image and the theoretical concept of an introjected object. Simple situations like the one described might prove convenient starting points for final elucidation of these divergencies.

MISS E. F. SHARPE: I wish to thank Mrs Isaacs for the exhaustive work her paper represents. The only adequate response is to state as clearly as possible one's own views in the spirit of Freud's quoted words. Only apparent completeness, finality, and certainty need perturb us, not the gaps and uncertainties of our knowledge.

Mrs Klein has immensely enriched our knowledge of the details of infantile phantasies. I have acknowledged this in the past. In my review of Branson's book on King Lear (Sharpe 1934) this acknowledgement is explicit. If my views are taking a long time to clarify, that too is an acknowledgement. In ten minutes I can only deal with one point.

Freud gave us his monumental work on dreams and I do not understand any difficulty about the existence of unconscious phantasy starting from infancy. Any dream analysed to its infantile roots reveals it. What difference is there between unconscious phantasy and the stuff dreams are made of?

Freud says in 'Introductory Lectures', page 312, 'Objects and channels which have been forsaken by the libido have not been forsaken in every sense: they or their derivatives are retained to some degree of intensity in the conceptions of phantasy. The libido has only to withdraw on to phantasies in order to find the way open to it back to all repressed fixations' (Freud, S. 1916–17: 312; SE 23:272).[3] He indicates his belief that the ego tolerates phantasies, develops no strong opposition as long as a certain condition of a quantitative nature is preserved. When this quantitative factor is disturbed the libido returns to phantasies, and this condition occurs when reality satisfaction fails.

I will deal with one phantasy to which the libido returns when reality satisfaction fails.

Freud also says: 'Let us be clear that the hallucinatory wish-psychosis in dreams or elsewhere performs by no means identical functions. Not only does it bring into consciousness hidden or repressed wishes, but it also represents them as fulfilled, and that in such a way as *to command entire belief.*' [Freud, S. 1917c:145; SE 14:230][4]

Freud, Mrs Klein, all of us, agree that the infant's breast hallucination is the initial wish psychosis. The wish is represented as fulfilled and commands entire belief. Dreams and unconscious phantasies regress to this level of perception.

The breast phantasy is a rudimentary psychical process, but the belief is that the infant possesses the real tangible breast, i.e. an actuality. In this phantasy the infant achieves a reunion with the body of the mother.

The phantasied introjection of the breast, the entire belief that the actual breast is inside, is the next stage of wish-psychosis. The illusion or delusion this achieves is that still there has been no bodily separation from the mother. There is no mental imagery in this process. It is the hallucinatory perception inside not outside. She is within the child in place of the child within her as in pre-natal days.

The entire belief in the good concrete object within, or the bad object within, preserves the illusions of non-bodily separation. Primitive introjection and projection alike are attempts to deny the reality of bodily separation.

From this core of belief in the actual good object within proceeds the belief in God immanent, the dweller in the innermost, the ultimate certainty and reality. It is the secret of the contemplative life, the heart of mysticism. She is in me and I in her. It is immaterial if one says God instead of Mother. 'One altogether, not by confusion of substance but by unity of Person.' It is in an ultimate psychotic belief in a non-bodily separation from the first object and this is wish-psychosis.

Dr John Pratt, one of our candidates remarked to me one day: 'Analysis is the accomplishment of mourning, the detachment of the libido from every infantile fixation point.' Detachment begins with the bodily expulsion from the mother's body; there follows the semi-uterine existence of infancy, with the breast hallucination of non-separation. Weaning detaches the baby from the nipple, while the ability to walk means the final physical hold of mother on child, of child on mother is ended. But the child who is still tied to his mother's apron strings is attached by the umbilical cord as unsevered for the mother as for the child. There is for both no separation, they are of one bone, one flesh. The work of mourning is not accomplished by retaining the belief in the actual good object within.

338

There is no relinquishment of an intimate ideal, a mother who ministered to us alone. Our troubles start with reality, with separation, and a mother who was sexual and bore other children by a father, the recognition of which realities is the blow to narcissism and idealism.

I see the depressive position of Mrs Klein's theory, if all the important factors are admitted, as almost the last of the external physical birth throes. It follows that the strength of the psychotic mechanisms will give to Mrs Klein's early Oedipus setting a psychotic quality, something quite different from the Oedipus complex in the Freudian sense. Following the breast hallucination and the incorporation of the actual breast there can be the delusion of incorporation of the actual pregnant mother and the father together with the belief that the new baby is magically the child's own. That is the whole world is inside, upon the basis of the original wish-psychosis, a refusal of separate existence. This is the Trinity: Father, Son and Holy Ghost and yet not three but one. The Freudian Oedipus complex is of a different nature altogether, involving ego organization and repression which is inseparable from reality adaptation. The Oedipus complex is bypassed when the wish-psychosis is retained to any strength.

The term 'super-ego' is only correctly used when it designates what it says: a super*ego*. This superego is inseparable from the Oedipus complex of Freud. Some other term should be found such as 'id-ideal' in contrast to ego-ideals for those derivatives of the incorporation of the actual object when ego differentiation has hardly begun. The superego in the Freudian sense is accessible to influence and amelioration, that which derives from the belief in actual incorporation is inaccessible and adamant, the belief in righteousness as adamant as implacable evil.

In his 'Metapsychological Supplement to the Theory of Dreams' Freud says that on our capacity to distinguish perceptions from mental images depends our whole attitude to the outer world, to reality. It did not always exist. At the beginning we hallucinated the satisfying object when we needed it. [Freud, S. 1917c: 147; SE 14:231]

The ineradicable infantile wishes for concrete realization never cease. The acceptance of a symbol, the capacity for mental imagery, means not that infantile wish and hope are relinquished, but that belief in reality separation has occurred and substitutes must be found. The introjected corporeal object no longer commands entire belief. Reality is reached via mental image.

It may well be that in all of us something of this wish-psychosis

339

returns, it is the degree that matters. We have to reckon with its far-reaching consequences. For a belief in the actual good object the actual bad one results in world affairs with a Hitler-ridden Germany and pipe-smoking optimists elsewhere who say 'God's in His Heaven, all's right with the world'.

Freud showed us the way to individuality out of mass psychology, the way of emergence from that matrix, called by some 'the racial unconscious'. It is by shedding illusions about ourselves and others, and the first and deepest illusion is the belief in the actual incorporated object.

The bearing on practical analysis in relationship to this one phantasy is the imperative task we have of attempting to achieve as far as we can a psychical delivery. As far as we can. I do not believe in the omnipotence of the analyst or of psychoanalysis. That is still illusion that ignores many facts. The *psychical* delivery of the patient (no matter what magical results are achieved) is only brought about by the patient: relinquishing the belief in the incorporated analyst. For if not, the fundamental wish psychosis remains.

My difficulty is not disbelief in the existence of illusions of bodily incorporation, nor illusions of actual objects inside, but the problems of technique involved as how best to dispel or weaken these illusions, to bring the patient to face realities and grow to the stature of an individual separate existence.

DR MELITTA SCHMIDEBERG (read by the Chairman in absence of Dr Schmideberg): As Dr Isaacs' paper contains no clear statement of the controversy in question, I see no point in discussing her paper. But as my name has been mentioned, I wish to make a protest. I am quoted as belonging to the English School (presumably an adherent of Mrs Klein!) on the strength of a passage from a paper published more than ten years ago, in which I used the words 'introjection' and 'projection' in the vague ambiguous manner which was then the fashion both in the Continental and English analytic literature. Dr Isaacs omits to take notice of my numerous contributions in which I have since criticized Mrs Klein's theories and objected to the ambiguous use of the above terms. Such a blatant omission is contrary to scientific tradition and spirit. It is the lack of these that makes it impossible for me to take Dr Isaacs' paper seriously.

DR HEDWIG HOFFER: We are indebted to Mrs Isaacs for her accomplished presentation of her thesis. But to my mind her exposition of Freud's theories has not been handled with the same skill. Such an inequality in presentation might perhaps give rise to misunderstandings and I should therefore like to comment on it. Let me illustrate my objections with a few examples.

Mrs Isaacs deals with psychic reality on pages [269–71] and uses it as an introduction to her topic. She quotes Freud in order to demonstrate the importance he himself attributed to psychic reality. I naturally do not deny this fact but I wish to comment on the way this quotation is used. When you read the quotation please do not omit reading the passage in the middle of it as well. The quotation is taken from Freud's paper 'The Unconscious', page 123, 'Coll. Papers', vol. IV, and deals with the derivatives of the unconscious instinctual impulses. Freud describes them as highly organized, exempt from self-contradictoriness and capable of uniting in themselves opposite features. In the omitted passage Freud says concerning such derivatives: 'Their origin remains decisive for the fate they will undergo.' [Freud S. 1915b:123; SE 14: 191][5] And in order to make what he has in mind quite clear and unmistakable Freud illustrates the importance of the origin of such derivatives, comparing them to coloured people who resemble white men but betray their coloured descent in some striking feature. And only after this does he continue where the quotation continues, with the sentence about the nature of phantasy-formation.

Freud's quotation is taken out of his context and fitted into an entirely different subject-matter. In this way the accent is shifted from one aspect of the whole to another one. In the quoted paragraph Freud is dealing with the differentiation between one mental system (Pcs) and the other (Ucs). In order to get this differentiation clear he describes the character of the derivatives of the instinctual impulses in the Ucs. In the omitted passage he expresses his view that their origin decides their fate. This statement, which is stressed with a comparison, shows the weight Freud attributes to evolution.

The connection between Freud's argument about the communication between the two systems and Mrs Isaacs' subject is not so easy to see. Mrs Isaacs centres her quotation round Freud's insertion about phantasy-formation. As time is pressing I refrain from going into details but here again Freud refers to the content of the repressed in the Unconscious, not to phantasy-formation in particular or psychic reality in general.

I doubt whether it is permissible to quote Freud in this manner, since the result gives a meaning which was not intended by the author.

The same objection is valid for the next example.

On page [278] Mrs Isaacs states her view that the infant's capacity to hallucinate is 'either identical with phantasy or the pre-condition for it'. She describes in some length what the infant hallucinates and then without further comment she goes on: 'but let us again consider what Freud himself has to say about this'. But the quotation taken from 'Instincts and their Vicissitudes' is not concerned with the infant's hallucinations, but with the libidinal development and the development of object relationship under the rule of the pleasure principle. Also in this quotation I regret the omission of half a sentence which runs: 'in consequence of experiences undergone by the instincts of self-preservation it [the ego] tends to find objects there'. [Freud, S. 1915a: 78; SE 14: 135][6] This part of the sentence is not indifferent to the whole context because it mentions the influence of experience, an essential element of Freud's conception.

Let us have one last example taken from the 'New Introductory Lectures'. In the lecture about the psychology of women Freud deals with the girl's antagonism against her mother. In the passage to which Mrs Isaacs refers, Freud gives 'as a potent source for this antagonism the child's many sexual wishes which change with its libidinal phases'. [Freud, S. 1933a: 158; SE 22: 123][7] The quotation which you may read on page [281] of Mrs Isaacs' manuscript again suffers from an omission. The omission and the whole context, which is too long to be quoted here, leaves no doubt that Freud is referring to regression, and the motivating of animistic thinking and infantile reasoning. The last certainly cannot occur before the acquisition of verbal images. And one page after the quotation, Freud ends the paragraph, 'All of these factors – slights, disappointment in love, jealousy and seduction followed by prohibition – operate as well in the relationship between the boy and his mother, and yet are not sufficient to alienate him from the mother-object'. [Freud, S. 1933a: 159; SE 22: 124][8]

Mrs Isaacs quotes Freud in order to illustrate Mrs Klein's adherence to Freud's findings and to back Mrs Klein's hypothesis of early frustration and early projected hate. It seems somewhat misleading to preface the quotation in this way – 'again, when speaking of oral frustration Freud says' – because Freud mentions oral frustration in connection with the make-up of the female character and speaks neither of early childhood, nor of the child in general, nor of projected hate. So the context shows that Freud is concerned with another topic altogether, and therefore his arguments are unfit for Mrs Isaacs' purpose.

Advance in science is based on the freedom of every worker in the field to follow up his own thoughts. The presentation of his own findings and the checking of his particular experience with that of his fellow workers establishes in the long run the validity of his recent findings. There need be no haste for such a conclusive test, but it is an ill service to science to readjust former accepted theories in order to make them apply to later ones.

DR K. FRIEDLANDER: I want to concentrate today on the question of regression. Some of you may remember that in the discussion after Wälder's paper Jenny Wälder drew attention to the fact that phantasies of oral character expressed in the third or fourth year of life need not be old phantasies formed during the oral phase but may derive their oral character from regression. Dr Jones refers to this same occurrence when he mentions the phantasy of the child of 4 who wants to bite the mother's breast. This phantasy could originate (a) from the wish to bite the mother, an instinct derived from the genital and anal-sadistic phase, (b) the wish to bite the breast may be due to regression to the oral stage, recalling the old dim wishes and frustrations concerned with feeding. This controversy has played a role in our discussions here ever since.

Mrs Isaacs when talking about regression admits the difference in Mrs Klein's view as compared with the psychoanalytical theory, but her statement does not make the significance of this difference clear. This statement rather conveys the idea as if there were an incompatibility between recognizing the importance of the psychological happenings in the first years of life and recognizing the mechanism of regression.

As far as is possible in so short a space of time I want to show that the mechanism of regression is indispensable in Freud's theory of the aetiology of the neuroses and intimately bound up with the theory of libidinal development. I also want to show that Mrs Klein's view of the 'early mental development' must necessarily lead to a depreciation of the importance of the mechanism of regression because Mrs Klein has given up Freud's theory of the development of libido.

What I cannot show, owing to lack of time, is the fact that regression is not merely a theoretical conception but a process which can be observed in every dream and the undoing of which is often the most important step in therapy, for instance of obsessional neurosis. That is to say that the depreciation of the mechanism of regression must also necessarily have an important bearing on the change which the technique of psychoanalysis has undergone by Mrs Klein and her followers.

I cannot talk about regression without referring shortly to some aspects of libidinal development. We know that the libido has the inherent, that is to say biological, tendency to pass through certain stages of development. Without this tendency of the instincts to develop, our therapeutical efforts would come to nothing. Whatever educational methods are adopted, children do not remain in the oral stage of libidinal development but pass through the anal-sadistic and phallic phase until the component instincts become united under the primacy of the genitals. Not the whole of the instinctual drives undergo this development. Owing partly to constitutional, partly to environmental factors a greater or lesser amount of libido may get arrested at the one or other stage; we talk of fixation points. In rare instances, the genital phase may not be reached at all although that is more of an assumption than a certainty. There are therefore many individual variations, for instance as to the strength of instinctual drives which remain in the unconscious in their original form or which although they have not developed towards the genital stage yet have been altered, desexualized by the various mechanisms of sublimation and reaction formation.

Of course the strength of the primary impulses in the unconscious will be different in different people and, whether regression has taken place or not, will depend on the amount of libido which has either been collected under the primacy of the genitals or has been desexualized. But there is no doubt that some of these original instincts remain always in the unconscious and exert their influence in their unaltered form.

It is to these instinctual trends that Freud, quoted by Mrs Isaacs on page [297], refers when talking about the first, most primal libidinal impulses. He is then not referring to Mrs Klein's early phantasies, as we are made to believe from the setting of the quotation in Mrs Isaacs' paper, but to the whole of the unconscious pre-genital instincts and phantasies up to the fifth year of life. This is made quite clear by the preceding paragraph, in which Freud, far from agreeing, even criticizes Mrs Klein's view of the early Oedipal conflict: he states that this theory is disproved not only by experiences on adult patients but mainly by the fact of the long-lasting pre-Oedipal mother-relationship of the little girl, which reaches at least into the fifth year. Freud's emphasis on the importance and strength of these primary libidinal impulses, especially the pre-Oedipal mother-relationship of the little girl, with which we all fully agree, is used in an argument against Karen Horney who denies the primary character of the girl's penis envy. In a way this argument would also apply to Mrs Klein who considers the penis envy not to be a primary formation but a defence mechanism.

Freud's argument then, as is seen quite clearly and unmistakably when taking into account not Mrs Isaacs' somewhat misleading quotation, but the contents of the last paragraphs of Freud's paper on 'Female Sexuality', is simply that the energy behind these libidinal wishes does not derive its whole strength from later regressions, 'later' meaning regressions in adult life, but that there always remain primary instinctual drives in the unconscious.

The fact therefore of the recognition of the lasting importance of the libidinal development up to the fourth or fifth year does therefore in no way infringe upon the importance of the mechanism of regression, and the aforementioned quotation of Freud does certainly not strengthen Mrs Isaacs' view on the subject.

To come back to regression: certain conditions, either environmental or inner psychic or a combination of both, may at any time during life arouse a conflict between the instinctual drives and the ego. As a way out of this conflict the forward movement of the libido may be checked and a retrograde movement may take place. The whole of the libido already advanced to the phallic or even genital phase or only part of it may be included in that retrograde movement which will stop at the strongest fixation point. This process is described as regression of the libido to a former stage of development. This former stage of development, let us say the anal-sadistic phase, will now be reinforced by the already further developed libido and it will be extremely difficult to say in any given case which amount of the instinctual drives is derived from the original fixation and which from the regressed libido. If a regression takes place from the genital to the anal-sadistic phase, the result will be an obsessional neurosis, where to love a person is equated with destruction of some kind. If, on the other hand, the disturbance at the genital phase leads to a repression of the instinctual drives with a regression not of the libido but of object choice, the resulting illness will appear under the picture of hysteria. Again fixation at the still earlier phases of libidinal development may have been very strong, large quantities of libido having been excluded from further development and remaining in the unconscious unaltered in their original form. A breakdown with a regression to these still narcissistic stages of development will give rise to the outbreak of a psychosis.

At one time it was thought that in perversions the development to the genital stage had been completely arrested and the whole of the libido remained fixated to the one or other component instinct. But since Freud's paper on fetishism we have seen that even in perversions the beginnings of a genital phase, however weak, can be observed and the regression plays an important role even in these conditions.

I hope with these few words to have recalled to your minds the connections between primary libidinal development to the genital stage, the varying strength of fixations on the different levels of development, repression, and regression of the libido to earlier stages or regression of object choice, which in their variations bring about the different pictures of mental illness. Not only is the aetiology of neuroses based on the conception of these mechanisms, but we are also influenced in our prognostic views by the completeness and depth of regression which we think has taken place.

This is, simplified, Freud's theory of the aetiology of neuroses and of the part which regression plays in it. We see that the conception of regression is of course intimately bound up with Freud's conception of the libidinal development up to the genital phase. This conception is based on the biological tendency of the instincts to develop.

Contrariwise, in Mrs Klein's view the libido has no inherent or biological tendency to develop in the described way. The so-called early phantasies, which we can only perceive as either being inborn or universally formed in the first months of life and which already contain oral, anal-sadistic, and phallic impulses as well as guilt feelings and defence mechanisms, are thought to be of primary importance in so far as the further development occurs as a flight from too great a fear or too great a guilt feeling aroused by these phantasies. The process of development is seen in a more static form. There are those tormenting, highly organized phantasies in the small infant, and everything which occurs later on, be it an environmental happening or an inner psychic process, is used to mitigate these terrifying sadistic phantasies. Development, in Mrs Klein's view, consists in an alteration by various means, for instance by introjection and projection, of these original phantasies.

Naturally, therefore, the conception of regression has no place in this theory. The whole of the libido remains fixated to these early phantasies throughout life, without undergoing the biological developmental phases described by Freud and observed over and over again in children, and therefore regression is not necessary; there is nothing more primary to regress to. The important fact which emerges from these ideas in my opinion is not that Mrs Klein lays less stress on a mechanism on which we lay more stress.

The importance of the depreciation of the mechanism of regression, which Mrs Isaacs as such admits, is the fact that it is the result of giving up Freud's conception of the biological development of the libido.

DR M. BALINT: (1) One of the main tenets of the psychoanalytical theory from the beginning has been that the Oedipus complex is the nuclear complex of every neurosis. I do not wish to investigate now how far this statement is true in its classical form or whether it needs amplification. But it is certainly true that we meet neuroses well below the age of the 'proper' Oedipus complex: e.g. neurotic feeding disturbances, even in breast-fed babies, and still more frequently in and after the period of weaning; night terrors and sleeping difficulties at a very early age. Our classical theory still cannot offer a satisfactory explanation for these phenomena. It is certainly a lasting merit of Mrs Klein that she was one of the first to call our attention to this unsatisfactory state of affairs and to suggest some theoretical considerations as a basis of these.

(2) The use of the word 'phantasy' by Mrs Klein and her followers has met with objections from many quarters, which is understandable. Still I wish to point out that the term 'phantasy' has certain advantages: (a) The term 'instinctual derivatives' which was used by Freud and suggested by many of the speakers in place of phantasy is likely to give the impression of an almost mechanical process, whereas 'phantasy' suggests 'meaning' and the working of mental tendencies. (b) 'Phantasy' expresses clearly that we have to do with something resulting from an intimate interaction of real experience and wishful shaping. (c) Lastly, 'phantasy' denotes that these mental phenomena are individual, i.e., connected with the particular mental make-up of a particular child.

Where I do not follow Mrs Klein is in regard to the content of these phantasies. Every observer who has to do with quite young children states that in the first few months of life we may see signs of irritation, pain, anger, or fright, but none of hate and anxiety, which seem to appear only in the latter half of the first year. Further, it is true that especially in the first weeks of life even the normal child appears to be frequently irritated and experiencing discomfort, but one should bear in mind that most of his waking hours are spent in feeding, when his satisfaction is quite obvious. Therefore, if one takes the sum total of the waking hours into consideration the proportion of irritation versus satisfaction is approximately the same as in later life. This is one of the reasons why I feel that perhaps Mrs Klein is laying undue emphasis on the role of hatred, frustration, and aggression in the infant.

(3) With regard to defensive mechanisms involved in 'phantasy' building we know, unfortunately, but little. It is generally assumed that repression has not the important role in the first year as in later life. The probable explanation is that the prerequisite of repression is some degree of ego integration. So we have to look for more

primitive forms of defensive mechanisms which could operate without, i.e. before an integrated ego, such as projection and introjection which form the basis of many of Mrs Klein's findings.

(4) A few more words about regression in reply to Dr Friedlander's criticism. The term 'regression' was used by Freud in three different senses:

(a) To denote a backward movement along the stages of development of libidinal aims and/or objects.
(b) To denote a process moving against the normal direction of the mental apparatus: i.e., as against the normal perception → thinking and feeling → action, the regressive trend is thinking and feeling → perception, as e.g., in hallucinations and dreaming.
(c) To denote that a mental element which has been subjected to the secondary process is now again subjected to the primary process.

Notions (b) and (c) were originally described in the *Interpretation of Dreams* whereas notion (a) came somewhat later. Dr Friedlander was right in showing that Mrs Isaacs does not use regression in sense (a), but it is obvious that sense (b) and (c) were extensively used in her paper.

In any case regression to older aims and objects cannot have a great role in the first years.

DR B. LANTOS: My remarks are concerned with primitive reactions, actions, and play of the child. I think a certain divergence in our views can be clearly demonstrated in the discussion of these questions. The paper gives detailed accounts of observations of such actions and plays in order to prove the thesis on early phantasies, and I shall refer to these accounts and the conclusions drawn from them. Before setting out to do that, however, I should like to remind you that there have been no controversies about the existence of phantasies from an early phase of life. The problem is and has always been (1) the specific content of these phantasies, (2) the actual age at which we can first detect them, and (3) the dynamic part they play in the child's development as well as in his actions and plays.

One illustration of the problem and of the way the paper deals with it, can be found on page [281] under the heading 'Phantasy and sensory experience'. To summarize it briefly, the author here acknowledges that organ-pleasure as well as some of the sensations coming from outside, such as sensations of warmth, the desired contact with the mother, satisfaction derived from sucking etc., bring actual experience of pleasurable sensations. These pleasurable perceptions begin to influence mental processes very early and the psyche deals with them under the dominance of the pleasure principle. The pleasurable interest in his body, his discoveries and experiments in this direction are clearly shown in the play of an infant of 3–4 months, in his play with his fingers, toes, limbs, his mouth, and so on.

So far we are in full agreement. Now we not only think that the pleasurable interest in his body is shown in this play, but we go even further in stating that this pleasure and interest is the motor of the described play as well as of many other plays during the next months and later. We estimate the dynamic force of this pleasure so highly that we don't feel the need to look for other explanations. We believe that bodily functions (such as moving, crawling, walking, jumping, etc.) and the functioning of the sensory apparatus (such as looking, hearing, touching, tasting, and smelling) are pleasurable in themselves. So is mental development with its gradual acquisition of knowledge and understanding. This pleasure we call auto–erotic, referring to the sensory apparatus, organ pleasure, referring to bodily functions, and intellectual pleasure – they all are the same in so far as they are pleasures in themselves, that is to say: pleasures without meaning. A meaning may become attached to them and actually is often attached in later age, but the essentially auto–erotic, organ or intellectual pleasure is, as we think, the most important stimulus to normal development, if such a stimulus be needed at all.

In the quoted passage of the paper the description of the infant's pleasurable interest in his body goes on like that: 'In this play the 3-months-old infant manifests his process of symbol-formation bound up with those phantasies' – and here comes the surprising turn – 'which we discover in the unconscious mind of young children during their analysis.' '. . . analytic work with children of two years and over shows how the child's play exemplifies the dream mechanisms – symbolization' etc., which 'must operate in the child's play more freely and fully in the earlier than in the later ages. To an older child, too, a box may symbolize his mother, but it has many practical uses for him in external life as well. For the tiny infant who first discovers the pleasures of dropping things into boxes and tipping them out again and so on and so forth, the symbolic meaning must far out weigh the "reality" value, which must at first be quite marginal in significance.' So far the paper. It brings in phantasy and symbolic meaning to explain a very simple play for which the auto-erotic pleasure derived from it by the baby is, in our opinion, quite sufficient explanation. But one might argue that even if it were

349

sufficient, this would not exclude the operating of other additional forces. We are quite prepared to accept that if we can get any proof – but unfortunately no such evidence has been forthcoming. As so often in the past we are told again that the analysis of children of two years and more is the proof of what is happening in the baby's mind. This kind of deduction is not new but it still fails to convince us.

In the second part of her paper Mrs Isaacs takes great pains to enumerate behaviouristic data from birth up to the second year. We are, of course, mostly concerned with the first year. On page [302] it is stated that the child during the first few months of his life reacts with anxiety – we would call it displeasure – to the majority of outside stimuli. (I don't know whether all behaviourists have come to the same result but it does not make much difference.) Taking this for granted we understand that the baby has to get used to the conditions which are so completely different from his existence in the mother's womb (light, sounds, temperature, circulation, nourishment, etc.). That this is a source of much displeasure, that it leaves its marks deep down in the unconscious we know and never doubted. We agree that it is general and normal for the waking infant to find the world disagreeable. Whether that is far more general than we have allowed – as the paper points out – we don't know. Actually there are well-cared-for and healthy babies who show joy of life and contentedness from the very beginning. But however that may be, the fact that the infant shows signs of discomfort and the tendency to flee back to pre-natal peace and uninterrupted satisfaction is in no way the same as to feel the outside world actively hostile with all the consequences implied by such a feeling; these consequences, according to the paper, being persecutory fears, phantasies of being attacked by a 'bad' mother and, in response to it, destructive wishes to attack her. But it doesn't stop there: the destructive wishes of the infant are supposed to be projected on to his mother, increasing his primary fears of being attacked by her. 'And every frustration, every failure on her part to remove any source of pain as well as to feed and comfort him, reinforces his picture of her as a "bad mother".' To our mind too elaborate a process for a tiny infant of some weeks; and when as a proof of it we read again 'as we know from later analysis', we feel that we have been left without any proof once again.

On page [303] there is Shirley's report about the first active social responses of the child (how he watches faces, feels soothed by his mother's voice, begins to smile and to express joy in the society of adults, shows signs of affection, and wants to touch and manipulate persons). Actually a rather idyllic description, without a sign of aggression of any kind. So we are rather taken aback when we suddenly are faced with the following conclusion: 'In these observations as to the infant's active concern with his mother's body – both loving and aggressive – we have full confirmation of Melanie Klein's hypothesis as to his early wishes and phantasies towards his mother. We see the first dawn of the epistomophilic impulse, as well as of the wish to control and master, and we have clear hints of the way in which, by means of his play, the child libidinizes his aggressive wishes and anxieties.'

The same happens with the next set of behaviouristic data on page [305]. I wonder whether some could be found which would serve better to support the thesis – those brought forward here certainly don't. We are given a harmless and rather gay picture, a rather charming description of the infant's play at the breast. I looked up the most negative signs and enumerate them here without omitting one. They are: The infant shows that he recognizes a changed situation by frowns and other slight signs of anxiety. He shows distress when mother goes away. He shows eagerness or annoyance by vocal changes. He frowns or smiles in response to angry or friendly looks. That is all, and these data would never lead us to the conclusion that 'in both the manipulative and the linguistic play of the first half-year, thus, we see at work the mastering of anxiety and aggression by libidinization, by the spreading out of pleasure from the oral nucleus of primary satisfaction'.

From 6 to 12 months [see p. 307] the child shows rapid development in perception, skill, memory, and imagination. The actions he performs show in our opinion – his growing intelligence. The plays called 'manipulative plays' serve to sharpen his sensory and motoric apparatus, while giving him auto-erotic pleasure in the wider sense – including organ pleasure and intellectual pleasure. But they do not suggest to us that he has explicit phantasies. Even his thumb-sucking, masturbation, hair pulling and other habits are at that age still auto-erotic. (The occasional presence of night-terrors are just a repetition of the fears he experiences while being awake, such as direct fears of strangers, and unknown dangers, and may be an archaic inheritance.) Here I do not believe that masturbation makes him feel: I shall bring my mother back. We do not believe that he wants to eat her up, to tear her to bits, to drown and burn her – all that would be of no use to him – and consequently he does not need to restore her, to make her better, to feed her, or to put the bits together again [pp. 309–11]. The fact that he is able to recognize persons, that he is aware of their coming and going and afraid of their loss, and that he reacts accordingly, is in our opinion bound up with the development of the sensory and mental apparatus without

351

suggesting the existence of phantasies. But this is a quotation which other speakers have already dealt with. I wanted to refer only to the evidence brought forward by facts.

As we read on page [309], 'Melanie Klein's views as to the early phantasy life of the infant, and concept of the "depressive position" take full account of all these facts. The concept of the depressive position was based upon these facts, as she came to understand them through her work in the analysis of children of two to three years of age.'

Now if these are the facts on which her views are based, we are discouraged and without hope of coming to an understanding. These facts are really not new at all, but they did not and don't suggest to us anything like the thesis. The difference quite clearly is not that we are building on different facts but that we are interpreting the same facts differently. The announcement that her views are based upon facts, as she came to understand them through her work in the analysis of children of two or three years of age, is in no way helpful in clearing up the question when the mentioned phantasies are really first produced. We still wonder why the baby, longing for milk, should wish to dismember his mother, or should even want to separate her from the father, but it is incomprehensible for us. All that may occur to him at a later age, but that does not solve the problem and answer our question.

DR W. C. SCOTT: I first want to say something that was suggested to me by listening to Miss Sharpe. I am sorry to have to come to a meeting like this. One comes to learn something with which Miss Sharpe only ended, to learn something about technique. I am sorry that so much time should be taken up by other problems. There are certain problems of unconscious content which are too difficult for analysts to tackle. Freud has tackled some and he must have had difficulties, also Mrs Klein has tackled some, and I know from my experience with children and psychotics that they exist. I was stirred by the end of Miss Sharpe's paper.

Mrs Isaacs has well summarized the facts and views which are the necessary basis for any discussion of phantasy in the psychoanalytical sense. With all that she says I fully agree in principle. In detail I might differ slightly with a few interpretations. For instance, the child who is annoyed by a neutral stranger at 5 months may not be showing his attempted solution of ambivalence but rather may be annoyed at the dawning of the breakdown of his omnipotence – he may feel that the hallucinated wish-fulfilment of seeing his mother has been interfered with by the appearance of the stranger.

In much discussion of phantasy or of the primary unconscious mental activity it is still disparaged instead of continually keeping before us the fact that the bounds of our knowledge are unlimited no matter how much we have already learned. We still mistakenly tend to carry back the common adult dichotomy of 'body–mind' to the infant when we take its sucking for granted and talk of rudimentary psychic behaviour or rudimentary phantasy. Unfortunately, as adults we can try to remember the sucking more easily than we can remember that part of the experience which we deign to call 'phantasy'. But surely infantile sucking is as different from the ritual of the ordinary several-course meal of the adult as is infantile phantasy from phantasy of the adult. We must study our facts in their own right and be willing to learn slowly.

The attempt to seek the chronology of the states of phases of development in their genetic continuity should always be before us. We will make mistakes but they will be corrected. The unalterable time sequence is one of those aspects of adult reality which is most important. The relationships of the 'whens' of experience only slowly become conscious. We have much evidence that the infant omnipotently manipulated his time scale and I think this is one reason why we have difficulty in discovering chronology.

The basis of early phantasy is often said to be sensation, feeling, etc., as if there were two aspects of experience which were from the first contrasted. Is it not a fact that our assumption is of a most direct continuity between the later explicit phantasy and the early implicit phantasy? Is not this early implicit phantasy that from which such aspects of experience as sensation, feeling, etc., emerge? And is it not these sensations, etc., which may be 'mere' experiences whereas phantasy either in infancy or adulthood is *never a 'mere' experience*.

The further understanding of a crucial assumption seems essential. Freud wrote in 1923 (*The Ego and the Id*), 'The ego is first and foremost a body ego.' [Freud, S. 1923b: 31; SE 19:26)[9] Concerning this we want to know more about what the body means in unconscious phantasy. Whether we talk of the ego or of other people as whole or part-objects; or whether we talk of ego nuclei, ego disintegration and integration, or whether we talk of organization of disorganization of subject functions as contrasted to object (that is, non-subject) functions, may be less important than the manner in which we describe new contents of experience. Concerning the early phantasy of the 'body' I think we might obtain help from neurologists or psychologists who are interested in the 'body scheme', just as we got some help from the behaviourists. We cannot be really sorry that the behaviourists give us nice examples that the

353

child is being angry, scratching, tearing up things, etc. We must be grateful to them for spending so much time on these observations. In many neuroses and all psychoses, hypochondriasis and even affect may be related to the vicissitudes of this unconscious body scheme or, as I would rather call it, 'the phantasy of the body'.

Mrs Isaacs stressed the first two months of a child's extra-uterine life as being marked by great variations in experience. Sometime I think we may live to attend heated discussions concerning the importance of experiences in these early weeks which we now barely recognize, let alone can describe in words which will have the same meaning to everyone. We will want to know the real age of the child, since a week may make a difference. We will want to know of his 24-hour behaviour since later experience shows that an experience need only happen once to make a difference.

This shows that we have difficulties of terminology ahead but we should at least be able to agree on the use of words now – and should only introduce new words or uses with good reason. I think there is excellent reason for using 'phantasy' as the historical equivalent of primary unconscious mental activity, remembering that this is dynamic and continuously developing. I might even say that we know as little about the end result of the development of phantasy as we do of the beginning of its development.

Notes

1 'Truly a matter of conceptions – that is to say, of introducing the right abstract ideas.' [SE 22:81]
2 'Analytic experience has forced on us a conviction that even particular psychical contents, such as symbolism, have no other sources than hereditary transmission, and researches in various fields of social anthropology, make it plausible to suppose that other equally specialized precipitates left by early human development are also present in the archaic heritage.' [SE 23:240–1]
3 'All the objects and trends which the libido has given up have not yet been given up in every sense. They or their derivatives are still retained with a certain intensity in phantasies. Thus the libido need only with-draw on to phantasies in order to find the path open to every repressed fixation.' [SE 23:272]
4 'Let us be clear that the hallucinatory wishful psychosis – in dreams or elsewhere – achieves two by no means identical results. It not only brings hidden or repressed wishes into consciousness; it also represents them,

with the subject's entire belief, as fulfilled. The concurrence of these two results calls for explanation.' [SE 14:230]

5 'Their origin is what decides their fate.' [SE 14:191]

6 'But, in consequence of experience undergone by the instincts of self-preservation, it acquires objects from that world.' [SE 14:135]

7 'The child's multifarious sexual wishes, which alter according to the phase of the libido.' [SE 22:123]

8 'All these factors – the slights, the disappointments in love, the jealousy, the seduction followed by prohibition – are, after all, also in operation in the relation of a boy to his mother and are yet unable to alienate him from the maternal object.' [SE 22:124]

9 'The ego is first and foremost a bodily ego.' [SE 19:26]

4

Second
Discussion of Scientific Controversies

British Psycho-Analytical Society

96 Gloucester Place,
London, W.1.

NOTICE TO MEMBERS AND ASSOCIATE MEMBERS

A meeting of Members and Associate Members will be held on Wednesday, February 17th, 1943, at 8 p.m., at 96 Gloucester Place, London, W.1. This is the second of the Series of Scientific Discussions on controversial topics.

Continuation of discussion of Mrs Isaacs' paper

A copy of the contributions to the discussion held on January 27th is enclosed.

Members are reminded that they should prepare their contributions beforehand and hand them to the Secretary. The Hon. Treasurer wishes to remind Members who have not yet paid their contribution to printing expenses that the sum due is £1.

EDWARD GLOVER
Scientific Secretary

January 3rd, 1943

**A Meeting of Members and Associate Members
was held on Wednesday, February 17th, 1943, at 8 p.m.,
at 96 Gloucester Place, London, W.1.**

(Second meeting in the series of Scientific Discussions on controversial issues existing within the Society: continuation of discussion of Mrs Isaacs' paper.)

Dr Glover was in the Chair and 33 Members and Associates were present (Glover, Payne, Weiss, Gillespie, A. Stephen, Rosenberg, J. Riviere, Isaacs, Reis, Lantos, Fleischer-Gero, Heimann, Klein, Hoffer, A. Freud, Burlingham, Stross, H. Hoffer, Balint, Money-Kyrle, Rubens, Frank, Low, Herford, Friedlander, Winnicott, Sharpe, Brierley, Franklin, Wilson, Taylor, Usher, Evans).

Eight candidate-guests were present (Schwarz, Milner, Cooke, Mannheim, Hollischer, Meynell, Bonnard, Dr Schlossberg).

The minutes having been circulated were taken as read.

Dr Glover read a contribution sent by Dr Fairbairn.

This was followed by contributions by Major A. Stephen and Dr Fuchs, the latter read by Dr Glover in Dr Fuchs' absence. Dr Isaacs replied to the speakers who read papers at the last meeting. A contribution sent by Dr K. Stephen was read by Major Stephen.

A discussion followed opened by Miss Low, carried on by Miss Freud, who asked for the opportunity to present considered questions not to be answered spontaneously but at another meeting. She did not think it the time for free discussion only.

Dr Balint suggested that the questions should be circulated beforehand. This would shorten the procedure. Dr Friedlander said that questions should be put forward in the meeting so that they could be elaborated. Dr Heimann said that time was too limited. Dr Rosenberg said other people wished to contribute. Dr Wilson suggested that Miss Freud and Dr Isaacs should conduct the next meeting. Dr Friedlander suggested that people should not be bound by limited time. Dr Glover asked whether the members wished to go on with the discussion of this paper. Mrs Riviere suggested that contributions should be circulated beforehand. Dr Glover said that the Secretary reminded him that for practical reasons it would not be possible to circulate multiple contributions before the meeting.

The following decisions were made:

1 that the discussion at the next meeting should take the form of

  prepared questions and if necessary exposition of the considerations leading up to them.
2 that all members wishing to contribute should notify the
  Programme Committee (c/o Institute of P.A.) of their intention
  and of the length of their paper within a few days of receiving
  the enclosed copy of the proceedings.
3 if it is likely that the amount of material would exceed the limits
  of one meeting, the Committee should be authorized to select
  certain contributions to be given at that meeting and to give the
  other Members opportunity of reading their contributions at a
  subsequent meeting.
4 That the meetings should close at 10.15 p.m.
5 That the next discussion meeting will be held on March 17th.

  (signed) Edward Glover

Discussion held on February 17th, 1943

**Continuation of Discussion on Mrs Susan Isaacs' paper
'The Nature and Function of Phantasy'**

DR W. R. D. FAIRBAIRN (Paper, read by Dr Glover in Dr
Fairbairn's absence): It seems to me that, in considering the role of
phantasy in mental life and the stage at which it comes into
operation, we can help to clarify our ideas to some extent by taking
into account the general classification of mental processes which
emerges from the non-psychoanalytical 'analysis' of mental processes undertaken by G. F. Stout (Stout 1927). Highly intel-
lectualized and preoccupied with the conscious as Stout's approach
is, he must nevertheless be credited with a remarkable capacity for
analysing psychological phenomena into their elements and reducing
these elements to order. According to Stout, mental activity
manifests itself in three modes and at three levels. The three modes
which he distinguishes are (1) cognition (knowing), (2) affection
(feeling), and (3) conation (doing) and the three levels which he
described are (1) the perceptual, (2) the ideational or imaginative, and
(3) the conceptual. These two classifications may be profitably combined in a table such as appears opposite.

Actually all these levels and modes are represented in some measure
in all human mental activity, but with the emphasis varying both as
regards level and mode according to circumstances in the adult. In the
infant, mental processes are conducted predominantly at the
perceptual level; and mental growth consists in a gradual development

	Cognitive	Affective	Conative
Perceptual level	Perception	Emotion	Impulse
Ideational level	Imagination	Sentiment	Desire
Conceptual level	Conception	Ideal	Purpose

from the perceptual through the ideational to the conceptual level. At the same time, although the mental life of the infant belongs characteristically to the perceptual level, it is not altogether devoid of ideational, and even conceptual elements. From this point of view it may, therefore, be claimed that phantasy, which is an ideational process, is present in some measure from the outset of life, although it is only when infancy is succeeded by early childhood that, with the establishment of the ideational level proper, phantasy reaches its zenith – only later to become submerged in part by processes belonging to the conceptual level as this becomes consolidated.

In terms of the above classification, one of the distinctive features of psychoanalytical thought is seen to lie in the importance which it attaches to mental processes belonging to the ideational level. Such a classification also enables us to understand how it comes about that analysts may differ regarding the stage at which phantasy makes its appearance. The fact would seem to be that phantasy is already operative in embryonic form from the earliest days of infancy, and that, as an ideational process, it plays an increasingly important part in mental life as the ideational level is reached. It would thus appear to be wrong to say that phantasy plays no part in the mental life of infancy. At the same time it would be equally wrong to say that infancy is the period of life during which phantasy manifests itself most characteristically and exercises its chief effects.

In conclusion, I cannot refrain from voicing the opinion that the explanatory concept of 'phantasy' has now been rendered obsolete by the concepts of 'psychical reality' and 'internal objects', which the work of Mrs Klein and her followers has done so much to develop; and in my opinion the time is now ripe for us to replace the concept of 'phantasy' by a concept of an 'inner reality' peopled by the ego and its internal objects. These internal objects should be regarded as having an organized structure, an identity of their own, an endopsychic existence, and an activity as real within the inner world as those of any objects in the outer world. To attribute such features to internal objects may at first seem startling to some; but, after all, they are only features which Freud has already attributed to the superego. What has now emerged is simply that the superego is not the only internal object. The activity of the internal objects, like that of the ego, is, of course, ultimately derived from the impulses originating in the id. Nevertheless, subject to this proviso, these objects must be regarded as having an activity of their own. Inner reality thus becomes the scene of situations involving relationships between the ego and its internal objects. The concept of 'phantasy' is purely functional and can only be applied to activity on the part of the ego. It is quite inadequate to describe inner situations involving the relationships of the ego to internal objects possessing an endopsychic structure and dynamic qualities. It would still seem legitimate, however, to speak of 'phantasies' in the plural (or of 'a phantasy') to describe specific inner situations (or a specific inner situation), so long as this limitation of meaning is appreciated.

DR ADRIAN STEPHEN: I want to say something about the part of Mrs Isaacs' paper in which she describes phantasy as the 'psychic representative' of instinct. To me she seems both to be in complete accord with Professor Freud and to be right. Some of her critics, however, think otherwise; they think that she both disagrees with Professor Freud and is wrong, and I want to describe what seems to me one cause of this difference of opinion.

There are others too, but I believe that one cause of disagreement lies in the difficulty which we all face of finding terms adequate to express our meaning. Freud did, indeed, build up for us what Dr Glover has rightly described as an 'orderly series of concepts' and he gave us a language in which we can discuss these concepts and their practical application. That is true; but it is also true as Freud would have readily admitted that these concepts are somewhat vague and tentative and that they are built up mainly on the observation of the minds of adults. If we treat them, therefore, as though they were as clearly defined as, say, the concepts of algebra, and if we regard phantasy for instance as the name of something static, something which must be of exactly the same nature in children and in grown-ups, something without a developmental history, then we are quite certain to fall both into disagreement with one another and into mistakes. If we want to avoid mistakes and disagreements that are founded on misunderstandings we must be continually referring back from the concepts and from the abstract words to the phenomena which they are meant to explain. Otherwise, though our pronouncements may sound impressive they will tend to be wrong even when they are not quite empty of all meaningful content.

To understand what Professor Freud and Mrs Isaacs have said we must first be as clear as possible about what they both mean by the technical terms 'instinct' and 'phantasy' and what Mrs Isaacs means by the term 'psychic representative'.

As to the word 'instinct', there are, so far as I can see, no great differences between the ways in which it is used by various analysts. I have no books by me to verify my references but Freud somewhere, if I remember right, calls it 'border-line concept'. [Freud, S. 1900: 105; SE 4: 122] Its main purpose in psychoanalytic theory is to provide a class name for the causes of certain processes of both a psychic and physical character. Physical processes might be, for example, those which lead up to and accompany sexual intercourse, and the psychic processes are the corresponding 'needs' or 'wants' and I take it that it is to these that Mrs Isaacs refers by the name of 'phantasies'. The question arises as to whether she is justified in using that term – or, rather, as to what is the nature of the psychic processes which occur, for if we know that it matters little what we call them.

To go back to Freud's writings, in a passage which is familiar to us all, at the very beginning of his 'Three Contributions to the Theory of Sex', [Freud, S. 1905: 78; SE 7: 136] he describes instincts as having aims and objects. 'Aim' is the word for the behaviour which an instinct impels us to take, for instance sexual intercourse, and object is the word for the person with whom the intercourse is to take place; or eating, I take it, may be the aim of an instinct and food the object. Freud in this passage was obviously thinking of cases in which the object is a concrete object, but he would certainly have agreed, as I suppose we all should, that the object may be imaginary or, if you like, phantastic.

It seems to me that when she is speaking of purely imaginary instinctual objects Mrs Isaacs is clearly justified in speaking as she does. In these cases the object must of necessity be phantastic, and very possibly the aim remains phantastic also. Here, surely, phantasy is the psychic representation of the instinct, but it does not seem to me that the case is much altered when the objects concerned are material, such as a human being or part of one.

It seems to me that, so far as we can tell, whether the object is concrete or not and whether the instinctual impulse is carried into action physically or not; in every case there is the imagination or, if you like, phantasy or fulfilment. Sometimes we use the word 'wish' in this connection, we call the impulses 'wishes' and often the phantasies which represent them are described as dreams (though dreams, of course, as we know them in adults at least, always represent several different wishes in conflict).

It seems to me that among adults phantasy is the psychic

representative of instinct in all cases; the question is whether this is true of children also. I agree with Mrs Isaacs that it is harder to be certain about this for one who has never analysed a child than it is for one who has, but in the absence of evidence to the contrary it seems at any rate more economical to suppose that in this way adults and children are alike.

Of course we all know that phantasies are built up on the basis of memories, memories of satisfaction and frustration and so on, and as we grow older, and as our instincts evolve and our store of memories becomes greater and more varied, no doubt our phantasies change considerably in the complexity and variety of their content, but it is difficult to suppose that instinctual impulses even in a small baby are not accompanied by phantasies of some sort of its fulfilment. To suppose this would be really to suppose that a baby can have a wish without wishing for anything – and to my thinking wishing for something implies phantasying the fulfilment of that wish.

Miss Freud has argued among other things that Mrs Isaacs tends by her view of phantasy to minimize the importance of the pleasure principle. If I understand her, she thinks that Mrs Isaacs must necessarily underestimate the importance of the pleasure that a child gets by satisfying its instinctual needs. Of course I do not know what answer Mrs Isaacs herself would give but to me the criticism seems based on the mistake which Freud has described as taking abstractions too rigidly. I will explain what I mean by an example. We all of us know what it is to be thirsty. In this condition we mostly try to get hold of something to drink and we probably have conscious and unconscious phantasies both about the drink we want and about how to obtain it. We can then describe our psychic processes in two ways. We can say that we want a drink or that we want to quench our thirst. In the one case we are describing a phantasy about the object, in the other we are describing our aim of reducing instinctual tension. In actual fact, though we are employing different words and different concepts, the facts we are trying to describe are really the same. What we want is not merely the drink and not merely the satisfaction of quenching our thirst. What we want is the thirst-satisfying drink – and our phantasy is that we get this drink and to say this is certainly not to deny the importance of the pleasure.

The phantasy and the impulse to get pleasure are not two separate psychic entities though it may be useful sometimes to separate them conceptually; they are two aspects of one psychic process and to assert the existence of one is not to minimize the importance of the other.

DR S. FOULKES (read by Dr Glover in Dr Foulkes' absence): In the first instance I want to express my gratitude and admiration for Mrs Isaacs' excellent presentation of the subject, with which I find myself in agreement on many points. It is, however, our present purpose to take up some points of disagreement and in particular to scrutinize the material as to essential deviations from Freud's own tenets.

My own position is briefly as follows: I can confirm most of Mrs Klein's clinical findings, the more so as I was familiar with them, in particular through psychoanalytical investigations on psychotics, long before I came to this country and learned that they are considered the prerogative of Mrs Klein and her collaborators. These clinical data have, in my opinion, a legitimate place inside psychoanalysis. I had looked upon them as common knowledge amongst analysts everywhere. I must confess that I was mistaken in this. Therefore it is undoubtedly still more a merit of Mrs Klein and her co-workers to have emphatically drawn the attention of analysts to them. There is a tendency, however, to make these new discoveries the backbone of analytical technique and theory to the detriment and omission of at least some of the fundamental analytical concepts. This is certainly not done intentionally and deliberately but should come out clearly when things are thought out to their ultimate conclusion, which we all hope will be the result of this series of discussions. Against this tendency analysts are right to make a firm stand, they would be poor analysts indeed if they gave up fundamental positions lightly.

On the present occasion I can take up only a few points, picking out those not so likely being dealt with by others. First a word to Mrs Isaacs' controversy with Dr Brierley, because it seems typical of a certain confusion. Mrs Isaacs is not correct in stating that words stand in the first place for concepts. A lot of work in modern psychology, in particular also in connection with the study of the aphanasis, has established the fact that conceptual thinking corresponds to the highest level of mental achievement, the latest to be attained in development, both phylogenetically and ontogenetically, and the earliest to be lost again. Words are in the first instance expressions of something emotional, when they come to have a meaning they are quite concrete, inseparable from the objects or situations to which they belong, in fact they are themselves concrete things in the mind and treated as such. Only very much later can they be used in the abstract as a designation, for instance, of a whole category of things or for an abstract idea. This so-called significative function of language is precisely the one exclusively to be used in scientific, rational thinking and this level must be attained if a scientific approach to the world is to be possible. It is this dehydrated, lifeless, skeletal use of words for which we aim, and for good reasons, if we want to compress our clinical experiences, for instance, into scientific terms to be used for a precise and short cut. It is a dry business, I know, but it would be silly to deny those of us who feel obliged to trouble about it, the capacity of a full and deep understanding of life experience for that reason. It would be just the same as to say that somebody who understands the theory of music cannot understand a concert. I mention this only because I have come up against such an attitude. Mrs Isaacs writes: 'But if there is any question of codes and decoding, it is surely the abstract term which has to be decoded into concrete experience, perceptions and images, as these are lived.' [p. 275] No, this is surely not so. Not if we are concerned, as we are in that context, with a scientific formulation as such. If we were concerned with the analysis of the person who makes that statement Mrs Isaacs would be perfectly right. It seems to me significant that this assumption is in fact all the time silently made, every statement or experience is treated as an epiphenomenon which has to be traced back to an underlying 'unconscious phantasy' to discover its true meaning. This is not even true always inside the procedure of an analysis and mostly absurd outside it. This brings me to another point, of still more general importance in Mrs Isaacs' paper. On pages [271–2], Mrs Isaacs writes: 'I wish to state here my opinion that the primary content of all mental processes are unconscious phantasies. Such phantasies are the basis of all unconscious and conscious thought processes.' Personally I agree with this statement, although the term 'phantasy' is somewhat oblique. Near the analytic circle, Schilder has pointed this out more scientifically as early as 1922 in his paper 'Ueber Gedankenentwicklung' (On Thought Development), and Bleuler has something to say on the matter in his book *Die Naturgeschichte der Seele und ihres Bewusstwerdens* (The Natural Science of the Mind and its Attaining Consciousness) (Bleuler 1921). But for all these people, as well as for Freud, the whole of mental life, conscious or unconscious, is suspended between the two material realities of body and outside world. The instinct, the conceptual representative of the life force, is firmly rooted physically in the body and always directed towards the outside world, to which in a certain sense the body itself belongs. Mental life, the ego and superego, develop by way of a compromise as retardation stations and redirecting points in the clash of these realities. Phantasies are significant and may be highly important nodal points. But in Mrs Isaacs' theory it would look as if they were primary motors, lords in their own rights, absorbing instinctual urges and physical reality as their material only. It looks as if we were back at the religious and spiritual level with an independent soul having energies of its own from another world. This is particularly

364

so when these phantasies have attained the dignity of 'inner objects'. This came out beautifully in Dr Heimann's recent paper, in which it looks as if the inner devils lastly decide what is going to happen to the patient. Now many people, I am sure, knew long before Freud that the devil was the projection of man's bad and God of his good impulses but they would not therefore have taken them as existent in reality. On the contrary, those who naïvely believe in God and the Devil would not recognize them as personifications of man's impulses. By the way, with Mrs Isaacs' views one cannot even hope to attempt the solution of such an important problem as to why in the Middle Ages all the inner objects were in the outside world whereas in the modern world they are mostly found inside, whereas I with my view, can. Why is it that according to hers and others' observations children form a typically western European, Puritan, Christian super-ego as early as, say, in the second year of life? To put it very briefly, inner objects and unconscious phantasies are to be analysed and analysis does not consist in tracing mental phenomena to the unconscious phantasy level and leaving it at that. I repeat that these percepts have a legitimate place in psychoanalytical thought and technique – what place I hope to point out another time – but to base our theory on them would seem to me a regression to pre-scientific thinking.

DR KARIN STEPHEN (Paper read by Dr Adrian Stephen in Dr Karin Stephen's absence): I am in hopes that the result of these discussions of our scientific differences will lead to a real clarification at least of our recognition of the points about which we do not agree, and perhaps even that they may lead to such an improvement in our understanding of each other's meaning that some at any rate of our apparent differences will be resolved by the discovery that they rested on misunderstandings.

But if we are each to get our own ideas clear to ourselves, and still more if we are to make them clear to each other, one thing is very important, that we should take the greatest care that the sense in which we use our words is unambiguous and always consistently the same, otherwise we shall get confused in our own minds and argue at cross purposes with each other.

It is in order to forestall this danger, not in order to carp or split hairs, that I want to say a few words about Mrs Isaacs' use of the word 'phantasy'.

In reading her extremely stimulating paper, with much of which I found I agreed, I had the feeling that even she had not escaped some ambiguity and inconsistency in her description of what she meant by phantasy. A large part of the paper was, as she explained, devoted to

365

defining phantasy. To begin with she pointed out that, spelling the word with a '*ph*' it was to be taken to refer to 'unconscious mental content, which may seldom or never become conscious'. She then goes on to describe what kind of mental contents she means by these unconscious phantasies. She says that there are 'the primary contents of all mental processes' and that 'phantasy is the mental corollary, the psychic representative of instinct, and there is no impulse, no instinctual urge, which is not experienced as unconscious.

What is meant here, I take it, is that instinct is always accompanied by the feeling of doing what the instinct demands, a feeling which may be based on rudimentary motor activity. This agrees with Mrs Isaacs' quotation from Mrs Riviere when she says, 'When we speak of "phantasies" in babies or small children . . . we surmise that the child feels as if it were carrying out the desired action and that this affective feeling is accompanied by a corresponding physical excitation in certain organs'. [pp. 283–4]

Mrs Isaacs explains that what she and Mrs Riviere mean by phantasy in calling it the psychic representative of instinct, this feeling, that is, of carrying out the instinct, is very like what Freud meant when he spoke of 'the attempt at satisfaction by hallucination', and she says 'the capacity to hallucinate is, in my view, either identical with phantasy or a precondition for it'. Taken all together I think Mrs Isaacs makes it clear what she means by her description of phantasy as the psychic representative of instinct, except that it is left uncertain whether this unconscious mental content is simply *not* conscious or is unconscious in the sense of being repressed.

But elsewhere Mrs Isaacs gives an alternative description of phantasy which seems to me to go considerably beyond this description of it as the psychic representative of instinct. She quotes Mrs Riviere again when she says, 'I wish especially to point out that, from the very beginning of life, on Freud's own hypothesis, the psyche responds to its experiences by interpreting them – or rather *mis*interpreting them, in a subjective manner that increases its pleasure and preserves it from pain. It (phantasy) consists of true perceptions and false interpretations.' [p. 282]

Now it is true that this could be applied to the interpretation of rudimentary motor activities of the kind which would be used to carry out an instinctual urge, little sucking movements for instance, subjectively experienced as being the actual carrying out of the instinct in reality. But in many of the illustrations she gives of this sort of 'subjective interpretation', or misinterpretation, of experience, Mrs Isaacs widens the meaning beyond this so as to include phantasies which have reference to external objects and events and presuppose the power to distinguish between me and not-me, for instance when she says that the child in an anxiety state experiences mental disintegration as 'my-mother-inside-me-is-in-bits'. It may be that infants, even at a very early age, are capable of both these kinds of phantasy, or it may be, as I think Mrs Isaacs' critics would maintain, that they are only capable of the former, simpler kind. This is not the point I want to discuss here. My point is just this, that although of course there would be genetic continuity between these two meanings of phantasy, which must not be forgotten, this does not, it seems to me, exonerate us from the need to keep the distinction clear between the first description of phantasy, which may be regarded as a mere subjective misinterpretation, under the influence of the pleasure principle, of the somatic accompaniment of instinct itself, and this other way of using the word to apply to subjective misinterpretations which presuppose such more highly developed perceptual and discriminative powers.

I recognize the difficulties of precision and also the dangers of too great pedantry but still I feel that the more we are able to keep clear of ambiguity in the use of such key words as this one, 'phantasy', and the more precisely and consistently we manage to use them, the more clearly our real differences will come to light and the less our efforts will be wasted by arguing at cross purposes.

MRS SUSAN ISAACS — *Reply to discussion* I have appreciated all those speakers in the discussion who put forward their queries and doubts and suggestions in a co-operative and thought-provoking manner. I believe we have all felt a great pleasure in the frank exchange of our views. Many interesting points arose, which merit careful attention.

As I said before the discussion, I do not propose to enter in my present reply into the various questions which relate to the problem of regression. It has been agreed that I shall do so in a full paper, to be read at a meeting in April or early May. I have noted the various comments on this subject made by Dr Jones, Dr Payne, Miss Freud, Miss Sharpe, Dr Friedlander, and Dr Balint.

I was encouraged to find that Dr Jones was in agreement with the procedure and with the main content of my paper. I certainly accept his view that defence phantasies are in the last resort also wish-fulfilments and are derived from instinctual sources. They are special modifications of instinctual aims and energies. In my paper [p. 278] I said: 'in a wider sense all these mechanisms which aim at diminishing instinctual tension, anxiety, and guilt, also serve the aim of wish-fulfilment. But it proves helpful to discriminate the specific modes of these different mechanisms and their particular aims.'

I welcome, too, the emphatic view of Dr Jones and others that a priori arguments upon the question of phantasy are of little use, and that only a close observation and discussion of empirical data can carry us further. What we want to know is what does go on in the infant's mind, and how these early processes develop into the later ones with which we are more familiar.

I appreciate Dr Brierley's re-statement of her earlier comments on Mrs Klein's terminology. I fully accept her emphasis on the importance of a proper formulation, for the purposes of abstract thinking, of our discoveries about the child's experiences. I am sure Dr Brierley is right that we have not paid enough attention to the terms of our formulations. But I still feel that 'phantasy' is a better term than the word 'meaning' for describing the manifold facts which I have grouped under it.

I agree with Dr Brierley, too, that the infant's hallucination of the wished-for sensations aroused by his first experience of the nipple is his first memory as well as his first phantasy. I have long thought that we as analysts should consider the phenomena studied by Jaensch and other experimental psychologists under the term 'eidetic imagery', and see where these fitted in with our own views. This is one of the many tasks which lie around us, waiting to be taken up.

The whole problem of the relation between phantasy and perception, phantasy and thinking, calls for much further study. I would not say that thinking is a variety of phantasy, but I should say that it is derived from phantasy – or, rather, from the inter-play between phantasy and external reality. This problem, the inter-play of internal and external reality, is one which I hope we shall be able to persuade Melanie Klein to discuss in some future paper in this series.

The external world certainly forces itself upon the attention of the child, in one way or another, early and continuously. But, as Freud pointed out and the various facts of experience during the first few weeks confirm, the external world which does not at once satisfy our wishes, which frustrates or interferes with us, is hated and rejected. We may fear it and watch it and attend to it, in order to defend ourselves against it; but not until it is in some degree libidinized, receives some measure of love, can it be played with and learnt about and understood. The postponement of satisfaction and the suspense involved in the complicated learning and thinking, about external reality which the child presently accomplishes, can only be endured and sustained when it itself satisfies instinctual urges, expressed in phantasies, as well. Learning depends upon interest, and interest is derived both from desire, curiosity and fear; but desire and curiosity must predominate. I reminded you in my paper of Melanie Klein's work on symbol-formation. The external world is libidinized through the process of symbol-formation. Almost every hour of free association reveals to us something of the phantasies which have sustained the development of interest in the external world and the process of learning about it is drawn. It is a familiar fact that, from one point of view, every instance of concern with reality, whether practical or theoretical, is also a sublimation. I may remind you of Miss Sharpe's paper on 'Similar and Divergent Unconscious Determinants Underlying the Sublimations of Pure Art and Pure Science'. (Sharpe 1935: 186–202)

Dr Payne reminded us very appositely of the fact that both Freud and Ferenczi held that conversion symptoms in the hysteric make use of sensations, movements, and visceral changes, as an archaic mode of expression of feelings, phantasies, and object-relationships.

Dr Payne also remarked that phantasy does not occur until there has been psychic experience. I agree. Indeed I thought I had made this clear in the passage which I quoted from Mrs Riviere's paper, and my comments upon it. Phantasy is a 'subjective interpretation' of experience, as well as the mental expression of instinctual trends.

The first psychical experiences result from the massive and varied stimuli of birth and the first intake and expulsion of breath followed presently by the first feed. Those considerable experiences during the first twenty-four hours must already evoke the first mental activity, and provide the material for both phantasy and memory. Dr Middlemore's studies of the effect of the earliest feeding experiences are relevant here.

Dr Payne's further points will be discussed in the paper on regression, but I might say now that I certainly do not suggest, nor have I ever heard it suggested, that these early phantasies are immutable, always 'fixated', or dynamically different from those which develop later on. I stressed their importance only because their existence and their dynamic influence have so often been and still are being denied altogether.

With Dr Scott's valuable suggestions as to the unity of body-mind experience in the infant, the emergence of distinct sensations, feelings, etc. from the matrix of implicit phantasy, and the need to know much more than we do now of the body-ego, I am in full agreement, and consider these points to be of great importance. I hope Dr Scott himself will before long have leisure enough to develop them more fully for us.

Dr Balint's point that we should take into consideration the large amount of time spent by the infant in feeding, when discussing the relative amount of satisfaction and dissatisfaction in his waking hours, is of course an important one. This consideration is part of the view which I quoted from Bernfeld, and with which Melanie Klein's conclusions are in harmony, that oral satisfactions are the source of the progressive libidinization of the stimuli and bodily experiences which at first bring only irritation and anxiety.

Dr Balint's query as to the actual feelings of the infant in the first few months of life is one which can only be settled by more detailed study and records, such as the work of Merrell Middlemore.

I appreciated Miss Sharpe's contribution, a large part of which amplified with vivid material many of Melanie Klein's views as to early phantasy. The questions she raised, and a certain degree of misunderstanding of Mrs Klein's position, I shall consider more fully in the paper on regression.

Miss Sharpe seems to me to make far too distinct a separation between the early Oedipus setting, with its phantasies of incorporation and the later developed ego with the Oedipus complex as Freud saw it. It is in the understanding of the steps between these two, all the varied paths of development from the earlier to the later phases, and all the phantasies and experiences encountered and lived through on the way, that the key to the question of technique lies. The patient's ego will dispel its own illusions and accomplish its own work of mourning – as Miss Sharpe and Dr Pratt so vividly express the problem – if only we can see and can show him each situation which has been felt and experienced, been fled from or denied or overcome or accepted, as he grew from the earlier to the later stages of life; if we can help him to put all these phantasies and experiences into words as they come up again in the transference situation.

To turn now to Miss Freud's contribution. It would certainly mean a great advance in our whole approach to the questions at issue if our differences were in fact narrowed down to the subject of mental functioning in the first year of life. But it does not seem to me that this has yet happened. Some of the passages from the Report by Miss Freud and Mrs Burlingham on which I commented, and to which Mrs Burlingham refers, dealt with the second year. The views of Dr Wälder which Dr Friedlander quotes with approval, and the position so tenaciously held by Dr Lantos, still assume that phantasies come into operation and are traceable only in the third and fourth years. So that mental life in the second year is certainly as much in debate as the first year.

With regard to Miss Freud's comments upon my quotation from the Preface to the *New Introductory Lectures*, I shall ask you to note that I said: 'the spirit of our enquiries should be that of Freud's own when he wrote' the quoted passage. I might perhaps have quoted the following passage: 'You know that we have never been proud of the fullness and finality of our knowledge and our capacity; as at the beginning, we are ready now to admit the incompleteness of our understanding, to learn new things and to alter our methods in any way that yields better results.' [Freud, S. 1919: 392; SE 18:159][1]

I wish to add that I myself have never accepted Dr Glover's suggestion that this series of meetings should confine itself to arguing about controversial points only, taken in a narrow sense. In my view and that of many other Members (and in agreement with the report of the Programme Committee), the aim of these discussions is the clarification and better formulation and understanding of the different scientific theories held by different people. As Dr Jones put it, we need to find first a basis of agreed conclusions, from which to explore the more difficult points of divergence.

As regards Miss Freud's second objection, I would point out that Freud said we all have an inveterate prejudice in favour of external reality, and have constantly to exercise great self-control not to fall into this error. Dr Jones, too, agreed how necessary it is to remind ourselves not to underestimate psychical reality.

I cannot help regretting very much that Miss Freud does not consider it possible that these discussions should provide an opportunity for establishing the truth or untruth of the views put forward, especially as definite evidence has been offered. It seems unsound to concentrate first on the secondary question of compatibility or incompatibility, and the formalistic considerations such as those to which she devoted herself.

I do not accept her contention that Melanie Klein's views 'explicitly retain' and 'implicitly deny' existing analytic conceptions. Where we deny or wish to revise existing conceptions, we say so. Let us look at each of Miss Freud's points in turn – omitting point (v) [pp. 328–9], which deals with regression and to which I shall return in my paper on that subject.

Regarding my use of the term 'phantasy', I may point out that Freud has repeatedly said that *everything* is unconscious to start with, whether or not it become conscious later on, under certain conditions. And in the inimitable phrase which I quoted, Freud spoke of our need to 'learn to emancipate ourselves from our sense of the importance of that symptom which consists in being conscious'.

Points (ii) and (iii) I shall take together, as they are closely related. I know of no evidence to show that in the earliest stages we can distinguish between mental processes which are instinct-derivatives and those which are not. As Dr Brierley suggested, the infant's hallucinatory wish-fulfilment is probably the first memory as well as the first phantasy. And as Dr Scott put it, the earliest 'implicit phantasy' which is so intimately bound up with sensations and interprets sensations, is the matrix from which distinguishable sensations, feelings, and images, etc. gradually emerge. And, as I have already agreed, the details of the way in which perception and knowledge of external reality become differentiated from phantasy and internal reality await much fuller study.

Phantasy as the imaginal corollary does not take the place of the sensorial corollary in our views. It seems to me that, both in these remarks of Miss Freud's and in Mrs Burlingham's comments, there is a marked tendency to treat sensations as if they were solely a bodily matter, were non-mental. But if, as Freud maintained, they are psychical experiences, then from the beginning, phantasy and images are inherent in sensations and grow out of them. (Here, once more, we are on the same ground as the great academic psychologists, such as Ward, James, and Stout.) Dr Scott's point about the infant's 'phantasy of the body' is a very important one in this connection. How much we have yet to learn about these things.

In my paper I explicitly emphasized the importance of pleasurable sensations, as well as the way in which the infant interprets his actual experiences, his real internal and external sensations, in order to increase pleasure and diminish pain. And throughout Melanie Klein's clinical studies she has emphasized the importance of pleasurable bodily experiences.

In connection with this point, Miss Freud referred to the 'pleasure principle' as 'the sole governing principle within the unconscious'. But after all there is Freud's own book *Beyond the Pleasure Principle*. And on pp. 37–8 of that book, speaking of the dreams of traumatic neurosis, he says: 'they thus afford us an insight into a function of the psychic apparatus, which without contradicting the pleasure-principle, is nevertheless independent of it, and appears to be of earlier origin than the aim of attaining pleasure and avoiding pain.' [Freud, S. 1920: 37–8; SE 18: 32][2] Now here we have in fact one of the actual differences between the work of Melanie Klein and some other analysts. Melanie Klein has paid attention to these later developments of Freud's own theory regarding e.g. the death instinct, and found them fruitful in her investigations. I believe that Dr Heimann, in her paper on introjection and projection, will bring out the bearings of this point.

Miss Freud's fourth point is that 'the nature of the unconscious phantasies described by Melanie Klein as existent in the first year of life completely alters the conception of unconscious life as such'; and this point is elaborated in some detail.

First, Miss Freud takes my remark that the infant identifies the mother who does not remove a source of pain with the pain itself. Now I would agree that my way of stating this fact was open to her interpretation, although I did not intend it. I was condensing in this \ statement the observer's knowledge and the infant's experience. Anna Freud is quite right that in the early days the infant does not experience the negative fact of the mother's not removing the source of pain. That is a later realization. The pain itself is positive, the 'bad' mother is a positive experience. When at 6 months or so, the infant sits up and *sees* that she does not come when he wants her, he may make the link between what he sees of her not coming and the pain or dissatisfaction he feels. But in the earliest days and the level of the primary process, loss and dissatisfaction or deprivation are felt in sensation as positive experiences. A patient of mine said recently, in the common phrase, that she was 'full of emptiness' and we are all familiar with similar examples. Emptiness is positive, in sensation; just as darkness is an actual thing, not the mere absence of light. Indeed we never feel darkness to be the absence of light, whatever we may know. Darkness falls, like a curtain or a blanket. When the light comes it drives away the darkness. And so on. I certainly do not mean to suggest that the infant's early experiences include the idea of negation.

But I do not see how Miss Freud arrives at the notion that I attribute a sense of time to the young infant or include this in my idea of the primary process. I do not use the phrase 'the phantasy of the mother's permanent absence'. It is *Freud* who says of the infant, 'as soon as he misses his mother he behaves as if he were never going to see her again'. All I add is: 'He behaves as if', to my mind, is the same thing as saying 'he has phantasies that . . .' etc.

I have not suggested that the primary process itself includes integrative functions, or that the concept should be altered so as to include integration.

But I certainly do not consider that the primary process can be held to operate over the whole field of the infant's mental life and behaviour for more than the first few weeks of life – if so long. I should be interested to know when Miss Freud and Mrs Burlingham believe that the secondary processes *begin* to operate. Freud himself says in a passage which I shall quote in a moment: 'So far as we know, a psychic apparatus possessing only the primary process does not exist.' The progressive alterations in the infant's responses during, for example, the second month onward show that there is a very considerable degree of integration in behaviour and perception. I drew your attention to the first signs of memory, anticipation, etc. by the time the infant is 5–6 months of age, there is a high degree of integration and co-ordination. It seems to me entirely against the observable facts to hold that his mental life – even from 3 months on – is dominated wholly and entirely by the primary process and the 'free and independent flow of instinctual urges', without conflict or integration.

I was indeed puzzled by Miss Freud's assumption that the first year of life was devoted to 'the kind of uncorrelated mental life to which dream-function regresses' [p. 331]. I remember no passage in Freud's writings which shows that he held this view. If there is one, I hope she will point it out. (In passing, I draw attention to the contradiction between such a view and that of Dr Lantos, who emphasizes the infant's intelligence and adaptation to reality – or that of Mrs Burlingham, with her emphasis on memory-images.)

I have been re-reading *The Interpretation of Dreams*, and shall quote a passage bearing on this question. It is rather a long passage, but we need the whole of it.

On p. 555 of the last English edition, Freud writes:

> When I termed one of the psychic processes in the psychic apparatus the primary process, I did so not only in consideration of its status and function, but was also able to take account of the temporal relationship actually involved. So far we know a psychic apparatus possessing only the primary process does not exist, and is to that extent a theoretical fiction; but this at least is a fact, that the primary processes are present in the apparatus from the beginning, while the secondary processes only take shape gradually during the course of life, inhibiting and overlaying the primary, while gaining complete control over them perhaps only in the prime of life. Owing to this belated arrival of the secondary processes, the essence of our being, consisting of unconscious wish-impulses, remains something which cannot be grasped or inhibited by the preconscious; and its part is once and for all restricted to indicating the most appropriate paths for the wish-impulses originating in the unconscious.
>
> [Freud, S. 1900: 555; SE 5: 603][3]

Now you will note that Freud says that a psychic apparatus possessing only a primary process is a 'theoretical fiction'. But later on, he speaks of the 'belated arrival' of the secondary processes, which seems somewhat contradictory. The contradiction is resolved if we take the 'belated arrival' to refer not so much to the *onset* of the secondary processes, their rudimentary beginnings, but rather to their full developments. And such a view would best accord with what we can see of the infant's actual development, in adaptation to reality, in control and integration. We can certainly say that Freud does not postulate a definite period of time during which the primary processes hold complete sway – indeed, he expressly rules this possibility out.

From about the second month on, the infant spends an increasing amount of time in experimentative play, which is, at one and the same time, an adaptive, integrated activity, adapted to a limited reality, and a means of expressing phantasy, a wish-fulfilment. But from about this time he also spends a growing amount of time in quiet dozing or semi-dozing, or lying peacefully awake. It seems likely that in these quiet waking moments he is day-dreaming and that the pleasure-ego is being built up and enjoyed.

But all these detailed problems need to be considered more fully by careful observations and discussion.

Miss Freud suggests that only an 'active centre', a 'central personality' in the unconscious, could account for the presence of a 'so-called early defence'. But the child is born with the capacity for reflex defences against painful or disagreeable stimuli. He shows such reflex defences from the beginning, and could not survive without them.

One final comment on Miss Freud's points. She says: 'Unconscious life, according to this paper, thus combines qualities of the primary with important characteristics of the secondary process' [p. 330]. But so it does, indeed – in certain aspects, as Freud himself shows us. You will remember the passage which I quoted from Freud about unconscious phantasy-formations in normal people, which Mrs Hoffer completed for you in her reply.

Amongst the derivatives of the unconscious instinctual impulses, the character of which we have just described, there are some which unite in themselves opposite features. On the one hand, they are highly organized, exempt from self-contradictoriness, have made use of every acquisition of the system Cs, and would hardly be distinguished by our ordinary judgement from the formations of that system. On the other hand, they are unconscious and are incapable of becoming conscious. Thus they belong according to their qualities, to the system Pcs, but in actual fact to the Ucs. Their origin remains decisive for the fate they will undergo. We may compare them with those human half-breeds who, taken all round, resemble white men, but betray their coloured descent by some striking feature or other, on account of which they are excluded from society and enjoy none of the privileges of white people. Of such a nature are the phantasy-formations of normal persons as well as of neurotics, which we have recognized as preliminary phases in the formation both of dreams and of symptoms, and which, in spite of their high degree of organization, remain repressed and therefore cannot become conscious. They draw near to consciousness and remain undisturbed so long as they do not become strongly cathected, but as soon as a certain degree of this is exceeded, they are thrust back.

In other words, the Ucs does include different sorts of processes, and must not be taken to refer *only* to the earliest most primitive aspects of the mind, the primary processes.

I am inclined to think that some at least of the doubts and difficulties as to my views expressed in this discussion arose from the fact that in my paper I did not yet develop fully the truth which I mentioned in my Summary – item (h), regarding differences in the elaboration of phantasies. Phantasies are of many sorts and function at various levels of the Ucs, as well as in the preconscious and conscious minds. All this is implied in what I said and is an integral part of Melanie Klein's views; but it needs to be brought out more clearly and amply than I did in my paper.

I would again remind you of another of the quotations from Freud, one which I personally feel to be extraordinarily illuminating and significant.

It would certainly be wrong to imagine that the Ucs remains at rest while the whole work of the mind is performed by the Pcs, that the Ucs is something finished with, a vestigial organ, a residuum from the process of evolution; wrong also to assume that communication between the two systems is confined to the act of repression, the Pcs casting everything which disturbs it into the abyss of the Ucs. On the contrary, the Ucs is living and capable of development and maintains a number of other relations to the Pcs, amongst them that of co-operation. To sum up, we must say that the Ucs is continued into its so-called derivatives, is accessible to the influence of life, perpetually acts upon the Pcs, and even is, on its part, capable of influence by the latter system.

[Freud, S. 1915b: 122–3; SE 14: 190][4]

What I have said so far about the primary processes, integration, etc., bears also upon Mrs Burlingham's contribution. But I will add two further points. Her comments seem to me to outline a position which is untenable for the psychoanalyst, who can and does say that in the first few months, regarding the infant's instinctive wishes towards his mother 'whilst she is breast-feeding him, he wants to "eat" her'. [Freud, A. 1942: 182] Such a position could only be logically held by a psychologist who rejects the notion of cannibalistic impulses and oral sexuality at any age, and considered sucking to be purely a nutritive reflex. To credit the infant with oral wishes of a sexual character, with all the primary processes of the unconscious, to allow him conscious memory images and yet deny him phantasies, seems to me a theoretical *tour de force*, incapable of any logical justification.

I note also that neither Miss Freud nor Mrs Burlingham make any comment upon my view that it is inconceivable that the child should experience a 'deep and serious grief' when the mother is absent, without phantasies regarding her absences and her longed-for return.

Now I come to Dr Glover's comments. As regards his first point, it is my considered opinion that the present discussions are concerned with the differences between two developments of the many-sided discoveries and teachings of Freud. Freud opened up many possible lines of research, not all of which have been taken up and explored by every psychoanalyst. Notably his views on the death instinct and his concept of incorporated objects have been left on one side or rejected by many workers. And his insight into the possibility of understanding the play of a child in the second year of life has been neglected by many. Melanie Klein responded to this hint, as well as appreciating the profound significance of Freud's reflections upon the death instinct.

Again, I do most definitely claim that Melanie Klein's views are derived from Freud's own theories and observations. They are in large part identical with his. Where they differ, they are a necessary development of his work, arrived at by making use, with very young children, of Freud's own instrument of discovery, the study of the transference situation.

As regards my emphasis upon the need for first-hand acquaintance with the methods of child analysis, I shall let Dr Glover himself answer his own present objection.

In his contribution to the Symposium on Child Analysis, Dr Glover stated my position in a more extreme way than I myself have done. He wrote:

in discussing the subject of child analysis . . . I think it is possible that the idea of radical interference with the mental functioning of young children is calculated to arouse faint echoes of outworn conflicts. Otherwise I find it difficult to account for the fact that although the work on early analysis has been produced by one single investigator (Melanie Klein), it has been subjected to vigorous criticism by other analysts whose labours have been in quite distinct fields. Those who deal solely with adolescents and adults are of course entitled to hold theoretical views on the subject, but these are at best pious opinions. Even the work of Anna Freud, dealing as it does with the analysis of children in the latency period, can scarcely be regarded as a satisfactory basis of criticism of methods and findings, in a pre-latency grouping. Indeed it is striking to observe that many of Anna Freud's criticisms of Melanie Klein's methods are based on theoretical grounds. By the same token, I feel that I have little or no right to take part in a symposium on child analysis; the few male children I have analysed have been in the latency period. Nevertheless, whilst I should prefer to await the findings of investigators, who have used Melanie Klein's methods on children under the age of six, there are two aspects of the discussion on which the ordinary analysts may hold a legitimate if not too emphatic opinion.

[Glover, E. 1927: 385]

So far Dr Glover. I did not myself suggest that those without first-hand experience of early analysis could hold only 'pious' opinions about matters arising from it, but only that they were not in a favourable position to reject evidence with which they have not acquainted themselves in close detail.

In this paper on child analysis, Dr Glover goes on in a way which shows that at that time he also held that the issue between Anna Freud and Melanie Klein was between two different developments of Freud's work, and that Melanie Klein's was in the more direct line of descent. He discusses and criticizes Anna Freud's view that a transference neurosis does not occur in children, and her notion that because the child cannot give word-associations a 'radical difference in the approach' to children is required. He says:

But, after all, is there such a difference between the analysis of children and the analysis of adults? The adult plays with the association technique in much the same way as Melanie Klein's cases play with her toys. We do not obtain analytical material from the adult because the latter says 'I am prepared to co-operate with you by saying what is in my mind', but because, willy-nilly, as soon as the patient starts saying what is 'in his mind', it is magnetically distorted by what is 'not in his (conscious) mind', i.e., by unconscious phantasy, etc. The same seems to happen in child analysis, making allowance for what is practically only a difference in dialect.

[Glover, E. 1927: 386]

These are, you will note, Dr Glover's own words.

Among his other criticisms of my paper, Dr Glover complained that I did not mention many of Freud's concepts, which, he said, 'have fallen by the wayside'. In other words, he is in great haste to deny the necessary limitations of the contents of my paper by time and space, and leaps forward to assume that what has not yet been dealt with has been or will be denied. But he has no grounds whatever for such a leap, such an assumption. At no point in my paper did I make the absurd suggestion that I was offering a complete account of psychoanalytical theory, of Freud's or of Melanie Klein's views, not even a description of the unconscious, as Miss Freud implied. It was stated explicitly that the paper was of a preliminary character.

It is easy enough to enumerate a long string of concepts and ask that these should be considered in relation to the subject of phantasy. Of course they should be thus considered; and until we have gone into them, we cannot claim to have fully understood or expounded the nature and function of phantasy. Our whole discussion has brought out once again the real importance of formulating any new discoveries and hypotheses, not only clearly, but also so as to show their relationships with previously established conclusions. But to consider these matters is very different from merely enumerating them. Such a task requires time, co-operative effort and attention, open minds and the will to understand. This task is in the minds of most members the true purpose of this whole series of discussions.

Dr Glover, like Dr Friedlander, makes some definite assertions about my views and those of Melanie Klein which he could not substantiate by any quotation, and which have no foundation in fact. Both of these speakers asserted that we have abandoned Freud's conception of the biological development of the libido. There is not the slightest evidence for the assertion. We have only to turn to chapters 9, 10, and 12 of Melanie Klein's book (Klein 1932: 147, 176, 240) to see its untruth. In these chapters Mrs Klein makes it quite clear that she adheres to the concept of successive biological stages of the libido, but that she considers these phases to be less spread out in time than was originally thought. It was always held that there was considerable overlap between the successive phases; but, on Melanie Klein's evidence from early analysis, the anal-sadistic and the genital phases set in much earlier than had been appreciated before her work. Whilst the child is still predominantly in the oral stage – the time of maximal sadism – anal and even genital trends begin to make their appearance; and this early link between the oral and the genital trends intimately affects the later stages of development of the genital impulses themselves.

I myself would comment here that it is a well-known fact that erections occur early in infancy, and that Melanie Klein's views are thus once again in close accordance with observed facts. Full genital development does not, of course, come until much later.

Mrs Klein also shows the changed perspective in which the development of the libido has to be considered, in view of Freud's later work on the death instinct, and her own observations on the preliminary cathexis of the genital impulses at the time of the oral–biting stage. For instance (on p. 150 of her book) (Klein 1932), she points out that the libido enters upon a struggle with the destructive instincts, consolidating its own position only gradually. She says:

> Side by side with the *polarity* of the life–instinct and the death–instinct, we may place their *interaction* as a fundamental factor in the dynamic processes of the mind. The emergence of the states of organization with which we are acquainted corresponds, I should say, not only to the positions which the libido has won and established in its struggle with the destructive instinct, but, since these two components are for ever united as well as opposed, to a growing adjustment between them.

Later in the book (e.g., pp. 276–7), Mrs Klein goes on to show the intimate connection between the early sadistic phantasies and specific anxiety situations and libidinal development and gratifications. On the one hand, anxiety intensifies libidinal needs; but, on the other, gratification of his various erotogenic zones enables the child to master anxiety, and thus fosters libidinal development. Finally, she considers the interaction between libido, superego and object-relationship, in the whole course of development. What analysis does, Mrs Klein says (pp. 235, 280), is to relax the pre-genital fixations by diminishing anxiety, and thus assist the superego to move forward from pre-genital stages to the genital stage.

I wish further to comment upon what was said by four speakers, Dr Glover, Dr Friedlander, Mrs Hoffer, and Dr Schmideberg, about my use of quotations from the writings of Freud and others. These criticisms are of three sorts. First, that I have left out the context of the quoted passages, context which would show that the authors did not in fact support the views I am putting forward. Dr Glover asserts this, but supports his assertion by no example. Mrs Hoffer does give more of the careful attention to the passages quoted which I urged my readers to give, since I was writing for an informed audience which has access to all the literature from which I quoted.

Mrs Hoffer has a second complaint, interwoven with the first, which is that Freud is not *discussing* phantasy as such in the papers from which I quote, but is talking about other subjects, such as the communication between the Pcs and the Ucs, or instincts and their vicissitudes. Certainly he is. But we are entitled, nay, we are *compelled* (if we wish to understand his work) to examine the instruments of his thinking on any subject, the concepts he uses and the way in which he uses· them, as well as what. he says on the specific subject under discussion. We can learn what Freud's instruments of thinking are, and how he uses them, in each of his essays and clinical papers. If we do not, but confine our attention to one specific topic, we shall miss much that we might learn and need to learn, of Freud's view on the manifold complexity of the human mind.

The fact that Freud later goes on (after one of the passages I quoted) to speak of the problem of the differences between the attitude of the girl and that of the boy to the mother – a difference which of course has to be fully considered – does not alter the fact that when he is speaking of the child's feelings of 'being dethroned, robbed', etc. he explicitly refers to the age of 11 months. And – in the very quotation which Mrs Hoffer adds to mine – he says that these things occur with the boy as well as with the girl. The outcome at a later date is different because of the fact that the boy has a penis and the girl has not; not because the *earliest* feelings and phantasies are different.

I ask my hearers and readers to look again at the passages I quoted, together with the parts omitted, and consider closely in each case whether or not I am justified in taking those passages as evidence of Freud's views about phantasy in general, as well as about the particular topic he is discussing at the moment. (Remembering that Freud did not necessarily and always use the *term* 'phantasy'. He sometimes spoke of 'the mental expression of instinctual urges', as I pointed out in my paper; but that, to my mind, is a distinction without a difference. The real question is, are the facts of early mental activity to which Freud did refer the same facts as those to which I am applying the term 'phantasy'?)

One may wish to quote whole papers, whole chapters, at the very least, whole paragraphs. But we know this is not practicable. We can only refer readers to the original papers.

I wish Dr Scott had included in the circulated version of his contribution the excellent extempore comments he made on this question of quotations. You remember that he pointed out that if a later writer has nothing to add to an earlier writer's views, he does not need to write at all. But when a later author is reporting upon further investigations, it is informative and valuable to find that earlier workers held views which point in the direction of the new discoveries, or actually support them, even though the earlier investigator had not fully explored the possibilities he had glimpsed, or seen the whole significance of his own data and his own theories when viewed in the light of the further discoveries and conclusions now reached.

I cannot avoid the impression that some of the contributions to this discussion imply that Freud's work and his conclusions are never to be developed any further – and that no one is to formulate theories which he himself had not yet framed or fully developed. But nothing could be more un-Freudian than such an attitude, which would certainly have horrified him.

I said above that all the literature from which I quoted is accessible to all Members. It is possible that there is one exception to this. Not every Member may possess or have read Dr Glover's paper on 'A Psycho-analytical Approach to the Classification of Mental Disorders'. [Glover, E. 1932] I wish they could and would read it, because in it – a long and important paper – there is not one reference to the Oedipus complex! Yet when I read the paper at the time of publication, it did not occur to me to say that Dr Glover had thrown the Oedipus complex over, or let it fall by the wayside! I do not suggest that now. He was dealing with other aspects of development, that is all.

A third criticism of my use of quotations is Dr Schmideberg's complaint that whilst I quote from a paper which she wrote ten years ago, I do not quote from her more recent writings in which she expresses different views. Now I believe that this is the first time that Dr Schmideberg has told us that she herself has changed her opinions. Hitherto, like Dr Glover, she has, in recent years, heavily criticized those analysts who still hold the views she herself held ten or more years ago, but has not told us that she now considers her own earlier views to have been erroneous.

We are all entitled to change our views at any time. We are likely to do so if our science advances. But if and when we do, especially upon important and hotly debated subjects, we should say so, as Freud himself did. We are not entitled to join in a controversy as if we ourselves had never taken up the position we now reject, and to leave it to be imagined by those new to our discussions or those with short memories that our views have always been what they are today.

It is common knowledge which hardly needs re-stating that Dr Schmideberg and Dr Glover have for some years been opposed to Melanie Klein's views; but this need not prevent me from quoting statements of theirs which in my opinion aptly express views which I still think true.

I wish to express once again my appreciation of all those speakers, whether they agree with me in part or disagree, who have stated their criticisms and questions freely and frankly. I shall take up in my paper on regression the many points touching upon this question, and the development of the libido, which I have not dealt with now.

In quoting at length from Freud, I wished not only to show how Melanie Klein's work is derived from Freud's own. I wanted also to emphasize that we all have a common relation to Freud's work, a common basis for our further researches, in his discoveries and formulations. I hoped thus to make it easier for us to co-operate in the mutual understanding of the special directions which different groups of workers have taken, and will no doubt continue to explore.

I look forward to our future discussions in the hope of resolving or narrowing at least some of our differences.

Notes

1 'As you know, we have never prided ourselves on the completeness and finality of our knowledge and capacity. We are just as ready now as we were earlier to admit the imperfections of our understanding, to learn new things and to alter our methods in any way that can improve them.' [SE 18: 159]

2 'They thus afford us a view of a function of the mental apparatus which, though it does not contradict the pleasure principle, is nevertheless independent of it and seems to be more primitive than the purpose of gaining pleasure and avoiding unpleasure.' [SE 18: 32]

3 When I described one of the psychical processes occurring in the mental apparatus as the 'primary one', what I had in mind was not merely considerations of relative importance and efficiency; I intended also to choose a name which would give an indication of its chronological priority. It is true that, so far as we know, no psychical apparatus exists which posseses a primary process only and that such an apparatus is to that extent a theoretical fiction. But this much is a fact: the primary processes are present in the mental apparatus from the first, while it is only during the course of life that the secondary processes unfold, and come to inhibit and overlay the primary ones; it may even be that their complete domination is not attained until the prime of life. In consequence of the belated appearance of the secondary processes, the core of our being, consisting of unconscious wishful impulses, remains inaccessible to the understanding and inhibition of the preconscious; the part played by the latter is restricted once and for all to directing along the most expedient paths the wishful impulses that arise from unconscious.   [SE 5: 603]

4   It would nevertheless be wrong to imagine that the Ucs remains at rest while the whole work of the mind is performed by the Pcs – that the Ucs is something finished with, a vestigial organ, a residuum from the process of development. It is wrong also to suppose that communication between the two systems is confined to the act of represssion, with the Pcs, casting everything that seems disturbing to it into the abyss of the Ucs. On the contrary, the Ucs is alive and capable of development and maintains a number of other relations with the Pcs, amongst them that of co-operation. In brief, it must be said that the Ucs is continued into what are known as derivatives, that it is accessible to the impressions of life, and that it constantly influences the Pcs.   [SE 14: 190]

5

Third
Discussion of Scientific Controversies

British Psycho-Analytical Society

NOTICE TO MEMBERS AND ASSOCIATE MEMBERS

A meeting of Members and Associate Members will be held on Wednesday, March 17th, 1943, at 8 p.m., at 96 Gloucester Place, London, W.1. This is the third of the Series of Scientific Discussions on controversial topics existing within the Society.

Continuation of discussion on Mrs Isaacs' paper

A copy of the contributions to the discussion held on February 17th, 1943, is enclosed herewith.

At the last meeting held on February 17th questions of technical procedure were discussed. It was felt that limitation of contributions to the discussion in regard of both time and length was a drawback. It was therefore decided that:

(a) the discussion at the next meeting should take the form of prepared questions and if necessary exposition of the considerations leading up to them.

(b) all members wishing to contribute should notify the Programme Committee (c/o Institute of Psycho-Analysis) of their intention and of the length of their paper within a few days of receiving the enclosed copy of the proceedings, i.e. by *Tuesday, March 2nd*.

(c) if it is likely that the amount of material would exceed the limits of one meeting, the Committee should be authorized to select certain contributions to be given at that meeting and to give the other Members opportunity of reading their contributions at a subsequent meeting.

(d) the meetings should close at 10.15 p.m.

Members are again reminded that all contributions to the discussion should be prepared in writing and handed to the Secretary for the purpose of circulating full minutes. Also those Members who have not yet paid their contribution to printing expenses of £1 are asked to do so as the cost of duplicating is heavy.

EDWARD GLOVER
Scientific Secretary

February 24th, 1943

Minutes of the Third Scientific Discussion Meeting
held on March 17th, 1943, at 8 p.m.
at 96 Gloucester Place, London, W.1.

Dr Glover was in the Chair and 29 Members and Associates were present (Payne, Weiss, Friedlander, Lantos, W. Hoffer, Stross, H. Hoffer, Burlingham, A. Freud, Mrs Schmideberg, Herford, Fleischer–Gero, Frank, Ruben, Franklin, Winnicott, Ries, Sharpe, Usher, Riviere; Klein, Evans, Isaacs, Money-Kyrle, Rickman, Heimann, Rosenberg, Taylor).

Nine candidate-guests were present (Schlossberg, Little, Bick, Mannheim, Bonnard, Gompertz, Milner, Hollitscher, H. Schwarz).

The Secretary, Dr Payne, read the minutes of the last discussion meeting held on February 17th. The minutes were approved and signed.

Dr Glover opened the meeting and proposed before going into the main purpose of the evening, to settle one practical point arising out of previous experience in case of an air-raid warning. Various suggestions had been made. After discussion it was decided (a) to stop the meeting to allow Members who had responsibilities at home to return there, (b) to ask Members to carry their chairs to the basement and to continue the meeting there.

DR GLOVER: As regards our programme for tonight, like many of those carefully prepared schemes some facts have spoiled our plans. The notifications of discussion papers were quite numerous and it was obvious that it would not be possible to deal with all of them in one evening.

Though there had been the suggestion that members should not be limited in regard to time if they wanted to expand on themes leading up to questions, the notifications of papers were rather on the short side. But even so it would have been impossible to deal with all of them in one evening. We might have been able, however, to deal with a good number of them. We tried to see whether those left over could have their contributions prepared so that their contributions could be circulated with the papers given this evening, but this did not prove practicable.

The next thing for the Committee was to arrange the orders of papers. As only one notification of a longish paper – my own – has been received we tried to arrange this point by telephone. Today again we had a number of disappointments. Our intention was to start with those Members reading their contributions who have not yet spoken. This would have been Mrs Rosenfeld, Dr Heimann, Miss Low, Dr Melitta Schmideberg. Then we had a message tonight from Mrs Rosenfeld that she cannot come to the meeting. We have not received her paper to read it to the meeting.

Dr Brierley's idea was that we should roughly take the order of speakers in the previous discussion for all those who have already spoken before. This again was spoiled by Dr Brierley developing a flu so that she cannot give her communication. Also Miss Freud is unable to give her contribution this evening.

So I feel it is the best thing to call on those who have not yet spoken before, then on as many of the others as can speak tonight. This means that Dr Heimann will start and Miss Low and Dr M. Schmideberg will follow. Now Miss Low is prevented by indisposition from attending tonight and has been unable owing to her trouble to write out an expansion of the considerations leading up to her questions. She has only been able to give me just before a few sheets which contain the specific questions which she would like to put. I hope that she will have an opportunity to expand another time.

DR HEIMANN (Paper, see circulated minutes).

MISS LOW (written statement, read by the Chairman in Miss Low's presence. For text see circulated minutes.)

MRS ISAACS (interrupting): Does Miss Low say that I agreed with Dr Fairbairn or does she mean that she agrees?

DR GLOVER (reading the sentence to the meeting again): It must refer to you, I think.

MISS LOW's contribution continued.

DR MELITTA SCHMIDEBERG (Paper, see circulated minutes).

387

DR GLOVER: That completes the contributions from the side of those who have not spoken already. As regards the next set of contributions, I think we might keep roughly to the order we had before except some of the members, like Mrs Hoffer, who would not have time this evening. The next after Dr Jones's would be my contribution and I propose that Dr Payne takes the Chair in the meantime.

DR GLOVER (Paper, see circulated minutes).

DR GLOVER: This would be Dr Payne's turn but she has not had time to prepare her contribution.

(Short interruption for refreshments.)

DR GLOVER: One point arises about Dr Brierley's contribution. Dr Brierley phoned at the last minute to say that she could not give her paper owing to illness. She was anxious however that contributions which are completed should be included in the circulation of minutes. We might take Mrs Isaacs' advice on this matter. If she would prefer to have it done this way I would suggest that the meeting approves. There are no objections; in that case we will arrange that Dr Brierley's contribution be included in the minutes to be circulated. We hope to receive it tomorrow. (For Dr Brierley's contribution, see circulated minutes.)

MISS SHARPE (Paper, see circulated minutes).

MRS ISAACS: May I ask a question? Three or four sentences ago you asked do we believe in the actual objects inside and if not how is the technique justified. Can you make that clear, Miss Sharpe?

MISS SHARPE: That is what I want to know. I was thinking of the pattern of Freud's technique.

DR FRIEDLANDER (Paper, see circulated minutes).

DR LANTOS (Paper, see circulated minutes).

DR GLOVER: That brings us to the end of the contributions prepared for this evening. As I indicated before some people have been unable to bring their contributions forward today. They will have to be dealt with at the next meeting. We have now a few minutes left. This may give Members opportunity to bring forward any questions they may want to put. Do Members wish to add any to the existing questions brought forward?

MRS ISAACS: May I ask Dr Glover how many more contributions are to be expected?

DR GLOVER: Dr Brierley's paper will not be read, as it will be included in tonight's minutes, but here are Mrs Rosenfeld, Miss Freud, Mrs Hoffer. Miss Low should be given opportunity if she can to expand on her questions, and there is Dr Payne who is not sure if she can prepare a contribution for the next meeting.

The date of the next meeting dealing with the Scientific Discussion was then decided to be *April 7th, 1943.*

MRS ISAACS. I should like to make a suggestion. We all feel it was an excellent thing that the papers have been written and circulated, but it turns out to be inhibiting our discussion. I feel it might be favourable to have a spontaneous discussion occasionally as well, which is not to be written down. The last time when Members were [given such opportunity], they did not want to make use of it. They might be glad now of being given another opportunity.

DR GLOVER: Do you mean that we should fill up the time at the next meeting after the three or five contributions have been read?

MRS ISAACS: I was wondering what Members feel about it.

DR M. SCHMIDEBERG: Is it necessary to read the next contributions or can they be circulated?

DR GLOVER: There is a proposal: to have an extra meeting on the first Wednesday in April to bring up to date all outstanding contributions. As they will not take more than approximately one hour, to reserve the remainder of time for spontaneous discussion.

MRS ISAACS: Could the papers be sent to me beforehand so that I can prepare my reply? (It is pointed out by Dr Payne that time would be too short for the office to cope with this task.)

DR GLOVER: Are there any further suggestions?

It was decided to have a meeting on the first Wednesday in April to produce the regular discussion papers and have a spontaneous discussion if any time remains.

Discussion held on March 17th, 1943

Continuation of discussion on Mrs Susan Isaacs' paper
'The Nature and Function of Phantasy'

DR P. HEIMANN: In his contribution to the discussion on Mrs Isaacs' paper 'The Nature and Function of Phantasy' Dr Foulkes first states his familiarity with Melanie Klein's clinical findings, and from the context it is clear that he refers to her work on unconscious phantasy and internal objects. He seems, however, to be unconvinced as to the importance and the dynamics of these clinical data, and to disagree with the significance which Melanie Klein and her co-workers attribute to them. He further expresses the view that Mrs Isaacs' theory treats phantasies 'as if they were primary motors, lords in their own rights, absorbing instinctual urges and physical reality as their material only'. [p. 364]

Now I shall leave it to Mrs Isaacs to deal with the fact that Dr Foulkes apparently did not notice that she had pointed out in her paper that unconscious phantasy is the mental representative of instinct; the conclusion being that unconscious phantasy is charged with instinctual energy.

Dr Foulkes ends with the suggestion that 'inner objects and unconscious phantasies are to be analysed', an excellent, though hardly original idea, which becomes somewhat spoilt when he goes on to say 'and analysis does not consist in tracing mental phenomena back to the unconscious phantasy level and leaving it at that'. [p. 365] It is not clear to me what he means by this remark. It is a pity that he did not say in what analysis does consist in his view. But he seems to imply that Melanie Klein and her co-workers do not know how to analyse such phantasies, and as he quotes my paper on 'Sublimation and Internalization' as an example for such failure, I want to say a word or two in reply.

In referring to this paper Dr Foulkes says: 'It looks as if the inner devils lastly decide what is going to happen to the patient.' Dr Foulkes seems to have confounded my presentation of my patient's feelings with my theoretical evaluation of these feelings, a remarkable misunderstanding, as at one point I explicitly stated that I tried to use my patient's own words and throughout the paper I made it clear that I aimed at getting the truest and most vivid reproduction of her feelings and her emotional state. In passing I may remind Dr Foulkes that in psychiatric case histories it is thought desirable to reproduce the patient's own expressions and to represent the mental picture as the patient feels it to be. According to my patient's feelings before the analysis the devils did decide what was going to happen to her. But where I describe that my patient attributed such powers to her inner devils, it does not follow that I share her belief or do not analyse it.

In the paper referred to above I was concerned to show the connection between phantasies of internal objects and sublimation, and therefore I did not give instances of the technical procedure of the analysis of these devil phantasies. But the result of the analysis as regards those phantasies was shown clearly. To quote from a passage in which I summarized some of the factors by which the patient's insight into her psychical reality came about: 'she then no longer felt inhabited by persecuting devils, and this type of phantasy practically ceased to exert any influence over her' (p. 12). Thus it would appear to be a mistake to assume that those unconscious phantasies and inner objects were not analysed, 'but left at that' [Heimann 1942: 12]

As regards technique the paper shows that this result was achieved by employing the ordinary principles of analytic procedure: the working through in the transference situation of present and past experiences, which brought home to the patient the fact that these devils whom she had felt as existing concretely inside her body and dominating her like 'lords in their own rights' (to use Dr Foulkes' very apposite description) were a creation of her mind, an outcome of her unconscious conflicts, a peculiar blend of love and hate, anxiety and guilt, punishment and reparation. It is therefore impossible to understand what he can have meant in his reference to my paper by assuming that in such a case we trace the mental phenomena back to unconscious phantasy level and *leave it at that*.

MISS BARBARA LOW: (As Miss Low was prevented by indisposition from being present at the meeting her contribution was read by the Chairman.)

Owing to inability to use my eyes much just now, I have been unable to collect material necessary to enlarge upon my points. So I can only put the *questions* at present.

They may seem elementary questions, but I believe they are matters on which some of us feel there is confusion. It seems to me important to get these points clear because they must affect our understanding – of the patient's situation, and our analytic technique. I shall be grateful if Dr Isaacs will deal with them.

QUESTIONS FOR DR ISAACS

(1) *What is the exact distinction between 'phantasy' and 'the inner psychical reality'?*

I find that at times Dr Isaacs uses the terms *interchangeably*, and at other time *makes a distinction* between the two things – this is confusing.

Further, she declared herself in support of *Dr Fairbairn* who stated in his paper (read by Dr Glover) the following: '*The concept of "phantasy" has now been rendered obsolete by the concepts of "psychical reality" and "internal objects".*' (Fairbairn, p. [359]) Clearly this makes a definite distinction between phantasy and psychical reality.

If there are differences between the the two mental states,

(a) *by what process does phantasy develop (or has developed) into 'inner psychical reality'?*

(b) *What is the relationship, in Dr Isaacs' view, between ego-perception and this inner psychical reality?*

(2) In Dr Isaacs' papers and those who think with her there often seems the *implication* (not explicitly expressed) that the inner psychical reality is an entity which remains untouched by the external situation. I should like to know more about this.

(3) Does Mrs Isaacs interpret Freud's theory of phantasy as a developing situation, dependent upon new psychic situations as they arise? For example, the phantasy of the introjected mother (good or bad) must surely be modified (and perhaps completely changed) with the onset of the Oedipus conflict.

I am not at all clear as to Dr Isaacs' view.

DR MELITTA SCHMIDEBERG: (1) I am glad to learn from Dr Isaacs' statement that 'it is common knowledge that Dr Schmideberg has for some years been opposed to Melanie Klein's views' [p. 382], but surely it would have been fairer to state this straight away when she quoted me as belonging to the 'English school'.

(2) Dr Isaacs believes that my recent statement was the first occasion on which I said that I have changed my opinions. In 1941 I gave a lengthy paper discussing the fallacies that arise out of the ambiguous use of the terms 'introjection' and 'projection'. It seems rather obvious that after that I would not go on using those terms any more in the ambiguous manner in which I myself – and most English and Continental authors – had hitherto used them.

(3) I object to Dr Isaacs' statement that 'Dr Schmideberg heavily criticized those analysts who still hold the views she herself held ten or more years ago, but has not told us that she now considers her own earlier views erroneous.' [p. 382] Even Dr Isaacs will find it difficult to substantiate that I ever believed in the 'manic defence', the 'depressive position', or the 'internal object' psychology as propounded by Mrs Klein and her adherents since 1934.[1]

Dr Isaacs omits to define Mrs Klein's views in detail, and thus saves herself the trouble of having to substantiate them, and of distinguishing which part of them is original. Having disposed of this scientific safeguard she feels justified in claiming anybody as adherent who ever took an interest in introjection or used the term in as ambiguous a manner!

I have not heard Dr Scott's impromptu remarks: I read only Dr Isaacs' allusions to them. It seems important to distinguish between the expression of new ideas and free development of a science, and between quoting tendentiously from accepted authors. If I were allowed to neglect the context and were quoting only verbatim, I would have no difficulty in finding many sentences in the Bible, *Mein Kampf*, Shakespeare, or any other famous book 'which point in the direction' of Mrs Klein's theories, or of the theories of any other author, – but I would not regard such quotations as proving anything whatsoever.

I must confess I was most reluctant to take part in this discussion, but as I am now here, I would like to make a few general remarks.

Dr Isaacs has been reproached by some critics for not having stated clearly the existing divergences. Her answer is that the aim of these discussions is to clarify the different theories. This is not exactly my own opinion, but it is an aim that can be regarded as legitimate. However, she has not done much towards this aim either. She has made no attempt to describe and substantiate in detail Mrs Klein's theories. Again, if her aim is to elucidate the mental life of the young baby, then she should have stated what we know about it, and from what sources this knowledge is derived.

We have, in my opinion, no way of ascertaining directly what a small infant feels or thinks. We can only draw certain deductions from a number of sources, for instance: (a) behaviouristic observations, (b) observations as to how infants react to changes of environment, differences in handling, analysis of the mother, etc., (c) observations of psychotics, defectives and other regressive conditions, (d) deductions from the general analytical theory of development, (e) conclusions drawn from the analysis of adults and older children, (f) from the analysis of younger children, etc. (Incidentally, if Dr Isaacs attaches such importance to this last method, she should be interested in my opinion as I believe that my record of having analysed the youngest children hitherto analysed – 3 infants between 12 and 21 months – is still unbroken!) I myself, however, would regard this last avenue of approach only as one of many possible ones: deductions drawn from it should be accepted only if they tally with those gained from the other sources.

To arrive at a few examples. The baby of a patient of mine, a few weeks old, cried a lot and was in a 'difficult' state. It cried for the comforter and when given it would push it back. It wanted a certain thing, and when given refused to take it. The mother was in an acute obsessional state. As soon as the mother improved, the baby became normal though remained oversensitive. Second, I analysed a boy aged 21 months suffering from numerous symptoms, and also from pathological disgust. The mother told me that at the age of 9 months, before he could walk, he would not want others to see his excretions and made great efforts to crawl into a corner to defecate. Third, I analysed a girl of two and a half who had taken the breast only with difficulties and was unusually inhibited in eating as well as in all activities practically from birth. During analysis the mother observed that the child suddenly started to play with her breasts – a thing she did not do at its proper time. She also started during her analysis to crawl like babies of about 9–12 months do. She had learned to walk without ever crawling. Fourth, an adult patient started the analysis with conscious hostility against his father and idealization of his mother. In the analysis he developed quite vicious hostility against me and became more friendly towards his father. I do not want to discuss the various reasons for these reactions, but it is interesting to note that according to his mother he used to push away the bottle in his first year of life when the mother gave it, but be 'as good as gold' if the father looked after him. I could mention, of course, many more observations on babies about various environmental factors affecting them, about their likes and dislikes, about individual differences, about their reactions to their parents and others, about manifestations of anxiety, guilt, shame, and self-control, about early neurotic symptoms and phobias, the persistence or disappearance of these as the children grew older, etc.

My point, however, is to show that these examples are empirical observations, from which we may draw various conclusions with a varying degree of probability. None of them tells us with absolute certainty what exactly goes on in a baby's mind, or in his unconscious.

One weakness of the Kleinian authors is that they do not draw sufficient distinction between empirical observation (analytic or otherwise) and conclusions, and between conclusions of varying degree of plausibility. Material of child analysis should be so presented as to enable other analysts too to form an opinion.

Dr Isaacs' aim in her present paper is to substantiate that already infants of less than 12 months have some sort of phantasies (using this term in a very wide sense), an assumption which few analysts will challenge. But we all know that Mrs Klein holds that babies have specific phantasies and reactions which are of great importance for development and later neurosis. This is a very different assumption from Dr Isaacs' thesis; even if the first assumption were proved, it would not prove the next one. Mrs Klein's assumptions are derived in the first place from the analysis of adults and of children older than two and a half years. To convince us of the existence and importance of the specific phantasies she attributes to babies, she must give us the analytical material from which she draws her conclusions, and the method step by step by means of which she has arrived at the conclusion. We must discuss the criteria that justify 'reconstruction', and the varying degrees of plausibility achieved in each individual attempt. To be told, as we had been more than once, 'we found in analysis' or 'the material proved' is no argument. We must be careful to avoid false analogies. For instance, I have heard Mrs Klein claim that as Freud drew conclusions from adults to children, so she is entitled to draw conclusions from the analysis of children to infants. There are important differences, however: (a) Freud based his conclusions largely on actual recollections of patients; (b) the conclusions (e.g. concerning manifestations of infantile sexuality) could be checked by direct observations on children; (c) they were to quite a degree borne out by observations of a different type, e.g. on psychotics, perverts, etc. Children have no direct memories of infancy, and the 'constructions' made by analysts must be very carefully checked. In those recent discussions and on other occasions various speculations about infants have been put forward (incidentally Ferenczi should have been quoted), some of which are quite interesting. But it is important to stress that these are only speculations which are difficult both to prove and to disprove. Needless to say it is not possible to observe the unconscious phantasies of babies directly. It is possible to observe their expression of emotion, their actions, etc., but again we must distinguish strictly between such observations and the speculations derived from them.

DR E. GLOVER: I should like to intervene at this state of the discussion of Mrs Isaacs' paper. I do not intend on this occasion to answer the debating points raised by Mrs Isaacs in her reply to my previous criticisms. I shall deal with these later and, I think I may promise, adequately. My immediate object is to clarify some of the differences between Freud's metapsychology and the system offered us by Mrs Isaacs. May I say, however, that although I am in favour of the accurate distinction and use of basic psychoanalytical concepts, I see little prospect of solving the present controversies between Freudians and Kleinians by this means. As I have pointed out, the validity or otherwise of Mrs Klein's views and techniques do not depend on the accuracy of Mrs Isaacs' metapsychology. Nor, for the matter of that, do they depend on such pronouncements of Freud's as have been taken over by Mrs Isaacs (and others) with open enthusiasm. I think, for example, that her laudatory references to Freud's great discovery of the nature of 'psychic reality' indicate merely her hope and belief that Freud's views on this subject can be made to support her own theories, viz., that phantasy is the primary content of all mental processes and the psychic representative of instinct and that there is no impulse, no urge which is not experienced as (unconscious) phantasy. I hold, on the contrary, that Freud's views on psychic reality do not support Mrs Isaacs' theory of phantasy, that they had an entirely different clinical content and connotation to that given them by Mrs Isaacs (i.e. in the context of symptom formation), and finally that Mrs Isaacs' concept of phantasy is in opposition to Freud's basic concepts of the function of the psychic apparatus. Incidentally I don't agree with these contributors to the discussion who suggest that Freud's basic concepts were mere tentative formulations which he would himself have played about with or modified freely at some later date. The outstanding fact about the theoretical chapter in his *Interpretation of Dreams* and about the formulations contained in his paper 'Instincts and their Vicissitudes' is that they have stood the test of time. They are in fact basic. They are not reconstructions of mental content, or sketches of phases of development, still less are they interpretations of specific clinical data such as those on which Mrs Isaacs, following Mrs Klein, bases her definition of phantasy. They are basic operational concepts concerning the psychic apparatus. They describe in dynamic, economic, and structural terms those functions of the mind dealing with instinct excitation. Freud's whole system is built up on the dynamic nature of instinct excitation, which, in distinction to the independent stimulations of the external world, he re-arranged as continuous. First comes the organization of memory-traces in the various systems. This is bound up with a pleasure–pain series of experiences which in turn represent various degrees of gratification or frustration of impulse. The ultimate aim of all instincts is gratification, and memory traces are primarily concerned with those images which extend the aim, i.e. with those images which are, as it were, buried into the mind through their respective association with psychic pain or pleasure. The function of these images is an adaptation function first and mainly developed in association with frustration. But so long as (that ultimately proves to be) the object of the instinct promotes the gratification of the subject's aim (as in the case of most infantile needs), this function remains larval. When frustration becomes acute the cathecting of pleasure and pain image associations develops reality value, inasmuch as images promoting activities that accelerate gratification and images leading to avoidance of activities that increase frustration, increase the probability that instinct tension will be reduced. This reality process develops by an assumption of experiences until the faculty of reality proving is established. Reality proving promotes correlation between the subject, the aim, and the object of any given instinct. I repeat, the basic function here is a reality function, i.e. reality in terms of instinct gratification and frustration within an undefined but no doubt short space of time, that is to say as soon as the larval state is passed, the baby has as good (that is to say, adequate and effective) a sense of reality for any given instinct as any of us in this room have for ours, in some respects probably a better (more wholehearted) reality sense.

Now owing to a number of factors that have not yet been fully elaborated, but in particular to the symptom-specific intensity of excitation charges, also to that mental tendency which when fully developed can be described as regression, and again to the peculiar nature of frustrations existing when the regressive need for sleep is paramount and gratified, i.e. in sleep, a regression series occurs. This is characterized by backward flow of frustrated instinct energy from the motor to the sensory end of the psychic apparatus. The qualitative aspects of this instinct tension have also not been fully examined but we may be sure that a certain amount of condensation or fusion of various instinct charges occurs which gives rise to acute quantitive damming up. Anyhow the result is an attempt at hallucinatory gratification. The psychic pleasure secured or sampled in this attempt varies of course in accordance with the depth of sleep and the intensity of frustration, but when earlier pleasure experiences have been intense or when earlier frustrations have been acute the hallucinatory process is no doubt compensatory as well as being an unsuccessful attempt at reality adaptation. Incidentally this compensatory pleasure is heightened when the hallucinatory regression frees energy once more in the direction of motility: and some actions appropriate to the hallucination occur – as in sucking movements during sleep. But this is possibly only a marginal increase. The part release of appropriate motility is in itself a proof of the reality nature of the aims, cathected in the regression to the sensory end of the apparatus. There are, of course, many variations in the series of hallucinatory processes but I have only time to deal with the commonest. The immediate point is that although the process fails to gratify the instinct it is regulated along reality lines. The hallucinatory regression is an attempt at gratification initiated by frustration but arrested at the imaginal level and so doomed to failure. It is a frustration product characterized by its extreme imaginal intensity, but the imaginal element is in no sense a phantasy. *There is as yet no question of using the term 'phantasy' for such psychic events.* Phantasy in the sense in which it is used by Freud is a much later, more complicated, and from the point of view of reality a more revolutionary development. It is later and more complicated because it presupposes some psychic cognizance, however primitive, of the relation of subject to aim and object of an instinct. No psychic product is entitled to the label 'phantasy' that does not come up to this instinctual standard of correlation. I think also that some appreciation of the different quality of different degrees of frustration is a prerequisite of phantasy formation. By those definitions it is possible, without prejudicing theories of origin, to draw an essential distinction between on the one hand psychic image presentations whether associated with reality gratification or hallucinatory gratification and on the other hand any variety of phantasy, either conscious or unconscious. This distinction will be lost if we accept Mrs Isaacs' views. Mrs Isaacs' theses, so far from clarifying our ideas, would if accepted set them back more than 40 years. Following her reckoning the distinctions between images, ideational representations, end-presentations of instinct, reality thinking and phantasy (in the accepted Freudian sense) are confused if not completely blurred and the reality (adaptation) function of memory is placed in a secondary category. Mrs Isaacs does nothing to distinguish a cathected image memory from a phantasy. And despite her demurrers there seems to me no end to this process short of abolishing the distinction between the perceptual aspects of consciousness, the imaginal aspects of consciousness, the preconscious, and the unconscious. Not only so, Mrs Isaacs' metapsychology implies that thought and phantasy are primarily indistinguishable. If these views are accepted Freudian basic concepts must be rejected. Nor is it solely a question of confusion. Mrs Isaacs' modes of thinking are positively infectious. Even Dr Adrian Stephen (who in his contributions to the work of this Society has openly displayed an interest in the application of Occam's Razor to psychoanalytical concepts) who apparently accepts Mrs Isaacs' views of phantasy, goes on to say apropos of the nature of objects of instincts that Freud would certainly have agreed 'the object (of an instinct) may be imaginary or, if you like, phantastic' [p. 361]. I am quite sure Freud would most certainly have disagreed and I for one certainly do not like this connotation of the word 'phantasy'. It is a connotation which fails to distinguish between the terms 'imaginary', cathexis of memory-traces, and presentations. To put it briefly: by these premises an abstract object of an instinct would be a phantasy. The drive to study Greek (i.e. love of Greek) translated in these terms would imply that Greek (the object) is imaginary – a phantasy. But I think perhaps, Dr Adrian Stephen was confusing different and particularly later levels of object-displacement and had in mind also some problem of sublimation, and of aim-inhibited instinct in relation to phantasy.

To return to Mrs Isaacs: phantasy in the Freudian sense will occur at any level of the psychic apparatus and of course different types of phantasy can be merged, fused, or condensed and can be linked on in different ways and at different levels with reality thinking. Incidentally, do not let it be imagined that because I reject Mrs Isaacs' theorem of phantasy, I am thereby rejecting the existence of unconscious phantasy or that I am rejecting the existence of phantasy in the first years of life, or again that I am denying that phantasy formation once established does not pass through a complicated development to serve various ends. This type of argument has already appeared too frequently in this series of discussions. I am merely rejecting Mrs Isaacs' metapsychology. Nor do I disbelieve in the existence of the dynamic unconscious because I reject her implied new unconscious enclave exists at the core of Freud's unconscious. I am simply maintaining that Mrs Isaacs' views are on that subject incompatible with the views of Freud. In short, Freud's use of the term 'phantasy' and its relation to other forms of psychic representation (whether these be earlier or later in development, conscious or dynamically unconscious) is the only one which gives us the necessary accuracy and freedom to tackle the problem of infantile mental development. It also has the advantage of emphasizing what I have called the revolutionary aspects of phantasy formation, namely the breakaway from primitive and rigid laws of reality proving, as well as a breakaway from the comparatively effortless but inadequate regression to hallucinatory thinking during sleep. In terms of reality reward, phantasy has in common with hallucinatory thinking an ultimate lack of reality gratification of the instinct stress, but we fall into error in thinking that it spares psychic expenditure. The divorce of early forms of thought from their original adaptation function can only be achieved through violent strains to the psychic apparatus, as is indeed obvious in the case of regression in the psychoses. It is as difficult to achieve as the displacement of instinct energy from its original cathexes – a process, by the way, which has much to do with early phantasy formations. Phantasy, however early, is a complicated end product to be set off against reality action. To my mind it would be a retrogressive step to accept Mrs Isaacs' theory of phantasy-meaning from which, according to her, later reality thinking is derived. And I am glad to say that although I have frequently considered the amount of ego development as distinct from ego inhibition that can be promoted through conflict between superego and id, I have always insisted on the necessity of postulating the primary reality function of the primitive ego. Indeed, without such a postulate, there is nothing to prevent us falling into a primitive variety of mysticism. It is my own impression, for example, that a good deal of the complicated system of interpretation occasionally described by Mrs Klein and her adherents constitutes a variety of mysticism. And I think that when Anna Freud made her point about Mrs Isaacs confusing the primary and secondary processes she might have gone much further. She might have suggested that in Mrs Klein's and Mrs Isaacs' attempts at reconstruction of the mental content of the infant, there was injected a complicated set of imagined relationships, which, although apparently primitive in nature, are to some extent the product of the superficial preconscious layers of the analyst's mind, rather in the way that a mathematician can preconsciously elaborate relationships through a haystack formula.

To sum up, phantasy is essentially a frustration product and even in its most primitive forms shows a high degree of complication in the sense of correlation between the subject, aim, and object of an instinct. At its primitive levels it is a direct derivative not just of instinct urge but of instinctual frustration. The term therefore cannot function as a ruling concept in the sense that 'ideational presentation', 'cathexis of memory-traces', etc. can function as basic concepts in Freud's metapsychology. On the contrary, Mrs Isaacs' use of the term confuses the whole Freudian system of psychic representation of instinct. And despite all the talk of instinct derivatives and of the relation between psychic reality and so-called external reality, there is no difficulty in either the statement or the comprehension of these ideas which has not already been met in Freud's basic formulations. I think a good deal of the discussion of the relation between psychic and external reality must be bound up with some difficulties inherent in the Klein system. Freud's clear-cut statement that the derivatives of instinct are ideational and affective specifically include the perception of sensory (somatic) expressions of affect, whether these expressions are derived from primary affects or from secondary, 'reaction' affects. As I said before, the external world, the Himalaya Mountains for example, in the psychic sense is not something spatially outside the mind. It is perception of which there are memory-traces in the psyche. But neither the Himalaya Mountains nor the psychic perception of them nor the cathexis of the Himalayan system of memory trace is a phantasy.

DR MARJORIE BRIERLEY (As Dr Brierley was prevented by indisposition from being present at the meeting, her contribution was not read, but it was unanimously agreed to include it in the minutes).

One of the difficulties the present discussion has brought to light might be described as that of finding room in the same mind for 'internalized objects and memory images'. I have heard this difficulty put in a question, 'What is the relationship between the internalized object and the memory images?'

We cannot at this stage discuss the specific theory of internalized objects. We must wait at least for Dr Heimann's paper before we can do this with advantage. In any case the detailed answer to such a question should come from a primary speaker. In so far as this particular difficulty is a purely conceptual one, we can try to decide at once whether or not there is room for both concepts in a consistent theory or whether they are mutually exclusive and can have no common basis.

When Mrs Burlingham talks about the memory image of the mother in the mind of the two-year-old child who is able to retain a memory of the mother in her absence, she is talking of conscious memory. She would not, I imagine, maintain that conscious memory of the mother precluded the coexistence of unconscious memories, or that the conscious memory is not the resultant to date of the child's two years of life with its mother. She makes it quite plain that this conscious memory is only retained as long as it is predominantly a source of pleasure. When it becomes too painful it is 'rejected from consciousness' and the mother is forgotten. But the now painful unconscious memory continues to influence the child's behaviour. When the mother reappears, the child not only fails to recognize her but regards her with hostile 'stony indifference'.

If we now consider the concept of an internalized object in an artificially simplified form – what is it? It is the concept of an unconscious phantasy gratifying the wish to have the mother constantly present in the form of a belief that she is literally inside the child's body. Is there any reason why such an unconscious phantasy cannot be conceived as existing in the mind of a child capable of conscious memory, or co-operating with conscious or unconscious memories in determining behaviour? Might not such a phantasy help the child to retain conscious memory of its mother during temporary absences though it might fail to bridge a long gap? One may legitimately enquire into the evidence for the existence of internalized object phantasies but, in so doing, one will be enquiring into the existence of a special class of unconscious phantasy, not into some strange new phenomenon that has no precedent in psychoanalysis.

The terms of the question – what is the relationship of the internalized object to the memory image? – rather obscure the fact that memory and phantasy both involve memory images. All images are essentially memory images. On one point there appears to be common agreement, namely, that the infant cannot hallucinate or have a mental image until it has had sensori-affective or perceptual experience. We do not know precisely what the processes concerned in retention are, but we do know that experience registers in the psyche. It registers in such a way that it can be revived in hallucination or in imagination under certain qualitative conditions and in such a way that subsequent experience is modified by preceding experience. Freud called these registrations 'memory-traces' and assumed that they are themselves unconscious, but that their activation gives rise to images. Thus, all images, whether they occur in conscious or unconscious memories of phantasies, are memory images in so far as they derive from memory-traces laid down in the first instance by perceptual experience. Once images are available, imaginary experiences will play a part in organizing trace systems, since they are psychologically real experiences.

There are two points to bear in mind about memory-traces. The first is that memory-traces are probably better thought of as experience or reaction traces rather than isolated sensory traces. What is revived is not the sensory image alone but the image, along with its related affects and impulses. The most fundamental contribution made by Freud to general theory, the basis of his theory of the unconscious, lay in his recognition of the dynamism of mental life. Mental life is a sequence of mental processes each of which, as he said, normally follows a definite course from stimulus to innovation. The functional units of psychic life are responses to stimuli (internal or external). The unit of experience is not an isolated element, a separate impulse, feeling or image, but always a definite relationship of impulse, and feeling to presentation. The conception is indispensable, and is embodied in Freud's use of the word 'wish'. The phraseology of the old Associationist psychology was also to hand and Freud, on occasion, used it. It still has value in as much as it distinguishes between the cognitive, affective, and conative aspects of experience. But it is safer to think of memory-traces as experience or reaction traces rather than as isolated image traces, or at least to remember that revival of an image involves some revival of the impulses and feelings originally related to it.

The second point to bear in mind about memory-traces is that they not only permit past experience to be revived but to modify subsequent experience. They are both the agents and the structural units of mental organization. (Their relation to Dr Glover's ego nuclei will be evident.) The nature and variety of the child's experiences with his mother will be reflected in the number of and character of the memory-traces, and the reaction patterns that develop among them in relation to her. Pleasurable experiences will lay the foundations for pleasurable memories and phantasies. They will promote the organization of friendly mother systems, whereas painful experience will promote hostile mother systems. Cutting out all details, no relatively integrated object system such as the two-year-old's memory of his mother will be a unitary mental system, it will be a synthesis or resultant of two years' life with her. The conscious memory will be the apex of a complicated unconscious mother system, going back to the earliest reactions both actual and phantasied, and containing all the reaction patterns so far established. Considering our inveterate anthropomorphism, I do not, myself, find it difficult to conceive that animistic phantasies about incorporated mothers find place amongst these unconscious reaction patterns.

I do not know whether I have succeeded or not, but what I have tried to do is to show that whatever one's views about Mrs Klein's specific theories, it is possible to conceive of the existence of internalized object phantasies in a way that is consistent with Freud's basic concepts of psychic activity and to relate phantasy and memory to a common foundation in memory-traces. And this without accepting the suggested expansion of the definition of phantasy. I do not think that the true value of Mrs Klein's work is bound up with this definition. I still think it is less a true expansion, comparable as Dr Jones suggested, to Freud's expansion of the term 'sexuality', than an oversimplification comparable to the fallacious assertion that sexuality was the only instinct recognized by Freud. Of course, we do habitually use the terms 'phantasy' and 'phantastic' loosely to describe any mental content that does not correspond with our adult assessment of the facts. But it seems to me that the equation of phantasy with subjective interpretation and unconscious psychic content is an extension of this habit masked by compensatory emphasis on the psychological reality of subjective experience. If we do agree to this expansion we lose the only criterion which adequately distinguishes phantasy from other forms of mental activity, the criterion not of wish-fulfilment but of the *mode* of wish fulfilment. For purposes of theory, I continue to find it more useful to define 'phantasy' as a specific (fundamentally reflex) mode of dealing with the painful tension of frustrated need by regression to imaginary gratification. In the adult, phantasy thinking where discharge is blocked and reality thinking directed to procuring discharge in the outside world, constantly blend and interweave in the patterns of current mental activity. Surely this blending and interweaving of modes of activity is also characteristic of infantile and unconscious mental life.

MISS ELLA F. SHARPE: In the report of my remarks made on January 27th one important word was missing in the typescript due to the very rough copy I gave to Mrs N. The passage should run: 'The depressive position of Mrs Klein's theory I see (if the all-important *quantitative* factors are admitted) as almost the last of the external physical birth throes.' The omitted word was 'quantitative'.

Will Mrs Isaacs say something on this point?

It is my experience in psychoanalytical work that the separation from the mother's breast is felt as a much greater trauma by some children than by others due both to unknown instinctual factors within and external factors such as bad management by the mother and the birth of another baby within twelve months after the first.

One gets the impression, perhaps wrongly, that Mrs Klein's depressive position postulates that the loss of the breast has the same determining significance for all children, i.e. a 'depressive' significance. Now I can accept even this if the weaning separation from the mother is thought of as the last birth throe. For if we are looking for *one* root cause of all the ills of mankind it surely is being born at all, and weaning is its last stage. I assign to Mrs Klein's depressive position the same kind of significance that I gave to birth anxiety, namely an initial pattern of anxiety, but Freud said all later anxiety was not birth anxiety.

I have the clearest example in a woman of 40 that the trauma which caused regression to an oral state was the birth of her sister when she herself was not quite a year old, i.e. that it was not the separation from the breast as such that fostered subsequent denials of reality.

The strength and persistence of psychotic trends is surely much greater in the development of some people than others, but rightly or wrongly I get no impression from the work of Mrs Klein and her colleagues of these quantitative factors.

Secondly, I shall be glad to know from Mrs Isaacs in what way she thinks I make too great a distinction between Mrs Klein's early setting of the Oedipus complex with its phantasies of incorporation and the Oedipus complex of Freud. The development of the ego at the latter stage seems to me rather a momentous distinction, implying as it does a reality knowledge of sex differences and an orientation to a biological destiny.

Thirdly, with regard to technique I should like to have my misapprehensions corrected.

Mrs Isaacs says that the key to technique lies in understanding all the steps between two phases of development from the earlier to the later, all the phantasies and experiences encountered and lived through on the way. Perhaps we mean the same thing, but I should put my experience this way, that it is by technique that phantasies and experiences are brought to light and that understanding is gained as a result of these revelations in due course. That is technique is the key to evoking the data on which alone understanding and interpretation depend.

But my query about technique concerned one specific problem. I will make it explicit by an illustration.

If an hysterical patient believes she was sexually assaulted as a child, I believe she believes it. Her belief is her psychical reality. I, as the analyst, neither believe nor disbelieve in that external assault. Analysis will reveal the truth. If it reveals a phantasy we find why and how this belief was necessary. Never once shall I refer to this assault as a reality, only as *her* belief.

A young male patient believed he had the devil inside him. On occasions he exorcised the devil in my consulting room and got him out by tremors and shudders and deep sighs and expulsion of breath. Extreme pallor then slowly changed to a natural hue and he became himself again, the devil had gone. Now I as his analyst believed that he believed in an actual devil inside him, that was his psychic reality. I took his belief seriously, but never from any words or phrases of mine could he have thought that I believed he had a concrete bad man inside.

My query about technique concerns the psychotic belief of actual objects inside, breasts, penises, parents, evil, and good.

Sometimes I get the impression that some analysts who deal with these beliefs, interpret to their patients as if they themselves believed not only their patients' beliefs, but in the actuality of the concrete objects inside.

If my impression is wrong I shall be glad of correction.

The ritual of the young male patient gradually disintegrated, revealing in course of time the condensation that had taken place of abstracted elements from several repressed affective experiences (with phantasies) that occurred in early childhood. He no longer believes in a devil inside him but he does believe in his own rage, jealousy, and desire concerning people external to himself in the past and in the present.

DR KATE FRIEDLANDER: The question I want to ask Mrs Isaacs is whether there is any evidence available for the occurrence of phantasies during the first year of life like the one mentioned for instance on page [277] of her exposition: 'I want to suck the nipple, to stroke her face, to eat her up, to keep her inside me, to bite the breast, to tear her to bits, to drown and burn her, to throw her out of me.' I have no special reason for selecting this particular phantasy, I could have taken any of the others mentioned.

The question implies that we are not satisfied with the evidence so far put forward and further that we do not believe that phantasies of that kind do occur in children as young as that. In order to avoid further useless controversy I have to mention first of all an intentional misunderstanding in Mrs Isaacs' reply to my former contribution: I have neither said nor implied that phantasies do only occur in children in the third or fourth year and nothing in my contribution can possibly suggest this idea which I do not hold. Children certainly have phantasies very early, probably already in the second half of the first year, but so far all the available evidence goes to suggest that these phantasies are of a very simple nature, still connected with the child's most primary needs. It does not facilitate these discussions if such statements are made without foundation. What I did say was that oral elements contained in a phantasy do not necessarily prove that this particular phantasy has developed during the oral stage.

To come back to my question and to the reasons why I attach such importance to a clearly stated answer.

The occurrence of such highly organized phantasies necessitates not only the capacity for dim feelings and sensations in the baby, but rather the perception of a great variety of experiences as well as conceptual and even abstract thinking. 'To keep her inside me' involves a clear distinction between the ego and the non-ego, the outside world. 'To tear her to bits' involves the conception of the mother as a whole person and the knowledge that tearing a person to bits means killing. 'To drown and burn her' would necessitate experiences of that kind, of drowning and burning with the consequences it involves, which the baby, exceptions excluded, could not possibly have had.

The conception of the occurrence of these complicated phantasies during the first year of life is in direct contradiction to analytical as well as non-analytical observations and theories about this period of life.

Analytical knowledge about the first year of life is gained in two ways. Firstly, it has been inferred from the analysis of grown-ups and children; also Mrs Klein's conception of the processes going on in the mind of the child in the first year of life is inferred knowledge, because children, even if they are only two years of age, do not talk about and do not show directly any memory-traces of the first year of life, although I do of course believe that memory-traces are formed from birth onwards and increasingly during the first year. Secondly, knowledge has been gained by direct analytical observation, work which has been undertaken and carried out for years now by Anna Freud and Mrs Burlingham.[2]

The analytical theory based upon the above means of ascertainment of the mental processes during the first year of life assumes that impulses and emotions are still under the predominance of the pleasure–pain principle, not the death instinct, as Mrs Isaacs seems to believe; that towards the second half of the first year the first signs of an object-relationship to the mother appear; and that the precondition for the formation of this object-relationship is the growing perception of the outside world based upon the memory-traces from birth onwards. This, of course, is only a rough summary, but I want to emphasize mainly that it is a basic principle in this analytical conception of the first year of life that the first object relationship to the mother has not been there from the beginning but is the result of a process of development going for months before the high achievement of object relationship of a still primitive kind of course is apparent at all.

Mrs Klein's theory is in contradiction to this current analytical theory, because it ascribes phantasies with contents far beyond this stage of development to the baby during the first months of life already.

Now to the non-analytical conception of the mental processes during the first year of life. There are mainly two sciences to which we have to turn for information: brain-anatomy and physiology, and behaviouristic psychology. For my present purpose we can deal with these two sciences together, as behaviouristic observations are based upon and in full agreement with the physiological and anatomical development of brain and senses.

The brain of the child at birth is not yet fully developed. The myelinization of the white matter of the brain and the formation of the cortex are by no means finished even at the end of the first year of life. It is known from the anatomical and physiological studies on anencephali and from psychological and anatomical examinations of organic brain lesions in the grown-up, that the mental functions, as for instance the formation of conceptions and abstract thinking as well as many faculties which we ascribe to the function of the superego, are correlated to the normal function of the fully developed cortex and the association-fibres between the cortex and the midbrain. We know and appreciate this fact in relationship to the motor functions, for instance. We would not say that the child does not start to walk in the first weeks of life because it is prevented from doing so by some mental process, but on account of the fact that the motor tracts are not fully developed yet. The same holds good for speaking, which also starts at a definite time, and reading, which starts very much later, only to mention a few of these functions. There are individual variations as to the beginning of these mental and physical activities, but they are within limits of a short space of time. No infant has been known to start walking shortly after birth.

Mrs Klein's theories of phantasies of the described complicated order, concerning a variety of perceptions, conceptual and abstract thinking, during the first year of life are in complete contradiction to the anatomical and physiological knowledge of the development of the brain during the first year of life, in so complete contradiction that if we would translate these ascribed mental functions of the baby into motor functions it would mean that the child starts to walk within the first weeks of life, before it has been sitting up and crawling.

Our analytical knowledge about the first year of life is still very incomplete, and theories and hypotheses about it should be welcomed. But these theories would have to comply with the criteria which Dr Brierley has set out in her last paper. The more so as Mrs Klein's theories are not complementary to old theories but, as I have shown just now, in complete contradiction to them and to all the objective knowledge which we can get from other sciences. Also Mrs Klein does not only want to explain with her new conceptions, let us say a certain disturbance seen in a few cases, but these theories are already used to formulate new hypotheses about mental life in general. So that one is perfectly justified in asking that the evidence put forward in support of these theories should be particularly clear and convincing.

What is the evidence which has been given so far? On page [298] in Mrs Isaacs' first contribution we find the evidence divided into categories.

(1) 'Considerations regarding the relationships between established facts and theories. When considered fully, these relationships, in my view, require the postulates I have put forward, and by means of these postulates become better integrated and more fully understood.'

This point coincides probably with what Dr Brierley states about scientific theories in general: 'The criteria of a new hypothesis are: is the hypothesis necessary? Is it a fuller or better explanation of a certain range of facts? Does it cover more facts? and so on.'

Mrs Isaacs therefore implies that her conception of phantasy as the psychic representation of instinct, one of the main statements in her contributions, serves this end. Of course technical terms are a matter of convention. But it does not clarify one's views if two conceptions are called by the same term. Mrs Isaacs maintains that the mental corollary to instinct and what we are used to call 'phantasies' are intrinsically the same processes. It has already been pointed out by Miss Freud, Dr Glover, and others, that this is not so and I do not want to go more fully into this question now although I believe it to be one of the key points of disagreement. It has also been pointed out by both Drs Stephen, who would not mind applying the term 'phantasy' to the mental state caused by instinctual need, that Mrs Isaacs talks about two quite different kinds of phantasies, namely the complicated phantasies I have discussed and the mental processes accompanying instinctual needs. As a matter of fact, I believe that Mrs Isaacs is only talking about one kind of phantasy in practice, the complicated phantasies, but that in order to explain why those phantasies are there at this early stage she has to extend the term 'phantasy' to the mental representation of instinct and thereby alter the conception in a way which does not help to clarify matters, as Miss Freud has pointed out in her contribution.

So we see that, far from explaining old theories in a better way, Mrs Isaacs has to alter old conceptions; the term 'phantasy' has to be applied to two different phenomena in order to explain certain points in the new hypothesis. So that certainly Mrs Klein's hypothesis does not comply with the criteria which hold good for any new scientific theory, that it has to explain plain old facts and theories in a more comprehensible way. Actually, it is the other way round. This is the reason why I think that the evidence put forward in this first point does not do what is indicated in the title.

In this connection I want to point out that it is possible to apply the analytical theory to many other fields of knowledge, whilst the same does not hold good of Mrs Klein's theory. I should be quite willing to substantiate this statement at a later date. But again we see here a restriction of the horizon and not a widening as one should expect from a new hypothesis.

Point (2) of Mrs Isaacs' evidence: 'Behaviouristic data'. Dr Lantos has at least started to analyse these data and conclusions drawn from them and as yet Mrs Isaacs has not answered to these points. The gist of it is that the data are interpreted in much the same way as if they were analytical material and not as such correlated. Still, we have to wait for Mrs Isaacs' answer.

As to point (3): 'Clinical evidence, gained from the actual analysis by strictly analytical methods, particularly of the ages of two and three.' I have already mentioned that the analysis of children over two can only give us inferred knowledge about the first year of life and is as such not much more valuable as evidence than data gained by other analysts with older children and grown-ups.

(4) 'Confirmatory experience in the analysis of adults.' As far as the development in the first year of life is concerned these experiences have only been put forward by adherents of Mrs Klein's view. That phantasies of this kind occur in grown-ups, especially in psychotics and borderline cases, is known, but does in itself not prove their development in the first year of life.

These are the four points, and in my opinion in none of the points Mrs Isaacs has put forward what one could call conclusive evidence.

Still, even if Mrs Klein's theory is in complete contradiction to the known facts and theories, even if so far we do not see that it explains the known facts and theories better than the old hypothesis does, that would not be sufficient reason to reject these theories. The criterion is whether enough evidence is forthcoming to support the new view and to explain the contradictions to existing theories, analytical and non-analytical, in a comprehensive way.

We should be very grateful if Mrs Isaacs in her reply would concentrate on answering the question in a positive way, namely in giving the evidence and not only criticizing my exposition. I cannot in this short space of time go into more detail, for instance about the current analytical theory about the first year of life, which I have put into two sentences, but I am quite certain that Mrs Isaacs is familiar with this current theory, and my exposition serves only the purpose to substantiate why I ask the question.

What is the evidence, other than has been given so far, for the existence of complicated phantasies like the one mentioned during the first year of life?

DR BARBARA LANTOS: I was rather surprised to find myself accused by Mrs Isaacs of holding – and even tenaciously holding – the view 'that phantasies come into operation and are traceable only in the third or fourth years' [p. 370]. I really wonder how Mrs Isaacs could misunderstand my contribution in that way? And as, according to her, these alleged views of mine are also those of Miss Freud, Mrs Burlingham, Mrs Wälder and Dr Friedlander, I want very much to clear up this misinterpretation.

I *never* said – for I don't believe it – that phantasies are coming into operation only as late as the third or fourth year. What I said was that the analysis of two- or three-year-old children cannot be accepted as proof for the existence of early phantasies in infants of only a few months. Therefore we regretted very much that Mrs Isaacs, as so often before, again just hinted at the fact that Mrs Klein understood the early phantasies from her work in the analysis of children of two to three years . . . calling that evidence.

That was the only connection in which I mentioned the age of two to three (not even three to four) in my contribution. And I would like to stress that this is something vastly different from the alleged statement that phantasies are coming into operation in the third or fourth year. I actually started my remarks with the statement that there have never been any controversies about the existence of phantasies from an early phase of life. To state it clearly and unmistakably: 'early phase' means the age of about one year, but in no case the third or fourth year.

Well, if that is so, you may argue, why not say so at once? One year or three months are still different, of course – but is it, after all, such a big difference and can it account for such diverging views! There I have to remind you that the difference does not only concern the onset of phantasies in general, but the very specific content and organization of the first, so-called early phantasies. To state it again quite precisely: we think that phantasies of a rudimentary kind are starting as early as perhaps the first year, phantasies which hardly differ from recollections, really sensations connected with memory images and experiences. But we do *not* believe that all the highly organized phantasies which are meant by Mrs Klein when she uses the term 'early phantasies', including the depressive position and so on, can be experienced in the first year or even in the first few months of life.

When we doubt the existence of highly organized aggressive phantasies in the infant with all the complicated mechanism of defence, guilt feelings, remorse, and reparative tendencies, that does not mean that we doubt the existence and presence of oral impulses of a sexual character, but as we don't think that 'phantasy is the mental corollary of instinct', at least, not necessarily, there is no contradiction for us in accepting the existence of impulses or instincts without finding at the same time, necessarily, phantasies. Others have, probably, dealt with the question of phantasy more exten-sively, so I don't want to bore you by repetition. (I am thinking, especially, of Miss Freud's, Dr Glover's, and Dr Friedlander's remarks about that and I would like to state that I am using the term 'phantasy' in the way they described it.) Yet it is not a terminological argument I want to enter into, but I have to remind you that we mean something very different when we are speaking about phantasies. And we think we can describe mental life as well as the

411

activities of the infant much better if we do *not* replace life as a whole by phantasy, but by observing very distinctly the different stages of mental development. Phantasy processes are built up by a combination of perception, memory, ideation, and conception, and they are only imaginable on a higher level of mental development. This level is not reached on the first day of life. It cannot be reached then, for the physical apparatus of mental life is not yet developed to that extent, nor can it be developed without certain experiences which the infant gains in the course of his post-natal life.

I had to say all that before I could answer another charge which Mrs Isaacs brings forward against Mrs Burlingham and myself on page [374], namely that my emphasis on the infant's intelligence and Mrs Burlingham's views on memory images are in contradiction to Miss Freud's views concerning the domination of the primary process in the first year of life. As I think that Miss Freud will go into this in detail, I only want to stress that intelligence, that is perception, acquisition of knowledge by perception and sensory experiences, sensory skill, understanding of and adaptation to reality are in no way contradictory to uncorrelated mental life especially in an emotional respect. The primary process, as we know it best by the study of dreams, is a working method of the mental apparatus and has nothing to do with the presence or lack of intelligence. Although gradual changing over to the secondary process is certainly helped by, probably not even possible without making use of, intelligence, yet they are different categories. By the way, Miss Freud never said – in contradiction to Freud, as Mrs Isaacs thinks – that there is a mental apparatus possessing only the primary process. But there certainly is a phase in life when the primary process is dominating every activity to an overwhelming degree, leaving only very little space to the secondary process, which is growing gradually from its rudiments at the cost of the primary process. But intelligence does not prevent the effectiveness of the primary process – it even breaks through occasionally in adult life, as we all know. Nor is the presence of memory images in contradiction to the domination of the primary process. The primary process makes use of the memory images when building phantasies, in the bizarre way of the dream, neglecting, ignoring, or denying connections and consequences which are well known to the child and adult intellectually and are taken into account in a different mood or a different state of mind.

The contradiction between Miss Freud and myself, however, which Mrs Isaacs discovered to my surprise, almost sidetracked me from the central question of my contribution, namely from the question of erotic pleasure. I quoted in my remarks the example brought forward by Mrs Isaacs, about the 3- to 4-months-old baby who is dropping things into a box, anyhow rather an early age for this game, but that is not the point here. With the help of this example I pointed out that in our opinion the pleasure of sound and movement, that is to say auto-erotic pleasure, is the dynamic force which stimulates the child to try and repeat this game, and that auto-erotic pleasure in the wider sense, including organ pleasure and intellectual pleasure, are the most important stimuli of bodily and mental development at a time when we hardly believe in the existence of phantasies at all.

It is only fair to state that Mrs Isaacs acknowledged the influence and importance of pleasurable sensations in mental processes explicitly in her first paper as well as in her discussion. What I would like to ask her now is to give us a precise statement concerning auto-erotic pleasure in the following connection: Does she think – as we do – that there are activities which are carried out just for the sake of auto-erotic pleasure without any phantasies being attached to them? Does she agree that the normal running about of the child, for instance, is carried out without phantasies just for the sake of the organ pleasure which is gained? That babbling primitive speech, moving things, listening to noises, and all primitive plays, which are hardly more than training and indulging of growing bodily and mental abilities and skill, are all experienced with and driven by auto-erotic pleasure, without phantasies attached? Please let me emphasize that we are quite aware of the fact that very soon phantasies expressing object relationships can be attached to all these activities, helping or disturbing them. But my question is, quite clearly, and I would be grateful for an answer: Is she sharing our opinion, that

(1) in the first few months auto-erotic pleasure – that means pleasure without phantasies – is the only stimulus to the infant, and

(2) that even in later age there can be activities or plays which are carried out only or mostly for the sake of auto-erotic pleasure?

To bring it under one denominator: we would like to know whether she believes in the driving force of pure auto-erotic pleasure, without any blending with phantasies.

Note

After discussion of future arrangements it was decided that contributions already notified but not given should be given at the next meeting, and that afterwards whatever time was available should be devoted to spontaneous discussion. The relevant points in this spontaneous discussion will however be included in the next set of minutes.

Notes

1 In the above paper ('Introjected Objects: A Terminological Issue or a Clinical Problem?') [Schmideberg, M. 1941] I pointed out that I interpret phantasies about objects within the body in schizophrenic and other patients – following Freud and Abraham – as flights from a painful reality and as regressive distortion of libidinal and sadistic phantasies, whilst Mrs Klein regards 'introjected object phantasies' as primary, and even interprets reactions to real external persons in terms of such phantasies. The difference is a fundamental one.
2 Kate Friedlander is referring to Anna Freud's and Dorothy Burlingham's work on 'Infants without Families and Reports on the Hampstead Nurseries' (1942).

6

Fourth
Discussion of Scientific Controversies

British Psycho-Analytical Society

96 Gloucester Place,
London, W.1.

NOTICE TO MEMBERS AND ASSOCIATE MEMBERS

A meeting of Members and Associate Members will be held on Wednesday, April 7th, 1943, at 8 p.m., at 96 Gloucester Place, London, W.1. This is the fourth of the Series of Scientific Discussions on controversial topics existing within the Society.

Continuation of discussion on Mrs Isaacs' paper

A copy of the contributions to the discussion held on March 17th, 1943, is enclosed herewith. In reference to the procedure at this meeting attention is called to *page 16 of the minutes*.

EDWARD GLOVER
Scientific Secretary

March 25th, 1943

415

A Meeting of Members and Associate Members
was held on Wednesday, April 7th, 1943, at 8 p.m.,
at 96 Gloucester Place, London, W.1.

(Fourth meeting in the series of Scientific Discussions on controversial issues existing within the Society: continuation of discussion of Mrs Isaacs' paper.)

Dr Glover was in the Chair and 28 Members and Associates were present (Glover, Payne, Friedlander, Lantos, Weiss, Mrs Hoffer, Mrs Burlingham, Dr Stross, Frank, Fleischer-Gero, Herford, Macdonald, Ries, Sharpe, Gillespie, Taylor, Evans, Usher, Klein, Isaacs, Winnicott, Wilson, Rickman, Riviere, Heimann, Franklin).

Eleven candidate-guests were present (Hollitscher, Schlossberg, Pratt, Bick, Little, Mannheim, Frankl, Schwarz, Gompertz, Milner, Bonnard).

Minutes of the last discussion meeting were read and signed.

Dr Glover opened the meeting. The Secretary raised the question of the expenses for the circulation of full minutes, as the contributions received from Members so far will be exhausted after this meeting. After discussion it was decided to circulate a further appeal to Members who have not yet paid the first contribution of £1 and later to call on Members to put up a further 10s. when necessary. Duplicated minutes should in future only be sent to those Members who either contributed to the cost or are not in a position to do so.

Dr Glover then explained that a number of contributions to the discussion were left over from the last meeting and that Mrs Rosenfeld had intimated that she would not give her contribution at this point. This left two main contributions and three others which in the meantime had been notified.

Consequently the following Members spoke in turn: Miss Anna Freud, Mrs Hedwig Hoffer. Then two papers sent by Major Adrian Stephen and Dr Foulkes respectively were read in absence by Dr Payne. Dr Payne then took the Chair while Dr Glover read his contribution. (Full minutes of all these papers to be circulated to Members.)

As agreed at the last meeting, Dr Glover then opened the spontaneous discussion.

Dr Payne and Mrs Isaacs raised questions in connection with Miss Anna Freud's paper. Dr Glover, Miss Freud, Dr Payne, Mrs Isaacs,

Dr Friedlander, Dr Lantos took part in the discussion and Dr Glover summarized. (Full minutes attached here and abstract circulated.)

A discussion of arrangements of future meetings took place and the following was decided:

May 5th: ordinary Scientific Meeting, paper Miss Freud.
May 19th: Scientific Discussion Meeting: reply Mrs Isaacs to discussion.
June 16th: Scientific Discussion Meeting: Dr Heimann to comment upon it and discussion.
June 30th: Scientific Discussion Meeting: further discussion of Dr Heimann's paper.

(signed) Edward Glover

Discussion held on April 7th, 1943

Continuation of discussion on Mrs Susan Isaacs' paper
'The Nature and Function of Phantasy'

MISS ANNA FREUD: When several weeks ago I specially asked for this second round of remarks and questions to be addressed to Mrs Isaacs, I was led by a feeling of dissatisfaction with our preliminary results. A danger which I had underestimated in the beginning was that of misapprehension of remarks made in discussion which proved misleading. My contribution today is prompted by one feeling only: a disinclination to enter upon our next topics (introjection and projection; the pathogenic role of phantasy) before the present subject has been clarified. The opportunity of discussing certain basic concepts, which will be indispensable for a continuation of this discussion, may never return. But to enter into future discussions without such clarification seems futile.

The points which I have in mind in this respect are the following:

(a) The beginnings of object relationship and early object phantasies.
(b) The synthetic function of the ego and early phantasies of guilt and reparation.
(c) Some reasons for disagreement about 'early phantasy'.

If a lengthy explanation is attached to each, it is only meant to serve the purpose of avoiding misconceptions of my own views about these matters.

(a) THE BEGINNINGS OF OBJECT RELATIONSHIP AND EARLY OBJECT PHANTASIES

The following seems to me an outstanding difference between Mrs Klein's theories and psychoanalytical theory as I understand it. For Mrs Klein object relationship begins with, or soon after, birth, whereas I consider that there is a narcissistic and auto-erotic phase of several months' duration, which precedes what we call object relationship in its proper sense, even though the beginnings of object relation are slowly built up during this initial stage. According to Mrs Isaacs' descriptions, the new-born infant, already in the first six months, loves, hates, desires, attacks, wishes to destroy and to dismember his mother, etc. He has feelings of guilt towards her, commits acts of aggression, of reparation, and does things on her behalf or against her wishes. This means that his attitude towards her is that of a fully developed object relationship.

According to my own conception of this same period, the infant is at this time exclusively concerned with his own well-being. The mother is important, so far as she serves or disturbs this well-being. She is an instrument of satisfaction or denial, and as such of extreme importance in the child's narcissistic scheme of things.

To make this divergence of views still more explicit, I refer to Dr Adrian Stephen's contribution, in which he uses, in criticism of what I said about wish-fulfilment, the example of the 'thirst-satisfying drink' [p. 362] I should not like Dr Stephen to think either that I fail to see the close connection between the aim and object of an instinct, nor that I have really made the mistake of taking an abstraction too rigidly. Dr Stephen is of course right in assuming that at later stages the desire for the drink and the desire to satisfy thirst coincide. But what I mean to imply in my description of the child's narcissistic state, is a stage in which the aim of the instinct (Dr Stephen's terms 'satisfying the thirst') is of overwhelming importance, whereas the object (in Dr Stephen's example 'the water') is only dimly taken into account. I do not mean by that, as Mrs Isaacs thinks, that for the infant sensations of pleasure are merely a bodily matter, are non-mental. But I believe that the psychic processes of the child are governed by the urge for satisfaction, that is by the aim of the instinct, and not by phantasies of its object. It seems to me that the infant desires (and hallucinates) satisfaction as ardently and insistently as the older child, for instance, desires (and phantasies) the presence of the mother. To express it once more in the simple terms of Dr Stephen's example: in the beginning of life the infant only cares about the satisfying of the thirst; it is an all-important step in his development towards object relationship when he begins to care about the water.

The interpretation of this narcissistic state between birth and object relationship has always seemed an important part of psychoanalytical theory. It has been under discussion many times, and arguments have been brought forward repeatedly to disprove or to diminish either the length or the importance of that period. Ferenczi and his followers in Budapest, for instance, collected evidence to prove that during this narcissistic period the infant is open to influence exerted by the object. I am very ready to accept such evidence. There is not the slightest doubt in anybody's mind about the complete dependence of the infant on his surroundings. His state of health and his state of contentment are continually influenced by the mother's mood, the mother's emotions, and the mother's behaviour. But this does not alter the fact that the infant's object relationship is still an indirect one: changes in the object reach him by way of difference in the satisfaction given. The person of the object remains interchangeable so long as the gratification remains the same.

According to analytic conceptions an object relationship is built up slowly during a period of several months. Perception and reality testing in connection with experiences of satisfaction and frustration of wishes furnish the means by which the object becomes the centre of interest and, during the next year of life, equals in importance, sometimes even supersedes in importance, the gratification received. This new state of affairs, which puts an end to infantile narcissism, continues all through life, though there are certain conditions under which the individual may regress to the former state. One of these conditions has been described in the report on young children, written by Mrs Burlingham and myself, which Mrs Isaacs has referred to several times. We gave examples which showed that children in the second year of life, who are deprived of their first objects, have a tendency to revert to the state where satisfaction counts for everything and objects count for nothing. The same thing occurs in adults in certain abnormal states (for instance, perversions), in which the individual is firmly fixated to a specific form of gratification, not to a specific object of the past. Attainment of this gratification is of overwhelming importance and the object merely serves the purpose of bringing it about. The lack of real object relationship in these cases sometimes resembles that in psychotic states.

This lengthy explanation is merely meant as an introduction to a simple question. Would Mrs Isaacs agree with the following formulation?

One of the outstanding differences between Freudian and Kleinian theory is that Mrs Klein sees in the first months of life evidence of a wide range of differentiated object relations, partly libidinal and partly aggressive. Freudian theory on the other hand allows at this period only for the crudest rudiments of object relationship and sees life governed by the desire for instinct gratification, in which perception of the object is only achieved slowly.

I know that Mrs Isaacs' answer could easily be that just this is the progress and advance of Kleinian theory, that it has filled a dark and otherwise empty period with the psychic content which rightfully belongs to it. But to me it seems that this is not an empty period and that its real content is not the object relationship of later stages. It is certainly true that the first months of life are a dark period, since we know so little about the real reactions of the child to the processes of instinctual urge and its gratification and frustration. But further research into the infant's states of contentment and distress should bring enlightenment.

If Mrs Isaacs agrees with this formulation, it would then be easier to understand the differences of opinion about auto-erotism, as discussed by Dr Lantos. For anybody who holds the theory that object relationship begins with birth, auto-erotism would naturally play a part in the scheme of object relationship. The part of the body which furnishes pleasure might be conceived as a substitute or symbol for the object, or, as a colleague suggested to me in a private discussion, the child might love his own body because the mother handled it, or because it is filled with the mother's milk. It is on the other hand in agreement with the Freudian conception of a narcissistic beginning of life, to conceive of auto-erotism as an intrinsic source of pleasure, independent of relations to the object, its importance diminishing and rising with the rise and fall of object relationship.

It is easy to see where this subject touches on the problem of early phantasy. Owing to the limited possibilities for expression which the infant possesses, there is no direct evidence about phantasy in the first year of life. Its existence is inferred from circumstantial evidence collected in the later years of childhood. That means that the inferences drawn from the later material are necessarily influenced by the theoretical views held by the various analysts.

The 'early phantasies', described by Mrs Klein and other authors of her school, all concern libidinal or aggressive wishes directed towards the mother. Since, in Kleinian theory, object relations to the mother exist in rich variety from the very beginning, this characteristic of the phantasies is no objection against placing them in the first months of life. Contrary to this, with people who feel convinced of the existence of an initial narcissistic phase, the fact that a phantasy is concerned mainly with object relations immediately places it outside that first phase, in the period after such object relationship has been established. In a similar way, Freud, on the basis of his views about a narcissistic phase, merely ascribed hallucinatory wish-fulfilment to the infant and no 'phantasies' containing elements of complex attitudes towards an object. The dating of all phantasies found later as to the time of their origin thus naturally depends on our ideas about the date when all the various elements used in the phantasy can legitimately be expected to have been at the disposal of the child.

This explanation merely serves to introduce my second question. Does Mrs Isaacs agree with the following formulation? 'The assumption of early object phantasies in Mrs Klein's theories is bound up with the theoretical substitution of a very early stage of rich and varied object relationship, for the early phase of narcissism and auto-erotism as described by Freud.'

(b) THE SYNTHETIC FUNCTION OF THE EGO AND EARLY PHANTASIES OF
GUILT AND REPARATION

A second outstanding difference between Mrs Klein's theories and psychoanalytical theory as I understand it concerns the role and date of origin of the synthetic function of the ego. I have made an attempt to clarify this point in my former contribution in a paragraph dealing with the primary and secondary modes of mental functioning. This attempt failed owing to a misapprehension on Mrs Isaacs' part which was evidently due to lack of clear expression on my part. I therefore try to re-state the position in less misleading terms.

I consider, in agreement with Mrs Isaacs, that correlation or synthesis of perception and reality-testing is achieved in degrees from birth onwards. It would not be accurate to say that this is achieved by the ego, since no ego exists as yet; it is more accurate to say that this synthetic function builds the ego or constitutes the first ego-nucleus. There would be no growth of intelligence in the child without the steady growth and increasing power of this function. So far Mrs Isaacs is right in asserting that it is nonsense to speak of uncorrelated mental activity in the first year of life.

Only, as is abundantly clear from the context of my remarks, I did not deal in that paragraph with the correlating function, as applied to perception and reality testing, but as applied to impulses and wishes. (See what I said about 'conflict between impulses', 'co-existence of ambivalent feelings', 'independent existence of all urges', 'disregard of mutual contradiction'.) I consider, not only on the basis of psychoanalytical theory, but on the basis of my own observations and experiences, that this synthetic function is not exercised on instinctual urges during the first year and, in fact, not until considerably later. Even though correlation of perception grows continually, wishes and impulses continue to be governed by the primary process with its characteristic lack of unification.

After an ego has been formed, wishes and impulses are subjected to the synthetic function in slow stages. To describe it in greater detail: The first step in correlation to be observed is that between inner urges and memory of outside prohibition. This occurs from the first year onward, but it is hardly to be called synthesis in the proper sense of the word, since what is correlated is an inner urge with an outside force. It is usually not effective enough to check the child's action, though it can produce fear and discomfort. The second step in correlation is that between two contrasting inner urges, for instance between love and hate. Such synthesis is frequently observed in the second year, though it is at that time by no means a regular occurrence. If children in the second year are not checked by fear of outside prohibition, their contrasting wishes and emotions can still flow freely. It is usual that conflicting inner urges succeed in finding successive expression, without the one necessarily influencing the other. I distrust all explanations which automatically interpret the quick changes from love to hate or hate to love-reactions of the infant as acts of reparation. I consider that these various reactions may be adequate and independent expressions for the respective sides of the child's ambivalence. The child between one and two actually possesses a wide range of libidinal and aggressive relations to objects. But the conflicting acts and emotions which arise on the basis of these relations can still coexist in his mind and in his behaviour without adding to or detracting from each other. There would be a great deal more to be said on this subject on the basis of direct observation. In watching the behaviour of children at this stage, one is reminded of the popular saying, 'to eat one's cake and have it too', which expresses the lack of synthesis between two equally ardent desires. Whenever correlation between contrasting urges occurs at this stage, it makes itself felt rather in feelings of discomfort and unhappiness which accompany action than in an inhibition of action. (Special reference to children with an obsessional constitution.)

The third and final step in development of the synthetic function consists in correlation between an inner urge and an inner prohibition. This achievement which, in Kleinian theory, is ascribed to the very beginning of life, belongs, in the Freudian view, to the development of the Oedipus complex and its consequences for the formation of the superego. The affect which accompanies this unification is guilt. I cannot see evidence of this reaction before the third year.

It is easy to see how our conception of the slow development of the synthetic function influences our attitude towards acceptance or non-acceptance of certain phantasies for certain stages. I repeat once more what I have said earlier concerning phantasies of object relationship. Phantasies are not observed in the first year of life; they are inferred. That means that they are not clinical data which can be demonstrated in a convincing way, but the result of interpretations of clinical material which is found later. An analyst who is not convinced of the existence of a synthetic function in the first year of life will not date back to that period phantasies which include elements of guilt and reparation. An analyst who believes in such synthetic function exercised over impulses and wishes from birth will not hesitate to ascribe phantasies of this kind to the first year of life.

(c) SOME REASONS FOR DISAGREEMENT ABOUT 'EARLY PHANTASY'

The papers presented so far by the various speakers in the discussion have at least clarified one point, namely, that disagreement about 'early phantasies' does not arise from the causes to which Mrs Isaacs ascribes it. Mrs Isaacs believes that we object to the concept of early phantasy because of a prejudice against psychic reality as such; if it were so, this would disqualify us as psychoanalysts. Or Mrs Isaacs believes that we object to the concept of pre-verbal phantasy. Dr Payne aptly refuted this accusation by referring to hysterical symptoms as a well-known non-verbal expression of phantasy. Mrs Isaacs is even under the misapprehension that some of us postpone the date for phantasy activity until the age of four. Dr Lantos has refuted this accusation as a misunderstanding, the origin of which is difficult to conceive.

In contrast to Mrs Isaacs I consider that as an outcome of the present discussion, the disagreements expressed with Mrs Klein's conception of early phantasy can be grouped according to their reasons as follows:

(i) DISAGREEMENT DUE TO THE EXTENSION OF THE TERM 'PHANTASY'

As Dr Glover and Dr Brierley have pointed out in their contributions, the term 'phantasy', in its new use in Kleinian theory, covers modes of mental functioning for which we use other terms: thinking, reality-thinking, remembering, wishing, longing, in short all mental activities of the infant. Since we continue to use our own terminology, we declare every so often in given cases, that a certain process in the child's mind is not phantasy, which to Mrs Isaacs means that we deny its existence altogether. Much of the disagreement between Mrs Isaacs and Mrs Burlingham is of this nature.

(ii) DISAGREEMENT CONCERNING DATING OF PHANTASIES

I have attempted to make this particular point clear with the help of two instances, that of early object phantasies and that of early phantasies of guilt and reparation. I hope that I have conveyed the meaning that there is little disagreement between Mrs Isaacs and myself about the existence of such phantasies. Disagreement is confined to their date of origin. That means that the divergence of opinion in these cases only appears to concern phantasy activity. What lies behind it is the serious divergence of views about the sequence of development and the dating of certain all important events and functions: the beginning of object relationship; the onset and climax of the Oedipus complex; the formation of the superego; and the dating of various ego-functions, as, for instance, the synthetic function of the ego, exercised on existing urges. We all know that our views on these matters go rather far apart.

(iii) DISAGREEMENT CONCERNING CONTENT OF PHANTASY

To my astonishment, this very important point has so far found no speaker and has only vaguely been referred to in various places. The early phantasies most frequently described in Kleinian theory are violently aggressive phantasies. This seems logical to the analysts who are convinced of the preponderance of the death instinct at the beginning of life. The existence of these same phantasies is widely questioned by those to whom the libidinal impulses seem of overwhelming importance for this time of life. Again, the underlying difference of opinion does not refer directly to phantasy activity but, partly to dating as before, and partly to a divergence of views about instinct theory.

424

(iv) DISAGREEMENT OWING TO CONFUSION BETWEEN THE CONTENT OF
CERTAIN PHANTASIES (I.E., CANNIBALISTIC PHANTASIES)
AND THE PROCESS OF INTROJECTION

This point has been touched upon by Miss Sharpe and Dr Brierley.
When Miss Sharpe complained in her last contribution that in Mrs
Klein's technique of analysing phantasies the content of the phantasy is
treated, not as psychic reality, but as 'real', she deals, I believe, with
this particular confusion. What is considered real is evidently not the
result of the phantasy of introjection, but the process of introjection
itself, which in Kleinian theory becomes the basis of all object
relationship. It has always puzzled me how it was possible in Kleinian
technique to interpret deeply repressed cannibalistic phantasies in the
beginning of analysis without meeting absolute disbelief in the patient
or without strengthening his resistance. I seem to understand as a
result of this discussion, and I wonder whether Mrs Isaacs would agree
with this formulation, that what is pointed out to the patient is not the
content of a phantasy but a mechanism of psychic functioning.

I do not think, that Dr Brierley's article, [Brierley 1937] excellent as
it is, has done enough to solve this confusion or to clarify the
disagreements which she caused by it. Dr Brierley shows that it is
perfectly possible for memory images of the mother and cannibalistic
phantasies concerning the mother to exist at the same time. I am quite
convinced that this is the case and also that cannibalistic phantasies,
like all phantasies, involve the use of memory images. But Dr Brierley
only deals with the cannibalistic phantasy of taking the mother inside
and not with the process of introjection built on it. Disagreement does
not arise concerning the phantasy that the mother has been swallowed
up, but concerning the role given by Kleinian theory to the
mechanism of introjection. Kleinian theory seems to assert that all
early mental functioning of the infant proceeds on the lines prescribed
by introjection. The question which Dr Brierley tried to answer in her
contribution was originally put by myself and it really should have
run: What is the role of memory images in a scheme of mental
functioning which is completely governed by the mechanism of
introjection?

It is again clear that the underlying difference of opinion does not
concern phantasy activity itself, but our views about the various
mechanisms of mental functioning, their dating, their sequence, and
their importance for governing mental life.

MRS HEDWIG HOFFER: It is not my intention to widen the scope of
our discussion on early phantasies. What I will say is more in the

nature of a working through and was already touched upon in various contributions.

My question is simply this: what makes us feel so extremely uneasy when we read statements such as the following, 'The capacity to hallucinate is, in my view,. either identical with phantasy or the pre-condition of it'. (The quotation is taken from Mrs Isaacs' first paper, page [278].) Or on page [281] of the same paper, 'Now what does Freud mean by "dim impulses which it was impossible for the child to grasp psychically at the time and which were only interpreted later"? This can only be the same thing as Melanie Klein describes.' Or, to take a last quotation from Mrs Isaacs' reply, page [375], when she describes 'a baby from about two months on' 'daydreaming'.

Let me try to answer the question myself. Such statements ignore all the differentiations we have learnt to make. But the differentiations are the landmarks which guide us through the dark landscape of early development. Psychoanalytical understanding is based on the observation of others more or less like ourselves and on introspection. It is more than a coincidence that such a revealing work as Freud's *Interpretation of Dreams* or Varendenck's interesting research on the 'Psychology of Day-dreams' is based on introspection.

The analysis of comparatively small children is, to my mind, of little help in this respect. Because a child of two or three is unable to formulate earlier experiences and even at that stage his clumsiness in describing emotional data and his high degree of suggestibility make him a very unsuitable collaborator for psychical research. Too much depends on the analyst's interpretation. The conditions of adult analysis which allow us to carry out therapeutic aims and at the same time lend themselves to the needs of psychological research are not present to the same degree in child analysis.

So our possibilities of knowing are restricted to direct behaviouristic observations and to the conclusions which the study of dreams and regressions allow us to draw.

Hallucinations are an archaic mode of mental activity and our knowledge of it comes from the regression to it in dreams or in different psychotic states. On the behaviouristic side we can infer from the infant's attitude that it tries to satisfy instinctual needs in this way.

The brain is an organ which is at work from birth to death – constantly receiving stimuli from within and from without. Empirical and theoretical considerations force us to assume some kind of precipitate of all this activity. But I need not go into details as Dr Glover and others have dealt with this topic thoroughly.

What one might call the awakening of the mind starts slowly. In

Inhibitions, Symptoms, and Anxiety Freud warns us not to overestimate the fact of birth as a step in development. He says, 'there is much more continuity between intra-uterine life and earliest infancy than the impressive caesura of the act of birth allows us to believe.' [Freud, S. 1926: 109; SE 20:136]

We do not know of any state of mind where the pleasure–pain principle is not at work. The first utterances are pain signals. But there is nothing to lead us to call this initial stage of mental development 'phantasy'. In the second half of the first year the baby begins to behave humanly. But even then when the emotional fog brightens and a kind of mental life in some way similar to our own begins to set in, I would be very reluctant to call this uncorrelated mental activity 'phantasy'. Nobody doubts the possibility of some very simple conceptions which contain elements of the same thing as we call in more differentiated stages phantasy. But the wholesale use of the term seems to me of no advantage. My view here coincides with that of Dr Brierley, Miss Freud, Dr Friedlander, Dr Glover, and others.

Freud widened the scope of the term 'sexuality', because the exclusive application of this term in pre-Freudian times was based on prejudice, convention, and moral evaluation, not on biological facts. But the case of phantasy is not the same. Phantasy is one specified mental activity. It is connected with the unpleasure-principle and with reality testing.

Starting from dream-thoughts Freud describes day-dreaming in analogy to nocturnal dreams stressing the point that they have essential features, especially wish-fulfilment, in common. And he goes on some sentences later to point out that these phantasies or day-dreams are the immediate predecessors of symptoms. Whenever Freud speaks of phantasies he does so with reference to regression. He deals thoroughly with the subject in 'The Poet and Day-dreaming' and, if I may quote at some length,

> One may say that a phantasy at one and the same moment hovers between three periods of time – the three periods of our ideation. The activity of phantasy in the mind is linked up with some current impression, occasioned by some event in the present, which had the power to rouse an intense desire. From there it wanders back to the memory of an early experience, generally belonging to infancy, in which this wish was fulfilled. Then it creates for itself a situation which is to emerge in the future, representing the fulfilment of the wish – this is the day-dream or phantasy, which now carries in it traces both of the occasion which engendered it and of some past memory.
>
> [Freud, S. 1908:177; SE 9:147][1]

In 'Formulations Regarding the Two Principles of Mental Functioning' Freud defines phantasy once more, without widening or changing the scope of the term. I quote 'with the introduction of the reality-principle one mode of thought-activity was split off; it was kept free from reality-testing and remained subordinated to the pleasure principle alone. This is the act of phantasy making.' [Freud, S. 1911a:16; SE 12:122][2] Freud uses the word 'day-dream' in this strict sense alone. The complicated make-up of such mental phenomena makes it unlikely that they occur in this form very much before the third year. I believe that some of us have kept to this definition of the term 'day-dream'. Maybe this fact is partly responsible for Mrs Isaacs' assumption that any one of us might date the beginning of phantasy life as late as this. In the same way as a child's simple night-dream is governed by the same rules as the unintelligible and disconnected dreams of adults, we may assume that day-dreams too have earlier editions which exist before the stage of clearly differentiated systems is reached and which are based on visual memory-traces. The term 'phantasy', if we use it as a term and not only as a description, includes much more primitive phenomena as well. We have to come back to these facts when we deal with regression, but I think in this respect we should hear Mrs Isaacs first.

Freud makes a strict distinction between these day-dreams, however simple they may be, and the child's phantasy game. He stresses the fact that the child links his imaginary world with the tangible and visible things of the real world and that this link distinguishes the child's game from day-dreaming.

Before I finish let me mention one further point. The existence of an omnipresent phantasy-life in adults and its importance in the psychical make-up was a psychoanalytical discovery of the first order. We understand that the pioneers in this new-found land were fascinated and that their interest in the meaning and the content of such phantasies was paramount. But this phase of our science belongs to the past. I do not underestimate the therapeutic value of the meaning of phantasies, but do not let us overestimate its importance for psychological research.

If we stick to Freud's elaborated categories we are able to correlate the different stages of regression in psychopathology to the different stages of normal development. And we are able to conceive the primitive psychical make-up of an infant and the elaborate organization of an adult personality as a lawful continuity.

These are some of the reasons why I disagree with Mrs Isaacs' picture of early mental activity.

In evolution more primitive organisms are followed by more

complicated ones. I should suppose that science obeys the same laws. We progress from simple generalizations to specified definitions.

DR ADRIAN STEPHEN (read in absence of Dr A. Stephen by Dr Payne): Had I received notice of the meeting on March 17th which, unluckily, I did not, or had circumstances allowed me to be present tonight I might have had the chance of replying verbally to the criticisms levelled at me by Dr Glover. As things are I must ask leave to submit a few remarks in writing.

On page [396] of the circulated minutes Dr Glover expresses his disagreement with those who, as he puts it, 'suggest that Freud's basic concepts were mere tentative formulations which he would himself have played about with or modified freely at some later date'. Now, no one, so far as I can discover, has suggested that Freud would have 'played about' with his concepts but I, and I alone, I think, have used a phrase about 'tentative formulations' and I suppose that Dr Glover was referring to me, at any rate among others.

Now the curious thing to notice about Dr Glover's phrase is that one would be inclined on reading it to suppose that he was defending Freud against an attack by me, whereas the real fact is that I am in agreement with Freud and it is Dr Glover who is attacking him. In his paper on 'Instincts and their Vicissitudes' Freud speaks of the need for elasticity in psychoanalytic concepts and he adds these words: 'The science of physics furnishes an excellent illustration of the way in which even these basal concepts which are firmly established in the form of definitions are constantly being altered in their content.' [Freud, S. 1915:61; SE 14:117][3]

Even if Freud had not spoken in this manner himself what he said was obviously true, and even the basal concepts of such an old and widely studied science as physics are frequently found to need revision how is it to be expected that our own concepts should be anything but extremely tentative?

In another passage Dr Glover takes me to task by name. His complaint appears to be that I use the words 'phantastic' and 'imaginary' as though they were synonymous and he produces some elaborate arguments to prove how wrong I am. Now these arguments are, I think, full of logical fallacies but I need not weary the Society by proving it for I never upheld the opinion which Dr Glover intended them to refute.

The phrase that Dr Glover selected from his onslaught is one in which I suggest that Freud would have agreed that an instinctual object may be, as I say, 'imaginary, or if you like phantastic'. Certainly taken by itself, isolated, this sentence or rather this part of a sentence does seem to bear the interpretation which Dr Glover puts on it. It does look as though I meant that 'imaginary' and 'phantastic' were two synonymous epithets. The phrase, however, did not occur in isolation. I had been giving a short account of Freud's concept of an instinctual object, as he describes it in his 'Three Contributions to the Theory of Sex'.[4] I pointed out that there Freud spoke of objects as if they were always concrete. Now a concrete object, though it may stimulate a phantasy, is not in itself phantastic. I wanted, however, to speak of phantastic objects as to the nature of which there has been so much disagreement and I therefore introduced the notion of an 'imaginary' object for it seemed to me clear that the imaginary object of an instinct must by its very nature be 'phantastic' too. While, therefore, the two words 'imaginary' and 'phantastic' are not synonymous it so happens that to agree that an object is imaginary is also to agree that it is phantastic. Since, then, Freud constantly wrote of objects that are 'imaginary', I think he would have agreed that they were phantastic too.

This is all that the phrase meant which so excited Dr Glover's wrath. I am sorry to have had to explain it in such tedious detail but Dr Glover's outburst really left me no alternative.

DR S. H. FOULKES (read in absence of Dr Foulkes by Dr Payne): I am writing in a military atmosphere, in which I am very much absorbed, and it is therefore not easy to switch my mind back to the discussion in which you are engaged. Therefore only a very short reply to Dr Heimann's remarks, which reached me today.

To put the least important in a summary way: She can take it that I have not committed the oversights nor the confusions with which she credits me.

I can see that unconscious phantasy is in Mrs Isaacs' view, the mental representative of instinct. The question is one of emphasis: notwithstanding the great dynamic power of phantasies, are we to regard them as primary motor directing instinctual energy and reality, or are instincts and their reality-objects the primary agents, leading to the formation of phantasies under conditions of conflict, frustration, etc.? Dr Heimann's suggestion that I should have pointed out in what analysis consists is rather unfair in reference to discussion remarks limited to ten minutes. Nor should it be necessary to point this out to a meeting of seasoned analysts of the foremost analytical society still in existence. I presume I mean the same as she does, when she refers, e.g., to 'the ordinary principles of analytic procedure'. I shall, however, be glad, when peace comes, to tell her precisely in what analysis consists in my view.

It was not necessary to remind me 'in passing' 'that it is thought desirable in psychiatric case histories to reproduce the patient's own expressions', etc. – I am quite familiar with that. But we are always given to understand that the elucidation of the patient's unconscious phantasies, inner objects, etc., is the result of painstaking labour on the part of the analyst, belonging as they do to the deepest unconscious levels. Surely, what Dr Heimann describes is the outcome of her own interpretative work with the patient and not comparable to the spontaneous conscious statements, reactions, etc., with which the psychiatrist is concerned. If Dr Heimann thinks too that these phantasies are the raw material which must be submitted to further analysis, by which I mean in this connection the redressing of displacements, substitutions, and other distortions and the ultimate re-establishment of the pregnant original situation or situations and the laying bare of primary instinctual urges and their conflicts, and if she furthermore means by 'the ordinary principles of analytic procedure' the same as I and other analysts, well, then, we are in agreement. If not, she would better describe her technique as well another time. But I am not alone under the impression that she means and does something different and I am afraid that she pays lip service either to Freud or to Mrs Klein. May be that I am wrong, of course, time will show.

From Dr Heimann's pointed tone it would seem that she felt attacked. Let me therefore say in conclusion that this was not my intention and that I found her paper interesting and stimulating. But perhaps I have become identified with one of the bad objects she might still harbour in her mind, who knows?

With my best wishes to all! S.H.F.

DR EDWARD GLOVER: Since the last meeting I have been asked to explain more fully the following sentence occurring in my contribution to the discussion of Mrs Isaacs' paper. I said on that occasion: 'Despite her (Mrs Isaacs') demurrers there seems to be no end to this process (i.e. confusing cathected memory images with phantasy) short of abolishing the distinctions between the perceptual aspects of consciousness, the imaginal aspects of consciousness, the pre-conscious and the unconscious.' Why, I have been asked, bring in at this point the preconscious and the unconscious? Am I merely repeating Anna Freud's criticism, which was, you may remember, that to judge from her examples, Mrs Isaacs' primary unconscious phantasies show some of the hallmarks of the 'secondary', as distinct from the 'primary' process? Actually my argument, although complementary to that of Anna Freud, is based on considerations of a different order. Mrs Isaacs' view that reality thinking is a derivative of primary phantasy thinking would involve a complete recasting of our accepted ideas of unconscious defence mechanisms, of their function, their timing, and their psychic locality. It would imply, e.g., that ego-syntonic as well as ego-dystonic presentations are subject to repression and that in some way or another the ego-syntonic impulses develop the capacity of escaping this censorship. On the contrary I maintain that reality thinking is primary and must always be distinguished from that organized product of frustration to which Freud applied the term 'phantasy'. It is to my mind unthinkable that presentations of instinct which are capable of gratification and therefore capable of becoming conscious without interference from unconscious defence mechanisms (Bewusstseinsfahig), should, as Mrs, Isaacs would have us think, begin to be distinguished at a later date from an original phantasy nexus. The whole weight of biological evidence of survival is against the assumption. Reality thinking is the primary product of psychic adaptation. Moreover since Mrs Isaacs is unable to distinguish between re-cathected memory traces and phantasies, she not only abolishes the economic function of repression but also obliterates the distinction between the dynamic unconscious and the preconscious. By the same token she alters our (structural) concepts of psychic boundaries. I had already referred to this obliteration of boundaries in my earlier contribution to this discussion. On that occasion I pointed out that Mrs Isaacs' postulates implied the existence of a new and dynamically independent core to the Freudian unconscious, even if she did not indicate by what means these representatives of instinct retained their active capacity to influence later developments. If this were the case the relation of what Freud called the dynamic unconscious to Mrs Isaacs' primary enclave would be similar to that now regarded as existing between the preconscious and the dynamic unconscious.

And here I would like to answer one of the debating points made by Mrs Isaacs in her reply to my first contribution. According to Mrs Isaacs I had no good ground for suggesting that if her views were correct, the theoretical and clinical importance of the Oedipus complex would disappear. Her reply was that because she hadn't mentioned the Oedipus complex in her paper it didn't follow that she ignored it. Now this was not my argument. What I did say was that her assumption of a primary active core to the unconscious based on the persisting cathexis of instinct presentations existing in the first two years – a core which, according to Mrs Isaacs, retains its powers to influence all later mental development – committed her to a depreciation of the specific significance of the classical Oedipus complex. Even if Mrs Isaacs at some future date should seriously maintain that she does not depreciate the significance of the Oedipus phase, such assurance would be incompatible with the theories already outlined in her own paper. Her views on the dynamic significance of what she would call early phantasy and her views on regression, may enable her to plead that the Oedipus phase acquires a secondary significance. But Freud's view was that whatever the pre-genital phases of infancy contribute, the Oedipus complex is nevertheless of primary significance.

To end in a lighter vein: I would like to take this opportunity of commenting on the second of the points raised by Mrs Isaacs in reply to my earlier criticisms. I had pointed out that if, as Mrs Isaacs evidently held, only child analysts were in a favourable position to judge as to the validity of reconstructions of child mental development, there was little point in this Society continuing the present discussion. To which Mrs Isaacs perfectly legitimately pointed out that many years ago, in the symposium on child analysis printed in the Journal, I had myself gone very much further than she had. I had said bluntly that other analysts were not in a position to judge. That is perfectly true. But I am afraid that under present circumstances my retort is only too obvious. If any proof were needed that my former belief was much too optimistic if not indeed profoundly mistaken, it is to be found in the present discussions between child analysts in our Society. We are in fact faced with the spectacle of one group of child analysts on the strength of their analytic work with children advancing views which other child analysts regard as profoundly wrong if not indeed anti-analytical in content. Under these circumstances I am however reluctantly compelled to retract my earlier oversanguine judgement. Events have not justified my belief and I am afraid that it is no longer possible to maintain it.

But debating points apart I should like to add that I have often regretted being prevailed on to take part in that particular symposium. It was, as events have shown, much too precipitate, and had all the scientific disadvantages of concerted discussion. Possibly in the course of this present series I may have an opportunity of stating my views on the subject more clearly. At present I am concerned to rectify my earlier misjudgement.

(Completion of minutes to follow.)

433

Abstract of spontaneous discussion

held on April 7th, 1943

(Completion of minutes circulated)

As arranged, Dr Glover invited Members to put any questions dealing with subjects that had been under consideration in the previous meetings. Two questions only were put forward, one by Dr S. M. Payne, and one by Mrs S. Isaacs.

QUESTION (1) DR PAYNE

Dr Payne questioned Miss Anna Freud's statement that she did not think the mother was regarded by the child as an object in the first year of life, and based her criticism on behaviouristic differences in reactions to mother, nurses, strangers, etc., observed during feeding. Miss Freud first of all pointed out that her remark referred to the first half year. She agreed that behaviouristic differences existed but held that these are caused by changes in the form in which satisfaction is presented. She held further that there are qualitative differences between attitudes towards an object during this narcissistic phase and object attitudes at later stages. Dr Glover summarized as follows: 'For the sake of clarity in the records, may I summarize the question and answer. Dr Payne asks whether the varying behaviour of the child when fed by different objects does not imply the existence of an object relationship in embryo, to which Miss Freud replies that these variations are due to differences in the conditioning and do not imply that an object relationship exists in the first half year.'

QUESTION (2) MRS ISAACS

Mrs Isaacs raised various points concerning a statement in Miss Anna Freud's contribution which dealt with an alleged misapprehension on her part about dating of early phantasies. A discussion developed between her, Miss Anna Freud, Dr Friedlander, and Dr Lantos. Mrs Isaacs maintained that, according to statements made by Dr Robert Wälder, Dr Friedlander, and Dr Lantos, she had ample grounds for assuming that members of Continental groups postpone the beginning of phantasy-activity to the third or fourth year. The three last-named speakers replied that the various passages quoted refer to

434

specific phantasies and not to phantasy-activity as such, the existence of which in the second year is not a matter of controversy. Dr Glover summed up as follows: 'that there is controversy about the existence of phantasies up to, roughly speaking, the end of the first 12 months, and that, as regards phantasies which occur afterwards, the existence of these is not disputed; but there is controversy about the content ascribed to them.'

Minutes of spontaneous discussion on April 7th, 1943

DR GLOVER: I think that concludes the formal contributions and you may remember that we agreed to use the time remaining in a spontaneous discussion, dealing of course with the subject we have been considering in the previous meetings. As I imagine we will be completing this discussion with Mrs Isaacs' reply, this is obviously an opportunity for Members to put any questions they would like to have included in the list.

DR PAYNE: I should like to ask Miss Freud a question. She said she did not think that the mother was regarded by the child as an object in the first year of life. (Miss Freud: 'First half year') There are behaviouristic facts, for instance, that the child may be given the bottle by a stranger and refuse it, just as it may be given a wet nurse and would not take the breast from her. Such facts suggest that the child differentiates between objects.

DR GLOVER: Would Miss Freud like to answer this question now?

MISS FREUD: Yes, this is a question that should certainly not be answered too quickly or without preparation, but I would not have made the remarks I made without considering such facts. There is no doubt that the child notices differences and even the slightest differences in atmosphere, position, behaviour, mood of the person who gives the bottle. But, as I said before, these differences reach the child because there is a change of the form in which the satisfaction is presented. It is not the same as the beginning object relationship we find in the second half year where the child will refuse just because it is a different person. What we call change of atmosphere, change of mood, it is not the tie to the person. If one could imitate the form in which the satisfaction is given completely, the child would accept it. Experience shows that it is surprisingly easy to interchange objects at that time, just as it is surprising how difficult it is later.

DR PAYNE: It seems to me the difference is one of degree.

MISS FREUD: It seems so absolutely different in kind when one watches it closely.

DR PAYNE: But I have watched it too.

DR GLOVER: The question seems to be whether in Miss Freud's opinion in this early behaviour conditioning plays a role. Alterations of behaviour do not imply that an object relationship in the full sense exists.

DR PAYNE: In embryo, if you like –

MISS FREUD: To me the difference seems qualitative and not quantitative.

DR GLOVER: For the sake of clarity in the records, may I summarize the question and answer. Dr Payne asks whether the varying behaviour of the child when fed by different objects does not imply the existence of an object relationship, to which Miss Freud replies that these variations are due to differences in the conditions and do not imply that an object relationship exists.

MRS ISAACS: As nobody puts any more questions, there are one or two points which I think it would be useful if we could get clear. If Miss Freud would confirm me by re-reading the sentence in which she referred to my statement about her dating early phantasies.

MISS FREUD: 'Mrs Isaacs is even under the misapprehension that some of us postpone the date for phantasy activity until the age of 4.'

MRS ISAACS: I have not said that. I said the third or fourth year. That means the age of 2–3. Here there is a question of misunderstanding. We should get it really clear what everyone said. First I should quote Wälder, because I said in my first paper what I believed then that Wälder held and he, on page 112 in his article says: 'But apart from the simple inference as to his instinctual and affective situation we learn nothing: we have no evidence in his behaviour of any phantasy.' [Wälder 1937]

MISS FREUD: Does he name any age there?

MRS ISAACS: He says on page 428: 'All phantasies which have been described as belonging to this early period have been abundantly proved to occur at a later age, in children of about three years old. I believe that we shall obtain evidence that they occur even during the course of the third year. Their existence is not in question, only their occurrence in the first year.' Wälder takes the view that phantasy does not exist in the first year.

DR FRIEDLANDER: Wälder says that phantasies of the kind described by Mrs Klein do not exist at this time, that we have no evidence in the child's behaviour that such phantasies occur in the first year.

436

MRS ISAACS: Anybody who reads that would think that no phantasies exist in the first year.

MISS FREUD: This is what I tried to say today, that phantasies are not found at the early age, they are interpreted. What Wälder says is that there is no evidence.

MRS ISAACS: The whole trend of his paper is to say that phantasies can surely be found in the third and fourth year, but not in the first year.

Mrs Isaacs then referred to Dr Friedlander's first reply to her paper, in which she began by referring to Jenny Wälder's statement that phantasies of oral character expressed in the third or fourth year of life need not be old phantasies formed during the oral phase but may derive their oral character from regression.

Then Dr Lantos in her first reply to me says: 'I should like to remind you that there have been no controversies about the existence of phantasies from an early phase of life. I must say, that was news to me. People other than the Viennese Society would agree . . . [Editor's note: The transcript of the reply is incomplete.]

DR FRIEDLANDER: Yes, there is no controversy. Not about the existence of phantasy, but about the specific content attributed to it.

MRS ISAACS: We are not discussing the content.

DR FRIEDLANDER: That is just the point.

MRS ISAACS: If we say they exist and are important, and you take the view that . . . [Editor's note: The transcript of the reply is incomplete.]

DR FRIEDLANDER: There is a controversy whether this importance exists in the first year of life.

MRS ISAACS: Then Dr Lantos goes on: 'The problem is and has always been (1) the specific content of these phantasies, (2) the actual age at which we can first detect them, and (3) the dynamic part they play in the child's development as well as in his actions and plays.' Then I referred in my reply to what Dr Lantos had said, that 'the views of Mrs Wälder which Dr Friedlander quotes with approval, and the position so tenaciously held by Dr Lantos, still assume that phantasies come into operation and are traceable only in the third and fourth years.'

There are the various statements and they don't justify of course anything like what Miss Freud said just now. There is considerable controversy.

DR GLOVER: Are there any other points Members wish to state or questions Members would like to bring up?

MISS FREUD: I am not quite clear what the question is. Does Mrs Isaacs mean to say she has raised evidence enough to believe that phantasies of the kind described by Mrs Klein occur in the first year of life? I think what Wälder tried to say is that, at the later stages, phantasies can actually be found because the child already possesses verbal expression, and that from that date on there can be no controversy about existence or non-existence of phantasy. But verbal expression is of course much earlier than at 3 or 4 years.

MRS ISAACS: But he refers to it.

MISS FREUD: He refers to specific phantasies.

MRS ISAACS: That does not fit with the passages I read. He refers there to something more general than the example.

It seems to me a very important point to establish if it is generally agreed that phantasies do occur in the first year of life.

MISS FREUD: There is certainly controversy about the first year, but no controversy about later years.

DR GLOVER: Is that point clear that controversy exists about the first year of life?

MISS FREUD: Yes, and it is difficult to clear it up because there is no evidence in the first year and so, as I tried to show, it depends on other opinions.

MRS ISAACS: May I ask then on what grounds you say that phantasy exists in the first year?

DR LANTOS: Primitive phantasies may occur towards the end of the first year because then we have certain expressions from which we can conclude their existence. We are not agreed that phantasies exist before. We believe that in the second year phantasies of such complicated kind may exist.

DR GLOVER: Can we accept the following summing up: that there is controversy about the existence of phantasies up to roughly speaking the first 12 months, and that, as regards phantasies that occur afterwards, the existence of these is not disputed. But that there is controversy about the content ascribed to them.

A discussion of arrangements of future meetings took place and Dr Payne pointed out that owing to the amount of secretarial work the first meeting in May should be an ordinary Scientific Meeting, to be held on the 19th of May.

Miss Freud offered, as there was no paper notified for the Scientific Meeting in May, to give a report on some material which is the outcome of observations on children between 1 and 2 years, particularly social reactions. But she would have to say it is not from analytic observations but from direct observation, which of course limits its interest for analysts. This proposal was accepted. Date: *May 5th.*

It was then decided to have Mrs Isaacs' reply to the discussion at the second meeting in May. Date: *May 19th*.

At the first meeting in June, after Dr Heimann's paper was circulated beforehand, Dr Heimann would comment upon her paper and a few contributions to the discussion of it given. Date: *June 16th*.

At the second meeting in June more extensive comments on Dr Heimann's paper would be given. Date: *June 30th*.

The meeting was closed at 10.15 p.m.

Notes

1 We may say that it hovers, as it were, between three times – the three moments of time which our ideation involves. Mental work is linked to some current impression, some provoking occasion in the present which has been able to arouse one of the subject's major wishes. From there it harks back to a memory of an earlier experience (usually an infantile one) in which this wish was fulfilled; and it now creates a situation relating to the future which represents a fulfilment of the wish. What it thus creates is a day-dream or phantasy, which carries about it traces of its origin from the occasion which provoked it and from the memory. [SE 9:147]

2 'With the introduction of the reality principle one species of thought-activity was split off; it was kept free from reality-testing and remained subordinated to the pleasure principle alone.' [SE 12:122]

3 'Physics furnished an excellent illustration of the way in which even "basic concepts" that have been established in the form of definitions are constantly being altered in their content.' [SE 14:117]

4 Probably Adrian Stephen is referring to the paragraphs entitled 'Object finding' in 'Three Contributions to the Theory of Sex' (Freud, S. 1905).

7

Fifth
Discussion of Scientific Controversies

British Psycho-Analytical Society

The next meeting in the Series of Scientific Discussions on controversial issues existing within the Society will be held on Wednesday, May 19th, 1943. Notification will be circulated after the Easter holidays, together with an abstract of the spontaneous discussion held on April 7th.

With regard to the expenditure involved in circulating the minutes of Scientific Discussions to Members, it was decided that a final application be made to those Members and Associate Members who have not yet paid the first subscription of £1. Failing a reply from any Member the minutes would no longer be sent to that particular Member. It was agreed, however, that exceptions should be made in cases where payment of a subscription would prove a hardship.

EDWARD GLOVER
Scientific Secretary

Note attached by Committee to Minutes of May 19th, 1943

The attention of the Committee has been called to the following passage on p. 4 of the above minutes: 'Another example of the question-begging attitude is the continued use of the terms "Kleinian" and "Freudian" theory. . . . Dr Glover often uses these labels, *in spite of the fact that he is acting as Chairman in these discussions.*'

With reference to the italicized phrase the Committee wish to remind Members that the technical procedure at meetings in regard to the public expression of personal opinion by the Chairman has been correct. The last paragraph of their original 'Report' runs:

> In conclusion the Committee would like to make it clear that while it will of course willingly continue to act as a whole as organizer of the discussions, its individual members feel at liberty to make their personal contributions to the discussions themselves.

This paragraph, inter alia, was approved by the Society on 21st October, 1942. On each occasion on which the Chairman has made personal contributions to this series of discussions he has vacated his Chair in favour of the Acting-Secretary and has stated explicitly his reason for so doing, viz: that he wished to exercise his right to speak as an *ordinary Member* of the Society.

(signed)　　Marjorie Brierley
Edward Glover
James Strachey

Discussion held on May 19th, 1943
Conclusion of Discussion on Mrs Susan Isaacs' paper 'The Nature and Function of Phantasy'

MRS SUSAN ISAACS (formally replying to previous discussion): Since my last reply to comments upon my paper, there have been 17 contributions by other Members. The task of dealing with these is considerable, and requires a reply of some length.

It is not possible for me to deal with every important point. I must select those which seem to me either the most urgent or the most re-paying.

What I wish to say falls into two categories; the first concerns the mode of approach to these problems; the second, certain factual issues of central significance.

I THE MODE OF APPROACH

(1) A number of speakers have referred to particular phantasies, arguing as if my original paper had been concerned to establish those actual examples of phantasy activity. E.g., Dr Glover speaks of a 'primary enclave' which I have introduced into the Freudian Ucs. Dr Friedlander and Dr Lantos (on March 17th) refer especially to phantasies of aggression. So does Miss Freud (April 7th), expressing

surprise that no one raised this issue more directly. Miss Sharpe (January 27th) spoke in particular of the phantasy of the 'good object'.

My paper, however, was not primarily concerned to establish any particular content of phantasy, either in general or at any given age. It dealt with the nature and function of phantasy as a whole, and its place in the mental life. This is shown quite clearly in the summary of conclusions, at the end of my paper.

At various points I mentioned actual examples of phantasy [e.g. on p. 277] for illustrative purposes. I did not suggest that these examples covered the whole field of phantasy, nor refer them to any particular age.

Now I do of course consider that the very same evidence which establishes the existence of phantasies, even at the earliest ages, gives us some indication of their character. If we could not get any inkling of their nature and content, the evidence for their activity would certainly be negligible. Nevertheless, to accept the general evidence for phantasy activity from the beginning of life, and the place of phantasy in the mental life as a whole, does not automatically imply accepting any particular phantasy content at any given age. Each age and each phantasy ascribed to it must be considered in detail on its own merits, according to the particular evidence.

And this I was not discussing. My paper was explicitly of a preliminary nature, intended to pave the way for a detailed discussion of specific problems, such as introjection and projection, which Dr Heimann will bring before you at the next meeting.

(2) As, however, the question of aggressive versus libidinal phantasies has been raised, I wish to say something about it.

In her contribution on page [424] (April 7th) Miss Freud says: 'The early phantasies most frequently described in Kleinian theory are violently aggressive phantasies. This seems logical to the analysts who are convinced of the preponderance of the death instinct at the beginning of life. The existence of the same phantasies is widely questioned by those to whom the libidinal impulses seem of overwhelming importance for this time of life.'

And Dr Friedlander, 'The analytical theory' (held by her and Miss Freud, etc.) 'assumes that impulses and emotions are still under the predominance of the pleasure–pain principle, not the death instinct, as Mrs Isaacs seems to believe.' [p. 407]

Now Mrs Klein has nowhere stated that the death instinct predominates in early infancy, *as a general condition,* and does not hold that view.

In my former reply to Dr Friedlander and Dr Glover regarding

Mrs Klein's views on the biological development of the libido, I quoted passages from her book which made it abundantly clear that Melanie Klein gives quite as much importance to the libidinal as to the aggressive elements in early instinctual life. E.g.: 'Side by side with the polarity of the life-instinct and the death-instinct, we may place their interaction as a fundamental factor in the dynamic processes of the mind.'

The quantitative aspect of the fusion of life and death instincts is one about which we have little or no knowledge at the present time. Mrs Klein certainly thinks there are moments or periods of defusion during the first year, when the death instinct may be relatively dominant, and that such periods correspond to the occurrence of aggressive phantasies and sensations, varying, of course, in each individual child.

We do not forget that Freud said that the repetition compulsion, expressing the death instinct, 'appears to be of earlier origin than the aim of attaining pleasure and avoiding pain' (Freud, S. 1920; SE 18: 23). Or again, 'The relation of hate to objects is older than that of love. It is derived from the primal repudiation by the narcissistic ego of the external world whence flows the stream of stimuli' (Freud, S. 1915a: 82; SE 14: 135).[1] And in 1915, long before *Beyond the Pleasure Principle*, Freud made clear the sadistic character of early love impulses. In 'Instincts and their Vicissitudes' he wrote: 'First among these (the sexual instincts) we recognize the phase of incorporating or devouring, a type of love which is compatible with abolition of any separate existence on the part of the object.' (Freud, S. 1915a: 80; SE 14: 138)[2]

Dr Glover, in his paper on Drug Addiction (1932), pointed out quite truly that, whilst in the earliest theories regarding aetiology, libidinal factors predominated, yet in later years Freud came increasingly to recognize and emphasize 'the general importance of hate, aggression and destructive impulses in ego-development'. This was also true of Abraham and many other workers.

Melanie Klein, thus, neither discovered the destructive elements although she gives them greater weight, nor neglects the libidinal components in early impulses and phantasies. Her specific contribution has been to trace out in greater detail than had been done before the precise character of the aggressive components, and the intimate way in which these influence the course of libidinal development, the Oedipus complex, and the structure of the ego. She gives more weight to aggressive phantasies than had been done by previous analysts; but that is not the same thing as giving more weight to aggressive than to libidinal phantasies.

(3) Regarding my general thesis, the arguments of several contributors beg the questions at issue.

Some of Miss Freud's supporters express a high degree of negative
preconception about the non-existence or even the impossibility of
evidence concerning the psychic happenings and phantasies of the
first 12 months. I draw attention to this, because Mrs Klein is often
charged by some people with using *her* preconceptions, of a positive
kind; indeed, with having invented or imagined the evidence.
Negative preconceptions are, however, quite as unscientific as
positive ones, and may even be more damaging to scientific work,
since they lead to a dead end; whilst positive ones can much more
easily be tested and corrected by the facts.

Dr Lantos, Dr Friedlander, and Mrs Hoffer will not accept any but
direct evidence – direct meaning either contemporary verbal statement by the child, or definite and conscious memories. Miss Freud
and her pupils have themselves no analytic evidence to offer and
recognize none, because Miss Freud holds the a priori view that transference does not occur in young children, and analysis in the strictly
Freudian sense is therefore not possible with them (Freud, A. 1927).

Mrs Klein, having approached the question with an open mind,
found that transference does occur with young children, and that
strictly Freudian analysis is both possible and practicable. It is from
the repetition and acting out in the transference situation that we are
able to infer both psychic happenings and external events. Her
findings as to early phantasies have been reached on the basis of such
analyses, taken along with the facts of behaviour.

Dr Friedlander [p. 406] refers to the fact that Mrs Klein's views as
to mental life in the first year is 'inferred knowledge' as of course it
is. In this passage, Dr Friedlander, like some other speakers,
questions the validity of inferred conclusions. Actually, the technique of psychoanalysis itself is based almost entirely upon inferred
knowledge. Freud's writings contain more than one well-known
passage where he deals faithfully with those who decry its value, and
points out that the capacity to accept and rely upon inferred
knowledge was one of the major advances made by man in his
intellectual development.

Ucs phantasies are *always* inferred, never observed as such. As Dr
Glover pointed out in the passage I previously quoted from the 1927
Symposium, the patient does never *tell* us his Ucs phantasies – or for
that matter, his preconscious resistances. He says or does things in
such a way as to make it possible and necessary for us to infer that
such and such Ucs phantasies or resistances are operating. And
this is true whatever his age. The language of the first year is a

different, and a somewhat more meagre and cryptic language, that is all.

Dr Friedlander rejects the inferences of Mrs Klein, but asserts that 'current analytical theory' – please note that she does not speak of her own views, or Miss Freud's views, but of 'current analytical theory' – is 'gained in two ways'. 'Firstly, it has been inferred from the analysis of grown-ups and children. . . . Secondly, knowledge has been gained by direct analytical observation, work which has been undertaken and carried out for years now by Anna Freud and Mrs Burlingham' [see pp. 406–7].

Now, Miss Freud and Mrs Burlingham do not analyse the children they observe in their Nurseries. In what sense, then, are their observations 'analytic' as well as 'direct'? Presumably, they make inferences from what they observe. But if this is so, we do not understand why this can be done by Miss Freud and Mrs Burlingham, and not by Mrs Klein and her co-workers, a number of whom have also made systematic observations and published the inferences based upon them. For instance, there is Dr Winnicott's work, based upon 20 or more years of work as a physician observing infants and young children. Some of his conclusions have been published in his book on *Disorders of Childhood*, and his paper 'The Observation of Infants in a Set Situation' (Winnicott 1941). Ten years ago I published my own book *Social Development in Young Children* (Isaacs 1933), containing a large number of first-hand records of the social and emotional responses of young children, mostly from two years of age onwards, but including a number of the first and second years of life. There is also Dr Middlemore's work, from which I quoted in my paper.

(4) Miss Freud says (April 7th, p. [423]), 'An analyst who is not convinced of the existence of a synthetic function in the first year of life will not date back to that period phantasies which include elements of guilt and reparation. An analyst who believes in such synthetic function . . . will not hesitate to ascribe phantasies of this kind to the first year of life.' There are other similar passages concerning the influence of preconceived theories upon people's opinions in these matters. Unfortunately, it is true that in all our minds theories have a way of becoming rigid and blurring our vision of new facts. But we ought not to rest content with such a state of affairs. There is no virtue in it. We should struggle against such tendencies in our scientific thinking. Freud has always emphasized the empirical character of psychoanalysis. E.g. in the Encyclopaedia article, he says, 'Psycho-analysis is not . . . a system starting out from a few sharply defined fundamental concepts . . . and having no room for fresh discoveries or better understanding. On the contrary,

it keeps close to the facts in its field of study, seeks to solve the immediate problems of observation, gropes its way forward by the help of experience, is always incomplete and always ready to correct or modify its theories.' (Freud, S. 1923a; SE 18:253)[3]

Now anyone who traces the course of Melanie Klein's work, from her earliest contributions to the present day, will see that her conclusions were formed step by step, in close accordance with the facts available at the time. She had tentative theories in her mind, based on former work, as Freud did and we all must do; but she held them in suspension. She did not regard them as touchstones of fact, but as explanations of the facts when these were brought together, and modifiable by new facts.

This view of Mrs Klein's general procedure can be verified by anyone who will take the trouble to follow out the development of her work in her published contributions.

I would also suggest that some at least of the so-called 'theories' to which Miss Freud refers are themselves matters of fact, not of theory. Whether or not the synthetic function of the ego develops slowly, and how far it is developed at any given age, whether or not the infant's impulses are predominantly libidinal or aggressive, are matters of fact rather than theory. The facts may be difficult to discover. They may require patient study and constant correction of our observations; but they are there to be won.

(5) Another example of the question-begging attitude is the continued use of the terms 'Kleinian' and 'Freudian' theory, the preconception here being that Kleinian cannot be Freudian and is opposed to it. Dr Glover often uses these labels, in spite of the fact that he is acting as Chairman in these discussions. But that does not justify Miss Freud's doing so. Miss Freud began by saying, 'Psychoanalysis, as I understand it', and passed from that correct scientific attitude to speak of 'Freudians' in contrast with 'Kleinians' [p. 420]. Miss Freud thus not merely seeks to substantiate by reasonable argument, as she has every right to do, that her own views are the correct representation of psychoanalysis; she also wishes to imply, by the use of these labels, which like all labels have an affective character, that the whole matter has already been settled in her favour. It is, however, both safer and fairer, when difficult controversial matters are under discussion, to refer to the work and statements of individuals, rather than to adopt terms which denote groups. I suggest that we should follow this practice. Mrs Klein accepts responsibility for her views; why does not Miss Freud – and Dr Friedlander and Dr Lantos and others – refer to their other views as their own?

With regard to Dr Glover's repeated use of these terms 'Freudian' versus 'Kleinian', there is something more to say.

In his last contribution, Dr Glover acknowledged my right to quote from earlier statements of his, strongly opposed to his present views, and said that he had 'often regretted being prevailed upon to take part in that particular symposium' (1927) [p. 433]. He is, of course, entitled to take back his former position. But this admission that he could be 'prevailed upon' to commit himself to such sweeping and dogmatic views in scientific matters as he then presented does not increase our confidence. One might imagine that such grave errors, once seen and admitted, would lead any scientific worker to be more cautious and tentative in his later pronouncements. But that does not seem to hold in his case.

Moreover, Dr Glover's position remained what it was in 1927 until quite recently, and he has not yet entered upon the necessary and extensive revision of his own writings, so many of which have been greatly influenced or even based upon Melanie Klein's 'inspired stimulus', as he called it in 1932, in the paper I have already quoted from ('A Psycho-Analytical Approach to the Classification of Mental Disorders').

E.g., his paper on Drug Addiction (1932), his review of *Inhibitions, Symptoms and Anxiety*, and his 'Note on Idealization', both as recently as 1938. I hope that you will all turn back to these papers, and re-read Dr Glover's part in the present discussion, in the light of those pronouncements.

In the review of *Inhibitions, Symptoms and Anxiety* in particular, you will note that Dr Glover not only accepts and makes good use of Melanie Klein's views as to the early onset and the character of the primitive superego, but he is very critical of Freud himself in various ways. He rightly draws attention to the changes which had occurred in Freud's views to the time of the publication of '*Hemmung, Symptom und Angst*', saying, e.g., that 'Freud was faced with the task of readjusting and amplifying his earlier and over simple metapsychology' – compare this, by the way, with Dr Glover's present claim that Freud's 'basic concepts' have never been altered or questioned [p. 396]. He then expressed his opinion that further changes are required to fit the newer facts. E.g. he speaks of 'the old-fashioned nature of the clinical material from which Freud's thread of argument is drawn'. He says that 'old views on pre-genital stages, on the etiology of hysteria and obsessional neurosis etc. were taken over (in Hemmung) without any modification'. And he corrects Freud's 'old fashioned classification' of primary phobias, saying that 'Freud . . . jumps from these early stages to the

447

symptomatic phobias of a five-year-old'; but, he says, 'the simplest behaviouristic observation of infants shows that by the time they can talk they exhibit a considerable number of phobias'. And then: 'In short it may be said that Freud's analysis of anxiety situations was handicapped by lack of sufficient clinical observation of children and by bias in favour of those analytical conclusions derived from study of adults.' [Glover, E. 1938: 111]

I agree with some of these criticisms of Dr Glover's, though not with his way of expressing them. But how is it possible for one who, only five years ago, was writing so extensively in this way, now always to refer to Mrs Klein as if she were wholly opposed to Freud, whilst he himself is (by implication) a Freudian and not a Kleinian?

On the other hand, Dr Glover refers to the fact that Mrs Klein's work on restitution tendencies is related to Freud's earlier concept of 'undoing', although he does not show what the true relation is between those concepts.

Why do I draw your attention to these matters? Because the course of the present discussion shows that our deliberations on the objective facts are so often deflected and obscured by 'political' issues, on the one hand, and by faulty methods of discussion, on the other. I am hoping that we can reduce these disturbances in our future discussions.

Dr Glover, in his last comments, called my quoting from his earlier writings, 'debating points'. They are very far from being debating points. I am not concerned to score. I am deliberately protesting against the attempt to force the discussion of scientific differences into personal and 'political' moulds. I have quoted, and shall quote further, from Dr Glover's published writings, whenever I consider them to be just and true. But these quotations do also serve to show how inappropriate it is for Dr Glover in particular to imply a wholesale antithesis between 'Freudian' and 'Kleinian' views.

Finally: it seems that whilst Dr Glover is willing to make a large-scale renunciation of his views of 1927, he is not willing to acknowledge a false or misjudged statement made so recently as January 17th. Neither he nor Dr Friedlander have taken any notice of the evidence given in my reply of February 17th, by way of actual quotations from Mrs Klein's book, showing that their statements that she had abandoned Freud's conception of the biological development of the libido were untrue.

(6) One particular point requires comment: In those discussions Dr Glover has insisted that if my views and those of Mrs Klein are correct, 'the theoretical and clinical importance of the Oedipus complex would disappear . . . her assumption of a primary active

core to the unconscious based on the persisting cathexis of instinct presentations existing in the first two years . . . committed her to a depreciation of the specific significance of the classical Oedipus complex, . . . Freud's view was that whatever the pre-genital phases of infancy contribute, the Oedipus complex is nevertheless of primary significance'. [See pp. 432–3.]

Now it might well be said that Mrs Klein, so far from lessening the importance of the Oedipus complex, extends its sphere since: (a) she sees it in action over a greater period of time and influencing a greater variety of phenomena in development, and in particular (b) she recognizes its presence and its influence in the development of the girl at those ages when Freud believed that the girl child was still simply and exclusively attached to her mother.

Once again an effective answer to Dr Glover's criticisms is provided by his own previous useful statements on the same issue. I draw your attention to the following passages from his paper on Drug Addiction (Glover, E. 1932: 306–7):

> But I cannot find any adequate explanation of drug-addiction which does not assume an active Oedipus situation at a stage when object-relations are little more than the psychic reflection of organ relations; . . A psychic situation contains the essential ingredients of an 'Oedipus complex' provided: (1) a state of instinctual frustration exists, (2) this state of frustration is related by the subject to more than one object (or part object, i.e. organ–object), (3) some degree of genital interest exists (whether directly frustrated or not), and (4) the state of frustration involves an aggressive reaction to one or more objects (or part-objects).

Later on:

> Genital interest exists from the first year of life in both sexes, and is bound to play a part directly or indirectly in all frustrations. In this sense all frustrations have an Oedipus component. If the argument is advanced that in early stages the genital element is quantitatively negligible, there is no objection to the use of some other term, e.g. 'Oedipus prototype' or 'fore-runner', 'pre-Oedipus', etc. There would, however, be a very definite objection if such terms were used to gloss over the dynamic significance of the earlier conflicts. If we can show that earlier conflicts play a part in the etiology of, say, the psychoses, similar to the part played by the model genital Oedipus situation in hysteria, why not reduce complications by calling all infantile conflict over frustration 'Oedipus' conflict?
>
> In supporting these views, which are in most essentials the views of Melanie Klein, I do not intend to suggest that the

importance of later and more organized systems can be glossed over in drug-addiction.

As Dr Glover rightly suggests here, the importance of later phases of development is not lessened, although it may be altered, when earlier phases, and the relation of earlier to later phases, come to be understood. It seems to me quite unsound to assert that the Oedipus complex suffers depreciation because we learn how it develops and what leads up to it.

(7) Another point: Dr Friedlander says: 'now to the non-analytical conception of the mental processes during the first year of life. There are mainly two sciences to which we have to turn for information: brain-anatomy and physiology, and behaviouristic psychology. . . . behaviouristic observations are based upon and in full agreement with the physiological and anatomical development of brain and senses.' [See p. 407.]

Now: (a) There is still a great deal to be learnt about the functions of cortical areas and the cortex as a whole. Brain physiology can lay down broad limits, but cannot settle the details of the infant's potentialities or experiences.

(b) Even the study of the behaviour of the infant and young child (let alone its inner psychic life) is an independent science, with its own highly developed technique, procedures and safeguards. This view is fully accepted amongst those who are doing careful and fruitful investigations with modern methods of research – such as the members of the Society for Research in Child Development in USA, which includes anatomists, physiologists, and psychologists. Reliable and far-reaching studies have been made by those who follow this independent science of child behaviour: such as the work of Shirley on the development of posture, revealing detailed facts which no brain anatomist knew or could have discovered without the special and proper technique of this independent science. So with regard to Charlotte Bühler's work on the first year of life, or on mental tests for infants and young children. So with regard to Gesell's studies of norms of general and specific mental development.

If this be true with regard to the external facts of behaviour and child development, it is even more true with regard to the development of the inner psychic life. Freud himself expressed this forcibly in his *Introductory Lectures* (p. 16). He said: 'it (psychoanalysis) must dissociate itself from every foreign preconception, whether anatomical, chemical or physiological, and must work throughout with conceptions of a purely psychological order.' [Freud, S. 1916–17:16; SE 15–16: 18][4]

450

(c) That there is a continuity in phases of development (as I brought out in my paper) would not surprise the brain anatomists; but what the details of the sequence are and what the child's psychic experience is, these facts have to be discovered by direct study. We can then go on to correlate these facts with the development of the brain structure. Brain physiology, indeed, needs the co-operation of the independent sciences child development and child psychology, if the correlations between the bodily and the mental life are to be established.

(I might perhaps say, in passing, that of all Members of this Society, I am probably the least likely to forget or overlook these considerations, since in my academic work I have for so many years been occupied with precisely these scientific studies of child development and child behaviour.)

(d) I should fully agree, as Mrs Klein would also, that the specific content of early phantasies, no less than the ways in which they are experienced by the child and their modes of expression, are bound to be in accordance with his bodily development and his capacities for feeling and knowing at the given age. They are a part of his development, and are expanded and elaborated along with his bodily and mental powers, influencing and being influenced by his slowly maturing ego.

Dr Friedlander has overlooked – or else really does not understand – that early phantasy is, in our view, intimately bound up with bodily functions and experiences. In my paper, I emphasized strongly that the earliest phantasies were implicit in impulse, affect and sensation. They are simple, but intensely affective; they are feelings and sensations, not ideas. I emphasized, also, the continuous development from those simplest and most implicit phantasies, through 'free' plastic images – visual, auditory, kinaesthetic touch, taste and smell – to verbal representations.

We have to put them into words, in order to discuss even the simplest phantasies; but that does not mean they are *experienced* in that form.

For Dr Friedlander, Mrs Hoffer, and Dr Lantos, a phantasy does seem to be a complicated, organized conscious and intellectual process.

This was clearly shown on page [406] of Dr Friedlander's contribution on March 17th. She said, e.g.: The Ucs phantasy 'to tear her to bits' involves the knowledge that tearing a person to bits means killing; 'to drown and burn her . . . would necessitate experiences . . . of drowning and burning with the consequences it involves' [p. 406]. And so on. But such a view is really absurd. It

451

overlooks the phylogenetic sources of knowledge, the fact that such knowledge is *inherent* in bodily impulses as a vehicle of instinct, in the *aim* of instinct. When Freud says that the aim of oral love is 'incorporating and devouring, with abolition of any separate existence on the part of the object', does he mean that the infant has seen objects eaten up and destroyed, and then comes to the conclusion that he can do this too, and so wants to do it? No! He means that this aim, this relation to the object, is inherent in the character and direction of the impulse itself, and its related affects. [Freud, S. 1915a: 78; SE 14: 138]

From whence does the child draw the material for his 'infantile' sexual theories? From his own bodily impulses and wishes. He has never observed that babies are made from food or faeces! He has never seen father urinating into mother! His conceptions of these matters are derived from his bodily impulses, not the other way about. To 'drown and burn mother' means, in the first instance, to flood her with urine in burning anger; the 'burning' is an expression both of the bodily sensations and of the intensity of his rage. The 'drowning', too, expresses the feeling of intense and omnipotent hate, when the infant floods his mother's lap. The rush of water from the tap, the flooding river or stormy sea when these are seen or known about as external realities, link up in his mind with his early bodily experiences, instinctual aims and phantasies. And when he is given names for those things, he can then sometimes put his phantasies into words.

Dr Brierley has pointed out that the language of affect is older than that of words, in the individual and the race. [Brierley 1937: 256–8] And Freud said of visual images, which represent an intermediate stage between phantasies implicit in sensation and movement, and phantasies expressed in words: 'it (visual memory) approximates more closely to unconscious processes than does thinking in words, and it is unquestionably older than the later, both ontogenetically and phylogenetically'. [Freud, S. 1923b: 23; SE 19: 21][5]

(8) In passing, I might here refer to the point raised by Dr Karin Stephen, who would like us to keep the word 'phantasy' for the simplest kinds only, and find some other word for the more developed and elaborated types. For some purpose it might be useful to do this, but there would be disadvantages. It would blur that essential point of genetic continuity. The simplest sort of pre-verbal phantasy is only the beginning point of a continuous series. As I have tried to make clear, and as Dr Brierley showed, sensations and memory images, and later on perceived objects enter into the

elaboration of phantasies, in a continuously developing series, from the earliest phases onwards.

(9) Various statements have been made (e.g., by Dr Glover, Miss Freud, Dr Friedlander) as to Freud's views on particular matters. In especial, Dr Glover made a long exposition of his interpretation of Freud's metapsychology. These contributors do not quote Freud's own statements, with the dates at which they were made. This re-statement of Freud's views in their own words, however, tends to make things appear much more rigid and one-sided. Compare, for instance, the passages regarding the 'primary process' in Miss Freud's first comments on my paper, [p. 330] with the more openly hypothetical character of Freud's own words, quoted by me in my reply [p. 373] of February 17th: 'So far as we know, a psychic apparatus possessing only the primary process does not exist, and is *to that extent a theoretical fiction.*' (My [Isaacs'] italics.)

Or note, again, the fixed and rigid character of Freud's metapsychology as presented by Dr Glover in his contribution of March 17th. He explicitly claimed it to be unchanged and unchangeable. I shall refer to the content of this later on. Here I suggest that you read again the relevant passages in *The Interpretation of Dreams*, and see how much more cautious, exploratory and tentative is Freud's own temper; and how openly hypothetical his formulations. Read, too, this passage from 'Instincts and their Vicissitudes' to which Dr Adrian Stephen drew our attention:

The view is often defended that sciences should be built up on clear and sharply defined basal concepts. In actual fact no science, not even the most exact, begins with such definitions. The true beginning of scientific activity consists rather in describing phenomena and then in proceeding to group, classify and correlate them. Even at the stage of description it is not possible to avoid applying certain abstract ideas to the material in hand, ideas derived from various sources and certainly not the fruit of the new experience only. Still more indispensable are such ideas – which will later become the basal concepts of the science – as the material is further elaborated. They must at first necessarily possess some measure of uncertainty; there can be no question of any clear delimitation of their content. So long as they remain in this condition, we come to an understanding about their meaning by repeated references to the material of observation, from which we seem to have deduced our abstract ideas, but which is in point of fact subject to them. Thus, strictly speaking, they are in the nature of conventions; although everything depends on their being chosen in no arbitrary manner, but determined by the important relations they have to the empirical material – relations we seem to divine before we can clearly recognize and demonstrate them. It is only after more searching investigations of the field in question that we are able to formulate with increased clarity the scientific concepts underlying it. . . . The progress of science, however, demands a certain elasticity even in these definitions. The science of physics furnishes an excellent illustration of the way in which even those 'basal concepts' that are firmly established in the form of definitions are constantly being altered in their content.

[Freud, S. 1915a: 60–1; SE 15: 117][6]

In actual fact, Freud greatly expanded and revised his metapsychology in successive contributions – although he did not always re-write every part of his earlier work in the new light of his later discoveries and later developments of theory. In Dr Glover's account of Freud's views he refers only to *The Interpretation of Dreams* (1900) and 'Instincts and Their Vicissitudes' (1915). But many other parts of Freud's works have to be considered if we wish to gain an adequate idea of his whole metapsychology. For instance, among others, 'On Narcissism' (1914), 'Mourning and Melancholia' (1917), *Beyond the Pleasure Principle* (1920), 'Group Psychology' (1921), *The Ego and the Id* (1923), 'Negation' (1925), and *Hemmung, Symptom und Angst* [*Inhibitions, Symptoms and Anxiety*] (1926).

As I pointed out in my first paper, Melanie Klein's work is more closely related to these later developments of Freud's views than to his earliest formulations. She was more able to accept his later work and to make full use of it than many other analysts have shown themselves to be – for instance, the Vienna group.

Listening to the selective accounts of Freud 's theories offered by some of the contributors to this discussion, and noting their dogmatic temper, I cannot help wondering what would have happened to the development of psychoanalytic thought if for any reason Freud's work had not been continued after 1913, before his work on Narcissism and Mourning and Melancholia; or after 1919, before *Beyond the Pleasure Principle* and *The Ego and the Id*. Suppose some other adventurous thinker had arrived at these profound truths and had dared to assert them! I fear that such a one would have been treated as a backslider from the strict path of psychoanalytic doctrine, a heretic whose views were incompatible with those of Freud, and subversive of psychoanalysis.

I come now to the last point in the first part of my reply; one which I consider very important.

In my extempore remarks on April 7th, I drew attention to the sentence in Miss Freud's communication of that day, in which she said: 'Mrs Isaacs is even under the misapprehension that some of us postpone the date for phantasy activity until the age of 4. Dr Lantos has refuted this accusation as a misunderstanding, the origin of which it is difficult to conceive.'

Now in fact, as readers can ascertain, I had always quoted the age given by Robert Wälder, and by Dr Friedlander who quoted Jenny Wälder, viz: the third and fourth year, i.e. two and three years of age. And apart from this error about my own remarks, I must say that it is on the contrary difficult to conceive how anyone could be expected to know that any member of the Vienna Society has yet entertained the existence of phantasies before the third year – until these discussions. Wälder said, e.g., 'But I see no grounds which compel us to conclude that the phantasies themselves belong to those early periods' (i.e. before the third year, p. 429).

Since Wälder's paper, nothing has, to my knowledge, been published by the Viennese Members on this topic. The private discussions held by Dr Jones, Mrs Riviere and other Members on their visit to Vienna in 1936, and during Wälder's visit here in 1937, left no doubt in our minds both that Wälder's paper was fully representative of the views of the Vienna group, and that Mrs Klein's conclusions about the existence of phantasies before the third year found no acceptance whatever by any Vienna Members.

Wälder in his (1937) paper explicitly rejects the possibility of phantasy formation antedating verbalization. (Incidentally, hysterical symptoms have no bearing on the *dating* of phantasy. Hysterical cases investigated have always been of an age subsequent to verbalization. Dr Payne's remarks on this point support the possibility of non-verbal phantasy, but they do nothing to prove to us that the Vienna Members would accept *pre*-verbal phantasy, as Miss Freud claimed in her observation on [p. 424] April 7th.)

I have therefore been entirely justified in assuming that the views of the Vienna Members were still as stated by Wälder in 1937.

Besides Miss Freud's remarks on this point, Dr Lantos (March 17th) now expresses surprise that I attribute to her the belief that phantasies only come into operation and are only traceable in the third and fourth years, and says she never stated this and does not believe it to be true. She states: 'there have never been any controversies about the existence of phantasies from an early phase of life . . . "early phase" means the age of about one year, but in no case the third or fourth year.' [p. 411] I beg to point out here that these statements are completely at variance with the facts. Wälder's paper alone is a complete refutation of the statement that there has never been any controversy about the existence of phantasies at about one year, whilst no other publication has expressed any modification of his view. If, however, readers will compare the various statements made by Miss Freud, Dr Friedlander and Dr Lantos with the definite views of Robert Wälder in his paper of 1937, there stated to be largely representative of the Vienna group, they will see that there is now a strong tendency to place phantasies much earlier than was previously done. And in her extempore remarks on April 7th, Miss Freud [p. 420] agreed with the possibility of phantasy in the second half of the first year. There is thus a definite change of position, an approximation to the views of Melanie Klein which is to be welcomed. But this should, of course, be stated as such.

In my first paper, I also asked you to note how Miss Freud and Mrs Burlingham were now willing to recognize the existence of 'deep and serious grief' in the second year of life. Let us note just now that such emotions in children during the second year had not been observed or recorded or studied in psychoanalytic literature before the work of Melanie Klein on depression. Moreover, in her last contribution [p. 424], Miss Freud refers to 'early phantasies of guilt and *reparation*', (My italics) and says there is 'little disagreement about the existence of such phantasies. Disagreement is confined to the date of origin.'

Now this is the first time I have heard Miss Freud acknowledge the existence of phantasies of reparation. There is no reference to this in her book, *The Ego and the Mechanisms of Defence* (Freud, A. 1936: 132). Even in her chapter on 'A Form of Altruism', where I myself should have thought that reparation phantasies would play some part in the cases and situations described, there is no mention of reparation.

In her report of Nursery Children (Freud, A. 1942) on May 5th, however, Miss Freud did give us vivid illustrations of reparation wishes. Here again, we have a definite change of position, in the direction of Melanie Klein's work.

Mrs Klein has been an exponent of this concept for many years. As Dr Glover pointed out, the concept of reparation is derived from Freud's concepts of reaction-formation and obsessional undoing. But it neatly expands and clarifies these earlier notions, and shows more clearly the relation of these mechanisms to aggressive and libidinal tendencies. Mrs Klein's view of reparation wishes is bound up with the greater weight placed upon early aggressive phantasies, their complex interweaving with early libidinal wishes, and the anxiety and guilt resulting from their inter-play. Reparation involves more –

love for the object, and the fear of injuring or losing it – than do the earlier notions of reaction-formation and undoing.

Mrs Klein first elaborated this theme in her paper 'Infantile Anxiety-Situations Reflected in a Work of Art and in the Creative Impulse' (Klein 1929). A number of English analysts have made use of these views, in particular Miss Sharpe. Her Oxford Congress paper, for example, 'On Certain Aspects of Sublimation and Delusion', (Sharpe 1930) was one of the first to take up these contributions and use them illuminatingly.

But the concept of reparation, as Mrs Klein expounded it, had not been accepted by the Vienna Members, and not (so far as I know) by Freud himself. It has not been mentioned in their publications. And yet here it is, in Miss Freud's paper of April 7th referred to as indisputable. That it should be accepted as an integral part of 'current psychoanalytical theory' is to be welcomed; but an explicit acknowledgement is called for.

Furthermore, in her paper on April 7th, Miss Freud spoke of feelings of guilt in *children of the third year*, i.e., of two years of age. (My italics.) [See p. 423.]

Now on the classic view, guilt is the hallmark of the superego, which in its turn was postulated to be the outcome of the *passing away* of the Oedipus complex. Are we now to hold that the Oedipus complex passes away, or begins to pass away, in the third year? Or can we take it that Miss Freud has come to recognize that all these developmental processes are much more complex and fluid, and cover a much longer period of time, than was previously realized – and as Mrs Klein's work has demonstrated? It is now allowed that feelings of guilt and hence the early superego are experienced even while the (classic) Oedipus complex is maturing, and long before it begins to pass away? As it stands, Miss Freud's statement is a modification of Freud's own views, far in the direction of Melanie Klein's.

Miss Freud suggested that I might say that Mrs Klein's work has 'filled a dark and otherwise empty period with the psychic content which rightfully belongs to it'. I do, indeed, say that Mrs Klein's observations and conclusions have filled this 'dark and empty period'. And that it was such, before her work, should be acknowledged.

Now, make no mistake! this question has nothing to do with priority as such. It does not matter who discovers which truth, provided that all truths are shared and acknowledged, that no group of workers claims to have dogmatic and private possession of the innermost secrets of truth, and that all this nonsense about

'Kleinians' and 'Freudians' is given up. The scientific freedom to oppose and dispute the details of new discoveries or new theories carries with it the obligation to admit mistakes and to acknowledge any change of views. It is not allowable to accept other people's contributions tacitly whilst openly asserting that their views are radically wrong or 'unorthodox'.

II CONCERNING THE FACTUAL ISSUES

I come now to some of the factual issues:
(1) I shall first take the points raised by Miss Low and Miss Sharpe, these being related.
(a) I do not know in what passages of my paper Miss Low thinks I make a distinction between phantasy and inner psychical reality. To be precise, I would say that 'inner psychical reality' includes affects as well as phantasies, but is otherwise indistinguishable.

I have not declared myself in support of Dr Fairbairn's notion that that the concept of phantasy has been rendered obsolete by the concepts of psychical reality and internal objects. I would not subscribe to such a view. Neither the concept of psychical reality nor that of internal objects is a new one. Both are Freud's discoveries. Dr Fairbairn, to my mind, overemphasizes and distorts certain parts of Mrs Klein's theories to the point of caricature. He over-substantifies internal objects and makes them far too independent, leaving wishes and feelings and the id generally out of account, on deliberate theory. Dr Fairbairn's position is not to be taken as representing Mrs Klein's work or conclusions.
(b) Miss Low's second question, whether inner psychical reality is affected by external situations, is related to Miss Sharpe's first query regarding quantitative factors.

Mrs Klein and all her collaborators certainly agree that quantitative factors are very important. There is plenty of evidence of this in our published work, note, for instance, Mrs Klein's discussion of the differences between the 'Wolf man' case and 'Little Hans' in her book. Or her contribution to the Symposium on Etiological Factors in 1933;[7] the descriptions of her cases in her book and various papers. She has always emphasized the interaction of constitutional and external factors.

Is not this question of quantitative factors exactly the same in respect to the earliest phantasies as in respect to the Oedipus complex? We know that every child passes through the Oedipus complex. We find it determining the character and history and

458

neurosis of every adult patient. But the outcome of it, the post-Oedipal history, the actual character or actual symptoms, vary over the whole range of human possibilities. Exactly the same applies to the 'depressive position' and early psychotic phantasies, which influence the course the Oedipus situation will later take. On Mrs Klein's view, every infant and young child experiences this phase of development; the outcome of it, both in immediate and in later history, varies greatly – according to those quantitative factors to which Miss Sharpe refers.

These quantitative factors may be due to inherent differences in instinctual endowment (such as greater or lesser degree of aggressiveness, greater or lesser degree of capacity to tolerate frustration, and so on). Or to early environmental influences. These are referred to in the above-mentioned contributions of Mrs Klein. Of my own publications, I shall refer to my paper on Temper Tantrums [Isaacs 1940] in which I point out the influence of actual events in the patient's life on his symptoms, particularly his anxieties about incorporated objects. Moreover, in 1938, I read a paper to this Society, 'An Acute Psychotic Anxiety in a Four-Year-Old Boy', the *main thesis* of which was a detailed study of the effect of the general environmental setting and particular external events upon the inner psychical reality of the patient, his phantasies and anxieties and the changes in his defences concurrent with those events.

The answer to Miss Sharpe's third query, whether Mrs Klein and her collaborators interpret to the patient as if we ourselves believed he had actually incorporated concrete bodily objects, is that we do not. Like Miss Sharpe, we believe that the patient believes he has concrete objects and part-objects inside him. And we accept the full weight of his belief, without evasion, we do not, however, ourselves believe that he has, nor give the patient reason to suppose that we believe it.

I shall leave my discussion of Miss Sharpe's second question, concerning the degree and sort of distinction between the earlier and the later phases of the Oedipus complex, for my paper on Regression.

(2) Miss Freud and Dr Lantos have raised the topic of object relationships. This belongs more fully to Dr Heimann's subject of Introjection and Projection, but I wish to say something in answer to the questions put to me.

(a) I find many elements of truth in what Miss Freud says, but also much contradictory thinking, with a failure to follow through to their full consequences many of the facts which she discerns. Some of her comments suggest that the difference between us is one of degree, precise dating, etc. But then again, she has recourse to sharp antithesis, preferring to emphasize contrasts rather than to seek approximations.

(b) I cannot accept this sharp antithesis in the formulation she offers me on page [418]. These two views are not so contrasted, if they are looked at more closely and the precise meaning of their terms examined. Mrs Klein does *not* hold that there is 'a wide range of differentiated object relations' in the first months, *if* (1) by 'first months' is meant actually from birth onwards; and (2) by 'differentiated' is meant intellectually differentiated – involving developed perceptions.

Miss Freud's more moderate statement on page [418] that 'for Mrs Klein object relationship begins with, or soon after, birth' is correct. But then *this* statement is *not* in contradiction of Freud's own view that there are 'only the crudest rudiments of object relations, and life is governed by the desire for instinct gratification, in which perception of the object is achieved only slowly'.

(c) Miss Freud speaks of object relationship 'in the proper sense'. I do not think there is a 'proper' sense. There are many varieties of object relationship, over the whole range of life, many degrees of definition and differentiation, from the most rudimentary to the most highly developed. But none of these is a 'proper' sense.

We should fully agree that the earliest object relationships are very rudimentary and primitive, and that they become differentiated and articulated only gradually. But a primitive object relationship is still an object relationship, in just the same way as the child is still human, although he is an undeveloped man. The only logical meaning of the statement that 'an object relationship is built up slowly during a period of several months' [see p. 419] is that there *is* an object relationship there from the beginning of this period, but that it is 'crude' or primitive, and changes in its character as the building-up proceeds. Which *is* what we hold.

The problem then is, what are the precise characters of the earlier and later phases?

(d) In answer to Dr Lantos' question, I do not believe that 'in the first few months auto-erotic pleasure, which means pleasure without phantasy, is the only stimulus to the infant'. [See p. 413.]

The full grounds for my view again belong to the topic of introjection and projection, since auto-erotism cannot be understood without reference to internal objects, with which I cannot now deal.

It does not seem reasonable to me to emphasize auto-erotism so strongly whilst at the same time drawing attention, as Dr Lantos does, to the development of perception and intelligence. Perceptions cannot be developed apart from object relationships, and libidinal and intellectual development are intimately related.

(e) But as to this notion of a period of auto-erotism, devoid of object relationship, 'of several months' duration' after birth, let us see what Freud has to say. In many places he has made it clear that the new-born infant has an object relationship to the breast, of a rudimentary kind. For example: (*Three Contributions to the Theory of Sex*, pp. 43–4)

> the action of the thumb-sucking child is determined by the fact that it seeks a pleasure which has already been experienced and is now remembered. . . . It is also easy to conjecture on what occasions the child first experienced this pleasure which it now strives to renew. The first and most important activity in the child's life, the sucking from the mother's breast or its substitute must have acquainted it with this pleasure. . . . To be sure, the gratification of the erogeneous zone was at first united with the gratification of taking nourishment. He who sees a satiated child sink back from the mother's breast, and fall asleep with reddened checks and blissful smile, will have to admit that this picture remains as typical of the expression of sexual gratification in later life. But the desire from the repetition of the sexual gratification is separated from the desire for taking nourishment. . . . The child does not make use of a strange object for sucking but prefers its own thumb ·because it is more convenient, because it thus makes itself independent of the outer world which it cannot yet control.
>
> [Freud, S. 1905: 43–4; SE 7: 181–4][8]

Again in his Encyclopaedia article Freud writes: 'In the first instance the oral component instinct finds satisfaction anaclitically – on the basis of the satisfaction of the desire for nourishment; and its object is the mother's breast. It then detaches itself, becomes independent and at the same time auto-erotic, that is, it finds an object in the child's own body.' [Freud, S. 1923a: 42, 101; SE 18: 245][9]

There are other passages in Freud where he speaks of a 'primary narcissism', and where, if we did not take them in conjunction with the unequivocal passages just quoted, we might easily be led to believe that Freud takes the position outlined by Miss Freud that there is a period of unbroken auto-erotism from birth onwards.

But it should be noted (just as I pointed out regarding the primary process) that Freud himself nowhere insisted a time period to the duration of unadulterated 'primary narcissism'. He does not say that

461

it persists unchanged or practically unchanged for several months from birth onwards. For him it is, like the 'primary process', a limiting concept. Some degree of unchanged narcissism there remains throughout life in all of us – variable according to age, to state of health, degree, or satisfaction or frustration, etc., etc. But there is no evidence that it occupies the *whole field* of mental life in the infant beyond the first few hours, or that Freud held that it did. As soon as there is a response to the smell and contact with the breast, as soon as sucking is established, there is some degree – it may be very slight, but it is actual – of object relationship.

I agree with Dr Adrian Stephen's excellent remarks on this subject. What the infant wants (after the first two or three days, at least) is the thirst-and-libido-satisfying-something, which later on becomes re-cognized as the nipple. His feelings of satisfaction (the pleasures of sucking, the warmth inside, the stilling of hunger-pangs, the general feeling of well-being) are bound up with the touch–smell–movement nucleus of sensation and impulse which means the experience of 'the nipple'. What 'the nipple is in sensation and perception must change and extend and become more elaborated day by day'.

(f) Miss Freud vividly and rightly emphasizes the infant's ardent desires for bodily satisfaction. The importance of bodily satisfac-tions, and the intensity and depth of feeling which the infant experiences towards his early objects, can hardly be overstressed. The passionate emotions and intense desires felt towards his primitive objects is just what gives these early object relationships of the infant their great significance. As Freud said and Dr Jones emphasized, the earliest impulses have an intensity greater than anything that comes later and incommensurable with any other. In this sense, early object relationships are 'rich', full of meaning, and influencing the course of later development.

Another important difference between earlier and later phases of object relationship concerns the *kind of object* perceived. This is not at first 'something-which-looks-so-and-so'; or is called so-and-so; but 'something-which-feels-and-smells-and-tastes-so-and-so'.

I cannot agree that the infant's relation to the breast or to his mother is 'indirect', as Miss Freud puts it. It is direct enough, but in terms different from those of later perception. The breast is at first experienced not through seeing but through touch (of the lips) and smell and taste, visceral and kinaesthetic experiences. Only later do visual elements begin to come in. (Experiments reported by Dr L. Frankl showed that the first element of visual recognition is a *pointed shape*.) All these elements of perceptual experience, extend and become elaborated and integrated with wide variety of new stimuli as the days and months go on. E.g. the mother face is smiled at and attentively regarded at one month.

The first object is not the mother, but the nipple-breast. Presently the infant perceives and desires her face, her hands and arms. Gradually, these discrete perceptions are unified into an awareness and feeling for the mother as a whole – by 4–5 months, as I showed in my paper.

The fact that the infant's early libidinal and perceptual relationships are with part-objects – nipple, breast, face, hands etc., together with the intensity and depth of his feelings, means that his world is a very different world from our own – or from what it becomes in the second half of the year, when he responds to his mother as a whole person. But it is none the less a world of object relationships – *alongside auto-erotic satisfactions.*

(g) Now Miss Freud, Dr Friedlander and Dr Lantos may reply to me, 'But you have been talking about the perception of the external world, which is quite a different thing from object relationship!' Miss Freud agrees that 'a synthesis of perception and reality-testing is achieved in degrees from birth onwards', but holds that 'this synthetic function is not exercised on *instinctual urges* during the first year and, in fact, not until considerably later'. (My italics.) [See p. 422.]

This position seems to me quite untenable. Freud himself has repeatedly shown that in his view *the ego is a differentiated part of the id*. He did not put it in those words when he first formulated his views about memory-traces in *The Interpretation of Dreams*, but he has done so since in several of his writings. Note, for instance, the following: 'one must not take the difference between ego and id in too hard-and-fast a sense, nor forget that the ego is a part of the id which has been specially modified.' [Freud, S. 1923b: 51-2; SE 19: 38][10]

> Originally, of course, everything was id; the ego was developed out of the id by the continual influence of the external world. In the course of this slow development certain material in the id was transformed into the preconscious state and was thus taken into the ego.
>
> [Freud, S. 1940: 43; SE 23: 163][11]

The ego is thus not to be thought of as a mere system of marks; a wraith or a shadow of experience. It is a living part of the id which has become modified by experience of the external world, in its search for satisfactions from objects in the external world.

And what are those seekings, those satisfactions? They are (at first) oral seekings, oral pleasures. All learning is oral learning, at first. All through the middle part of his first year, the infant's hand reaches out to everything he sees in order to put it into his mouth, to feel and explore it. Later on his hand becomes independent of his mouth. But hand and eyes retain an oral significance throughout life, in conscious metaphor and Ucs phantasy.

This means that the objects which the child touches and manipulates and looks at and explores are invested with oral libido. He could not be interested in them if this were not so. If he were entirely auto-erotic, he could not learn. The instinctual drive towards taking things into his mind through eyes and ears and fingers, towards looking and touching and exploring and experimenting, satisfies some of his frustrated oral wishes. Perception and intelligence draw upon this source of libido, for their life and growth.

But, in its turn, this means that *pari passu* there *is* some measure of synthetic function exercised upon instinctual urges. The child could not learn, could not adapt to the external world (physical or human) without some sort and degree of control and inhibition, as well as satisfaction, of instinctual urges.

Many of these points were made by Dr Brierley, in her valuable and illuminating contribution on March 17th. She brought out very clearly the fact that perception and knowledge involve the modification of instinct, and that the child's conscious awareness of his mother at, say, two years of age 'will be the apex of a complicated unconscious mother system, going back to the earliest reactions, both actual and phantasied, and containing all the reaction patterns so far established' [see p. 403].

(h) On page [422] of her last contribution, Miss Freud states that from the first year onward we can see 'the first step in correlation', that between inner urges and memory of outside prohibition. The synthesis between two controlling inner urges such as love and hate, she thinks, is frequently observed in the second year, although not a regular occurrence by then. 'If children in the second year are not checked by fear of outside prohibition, their contrasting wishes and emotions can still flow freely.' The third and final step of correlation between an inner urge and an inner prohibition, the affect belonging to which is guilt, Miss Freud (now) puts in the third year.

But there are many recorded observations of conflict of feelings, of anxiety and guilt at earlier ages than these. Neurotic symptoms (feeding difficulties, tantrums, head knocking, and body rollings, sleep disturbances, phobias and night-terrors, etc. etc.) frequently occur during the second year, and often earlier still. (See e.g. my own book *Social Development in Young Children* [Isaacs 1933].)

Indeed, many of the observations of the social behaviour of children reported to us by Miss Freud herself on May 5th last, support the view that the synthesis of the instinctual life of the child begins and even reaches a complex level, much earlier than Miss Freud has allowed in her theoretical statements.

She described, for instance, the behaviour of the twins who were taken away from their mother at ten months of age and proved completely irreconcilable when they returned to her at two and a half years. Miss Freud said she had no doubt, from the behaviour of the children, that this was not a case of their having forgotten their mother, but of their 'being cross with her'. The details of their rejection of her were dramatic and most interesting. At ten months of age, then, these twins had so intense and so well-organized an object relationship to their mother that they could maintain a bitter resentment and unforgivingness to her when they returned at two and a half years, making their return a complete failure.

Again, Miss Freud, referring to the 'educative influence' which the children exert upon each other, described how a number of children even in their second year became 'strict and cruel' to each other, especially when they engaged in 'habit-training' each other [Freud, A. and Burlingham 1942]. Very often they also soothed and helped each other, in the manner of the nurses to whom they were accustomed. The 'strict and cruel' habit-training was not something the children had experienced from their nurses; it came spontaneously to them. Now to my mind it is impossible to resist the conclusion that this strict and cruel behaviour when 'training' each other is an expression of the early and severe superego. Such behaviour is completely in line with Melanie Klein's analytic studies and observations (and my own observations of young children), as well as with her conclusions as to the early development of the superego – closely connected in this example with anal-sadistic impulses and phantasies.

(3) I have now to deal with Dr Glover's serious misrepresentation of Freud in his statements (of March 17th and April 7th). Dr Glover asserts that reality-testing and reality-adaptation are quite independent of phantasy and prior to the latter in time of development. He said, e.g., 'Reality thinking is primary . . . is the primary product of psychic adaptation', and so on, at great length (April 7th). But this is quite contrary to Freud's own views. There are many passages which show that Freud regarded the reality-principle as a secondary one, coming into operation because the infant finds phantasy unsatisfying, e.g. in 'Formulations Regarding the Two Principles in Mental

Functioning' [Freud, S. 1911a: 14–16; SE 12: 219–221][12] Freud says:

> This attempt to find satisfaction by means of hallucination was abandoned only in consequence of absence of the expected gratification, because of the disappointment experienced. *Instead,* the mental apparatus had to decide to form a conception of the real circumstances in the outer world and to exert itself to alter them. A new principle of mental functioning was thus introduced. This institution of the reality-principle proved a momentous step.

Freud then speaks of the way '*the new demands*', as he calls them, affected mental development, and refers to the '*suppression*' of the pleasure-principle by the reality-principle, which is not accomplished all at once. (My italics)

Could anything be clearer? I shall quote other passages on the same theme in a moment.

(4) This brings me to an important point of Dr Brierley's. She would, I think, agree that both phantasy and reality-testing are present from the earliest days. She points out that 'phantasy thinking . . . and reality thinking constantly blend and interweave in the patterns of current mental activity' in adults, too. But she emphasizes that they are quite distinct modes of wish-fulfilment, and rejects my extension of the term 'phantasy' to include the subjective interpretation of experience and the primary content of Ucs mental processes, because she feels this blurs the distinction between phantasy and reality-thinking.

Now I fully agree that phantasy-thinking and reality thinking are distinct mental processes, different modes of wish-fulfilment. But to recognize their distinct character does not necessarily imply that they are entirely independent of each other in origin and operation. And here, I do not mean merely that they blend and interweave; I mean something less adventitious. *What I believe is that reality-thinking cannot operate without concurrent and supporting Ucs phantasies.*

I have already reminded you that all early learning is based upon the oral impulses, and have referred to the way in which the seeing and mouthing and grasping of the breast is gradually shifted on to other objects, and hand and eye only slowly attaining independence of the mouth, as instruments of exploration and knowing.

Here I must touch upon the subject of introjection and projection. Dr Heimann has reminded me of passages in Freud's essay on 'Negation', which perfectly express what I am now trying to say.

> The function of judgment is concerned ultimately with two sorts of decision. It may assert or deny that a thing has a particular

property; or it may affirm or dispute that a particular image exists in reality. Originally the property to be decided about might be either good or bad, useful or harmful. Expressed in the language of the oral, instinctual impulses, the alternative runs thus: 'I should like to eat that, or I should like to spit it out'; or, carried a stage further: 'I should like to take this into me and keep that out of me.' That is to say: it is to be either *inside* me or *outside* me. . . .

The other sort of decisions made by the function of judgment, namely as to the real existence of something imagined, is a concern of the final reality-ego, which develops out of the previous pleasure-ego (a concern, that is, of the faculty that tests the reality of thinking). It is now no longer a question of whether something perceived (a thing) shall be taken into the ego or not, but of whether something which is present in the ego as an image can also be re-discovered in perception (that is, in reality). Once more, it will be seen, the question is one of *external* and *internal*; what is not real, what is merely imagined or subjective, is only *internal*; while on the other hand what is real is also present *externally*. When this stage is reached, the pleasure-principle is no longer taken into account. . . .

Thought is to be regarded as an experimental action, a·kind of groping forward, involving only a small expenditure of energy in the way of discharge. Let us consider where the ego can have made a previous use of this kind of groping forward, where it can have learnt the technique which it now employs in thought-processes. It was at the sensory end of the mental apparatus, in connection with sensory perceptions. For upon our hypothesis perception is not a merely passive process; we believe rather that the ego periodically sends out small amounts of cathectic energy into the perceptual system and by their means samples the external stimuli, and after every such groping advance draws back again.

The study of judgment affords us, perhaps for the first time, an insight into the derivation of an intellectual function from the inter-play of the primary instinctual impulses. Judging has been systematically developed out of what was in the first instance introduction into the ego or expulsion from the ego carried out according to the pleasure-principle.

[Freud, S. 1925: 368–70; SE 19: 236–8][13]

Thus, on Freud's own view, the mechanism of introjection, which in its turn arises out of and rests upon the Ucs phantasy of incorporation, underlies not only the retention of memory-traces, but also the function of reality-testing and judgement.

You may note how far, in this 1925 essay on 'Negation', Freud had travelled from the metapsychology of *The Interpretation of Dreams* – how much more deeply and intimately his clinical knowledge had entered in and given life to his theoretical formulations by this date.

On Freud's own teaching, therefore, if we are to understand either phantasy or reality-testing and 'intelligence', we must look at mental life as a whole and see the relation between these various functions during the whole process of development. To set them apart and say 'that is phantasy but this is perception and intelligence' is to miss the developmental significance of both.

(5) Finally; this principle of looking at the mental life as a whole bears closely upon the question of evidence, which Dr Friedlander raised in her question to me. Merely cataloguing the facts of behaviour (whether of the child's play or the adult's speech) cannot convince anyone who is not willing to look at the inter-relationships of the facts, in the light of our knowledge of Ucs mental processes.

I cannot now re-state, nor even amplify, the evidence already adduced, although it needs, of course, to be greatly filled out in detail.

I want to suggest to Dr Friedlander that she considers the evidence I offered in the light of the various considerations I have here brought forward, which I shall now sum up very briefly:

I have pointed out:

(1) That Miss Freud, Dr Friedlander and others approach these questions with preconceptions of a negative sort.

(2) That in especial they greatly undervalue pre-verbal forms of phantasy, and fail to appreciate the way in which this develops continuously into verbal forms.

(3) That the particular formulations of Freud's views which they offer are far from being representative of his conclusions; in particular, they appear to ignore the views he expressed in 1925 about the phantasies underlying the functions of reality-testing.

(4) That all knowledge of Ucs processes is inferred knowledge, not only that regarding the infant.

(5) That Miss Freud, Dr Friedlander and others are greatly handicapped in their appreciation of Ucs processes in very young children by Miss Freud's preconceived view that the transference neurosis does not occur in children, which precludes her from access to the facts. It is by means of repetition and acting out in the transference situation that we

gain our most intimate knowledge of the phantasy life of the young child, as well as of his early history. We are able to infer back to what the child felt and imagined, no less than what he experienced, in his early months and years, when we take his responses in the transference situation along with the content of the known facts (a) about this particular child and (b) about the development of infants and children in general.

(6) That nevertheless the gradual changes in recent years in the views of many analysts, including Miss Freud and her group, are a result and a vindication of Melanie Klein's work, and should now lead these analysts to be more openly receptive to her methods and conclusions. Examples of such changes are: the full acceptance; of oral- and anal-sadistic phantasies about the mother's body, at 2–3 years; the presence of 'deep' and 'serious grief' in the two-year-old; the earlier age of onset of the Oedipus complex; signs of guilt and reparation wishes at two years (or earlier); phantasy activity in general in the second half of the first year. (I may remind you that one important contribution which Melanie Klein made to the understanding of the superego has been acknowledged by Freud, viz: the fact that the severity of the superego is due not only to the actual treatment he receives from his parents, but also to his own aggression.) [Freud, S. 1930: 53; SE 21: 78]

(7) That many of the facts of social behaviour in the second year of life reported to us by Miss Freud on May 5th bear out Mrs Klein's conclusions regarding, e.g., early object relations and the early superego.

Mrs Klein has been accepted about so many things; she may turn out to be right about her most recent contributions!

DR M. BRIERLEY (Contribution, read in Dr Brierley's absence by the Chairman): Miss Freud made it very clear that our views on the genesis and development of object relations are crucial in these discussions but I cannot, here and now, condense all that I should like to say on this subject. I can only itemize certain lines of approach, which I hope to expand later in a paper, which still seem to me to offer some prospect of constructive accommodation. I may make what appear to be positive statements in order to save time but they are to be understood as tentative rather than dogmatic.

We seem to agree that the unit of psychic life is the reaction and that the initial reactions of infants are undifferentiated. The infant responds to the total situation resulting from the internal and external stimuli operating at any given moment. We, as adults, can say that the sensory component in the unit reaction is the basis or forerunner of later object-development, an object-rudiment, and we can distinguish internal and external sources of stimulation. Not so the baby. For the baby there are just happenings. The baby, however, can and does discriminate between pleasurable and painful situations. The distinction between pleasurable and painful reaction is definite, and the motor responses are obviously divergent. In other words, infantile relationships to situations are of two types: definitely affirmative or appetitive, or unambiguously negative. Possibly, in terms of instinct, we should say that the baby's first libidinal relationship to situations is primary identification, and its first aggressive relationship primary repudiation. 'Yes, yes' situations are the matrix of the pleasure 'me' of ego-synthesis and love objects; 'no, no' situations the matrix of ego differentiation and of hate-objects.

Leaving out the time factor, the transition from the earliest unorganized and sporadic reactions to organized ego-object reaction-systems will lie through various stages of partial organization. All the evidence appears to suggest that the first partial organizations occur along lines of similarity and that they are relatively autonomous. They take the field in succession, i.e., they alternate. If this be so, one would expect two consequences: (a), one would expect early behaviour to show the very features reported by Anna Freud, and (b), one would expect early object discrimination to be highly selective and to yield sharply divided types of mental object corresponding to the sharp division between pleasure and pain. In fact, one would expect something like Mrs Klein's good and bad imagos. One would also expect ego-integration, true object relationship, and true ambi- or multi-valence as distinct from alternation, to emerge together as the result of processes similar to those described by Freud in more purely ideational terms in 'Negation'.

The problem of precocity can only be settled satisfactorily when we can estimate the normal rate of progress in organization. There would appear to be scope for great individual variation in this rate. In trying to arrive at some average norm we should take into account relevant physiological data, as Dr Friedlander suggested, but the problem of precocity has other aspects. I can only agree with Miss Freud that Kleinian descriptions of early phantasy often sound precocious. The point which has to be settled is how far this precocity is apparent and how far it is real. Mrs Isaacs will already have clarified this and we shall be on still firmer ground when we have heard Dr Heimann and Mrs Klein herself. A difficulty arises in the fact that we have to describe pre-verbal experience in words in order to discuss it, but we know perfectly well that the use of words and the construction of sentences imports a kind of degree and organization into our description that is not native to the primitive experience itself. I think, personally, that some of the precocity attributed to Mrs Klein's infant is due to this simple fact, that an adult cannot make any content of infantile experience intelligible to other adults without subjecting the experience itself to some degree of falsification or retrospective sophistication. Where I think Mrs Klein may sometimes err is in forgetting that this process of retrospective sophistication is not limited to adults but, presumably occurs in every phase of development with reference to preceding phases. Phantasy systems which emerge from repression in adults contain many elements derived from post-infantile life which, in their turn, have succumbed to repression and have become assimilated to systems of infantile origin. These infantile systems may themselves give signs of developmental stratification. Thus, they often show a number of different versions of the same plot. One may find a primitive oral theme in an anal-oral version, and this may again be repeated in a genital version. In other words, revival of the same primitive experience assumes novel forms corresponding to the stage of development and the current life situation. This ·kind of experience with adults leads me to think that a phantasy which can be demonstrated in a child of two years may have unmistakable reference to suckling or weaning experiences and may, in fact, revive such experiences. But in the two-year-old this re-editing or retrospective sophistication will be operative. His phantasy may have a form corresponding to his current development rather than to the stage to which its content refers. It may well show a considerable degree of subject–object differentiation, but such differentiation may be largely retrospective; it need not be taken for granted that it was present during the original experience.

I can only say a word or two regarding content. Abraham used 'cannibalistic' to denote oral-sadistic phantasies but libidinal oral phantasies also exist and are clearly of great developmental importance. Libido and aggression both operate from the start. What is important at each stage is not so much the absolute quantity of each involved as the ratio of libido to aggression. Clinical evidence shows how often too much pain and too little pleasure may blight early libidinal development. How can an infant comfort itself with libidinal hallucinations unless it has adequately satisfactory suckling experience? Or how can a baby come to terms with its own instincts if its libidinal development is frosted in the bud by sudden premature weaning?

I must leave the questions of organization of instincts and of the confusion between mental mechanization and phantasy for another time.

DR PAYNE: I should like to put a question to Mrs Isaacs. I think I have not quite understood one part of what she said about introjection and projection at the end of her paper. I got the impression that she was saying that all mental development depended upon introjection; namely, that perception followed by ideation was another way of talking of introjection, but that mental experience always relied on introjection.

MRS ISAACS: Is not that what Freud said?

DR PAYNE: Surely that is using 'introjection' in a very wide meaning?

MRS RIVIERE: Freud links it up there with instinct.

MRS ISAACS: I have no doubt there is much more to be worked out about that. Dr Heimann will in her paper go deeper into that.

MISS FREUD: May I just make a remark, not about the subject matter, but about a question of procedure. When we decided upon the programme we said there would not be enough time to answer to Mrs Isaacs' reply to the discussion, because it would mean a re-opening of all the questions already discussed. Is there any way of stating for the records that not answering Mrs Isaacs now does neither mean that we are satisfied with the answers she has given nor that we now agree with the views she has expressed?

DR GLOVER: The statement Miss Freud has just made will of course go into the minutes and be circulated.

MRS ISAACS: I don't think it is usually understood in scientific procedure that the last speaker is taken to be unchallenged.

DR PAYNE: It might be possible to take up special points later either by people reading a paper or writing in the Journal.

DR GLOVER: Would you be satisfied with Mrs Isaacs' reassurance, Miss Freud, or would you rather have it recorded in the minutes?

DR PAYNE: It will go in the minutes automatically.

DR FRIEDLANDER: I should like to state that I am rather disappointed that Mrs Isaacs has not answered my question but leaves me to look for an answer myself. I have looked for it for years and not found it although I want to stress that I am familiar with the literature on the subject.

The discussion was then closed and it was decided that the next discussion meeting should be held on Wednesday, *June 23rd,* 1943, when Dr Heimann will present her paper on Introjection and

Projection. This paper to be circulated beforehand. It was also agreed to hold a further discussion meeting on *July 7th, 1943.*

Notes

1 'Hate, as a relation to objects, is older than love. It derives from the narcissistic ego's primordial repudiation of the external world with its outpouring of stimuli.' [SE 14: 139]

2 'As the first of these aims we recognize the phase of incorporating or devouring – a type of love which is consistent with abolishing the subject's separate existence which may therefore be described as ambivalent.' [SE 14: 138]

3 '*Psycho-Analysis in Empirical Science.* – Psycho-analysis is not, like philosophies, a system starting out from a few sharply basic concepts, seeking to grasp the whole universe with the help of these and, once it is completed, having no room for fresh discoveries or better understanding. On the contrary, it keeps close to the facts in its field of study, seeks to solve the immediate problem of observation, gropes its way forward by the help of experience, is always incomplete and always ready to correct or modify its theories.' [SE 18: 253]

4 'It must dissociate itself from every foreign preconception, whether anatomical, chemical or physiological and it must work throughout with conceptions of a purely psychological order.' [SE 15–16: 18]

5 The quotation is slightly incorrect. [Ed.] Freud even in this translation is referring to 'Thinking in pictures' and not to 'visual memories': 'Thinking in pictures is therefore, only a very incomplete form of becoming conscious – in some way, it approximates more closely to unconscious processes', etc. [Freud, S. 1923b: 23]

'Thinking in pictures is, therefore, only a very incomplete form of becoming conscious. In some ways, too, it stands nearer to unconscious processes than does thinking in words and it is unquestionably older than the latter both ontogenetically and phylogenetically.' [SE 19: 21]

6 We have often heard it maintained that science should be built up on clear and sharply defined basic concepts. In actual fact no science, not even the most exact, begins with such definitions. The true beginning of scientific activity consists rather in describing phenomena and then in proceeding to group, classify and correlate them. Even at the stage of description it is not possible to avoid applying certain abstract ideas to the material in hand, ideas derived from somewhere or other but certainly not from the new observations alone. Such ideas – which will later become the basic concepts of the science – are still more indispensable as the material is further worked over. They must at

473

first necessarily possess some degrees of indefiniteness; there can be no question of any clear delimitation of their content. So long as they remain in this condition, we come to an understanding about their meaning by making repeated references to the material of observation from which they appear to have been derived, but upon which, in fact, they have been imposed. Thus, strictly speaking, they are in the nature of conventions – although everything depends on their not being arbitrarily chosen but determined by their having significant relations to the empirical material relations that we seem to sense before we can clearly recognize and demonstrate them. It is only after more thorough investigation of the field of observation that we are able to formulate its basic scientific concepts with increased precision and progressively so to modify them that they become serviceable and consistent over a wide area. Then, indeed, the time may have come to confine them in definitions. The advance of knowledge, however, does not tolerate any rigidity even in definitions. Physics furnishes an excellent illustration of the way in which even basic concepts that have been established in the form of definitions are constantly being altered in their content.   [SE 15:117]

7 Isaacs is referring to M. Klein's *The Psychoanalysis of Children* (Klein 1932: 158–61) and to 'On Criminality', a paper by Klein read at a symposium on crime, now published in *Love, Hate and Reparation and Other Works* (1921–45: 258–61).

8   It is clear that the behaviour of a child who indulges in thumb-sucking is determined by a search for some pleasure which has already been experienced and is now remembered. It is also easy to guess the occasions on which the child had his first experience of the pleasures which he is now striving to renew. It was the child's first and most vital activity, his sucking at his mother's breast or a substitute for it, that must have familiarised him with this pleasure. The satisfaction of the erotogenic zone is associated, in the first instance, with the satisfaction of the need for nourishment. No one who has seen a baby sinking back satiated from the breast and falling asleep with flushed cheeks and a blissful smile, can escape the reflection that this picture persists as a prototype of the expression of sexual satisfaction in later life. The need for repeating the sexual satisfaction now becomes detached from the need for taking nourishment. . . . The child does not make use of an extraneous body for his sucking, but prefers a part of his own skin because it is more convenient, because it makes him independent of the external world, which he is not yet able to control.
                    [SE 7: 181–4]

9 'In the first instance the oral component instinct finds satisfaction by attaching itself to the sating of the desire for nourishment; and its object

is the mother's breast. It detaches itself, becomes independent and at the same time auto-erotic, that is, it finds an object in the child's own body.' [SE 18: 245]

10 'Moreover, one must not take the difference between ego and id in too hard and fast a sense, nor forget that the ego is a specially differentiated part of the id.' [SE 19: 38]

11 'Originally to be sure, everything was id; the ego was developed out of the id by the continual influence of the external world. In the course of this slow development certain of the contents of the id were transformed into the preconscious state and was thus taken into the ego.' [SE 23: 163]

12 'It was only the non-occurrence of the expected satisfaction, the disappointment experienced, that led to the abandonment of this attempt at satisfaction by means of hallucination. Instead of it, the psychical apparatus had to decide to form a conception of the real circumstances in the external world and to endeavour to make a real alteration in them. A new principle of mental functioning was thus introduced.' [SE 12: 219–21]

13 The function of judgement is concerned in the main with two sorts of decisions. It affirms or disaffirms the possession by a thing of a particular attribute; and it asserts of disputes that a presentation has an existence in reality. The attribute to be decided about may originally have been good or bad, useful or harmful. Expressed in the language of the oldest – the oral – instinctual impulses, the judgement is: 'I should like to eat this', or 'I should like to spit it out'; and, put more generally: 'I should like to take this into myself and keep that out'. That is to say: 'It shall be inside me' or 'It shall be outside me'. . .

This postponement due to thought has also been discussed by me elsewhere. It is to be regarded as an experimental action, a motor palpating, with small expenditure of discharge. Let us consider where the ego has used a similar kind of palpating before, at what place it learnt the technique which it now applies in its processes of thought. It happened at the sensory end of the mental apparatus, in connection with sense perceptions. For, on our hypothesis, perception is not a purely passive process. The ego periodically sends out small amounts of cathexis into the perception system, by means of which it samples the external stimuli, and then after every such tentative advance it draws back again.

The study of judgement affords us, perhaps for the first time, an insight into the origin of an intellectual function from the interplay of the primary instinctual impulses. Judging is a continuation along lines of expediency of the original process by which the ego took things into itself or expelled them from itself, according to the pleasure principle.   [SE 19: 236–8]

8

The Medical and Child Welfare Committees

The Medical and the Child Welfare Committees
(1943 Annual General Meeting)

Addition to the Agenda for the Annual Meeting on July 21st, 1943

The following resolution has been sent in by two Members for consideration at the Annual Meeting: 'In view of the fact that proposals are being considered by various public bodies for the post-war organization of the medical profession it is resolved that the Institute shall set up a Medical Committee immediately to consider the position of the Institute and to make contact with authorities concerned in the interest of Members.'

(Proposed by Dr W. H. Gillespie and Dr John Bowlby)

Members should come to the meeting prepared with nominations for the proposed Committee on the Agenda to be usualised [*sic*] if the Meeting passes the resolutions concerned. Nominees should be consulted before their names are put forward.

June 30th, 1943   S. M. Payne,
                                                                   Hon. Secretary

**The Annual Meeting of the British Psycho-Analytical Society
was held at the home of the Society,
96 Gloucester Place, London, W.1., at 8 p.m.,
on Wednesday, July 21st, 1943**

Dr Jones was in the Chair.
Members present: Drs Jones, Glover, Payne, Friedlander, Lantos, M.
Schmideberg, Thorner, Miss Sharpe, Miss Freud, Mrs Burlingham,
Mrs Hoffer, Drs Macdonald, Gillespie, Bowlby, Franklin, Win-
nicott, Mrs Klein, Drs A Stephen, Herford, Rickman, Mr James
Strachey, Mrs Isaacs, Mrs Riviere, Drs Heimann, Scott and Wilson –
27 Members.

1 The minutes of the last meeting were read and approved.
2 Presentation of Reports.

(a) (i) Report of the Scientific Secretary 1942–1943

During the year 12 Scientific Meetings of the Society were held.
According to the decision taken at the last Annual Meeting roughly
one meeting per month was devoted to the discussion of controversial issues existing within the Society. Of the 12 Scientific Meetings
held 6 were therefore devoted to organized discussion, one of which
was a preliminary meeting dealing with questions of programme and
procedure; at the other 6 meetings scientific papers were given by 6
Members and one guest, who gave a paper on shock therapy.

The average attendance by Members was 29, the average
attendance at ordinary Scientific Meetings being 26 and at Discussion
Meetings 32. The highest attendance was 38, the lowest 18. A
number of Members who in the previous war years had not been
able to attend meetings have been able to re-establish contact.

During the year 95 guests were present at the Society's meetings,
of whom 86 were present on more than one occasion. 6 of the guests
took part in discussion. There are now 10 permanent guests on the
Society's lists.

38 Members and Associates took part in general discussion, 11
participated regularly.

E. Glover

(a) (ii) Interim report of the Committee for the Organization of Special Scientific Discussions (appointed at the Annual Meeting July 29, 1942)

During the year 6 of the Scientific Society Meetings were devoted to the above series. The first was a preliminary meeting to receive the report of the Organizing Committee and discuss procedure. At the second meeting Mrs Isaacs' paper on 'The Nature and Function of Phantasy' was presented with additional comments by the author. Discussion followed on the third, fourth, and fifth meetings. On the sixth meeting Mrs Isaacs replied and the discussion was closed.

The Committee held that no useful purpose would be served by attempting to summarize the state of the discussion at this juncture.

With regard to future discussions the next Paper will be by Dr Heimann on 'Some Aspects of the Role of Introjection and Projection in Early Development' and will be followed by a paper by Mrs Isaacs on 'Regression', after which it is probable that Mrs Klein will give at least two consecutive papers. Further more detailed arrangements will be put before the Society in the autumn session.

Marjorie Brierley
Edward Glover
James Strachey

(b) (i) Business Secretary's Report on the Year ending June 30, 1943

In accordance with the resolution passed at the last Annual Meeting held on July 29th, the Emergency War Committee had carried on the administration with the aid of Dr Friedlander who was co-opted to act as Treasurer. The Emergency Committee, however, has not taken full authority, as the Council has met on three occasions.

Two Business Meetings have been held during the year to elect trainees who have been passed by the Training Committee to Associate Membership, namely Dr Usher in November 1942 and Mrs Milner and Mr Hollitscher in May 1943.

One Member, Dr Hugo Staub, died in America, and Miss Mary Chadwick, an Associate Member since 1923, died suddenly in May 1943.

The number of Honorary Members is	2
Members	62
Associate Members	30

S. M. Payne

(b) (ii) Interim Report of the Committee appointed to investigate questions of tenure of office and the holding of multiple positions

The ad-hoc Committees elected at the last Annual Meeting have not been able to conclude their work for various reasons. The Scientific Secretary has reported on the work of the Committee elected to organize the Scientific Discussions. It is necessary for me to point out that the fact that the scientific problems were still under discussion influenced (rightly or wrongly) the attitude of members of the committee elected to investigate the questions of tenure of office and the holding of multiple offices, so that an interim report only is available.

This Committee was unfortunate owing to unforeseen events; in the first place one member serving in the RAMC was moved to Scotland temporarily directly after his election, and as his return was expected immediately a meeting of the Committee was postponed to allow him to attend. Two meetings were held at which concrete proposals were put forward to form a basis for discussion. Three members, Dr A. Stephen, Miss Low, and Dr Payne, proposed (1) the limitation of tenure of office in principle, opinions differing slightly in respect of time and application; (2) the election of all committees by the Society, and a rotation of retirement with eligibility for re-election after 2 years. Miss Low proposed that not more than 2 offices should be held simultaneously. Counter-suggestions were brought forward by Miss Freud and Dr Glover pointing to the inadvisability of such a course in the present indetermined state of the Society.

Dr Glover made a proposal that the Committee should preface a constitution to meet the possibility of running the Society in two separate sections to meet the requirements of two different groups. When it was ready to proceed to the formulation of recommendations the latter proposal was not discussed.

It was agreed at the meeting held in February to defer drawing up resolutions for the time being until the Scientific Discussions had gone further. Unfortunately the prolonged illness of another member has delayed further work. It is for the Annual Meeting to decide what the policy of this committee is to be, if it is to continue to function, and whether it shall or not be influenced by the progress of the Scientific Discussions.

S. M. Payne

3 THE CHAIRMAN mentioned that a year ago the Annual Meeting had appointed the Special Committee to investigate questions of

tenure of office and the holding of multiple positions, that this Committee had been investigating under the difficulties Dr Payne had just described, and that the Committee felt they would find their work much easier when the Scientific Discussions had gone further.

DR A. STEPHEN said that he gathered that Dr Jones held the opinion that the Committee were unanimous in thinking that alterations in the rules should wait until scientific divergencies of opinion were settled. He wished to protest against this point of view, as he considered that the alterations of the rules should be independent from scientific opinions and he held the opinion that a decision should be come to at once.

MISS FREUD said that she thought that the present state of the Society was not favourable to alterations in rules and that the experiences of the American Psychoanalytic Association which resulted in the formation of several separate societies were an argument against decisions being taken when there were strong scientific differences.

MR ADRIAN STEPHEN replied that it depended on how remote the possibility of the Society splitting into two is.

DR RIVIERE said that it seemed to her a hypothetical case which did not affect the decision of the moment, and that she did·not see why the Society should not have the best rules until it decided to split.

DR MACDONALD suggested that since the meeting had a majority report it might be possible to proceed on it in the meantime.

DR PAYNE mentioned that no vote had been taken in the Committee and that another meeting would have to take place before a report could be given, but probably 3 out of 5 Members would vote in favour of the proposals.

DR M. SCHMIDEBERG suggested asking the organizing committee to hurry up the Scientific Discussions in order to come to conclusions, and that it might be possible to finish these discussions in one year.

THE CHAIRMAN then asked the members to vote on the following proposal:
'To recommend the Committee elected to investigate questions of tenure of office and the holding of multiple positions, to proceed as quickly as possible, and to announce a decision by Christmas.'

A vote was taken and the resolution accepted by a large majority.

(c) The Acting Treasurer presented the balance sheets of the Society which were passed by the meeting

All reports presented to the meeting were passed.

4 The Council informed the meeting that owing to the persistence of conditions which existed at the time of the Annual Meeting of 1942 the Council had not up to the present time asked Members for nominations of new officers. The Council thought it probable that Members would prefer to leave unchanged the present war emergency administration because of the absence of many Members on war service and the fact that the two Committees (a) for the discussion of scientific differences, (b) for possible alterations in the constitution, had not concluded their investigations and could only present interim reports to the Annual Meeting. If, however, a majority of Members attending the Annual Business meeting wished elections to be held this year an extended Annual Meeting could be held in the autumn. Members had been asked by circular notice to send resolutions to this effect to the Secretary. No resolutions had been received.

A resolution was put to the meeting by the Chairman suggesting that the War Emergency Committee should continue to function for another year. This was seconded by *Miss Sharpe* and *carried unanimously*.

5 All the Associate Members were re-elected:
Dr Mary Barkas, Dr Mendel Brunner, Dr M. Burke, Dr M. Culpin, Dr G. Debenham, Dr H. W. Eddison, Miss M. G. Evans, Mrs E. Fleischer-Gero, Dr Klara Frank, Mr Martin Freud, Dr D. N. Hardcastle, Mr Walter Hollitscher, Dr Pryns Hopkins, Dr W. Inman, Miss Gwen Lewis, Dr J. Strafford Lewis, Dr Hilde Maas, Mrs Marion Milner, Mr Money-Kyrle, Dr G. W. Pailthorpe, Dr L. S. Penrose, Mrs Hannah Ries, Dr E. Rosenberg, Dr Max Schur, Miss Elisabeth Schwarz, Dr Josefine Stross, Dr J. M. Taylor, Dr Rees Thomas, Dr R. D. Usher, Dr R. C. Winn, Prof. F. R. Winton.[1]

It was decided to write again to Dr Max Schur with regard to his subscriptions which had not been received for several years, and to send a copy of this letter to another Member resident in the USA.

6 Miss Barbara Cooke and Miss Hedwig Schwarz, proposed by the Training Committee, were elected to Associate Membership.

7 Dr Elisabeth Rosenberg's name was put up for election to Membership by the Council and a secret ballot was taken. She was elected to Membership.

8 THE SECRETARY (DR PAYNE) gave a report on the situation in regard to the two resolutions received:
(a) 'In view of the fact that proposals are being considered by various public bodies for the post-war organization of the medical profession it is resolved that the Institute shall set up immediately a Medical

Committee consisting of 7 members to consider the position of the Institute and to make contact with authorities concerned in the interest of Members.'

(b) 'That a Committee should be appointed to consider the part which the Institute can take in the future in the training and education of various classes of workers interested in child welfare.'

Although the two resolutions which the Society is about to discuss may not seem to have connection with each other it is my opinion that they are closely connected; and I want to make a few introductory remarks about the two together.

In my opinion the future position of the Society and Institute has become extremely precarious as the result of social reorganization arising out of war conditions. It may be that we are not equipped to meet the situation because of our policy in the past, but spending time on recriminations will not solve the problems of the future. The proposal to constitute a Medical Health Service, which is the part of the Beveridge Report to which the Government is already committed, has brought into being a number of committees associated with various medical organizations for the purpose of considering the problems which have to be faced and bringing influence to bear on the authorities who will eventually frame the necessary legislation. Some Members have served as private individuals on some of these committees but the Institute and Society as a recognized body has not been approached and the medical Members have not been consulted as to the policy to be adopted. For this reason when I was approached by some of the younger medical Members and was asked to circulate a resolution to elect a medical committee to consider what could be done to strengthen our position I did so gladly, and take full responsibility for the note added to the Agenda on the subject of nominations, as Dr Glover held the opinion that there was no precedent for this additional note.

My opinion is that this is an unprecedented situation in which red tape must be ignored. At the present moment reports have been reaching the ears of our medical Members that the Institute of Psycho-Analysis is not considered to be of sufficient importance to merit consideration. It is impossible of course, to judge the truth of these reports but it is essential for us to decide whether we can or not put forward constructive proposals of a kind which could enable us to co-operate in some way with other institutions concerned with mental health.

If we do not do this, in a few years' time we shall get no medical men or women applying for training unless they are seriously incapacitated themselves and it is probable that our younger medical

Members will tend to drift away. The result will be that if the Institute continues to exist it will be divorced from the medical profession as a whole. It has been argued that this would not matter and that the Institute and Society could carry on in touch with a limited section of the public. If this happened it would be inevitable that a preponderance of Members interested in the application of analysis to education would limit the amount of research work which could be done on psycho-pathology. Personally I regard a prospect of this kind as a threat to the progress of medicine and especially of psychiatry. Hence if the majority share my views it is essential that we should take all the means in our power at the present time to promote co-operation without losing identity. I will remind the Society that Professor Freud made his discoveries after years of work amongst the mentally sick. Without co-operation with those working in the medical profession on the problems of psycho-pathology we cannot get sufficient access to material to carry on scientific research work of value. Indeed some of the fallacies arising in new work at the present time are due to lack of opportunity to observe and study a sufficient number and a sufficient variety of cases.

I have put the question of our co-operation with the medical profession first but I regard the resolution concerning the provision for the teaching of psychoanalytic knowledge to groups of people concerned with the needs of children as equally important. In a paper which I read at the first meeting in November 1942 called to discuss the public activities of the Institute I put forward a proposition that there should be a separate branch of the Institute devoted to the teaching of applied psychoanalysis to various groups of people concerned in the care and education of children. We all know that the attention of the thinking public is occupied with the reorganization of welfare and education of children and that many people are asking for instruction in the psychology of the child and that where the need is great a supply will always be forthcoming.

Individual members are working in various ways. Miss Anna Freud and Mrs Burlingham's war nurseries are outstanding examples of individual effort. Dr Winnicott is associated with many bodies interested in child psychology and has recently drawn up a valuable memorandum entitled 'The Relation between Clinical Paediatrics and Child Psychology', which was adopted by the British Paediatric Association. In this he was supported by Major Mildred Creak and Dr Alan Maberley. Dr Friedlander has been lecturing to social workers and other groups of workers interested in delinquency. There are also other Members doing work of various kinds.

Perhaps the greatest evidence of the need for the Institute and

Society to do something as a group lies in the number of applications for training or teaching in psychoanalysis which, as Training Secretary, I receive from well-educated women interested in the psychology of children or in work connected with social problems. We already have more unqualified analysts than our position in the medical world justifies and we are bound to refuse the majority of these applicants. Many of them would be much benefited by organized teaching and a form of training of a less intensive kind than that required by the therapist. I am aware that there are difficulties, but if there was sufficient recognition of the fact that there are differences in needs and that there is room also for different degrees of training I believe something valuable could be achieved. I would suggest that a committee be set up that has no connection with the Training Committee. It could have the function of sending representatives to serve on other bodies studying these problems as well as the organization of lectures on child-psychology. Analyses carried out by the members of the committee would not qualify the trainee as a psychoanalyst but would qualify for observation work and many other kinds of valuable psychological activities.

The foundation of a department of this kind would show the medical profession and public health authority and educational authority that the Institute is strong enough to recognize and utilize scientific groups according to their specialities and is therefore able to make full use of the special knowledge of each group with full recognition of the variety of qualification and knowledge in the different groups.

Lastly, if we do not do our share in attempting to satisfy the demand for knowledge of the psychology of the child others will take our place as they are already doing and the Institute will not keep pace with organizations which in the past have been regarded as less efficient than our own.

DR M. SCHMIDEBERG said that she had recently been in touch with various probation officers, officers of care committees, and other such bodies and that she had the impression that medical psychology was becoming increasingly appreciated and advice and teaching sought for by such bodies and individual officers. She did not think, however, that it would come from this Institute first of all, that our training is still too expensive and taking too long so that a training lasting 5 years comes to 2,000 guineas. One could not expect medical people to go in for it unless they were very neurotic. They can get their training cheaper from other bodies and also shorter and with better prospects of earning. Secondly the Institute could not take the responsibility of training people unless there was unity about scientific views. Thirdly, social workers are in charge of 60–100 cases on the average. On the other hand, for years the dominating idea in this Society had been of deep and long analysis, that at a time even all cases treated under 100 sessions were omitted from the statistics. After the war a great number of child guidance clinics would be established and juvenile courts would have their own psychologists, etc, all these in order to give service to as many people as possible with the expense of very little time and money in the individual case. If there would be State Medical Service they would not be able to afford much time and money. Dr M Schmideberg could not see how the Institute could train people for that service.

MISS SHARPE said: I think it is eminently desirable that we should appoint a committee to consider the part which the Institute can take in the training and education of various classes of workers interested in child welfare. I think it would be lamentable if the knowledge and experience this Society represents in its Members were not made available and used for the benefit of the post-war world. I think such a committee should consist of Members who have had educational experience and those who have the widest contacts with different types of social and educational organizations.

DR JONES said that in his opinion there were three issues involved: First, the question of appointing a medical committee to co-operate with other medical bodies. Second, a committee to co-operate with child psychology or child welfare bodies. Thirdly, about actually extending our teaching work amongst child welfare or social workers. The third must come logically after the second. In regard to the first issue, i.e. to appoint a special public relations committee on the medical side, either the medical Members on the Council could function or a special committee could be appointed. In the second case there might be clashes, i.e. if the Institute were approached officially there would be the committee and the Council to deal with.

DR K. FRIEDLANDER suggested first to discuss what is going on in the BMA to see whether Members take part and the various points of view taken.

MR STRACHEY said that he considered the present discussion out of order as the proposer and seconder had not yet spoken to the resolution.

THE CHAIRMAN asked these two Members to speak to their resolutions.

DR GILLESPIE: No doubt you are aware that various bodies are at present considering the future of medicine but I doubt if many Members have any clear idea of what is going on in this sphere. There is a considerable number of bodies dealing with psychological medicine alone; the principal ones I know of are the Psychological Medicine Group of the BMA, which has recently held a conference to which I understand Dr Glover and Dr Carroll were invited; the BMPA Planning Committee; the Royal College of Physicians Committee on Psychological Medicine; the Langdon-Brown Committee. The Combined Colleges of Physicians and Surgeons are concerned with defining the status of consultants and I understand are actually making a list of those to be recognized as such under the new national scheme. Also to be considered are the group known as Medical Planning Research; the Socialist Medical Association; the Medical Practitioners' Union, and the National Provisional Council of Mental Health.

The recommendations of these bodies are likely to have a profound effect on what happens after the war. Soon we as a Society shall find ourselves faced with a *fait accompli* in which we have expressed no opinion and brought no influence to bear. It is time we shook off this apathy that we have shown about public matters. While we have been absorbed in the discussion of scientific differences, the whole face and structure of medical practice may well have changed fundamentally. Most Members probably know that it is the government's intention to introduce a state medical service, and they favour a salaried one, eventually on a full-time basis. The BMA is fighting a rearguard action on some of these points. This is not the time or place to express an opinion on the merits of these proposals, but surely it is clear that such a change will affect the prospects of analytic practice profoundly. It is hardly to be expected, for instance, that many medical analysts can be expected to outlaw themselves from the profession by refusing to join the new service.

In putting forward this resolution, I am merely making the very modest proposal that we should have some voice in events that so profoundly affect, indeed threaten, our future as analysts. In common with many other medical Members, I do not depend on analysis for my livelihood, and have no anxieties about finding a suitable niche in a state service; such a niche, however, is most unlikely to be wide enough to admit of the practice of analysis, and it is only on this score that I personally have anything to fear. But the case is very different for the lay analysts – what role will be assigned to them in an all-embracing scheme of state medicine? For them, it would seem to be much more a matter of life and death. On the other hand, it would appear likely to provoke less prejudice and animus if the other medical bodies dealing with the future of medicine are approached by a purely medical committee of the Society, whose advocacy is likely to carry more weight than would be the case were the lay analysts to plead in their own cause. It is for this reason that we are proposing the setting up of a medical committee for the purpose of making the necessary contacts.

In the past, the Society has followed a policy of deliberate self-isolation. We need not discuss whether that policy expressed the will of the majority of the Society, but in my personal view it was most unfortunate that this policy should be pursued consistently over such a long period. To continue along the same lines now appears to me to be sheer suicide. In view of the fact that the Society's health has obviously been somewhat precarious recently, even a half-hearted suicide attempt might well prove fatal. One of the most serious symptoms of the Society's unsatisfactory state of health is the fact that the supply of younger medical candidates has almost completely dried up. There must be reasons for this, and they are not far to seek when one considers the kind of external relations that have been cultivated by this Society. Clearly, as time goes on the medical membership will diminish from this cause, and the Society will present less and less attraction to the medical man. I would remind you also that at present it is clearly the government's intention that newly qualified doctors should join a whole-time salaried state service without option, so that here we have an external threat to the future of our Society. The internal threat, due to the Society's failure to appeal to the young medical men, was already serious enough; he would be a bold man who would predict that we could survive a double attack. It may be that it is already too late to do anything effective, or this may be only the eleventh hour. But if we continue our isolationist policy, I can see no hope for the Society. I therefore beg to put forward the following resolution:

'In view of the fact that proposals are being considered by various public bodies for the post-war organization of the medical profession it is resolved that the Institute shall set up a medical committee immediately to consider the position of the Institute and to make contact with authorities concerned in the interest of Members.'

DR BOWLBY: In seconding the resolution that a medical commit-tee should be set up to approach and negotiate with the various bodies now planning the future of the medical profession, and more especially the psychiatric side of the profession, I wish to emphasize two points which Dr Gillespie has already mentioned. First, we are at the moment on the threshold of drastic changes in the organization of the medical services of the country. Secondly, the psychiatric side of these services has ceased to be a Cinderella and is now taking its place on an equality with medicine and surgery.

The reorganization of the medical services of the country is on a scale such as occurs only once in a century. It is probable that the changes likely to follow in the next decade will be equal in importance to the changes following on the introduction of the Medical Register. The position of voluntary clinics, of teaching centres, and of private practice will all be deeply affected. It seems extremely probable that some form of National Medical Service will be set up and that all medical practitioners will be in some way or other associated with it. The exact nature of the new service is, to my mind, irrelevant to our present discussions. At this late hour we are powerless to alter the course of the negotiations, even if we wished to do so. Indeed it is probable that final decisions will be reached during the course of the next 12 months.

But even if we cannot influence the basic structure of the National Medical Service, we may be able to do much towards shaping the niche into which our Institute and Clinic will fit. By proper action we can ensure that psychoanalysis is recognized as being of value to the community, as a therapy, as a method of research, and as the most fruitful theory of psychopathology yet formulated. Nevertheless such recognition will not follow automatically. It is up to us to negotiate with the proper authorities to see that this recognition is given.

But in addition to this drastic reorganization of the medical services, it so happens that psychiatry is itself undergoing a revolution. This is my second point. If in the last war psychopathology and psychotherapy forced themselves on the public attention it may be said that in this war they have come of age. Psychiatry is now claiming for itself a place equal to those long occupied by medicine, surgery, and more recently by gynaecology and obstetrics. The organization of a Mental Health Service to cover the whole country is being envisaged; and so that there should be an adequate supply of trained personnel the formulation of a syllabus and the provision of facilities for the training of psychiatrists is the subject of lively debate. Once again it is imperative that our Society should see to it that its views are considered so that psychoanalysis comes to play a leading part in this reorganized and expanded psychiatric service.

Dr Gillespie has already listed some of the bodies which are considering these matters. There is the Psychological Group of the BMA concerned principally with the planning of a National Psychiatry Service. There is the Committee of the Royal College of Physicians and also the Langdon-Brown Committee, both concerned with the training of psychiatrists. There is the Committee of the Royal Medicopsychological Society, about which I personally know nothing, and, for all I know, there are other bodies.

This brings me to my next point. Many of us do not know what is going on or where. I wonder how many in this room this evening could say which of our Members is on which of these committees, what schemes he has advocated, and what resolutions he has opposed. I know some names myself, but I am certain I have not a complete picture. For instance I have no idea whether we have any Member serving on the very important Committee of the Royal College of Physicians and I naturally do not know what policy he is following, if we have such a Member.

This state of affairs is not altogether surprising, for the Society grew up on its own and adopted a policy in which relations with other bodies were not cultivated. It has been a self-sufficient Society. I am not concerned tonight with the wisdom of this policy, but only with its effects. It has resulted inevitably in the Society having no machinery for representation on other bodies, nor arrangements whereby policy is co-ordinated or the Members consulted on matters of principle. It is significant that tonight, so far as the Agenda tells us, no report will be made by any of our Members who happen to be members of any of these committees. In saying this I am not considering any one or two persons. There are, I believe, several of us, of different shades of opinion, concerned, and I am quite sure that the absence of such reports is not due to any desire to keep the Society in the dark, but simply to a lack of machinery and a lack of precedent. It is not easy to change the ways of two decades overnight.

For all we know, as a result of the absence of any co-ordinating machinery, the policy being advocated by one Member on one committee is inconsistent with that being advocated by another Member on another committee. Furthermore, the politics followed by individual Members may not represent the opinions of the majority of the Society, and in becoming members of committees it must be remembered that we cannot escape being considered in some ways to represent psychoanalysis and the Psycho-Analytical Society. It is impossible for a Member, especially an office holder, to sit on a committee discussing the future of psychiatry without his or her being taken to represent the views of the Society as a whole. Whether we encourage it or not, we cannot escape this responsibility.

I would ask Members to ponder this situation for a moment, and to reflect on our position. We find ourselves in a rapidly changing world and yet, as a Society, we have done nothing, I repeat nothing, to meet these changes, to influence them or to adapt to them. That is not the reaction of a living organism but of a moribund one. If our Society died of inertia it would only have met the fate it has invited.

But there is no reason for this ignorance and inertia and incoordination to continue. We can, if we will, decide and decide now to set up machinery for dealing with these problems. It is to meet these circumstances that Dr Gillespie has proposed that a committee of medical Members should be appointed. There will be few Members, I believe, who will not recognize the urgent need for such a committee and support the proposal.

It is, of course, necessary that the committee should be a strong one and representative of the different aspects of our work. Two or three Members cannot deal with the many forces at present influencing the future of the different branches of psychiatry in this country. There is, for instance, child psychiatry, the psychiatry of the Emergency Mental Service, private practice, research, and the psychiatric sides of selection, now extending beyond the Army in significant ways. In addition, there are the numerous committees of which we have already spoken. It is apparent that one or two members cannot possibly represent the Society in all these different fields. It must be a team effort and for this reason I believe flat a committee consisting of about seven Members, of which our two principal active officers should be two, is essential.

I conceive the duties of such a committee to be threefold. First, it must explore the ground and discover what are the professional conditions in which we are likely to be living and working in the future. Secondly, it must consult the Society regarding the policy which it should advocate. Thirdly, when this has been agreed to, it must see to it that the Society's policy is represented in an effective way. I need hardly say that the committee must, on every matter of principle raised, lay the position before Members so that full discussion is possible. All Members, medical and lay, must know what is being said in their name and must play responsible parts in framing the policy of the Society.

Further, I wish to emphasize with Dr Gillespie that such a committee, though medical in constitution, will act no less in the interest of the lay Members. It is evident that a supplementary register of psychotherapists not medically qualified will sooner or later be prepared. It is most desirable that the medical Members of the Society should represent the views and interests of the lay Members when such a supplementary register is made and the powers and responsibilities of its members formulated. Without this medical support the interests of lay Members may suffer very seriously.

Nevertheless I feel that it is the furtherance of psychoanalysis as a science and a therapy rather than the interests of individual Members that must be our principal aim. There are at present only two countries where psychoanalysis flourishes. One is the USA, the other Great Britain. It will be another generation before psychoanalysis lives again on the continent of Europe. Until that day our Society will remain the only bulwark of analysis on this side of the Atlantic. It is thus all the more essential that our Society should grow in size and its influence expand so that analysis ceases to be a backroom boy but comes instead to play a leading part in the scientific, medical, and social life of our community. Only if this is accomplished here can we expect analysis to become once again a live force in Continental countries.

It is because of these immense responsibilities which we as a Society bear, that I appeal to Members to support the resolution. Without this Committee I see no prospect whatever either of the interests of individual Members being safeguarded or of analysis attaining the position which we wish it to attain in the medical services of the future.

DR JONES thanked Drs Bowlby and Gillespie, and expressed the gratification of the Society about the part they were playing. He said he did not want to diminish the weight of the statements but that he was inclined to say that Dr Gillespie's picture of the future was a little terrifyingly dark; e.g. in discussions by the College of Physicians on the subject of consultants it was decided that the honorary staff of hospitals must hold consultant's degrees, but this condition did not apply to specialists.

DR RICKMAN said that he was in favour of the resolution proposed.

DR GLOVER agreed that whatever committees we have must represent the policy of the Society. For instance, in regard to child welfare workers it was most important that this should be so. In regard to the medical committee which, as pointed out, would also include the interests of lay Members, he felt that it would be a very active body with a very great deal of work to do for every individual member and with the necessity for everyone to be ready at a day's notice to attend a meeting, a lunch, etc. Whatever committee was appointed should be a mobile body who could move at a day's notice, ready to devote their time to the matter and also money, as it was quite a costly business really at times. (This as far as the practical side was concerned.) Dr Glover also said that regarding the point made that the policies of the Society should be clarified concerning extension of its activities, he did not know who should do that. It should be settled, to begin with, what the relationship of this committee to the Society was.

Dr Glover then proceeded to report on the activities of the BMA Committee in which he took part and reported that its first production was what was called the Grey Book (recommendations on the organization of psychiatry in the country on children, etc.). The procedure then was to invite a number of people representing various interests, to participate in discussions on state medical service. These members, although their credentials were taken, did not speak for their respective clinics, but were there as personal members. The trend was essentially with the stress on service institutional psychiatrists. From our Institute there was myself, Dr Carroll was there as Director of the ISTD, Dr Maberly from the Child Guidance Council, etc. The state medical service was visualized as an extension of existing services. The Ministry had not proposed state medical service in regard to psychiatry, because of the uncoordinated state of the lunacy laws. The result of the Committee's endeavours was that within a fortnight the Minister consented to do so. In regard to child services they had to take other bodies into consideration. Another tendency was Dr Glover's own impression that it was influenced by the conditions in the Army; that the Committee was concerned from the beginning with the organization of the state service without view to existing voluntary services. Part of his work on this committee referred to this. A gradually increasing tendency developed for a minority to get together on this point. The Society would have to take into account what degree of co-operation – without regard to the different methods – was possible on matters of ideals and policy. Dr Glover's point was to get the Committee to instruct the negotiating body to consider the voluntary services outside the state medical service. That was to a certain extent secured, mainly by protest. It also changed the opinion of the Members concerned with the drawing up of the scheme.

The only other committee Dr Glover was concerned with was the Langdon-Brown Committee. Dr Glover on that occasion paid tribute to Dr Wilson for taking the first steps for the formation of this Committee. It had its origin in the War Emergency Committee of the British Branch of the International General Medical Society for Psychotherapy and by co-option finally included 16 members. Dr Glover's intention was to make it an *ad hoc* Committee. The Committee came together regularly since October 1941 until recently and produced a printed report, the purpose of its activities being to get as much teaching in psychological medicine into the syllabus as possible. There was a split between the neurologically minded members and the psychologically minded. This split was never resolved. Finally it became a majority question. The British PA Society contributed £10 to the expenditure of the committee and Dr Glover also arranged for private contributions. Dr Glover stressed that it was obvious that we must safeguard our own training whatever relation we have with other bodies. Members will get copies of the printed report. This Committee was entirely concerned with the training of postgraduates and specialists.

DR JONES then suggested to take a list of Members who were already taking part in various such committees, and of such committees as exist:

BMA Committee: Drs Glover and Carroll
Langdon-Brown Committee: Drs Glover and Karin Stephen
Royal Medico-Psychological Association: (Dr Scott was trying to find out about it)
Royal College of Physicians: Dr Rickman

DR BOWLBY added that there was a special conference of the BMA and a Psychological Sub-Committee.

DR GLOVER remarked that the Group Committee was weak and gave recommendations to the conference, and that we had no Members on the committee.

DR SCOTT said that any member of the BMA could become a member of the psychological group. He suggested that any Member who has not a full-time state job should join the specialist group.

DR RICKMAN reported that the Royal College of Physicians Committee had a Psychological Committee concerned with (1) the training of undergraduates, (2) the training of specialists, (3) the question of qualifications, (4) future measures.

The Committee's deliberations for 7 months were solely concerned with the training of undergraduates and were concluded on this point. Dr Rickman's part was mainly to get certain points put forward with the greatest possible emphasis, e.g., that the undergraduate must be so instructed in psychological medicine that he will see the patient as an individual living in the society from the beginning: the sociological along with the biological point of view. It was achieved that the Committee suggested that 36 hours in the second half of the third year should be devoted to this. In the final report of the Committee it was stated that the undergraduate should be required to go round to the various clinics, not be confined to his teaching hospital and one mental hospital. This was very little for such a long time of deliberations.

493

DR M. SCHMIDEBERG suggested that another meeting should be held to discuss these points, as it was now 11 p.m.

DR K. FRIEDLANDER reported that she had certain experience with bodies working in the welfare field on the training of social workers in psychoanalysis and had been asked to draw up a syllabus for the London School of Economics on the application of psychoanalysis. It was decided that this question should be dealt with when the possibility of appointing a committee for the training of child welfare workers is discussed.

DR M. SCHMIDEBERG proposed that another meeting to discuss the question of a medical committee should be held.

DR GLOVER said that as we had to have a medical committee, the Society could proceed to get ahead with that.

THE CHAIRMAN then put to the Society the resolution of Drs Bowlby and Gillespie with the addendum of Dr Bowlby, that the committee should have 7 members.

A vote was taken on this point and the Members agreed unanimously.

The following Members were nominated for election to this Committee: Dr Bowlby, Dr Gillespie, Dr Rickman, Dr Payne, Dr Glover, Dr Winnicott, Dr A. Stephen, Dr Wilson, Dr Carroll.

The Chairman reported that one name had been proposed in writing, the name of a Member without a British medical degree. The meeting decided that it would not be desirable for the Committee to include a Member without a British degree.

A Secret Ballot was taken and the following Members were elected to serve on the Medical Committee: Dr Bowlby, Dr Gillespie, Dr Payne, Dr Winnicott, Dr Adrian Stephen, Dr Glover and Dr Rickman.
(Dr Wilson had left the meeting before this vote was taken.)

The Chairman then stated that it had been decided that the question of the other committee on the Agenda, viz. about the training of child welfare workers, should be postponed to a Business Meeting in October.

(signed) Edward Glover

Editorial note: After this meeting Klein wrote to David Matthew, on 27 July 1943 as follows:

Just a note to let you know about the meeting, because I am sure you will be interested to hear how it went off. It showed a very different situation in the Society from that which existed a year ago. The resolution put forward by Gillespie and seconded by Bowlby was very strong, firm and impressive. It not only proved that there is a great need for the Society to be more in touch with medical bodies and to represent analysis at its best with them, but it was a clear expression of what Glover (and Jones in the past) have missed on this line. It was also a clear expression of disapproval of the autocratic methods of Glover, who has not consulted anybody else and seems to do what he likes about these things. Scott, too, made a very good impression by asking for a special point about which the Ministry of Health had been enquiring from various bodies. He expressed a wish that the answer, which was provided only by Glover, should be read out, and here again disapproval was expressed that other people had not been asked to co-operate. But apart from this special though very important point, the whole tenor of the meeting and the attitude of the members showed the way in which Glover had conducted those discussions, and there was universal demand that the committee of investigation into the tenure of office should proceed more quickly, in spite of the fact that there has been no decision about the result of the discussions. Bowlby said that it might help the discussions very much if there was a change in the constitution. All that was done without particular emotions, and coming as it did from a different side, impressed, I think, the whole meeting as well as Glover himself. He was rather subdued and did not react, at least not at the time, with any aggression to those statements. It would also be very difficult for him to do so, because as things stand it would really mean his being in opposition to the majority of members. . . .

(Note: Continuation of the AGM held on 21 July 1943)

**Abstract of Minutes of Extended Annual Meeting
of the British Psycho-Analytical Society
and the Institute of Psycho-Analysis
held at the home of the Institute and Society,
96 Gloucester Place, London, W.1.,
at 8 p.m. on Wednesday, November 3rd, 1943**

DR GLOVER was in the Chair and 23 Members were present (Dr Payne, Dr Lantos, Dr Friedlander, Mrs Hoffer, Miss Low, Miss Anna Freud, Mrs Burlingham, Dr Franklin, Mrs Ruben, Dr W. Hoffer, Dr Brierley, Dr Macdonald, Miss Sharpe, Mrs Klein, Dr Winnicott, Dr Isaacs, Dr Heimann, Mrs Riviere, Dr Bowlby, Dr Adrian Stephen, Dr Karin Stephen, Dr Gillespie).

1 It was decided to take the minutes of the Annual Meeting as read except that part of the minutes which had a bearing on the Agenda of the present meeting, namely the resolutions concerning:
(i) The election of an *ad hoc* Medical Committee.
(ii) 'The proposal that a Committee be elected to consider the part which the Institute can take in the future in the training and education of various classes of workers interested in Child Welfare.'
    The Secretary read the resolution to the meeting and the result of the voting on the election of the Medical Committee. The minutes were signed by the Chairman. Members were informed that the full minutes can be seen in the office of the Institute.

2 The Chairman introduced the Agenda and informed the meeting that under item (3) 'Any other business', a report would be read by Dr A. Stephen on the deliberations of the Medical Committee.

3 The Secretary (Dr Payne) was asked to introduce Resolution (2) on behalf of the Council.

DR PAYNE affirmed that the Council put forward the resolution owing to the necessity for Members to decide what part, if any, the Institute wishes to play in the reorganization of social services which is contemplated after the war.
    DR GLOVER suggested that Dr Payne should open the discussion by describing the possible function of the proposed committee in more detail.
    DR PAYNE said she would mention two ways in which a committee dealing with child welfare problems could be utilized:
(a) To keep Members in touch with other bodies interested in the same problems and to inform the Institute when the need for representation of the Institute on other bodies arose. Recent discussions at the British Psychological Society and in other places have shown the need for work of this kind.
    The fact that child welfare involves both the medical and educational authority creates a problem of administration in itself which is being discussed on all sides. The Institute should formulate its own policy and the proposed committee should advise the Members.
(b) To advise on the training or teaching of women interested in child welfare who are unsuitable to be psychoanalysts but need psychoanalytical knowledge.
    DR GLOVER gave examples of the activity of educational psychologists who are trying to get child guidance under their control.
    MISS LOW spoke strongly in favour of the proposal, and

496

suggested the formation of an Educational Section of the Society.

DR PAYNE said that the Report of the Medical Committee might influence the discussion, and it might be well to hear it first.

DR GLOVER said it would touch on the subject of lectures. Miss Low's suggestion of organizing an educational section could be discussed but it would be a matter for the new committee to consider. He suggested that Dr Stephen should read part of his report.

DR A. STEPHEN said that the report of the Medical Committee contained 3 recommendations:

(i) That a course of instruction in the principles of psychoanalysis suitable for those professionally engaged in the study of psychological medicine should be arranged as part of the Institute's regular programme of work.

(ii) That the Board should be asked to appoint a special committee to arrange for this course, its members to be elected by the Members of the Institute. It is suggested that it will be advisable for the membership of this new committee to overlap with that of the present committee in order that the two may act in the closest co-operation.

It should be observed that there is of course no intention to interfere with the work of the Training Committee. It is not proposed that these lectures should be given immediately. A committee should be appointed to consider the syllabus and have it ready.

DR GLOVER said the Medical Committee could make suggestions but could not be responsible for carrying them out. It would be best to discuss the relationship of training to pedagogues and social workers next.

MRS ISAACS said that the British Psychological Society had a Sub-committee considering the question of people doing child psychology. There is a movement towards a definite qualification in psychology of a more advanced kind than a Hons. degree. It is desired that psychotherapy shall be included. She went on to say that she had ample evidence of the demand for more knowledge of psychoanalysis amongst educational and psychiatric social workers and she welcomed the proposal.

MISS FREUD asked whether this was the time to form either a committee or section whilst the scientific differences were unsettled.

DR GLOVER said it depended on whether we were discussing the formation of an educational section or an observation committee. Personally he thought that the state of internal dissension made new projects undesirable.

DR PAYNE said that in spite of differences there should not be a split. Secondly, if we are going to take part in what is going on outside we cannot wait.

MISS LOW suggested that new developments might heal old differences.

DR HOFFER reminded Members that in the past in reviews of books of Members of the Vienna Society some British Members had been prejudiced against the Viennese views on the teaching of psychoanalysis to pedagogues. He thought these differences should be settled first.

DR BOWLBY spoke in favour of a committee and agreed with Dr Isaacs' remarks.

DR FRIEDLANDER said that different views might interfere with the teaching of pedagogues and gave an example which occurred when she was lecturing.

DR GLOVER said the question raised was 'In the current state of differences of opinions is it the best time to start on new activities?'.

MISS FREUD said she was clear that there was an external necessity, but she thought it better to concentrate on clearing up differences.

DR K. STEPHEN suggested that it could be found out whether it was possible for Members who have different views to act together.

MISS SHARPE asked a similar question.

MISS LOW pointed out that people with different views lectured at the London School of Economics. Child workers would not want theories.

DR BOWLBY said that we all held fundamental principles in common which differentiated us from all other schools of psychiatry, and that it was on these common grounds rather than on our differences that this type of public work can be undertaken. He suggested that in view of the time it might be desirable to consider taking a vote on the Child Welfare Committee.

DR GLOVER said there would be 3 committees

(1) Medical Committee
(2) Child Welfare Committee
(3) Lecture Committee.

He asked Miss Freud if she was in favour of a Child Welfare Committee with general terms of reference.

MISS FREUD said she would like to limit her activities to the Scientific Discussions.

DR GLOVER proposed to put the resolution proposed by Dr Payne and seconded by Dr Bowlby to the meeting. MISS FREUD suggested that the word 'now' should be inserted in the resolution. DR GLOVER suggested the Resolution:

> That a Committee should be elected forthwith to consider the part which the Institute can take in the future in the training and education of various classes of workers interested in child welfare.

This was passed by 14 to 6 votes. DR GLOVER proposed that voting should be by post. *This was agreed.*

It was also *agreed that the Committee should consist of 7 members, 2 of these to be elected from the Medical Committee. It was decided that the terms of reference should be as stated in the resolution.*

4 DR ADRIAN STEPHEN then proceeded to point (iii) of his report of the Medical Committee:

(iii) That the Board should be asked to get in touch as soon as may be with the Inter-departmental Committee which has been appointed by the Ministry of Health to consider the organization of medicine after the war, in order to place before that committee the views of our Institute on Postgraduate Instruction in Psychological Medicine.

It was stated that the matter was urgent as the Interdepartmental Committee had almost completed its work. A memorandum on the subject had been drawn up and discussed by the Medical Committee.

A discussion followed in which Drs Bowlby, Payne, Friedlander, Glover, Heimann, Isaacs, and Riviere took part.

It was decided to authorize the Council to forward the memorandum.

5 THE CHAIRMAN, DR GLOVER, pointed out that there was a suggestion from the Medical Committee that a Lecture Committee be appointed to consider proposals for lectures from the other committees and with the task of implementing recommendations.

MRS RIVIERE proposed that some members of the two committees should serve on the Lecture Committee.

A discussion followed in which Drs Glover, Payne, and Isaacs took part.

DR BOWLBY proposed that two members from each of the *ad hoc* committees should be included in the Lecture Committee to ensure continuity of work. This was seconded by Mrs Isaacs.

DR GLOVER said he considered it improper to elect an administrative committee of the Society in which 4 out of 7 members were elected from *ad hoc* committees.

It was not possible to follow the discussion here.

DR PAYNE pointed out that the Lecture Committee could only have an *ad hoc* status.

DR GLOVER agreed that this fact diminished the importance of the precedent.

Vote being taken it was decided that a committee be elected to be called an Ad-hoc Lecture Committee. That it consist of 7 members, of whom 4, viz. 2 each, be elected by the Medical and Child Welfare Committees respectively, the remaining 3 members to be elected by the Society. It was decided to hold elections for the Ad-hoc Lecture Committee by post.[2]

(signed) S. M. Payne

Notes

1 Ever since Jones had founded the British Psycho-Analytical Society, following his experience in the London Psycho-Analytical Society, Associate Members had to be re-elected each year. If they or their work was not satisfactory, they could just not be re-elected, as obviously had happened to Max Schur.
2 On 19 January 1944, the Society was notified that the following Members had been elected to the Child Welfare Committee: Major John Bowlby, Dr Marjorie Franklin, Dr Kate Friedlander, Dr W. H. Gillespie, Mrs Susan Isaacs, Major Clifford Scott, and Dr D. W. Winnicott.

9

Paper by Paula Heimann on
'Some Aspects of the
Role of Introjection and Projection
in Early Development'

British Psycho-Analytical Society

96 Gloucester Place,
London, W.1.

NOTICE TO MEMBERS AND ASSOCIATE MEMBERS

A meeting of Members and Associate Members will be held on Wednesday, June 23rd, 1943, at 8 p.m., at 96 Gloucester Place, London, W.1. This is the sixth of the Series of Scientific Discussions on controversial topics existing within the Society and the second paper given in that series.

Copy of the paper is enclosed herewith. For rules governing procedure at this meeting see [page 502]. This discussion on Mrs Susan Isaacs' paper was concluded at the meeting held on May 19th. Copy of Mrs Isaacs' reply and the ensuing discussion is enclosed herewith. A note to Members from the Organizing Committee is attached to these minutes.

It was decided at that meeting that Members and Associate Members should be asked to make a further contribution of 10/-d to the cost of duplicating at their earliest convenience. (Cheques should be made payable to the Institute of Psycho-Analysis and not combined with Clinic fees or other payments.) Members are reminded that the Society has decided not to distribute copies of the minutes to those who have not subscribed to the cost.

Edward Glover
Scientific Secretary

RULES GOVERNING DISCUSSION

1   That the principal paper(s) having been previously circulated should be taken as read, but that in the case of papers of 45 minutes' length the author be allowed a period not exceeding 20 minutes to comment on it without however introducing fresh material in this commentary.
2   That those participating in discussion should in the first instance be allowed 10 minutes for this purpose with the right to participate again if time permits.
3   That Members taking part in discussion should bring written statements of their contributions and hand them to the Secretary to enable her to keep as correct records as possible.

'Some Aspects of the Role of Introjection and Projection in Early Development'
by Dr Paula Heimann

(Being the second paper in the series of discussions on controversial topics. As on the previous occasion, this paper will be taken as read at the meeting to be held on June 23rd, 1943)

Introduction

For this paper I have singled out a few essential considerations which appear to some of us as inescapable conclusions arising from the fundamental principles of psychoanalysis. Freud's discoveries are the basis of psychoanalysis; consequently, I shall attempt to show how the views I am representing have developed from the application of principles discovered by Freud, though in some instances these were not pursued far by himself. It would be impossible within the scope of this paper to establish adequately all the connections between the concepts of introjection and projection and the many other problems in our work.

For this reason I considered that it would be best to aim at showing the relation of introjection and projection to certain of the fundamental theories and working hypotheses with which psychoanalysis operates: namely,

     I the theory of the Mental Structure;
    II the principle of the Life and Death Instincts;
   III the theory of Object relations.

If this paper throws light on a few fundamental theoretical issues, it may help to pave the way towards detailed clinical discussions in reference to introjection and projection.

I have to add here that since writing my paper I found that even to deal with these topics adequately would make it far too long. It has been necessary, therefore, to omit entirely many considerations which have important bearings on my theme, and to present my material in a manner which cannot avoid appearing both dogmatic and brusque. I regret this, for it will be a handicap both to my theme and to my audience.

In psychoanalytic literature we find a number of terms which are often used as synonyms and yet have slightly different meanings, such as: 'introject', 'establish inside', 'incorporate', 'internalise', 'identify', 'take in', and, conversely: 'project', 'expel', 'reject', 'externalize', 'push out', 'discharge'. Foulkes (1937) made some suggestion as towards determining the use of the various terms, but as no decision has been made I shall use the terms 'introject' and 'project' when referring to the mental mechanisms which are modelled on and correspond to the bodily experiences of taking in and expelling respectively.

i The relation to the mental structure

The psychoanalytical concept of the mind[1] regards it as composed of three main parts differentiated by their functions. The id is the reservoir of the instincts and thus the source of all the instinctual energies: the ego, the interpreter and intermediary between the various parts of the mind and the outside world: and the superego, the internalized representative of the most important objects, the parents. These differentiations are brought about by the fact that the organism exists in a world on which it is dependent by virtue of its instincts: its desire for pleasure, and its need to keep alive and to deflect the death instinct outward.

It seems evident that such an organism, which depends to a great extent on other organisms for attaining its purposes, must become influenced and changed by such contacts. Now what are the mechanisms by which these alterations and changes (differentiations of the original substance) are brought about? Freud gave us the answer to this question in some detail.

Considering the ego first, the following passage from *Beyond the Pleasure Principle* (p. 29) illustrates the change in the ego consequent upon its position:

> Let us imagine a living organism in the simplest possible form as an undifferentiated vesicle of sensitive substance: then its surface, exposed as it is to the outer world, is by its very position differentiated and serves as an organ for receiving stimuli. . . . It would then be easily conceivable that, owing to the constant impact of external stimuli on the superficies of the vesicle, its substance would undergo lasting alterations. . . .
>
> We have more to say about the living vesicle with its receptive outer layer. This . . . operates as a special integument or membrane that keeps off the stimuli. . . . For the living organism, protection against stimuli is almost a more important task than reception of stimuli. . . . The reception of stimuli serves above all the purpose of collecting information about the direction and nature of the external stimuli, and for that it must suffice to take little samples of the outer world, to taste it, so to speak, in small quantities.

He goes on to say that in highly developed organisms portions of the receptive external layer form the sense organs, and 'it is characteristic of them that they assimilate only very small quantities of the outer stimulus, and *take in only samples* of the outer world' (my italics). [Freud, S. 1920: 367; SE 18:27–8][2]

What Freud describes in these and other passages is that the ego, the surface part of the id, comes into being and functions by means of both *taking things into itself and, conversely, rejecting them from itself* (as other quotations will show). The surface part of the organism on which the stimuli from the outer world impinge is equipped with the capacity of receiving or rejecting them; or, if you like, it comes to develop such capacity. This is its main function for the whole organism. It discharges this function by what might be called the *pars pro toto* principle, namely, by sampling the stimuli, taking in small quantities first, and in this way testing their nature.

The concept of the ego as an organ of reception necessarily led Freud to attribute perception to it; the Pcpt system is the nucleus of the ego. 'It clearly starts out from its nucleus, the system Pcpt.' . . .

'In the ego perception plays the part which in the id devolves upon instinct.' [Freud, S. 1923b: 27,30; SE 19:23,25][3]

How does perception work? 'Upon our hypothesis perception is not a merely passive process; we believe rather that the ego periodically sends out small amounts of cathectic energy into the perceptual system and by their means samples the external stimuli, and after every such groping advance draws back again.' [Freud, S. 1925: 370; SE 19:238][4]

The function of perception is bound up with consciousness, which heightens perception and vice versa. In their service various other mental operations develop after the institution of the reality-principles: attention, notation, memory. [Freud, S. 1911a:15; SE 12:18] Attention leads to a familiarity with the data in the outer world and it serves as a precautionary measure. This 'searching' of the outer world in order to obtain familiarity has to be ranged alongside the reception of stimuli, which 'serves above all the purpose of collecting information'. Thus the mechanism of taking in recurs in the operation of attention. Notation and memory appear as further steps, subsequent to the taking in; what has been received is stored and deposited for further use. Perception appears as the first mode of intake of a stimulus, engendering attention to obtain familiarity; notation and memory represent the storing of the collected information.

The function of keeping out dangerous stimuli ascribed to the barrier against stimuli is akin to the function of discharge and expulsion, etc. It forestalls an intake which would later necessitate expulsion. (Actually it *is* an expulsion, in so far as the decision not to let in the dangerous stimulus presupposes that a small sample of it has been taken in, decided upon as being bad and expelled, and the whole from which the sample was taken kept out, in consequence of the judgement. Freud actually compared this with eating, as follows:

'Originally the property to be decided about might be either good or bad, useful or harmful. Expressed in the language of the oldest, that is, of the oral instinctual impulses, the alternative runs thus: "I should like to eat that, or I should like to spit it out"; or, carried a stage further: "I should like to take this into me and keep that out of me".' [Freud, S. 1925: 368; SE 19:238][5] This passage goes on to show that the original pleasure-ego tries to 'introject' into itself everything that is good, and to reject from itself what is bad. Thus eating and spitting out, taking in or keeping out, introjecting or projecting are the fundamental patterns, the original instinctual activities and mental mechanisms on which the life and development of the organism is based. 'The objects presenting themselves, in so far as they are sources of pleasure, are absorbed by the ego into itself, "introjected" (according to an expression coined by Ferenczi); while, on the other hand, the ego thrusts forth upon the external world whatever within itself gives rise to pain (the mechanism of projection).' [Freud, S. 1915a:78; SE 14:136][6] Ferenczi (1913:213–14), who introduced the concept of introjection, held that every expansion of the circle of interest represented an introjection, in which Mrs Klein follows him.

Observation of the baby shows quite directly how he gets to know the outside world. He devotes an intense attention to his surroundings (to the objects around him) and gets to know them step by step and bit by bit. The modification of his mental apparatus through this function of attention and of his 'tasting' the stimuli comes about by his taking in with his mouth and hands and eyes and ears, every object which attracts his attention. It did not need psychoanalysis to discover that a baby takes everything into his mouth! His first attempts to make acquaintance with any new thing are expressed in efforts to take hold of it and suck or taste it. As he does so, he actually introjects it; in his experience he incorporates it, sucks it in, eats it up. (Cp. Freud: 'I should like to eat that'. . . . 'I should like to take this into me. . . .') The evidence of this familiar observation is that the way in which the baby takes in the outer world is on the oral pattern and is bound up with introjection. Thus the function of attention, which, according to Freud, is instrumental for the modification of the mental apparatus, follows the pattern of oral incorporation. And this is not surprising since the oral libido is in the ascendant at this time of life.

In *The Ego and the Id*, Freud states that when he explained the disorder of melancholia by means of the concept of introjection, it was not known how common and how typical this process (of introjection) is. He goes on to allot to introjection a great share in determining the form taken on by the ego and states that it contributes materially towards building up its character. The next sentence deals with the primitive oral phase in which object-cathexis and identification (introjection) can hardly be differentiated from each other. It seems very significant that Freud brings into such close connection the building up of the character of the ego, to which introjection materially contributes, the 'very beginning' of the individual's existence, and the oral phase. (This connection between character and introjection is emphasized at various places in Freud's writings.) He goes on to say that the *introjection* of melancholia 'is a kind of regression to *the mechanism of the oral phase*', and that 'the process, *especially in the early phase of development,* is a very frequent one, and it points to the conclusion that the character of the ego is a *precipitate* of abandoned object-cathexes and that it contains a *record* of past object-choices' (my italics). [Freud, S. 1923b:35; SE 19:29–30][7] Melanie Klein's researches fully confirmed this conclusion; her work with young children has shown that the earliest relation to an object is effected by means of introjecting it.

Our understanding of the complicated processes and conditions of the mind has been made easier by Freud's comparison of it with the simplest organism, the amoeba, [Freud, S. 1914:33; SE 14:74] and by his showing us that the mind is to be regarded as a living organism subject to the same general biological laws. The amoeba is an undifferentiated mass of living substance which accomplishes the intake of food and excretion of the products of metabolism by means of forming temporary organs which disappear again when the function has been carried out, and by movements – functions which corrrespond to the processes of perception, sampling, and rejection. The human being, the highest form of the species of living substance, strikes us as being very different from such a unicellular organism; yet it is useful to remember genetic development and to apply the laws of life, which are so clear in a simple organism, to the highest form of life.

I mention this in order to throw into relief my main point, namely, that the most fundamental vital processes of any living organism consist of intake and discharge. The mind, also a living organism, is no exception to this rule: it achieves adaptation and progress by employing throughout its existence the fundamental and basic processes of introjection and projection. Consequently, the mechanism of taking in and expelling, or if we think of their psychical correlates, introjecting and projecting are vital processes of the first magnitude. It may well be that they are the basic processes, not only for maintaining life (as with physical metabolism), but for all differentiations and modifications in any given organism. Such taking in and expelling consists of an active interplay between the organism and the outer world; on this fundamental pattern rests all intercourse between subject and object. I believe that in the last analysis we may find it at bottom of all our complicated dealings with one another. The patterns Nature uses seem to be few but she is inexhaustible in their variation.

It is on the basis of these considerations that Melanie Klein and her co-workers regard these processes as having such very great significance; it is their derivation from inherent biological facts that leads us to attribute such essential effects and functions to them (which single them out from other mechanisms) and hence to devote

507

special attention to them in the investigation of mental development. We find them active at any point and any period of development, though differently accentuated at different periods, according to the phase of the libido dominant at the time, namely, to the varying primacies of the instincts. Accordingly they are destined to discharge different functions and to pursue different aims at different periods of development. From the primitive aim of 'eating and spitting out' (Freud), to the nature and super-personal function of procreation, there is a long road to go which involves such modifications that it may be difficult in the final stage to recognize the initial phase, the original pattern.

Only in passing will I mention the necessity for clinical reasons to keep genesis and development in mind. In the Ucs the oral significance of growth and acquisition and the anal significance of loss and gift are maintained; so that under circumstances in which this fundamental pattern becomes reactivated all acquiring means devouring, all giving means spitting, or defecating with the result that guilt and anxiety arise along with these activities. Only if analysis of the Ucs phantasies related to the introjective and projective mechanisms, their interplay with each other and with the many other modes of mental and instinctual activity is never neglected, can one hope to do justice to the complicated context of mental life. The facts of displacement and variation must not deflect attention from the original pattern. I refrain from going into details, but I may just point to the invariable equation between breast and penis, penis and child, child and faeces, and the universal oral theory of sexual intercourse and the anal theory of birth. We know how important these facts are; one of the reasons for their existence is the universal operation of introjection and projection.

Introjection, moreover, according to Freud's explicit statements, is the decisive factor in the formation of the superego, another differentiation within the mind. It is significant that he arrived at his formulation of this mental institution by way of the phenomenon of introjection. There are, however, many direct and emphatic statements in his writings about earlier phenomena of introjection: its frequency, its typical occurrence in early childhood, the modifications in the ego resulting from one ego 'becoming like another' and 'as it were, taking it into itself', introjection as the earliest form of tie to an object, and the lasting effects of the earliest identifications surpassing in importance any which occur later, and so on. (It must be kept in mind that Freud often uses the terms 'introjection' and 'identification' interchangeably.)

Freud assigns superego formation roughly to the fifth year of life, while he places ego-formation very early (the ego is already in existence at the second oral, the narcissistic stage). Thus, according to Freud there would appear to be a gap in the structural development of the child's mind. Yet the abundant references to the earlier phenomena of the same order tell another story, the truth of which is demonstrated by the observations made in early analyses. The conclusion forced upon us (which embodies the general law of the gradual development of all human functions) is that the superego, as described by Freud and distinguished by him with its special name, is the *end-result* of a long process undergoing different phases in close relation to the succeeding phases of instinctual development: '. . . to compensate for this loss of object (parents), its identifications with its parents, which have probably *long been present*, become greatly intensified' (my italics). [Freud, S. 1933a:87; SE 22:64][8]

Freud constantly emphasizes the relation of introjection to the loss of the object. Observation tells us – Freud emphatically describes it – that the experience of early childhood is fraught with the danger of loss of the object (subjectively felt). The subjective experience of losing the mother occurs so frequently for the infant, since 'as soon as he misses his mother he behaves as if he were never going to see her again'. [Freud, S. 1926: 167; SE 20:169][9] That is to say that the younger the child, the more will he be compelled to compensate for the loss of the object (mother) by increasing and utilizing his introjections of her. In such situations the already existing identifications with the object (mentioned by Freud) become increased and the 'becoming like' the other person takes place. Thus we have ample ground to assume on Freud's own statements that the mechanisms which he described explicitly for the formation of the superego at five years of age are in operation throughout early childhood; and to expect that the rudimentary beginnings of a superego will occur in this early period. This is the view of Melanie Klein and her co-workers.[10]

It is true that the early introjected objects differ materially from the later superego. Nevertheless they lead us to it and have certain features in common with it. The earliest introjections establish a protective and a persecuting agency within the mind ('good' and 'bad' breast). This very primitive stage of the superego function is in keeping with the primitive state of the ego. When the ego advances to a perception of the mother as a whole person, and the whole mother is the object of the infant's love, a new element enters into the infant's relation to his incorporated object; guilt (though as yet of a rudimentary kind) and dread of losing the loved object arise, a

509

condition which is characteristic of the superego, as Freud described it.

The prohibitions emanating from the introjected object or objects correspond to the impulses actually dominant at the time; e.g. in the classical Oedipus phase the prohibition is directed against the genital desires for the one parent and the aggressive rivalry against the other; in the anal phase the anal-sadistic, in the oral phase the cannibalistic impulses will be prohibited. (Certain feeding difficulties in early childhood argue an inhibition of greed, i.e. of oral-sadistic impulses.) As regards the anal impulses, Ferenczi pointed out the fact of 'sphincter-morality' and coined the term. The early introjections thus represent the early stages of the later genital superego, which in our view forms the 'apex' of a complete superego system, developing through a long period (to paraphrase an apposite expression which Dr Brierley recently used in respect of the early relation to the mother).

Amongst the many aspects of this exceedingly important problem, which await further discussion, I will select one which relates to my subject-matter. In the superego the identification resulting from introjection is not a complete one, since in some very essential respects the child must *not* be like the parents. Here we see that the process resulting in the institution of the fully developed superego follows the original pattern laid down in the earliest 'sampling' of the external world: the introjection of the parents is a selective process and is not carried out in relation to the whole of them. Some of their aspects become excluded. It seems that this exclusion (so necessary if the purposes of the process – superego formation – are to succeed) must be regarded as akin to projection, following the primary law of expelling or excluding from the organism whatever is harmful. This would be another instance of the structural effect of the introjection–projection pair of opposites.

The role of introjection and projection processes in relation to Freud's scheme of the mind acquires even greater significance when they are considered in their bearing on the primary life and death instincts. If Freud's view of the synthetic and structural function of these processes, particularly at the beginning of life, is taken together with his view of the defence which the life instinct has against the death instinct (deflection outward) a considerable measure of correlation and interrelation begins to emerge.

The life instinct maintains itself in the organism from the beginning and during its development by means of introjection and projection processes. Freud described one of the most momentous of such phenomena with his insight into the derivation of the intellectual function (judgement) from the interplay of the primary insincts, when he showed its systematic development by way of affirmation or denial (of goodness or badness, usefulness or harmfulness in the object), from the primary acts of 'introduction into the ego or expulsion from it' (introjection and projection) – in instinctual terms from 'eating and spitting out'. As regards projection the ultimate *aim* of the life instinct in its struggle with the death instinct would be expulsion; the death instinct, however, cannot be expelled, since it is an inherent component of the organism. The next thing to expulsion is deflection outward. Only the direction or the instinctual drive can be changed. Thus deflection outward became, as Freud showed, the ultimate defence of the life against the death instinct. Introjection and projection are the essential basic mechanisms on which life depends.

Structure and death instinct are antithesis, since the latter aims at a return to an earlier, inanimate condition, whilst the former aims at progress and promotion of life. The mental structure is indeed a means of life, and a very essential means of promoting and safeguarding life. It is hence to be expected that these mechanisms which are most suitable for the maintenance of life and the deflection of the death instinct, i.e. introjection and projection, occupy a special place in the building up of the structure of the mind and find ample occasion to operate and undergo rich variation. The pattern of taking in the good and keeping out, rejecting, deflecting the bad is fundamental for life and the structure of the mind.

ii The life and death instincts

The role of the inner stimuli ('needs') must now be considered, particularly since the instincts play an essential part in the operation of introjection and projection. Both the formation of the mental structure and its subsequent functioning depend upon a balance being kept between the primary instincts. Here we have to face the fact that the aims of the instincts to which the organism is subject are in opposition to one another; in other words, that we deal with an organism which is by its very nature in a condition of conflict.

At the beginning of his clinical work, Freud discovered that psychical conflict is at the root of all neurotic symptoms – a discovery which was destined to alter the face of psychology. He came to postulate the existence of antithetical instincts, whose operation compels the mental apparatus to adopt various strategic techniques; mechanisms of defence, of adaptation, modification, and compromise. These antithetical instincts he ultimately formulated as

511

the two primal instincts of life and death. Freud himself, as we know, hesitated to give full recognition to his last discovery; yet he was driven on inexorably by its inherent impelling truth to perceive the implication of a primal antithesis between a life instinct and a death instinct, whose fusion and defusion account for the phenomenon we call life.

Here I would place a first and fundamental point of divergence in analytic thought and word. Acceptance of the theory of the death instinct brings about a different approach to the manifestations of destructiveness, the inter-play of love and hate, in fact, to all psychological phenomena, from that obtaining when psychical conflicts are not traced back to an antithesis as final and cardinal as that of these inherently conflicting primal instincts. One conceives of the human mind as being by its very nature compelled to manipulate constantly between two fundamentally opposed instincts, from which all emotions, sensations, desires, and activities derive. It can never escape conflict, can never be static, but must always go on, one way or another, must always employ devices to mediate between its antithetical drives. And since the instincts are inborn, we have to conclude that some form of conflict exists from the beginning of life.[11]

Our assessment of environmental factors is different, too, from this standpoint. The impact of external stimuli falls upon a subject who is assailed by stimuli from within, and the significance of accidental experiences can only be appreciated if the intrapsychic background of conflict is taken into consideration as well. In the same way in which the imperative nature of the sexual instincts can only be grasped after recognition of them as the carriers of the life instinct, so the destructive manifestations can only be seen adequately in perspective when we keep in mind that they are ultimately a 'deflection outward' of the death instinct. Our understanding of the position of the individual with whom we are dealing becomes more poignant when we become aware of the source from which his destructiveness springs. It is by no means merely an academic question whether we accept the theory of the death instinct, for it cannot fail to influence profoundly our practical work; e.g. our understanding of the negative transference rests on a different basis in the light of this theory, which also holds out a prospect of fuller comprehension of the difficult problems of projection and persecution symptoms.

Aggressive instinctual manifestations were, as we know, soon discovered by Freud, and Abraham added greatly to our knowledge of them; but even so they never received that full investigation which

512

the libido and its development had found. Analytic theory has treated the two instincts in an unusual manner: the libido is the first-born and privileged child, the destructive instinct is the late-comer, the stepchild. Libido was recognized as such from the first; the other instinct, its adversary, went under various disguises, and had several names before its true identity was established.

One of the foundation-stones of psychoanalysis is the principle that in its operation the libido is attached to the physiological functions. This discovery, though readily enough accepted and though its usefulness is established beyond doubt, appears to have implications which are not yet fully worked out. I shall return to this point in a moment. All the familiar phenomena of oral, anal, muscular, etc. erotisms, as well as those of the libidinal ties formed towards the object who satisfies the physiological needs, exemplify, as we know, the libido's attachment to bodily functions. But when, from the analytic evidence of acute conflicts in very young children, Melanie Klein came to devote full attention to the destructive impulses, she was led directly to the conclusion that these impulses behave exactly as does the libido. She realized that they are the expression – deflected outwards – of the otherwise inarticulate death instinct operating the same way as the libido through the bodily functions and towards the objects of the bodily needs. Thus it became necessary to apply the same which concerns the libido also to the destructive instinct, and to recognize it in the sadistic elements of bodily function, and in the sadistic relation to the object satisfying these functions.

In the light of these findings it can be seen that Freud here did more than discover a character of the libido: he stated a special case of a broader principle, which concerns the mode of operation of instinct in general and which rests upon the fact that the human organism is a mind–body entity. The instincts are the source of the energies on which all the mind–body processes depend. They lie, as we know, on the borderland between soma and psyche; they are Janus-faced, one face turns to the bodily, the other to the mental facet of the organism. Both the instincts – the libido and the destructive instinct – seek to fulfil their aims in bodily activities, just as, conversely, the mental functions derive from them both (as Freud described in detail in 'Negation'). In the same way, because the instincts are mind–body processes, mental experiences are bound to take place alongside the operation of the instincts in the body, and a mental–emotional relationship must follow in the wake of the bodily activities towards the object who gratifies them, i.e. ties of both a libidinal and a destructive kind are formed towards the first object. As we know,

513

the mental emotional relation to the object develops 'anaclitically', that is, in dependence on the physical satisfaction which the object gives (or does not give) to the child, and it reflects in turn the object's attitude, which too combines a physical with a mental activity. It goes without saying that the mother who feeds a child experiences not only a physical sensation, nor does she offer the child a physical substance only. First love and first hate are closely knit with the sensations aroused when bodily needs demand satisfaction. Indeed, the terms 'oral-sadistic' and 'anal-sadistic', though coined at a time when cruelty was regarded as a component impulse of the libido and before it was recognized as a derivative of a primary instinct of destruction, would actually imply that the destructive instinct is attached to the same functions as the libido.

These considerations should, I believe, make it easier to understand both the libidinal and the destructive phantasies bound up with, let us say, eating and excreting, which Melanie Klein has found in her analyses of young children. The theme would lead on to the considerations adduced by Mrs Isaacs in discussing the nature and function of phantasy as the mental correlate of instinct; the view she put forward rests ultimately on the observed fact that libido attaches itself to the physiological functions. In other words, this observation tells us that love and desire for love accompany bodily needs.

There is another basic contention in the libido-theory which is intimately bound up with the attachment of the libido to the physiological functions, namely, that of erotogenicity of practically all organs. Here, too, Melanie Klein's discoveries show that what holds good for the life instinct also holds for the death instinct, i.e. that those organs capable of producing libidinal sensations will also be the seat of those which accompany the discharge of destructive instinctual tensions. Joan Riviere (Riviere 1936) has described some of the destructive charges of various organs: 'Limbs shall trample, hit and kick; lips, fingers and hands shall suck, twist, pinch; teeth shall bite, gnaw, mangle and cut; mouth shall devour, swallow and "kill" (annihilate); eyes kill by a look, pierce and penetrate, breath and mouth hurt by noise, as the child's own sensitive ears have experienced.' We might say all bodily functions are based on instinctual activities, bound to serve two masters, the life instinct and death instinct. Full recognition of the theory of the primary instincts leads to the conclusion that, since these instincts operate in a condition of fusion, each part of the body will partake of both, or will be utilized by both. It may well be that the predominance of either instinct decides the issue, whether the activity is 'healthy' or a 'morbid' one.[12]

514

It might be objected that my remarks about these basic principles of instinct-theory have nothing to do with my theme. But their bearing on the problems of introjection and projection will become clearer, when the relation of objects is under consideration, for these mechanisms are both prompted by instinctual urges and also presuppose objects.

In the frame of Freud's libido-theory introjection occupies the first place amongst the mental mechanisms of the oral phase, and projection (expulsion) does so in the anal phase of the libido. Keeping in mind that the general character of instinct is that it occurs in pairs of opposites, however, we shall be warned against a too dogmatic separation of mechanisms based on them. Moreover, the aim of these processes is complementary: '. . . the original pleasure-ego tries to introject into itself everything that is good and to reject from itself everything that is bad.' [Freud, S. 1925: 369; SE 19:237][13] Freud's words here depict the aim of introjection and projection on the basis of a predominance of the life instinct. It is against the background of these principles that the significance of the phenomena of introjection and projection is thrown into proper relief.

iii The early relation to objects

No chapter of the intricate book of human problems has been enriched so much by Melanie Klein's researches as that which deals with the individual's relation to objects. Dr Brierley recently expressed the view: 'Taken in conjunction with the earlier quoted statement that the "ego is a precipitate of abandoned object-cathexes" we have grounds in Freud's own work for thinking that the object-aspect of instinct calls for close scrutiny.' (Brierley 1942: 111) It is precisely this 'close scrutiny' which Melanie Klein has devoted to the investigation of mental processes, and which has thrown into relief the paramount significance of object-cathexes from the beginning of life.

It must be borne in mind that the child's perception and conception of an object varies considerably according to his stage of development. His relations to objects are in the beginning distorted by subjective urges and phantasies, and proceed gradually through the whole course of development to the true perception and mature conception of another being as another individual in his own right, independent of the subject's needs and wishes. This development is concurrent with that of the instincts.

One essential aspect of Melanie Klein's work concerns 'internal

515

objects'. In order to present her views on this topic and on the introjective and projective mechanisms in the earliest stages of development, I wish first to summarize Freud's view on auto-erotism and narcissism.

Freud describes auto-erotism as the first phase of infantile sexuality. In this phase the child's libido turns to a part of his own body, an erotogenic zone, and he derives libidinal gratification from it, independently of another person. The most frequent example of such auto-erotic activity is that of the infant sucking his thumb. Freud states: 'It is, moreover, clear that the action of the thumb sucking in a child is determined by the fact that it seeks a pleasure which has already been experienced and is now remembered. . . . The first and most important activity in the child's life, the sucking from the mother's breast (or its substitute) must have acquainted it with this pleasure.' [Freud, S. 1905: 42; SE 7:181][14]

In his recently translated Encyclopaedia articles Freud says: 'In the first instance the oral component instinct finds satisfaction "anaclitically" – on the basis of the satiation of the desire for nourishment; and its object is the mother's breast. It then detaches itself, becomes independent and at the same time auto-erotic, that is, finds an object in the child's own body.' [Freud, S. 1923a: 101; SE 18: 245][15]

But whilst the child is capable of these intense auto-erotic gratifications, he still maintains his capacity to turn his libido to the external object. Many non-analytic authors record observations which would support this view. Among analytic writers Bernfeld says: 'the primary form of organisation of the libido is narcissistic, a given condition in the infant. . . . *But one need not succumb to the idea that the entire libido is narcissistic even in the grasping period.*' (My italics.) [Bernfeld 1929:202]

The libido is not entirely withdrawn from objects in the outer world, for throughout the auto-erotic phase a part of the libido adheres to objects, it is not for food only that the infant turns to the breast.[16] The separation of the desire for food from that for libidinal gratification which Freud postulated (as a step in development) does not mean that the activity of feeding is altogether divorced from libidinal gratification. We know that eating maintains throughout life a libidinal element – indeed the close affinity between the self-preservative instincts and the libido is explicitly stated in Freud's concept of the primary life instinct.

Thus, according to Freud, at the beginning there is an object relation, for the instinct 'in the first instance' attaches itself to an object in the outside world. At many places Freud emphasizes the paramount significance of this object for the individual's whole life.

He calls the pleasure experienced at the breast the 'unattainable prototype of every later sexual satisfaction'. [Freud, S. 1916–17:264; SE 20:314][17]

What is the fate of this first instinctual experience of the libidinal cathexis of the breast? The inference from Freud's own pronouncement is that the auto-erotic phase follows a period in which the infant's libido is attached to an external object, the mother's breast. Freud left unsolved the problem of what happens to this intense and fundamental relation when the child enters upon the auto-erotic phase.

Melanie Klein holds that this relation which provides the most intense libidinal gratification, and a gratification which (according to Freud) is retained for ever in the unconscious, is not given up in the auto-erotic phase. Wnat happens is that the breast is introjected and the intense sensations and feelings, experienced when sucking at it, become attached to the introjected breast. This internalized breast forms a core for all further object relations. The conclusion that the earliest object relations are bound up with introjection is in accordance with views expressed by Freud in many places of his writings. When referring to the superego Freud says: 'The basis of the process is what we call an identification, that is to say, that one ego becomes like another, which results in the first ego behaving itself in certain respects in the same way as the second; it imitates it, and as it were takes it into itself. This identification has been not inappropriately compared with the oral cannibalistic incorporation of another person. Identification is a very important kind of relationship with another person, probably the most primitive.' [Freud, S. 1933a: 87; SE 22:63][18]

Introjection, however, appears to be the condition on which the withdrawal from an object in the outer world can take place. 'It may be that by undertaking this introjection, which is a kind of regression to the mechanism of the oral phase, the ego makes it easier for an object to be given up or renders that process possible. It may even be that this identification is the sole condition under which the id can give up its objects. At any rate the process, especially in the early phases of development, is a very frequent one.' [Freud, S. 1923b:24; SE 19:29][19]

In our view the introjected breast is the object of the infant's auto-erotic wishes and experiences. When turning away from the external object, the infant turns to the object which he has taken into himself. He can now behave as if he himself (i.e. parts of his own body) were this object; that is to say, he can now satisfy himself, as previously the external object satisfied him.

517

Turning now to narcissism: this represents a somewhat later stage than auto-erotism, since 'it is impossible to assume that a unity comparable to the ego can exist in the individual from the very start; the ego has to develop. But the auto-erotic instincts are primordial; so there must be something added to auto-eroticism – some new operation in the mind – in order that narcissism may come into being.' [Freud, S. 1914:34; SE 14:77][20]

What is this 'new operation'? In order to answer this question we have to look at the history of psychoanalytic thought. The concept of narcissism was introduced in 1914, that is to say long before the theory of the structure of the mind (and hence of the mental operations leading to that structure) was formulated in *The Ego and the Id*, 1923; before the mechanism of introjection was embodied in 'Mourning and Melancholia', 1917; and further before the classification of the instincts was achieved in *Beyond the Pleasure Principle*, 1920.

Thus the theory of narcissism was established long before Freud had found the solution to some of the most crucial problems. In our approach to narcissism (and auto-erotism for that matter) today we have at our disposal many more facts than were available in 1914. It is evident that the 'new operation in the mind' which changes auto-erotism into narcissism concerns the formation of the ego. Now from Freud's later work we know that the ego, 'the precipitate of abandoned object-cathexes', comes into being by introjection (and projection). Since in narcissism there exists an ego, it follows that objects have already been established within the mind. In our view the introjective processes involve a displacement of the libido from the external (abandoned) object on to the internal object, and the narcissistic condition is bound up with a libidinal cathexis of internal objects. We also differ from Freud's view in another point, since we assume that the ego-formation is a continuous process, and one initiated by the first introjections. On this account, therefore, we should not draw a sharp line between auto-erotism and narcissism. As far as ego-development is concerned, we see the difference between the two conditions in terms of degree; they are at variance in all those respects which depend on the stage of ego-development.

I wish to consider now the distribution of libido and aggression in auto-erotism and narcissism. Auto-erotism is characterized by the predominance of the libido (as the term denotes), whereas narcissism shows a stronger admixture of aggressive trends. Some of Freud's statements seem to support this view; for example:

The relation of hate to objects is older than that of love. It is derived from the primal repudiation by the narcissistic ego of the external world whence flows the stream of stimuli.

[Freud, S. 1915a:82; SE 14:139][21]

Further:

. . . it seemed as though this kind of narcissistic attitude in them [the patients] was one of the factors limiting their susceptibility to influence.

[Freud, S. 1914:30; SE 14:73][22]

This limitation of the susceptibility to influence led to the long-maintained opinion that narcissistic patients could not be analysed; but later work, done particularly in this country, showed that this narcissistic repudiation is due to hostility, which expresses itself as negative transference and proves – in many cases – accessible to analysis.

Viewed from another angle, auto-erotism belongs to the oral-sucking stage (Abraham), and narcissism to the later, the oral-biting stage which coincides with the 'phase of maximal sadism'. (Klein 1936:123–48) Since auto-erotism is the earlier of the two phases, the object of the libido is still a part-object, whereas in narcissism the relation to whole objects has already started. This fact accounts to some extent for the greater hostility of this later period, as the reality-principle is now more strongly established including the important relation to whole objects with full ambivalence. (Klein 1935: 173) The increased reality sense means that the narcissistic ego has a more advanced capacity for perception which includes that of the unpleasant inner stimuli and a lessened capacity for hallucinatory gratification.

Hallucinatory gratification may be considered as the supreme instance of auto-erotic activity. The baby who screams in hunger and discomfort will suddenly stop screaming and start sucking his finger or another part of his body, and the expression on his face leaves no doubt as to the intense gratification which he experiences. But when Freud gave to such behaviour the name 'Hallucinatory gratification', he clearly did not think that the baby was merely experiencing pleasure. This auto-erotic gratification is evoked by pain, and the pain is not combated by real means, but by hallucination. The infant thus copes with frustration by a method which is determined by the pleasure principle, and in which 'whatever was thought of (desired) was simply imagined in an hallucinatory form'. [Freud, S. 1911a: 14; SE 12:219.][23] Freud defined the difference between recollection and hallucination: an hallucination occurs when the cathexis passes over

519

entirely from the memory-trace to the Pcpt. element. [Freud, S. 1923b: 22; SE 19:20]

In speaking of 'hallucination', therefore, we imply that in the past the infant really experienced such gratification from his mother, and that the memory of this experience – which is the basis of the hallucination – plays a decisive role in the whole process. As soon as the infant experiences gratification at the breast, a memory-trace of this experience is laid down which subsequent repetitions carve out ever deeper. But at the same time he also introjects the breast. This gratification, feeding and libidinal pleasure at the breast, is what is thought of (desired) in an hallucinatory form. Melanie Klein maintains that hallucinatory gratification is based on the relation to a 'good' inner breast, which the infant rediscovers in a part of his own body. The breast, this 'source of pleasure', has been 'absorbed by the ego into itself'; the infant feels this 'good' object inside himself, and therefore he has it at his beck and call, can omnipotently manipulate it and deny the actual condition of pain. This inner 'good' object has such a strong psychic reality that for the time being the peremptory need for the real breast can be stifled, overpowered, successfully denied, and/or projected outside. The inner breast accounts for the independent character of the auto-erotic gratification.

In this connection we must have regard to an economic consideration. It seems plausible to assume that the hallucinatory gratification is stronger when its object is a part, i.e. the nipple, than when it is a whole person; for the nipple was really 'inside' the infant, completely enclosed by the lips, the gums, and the tongue. It may well be that in the earlier phase (part-object relation) a greater quantity of libidinal gratification is experienced than in the later phase when the whole object is cathected and tactual sensations are more dispersed.

Hallucinatory gratification is thus only apparently lacking an object. In fact only the external object is given up, but in phantasy there exists an object.

I would say that the phenomenon of hallucination in general loses much of its strangeness if we connect it with introjection and projection. The person who hallucinates an object would thus be able to do so, because he feels actually this object inside himself and projects it outside, where he perceives it as if it were really there.

To summarize a few essential points in which our views concur with Freud's concept of auto-erotism and narcissism:

1 Object-libidinal experiences precede the auto-erotic phase [see p. 516];

2 Auto-erotic gratification is based on memories [see p. 516];
3 Narcissism presupposes a more advanced stage of ego-development [see p. 518] which is responsible for the greater element of aggression (destructive instinct).

Our views differ from Freud's explicit statements in the following points:

1 that in auto-erotism and narcissism libido is turned upon an introjected object which is represented by the infant's own body;
2 that in both conditions unconscious phantasy is operative;
3 that as regards ego-formation the difference between auto-erotism and narcissism is in terms of degree. We do not believe that narcissism comes into being by a sudden 'new operation in the mind'.
4 We hold that the libido is not entirely withdrawn from the external object.

Consequently, in our view, the auto-erotic and narcissistic phases are less absolute, that is to say, not so completely devoid of *external* object relations as the terms auto-erotic and narcissistic 'phase of development' seem to imply. We do not believe that there is a clearly demarcated phase of several months (Miss Freud recently suggested the first six months of life) in which the libido has an exclusively auto-erotic or narcissistic character. We do believe that the first few months are distinguished by the occurrence of transitory states of an auto-erotic or narcissistic nature, which attain their peak during this period. The infant's auto-erotic and narcissistic withdrawal is not continuous, he returns again and again to the breast, and his relation to his real mother steadily develops during those early months, as everyday observation shows without doubt.

I wish to remind you here of that narcissistic condition which is never given up, namely sleep. Here we have a withdrawal from the outer world, and an egoistic concentration upon ourselves – we, the dreamers, are always the leading figures. But does this narcissistic condition lack objects? What a multitude of objects there are in our dreams and what a complexity of relationships is revealed in the midst of a highly narcissistic hallucinatory activity!

One might say that auto-erotic gratification associated with phantasies of having a good breast (mother) inside, paves the way for the return to the external object because these phantasies alleviate the frustration caused by the mother's absence, and thus help the infant to preserve the memory of a 'good' breast which he rediscovers in

521

the outer world again and again. Up to a point the relation to the internal object thus promotes that to the outer world.

As both memory and hallucination are ultimately derived from the external object, they can lead back to it. This is one of the many aspects (beneficial or detrimental) of the interplay between the phantasies about internal objects and the relation to real people, whose exploration is an essential part of Mrs Klein's contribution to psychoanalysis.

Introjection proves a fateful step in development. With regard to its effects on physic dynamics it may be compared to regression: in that it necessitates a constant expenditure of mental energy. It is not an event which is over and done with. Once it has taken place, for it starts processes which involve all spheres of mental life (and even influence physical life to some extent), an inner world comes into being. The infant feels that there are parts of people and whole people inside his own body, who are alive and active, and affect him and are affected by him. Sensations, feelings, moods, affects are dominated by his relation to his inner objects. In fact, these phantasies exert an influence on all his mental functions: perception, attention, judgement, reality testing, and the relation to people and things. Ultimately these phantasies are based on the infant's impulses and during the early phase when the instincts are polymorph, they are uncoordinated, contradictory, and change swiftly from one extreme to the other, and reflect the outer world in extreme distortions. They become modified in accordance with the modifications which the instincts undergo and with the progressive organization of the ego.

In auto–erotism it is predominantly a 'good' inner breast to which the infant withdraws from his condition of frustration. But this victory of mind over body of a pleasurable phantasy over a painful reality is only short-lived; the painful reality reasserts itself. I think it not unlikely that the moment at which the hallucination comes to an end, and the ego is compelled to perceive the painful inner stimulus, coincides with a change in the phantasies about the inner breast. There is no longer a 'good' inner breast, there is a 'bad' breast, and the infant turns from it to the external breast. Thus 'good' breast and 'bad' breast, inner breast and outer breast appear in his feeling and phantasy in close alternation. The whole mental life of the infant revolves about and develops from the phantasies of a 'good' and a 'bad' breast in the inner and the outer world. Primitive though this intense and exclusive concern may appear, measured by the standards of adult interests and relationships, it is rich in affect and full of meaning to the infant.

The quick changes from good to bad feelings, good to bad objects and vice versa – both probably to an extreme degree – are specific for the experiences of early infantile life. But the capacity to accept a good and satisfactory object after frustration depends on a satisfactory balance between projective and introjective mechanisms. The experience of gratification at the mother's breast after frustration has far reaching effects in developing the infant's confidence that bad things go and good things come. Alternation between frustration and gratification is repeated again and again, and thus the pattern becomes established of a turning from the inner to the outer world and vice versa; and as the earliest experiences lay the foundations for the type of response to people and events, those who have learned in infancy that frustration and anxiety can be quickly removed approach life with an optimistic attitude, and are capable of recovering from disappointments.

Normally the feeling of persecution by a 'bad' inner breast stimulates the wish to expel the 'bad' breast and to take in a 'good' breast and so helps to establish contact with the outer world. But disturbances of various kinds may arise. The capacity to expel 'bad' objects and feelings may be inhibited. (We regard such inhibition as the result of a failure to turn aggression outward ultimately a failure on the part of the ego to cope with – master – the death instinct.) This leads to a feeling in the baby that his inside is filled with powerful 'bad' objects, which is one of the phantasies associated with the sense of intolerable inner tension, as we see clearly in the analysis of children and adults. But when everything within has turned bad there may seem to be no hope of something good from outside either. In the infant this is shown by a reduced capacity to introject so that a vicious circle is created: the continuance of the bad inner condition due to failure of projection leads to failure of introjection and so further increases the fear of persecution.

In our view the disturbances in introjection and projection play a decisive role in early neurotic symptoms, phobias, and inhibitions in feeding (feeble, listless sucking, incapacity to hold the nipple, refusal of the breast, exaggerated response to slight obstacles, difficulties in the excretory functions, etc.). In some cases disturbances in introjection and projection, observed in early infancy, persisted in such a way that those functions which are built upon or closely connected with these processes become affected. Development as a whole may become retarded, since perception, attention, interest, together with the ability to be influenced by people and things, are largely dependent on introjection and projection. An extreme case of this kind has been described by Melanie Klein in her paper 'The

523

Importance of Symbol-Formation in the Development of the Ego'
(Klein 1930).

The strength of inner needs, the immaturity of the mental
apparatus, and the weakness of the sense of reality dovetail to
produce a characteristic relation to objects; gratification is attributed
to a good, pain to a bad breast; it is always an object which is made
responsible. This is an example of the animistic thinking which
Freud describes as characteristic both of primitive men and of
infants. (*Totem and Taboo*) That this mode of thinking is not confined
to savages and infants need hardly be stressed. 'In many social strata,
even to this day, no one can die without having been done to death
by someone else, preferably by the doctor.' [Freud, S. 1933a:33; SE
22:122][24] The infant who knows only one object, the breast, ascribes
his pain to persecution by a 'bad' breast, and his pleasure to love
emanating from a 'good' breast.

There is another primitive conviction which, I think, originates in
this period of life, i.e. the belief in the omnipotence of feelings,
wishes and thoughts. The belief that there are objects in one's own
inside equates mental operations with motor actions. In this phantasy
world the inner objects are as much affected by inner processes
(feelings, wishes) as are people in the world of objective reality by
actions. In subjective experience, therefore, it is true that feelings are
all powerful; e.g. hostile feelings constitute an attack on the inner
object which retaliates as a real person would for hostile actions. The
strength of the character of such retaliation corresponds to those of
the primitive sadistic attacks.

We assume that during the first few months of life there exists in
phantasy a 'good' breast side by side with a 'bad' breast, and the
introjection and projection mechanisms work in a relatively simple
manner: the 'good' breast is introjected and kept inside, the 'bad'
breast projected. With the growth of the ego and of its perceptive
and synthetic functions, object relation advances gradually to the
level of whole objects. This step complicates the introjection and
projection mechanisms because it gives rise to new anxieties which
devolve upon the loss of the 'good' object. Whenever 'good' and
'bad' are not distributed to two different objects, but are aspects of
one and the same, the fear of expelling the 'good' with the 'bad'
comes into being, and conversely, of taking in the 'bad' with the
'good'. Such anxiety may either impede introjection and projection
and retard mental development, or cause a rapid alternation of these
processes – a frantic taking in and expelling of objects which
interferes with the establishment of a stable attachment to the
surroundings. Anxiety also arises in connection with the fuller love

which develops with the perception of the mother as a whole person. We believe that the infant feels a rudimentary love towards the gratifying breast, but that the affection for the whole person adds to this love and develops it greatly. The oral libido, however, is still predominant, and the desire of this period is to incorporate the loved object. The mouth at the same time is the main organ for the discharge of the destructive impulses, and the more the destructive capacities of the introjecting organ are felt, the greater is the fear of losing the loved object in the very process which aims at its possession. (Some elements of this early situation are present in tantrums with which we are familiar in the older child and which are characterized by simultaneous craving for comfort and gratification and impossibility of acceptance.) The fear of losing the loved object may be aroused in a variety of ways. The introduction of the mother as a whole person into the scene widens the whole field of the infant's conflicts while at the same time the complexity of the interacting factors is greatly increased and creates a critical situation, in which the child must deal with guilt, grief, reparation – wishes, etc. while he is trying to incorporate and still preserve his loved mother. The earlier anxiety of damaging the 'good' breast and of retaliation develops into the far stronger and more complex guilt anxiety of destroying and losing the loved mother. These are some of the elements which constitute the 'infantile depressive position', to deal with which, however, is beyond the scope of this paper. It is noteworthy that introjection and projection which have been the predominant means of protecting against object-loss (Glover 1932:15)[25] lead at this point to such severe anxieties that the ego is compelled to devise and employ various other defence mechanisms which are of great significance for the development. To mention a few of the early defence mechanisms: various forms of denial of psychic and objective reality, scotomization, splitting and re-uniting of objects, stifling of love feelings and of emotions in general. These again are outside the limits of this paper.

The picture of the instinctual and emotional life at this stage is, as I said, of the utmost complexity. The relation to and introjection of whole objects introduces love feelings of a more advanced kind with feelings of concern for the object; but the relation to part-objects still goes on, with the primitive oral impulses, both greedy and sadistic, dominating the scene. More and more objects are drawn into the circle of the child's interest, and the father and the important mother–father combination play an ever increasing part.

In seeking gratification from his own body the infant discovers more of his erotogenic zones, and anal and genital sensations and phantasies make their appearance. The father's penis becomes a new object of desire, but this desire is shaped in an oral mould, that is to say the leading aim is to incorporate it. The inevitable oral frustrations, experienced in relation to the mother, further impel the child to turn to his father, whose penis becomes introjected along the unconscious equation: breast–penis. This simultaneous relation to both parents (and their most characteristic parts, breast and penis) introduces jealousy and rivalry which derive from oral envy and greed. (Freud described the intense jealousy of a child of eleven months in relation to a new brother or sister. [Freud, S. 1933a: 157–8; SE 22:123] In our view, such rival hatred is felt also to the parent to whom the infant ascribes the possession of the organ which is withheld from him.) Melanie Klein regards this situation, which is characterized by libidinal desires comprising genital trends towards one parent and rivalry hatred against the other, as the early stage of the Oedipus complex, and since she lays stress on the accompanying introjections of the parents she places the superego formation side by side with the Oedipus complex. According to this view, the first roots of the superego are to be found in the introjected 'good' and 'bad' breast, to which are added the 'good' and 'bad' parents and the 'good' and 'bad' penis; the building up of the superego proceeds in stages concurrently with the development of the integrating function of the ego, until it takes the shape under which Freud discovered it.

Before concluding my paper I would like very briefly to indicate what I believe to be the role of introjection and projection in further development. I hope I made it clear that we regard these mechanisms as being of unique significance for the structure and progress of the mental apparatus, and that we see them at work throughout life.

Although these processes retain the function of introducing into the ego what is 'good and useful' and removing what is 'bad and harmful', yet in the course of development other functions are added to this primary one. With the widening of the object world, the expansion of the ego and the increasing mastery of the destructive instinct, the attitude towards the desired object changes so that the wish to give gains in strength and the gratification of giving rivals that of receiving; projection can now refer to something good as well. In adult sexual intercourse and procreation I would see the physical pattern of this mental attitude. To project something good, or even to introject something bad, out of love, is very different from doing the same thing because no discrimination can be made. The former is in the service of the life instinct whereas in the latter we see the predominance of the death instinct. The criterion of normality and maturity in terms of introjection and projection appears to be the ability to maintain a balance between the fundamental original mode of operation and its later modifications.

This change in the picture is furthermore due to a widening in the range of desire and hence of introjection; for the concept of 'good' increasingly includes intellectual, artistic, and other values, notwith-standing the fact that in the unconscious such things are felt ultimately to be something physical. It is with good reason that metaphor calls science the 'Alma Mater'. While introjection of non-material things proceeds with the help of various mechanisms (displacement, symbol-formation, sublimation), the early animistic inner world becomes modified and the assimilation of internal objects leads to an integrated and rich personality.

Notes

1 (Original footnote) See Freud's 'The Interpretation of Dreams', 'Formulations Regarding the Two Principles of Mental Functioning', and 'Narcissism', CP IV; 'Beyond the Pleasure Principle'; 'Group Psychology'; 'The Ego and the Id'; 'Negation', *IJPA*, VI: 367. ·

2 Let us picture a living organism in its most simplified possible form as an undifferentiated vesicle of a substance that is susceptible to stimulation. Then the surface turned towards the external world will from its very situation be differentiated and will serve as an organ for receiving stimuli. (It would be easy to suppose, then, that as a result of the ceaseless impact of external stimuli on the surface of the vesicle, its substance to a certain depth may have become permanently modi-fied.) . . . But we have more to say of the living vesicle with its receptive corticle layer, this functions as a special envelope of membrane resistant to stimuli. . . . (Protection against stimuli is an almost more important function to the living organism than reception of stimuli.) . . . (The main purpose of the reception of stimuli is to discover the direction and nature of the external stimuli; and for that it is enough to take small specimens of the external world, to sample it in small quantities.)   [SE 18:27–8]

3 'It starts out, as we see from the system Pcpt., which is its nucleus. . . . For the ego, perception plays the part which in the id falls to instinct.' [SE 19:23,25]

4 'For, on our hypothesis, perception is not a purely passive process. The ego periodically sends out small amounts of cathexis into the perceptual system by means of which it samples the external stimuli, and then after every such tentative advance it draws back again.' [SE 19:238]

5 'The attribute to be decided about may originally have been good or bad, useful or harmful expressed in the language of the oldest – the oral – instinctual impulses. The judgement is: "I should like to eat this", "I should like to spit it out"; and, put more generally: "I should like to take this into myself and to keep that out". That is to say: "It shall be inside me" or it shall be outside me.' [SE 19: 238]

6 'Insofar as the objects which are presented to it are sources of pleasure, it takes them into itself, "introjects" them (to use Ferenczi's 1909 term); and, on the other hand, it expels whatever within itself becomes a cause of unpleasure.' [SE 14:136]

7 '. . . the process, especially in the early phases of development, is a very frequent one and it makes it possible to suppose that the character of the ego is a precipitate of abandoned object cathexes and that it contains the history of those object-choices.' [SE 19:29–30]

8 '. . . as a compensation for this loss of objects there is such a strong intensification of the identifications with his parents which have probably long been present in his ego.' [SE 22:64]

9 'As soon as it loses sight of its mother it behaves as if it were never going to see her again.' [SE 20:169]

10 (Original footnote) Freud as we know, defines the superego as the heir of the Oedipus complex. In this connection, however, I am dealing only with the mechanism of the superego formation – i.e. introjection – and not with the complex dynamic factors involved in its formation, which would require another paper.

11 (Original footnote) It was the existence of such intense conflicts at an early age, which Melanie Klein came to understand through her analyses of young children, that led her in course of time to see the validity and clinical significance of the theory of the life and death instincts.

12 (Original footnote) I do not wish to imply that such predominance is purely quantitative. Many clinical observations recommend the view that quantitative terms alone do not do justice to the complex situation.

13 'The original pleasure ego wants to introject into itself everything that is good and to reject from itself everything that is bad.' [SE 19:237]

14 'Furthermore it is clear that the behaviour of a child who indulges in thumb sucking is determined by a search for some pleasure which has already been experienced and is now remembered. It was the child's first and most vital activity, sucking from his mother's breast, or at substitutes for it, that must have familiarized him with this pleasure.' [SE 7:181]

15 'In the first instance the oral component instinct finds satisfaction by attaching itself to the sating of the desire for nourishment; and its object is the mother's breast. It then detaches itself, becomes independent and

at the same time auto-erotic, that is, it finds an object in the child's own body.' [SE 18:245]

16 (Original footnote) In order to simplify the presentation I am referring throughout to breast-fed children. My views, however, about early development do in fact apply also to children who were never fed at the breast, because I believe that, although breast-fed children have a more favourable start in life, there are ways in which the substitute can be tendered to the child to make up for disadvantages, by approximating the feeding situation as far as possible to that at the breast. If the mother herself feeds the child, takes him into her arms, gives him physical contact, etc., she can establish that mother–child closeness which is an integral part of breast-feeding. But with regard to the child's phantasies about the breast, they are in my view not dependent on the experience of feeding from the breast. There are good reasons to assume that the child possesses an unconscious knowledge about the breast – in the same way in which there is an unconscious knowledge about sexual intercourse (primal phantasies).

17 'The unmatched prototype of every later sexual satisfaction.' [SE 20:314]

18 'The basis of the process is what is called "identification" – that is to say, the assimilation of one ego to another one as a result of which the first ego behaves like the second in certain respects, imitates it and in a sense takes it up into itself. Identification has been not unsuitably compared with the oral, cannibalistic incorporation of the other person. It is a very important form of attachment to someone else, probably the very first.' [SE 22:63]

19 'It may be that by this introjection, which is a kind of regression to the mechanism of the oral phase, the ego makes it easier for the object to be given up or renders that process possible. It may be that this identification is the sole condition under which the id can give up its objects.' [SE 19:29]

20 'We are bound to suppose that a unity comparable to the ego cannot exist in the individual from the start; the ego has to be developed. The auto-erotic instincts, however, are there from the very first; so there must be something added to auto-erotism – a new psychical action – in order to bring about narcissism.' [SE 14:77]

21 'Hate as a relation to objects is older than love. It derives from the narcissistic ego's primordial repudiation of the external world with its outpouring of stimuli.' [SE 14:139]

22 '. . . it seemed as though this kind of narcissistic attitude in them constituted one of the limits of their susceptibility to influence'. [SE 14:73]

23 '. . . whatever was thought of (wished for) was simply presented in a hallucinatory manner'. [SE 12:219]

24 'Even today in some strata of our population no one can die without having been killed by someone else, preferably by the doctor.' [SE 22:122]

25 'Introjection is essentially a mechanism for dealing with lost or disappearing objects.' [Glover 1932:15]

10

Sixth
Discussion of Scientific Controversies

Discussion held on October 20th, 1943

Commentary by Dr P. Heimann

preliminary to discussion of her paper
(compressed from paper circulated to Members in June 1943)

Mr Chairman, Ladies and Gentlemen,
Since time is short and by the rules we must confine ourselves to our
written statements, I shall give a brief summary of the paper that was
circulated in June. I am told that it was difficult to read, because it
was so compressed. I hope that this will not be difficult to listen to as
it is still more compressed.

I shall use the root terms 'introject' and 'project' when referring to
the mental mechanisms which are modelled on and correspond to the
bodily experiences of taking in and expelling respectively.

We regard the mind as composed of 3 main parts differentiated by
their functions: the id is the source of all instinctual energies; the ego
is the interpreter and intermediary between the various parts of the
mind and the outside world; the superego is the internalized
representative of the most important objects – the parents.

Further, we regard the mind as being capable of change by its
contacts. Now, what are the mechanisms by which these alterations
are brought about? Freud has given us the answer, and most clearly,
in *Beyond the Pleasure Principle* in 1920. Making an analogy of the
mind with a living vesicle, there is a receptive outer layer, which not
only wards off but also receives stimuli, it collects information about

531

the direction and nature of stimuli by *taking in* small samples. The function of the outer layer is also to *expel*.

'Originally the property to be decided about might be either good or bad, useful or harmful. Expressed in the language of the oldest, that is of the oral instinctual impulses, the alternative runs thus: "I should like to eat that or I should like to spit it out." . . . "I should like to take this into me and keep that out of me".' [Freud, S. 1925:368–9; SE 19:236–7)[1] Thus eating and spitting out, introjecting and projecting, are the fundamental patterns on which the life and development of the organism are based.

'The objects presenting themselves, in so far as they are sources of pleasure, are absorbed by the ego into itself, "introjected" (according to an expression coined by Ferenczi) [in 1909] while on the other hand, the ego thrusts forth upon the external world whatever within itself gives rise to pain (the mechanism of projection).' [Freud, S. 1915a:78; SE 14:136][2]

Freud stated in *The Ego and the Id* [1923] that when he explained the disorder of melancholia [in 1917] by means of the concept of introjection it was not known how common and how typical this process of introjection is. He allotted to introjection a great share in determining the form taken by the ego and states that it contributes materially towards building up its character. The introjection of melancholia is a kind of regression to the mechanisms of the oral phase: '. . . the process *especially in the early phases of development* is a very frequent one, and points to the conclusion that the character of the ego is a precipitate of abandoned object cathexes and that it contains a record of past object choices'. [Freud, S. 1923b:36; SE 19:29][3] I emphasize this to throw into relief two points, first that the basic processes are those of taking in and expelling objects from the ego, and secondly that this is the earliest process in the intercourse between subject and object.

These processes of introjection and projection are differently accentuated at different periods, according to the varying primacies of the instincts. They are destined to discharge different functions and to pursue different aims at different periods of development.

Introjection, according to Freud's explicit statements, is the decisive factor in the formulation of the superego, another differentiation within the mind. He assigns superego formation to roughly the fifth year of life, while he places ego-formation very early (the ego is already in existence at the second oral, the narcissistic stage). There are, however, many direct and emphatic statements in his writings about earlier phenomena of introjection: its frequency, its typical occurrence in early childhood, the modifications in the ego resulting from one ego 'becoming like another' and 'as it were, taking it into itself', introjection as the earliest form of tie to an object, and 'the lasting effects of the earliest identifications surpassing in importance any which occur later', and so on. The truth of these statements is demonstrated by the observations made in early analyses. The conclusion forced upon us is that the superego as described by Freud and distinguished by him with its special name, is the *end result* of a long process undergoing different phases of development. The earliest introjections establish a protective and a persecuting agency within the mind ('good' and 'bad' breast), a very primitive sort of superego consonant with the very primitive sort of ego then existing. Nevertheless these primitive processes lead up to and have features in common with the later superego. When the ego advances to a perception of the mother as a whole person and the whole mother becomes the object of the infant's love, a new element enters into the infant's relation to his introjected object.

Guilt, at first of a rudimentary but none the less important kind, and dread of losing the loved object arise at this early stage – these are characteristics of the superego as Freud described it.

Similarly the prohibitions emanating from the superego correspond with the impulses and the ego–development at any age under consideration.

But, as Freud has shown, the superego resulting from introjection is not a complete replica of the parents; in some essential respects the child *must not* be like the parents. The excluding process can be regarded as akin to projection, following the primary law of expelling or excluding from the organism whatever is harmful. This would be another instance of the structural effect of the introjection–projection pair of opposites.

At this point we can with profit turn to a consideration of the life and death instincts. Freud's earliest clinical work discovered conflict at the root of all neurotic symptoms. He came to postulate antithetical instincts which are in the last resort responsible for such conflicts, and ultimately he formulated these two opposed instincts as life and death instincts.

When, from the analytic evidence of acute conflicts in young children, Melanie Klein came to devote close attention to the destructive impulses, she was led to the conclusion that they behave exactly as does the libido, in so far as they too operate through the bodily functions and towards the objects of bodily needs. Both instincts, the libido and the destructive instinct, seek to fulfil their aims in bodily activities, just as conversely the mental functions derive from them both (as Freud described in detail in 'Negation'). In the same way, because the instincts are mind–body processes, mental experiences are bound to take place alongside the operation of the instincts in the body, and a mental, emotional relationship must follow in the wake of the bodily activities towards the object who gratifies them. First love and first hate are closely knit with the sensations aroused when bodily needs demand satisfaction. The child's relation to objects develops gradually concurrent with the development of instincts. We come now to the problem of auto–erotism and narcissism. This is a point which I developed at great length in my paper. Here I shall only remind you of our view that in auto–erotism and narcissism libido is turned upon the introjected object which is represented by the child's own body; in both conditions unconscious phantasy is operative; auto–erotism is characterized by the predominance of the libido, whereas in narcissism there is a stronger admixture of aggressive trends; as regards ego formation the difference between auto–erotism and narcissism is in terms of degree; the libido is not entirely withdrawn from the external object.

To return to introjection. With the growth of the ego and its perceptive and synthetic functions, object relation advances to the level of whole objects. This step complicates the introjection and projection mechanisms, because it gives rise to new anxieties devolving upon the loss of the 'good' object. When 'good' and 'bad' are not distributed to two different objects, but are aspects of one and the same object, the fear of expelling the 'good' with the 'bad' comes into being, and conversely, of taking in the 'bad' with the 'good'. Such anxiety may either impede introjection and projection and retard mental development or cause a rapid alternation of these processes which interferes with a stable attachment to the surroundings. It is noteworthy that introjection and projection which have been the predominant means of protecting against object-loss lead at this point to such severe anxieties that the ego is compelled to devise and employ various other defence mechanisms.

The instinctual and emotional life at this stage is of the utmost complexity. More and more objects are drawn into the circle of the child's interest, and the father and the important father–mother combination play an ever-increasing part. The father's penis becomes a new object of desire, but this desire is shaped in an oral mould, that is to say, the leading aim is to incorporate it. The inevitable oral frustrations experienced in relation to the mother further impel the child to turn to his father whose penis becomes introjected along the unconscious equation; breast–penis.

The processes of introjection and projection retain the function of introducing into the ego what is 'good and useful' and removing what is 'bad and harmful', yet in the course of development other functions are added to this primary one. With the widening of the object world the expansion of the ego and the increasing mastery of the destructive instinct, the attitude towards the desired object changes so that the wish to give gains in strength; projection can now refer to something good as well. Adult sexual intercourse and procreation would be the physical pattern of this mental attitude. Progressively in the course of development the early animistic inner world becomes modified and the introjected objects prove a source of widening and enriching the ego.

Discussion held on October 20th, 1943, on Dr Paula Heimann's paper 'Some Aspects of the Role of Introjection and Projection in Early Development'

DR M. BRIERLEY: There is a great deal in Dr Heimann's paper which seems to me to call for very serious criticism. Since it is impossible to comment on the whole paper in 10 minutes, I propose to concentrate on a single topic which is not the main argument but which is for me a fundamental issue. This topic is the *treatment of perception and, by inference, image formation, as introjection.* Such treatment would seem to equate images with 'internalized objects'.

Dr Heimann begins by defining the sense in which she intends to use her title words. She says, 'I shall use the terms "introject" and "project" when referring to the mental mechanisms which are modelled on and correspond to the bodily experiences of taking in and expelling respectively.' I think we shall avoid unnecessary confusion if we recognize that this is a subjective definition, i.e., a definition formulated, not merely from the data of experience, but from the standpoint of subjective experience. A mental mechanism modelled on and corresponding to bodily experience is an imagined action, a mode of imaginary behaviour patterned on foregoing actual behaviour. Such a definition goes with the subjective concept of mind as the ever-growing whole of personal experience as lived by the individual. The structure of mind, from this point of view, is the complex system of reaction patterns resulting from experience.

Subjective definitions of mental mechanisms and subjective concepts of mind are perfectly legitimate. They are of more immediate practical use in therapeutic and other direct contact work than objective types. At any rate at the sensory-affective and perceptual levels, mental activity, as we experience it, is essentially imaginary action. At these levels we deal with people and things in imagination in the various ways in which we are used to dealing with them in the outer world. This holds good whether we are remembering past events, rehearsing future ones, or merely day-dreaming, and whether our reactions are conscious or unconscious. In everyday life, the specific personal meaning of any current situation will govern both our mental and our motor reactions to it. Subjectively, life as a succession of reactions to the meanings of situations and therapy is mainly concerned with tracing the patient's reaction patterns in the terms of his own experience, conscious and unconscious. Hence, subjective definitions have a necessary and proper place in practice. But if Freud had confined himself to the subjective approach he might never have arrived at the concept of the Unconscious as a psychic system and could never have written *The Ego and the Id.*

Mental mechanisms can also be defined *objectively* as specific mental processes giving rise to specific modifications of the mental organization. Such definitions are also formulated from the data of experience and from the standpoint of the observer seeking knowledge about the mental factors that condition the nature of experience itself and the development of reaction patterns. The difference in standpoint is related to the difference between first and third persons, between identification and object relationship. Such impersonal definitions of mechanisms go with correspondingly objective concepts of mind, such as that given by Freud when he described mind as an apparatus for the regulation of instinct tension. The structure of mind from this angle is its organization.

Although their data are the same, the subjective and objective *approaches to it* are distinct. Since it is so necessary and yet so difficult to keep them distinct, I think we should gain by using different terms corresponding to the different angles of approach. Personally, I should prefer to keep the word *introjection,* in association with mental mechanism, for the function of the psychic apparatus and the term *incorporation* for imaginary taking-in through any physical channel. What happens when the distinction is lost is illustrated by Dr Heimann's treatment of perception and hence, by implication, of image formation.

Perception and image formation are functions or capabilities of the mental apparatus which make the activity we call 'imagination' possible. It is the development of imagery that makes it feasible to swallow anything in imagination. To make introjection, defined as modelled on bodily behaviour, responsible for image formation is to

536

put the cart before the horse. If we wish to call image formation introjection, then we should find some other term for the defence-mechanism of introjection, and continue to distinguish sharply between that mechanism, as mechanism, and the subjective behaviour of imaginary incorporation that may be its concomitant in experience.

If the equation of image formation with introjection, as defined by Dr Heimann, is a fallacy, what kind of a fallacy is it?

In the first place, it is very difficult for anyone to emphasize anything without exaggerating. This paper, and Mrs Klein's work as a whole, emphasizes many things that to my mind need emphasis. It underlines, for instance, the developmental importance and continuing influence of oral experience and the extent to which oral interests tend to mould our mental life because it begins in a phase which is justifiably called an oral primacy. Nevertheless, oral primacy is never oral monopoly. Exaggeration creeps in when the oral interpretation of mental functions, such as perception and image formation, is accepted as a complete and sufficient explanation. When the baby is trying to put everything into its mouth, it comes across many things that won't go in. Image formation as a function of mind will not go into subjective incorporation.

In the second place, Dr Heimann takes Freud's analogy of stimulus 'tasting' literally. [See p. 504.] In the passage she quotes, Freud writes 'it must suffice to take little samples of the outer world, to taste it, so to speak, in small quantities'. Those three words 'so to speak' appear to me to show that Freud knew exactly what he was doing, namely describing by analogy. I do not think there was any confusion in his mind between the process he was trying to apprehend and to explain and the particular form of his explanation. To take an analogy literally is to confuse the process one is thinking about with the form in which one apprehends it.

An analogy is an unconsciously favoured preconception. Since 'the ego is first and foremost a body ego', it is inevitable that when we first begin to think about thinking and mental processes, we should think of them as analogous to bodily processes and that they should lend themselves readily to expression 'in the language of the oldest, i.e., of the oral instinctual impulses'.

I do not know when the baby attains what we should recognize as definite imagery. The balance of improbability seems to me to favour the notion that the breast is at least one of the earliest objects to be recognized as such. I think it likely that early imagery loses its hallucinatory vividness only gradually and, hence, it does not seem to me incredible that early images of the breast may occur as parts of experiences that we should call imaginary incorporation. In the same way I think that the frequent association of identification with regression to the oral phase and imaginary incorporation may be due to the fact that the original or primary identification is re-established for the infant during suckling. But such considerations do not affect my argument. They only help to explain why it is so easy and so tempting to think of mental processes in terms of oral experience. But to understand the subjective significance of a given process does not necessarily throw much light on the nature of the process itself. Nor is the nature of the process itself to be confused with the purposes for which we use it.

There is abundant clinical evidence that thinking can satisfy oral wishes, that one can have a 'thirst' for information and a 'hunger' for facts, and a further abundance of evidence showing how much intellectual activity may be impeded by adverse oral linkage. Just as it has to be underlined that primacy is never monopoly, so it must be emphasized that thinking can subserve, or be impeded by, any instinctual impulse and that the whole field of bodily experience can provide analogies for mental processes. If we have a 'feast of reason' we have also a 'flow of soul'; we speak of 'fertile' theories and are 'pregnant' with thought; we also 'grapple' with ideas and 'wrestle' with problems.

To limit ourselves to understanding the subjective meaning of our unconscious preconceptions about mental processes and to equate these with the processes themselves would be comparable to limiting our knowledge of the outer world to perceptual knowledge. If that had happened in the natural sciences we should still think the earth was the centre of the Universe and that the sun literally rose and set. Psychoanalysis is a very young science and objective knowledge about mental life is very hard to achieve just because we are so strongly conditioned by our primitive corporeal preconceptions about it. Things are not necessarily what they seem in the realm of mind, any more than in the outer world. So long as we fail to distinguish between process and analogy, between objective facts and subjective meanings, we shall only move in circles. We shall describe the mental process in terms of its unconscious significance and then equate the unconscious significance with the objective process, a most pernicious type of solipsism.

Thus, while I regard it as imperative to recognize the continuing influence of oral experience in shaping our thinking, I do not think that intrinsic functions of the mental apparatus, such as perception and image-formation, can be adequately defined in the terms of oral experience. Indeed, if we persist in equating mental functions with our subjective interpretations of them, we forfeit our claim to be scientists and revert to the primitive state of the Chinese peasant who interprets an eclipse as the sun being swallowed by a dragon. His subjective logic may be unanswerable but his explanation of the event is erroneous.

DR K. FRIEDLANDER: Dr Heimann's paper states clearly certain divergences from Freudian theory in regard to the conception of auto-erotism and narcissism.

But what is of even greater importance is that the fundamental difference between Mrs Klein's approach to instinct theory and the scientific principles on which the psychoanalytic conception of mental life is based has for once become clear though Dr Heimann did not regard the statements which I shall presently discuss as different from those usually accepted amongst analysts. But the divergences in libido theory which she explicitly names are already the logical sequence of this fundamental difference of approach.

This basic difference is to be seen in Mrs Klein's interpretation of the nature and function of primary instincts. This difference is brought about by the free interchange in Mrs Klein's theory of biological and psychological conceptions.

If I may be allowed to illustrate this different approach to biological facts with an example from another field. If we consider an illness like senile dementia we have certain biological or physiological facts: the brain is shrunken, there are fewer nerve cells and fibres, and so on. Then we have certain psychological facts: memory is poor, unpleasant events are remembered better, there are hypochondriacal delusions, depression, and so on. That is to say, one can define senile dementia either in physiological or in psychological terms and one can try to find out whether there is any correlation between these two findings, and to keep that correlation, whatever it may be, in one's mind will be very important. But to say the brain cell's damage is equivalent to the patient having delusions would lead to the erroneous assumption that delusions are caused by a damage to cells in a certain area of the brain, and that as we all know is not correct.

I have given you this simple example in order to illustrate this law of modern psychopathology; that one can define a condition either in biological or psychological terms and that one can correlate the respective findings. But the straightforward exchange of biological and psychological conceptions leads to erroneous conclusions. In the given example the mixing up of conceptions impresses all of us as most undesirable. In the very complicated question of the development of certain functions in early childhood where the scientific methods of establishing facts are so far more or less absent, a confusion caused by such indiscriminate use of explanations is less obvious and less easy to prove than in the aforementioned example, where biological and psychological findings can be ascertained by direct observation. Nevertheless I believe that the indiscriminate use of biological and psychological explanations leads to the same undesirable results.

The advance in psychopathology due to Freud's work has been made possible by an entirely new approach to the problems of mental life. Before Freud the attempt had been made to translate psychological findings into physiological terms; therefore Charcot's and Janet's work did not lead very much further than to the usual psychiatric description. Freud, always keeping biological facts in mind, developed new psychological conceptions, which he solely used when discussing psychological phenomena. When using biological conceptions to illustrate or compare them with psychological facts he does it in an 'as if' way. The result of this modern approach was that Freud was able to build up a consistent theory of the structure of the mind which fitted the observed facts and threw light on occurrences hitherto quite inexplicable.

Going back to the old approach of a translation of biological phenomena into psychological terms, we are apt to end in the same blind alley as workers did before Freud.

There is, amongst others, one point in Dr Heimann's paper where the result of using in the same explanation biological and psychological terms becomes very obvious. Dr Heimann states: 'I wish to remind you here of that narcissistic condition which is never given up, namely sleep. Here we have a withdrawal from the outer world, and an egoistic concentration upon ourselves – we, the dreamers, are always the leading figures. But does this narcissistic condition lack objects? What a multitude of objects there are in our dreams and what a complexity of relationships is revealed in the midst of a highly narcissistic hallucinatory activity.' [See p. 521.] In this statement a biological condition, sleep, has been equated with a psychological condition, the dream, with the result of a misapprehension of Freud's theory of the dream. In Freudian theory we would express the same situation in the following way: sleep is a biological condition. Regarded psychologically, this condition can be expressed as one in which the libido is entirely withdrawn from the objects on to the own self. The relationship to the outer world ceases to exist. This biological condition, described psychologically as a narcissistic state, can be disturbed by external and internal stimuli, which threaten to awake the sleeper. The dream is to be regarded as a compromise between the wish to sleep and the disturbing forces. Object relationships appearing in the dream belong of course to the intrapsychic forces trying to gain consciousness in the sleeper and not to the sleep. The conception of narcissism certainly plays a role in the psychology of the dream as well. According to the regression which takes place in the dream narcissistic traits are pronounced. The term 'narcissism' is used in a different sense when we apply it either to the sleep or to the dream. Applied to sleep it does not mean more than a description. If we apply 'narcissism' to the dream it signifies a psychological happening. We need not explicitly state this difference as long as we are aware of it in our minds. But if the application of a psychological term to a biological condition is meant to imply that this biological condition is now a psychological one, then a conclusion like Dr Heimann's, namely, that sleep is a highly narcissistic hallucinatory activity, may result. And that very clearly is not Freudian theory any longer. It therefore, in our view, does not strengthen Dr Heimann's point of the importance of object relationships during the narcissistic phase.

This kind of approach, that is to say the translation of biological conditions into psychological terms, and operating with these terms as if they were psychological conceptions, is in my opinion the basis for the divergence in the interpretation of the theory of the primal instincts, which I regard as the starting point for the divergences in instinct theory and the theory of neuroses.

Dr Heimann states [see p. 511] that acceptance or non-acceptance of the theory of the death instinct brings about a different approach to various psychological manifestations as well as to the significance of the assessment of environmental factors, and so on.

In our opinion it is not the acceptance or non-acceptance of the death instinct but the different interpretation of the theory of the primal instincts which brings about this obvious divergence between the Freudian and the Kleinian theory.

Dr Heimann states: 'the aims of the instincts to which the organism is subject are in opposition to one another; in other words, that we deal with an organism which is by its very nature in a condition of conflict' [see p. 511]. This is the statement with which the divergence starts. I shall come back to it presently. I want first of all to summarize Dr Heimann's deductions from the statement, which are a logical sequence if one agrees with its content. Dr Heimann states that these opposing instincts have the aim to assert themselves. The life instinct has to predominate, so it has to devise means to overcome the death instinct. It does it by way of deflection outward, which Dr Heimann equates with projection. She says 'that as regards projection, the ultimate *aim* of the life instinct in its struggle with the death instinct would be expulsion; the death instinct, however, cannot be expelled since it is an inherent component of the organism. The next thing to expulsion is deflection outward.' We already get the notion of two equally strong instincts of the same quality, but with different aims. This idea becomes clearer when Dr Heimann discusses the further development of the libido, with object cathexis and so on. I refer to her statements [see p. 511]. There the impression is still more pronounced that the life and death instincts behave like two component instincts, having the same fate but with opposite aims. I refrain from further quotations out of Dr Heimann's paper as I can assume that everybody is familiar with it.

The view expressed about the primal instincts as regards this first time of life by Mrs Klein is therefore that the child is born with these two opposing instincts in a state of conflict. That these instincts fight for predominance, that the life instincts by means of projection get the upper hand and that all the infant's first experiences are tainted by this struggle. That it perceives the first objects, almost at once, that introjection of these objects takes place, and that the further·conflict between these two instincts takes place around these introjected objects. The two instincts are in their appearance similar to component instincts.

May I, before I examine this theory, state briefly our view of the theory of the primal instincts. In doing so I refer to Freud's theories as given in *Beyond the Pleasure Principle* and all subsequent papers which have any reference to the subject, as for instance *The Ego and the Id, Civilization and its Discontents*, 'Negation', *New Introductory Lectures*, etc. I shall refrain from giving quotations not only because it would lengthen my contribution unnecessarily but also because we have seen recently how misleading it is to take out single sentences from their context. The theory of the primal instinct can certainly not be grasped from single quotations.

Always keeping to the dualistic theory of instincts Freud has from very early onwards tried to give his observations a theoretical foundation which, as he always pointed out, has to be taken from the field of biology. As the first theoretical assumptions of self-preservative and sexual instincts did not appear to be wide enough in view of certain clinical findings he arrived at last at his theory of the primal instincts, in which he believed to see a fundamental biological law governing organic as well as inorganic matter. He arrived at this theory by speculative and theoretical considerations, always em-

542

phasizing that psychological facts alone would not be a basis for arriving at a theory of instincts. I need not go into the reasons for that statement with which we are all familiar. These primal instincts, the life instinct and the death instinct, he describes as antithetical tendencies of a different quality, and naturally therefore also of a different aim. The aim of the life instinct is to unite, to build up greater communities, originally of cells. The death instinct is the conservative tendency to return to a former state of development, which for organic matter would be to return to the inorganic state. Biologically these tendencies work against each other, and life became possible millions of years ago by a deflection outward of the death instinct when organisms with one cell combined to form organisms consisting of a community of cells. Since then the interplay between these two tendencies causes the appearance which we call life. This life cycle, an interplay between two tendencies, has in historical times already achieved a certain unalterable form, and the human being is very apt to fight against any interference which may alter this prescribed way. This is a purely biological theory in which psychological conceptions so far have no place. How does this theory help to explain the clinical facts which were observed?

Freud sees in the instinctual drives which we meet in the human being derivatives of these libidinal tendencies. In certain manifestations the one, in others the other, may be more pronounced so that one can assume their derivation being more pronounced from the one or other tendency. Normally these tendencies, or instinctual drives, are fused, but there are certain conditions of a pathological kind when a partial diffusion may take place. Or certain instinctual drives may have more of the one or other tendency at the beginning and mix more extensively with the other tendency later on. We may have the impression that we can observe derivatives of the life instinct in a pure form in the sexual instinct, but even that assumption is fallacious and only due to the fact that the life instinct manifests itself in more noisy actions than the death instinct, which is always quiet and in the background. Even in the reversal of sadism, the nearest approach to a derivative of the death instinct, the admixture of the derivatives of the life instinct is unmistakable.

Now what did this theory do and in what way was it superior to the former theoretical assumption? As you all know, it explained the appearances of masochism in its various forms, it established the possibility of a primary masochism, in so far as some derivatives of the death instinct might have escaped the deflection outward which occurred in very old times. It affirmed the dualistic theory of instincts. In other words, this theory was able to put the psychoanalytical assumptions as formed before on a firmer theoretical basis. It did not lead Freud to alter anything with regard to the libidinal theory or the theory of neuroses, to name only two fields of psychoanalytical investigation.

How is it possible that Mrs Klein's interpretation of the theory of instincts leads her, as Dr Heimann pointed out [see p. 521], to alter the conceptions of auto-erotism, narcissism, object relationship, superego formation, to alter the relative importance of defence mechanisms, to give certain mechanisms prevalence before others and so on?

I think the reason for this is the different interpretation of the theory of the primal instincts by making an equation of the kind described in the beginning between biological and psychological conceptions. To come back to the statement mentioned in the beginning. Dr Heimann says: 'The aims of the instincts to which the organism is subject are in opposition, to one another; in other words, that we deal with an organism which is by its very nature in a condition of conflict.' We agree with the first sentence, that the instincts to which the organism is subject are in opposition to each other; this is a biological theory, exemplified by many facts. We entirely disagree that one is justified to conclude that this organism is therefore in a state of conflict. It might be, but the biological facts do not necessitate this assumption. If one regards conflict as a psychological conception in our sense it can only be applied to biological facts as a description or in an 'as if' form. But it cannot form the conclusion of a biological statement. Unless one would also say that the amoeba is in a state of conflict too. But then the conception of conflict loses its meaning altogether. This misconception leads at once to a further psychoanalytical impossibility, namely to the fight of two instincts without intervention of what we call the mind. It is one of the most fundamental principles of psychoanalytic doctrine that in the id, which is the instinctual part of the personality, antithetical instincts live one by the other without disturbing each other, each striving for satisfaction. A struggle ensues if this satisfaction of antithetical instincts is withheld, but the level of the struggle is not the primary unconscious. The further result of this misconception is the theory that the life instinct employs a defence mechanism, namely projection, against the death instinct. In Freudian theory defence mechanisms are employed by the ego against the instincts. This is the very nature of the defence mechanism in psychoanalytic thinking.

All the further modifications are now easily to be understood as logical sequence to this first difference in interpretation. In this fight between the instincts an object is being called for. This is seen in the introjection of the breast which is regarded as the first object relationship. This conception contradicts Freud's explicit statement that important though this first relationship will remain throughout life, in the beginning the breast is not perceived as not belonging to the own body. The libido with which it is cathected is governed by the same principle as as the cathexis of the own body. In consequence to the assumption of this first object relationship, the phases of auto-erotism and narcissism lose their significance and are in Mrs Klein's theory in no way different in their psychological content from later stages. We shall probably hear about further divergences in the coming contributions.

I believe that the fact that from Dr Heimann's paper the conception of introjection–projection has not really become clearer depends again on the application of psychological conceptions to biological facts. In the first pages of her paper Dr Heimann talks about intake and output as the most fundamental factors in physical life. Everybody would agree to that, it is a very well-known biological law. In these discussions she equates introjection–projection with this biological pattern. This is also understandable. Then, on page [508], she states: 'In the Ucs the oral significance of growth and acquisition and the anal significance of loss and gift are maintained; so that under circumstances in which this fundamental pattern becomes reactivated all acquiring means devouring, all giving means spitting, or defecating, with the result that guilt and anxiety arise along with these activities.'

In our view, as long as introjection–projection is equated with intake and output it has no psychological significance at all. The fact that this fundamental pattern is present does not explain the psychological happening of guilt and anxiety; in the same way as the presence of antithetical instincts need not necessarily lead to conflict.

I have tried to show the fundamental differences in Freud's and Mrs Klein's views in regard to the interpretation of the primal instincts. I have tried to show that this difference of theoretical views is the result of the direct application of psychological conceptions to biological ones and vice versa in Mrs Klein's theory.

A further result of this difference in the basic approach to mental life is the fact that Mrs Klein regards the mental life of the infant as qualitatively the same as that of the older child or grown-up, the differences being of a quantitative nature only, while we believe that psychic structure has an ontogenetic development and that there is a qualitative difference in mental life of the new-born and the child of two for example; whilst in the new-born biological tendencies govern predominantly, in the older child psychological tendencies are equally strong. The relationship to the mother is therefore a biological one in the beginning and by the awakening of psychic life is slowly altered into a more and more psychological one.

If we meet with sucking disturbances in a new-born child we would enquire into the functional disturbance of this inborn reflex mechanism rather than build up a hypothesis about the child's mental state at the time, whilst if we meet an eating difficulty in a child of two we would not only take the temperature but enquire into the psychological basis for the disturbance. I gave this example in order to demonstrate that this divergence in instinct theory the basis of which I have tried to discuss leads to very far-reaching differences in its practical applications. As we all know these practical differences have led to the present discussions in the first place.

DR S. M. PAYNE: I read Dr Heimann's paper with great interest and found it stimulating. The subject matter confronts us with some of the most obscure and neglected problems of dynamic psychology and she approaches these problems with the aid of the work done by Mrs Klein and her co-workers.

The work referred to has already increased our insight into the mechanisms employed in the earliest phases of ego development and has led to the extension of previous theories concerning the structure of the infantile ego and to the formulation of new theories. I think that it is inevitable and perhaps it it is platitudinous to note that new insight always tends to seem to obliterate temporarily older facts and has to find its own level.

That the mechanisms of introjection and projection play an important role in early mental development is accepted by all who believe in Freud's theories. In her paper, however, Dr Heimann makes claims for the importance of these mechanisms at the expense of other well-recognized and established psychological phenomena. I can only take up a few points in this connection in a short contribution.

In the first place I think some of the false claims arise out of the indiscriminate use of the terms 'introjection' and 'identification'. It is true, as Dr Heimann says, that in a few passages Freud and other analysts apparently use these terms to mean the same thing, but it is clear that in his description of different types of identification Freud is speaking of a totally different psychological concept. Introjection is a mechanism. Identification is a type of relationship between an object imago system and the ego system. If therefore the two terms are used synonymously in an exposition of theory it means that the

546

dynamics of the genesis of object relationships which form such an important part of the libido theory are omitted.

Secondly, the aim of Dr Heimann's paper seems to be to stress the importance of the oral phase of psychological development rather than to describe the part played by certain mechanisms and the fallacy lies in my opinion in the fact that she identifies eating and introjection.

I think that it can be shown that important psychological facts are either masked or ignored by (a) making the terms identification and introjection interchangeable and (b) by regarding eating and introjection as different forms of the same reaction by glancing briefly at what we know of the formation of the body ego, which occurs at a time in which introjection mechanisms first operate.

The pre-natal infant is presumed to be psychically one with the mother, and at present we find it hard to formulate the rudimentary psychical world which must be present. The relationship can be described as one of primary identification. Actually the pre-natal infant is taking in from the mother, but not from the mouth, and the discharge of waste products takes place by blood changes which go into the maternal blood stream. The trauma of birth suddenly alters this and psychical awareness of tensions arises, which ushers in an awareness of something external, 'not me', and therefore also awareness of 'me'. What is first apprehended as external is a part of the body, bodily processes, the surface of the body, orifices, particularly the mouth but not exclusively. Thus the first external object to be libidinized is the body ego. Freud says, 'The ego is first and foremost a body-ego.' It is ultimately derived from bodily sensations, chiefly from those springing from the surface of the body.

The process by which the body ego is formed is well described by Tausk. He says 'This must be the time when the infant is discovering his body, part by part, as the outer world, and is still groping for his hands and feet as though they were foreign bodies. At this time everything that happens to him emanates from his own body, but acting upon it as if produced by outer objects. The "disjecta membra" are later on pieced together and systematized into a unified whole under the supervision of a psychic unity that receives all sensations of pleasure and pain from these separate parts. The process takes place by means of identification with one's own body.' (Tausk 1919)

Schilder (1935) has drawn special attention to the fact that it is to a certain extent due to external physical contacts that the body is discovered. The mother's handling of the infant's body excites sensations and directs the child's attention to its body. All the orifices receive stimulation in various degrees, and the mother again plays an active role. So do stimuli coming in the form of light, and heat and sound. The hands and eyes of the infant play a leading part in the discovery of the body and obviously at first are outside the world of the body which is discovered, just as the hands, eyes of the mother are outside. The result is that the first external relationships are experienced to a great extent in terms of physical sensation. Sensations connected with sucking may be the most important. Awareness of the inside of the body is more likely to depend on unpleasant excessive tensions and must play an analogous part in the formation of the body ego.

The points I want to make briefly are these:

1   The psychical relationship to the mother comes about not only through feeding but by means of all bodily contacts.

2   At this early phase of psychical development there can be no fixed boundaries between the 'me' and 'not me' – and there is a tendency to re-establishment of the primary identification. The question is, does this take place by means of an introjection, or is it by means of withdrawal of cathexes from the developing 'not me'? The infantile body ego is in an ill-defined state of flux.

3   It seems obvious that perceptions of external people, particularly the mother, are bound up with the perceptions of the body and the two must be intimately connected together in the formation of the body ego.

4   If we turn to the dynamics of primitive ego formation we must recognize the fact that the psychical cathexes by means of which the ego structure is built up will be predominantly of presentations connected with physical sensations which occurred at the time of the perception of the external object rather than the cathexis of presentations connected with the external object. In other words there is a vast difference between the image of an external object, say the mother or part of her, which is introjected as the result of a physical experience of this kind and identified with part of the body, and one that is introjected when the ego has developed to a stage in which the external object is differentiated from the self.

We are accustomed to recognize these differences when speaking of regressions which take place on the outbreak of a psychosis; namely, that object love is abandoned and cathexes are withdrawn from object presentations, that is from the image of the object and from thoughts, ideas, wishes, and memories connected with the object. The cathexes thus withdrawn from one part of the ego structure return to primitive ego presentations connected with organs, parts of the body, and primitive phantasies associated with the primitive images connected with the body ego.

Owing therefore to the great psychical differences between relationships to objects at different stages of psychological development it seems to me to be of paramount importance not to mask these differences by oversimplification or confusion in the use of terms.

I repeat that it is true that Freud himself and many other analysts have used the terms 'introjection' and 'identification' interchangeably, but Freud obviously did not do this systematically. In fact it is clear that he and other leading analysts such as Abraham came to use 'introjection' as applicable to a mechanism characteristic of primitive oral relationship to an object, while he developed the meaning of the term 'identification' and applied it to certain types or relationships to objects not only people but things. At the same time he distinguishes between identification and what I shall call full object love.

I do not think that this confusion in the use of terms can be hastily dismissed because it has led to the increase of misunderstanding of Mrs Klein's work and has retarded the assimilation of new ideas to old.

Perhaps I should have noted before in this paper that when the terms are used in what I regard as the right sense it is obvious that the mechanism of introjection does not necessarily lead to identification; in fact where the term 'introjection' is most appropriately used the imago formation which follows often tends to be regarded by the ego as a foreign body .

I note that Dr Heimann quotes freely from Freud's article on negation when she is dealing with the mechanisms of projection. In this article Freud is talking about rejection from the ego by means of *repression*, not by projection. He says, 'the pleasure ego tries to introject into itself everything that is good, to reject from itself everything that is bad. From its point of view what is bad, what is alien to the ego, and what is external are, to begin with, identical.' [Freud, S. 1925:368; SE 19:237][4] The *rejection* to which Freud refers relates to the positive assertion which has been repressed and is represented in consciousness by a negation.

It was customary at one time, except in cases of psychosis, to regard the repression of a presentation as a preliminary to its projection. This is exemplified in cases of phobia in adults. It is the repressed dangerous imago which is projected on to the substitute object.

My reason for stressing this again is that oversimplification is a real danger to progress in the study of these complex psychological states.

Lastly Dr Heimann says that Freud compares the mind to an amoeba which accomplishes the intake of food and excretion by means of forming temporary organs which disappear when the function has been carried out. I confess that I think she is incorrect in her reading of Freud, in this matter. Freud does not compare the mind to an amoeba, he says, 'Thus we form a conception of an original libidinal cathexis of the Ego, part of which cathexis is later yielded up to objects, but which fundamentally persists and is related to the object cathexes much as the body of a protoplasmic animalcule is related to the pseudopoda which it puts out'. [Freud, S. 1914: 33; SE 14:75][5] There is no reference to taking in food or excreting. Further, the analogy is concerned with the cathexes of presentation in the ego, i.e. whether object presentations are cathected or whether cathexes are withdrawn to more primitive ego presentations. The point being that object presentations can be cathected at the expense of other ego presentations relating to the body, etc., and that these cathexes under certain circumstances can be withdrawn and return to the original ego presentations. The cathexis of external objects sounds to the uninitiated as if something was actually projected into the external world. We know of course that what is cathected when object love takes place is the image of the object in the mind and presentations associated with that image. The whole process is intrapsychic.

MRS HEDWIG HOFFER: Dr Heimann's candid and consistent representation of her views constitutes a perfect basis for discussion. My appreciation of this painstaking work will be best expressed in an endeavour to be equally consistent and clear. I will deal with two points only because I consider these points interesting from a more general standpoint.

My first question is: Did Mrs Klein succeed in her attempt to demonstrate on clinical material the working of the death instinct? My second point concerns Mrs Klein's idea of the earliest libidinal stages and earliest object relationships.

The assumption of the death instinct is a biological not a psychological hypothesis. Based on considerations of a phylogenetic and ontogenetic nature, it gave Freud the possibility to correlate psychological facts to a physical law.

The libido theory too is a biological hypothesis but unlike the death instinct theory it lends itself comparatively easily to correlation with psychological facts.

After the foundation stone of all psychoanalytical knowledge had been laid by the discovery of the Unconscious nothing has proved more productive for further investigation than the application of the libido theory. This theory enabled Freud and his co-workers to build up a comprehensive doctrine of neurosis and a psychological psychology. But in spite of this too many questions in the field of normal and pathological psychology have remained unanswered.

Freud himself explains the late discovery of the death instinct on emotional grounds.

Certainly the new finding did not facilitate matters for the analysts, and the analytical literature following *Beyond the Pleasure Principle* demonstrates how different authors tried to make good use of this addition to our knowledge. Simultaneously Abraham pursued his own course. He tried to show 'the development of the libido viewed in the light of mental disorders'. Let us stress the restricted scope of these studies. Abraham only endeavoured to trace 'the aetiology of manic–depressive disorders on psychoanalytical lines'. [Abraham 1924:418]

Inspired by his findings Mrs Klein based her research on his discoveries and tried to link them to Freud's newly formulated instinct theory.

Such a scientific task can be approached in various ways. For instance one investigator may start from the differences in the libidinal development and may try to obtain results by this comparison. Another may do the opposite and stress the common factors in the various clinical pictures.

Mrs Klein does not attempt to demonstrate in detail how she came to the conclusion that Abraham's findings on the special role that hate and love play in the object relations of melancholia are equally valid in a variety of other cases. This assumption is responsible for her postulate of the infantile Depressive Position.

All of us know how difficult it is to present analytical case material. But it is equally difficult to agree with something which has not been put to the test. Mrs Klein will object to such a statement. She will claim, I believe, that every analyst can see these things for himself. So it is perhaps more to the point to ask why our interpretation and evaluation of our case material differs so.

This divergence of opinion makes me question the correctness of the following statement, taken from Dr Heimann's paper. 'But when . . . Melanie Klein came to devote full attention to the destructive impulses she was led directly to the conclusion that these impulses behave exactly as does the libido.' How was it possible for Mrs Klein to devote her full attention to the death instinct? [See p. 513.]

If she speaks about the destructive impulses and means the deflected instinct derivatives, we are on familiar ground and we see the usual interplay of love and hate. On the other hand if she means the instinct proper, then the difficulty arises as to how we are able to isolate the different instinct components. To my mind this cannot be done by psychoanalytical investigation limited to verbal contact. I assume biochemistry will one day step in and detect the specific characteristics of the death instinct. It is most unlikely that our means of observation grant us anything like a complete picture of instinctual life. Our therapeutic results may seem to contradict me but they only prove the power of our libidinal forces. Freud's conception (quoted from *Beyond the Pleasure Principle*) 'that there is a tendency innate in living organic matter impelling it towards the reinstatement of an earlier condition' [Freud, S. 1920:44; SE: 18:36][6] leaves no doubt as to the fundamental difference between this instinct and the libido.

We understand that the libido, which is constantly on the move, constantly ready to melt into new units, is an articulate force and a shaping force. Moreover our theoretical deductions impel us to believe that whenever contact with the outer world and especially with other human beings is established, the libido takes the lead.

Freud himself did not investigate detailed clinical facts in the light of his new theory and his laconic remark, [Freud, S. 1940: 32; SE 23:150][7] 'It becomes relatively easy for us to follow the late vicissitudes of the libido; but this is more difficult with the destructive instinct', does not sound too encouraging.

A second point which I want to raise concerns Dr Heimann's summary in her paper. 'To summarize a few essential points in which *our views* concur (my italics, H.H.) with Freud's concept of auto-erotism and narcissism.' [See p. 520.]

The first point of her summary demonstrating this concurrence runs: 'Object-libidinal experiences precede the auto-erotic phase.' Dr Heimann's first quotation in support of her concurrence with Freud is: 'It is, moreover, clear that the action of the thumb-sucking child is determined by the fact that it seeks a pleasure which has been already experienced and is now remembered. . . . The first and most important activity in the child's life, the sucking from the mother's breast (or its substitute) must have acquainted it with this pleasure.' That might sound like a statement about a first object relation and Dr Heimann interprets it in this way. In her view the thumb-sucking of the child after the earlier experience at the breast is a withdrawal from objects. However, if we continue the quotation but one sentence further Freud's conception becomes explicit. He adds: 'We

552

would say that the child's lips behaved like an erogenous zone, and that the excitement through the warm stream of milk was really the cause of the pleasurable sensation.' [Freud, S. 1905:43; SE 7:181][8] The whole content of this statement, revolutionary as it was in 1905, is an analytical truism in 1943. Nothing more is stated than the well-known fact that the child is born with erotogenic zones.

Dr Heimann's second quotation too does not seem to me evidence of her theory. I repeat the quotation of Freud: 'In the first instance the oral component instinct finds satisfaction "anaclitically" – on the basis of the satiation of the desire for nourishment; and its object is the mother's breast. It then detaches itself, becomes independent and at the same time auto-erotic, that is, finds an object in the child's own body.' [Freud, S. 1923a:101; SE 18:245][9]

We are in perfect agreement that the pleasant experience at the breast leaves memory traces and paves the way to later object relation. The gist of Freud's considerations lies in the statement that the pleasurable experience is mixed with the satisfaction of a bodily need. And this oneness of a psychological incident, receiving pleasure, together with a physiological incident, satiation, is the phenomenon which Freud stresses.

In this connection the breast is no more than the source of this pleasure at a time when the infant is quite unable to connect cause and effect. That in a later elaboration of such early experiences the breast becomes cathected is no contradiction. Abraham shares Freud's view that the infant has no capacity for building up an object relationship. Freud describes in subtle and definite differentiations these first steps in emotional experience. In his 'Outline of Psycho-Analysis' he says: 'A child's first erotic object is the mother's breast that feeds him and love grows upon the prop of a satisfied need for food. To begin with, the child certainly makes no distinction between the breast and his own body, when it has to be separated from his body and shifted to the "outside" because he misses it so often, it carries with it as an "object", part of the original narcissistic cathexis.' [Freud, S. 1940:66; SE 23:188][10] I have quoted this passage because Freud's words sound somewhat similar to Mrs Klein's, but I think the similarity ends in sound. Freud sees in the new-born child an undifferentiated ego-id in which the whole libido and the whole death instinct are present at one and the same time. Several times he uses the analogy of pseudopoda, which are sent out and withdrawn, to illustrate the mobility of the libido. This quality of the libido works from the first day. In that sense Freud regards the mother' s breast as the first erotic object. But object relation in Freud's terminology is a more centralized and more stable psychic

553

phenomenon. It presupposes the capacity of the individual to distinguish between personalities, to associate particular memory-traces of a particular individual with new experiences with the same person and, most important of all, the fixation of the libido to a particular object. The first instant at which we get a more or less consistent picture of a definite libidinal position is in auto-erotism.

DR SUSAN ISAACS: The remarks which follow are highly condensed and of a preliminary nature. I intend to expand them at some future date.

In defining the sense in which she would use such terms as 'incorporation', 'introjection', Dr Heimann touched momentarily upon a focal problem, that of *the relation between instincts, phantasies, and mechanisms*.

In his useful survey of the classic views on introjection ('On Introjection'), Dr Foulkes [Foulkes 1937:278] suggested, perhaps rather hesitatingly, that particular ego mechanisms are derived from and modelled upon the various id impulses. Many of Freud's own statements, however, are explicit on this point, which is in accordance with his view that the ego is a differentiated part of the id.

Moreover, Freud actually takes us further than this. In the essay on 'Negation', from which both Dr Heimann and I have quoted, Freud not only states that even the intellectual functions of judgement and reality-testing 'are derived from the interplay of the *primary instinctual impulses*' (my italics), and rest upon the *mechanism* of introjection: he also shows us the part played in this derivation by *phantasy*. Referring to that aspect of judgement which asserts or denies that a thing has a particular property, Freud says: 'Expressed in the language of the oldest, that is, of the oral instinctual impulses, the alternative runs thus: "I should like to eat that, or I should like to spit it out"; or, carried a stage further, "I should like to take this into me and keep that out of me". That is to say, it is to be either *inside me or outside me*.' [Freud, S. 1925:369; SE 19:237][11]

Freud refers here to '*the language* of the oral impulse'; that is to say, to the phantasies which are the psychic representatives of the bodily aim. (He does not mean that these wishes are experienced in these words, but that, if they were put into words, these are the words which would express them.) In this actual example, Freud is showing us that phantasy is the mental expression of an *instinct*. But he is at one and the same time expressing the subjective side of the mechanism of introjection (or projection). In Freud's view, thus, *phantasy is the link between the id impulse and the ego mechanism*, the means by which the one is transmuted into the other. 'I should like to eat that' is the phantasy which represents the id impulse in the psychic life; it is at the same time, the subjective *experience* of the mechanism or process of introjection.

An instinct is conceived as a border-line process. It has a bodily aim directed to a concrete external object. It is represented in the mind by a phantasy. The phantasy is about the body, about bodily aims, pains, and pleasures. But *it is itself psychic*. It is a figment, when contrasted with bodily realities. It cannot itself be touched or handled or seen. Yet it has 'real' effects. [Freud, S. 1933a:154; SE 22:120][12] It helps to build character and personality, it makes possible knowledge of the external world and reality-testing, as Freud has shown in 'Negation'. The ego could not develop without phantasy. The effects of phantasy, of the 'figment', may even be – and indeed often are, in conversion symptoms, mannerisms, the bodily expressions of character and personality, the material bodily changes. They may lead to life and to death.

A phantasy is *both* a 'figment' and a function. The mechanism of introjection *operates through* phantasy.

In her last contribution to the discussion on phantasy, Miss Freud said: 'What (in Mrs Klein's view) is considered real is evidently not the result of the phantasy of introjection, but the process of introjection itself'. [See p. 425.]

Now, one of the 'results of the phantasy of introjection' is the process of introjection. It is not an actual bodily eating up and swallowing, but it does lead to actual, 'real' alterations in the ego. These come about as a result of such a phantasy as, e.g.: 'I have got a good breast inside me'. Or it may be 'I have got a bitten-up, torturing bad breast inside me – I must kill it and get rid of it' and the like. These beliefs, which *are* figments, yet lead to real effects to profound emotions, actual behaviour towards external people, profound changes in the ego, character and personality, symptoms, inhibitions and capacities. Materially, phantasies are fictions: psychically, they are realities, having real effects.

The problem has often been dealt with by saying that what *is* introjected is an image or 'imago'. This is surely quite correct; but it is too formal and meagre a statement of a complex phenomenon to satisfy us.

For one thing, this statement is the language of the preconscious, not of the unconscious. How do we come – you and I, psychologists and ordinary people alike – to know this distinction, to realize that what we have 'taken inside' is an image and not a bodily concrete object? By a long and complex process of development. Its broad outlines must include the following steps, among others:

555

(a) The earliest phantasies are built mainly upon smell, touch, taste, kinaesthetic and visceral sensations, which at first are more closely linked with the experience of 'taking things in' (sucking and swallowing) than with anything else. The visual element is extremely small.

(b) These sensations (and images) are a part of bodily experience, scarcely capable of being referred to an external, spatial object. The kinaesthetic and visceral elements are never capable of this. They give phantasy a concrete bodily quality, a 'me-ness'. They are experienced in the body and on this level, *images* are scarcely if at all distinguishable from actual sensations and external perceptions. They refer to the inside. Perceiving is introjection.

(c) The visual element in perception slowly increases and presently becomes spatially differentiated. But the early visual *images* are 'eidetic' in quality – probably even up to three or four years of age. They are intensely vivid, concrete and often confused with perceptions. Moreover, they remain for long intimately bound up with visceral and kinaesthetic responses: they are closely linked with emotions and tend to actions. (Many of the details referred to here so summarily have been well worked out by academic psychologists.)

(d) During the period of development when the visual elements in perception (and in corresponding *images*) begin to predominate over the visceral and kinaesthetic, becoming differentiated and spatially integrated, and thus making clearer the distinction between the inner and the outer worlds, the concrete bodily elements, visceral and kinaesthetic, in the total experience of perceiving (and phantasying) undergo *repression*. The visual externally referred elements in phantasy become relatively de-emotionalized, de-sexualized, in-dependent, in the preconscious of bodily ties. They become *images* in the narrower sense, representations in the mind but not in the body of external objects recognized to be such. It is 'realized' that the objects are outside the mind, but their *images* are 'in the mind'.

In 'Negation', it may be noted Freud points out the part played by frustration and loss in this process. After saying 'What is not real, what is merely imagined or subjective, is only *internal*; while on the other hand what is real is also present *externally*', he later adds: 'But it is evident that an essential pre-condition for the institution of reality testing is that objects shall have been lost which have formerly afforded real satisfaction.' [Freud, S. 1925:369–70; SE 19:236–7][13]

(e) Such *images*, however, *draw their power to affect the mind* by being 'in it', their influence upon feelings, behaviour, character and personality, upon the mind as a whole, *from their repressed unconscious visceral and kinaesthetic associates,* the unconscious whole of phantasy, *which form the link with the id*; and which do mean, in Ucs phantasy, that the objects to which they refer are inside the body, are incorporated.

In psychoanalytic thought, we hear more of '*imago*' than of *image*. I take it that the distinctions between an '*imago*' and an '*image*' are: (a) '*imago*' refers to an *unconscious* image (b) '*imago*' refers (exclusively?) to a person or part of a person, the earliest objects, whilst '*image*' may be of any object or situation, human or otherwise: and (c) '*imago*' includes a reference to the visceral, kinaesthetic and emotional elements in the subject's relation to the imaged person, the bodily links in ucs phantasy with the id, the phantasy of incorporation which underlies the process of introjection.

In sum: (a) Unconscious phantasies are *about* the body, and express instinctual aims. (b) They are psychic phenomena. (c) They have both psychic and bodily 'real' effects. (d) They form the *operative link* between instincts and mechanisms; e.g., the 'result' of the phantasy of incorporation *is* the psychic process of introjection.

DR EDWARD GLOVER: Throughout the years during which Mrs Klein and her adherents have put their views and interpretations before this Society, it has become increasingly obvious that they would sooner or later be compelled to produce a metapsychology to fit their views. For a time however it was not certain whether they would treat Freud simply as a pioneer who was in many respects out of date or whether they would seek to engraft their own theories on Freud's psychology. In the first paper of this series Mrs Isaacs made clear that the second of these policies was to be followed. She set herself the twofold task of giving a Kleinian version of the concept of phantasy as used by Freud and at the same time of trying to prove that the new concept was nevertheless a sound Freudian concept, one which had the additional advantages of expanding and enriching the original. But apart from the fact that her efforts ended in failure, in that she confused utterly the Freudian distinction between an imago and a phantasy and, to my mind, blurred also the distinction between the preconscious and the true unconscious, Mrs Isaacs developed a line of approach and a technique of argument which are not only unscientific but in some respects definitely unpsychological. It is important to note this point because in the second paper of the series Dr Heimann not only follows this technique but provides us with its *reductio ad absurdum*. This is not altogether Dr Heimann's fault. Having taken as her subject some early mechanisms and in effect early structure of the ego, she was faced with the necessity of expanding the Klein metapsychology and at the same time of linking to it the clinical interpretations and formulations which were the original cause of the present controversy. And since the basis on which she builds is unsound it follows that flaws must be even more evident in the superstructure.

Although some of the Kleinian methods of argumentation have already been subjected to severe criticism in these discussions, I think it is important to outline these methods in more detail. The main features are as follows: (1) Having quoted passages from Freud the lecturer proceeds to point out what she takes to be their meaning, as if this meaning followed naturally from the quotations. On closer examination however these conclusions prove to be Kleinian assumptions, in most cases unjustifiable assumptions. (2) A Kleinian assumption, in itself unproven, is followed by a Freudian quotation alleged to be in support of it. These two methods can be further subdivided (a) either the assumption refers to the same phase of development with which Freud was concerned or, more frequently (b) the assumption has reference to a phase of development, or to a clinical fact or to a subject entirely different from the phase, fact or subject with which the quotation from Freud is concerned. Unless one is at pains to correct this 'hop, skip and jump' method, disciplined argumentation is impossible. To take a simple instance from [p. 504] of Dr Heimann's paper: Having quoted passages from Freud's *Beyond the Pleasure Principle* about the differentiated outer layer of the living vesicle, whose protective functions (protective, that is, against outer stimuli) are almost more important than that of the reception of stimuli, Dr Heimann goes on to say, 'What Freud describes in these and other passages is that the ego, the surface part of the id, comes into being and functions by means of both taking things into itself and conversely rejecting them from itself'. Now in these passages Freud was *not* considering *taking things* into the ego, he was considering the *living vesicle* in order to illustrate the *biological function* of a layer protecting against *outer stimuli* (the concept of the Reizschutz) and he goes on to point out that in more highly developed organisms the sense organs constitute such a protective layer. But you may ask, why not permit Dr Heimann (or Mrs Klein) also to use such biological analogies in dealing with psychic structure and function? The answer is: simply because neither Dr Heimann nor Mrs Klein are content with analogies. They convert analogies into literal identities. According to them 'taking in things' and 'rejecting' them are, as Dr Heimann's later argument indicates, *identical* with 'introjection' and with the actual taking of the nipple into the mouth or spitting out of the mouth. In the very next paragraph Dr Heimann says '*Thus the mechanism of taking-in*' (note that this is now a mechanism) 'recurs in the operation of attention'. In the next paragraph the adverb is altered. The function of keeping out dangerous stimuli 'is *akin* to the function of discharge and expulsion. However', she goes on immediately to say, 'it *is*[14] an expulsion in so far as the *decision* not to let in the dangerous stimuli, presupposes that a small sample of it has been taken in, *decided upon* as being bad and expelled and the *whole* from which the sample was *taken*, kept out in consequence of the *judgement* to which the sample was subjected'. (Note incidentally the preliminary use of the term 'bad' which later on is used in a moral sense.) The end of this paragraph illustrates method 2. Likening the 'tasting', of stimuli to eating, Dr Heimann goes on, 'And I would suggest that the barrier against stimuli *involves the same process* (my italics) as that of judgement, which Freud actually *compared* (my italics) with eating.' Here she quotes Freud's paper on 'Negation', with a cross-reference to 'Instincts and Their Vicissitudes'.

The paragraph following these quotations contains a confusion between psychic objects and external objects such as might be taken into the mouth. The baby's first attempts (I quote again) 'to make acquaintance with any new *thing* are expressed in efforts to take hold of it and suck or taste it. *As he does so he actually introjects it;* in his experience he *incorporates* it, sucks it in, eats it up.' (All italics mine.) And note the next quotation, 'The *evidence* of this familiar observation is that the way in which the baby takes in the outer world is *on the oral pattern* and is *bound up with* introjection. Thus', she continues, 'the function of *attention . . . follows the pattern* of oral incorporation.' (My italics.) But at the beginning of this paragraph Dr Heimann asks how the baby *gets to know* the outside world and answers by saying: 'he devotes an intense attention to his surroundings'. [See p. 506.] This sample of Dr Heimann's methods of argument is already lengthy enough, but the same processes of faulty reasoning, confusion of biological analogies with psychological facts, inconsequent mixing of phases, jumping from one to another whether they have any connection or not, confusion of subjective and objective, goes on throughout the whole paper. Dr Heimann in fact plays with Freud's theories as a kitten plays with a ball of wool.

This brings me to the third feature of Kleinian methods of argument. (3) It consists in referring to Mrs Klein's work and its importance as if the work and the conclusions must be taken as self-evident and true, the work proving the conclusions, the conclusions equally supporting the work – *whereas the fact is that we are at present investigating the validity of both the work and the conclusions.* For example 'her (Mrs Klein's) work has shown', 'Melanie Klein came to understand through her analysis', 'in the light of these findings'. 'Here, too, Melanie Klein's discoveries'. 'No chapter . . . has been enriched so much by Melanie Klein's researches'. [See pp. 514–15.] I don't think it is worth while to quote these passages *in extenso*. I am only concerned with the technique of presentation which is to suggest by implication that the subject of controversy is already an accepted fact.

(4) A fourth feature of the argument is the dovetailing of controversial metapsychological assumptions with portions of Mrs Klein's systems of interpretation, the validity of which, I would again remind you, we are at present discussing. Her metapsychological series includes such unproven assumptions as the following: the identity of external and of psychic stimuli (hence the identity of sensory experience and ideational cathexis), the identity of 'taking in', introjection, incorporation, and eating: the equation of traumatic stimuli with what, it is alleged, the child regards as 'bad', later with a moral appreciation of 'bad' as opposed to 'good'; the equation of psychical projection and somatic rejection: the postulation of 'whole' objects (whatever whole may mean): the *maintenance* of life instincts, indeed of life itself, by means of introjection and projection (my ital.): the view that structure has an aim like an instinct: that the organism (whether psychic or somatic is not made clear) is in a condition of conflict from the beginning of life and that external stimuli are accidental; the theory of 'internal objects' in general and in particular of an 'introjected breast' which forms 'the core for all further object relations', and which is 'the object of the child's auto-erotic wishes and experiences'; the abolition of the distinction between auto-erotism and narcissism (hence the implication of an identity between organ excitation and psychic cathexis of the ego). (In passing it is significant that Dr Heimann has no sooner abolished the distinction than she proceeds to establish a distinction of her own or Mrs Klein's, the postulation of an early phase of 'maximal sadism', the identity of hallucinatory gratification and (a) auto-erotism, (b) the child's alleged relation to a 'good' inner breast 'felt' as such (whether consciously or not is not stated) and subsequent projected, the association of mental tension with powerful bad objects felt by the baby to be in his inside, the identity of these so-called inner objects alleged to be felt by the baby with psychic objects, the view that the mouth is the main organ for the discharge of destructive impulses and again that it is the 'introjecting organ': that projection is one of two main protections against organ loss, that memory is ultimately derived from the external object. And so on.)

This formidable list of misconceptions, only a few of which if sponsored by a candidate in training would give rise to grave misgivings as to his qualifications, is not compiled merely to point out what a whirl of confusion can be caused by undisciplined psychological thinking. Nor am I concerned solely with the fact that their tendency is opposed in many vital particulars to accepted Freudian theory. But I do wish to point out that running in parallel series, we find the familiar Kleinian interpretation built up piecemeal: the 'introjected' 'good' or 'bad' breast (or nipple), the inner persecuting bad breast, and at the same time the view that hostile feelings constitute an attack on the 'inner object', fear of expelling the 'good' with the 'bad', frantic taking in and expelling of psychic objects, the 'whole' mother, reparation wishes, anxiety of destroying and losing the loved mother, the 'infantile depressive position', the 'introjected penis', in fact the whole Klein nexus of interpretation. Now it seems that this method is regarded as a process of proof – a new kind of evidence. Assertions are piled on assumptions, the assumptions prove the assertions and the assertions the assumptions!

One last feature of the argumentation calls for attention. It is a feature that might escape the attention of the unwary because at first sight it appears quite natural. Sandwiched between layers of quotation, assumption and interpretation are a number of statements, some of which are familiar Freudian views without any particular reference to indicate their original bearing (e.g. the equation between breast and penis, penis and child, child and faeces), some general statements having no particular psychological bearing but purporting to do so ('the most fundamental vital processes of any living organism consist of intake and discharge'). The first of these two types is of course the commoner but it must be observed that the object of this procedure is not to expound Freudian psychology but to support Kleinian interpretations and generally to create an impression of their plausibility.

Faced by these methods of technique of argumentation and by the complexity of the interweaving process one is compelled not only to isolate the individual flaws but to restate fundamental differences. The fact is that Dr Heimann, speaking as a Klein adherent, has continued the disintegrating process started by Mrs Isaacs in the first paper of the series. Amongst the many serious flaws which she presents to us as Kleinian discoveries I would single out (1) her incapacity to distinguish between the concept of the psychic apparatus, the structure of the ego and the subjective experiences of the child and (2) the gradual disappearance of the psychology of the unconscious. Dr Isaacs in effect attacked the Freudian concept of the

561

unconscious by confusing the true unconscious and the pre-conscious.

Dr Heimann has gone farther: she has equated the unconscious with the experiences of consciousness. I emphasize this latter point because it seems to me to confirm a suspicion I have long held regarding many of Mrs Klein's interpretations, viz. that they carry the hallmark of secondary or even conscious elaboration. What Mrs Klein projects into or, perhaps better, attributed to the child's mind will, I think, prove in many instances to be simple, adult conjectures about the child's subjective reactions, in other words what she thinks the child ought to think.

Notes

1 'The attribute to be decided about may originally have been good or bad, useful or harmful. Expressed in the language of the oldest – the oral – instinctual impulses, the judgement is: "I should like to eat this", or "I should like to spit it out": and, put more generally, "I should like to take this into myself and to take that out".' [SE 19: 236–7]

2 'Insofar as the objects which are presented to it are sources of pleasure, it takes them into itself, "introjects" them (to use Ferenczi's 1909 term): and, on the other hand, it expels whatever within itself becomes a cause of unpleasure.' [SE 14:136]

3 'At any rate the process, especially in the early phases of development, is a very frequent one and it makes it possible to suppose that the character of the ego is a precipitate of abandoned object cathexes and that it contains the history of those object choices.' [SE 19:29]

4 '. . : the original pleasure-ego wants to introject into itself everything that is good and reject from itself everything that is bad. What is bad, what is alien to the ego and what is external are, to begin with, identical.' [SE 19:237]

5 'Thus we form the idea of there being an original libidinal cathexis of the ego, from which some is later given off to objects, but which fundamentally persists and is related to the object cathexes much as the body of an amoeba is related to the pseudopodia which it puts out.' [SE 14:75]

6 '*It seems, then, that an instinct is an urge inherent in organic life to restore an earlier state of things* which the living entity has been obliged to abandon under the pressure of external disturbing forces.' [SE 18:36]

7 'At a later stage it becomes relatively easy for us to follow the vicissitudes of the libido, but this is more difficult with the destructive instinct.' [SE 23:150]

8 'The child's lips, in our view, behave like an erotogenic zone, and no doubt stimulation by the warm flow of milk is the cause of the pleasurable sensation.' [SE 7:181]

9 'In the first instance the oral component instinct finds satisfaction by attaching itself to the sating of the desire for nourishment; and its object is the mother's breast. It then detaches itself, becomes independent and at the same time auto-erotic, that is, it finds an object in the child's own body.' [SE 18:245]

10 'A child's first erotic object is the mother's breast that nourishes it; love has its origin in attachment to the satisfied need for nourishment. There is no doubt that to begin with, the child does not distinguish between the breast and its own body; when the breast has to be separated from the body and shifted to the "outside" because the child so often finds it absent, it carries with it as an "object" a part of the original narcissistic libidinal cathexis.' [SE 23:188]

11 'Expressed in the language of the oldest – the oral – instinctual impulses, the judgement is: "I should like to eat this", or "I should like to spit it out": and, put more generally, "I should like to take this into myself and to take that out". That is to say: "It shall be inside me" or "It shall be outside me".' [SE 19:236–7]

12 (Original footnote) '. . . hysterical symptoms spring from phantasies and not from real events.' [Freud, S. 1933a:154]

'. . . hysterical symptoms are derived from phantasies and not from real occurrences.' [SE 22:120]

13 'What is unreal, merely a presentation and subjective, is only internal; what is real is also there outside . . . but it is evident that a precondition for the setting up of reality-testing is that objects shall have been lost which once brought real satisfaction.' [SE 19:236–7]

14 (Original footnote) Only the word 'is' is underlined in the original. The other italicized words are underlined by me to call attention to the fact that even in elaborating a biological analogy Dr Heimann falls into confusion between biological and psychical function. Also that this confusion is anthropomorphized and expressed in terms of consciousness.

Seventh
Discussion of Scientific Controversies

**A Meeting of Members and Associate Members
was held on Wednesday, November 17th, 1943, at 8 p.m.,
at 96 Gloucester Place, London, W.1.**

(Seventh meeting of the series of Scientific Discussions on controversial topics existing within the Society.)

Dr Glover was in the Chair and 19 Members and Associates were present (Payne, Sharpe, Friedlander, Weiss, Klein, Heimann, Riviere, Money-Kyrle, Wilson, Low, Ruben, Stross, Hedwig Hoffer, Reis, Fleischer-Gero, Mrs Milner, Dr Usher, H. Schwarz, Dr Hoffer)

Three candidate-guests were present (Gompertz, Dr Little, Dr Pratt.)

Dr Glover opened the meeting. The Secretary read the minutes of the previous meeting which were passed and signed.

Miss Low asked to be allowed to make a statement.

MISS LOW made the following statement:
I want to make a strong protest in reference to the proceedings concerning the Lecture Committee at the meeting held on November 3rd. The subject of the Lecture Committee had not been placed on the Agenda for this evening. Therefore I hold it to be quite out of order to make any decisions on the matter. (A discussion was quite admissible under 'any other business'.) Dr Payne tells me there is no rule to forbid such decisions without the matter being placed on the

Agenda. That does not answer my point. One cannot always have a rule applying to every point. Though it is a fundamental principle of all societies never to take decisions or vote on any matter until it had been put on the agenda and duly notified to all members. There is an order of tradition and fair procedure even if by oversight an actual rule has not been drawn up. In this case the procedure was undemocratic, unfair, and very discourteous.

I am primarily concerned, as I said, with the procedure. But it is obviously quite improper that sub-committees, in this case the Medical Sub-committee, should be allowed special privileges in placing individuals from their own committee without free election on the Lecture Committee. We must have a free independent committee, elected in the ordinary way by votes of all Members on an equal footing. The present arrangements would give the Medical Sub-committee a special position, which is undesirable.

Several people were obliged to leave the meeting early. A large number of Members were absent owing to war service and a number present have informed me that the discussion was so sprung upon them and so confusing that they were unable to vote at all. It seems almost unbelievable that even the Secretary of the Lecture Committee was neither informed nor consulted concerning the discussion and the subsequent decisions (he was absent owing to fire-guard duties).

Therefore the correct procedure is for all the decisions made, of which notice has been sent to Members, to be cancelled entirely and for a fresh meeting to be called at a convenient time for which a discussion on the Lecture Committee shall be placed on the Agenda. All absentee Members to be asked to send in their views in writing. One month should be allowed to elapse between the notice and the meeting itself.

DR W. HOFFER: I should very much like to support Miss Low's proposal that this special Lecture Committee should be discussed here. Is this Lecture Committee to be the same as that I remember was chosen in 1938 or 1939 at the Annual General Meeting? I understood that the Lecture Committee proposed last week is the one Miss Low now says was not correctly decided upon. For us who are less acquainted with parliamentary procedure it was surprising that this Public Lecture Committee was linked up with that committee elected last time, the Child Welfare and the Medical Committee.

DR PAYNE made the following statement:
I am surprised at Miss Low's protest as it amounts to a vote of censure of the Chairman. He did not rule the election out of order at

the time and if it was out of order he should have done so. Miss Low speaks of changes being introduced without notice being on the Agenda. To have a Lecture Committee is a settled policy of the Institute, and it existed for at least ten years before the war, when it was temporarily suspended. It has to be elected by the Board if it is a standing committee. A committee elected as suggested is an *ad hoc* committee only, as the Chairman pointed out.

If we go back to the annual meeting you will remember that there were two proposals, one to elect a Medical Committee to (a) consider the position of the Institute in relation to post-war medical reconstruction, (b) consider methods of co-operation with the medical profession. This Medical Committee gave a report at the meeting under discussion in which it was recommended that lectures on psychopathology should be given regularly to psychiatrists and medical practitioners. This is not a new policy; all that is new is the specialized form of the lectures to be given. It was felt that a committee should be formed at once not to give lectures immediately but to consider the syllabus, and arrange lecturers so that they can be started directly the war is over. The proposal for a lecture committee arose out of this report.

MISS LOW AND DR HOFFER say that they see no relation between the Medical Committee and a lecture committee.

(MISS LOW, interrupting: I did not say that there was no relation, I said there was no ground for giving the Medical Committee special privileges.)

DR PAYNE (continuing): The Medical Committee was elected by the Society. The main point arising out of their considerations was the giving of lectures. Presumably Miss Low would consider that medical Members should deal with lectures to the medical profession. Unless the Medical Committee has representatives on the Lecture Committee the work already done will have to be wasted. The only reason for the suggestion is to ensure continuity. The same arguments apply to the Child Welfare Committee the election of which was discussed at the meeting.

MISS LOW: Dr Payne has not answered a single point I raised. It is not true that these decisions were made in a democratic way by the Society. They were not discussed, there was no time for it and all absent Members were ruled out by it not having been put on the Agenda. I went home early because I did not want to be stranded at night. If I had had an idea that this matter was going to be discussed I should have stayed, of course. For Dr Payne to reply that it was an open meeting – it is not true, because it was not put on the Agenda as it should. The Medical Committee was elected for its own business and its own work.

(DR PAYNE: But there are only two of its members to represent it on the Lecture Committee.) [MISS LOW:] I don't care whether it's two or two hundred. It is a matter of principle whether the Medical Sub-committee has a right to have its two members on the Lecture Committee unless elected by the whole of the Society. The Society elected the Medical Committee, but not for the Public Lecture Committee.

DR PAYNE: It is not a Public Lecture Committee, it is an *ad hoc* Committee to organize special lectures.

MISS LOW: I don't think you have answered a single point.

DR GLOVER: As I have to give a ruling as far as this meeting is concerned, I think that we are not in a position to deal with the matter under discussion. As regards the issue raised, some of you may remember the last utterance of mine at the last meeting, viz. that there had been enough irregularities at that meeting. It is true, the original suggestion to have a Lecture Committee was altered by a suggestion to make it an *ad hoc* committee. Nevertheless in so far as neither suggestion was on the agenda, I am ready to accept criticism on this point. As regards the method of selection of the *ad hoc* Lecture Committee, however, I protested quite vigorously but my protest was overruled. It seems to me that Miss Low's only means of redress is to invoke the clause calling an extraordinary meeting of Members.

The Chairman then opened the subject of the meeting, viz. continuation of the discussion on Dr P. Heimann's paper, 'Some Aspects of the Role of Introjection and Projection in Early Development'. Miss Ella Sharpe gave a contribution and then Dr Heimann replied to the previous discussion. In a spontaneous discussion Dr Kate Friedlander and Dr Glover spoke in turn.

(All papers read in the discussion were recorded, duplicated, and circulated to Members.)

(signed) Edward Glover

Discussion held on November 17th, 1943

Conclusion of Discussion on Dr P. Heimann's paper 'Some Aspects of the Role of Introjection and Projection in Early Development'

MISS ELLA SHARPE: 'A Clinical Reference'. I would like to give a simple clinical example bearing upon the present discussion.

Dr Payne pointed out in her contribution that the mechanism of introjection does not necessarily lead to identification. What follows often tends to be regarded by the ego as a foreign body. She further noted that Dr Heimann quoted Freud's article on 'Negation' in dealing with projection, while Freud himself was talking about rejection by means of repression, not by projection. The pleasure ego tries to introject into itself everything that is good, good meaning pleasurable and not to be equated with the morally good, and it tries to reject all that is bad, that is the unpleasurable which is not to be equated with the morally evil.

Over and over again in clinical work it has occurred to me that perhaps what I regard as a problem of repression on the part of the ego, i.e., rejection because of displeasure, would be attributed by Mrs Klein to introjection. I am speaking of psycho-neurotics, of course.

Take as an example the phantasy of two people fighting inside, which I have had revealed to me often enough especially in dreams. The attitude of the ego has varied, sometimes the onlooker has been dispassionate, sometimes there has been fearful apprehension lest one of the two combatants should be vanquished. In terms of projection or displacement instead of introjection this phantasy reveals itself in patients incapable of identifying themselves with one or other side in national disputes.

Now for me the mechanism of dynamic importance in this phantasy is repression. The ego rejected, i.e. repressed reality experiences because they caused displeasure, frustration aroused rage. My opinion is that such repression reached its zenith when the ego had learned through reality experiences that external dangers to the body were to be feared and avoided. For along with the knowledge of parental intercourse there goes into the limbo of the forgotten the pre-latency masturbation.

For me the phantasy is possible entirely through repression of early masturbation, which itself was inseparable from some type of knowledge concerning parental intercourse.

I have found in cases where anxiety was manifested lest one or other of the partners should be vanquished the clearest evidence that the child masturbated *while* the intercourse of the parents proceeded. The anxiety felt was lest the parents should discover his activities, while the war lasted he was safe.

I am not concerned here with the re-activation of magical and omnipotent modes that possibly follow repression, only with the purpose such a phantasy serves, namely as an ego defence. The mechanism of paramount importance is repression. To speak of 'introjection' of the two parents is in my view to miss the realities that made the phantasy both possible and necessary.

DR PAULA HEIMANN (formally replying to previous discussion): I shall not be able to reply to all points of criticism made by the various contributors to the discussion. I shall select those which seem to raise problems of general importance or are of special interest to me. (I am adding here that I am not replying to Miss Sharpe's contribution, as I have only just heard it.)

I shall start by taking up the important point raised by Dr Brierley, viz. her view that my definition of introjection and projection is a 'subjective' one. Now I should fully agree with Dr Brierley, that it is the aim of psychological science to reach objective truths about the mind, that is to say, about subjective experience. We arrive at such knowledge on the basis of what we observe of the subject's actions, including his signs of feeling and what he tells us in words of his experiences, memories and conscious imaginings. By means of such data, Freud reached irrefutable proof of the existence of unconscious wishes, feelings and phantasies. Our knowledge of these Ucs processes is always inferred, never direct, and there is always the possibility of error. Repeated recurrences of data of the same kind, however, in our own and other workers' experience, yield a relatively trustworthy conviction of inherent psychological laws, both general and individual. That is to say, we come to know that when such and such a desire is aroused the individual takes such and such steps towards its fulfilment. When he is frustrated, he behaves in such and such ways. When he is anxious, he tries to protect himself in some specific manner. Whilst formulating our conclusions about these and similar phenomena in our objective theories, we are nevertheless always fundamentally concerned with 'subjective' data, 'subjective' processes. The mind is essentially something which feels, wishes, fears, phantasies, and thinks, and cannot be known apart from these phenomena.

Dr Brierley remarks that 'if we persist in equating mental functions with our subjective interpretation of them, we forfeit our claim to be scientists and revert to the primitive state of the Chinese peasant who interprets an eclipse as the sun being swallowed by a dragon. His subjective logic may be unanswerable, but his explanation of the event is erroneous.' Dr Brierley is here being led far astray by her own analogy. The science of psychology is not to be equated with the science of astronomy. What *we* are studying is *not* the solar system, but the mind of the Chinese peasant, not the eclipse but the belief of the peasant concerning the eclipse. How do such beliefs arise, what function have they in mind, how are they related to other mental phenomena, such as sensation, feeling, and perception? And further, how does the knowledge that the sun is *not* swallowed by a dragon develop in the mind of peasants and philosophers? The function of reality-testing and its relation to early experience and Ucs phantasies is itself an essential part of our subject-matter, but has for the psychologist no claim to priority of importance over the more primitive mental processes from which it is derived.

Dr Brierley often asks us to describe and discuss the 'nature of the process itself' and not its content or subjective aspect. She says: 'But to understand the subjective significance of a given process does not necessarily throw much light on the nature of the process itself. Nor is the nature of the process itself to be confused with the purposes for which we use it.' [See p. 538.] Here it seems to me that Dr Brierley is not satisfied with strictly psychological knowledge. She wants something beyond psychology, something absolute and ultimate which is outside the scope of empirical science. The distinction between the so-called subjective and the so-called objective approach, between the 'nature of the process itself' and its content is one which belongs to the philosophy of science rather than to our empirical studies within the field of psychology as such. These ultimate problems of the philosophy of science are full of interest, and I should like to follow them with Dr Brierley, but they are altogether outside our present scope and are not relevant to my paper.

If, however, I were to follow Dr Brierley into these problems of the philosophy of science, I should have to question most seriously her apparent suggestion that there are psychological concepts and theories which have been proved to be of use in 'therapeutic and other direct contact forms of work' and which yet are somehow scientifically inferior. Surely one of the most distinctive tests of sound scientific theory is that it operates successfully in practice and promotes new discoveries.

Keeping within the strict field of empirical method, the suggestion that we should discuss 'the nature of the process itself' rather than its content seems to rest upon a false assumption. The nature of mental process, as well as of the structure and mechanisms of the mind, is partly determined and characterized by phantasies, that is to say, by the subjective content of the mind which has a variety of effects at different times. (This subjective content itself is largely determined by biological conditions, the workings of the instincts.) When the mind itself, which is the domain of the subjective, is the object of study, we still have to be objective in our attitude towards the phenomena we are studying; but we have to accept and to remember that the nature of the object is to be 'subjective'. 'We cannot dictate to things their characteristics', as Freud said in connection with dreams being indefinite or nonsensical. [Freud, S. 1916/17:68; SE 15:85][1] If the formation of the mental organization is influenced by phantasy, we cannot protest. It either is or is not, and our business is to ascertain the facts. It may be a false *assumption* to assert a priori that 'image-formation will not go into subjective incorporation'. Perhaps it will, although we should not consider this a good way of describing the phenomenon.

Dr Brierley draws our attention to the extremely important experience of frustration. It is a fact, as she says, that 'when the baby is trying to put everything into its mouth, it comes across many things that won't go in'. [See p. 537.] But what is the conclusion? This fact does not contradict the existence and significance of the oral impulse to incorporate; it changes the baby's experience and therefore his phantasies by frustrating his impulses. We know that the result of such frustration is the modification of impulse, the search for other modes of gratification, the utilizing of other means of discharging tension and gaining pleasure, the progressive cathexis of other and non-oral objects, the substitution of the reality principle for the pleasure principle, and so on and so forth. Frustration is an extremely important factor in development. But to appreciate the part it plays, we cannot neglect the function of phantasy. When things will not go into his mouth, the baby is deprived of bodily pleasures and actual satisfaction. But in his Ucs phantasies he is omnipotent and does get things into his mouth. Mentally, anything can go into anything; we cannot overlook the importance – shown by Freud – of the primitive function of hallucinatory manipulation of frustration. We are considering here an extremely complex situation. The real frustration is felt as a sensation of pain (Unlust), and this colours the perception of the external object as well as the feelings about the internal object which in phantasy he has swallowed. It has become a 'bad' object inside, because it frustrated him, and since *ex hypothesi* the baby is under the sway of oral primacy, he equates the painful sensation of being frustrated with a phantasied 'bad' breast. In my paper I showed how such a situation sets into operation both introjective and projective mechanisms. The frustration of oral impulses leads on the one hand to the phantasy system of bad internal objects and on the other to the marshalling of other instinct components and other mental mechanisms, including reality development and reality differentiation.

A further important point is the relation between images and phantasies. Dr Brierley says: 'It is the development of imagery that makes it feasible to swallow anything in imagination.' [See p. 536.] But how does imagery develop? From the sensations and feelings which are the result of primary impulses acting towards the external world and the external world acting on impulses. Mrs Riviere expressed this view in her paper, 'The Genesis of Psychical Conflict in Earliest Infancy'. [Riviere 1936:399] I quote: 'that from the very beginning of life . . . the psyche responds to the reality of its experiences by interpreting them – or, rather, by *mis*-interpreting them in a subjective manner that increases its pleasure and preserves it from pain . . . phantasy-life is never pure phantasy: It consists of true perceptions and of false interpretations; all phantasies are thus mixtures of external and internal reality.' Primitive impulses are expressed first in visceral and kinaesthetic sensations with accompanying affects. The mouth can want to take in and the wish can be felt in the mind before the formation of explicit imagery. It seems to me that Dr Brierley is using the term 'image' too narrowly. She seems to have only or mainly preconscious images in mind, and moreover mainly images of the visual order. But perception and image-formation cannot be sharply separated from Ucs phantasy. As Mrs Isaacs pointed out in her contribution to this discussion the earliest sensations and images are predominantly kinaesthetic, visceral, touch, taste and smell, the visual element being very small. The visual element in perception and imagery becomes gradually differentiated and grows in extent and significance, but it long remains closely associated even in the preconscious with bodily experiences. Later on, the visceral and kinaesthetic elements with which early visual imagery is bound up become repressed. Visual images then become in the preconscious relatively independent, de-sexualized and de-emotionalized. 'They become "images" in the narrower sense, representations "in the mind", but not in the body, of external objects, recognized as such. It is "realized" that the objects are outside the mind, but their images are "in the mind".' (In passing I may remind you of instances which show the connection between perception and bodily sensation: even in adult life the perception of appetizing food 'makes our mouth water'.)

It will be seen therefore that Dr Brierley is under a misapprehension in thinking that in our view 'images' are equated with internal objects. They are seen to develop from Ucs phantasy in interplay with perception of the external world. They are a preconscious phenomenon, though in Ucs phantasy they may be associated with internal objects.

I shall now take up the comments made regarding oral primacy. I agree with both Dr Payne and Dr Brierley that oral primacy is not oral monopoly. In fact Mrs Klein has frequently emphasized the overlapping of the different impulses, which shows that she does not think in terms of any monopoly. The child gains experience from other parts of his body as well as his mouth, but these are brought to a focus by his oral impulses. By 'oral primacy' we mean that at the beginning of life oral impulses and sensations predominate over all others, and bring a greater intensity of pleasure and therefore greater possibilities of frustration. They lay down a pattern of experience, and colour and influence other experiences of the body, as well as the way in which the child reacts to these. I fully agree that many problems still remain with regard to these earliest phases of development and that there is much that is obscure or conjectural, but so far I have seen no reason to modify the view of the predominance of the oral phase of libidinal development at the beginning of life. It may be that Dr Payne and Dr Brierley attribute somewhat less importance to the oral elements, and this would necessarily lead to a different valuation of introjection. It may be that the apparent difference between us, however, is due rather to a misunderstanding. (Perhaps Dr Payne and Dr Brierley momentarily forgot the perspective of my paper.) I may remind you that I was specifically asked to discuss 'The Role of Introjection and Projection in Early Development'. The necessary limits of length made it possible to deal only with *some aspects* of these questions, and I embodied this limitation in my title. Nevertheless, I did point out that other early defence mechanisms, of which I mentioned a few, also had a decisive influence upon development. I fully agree that these other aspects of mental life and other mechanisms would require to be far more thoroughly described in any account of mental development which claimed to be comprehensive.

I shall turn now to an important point in Dr Friedlander's contribution, one which was also raised by Mrs Hoffer and referred to by Dr Glover. This concerns our views on the death instinct.

In the first place I must express my astonishment that it is so often asserted that Freud arrived at his concept of a death instinct merely by speculation and biological considerations. This is not so in fact, and it seems strange how it can be forgotten that Freud in *Beyond the Pleasure Principle* starts from clinical observations: the dreams of people suffering from traumatic neuroses (which repeat the traumatic event), and the play of children. It is true that he breaks off the discussion of both these phenomena, but it becomes clear that in showing the element of repetition in both he has already made the essential point. He goes then on to describe the observation that patients instead of recollecting the repressed events repeat them as a current experience. At this point Freud introduces the concept of 'repetition-compulsion' and demonstrates the existence of a repetition compulsion also in the lives of non-neurotic people. 'It here gives the impression of a pursuing fate, a daemonic trait in their destiny. . .' [Freud, S. 1920:22; SE 18:21][2] This concept served as a springboard to the concept of the death instinct which Freud then proceeded to elaborate with the aid of biological speculation. The repetition-compulsion, however, is the connecting link between the death instinct and observable clinical data (certain dreams, play of children, acting-out of patients under analysis, daemonic trait in people's destiny).

I quote from *Beyond the Pleasure Principle*, 'In the light of such observations . . . . drawn from the behaviour during transference and from the fate of human beings, we may venture to make the assumption that there really exists in psychic life a repetition-compulsion, which goes beyond the pleasure-principle. We shall now also feel disposed to relate to this compelling force the dreams of shock-patients and the play-impulse in children. We must of course remind ourselves that only in rare cases can we recognize the workings of this repetition-compulsion in a pure form, without the co-operation of other motives. . . .' [Freud, S. 1920:24; SE 18:22][3]

I wish to emphasize the fact that Freud proceeded from clinical observations when he embarked on his journey to discover the death instinct and that on his way he arrived at a most important psychological discovery, viz: the repetition-compulsion; moreover throughout he returned to clinical facts. It is true that he later entered into the field of speculative biology and it is also true that he never made the acceptance of the death instinct theory a sine qua non of psychoanalysis. He described his own attitude as that of a 'mild goodwill'.

We have already pointed out in various places the fact that Freud did not himself explore all the avenues of research which his observations and his imaginative intellect opened to the work of scientists. We may take *Beyond the Pleasure Principle* as an example of the pursuit of scientific ideas which have grown out of observation, regardless of any other consideration than scientific interest. The fact mentioned by Dr Friedlander that Freud did not revise his theory of libidinal development in the light of his concept of the death instinct does not preclude our bringing them more closely together, if our own clinical observations appear to call for such a step. When new researches provide us with further facts, not available when particular theories were first formulated, we cannot refuse to expand our theories so as to cover the new material.

But to come back to my main point: it cannot be denied that Freud was led to his view about the death instinct from his clinical observations. To assert otherwise is both untrue and disadvantageous since it appears to put the theory of the death instinct a priori out of the bounds of psychoanalytical research.

Moreover Dr Friedlander seems to be incorrect also in her account of the theory as such. According to her, the death instinct was deflected outward millions of years ago. I do not quite understand how she then can go on to say: 'Since then the interplay between these two tendencies causes the appearance which we call life'. If life became possible by the deflection outwards of the death instinct, how does she reconcile this with 'the interplay between these two tendencies' [see p. 543] – presumably inside the organism – causing 'the appearance which we call life'? But whatever Dr Friedlander's concept of the death instinct may be, Freud's hypothesis is that by cosmological events life was created from the inorganic substance and simultaneously the death instinct (the instinct to return to the inanimate condition) came into being. 'At one time or another, by some operation of force which still completely baffles conjecture, the properties of life were awakened in lifeless matter. Perhaps the process was a prototype resembling that other one which later in a certain stratum of living matter gave rise to consciousness. The tension then aroused in the previously inanimate matter strove to be at an equilibrium; the first instinct was present, that to return to lifelessness.' [Freud, S. 1920:47; SE 18:38][4] And in discussing the interrelation between the two instincts Freud says: 'If, then, we are not to abandon the hypothesis of death instincts, we must associate them with life-instincts from the beginning.' [Freud, S. 1920:73; SE 18:57][5] Dr Friedlander's statement that 'life became possible millions of years ago by a deflection outward of the death instinct' thus differs materially from Freud's exposition. It suggests, moreover, the mistaken idea that once upon a time the death instinct was successfully tackled and settled. I presume, however, that this is not what Dr Friedlander really means to imply. Dr Friedlander questions my correlating the existence of primary antithetical instincts with the existence of psychic conflict, and seems to regard such procedure as a 'psychoanalytic impossibility'. I cannot quote her lengthy discussion and must ask you to look it up for yourselves.

In reference to Dr Friedlander's view that 'the interplay' between the life instinct and the death instinct has not to be correlated with psychic conflict, I wish to remind her of the following two quotations from *Beyond the Pleasure Principle*. Freud says: '. . .the fact that they [refers to the life instincts] runs counter to the trend of the other instincts which lead towards death indicates a contradiction between them and the rest on which the *theory of the neuroses* has recognized as full of significance'. (My italics.) [Freud, S. 1920:50; SE 18:40][6] And again, 'Our recognition that the ruling tendency of *psychic life*, perhaps of nerve life altogether, is the struggle for reduction, keeping at a constant level, or removal of the inner stimulus tension (the Nirvana-principle, as Barbara Low terms it) – a struggle which comes to expression in the pleasure principle – is indeed one of our strongest motives for believing in the existence of death instincts.' (My italics.) In both these passages Freud clearly attributes psychological affects to the existence of antithetical instincts. The second, moreover, shows that in his considerations Freud comes to the death instinct also from the other, the psychological side, as he says that 'our recognition of the ruling tendency of psychic life. . . : is one of our strongest motives for believing in the existing of death instincts.' [Freud, S. 1920:76; SE 18:55–6][7]

Dr Friedlander and Mrs Hoffer seem to think that Mrs Klein does not recognize the fundamental difference between the life instinct and the death instinct. Dr Friedlander says in her account of my views: 'We already get the notion of two equally strong instincts of the same quality but with different aims.' And Mrs Hoffer says: 'Freud's concept (quoted from *Beyond the Pleasure Principle*, [Freud, S. 1920:44; SE 18:115] "that there is a tendency innate in living organic matter impelling it towards the reinstatement of an earlier condition" leaves no doubt as to the fundamental difference between this instinct and the libido'. Now, I thought that in my paper I had emphatically stated the fundamental primary antithesis between the two instincts. I am puzzled to account for these misunderstandings. I can only think that they must have arisen over my claim that (I quote from my paper) 'Freud here did more than discover a character of the libido: he stated a special case of a broader principle, which concerns the mode of operation of instinct in general and which rests upon the fact that the human organism is a mind–body entity. The instincts are the source of the energies on which all the mind–body processes depend. They lie . . . on the borderland between soma and psyche; . . . Both the instincts – the libido and the destructive instinct – seek to fulfil their aims in bodily activities. . .' [See p. 513.]

In this passage I expressed my view concerning the mode of operation of these two instincts, i.e., that they both operate through bodily function. But when I thus said that the mode of operation is the same for both instincts, it does not follow that their aims are the same. Indeed there can be no doubt that I saw and described their aims as antithetical. That there is a common nature between the instincts has been stated by Freud, as follows: 'No knowledge would have been so important for the establishment of a sound psychology as some approximate understanding of the common nature and possible differences of the instincts. . . .' [Freud, S. 1920:64; SE 18:51][8] Thus Freud expected that the instincts in spite of their antithetical aims have something in common with each other. With my suggestion that they have in common the mode of operation I am closely following Freud's view. Mrs Hoffer, I take it, does not agree with me. Yet she quotes a passage from Freud which fully warrants my suggestion. Let me quote the relevant words again in the quotation which Mrs Hoffer chose, '. . . that there is a tendency *innate in living organic matter* impelling towards the reinstatement of an earlier condition' (my italics). 'Living organic matter' – is this not the body? And if there is innate in the body such a tendency, how else than through bodily function can it express itself and pursue its aim of the reinstatement of an earlier condition, i.e., death and the breaking up of the unity of the cells comprising the body. We know that this destructive tendency becomes deflected outward under the influence of the libido; how else than through bodily function which discharges tension, does such deflection take place?

Mrs Hoffer reminds us that in Freud's view emotional factors account for the late discovery of the death instinct. But this is no reason for withholding any attempt to carry on research into its operations, its interplay with the libido, its effect on emotions, object relations, and the whole personality. We have to overcome emotional obstacles and be objective. Freud's 'laconic remark', 'It becomes relatively easy for us to follow the late vicissitudes of the libido; but this is more difficult with the destructive instinct', is in Mrs Hoffer's view 'not too encouraging'. That may be so, but this is not the point. I would say not only have we the right to go on with research as far as we are able, but that it is *incumbent* upon us to do so and to make use of the working tools which Freud gave us.

Incidentally an inaccuracy of statement slipped into Mrs Hoffer's discussion. She quotes from my paper: 'But when . . . Mrs Klein came to devote full attention to the destructive impulses. . .' [see p. 551] and then proceeds to ask: 'how was it possible for Mrs Klein to devote full attention to the *death instinct*?' (My italics.) Now I spoke of devoting attention to the destructive impulses; Mrs Hoffer, however, speaks of the 'death instinct'. This makes a difference. As you may have noticed, I have used the term 'death instinct' when referring to theoretical deductions, and the term 'destructive impulses' when dealing with clinical considerations. I believe we are all agreed on the fact that what we are actually observing and dealing with in the analysis of a patient is his impulses, the derivatives of instinct, not the instincts themselves. When we think about the origin of the impulses and when we formulate our theories, then we are wont to speak of instincts. Mrs Hoffer's question thus should read: 'How was it possible for Mrs Klein to devote full attention to the destructive impulses?' The answer is not difficult. Mrs Klein did so when she applied strictly analytic technique in her analysis of young children whom she provided with adequate means – toys – to express themselves. By approaching the material which presented itself to her without any particular preference she came to see the strength of the destructive impulses in the young child, the phantasies connected with them, and the anxieties which they arouse. In this she followed Freud's example in his work with adults.

Many of the points dealt with so far have touched incidentally upon the broad question raised by Dr Friedlander, Mrs Hoffer, and others, namely, the relation between biological and psychological considerations. Dr Friedlander and Dr Glover believe that I confused the two sets of notions (and 'jumped about' between them). Dr Friedlander criticizes my reference to dreaming in this connection. She says, '. . . a biological condition, sleep, has been equated with a psychological condition, the dream, with the result of a misapprehension of Freud's theory of the dream.' [See p. 540.] My answer is: I was not dealing with the theory of dreams. I referred to the 'egoistic concentration upon ourselves – we, the dreamers are always the leading figures.' And when I spoke of 'a highly narcissistic hallucinatory activity' this obviously referred to my words 'our dreams' not to the state of sleep. On second thoughts, however, I would myself demur against giving dreams as an example of an object relation in the infantile narcissistic state, since it might well be argued that objects do not belong to the period *to* which the dreamer regresses, but to the one *from* which he regresses. On these considerations I would agreed that it is not a well-chosen example and does not illustrate my point about the existence of phantasies concerning introjected objects in the narcissistic condition of the infant. However this example was not meant to do more than to illustrate my point and its failure to do so does not affect my argument. Nor does it serve Dr Friedlander's argument. As regards her criticism that I confound a biological with a psychological condition, I must remind her of the fact that Freud elaborated his concept of narcissism on the basis of his investigation of organic illness and physical pain. He goes on to discuss sleep and says: 'The condition of sleep, like illness, implies a narcissistic withdrawal of the libido away from its attachments back to the subject's own person, or, more precisely, to the single desire for sleep. The egoism of dreams fits in very well in this connection. In both states we have, if nothing else, examples of changes in the distribution of the libido which are consequent upon a change in the ego.' [Freud, S. 1914:40; SE 14:83][9] This quotation suffices to show that in calling sleep a 'narcissistic condition' I did not introduce any new notions, but kept quite close to Freud's own words in which he says 'the condition of sleep implies a narcissistic withdrawal. . .'. My description however was certainly condensed.

With regard to the general question, it is certain that psychological concepts are always most intimately bound up with biological considerations. Our subject-matter is the living human being, a psycho-physical entity whose bodily and psychical processes influence each other reciprocally. Freud has said that the concept of instinct is indispensable in psychology, a concept which he has repeatedly described as a borderline concept between mind and body. As I said, he arrived at his biological speculations about the death instinct through his clinical observations and strictly psychological data. On this point, the death instinct is on exactly the same footing as the theory of the libido and instinct theory in general. As Mrs Hoffer indicated that the theory of libidinal development is as biological as it is psychological: and neither more nor less so than the hypothesis of the death instinct.

We follow Freud in using a biological approach to the psychological formulations required by the observed clinical data, and in his attempts to relate psychological phenomena to the wider field of biological processes.

Since Freud derives the ego from the id, which is the reservoir of instinct, and conceives of instinct as a borderline phenomenon, partaking of both bodily and mental processes, it cannot be true that his application of biological notions to psychological data is purely analogical and 'as if'. He does not conceive the actual relationship of psychology to biology as being merely analogical, although he sometimes uses an analogy to elucidate some particular knotty problem. His whole approach to the mental life is based on the view that psychological phenomena are *genetically and functionally* related to biological facts.

Here we may return for a moment to Dr Brierley's points about objectivity and analogy. Dr Brierley is anxious that we should not take analogies too seriously. And yet she seems to treat the notion of the 'psychic apparatus' as if this were not an analogy. But it is an analogy, a very useful one, providing us with tools for the ordering of certain aspects of mental phenomena. But it is not to be taken as a literal description, nor as a tool free from limitations and dangers. It is too concrete an image, and it is drawn from a sphere of concrete reality which is remote from psychological data. It tends if we are not careful to lead us astray into mechanistic notions which are not applicable to our subject-matter such as too sharp a separation of mechanism and content.

In 'Instincts and Their Vicissitudes' Freud wrote:

> Even at the stage of description it is not possible to avoid applying certain abstract ideas to the material in hand, ideas derived from various sources and certainly not the fruit of the new experience only. . . . So long as they remain in this condition, we come to an understanding about their meaning by repeated references to the material in observation, from which we seem to have deduced our abstract ideas, but which is in point of fact subject to them. Thus strictly speaking they are in the nature of conventions; although everything depends on their being chosen in no arbitrary manner, but determined by the important relations they have to the empirical material relations that we seem to divine before we can clearly recognize and demonstrate them.
> [Freud, S. 1915a:60; SE 14:117][10]

I wish to emphasize here Freud's point that everything depends on our abstract ideas being chosen *'in no arbitrary manner, but determined by the important relations they have to the empirical material'*. (My italics.)

When we speak of a 'mechanism' in the psychic apparatus, the usefulness of this analogy is lost, if we forget to have immediately in mind the question: 'A mechanism for what? or against what? For what purpose is it employed? Against what pain is it meant to defend the person?' A rigid separation between 'mechanism' and 'content' is a danger to psychological understanding. It is not in line with Freud's approach and it springs from a basic fallacy: a rigid divorce between the id and the ego. Freud urged us never to forget that the ego is a differentiated part of the id, differentiated under the influence of external stimuli. In dealing with the mind, we are not dealing with an abstract entity which we can separate from its interplay with the body, that is, with the instincts, and study as 'a process' in itself.

There is another point regarding analogy. Dr Brierley says: 'Dr Heimann takes Freud's analogy of stimulus "tasting" literally. In the passages she quotes, Freud writes: "it must suffice to take little samples of the outer world to taste it, so to speak, in small quantities".' These words – Dr Brierley goes on – 'so to speak' appear to me to show that Freud knew exactly what he was doing, namely describing by analogy.

Since Dr Brierley builds so much on these three words 'so to speak' I must point out to her that these three words do not occur in Freud's original writing, which runs: 'Die Reizaufnahme dient vorallem der Absicht, Richtung und Art der äusseren Reize zu erfahren und dazu muss es genügen, der Aussenwelt kleine Proben zu entnehmen, sie in geringen Quantitäten zu verkosten.' ['Jenseits des Lustprinzips.' 1920] 'Bei den hochen entwickelten Organismen hat sich die reizaufnehmende Rindenschicht des einstigen Bläschen längst in die Tiefe des Körperinnern zurückgezogen, aber Anteile von ihr sind an der Oberfläche unmittelbar unter dem allgemeinen Reizschutz züruckgelassen. Dies sind die Sinnesorgane . . .' How the words 'so to speak' came into the English translation by C. M. Rubback I do not know. But this is not my whole answer to the criticism that I take analogies literally. This criticism can only be made on the basis of too sharp a distinction between instinctual impulses and intellectual activities, disregarding the fact shown by Freud that the latter are derived from the former, too sharp a line between id and ego. This sharp demarcation between phenomena which are in fact genetically related corresponds also to the point I mentioned before: the too hard and fast distinction which in my view Dr Brierley makes between psychoanalysis as a therapy and field of observation and psychoanalysis as a theoretical science.

I can reply quite shortly to a point raised by Dr Payne who does not think that Freud did compare the mind to an amoeba. I did not draw this conclusion merely from the passage in 'On Narcissism' referred to by Dr Payne. Throughout *Beyond the Pleasure Principle* Freud uses comparisons with a one-celled organism, unmistakably an amoeba-like creature, though he does not use the word 'amoeba'. This is so also in the quotation which I mentioned before when explaining that in the original writing there is no 'so to speak'. In my view Freud had the amoeba in mind, and not just a hypothetical vesicle.

Another point of Dr Payne's was to the effect that in 'Negation' Freud deals with repression and not with projection. But whilst Freud says that a negative judgement is the intellectual substitute for repression, his whole thesis is that the negative judgement itself derives from projection. He says, 'Judging has been systematically developed out of what was in the first instance introduction into the ego or expulsion from the ego. . .' [Freud, S. 1925:370; SE 19:239][11] At the same time he demonstrates that intellectual functions are derived from the interplay of the primary instinctual impulses. As regards Dr Payne's remarks about identification I fully agree with her that it is desirable to clarify the various terms used in psychoanalytic literature. In fact, I *pointed* out that no definite decision has as yet been made in this matter. On the other hand this fact made it imperative to me to define in what way I used the terms 'introjection' and 'projection'. But it was not my task to investigate the general question of nomenclature, and to discuss where the various terms used coincided, diverged, overlapped, etc. Nor was I dealing primarily with identification. I felt entitled to adduce those particular passages in Freud's writing in which the whole context makes it clear that he deals with introjection, although he uses the term 'identification'. I am not alone in my impression that Freud sometimes uses the two terms interchangeably. Foulkes, from whom I will now quote more fully, says:

> Freud does not care too much about keeping identification and introjection apart. He seems, roughly, to consider complete identification, based on a true, total introjection of the object as the pre-genital object relation, and to correlate a later, partial identification with the preservation of the object, with the genital level. There is however no doubt that he continually connects the notion of introjection with an oral incorporation on a mental plane, an introjection forming the basis of identification, from which it is not always kept strictly apart. On arriving at the formulation that our character is based upon introjected objects he makes it clear that there is perhaps more than an analogy in the primitive belief that we acquire the properties of things which we eat (such as animals), and that we become identified by the taking in of the same substance (for instance, through Holy Communion). His wording, however, remains cautious, and we can never be too sure whether he means that introjection actually is an oral incorporation, or that it can only be compared to it on the basis of a distinct, but not yet fully established correlation.
>
> [Foulkes 1937:274]

A full investigation of the problems connected with introjection and projection, it may reasonably be hoped, will result in establishing such correlation.

You may have noticed that I did not quote the identification processes described in *Group Psychology*. I did not include this type of identification since it is not directly equivalent to introjection, although introjection in fact plays an important role in bringing about the identification between the members of a group. I did not deal with it since it does not strictly belong to my theme. Such deliberate omissions on my part show that I carefully restricted my use of Freud's remarks on identification. As regards the feeling of a 'foreign body' within the boundaries of the self which Dr Payne mentions, I would remind you of my paper on Sublimation, in which I described such a situation in a patient. Such feeling is closely connected with a paranoid relation to the introjected object, a situation in which the introjected object is conceived of as a persecutor. It seems to me that Dr Payne here touches on the problem of ego-syntonic and ego-dystonic introjections, of wished-for identifications and hated identifications, but the problem of identification, as I said, is beyond the scope of my paper. It certainly is a most important problem. I agree with Dr Payne also that there is a vast difference between the imago of the object at the different stages of ego-development, but I thought I had emphasized this point in my paper. That the vast difference in object relations applies also to the introjected objects, I discussed especially when dealing with the superego.

I fully agree with Dr Payne that the phenomena of introjection have also to be investigated from other aspects than that of identification; in fact my paper dealt with some of these other aspects, such as the influence of introjection and projection on the development of the mental structure.

I agree with much of what Dr Payne has said about the development of the body ego, and with the views of Tausk and Schilder. [See p. 547.] But the idea that the hands and feet are ever 'outside the world of the body which is discovered' seems to me a difficult one to accept. I would agree that the hands and feet *as seen* must be at first outside the body as this is felt in kinaesthetic and contact sensations.

Dr Brierley says: 'Personally, I should prefer to keep the word *introjection*, in association with mental mechanism, for the function of the psychic apparatus and the term *incorporation* for imaginary taking-in through any physical channel'. [See p. 536.] We should agree with this. Indeed, this is what I suggested. We do not want the *distinction* lost, either. But we do also want the *relationship* between the mechanism and the phantasy, the ego activity and the id impulse from which it is derived, to be kept in mind. It does not seem to us that either the one or the other, ego or id, can be understood without appreciating the relationship between them. In my view introjection like any mental activity has to be regarded from at least three angles: it is an instinctual derivative and serves the gaining of pleasure; it protects against pain (Unlust) and thus has a defensive function as it serves the developmental process.

A further point can only be touched upon. Dr Friedlander said, 'How is it possible that Mrs Klein's interpretation of the theory of instincts leads her, as Dr Heimann pointed out, to alter the conceptions of auto-erotism, narcissism, object relationship, super-ego formation, etc.' [See p. 544.] As it happens, I did not point this out. On the contrary, I emphasized that Mrs Klein came to her conclusions through her clinical findings, but found a theoretical explanation for many of her data in Freud's concept of the death instinct.

Another point in Mrs Hoffer's comments concerns the erotogenic zones. Here she seems to me to be in error. She thinks I have failed to grasp the meaning of the quotation: 'It is, moreover, clear that the action of the thumb-sucking child is determined by the fact that it seeks a pleasure which has been already experienced and is now remembered. . . . The first and most important activity in the child's life, the sucking from the mother's breast (or its substitute) must have acquainted it with this pleasure', since I did not go on to quote the next sentence: 'we would say that the child's lips behaved like an erogenous zone, and that the excitement through the warm stream of milk was really the cause of the pleasurable sensation'. Mrs Hoffer comments on this by saying: 'Nothing more is stated than the well-known fact that the child is born with erotogenic zones.' [See pp. 552–3.] From the whole context in which she quotes this passage, it seems that Mrs Hoffer believes that the infant has no object relation to the breast, because he derives his pleasurable sensation from his own erotogenic zone. I do not see that this follows at all. Surely Mrs Hoffer will agree that the supreme form of a sexual object relation – adult heterosexual intercourse – is effected by means of erotogenic zones, i.e., the genitals. The possession of erotogenic zones is no distinctive characteristic of the infant, and therefore does not prove anything with regard to the question whether or not the infant has object relations. If the pleasurable sensations provided by erotogenic zones were a criterion of a lack of object relation, we would have to say that the partners in adult sexual intercourse have no relation with each other, since they experience intense pleasurable sensations from their genitals. And such a conclusion *would be a fallacy*.

In concluding my thanks are due to those speakers who by their contributions have helped to clarify and amplify certain points which are of general interest. I would like to add that the discussion has confirmed my own view that the fundamental processes of introjection and projection offer a wide field for further work and study.

Spontaneous Discussion

DR FRIEDLANDER: Perhaps I could just mention one or two points to make my contribution clear. When I speak of deflection outwards of the death instinct I do not mean projection. Secondly, I am very sorry that Dr Heimann has not really answered my point about conflict aroused by the presence of two antithetical instincts. Of course neurosis is caused by internal conflict. The fact, however, that the human being is born with these two antithetical instincts does not prove that it is in a condition of conflict from the beginning. For conflict we need the presence of the mind. That was the point I pressed in my contribution and this point has not been answered.

For these discussions we need to keep apart theory and clinical experience. The validity of a theory cannot be proved, at least in our science, by its application to therapy. For instance, mesmerism and the spring in Lourdes had much better therapeutic results than psychoanalysis. That, however is no proof for the correctness of the theory behind it.

DR EDWARD GLOVER: I think that from one point of view Dr Heimann is to be congratulated on her reply to the discussion. She has at least made some attempt to argue the issues raised. In this respect her reply differs from that made by Mrs Isaacs to the discussion on her (Mrs Isaacs') paper. Mrs Isaacs, you may remember, adopted what I would like to call the 'What did Gladstone say in 1864?' method of reply: that is to say, she was at pains to quote from the earlier writings of her critics with a view to shewing that if these opinions had subsequently altered, the critics' current criticisms were not valid. This is called in legal circles 'damaging the credibility of the witness'. But the method is a two-edged weapon and in any case cannot be accepted as a reply to criticisms on her paper.

But although Dr Heimann's reply differs in this respect from the reply of Mrs Isaacs, I am afraid the result is no more satisfactory from my point of view. For in her arguments she repeats the same confusions of thought and exhibits the same lack of psychological grasp that characterized her paper. It is, of course, difficult to take up her argument in detail. That would require a commentary as lengthy as Dr Heimann's paper. Also, it is not always possible listening to a paper to be quite sure that one has grasped accurately the exact significance of the points raised. But I have made a list of points that seem to me to illustrate my contention and I should like to deal with some of these now.

585

In the first place Dr Heimann takes Dr Brierley to task for insisting that we should distinguish between mental functions and our interpretation of them, a point Dr Brierley illustrated by reference to the reactions of a Chinese peasant to the solar system. Dr Heimann thinks that Dr Brierley is going beyond psychology to ask for some absolute distinctions. Whereas the fact is that Dr Brierley only goes beyond psychology in the sense that she takes up a – legitimate – metapsychological approach. *She simply asks that we should stick to our metapsychological concepts of mental processes, not vary them in accordance with subjective predilection.* The fact that the nature of subjective belief is also part of metapsychological study does not debar her from distinguishing subjective phantasy from concepts of the mental apparatus and of its mechanisms. Incidentally I see Dr Heimann goes on to repeat the old fallacy that we judge of the *validity of subjective interpretations of mental phenomena by their therapeutic effect in analysis.* I was under the impression that I had finally exploded this fallacy in a paper given many years ago, 'The Therapeutic Effect of Inexact Interpretation'. [Glover, 1931] But it seems that this is not the case.

This brings me to the next point. Dr Heimann in her discussion of image and phantasy has – if I have grasped her correctly – put forward the view that *mental mechanisms are partly determined by phantasy.* Expressed in theoretical terms this would mean that the end results of mental processes determine the processes themselves, which is absurd. Dr Brierley's concern was with the necessity of distinguishing mental images from phantasy products.

Again, in stressing the fact that phantasy is caused by frustration, Dr Heimann brings forward an old view on which everyone is agreed. Frustration is certainly one of the stimuli to phantasy formation. But this does not justify any of the confusions of which Dr Heimann is guilty – e.g., the confusion of images and phantasies, or of images and object images. At this point Dr Heimann simply repeats her subjective interpretations about bad internal objects etc. without bringing forward any evidence in support of them.

Coming now to Dr Heimann's lengthy consideration of the death instinct and its functions (although this is strictly speaking Dr Friedlander's concern), there are one or two points that occurred to me. Leaving out of account the issue of the relation of clinical data to (a) the postulation of a repetition compulsion, (b) the characteristics of instinct in general, and (c) to the concept of a death instinct in particular I should like to go straight to a crucial point which, if I followed Dr Heimann rightly, she herself makes at a later stage of the argument. Dr Heimann states that she uses the term 'death instinct' when discussing theoretical matters but that when dealing with clinical considerations she uses the term 'destructive instinct'. By this confession Dr Heimann has provided the complete refutation of her own remarkable theory, viz., that 'conflict' exists from the very beginning of life. For the term 'conflict' as used by Freud is a *clinical* term. It refers to processes that gradually develop as the ego becomes differentiated and moreover it has specific correlations with symptom formation. The term loses its meaning when used to illustrate biological speculations as to the nature of instincts existing at birth, e.g. the 'aims' of the 'life' and 'death instincts'. Incidentally I observe that Dr Heimann discussing Mrs Klein's views on this subject states that Mrs Klein formed ('came to see') her conclusions as the result of applying strictly analytical technique to the analysis of children. *But surely this is precisely the matter we are concerned to discuss in the whole of this series, viz. whether these conclusions are valid or are subjective ideas*, in other words, *how far Mrs Klein's ideas affect her conclusions and techniques*.

To turn now to the question of 'biological' and 'psychological' approaches to mental phenomena. I would like just to draw attention to a confusion in Dr Heimann's discussion of the phenomena of sleep. Her point seems to be that because in sleep and in narcissism a withdrawal of object libido takes place, the two conditions are identical and that conclusions about the one state are valid for the other. This is surely an illogical process – viz. *to identify two conditions because they have one factor in common*.

But in the whole 'biological-psychological' issue and its relation to 'psycho-physical' processes, Dr Heimann seems to leave out of account that *the primary concern of psychology is the study of mind* and that, however interesting and stimulating biological analogies may be, they cannot be grafted on to concepts of the mental apparatus.

On this question of the use of analogies Dr Heimann tries to make a point, viz., that *the basic concepts of mental structure and function are themselves based on analogies*. Thereby presumably she seeks to justify her conversion of biological analogies into metapsychological concepts. Now in a sense this is true but in a strictly limited sense. It is true, for example, that in adopting terms such as 'repression' or 'projection' Freud took over words in common use. But he gave them a specific scientific connotation. He used them to describe and identify certain unconscious mental processes. In addition to defining these basic concepts, he developed a threefold metapsychological approach to mental phenomena (topographic, dynamic, and economic) by means of which slipshod use of these terms can be avoided. In other words, he introduced metapsychological 'safeguards'. But this is an entirely different thing from taking over

587

biological analogies (or for that matter any form of analogy) and without the slightest evidence, incorporating them in the actual body of psychological theory.

It is just this slipshod habit that gives rise to many of Dr Heimann's confusions of thought, in particular her confusion between 'mechanism' and content of phantasy. In this connection I note that Dr Heimann has seen a little light. I may be wrong here but if so I shall be glad to be corrected. Having first of all confused 'swallowing', 'incorporation' and 'introjection', she is now ready to admit that it is necessary to distinguish incorporation from introjection. Now this is a step in the right direction. But it is a very small step when one remembers the number of misconceptions she has adopted. In any case Dr Heimann immediately detracts from the value of this admission by coining yet another misconception. She makes the plain assertion that *introjection is an instinctual derivative*. And having called attention to this final flaw, I must bring to an end this selection from amongst Dr Heimann's confusions of thought.

Notes

1 'We cannot lay down for things what their characteristics are to be.' [SE 15: 85]
2 'The impression they give is of being pursued by a malignant fare or possessed by some daemonic power . . .' [SE 18: 21]
3 'If we take into account observations such as these, based upon behaviour in the transference and upon the life histories of men and women, we shall find courage to assume that there really does exist in the mind a compulsion to repeat which overrides the pleasure principle.' [SE 18: 22]
4 'The attributes of life were at some time evoked in inanimate matter by the action of a force of whose nature we can form no conception. It may perhaps have been a process similar in type to that which later caused the development of consciousness in a particular stratum of living matter. The tension which then arose in what had hitherto been an inanimate substance endeavoured to cancel itself out. In this way the first instinct came into being: the instinct to return to the inanimate state.' [SE 18: 38]
5 'If, therefore, we are not to abandon the hypothesis of the death instincts, we must suppose them to be associated from the very first with the life instincts.' [SE 18: 57]
6 'This fact indicates an opposition whose importance was long ago recognized by the theory of the neuroses.' [SE 18: 40]
7 'The dominating tendency of mental life, and perhaps of nervous life in

general, is the effort to reduce, to keep constant or to remove internal tension due to stimuli ("the nirvana principle"), to borrow a term from Barbara Low [1920: 73] – a tendency which finds expression in the pleasure principle; and our recognition of that fact is one of our strongest reasons for believing in the existence of death instincts.' [SE 18: 55–6]

8   'No knowledge would have been more valuable as a foundation for true psychological science than an appropriate grasp of the common characteristics and possible distinctive features of the instincts.' [SE 18: 15]

9   'The condition of sleep, too, resembles illness in implying a narcissistic withdrawal of the positions of the libido on to the subject's own self, or, more precisely on to the single wish to sleep. In both states we have, if nothing else, examples of change in the distribution of libido that are consequence upon a change in the ego.' [SE 14: 83]

10   Even at the stage of description it is not possible to avoid applying certain abstract ideas to the material in hand, ideas derived from somewhere or other but certainly not from the new observations alone. So long as they remain in this condition we come to an understanding about their meaning by making repeated references to the material of observation from which they appear to have been derived, but upon which, in fact, they have been imposed. Thus, strictly speaking, they are in the nature of conventions – although everything depends upon their not being arbitrarily chosen but determined by their having significant relations to the empirical material, relations that we seem to sense before we can clearly recognize and demonstrate them.   [SE 14: 117]

11   'Judging is a continuation, along lines of expediency, of the original process by which the ego took things into itself or expelled them from itself, according to the pleasure principle.' [SE 19: 239]

Scientific Controversies and the Training of Candidates

Discussions by the Training Committee on the possible effects of Current Scientific Controversies on the training of Candidates

Editorial comments (1)

PEARL KING

In this section of the book we have put together the memoranda, statements, and reports dealing with the attempts of the members of the Training Committee to explore the effects of the scientific differences on the training of Candidates, the extent to which the Candidates were being drawn into the controversies, and being taught a version of psychoanalytic theory and technique, which to members like Edward Glover, Anna Freud, and her colleagues from Vienna, seemed incompatible with 'Freudian' psychoanalysis as they understood it.

As far as can be ascertained from the minutes of the Training Committee, Glover's memorandum was written during September 1942, following the AGM in July 1942 when it was decided to refer this topic to the Training Committee for them to discuss and to report their conclusions back to the Society. During the discussions reported in Section 1, various accusations had been made, especially by Glover, to the effect that the Kleinians were taking a dominant part in training activities. Statistics which were eventually produced by Sylvia Payne, to show the number of Candidates each training analyst had in analysis or as controls (supervisions) are included in Section 1, Chapter 7. The circulation of these figures must have done something to reduce the exaggerated claims of those who were attacking the Kleinians for trying to dominate the Society by taking as many Candidates as possible. It was not until October 1942 that the meeting to decide how to explore the scientific and theoretical differences took place, and Anna Freud was particularly keen to get a decision on these issues before turning to their effect on current training problems.

In February 1943, following the second Discussion of Scientific Controversies (Section 2, Chapter 4) Strachey wrote his memorandum (Chapter 2) on how to decide whether or not a new way of conceptualizing a patient's material was or was not to be regarded as approved psychoanalytic technique.

Mr Strachey read a short paper on the relationship between current theoretical controversies and the problems of training. This was followed by a discussion. It was decided that members of the Training Committee should each record short memoranda of what they consider the salient points in technique before the next Training Committee. Meanwhile Mr Strachey's memorandum should be circulated and used as the basis for further discussion. He was also asked to develop certain points in his paper for the benefit of the extended discussion. It was decided that decisions should not be reached in any hurry.

(Extract from the Training Committee minutes,
24 February 1942)

Glover was critical of some aspects of this memorandum (Chapter 3) particularly Strachey's suggestion that 'the essential criterion of whether a person is fit to conduct a training analysis is not whether his views of aetiology or theory are true but whether his technique is valid', therefore 'we should decide what are the essentials of a valid psychoanalytical technique'. Glover felt that an analyst's technique was more closely related to his theoretical position than did Strachey. On 7 June 1943 'It was decided that a report should be placed before the annual meeting to the effect that the Training Committee had not concluded their discussions on controversial matters connected with changes in technique, but were keeping pace with the scientific discussions and would postpone their report until the scientific discussions were concluded' (Extract from T. C. minutes).

Nevertheless, when the Training Committee eventually discussed these issues, both Marjorie Brierley and Sylvia Payne agreed with Strachey's proposal that each member of the Training Committee should be asked to write a short statement describing their technique and their way of analysing, in an attempt to see if the differences between them were or were not related to their particular theoretical standpoint. However, the decisions reached at the AGM which took place on 21 July 1943 (Section 2, Chapter 8) considerably changed the mood of the Members of the Society, and the Training Committee were urged to conclude their deliberations.

Accordingly, on 25 October 1943,

Dr Glover asked what members had brought memoranda on the fundamentals of technique and it was agreed to start with Dr Brierley's memorandum which was read. This was followed by Mrs Klein's and Miss Anna Freud's memoranda. As the hour was late and it was not possible to continue work it was decided that the memoranda should be circulated to the members of the Training Committee and that the agenda for the next Training Committee to be held on November 24th should consist of a discussion on the opinions arising out of these memoranda. (signed) S.M. Payne.

(Extract from T. C. minutes)

There are no available minutes of this next meeting which took place on 24 November 1943 to discuss the other memoranda which the members of the Training Committee had written. Based on this discussion a Draft Report[1] was written by Strachey (Chapter 9). Among the recommendations were 'That, in choosing the members of the Training Committee, the Society should deliberately bear in mind the undesirability of appointing persons who are prominently involved in acute scientific or personal controversies'. The·recommendations for the selection of training or control analysts were also along these lines. Anna Freud considered these recommendations an insult and resigned from the Committee at its next meeting.

The draft report was reacted to by Glover with another memorandum (Chapter 10), in which he expressed his opinion that the main issues had not been dealt with, and he strongly attacked not only the Kleinians[2] but he also attacked 'his English colleagues' on the Training Committee; namely, James Strachey, Sylvia Payne, Ella Sharpe, and Marjorie Brierley. This chapter also includes Ella Sharpe's response to this attack and other extracts from Training Committee minutes. Melanie Klein was also unhappy about this report, and it was amended for the final report, which did not include such recommendations.

The discussions that took place on the Training Committee overlapped in time with the Sixth and Seventh Discussions of Scientific Controversies (Section 2, Chapter 10 and Chapter 11). The discussion by the Members of the Society of the Final Report of the Training Committee (Chapter 11) did not take place until the Extraordinary Business Meeting on 8 March 1944 (Section 5, Chapter 3).

Notes

1 I am indebted to Anne Hayman for discovering a copy of this draft report in the Archives of the British Psycho-Analytical Society.
2 John Rickman was in the Army during the period when these discussions took place, but he would however have received copies of the various memoranda and reports. He was available as a signatory of the final report.

1

Introductory Memorandum
by Edward Glover
Chairman of the Training Committee –
September 21st, 1942[1]

Some of the confusion arising out of the present discussion might be reduced if preliminary agreement could be reached on as many points as possible. There are three main problems to consider. (1) *What to teach*, (2) *Who should teach*, (3) *How they should teach*. In order to facilitate possible agreement along these lines I have set down what I personally regard as essential points in any training scheme. I would suggest that all other members of the Committee should follow suit.

1 *What to teach*. There is to my mind only one answer to this question, viz. the main body of psychoanalytic knowledge, in a word mainly Freud. This should be, indeed must be, in future expanded in *every possible and legitimate direction* to include contributions by any other analytic worker provided these are generally accepted by the competent authorities. Controversial views should also be put before candidates but only in an advanced course. This course should be comprehensive and include all varieties of controversial view, not just a few mutually opposing or exclusive views. *Reasoned criticism* of all such controversial views should be an essential part of this course. Even when a teacher's own views are what might be called 'legitimately' controversial (i.e. views and methods which though giving rise to differences of opinion *do not appear to contradict* any essential Freudian principles) they should *not* be *taught* until they have been fully discussed and generally accepted by the Society electing the Training Committee. Candidates should also be orientated as to the most important views running counter to the teachings of Freud, whether these arising within or without the

Society. This should be an orientation course for purposes of training in 'analytical thinking'.

2 *Who should teach?* Only analysts whose views do not contradict in any important respect the main body of Freud's teaching. Should any appointed teacher find himself developing an important disagreement with Freud's teaching he should inform the Training Committee of the fact. In all cases of doubt the Training Committee in the first instance should decide whether or not the particular views are against the accepted teachings of Freud. If they are unable to decide, the particular issue should be referred first to the International Training Commission for discussion. [See also Section 1 for functions of the Branch Society.][2]

3 *How to teach*:

A   *Positive aims*

In such a way that

(1) Candidates are thoroughly familiarized with Freud's work and with the importance of studying that work,

(2) Candidates are allowed to learn from their own experience and are not intimidated by fear of error.

(3) Candidates are permitted and encouraged to form their own opinion on 'legitimate' controversial issues and, if possible, to pursue researches on them.

B   *Methods of eliminating error*

(1) *Subjective error on part of Candidate*. These are either emotional or ideational. Training analysis is supposed to eliminate emotional error, and other instructional courses to eliminate ideational error. But it is perfectly obvious that residual transferences of Candidates (either 'open positive' or 'concealed negative') frequently remain operative throughout the later part of their training and continue in operation when the Candidate is admitted to the Society. In view of the existence of these 'training transferences' every effort should be made to counter them (a) by well-balanced teaching, (b) by frequent reminders to candidates of this possible source of error.

(2) *Error due to bad teaching*. This should be clearly distinguished from emotional bias on the part of the Candidate although obviously it can strengthen such bias. The fact has to be faced that analysts are not necessarily born teachers, much less trained teachers, and hence may either hamper or intimidate their pupils. Apart from this, teaching may be bad because it is wittingly tendentious.

The main pitfalls in this direction are:-

(a) Underemphasizing the central and accepted teachings of psychoanalysis.

(b) Overemphasizing certain *aspects* of accepted teaching.

(c) Overemphasizing material which is still in the stage of being legitimately controversial or

(d) Emphasizing views or adopting analytic procedures which are either not a legitimate part of psychoanalysis or which may be in opposition to the accepted views of psychoanalysis.

The existing situation

The most significant fact (and one that is not without its humours) is that, if, for the sake of convenience, we divide the members of the Training Committee or Society into three groups, all three would claim, no doubt with sincerity, that they subscribe to most of the views I have set out above. Now either we are all talking nonsense and making little personal storms in tea cups or there are genuine differences which it would be both hypocritical and inadvisable to conceal. The question is: can any agreement be established as to these differences?

As I see it the position is as follows.

1 The 'Vienna' Group[3] regard themselves as a typical Freudian nucleus differing in no way from any other Freudian group.

2 The 'Klein' Group regard themselves as a Freudian nucleus but consider that they have added vital knowledge and expanded Freudian teaching in many if not most directions.

3 The Vienna Group consider that the work of the Klein Group is in many important respects (I am not sure in how many respects) a deviation from and sometimes in opposition to classical Freudian theory and practice.

4 The (?middle, ?moderate, ?compromise, ?composite, ?remaining) Group (title uncertain) regard themselves also as a Freudian group. As regards contributions made by analytic workers other than Freud, they reserve the right to accept or reject such contributions after they have been freely and fully discussed in a proper scientific atmosphere. The reactions of members of this group to the work of Mrs Klein vary. All think that she has made contributions to psychoanalysis, but some think only in her earlier work. Others think that her later work too contains ideas of value, but that these cannot be regarded as a valid enough or broad enough basis for a new metapsychology. Others again think that her later work neglects or depreciates or deviates from some of the classical Freudian findings. But they would all agree that there is no justification for regarding her views as a total advance in every direction. In short they would

regard such of her findings as they believe can be fitted into the general structure of psychoanalysis as, on the whole, rather specialized contributions, and according to taste rate them with the contributions of Abraham, Ferenczi, Jones, etc. On the other hand, they would agree with the attitude of the 'Vienna' Group in regarding Freud's teachings as the main concern of psychoanalysis.

Finally they would regard the present issue of analytic teaching as having been somewhat artificially restricted. They feel that the correctness or incorrectness of Mrs Klein's views should be assessed in the proper (scientific) manner and place, bearing in mind that these particular issues are only one of many analytical problems; but they would say that the most important issue is one of *scientific freedom*.

Do existing methods of teaching, of investigation, and of discussion hamper the development of students and the progress of psychoanalysis? My impression is that they are all agreed the existing methods do hamper both.

In conclusion I would add some general observations of my own. In distinguishing between the validity or relative importance of Mrs Klein's views and, on the other hand, the methods of propagating them, the only practical test seems to me to be a behaviouristic one, viz. the reactions of candidates during training and after they are admitted to the Society or themselves become teachers.

If one judges from the history of scientific discussion in the Society, from say 1923 onwards, three stages can be roughly distinguished

(a) from 1923 to 1928 or 29, where discussion, even if uninspired, was comparatively free,

(b) from 1928–29 to roughly 1933–34, when it was increasingly stereotyped and monotonous, and

(c) from 1934 to the present day, when it became sporadically more lively, but much more in terms of allegiances and in some respects at any rate even more unscientific than when it was merely stereotyped.

This seems to me to call for a radical revision of our methods of teaching. More than at any other stage of the development of psychoanalysis it is necessary now to secure sound Freudian teaching and at the same time freedom from all factors of prestige-suggestion or timidity which tends to paralyse the individuality of students and consequently their capacity for useful research.

Notes

1 Glover's statement, as chairman of the Training Committee, was circulated to the members of the Training Committee a year before the committee got down to discussing the training situation in detail in October 1943.
2 There are at present four competent authorities, varying in the amount and directness of influence they exert. (a) The Branch Society is competent through votes of full Members but it must be recognized by (b) the International Psychoanalytical Association. The latter also appoints (c) the International Training Commission which in practice consists mostly of (d) local Training Committees elected by Branch Societies. Whilst therefore the Branch Society is the forum for scientific discussion of all psychoanalytic material, prior to its being accepted and, if accepted, incorporated in psychoanalytic teaching, immediate exercise of teaching authority rests in the Training Committee and the International Training Commission for discussion.
3 These labels are for convenience only. In the case of the Society the so-called 'Vienna' Group would certainly include some former Berlin Members and possibly a few English colleagues of an 'expectant' type.

2

Discussion Memorandum
by James Strachey

Member of the Training Committee –
February 24th, 1943

The Training Committee have been instructed by the Society to consider the ways in which current theoretical controversies affect matters of training. I want to begin by pointing out that this problem which has been confided to us is ultimately a *political* and *administrative* problem and not a scientific one. A student of psychology, having arrived at what seemed to him the truth about certain phenomena, might quite well, like Henry Cavendish in the field of physics, be satisfied with leaving things at that – and decide to keep his conclusions to himself. The Members of the Psycho-Analytical Society, for various reasons, have decided on the contrary that they wish to disseminate their conclusions as widely as possible, and the business of this Committee is to consider how best to carry that decision into effect. We are thus concerned with problems not of theory but of practical expediency.

This does not in the least imply that our problems are unimportant. On the contrary, it is quite likely that upon our decision the whole future of psychoanalysis in this country will depend. For, if we decide unwisely, one of two equally bad consequences may in the extreme case follow. On the one hand, the dissemination of psychoanalysis may become so extremely restricted that something like a Henry Cavendish position may actually be brought about. Or, on the other hand, we may effect a very wide dissemination of views, and yet, if those views bear only a faint resemblance to those of psychoanalysis or are actually opposed to them, our policy will have been no less of a failure. Between these two equally undesirable extremes it is our business to find an optimum mean. But you will already see from this that though a political problem is not necessarily less important than a scientific one, it requires an entirely different manner of approach. Scientific problems must be faced with ruthless logic and clear-cut consistency: there is no half-way house between truth and falsehood. Administrative problems, with their considerations of expediency, their constant balancings of probabilities, call for flexibility and compromise. Yet there is no contradiction here. Political adaptability is not in the least incompatible with the strictest regard for scientific truth; nor for the matter of that, is rigidity in the application of a belief any evidence that the belief so applied is a true one.

Before we embark upon this political discussion, however, there is one preliminary question to be settled concerning the kind of truths involved in psychoanalysis, the answer to which must profoundly influence all our decisions. There are two possibilities. On the one hand, psychoanalysis may choose to regard itself as a closed system of immutable and all-inclusive verities, incapable of extension or correction. In that case the problem of the training of its practitioners will in many ways be greatly simplified: their proficiency will be judged wholly by their approximation to the beliefs and practices laid down by the system, and discussion will be mainly centred upon the precise meaning of the dogmatic propositions contained in it. On the other hand, psychoanalysis may prefer to adopt Freud's own view of its character, as he expresses it in an article of which a translation will be found in the current number of the *International Journal*: 'Psychoanalysis', he says, 'is not, like philosophies, a system starting out from a few sharply defined fundamental concepts, seeking to grasp the whole universe with the help of these and, once it is completed, having no room for fresh discoveries or better understanding. On the contrary, it keeps close to the facts in its field of study, seeks to solve the immediate problems of observation, gropes its way forward by the help of experience, is always incomplete and always ready to correct or modify its theories.' [Freud, S. 1923a: 105; SE 18:253][1] This alternative view which Freud gives us of the nature of the truths of psychoanalysis promises us a far harder administrative task. Nevertheless I shall resist the temptation to follow the well-trimmed vistas of the former prospect and I shall assume without further discussion that we are agreed in choosing the second and thornier path.

What, then, are our difficulties?

I will begin with a very slight one. And indeed I only mention it in order to show the sort of spirit in which, as it seems to me, administrative problems have to be met. Since what the Society has instructed us to spread abroad is not *all* truth but the truth about a particular limited set of events, we shall start off by being selective and exclusive. There are a number of people who are interested in the phenomena of geophysics; but we shall not insist upon all Candidates mastering the truths about the surface-tension of the earth, and indeed we shall discourage those who conduct our seminars from expatiating too freely upon the laws determining the epicentres of earthquakes. But again, there are a number of sciences which actually shade off more or less closely into ours: other specialized branches of psychology, certain departments of medicine and physiology, education, anthropology, and so on. Knowledge in *these* branches of learning we shall obviously *encourage* in our Candidates, though it seems improbable that, since each of them is a whole-time job in itself, we shall be able to insist upon every Candidate being proficient in all of them: we shall have to content ourselves with aiming at having some practitioners in contact with each of these neighbouring fields. But this question and the question of precisely which fields are and are not included in our scope are clearly matters for what may be described as a *quantitative* solution, in which the quantity will be determined upon grounds of expediency and need not be fixed precisely but may be allowed to vary between certain limits without any harm being done.

I shall now go on at once to our main difficulty as organizers of psychoanalytic diffusion. It is one which is inherent in Freud's view of our science as something incomplete and susceptible to modification. For who is to decide whether a particular extension is justifiable or a particular correction necessary? Only if we had an omniscient leader who could impose his opinion on us, or if by some miracle we all of us always arrived at the same conclusion, could this difficulty be avoided. And neither of these ways out seems likely to be offered us. A division of opinion of this kind upon a proposed extension and correction of our views is, as we all know, the actual occasion for these remarks; so that we are all familiar with the way in which a difference in theoretical opinions can come to affect us here in the Training Committee. The danger arises that those who hold one set of views may feel tempted to declare that those who hold the contrary set of views are on that account incompetent to carry out training activities; and such an attitude, if persisted in, must quite inevitably lead to an unbridgeable cleavage in the practical side of our work.

There is a further important point to observe. Some of us may be inclined to think that the present difference of opinion is of extraordinary or even unique importance – the like of which we shall probably never experience again; and that therefore if only we can surmount *it* (by violent means, if necessary) the situation will be saved. This, of course, will be pure delusion. This particular sort of crisis is one which, from the nature of things, is bound to be recurrent. We must actually, if we accept the words of Freud which I have quoted, look forward to a constant succession of such situations. We may be quite certain that important suggestions for the extension or correction of our views – and we must hope that there will be many such – are seldom likely to be accepted without dispute; and if upon each such occasion the disagreement is carried over into the field of training we must look forward to a perpetual succession of disruptions. The political future of psychoanalysis under such conditions can hardly be described as rosy.

It is therefore the clear duty of anyone who has the interests of psychoanalysis at heart to hesitate before he acquiesces in a programme of avalanches, and in particular to scrutinize its underlying assumptions. Above all, it seems important to find an answer to this question, around which so much of the trouble seems to revolve: 'To what extent and in what respect do false or *defective* views about the findings or theories of psychoanalysis imply incompetence to carry out a training analysis, to do control work, to conduct a seminar or to give a course of lectures?' This, of course, is not a single question but a number of questions lumped together and I have no intention of tackling them systematically. I shall merely say something upon what is evidently the core of the business – that part of the question which concerns possible disqualifications for carrying out a training analysis.

'Your views are so *defective* that you are incompetent to carry out a training analysis or for the matter of that any analysis at all,' says one protagonist.

'Your views are so *false* that you are incompetent to carry out a training analysis or for the matter of that any analysis at all,' says the other protagonist.

It is essential not to mince matters but to state the problem in these extreme terms, since this is how the situation is bound to be regarded by the convinced supporters of a new view and by its convinced opponents respectively, and theirs are the positions with which we have to deal.

First of all, though, this difficulty, like the one I have already discussed, about exclusiveness or inclusiveness of subject-matter, can also be treated to some extent along quantitative lines. There are certain *maxima* of defectiveness and falseness about which there will in fact be unanimity. Thus we shall all agree in refusing to recognize as a training analyst a person who has never heard of the Oedipus complex or one who believes that claustrophobia is caused by the action of moonbeams upon the scalp. And again there are certain *minima* of defectiveness and falseness about which there will also be practical unanimity. Thus we shall all agree that failure to have read an article by Federn published in the *Zeitschrift* in 1926, though regrettable, is not a ground for exclusion. And someone who believed that the latency period set in more often during the first half of the sixth year of life than during the last half of the fifth year of life would perhaps be regarded as competent to carry out a training analysis even by someone who believed that the latency period set in more often during the last half of the fifth year of life than during the first half of the sixth year of life.

Here then, as in the case of the difficulty about exclusiveness of subject-matter, the line between the *maxima* of error which involve exclusion and the *minima* of error which allow of inclusion must be drawn according to the dictates of expediency.

But the drawing of this line is not an easy one. Freud himself has attempted it more than once. For instance, in the same article from which I have already quoted, he says that 'the principal subject-matter of psychoanalysis and the foundations of its theory' are 'the assumption that there are unconscious mental processes, the recognition of the theory of resistance and repression, the appreciation of the importance of sexuality and the Oedipus complex', and adds that 'no one who cannot accept them all should count himself a psychoanalyst'. [Freud, S. 1923a: 102; SE 18:247][2] Would all of us regard this is an adequate criterion? Or would some of us think that it needed extension or qualification or precision before it was sufficiently exclusive? Above all, there is the question of date. Freud wrote that passage in 1922. Would he himself have been satisfied with the same test 15 years later?

We may indeed find it instructive if, for a moment, we try to picture what would have happened if the whole chain of Freud's own discoveries and theories had been made, not by a single man in the course of one lifetime, but by a succession of men over a longer period of years. What would have been the attitude of analysts who had been brought up in the straightforward 'libido–ego conflict' theory of the neuroses to the man who first adumbrated the concept of narcissism? In what terms would analysts who were accustomed to lay very great stress upon the primary passive feelings of their male patients – in what terms would they be inclined to characterize the treatments carried out in the old days when everything had by hook or by crook to be accounted for in terms of the direct Oedipus complex? It is not very fantastic to suppose that every one of such modifications as these would have provoked crises exactly comparable to our present one and to the many others which may be ahead. Nevertheless, as things in fact turned out, there were no such disruptions: the innovations and corrections succeeded one another with the utmost smoothness. Is there any possibility, then, of our being able to profit by this object-lesson?

I am inclined to think that one of the main causes of our trouble is a confusion over the relations between findings and theories on the one hand and technical procedure on the other. I have already remarked that people are inclined to say of their opponents: 'His views are wrong, so his technique must be wrong.' This is, in fact, the starting point of our investigation. If one presses the matter a little and asks how the speaker *knows* that his opponent's views are wrong, the result is sometimes a trifle circular: 'Oh, he uses a wrong technique, so his views *must* be wrong.' The truth is, of course, that the inter-relations between technical procedure, findings and theory are very complicated. It is quite possible, for instance (as I just said now), to make use of a faulty technique and yet to hold correct views. So, too, as I think the changes in Freud's opinions show, it is possible to use a valid technique and yet to arrive at false conclusions. Nevertheless, I am prepared to insist that upon the whole a valid technique is not necessarily or even chiefly the *product* of our scientific findings and theories, but that it is rather the most efficient instrument by which they can be reached. And I suggest that the essential criterion of whether a person is fit to conduct a training analysis is not whether his views on aetiology or theory are true, but whether his technique is valid. If his technique is valid, then any gaps in his knowledge (and there are sure to be many) and any mistakes in his deductions (and they are not likely to be few) will have only what I may call a *local* effect, they will not lead to any *generalized* distortion of the analytic picture, and it will moreover always be possible for the gaps to be filled in and the mistakes corrected.

It will no doubt be argued that things must also work in the opposite direction: that anyone who has incomplete or false views upon the subject-matter of psychoanalysis must necessarily come to make use of a faulty technique. I agree that this is so up to a point; but I believe it should be possible to make a distinction between two different kinds of faultiness, of which one is much more fundamental than the other. To take a concrete example, let us imagine the analyst who was conducting an analysis of a male patient, for instance an obsessional neurotic, before the importance of the inverted Oedipus complex was adequately appreciated. His technique would undoubtedly be very faulty: he would leave a large amount of unconscious material uninterpreted and he would tend to lay a wrong emphasis upon much of what he did interpret. Nevertheless, provided he used what I call a valid technique, what work he *did* do would, in my opinion, be unobjectionable as far as it went, and he might, owing to a thorough analysis of that limited part of the patient's mind which he *did* understand, produce indirectly a salutary effect upon the patient's mind as a whole, including those parts of it of which he was actually in ignorance. It is, indeed, in some such way as this that we must account for all the successful analyses carried out in the period before Freud made his later discoveries and also for all of our own successful analyses today – since I am rash enough to believe that in the course of the next few hundred or thousand years some further facts will be discovered about the human mind of which we are ignorant today. On the other hand I think it would be possible for an analyst with a full and correct knowledge of the nature of the inverted Oedipus complex to make use of that knowledge in order to conduct an analysis with a technique so wrong (for instance, in its handling of the transference) that we should hesitate to allow him to act as a training analyst. Thus the kind of more fundamental validity that I have in mind is more a matter of *form* than of *content*: it is a question of the sort of way in which the analyst behaves rather than of the knowledge he possesses.

I am aware, of course, that this only shifts the ground. We must now consider – though I don't propose to do so today – what are the essentials of this valid technique. That must be our first and principal task. It is one which, in spite of the greater attention it has received in the last ten years, is still far too much neglected. Its actual details continue to be wrapped in an unholy mystery. In spite of Dr Glover's questionnaire, what do we really know about one another's actual way of behaving as analysts? Maybe we should be shocked if we did. Maybe it would turn out that our basic methods are more in agreement than we fear. At all events, if there are to be divisions in this Committee, it is surely at that point that they must be focused and not in the realm of inference and theory. And, finally, after we have elucidated such differences as may appear, it will even then still be our duty to treat them as a matter of politics, that is, to consider yet another quantitative question – of how far these particular differences are likely to produce results so distorted as to be untrustworthy in really serious respects.

But there remains a possibility which I have not yet approached. So far I have been assuming that in connection with disputed findings or disputed theories each of us is absolutely and positively certain that he is right and his opponent wrong. What I have so far been discussing is how far, granted that I am absolutely and positively certain that I am right, I may nevertheless be ready, for political reasons (that is, on grounds of expediency) to allow my opponent to function as a training analyst although I am absolutely and positively certain that he is in the wrong. This, I have suggested, I may be willing to do if the matter under dispute is a not too important one, and also if I can convince myself that the technique which he uses is sufficiently valid for the error to be limited in its scope and susceptible of being corrected.

But how about the extraordinary and wildly unlikely situation that would arise if I were *not* absolutely and positively certain of these things but merely considered them on the whole probable or was ever, horror of horrors, in complete doubt as to where the truth lay?

This much at least is certain. If each of us were even a little sceptical about his own conclusions and a little ready to consider other people's and if each of us could put up with a little uncertainty upon a few questions, the administrative difficulties of the Training Committee would be a good deal diminished. On the other hand its immediate task would not differ from that which I have already proposed: namely, a rigorous investigation of the essentials of a valid technique. For there is in the last resort no way of resolving doubts and uncertainties except by the accumulation of new facts, and the credibility of those facts is bound to rest upon the trustworthiness of the instrument by means of which they are observed.

In my opinion, therefore, the action to be taken by the Training Committee falls into three parts:

First, we should decide, to the best of our ability, what are the essentials of a valid psychoanalytic technique.

Secondly, we should try to discover whether and in what respect the parties to our current controversies diverge from those essentials.

Thirdly, with this knowledge before us, we should proceed to the purely political question of whether it is expedient to inhibit any of those concerned from functioning as training analysts or in any other educational capacity.

Notes

1 'Psycho-analysis is not, like philosophies, a system starting out from a few sharply defined basic concepts, seeking to grasp the whole universe with the help of these and, once it is completed, having no room for fresh discoveries or better understanding. On the contrary, it keeps close to the facts in its field of study, seeks to solve the immediate problems of

observation, gropes its way forward by the help of experience, is always incomplete and always ready to correct or modify its theories.' [SE 18: 253]

2 'The Corner-Stones of Psycho-Analytic Theory'. 'The assumption that there are unconscious mental processes, the recognition of the theory of resistance and repression, the appreciation of the importance of sexuality and of the Oedipus complex – these constitute the principal subject-matter of psychoanalysis and the foundations of its theory. No one who cannot accept them all should count himself a psychoanalyst.' [SE 18: 247]

3

Edward Glover's response
to Memorandum by James Strachey

Mr Strachey's approach to the problems with which the Training Committee is faced was evidently influenced by two factors, his concern that teaching methods should not infringe scientific traditions at any point and his interest in the technique of psychoanalysis. In his view 'the essential criterion of whether a person is fit to conduct a training analysis is not whether his views of aetiology or theory are true but whether his technique is valid'. His practical recommendation is that before touching on the political problems of training, i.e., who should teach and what he should teach, we should decide what are the essentials of a valid psychoanalytical technique. With Mr Strachey's general approach I am of course in entire sympathy; and I believe also that an investigation of technique, in particular of the technique and content of interpretation, would bring to light many important divergences of outlook and method, bearing on our present controversies.

But I do not agree that the training problem is one that can be solved by investigations of technique alone. And this not simply because, in my view, the technique of the teacher is very considerably influenced by his theories but because our practical problem is not concerned solely with technique. There are four main factors in the analytic situation, the analyst, the technique, the transference, and the analysand. To measure the technique without at the same time observing the other factors in the training situation, viz. the training analyst, the transference, and the Candidate would in my opinion be an error in method. It seems to me therefore that Mr Strachey has not fully appreciated the exact nature of the impasse in which the Committee finds itself. And so, before we discuss his

611

practical recommendations in detail I would like to summarize briefly my 15 years' experience as a member of this Training Committee.

My first conclusion is that for all scientific and practical purposes, the training system of this Society has already broken down.[1] And my main recommendation is that the Committee should report this fact to the Society. I have my own theories as to the cause of this breakdown; and though I do not wish to become involved in a theoretical discussion, I would like to offer briefly my favourite explanation. It is simply this: *so far, it has not been possible to eliminate adequately the vitiating factors of transference and counter-transference arising during analytic training.* In theory, of course, one of the aims of the 'training analysis' is to resolve the candidate's transferences even more thoroughly than is done in the case of, say, a neurotic patient. As far as the training analyst's counter-transferences are concerned it is merely assured that he will be able to resolve those himself.

Now we know from clinical experience that the practical test of resolution of a transference does not differ from the test of resolution of a symptom, namely, that it should not be capable of reactivation under stress. And this brings me to my second conclusion, namely, that whereas, with reasonable luck, the neurotic patient may not experience stresses liable to reactivate his symptoms, the Candidate both during and after analysis works under professional conditions calculated not only to prevent resolution of his transferences but to promote their reactivation. These professional stresses tend to go unobserved partly because they have not the dramatic quality of neurotic stresses, but mainly I think because we turn a blind eye to them. I am not prepared to say whether this blind eye is turned voluntarily or whether it is a myopia of unconscious origin. What I can say is this: never in my experience of committee work or of teaching institutions have I come across a committee that was so obviously hampered and intimidated by what might be called either 'unrealistic idealizations' or 'pedagogic perfectionism'. It is true, of course, that this form of defensive timidity is not confined to Training Committees. Nevertheless it is a fact that in the work of the Training Committee the cult of perfectionism has gone far to prepare the ground for our present stalemate. At any rate I could go so far as to say that the professional trainee – so long as he continues in active work and so long as his training analyst remains in active work – has little opportunity of emancipating himself from the transference situation. Although his analysis may be longer than that of a patient and although it is actually brought to an end in the same way as that of a patient, he does not, as the ordinary patient does, resume an independent existence. The analysis may stop but the Candidate remains in an extended or displaced analytic situation. He cannot even speak at an ordinary meeting except under the shadow of his former transference.

I do not suggest that this is a complete account of our main training problem: nor, as I have said, do I wish to become involved more than is necessary in a theoretical discussion. My immediate aim is a purely practical one. I am even ready to agree that for most therapeutic purposes, the Candidate's 'training transferences' may have been well enough analysed in the past. Even his reactions to professional contacts with colleagues in the Society were on most occasions satisfactory enough – though, let it be said, by no means so good as the reactions of most unanalysed scientists in other societies. In short, under ordinary conditions, the stresses peculiar to analytical life used not to lead to violent eruption of transference reactions. It is true that minor manifestations were plentiful enough. No objective observer of discussions at Scientific Meetings of the Society could fail to note the existence of training allegiances, even of the phenomenon of postponed obedience. But so long as no major scientific divergences existed in the Society the most that could be said of those allegiances was that they gave rise to monotony in discussion and to a low level of spontaneous research. When, however, major divergences arose regarding the validity of Mrs Klein's views, a situation of stress developed that increased existing training transferences and reactivated old transferences. On this occasion I shall not attempt to give personal illustrations: I shall content myself rather with the blunt assertion that for some years past transference eruptions have occurred so powerful that it not only makes scientific discussion impossible but reduces analytical training to an unscientific level. Moreover I believe that unless we admit this fact and recognize that the difficulty is not confined to the reactions of the Candidate but depends also on the reactions of his training analyst, there is little chance of re-establishing scientific standards of training.

In earlier days I used to think that these sources of emotional bias might be reduced by a balanced curriculum of instruction, in lectures, seminars, in analytic controls, and later in society discussions. But this I can see was a naïve hope. There is little evidence that the curriculum brings about correction of bias except in those Candidates who have a temperamental inclination to eclecticism or in Candidates whose analysts have kept aloof from controversy or have no strong feelings on differences of opinion within the Society. Such Candidates are certainly in the minority.

As I have indicated the problem is not confined to the reactions produced in Candidates. At every point of organization, including even the initial selection of Candidates, difficulties arise. To whom, for instance, is the Candidate to be allocated for training analysis? If the rota of training analysts includes, as it does, a number of analysts who differ on important points of theory and practice, the responsibility of the Training Committee is a heavy one. For it is morally certain that the Candidate's future opinions, allegiances, and professional life will be determined by that first choice. The same applies, though no doubt to a lesser extent, to the choice of control analysts, to the organization of lecture courses, and to seminars. Nor does the matter stop there. Although postgraduate training is not compulsory – a good deal of unobtrusive and unorganized post-graduate training goes on, e.g., secondary analysis of Associate Members and Members, private controls, and private group discussions. The immediate effect of these activities is to increase the cleavages in the Society, and this in turn affects, sooner or later, the training situation. For the training analysts of the future will in the natural course of events be chosen from amongst analysts whose training allegiances are at present being formed – and in the meantime a number will be chosen from those unofficial post-graduate trainees who will inevitably bring their allegiances with them. This is only natural. Firmly convinced that their views are correct and that their techniques are justified by their views, they are bound to feel that their teaching is entirely legitimate. To cut a long story short this is in my opinion the present situation of training in the Society. For all scientific purposes our training system has broken down.

The obvious question is: can this situation be put to rights? If so how can we set about it? Here again a distinction must be drawn between principles and practice. In principle, of course, the remedy should lie in more thorough training analyses, more thorough resolution of training transferences, and more thorough analysis of the identifications with and introjections of the analyst which the Candidate builds up. In practice, however, there is, as I have suggested, little sign of these radical changes, still less that the influence of varied controls counteracts the original bias. We must face the fact that so long as important divergences exist in our Society, the immediate aims of training are bound to be influenced by the more distant aim of securing converts to any given set of views. And this in turn is bound to affect the selection of members of the Training Committee, the appointment of training analysts, and the advancement of Members in the Society. It seems to me quite obvious that the logical end of such a situation is a fight for control of the Psycho-Analytical Society.

No doubt, so long as there exists a solid group of training analysts who are opposed to extremist views or who do not countenance the teaching of controversial views as a natural or essential part of technical training, this end can be delayed. But in my experience such groups are too indifferent to take effective action to counter or even to modify extremism. They do not appear to be coherent enough or organized enough to withstand the influence of more enthusiastic groups.

Nevertheless we might well consider whether the situation could be improved by increasing the numbers of training analysts, control analysts, seminar leaders, and lecturers who do not hold extreme or controversial opinions: possibly even by excluding from teaching activities those whose extreme views handicap their teaching capacity. I thought once that extremists might be prevailed on not to obtrude their personal convictions in their training activities and I still think this ideal could be attained by lecturers, possibly even by seminar leaders. But I now admit that it is unreasonable to expect the training analysis to follow these more balanced lines. And since the training analysis is the Achilles' heel of our system there is no escaping the fact that modifications in training can only be effectively secured through selection of training analysts. The only other alternative I can think of is to abolish the designation of training analyst, to return, for a time at any rate, to our previous system of accepting Candidates from amongst those analysed by any recognized member. This would no doubt reduce extremism for a time at any rate.[2]

Finally, what course should be followed if neither of these expedients is adopted? It seems to me that two alternatives exist. Either the Society adjudicates on the respective validity of opposing views and prohibits the teaching of views that are held to be either invalid or controversial: or the Training Committee organizes two or more systems of training whereby Candidates can be trained exclusively in any given system. However absurd such a system might appear to a casual observer, it is the only one that would prevent for a time official splitting of the Society. I came to this conclusion with regret. For a long time I held the view that Candidates should have sufficient gumption to see through the idiosyncrasies of their teachers. Evidently this is too much to expect.

As for the teachers, I find it hard to abandon the view that these at least should have sufficient gumption not to make controversial views an essential and binding part of their instruction. It follows therefore that in my opinion the main flaw in our training system has been the selection of teachers who are strictly speaking unqualified to teach that most impressionable creature – the student in training.

Notes

1 Glover's accusation that 'the training system of this Society has already broken down' was strenuously denied by Miss Ella Sharpe in her statement to the Training Committee on 24 January 1944 (p. 665).
2 (Original footnote) A training committee could still function for interviewing the Candidate's *analyst* before acceptance of the Candidate and for providing a variety of pedagogic lectures and seminars. The analyst would however select the Candidate's 'controls' from amongst the general list of *Members*.

4

Memorandum on her technique by Marjorie Brierley

Memo on valid technique for the Training Committee, October 25th, 1943

1 Introduction

Mr Strachey noted that the details of individual technique 'continue to be wrapped in unholy mystery'. Unless this mystery is substantially reduced I do not see how we are to find out what the limits are within which technique may vary and yet retain validity, in particular for training purposes. At this juncture we need to discover what techniques are in use in current practice in order to establish empirical rather than theoretical criteria. Some consideration of general principles will be necessary but we must state frankly what we do and why we do it if we are to get the data we require. At the same time, it is obviously impracticable for anyone of us, let alone all, to give a complete account of our individual methods. Leaving out of account all deliberate modifications in war emergency cases, etc., in routine analysis my own behaviour varies so much in detail from patient to patient that I often feel I have no technique. Nevertheless, I think it may help to keep discussion on the level of the actual conduct of cases if I state as briefly as possible the gist of what I do myself about a few selected topics. Such a course may tend to prevent our losing ourselves in generalities by providing a few solid bones of contention.

I propose then to begin by stating as shortly as possible what I consider my aim and my task as an analyst to be, how I pursue them, and what guides me in this work. I shall then give one instance of handling of a patient at the beginning of treatment. I have chosen this illustration partly because it was at the beginning, and it is therefore easier to summarize the information I had at the time, and partly because its validity seems to me to be debatable and it has some bearing on current issues. After a note on training aims, I shall then state how far and in what way I consider my technique has been influenced by Mrs Klein's work. I will conclude by stating, with equal frankness, and, I trust, equal brevity, the misgivings I entertain about my own methods, about classical or conservative Freudian technique and about Mrs Klein's technique.

2 Aim and task of analysis

The aim of analysis condenses for me in to the single phrase 'ego-redintegration on a reality basis'. This blanket phrase covers for me the numerous other ways in which the aim can be described, e.g. re-adaptation, re-distribution of energy between psychic systems in favour of the ego, re-solution of conflicts, revision and re-edition of defences, reclamation work, etc., etc. It has the advantage that it expresses what I take to be the essence of the analyst's task. This is to help the patient to free himself from id and/or superego tyranny and to support his ego until such time as it has acquired sufficient mastery in its own house to dispense with my services. I regard myself as the ally of the ego in the task of mediation between id, superego and environmental demands and in bringing about the increase in both internal and external reality tolerance which is necessary if faulty automatic controls are to be corrected and voluntary control increased. I think it is true that ego-support is most effectively provided, at least in early stages of analysis, when the analyst is accepted as an auxiliary superego. But, to my mind, the value of this favourable situation is lost if the analyst sides with the pre-existing superego. It is impossible to bring about a greater degree of co-operation between psychic systems under the leadership of the ego, or to the benefit of the ego, by reinforcing a reactionary superego. Judging from cases I have seen myself, some Tavistock Square people are liable to make this mistake. They analyse unconscious content in preference to conscience controls. In this respect they are partial realists, whereas it seems to me technique is the more valid, the more it achieves all-round realism. It happens that I am not, by nature, sympathetic to reactionary superegos and I am, perhaps, over-indulgent towards id wishes, and I am well aware of the kind of error to which this predisposes me. Nevertheless, it is a fact that I do consistently regard myself as the ally of the ego and its guide to realism and seek to behave as such.

3 Process of analysis and analytic relationship

The foregoing remarks do not of course mean that I regard the analytic process as an ego process, or the dynamic relationship between analyst and patient as limited to an ego-relationship. The process affects the whole psyche and the relationship which promotes it is a total relationship in which unconscious interaction is, for the most part, of greater importance than ego-contact. Dynamism depends upon unconscious rapport. For the analyst, rapport seems to require a sufficient degree of identification with the patient to make empathy possible but not such a degree as to impair his judgement and perspective. Evidence that one is in touch comes to light in various ways, as does evidence of inadequate rapport, but it makes itself felt in me, at any rate, as affective resonance.

4 Method of work

I began to practise with rather over-optimistic and over-passive notions. Thus, I thought of analysis as a process which would automatically benefit the patient if I could help to clear the resistance-obstacles out of the way so that it could run its course. I regarded myself as a passive recipient of transference. I still think that one can only help patients to cure themselves but have come to realize that the analyst is more than a passive recipient and reflector. Today I regard the analyst rather as an active and responsible partner in a living process whose end-result, in favourable cases, is a more or less adequate degree of ego-redintegration. I don't impose myself upon the patient, but I realize he needs active co-operation in his search for himself. Indeed, I think I went through a short phase of over-activity but all that remains of that in my routine is a tendency to interpret too soon rather than too late and to do something under the spur of therapeutic anxiety when it would really be better to do nothing at all. But I do not act except in response to the patient; my receptivity is not diminished. In working, my conscious judgement is constantly in use, particularly in assessing and reviewing the impressions I receive and my impulses to react. But the real work always seems to me to be done by unconscious inference and empathy far more than by conscious thinking. For me, counter-transference phenomena fall into two classes, object-reactions to the patient, and identification-reactions with the patient. Just as affect in the patient is a clue to his immediate focus of interest, so I find empathy a useful indicator for timing and type of interpretation.

Naturally, I approach every patient with a full quota of implicit rather than explicit theoretical and technical preconceptions. On the whole it seems to me that these pre-conceptions are of the nature of a chart on which the patient plots his own pattern. They don't force any shape on the pattern itself but they certainly influence the ways in which I apprehend the pattern and the terms in which I can describe it to him. But I am more inclined to alter my preconceived notions to fit the patient's new pattern than to cut the pattern to fit my notions. The effort to understand in order to help is also a continuous process of learning from the patient. I find the conjunction of therapy and research most disadvantageous because therapeutic anxiety interferes with learning. I should learn more and more quickly, if I could think of the patient as a guinea-pig and for all I know the patient himself might do better. But from beginning to end he obstinately remains a fellow human being, whose therapeutic needs demand priority over research interests.

I have no rule as to type or depth of interpretation other than consideration of what the patient appears to need at the time. Some patients ask for deeper interpretations much earlier than others. I have had little experience of true psychotics but, judging by borderline cases I have seen, I should imagine they would need deep interpretation early more often than the ordinary run of psycho-neurotics. To my mind the validity of any given interpretation, superficial or deep, depends upon its immediate suitability to the patient as much as upon its accuracy. Faulty timing of an accurate interpretation, e.g., a true picture of an unconscious situation which cannot yet be tolerated, can have all the hindering effects described by Dr Glover as results of inexact interpretation.

While I agree with Mr Strachey that the type of interpretation he calls mutative are most effective, I seldom find myself in a position to give a transference interpretation of a complete drama with all the cast present. I am more accustomed to transference revivals, scene by scene, or even phrase by phrase, and to frequent absenteeism. I do not limit transference-interpretation to transference to me; I pursue it into the outer world in pursuit of derivatives and displacements of instinct but, whenever possible, I bring extra-analytic interpretation into relation with the current analytic situation. I go very cautiously with patients who are intolerant of direct transference interpretation and take every opportunity of analysing this resistance until some degree of toleration is brought about. I find it useful to follow, not only the succession of transference phases, but the changing significance of the analytic situation in relation to transference phenomena. For instance, if a patient greets me with the scowl of which his mother used to complain, and on that day grumbles about having to come at the same time every day and is otherwise grudging of associations, I count that scowl as a dose of hostility belonging to a lavatory situation. On another day I might be greeted with precisely the same scowl but it would refer to a different life-situation if the significance of analysis had changed, e.g., if it had become a school-room or his parent's bedroom. I am not satisfied with any emotional picture until I can put it in its environmental frame.

This has a bearing on interpretation relating to 'internalized objects'. Over and over again I find that preoccupation with internalized objects and anxieties of a type attributed by Mrs Klein to a 'depressive position' come to the fore and have to be interpreted in relation to the acquisition of sphincter control. The object stories mirror the tribulations of that period of life though of course these are not the only events reflected in them. Nevertheless, a patient who was very firmly convinced that there was no good in her, that she would always make a mess of anything she undertook, and never be or do anything worthwhile was a young woman who had dysentery sometime between 1 and a half and 2 and a half years of age. There is some uncertainty about the actual date but the internal evidence places the illness in the period during which she had begun to achieve some security of control, a security which was most thoroughly shattered. Teething, learning to walk and to speak, also come in. Hence I rarely give internal object interpretations solely in terms of affective relations to objects, but, whenever possible, in relation to a life-situation which seems to be their setting. I do not know how it may be with true psychotics, but psycho-neurotics who talk freely in internal-object terms have usually regressed; they are in flight from Oedipus situations. Nevertheless, when the Oedipus story is told, it turns out to be an abnormal story, and it seems likely that positions to which the patient regresses are, more often than not, positions in which some hitch occurred which impaired both the development of an adequately heterosexual Oedipus situation and a favourable issue from it.

5 Illustration

A married woman in her 30s told me in her first interview she had a kind of devil she wanted me to exorcise and she hoped to get something good from me to put in its place. The remainder of that time and the next few interviews were spent either in describing the history of her illness (obsessional preoccupation with death and fear of compulsive suicide) or in telling me about her life and family history. This included the early loss of her mother and her childhood devotion to her father. Whenever she talked about her husband she emphasized and re-emphasized his goodness to her in such a way that I received a very strong impression that she was choking with suppressed hostility to him. She also told me she was frigid and had never yet succeeded in becoming pregnant though she always felt she wanted a large family. She talked very freely and I did not intervene until she began to repeat herself. My first interpretation was then along the lines that she hoped to re-find in me the mother she had lost too soon and that what she wanted to confide to me, but felt it as both outrageous and unjustifiable, was her accumulated irritation with and bitter disappointment in, her husband and her married life. In spite of all his very real goodness, he fell short of the standard set by her father. This opened the flood-gates of her discontents. On the one hand, her affection for her husband revived and on the other, her grudge against her father for re-marrying in her teens and her hatred of her stepmother came to the surface, together with the fear that I might prove a stepmother. In short, the analysis appeared to be getting under way. To our mutual astonishment, we found out some time later that she must have become pregnant during the fourth week of analysis.

? Was my handling valid or was it a supreme example of 'connivance' with the patient's wishes. (What would have happened if analyst had been a man?)

6 Training analysis

Training analysis is, in all essentials, the same as therapeutic analysis. Both for his own and his patient's sake it is desirable that a Candidate should have a good degree of insight into his own mentality and sufficient anxiety tolerance. But once the process of ego-redintegration is well begun, and there is reason to suppose that the practice of analysis is an appropriate sublimation for the Candidate, work with patients may assist the later stages of analysis and may, indeed, shorten the period of personal analysis. I should think the length of training analysis is bound to remain a moot point because its optimum duration, like the optimum duration of a therapeutic analysis, must vary considerably from Candidate to Candidate. The most important general condition is that the analysis should have progressed to the point at which the Candidate has begun to find himself and is capable ultimately of becoming relatively independent of his analyst in regard both to his life and his work. If this point is reached, post-analytic association with the analyst will help to humanize the analysis and weaken the infantile transference bonds, to the point at which, though their influence will continue to be felt, they will not dominate feeling and behaviour.

Objectivity about oneself is never complete and objectivity about one's analyst more relative and more difficult to attain. But it is a necessary training aim. A degree of dependence at first, asking advice, conscious or unconscious imitation of method, etc., is only natural, just as it is natural to look for guidance to control analysts. But if the training analyst can get the candidate to a point from which he can continue to grow and to learn from experience and his controls give him sound directions with a view to helping him to develop his own technique, his best teachers thereafter will be his patients. Every new patient will continue his education and probably also continue his personal analysis with the utmost ruthlessness. All that training should hope to provide is a good start. Only by releasing trainees from tutelage when they are able to work on their own, and encouraging them to mature along their own lines, can we hope to ensure any steady progress in technique from generation to generation.

7 Effect of Mrs Klein's work on technique

If I ask myself in what way has Mrs Klein's work influenced my own technique, the answer is very little in principle but considerably in range. For instance, I give as many interpretations relating to the Oedipus complex as I did when I first started, probably more. The only difference is that I can now sometimes relate the peculiarities of specific Oedipus situations to foregoing experiences. Thus an adult hysteric's capacity for love with exclusion of the genitals and exaggerated need to be loved, may represent a failure to surmount an Oedipus situation which is pathological in itself because it is the heir of earlier miscarriages of development. I now have a much clearer appreciation of the complicated interrelationships between oral, anal, and genital aspects of experience and of the interplay between libido and aggression. In general, I have a much greater respect for some of Mrs Klein's clinical findings than I have for the way she reports them or the deductions she draws from them. I think she feels what certain babies feel like in certain circumstances. I do not think she necessarily

623

knows what all babies feel like in all circumstances. I often think she concentrates on some aspects to the neglect of others. Nevertheless, I think she has greatly extended the area of research and thrown light on many obscure problems. It does not seem to me to matter whether we accept or do not accept her point of view provided we study our own case material in order to determine how far it supplies confirmation or disproof. From the point of view of practice and training, it is the validity of clinical findings that has to be assessed and this can best be done by comparison with other clinical findings.

8 Misgivings

(a) *Personal technique* The most likely sources of error in my own technique will be apparent and need not be further elaborated here.

(b) *Conservative Freudian technique.* It is inevitable that our Viennese colleagues should feel a special responsibility for maintaining 'true' psychoanalysis; hence I find their misgivings about Mrs Klein's work natural and comprehensible. At the same time there is a risk that concern to keep analysis 'sound' may tend to ultra-conservatism and over-rigidity. To those of us who have profited by Mrs Klein's work without becoming her disciples 'Vienna teaching' seems rather to lack vitality and to be limited in scope. It seems inadequate in the same way that Freud's encyclopaedia article seems inadequate since the publication of *The Ego and the Id.* Their errors, if any, are negative errors of omission not errors of commission. There is no hint of any 'wild' psychoanalysis; only the potential dangers of over-conservatism leading to undue restriction of outlook and technique.

(c) *Mrs Klein's technique* As you all know I am greatly interested in Mrs Klein's work and have found it both illuminating and useful. But I have always felt that it lacked perspective and that she was too prone to over-simplification and to over-emphasis. I was alarmed by the wave of enthusiasm which swept the Society some years ago, a wave which sent Members rushing to Mrs Klein to consult her about their cases. I felt it to be so far from healthy that I remain one of the few Members who never has consulted Mrs Klein in this way. The most immediate disadvantage is, of course, that I have no first-hand knowledge of her actual methods. Impressions that her technique and that of her close colleagues may tend to stereotypy, to selective emphasis and various forms of transference suggestion, are all at second, third and fourth hand, apart from statements made in meetings.

The main root of my own misgivings has always been the direct first-hand impression that neither Mrs Klein nor her closest adherents are sufficiently realistic about her work. I am prepared to make every allowance for the various unfortunate circumstances which have combined to favour intolerance of criticism and over-protective aggrandizing of her work. I do not feel sure that these unfavourable circumstances completely explain the apparent lack of realism. Bad conditions existed in our Society before the arrival of our colleagues from Vienna. Indeed, a number of us hoped that their arrival would help us to achieve a more genuinely realistic spirit in the Society. The paper I read on scientific method in 1939 was, in effect, both an expression of this hope and an appeal. [Brierley 1939] The suggestion for a series of symposia I then made was premature. Whatever may be said about the defects and difficulties of the present series of Special Scientific Meetings and this TC enquiry into technique they represent an attempt to deal with our current controversies in a realistic, i.e., scientific way. They also represent an attempt to deal with our crises in a democratic way. It is at last possible to say what we think and Mrs Klein is now receiving in large quantities the criticism she might with advantage have had in graded doses from an earlier date. Science, like anything else, can be idealized but science in itself is only systematized knowledge. Scientific procedures are not counsels of perfection, they are only special developments of reality testing, designed to establish the maximum of probability and the minimum of error.

I have not in the least changed my opinion that there is a great deal of real value to be extracted from Mrs Klein's work. The papers we have heard so far, on the other hand, have done nothing to reassure me that her colleagues' estimate and exposition of her work is sound. We are bound to ask ourselves how far the type of error exhibited in their theory is, or is not, reflected in their practice. This is a matter on which we should not take anyone else's word but should try to estimate for ourselves on the evidence with which Mrs Klein can provide us if she will. What I call the inadequate realism displayed by enthusiasts about Mrs Klein's work is felt by a number of other Members and has been expressed at different times in different ways. The simplest and most direct way I can put it now is this: they tend to treat Mrs Klein's work as an idealized object. I hope Mrs Klein will realize that I am not making accusations and not trying to be rude and unkind. I regard it as urgent to make plain, particularly to Mrs Klein herself, what the disturbing impression is that I constantly receive and why it raises doubts in my mind about technique. The essential doubt is, do they or do they not promote a realistic solution of infantile problems of ambivalence, especially ambivalence regarding the mother?

To my mind, an 'idealized object' is something very different from an adequately libidinized 'good object'. Personally I am convinced that adequate satisfaction during the suckling phase is a major predisposing factor to libidinal object formation and stable ego-development, i.e.,sufficiently comprehensive ego-integration. I am fairly sure that libidinal and ego-development can be prejudiced from the start by undue privation during suckling life, let alone by traumatic weaning. Also, I think the baby's first all-or-none experiences have an affective intensity seldom equalled and perhaps never surpassed in later life. They are sporadic but, in so far as pleasurable and painful experiences are distinct from one another, they may be said to alternate. Whether the object of instinct is psychologically objectified in very early experience seems to me very doubtful, but I do not doubt that these early experiences are the matrices, the experiences differentiated by feeling, out of which good and bad object systems eventually develop. The point I want to stress is, that good infantile experience, however extravagant by adult standards, is realistic in that it is a response to actual satisfaction, either immediate or hallucinated, just as bad experience is a response to actual deprivation. True ambivalence, as distinct from successive affective experiences, true ambivalence in the sense of recognition of the fact that the same person is both lovable and hateful can surely only develop when ego and object integration are fairly well advanced. From internal evidence in adult cases, in which the analyst suddenly looks quite a different person to the patient, I inclined to think the cannibalistic object still alternates with the comforting feeding object and that unconscious theories, such as that one has been weaned as a punishment for cannibalism, gain coherent form some time after the event.

But we know beyond any doubt that ego and object systems emerge sufficiently early to be well established somewhere about the end of the 2nd year, and that the period of life during which the child is gaining sphincter control, which of course overlaps with teething, learning to walk, and beginning to understand words and to speak, and with the beginning of personal sexual interest, may be characterized by intense and intolerable true ambivalence. One attempt to solve this problem is by regression, by re-dividing the object of the ambivalent feelings into two objects, corresponding to the two series of earlier alternating good and bad experiences. Where this happens, the good half-object is no longer simply an object invested with intense primary libidinal suckling affects; it is an object which is maintained to be better than it is in reality, and the bad half-object is correspondingly worse. Various things may happen by way of displacement, distribution of identifications, etc., which may tend to stabilize this solution, but it is potentially dangerous because the ambivalence itself persists and the idealized object is forever in danger of becoming its denigrated opposite, unless its goodness is constantly inflated by over-compensatory love and it is constantly sheltered from aggression. It is this idealized object which has to be protected from destruction by biting, etc. The question is, does Klein technique in relation to good object, especially good mother objects, promote this kind of unrealistic solution of problems of ambivalence, or does it promote the surmounting of ambivalence along realistic lines? Do they take sufficient account of the fact, for instance, that the little girl's future development is best safeguarded if she comes really to love her father more than her mother? I am well aware that this idealization–denigration defence is deeply rooted in human nature and that some use of it is probably normal. It is the quantitative factor which may be decisive here, as so often in other situations. As a partial or a transitory solution, which may revive temporarily at adolescence, it may be considered normal, and its persistence as a religious solution would still be considered normal by millions of people. Nevertheless, it is an unrealistic solution which analysis may have to accept for some people, but which it has no business to promote. It is just the ready discipleship of Mrs Klein's adherents, their too-tender care and hyper-sensitivity, that rouses such doubts and makes one wonder whether their handling of certain phases of transference is more or less valid.

The relevance to training is twofold. In the first place, we cannot afford to train Candidates to promote unrealistic solutions of their own or their patient's ambivalent conflicts. In the second place, if Klein trainees did finish training identifying their analysts with 'idealized' objects, they would inevitably tend to identify themselves totally with their trainers and would have to become follow-my-leader copyists. They would remain under the psychic necessity of swallowing their training whole and never using their teeth upon what they are taught. In such circumstances there could be no hope of steady progress; only the chance of revolution. But while the trainee remained the echo of the trainer the result in both theory and practice could only be sterile repetition.

I should like to emphasize that for my own part, I am grimly determined not to pre-judge this issue. On the contrary I propose to insist upon my right to make up my mind on the evidence that I hope Mrs Klein will be good enough to provide, both in this enquiry and in her forthcoming papers. I should also like to emphasize that we cannot crystallize psychoanalysis; we cannot keep it fixed in any shape or form, however desirable these may appear at any given time. Analysis cannot live unless it grows, and it cannot grow without undergoing modification. The essence of analysis, as of any science, is realism. We can safely release analysis to the care of oncoming generations if we train them as realists, but only if we train them as realists.

5

Memorandum by Anna Freud

Statement for
the Training Committee dated 29th September 1943,
concerning the bearing of the present controversies on
the training of Candidates by Anna Freud

The Training Committee has lately been criticized by the Society for delaying the report about the bearing of the present controversies on training, as if such postponement were a deliberate attempt to sabotage the efforts made to clarify the situation in the Society. It seems to me that these criticisms were unjust and that according to the present policy of the Society no considered statement can be made about these matters except on the basis and in close conjunction with the outcome of the discussions about these Scientific Controversies.

But if our recommendations have to be presented to the Society regardless of this fact there are, as far as I can see, two points for the Training Committee to consider:

1 Whether Mrs Klein's new findings and theories necessarily lead to transformations and innovations of technical procedure, and
2 If this should be the case, whether the Training Committee considers it as its task to teach one main analytic theory and technique or whether it desires to create an open forum for the free teaching of all current analytic theories and consequent techniques.

Ad point 1

It is unnecessary to remind analysts of the fact that, during the whole development of psychoanalysis, theory and technique have been found to be indissolubly bound up with each other, so that every new step in theory produced changes of the technique and every

629

technical innovation produced new findings which could not have been unearthed by the former methods.

The two main foundation stones of psychoanalytic technique were the substitution of free association for hypnosis, and the control and reduction to a minimum of the real relations between analyst and patient. The first followed on the discovery of the dynamic importance of resistance; the second on the discovery of the facts of transference. The technical rule of free association has remained more or less undisputed through the development of psychoanalysis. The technical rules governing the behaviour of the analyst, and thereby the whole analytical setting, have been repeatedly under discussion and have undergone or withstood a series of attempts at revision and transformation, following on various theories about the paramount importance of any one among the pathogenic factors responsible for the formation of neuroses. Technical innovations mostly took the direction of especially preparing the ground for the re-emergence of this particular pathogenic factor in the transference neurosis.

To enumerate some instances:

1 Special valuation of the damming-up of libido as a pathogenic agent was responsible for the so-called 'active therapy' by Ferenczi and Rank.
2 Rank's birth trauma as a main pathogenic factor resulted in the technical rule of planned termination of analysis.
3 The great significance which Ferenczi ascribed to certain frustrations suffered by the infant in early phases of its mother-relationship, led to technical prescriptions concerning an indulgent attitude of the analyst, which was deliberately planning to invite reproduction of a mother–child relationship between analyst and patient.
4 Reich, who attributed the failure of normal development of genital faculties to an early repression of aggressive attitudes, evolved a set of technical rules which were specially designed to reproduce aggressive scenes between analyst and patient, etc.

To return to the bearing which this enumeration may have on the present controversy about Mrs Klein's theories. So far Mrs Klein has not expressly stated which changes of technique follow on her new outlook on the theory of neurosis. It seems therefore that discussion of this point is not profitable until such time when this subject has been included in the programme of the Scientific Discussions of the Society. Before that happens all one can do is to touch on certain points where differences of technique between Mrs Klein and so-called orthodox analysis have become known or can be inferred from Mrs Klein's writings. The most prominent of these differences seems to me the almost exclusive emphasis given by Mrs Klein to all transference material, compared with material which emerges in dreams, in verbal associations, in memories and screen-memories. In Freudian technique the value of these various sources of material was considered to be fairly equal, though it was assumed that memories which belong to a pre-verbal era cannot emerge in any other form except in transference behaviour. The interpretations of transference behaviour, though important from the beginning of an analysis, thus became increasingly so towards the later stages of the treatment when interpretation attempts to reach down to ever deeper levels. According to Mrs Klein's theory the importance of pre-verbal phantasies is overwhelming compared with the pathogenic role of happenings which occur after the acquisition of speech. Consequently in her technique the contributions from all other sources of material dwindle in importance until interpretation of transference behaviour remains as the main technical weapon of the analyst from the beginning to the end of a treatment. The displacement of importance in her theory from later stages of development to the earliest one thus results in the accompanying displacement of importance in her technique.

To refer to other differences: interpretation of transference on Freudian lines is based on the theoretical assumption that the first and superficial contact with the analyst (as with any other object) is governed by normal rational attitudes, and that transference of emotion from deeper layers occurs in increasing strength when contact deepens and the so-called transference neurosis has had time to establish itself. Mrs Klein's interpretation of transference reactions in the beginning of an analysis seems to be based on a theoretical assumption of the opposite kind: that the powers of transference reactions are greater where the partner is still an unknown quantity, i.e. a phantasy object, and that the distortions of such a transference are slowly corrected and diminished by real experience where the object becomes known and familiar. It is clear that the technical handling of a situation must be different according to the underlying theoretical assumptions.

The aim of the Freudian technique is, above all, to undo repressions and is based on the conviction that the widening of consciousness which brings more psychic matter under the control of the ego is the main therapeutic agent. Mrs Klein's theory attributes the greatest pathogenic importance to the mechanisms of introjection and projection and consequently expects beneficial results mainly from the reductions and transformations of the so-called internalized objects and their interrelations with outside reality. It is difficult to see how the same technical devices can serve both purposes.

There are other differences in technique which, I think, must arise out of Mrs Klein's assumption that reactions which play a part in the earliest (pre-psychological) phase of the infant's existence are still in action in adult life and re-emerge in the state of transference. Reactions to the analyst will thus be interpreted as a wish to 'keep him inside', to expel him, etc., reactions which in this pre-psychological phase may have taken the place of later love and hate feelings.

As stated before, it does not seem fair to enter into discussions of this kind before Mrs Klein herself has given the lead by stating the interrelations between her own theories and her own technique, and before we have heard more about the role ascribed by her to repression and regression in the formation of neuroses. It is especially the theoretical concept of regression which, in Freudian analysis, has the greatest bearing on technique.

Ad point 2
The Institute as an open forum

In a former meeting of the Training Committee Mr Strachey has put forward the suggestion that the analytic Institute might form an open forum where current analytic theories and techniques are taught without giving preference to any one among them. This seems a possible solution at a time like the present when various analytic theories exist side by side and claim equal rights as being genuine attempts to arrive at the truth.

I should like to point out that such a change of programme, far from diminishing the present difficulties, presents the Institute with a whole series of new problems for the solution of which the Training Committee is at present hardly equipped. Which would be the current theories to be taught? Would they be merely theories which are originated by authors who are Members of the Society, or of the Training Committee, or of the International Psychoanalytical Association, or would the programme include outsiders? (At present there is hardly any instruction given to Candidates of this Institute concerning new developments in psychoanalytic theory and technique in other countries, for instance by Alexander, Rado, Horney, etc.) Where would the line be drawn between current theories to be included in the teaching programme and others which are disregarded? Who would assume the responsibility for distinctions of this kind and would they be less difficult to make than it is now to assess the relative value of the conceptions of analysis held by the two main groups of this Society? But even leaving aside the choice of theories to be included, the arrangement of such a new teaching programme (an open forum) could only follow on the theoretical work necessary to distinguish such theories clearly from each other, to define their points of contact and points of divergence; to avoid confusion the theories would have to be named either according to their authors or according to some central principle involved in them. Since a close connection between theory and technique is the generally accepted point of view, each theory would have to be taught together with the therapeutic procedure based on it.

Though the idea of an open forum for psychoanalytic teaching may seem tempting at a first glance, I personally doubt whether it could be carried out effectively and whether the result would not fall far short of the intentions, would not in effect turn out to be similar to institutes like the Tavistock Clinic with all their well-known shortcomings. If such a teaching procedure had been adopted from the beginning of psychoanalytic development, psychoanalysis of the present day would include the theoretical and technical teachings of, for instance, Stekel, Adler, Jung, Rank, etc. (A psycho-therapeutic institute of this type was actually set up in Berlin in 1934 [The Goering Institute] under the pressure and according to the express wish of the Nazi regime.)

If the development of psychoanalytic institutes should, in spite of those and similar arguments, go in this direction, this would probably lead to the gradual dissolving of psychoanalytic societies which, after all, were founded for the propagation and development of a more or less unified and consistent theory and method. Such disintegration of psychoanalytic societies and psychoanalytic teaching may on the other hand be inevitable. In this case further progress and development will again, as in the earliest times of analysis, have to be expected from the efforts of single individuals and not from the activities of societies and institutes. There are many factors in the psychoanalytic circles of all countries which point in this direction.

The findings and recommendations to be put before the Society should, so far as I am concerned, be of the following nature: it should be pointed out to the Society that, under the present conditions, the Training Committee is confronted with a task which cannot be fulfilled to satisfaction. The training of Candidates wavers between the two principles of unified teaching on the one hand and the

633

establishing of an open forum on the other. It is impossible to carry out a teaching programme which is based on one main theory, since the divergences of opinion between members of the Training Committee is too far-reaching to allow of such unification. It is on the other hand impossible to give equal status to two or more theories since the points of coincidence of divergence between such theories are still undefined and techniques are not clearly apportioned to the theories to which they organically belong. The first step of disentangling matters was taken when the Training Committee decided that the training analyst and control analyst of a given Candidate should hold at least similar theoretical views, which means that no Candidate should be expected to handle a case technically except on the basis of his experience in his own personal analysis. Before that step was taken, Candidates were sometimes placed in the position to work with patients on the basis of one analytic theory while their own analysis had been conducted on the basis of another.

It should be pointed out to the Society that the allocation of new Candidates remains now more or less a matter of chance, except in those cases where the new Candidate arrives equipped with knowledge which enables him to discriminate between the various schools of thought in analysis. This happens rarely and is made more difficult by the fact that 'orthodox' analysis and Mrs Klein's theories are not distinguished from each other by any name. Still, this haphazard allocation of a Candidate to any particular training analyst usually determines the theoretical orientation of a future analyst.

It is a further grave disadvantage, which should be pointed out to the Society, that under the present conditions, members of the Training Committee have, of necessity, the right to judge the status of Candidates in whose training they have had no hand, because it has been carried out by training and control analysts of another school of thought, with which they themselves are not in agreement. Similarly they have to take part in the election of training and control analysts though those belong to a school of analytic thought which they oppose. In both these instances there is hardly the possibility for them to exercise their functions in the right spirit. Either disagreement about theoretical matters will be fought out over individuals, or, to avoid deadlocks, and to reach necessary practical agreements, the decisions of the Training Committee will be arrived at by petty bargaining, instead of being based, as they should be, on the ideas, opinions and convictions of its members.

6

Memorandum on her technique by Melanie Klein

Melanie Klein – 25th October 1943

In order to find out where differences in technique lie, we must discuss the way in which we apply the fundamental principle of analysis, that is to say the kind of approach each of us has in analysing unconscious mental processes, transference, resistance and repression, infantile sexuality, the Oedipus complex, etc. Since we have agreed that this first statement should be a short one, I am selecting only two characteristics of my technique; even so I shall have to do this in an epigrammatic way.

From my work with young children I came to certain conclusions which have to some extent influenced my technique with adults. Take transference first. I found that with children the transference (positive or negative) is active from the beginning of the analysis, since for instance even an attitude of indifference cloaks anxiety and hostility. With adults too (*mutatis mutandis*) I found that the transference situation is present from the start in one way or another, and I came, therefore, to make use of transference interpretations early in the analysis.

In my experience, the transference situation permeates the whole actual life of the patient during the analysis. When the analytic situation has been established, the analyst takes the place of the original objects, and the patient, as we know, deals again with the feelings and conflicts which are being revived, with the very defences he used in the original situation. While repeating, therefore, in relation to the analyst some of his early feelings, phantasies, and sexual desires, he displaces others from the analyst to different people and situations. The result is that the transference phenomena are in part being diverted from the analysis. In other words, the patient is

635

'acting out' part of his transference feelings in a different setting outside the analysis.

These facts have an important bearing on technique. In my view, what the patient shows or expresses consciously about his relation to the analyst is only one small part of the feelings, thoughts, and phantasies which he experiences towards him. These have, therefore, to be uncovered in the unconscious material of the patient by the analyst following up by means of interpretation the many ways of escape from the conflicts revived in the transference situation. By this widened application of the transference situation the analyst finds that he is playing a variety of parts in the patient's mind, and that he is not only standing for actual people in the patient's present and past, but also for the objects which the patient has internalized from his early days onwards, thus building up his superego. In this way we are able to understand and analyse the development of his ego and his superego, of his sexuality and his Oedipus complex from their inception.

If during the course of the analysis we are constantly guided by the transference situation, we are sure not to overlook the present and past actual experiences of the patient, because they are seen again and again through the medium of the transference situation.[1]

Provided the interplay between reality and phantasy, and thus between the conscious and the unconscious, is consistently interpreted, the transference situation and feelings do not become blurred and obscured.

This constant interaction between conscious and unconscious processes, between phantasy products and the perception of reality, finds full expression in the transference situation. Here we see at certain stages of the analysis how the ground shifts from real experiences to phantasy situations and to internal situations – by which I mean the object world felt by the patient to be established inside – and again back to external situations, which later may appear in either a realistic or phantastic aspect. This movement to and fro is connected with an interchange of figures, real and phantastic, external and internal, which the analyst represents.

There is one more aspect of the transference situation which I should emphasize. The figures whom the analyst comes to represent in the patient's mind always belong to specific *situations*, and it is only by considering those situations that we can understand the nature and content of the feelings transferred on to the analyst. This means that we must understand what in the patient's mind analysis unconsciously stands for at any particular moment, in order to discover the phantasies and desires associated with those earlier

636

situations – containing always elements of both actuality and phantasy – which have provided the pattern for the later ones.

Moreover, it is in the nature of these particular 'situations' that in the patient's mind other people besides the analyst are included in the transference situation. This is to say, it is not just a one to one relation between patient and analyst, but something more complex. For instance, the patient may experience sexual desires towards the analyst which at the same time bring up jealousy and hatred towards another person who is connected with the analyst (another patient, somebody in the analyst's house, somebody met on the way to the analyst, etc.) who in the patient's phantasy represents a favoured rival. Thus we discover the ways in which the patient's earliest object relations, emotions, and conflicts have shaped and coloured the development of his Oedipus conflict, and we elucidate the various situations and relationships in the patient's history against the background of which his sexuality, symptoms, character, and emotional attitudes have developed.

What I want to stress here is that it is by keeping the two things together in the transference – feelings and phantasies on the one hand and specific situations on the other – that we are able to bring home to the patient how he came to develop the particular patterns of his experiences.

To turn now to my technique in analysing defence mechanisms (this obviously has a bearing on the analysis of resistance; but this is not my point here). I owe to the analysis of young children a fuller understanding of the earliest object relations, and a new insight into the origin of anxiety, guilt, and conflict. These findings enabled me to develop a technique by which children from two years onwards are being analysed. This technique not only opened up a new and promising field for therapy and research, but had also a strong influence on the technique with adults. The view that it is the destructive impulses directed against the loved object which give rise to anxiety and guilt, led me in my work with adults to take particular account of anxiety and guilt and to regard the defence mechanisms as primarily developed by the ego against anxiety from these sources.

Every step in analysing anxiety and guilt and the defence mechanisms from this point of view leads in my experience to a fuller understanding of all other emotions as well. This implies an extensive analysis of the phantasy life and of the unconscious generally, as well as of the defence mechanism and the ego, that is to say of the whole personality. Not only is such an approach not incompatible with the full analysis of the libido – it is, in my experience, a condition for it. For the anxieties stirred by the destructive impulses constantly influence the libido – at times inhibiting, at times increasing the libidinal desires – and thus the vicissitudes of libido are fully comprehensible only in relation to the early anxieties with which they are intimately bound up.

With some adults there may be a lengthy period in which we can detect no manifest anxiety, nor are able to make intent anxiety manifest. Then, in my experience, the analysis proceeds by uncovering in the material the defences against anxiety and guilt. The more we know about the early defence mechanisms, the more we are able to detect them and also to see the later ones at work in the material of our patients, and thus to find access to anxiety and guilt, depressive feelings, and all the other emotions. Needless to say, my technique varies in different types of cases and illnesses; though this particular approach to anxiety and guilt remains one guiding principle. I should wish to illustrate this here by instances but must limit myself to stating the general principle.

Note

1 (Original footnote) I am in full agreement with James Strachey's paper on 'The Nature of the Therapeutic Procedure'. [Strachey 1934]

7

Memorandum on her technique
by Ella Freeman Sharpe

Concerning the problem of technique and training
by Ella Freeman Sharpe (November 24th 1943)

In the Collected Papers Freud says concerning the technical rules which he evolved out of his experience.

> My hope is that compliance with them will spare physicians practising analysis much unavailing effort and warn them of various possibilities which they might otherwise overlook. I must however expressly state that this technique has proved to be the only method suited to my individuality: I do not venture to deny that a physician quite differently constituted might feel impelled to adopt a different attitude to his patients and to the task before him.
> [Freud,S. 1912: 323; SE 12:111][1]

How far removed Freud is, in his vision, tolerance, and sanity from the fears and the necessity for complete certainty that beset those of his followers, who would crystallize and impose a hard and fast technique upon others. Practitioners are called analysts who do not adopt Freud's technique, and he frankly says the technique suited his individuality.

I would make this comment. Freudian technique is only a vital method when it is employed by people who have found that as individuals it is the only method that suits them. Certain rules of Freudian technique can be taught and be applied, but that is a very different thing from the finding of a technique that is suited to the individuality of the practitioner.

Freud's technique as a method that suited him individually would carry little weight if that method had not revealed those fundamental truths upon which the science of psychoanalysis rests. Freud did not invent those truths, they existed before Freud. He discovered them by empirical methods. He went on discovering, but I have not gathered that as a result of the more intricate structure of the mental apparatus he revealed in course of time that his methods of approach and research were thereby altered. The claim on us of Freud's technique is that his technique and his discoveries are inseparable. We believe by no other method could the foundations of a dynamic psychology have been laid. Just as he did not 'invent' his discoveries, so his technique was not 'invented', it 'evolved'. The procession of his revelations concerning the psychical life conveys in perspective the effect of witnessing an evolutionary process, and his concept of analysis achieved by his technique is of a 'process'. He says analysis sets a process in motion, or sets a process in operation.

The process, he says, goes its own way, the process being repetition of psychical history with the analyst as the substitute for parental and family figures. But this process, Freud maintains, can only go at its own rate, it cannot be forced because it is determined by a totality of factors, all of which can never be gauged. 'Thou seest the end from the beginning' is spoken of God, but a scientist is content to discover from end results the course of such threads in a pattern as he can follow and only so far as he can follow with clarity.

The concepts of 'pace' and 'process' seem to me to be vital ones for a valid technique, checking as they do our hurry and hope of magical results. Profound changes come slowly involving as they do redistribution of psychical energies. It matters little how great the intuitive insight of the practitioner may be, nor how much of it he communicates to the patient, for the fact remains that genuine psychical development depends upon what a person emotionally realizes for himself. The analyst may help to clear the path, but he cannot do the task required of the patient.

In an attempt to understand some of the reasons for successful analyses I have recalled and studied from this angle three patients of whom I have been able to get reports up to date.

I conducted the analysis of one, twenty-two years ago. Another seventeen years ago, a third fifteen years ago. The first was a girl of 16, suffering from a complete nervous breakdown with periods of psychical deafness, the second a paranoid woman with a family history of insanity. The third was a delusional case, a young woman in her twenties who had hallucinations and came to me after emerging from a confusional state.

If cure is any criterion of a valid technique these cases have stood the test of time; 15, 17, 22 years and the patients have not had any analysis in the interim. The girl of 16 is a married woman with 3 children. They remained in Bristol throughout the Blitz without untoward results, the paranoid woman is teaching in her 70th year and enjoying a comparatively serene old age after half a life time of mental suffering, the delusional young woman now in her forties leads an active reality life along lines she developed for herself. Like all of you I could cite other cases, but I choose these because only one case of the three was strictly speaking psycho-neurotic, and I treated these people when I knew comparatively little of the structure of such mental illnesses. I know a great deal more today, I could hope for no better results therapeutically, though I could hope for better intellectual understanding. What equipment had I then?

The first thing I had was an absolute belief in psychic determination. The second was a belief in 'process'; that one set a process in motion. One had to evoke from the patient, in a favourable atmosphere, the secrets so jealously guarded. I call this now, 'dealing with resistances'.

Knowing as I do now much more about ego defences, I do not actually deal with resistance more effectively than I did twenty years ago when I had only the vivid realization that the patient was *mortally* afraid, which is after all the cause of repression. It is only the emotional realization of the patient's fears that can subtly direct technique to assuaging them, otherwise 'resistances' can well be interpreted into wilful lying and deceit.

My belief in 'process' has deepened not lessened during the passing years. That the 'pace' of the 'process' can be hindered by lack of skill in handling transference resistances one admits, but with the exercise of expert skill, I still believe in a 'pace' that is ultimately set by the individual psyche in question and that the analyst's 'pace', if not attuned to it, can throw the 'process' out of gear. Results may be obtained, I do not deny, but they are not the *patient's* results. The first spontaneous transference affect towards myself as a separate individual from herself evinced by a woman patient lately, occurred exactly fourteen months after the beginning of her analysis. She decided to adopt a child, and in telling me of this expressed the first signs of ambivalence towards me. The day she informed me proved to be the birthday of her only sister who was born when she was fourteen months old. During that fourteen months of analysis the patient had reached a pseudo-stabilization, necessary and inevitable for further analytical progress, based entirely on the magical one-ness with the mother before disillusion set in with the arrival of the next child. This patient's slow awareness of myself as a different entity, made me once more realize this 'process' set going by analysis, a profound 'repetition', which, in this instance at any rate, all my interpretations for fourteen months neither hastened nor delayed, nor obscured.

Twenty-two years ago I was never dominated by the desire to cure, only to understand. Cure was for me an accompaniment of revealing the hidden causes of illness. Interpretations were simple and went no further than my direct understanding of the bit of work I was engaged upon. I regarded transference as the meeting place of present and past emotional fixations and the expression of hostile transference even more liberating to the psyche than the infantile positive one. Transference was to be used for one purpose only, the levering of the repressed into consciousness, one had no other use for it. I believed in real parents, as well as imagos, in real events as well as imaginary ones. I believed, as I still do, that phantasy, however horrific, must be easier for the person ridden by phantasy, than reality. I had to understand why and where and how the two were associated in a space–time world.

I believed and still believe in Freud's recommendation that the analyst should content himself with the motto of an old surgeon: 'Je le pansai, Dieu le guérit'. There is something not due to us, however skilful we may be, when a patient achieves a cure, and we must bow to reality and acknowledge there are illnesses that cannot be cured. An analyst of our Society said to me quite seriously not long ago, 'Only the limitations of time prevents the cure of all psychical disorders'. That belief is not consonant with reality, its reference is to eternity.

Alongside these three successful cases I place two major failures, an alcoholic and a conversion hysteria with a psychotic foundation. These patients may have been curable, they may not. Early technique was ineffectual if they were, I do not say 'invalid' technique, but 'ineffectual' and I should be arbitrary indeed, if I did not consider the possibility that a different technique might have brought more successful results.

Freud says that every analyst's achievement is limited by what his own complexes and resistances permit. How rarely one hears today that technique and success or failure are conditioned at all by any individual analyst's complexes and resistances! Yet he who thinks otherwise is surely blind to the specific limitations set by his own total personality. Resistances and complexes vary in nature and intensity. I speak of 'analysed' practitioners, not 'unanalysed'. So also do analysts differ in the nature and quality of their insight for the same reason – resistances and complexes. I do not believe one person sees 'the whole truth and nothing but the truth' of a single patient. The degree of insight a person has, in one direction, is often accompanied by corresponding blindness in other directions. Perhaps nothing marks Freud's work with the stamp of genius more than the comprehensiveness of his range of discoveries, the awareness of so many different factors in psychical phenomena, the complexity, not the simplicity that challenges technique.

Freud says, 'I appreciate that various forms of disease cannot all be dealt with by the same technique.' [Freud, S. 1919:399; SE 17: 165][2] There again speaks the man who out-strides his followers. A 'different' technique can be a valid psychoanalytical technique if it is evolved to deal with different diseases. People are individuals with individual histories. A technique based on a priori assumptions that all people suffer from the same disease is static and therefore dead. It has rules and phraseologies that can be learnt and applied mechanically. A valid technique is adaptable to specific needs of an individual, it is not a yardstick. It is not settled beforehand, but evolves alongside the unfolding 'process', even though that 'process' will certainly show that all patients suffer from castration anxiety and fear their own instincts.

A year ago I paced up and down Devonshire Place with a patient whose anxiety had reached a climax of frenzy in which murder and suicide were imminently possible. The crisis had been unpredictable through a synchronization of a repressed trauma nearing consciousness and an unforeseeable external event. Free association methods on the couch were out of the question. I had to rely on my unconscious mind to bring out from all it had stored in previous analyses, conducted on classical lines, the apt interpretations. They came seemingly out of the blue and anxiety slowly lessened. My technique in this case was valid. But I should not teach a student from a specific exception of this sort, happening once in 20 years. I should relate it as an experience and all the details associated with it. I should deduce no general rules from it for the guidance of students in dealing with their cases. Such communicated experiences are helpful, if one's aim is to encourage students to acquire a pliant technique that is equal to a sudden emergency. In some such way my own work has been enriched by the special insight into the unconscious life Mrs Klein has demonstrated. I suspect her theoretical formulations, I await more details of her technique from herself. I assess phantasy differently, make a different use of it, but that much of the phantasy life of the unconscious she has detailed is accessible in an analysis conducted on general classical lines I can verify.

When a young student of 19 tells me during the course of one hour the following data I find this verification. He recalls stealing from his mother's pantry with the fears he experienced while so doing. He recalls a certain cupboard on the nursery stairs, of how sometimes he dared to put his head into it, but never long enough to dispel his fears. Sometimes he went past it with his head in the air and pretended to ignore its presence. Sometime later he dared again to put in his head. Then he refers to the number of girls with whom he had intercourse, and with not one of them has he been able to establish a love relationship of even a temporary kind. He has in fact just dared to put his head in cupboards. He then feels cold, he sees the rug on the couch. He says, 'I'm not going to put it over me. I'm ignoring it.'

The meaning is obvious, and I acknowledge that Mrs Klein's clinical work has aided and deepened such understanding. I might add that this young student has read no books on psychoanalysis.

Insight into the unconscious phantasy life such as Mrs Klein has, is a specific gift, which I venture to say has proved of value in some way or other to many of us.

But I believe that every analyst's achievement is limited by his own complexes. Mrs Klein's as well as all other analysts', and specific gifts of insight into one aspect of mental life do not necessarily mean a comprehensive insight into the whole field of mental phenomena.

A student who is going to be a valid technician will discover for himself *anew* by scientific method what Freud discovered, and by the same approach Mrs Klein's discoveries if valid will be rediscovered – not her formulations but her discoveries. We believe there will be other discoveries, but since only one genius so far has arisen who could both discover and formulate principles we must trust those who have cool scientific judgement to check up on the theories evolved by discoverers.

For me it is an illusion that a valid technique can be taught in the way that facts are taught. To make valid deductions from the phenomena we observe in the consulting room depends upon a special order of knowledge and awareness limited and conditioned always by the practitioner's personality.

Nobody can hand over a ready made technique except as an artefact. Knowledge can be handed on from one generation to another, whether profitable or not depends upon other factors than intellectual comprehension. As a body of knowledge P.A. science will do no more to make a saner world than any other science. It is as applied knowledge only that it will work to that end. So I believe we cannot hand on 'technique' for it depends upon other factors that outweigh the conscious application of some one else's rules and regulations. Every generation of psychoanalysts will have to evolve it for themselves and from 'scratch'. One has to tread Freud's path after him, start as he started not where he left off. There is no short cut. Experience must be vital and first-hand to be convincing. I have no reason to think many will move any faster than Freud in collecting data from which to evolve theory, especially if they brood over it as long as Freud found necessary, even though they may have stored in their heads all Freud's accumulated knowledge. A technique is dead if it is based upon a static outlook or inlook fixed upon the earliest discovery of Freud's or that of the latest discoverer.

What are the essentials of a valid technique? Belief in psychic determination through emotional conviction of the fundamental truths of psychoanalytical science.

A belief in a 'process' set going by the method of free association, in which the psychical patterns will be repeated and that this process has an inherent pace of its own, even when resistances are handled with all skill. A belief that cure if it is obtainable, goes alongside the practitioner's efforts to reach an understanding of the patient's problems. A belief that the handling of transference is the most vital problem in analytical method, errors in which outweigh all inadequacies of interpretation of material as such. There is only one legitimate use of transference, viz., for the benefit of the patient. In the transference affects the meaning of the patient's malaise is demonstrated and its chance of solution alone possible.

As far as attitude towards the analytical work is concerned, I revert to Freud's words on psychoanalysis itself. It does not start out from a few sharply defined fundamental concepts, seeking to grasp the whole universe with the help of these. On the contrary it keeps close to the facts in its field of study, seeks to solve the immediate problem of observation, and gropes its way forward by the help of experience.

A valid technique is slowly evolved from first hand experience involving error in its acquisition. A valid technician will neither deny nor be discouraged by the fact that his achievements will be limited by his own resistances and complexes.

A valid technique will admit of adaptation to specific needs of specific cases. It will be valid, whatever the departures from standard rules, if the foregoing assumptions underlie the departures. But the general principles of technique cannot be formulated from such departures. Different diseases admit of different techniques.

A valid technique is not directed to finding support for any theory, it is directed to only one object, the investigation of the psychical problems of a given individual, without a priori assumptions.

My criterion of the function of a 'control' analyst is this. Is he evoking the student's powers of observation, drawing attention to what is being overlooked, helping the student to assess material for himself? Is he checking swift, glib, facile conclusions, helping him to bear uncertainties? Is he capable of the thought also that the student might possibly be right and that he may be wrong? Is he willing to let the student acquire technique at the *student's own rate* knowing that what the student is not convinced of, or is not on the point of appreciating for himself, is not of much value? I believe those who conduct seminars or give illustrations of technique should ask themselves, 'Am I showing how I work, how I arrive at conclusions from given data, or am I saying "This is how it should be done, and these are the correct interpretations"?' One attitude is scientific, the other is personal and arbitrary. It is the method and type of approach we need to communicate.

One final consideration. The amount of control work done under another analyst by any member of this committee must be very small. Most of us worked our way by acquiring what imperfect technique we possess by dealing directly and almost unaided with our problems. We learned first-hand by trial and error; we had the inestimable advantage of talking case material over with friends and contemporaries. There was no leader and no led; we were independent. Help was reciprocal. We met on a common footing and had a common zest. I attribute some of the freedom we took for granted, the freedom we felt, to the fact that we were separated from our own analysts by the English Channel, an important bulwark of independence in so many ways. The three patients whom I analysed so long ago all left London. The problem the Society is faced by is that of psychological inbreeding due to the small number of its Members and that small number consisting as it does of mainly analysts and the people they have analysed. It is almost inevitable in such a situation that younger workers should be unable to make approximately independent judgements for themselves, and enjoy the measure of freedom in analytical development that we older Members had. We did not gather round one person, neither one nor another as the source and fountain of truth. We liked, disliked, or tolerated each other as persons but we were wholehearted about the science of psychoanalysis. I do not advocate that our students should have no more help than *we* had, but help can be given at the cost of independence if students continue too long moving in the orbits of their analysts instead of their own. The dissolution of students' transferences is the only method to bring and maintain psychological health and independence in the Society as at present constituted.

We need the special gifts and insight any worker can bring. We need to know those variations in technique that have resulted in successful solution of specific problems. But the liberty of students must be safeguarded. Individual variations of technique must not be imposed upon them as the only valid method. There is only one thing we have the right *to insist upon* in training students, namely the conviction of those fundamentals of psychoanalysis which are beyond question and controversy and the acquisition of the technique that revealed those truths, for those truths and technique belong together and constitute the basic theory and practice of psychoanalysis.

Finally, I can see one possible test of any psychoanalyst's scientific rectitude. Is he ready to admit that his technique is the one best suited to his own personality? Does he believe that his achievements are conditioned by the nature of his own complexes and resistances? An answer in the affirmative precludes any claim to infallibility.

Notes

1 'My hope is that observance of them will spare physicians practising analysis much unnecessary effort and guard them against some oversights. I must however make it clear that what I am asserting is that this technique is the only one suited to my individuality; I do not venture to deny that a physician quite differently constituted might find himself driven to adopt a different attitude to his patients and to the task before him.' [SE 12: 111]
2 'Lastly, another quite different kind of activity is necessitated by the gradual growing appreciation that the various forms of disease treated by us cannot all be dealt with by the same technique.' [SE 17: 165]

647

8

Memorandum on her technique
by Sylvia M. Payne

*Contribution to
discussion on the fundamentals of technique
by S. M. Payne (24th November 1943)*

The main difficulty to me in writing this contribution to the discussion was to decide whether it was more important to bring forward details connected with the application of technique which I consider to be fundamental or whether it was better to concentrate on points of more general technical significance.

I came to the conclusion that my first task was to define what I considered the attitude of the analyst should be to psychoanalysis, as this attitude must actually determine the effect of the technique however that technique is applied. Hence I will say that no analytical technique is sound however applied if the analyst regards it as the only method of saving the patient and as an exact method depending on exactitude for its success.

In training we aim at preparing the Candidate to be able to observe and judge objectively, and the ideal is that they should observe with their own eyes eventually and not only through those of their analyst or control analysts.

It is obvious that what an individual analyst considers to be fundamental when the application of technique is considered must vary, with the type of case which is thought to be suitable for treatment. If treatment is to be confined to psycho-neurotics and people with slight character difficulties a technique can be applied with more rigidity and exactitude than if the treatment of borderline cases and psychopaths is undertaken. It may be obvious that these cases cannot be cured but they may be helped, kept out of asylums, and prevented from committing suicide and often obtain a limited adaptation which is compatible with relative health and happiness. The treatment is therefore justified. The first interview in my opinion should be conducted in such a way that a diagnosis can be made, and if the consultant intends to conduct the treatment himself, the beginning of a contact of a certain type is established. That is to say, the basis of a transference may be laid down which does not immediately revive anxiety producing imagos of the parents but which establishes the beginning of a belief in an understanding helping figure of a new kind. If the consultant is passing on the case, while sufficient contact must be made to further the making of a diagnosis, there is no need to do more than this and a swift dynamic transference if made may make the preliminary stages of the patient's analysis more complex. Of course it is often impossible to influence the patient in this respect, he determines the nature of the transference. In the conduct of the treatment itself I regard the position on the couch prescribed by Freud as fundamental for training and in the average case. Exceptions to the rule will occur and must be made as the result of experience. There is no doubt that lying on the couch is the favourable position for the development of dissociated states and this must be borne in mind when psychotic patients are being treated.

The aim of the analyst is to make the conditions favourable for the patient to be able to associate freely. In the opening phases as a rule interpretations are of preconscious material and are associated with a certain amount of explanation when it seems necessary. Transference interpretations in the earliest phase are given when indicated by a sudden hold-up of material, or when they are obvious from what the patient says or does.

I have no doubt that we shall all agree that the correct handling of the transference is the most important part of analytical technique. Freud advised that the transference should not be analysed until there is evidence that it determines the resistatnce. A dynamic unconscious transference resistance may be animated at the first interview, in this case it has a conscious representation. For example, a case comes for treatment in the sway of acute ambivalence expressed in terms of what friends and relatives say about analysis. It is necessary to interpret at once the conscious fear of being harmed, perhaps robbed and made licentious by analysts. In other words the patient is afraid of his id impulses and it will probably be possible to link the fear of the analyst with the fear of being at the mercy of primitive impulses. In other cases the transference at the beginning may be of a powerful critical figure which certainly has preconscious representations which can be detected and interpreted. I should not give the interpretation in terms of an unconscious situation unless something quite unusual occurs.

In a number of cases these transference resistances do not arise immediately. It is obvious that the differences of opinion connected with technique centre round the method of giving transference interpretations.

It may help us to be objective to recognize modifications which have taken place gradually in our technique as the result of progress of knowledge and experience, the interchange of ideas and the influence of individual characteristics which are bound to show themselves in preferences for quantitative variations in the application of technique after the analyst has gained confidence through experience.

When I started my training with James Glover in 1919 I sat in a chair facing him and he wrote down every word I said. We did a lot of useful work under these conditions. Then after he had had training with Dr Abraham in Berlin he changed his technique and the patient lay on the couch, the analyst sitting behind. Interpretations were given mainly at the end of the session but not exclusively. Transference interpretations were given when transference resistance occurred and there was evidence in the material. The analyst was very passive.

When I worked with Dr Sachs the technique was much the same except that interpretation was much more systematized. There was more reconstruction and again transference was only interpreted when it was a resistance.

In subsequent years before Mrs Klein came to London I observed that some English analysts used transference interpretations very much more actively than Dr Sachs had done and some tended to bring every relationship spoken of by the patient into the transference situation at once by interpretation from the beginning of the treatment.

I did not adopt this technique altogether but I tended to increase the amount of transference interpretation and indeed interpreted more actively than before, but I did not actively interpret transference at the beginning of the treatment unless the actual material was presented, which it often is.

Mrs Klein, I understand, advocates immediate and direct interpretation of unconscious transference in every situation from the outset; and considers it expedient to relate every experience internal and external to the transference.

As a doctor who has practised suggestion in the past both with and without hypnosis it seems to me quite impossible to deny that direct interpretation in terms of transference at the beginning must operate as a suggestion and if successful will reanimate the unconscious imagos of the parents which function when hypnosis is brought about.

Of course these imagos must eventually be transferred to the analyst, the question is are there advantages in bringing the transference about in this active way and should it be used for all cases or for selected cases only? In my experience in psycho–neurotic character cases the transference neurosis is very quickly established by the older method, as a result not only of transference interpretation depending on material presented, but also as a result of interpretation of the content of phantasy, dreams, and ego resistance by means of which insight is increased. The work done in this way includes the analysis of preconscious and unconscious material and the reconstruction of infantile experience.

It has two advantages:

1 The establishing of an identification with a helping figure on a reality basis;
2 The early analysis of preconscious material which is a substitute for the unconscious phantasy and must be analysed sometime.

The disadvantage of the more active technique may be:

1 The patient is more likely to break off in the earliest phases;
2 It seems to be possible that it may be more difficult to resolve a transference situation actively fostered by direct suggestion. During the period in which the direct suggestions are given the ego is being actively dominated by the analyst playing the part of the omnipotent imago of the parent. It is clear that at that time anyhow there can be little increase in the strength of the ego. I am fully aware that the aim is to resolve ultimately the anxiety situations associated with the primitive object relations in the ego, but does the resolution brought about in this way tend to promote the persistence of an omnipotent parent imago of a beneficent kind rather than an independent integrated ego? It is important to say there that this result in certain types of cases in which full genitality and adult independence cannot be hoped for may be much the best result that can be obtained. My question is should it be the accepted method for all?
3 In my opinion very frequent transference may become a formula and lose dynamic significance, if an inevitable and regular accompaniment of all interpretations.
4 I have known direct interpretation of transference to be regarded by the patient as a disguised method of carrying on a love relationship with the analyst which gives gratification to the patient and without which a deprivation is experienced.

651

I am putting forward these queries to invite discussion, not to reject the direct and immediate method of transference interpretation. I am of the opinion that it must be used in cases with psychotic trends and in other cases in which pre-genital difficulties predominate and the patients are dominated entirely by the unconscious imagos. Further it is far more the question of when this mode of interpretation should be used than if it ever is correct which interests me. When experience has proved the rapidity of the development of the transference with a less active approach, and the great advantage of the analysis of preconscious material both from the point of view of the transference and the ego, any technique which appears to diminish the importance of or curtail this aspect of the work, in my opinion cannot be accepted without the most careful consideration.

Differences in technique occur not only between individuals in the same group but also between groups. In my opinion there are differences between the technique of all the British analysts and that of our Viennese colleagues. The British analyst is more active in the interpretation of transference and in the interpretation of pre-genital material. I have the impression also that British analysts do not consider it so important to concentrate on the interpretation of ego resistances before the interpretation of the content of phantasy.

Personally I think such differences are inevitable and I do not think it possible at present to make judgements as a result of comparing results. Of course students recognize even slight differences of technique but provided they understand the method and the differences are not fundamental, their training is not greatly impeded although it may be temporarily more difficult. The differences are comparable to the differences of opinion which exist amongst doctors in every form of therapy. Therapy cannot be an exact science.

9

Draft Report of the Training Committee

*Draft report of the Training Committee upon
the effects of current Scientific Controversies
on the training of Candidates*[1]

I Instructions to the Training Committee

At its General Meeting on July 29th, 1942, the British Psycho-
Analytical Society directed the Training Committee to consider and
report upon the effects of current Scientific Controversies, upon
questions of training. At the General Meeting on July 2lst, 1943, an
Interim Report was presented by the committee, which was then
requested by the Society to present a Final Report at the earliest
possible opportunity.

In the meantime the Committee has received written memoranda
upon the subject from the majority of its individual Members and
has had a number of lengthy and frank discussions upon it. As the
outcome of these, it begs to report as follows to the Society.

II Preliminary survey of the problem

The problem submitted to the Training Committee is ostensibly
restricted to the immediate controversy in the Society. Nevertheless,
the Committee feels that to suggest the adoption of a superficial, *ad
hoc* solution would be unsatisfactory. It would be a mistake to
imagine that the current situation is of extraordinary or unique
importance. The underlying causes that have produced it are, on the
contrary, almost certain to lead to a succession of similar difficulties,
and it is only by examining those underlying causes that there can be
any prospect of arriving at a more permanent remedy.

The Training Committee is an executive organ of the Society, charged with planning and supervising the education of future practitioners (and to a less extent of future research workers in psychoanalysis). The Committee is thus not directly concerned with the truth, or falsity of the views upon theory and practice held by Members of the Society. It is concerned only to judge which of those views most fully represent the general opinion of the Society and how best to incorporate them into the educational scheme. Its functions, in short, are administrative rather than scientific.

But there is one preliminary question upon the answer to which the whole character of the Committee's executive functions must depend. Are the opinions of Members of the Society a closed system of immutable and all-inclusive verities, incapable of extension or corrections? Or are they a body of generalizations, based upon observation, and constantly subject to expansion and modification in the light of increased experience? If the former view were accepted, the Committee's functions would be much simplified and it could devote itself quietly to the task of expounding the dogmatic assertions with which it would be concerned. Nevertheless, the Committee unhesitatingly follows Freud in accepting the second view of the principles of psychoanalysis as the correct one.

From this there seem bound to follow the difficulties of which the present controversy is only an example. For with every addition to our knowledge there will inevitably be demands for a revision of views that have hitherto been generally held, and those demands will inevitably be disputed and resisted. If our Society were a purely scientific one, we could cheerfully leave the settlement of such problems to the passage of time and to the amassing of more facts; but the educational side of our work, for which the Training Committee is responsible, requires more than a merely expectant policy.

It has, indeed, been suggested that the existence in the Society of two mutually contradictory sets of theoretical opinions must inevitably preclude any effective functioning of the Training Committee. How, it has been argued, is the Committee to decide whether a particular Candidate is to be sent for his training analysis to a holder of the one set of opinions or of the other? If it sends all the Candidates to the holders of the one set of opinions (whichever that set may be) it will in effect be passing a sentence of excommunication upon the other. While if it sends the Candidates impartially in equal numbers to holders of both sets of opinions, it will be dividing the future Members into two incompatible parties and thus bringing about an unbridgeable schism in the Society. The Training Committee is of the opinion that this dilemma is an unreal one; but, in order to dispose of it, a more detailed examination of the purposes of training must be undertaken.

The training of Candidates falls under three heads: (a) training analyses, (b) control analyses, and (c) seminars and lectures. These will now be considered separately.

III The purposes of training analyses

It has been affirmed with authority that a training analysis should differ in no respect from a therapeutic analysis – a postulate which the Committee fully accepts. But this postulate suffices in itself to invalidate the supposed dilemma which has been put forward in the last paragraph. For it will hardly be disputed that in a therapeutic analysis the analyst will neither anticipate nor desire the acceptance by his patient of his own theoretical views upon psychoanalytical questions. If this should in fact come about, it would only be as an incidental by-product of the analysis – a by-product, moreover, which might be viewed with suspicion rather than satisfaction. All of this applied, in the Committee's view, with special strength to a training analysis. The primary purpose of a training analysis, like that of a therapeutic analysis, must be to facilitate normal mental functioning. It would thus include amongst its aims the liberation of the Candidate so far as possible from the influences of unconscious prejudices, including those arising from transferences, so that he might be free to make independent observations and unbiased judgements and to draw valid inferences from what he observes. This would afford the best guarantee against the inevitable insufficiencies and errors to which the theoretical knowledge of even the most adequate of training analysts must be prone. For the Candidate, in proportion as he has been freed from his unconscious prejudices, will be able to accept those of the analyst's views which can be confirmed, to supplement those which prove incomplete, and to correct or reject those which seem false. On the other hand, an automatic and uncritical adoption by a Candidate of the theoretical views of his training analyst could only be regarded as an indication that his analysis had failed in one of its chief purposes; while an inclination on the part of a training analyst to bring about such a result would be evidence of the presence in his mind of unresolved counter-transferences and of a consequent incorrectness in his technique. There can be little doubt, in the Committee's opinion, that there is in fact a much greater temptation towards influencing an analysand's theoretical views in the case of a training analysis than in the case of a therapeutic analysis; and this tendency should therefore be especially guarded against in the selection of training analysts. It would seem to follow from this that persons who have a strong emotional interest in the prevalence of their own theoretical views among the present and future generations of psychoanalysts – however eminent their services to the science of psychoanalysis may have been – are not likely to be best fitted to carry out the particular tasks of a training analyst. Thus at any juncture, such as the present one at which an acute theoretical controversy is active in the Society, it would seem reasonable, in the appointment of training analysts, to pass over those principally concerned on both sides of the controversy.

IV The purposes of control analyses

Many of these considerations apply with equal force to the selection of control analysts, whose duties, though less fundamental, have an importance as well as a difficulty of their own. For the control analyst may be regarded as being responsible in the first instance for educating the Candidate at the conscious level and so enabling him to derive the greatest possible benefits from the deeper charges produced in him during the training analysis. The control analyst will naturally avoid trespassing upon the sphere of the training analyst, and for that very reason it would be undesirable that their outlook upon analytical problems should be violently discordant. But at the same time it must be one of the aims of the control analyst to enlarge the Candidate's horizon, to draw his attention to possibilities that have escaped him, and to discuss with him alternative explanations of the phenomena which he has observed.

(In this connection he will be in a position to recommend courses of reading to the Candidate or to indicate where gaps in his knowledge of the literature require to be filled.) It will thus almost inevitably fall to the control analyst to help the Candidate, in the course of impartial discussions and without unduly confusing him, to weigh the merits and demerits of differing opinions upon matters of theory held by various members of the Society. When it is remembered that, in addition to all of this, the control analyst is ultimately responsible for safeguarding the interests of the control patient, it will be evident that quite peculiar qualities of judgement, balance and tact are required for the proper fulfilment of his task, qualities which are unlikely to be associated with a rigid or extremist outlook upon psychoanalytical problems.

V The purposes of seminars and lectures

The position is very different, in the Committee's opinion, as regards seminars and lectures. Here there would seem to be no reason whatever for the exclusion of controversial issues. On the contrary, the Committee believes it to be important that no attempt should be made to shield the Candidate from the impact of what may be regarded in one quarter or another as heterodox beliefs. It should be an essential part of every Candidate's training to attend seminars and lectures given by partisans, and even by extreme partisans of any conflicting trends of thought that may be active in the Society.

VI The functions of the Training Committee

The supervision of the various educational processes which have just been enumerated is the responsibility of the Training Committee, and the question of whether that supervision is performed adequately or inadequately must obviously depend upon the personnel of the Training Committee itself, which depends in turn upon the votes of the Society as a whole.[2]

The Committee cannot avoid a suspicion that the Society in exercising its choice of members of the Training Committee has in the past been governed by inappropriate considerations. Hitherto the Society has been inclined to appoint to the Training Committee Members distinguished in various ways – for their prominent positions in the analytical movement, for their intellectual powers, for their contact with the main line of analytical tradition, for the originality of their contributions to our science, even for the very fact of their being leading exponents of some controversial tendency in analytical thought. A consideration of the actual functions to be performed by the Training Committee suggests that none of these characteristics (however admirable in themselves) are in fact good qualifications for its quite special task. Some of them, indeed, seem rather the reverse and in particular it may be asked whether those who have taken or are taking an active part in controversies and are both bitter and personal can reasonably be chosen to superintend the education of young practitioners. There is even a risk of training analyses being generally regarded as a means of diffusing particular sets of opinions so that the Training Committee may cease to be an organ of education and become instead a battle-ground for warring

657

parties and a political key-point, the control of which will decide the fate of this or that faction in the Society.

If the appointments to the Training Committee came to be regularly made upon lines such as these, it would seem scarcely possible for the Society to avoid a succession of disruptions both in its training activities and in its work as a whole.

VII Remedies

The means of preventing these unfortunate results would thus seem to be in the Society's own hands, and in particular in its choice of members of the Training Committee. If training analyses are to be conducted with complete concentration upon the one essential of improving the Candidate's mental functioning, if control analyses are to give him sympathetic but non-dictatorial help in his early efforts, if seminars and lectures are to offer him a truly impartial field of controversy – then the Training Committee itself must be possessed of such qualities as patience, moderation, tolerance, open-mindedness, and (in practical affairs) a taste for compromise. And it must be added that there seems to be no place in it for such ingredients as over-enthusiasm for innovation or over-rigidity in opposing it, to say nothing of personal enmity and resentment.

The remedy proposed by the Training Committee will no doubt appear too drastic to some and too half-hearted to others. In particular it will be disappointing to those who have at heart the acceptance or rejection of some particular set of opinions. The Committee would nevertheless venture to point out that the use of the machinery of training for the purpose of establishing or of eliminating scientific belief is unlikely to be effective in the long run. The Committee's proposals offer a postponement of hopes but not necessarily their ultimate disappointment. In time, and it may be in a very short time, what is now an innovation may become so firmly established as no longer to give rise to controversy; or before long, on the other hand, that innovation may be recognized as a mistaken or superfluous hypothesis and the whole dispute may be regulated to oblivion. But whether one or other of these consequences follows, or whether the matter continues to hang in suspense, can only be properly determined by the changing consensus of opinion in the Society as a whole – a consensus which will be based upon the gradual accumulation of scientific data and which will find its reflection in a shifting but measured choice of the membership of successive Training Committees.

VIII Recommendations

Before proceeding to set out their specific recommendations, the Committee desires to refer to the question of the date at which those recommendations should come into force. Although on the one hand it is undesirable that the present somewhat uneasy situation should continue longer than is necessary, on the other hand the middle of a World War is not the most suitable moment for holding an election, even of a Training Committee. The Committee would also point out that the book of training has in fact been proceeding during the last difficult years – on a reduced scale, it is true, and with some friction, but nevertheless, considering all things, with not unsatisfactory results. It therefore believes that (bearing in mind the probability of a relatively early clarification of the whole issue) it should be possible to carry on the work of training on its present basis until the end of the war.

The Training Committee accordingly recommends:

1 That as soon as practicable after the end of the war in Europe, the Society should proceed to the election of a new Training Committee.[3]

2 That, in choosing the members of the new Training Committee, the Society should deliberately bear in mind the undesirability of appointing persons who are prominently involved in acute scientific or personal controversies.

3 That it should be a definite instruction to the new Training Committee that it should so far as possible avoid selecting for the functions of training or control analysts persons whose desire to enforce their own extreme or rigid views shows signs of impairing the correctness of their technical procedure or of interfering with the impartiality of their judgement.

4 That, on the other hand, it should be a definite instruction to the new Training Committee that every Candidate should, by means of attending Seminars and Lectures, be given an opportunity of obtaining the closest and most extensive knowledge of all sections of opinion in the Society, including the most extreme.

Notes

1 This Draft was discussed at a special meeting that took place on, 24 November 1943, along with papers by Ella Sharpe and Sylvia Payne,

which must have been circulated prior to that meeting. This draft has been included because of the responses it evoked from Anna Freud and Glover (Section 3, Chapter 11).

2 At this period the Training Committee was elected each year during the Annual General Meeting of the Society, according to the decision reached at the Bad Homburg of the IPA in 1925. In 1968 the Council decided, for some of the reasons outlined here, to appoint the Training Committees itself (King 1981).

3 The Society did not wait until the end of the war, but elected a new committee at the AGM in 1944, alongside a new President.

10

Repercussions of the
Draft Report of the Training Committee

*Comments from Edward Glover
and other members of the Training Committee of
the draft report on training in the Society*

1 Comments of the draft report of the Training Committee by Edward Glover[1]

(1) *On terms of reference*: A report on the effects of the present controversies on training *must* point out the fact that the Committee is itself hopelessly divided into (i) the Klein Party (Klein, Rickman), (ii) the Freud Party (A. Freud, Glover), (iii) the party once designated 'Middle Groupers' (Brierley, Payne). Miss Sharpe's position is uncertain but she is much more Freudian than Kleinian. Nevertheless I think she could still be called a 'Middle Grouper'. In other words, the majority of the Committee are at complete loggerheads. If that hasn't some bearing on questions of training, I'm a Dutchman.

(2) Mr Strachey says: '*It would be a mistake to imagine that the current situation is of extraordinary or unique importance.*' – to which I say: schisms in the psychoanalytic movement may not be unique, but the present Klein schism is certainly of extraordinary importance to the British Society, if for no other reason than that, under present conditions of training, the schismatic views may in course of time and because of training transferences and the consequent policies of election and selection, be made the orthodox analytical teaching.

(3) I quote: '*The Committee is not directly concerned with the truth or falsity of views held by Members.*' – But this burkes the issue: the Committee is most assuredly *directly* concerned with the truth or falsity of the views which it officially permits to be taught as psychoanalytic views. For example it has appointed Mrs Klein, Dr Rickman, Mrs Isaacs, etc., etc. as official training analysts, control

661

analysts, lecturers, etc. It therefore not only sanctions their views but provides them with unique opportunities of teaching them.

(4) *On open or closed systems of training:* The question is not whether Mrs Klein's views can be taught on an 'open system' basis, but whether they are valid. The implication of this paragraph is that Mrs Klein's views are not incompatible with Freud's teachings. An important section of the Committee say they are incompatible. The whole of page 2 (of the draft report) exemplifies what I would call a 'head in the clouds' attitude to a very practical difficulty, viz. the breakdown of our training system.

(5) I quote: '*The Training Committee is of the opinion that this dilemma*' (the dilemma in question was the effect of allocation of Candidates to analysts holding only one set of views as against distributing the allocation between analysts representing opposing sets of views) '*is unreal.*' This is in flat contradiction of the facts. The Committee is in a dilemma: the training staff is in a dilemma; the Candidates are in a dilemma. The above statement itself is the only 'unreal' thing in the situation.

(6) I quote: '*This postulate suffices in itself to invalidate the supposed dilemma.*' (The postulate was that the training analysis should differ in no respect from a therapeutic analysis.) No postulate can invalidate a real dilemma. There is, of course, nothing wrong with the aspiration suggested in the postulate. There 'should' be no difference between a therapeutic and a training analysis. *But there is* (in this country at any rate). The real conclusion is that training analyses in this country as judged by results differ from therapeutic analyses. Incidentally patients are not analysed in order to become analysts but because they are ill. Patients may hold any views they like on the theory and practice of analysis: it doesn't matter. But it does matter when Candidates are taught inaccurate interpretations and are unable (because of transference) to gain their scientific freedom.

(7) *On the purposes of a training analysis.* All this argument is sheer 'idealization' of training analyses. If 'automatic and uncritical adoption by a Candidate of the theoretical views of his training analyst' is an indication of failure, then most of the training analyses carried out in the past 10 years have 'failed' and often 'failed conspicuously'. If all these idealizations were true the Candidate would be a stage further on than his training analyst and capable of analysing his analyst with some benefit to the latter.

(8) I quote: '*Thus at any juncture, such as the present one, at which an acute theoretical controversy is active in the Society, it would seem reasonable, in the appointment of training analysts, to pass over those*

principally concerned on both sides of the controversy.' And what is the good of suggesting that 'partisan' analysts should not *be appointed* to train so long as the most violent partisans are not only on the Committee but *already* on the *training staff* and likely to *remain* there? If this were the real mode of cure it could only be effective if *present teaching partisans* were dismissed from the training staff. But again the presumption is that the partisans are just legitimate hotheads differing over minor matters. The issue is, however, quite otherwise – viz. a question of the validity of Mrs Klein's views. The same applies to the remarks on control *analyses* – idealization is again a feature and the remedy is quite inadequate and implies that Mrs Klein's views are potentially valid.

(9) The draft talks of the disadvantage in a control analyst of a 'rigid and extremist' outlook. But the issue in the present controversy is neither 'rigidity' nor 'extremism' but whether the views taught by Mrs Klein are a part of psychoanalysis.

(10) I quote: *'Some of them, indeed, seem rather the reverse; and in particular it may be asked whether those who have taken or are taking an active part in controversies that are both bitter and personal can reasonably be chosen to superintend the education of young practitioners. There is even a risk of training analyses being generally regarded as a means of diffusing particular sets of opinions: so that the Training Committee may cease to be an organ of education and become instead a battle-ground for warring parties and a political key-point, the control of which will decide the fate of this or that faction in the Society. If the appointments to the Training Committee came to be regularly made upon lines such as these, it would seem scarcely possible for the Society to avoid a succession of disruptions both in its training activities and in its work as a whole.'* – The comments *on the Society's method of election* are sound enough in themselves but they lead on to the assumption that voters will vote in some other way. How can voting be anything else but partisan so long as the innovators regard their views as essential to the progress of psychoanalysis and the orthodox Freudians regard them as non-analytical and deleterious to psychoanalysis? The issue can only be settled by examining the views and if they are found inaccurate, preventing their being taught as accurate.

(11) *On remedies.* The opening sentence is pure over-idealization based on pure supposition.

(12) I quote: *'The Committee would point out that the use of the machinery of training for the purpose of establishing or eliminating a scientific belief is unlikely to be effective in the long run.'* – How long a run? The plain fact is that in a short run of, say, 50 years the machinery (which in practice lives on transference and counter-transference) *can* establish

and *can* eliminate scientific belief in Candidates. Do, for goodness sake, look at the facts as they present themselves in the finished products of training, viz. Society Members. So long as we had no 'extremists' in the Society, the Members were reasonably restrained if not particularly inspiring. As soon as 'beliefs' became the rage, the Members trained by 'extremists' became devoted partisans behaving with pseudo-religious fervour, and unless you sack the staff and appoint non-partisans you will never alter the situation. I doubt if you'll alter it even by sacking the partisans. That was why I suggested abolishing the training staff, for a time at any rate, and letting any qualified analyst do the work of analysing Candidates.

(13) *The belief that the Society's judgement will be formed by accumulation of scientific data.* What a hope that is at present (see discussions in the controversial series).

(14) *On recommendations.* It is suggested that training in the last difficult years has been proceeding with some friction but *'nevertheless considering all things, with not unsatisfactory results'.* There is an 'illuminating confusion' here. The Committee worked smoothly and without friction *only* during the Blitz year when the Klein party was absent. Before the war the Committee was already at a dead end and it has been in a state of violent friction ever since the return to pre-war committee conditions. Already *it can't carry on without dividing the training into at least 2 sections* (Kleinian and non-Kleinian) if not 3 (Kleinian, Freudian and Middle group). *The first decision to separate training has already been taken:* it is positively dishonest not to tell the Society so.

As regards the decisions recommended, I ask only one question: will the Committee say bluntly that present partisans should retire from training? If it will not, it is not a scientific committee.

Final comment: The Draft Report does not represent the opinions of members of the Committee or give an objective account of the deliberations of the Committee. It presents a temporizing account of the true state of affairs.

Edward Glover
Chairman

2 Extract from the minutes of the Training Committee held on Monday, January 24th, 1944

Dr Payne was in the Chair: Members present: Dr Payne, Miss Freud, Miss Sharpe, Mrs Klein, Mr Strachey.

Dr Brierley and Dr Rickman were absent, apologies had been received from both.

1 The minutes of the last meeting were read and approved.

2 Dr Glover had intimated that he was not going to attend the Training Committee and sent his comments on the draft report submitted by Mr Strachey. The Secretary reported that Dr Glover had written to her announcing that he was resigning his membership of the British Psycho-Analytical Society and the Institute of Psycho-Analysis.[2] It was felt by the Training Committee that it would be undesirable under the circumstances to consider the draft report, as Members would like time to think over the new situation created by Dr Glover's resignation. Mr Strachey proposed that the consideration of the report should be postponed and this was seconded by Miss Sharpe and carried.

Miss Freud asked if she was one of the parties alluded to in Mr Strachey's draft report and said that if so she considered it to be an insult, and she wished to resign from the Training Committee. The other members of the Committee asked her not to make up her mind tonight but to reconsider the situation.

Miss Sharpe intimated that she would like to read a short communication connected with Dr Glover's memorandum submitted at the last meeting:

I do not support Dr Glover's proposal to report to the Society that training has broken down scientifically and practically. Scientifically, the Training Committee awaits now a ruling from the Society on which aspects of Mrs Klein's work, theoretical and technical, are legitimate expansions of Freudian theory, which are wrong or subversive, which unproven. The Society should surely be told that fact and that the onus of electing a Training Committee that will implement their decision as to what Candidates shall be taught lies with them. This situation is in their hands, not in ours.

Practically training has not broken down. We can report its curtailment and the difficulties that beset us, difficulties that are at the moment insoluble. A true report of what has actually happened during four and a half years can be presented, the number of students who have been and are in analysis, the analysts of these students, and number of students under control and with whom, the number attending seminars, by whom conducted, the lectures given and by whom. That record of four and a half years will reveal some 10(?) to 12(?) Candidates who have been almost exclusively in close contacts with either Freudian experts or those who while valuing Mrs Klein's clinical data have never accepted as proven her theories as such.

I would like to separate what has actually happened during these years, *as a report,* from the difficulties that have to be solved in attaining a Training Committee with a unified policy based on the Society's decisions. It is a fact that at the moment I believe we have two students analysed by Mrs Klein or analysands of hers – the rest are all basically in touch with Freudian methods and principles. Dr Glover seems to leap over the last four and a half years and what may result from them to the period before that.

I wish Dr Glover had not allowed himself to attack his English colleagues, who during these years have given students and their welfare the most assiduous and unfailing attention, believing that in that way the securest foundation for sound judgements would be laid. It would seem that this unostentatious work, steady and non-remunerative work, done on sound Freudian principles, he deprives of influence and significance. 'Timid', 'indifferent', 'incoherent', 'unorganized', are the epithets he allows himself. That is as far as Dr Glover seems to see or understand. The worst of making unconsidered charges of this kind is that of provoking counter charges. I, too, have been on this committee fifteen years and with good reason could fling out at him the charge 'timid'. But it would get us nowhere concerning our problem. Let us deal with the problems presented to us now involving, as they may, a heritage of mistakes made by all of us in the past, Dr Glover included.

Again, personally I could take exception to Dr Glover's statement that the main flaw in our training system has been the selection of teachers who are strictly speaking unqualified to teach that most impressionable creature (which is only a half truth) the student in training. Is he there referring to the timid and incoherent and unorganized group who have done much of the actual training for the past four and a half years, or not? Dr Glover should surely make his meaning clear or he does injustice to some people who are in the widest and strictest sense qualified to teach.[3]

The problem of transference affects and allegiances in the Society is indeed a vital one but I would seriously submit that positive and negative manifestations do not emanate from one section alone. We must view it as a common problem, not a one-sided one.

I ask Dr Glover to realize during the last 4 and a half years he has had colleagues who have had no axe to grind, who have had no desire to 'capture the society', to further their own theoretical views, who are ready to relinquish their office at any moment, but who nevertheless have made according to their own gifts and shortcomings a solid contribution that may yet bear fruit in the future.

I therefore should not agree with any report suggested for presentation to the Society unless it embodied with a statement of our training problems, some account of what has practically resulted during four and a half years.

3 Extract from Training Committee minutes on 9 February 1944

Arising out of the minutes the Secretary said that in her opinion it had not been clear that Miss Freud had finally decided to resign and this view was also held by all the other Members except by Mrs Klein. It was agreed that Miss Freud must have intended that her spoken wish to resign should stand in spite of being asked to reconsider it, as she had subsequently informed her colleagues and Candidates of her action.

Mrs. Klein read a statement on her views of the draft report circulated to the members of the Training Committee. Copy of this statement[4] is attached to the minutes. After further discussion it was decided that Mr. Strachey should reconsider some items in his report and submit a draft of the revised version to the members of the Training Committee for criticism and comments.

The Secretary informed the Committee that the final report must be circulated with the minutes of the last Business Meeting because of the references to the training report in Dr Glover's statement in connection with his resignation.

4 Extract of letter from Melanie Klein to her group

After this meeting, Klein wrote to the members of her group on 25 January, 1944 as follows:

I am writing to tell you of an important piece of news. Dr Glover has resigned his membership of the Society. We were informed of that last night at the Training Committee, so this news is strictly confidential until the next business meeting when it will be announced.

The immediate cause for his resignation was the fact that the majority of the members of the Training Committee, not consulting me at all in this matter, had united against him and expressed their distrust of his partisanship. . . .

[Melanie Klein Archives, The Wellcome Institute, London]

Notes

1 A version of this draft report was first discussed at the Training Committee on 24 November 1943, and later circulated to its members.
2 For Glover's letters of resignation, see minutes of Business Meeting held on 2 February 1944 in Section 5 (pp. 850–3).
3 Miss Sharpe was herself a qualified teacher, unlike Glover, and her lectures to students show that she took endless care with her teaching.
4 Unfortunately, a copy of this statement was not attached to the minutes of this meeting, but the editors are grateful to a reviewer of the hardback edition of this book, Peter Rudnytsky, who discovered Melanie Klein's reply in the Melanie Klein Archives in the Contemporary Medical Archives Centre of the Wellcome Institute for the History of Medicine. With the permission of the Klein Trust, Melanie Klein's reply will now be found in the Appendix at the end of the book.

11

Final Report of the Training Committee

The effects of current Scientific Controversies on the Training of Candidates

(This report was adopted by a Business Meeting, March 8th, 1944.)

I Instructions to the Training Committee

At its General Meeting on July 29th, 1942, the British Psycho-Analytical Society directed the Training Committee to consider and report upon the effects of current scientific controversies upon questions of training. At the General Meeting on July 21st, 1943, an interim report was presented by the Committee, which was then requested by the Society to present a further report at the earliest possible opportunity.

In the meantime the Committee has received written memoranda upon the subject from the majority of its individual members and has had a number of discussions upon it. As the outcome of these a draft report was drawn up and submitted to the members of the Committee, but before it was considered or discussed by the Committee two of its members, Dr Edward Glover and Miss Anna Freud, resigned their membership of the Committee. The draft having been considered and amended by the Committee, it now begs to report as follows to the Society.

II Preliminary survey of the problem

The problem submitted to the Training Committee was ostensibly restricted to the immediate controversy in the Society. Nevertheless, the Committee has from the first felt that to suggest the adoption of a superficial, *ad hoc* solution would be unsatisfactory. And although recent events have put an end to any hope of an amicable settlement of the current dispute, they serve to emphasize the need for devising some plan by which similar situations in the future can be avoided or robbed of their catastrophic character. For it would be a mistake to imagine that the current situation is of extraordinary or unique importance. The underlying causes that have produced it are, on the contrary, almost certain to lead to a succession of similar difficulties. And it is only by examining those underlying causes that there can be any prospect of arriving at a more permanent remedy. In what follows, accordingly, the Committee thinks it will be more profitable to consider the deeper and more general causes of training difficulties rather than to concentrate upon the specific occasions which led to the recent disagreements.

The Training Committee is an executive organ of the Society, charged with planning and supervising the education of future practitioners (and to a less extent of future research workers) in psychoanalysis. The Committee is thus not *directly* concerned with the truth or falsity of the views upon theory and practice held by Members of the Society. It is concerned only to judge which of those views most fully represent the general opinion of the Society and how best to incorporate them into the educational scheme. Its functions, in short, are executive rather than scientific.

But there is one preliminary question upon the answer to which the whole character of the Committee's executive functions must depend. Are the opinions of Members of the Society a closed system of immutable and all-inclusive verities, incapable of extension or correction? Or are they a body of generalizations, based upon observation, and constantly subject to expansion and modification in the light of increased experience? If the former view were accepted, the Committee's functions would be much simplified and it could devote itself quietly to the talk of expounding the dogmatic assertions with which it would be concerned. Nevertheless, the Committee unhesitatingly accepts the second view of the principles of psychoanalysis as the correct one – the view taken by Freud himself.

From this there seem bound to follow the difficulties of which the present controversy is only an example. For with every addition to our knowledge there will inevitably be demands for a revision of views that have hitherto been generally held, and those demands will inevitably be disputed and resisted. If our Society were a purely scientific one, we could cheerfully leave the settlement of such

670

problems to the passage of time and to the amassing of more facts; but the educational side of our work, for which the Training Committee is responsible, requires more than a merely expectant policy.

It has, indeed, been suggested that the existence in the Society of two mutually contradictory sets of theoretical opinions must inevitably preclude any effective functioning of the Training Committee. Now, it has been argued, is the Committee to decide whether a particular Candidate is to be sent for his training analysis to a holder of the one set of opinions or of the other? If it sends all the Candidates to the holders of the one set of opinions (whichever that set may be) it will in effect be passing a sentence of excommunication upon the other. While if it sends the Candidates impartially in equal numbers to holders of both sets of opinion, it will be dividing the future Members into two incompatible parties and thus bringing about an unbridgeable schism in the Society. In spite of the fact that recent events may at first sight seem to confirm the validity of this dilemma, the Training Committee is nevertheless of the opinion that it is an artificial one – based, that is to say, upon emotional rather than realistic premises. But in order to dispose of it, a more detailed examination of the purposes of training must be undertaken.

The training of Candidates falls under three heads: (a) training analyses, (b) control analyses, and (c) seminars and lectures. These will now be considered separately.

III The purposes of training analyses

It has been affirmed with authority that a training analysis should not differ essentially from a therapeutic analysis either in its aims or in its methods. The Committee is in agreement with this postulate, and feels that, if it could be made certain that it was always accepted and acted upon, the corner-stone of a workable training system would have been laid. As will be seen from what follows, moreover, this postulate in itself suffices to invalidate the supposed dilemma put forward in the last Section. A training analysis, like a therapeutic analysis, is something in the nature of an experiment, an empirical investigation. The activities of the analyst must indeed be largely based upon theory, and theoretical conclusions will no doubt emerge from the investigation – with varying degrees of certainty – but, so far as the analysand is concerned, they will be by-products of the essential process. The supposed dilemma implies that a Candidate will necessarily adopt the theoretical views of his training analyst and that the training analyst will necessarily endeavour to bring this about; but these implications are quite inconsistent with the picture which has just been drawn of the part played by theories in an analysis.

The primary purpose of a training analysis, like that of a therapeutic analysis, must be to facilitate normal mental functioning. It would thus include amongst its aims the liberation of the Candidate so far as possible from the influence of unconscious prejudice, including those arising from transferences, so that he might be free to make independent observations and unbiased judgements and to draw valid inferences from what he observes. This would afford the best guarantee against the inevitable limitations and errors to which the theoretical knowledge of even the best of training analysts must from the very nature of things be prone. For the Candidate, in proportion as he has been freed from his unconscious prejudices, will be able to accept those of the analyst's views which can be confirmed, to supplement those which prove incomplete, and to correct or reject those which seem false. On the other hand, an automatic and uncritical adoption by a Candidate of the theoretical views of his training analyst could only be regarded as an indication that his analysis had failed in one of its chief purposes; while an inclination on the part of a training analyst to bring about such a result would be evidence of the presence in his mind of unresolved counter-transferences and of a consequent incorrectness in his technique.

There are, indeed, reasons for thinking that, although it is true that training analyses and therapeutic analyses are essentially similar, a training analysis offers greater difficulties to the analyst, especially in the vital matter of handling the transference and counter-transference. The fact, for instance, that extra-analytic contacts on a considerable scale are inevitable, at all events in the later stages of a training analysis, must complicate the situation. So, too, must the fact that the Candidate is aware that the real prospects of his career depend to a great extent upon his analyst's opinion of him. And, on the other side, a training analyst with strong theoretical interests – whether those happen to be of a conservative or of an innovating character – may feel a temptation to use the instrument of transference in order to further the prevalence of his own views among the coming generation of analysts, to found or to preserve a school of analysts with personal loyalties to himself.

But the existence of these special difficulties does not in any way alter the aims of the training analysis itself; they merely call attention to the fact that a training analyst must be an especially good analyst if those aims are to be attained. The question of what is meant by a good analyst will be more fully considered in a later section of this report. It is enough for the moment to remark that probably the most important as well as the most difficult of the Training Committee's tasks is the wise selection of training analysts.

IV The purposes of control analyses

The duties of control analysts, though less fundamental, have an importance as well as a difficulty of their own. For the control analyst may be regarded as being responsible in the first instance for educating the Candidate at the *conscious* level and so enabling him to derive the greatest possible benefit from the deeper changes produced in him during his training analysis. The control analyst will naturally avoid trespassing upon the sphere of the training analyst. But at the same time it must be one of the aims of the control analyst to enlarge the Candidate's horizon, to draw his attention to possibilities that have escaped him and to discuss with him alternative explanations of the phenomena which he has observed. It might well be advantageous, therefore, if one at least of a Candidate's control analysts were deliberately chosen as differing from the training analyst in his character, interests, and method of approach to psychoanalysis. If so, he should be especially well able to correct any tendency to one-sidedness in the Candidate's interpretations – to overemphasis upon some one set of factors or to neglect of others – whether this arose from a corresponding bias in the training analyst or from the particular structure of the Candidate's own mind. In this connection it may be added that the control analyst will also be in a good position to recommend courses of reading to the Candidate or to indicate where gaps in his knowledge of the literature required to be filled. So, too, it will almost inevitably fall to the control analyst to help the Candidate, in the course of impartial discussions, to weigh the merits and demerits of differing opinions upon matters of theory held by various Members of the Society. When it is remembered that, in addition to this, the control analyst is ultimately responsible for safeguarding the interests of the control patient, it will be evident that, besides a gift for imparting knowledge, quite peculiar qualities of judgement, balance and tact are required for the proper fulfilment of his task.

V The purposes of seminars and lectures

The position is a little different, in the Committee's opinion, as regards seminars and lectures. Here there would seem to be less reason for insistence upon a uniformly high degree of balance and sound judgement. The Committee believes it to be important that no attempt should be made to shield the Candidate from the impact of what might be regarded in one quarter or another as reactionary, heterodox, or unsubstantiated beliefs. It would be a useful part of every Candidate's training to attend at least some seminars and lectures given by partisans, and even by extreme partisans, of any conflicting trends of thought that might be active in the Society.

VI The functions of the Training Committee

The task of maintaining and supervising the various educational processes enumerated in the earlier sections of this report devolves upon the Training Committee. It has already been suggested that, of its many responsibilities, by far the most onerous is the duty of selecting training analysts. This (as has been proved by recent events) is the rock upon which, in the event of differences of opinion, the work of training and indeed the whole work of the Society is most likely to split. In the Committee's opinion the only possible way of avoiding such a disaster is the general acceptance of the fundamental principle that training analysts are to be appointed primarily because they are good analysts. There would then remain two further problems to be considered: firstly, what constitutes a good analyst? And secondly, how is a good analyst recognizable as such?

The Committee does not propose to enter here into any very elaborate discussion of these two questions. A good analyst for the present purpose would seem to be an analyst with a good analytic technique. And this, of course, raises the still further question of what constitutes a good analytic technique. Much would no doubt be said upon the subject, but the Committee believes that there will be a general agreement in the Society that the best criterion of an analyst's technique is his handling of the transference and counter-transference; and indeed it is only this which makes it possible to determine in the last resort whether and to what extent he is using psychoanalytical technique or some other psychological procedure.

Since even the best analysts are human beings (a fact which seems sometimes to be overlooked), it follows that even they will have imperfections in their technique. For instance, a concentration of interest, temporary or permanent, upon some particular aspect of mental functioning may make the analyst tend somewhat to overstress that factor in the analytic material, with a corresponding underemphasis upon some other factor. But the most universal sources of imperfection are to be found precisely in the region of the transference. It will not be disputed that at some time or other every analyst feels tempted to use the transference in a non-analytic manner. The perfect analyst's behaviour would, of course, be totally unaffected by such temptations – indeed he would never be subject to them. But the human analyst's behaviour will in fact be affected by them, though in many different ways. Two extreme cases are relevant to the present discussion. In one of these the analyst will in varying degrees make a direct use of the transference in order to influence the analysand towards an acceptance of his views; in the other the analyst, reacting against this inclination, will hesitate to put his own views before the analysand at all and will tend towards complete inertia. If these two extreme cases happen to operate in the sphere of psychoanalytical theory, we shall have on the one hand an enthusiast seeking for converts to his own way of thinking, and on the other hand a timid sceptic, paralysed by his insistence upon impartiality, moderation and compromise. Now these two extreme cases will clearly both be bad analysts; but, from what has been said, it seems probable that even the best analysts will to some small degree be subject to these same imperfections.

It is important, in the Committee's opinion, that the Training Committee should be fully conscious of these possible imperfections and should so far as may be guard against their effects. It is, indeed, one of the principal functions of control analyses, seminars and lectures to counteract such inevitable faults in the training analyst. But there is a further point worth considering in connection with the two contrary *directions* of defect described in the preceding paragraph. It has been laid down at the beginning of this report that there is no distinction in principle between training analyses and therapeutic analyses. This is true without qualification of the *ideal* analysis. But since in practice no analysis is perfect, it seems possible that different *kinds* of defect are more undesirable than others in certain *kinds* of analysis. Thus in a therapeutic analysis it may well be that a slight defect in the direction which may shortly be described as enthusiasm will do less harm than an equal defect in the direction of timidity. On the other hand it seems to be arguable that in the case of a training analysis the boot may be upon the other leg. The question, at least, is one for the earnest consideration of the Training

675

Committee and must necessarily influence their choice of training analysts.

It must be clearly understood that distinction between different kinds of defect does not contradict what was laid down earlier as the fundamental principle that training analysts are to be appointed primarily because they are good analysts. This must always be the overriding consideration; and it is only on occasions where there seems to be an equally balanced choice that account can be taken of the remoter effects of the various sorts of imperfection in technique.

There then remains the second problem: namely, how the Training Committee is to discover whether a given analyst is a good technician in the sense in which the term is here being used. There are evidently a variety of ways in which an opinion can be formed on this – by observing the results of the analyst's treatments, for instance, or the subsequent relations of the analysand with his analyst on the one hand and with his colleagues on the other, or again by carrying out control work with Candidates who are in analysis with him. Some of these methods, however, seem unsatisfactory and depend too much upon indirect and hearsay evidence. It is indeed one of the great handicaps to psychoanalytical work in general that there is such difficulty in obtaining really detailed knowledge of the technical methods of other analysts. It has been suggested (and the Committee warmly supports the idea) that it might be possible for members of the Training Committee to form a truer picture of the technique of training analysts if some of the Committee could from time to time attend case seminars given by one or other of the training analysts. It would further be highly advantageous if it became a recognized practice for members of the Training Committee and training analysts to have frequent joint discussions upon the actual details of their technical procedure.

Even with such additional help, however, it can never be easy for the Training Committee to decide with certainty upon a training analyst's technical qualifications. It might therefore be wise to discontinue the system which has hitherto been adopted of having a particular class of analysts who are definitely recognized as 'training analysts'. It might be preferable instead for the Training Committee to appoint a particular analyst *ad hoc* for each particular Candidate. In this way it would be possible for the Training Committee to observe the results of the work of a newly appointed training analyst and, if they should prove unsatisfactory, to remove him from the rota of training analysts in a much less drastic manner than the present arrangements would require. Indeed, the Committee feels that a certain fluidity in this respect would be of general advantage.

Finally, it is to be remembered that, in addition to the functions that have been mentioned, the Training Committee is also charged with the responsibility for accepting or rejecting Candidates in the first instance as well as for deciding when they can be regarded as qualified psychoanalysts. This side of the work of the Training Committee, though it is of prime importance, is not touched upon in the present report. But the Committee would like to take this opportunity of stating its view that one of the best guarantees of the smooth progress of the Society's work would be a large increase in the size of its membership. For, apart from the many other advantages which this would bring, there can be little doubt that internal differences which would completely disrupt a small Society could be digested with relative ease by a large one.

VII The responsibilities of the Society

The problem before the Society is how to devise a machinery of training which shall assure on the one hand the preservation of the essential structure of the science of psychoanalysis of which Freud laid the foundations, but which shall at the same time give ample opportunity for the modifications and extensions of that structure which increasing knowledge must demand. The Society itself can determine the principles which should govern the system of training, but the actual putting of those principles into execution, which is the crux of the matter, must necessarily be left in the hands of the Training Committee. Everything will therefore hinge upon an appropriate choice of personnel to serve on that Committee. It seems possible that the Society has been insufficiently conscious of its responsibilities in this respect. It may have been inclined to view the selection of the Training Committee as a matter of routine to which only perfunctory attention need be given. Or, again, it may have been inclined to base its selection upon irrelevant considerations, such as, to take one instance, long tenure of administrative posts in the Society. In particular, there sometimes appears to be a risk that, in electing the Training Committee, Members may give their votes to someone on account of the opinions he holds rather than on account of his personal qualities. Such a proceeding would seem to imply that the training system and even training analyses are to be regarded as a suitable means of diffusing particular sets of opinion. If this dangerously mistaken view found general acceptance, the Training Committee might cease to be an organ of education and become instead (as, indeed, it has threatened to do in recent times) an arena for theoretical disputes and a political key-point, the control of which would decide the predominance of this or that group in the Society.

It is therefore the Committee's opinion that the choice of membership for the Training Committee should be based primarily upon considerations of character and attitude of mind. The nature of the qualities required are sufficiently indicated by the tasks which the Training Committee is called upon to perform; but it may be suggested that among others they might with advantage include patience, moderation, tolerance of opposition and criticism, open-mindedness, width of outlook, good judgement of character, capacity for co-operation and (in practical, though not in theoretical, affairs) a taste for compromise. A Training Committee which could draw upon a reserve of such characteristics as these would have a good prospect of carrying out its difficult executive functions and would actually benefit rather than lose by any differences of opinion or outlook among its members.

VIII Recommendations

The Training Committee accordingly recommends:

(1) That the Society should pass a resolution endorsing in general terms the principles laid down in the present Report for the future regulation of training.

(2) That as soon as practicable the present Training Committee should be relieved of its functions and that the Society should thereafter proceed to the election of a new Training Committee.

(3) That, in choosing the members of the new Training Committee, the Society should deliberately bear in mind the qualifications indicated or implied in the present report.

(4) That it should be an instruction to the new Training Committee that, in its appointment of training and control analysts, in its organization of seminars and lectures, and in its supervision of training activities, it should so far as possible follow the lines suggested in the present report.

(Signed)   Marjorie Brierley
Melanie Klein
Sylvia M. Payne
John Rickman
Ella Sharpe
James Strachey

Editorial comments (2)

RICCARDO STEINER

The complexity of all the issues present in the Controversial Discussions and their repercussions on the future of psychoanalysis are also reflected in the scientific side of the documents concerning the training and the use of psychoanalytic technique. Here the reader will also find echoes of the particular historical situation in which those papers were written. Glover had accused Klein of having tried to take possession of the Society, through the training of the Candidates. Klein's defence of her position constituted one of the most painful and humiliating moments of the whole dispute. At that date Klein could show the groundlessness of the accusations by quoting the actual number of those she had in analysis as Candidates[1] and was supported by Sylvia Payne (Section 1, Chapter 7).

Yet what needed still to be clarified were the differences in technique and therefore in the actual practice of analysis and how that would affect the candidates and the future of the discipline. Anna Freud's paper on training is extremely well articulated and, besides describing in detail the 'classical' way of approaching the unconscious of the patient through a gradual analysis of the defences and resistances, explicitly touches upon political and educational issues. Here, to my mind, one can observe the repercussions of the particular historical moment I mentioned on page 238. I am thinking particularly of Anna Freud's apocalyptic statements concerning the risk of accepting Klein's views of psychoanalysis and Anna's mention of the situation that arose in Berlin after Hitler's coming to power and the pollution of psychoanalysis due to the introduction of all sorts of heretical schools of thought, such as, for instance, Jung's.

Anna Freud's paper is also important, because in her wise

emphasis on the dangers of the institutionalization of psychoanalysis, one has a glimpse of some of her future attitudes towards the British Psycho-Analytical Society. She would formally belong to it and respect the undertakings of the 'ladies' agreement' (to use Pearl King's words) and would not oppose the participation of people trained according to her views to the educational and administrative life of the Society, although with reservations and difficulties at times. Yet the creation of the Hampstead Clinic, immediately after the war, would guarantee Anna a sort of personal niche which would always remind people of her particular status of refugee in England. After all, Ernest Jones had promised her the possibility of continuing to work in London with the group of people she had in Vienna when she was preparing the emigration of her father and her friends and colleagues in 1938 (Steiner 1989).

The reader will find in the short but very condensed pages of Melanie Klein (pp. 635–8) some of the characteristics which were later on to constitute the specific approach of Klein and the post-war generation of her followers to their patients: the importance given to the presence of the transference, from the beginning of the treatment; and the importance given to the emergence of early primitive anxieties and processes of defence related to primitive object relationships. It is interesting to note that in her paper, beside the references to her own way of interpreting and developing Freud's ideas on the transference, Klein is referring to James Strachey's paper of 1934. He had been influenced by Melanie Klein and her views about unconscious phantasy and the role played in psychic disturbances and in normal development by the early superego in the 'here and now' of the analytical situation, in accordance with the tradition of a rather sophisticated British phenomenological empiricism. Klein avoids any hints at the institutional and educational implications of her technique, as if she wanted to be judged on the basis of what she actually was doing, more than on the hypothetical consequences that could be derived from her approach. Not only Anna Freud's criticism but also the fanatical statements against Mrs Klein of Edward Glover tended to concentrate on them. The reader will find particularly in Sylvia Payne's and Marjorie Brierley's documents and also in Ella Sharpe's memorandum and in the more general statements by James Strachey a different and very specific approach to the issues I have mentioned above. Here I think more than in the general discussions on Isaacs', Heimann's, and Klein's papers, Payne and the others seem to reveal their most characteristic qualities and originality.

In order to appreciate those qualities and characteristics one has only to think of all the cautious observation of Marjorie Brierley concerning what she accepted or rejected about Klein, or of her way of dealing with her patients, of her typical expression, 'learning from the patient', or of the historical approach of Payne in describing changes in the views on how and when to interpret. This, by the way, constitutes a brief and condensed history of the British approach to technique. Besides their personal differences and closeness to Klein, more pronounced in the case of Sylvia Payne than in others, what strikes the reader is their wish for flexibility, their disbelief in general assumptions or rigid preconceptions, their willingness to adapt their technique to the particular circumstances and to the individual patient. For good and ill one can foresee here many of the characteristics which later on would constitute the technical approach to the patient of the so-called Middle Group, to use Glover's expression, or of the non-aligned or independent British analysts. Yet one should not forget that their anti-dogmatic approach could become paradoxically dogmatic too, a special dogmatism of the self-professed eclectics which, in turn, could lead to conclusions quite as dubious as those obtained by someone who adhered rigidly to one approach to teaching, whether that of Freud or his daughter, of Klein or of any charismatic preceptor.

At one point in his comments which touch upon educational and institutional matters in a very sophisticated and tactful way, James Strachey recommended an open forum as the ideal solution for the discussions, where everybody could be allowed to express his or her views without being accused of heresy and being threatened with expulsion. Only time, according to Strachey, could decide that what 'is now an innovation may become so firmly established as no longer to give rise to controversy; or before long on the other hand, that innovation may be recognized as a mistaken or superfluous hypothesis and the whole dispute may be relegated to oblivion'.

Note

1 See for instance Melanie Klein to Sylvia Payne, letter dated 31 May 1942: 'What is important is that I have actually had only four candidates since 1929. . . . A second absolutely essential point would be to state definitely that the insinuation that I have used all sorts of underhand methods to gain power is untrue. You, as the Secretary of the Training Committee would necessarily know if something of the kind had happened and also while I had no opportunity to do so, Dr Glover was all along being in position of power.'

Second Series of Scientific Discussions on Controversial Issues

Editorial comments

PEARL KING

In the Introduction to this book, it was pointed out that the discussion of scientific controversies had been divided into two series, and had been placed in Sections 2 and 4, as other events taking place in the Society had changed character. However, it should be noted that 'The Background to the Scientific Controversies' by Riccardo Steiner (Section 2, Chapter 1) and his comments, cover the papers and discussions in Sections 2 *and* 4.

There was a gap of three months between the last discussion of the papers included in Section 2 and the commencement of this second series of Scientific Discussions of Controversial Issues. During that period the events included in Section 3 were taking place. In January 1944 Anna Freud resigned from the Training Committee and Edward Glover resigned from the British Psycho-Analytical Society and the Institute of Psycho-Analysis. Glover had delayed his actual resignation until after the meeting of the Training Committee on 24 January 1944, in order to make certain that he was eligible, while still a member of that committee, to make his comments on the draft report of the Training Committee (Section 3, Chapter 10).

The actual discussions included in Section 4 did not start until 16 February 1944, although the paper by Paula Heimann and Susan Isaacs on 'Regression' (Heimann and Isaacs 1943) and the three circulated comments on their paper by Edward Glover, Willi Hoffer, and Kate Friedlander (Section 4, Chapter 2) were circulated on 17 December 1944, before these resignations took place. Although Paula Heimann discussed their contributions in her opening statement, they did not attend that Scientific Meeting, nor did Anna Freud or any of her colleagues. By this time only a few Members

685

made written statements and the discussions took on the flavour of more spontaneous discussions.

In fact, this second series of Scientific Meetings, which were chaired by Sylvia Payne and not by Glover, as had been the case for the first series of discussions, developed into discussions between Melanie Klein and the indigenous members of the British Society, who were increasingly referred to as 'the Middle Group'. As such, the meetings became more explorative than concerned with proving the other person wrong, and the atmosphere became more conducive to scientific discussion. The numbers, however, of those attending the meetings were reduced. Only one meeting was held to discuss the paper on 'Regression'. The topic of phantasy (Hayman 1989) had proved far more central to the concerns of Klein's critics than was that of regression, which was more widely accepted. It did, however, lead to an interesting discussion on the death instinct.

Melanie Klein's first paper, on 'The Emotional Life and Ego Development of the Infant with Special Reference to the Depressive Position' (Klein 1944), was discussed at the ninth and tenth of the Special Scientific Meetings set up to discuss controversial issues, chaired now, as mentioned above, by Sylvia Payne. The main discussants, who made prepared statements, were Sylvia Payne, Marjorie Brierley, and Ella Sharpe. It was then agreed that the special series of discussions would be brought to a close after the tenth Special Meeting had taken place, as it was felt that these discussions were taking up too much of the Society's time and Members wanted more time for ordinary scientific papers.

It was agreed that the second paper from Melanie Klein, on 'The Oedipus Complex in the Light of Early Anxieties' (Klein 1945), would be given in the autumn, in October, as an ordinary scientific paper. In the event, this did not take place until 7 and 21 March 1945 (Klein 1945), as the deferred AGM had to take place on the date that had been set aside for that paper, so that the new officers could be elected following the changes in the constitution passed in June of that year (Section 5, Chapter 5). Following that meeting, the government of the Society came into the hands of the original Members of the British Society, with Sylvia Payne as President and a Training Committee that did not include Anna Freud or her colleagues from the Continent. The senior members of her group withdrew from active participation in Society activities for a while, until Sylvia Payne and Anna Freud began exploring the possibility of co-operation in relation to the reorganization of training arrangements to accommodate the needs of colleagues from the Viennese Society.

1

Paper by Paula Heimann and Susan Isaacs on 'Regression'

December 17th, 1943

I Introduction

The term 'regression' has been used by Freud and other writers in various senses.

In the sense which we shall discuss it in this paper, Freud refers to the backward movement of the libido, retracing to a certain point its former path of development, a process which occurs in characteristic forms in particular types of mental illness. This concept of the *regression of the libido* is intimately bound up with his conclusions as to the forward course of the development of the libido and its 'fixation points', conclusions which are complementary to the notion of regression and were formulated *pari passu* with it.

As we know, Freud discovered that the sexual instinct as met with in the adult is a complex set of component impulses and feelings, involving various membranes and organs of the body and having a complicated developmental history from the earliest days of infancy. Sexuality passes through various phases (oral, anal, and genital), in each of which one of the chief erogenous zones is predominant in aim. The earlier phases do not pass away altogether, they become more or less subordinated to the later aims. In the normal person, the libidinal life as a whole is eventually integrated under the primacy of the genital organ and its aims and satisfactions.

The order and essential character of this development of the libido is biologically determined, and springs from organic sources. It is not inherently dependent upon circumstance or experience. Yet it is at every phase of its history profoundly sensitive to psychical events, and responds to external and internal influences, both of a quantitative and of a qualitative order.

These internal or external factors may halt the forward movement of some of the libido at any point of development, to which this part then remains bound to a greater or lesser degree. Under certain conditions, the libido is liable to flow back to earlier stages of development and to such 'fixation points', which exert a pull on the forward-reaching libido.

Freud defines 'fixation' as 'a particularly close attachment of the instinct to its object'. (The object may be something external or part of the subject's own body.) He says that such fixation 'frequently occurs in very early stages of the instinct's development and so puts an end to its mobility, through the vigorous resistance it sets up against detachment'. [Freud, S. 1915a:65; SE 14:123][1]

Fixations not only hamper sexual development as such, by preventing the normal advance of libido from one erogenous zone to another, and from the earliest to later objects. They also limit the capacity of the subject to achieve sublimation, since sublimation depends upon the relinquishing of the primary objects and modes of instinctual satisfaction for substitute objects and derived (symbolic) forms of activity. Fixations also lead to inhibition of ego development, the ego renouncing those functions which are too closely bound up with early fixations.

Every mental illness involves some degree and some form of regression of the libido to early fixation points. Regression is a phenomenon of the utmost importance in the aetiology of neurosis, psychosis, and the involution of character. In hysteria, the libido regresses with regard to its objects, seeking again the earliest incestuous loves, whilst its aims remain (chiefly) genital. In obsessional neurosis (and certain forms of character deterioration), 'regression of the libido to an antecedent stage of the sadistic-anal organization is the most conspicuous factor and determines the form taken by the symptoms'. [Freud, S. 1916/17:288; SE 16:343][2]

In *Inhibitions, Symptoms and Anxiety*, Freud refers also to the effect of the regression of the libido upon the superego in obsessional neurosis: 'In order to effect the destruction of the Oedipus complex a regressive degradation of the libido takes place as well, the superego becomes exceptionally severe and unkind, and the ego, in obedience to the superego, produces strong reaction-formations in the shape of conscientiousness, pity and cleanliness.' [Freud, S. 1926:64; SE 20:114–15][3]

These regressive changes, thus, involve not only the sexual life itself; they affect the sublimations, the emotions, and the whole personality of the subject. The whole complex interplay and balance of the various mechanisms at work in the mental life are altered when regression occurs. This is patent in obsessional neurosis and the psychoses, but it is also true in hysteria, although less dramatically.

Freud's observations of these facts in adult mental life were confirmed by his more direct study of infants and young children. Every analyst rediscovers their truth in every patient, and many authors have amplified and extended the details of our knowledge. Abraham's contributions in this field were outstanding, and we shall discuss them in a later section. Ernest Jones's pioneer study of the effect of anal fixation upon the character influenced all later opinion. Space and time will not allow us even to mention in this paper valuable additions to our knowledge made by many other analysts.

The classic view as to the *causes* of regression laid stress upon the damming-up of the libido. This damming-up might arise either from external factors (frustration) or internal ones (fixations, inhibition in development, biological accession of libido at puberty and menopause). Both sets of influences give rise to an increase in libido which cannot be satisfied or disposed of, and which consequently disturbs the balance within the psyche and sets up an intolerable stress. The quantitative factor is considered to be of great importance.

These earlier formulations as to the *causes* of regression now require to be reconsidered in the light of Freud's own further work on the death instinct, as well as the added knowledge about early mental development which has been gained through the analysis of young children. Freud's theories were framed upon material obtained chiefly from the analysis of adults, supplemented by the analysis of a five-year-old and some observations of infants and young children. The work of Melanie Klein, in her much more extensive observations and analytic studies of very young children, has amplified the well-known facts of regression and thrown new light upon their interconnections. The outcome of these fuller observations conforms with the changes in our views about the causes of regression which is required by Freud's own later work.

II Data from infants and young children

In working directly with young children, whether in analysis or when observing them with an analytic eye, the opportunity is given of studying the experiences of the child in his earliest phases of libidinal development, *at the time when fixations occur.*

The relation of libidinal wishes to impulses of aggression can be directly noted. The anxiety stirred by different impulses in various circumstances, and the earliest defences against anxiety and ways of controlling impulse can be seen. The child's relations to his objects in particular situations of feeling and impulse, and the varied and changing expressions of his phantasies about his objects can be studied. The early processes of symbol-formation and displacement, the first sublimations, as well as the fixations, can be watched. Moreover, the setting of all these processes in their context of feeling can be noted, as the child's varied emotions – love, hate, fear, anger and guilt, joy and sorrow – come up in changing situations. Such contemporary studies of the changes in feeling and impulse and phantasy bring a far richer detail of fact about fixations than can be obtained when working back from the memories of adult life or later childhood. They yield also a juster perspective as to the relative emphasis which should be placed on different elements in the situation and a better sense of the complex interplay of factors.

As a brief illustration, we may consider one of the examples of play given at the end of the paper on phantasy, quoted there as evidence of early phantasy. A girl of sixteen months often plays her favourite game with her parents. She picks small imaginary bits off a brown embossed leather screen in the dining-room, carrying these pretended bits of food across the room in her finger and thumb and putting them into the mouth of father and mother alternately. She chooses the brown screen, with small raised lumps on it, from among all the other objects of varying colour and shape in the room, to represent the 'food' she wishes to give her parents. On the most familiar analytic lines, we are justified in concluding that these small brown lumps represent faeces and can thus link this play of feeding her parents with symbolic faeces with an earlier experience of the child's. Several times earlier (between twelve and sixteen months) the child had smeared herself with her faeces when lying in her cot in the early mornings, and put it into her mouth. She had been scolded and reproached by her parents at the time for doing this. Here, then, she is making a pleasurable game out of the situation of anxiety and guilt. The experience of eating and smearing her faeces is still at work in her mind: her libido is fixated. The reproaches of her parents are still causing her distress. When she is with them she fears they will frown and scold her again – as shown by her uneasiness if they will not play this game with her. Not only does the memory of the actual reproaches disturb her, however, but also the anxiety arising

690

from the aggressive impulses expressed in the original smearing, which (she feels) may have done them harm and turned them into enemies. (In *Civilization and Its Discontents*, Freud expressed his agreement with Klein's view that – as Freud puts it – 'the original severity of the superego does not – or not so much – represent the severity which has been experienced or anticipated from the object, but expresses the child's own aggressiveness towards the latter'.) [Freud, S. 1930:116; SE 21:120][4]

In her play now which, as can be seen in the child's manner, brings her great pleasure and libidinal satisfaction of various kinds – handling faeces again in symbolic form, winning the smiles of her parents, playing the part of the mother who feeds – she is overcoming the anxiety and guilt which bind her libido to the original smearing and eating. She is making an effort to sublimate her oral-sadistic and anal-sadistic aims. She shows her reparation wishes in her endeavour to 'feed' her parents: but in feeding them with 'faeces' she also makes them share her guilt and tries to prove that eating faeces does not poison and destroy.

Taking the occasions when the child actually ate and smeared her faeces together with this frequent and pleasurable game which soon followed, we can say that the game itself may be regarded as the birth of a sublimation: and yet, at the same time, it expresses a strong fixation. And we can see how the libidinal pleasure in fixation is used to overcome feelings of anxiety and guilt. (How intense and definite this particular fixation may turn out to be – which would doubtless be affected by later experiences as well – we cannot say without knowing more about the later history of the child.)

The original smearing and eating of faeces by the child was probably also an instance of the overcoming of aggressive impulses and anxiety by libidinal pleasure. Here we have the genesis of a fixation. It occurred when the child was alone in her cot in the early mornings, as such smearing and eating of faeces nearly always does occur. By doing this, the child was enabled to refrain from screaming and disturbing her parents – as the boy of 18 months described by Freud was enabled to let his mother leave him without protest by his repetitive game with the cotton reel. She thus kept at bay the fear of starvation and the dread of losing her parents, as well as the screaming attacks upon them, with all the anxiety these arouse. (Searl 1933:193)

We shall now formulate briefly certain general conclusions about the causes of fixation and regression to which we are brought by the closer study of infants and young children, conclusions which fill out the gaps in earlier views and correct their perspective.

CAUSATIVE FACTORS IN FIXATION AND REGRESSION

The history of the libido has long been appreciated as a focal aspect of development. We have now learnt that it has to be brought into relation with all other mental phenomena at every stage. Its successive phases affect not only the characteristic mechanisms at the time, but also other sources of instinctual energy, and every sort of emotion and intellectual activity; indeed, they shape the whole of the mental life at each phase.

(a) The quality and intensity of *feelings* are profoundly affected by the stage of libidinal development; and in their turn, emotions help to determine fixations and the further history of the libido. We would emphasize that feelings and the vicissitudes of feelings are always essential data for the understanding of any phase of libidinal development, or of development as a whole. In especial, we have learnt that the development of the libido cannot be understood without reference to feelings of anxiety and the situations and impulses which give rise to anxiety.

(b) The influence of *anxiety* upon libidinal development is highly complex, varying with the interplay of the child's psychical constitution and his circumstances at each crisis of his life. But one way or another, it is always a potent factor.

When stirred too intensely (by whatever situation), anxiety contributes to a fixation of the libido at that point, and may check further development. A fixation is thus partly to be understood as a *defence against anxiety*. It is a familiar observation that libidinal pleasure – whether oral, anal, or genital – may be used as such a defence: as, for instance, when anxious schoolchildren masturbate.

On the other hand, if in more favourable circumstances anxiety is aroused, but not overpoweringly, it serves to increase desire and acts as a spur to libidinal development. In many of her case studies, Melanie Klein has given evidence for these conclusions. In two chapters of *The Psychoanalysis of Children* (Klein 1932:194–278), she surveyed the role of anxiety in the sexual development of both male and female. She showed that specific anxieties not only contribute in both sexes to fixations and regressions, but also play an essential part in stimulating the libido to move forward from pre-genital to the genital positions. Space will not allow us here to refer to these facts in detail, but we wish to say that in our view neither fixation nor normal libidinal development can be understood without taking them into consideration.

In his study of early female sexuality, Ernest Jones (1927:489) also has shown the influence of anxiety in helping to determine both fixations and normal development.

— (c) Anxiety influences libidinal development. Anxiety itself, however, as many analysts would agree, arises from *aggression*. It is evoked by the aggressive components in the pre-genital stages of development. It is the destructive impulses of the child in the oral and anal phases (discovered by Freud and described more fully by Abraham) which are, through the anxiety they stir up, the prime causes of the fixation of the libido. These destructive components in the pre-genital impulses have to be overcome and neutralized by the libido, which, in so far as it is thus occupied, cannot move freely forward to new aims and the genital zone. The amount of libido which has to be kept back at the oral and anal levels – as in the example we have just discussed – in order to counter these aggressive elements (according to their intensity, whether this be due to innate strength or to adverse circumstances) makes so much the less available for genitality. This renders the genital aim so much the more precarious and regression so much the more likely an event, if further anxiety be evoked by frustration on the genital level and consequent further aggression and hate.

As Freud showed, it is frustration which initiates regression. But, in our view, it does so not only by a simple 'damming-up' of libido, but also by evoking hate and aggression and consequent anxiety. The newly evoked hate and aggression reactivate the hardly overcome pre-genital sadism, and this in its turn pulls back the libido to its earlier forms, in order to neutralize the destructive forces once again at work in the mind. Freud himself classed regression as a defence. We understand more fully now what it is a defence against. (We shall consider this matter again in a later section.)

— (d) But, further, the way in which impulses and feelings work to induce fixation and regression cannot be understood without appreciating the part played by *phantasies*. How do the libidinal and aggressive instincts operate *in the mind*? Through unconscious phantasy, which is their psychic representative – as was argued in the first paper in this series. (Freud said: 'hysterical symptoms spring from phantasies'.). [Freud, S. 1916/17:154; SE 15:223)[5]

It is the phantasies of loss and destruction arising from the sadism of the pre-genital levels which stir uncontrollable anxiety phantasies of the destruction of the desired object by devouring, expelling, poisoning, burning, etc., etc., with the ensuing dread of total loss of the source of life and love, the 'good' object, as well as the dread of retaliation, persecution, and threat to the subject's own body from the destroyed and dangerous 'bad' object.

In his comments upon Mrs Isaacs' paper on phantasy, Dr Balint drew attention to the well-known fact that phobias, night-terrors, and sleeping difficulties occur at a very early age, and that even at the breast some infants show neurotic feeding disturbances, whilst these are frequent during and after the period of weaning. Obviously, aetiological theories about such disturbances occurring in later childhood and adult life cannot be considered complete or adequate unless and until they embrace these earliest symptoms as well. In 1926 (p. 105) Freud said that the earliest phobias of infancy 'so far have not been explained' [Freud, S. 1926:105; SE 20:136][6] and added that 'it is not at all clear what their relation is to the undoubted neuroses that appear later on in childhood'. In our own view, these earliest phobias are an attempt to deal, by the projection of internal dangers on to the outer world, with the anxieties arising primarily from the cannibalistic phantasies characteristic of the oral-sadistic stage, phantasies which Freud himself discovered, although he did not bring them into relation with the early phobias.

The significance of animal phobias was discussed by Melanie Klein in her book *The Psychoanalysis of Children* (Klein 1932:178 *et seq.*). In her view, they are a mode of defence against the anxieties relating to the cannibalistic phantasies and to the earliest stages in the formation of the superego. Such projection is characteristic of the earlier anal stage. They provide a means for modifying the child's fears of his threatening superego as well as of his dangerous id.

> The first move is to thrust out these two institutions into the external world and assimilate the superego to the real object. The second move is familiar to us as the displacement on to an animal of the fear felt of the real father. . . . Regarded in this light, an animal phobia would be much more than a distortion of the idea of being castrated by the father into one of being bitten by a horse or eaten by a wolf. Underlying it would be not only the fear of being castrated but a still earlier fear of being devoured by the superego, so the phobia would actually be a modification of anxiety belonging to the earlier stages.

Melanie Klein then goes on to discuss Freud's two cases of Little Hans and the Wolf Man. Little Hans had overcome his earliest anxieties with considerable success. The object of the phobias was not very terrifying – a horse, not a wolf, represented his fear of his father and the anxiety persisting in this form was not too acute to allow him to play at horses with his father. In the Wolf Man, primitive anxieties were far more intense and unmodified. Melanie Klein takes the view that the passive feminine side which, as Freud described, was 'strongly accentuated', the tender passive attitude, covered up an overwhelming dread of the father. She points out that Freud's data show that the patient's whole development was abnormal and was governed by the dread of the wolf father. The early and rapidly developing obsessional neurosis which the patient had shown was evidence of very serious disturbance. And the later history of this patient – as described by Ruth Mack Brunswick – confirmed M. Klein's estimate of the nature and degree of the early cannibalistic anxieties lying behind the wolf phobia.

These primary anxieties are at one and the same time the source of the paranoid symptoms and of the homosexual emphasis in paranoia. 'Against a dangerous devouring father of this sort, they could not engage in the struggle which would naturally result from a direct Oedipus attitude and so they had to abandon their heterosexual position.' The primary oral and anal anxieties give rise to the homosexual fixation and to the regression to paranoia.

It is the anxiety stimulated by cannibalistic phantasies which is the most potent factor in oral fixations. We find in adults as well that these phantasies operate powerfully behind the various forms of oral and anal fixation – perversions, drug addictions, etc. The dread of the destroyed internal object (devoured and therefore inside) can only be allayed by continual oral pleasure, by constantly imbibing more good in order to counteract the bad already inside, and in this way also proving that the external sources of good have not been destroyed or lost irretrievably. It is this insatiable need which binds the libido to oral and anal forms.

We know that such fixations of the oral phase, with all its phantasies and anxieties, lead to profound disturbances of genital function. Yet this is far from being the whole story. The early phantasies by no means play a wholly retarding and fixating part in libidinal development. We pointed out above that when it is not too intense anxiety acts as a spur to libidinal development. (This depends, however, not only on the degree of anxiety, but also upon the specific nature of the phantasies involved – which, in their turn, are influenced by actual experiences as well as by primary impulses.)

It is now widely recognized that the earlier stages have definite and positive contributions to make to the genital phase.[7] For example, in certain respects, successful genitality in men and women alike is actually dependent upon specific impulses, feelings, and phantasies belonging to the oral phase. When the genital life is satisfactory in the man, the specific genital phantasies include an oral element. E.g. the phantasy of the penis as a giving and feeding organ, identified with the breast, is strong. And he feels the female genital to be safe and attractive, partly because he projects on to it, not so much the greed and destructive as the tender impulses of the suckling. Similarly, the woman's genital impulses and phantasies take over her happy experiences at the breast. Her pleasure in actively encompassing the penis, her freedom from the dread of engulfing it and destroying it and castrating her partner, is in part drawn from the unconscious memories of having loved and cherished and safely enjoyed the nipple in active sucking.

These memories also enable her to feel that the penis itself is a good and not a threatening object.[8]

These are, of course, only selected aspects of the highly complicated relationship between pre-genital and genital sexuality, but they may serve to illustrate our general point. Now, it is not enough to say with regard to these positive contributions of the oral phase that there is a displacement from certain elements in the oral phase to the genital function. This is true, but it is an incomplete statement. These oral phantasies and aims have remained uninterruptedly active in the unconscious mind exerting a favourable influence and promoting genitality. The oral libido has remained labile enough to be transformed to the genital and satisfied there.

This transfer comes about – and this is a most important point with reference to the theory of libidinal development and regression – partly because the earliest onset of genital impulses appears whilst the oral stage is still active. As was pointed out by Mrs Isaacs, replying to various remarks about Melanie Klein's views on the development of the libido made in reference to the paper on phantasy, there is actually much more overlap between the various stages than was formerly realized. We would add here that there is not only an overlap, but a movement backwards and forwards between the various phases of the libido, *within* those broad periods when one or other phase can be said to be predominant. It is, e.g., an observable fact that erections occur from time to time during the suckling period.

(e) The contribution of the oral phase to successful genitality cannot, however, be fully understood without reference to *phantasies of incorporation and the mechanism of introjection*. As was shown in the paper on 'Introjection and Projection', early oral satisfactions lead to the incorporation of a 'good' breast, as well as to a good relationship with the external mother. This good internal object (nipple, breast, mother) helps the subject to find a good external object once again in the genital phase, and to feel that his impulses towards it cherish and feed and give life.

Bound up with these phantasies, moreover, are the reparative

696

wishes. Genitality can be maintained when the reparative wishes can operate securely. Genitality breaks down and regression comes about when the reparative tendencies are disturbed (through frustration and the ensuing hatred and aggression), since the genital is then felt to be proved destructive and dangerous.

This brings into operation not only the fear of hurting and damaging the external loved object, but also the dread of the 'bad' internal object, the superego. In the passage we quoted earlier, Freud referred to the severe and implacable superego of the obsessional neurotic. He expresses his sense of the intimate interplay between the level of regression reached and the kind of superego when he says: 'the superego, originating as it does in the id, cannot dissociate itself from the regression and defusion of instinct which have taken place here'. [Freud, S. 1926:64; SE 20:115] We should fill this out by adding that the hate and aggression aroused by the frustration which starts the regressive process at once evokes the dread of the superego, the hating and vengeful internal object; and this in its turn stimulates the need to hate and fight again with all the weapons of pre-genital sadism.

In our view, the part played by internal objects and the superego is an essential factor in the regressive process.

Another important advance in the understanding of regression, gained chiefly from Klein's work with young children, together with the closer study of psychotic states largely stimulated by such work, is that fixations and other pathological states can be fruitfully approached from the angle of progression, as well as that of regression. This point of view, and its critical bearing on therapy, has been most clearly stated by Edward Glover, in his paper on drug addiction [Glover 1932:299] I may, therefore, quote him here. He wrote:

The approach to drug-addiction was (and still is) profoundly influenced by the concept of *regression*. The opposite view of a progression in psychopathological states has never been exploited to the same extent. The idea of progression implies that psycho-pathological states are exaggerations of 'normal' *stages in the mastering of anxiety* and can be arranged in a rough order of precedence. It is, of course, implicit in Freud's[9] original pronouncement regarding paranoid states: namely, that the symptom is in part an attempt at restitution, i.e., an advance from the unconscious situation it covers. Not only does it restore some link with reality, however inadequate, it performs also a protective function. The protective and restitutive aspects of other psycho-

697

pathological states have not been given the same attention. For example, we have long known that obsessional mechanisms function comparatively well in the remissions of melancholia: nevertheless, we are inclined to look askance at an obsessional neurosis *per se*, as a 'severe regression'. We think and talk of this neurosis as the result of a defensive flight backwards from the anxieties of an infantile genital system of relationships: rather than a remarkable impulsion forwards, a striking advance on the discomforts of an unconscious paranoid organization . . . if we study the numerous drug-habits which . . . are called 'idiosyncrasies' or 'indulgences' rather than addictions, we can see that drug-addiction is frequently a successful manoeuvre. The point is of considerable therapeutic interest. Obviously if we can grasp the progressive relations of psychogenetic states, our therapeutic energies can be directed with greater accuracy. For example, the cure of an addiction or even of a severe obsessional state may depend more on the reduction of an underlying paranoid layer than on the most careful analysis of the recognized habit-formation or obsessional superstructure.

From the study of young children, we should say that these opposite tendencies, progression and regression, are at work all the time in mental life. There is a constant ebb and flow between them during the whole period of development and at all times of mental stress. Any point of relative stability is actually a compromise between the two tendencies, depending upon the specific phantasies which are at work. Similarly, there is a constant movement of the mind between the various mechanisms which are available for disposing of anxiety and mastering instinct (introjection, projection, displacement, distribution, repression, isolation, undoing, and the rest). Eventually a certain compromise is reached, acceptable to the ego and yielding an optimal control of anxiety, between these various mechanisms, and between the forward and backward movement of the libido, together with the destructive components with which it is always more or less fused.

Certain of these points we shall now consider in more detail, particularly with reference to Freud's later work.

III Considerations arising from Freud's conclusions as to
life and death instincts

REGRESSION, FIXATION, AND THE DESTRUCTIVE INSTINCTS

The phenomena of progression and regression provide further evidence of the duality which underlies human life. They have ultimately to be traced to the life and death instincts. As has been pointed out in an earlier paper, the manifestations of the life instinct and the development of the libido were the first and have been the most thoroughly investigated subject of psychoanalysis. The study of regression was for many years almost entirely concerned with its libidinal aspect. It was Abraham especially who made a systematic study of the part played by the destructive instincts. He demonstrated that they also have a development, as shown in the successive changes in their aims. Building on Freud's theory of the three main libidinal phases, Abraham examined the phenomena of regression in certain mental illnesses and arrived at the conclusion that the destructive no less than the libidinal impulses undergo a change of aim in relation to objects.

Freud saw the first destructive aim arising during the primacy of the oral zone, namely, cannibalism. Abraham subdivided the oral phase into oral-sucking and oral-biting stages. He pointed out the force of the destructive impulses during the onset of teething, whilst he held that the first oral stage was free from aggressive impulses. (In this we do not follow him, since we hold that there is evidence of some destructive aims during the sucking stage. Abraham himself, when discussing the oral character, attributes an element of cruelty to the sucking stage, which makes people who have regressed to that stage 'something like vampires to other people'.) In his 'A Short Study of the Development of the Libido', Abraham [1924:418] described devouring by biting as the first destructive aim. This is followed at the first anal stage by the aim of destroying by expulsion. During the second anal stage, an important modification of the destructive instincts takes place, their aim being changed into that of control by retention. Whilst there is still a strong aggressive cathexis of the object, the mitigation of the destructive impulses is shown by the desire to preserve it. It is spared the full destruction of the earlier phases, on condition of being subject to control. At the final stage of instinctual development, the genital phase, the libido carries the field and – according to Abraham – there is full object-love without ambivalence (post-ambivalence).

Freud's theory of a primary instinct of destruction was published in 1920 (*Beyond the Pleasure Principle*), and was thus available to Abraham. Abraham must have known it when he wrote his 'Development of the Libido' in 1924. He did not link his own findings with the theory of the death instinct, although to us it appears that they are in line with it. It goes beyond the frame of this paper to deal with all the implications of Abraham's discoveries regarding the change of aim, i.e., the development of the destructive instinct. It is well known that Melanie Klein has built on his views, and that through her analysis of young children she has expanded and carried further the investigation of the working of the destructive impulses, the interplay of libidinal and destructive factors, their reflection in phantasy and the role which anxiety plays in development.

Bringing together what we have learnt from Freud, Abraham, and Melanie Klein about the instinctual aims of the pre-genital stages, we come to see the correlation between libido and aggression. The libidinal desire to suck is accompanied by the destructive aim of sucking out, scooping out, emptying, exhausting. The libidinal pleasure in biting is experienced along with the destructive impulse of devouring. To the pleasure of expelling corresponds the destructive aim of annihilating, whilst the pleasure of retaining coincides with the impulse to control and dominate. These considerations have an important bearing on the discussion of the role which the derivatives of the death instinct play in regression. Whilst some analysts think of regression predominantly in terms of the libido, we lay stress on the concurrent changes in the destructive impulse, i.e. their return to earlier, archaic aims. We hold that it is this recurrence of primitive destructive aims which is the chief causative factor in the outbreak of severe mental illness.

A precondition of regression is the formation of fixation points. On the basis of Abraham's findings referred to above, and Melanie Klein's extensive researches, we consider that a fixation point has not only a libidinal, but a destructive charge as well. Both become again operative when in regression the instinctual and emotional life of an earlier phase once more becomes dominant.

In this situation, violent anxiety is experienced which derives from several sources: (a) The present-day frustration which initiates the regression. It is common knowledge that frustration stimulates hatred and anxiety. (b) The specific anxieties (paranoid, depressive, and superego types of anxiety) which are revived by the return to primitive instinctual impulses (fixation points). Freud says in *New Introductory Lectures*: 'every stage of development has its own particular conditions for anxiety; that is to say, a danger-situation appropriate to it. . . . As development proceeds, the old conditions for anxiety should vanish, since the danger-situations which correspond to them have lost their force owing to the strengthening of the ego. But this only happens to a very incomplete degree.' [Freud, S. 1933a:116; SE 22:343][10] We have already mentioned Freud's reference to the extreme severity of the superego in regressive conditions. (c) The horror with which the ego reacts to being faced with the impulses and phantasies of a phase from which it had already removed itself. In describing the effect of regression at puberty in obsessional neurosis, Freud says: 'The ego will recoil with astonishment from promptings to cruelty and violence which enter consciousness from the id.' [Freud, S. 1926:68; SE 20:116]

In our view, thus, the facts just summarized, which include the breaking down of the sublimations and the modifications to which the destructive instincts were subjected in the course of development, have to be seen in operation together with the vicissitudes of the libido. There is another point at which our conclusions diverge from Freud's view of regression, in so far as this was still based on the earlier forms taken by his theory. Freud emphasized the damming-up of the libido as the cause of regression and of neurotic illness. Owing to the frustration which renders the discharge and satisfaction of the libido impossible, the libido becomes dammed up and this ushers in regression. 'The dissatisfied and dammed-up libido may now open the path to regression.' [Freud, S. 1911c:119; SE 12:236][11]

But if we accept Freud's theory of the life and death instincts, formulated in *Beyond the Pleasure Principle*, we are no longer justified in singling out the libido when considering regression and pathological conditions. The question now arises whether regression is not the outcome of a failure of the libido to master the destructive impulses and anxiety aroused by frustration. We believe that this is so: that the pathological condition of damned-up libido occurs only when the libido – in spite of its increase or apparent increase – proves unable to counter the destructive impulses which are evolved by the same factors which caused the damming-up of the libido, namely, the frustration.

As an example, we may briefly consider the problem of the menopause.

Many women fail to cope with conflicts of the menopause and regress at this point because the decline of sexual productivity deprives them of a redeeming factor of first magnitude. It is not only in devout Catholics that we meet with the feeling that sexual

701

intercourse is something bad and guilty for which only procreation can make amends. This attitude to sexuality, as is well known, exists in the unconscious of many women who believe themselves free of religious or ethical scruples about sexuality. Once this redeeming factor disappears, unabated guilt may flood a woman's mind. The knowledge that she can no longer bear children also opens the door to severe anxieties, particularly those centring upon a destroyed and barren inside, for which a persecuting mother is made responsible. Not to produce a live child is felt to be the same as to contain dead bodies inside (a phantasy which derives ultimately from the cannibalistic and destructive impulses of early instinctual life). These feelings stir up the fear of her own death. In the wake of these anxieties penis envy is stimulated, the possession of the penis becoming again so desired and needed since the feminine privilege of bearing children has ceased. Guilt towards the husband, partly for her impulse to castrate him, partly because now she deprives him of fatherhood, enters into the complicated picture. Moreover, the husband from whom she no longer receives a child assumes the role of the father who never satisfied her desire for a child, and thus the incestuous phantasies are revived which made sexual intercourse the primary crime. In consciousness these anxieties and conflicts may appear under the guise of being haunted by the fear of becoming unattractive and old. Women in the menopause often develop an increased demand for sexual intercourse, sexual gratification and success, affection and love. They are in the 'dangerous age'. Analytic investigation of such cases makes it evident that libidinal desires are vastly increased through anxiety and guilt.

Many other factors as well enter into the problem of the menopause, but these may suffice here, since we are concerned to show our approach to the problem of dammed-up libido rather than to investigate the psychology of the menopause as such.

In the situation in which the ego is confronted by the task of mastering the dammed-up libido, it is also faced with that of mastering destructive impulses and anxieties. These considerations are derived from clinical observations. In our view, their theoretical basis is to be found in Freud's theory regarding the fusion of the two opposed instincts, e.g., where he says 'the fact that what we are concerned with are scarcely ever pure instinctual impulses, but mixtures in varying proportions of the two groups of instincts'. [Freud, S. 1926:84; SE 20:125][12]

To sum up our conclusions on this matter. At the fixation point not only is libido immobilized, but the destructive impulses and anxieties specific for that period of development, which form a background of unsolved conflicts, also remain potentially active and ready to interfere with a firm establishment of the genital phase. The maintenance of pre-genital instinctual modes of behaviour and phantasies is not as such a pathological factor. We have referred above to their significance as stepping stones in the mastering of anxiety. Pre-genital aggressive and libidinal aims may contribute to genital ones and colour and enrich the genital activities, provided they are capable of subordination under the primacy of the genital. This, however, depends upon the balance between libido and destructive impulses, determining the type of phantasy which accompanies genital activity.

The breakdown of the genital phase involves the libido, the destructive instincts, and the *ego-achievements* alike. As is well known, deterioration in character and impairment of sublimations form part of the regressive process.

Another element in regression is that the *reparative aims* are interfered with. As already pointed out, we lay great stress upon the role which reparation and sublimation play in maintaining mental health. The instinctual processes of the pre-genital phases give rise to specific anxieties. The ego, built up by introjection and projection, is endangered in various ways by the destruction of its objects. Their restoration is a more urgent aim, giving impetus to sublimation. These ego achievements, thus, in addition to the gratifications which they provide, are prime factors in the fight against anxiety and guilt.[13] A certain degree and quality of guilt and anxiety stimulate reparation and thus encourage sublimation. An excess of these emotions, however, has a paralysing effect on sublimations. As long as the individual feels that his destructive impulses are kept in check or that harm done by him is being repaired, he can maintain the genital level, because he can then tolerate the actual frustration and his libido can be redirected on to other objects. And in so far as sublimation can be maintained and gratifications from other objects be sought, this in its turn helps him to bear frustration. Here we have a benign circle. But if reparation and sublimation break down, the ego's defences are overrun, gratifications of the aim-inhibited libido are lost, the strength of the destructive impulses is intensified, and pre-genital anxiety situations are revived. Persecution fears and despair make the actual frustration unbearable, partly because it has been augmented by these processes. Here there is a vicious circle involving both the re-emergence of archaic impulses with their associated anxieties, and the breakdown of sublimation and reparation – a circle which reflects the mutual influence of fixation and regression.

REGRESSION AND INHIBITION

Regression may result in symptom-formation or in inhibition, or in both. Freud held that the ego-function of an organ becomes inhibited if the sexual significance of that function, the erotogenicity of the organ in question, becomes too great. He says: 'As soon as writing, which entails making a liquid substance flow on to a piece of white paper, assumes the significance of copulation, or as soon as walking becomes a symbolic substitute for treading[14] upon the body of mother earth, both writing and walking are stopped because they represent the performance of a forbidden sexual act. The ego renounces these functions, which are within its sphere, in order not to have to undertake fresh measures of repression – in order to avoid coming into conflict with the id.' [Freud, S. 1926:16–17: SE 20:90]

In the light of the theory of the fusion between libido and destructive impulses the processes of inhibition come once more under discussion. We do not propose to deal with this problem thoroughly, but wish to show in broad lines our approach to it. The two examples mentioned in the quotation above (writing assumed the significance of copulation, and walking that of stamping upon the mother's body) are not on the same level. The latter definitely contains an element of violence, and we venture to think that it is precisely this, the phantasy of violence, derived from the admixture of destructiveness, which causes anxiety and guilt and enforces – by the intervention of the superego – an inhibition of that activity. We also think it likely that writing becomes inhibited only if its anal-sadistic and urethral significance predominates. The ego, as we know, uses defence mechanisms in order to combat anxiety. If in his phantasies the subject feels he would stamp on his mother's body, he comes to be afraid that he would destroy her and that she would retaliate, and it is these anxieties which bring about the inhibition of walking.

REGRESSION AND DEFUSION

Turning to the metapsychological aspect of regression, we find ourselves confronted with a great number of problems which cannot be regarded as finally settled, although Freud brought forward certain essential considerations. He put the phenomena of fusion and defusion into the focus of the problem and linked regression with defusion. 'Making a swift generalization, we might conjecture that the essence of a regression of libido, e.g. from the genital to the sadistic-anal level, would lie in a defusion of instincts, just as, conversely, the advance from an earlier to the definite genital phase would be conditioned by an accession of erotic components.' [Freud, S. 1923b:57–8; SE 19:43] And again: 'As regards the metapsychological explanation of regression, I am inclined to find it in a "defusion of instinct", in a detachment of the erotic components which at the beginning of the genital stage had become joined to the destructive cathexes belonging to the sadistic phase.' [Freud, S. 1926:63; SE 20:114]

These statements could be taken to imply that the fusion of the instincts is broken up when regression takes place, and that there is no fusion at the pre-genital stages which are re-occupied in the backward flow of the instincts. This implication could, however, scarcely be correct. Freud repeatedly emphasized that the two opposed instincts always occur in a state of fusion, and direct analytic observations fully bear out this view. We quote two passages from Freud. 'As a result of theoretical considerations, supported by biology, we assumed the existence of a death instinct. . . . This hypothesis throws no light whatever upon the manner in which the two classes of instinct are fused, blended and mingled with each other, but that this takes place regularly and very extensively is an assumption indispensable to our conception.' [Freud, S. 1923b:55–6; SE 19:40–1] And: 'what we are concerned with are scarcely ever pure instinctual impulses but mixtures in varying proportions of the two groups of instincts'. [Freud, S. 1926:84; SE 20:125]

These passages clearly exclude the idea of there being no fusion at the pre-genital stages. It seems rather that Freud did not envisage a complete, but only a partial detachment of the erotic components. Such partial detachment would suffice to bring about regression and a strengthening of the destructive impulses, although there is still a fusion of the instincts at the lower level to which regression proceeds. This view would be in accordance with Freud's statement about the varying proportions in the ever-present mixture of the two instincts, and with his differentiation of the pre-genital and genital phases with regard to the proportion of the two instincts.

This helps us over one difficulty, but still others have to be faced. The problem of the quantity of the libido and the destructive instincts, for instance, must be considered. Does the absolute amount of instinctual energy remain the same throughout life? Does the energy of one instinct, say that of the libido, increase, and that of the other decrease? Are such quantitative changes responsible for the prescribed order of instinctual phases? Or does the total amount of both instincts remain unaltered and have we to explain the changes in the primacy of the phases merely by the successful cathexis of one zone after another?

Some observations speak for the assumption of quantitative changes in the course of life. It would appear that Freud was inclined to this view. He says: 'As a result of reaching a certain period in life, and in accordance with regular biological processes, the quantity of libido in their mental economy has increased to an extent which by itself suffices to upset the balance of health and establish the conditions for neurosis. As is well known, such rather sudden intensifications in libido are regularly connected with puberty and the menopause, with the reaching of a certain age in women. In many people they may in addition manifest themselves in periodicities as yet unrecognized.' [Freud, S. 1911c:118; SE 12: 235–6][15]

On the other hand, there are observations which would be in favour of another view. We believe with Freud that libidinal satisfaction at the breast is the highest, never again attained, and that the child's first, most primal impulses 'have an intensity of their own which is greater than anything that comes later'. [Freud, S. 1931: 296; SE 21:243] These impressions do not suggest a weak instinctual life at the beginning, which becomes stronger in the course of development. It still might be possible that periodic increases occur, however, as for instance when the capacity for procreation is attained.

These are speculations to which we are tempted by the 'indefinite' character of the instincts. After all, Freud calls the instincts 'mythological beings, superb in their indefiniteness'. [Freud, S. 1933a:124; SE 22:95][16] We may remember that the instincts belong to the borderland between soma and psyche, and that our field is that of the psyche, whilst we look to the physiologist to provide us with the complementary data. We may speculate about the instincts, but our convictions are derived from psychological observations, from the investigation of behaviour, feelings, emotions, phantasies. It may be that not absolute quantities of instinctual energy, but specific features, inherent in the organ which has the lead, decide the issue between the fused instincts; and that the function of the organ stamps its character on the instinctual stage reached. By virtue of its superpersonal function of procreation, the genital would be best endowed to serve the purposes of the life instinct, so that by its operation a condition is brought about which amounts to an 'accession of erotic components'. But we cannot consider only the biological function of the organ which has the primacy. The *phantasies* associated with the various organs and their functions decide the issue psychologically. The first zones of instinctual experience are charged with phantasies of a strongly aggressive order. In advancing to the primacy of the genital, the primitive destructive impulses become modified and worked over, and the destructive phantasies become milder. Those phantasies associated with procreation are naturally and inevitably of a creative and reparative type.

Freud was inclined to the view that quanitative factors decide progression and regression, but he was also convinced of the significance of 'the manner in which the two classes of instinct are fused, blended, mingled with each other'.

It may well be that one of the functions of the libido is to bind the destructive instincts, to drain the sources of destructive impulses and thus to master them. At the genital stage, the libido would best succeed in utilizing the destructive impulses for its own purposes, thus attaining the overlordship in the fusion. That there is also a fusion of the instincts even at the genital phase is clearly demonstrated to us by the analysis of impotence and frigidity in which the fear of aggression leads to inhibition of the sexual act. As is well known, a certain degree and mode of aggressive elements, or to put it more specifically, a certain contribution from the derivatives of the destructive instinct are indispensable for the functioning of genitality. But the ego can allow the destructive impulses to enter into the genital act only if the mastery of the libido is assured; that is to say, if a far-reaching modification of their aims under the influences of the libido has already been attained.

To summarize: it cannot be doubted that there is a fusion of the opposed instincts at every stage of development. The character of that fusion, however, varies with the stages, but we are not yet in a position to say precisely in what this character consists. The safest hypothesis seems to be that it is not determined only by quantitative factors. We suggested in an earlier paper that the predominance of the life instinct could not be understood in quantitative terms only. The interrelation between the instincts, the manner of their 'blending and mingling' is at least as important, and may turn out to be the essence of the matter.

Defusion would then mean a break-up of that particular admixture, the overthrow of the rule of the libido in that form and not merely a detachment of the libidinal components or a diminution of their quantity.

If such detachment does take place, however, we have to account for the detached amount of libido. We know that Freud held that libido which becomes detached from objects is transformed into ego-libido and augments the primary narcissism. If we apply this conclusion to the defusion in regression, narcissism and regression have thus to be brought into relation with each other. As was pointed out in the paper on 'Introjection and Projection', [see pp. 517–19] narcissism is in our view bound up with the subject's relation to his internal objects. Regression would thus involve the internal object system of phantasies and feelings. We cannot however attempt to cope with this important problem within the framework of this paper. (We have drawn attention above to the role of the superego in regression.)

The phenomena comprised in 'regression' are thus, in our view, highly complex and fluid, involving a shifting equilibrium – and loss of equilibrium – of all sides of the mental life. As we suggested, the backward flow of libido and destructive instincts requires to be considered within the context of emotional experience and the phantasy life.

Notes

1 'This frequently occurs at very early periods of the development of an instinct and puts an end to its mobility through its intense opposition to detachment.' [SE 14:123]

2 'In obsessional neurosis, on the contrary, it is the regression of the libido to the preliminary stage of the sadistic-anal organization that is the most striking fact and the one which is decisive for what is manifested in symptoms.' [SE 16:343]

3 'In addition to the destruction of the Oedipus complex a regressive degradation of the libido takes place, the superego becomes exceptionally severe and unkind, and the ego produces strong reaction-formations in the shape of conscientiousness, pity and cleanliness.' [SE 20:114–15]

4 'But the essential difference is that the original severity of the superego does not – or does not so much – represent the severity which one has experienced from it; it represents rather one's own aggressiveness towards it (the object).' [SE 21:120]

5 (Original footnote) And in 'Negation', he spoke of 'the *language* of the oldest, that is, of the oral instinctual impulses' (my ital.). The whole essay on negation shows that, in his views, phantasy is not merely the mental expression of instinct, but is the link between an instinct and the psychic mechanisms specifically related to that instinct. (Freud, S. 1916/17:154; SE 15:223)

6 The same sentence as in the text.

7 (Original footnote) Among many other studies M. Brierley's paper, 'Some Problems of Integration in Women', is to be noted. [Brierley 1932]

8 (Original footnote) Ernest Jones's paper 'Early Female Sexuality', *IJPA* XVI, 1935, should be read in this connection.

9 (Original footnote) Freud: *An Autobiographical Account of a Case of Paranoia*. C.P. III, 1925.

10 'If we dwell on these situations of danger for a moment, we can say that in fact a particular determinant of anxiety (that is, situation of danger) is allotted to every age of development as being appropriate to it.' [SE 22:343]

11 'The unsatisfied and dammed-up libido can once again open up paths to regression.' [SE 12:236]

12 The same sentence as in the text.

13 (Original footnote) In his paper 'Fear, Guilt and Hate', *IJPA*, X, 1929, Ernest Jones made a comprehensive study of the interaction between these emotions.

14 (Original footnote) In the original the word used by Freud was 'Stampfen' which conveys more violence than is expressed by 'treading'.

15 'As a result of their having reached a particular period of life, and in conformity with regular biological processes, the quantity of libido in their mental economy has experienced an increase which is in itself enough to upset the equilibrium of their health and to set up the necessary conditions for a neurosis.' [SE 12:235–6]

16 'Instincts are mythical entities magnificent in their indefiniteness.' [SE 22:95]

2

Discussion on
Dr P. Heimann's and Mrs S. Isaacs'
paper on 'Regression'

(This discussion being circulated only, see notice dated December 17th, 1943.)

DR EDWARD GLOVER: In a controversial series of discussions like the present it is important to keep clearly and constantly in mind not only the central issues in dispute and the main thread of argument advanced by successive lecturers, but the main lines of criticism of that argument. Otherwise there is some danger of not seeing the wood for the trees. As far as the central issues are concerned, viz., the validity of Mrs Klein's theories and practice, and of the clinical evidence on which these are based, I need only remind you that so far we have not touched on these issues at all. So far the lecturers, Mrs Isaacs and Dr Heimann, have been concerned to develop a 'Kleinian metapsychology' on which presumably Mrs Klein's theories and clinical procedures can subsequently be based. This is of course a perfectly legitimate procedure but it is subject to certain disadvantages. For example: since we have not yet examined in this series either Mrs Klein's clinical theories or the clinical evidence on which they are based, we can assess the validity of her metapsychology only by comparing it with the metapsychology of Freud, and this has already given rise to a somewhat absurd situation, namely, that the discussion has sometimes turned not on the validity of Mrs Klein's basic concepts but on the validity of Freud's basic concepts. And I daresay some Members who have not realized the implications of Mrs Klein's theories are inclined to wonder what all the bother is about.

Apart from this, the metapsychology so far presented can be

710

boiled down to a few sentences: Mrs Klein's adherents propose to alter Freud's basic concept of phantasy by expanding it in a way which, the critics assert, is not only unjustifiable but gives rise to hopeless confusion. The latter say roundly that the Kleinian definition of phantasy includes mental activities which should be clearly distinguished from phantasy both descriptively and functionally. For example: 'Phantasy' is identified by Mrs Isaacs with perceptual experience, image formation, primary hallucinatory regression, and imago formation. The next stage in the Kleinian presentation involves a similar expansion and a similar confusion. The unconscious mental mechanism of introjection is identified with the formation of memory-traces, with the formation of an object imago with the subjective experience of corporeal activity and with true phantasy activity. This was subsequently corrected by Dr Heimann in so far as she was prepared to distinguish bodily incorporation from psychic introjection. Apart from this no other corrections have been made in the Kleinian presentation.

There is of course a certain consistency in this procedure. Mrs Isaacs' (or Mrs Klein's) extension of the concept of phantasy paves the way for Dr Heimann's (or Mrs Klein's) new definition of introjection, and the new definition of introjection could be used in support of the new definition of phantasy. The critics would say of course that the consistency is a consistency of error. But we must look ahead. *If these distortions of Freudian metapsychology were allowed to pass unchallenged it would be open to anyone to claim that whatever he or she has thought about the content of the unconscious is true.* Every surmise about unconscious content is of course true to the extent that every phantasy has its unconscious roots and has therefore a sound claim to have psychic reality *for that individual*; in other words, it is true to the extent that phantasy is, after all, phantasy. This point will be found to be of vital significance when we come to discuss the validity of Mrs Klein's clinical interpretations – a point which we have not so far reached. In the meantime therefore I will confine myself to these general comments: If we were to accept Kleinian definitions of phantasy and of introjection, all scientific control of psychoanalytical interpretation would disappear: for the matter of that it would be perfectly simple to prove that the moon is made of green cheese. Secondly, Mrs Klein's merging of concepts, so far from simplifying our approach to mental function, abolishes distinctions that are essential to our understanding of the mental apparatus.

Two other matters must be considered before we discuss the present paper on regression by Mrs Isaacs and Dr Heimann. In the first place, so long as we were concerned with basic concepts of the mental apparatus, discussion was essentially non-clinical. There was (or rather should have been) no possibility of confusing the metapsychological and the clinical use of terms. But as a matter of fact the most illuminating contribution to these discussions was contained in Dr Heimann's admission that when she was talking theoretically she used the term 'death instinct' but that when she was speaking clinically she used the term 'aggression'. Unfortunately this policy was not systematically pursued by either of the contributors. On the contrary, the confusion existing in Kleinian metapsychology could well be attributed to lack of discrimination between the concept of psychic apparatus and clinical descriptions of mental activity. The same lack of discrimination accounts for the inconsequent habit both lecturers displayed of giving extensive quotations from the writings of Freud which, they asserted, supported the new Kleinian concepts. As has been pointed out over and over again by the critics, the clinical content of most of the quotations had no reference to the reconstruction of primary stages of mental development with which Mrs Isaacs and Dr Heimann were concerned. When it comes to a subject like regression it is increasingly important to distinguish the metapsychological from the clinical aspects of the subject, the more so as it is increasingly easy to confuse these aspects. One may therefore anticipate that Freud will be more frequently cited in support of Kleinian hypotheses.

The second point is liable to go undetected by those who have not previously been particularly interested in these controversies. The closer we get to the discussion of stages of development with which practising analysts are familiar in their everyday clinical work, the more necessary it is to be closely familiar with the previous literature on these subjects and in particular with the contributions made by other psychoanalysts to current analytical theory. Otherwise we may fall into the error of believing that these contributions are an essential part of Mrs Klein's work. This is all the more urgent since Mrs Klein's work falls into two distinct parts, which, though they have a certain amount in common, must be clearly distinguished in any scientific discussion. Mrs Klein's earlier papers and contributions, i.e., those preceding her paper on depression, touched on a number of subjects, e.g. superego origin, the role of aggression or sadism, to which extensive contributions had been made by Abraham, Ferenczi, and others, to say nothing of Freud's own formulations. It is therefore necessary to single out from these the views for which Mrs Klein is solely responsible. No doubt there are some who supported this earlier phase of Mrs Klein's work particularly if they favoured the views of Abraham or Ferenczi but who would nevertheless reject

712

the theories she built up in her second period (e.g., the theory of a central depressive position). Others again would reject the interpretative technique of both phases. But unless we are clear both as to earlier literature and as to the two phases of Mrs Klein's work, this series of discussions will inevitably end in an inextricable confusion. I emphasize these points because it seems to me that in the present paper this confusion has already made its appearance and the casual reader may be pardoned if he does not see just how important for the future of psychoanalysis is the outcome of this controversial series of discussions.

To come now to the paper on regression by Dr Heimann and Mrs Isaacs, it should be noted that as far as Mrs Klein's views are concerned, the issues raised *in this paper belong for the most part to what I have called the earlier phase of Mrs Klein's work.*

Having reviewed briefly some of Freud's formulations on regression, the writers point out that the more extensive observations made by Mrs Klein would confirm the necessity for changes in our views about the causes of regression, which, they are careful to suggest, are required *by Freud's own later work*. The argument is of course that, as we can 'note' at first hand and 'directly' the relation of libido to aggression, can 'see' the infant's anxieties and defences, can 'study' the child's relations to its objects in certain situations of feeling, etc., and 'watch' symbol formations, displacements, sublimations, and fixations, we can arrive at 'a richer detail of fact'. At a casual reading the argument sounds convincing. But in fact, even allowing considerable latitude in the language of presentation, it is completely misleading. There are no such direct notes, views, studies, and observations. There are only *interpretations* of the child's behaviour and utterances from which *hypothetical reconstructions* of psychic situations or stages of child development are arrived at. *Other child analysts with precisely the same opportunities of observing child behaviour and utterance hold that Kleinian interpretations and reconstructions are inaccurate,* and that their own observations confirm the formulations set forth by Freud as the result of his study. Again and again this point has been made by the critics but it has not yet been openly admitted by adherents of the Klein position. The whole Klein system stands or falls on the evidence its adherents can bring forward that their interpretations are correct. Actually in the example of child 'phantasy' that follows this argument, the authors tacitly admit it. Proceeding to interpret a 16-month-old child's actions they say 'we are justified in *concluding* (all italics mine) . . . etc.' The child feeding them (the parents) with 'faeces' (an interpretation of part of the play) 'shows her reparation wishes'. 'She also makes them (the parents)

713

share her guilt. . . .' 'The original smearing and eating of faeces was *probably* also an instance of the overcoming of aggressive impulses and anxiety by libidinal pleasure.' '*Here we have the genesis of a fixation.*' 'By doing this the child was enabled to refrain from screaming and disturbing her parents.' 'She thus kept at bay the fear of starvation and the dread of losing her parents, as well as the screaming attacks upon them. . . .' The writers end, 'We shall now formulate briefly certain general conclusions about the causes of fixation and regression to which we are brought by the closer *study* of infants and young children.'

I should like to emphasize that for the moment I am not concerned with the validity of these interpretations or conclusions but with the scientific methodology of the writers. This can be described quite simply as 'begging the question'.

Now as to the conclusions. These have to be divided into two groups. For instance: 'We have now learnt that it (the history of the libido) has to be brought into relation with all other mental phenomena at every stage.' 'We would emphasize that feelings and the vicissitudes of feeling are always essential data for the understanding of any phase of libidinal development or of development as a whole.' So far so good. We have learned that in psychoanalysis, the history of libido is important and that affect is important! This indeed we learnt a long time ago. Then comes a conclusion of the second order: '. . . development of the libido cannot be understood without reference to feelings of anxiety and the situations and impulses which give rise to anxiety'. The crux of this statement is not the generalization but the significance of the term 'situations'. For who tells us of the situations but the analyst, who has first of all *interpreted* certain data and *postulated* the situations?

Then follows a discussion of the role of aggression as a prime cause of fixation: the anxiety caused by aggression induces libido fixation as a defence. Here is interpolated the usual process of Kleinian interpretation. We cannot, say the authors, appreciate this without understanding the 'phantasies'. Yes, but what do the authors mean by phantasy? Remember that they have extended the term beyond all scientific recognition. (And, by the way, it isn't relevant to quote Freud as the authors do at this point, i.e. that he said 'hysterical symptoms spring from phantasies': he did; but he attached a precise meaning to the word 'phantasy', one that the authors reject as incomplete.) And so we are again presented with the familiar Kleinian phantasies of destroying the desired object by devouring, expelling, poisoning, burning, etc., of the ensuing dread of total loss of the 'good' object, of the dread of retaliation, and of the threat to

714

the subject's own body from the destroyed and dangerous 'bad' objects – in other words *ex parte* interpretations and reconstructions. Going on, the authors quote from Mrs Klein's book *The Psychoanalysis of Children* [Klein 1932] on the significance of animal phobias. Underlying it (the animal phobia) would be 'not only the fear of being castrated but a still earlier fear of being devoured by the superego'. [See p. 694.] Coming events cast their shadow before. Looking back it is now clear that a more acute examination of these and many other earlier statements would have prevented the build-up of new metapsychologies such as those we are now discussing. And so the story goes on: It is a short step to the explanation of paranoia; the phantasy of the dangerous devouring father leading to the abandonment of the heterosexual position. The mixing of psychoanalytical commonplace passing apparently as a new discovery, the interpolation of interpretations, the forming of conclusions (discoveries) on the strength of interpretations is kept up throughout the paper. But on occasion the most controversial formulations consist of conclusions drawn from conclusions based on interpretations. Sometimes these further conclusions are openly stated: at others they are only suggested. For example: discussing the significance of oral fixation and describing how the dread of the 'destroyed internal object' can only be allayed by continual oral pleasure, the authors go on to dispense with one of the mixtures I have described. 'Successful genitality in men and women alike is actually dependent on specific impulses, feelings and phantasies belonging to the oral phase.' Now part of this formulation is a very old story, although formerly it was much more accurately expressed by Freud in other terms. But what are these 'phantasies'? None other than the familiar set of Klein phantasies. Anyhow, the writers go on, it is not enough to talk of oral displacement: 'the oral phantasies and aims have remained uninterruptedly active in the unconscious mind exerting (in the instance in question) a favourable influence and promoting genitality'. This is due to the incorporation of a 'good' breast. 'This good internal object helps the subject to find a good external object once again in the genital phase and to *feel* (my italics) that his impulses towards it cherish and feed and give life.' 'Bound up with these phantasies, moreover, are the reparative wishes.' 'Genitality breaks down and regression comes about when the reparative tendencies are disturbed.' This brings into operation also the dread of the ' "bad" internal object'. 'In our view, the part played by internal objects and the superego is an essential factor in the regressive process.' [See p. 697.]

Now here again I am not concerned for the moment with the

validity of the details, although it is to be noted that both biologically and psychologically they contradict what we know of genital development in the child. The important phrases are 'remained uninterruptedly active' and 'exerting' an 'influence' that is distinct from displacement. What precisely does this mean? You may perhaps remember that in my general criticism of Mrs Isaacs' first paper I said that she not only confused the unconscious with the preconscious but that she in effect postulated the existence of an enclave in the Freudian unconscious having the same relationship to the dynamic unconscious as, in Freud's view, the dynamic unconscious has to the preconscious. Well, here, expressed in more familiar terminology, or, as I would say, disguised by more familiar terminology is this remarkable theory, one which I hold subverts the whole of Freudian teaching. It is on this Kleinian formulation that I base my statement that Kleinians deny the primary significance of the Oedipus complex.

Now to come back to the details and to choose the factor of reparation, it is to be noted that this essentially obsessional mechanism is displaced backwards from the later phases of infancy and childhood to the phase of oral relations to objects. Interestingly enough the quotation from Freud given by the writers at this point in support of their own views is taken from a paper on the obsessional neurosis.

In the next part of the paper, the authors return to the subject of the life and death instincts in order to show that their views are merely a confirmation of changes required by Freud's own later work. The first significant statement is the following, 'Bringing together what we have learnt from Freud, Abraham, and Melanie Klein . . . *we come to see* (my italics) the correlation between libido and aggression'. No one of course objects to bringing together what we have learned from Freud and Abraham but I must, at the risk of tedium, repeat that what we are at present discussing is the validity of Mrs Klein's views and in particular of her later and more independent formulations. This 'bringing together' process has been one of the main sources of confusion in this series of discussions. Anyhow, the point adduced by the writers is that in regression there is, together with libidinal changes, a concurrent change in the destructive impulse, a return to earlier, archaic aims. They go on: 'The question now arises whether regression is not the outcome of a failure of the libido to master the destructive impulses and anxiety aroused by frustration. We believe that this is so.' They cite the reactions at the menopause: the decline of sexual productivity deprives women of a redeeming feature of the first magnitude. In

716

theoretical support of their views the writers quote Freud on the subject of fusion of instinct . . . viz., 'the fact that what we are concerned with are scarcely ever pure instinctual impulses, but mixtures in varying proportion of the two groups of instinct'. [Freud quoted, see p. 702.]

Now here again, apart from the details of the Kleinian position, there are a number of important principles at stake. One main consideration appears to be neglected by the writers although there is a good deal of biological as well as psychoanalytical evidence for it. Emphasis is frequently laid by the writers on the fact that analysts in the past put too exclusive emphasis on the role of the libido in regression because the libido was the first instinctual energy to be studied. Whereas the truth is that libidinal regression was singled out because of the *nature* of the libido. It is a commonplace that despite their adhesiveness, libidinal impulses are by comparison with other instincts remarkably labile. It is this lability which, together with the prolonged history of modification of the sexual impulse and of its components, prepares the way for subsequent regressions, in other words the reversal of this process is the main feature of regression. The sexual impulses can change their aims as well as their objects. Aggressive impulses may change objects but modify their aims to a comparatively small degree. It is true that certain varieties of fused impulse appear to behave as if the sadistic component had a specific aim but it should not be forgotten that the libido acts as the pilot impulse in the situation. It is therefore in the highest degree improbable that regression operates primarily through the aggressive series. This is supported by the constant reactive function preserved by aggressive impulses. It should be added that quite apart from the fact that Kleinian phantasy-systems are at present in dispute, phantasies alone cannot be taken as a proof of the significance or specificity of dynamic factors, and this for a number of reasons, in particular that the phantasies interpreted by analysts are frequently of an *ad hoc* variety having no great bearing on either fixation or regression.

Finally on this question of regression and defusion, the fact that fusion takes place 'regularly and very extensively' (to quote Freud) does not absolve us from the necessity of making a clinical distinction between recognized fusions such as anal-sadism and instinct drives in which the destructive or libidinal aims respectively predominate. It is here that clinical perspective is necessary. If arguments concerning regression are to be based on the study of instincts which, clinically regarded, represent an important fusion, the question of the specific influence of libidinal and of aggressive components must obviously be begged. Moreover the function of aggression in the service of libidinal drives, to say nothing of its general reactive function, would lose much of its accepted significance.

Some final quotations from Dr Heimann's and Mrs Isaacs' paper. 'We may speculate about the instincts, but our *convictions* (my italics) are derived from psychological observation, from the investigation of behaviour, feelings, emotions, phantasies.' But these phantasies, as I have said, are based on the interpretations, in other words are speculations. And as we have seen, Kleinian definition includes as phantasies, activities, and presentations that Freud designated quite otherwise. Let us therefore paraphrase the sentence: 'We may speculate about the instincts but our convictions are derived from speculations as to the meaning of behaviour, feeling, emotions.' And again: 'The *phantasies* (authors' italics) associated with the various organs and their functions decide the issue psychologically. The first zones of instinctual experience are *charged with phantasies* (my italics) of a strongly aggressive order.' And finally: 'Narcissism is in our view bound up with the subject's relation to his internal objects. Regression would thus involve the internal object system of phantasies and feelings.' [See p. 708.]

The foregoing are but a few of the points in Dr Heimann's and Mrs Isaacs' paper calling for criticism. A complete examination would require more space than the paper itself. It remains however to draw some general conclusions as to the method and *tendency* of the presentation, in particular its bearing on any future papers that may be given by Mrs Klein or her adherents. For in many instances the *policy* of even the most theoretical argument permits one to make accurate inferences as to the clinical validity of the conceptions on which the argument is based. Thus (to return for a moment to the Kleinian extension of the definition of phantasy) it is obvious that if interpretations of 'phantasy' require, as a necessary condition of (or preamble to) their acceptance, a major extension of the hitherto accepted definition of the term, then it is unlikely that the new 'phantasies' will conform to the scientific standards previously stipulated.

Assessing the paper in this way, and so far it is the only way one can do so, we come to see that, together with the earlier papers on phantasy and on introjection, it is intended to pave the way for the acceptance of whatever interpretations of clinical data Mrs Klein may care to present to us. The main difference between this paper on regression and the earlier metapsychological paper is that it has a more immediate bearing on current clinical problems. It is in fact more subversive of Freudian *clinical* teaching. The tendencies it manifests can be briefly summed up as follows: To ascribe a predominating influence to defensive (negative) systems in psychic development. This appears to be a general tenet of the Klein system. To the extent that this factor is singled out, the influence of the more positive (libidinal) factors is scaled down biologically as well as psychologically. The theory that fixation is a reaction to aggression is merely a special illustration of this main Kleinian viewpoint. For if fixation can be regarded as a reaction to (result of) aggression and if regression itself works backwards through an aggression series, it follows that progression must be attributed to the same factors.

The ascribing of a primary and *lasting* influence of oral aggression is however much more than mere emphasis on an early factor of aggression. This theory forms the basis of an entirely new 'system' alleged to operate in the unconscious. It implies the existence of an independent and dynamic core to the unconscious. This concept of a primary and independent core to the true unconscious is of course an inevitable consequence of the assumptions made regarding 'phantasy' and 'introjection'; i.e., even if the writers disclaimed any responsibility for this core theory, this could only be because they had not realized the implications of their own thesis. For if their 'phantasies', and 'internal object' formations and 'fixations' exist already at 12 months (as they imply in the case already quoted) and if regression works back to this period of oral, anal, and genital aggression (as they imply) and if, further, reality sense is *derived* (or split off) from the original phantasy nexus, it follows that there is an independent and permanently active core to the *unconscious* through which *all* instinct must always pass.

In addition to these tendencies, the Klein system is reinforced by some 'two-way' systems. One concerns the nature of instinct. Despite the emphasis laid on aggression, the writers are careful to emphasize this element of fusion with libido. By so doing they provide themselves with an avenue of escape, should their favoured thesis become inconvenient. The second two-way argument concerns the nature of anxiety. It is described as a primary reaction to aggression. Anxiety, they say, arises from aggression. This statement is covered by another, namely, 'It is evoked by the aggressive components in the pre-genital stages of development.' (Whether these are independent components or fused components is not stated at this point.) Anyhow, they go on to say that further anxiety can be evoked by libidinal frustration and consequent further aggression and hate. They would no doubt say that there is no contradiction in this, that the difference depends on the immediacy of the precipitating cause. But the system remains nevertheless a 'two-way' system in that the writers can say they do not neglect libidinal factors. Incidentally, it seems curious that libidinal energies which, according to the authors, have such effective power that they can neutralize the forces of aggression which are (again according to the writers) the immediate cause of so much anxiety, that these so effective forces cannot apparently give rise to direct anxiety when themselves frustrated. It is further true that in the next paragraph the writers say that frustration initiates regression, 'But, in our view, it does so not only by a simple "damming-up" of libido, but also by evoking hate and aggression and consequent anxiety.' But in view of the persistent emphasis on the factor of aggression this reservation does not seem to have much practical value.

Studying these tendencies we are in my opinion entitled to infer –

(a) that an entirely new and non-Freudian theory of neurosogenesis *must* be maintained by the Klein group;

(b) that the Oedipus factor in neurosogenesis *must* be regarded by them as a secondary factor in neurosogenesis;

(c) that the practice of interpretation followed by Mrs Klein and her adherents *must* differ radically from and be opposed to the accepted practice of Freudian interpretation. In all likelihood the practice will be more extensively non-Freudian than even the theories suggest;

(d) that the role of *actual* 'good' mother will nevertheless become a central assumption in all Kleinian arguments of the influence of environment (i.e., instinctual objects) on the child's development.

DR W. HOFFER: From discussions of controversial topics, which were our original intention, this series has developed into formulations about the fundamental principles of two sets of theories, the Freudian on the one hand and the Kleinian on the other. The two previous papers dealt with Mrs Klein's theory of the primary content of the unconscious (early phantasies) and with her new theory of instincts (special concept of the death instinct). This third contribution presents Mrs Klein's new theory of neuroses.

I realize from the previous discussions that disagreement with Mrs Klein's new theories may easily be taken as opposition against any change or progress in the theory of psychoanalysis. But the history of psychoanalysis shows that analysts have repeatedly been faced with new theories and conceptions and had to deal with this situation by either accepting or rejecting them. It has never been doubted that psychoanalytical theory, as any other theory, is open to emendation;

but, in every single case, the question remains whether new theoretical conception invalidates or enriches the accepted theory.

Comparison of the two sets of theories has shown already that, through the Kleinian approach, certain important elements of the Freudian conception have either been put out of action altogether or have been superseded in importance by new conceptions. This has been under discussion concerning the role of the primary processes, of auto-erotism in early childhood, of the pleasure principle, of the libido theory, and of the theories of anxiety and neurosis.

In my opinion it is the different conception of the onset and content of the Oedipus complex which is the basis of the deviations of the Kleinian from the Freudian view of neurosis, of fixation and regression. According to Freud's theory the Oedipus complex begins in the third year approximately; no doubt future observations under better conditions than hitherto possible will increase our knowledge of this central subject in many respects. The Oedipus complex, in its vivid and dramatic form, is a new constellation at this age, though it is, of course, built on the previous phases of the libido-development, the development of object relationship and of the ego. The claim that such a structure (an early stage of the Oedipus complex or an early Oedipus phase) exists and operates in the infant's mind from the beginning, is alien to Freud's theory and is entirely based on Mrs Klein's assumption of the so-called 'early phantasies'. Various contributors to these discussions have already rejected or at least thrown doubt on the scientific validity of this assumption. The Freudian concept of an Oedipus complex in the second half of the first infantile period is not assumed but based on observation and experience.

An essential prerequisite of the Freudian Oedipus complex is the attainment of the phallic phase. Phallic activities gradually take the place of the oral and anal-sadistic pre-genital activities utilizing for and subordinating to the phallic aims whatever has been left of the former. It is misleading when Dr Heimann and Dr Isaacs suggest that the first genital activities of the male infant (erections) should be considered as signs of an early onset of the phallic phase. Freud made it clear that – in his view – the primary phase of genital excitation (infant masturbation) is to be attributed to the general erotogenicity of the whole body surface and not to be considered as an activity of true phallic character. To distinguish between the penis as an erotogenic zone merely and the penis as an organ with active penetrating phallic characteristics, is not unimportant for the understanding of the various sexual disturbances of later life.

A second necessary step for the formation of the Oedipus complex in the Freudian sense is the ability to choose an object. There is, of course, no doubt that objects play a role in the infant's life long before the formation of the Oedipus complex. But it should be kept in mind that there is a fundamental difference between making use of an object for any kind of instinctual satisfaction and the real choice of an object. Between these two there lies an important step in development, the progress from auto-erotism and narcissism to object-love, from the mere wish to use to a desire to preserve the object. For the male child this means that the mother no longer plays only the role of giver and protector, she also becomes the receiver and the protected one. This is not achieved by a mere change from passivity (passive receiving) to activity (active giving) but is the manifestation of the preponderance of active male drives in the child of that age. It is genuine masculine activity, though usually short-lived under cultural conditions. The attitude towards the father (men) changes at the same time. So far he was either a stranger, causing fear, or he was used like the mother as a protector against fear and frustration. Now in the face of phallic activity and first object-choice, the father becomes, gradually of course, the centre of a double conflict. He is a competitor of the boy's desire to win the mother to satisfy his new instinctual phallic aims, and he is at the same time the source of a conflict of ambivalence. This ambivalence, love-hate-competition-admiration-fear, etc., will make its contribution to the further development of the male to inhibitions of phallic activity, to pleasure in passive traits and homosexuality.

The final outcome of the Oedipus conflict is the castration-complex. It signifies that the boy's wishes for contact with the mother have been frustrated. From now on he uses or may use this experience to combat instinctual desires by developing castration fear or by being threatened with castration by his superego. In the combination of the two facts, the acquisition of castration fear and the postponement of maturity until puberty (dichronous onset of sexuality) Freud saw the most direct aetiology and one of the three basic causes of neurosis.

According to Freud's view it is the happenings of this stage which decide about the onset of infantile neurosis. Under the strain of the Oedipus conflict the phallic organization may break down; due to anxiety caused by the intervention of the ego and superego the phallic aims are renounced and regression takes place to fixation points on former pre-genital levels. Thus it is impossible to decide whether a given pre-genital phase will prove pathogenetic or not before the phallic phase has given evidence of either its stability or instability. The comparative instability of the phallic phase has, in

Freudian theory, always been ascribed to an interaction of several factors, such as: the castration complex itself as the most recent agent; the pre-genital fixation points working from the past; and lastly (a) the constitutional differences in the comparative strength of pre-genital tendencies on the one hand and the genital organization on the other, (b) the bisexual constitution.

Mrs Klein in her earlier contributions had made it her task to collect ample evidence for the working of one of these three factors, namely the disturbances caused by pre-genital experience in the oral and anal-sadistic stage. At this time, though through Mrs Klein's findings in child analysis pathogenic emphasis was shifted to ever earlier levels of experience, her main theory of the formation of infantile neurosis remained the same as Freud's. Divergence of opinion about this central point arose when Mrs Klein, on the basis of the theory of the death instinct, formulated a new theory of neurosis (as outlined by Dr Friedlander). According to this theory the neurotic conflict, instead of taking place between the ego and the instincts, is rooted in the antagonism between the life and death instincts. Since this antagonism (unlike the Freudian conflict) is present in all living matter from the onset, it is only logical that the outbreak of infantile neurosis is in Mrs Klein's views not postponed until the onset of the phallic phase or the full development of the Oedipus complex or a certain stage of ego development, but can take place at any phase of the infant's life whatever its stage of libidinal or ego development. Thus the difference in the application of the theory of the death instinct accounts for the different dating of the outbreak of infantile neurosis.

A second and equally important point of divergence then concerns the pathogenic role of the sexual instinct as compared with the pathogenic role of the destructive instinct. As exemplified in the paper on Regression, the sexual significance of an action does not give rise to conflict with consequent neurotic development; such development is in Kleinian theory always taken to be due to the destructive admixture to the libidinal tendencies. According to Freud, the neuroses are the specific diseases of the sexual function, according to Mrs Klein's theory, the neuroses might be called the specific diseases of the destructive function. Since on all pre-genital levels and also on the genital level destructiveness and libido appear fused, this differentiation may be of minor practical value: it merely points to the specific element in the mixture which is mainly responsible for pathological development. But where theoretical considerations are concerned, this new point of view has the most far-reaching consequences. To name only one problem: is it to be understood that incest is forbidden and incestuous wishes become repressed because of the pre-genital destructive element contained in them and not because of the forbidden wishes for possession of the mother which bring the boy in conflict with the father (Oedipus complex)?

These main differences in the conception of the neurotic conflict are closely connected with other fundamental divergences, as for instance about the role and source of anxiety. In the Kleinian conception the conflict between the two primary instincts is the basis for the formation of anxiety since the destructive instinct continuously claims for oral primacy. 'Anxiety arises from aggression' (Dr Heimann and Dr Isaacs), thus sexuality as a source of anxiety no longer counts and the 'actual neurosis' so successfully upheld by Freud (1926) must be assumed to be definitely abolished. The Kleinian assumption that anxiety plays its part in the forward move of the libido has no counterpart in Freudian theory, which ascribes such progression to the normal biological forces operative in development. According to the Kleinian view the main pathogenic element in instinctual life is the tendency towards defusion which exists under all conditions.

DR KATE FRIEDLANDER: I have in my discussion remarks so far dealt with three aspects of the divergences in theory. I have first of all called attention to the fact that in Mrs Klein's theory the mechanism of regression has no place any more, and I have tried to show that this fact is the result of the giving up of the theory of libidinal development. I have then tried to show why the evidence put foward in favour of the so-called early phantasies is entirely inconclusive and that other evidence is called for, and I think you are all aware of the fact that this question of mine has never been answered. I have lastly tried to show the differences in the interpretation of the life and death instincts in Freud's and Mrs Klein's theory.

In the present paper on regression all these three aspects play a role again and their influence on the theory of neurosis becomes clearer than in the other papers. However, I shall not deal with the new theory of neurosis, which emerges in this paper, but rather concentrate on two points which are also connected with my former discussion remarks. The first will be to show the changes which the conception of regression undergoes in Mrs Isaacs' and Dr Heimann's paper from the beginning of the paper to the end and, secondly, I want to point out the differences in what Freud called the aggressive instincts and what Mrs Klein calls destructiveness.

In the beginning of the paper Freud's views on regression are summarized with special emphasis on the fact that the classic view regards the damming-up of libido as the cause for regression. It is then stated that the conception of regression needs to be reconsidered in the light of Freud's work on the life and death instinct and in view of Mrs Klein's work. I have already emphasized in my last contribution that Freud himself did not think it necessary to change his views in his formulations on regression after his work on the life and death instincts. He would have had ample opportunity to do so, but whenever after 1919 he referred to regression it was to his early conception which he still thought valid. That Mrs Klein's theories necessitate a review of the conception I have pointed out in my first contribution to these discussions.

What are the alterations in the conception of regression? We hear first [see p. 697] that frustration which causes in Freud's view regression does so not simply by the damming-up of libido, but by evoking hate and aggression and anxiety. This newly evoked hate and aggression reactivate the pre-genital sadism, and this in its turn pulls back the libido to its earlier forms, in order to neutralize the destructive forces. In this formulation we see already how the libido recedes into the background and is regarded not so much as the original driving force but as a neutralizer for the much more potent destructiveness. I want to point out that already in this formulation the conception of regression is not applied any more in its original sense, as it is apparently thought that pre-genital sadism can be evoked by aggressive feelings at the genital level directly if frustration occurs. Why that should be is not explained.

We then hear further [see p. 699] that progression is so to speak the complementary process to regression. If we hear that 'these opposite tendencies, progression and regression, are at work all the time in mental life' of young children, we become aware that again the term 'regression' is used with a different meaning to what the paper set out in the beginning. This sentence can only mean that in very young children, the normal development is disturbed by setbacks. Let us say that in the process of becoming clean times of good development change with a going back to bad habits. But when we take as a foundation for this discussion on regression the point of view set forth in the beginning of the paper, these developmental fluctuations are not yet regressions, and what is called progression would be regarded by us as the normal process of development.

Finally [pp. 704–5] when dealing with fusion and defusion of instincts, we hear still another explanation of regression. That seems to imply that there occurs first a partial defusion of instincts, and this defusion would bring about a strengthening of destructive instincts, and this in its turn causes aggression. Suddenly in the midst of a discussion of whether when regression has taken place a defusion of instincts follows, the whole process is turned round and we hear that the defusion of instincts is the primary cause which brings about the regression, and not the other way round.

So from the beginning of the paper where the conception of regression in Freudian terms is stated to the end of the paper, after this conception has been brought in contact with various other conceptions of Mrs Klein's theory we are left with nothing in our hand any longer. The conception of regression has vanished into thin air, first becomes an antithesis to progression and then a result of a partial defusion of instincts. The reason why this happens is very easy to see. Somehow the paper starts with the mistaken idea that when Freud described regression he was unaware that aggression exists. That he meant that only the libido regresses and the admixture of aggression does not. Therefore Mrs Klein cannot understand that Freud did not alter his concept of regression when he discovered the death instinct. This of course is an entirely wrong interpretation of Freudian theory. Freud, as also quoted by Mrs Isaacs and Dr Heimann on page [704] in this paper, has drawn attention to the aggressive aspect especially when he described the results of regression. 'The Ego will recoil with astonishment from promptings to cruelty and violence which enter consciousness from the Id.' [See Freud 1926:68.] Owing to the fact that the libido takes on pre-genital forms, the aggression is foreign to the ego and therefore has to be repressed. The discovery of the life and death instinct and even before that the description of the different nature of hate from love in 'Instincts and Their Vicissitudes' allowed of a theoretical explanation of processes which in their empirical form have long been known. Mrs Isaacs and Dr Heimann are of course justified in saying that regression was described in terms of libido. But at that time the aggression seen to be so predominant at the anal–sadistic level was still believed to come from the same source as the libido. So when Mrs Isaacs and Dr Heimann state that in their view there is a regression of destructive impulses as well, this idea is by no means original, but is contained in the classic view on regression. That also explains why Abraham in his 'A Short Study of the Development of the Libido' (Abraham 1924) does not especially refer to the death instinct, though the theory was of course known to him. This theory does not alter anything in the conception of regression, as the clinical facts which have led to the theory were known long before.

The fact that aggressive as well as libidinal instincts are modified

726

when regression takes place, belongs to the old Freudian theory, as I have just tried to point out. Nevertheless there is an important difference in Mrs Klein's theory on aggressions and in the Freudian theory, a difference which falls under two headings: the first is the relative importance of aggressive tendencies in the theory of the causation of a neurosis. Mrs Klein believes a neurosis to be caused by the awakening of aggressions, while we believe that the causation is still a libidinal frustration and the resulting aggressions a result of frustrated libido. This difference is of utmost importance, as it has a bearing not only on therapy but also on the prevention of neurosis. I shall not deal with this aspect today. The second difference is to be seen in the qualitative change which the aggressive instincts have undergone in Kleinian theory. In order to describe this qualitative change in what we call the aggressive or destructive instincts, I have to repeat what I have explained in my former contribution. If we were able to observe the death instinct directly it would appear to us in the form of a quiet force working against the wish to live. The aggressions which we can actually observe owe their noisy nature to the admixture of libido, and they owe their object-cathexis also to the libidinal admixture. It is certainly against Freud's description of the death instinct that something equivalent to object cathexis could take place. I refer to Mrs Hoffer's contribution who has dealt with this aspect in the last discussion. Now Mrs Klein does not deny, and Mrs Isaacs has devoted special attention in this contribution to the fact that we can only observe and have constantly to deal with fusions of instincts, even at the pre-genital level. So that we can assume that the so-called destructive phantasies of Mrs Klein's theory are considered by her to contain libidinal elements as well. Nevertheless it is certainly justified to try to compare the libidinal and destructive tendencies at each stage with one another, and Freud as well as Abraham have done so. On page [699] we hear what this comparison looks like in Kleinian theory. We hear first about the libidinal aim to suck as opposed to the destructive aim of sucking out, scooping out, emptying, exhausting. These destructive aims of the early oral phase are said to be contained in the so-called early phantasies, the existence of which is doubted by all but the Kleinian analysts. The reasons for this doubt have been given in the contributions to the paper on phantasy. What is so striking about these assumed early destructive aims is their complexity as compared with the structure of the first libidinal aims. To give an example: in sucking, irritation of the erogenous zone, the mucous membrane of the mouth, causes tension which is alleviated by the rhythmical movement. This is pleasurable and therefore calls for repetition. This

727

is a very simple mechanism of a predominantly biological nature at the very start. The psychological implications arise and develop later on from this primary aim. The mechanism of the destructive aim as postulated by Mrs Isaacs and Dr Heimann would be quite different. The tension caused by the instinct would drive to sucking out. Sucking out differs from sucking in that it implies the tendency of damaging the other person. That would presuppose a complete object relationship at the early sucking stage which we do not believe exists.

Most astonishing is the second opposition: 'The libidinal pleasure in biting is experienced along with the destructive impulse of devouring.' Now biting certainly contains an aggressive element and has so far always served as the example by definition for the first observable aggressive behaviour of the baby. It contains of course a libidinal element as well, we are agreed on the fusion of instincts, but it is certainly a definite modification of the theory of the instincts to set it in opposition to a destructive aim of devouring. And I think with this example I can show best the difference in the interpretation of aggressiveness in the two theories. Devouring sounds more destructive to the grown-up, it again contains the element of destroying the other person with the aim to do so. But again this expression of the aggressive instinct shows itself in its very first appearance by the intention to destroy the other person in the most sadistic manner, at a time when we believe that there is no conception yet of the outer world to that extent. The instinct behind that aim is not thought any longer to be a biological tendency, striving for relief of an organic tension, but a purely psychological tendency, which can be relieved by the physical action. The theory is not any longer that the complicated emotional life of the grown-up is built up by the vicissitudes of instincts, but that not only crude primary emotions but complicated emotional attitudes are in existence prior to and more important than biological instinctual urges. My main point in this connection is that what Mrs Isaacs and Dr Heimann describe as destructive aims as co-ordinated to certain libidinal aims is different in structure from a primary instinctual aim altogether.

Mrs Klein feels justified to nominate early destructive aims of that kind by referring to the so-called early phantasies. I have already pointed out that the existence of these phantasies at birth and in the first months of life is disputed and cannot be used as evidence if we take these discussions seriously.

To come back to regression: As was pointed out in Mrs Isaacs' and Dr Heimann's paper, regression does not play any role in the reactivation of destructive tendencies, as hatred experienced at the genital level re-activates pre-genital aggressions without the process of regression. The turning back of the libido to the former stage in order to mitigate the aggressive tendencies is still thought to be due to regression. But as Mrs Klein sees the important motive force in life in the destructive tendencies, for which she formulates primitive aims different in structure from what we know as instinctual aims, regression becomes an unimportant mechanism as dealing only with the libido. If that is so, the result will be, as I have pointed out in my first contribution, an entirely different theory of the neuroses.

That we are really dealing with a different theory becomes very clear at once when an actual example is given. Mrs Isaacs' and Dr Heimann's description of the unconscious content of the conflicts at the menopause are not in accordance with observations and certainly not with analytical experiences. We do not believe that the re-awakening of libidinal wishes at that time is caused by guilt and anxiety. We believe that libidinal wishes are increased, as observation shows, prior to the actual menopause owing to a hormonological upheaval. It is in accordance with this view that menopausal neurosis has decidedly diminished during the last two decades when sexual life prior to the menopause was under less restrictions, and also that menopausal neurosis was more common in virgins than in married women with children. That sexual satisfaction is more difficult to obtain at that time of life is due not, as Dr Heimann put it, to women being 'haunted by the fear of becoming unattractive and old' but to the fact that that really is so. If unable to cope with this conflict, a neurosis may be the result, but clinical experience against shows that one meets much more often with hysterical than obsessional symptoms at that time (in formerly healthy women). This again shows that only in rare cases does regression to the anal-sadistic stage take place. In even rarer cases an involutional melancholia may occur and then one might meet with the one or other of the unconscious phantasies as described by Mrs Isaacs and Dr Heimann. To take psychotic phantasies like the one of the 'barren inside' and present them as the normal occurrence in the menopause must necessarily lead to wrong conclusions. It seems to me that the old theory of the damming up of libido is much better able to explain the known facts in a comprehensive way than the theory of primary destructiveness as being the main force in psychic happenings.

Eighth
Discussion of Scientific Differences

*Discussion held on February 16th, 1944 –
conclusion of discussion on
Dr P. Heimann's and Dr S. Isaacs' paper
on 'Regression'*

Dr Payne was in the chair and 14 Members were present (Miss
Sharpe, Major Bowlby, Major A. Stephen, Dr Franklin, Dr
Gillespie, Dr Winnicott, Dr Usher, Mrs Milner, Miss Evans, Mr
Money-Kyrle, Dr Herford, Dr Heimann, Mrs Riviere, Mrs Klein).
Four guests were present.

Two announcements were made by the Chairman before the Agenda
was opened:

1 Members were informed that it had been decided to postpone
   Mrs Klein's second paper in the series of Scientific Discussions
   (on the 'Oedipus Complex') until after the summer holidays in
   order to have more time for scientific papers which Members
   want to read.
2 Dr Winnicott had informed the Chairman that a contribution he
   had made at a meeting of the Howard League for Penal Reform
   to a discussion on 'Birching' had been reported badly and
   without his permission in the *News Chronicle*. Dr Winnicott had
   copies of a correct version and can let Members who are
   interested have a copy.

DR P. HEIMANN (formally replying in her own and Dr Isaacs'
name to previous discussion. Dr Isaacs absent owing to illness):

Introduction

We have gathered from various quarters that the majority of
Members have grown weary of this 'controversy'. We ourselves

730

understand this feeling very well, and in large measure share it. In so far as these discussions have taken on the character of a mere 'controversy', they are not and cannot be fruitful. But such an approach to the discussions was not our intention nor that of the Committee. The value they should have in the long run would lie in their leading to clearer formulations of existing views, and of the relationships between earlier and later work, together with any modifications of earlier or later theories which may turn out to be necessary. As Mrs Isaacs said in her first contribution, 'The attempt to summarize and recapitulate a long series of researches . . . usually leads one not only to clarify obscure points and amplify what has perhaps been stated in too condensed a form but often also to see fresh angles of approach and new light upon particular problems. It is to be hoped that this will happen with these papers and discussions.' We ourselves would not have been willing to enter upon the discussions had we not had such a hope.

We associate ourselves here with Dr Brierley's remarks in her recent paper. She emphasized that every practitioner has something to contribute to theory. Moreover to keep an enquiring mind on theoretical issues makes one's practical work more fruitful.

We ourselves have wished our papers in these discussions to be a stimulus to scientific enquiry on the part of every Member. We have hoped that the Members as a whole would not only read the papers in succession, but would also be willing to study in detail the facts and theories put forward – to compare the papers with each other on detailed points, to compare them all with Freud's own writings, and to test them all with personal experience in practical work. Moreover, what matters in the long run is not so much whether any given view is 'new' or 'different', but whether or not it is true. The progress of psychoanalysis depends upon every Member's being willing to take the trouble to form his own judgement on the various theoretical issues which arise in the discussions.

Metapsychology and clinical facts

At various points, references have been made to metapsychology in general and to our views in particular.

We consider that two fundamental errors have been made by some contributors on this matter.
1 The distinction between metapsychology and clinical facts has been greatly over-emphasized; it has been sharpened so as to constitute a falsehood. Metapsychology, like scientific explanation in general,

consists in the systematic statement of *the relationships between observed data*. It is no less and no more than that.

How does Freud define metapsychology?

It will be only right to give a special name to the way of regarding things which is the final result of psychoanalytical research. I propose that, when we succeed in describing a mental process in all its aspects, dynamic, topographic and economic, we shall call this a *metapsychological* presentation. We must say beforehand that in the present state of our knowledge we shall succeed in this only at isolated points.

[Freud, 1915b:114; SE 14:181][1]

That is to say, in Freud's mind, metapsychology is merely a 'special name' for an exhaustive and systematic study of the relationships between observed clinical data. But it is the clinical data with which he is dealing. There is nothing mystic about metapsychology. It is not concerned with 'things-in-themselves' in the Kantian sense, but with exactly the same empirical facts as we deal with in the consulting room.

Freud has always insisted that psychoanalysis is an empirical science. We have previously quoted passages of his in which he emphasizes, with regard to the concepts 'introduced' for the purpose of systematization, that 'everything depends on their being chosen in no arbitrary manner, but determined by the important relation they have to the empirical material.' [Freud, S. 1915a:60; SE 14:117][2]

2 It is asserted that the views we have presented here were arrived at from an a priori theoretical starting point. We have already emphasized at several places that this is not true. We began from clinical experience with our patients and data observed in everyday life. Mrs Klein's views about early development were the outcome of the strictly analytic technique applied without presuppositions to the behaviour of young children. Similarly, Mrs Isaacs' suggested extension of the term 'phantasy' was based upon many years' practical analytic work, together with study and reflection upon the contributions of other analysts.

When we were asked by the Sub-committee to present our views for the purpose of these discussions, we were not requested to prepare clinical papers. We were expected to give a systematic account of our theoretical standpoint on particular issues, to compare them with other theories, particularly those of Freud, and to bring out the elements of agreement and differences. In such papers clinical data can only be used to illustrate or to make clear particular points of theory. To present the clinical data fully would occupy a far greater time and space than the framework of those discussions could possibly allow.

But the procedure required for exposition in these discussions does not warrant the conclusion – in our case any more than in Freud's or anyone else's – that our actual researches started from a priori assumptions. We very strongly hold, with Freud, that metapsychology 'is the final result of psychoanalytic research'.

One other point which seems often to be forgotten by other contributors is that we were not asked to give the total picture of our psychoanalytic views. We were asked to discuss specific theoretical problems, and have not attempted to do more.

Quotations from Freud

What is the purpose of quoting Freud?
(a) We do so because we were asked to show the links between Mrs Klein's work and Freud's. The Programme Committee specified one of the aims of these discussions is the consideration of 'the nature and degree of any incompatability of differing views'.
(b) Apart from this *ad hoc* purpose, it is for scientific reasons that we turn to Freud's writings. It is in order to learn, not only what he discovered, but also *how* he made his discoveries and how he established the relationship between the various facts he observed. With these aims in view, we think it far better to quote actual passages from Freud than to rely upon our general impressions of his theory. In this way, we enable our readers to see the precise grounds upon which we attribute a given view to Freud, and to examine the quotations in their whole context.

Several contributors have preferred to offer their general impressions on previously formulated accounts of Freud's theories. It seems to us, however, that such a method is less satisfactory because (a) it tends to blur the precise details of Freud's meaning; (b) (of special importance) it tends to blur or deny Freud's own development, the changes in his theories over the forty odd years of his publications, in response to his widening experience and deepening insight. · (Mrs Isaacs drew attention in her last reply to the development occurring in Freud's metapsychology.) And (c) it encourages rigid doctrines which are in the greatest possible contrast to Freud's temper of mind. On looking up the essay from which Dr Hoffer quotes in his present contribution, we noted the following passage from Freud: 'But if I should finally be convicted of erring in the theoretical question of the actual neuroses, I shall console myself with the progress of our knowledge which must devalue the standpoint of the single person.' [Freud, S. 1926:75; SE 20:123] How different this attitude of mind is from the rigid accounts of Freud's theory which some contributors offer!

We shall presently note some particular instances of the disadvantage of preferring general impressions to precise references.

The relation between
earlier and later phases of development

At many points, the relation between earlier and later stages of development has been referred to (e.g., with reference to object relationship, and genital erotism). In her first paper, Mrs Isaacs tried to show that the principle of genetic continuity is no empty generalization, but can be seen operating in detail in every aspect of development, e.g., bodily skill, perception, reasoning, phantasy, object relationship. In human development no mental abilities or functions appear suddenly. Each has a history and each has its primitive roots in the earliest phases. We are not yet able to trace out all the detailed steps of development in each function, but every increase of our detailed knowledge emphasizes the fact that there is continuity and that every function has its rudimentary form from the beginning of extra-uterine life.

Psychoanalysts are not alone in taking the view that the child's mental life is already active in the first days of life. There is a consensus of opinion amongst most psychologists that the new-born infant is far from being a creature of simple reflexes and that, e.g., the rudiments of perception and imagination are inherently present in his earliest responses to stimulus.

E.g., Hazlitt, the distinguished child psychologist and experimentalist, in her chapter on 'Retention, Continuity, Recognition, and Memory', says: 'The favourite game of "peep-bo" which the child may enjoy in an appropriate form from about the *third month* (our italics) gives proof of the continuity and retentiveness of the mind of the very young child. If impressions died away immediately and the child's conscious life were made up of a number of totally disconnected moments this game could have no charm for him. But we have ample evidence that at one moment he is conscious of the change in experience, and we can see him looking for what has just been present and is now gone.' (Our italics.) [Hazlitt 1933:78]

Hazlitt's whole treatment of these problems takes the line that explicit memory grows out of early recognition – i.e., 'any process of perceiving which gives rise to a feeling of familiarity'. She goes on:

> In speaking of the one-month-old child's sucking reaction to the sound of the human voice it has not been assumed that the child recognizes the voices, that there is a conscious experience corresponding to the idea 'voices again'. There may or may not be such conscious experience. . . . As the weeks go by, however, numberless instances of recognition occur in which the child's expression and good behaviour form a picture so like that which accompanies conscious experience of recognition at the later stages that it is difficult to resist the inference that the child is recognizing in the true sense of the word. Records tell of children from 8 weeks onwards appearing to be distressed by strange, and reassured by familiar faces.

And she takes the view that even *judgement* is present from a very early time, in the child's adaptive response, e.g., in the third and fourth months. Hazlitt has no doubt that the very earliest responses of the infant show the rudimentary qualities from which memory, imagination, thinking, etc. develop.

Dr Friedlander, however, in discussing the infant's sucking says: 'in sucking, irritation of the erogenous zone, the mucous membrane of the mouth, causes tension which is alleviated by the rhythmical movement. This is pleasurable and therefore calls for repetition. This is a very simple mechanism of a predominantly biological nature at the very start. The psychological implications arise and develop later on from this primary aim.' [See pp. 727–8.]

On such a view it is hard to see how psychological implications ever do arise. Why should they appear at two years, one year, six months, one month, if they are not inherently present in some rudimentary form from the beginning? Freud did not take such a view, since he so often referred to *instinct* as a 'borderland concept', partaking both of the soma and psyche and as being in existence from the beginning of life. He did *not* say '*first*, of the soma and *then* of the psyche'. And the psyche is not to be narrowed down to conscious images. The whole of Freud's work has demonstrated that the most significant elements are unconscious impulse, affect, and phantasy. If academic psychologists can see the rudimentary beginnings of memory, judgement, etc., in the earliest days, how can *we* possibly deny the rudiments of feeling and unconscious phantasy in the beginning?

735

We shall now take up the bearing of these general conditions upon the specific question of genital erotism.

Dr Hoffer says: 'It is misleading when Dr Heimann and Dr Isaacs suggest that the first genital activities of the male infant (erections) should be considered as signs of an early onset of the phallic phase. Freud made it clear that – in his view – the primary phase of genital excitation (infant masturbation) is to be attributed to the general erotogenicity of the whole body surface and not to be considered as an activity of true phallic character.' [See p. 721.]

On reading this very definite statement by Dr Hoffer, we wrote to him asking him if he would let us have references to the passages in Freud's writings on which it was based. Dr Hoffer replied, 'I had no particular reference in mind when I wrote my remarks but the following three passages in the German edition (Gesammelte Schriften) form the background of my argument.' [Freud, S. 1916–17:38; SE 16: 320–38 and 1905:63; SE 7:327]

We have read again these three passages, as well as Freud's writings generally. (We do not wish to take up space and paper by these long quotations, but ask our audience to look them up.) We ourselves are quite unable to see that they support such an absolute distinction between the earliest genital experiences of the boy and those in the phallic phase.

Now of course we agree that *full understanding* includes recognition of the differences between earlier and later phases; as well as the likenesses; i.e., it requires knowledge of *development*. We have not suggested that the phallic *phase* as such begins in the earliest days, but that phallic *trends* begin to make their appearance whilst the child is still predominantly in the oral phase. (See Mrs Isaacs' paper on February 17.) And there certainly is some overlap between the various phases of libidinal development. The differences between earlier and later genital erotism correspond to the differences between earlier and later stages in all fields of mental development. The fundamental difference is that in the earliest phase the oral libido has the primacy and genital erotism is sporadic and subordinate; whilst in the later phase, which Dr Hoffer calls the 'true' phallic phase, the aims and pleasures of the other erotogenic zones are subordinated to the primacy of the genital and integrated into its service. We know that this carries along with it great changes in the balance of the libidinal and aggressive instincts, as well as qualitative differences in their specific aims. There are also profound changes in the object relationship with which these aims are connected.

But none of these considerations justify the absolute distinction which Dr Hoffer attributes to Freud. Freud himself in various passages, particularly in *Introductory Lectures*, warns us against exaggerating the differences between the infant and the man (e.g., in the 'Three Contributions').

Dr Hoffer [see p. 721] draws attention to the erotism of the body surface as a whole, and we agree that this plays an important role in the child's total libidinal state. But in general psychoanalytic theory, the relation of skin erotism to the various stages of libidinal development has never yet been defined. Experimental studies by non-analytic investigators have, however, demonstrated that during the first ten days of life the sensitivity of the skin is subordinated to oral activity. The sucking reflex can be evoked by gentle touches on the skin of the cheek and by other stimuli. 'Stimulation of the lips of a newborn infant is followed by the sucking reaction in over 90 per cent of the infants of a given age, but a stimulation of the cheeks, eyes, temperature, taste, smell, and so forth, will also produce it. That is to say, sucking is a specific reaction to stimulation of the lips, but it is a reaction to many other stimuli also.' (Chapman Pratt) These experimental facts confirm Freud's theory of the early *primacy* of oral libido.

We do agree that the fully integrated phallic phase, with the primacy of the phallus, is bound up with the full development of the Oedipus complex. But we hold that both have their first rudimentary *beginnings* in the oral phase. Dr Hoffer seems to come very close to our view when he says [see p. 721]: 'The Oedipus complex, in its vivid and dramatic form is a new constellation at this age (i.e. the third year), though it is, of course, built on the previous phases of the libido-development, the development of object relationship and of the ego.' His next sentence, however, seems to suggest that we hold the view that the child is born with the Oedipus complex! This is surely a caricature of anything ever written by Mrs Klein or ourselves.

In reply to the various remarks of Dr Hoffer and Dr Friedlander on our views about object relationships, we do not think we need add anything to what we have previously said on this subject. We accept the fact that our arguments did not convince Dr Hoffer or Dr Friedlander. Meanwhile Mrs Klein's paper on the 'Emotional Life of the Infant' has been circulated which contains further material to substantiate our contention that object relations exist from the beginning of life, as well as references to a number of analytic and non-analytic observers who have arrived at the same conclusion.

We also ask our audience to compare in detail our former comments with such statements as Dr Friedlander's [p. 728] that our views 'presuppose a *complete* (our italics) object relationship at the early sucking stage'. A large part of all our contributions has been concerned with showing some aspects of the way in which object relationships develop from their *rudimentary beginnings*.

Biology and psychoanalysis

Dr Friedlander's remarks about the menopause raise again the general question of the relation between biology and psychoanalysis. She starts, however, from an error in her reference to our description of the menopausal conflict. Dr Friedlander says: 'That sexual satisfaction is more difficult to obtain at that time of life is due not, *as Dr Heimann puts it* [see p. 729] to women being "haunted by the fear of becoming unattractive and old" but to the fact that that really is so.' But we did not say that the fear of becoming old and unattractive made it more difficult to obtain sexual gratification. We wrote: 'in consciousness these anxieties and conflicts' (which we had just enumerated) 'may appear under the guise of being haunted by the fear', etc. Dr Friedlander's argument that the woman is really old and unattractive and for this reason finds it more difficult to obtain sexual satisfaction is thus beside our point. It could, however, be discussed for its own sake, since it is a psychoanalytic commonplace that anxieties and mental conflict tend to lessen the attractiveness of a person of *any* age and also for internal reasons may actually make it more difficult to obtain sexual satisfaction. But even if we leave this out of account and start from the fact that age and the bodily changes resulting from the menopause do in themselves tend to lessen sexual attractiveness, the psychoanalyst is still faced with the question of how and why these bodily effects and experiences are reflected in mental process, how and why these cause psychical conflict. A comparison between the situation in the menopause and the situation in adolescence is indicated. Why should the bodily and instinctual changes in adolescence stir up neurotic conflict? At this time the individual becomes more and not less sexually active, and yet as we all know, the gravest emotional conflicts may break out precisely at this time.

That a hormonological upheaval enters into the phenomena of the menopause no one can doubt, although this does not appear to be of the same intensity in all women and is in itself far from being a solved problem. But this fact does not preclude our psychological interest in the experiences, the anxieties and conflicts at that time – any more than the fact that depression may occur in response to a toxic factor after influenza, as well as in response to an external event such as the death of a loved person, and to endogenous conditions as in melancholia, precludes our interest in the unconscious psychological content of the depression. In each case – whether the immediate stimulus be internal or external – the psychological processes are a proper subject of psychoanalytic investigation.

In our endeavour to understand neurotic conflict at any age, or for that matter normal mental development and normal personality, we are *always* dealing with the mind–body entity. The prime movers of all mental life are the instincts, those borderland dynamic processes which relate both to body and to mind. It is quite possible that the internal secretions of our glands come very close to being the material vehicle of the instincts. They certainly are a vital part of those bodily processes which underlie and give rise to instinctual phenomena. We know that changes in the endocrine balance do affect moods and impulses and phantasies. We also know that things may act the other way round, that emotional conflict may disturb the endocrine balance and that strictly psychological treatment, the solving of emotional conflict by psychoanalysis, can itself act favourably upon the balance of hormones. We can only hope to correlate these two sets of complex phenomena – the bodily and the mental – in an exchange of knowledge with other scientists, such as endocrinologists, if we are willing to explore the psychological processes with the same thoroughness and dispassionateness as the endocrinologists give to their data.

Our problem lies in understanding the ways in which a woman deals with the changes in stimulation arising from the 'hormonological upheaval'. How does she cope with these changes in internal stimuli and with the actual responses of her husband or other people to the alteration in her appearance and personality which may occur at this period? What are the psychological factors that help one woman to overcome these difficulties – which to some extent are bound to arise – and what are the psychological factors that lead another woman to fall a victim to them? We cannot doubt that the degree and the manner in which every woman copes with the problems of the menopause depends in part upon her previous psychological history, for example the extent to which she has overcome her Oedipus complex and her castration phantasies, the ways in which she dealt with her earliest anxieties, as well as the width and stability of her sublimations. Dr Friedlander takes the view that the unconscious phantasies about the 'barren inside' would not be met with except in severe psychotic cases, such as involutional melancholia, and she asserts that our description of the unconscious content of the menopausal conflicts 'is not in accordance

739

with observations and certainly not with analytic experiences'. In her own observations and analytic experiences, Dr Friedlander may not have come across this unconscious content, but this is not true of many other analysts who are familiar with the anxieties and conflicts we describe. They do occur in normal women who cope successfully with the menopausal conflict. It is true that such phantasies and anxieties are much more pronounced in psychotics who – as we know – often give conscious expression to them; while with normal and neurotic women only the analysis of the deeper layers of the mind can reveal them. We hold that no sharp demarcation can be made between the complexes and unconscious phantasies of the normal, the neurotic, or the psychotic person. It is a well-established view in psychoanalysis that there is no difference in this respect between normal and neurotic individuals. Freud said in 'The Origin and Development of Psychoanalysis':

> Let me give at this point the main result at which we have arrived by the psychoanalytic investigation of neurotics, namely, that neuroses have no peculiar psychic content of their own, which is not also to be found in healthy states; or, as C. G. Jung has expressed it, neurotics fall ill of the same complexes with which we sound people struggle. It depends on quantitative relationships, on the relations of the forces wrestling with each other, whether the struggle leads to health, to a neurosis, or to compensatory over functioning.
>
> [Freud, S. 1910: 213; SE 11:50][3]

When speaking of the subdivision of the anal phase, Abraham said:

> In regarding this dividing line as extremely important we find ourselves in agreement with the ordinary medical view. For the division that we psychoanalysts have made on the strength of empirical data coincides in fact with the classification into neurosis and psychosis made by clinical medicine. But analysts, of course, *would not attempt to make a rigid separation between neurotic and psychotic affections.* They are, on the contrary, aware that the libido of any individual may regress beyond this dividing line between the two anal-sadistic phases, given a suitable exciting cause of illness, and given certain points of fixation in his libidinal development which facilitate a regression of this nature.
>
> [Abraham 1924:433 (Our italics)]

To summarize our argument: the combination of factors which Freud in the above-quoted passage mentions in respect of the difference between the normal and the neurotic, in our view explains also the difference between the normal and the psychotic person.

In normal women the anxieties about the 'barren inside' are dealt with and overcome in a great variety of ways, e.g., through the sublimations and the reassurance by good social and sexual relationships. Freud often made it plain that normal mental processes deserve to be analysed as well as the abnormal, for example, in his study of the unconscious mental processes involved in mourning. Freud, Abraham, and others have shown that the analysis of such normal processes of mourning for the loss of a loved person leads to far-reaching conclusions, and that there are many elements in common between mourning and melancholia.

Life instinct and death instinct

In the light of the known evidence, it seems to us a meaningless question to ask whether the libidinal or aggressive impulses are the more important. Dr Friedlander, when contending [p. 729] that we regard destructiveness as 'much more potent' than the libido, makes it clear that in her view the libido is 'the original driving force'. This is not Freud's view, since he speaks of their being always 'blended and intermingled' with each other. We have made it plain at every point of our discussion that we share with Freud this view that the two instincts are always active together in the human mind. They are fused to a greater or lesser extent at every stage of development, the degree of fusion or de-fusion varying in different phases. Each plays its own part and contributes its own characteristic share to every phase and every mental phenomenon.

In her paper, which has been circulated whilst we were writing this reply, Mrs Klein draws attention to certain passages in *Civilization and its Discontents* in which Freud not only emphasizes this omnipresent duality of instinct, but also links their conflict with neurosis. He writes (p. 121): 'guilt is the expression of the conflict of ambivalence, the eternal struggle between Eros and the destructive or death instinct'. And again (p. 122): 'an investigation of the sense of guilt – resulting from the conflict of ambivalence from the eternal struggle between the love and death trends'. [Freud, S. 1930: 121–2; SE 21:132][4] Now if there is an 'eternal struggle' between Eros and the death instinct, we see no significance in any attempt to decide which is the more important. What we have to decipher is the mode of their interplay and the degree of fusion or inter-fusion in each phase and each situation.

741

These passages from Freud may serve also as our answer to Dr Hoffer's question about the Oedipus complex [pp. 723–4 of his contribution]. After speaking (on p. 118 of *Civilization and its Discontents*) of guilt arising in the Oedipus complex, Freud says of the conflict of ambivalence: 'it must express itself in the Oedipus complex, cause the development of conscience and create the first feelings of guilt'. [SE 21:132][5] Then, as just quoted above, he refers both guilt and ambivalence to the 'eternal struggle between the love and the death trends' (p. 121). At another place in the same book he says: 'I am convinced that very many processes will admit of much simpler and clearer explanation if we restrict the findings of psychoanalysis in respect of the origin of the sense of guilt to the aggressive instincts'. [SE 21:138][6] Thus Freud clearly links guilt as it occurs in the Oedipus complex, arising from the murderous wishes of the son towards the father, with the innate conflict of ambivalence. It is thus shown that Freud assumes that the aggression of the son towards the father, stirred by the wish for sexual possession of the mother, and the dread of frustration, have their ultimate source in the primary instinct of destruction. The son wishes to castrate his father and possess his mother; hence he feels that his father will castrate him, rob him of his object of desire, and ultimately destroy all sources of pleasure for him.

This genital rivalry is a manifestation of the destructive impulses on the genital level in the Oedipus situation. Before this is reached, however, the primary instinct of aggression was already at work in other forms and other situations. As we know, hate, possessiveness, envy, and jealousy play a great role in the pre-genital stages.

Under certain conditions, the castration anxiety arising in the Oedipus situation leads to regression to these earlier levels. Among these conditions, as Freud has shown, a major factor is the degree to which fixation has occurred during development. When fixation on earlier levels, e.g., the anal-sadistic, has been marked, the attainment of genital sexuality is imperfect and precarious. Then the anxieties aroused in the Oedipus situation are very apt to lead to regression.

Dr Hoffer speaks as if Freud himself had never connected the neuroses with the destructive instincts. However, Dr Heimann, in her former reply, quoted a passage from *Beyond the Pleasure Principle* (p. 50) which leaves no doubt as to what Freud's view in this respect was: '. . . the fact that they' (the life instincts) 'run counter to the trend of the other instincts which lead towards death indicates a contradiction between them and the rest, one which the theory of the neuroses has recognized as full of significance'. [Freud, S. 1920:50; SE 18:40][7]

The discussion of these points about the relation of the 'eternal struggle' between love and death to the Oedipus complex, and to the theory of neuroses, illustrates once again the general remarks we have made about the value of quoting specifically from Freud's writings. We strongly recommend that contributors should always give the specific references upon which they base their general statements about Freud's views. There is ample evidence that his theories did change and undergo revision from time to time. We have just noted one example in the quotations above from *Civilization and its Discontents*. It is only too easy to forget this in making general statements and to crystallize his views in their earlier form as if this had been Freud's final and definitive theory.

In noting and pursuing such changes in Freud's views, we can also discern the directions in which further researches are required.

With regard to fusion and de-fusion, Dr Friedlander feels that we have at one point suggested that regression leads to de-fusion and at another point that de-fusion leads to regression [see pp. 725–6]. We do not consider the relation between de-fusion and regression to be one of cause and effect, either way. Regression and de-fusion are *different aspects* of the same highly complex phenomenon. We agree fully with Freud when he says in *The Ego and the Id*: 'Making a swift generalization, we might conjecture that *the essence of a regression of libido*, e.g. from the genital to the sadistic-anal level, *would lie in a de-fusion* of instincts' (our italics). [Freud, S. 1923b:57; SE 19:42][8]

It may be useful to state again briefly our views about the interaction of regression and fixation. We know Freud's view that regression becomes possible by virtue of the formation of fixation points. On the journey to genital sexuality, we pass through various points, as it were, stations, in development, and since some part of the libido – together with some part of the aggressive impulses, in our view – is left at these 'stations', we may return to them, may regress. It is worthwhile reminding ourselves that this journey is an internal process and that the stations are inside ourselves. The impulses 'left behind' are actually within ourselves – just as our memories are; and those, we know, are never lost by the psyche which has once experienced them, although they may appear to be. Thus, whilst we are maintaining our libido at the genital level, the earlier 'points' are still uninterruptedly active *in the unconscious*. The manner and the degree in which the pre-genital impulses and phantasies influence our lives depends partly upon the strength of the libido. We tried to show in our paper how, e.g., oral elements may enrich genital experiences, in that the penis, in addition to its genital function as such, may also take over the phantasy functions of feeding and comforting. Some of the pre-genital elements are, however, not suitable to enter genitality, as Freud pointed out in his Encyclopaedia article (e.g. the anal components). [Freud, S. 1923a: 101; SE 18:245]

In the example of menopausal conflicts, the question is not simply, as Dr Friedlander seems to think, that there is a regression to the anal-sadistic stage. Under the stress of the many conflicts involved in the loss of procreation, all the earlier impulses and phantasies may become active. This creates a hard task of psychical adjustment for every woman; yet she may pull through without definitely regressing. This process of combating the freshly stimulated activities of the pre-genital elements is a temporary and fluid condition which is not in itself a regression. The existence of the struggle and the need for a readjustment is a proof of the dynamic potentialities of the fixation points.

Dr Friedlander speaks as if it were Mrs Klein who had introduced the notion that the infant wishes to 'devour' the breast. She contrasts the term 'biting', as being a simple term, descriptive of the first observable aggressive behaviour of the baby, with the term 'devouring', of which she says 'devouring sounds more destructive to the grown-up. It again contains the element of destroying the other person with the aim to do so.' Now here Dr Friedlander has overlooked the fact that *it was Freud* who first introduced the concept of 'devouring' as the infant's primary aim in the oral phase. *In Instincts and their Vicissitudes* (1915) Freud says: 'First among these' (temporary sexual aims) 'we recognize a phase of incorporating or devouring, a type of love which is compatible with abolition of any separate existence on the part of the object.' This is sufficient evidence of the fact that Freud fully recognized an *object relationship* in the primary oral phase, and that he was the first to describe the aim of the oral destructive impulses, bound up with libidinal pleasure, as that of 'devouring', the 'total abolition of the object'. [Freud, S. 1915a: 81–2; SE 14:138][9]

A general remark about the trend of Dr Friedlander's arguments seems in place here. We have taken pains to deal with Dr Friedlander's points, but we think that our arguments cannot become clear unless the audience compares them with Dr Friedlander's contribution. The following assertion of Dr Friedlander illustrates our difficulties. On [p. 727] in the discussion she says: 'It is certainly against Freud's description of the death instinct that something equivalent to object cathexis could take place.' We find it difficult to understand the meaning of this sentence. If Dr Friedlander means that we suggest that it is possible for the death instinct

744

to effect an object cathexis without any participation of the libido, our reply would be: there can be no question of either the libido alone or the aggressive impulses alone effecting an object-cathexis, because this would presuppose hypothetical conditions which never arise, since the primary instincts are always fused. Our investigation can only be concerned with the question: which of the two instinctual components in the fusion is predominant in an object relationship, and thus determines its character? There is no doubt that sometimes the libidinal and at other times the aggressive impulses predominate in an object-cathexis. Regarding the predominantly aggressive object-cathexis, we may quote Freud. Speaking of the case 'in which feelings of love that have not yet become manifest express themselves to begin with by enmity and aggressive tendencies' he says: 'it may be that here the destructive components in the object-cathexis have outstripped the erotic and are only later on joined by the latter' (*The Ego and the Id*, pp. 59–60). And, in the same work: 'An ambivalent attitude is present from the outset and the transformation is effected by means of a reactive shifting of cathexis, by which energy is withdrawn from the erotic impulses and used to supplement the hostile energy.' [SE 19:43–4][10] Again, in *Instincts and their Vicissitudes* (1915), we have Freud's statement that 'the relation of hate to objects is older than that of love. It is derived from the primal repudiation by the narcissistic ego of the external world whence flows the stream of stimuli.' [Freud, S. 1915a:82; SE 14:139][11]

Dr Friedlander challenges our view that the opposite tendencies of progression and regression are at work all the time in the mental life during development, and suggests that this can only refer to 'setbacks' and 'times of good development', with regard e.g. to cleanliness. But the terms 'setbacks' and 'times of good development' are more paraphrases of the scientific terms 'regression' and 'progression'. The different use of terms does not disprove our contention of the fluidity of progressive and regressive elements in early development.

In conclusion, it will have been noted that both Dr Glover and Dr Friedlander have confirmed at several points that a large part of our views on regression are 'not original' but conform with accepted facts and with the views of Freud, Abraham, and other psychoanalysts. Throughout these discussions we have tried to show where on the one hand we are building on well-established theory, and where, on the other, we believe that newly gathered facts require some modification of earlier theories.

THE CHAIRMAN threw the meeting open to discussion.

DR PAYNE (paper): The main difference in the theory put forward in the paper by Mrs Isaacs and Dr Heimann and that postulated by Freud concerns the theory of the death instinct. Mrs Klein suggests that the death instinct plays just as important or a more important part in the causation of neuroses and psychoses than the libido. It is not clear which of these two opinions she holds. This view means that she regards regression and fixation to be caused more by the vicissitudes of the death instinct than by the libido, which is regarded as being mainly concerned in neutralizing the death instinct. Mrs Isaacs says that most analysts will regard anxiety as due to aggression. This is open to argument. I should like to say that in my opinion the value of Mrs Klein's work and insight into early phantasies, particularly the aggressive phantasies, cannot be measured by the suggestion she makes with respect to modification of Freud's metapsychology. Personally I cannot see that her findings require the theory of a death instinct. She has exposed the important role played by aggression and sadism, which Freud and Abraham had already begun to work on, and as she so often points out many of the phantasies and mechanisms which she lays stress on had been recognized by them.

There is no doubt that Freud recognized that libidinal frustration which leads to damming-up of the libido and initiates regression is accompanied by aggressive reactions which he describes in the case of the obsessional neurosis to be due to de-fusion of instinct. Hence he did not deny that aggressive reactions accompanied regression. He had not, however, shown the importance of aggressive phantasies in the way Mrs Klein has done.

The theory of the death instinct when taken out of its philosophical setting where Freud put it presents difficulties and paradoxes which it is hard for scientists to accept. In *Beyond the Pleasure Principle* Freud defines the death instinct as an urge to return to an inanimate state. Descriptively this implies a passive rather than an active state, an inertia, refusal to live, rather than an active destructive impulse.

If we turn to biology for evidence, the question arises as to whether we can observe a death instinct in animals. As a rule animals are aggressive in order to preserve life, they kill for food or because they expect to be killed, and not for the sake of killing.

New-born infants who, in favourable external circumstances, continually refuse food or who will not suck are as a general rule premature, physically weak, mentally deficient, or have experienced excessive shock at birth. They do not cry vigorously but show various degrees of inertia. The impression they give is lack of vitality, virility, or in other words of lack of libido. Manifestations of infantile aggression and anxiety develop and persist, maintaining their infantile characteristics longer than usual, and not undergoing modification as the result of the development of libidinal relationships to the external world of objects, because of lack of libido. But these babies do not scream so much or show as much vigorous aggression as the infant who resents interference with feeding or has to cope with frustration from the external world because his needs are great. In other words, active aggression in the simplest situation presents itself as an expression of a vigorous wish to live.

Very soon of course the psychological situation becomes complicated. Anxiety is aroused at a very early age by helplessness in the face of excessive instinct tension or the experience of pain, and psychical defensive mechanisms begin to operate.

In later life after the menopause when for physical reasons it is obvious that the libido is diminished quantitatively it is a fact that instead of the organism being more at the mercy of a death instinct and therefore liable to an increase of symptoms and anxiety, we find a great diminution in the intensity of psycho-neurotic symptoms such as migraine, claustrophobia, agoraphobia etc. We have instead an increase of involuntary states. I think if we examine clinical facts we shall find more direct evidence that aggression manifested actively is either a defensive reaction or in combination with the libido is manifested as a perversion than that it is a sign of the existence of an active death instinct. If this is true it does not seem to me to lessen the value of Mrs Klein's researches on the importance of aggressive phantasies, and the part they play in influencing psychical development. They only require to be put in the correct relationship dynamically to the libido.

In my opinion we need to weigh carefully the evidence produced by all workers with varying views on these subjects before we make new generalizations.

Free discussion (abstract):

DR WINNICOTT said that Dr Middlemore's observations suggested that inhibition of sucking in certain cases might be due to the infant's fear of its own aggression.

MRS KLEIN said that Freud had described the death instinct clinically in terms of aggression turned outwards. If aggression is directed outward the child will present a different appearance to an inhibited child who is not able to externalize aggression. Her conclusions did not stand or fall on the concept of the death instinct.

Many colleagues had come to conclusions similar to hers without believing in the death instinct. She did not think the difference of opinion need affect later conclusions. It is known that aggression is stirred by frustration, and that the first frustration occurs at birth.

MRS RIVIERE said that Dr Payne appeared to regard the death instinct as an instinct to kill. She regarded the death instinct as an impulse to regain the state of death. The manifest state was an inanimate one, but the instinct must be an urge. Freud called it a mute and a silent force but not a passive and inert one. Then the aggressive tendencies arose through – as Freud put it – the turning outward of that impulse. The aim was then deflected from the death itself into aggression and destructiveness outwards. And that leads to all the phenomena we are accustomed to deal with. The death instinct in action was always fused and could not be distinguished. As Mrs Klein says, in clinical work the two fused impulses struggling for mastery are met with.

DR PAYNE thought that Freud's concept was a philosophical one which made it hard to apply clinically. Of course manifestations of an aggressive instinct are observable everywhere; it is the idea of a link with a death instinct as defined by Freud which is obscure.

MRS RIVIERE said she would like a definition of a philosophical concept. She considered the concept of the death instinct to be biological.

DR BOWLBY said that whatever speculation led Freud to this concept, psychologically it had the character of a scientific hypothesis to explain data. The difficulties he had were: (1) Methodologically: he thought that the death instinct was a more complicated concept than that of an aggressive instinct stimulated by frustration, which explained phenomena fairly simply. A more complex theory to be justified must explain data which a simpler theory cannot explain. (2) The death instinct, as conceived by Freud, was an urge to return to a state of inanimate matter. This urge is experienced and turned into an impulse to destroy things in the external world.

DR A. STEPHEN said that the concept of the death instinct was put forward by Freud to explain why that child said again and again 'oh, oh'. It had nothing to do with aggression at all. It explained the repetition compulsion. Evolution is from the inorganic to the organic. The evidence for the concept is another matter. It was possible to substitute the theory of the death instinct for the theory that aggression was due to frustration.

MRS RIVIERE said that it is impossible to drop the concept of frustration. The point about frustration was precisely in its reference to life. Frustration is experienced as a threat of death. If the baby cannot get the breast the feeling it has is 'I shall die'.

DR BOWLBY said that it could be argued that the reason why the organism cannot bear the idea of dying was due to a strong life instinct.

DR PAYNE said that if frustration caused damming up of libido it did not follow that the aggressive activity which might accrue was due to the death instinct.

MRS RIVIERE: This point is considered in Freud's contribution.

MR MONEY-KYRLE said there were four aspects to the question:

1 The death instinct is the sense of return to inanimate matter.
2 The compulsion to repeat.
3 Aggression which results from frustration.
4 The nutritive impulse to devour, which in the first place is not intended to be destructive, but arouses anxiety as soon as it is found to be destructive in effect.

MISS EVANS argued for the necessity to postulate two forms of instinctual energy. She thought that there must either be two channels through which energy discharged or two different forms of energy from the beginning.

DR HEIMANN spoke on the same theme. She thought that without the concept of the death instinct a monistic conception of life was necessary. She thought that there were two questions to be considered. (1) The explanation of death. Is it the negation of life? (2) Clinical evidence of the death instinct in tendencies to self-destruction in the individual.

DR USHER said that she had had a patient who wanted to commit suicide but said it was too active.

MRS RIVIERE brought forward the argument that sleep was a state of death.

DR PAYNE and DR BOWLBY pointed out the significance of sleep for the renewal of life.

DR GILLESPIE reminded Members of the significance of the womb phantasy in connection with sleep.

MR MONEY-KYRLE said: Considered neurologically there is only one type of energy. There must be a correlation of what happens in the brain and in the mind. Psychologically one feels various urges but it is difficult to say if there is one or three or more.

DR GILLESPIE spoke of the monistic theory of instincts.

DR WINNICOTT considered that destructiveness manifested in the infant arose from primitive greed. There was no evidence of aggressiveness in the primitive baby.

749

DR PAYNE asked how he regarded screaming.

DR WINNICOTT said he did not regard screaming as a sign of a primary death instinct but of the destructiveness inherent in primitive love.

DR HEIMANN thought it was the turning outward of inner destructiveness. She also thought it important to define what is meant when it is said there is no conception of death in the Ucs, as there was pain, destruction, and terror.

DR PAYNE said that she thought it meant that there was no idea of non-existence in the Ucs.

MR MONEY-KYRLE spoke of the alternating states of mind in the manic-depressive, in which aggressive impulses were alternately operating externally and internally (mentally). He could not, however, get the concept of the death instinct in a more philosophical sense.

DR FRANKLIN referred to the relation of the older concepts of Freud connected with ego and object-cathexes and to his later concepts of life and death instincts.

DR HEIMANN said that Freud started from the monistic point of view and came to a dualistic point of view.

Further discussion took place on the same lines in which Mrs Riviere, Dr Gillespie, Dr Bowlby, Dr Heimann, and Mr Money-Kyrle took part.

The meeting was closed at 10 o'clock.

Notes

1 'It will not be unreasonable to give a special name to this whole way of regarding our subject-matter, for it is consummation of psychoanalytic research. I propose that when we have succeeded in describing a psychical process in its dynamic topographical and economic aspect, we should speak of it as a metapsychological presentation.' [SE 14:181]

2 '. . . although everything depends on their not being arbitrarily chosen but determined by their having significant relations to the empirical material, relations that we seem to sense before we can clearly recognise and demonstrate them.' [SE 14:117]

3 Let me at this point state the principal finding to which we have been led by the psychoanalytic investigation of neurotics. The neuroses have no psychical content that is peculiar to them and that might not equally be found in healthy people. Or, as Jung has expressed it,

'Neurotics fall ill of the same complexes against which we healthy people struggle as well. Whether that struggle ends in health, in neurosis, or in a countervailing superiority of achievement, depends on quantitative considerations on the relative strength of the conflicting forces.'   [SE 11:50]

4 '. . . the sense of guilt is an expression of the conflict due to ambivalence, of the eternal struggle between Eros and the instinct of destruction or death.' [SE 21:132] '. . . as a result of the inborn conflict arising from ambivalence, of the eternal struggle between the trends of love and death – there is inextricably bound up with it an increase of the sense of guilt'. [SE 21:133]

5 '. . . the conflict is bound to express itself in the Oedipus complex, to establish the conscience and to create the first sense of guilt'. [SE 21:132]

6 'I am convinced that many processes will admit of a simpler and clearer exposition if the findings of psychoanalysis with regard to the derivation of the sense of guilt are restricted to the aggressive instincts.' [SE 21:138]

7 'They operate against the purpose of other instincts, which leads, by reason of their function, to death; and this fact indicates that there is an opposition between them and the other instincts, an opposition whose importance was long ago recognized by the theory of the neuroses.' [SE 18:40]

8 'Making a swift generalization, we might conjecture that the essence of a regression of libido (e.g. from the genital to the sadistic-anal phase) lies in a defusion of instincts.' [SE 19:42]

9 'As the first of these aims we recognize the phase of incorporating or devouring – a type of love which is consistent with abolishing the object's separate existence.' [SE 14:138]

10 '. . . for it may be that here the destructive component in the object cathexis has hurried on ahead and is only later on joined by the erotic one . . . An ambivalent attitude is present from the outset and the transformation is effected by means of a reaction displacement of cathexis, energy being withdrawn from the erotic impulse and added to the hostile one.' [SE 19:43–4]

11 'Hate, as a relation to objects, is older than love. It derives from the narcissistic ego's primordial repudiation of the external world with its outpouring of stimuli.' [SE 14:139]

4

Paper by Melanie Klein on 'The Emotional Life and Ego-Development of the Infant with Special Reference to the Depressive Position'

Fourth Paper for Discussion of the Scientific Differences

(Being the fourth paper in the series of discussions on controversial topics. As on the previous occasions, this paper will be taken as read at the meeting to be held on March 1st, 1944.)

Introductory remarks

In previous contributions I described the infantile depressive position as a system of feelings, phantasies, anxieties, and defences arising in the first year of life. In so doing, I attempted to give a clear picture of certain early processes which, in my view, are of fundamental importance for the whole of mental life. I have not yet worked out in every detail the connections between infantile depressive feelings and later stages of development; but for many years I have been aware of the importance of this task. Indeed, ever since I began to understand more about the origins of depressive feelings, my investigations were also necessarily directed towards the connections between infantile depressive feelings and other aspects of mental life at different stages of development. This extensive ground will by no means be covered by the papers I shall contribute to this discussion; these will only be an instalment towards work which I hope will be forthcoming in future years.

The psychogenesis of depression has been a subject of particular interest to me for a long time, and the present papers are the result of experience accumulated over many years in the analyses of children at all stages of development, from twenty-one months onwards. I have had ample opportunity to compare this material with the material of adults – normal and abnormal – and to check it to some extent by the direct observation of infants and older children. My conclusions are thus based on much more evidence than I shall be able to produce in my exposition.

The present paper has two main purposes: I intend to correlate in more detail than I have done in the past my hypothesis of the depressive position with Freud's and Abraham's discoveries and concepts. At the same time I shall endeavour to show the part which early depressive feelings play in the whole of the emotional development during the first year of life. I shall assume that my audience is conversant with the papers which Susan Isaacs and Paula Heimann contributed to this discussion; this is to say, with the concept of unconscious phantasy and object relations from the beginning of life, and introjective and projective processes as fundamental mental mechanisms. For a detailed description of the infantile depressive position and its relation to manic-depressive states on the one hand and normal grief on the other, I refer to my two papers, 'A Contribution to the Psychogenesis of Manic-Depressive States' [Klein 1935] and 'Mourning and its Relation to Manic-Depressive States' [Klein 1940]. In those papers will also be found various references to defence mechanisms which the ego develops in its struggle to overcome early depressive feelings – defences which play an important part in building up the ego in the first year of life (and later on) and which are part of my subject-matter in the present paper.

Early object relations

Freud's hypothesis that there is no object relation in the auto-erotic and narcissistic phases has been discussed in Susan Isaacs' paper and particularly in Dr Heimann's contribution. I shall here only restate one or two of their arguments. Freud speaks of the early experiences of being fed at the mother's breast as the 'unattainable prototype of every later sexual satisfaction'. [Freud, S. 1916–17: 264; SE 16:314][1] The far-reaching effects of these experiences on later life are fully acknowledged by Freud. The concept of hallucination, for instance, which in turn has an important bearing on phantasy life as well as on illness, implies that hallucination comes about because the loss of this gratification (provided by an object – the mother's breast) is so painful for the infant that when he is deprived of it he must re-create this gratification in his mind.

Many passages in Freud's work go to show that according to his concept of primary narcissism there is an early stage without object relation. There are, however, other passages in Freud's work, as Mrs Isaacs pointed out in the discussion on May 19th, 1943, which substantiate the view that his concept of primary narcissism was a limiting concept. I now wish to draw attention to a footnote in the latest German edition of the *Three Contributions to the Theory of Sex* in which Freud refers to the theoretical gain derived from the analysis of little Hans. I am quoting this footnote in full in a later section of this paper and shall here only give one sentence which has a bearing on Freud's concept of primary narcissism. 'Moreover, my attention was drawn to a defect in the above exposition where, for the sake of clarity, I described the conceptual division between the phase of auto-erotism and the phase of object love as a division in time as well.' [Freud, S. 1910; SE 7:194][2] This remark seems to confirm Mrs Isaacs' argument that Freud did not apply the concept of primary narcissism to a definite state occupying a definite period of time in the way Miss Freud does.

Miss Freud, in her remarks on Susan Isaacs' paper on phantasy, specified the length of the phase without an object relation as extending to six months of age. She qualified this conclusion by saying that the infant up to six months has 'no object relation in the proper sense'. At the same time Miss Freud agreed with Susan Isaacs that 'correlation of synthesis of perception and reality-testing is achieved in degree from birth onwards' (discussion of April 7th, 1943). In another paragraph she stated: 'Ferenczi and his followers in Budapest, for instance, collected evidence to prove that during this narcissistic period the infant is open to influence exerted by the object. I am very ready to accept such evidence. There is not the slightest doubt in anybody's mind about the complete dependence of the infant on his surroundings. His state of health and his state of contentment are continually influenced by the mother's mood, the mother's emotions, and the mother's behaviour'. [See p. 419]

Now I should have thought that these various statements amounted to a description of some of the elements of the infant's object relation. However, Miss Freud concludes this paragraph – I think most surprisingly – with the sentence: 'But this does not alter the fact that the infant's object relationship is still an indirect one; changes in the object reach him by way of difference in the satisfaction given. The person of the object remains interchangeable so long as the gratification remains the same.' This seems to be a contradiction in terms, for it is an object relation if one is influenced by someone else's moods and attitudes and responds to them.

We cannot, of course, apply adult standards to the object relations of the infant, and it is clear that we must explain different object relations in infants at, say, two months, six months, twelve months, and so on. If, however, we take it a priori that the young infant has no object relation, instead of studying his mental life in all its particularities, we shall not get any further in our exploration of his object relations. Miss Freud's explanation that the 'psychic processes of the child are governed by the urge for satisfaction' and that it 'desires (and hallucinates) satisfaction as ardently and insistently as the older child, for instance, desires (and phantasies) the presence of the mother'; and again her speaking of 'the state where satisfaction counts for everything; and objects count for nothing' [see p. 419, discussion of April 7th, 1943] – this point of view leaves out of account the strong and emotional relation to the mother as a person, which can be clearly observed from at least the beginning of the second month. As early as this the infant shows an interest in the mother over and above the feeding process; often he interrupts his sucking to look at her face, to smile at her, to cuddle against her breast, to play with it; and his interest even extends beyond her person to other objects. The close understanding and contact between mother and child even at this early stage, the way in which the infant reacts and responds to the mother's attitude and feelings, the love and interest which he shows, constitute an object relation. No mother who has enjoyed feeding her children would doubt this, and many nurses and general practitioners share this view.

Early object love

In one of his last works Abraham [Abraham 1924] devoted only a few but very pregnant statements to the relation to objects in connection with the various stages of libidinal development, though it is clear from the way in which Abraham put forward these new hypotheses that in his own mind this relation needed much further exploration.[3] He said (p. 495): 'We regard the earliest, auto-erotic stage of the individual as being still exempt from instinctual inhibitions, in accordance with the absence of any real object relations.' Furthermore, on p. 488: 'On the level of partial cannibalism . . . the individual shows the first signs of having some care for his object. He may also regard such a care, incomplete as it is, as the first beginnings of object-love in a stricter sense, since it implies that the individual has begun to conquer his narcissism.' This phase can roughly be placed into the second half of the first or the

755

beginning of the second year. Thus, according to Abraham, we would assume the existence of love at a stage when its manifestations differ greatly from those which we connect with 'love in a stricter sense'; the logical conclusion would be to study the still more incomplete manifestations of love in the younger child.

Another important theoretical problem arises here. If we follow Abraham's hypothesis, there is an evolution of love, which starts with the phase of partial cannibalism (in his view coinciding with the early anal level), that is to say, at a stage when according to both Freud and Abraham the genital libido does not yet play a part. The question arises: does love exist in the infant prior to the emergence of genital libido? Or do genital trends, though covered up by the primacy of the oral and anal libido, form part of the child's sexuality and influence his emotional development much earlier than was accepted? I have for many years upheld the view, derived from my analyses of young children, that the libidinal stages overlap much more than was assumed, and that genital trends are present in the first year of life. In my view[4] genital trends play a part in the sexual and emotional development of the infant, and I think it possible that even from the beginning they influence, however dimly, the relation to objects. Whether it is due to the early activity of genital trends that elements of love are present even in the earliest relation of the infant to the mother's breast remains a theoretical problem to be further elucidated; but the fact that love in some sense is discernible within the earliest stages has been acknowledged by a number of observers approaching the study of the infant from various theoretical angles.

Bernfeld, in his valuable book on the infant, [Bernfeld 1929: 202] made some interesting suggestions. His observations led him to assume feelings of love in the young infant; this, of course, presupposes a relation to objects. When discussing the concept of the auto-erotic and narcissistic phases with which he theoretically fully agrees, he says that we can assert 'with almost complete accuracy, that from birth (from a few days after birth certainly) definite small quantities of libido are used for object cathexis'. Speaking of the mother, he says: 'She is not only the possessor of the breast but also the amplification, one might say, of the very earliest recognised and loved object, that object towards which the new-born first turns.' He then quotes Balzac's words: 'The small creature knows nothing besides the mother's breasts; it loves them with all its might, it thinks only of this fountain of life; it comes to them from and deserts them for sleep; it awakes only to return to them.'

Michael Balint, Alice Balint, and I. Hermann devoted a great deal of study to the earliest stages of development. M. Balint summarizes their various papers in *Imago*. [Balint 1937] To give shortly the main points their views have in common: they do not believe in a stage of primary narcissism, though they do not disagree with the theoretical concept of primary narcissism. In their view the first phase of extra-uterine life has an object and is characterized by a passive aim – the desire to be loved. Balint quotes a few authors who, in his view, support the concept of an early object relation, e.g., Edward Glover who said that the child quite early has 'some primitive objective reality of its own'. Balint furthermore quotes Glover as having said: 'the term "narcissism" has to some extent outworn its usefulness'. [Glover 1933: 489] Balint refers as well to Federn [Federn 1927: 392], Müller-Braunschweig [Müller-Braunschweig 1936], Isakower [Isakower 1936], E. P. Hoffman [Hoffman 1935], L. Rotter-Kertesz [Rotter-Kertesz 1934; 1936], and G. Roheim [Roheim 1940].

My experience has fully confirmed Abraham's discoveries that the relation to part-objects is the earliest in the infant's mind. First the whole interest and love focus on the nipple and on the breast; but very soon interest develops in the face and in the hands which attend to his needs and gratify them. Thus, step by step, the infant comes to perceive and love the mother as whole person. But, as I pointed out, we can assume that love towards the mother in some form exists from the beginning of life. I have on several occasions expressed the view that the relation of the infant to his mother is based on phylogenetic inheritance and is ontogenetically the most fundamental of all human patterns. If there are such fundamentals, acquired in the evolution of the race (and who could doubt this?), a relation of the infant to the mother who gives birth to him and attends to his first needs must be one of them.

Freud described unconscious sexual theories of children as a phylogenetic inheritance. The analysis of young children has not only confirmed this discovery, but revealed in many details the significance of these infantile theories in the intellectual and emotional life of children.[5] This interest in the sexuality of the parents is fundamental since it is so closely linked up with the child's own sexuality. It is obviously *still more fundamental* that, when he becomes separated from his mother at birth, the infant who was one with her body feels her to be his first and main object; and thus the phylogenetic inheritance is reinforced through his ontogenetic needs and experiences. One may assume that from the beginning the mother exists as a whole object in the child's mind, but in vague outlines as it were, and that this picture becomes gradually filled in as perception develops.

The origins of anxiety and guilt

Concerning the origin of anxiety, Freud revised only to some extent his earlier hypothesis that anxiety arises from the direct conversion of libido. He says,

> With regard to anxious expectation, clinical experience has taught us that there is a regular relationship between it and the disposition of the libido in the sexual life. The most frequent cause of anxiety-neurosis is undischarged excitation. A libidinal excitation is aroused, but is not satisfied or used; in the place of this libido which has been diverted from its use, anxiety makes its appearance. I even thought it was justifiable to say that this unsatisfied libido is directly transformed into anxiety. This view found some support in certain almost universal phobias of small children . . . it (the child) cannot control this libidinal excitation; it cannot keep it in a state of suspension, but turns it into anxiety. . . . Children's phobias, and the anxious expectation in anxiety-neurosis, serve as two examples of one way in which neurotic anxiety comes about; i.e. through direct transformation of libido.
>
> [Freud, S. 1933a:109–10; SE 22:82–3][6]

He states however in *Inhibitions, Symptoms and Anxiety* [Freud, S. 1926: 105; SE 20:136][7]: 'Only a few of the manifestations of anxiety in children are comprehensible to us, and we must confine our attention to them.' He then comes to the conclusion that anxiety is caused by the child 'missing someone who is loved and longed for'. Speaking of the fear of the loss of love, he says it is 'obviously a continuation of the fear of the infant at the breast when it misses its mother. You will understand what objective danger-situation is indicated by this kind of anxiety. If the mother is absent or has withdrawn her love from the child, it can no longer be certain that its needs will be satisfied, and may be exposed to the most painful feelings of tension.' [Freud, S. 1933a:115; SE 22:87][8] Once more, in *Inhibitions, Symptoms and Anxiety*, he speaks of the 'danger' against which the infant 'wants to be safeguarded' as one of 'non-gratification, of a growing tension due to need, against which it is helpless'. [Freud, S. 1926:106–7; SE 20:148][9]

Two conclusions can be drawn from these and similar passages: (a) in young children, it is unsatisfied libidinal excitation which turns into anxiety; (b) the earliest content of anxiety is the infant's feeling of danger lest his needs should not be satisfied because mother does not return.

Abraham, particularly in the work referred to above, threw much light on the earliest phases. His discoveries in the field of infantile sexuality were bound up with a new approach to the origin of anxiety and guilt. It is significant that the origin of anxiety remained a closed chapter until Freud discovered infantile sexuality, and we may find that the origins of guilt too can only be understood in connection with the early stages of infantile sexuality, i.e. the cannibalistic phase.

Abraham suggests that 'in the stage of narcissism with a cannibalistic sexual aim the first evidence of an instinctual inhibition appears in the shape of morbid anxiety. The process of overcoming the cannibalistic impulses is intimately associated with a sense of guilt which comes into the foreground as a typical inhibitory phenomenon belonging to the third (earlier anal-sadistic) stage' (loc. cit., p. 496). Abraham thus contributed materially to our understanding of the origins of anxiety, since he was the first to point out the connection of anxiety with cannibalistic desires. This was an essential step towards recognizing that anxiety arises from the aggressive impulses, although Abraham himself did not draw this conclusion. His hypothesis that guilt arises in the ego's struggle to overcome the cannibalistic impulses is no less revolutionary, for this implies a sense of guilt at a very early stage of development; whilst according to Freud's concept guilt originates (in connection with the superego) after the dissolution of the Oedipus complex. While Abraham's work in general has been fully accepted and recognized, these particular discoveries – though never disputed – have not been appreciated at their full value and have not been made much of in psychoanalytic theory.[10] My own findings, derived from the psychoanalysis of young children, not only corroborated Abraham's discoveries on anxiety and guilt and carried them further, but showed their importance in full perspective by bringing them together with a number of new facts discovered in young children. Abraham compared his brief survey of the psycho-sexual development to a 'time-table of express trains in which only the larger stations at which they stop are given' (loc. cit., pp. 495–6). He suggested that the 'halting-places that lie between cannot be marked in a summary of this kind' (p. 496). There is little doubt that had he been able to continue his work on the lines of his last books, he himself would have inserted some of the halting places which lie between, and he would certainly have welcomed other workers' suggestions in this direction. As it happened, his provisional survey gave pointers rather than a connected theory,[11] and they remained in need of further unification.

When I studied anxiety situations in young children, I recognized that sadistic impulses and phantasies are at the root of these anxieties. I was thus able not only to confirm Abraham's hypothesis that anxiety and guilt originate in connection with the cannibalistic impulses, but to carry these conclusions further in some directions.[12] I found that the early processes of introjection and projection lead to establishing within the ego (side by side with extremely 'good' objects), extremely frightening and persecuting objects which are conceived in the light of the infant's own aggressive impulses and phantasies, i.e. that he projects his own aggression on to his superego.[13] It is in these processes that the basis for paranoid anxieties can be found.

The projection of the infant's aggression on to his superego is in line with the processes underlying the unconscious sexual theories. In this connection Freud says: 'It can be stated in general about the infantile sexual theories that they are reproductions of the child's own sexual constitution.' [Freud, S. 1930:57; SE 7:125] Phantasies of this nature (for, as I see it, the unconscious sexual theories are inherently phantasies) extend according to my experience not only to the actual but to the internalized parents as well, and this explains the phantastic and terrifying nature of those early introjected objects. The anxiety arising from the aggressive impulses is thus multiplied by the fear of retaliating persecutors, both internal and external.

In a paper[14] presented to the Congress at Oxford (1929) I illustrated by an extreme case the pathological effects of the anxiety aroused by the destructive impulses in infants, and concluded that the earliest defences of the ego (in normal as well as in abnormal development) are directed not against the libido but against the anxiety aroused by aggressive impulses and phantasies.

Freud, as I have substantiated by quotations at the beginning of this section, did not, as far as young children are concerned (and in some other cases of anxiety as well), revise his early hypothesis that anxiety originates from the transformation of unsatisfied libido. This can also be seen from other passages in *Inhibitions, Symptoms and Anxiety* and in the chapter on 'Anxiety and Instinctual Life' in the *New Introductory Lectures*, which contains a résumé of his views on anxiety and guilt. As regards the origin of guilt, there is an unequivocal statement in *Civilization and its Discontents* in which Freud goes, as far as I know, further in his acceptance that guilt arises only from the destructive impulses than in any of his former writings. He introduces this passage by saying: 'This, I think, is the place to suggest that a proposal which I previously put forward as a provisional assumption should be taken in earnest.'[15] He then goes on to speak of the view propounded by some authors that frustration heightens the sense of guilt:

> How then is it to be explained dynamically and economically that a heightening of the sense of guilt should appear in place of an unfulfilled erotic desire? This can surely only happen in a roundabout way: the thwarting of the erotic gratification provokes an access of aggressiveness against the person who interfered with the gratification, and then this tendency to aggression in its turn has itself to be suppressed. So then it is, after all, only the aggression which is changed into guilt, by being suppressed and made over to the super-ego. I am convinced that very many processes will admit of much simpler and clearer explanation if we restrict the findings of psychoanalysis in respect of the origin of the sense of guilt to the aggressive instincts.
>
> [Freud, S. 1930:131; SE 21:138–9][16]

Though Freud, in this passage, clearly states that guilt only arises from the aggressive impulses, he has not altered his view about the stage of development at which guilt sets in, namely as a consequence of the Oedipus complex, and with the emergence of the superego.[17] There is thus a discrepancy of views between Abraham and Freud on the origins of anxiety and guilt. When Abraham put forward in 1924 his hypothesis that anxiety and guilt arise from the cannibalistic impulses (that is to say, in the infant) he could not foresee where these discoveries would lead, and there is no ground to assume that in his opinion they implied any divergence from Freud's views. Nor do I believe that there is necessarily any fundamental divergence. If we know more about anxiety and conflict in the young child, we can connect them with the guilt feelings of the older child, and are thus able to fill in the picture of early mental life. This has been done to some extent already, and has to be done even more in the future, by the analysis of young children. Here I may draw attention to the fact that Freud himself repeatedly mentions that he has not made a close and direct study of children. I shall quote here one passage from the *New Introductory Lectures*. Speaking of the application of psychoanalysis to education, and by implication obviously also to the study of children, Freud says: 'There is one subject, however, that I cannot pass by so easily, though this is not because I have any special understanding of it or have done much work on it myself. On the contrary, I have hardly ever occupied myself with it.' After giving credit to his daughter's work, he goes on:

> When, during the treatment of an adult neurotic, we tried to trace the determination of his symptoms, we were always led back into

his early childhood. A knowledge of the later aetiological factors was not sufficient either for our understanding of his condition or to effect a cure. The result was that we were forced to acquaint ourselves with the psychological peculiarities of the years of infancy; and we learnt a great many things which could not have been discovered except through analysis, and were in a position to set right a number of generally accepted beliefs about childhood.

[Freud, S. 1933a:168; SE 22:146–7][18]

When Freud did record observations of children, they were full of meaning; and the first analysis of a child undertaken under his guidance threw new light on some very important theoretical problems.[19] Had Freud himself been able to study children more closely, or had he analysed young children, he might have revised his view on the points which I have just discussed.

Here we return once more to facts. A number of workers have been able through the analyses of young children from about two years onwards to establish beyond doubt the operation at this stage – and going back to some time earlier – of feelings of anxiety and guilt which originate from sadistic impulses and phantasies and are bound up with superego development. These facts will in the future be checked by other workers when they use a technique which makes possible the approach to the unconscious and conscious mind of the young child. Direct observation as well proves that young children do not only suffer from the fear of loss of love (in the sense that their needs will not be satisfied) or fear of external authority,[20] but experience guilt and conflict in the full meaning of the word. As regards children in the third year of life, Miss Freud in one of her contributions to this discussion, and also on other occasions stated that there is evidence of guilt and reparation at this stage (she has also recorded observations of deep and serious grief in the second year of life). It is clear from the following quotation that she means guilt and reparation in connection with the superego. She said in the discussion of April 7th: 'The third and final step in development of the synthetic function consists in correlation between an inner urge and an inner prohibition. This achievement which, in Kleinian theory, is ascribed to the very beginning of life, belongs, in Freudian view, to the development of the Oedipus complex with its consequences for the formation of the superego. The affect which accompanies this unification is guilt. I cannot see evidence of this reaction before the third year.' This suggests that Miss Freud has altered her view that guilt as the function of the superego emerges only when the Oedipus complex has passed away, that is to say at about five years of age. Here I wish to repeat the question put to her by Mrs Isaacs: does Miss Freud now hold the view that guilt and tendencies to reparation arise before the superego emerges and the Oedipus complex has passed away, or does she think that the superego develops much earlier than Freud assumed?

Now I shall return to Freud's statement that anxiety is caused by the child 'missing someone who is loved and longed for'. [Freud, S. 1926:167; SE 22:169][21] This passage suggests deeper and more immediate sources of the infant's fear of loss than the mere anxiety that his needs will not be satisfied, that he may be 'exposed to the most painful feelings of tension'. [Freud, S. 1933a:115; SE 22:87][22] This intrinsic feeling of loss fits closely into the picture of the infant's mental life which is dominated by his emotions. We have also Freud's description of the young child's fear of loss in the following terms: 'He cannot as yet distinguish between temporary absence and permanent loss. *As soon as he misses his mother he behaves as if he were never going to see her again*; and repeated consolatory experiences to the contrary are necessary before he learns that her disappearance is usually followed by her re-appearance' (my italics). [Freud, S. 1926:167; SE 22:169][23] Here we have, I think, the most fundamental content of the infant's anxieties. This fundamental fear of loss of the loved object seems to me psychologically well-founded. As we know, the child's actual needs for attention and help dominate his life. But the ego experiences it as a psychic reality that the loved object has been devoured, or is in danger of being devoured, and therefore the loss of the loved and indispensable object is the immediate consequence of these cannibalistic desires.

Psychoanalytic theory recognizes fully the fundamental significance of oral libido and defences for normal and abnormal development and the links between the early and later stages. For instance the understanding of the aetiology of manic–depressive states and the concept of the superego with all the far-reaching implications of these discoveries for the whole of mental life are inconceivable unless we recognize the nature and impact of oral libido during the first year. Whilst full weight has thus been given to the effect of these early processes on later development, and their part in aetiology is firmly established in our science, these discoveries have found relatively little application to the actual emotional life of the infant; and this implies that the stage of development to which regression takes place in later life has not been studied and appreciated in its own right. The concept of regression has proved to be one of the corner-stones of psychoanalysis.[24] The fact, however, that the early workings of the mind were first discovered in the adult as they appeared through regression has led to an over-estimation of regressive as opposed to progressive processes. Thus, I think, it happened that Freud's great discovery of the cannibalistic impulses did not lead – until Abraham's suggestions – to further theoretical conclusions about the emotional experiences of the infant at the time when these impulses are dominant. We must, however, beware of undervaluing the immediate effect of these impulses, experiences, and phantasies on the infant's mental life, if our researches into what is still the most obscure region of human development are not to be abortive.

Feelings of loss and grief

The hypothesis that from the beginning the infant feels love towards an object leads to a different valuation of the impact of all his emotions while he experiences them. The strength of these emotions and their immediate effect can only be understood in relation to an object. If we fully appreciate the imperative need of the infant for his mother who alone can provide the gratification he craves for, we are bound to acknowledge that the emotion of loss he experiences has immediate and profound effects on his mental life. This element of loss is predetermined, one may say, in the infant from the experience of birth.

In *Inhibitions, Symptoms and Anxiety* Freud states that 'there is much more continuity between intra-uterine life and earliest infancy than the impressive caesura of the act of birth allows us to believe. What happens is that the child's biological situation as a foetus is replaced for it by a psychological object relation to its mother. But we must not forget that during its intra-uterine life the mother was not an object for the foetus, and that at that time there were no objects at all as far as it was concerned.'[25]

Miss Sharpe, in her contribution to this discussion (January 27th, 1943), suggested that the infantile depressive position starts with the separation from the mother's body at birth. She said:

The breast phantasy is a rudimentary psychical process, but the belief is that the infant possesses the real tangible breast, i.e. an actuality. In this phantasy the infant achieves a reunion with the body of the mother. The phantasied introjection of the breast, the entire belief that the actual breast is inside, is the next stage of wish-psychosis. The illusion or delusion this achieves is that still there has been no bodily separation from the mother. There is no mental imagery in this process. It is the hallucinatory perception inside not outside. She is within the child in place of the child within her as in pre-natal days.

[See p. 338]

The infant's introjection of the mother's breast is a process which comes into play both when gratification and when frustration are experienced. When he is suckling the infant takes in the breast in phantasy because it is 'good'. At times of frustration introjection is reinforced because the loss of the external loved object creates an urgent need to re-establish it inside. But when the infant thus deals with his feelings of loss because the mother frustrates him at the moment, he also deals with the loss derived from the separation at birth. His physical needs, chiefly his hunger, disturb this withdrawal into an internal situation and turn him back to the external world. At the same time, when he is being gratified by his mother, the actual physical nearness to her during feeding and when she 'mothers' him, helps him to overcome his longing for a former lost state.[26] Yet he derives from this longing a desire towards the physical closeness with her which increasingly (but never completely) takes the place of the desire for the lost pre-natal state. The various gratifications derived from the external world, and his growing interest in it, all help towards the gradual growth of his capacity to substitute an object relation for a lost situation.

In my earlier contributions to this topic, I suggested that the infantile depressive position arises when the infant perceives and introjects the mother as a whole person (between three and five months). The fear lest she be destroyed by his cannibalistic desires and phantasies gives rise to guilt. The relation to the whole person presupposes important steps in the integration of the ego and in the evolution of feelings of love. Thus, with the introjection of the whole object, elements of love, hate, anxiety, sense of loss and guilt come together more closely in the child's mind, and these experiences constitute the depressive position. However, the assumption seems justified, that the seeds of depressive feelings, in so far as the experience of birth gives rise to a feeling of loss, are there from the beginning of life. In the situation of again and again losing his bodily closeness to his mother, and above all to her breast, these feelings of loss are deepened; they become more complex and alter in strength and quality when the relation to the mother as a whole person develops.

While the unmistakable emotions of anger and rage have been fully recognized, grief in the infant has often been overlooked. Yet grief is at times clearly expressed on the infant's face, and many an observant mother is aware of her child's distress (though she might not express it in terms of grief). This is particularly evident when the child begins to shed tears. The face becomes more expressive, the lines deepen, and something in his eyes indicates that his range of emotions has widened.

We quote here an observer of whose objectivity and capacity for observation there can be no question. In his book, *The Expression of Emotions in Man and Animals* [Darwin 1872] Charles Darwin refers to the infant's shedding tears as a manifestation of mental as well as physical distress. He takes it so much for granted that even in the young infant tears are especially related to mental distress that it does not occur to him to look for any proofs for this assumption. He says: 'Weeping seems to be the primary and natural expressions as we see in children, of suffering of any kind, whether bodily pain short of extreme agony, or mental distress' (p. 156). Again, 'Infants whilst young do not shed tears or weep, as is well known to nurses and medical men. This circumstance is not exclusively due to the lacrymal glands being as yet incapable of secreting tears. I first noticed this fact from having accidentally brushed with the cuff of my coat the open eye of one of my infants, when seventy-seven days old, causing this eye to water freely; and though the child screamed violently, the other eye remained dry, or was only slightly suffused with tears' (p. 153). At another place he states:

The fact of tears not being shed at a very early age from pain or any mental emotion is remarkable, as, later in life, no expression is more general or more strongly marked than weeping. When the habit has once been acquired by an infant, it expresses in the clearest manner suffering of all kinds, both bodily pain and mental distress, even though accompanied by other emotions, such as fear or rage. The character of the crying, however, changes at a very early age, as I noticed in my own infants – the passionate cry differing from that of grief. A lady informs me that her child, nine months old, when in a passion screams loudly, but does not weep; tears, however, are shed when she is punished by her chair being turned with its back to the table. This difference may perhaps be attributed to weeping being restrained, as we shall immediately see, at a more advanced age, under most circumstances excepting grief. (p. 154)

The infantile depressive position

My concept of the infantile depressive position had its theoretical basis in Freud's and Abraham's discoveries of the factors underlying melancholia and normal mourning. We know the essential part introjection plays in melancholia. When a loved object is lost, or following a situation representing such loss, the object becomes installed within the ego. This introjection, however, is bound to miscarry if the cannibalistic impulses in the subject are excessive, and this leads to illness.

Both Freud and Abraham were led from these discoveries to important conclusions regarding normal mourning. In mourning as well the process of introjecting the loved object is carried out, but here it is successful. My experience showed me that depressive feelings arise in infants, and that these feelings originate in early introjective processes. When development progresses to the introjection of the mother as a whole person, the anxiety lest she be destroyed by his cannibalistic impulses (an anxiety which is stimulated by his love feelings and therefore sets going the whole conflict of ambivalence) confronts the infant with the danger of losing her forever. Freud's concept of primary introjection and of cannibalistic impulses and desires in the infant, as well as his view that the fear of loss underlies the early phobias, point to the conclusion that these processes play an important part in the infant's emotional life. *My contention is that the infant experiences feelings akin to mourning, and that these feelings arise from his fear of destroying and so losing his loved and indispensable object (as an external desire and through his greed).*

I can here only touch upon the vital part greed and the defences against greed play in the depressive position. The infant fears that his greed may cause the destruction of his loved object. Since he feels, particularly when he is frustrated and his hatred wells up, that his greed is uncontrollable, his anxieties lest the loved object be destroyed centre on his greed. It seems that the defences against greed are possibly the earliest of all, and their importance for later development cannot be overrated. As we know, greed is not only inhibited by anxieties but is also very much increased by them, and in particular the anxiety of losing forever the loved object tends to increase greed. It is part of the depressive position that the loved object which, in the infant's mind, is in danger of being destroyed is at the same time, for this very reason, all the more greedily desired.

As we know, this is one of the insoluble conflicts to which the melancholic is exposed.

In a later section of this paper I am discussing, though only in broad outlines, the feeding difficulties of infants, which I think can be explained if we accept the plausible hypothesis that they are caused by inhibition of greed.

Abraham, in discussing the special fixation of the libido at the oral level and some of the aetiological factors for melancholia, describes this fixation in a particular case as follows: 'In his depressive state he would be overcome by longing for his mother's breast, a longing that was indescribably powerful and different from anything else. If the libido still remains fixated on this point when the individual is grown up, then one of the most important conditions for the appearance of a melancholic depression is fulfilled.' [Abraham 1924:458][27] Abraham is actuated by his interest 'in the original emotional reactions of the child to such traumatic experiences' which cause the later melancholia. He goes on: 'We may justifiably assume that those experiences caused feelings of an unhappy character, but we have not up till now got any direct idea, any living picture, of the child's actual state of mind at the time.' This interest enabled him to discover in two cases of adults: 'A vivid picture in the patient's state of feeling at the early age of five. I should be inclined to speak of a "primal Parathymia" ensuing from the boy's Oedipus complex.' He concludes this description as follows: 'It is this state of mind that we call melancholia.' [Abraham 1924:469]

There remains a wide gap between Abraham's discovery of an actual melancholic phase at the age of five and my contention of the depressive position in the infant. However, the interest in the 'original emotional reactions of the child' is bound to take us back further than five years, namely to infancy and the phase of development in which the most important fixations for melancholia take place; these, as I wish to add, have a bearing on development in general. I am also aware that Abraham in his discovery of this phase in childhood refers only to melancholic parents, while I suggest that the depressive position in infancy is a universal phenomenon. This hypothesis is an extension of Freud's discovery that there is no structural difference between the neurotic and the normal; for my experience has led me to suggest that the same is true of the psychotic and the normal. A careful reading of Freud and Abraham shows that there are plenty of hints in their work which point in this direction. There are various passages in Freud's work which state this quite explicitly. For instance, he says in *The Origin and Development of Psycho-Analysis*, 'You must remember that our nightly dream productions show the greatest outer similarity and inner relationship to the creations of the insane, but on the other hand are compatible with full health during waking life.' [Freud, S. 1910:29; SE 11:33][28]

My hypothesis, propounded for many years, has been that young children develop phantasies and anxieties which in content are identical with the conscious and unconscious phantasies and anxieties of adult psychotics, and that the mechanisms and defences which we discover in adult psychotics are developed in infancy. It is thus in these early stages of development that I see the fixation points for all psychoses. Besides the similarities there are obviously a great number of differences between young children and psychotics (differences which I have pointed out in detail in my book and in other places). To put it in a nut-shell, these particular anxieties, modes of feeling and behaviour are normal in the infantile setting but pathological if they are maintained in the later years of childhood or adult life, or if regression to them takes place. However, even in young children there are variations in degree of intensity of anxieties and in the constellation of the factors at work, so that some children and even infants must be regarded as definitely ill. Normally the infantile neurosis is the means of working through, dealing with, and modifying these early psychotic anxieties and processes.

This hypothesis has sometimes been misunderstood and interpreted in the sense that I equate young children at certain stages with psychotics. This, however, as just explained, was never implied in my hypothesis. In fact, as can be seen from my book and papers,[29] I have always been careful when presenting my case material, to differentiate not only between psychotic traits and actual psychosis, but even between psychotic traits and, for instance, paranoid and hypochondriacal ideas.

The findings of Freud, Abraham, and Rado I think imply that depression originates in the first year of life. But to carry their views to their logical conclusion, we have to appreciate the immediate experience of the infant at its full impact (and if we do not allow for this impact, how can we explain the fixation?). My hypothesis of the infantile depressive position thus embodies a number of Freud's and Abraham's theoretical concepts about the early stages of development and carries them further – partly by unifying them (for to some extent these concepts had remained unconnected with each other) and partly by applying them to the emotional life of the infant as experienced at the time.

The approach to the infant's emotional life

The theoretical discoveries about the early stages of development
which we owe in the first place to Freud, and following his findings
to Abraham, Jones, and a few other authors, threw floods of light on
a young child's mental processes. There remained, however, a wide
gap between this theoretical knowledge and its direct application to
the understanding of young children. As a remnant from pre-
analytic days a tendency persisted in psychoanalytic theory to
consider the infant mainly from the biological and physiological
point of view; psychologically speaking he has been largely regarded
as the embodiment of phases, fixation points, instincts, etc.[30]
Theoretical conclusions, essential to the development of theory, have
been preserved *in vacuo*, as it were, because as a rule they have not
been applied to the infant as a living organism – which means
psychologially as well as biologically. Such rigid adhering to certain
fixed concepts without regard to observable facts is bound to lead us
in a retrograde direction. As an example I will quote Dr Friedlander's
statement in this discussion (October 20th, 1943): 'If we meet with
sucking disturbances in a new-born child we would enquire into the
functional disturbance of this inborn reflex mechanism rather than
build up a hypothesis about the child's mental state at the time, whilst
if we meet an eating difficulty in a child of two we would not only
take the temperature but enquire into the psychological basis for the
disturbance.' One might conclude from this statement not only that
in the case of a child under two there are no psychological causes for
his feeding difficulties, but even that he has no mental life at all. If Dr
Friedlander meant that with a younger child as well she would be on
the look-out for psychological causes, one would assume that she
would have given an earlier age than two. Such a point of view flies
in the face of some of Freud's and Abraham's most fundamental
discoveries about the early stages of development as well as of the
observable facts, and many non-analytic as well as analytic observers
would certainly oppose Dr Friedlander's point of view.

Freud's own recorded observations of infants are not numerous,
but they are extremely illuminating and, as we know, one of them
led him to a great discovery (repetition-compulsion). I shall now
quote fully Freud's description of the extremely complex mental
processes which imply a relatively advanced integrating capacity of
the ego, in one instance as early as eleven months. It is self-evident
that such processes could not have just begun at that stage, but must
have been developing for some time. Freud refers to the oral

770

frustration felt by children in connection with a new-born brother or sister: 'It is a remarkable fact that even when the difference between the children's ages is only eleven months, the older one is nevertheless able to take in the state of affairs. But it is not only the milk that the child grudges the undesired interloper and rival, but all the other evidences of motherly care. It feels that it has been dethroned, robbed and had its rights invaded, and so it directs a feeling of jealous hatred against its little brother or sister, and develops resentment against its faithless mother, which often finds expression in a change for the worse in its behaviour. It begins to be "naughty", irritable, intractable, and unlearns the control which it had acquired over its excretions. All this has been known for a long time, and is accepted as self-evident, but we seldom form a right idea of the strength of these jealous impulses, of the tenacious hold they have on the child, and the amount of influence they exert on its later development.' [Freud, S. 1933a: 157–8; SE 22:123][31]

As regards the early phobias, Freud repeatedly refers to them as 'altogether enigmatic' though he states that some 'such as the fear of being left alone and the fear of unfamiliar people can be definitely explained'.[32] *Pavor nocturnus* in older children is generally known as a symptom of the infantile neurosis. Yet night terror in infants has received little attention from either analytic or non-analytic observers, though it is by no means an infrequent occurrence. With healthy and happy infants, who as a rule enjoy good sleep, it is striking that under certain circumstances, such as a change of surroundings, and sometimes without any ostensible cause, they may wake up from their sleep with actual terror.

A mother reported to me that she found her infant, who was as a rule happy and slept well, sobbing in her sleep at the age of ten months; she had observed this once or twice before. The same mother, who has no theoretical bias of any kind and is a reliable observer, told me that when her infant was five months (and a few times on later occasions) she had been left crying longer than usual and was then found in what the mother described as a 'hysterical' state. She looked terrified, and the mother said she had no doubt that the child was frightened of her because she had not come when the child expected her. It took the child some time before she seemed to recognize her mother and re-establish contact with her. I have made similar observations on several infants at different stages from a few months onwards.

I pointed out earlier that grief and distress can be observed in infants. We may now add to this a fact less easily observed but which, I think, can be detected with close scrutiny: that is the severe though possibly short disturbance of the infant's relation to the mother, the complete withdrawal from her, which occurs in certain situations of anxiety. Provided we can appreciate fully the vacant look of his eyes, the movements of his body, the expressions in his features, we shall see besides his anger and rage also the disappointment, the loss of contact, the alteration in his relation to his mother. We must also remember that after such an anxiety situation, though the child has already calmed down, the next feed is often disturbed.

One of the outstanding features which I found in analysing young children was the child's sense of insecurity because the parents seem to him so very changeable. As soon as his fears come up, and particularly when he is alone, the child is apt to feel that the 'good' parents[33] have changed into the 'bad' ones, or else at times that they will never come back because they are destroyed by his own greed and hatred. This is one source of his early fears and conflicts; one of his defences against it is the splitting of the mother and father figures into 'good' and 'bad' mother and 'good' and 'bad' father, in order to obtain more security about his internal objects as well as his external ones. This insight led me gradually to understand the part which the child's aggressive impulses and phantasies play in the development of persecutory fears and feelings of guilt; and the extent to which the relation to the internalized parents contributes to all these developments.

Applying this analytic insight to the infant referred to above, we can say that her state, as described to me by the mother, was one of fear that the mother would never return because she was devoured or had turned into the 'bad' mother. This again helps us to understand what happens in a child's mind when the mother returns. Her very presence and signs of love re-establish the infant's belief in her as an unharmed and loving mother. This implies that his trust in his good internal and external objects increases and his fear of persecution by bad objects decreases. There is, as we know, no better means of allaying a child's fears than the presence and love of his mother, and the same holds good for the infant as for the older child. The accumulation of such beneficial experiences is one of the main factors in his overcoming the infantile neurosis. The interpretations suggested in this section are an instance of the way in which inference and observation support each other.

Feeding difficulties

The variety and frequency of feeding difficulties in infants have not escaped attention, but in classical theory have not found adequate explanation; we might therefore also call them 'enigmatic'. If we are not inclined to leave them as 'enigmatic', however, but endeavour – as is our scientific duty – to find the solution of such unsolved problems, my hypothesis of the infantile depressive position appears to be both workable and helpful. According to this view, feeding difficulties are a manifestation of infantile depressive feelings, they are not one of the ways in which the fear of loss of the mother expresses itself. It is not difficult to establish a connection between the feeding difficulties of the infant and his fear of loss of the mother – the link being his cannibalistic impulses which, as Freud discovered, arise in the young infant (according to Abraham at the onset of teething). In support of my view I adduce the fact that a rejection of food is also one of the outstanding symptoms in the depressive phase of manic-depressive states.

In my former writings I have referred to weaning and the period preceding and following it as the climax in the depressive position; but for the purposes of the present paper I want to consider it in connection with the infant's whole emotional life. Bernfeld, in his *Psychology of the Infant*, [Bernfeld 1929] arrived at new conclusions about the effect of weaning on infants. He refers to the fact that we have learnt from Abraham, Starcke, and one's own analyses that the 'role of weaning in the Ucs system . . . cannot be overestimated' (p. 255). He goes on to say that the experiences of the infant, or rather the manifestations at the time of weaning, last 'for such a short time' and are 'so weak' that they do not seem to confirm the expectations to which one would be led by the results of the analyses he refers to. In considering, however, these manifestations, he remarks that 'the available facts are scattered, acquired accidentally with insufficient exactness' (p. 256). (I think that this may well account for some of our difficulties in interpreting these facts at their full significance.)

He points out that 'varied individual differences underlie the child's concrete behaviour (at weaning). In many children longing and sorrow are scarcely noticeable; others show an obvious mood which can be interpreted in this way, but it continues only for a short time; while others maintain it for a relatively long time. Occasionally this apathy goes so far as to refuse nourishment completely (Hochsinger). (It is interesting to see that all through life sorrow shows a tendency to refuse food.) We need not speak of this form of behaviour, since it produces the correct clinical picture, the nutritional neurosis (Hochsinger)' (loc. cit., p. 357). It is interesting to note that Hochsinger, a well-known paediatrician, takes it for granted that these phenomena are neurotic.

Bernfeld compares the state of anxiety and restlessness, irritability, and a certain apathy which may take possession of an adult with a similar condition in the infant: 'it, too, becomes, to a certain degree, apathetic – "sad", one might say, resigned' (p. 256). Among the methods of overcoming the frustration of weaning he mentions the withdrawal of the libido from the disappointing object through projection and repression. Elsewhere he said: 'This means that recalling the breast as an instinctual aim, imagining the breast as an instinctual aim, is not merely forgotten but repressed. Of course, the term repression which is borrowed from the developed state of the adult ego is not precisely applicable here. Nevertheless, its essential properties exist in these processes which concern us and the detailed study of repression must be reserved for another connection' (p. 296).

In another place Bernfeld states that it is worthy of note 'that weaning is the first obvious cause which can be established and from which pathological mental development branches off – those nutritional neuroses which . . . in all cases, are contributory factors to the predisposition to neurosis' (p. 258). He also says:

> The mental processes which we call frustration, longing, sorrow, overcoming of sorrow, loss, resignation, cannot be objectively confirmed. They show themselves ambiguously and incompletely, or tardily and indirectly, after they have run their course. Moreover, the mechanisms, repression and identification, which are active according to psychoanalysis, work noiselessly during this overcoming, and as processes are imperceptible and only recognized when consummated. This means that a conclusion about the effects of weaning will have to be drawn from an intimate knowledge of the child's reaction to its world and its activities, which are the *expression of its phantasy life,* or *at least are the nucleus of it.* (p. 259) (my italics)

The conclusion that, even if facts were not as 'scattered' and acquired with 'insufficient exactitude' as they are, we could not expect by observation alone to get full proofs for the unconscious processes at work in infants seems a truism, but one which is worth while remembering, since the demand by a few contributors in these discussions for 'direct' proofs seems to ignore this fact. The intimate knowledge of the child's mind and particularly of his phantasy life to which Bernfeld looked forward in order to understand the effects of weaning has since been provided by the analyses of very young children.

To understand the effect of weaning on the infant, we have to consider his attitude towards his food and his mother during the whole of the suckling period, whether this be shown in actual feeding difficulties or in less striking but nevertheless significant phenomena.[34] There are infants who are not good feeders though the mother's milk is plentiful and satisfactory, and whose appetite improves when the bottle or other foods are introduced. (For the sake of clarity of argument I am not here dealing with those children whose feeding difficulties are obviously due to the mother's milk not being satisfactory.) I am particularly stressing the question of appetite as an expression of greed in this context, for some infants do quite well while they are being breast fed, but show a very much increased appetite when they are changed over to the bottle. In such cases the phenomena accompanying weaning often occur in connection with the bottle and come to a head when the last bottle is taken away. The way the infant accepts solid foods is of great significance, and here again we see the most different reactions in different children. There are infants who only begin to show appetite at this stage. Others develop at this point feeding difficulties which persist in some form or other throughout the early years of childhood. Again many infants find only certain tastes, certain textures of solid food acceptable and repudiate others.

When we analyse such children, particularly at two or three, we learn a good deal about the reasons for their predilections and dislikes. Here, however, I can only put forward a few general suggestions as to the reasons for the various feeding difficulties. Those children whose appetite improves when put on to the bottle prefer it because while the bottle symbolically stands for the mother's breast, it is further removed in their minds from the primary object − the breast − which they are afraid to destroy. If the anxiety is not too great (and much depends here on quantities of anxiety as well as on other factors) an infant might not refuse the breast and even thrive on it, and nevertheless his greed can be strongly inhibited. Some infants, however, do not succeed in the symbolic substitution of the bottle for the breast, and therefore even the bottle remains too vulnerable an object; this is one of the factors which contribute in my view to the inhibition in sucking. Some of such children can only allow themselves greed when solid food is offered.

The fact that in their apathy and sadness some infants can completely refuse food (which is one of their most fundamental desires and, could they accept it, would be their greatest comfort) is extremely striking. It is, therefore, surprising that so many analysts engaged in the study of young children should not have devoted more attention to it. Miss Freud's theory that with infants up to six months we find a 'state where satisfaction counts for everything and objects count for nothing' (discussion of April 7th, 1943) does not offer an explanation for this symptomatic refusal of food, nor for the equally significant feeding difficulties of all kinds which we meet in quite young infants.

In my view such persistent refusal of food in infants, so akin to the attitude of depressive adults, provides evidence for the struggle between the destructive impulses and the libido. Or, expressed in terms of primary instincts, for the struggle between the death instinct and the life instinct. We may conclude that in the case of such infants, as in certain types of melancholics, the death instinct at times prevails over the life instinct.

Once we understand this, and can detect the operation of the death instinct, we find that it does not even work as noiselessly as was assumed. In another place I suggested that the whole development of the libido (which is bound up with the development of the ego) needs to be considered in connection with the destructive impulses. 'The emergence of the stages of organization with which we are acquainted corresponds, I should say, not only to the positions which the libido has won and established in its struggle with the destructive instinct, but, since these two components are forever united as well as opposed, to a growing adjustment between them.' [Klein 1932:212]

The infant's relation to food and the relation to the mother, which are interdependent at the beginning of life, become to some extent divorced as development goes on. The progress in this differentiation and in the capacity to love the mother as a person depends on the successful building up of trust in good objects and in goodness within. This again is influenced by a number of internal factors which make possible a sublimation of oral greed. At the same time the importance of everyday experiences cannot be overrated in this connection, since difficulties arising over feeding, as well as persistent sensations of physical discomfort – particularly illness – in the early stages of life increase anxieties from all sources and thus interfere with the developing of trust and with the steps towards overcoming ambivalence.

To conclude this short summary of the feeding difficulties of infants, I shall remind you of a remark by Freud: 'It is probable, too, that the fear of poisoning is connected with weaning'. Here Freud not only clearly indicates a psychological cause of feeding difficulties but also points to a fact which I have myself drawn attention to for many years, namely that paranoid fears play a fundamental role in feeding difficulties in infants. His suggestion also seems to me to imply that the infant has unconscious phantasies about the 'goodness' and 'badness' of the breast, for otherwise how could he arrive at the feeling that the food is poisonous? [Freud, S. 1933a:157; SE 22:122]³⁵

Feelings of guilt and reparation wishes

I shall now consider some other everyday observations. It is common knowledge that infants expect praise and admiration for every new achievement. But it is less commonly recognized that he also wishes by means of these achievements to evoke love from his mother and to give her pleasure. How soon does he realize that his smile delights his mother, attracts her attention, keeps her near him, and at times serves this purpose better than his crying. There seems to be no doubt in analytic and non-analytic observers that when an infant cries, this is partly intended to bring his mother back to him; but that his smile and expressions of love could have a similar purpose has been less fully recognized.

I have seen a few infants, when they had woken with anxiety, using all their little tricks which they knew delighted the mother to keep her by their side. In one case an infant of ten months had woken with night terror, and the attempts on the part of her mother to put her to sleep were not successful. Every time the mother turned out the light, the little girl cried again with unmistakable signs of anxiety. When the light was turned on once more, she clapped her hands, smiled, and did everything which she knew was pleasing to her mother. The anxiety behind this liveliness was quite apparent, as this playfulness and cheerfulness were different from the usual happy mood with which they were associated in daytime; the infant was obviously trying to avoid being exposed once more to anxiety. Actually the mother decided to play with the child and to make her feel comfortable, and very soon the little girl went happily to sleep again.

In my view an infant knows intuitively that his smile and other signs of affection and happiness produce happiness and pleasure in the mother and evoke similar responses from her. With older children and in adult life, quarrels are often followed by expressions of friendliness, which are felt in the unconscious – if not consciously as the means of making amends and reparation. At the same time they are also an essential method of gaining reassurance against anxiety and guilt, and thus partly serve defensive purposes. I believe that the same is true, *mutatis mutandis*, of infants. One has only to watch the expression on an infant's face when his smile is not responded to and his attempts to please fail. The smile disappears, the light fades from his eyes, and something akin to sorrow and anxiety creeps into his expression.

We can also observe that the infant makes attempts to feed the mother in return for her feeding him. There are various things he expresses by putting his finger into her mouth. Sometimes he clearly wishes to explore the mouth, e.g. an infant of five months to whom I made noises corresponding to his own attempts to babble watched me with the greatest delight and interest and suddenly, while the sound came out of my mouth, he put his finger into my mouth – quite obviously an attempt to fetch the sounds out of it. At other times an infant indicates his wish for his mother to suck his finger or even playfully to bite it, which is partly an attempt to feed her. A little later on many an infant actually tries to feed his mother with his spoon. I am not concerned here with the extent to which the child imitates his mother, which no doubt he does; but my main point is that in this way he expresses his own feelings of love and gratitude towards her and his desire to feed her and give her pleasure as she gives him pleasure by feeding him. He also in my view makes reparation in phantasy and thus counteracts his feelings of guilt, which in a symptomatic way express themselves in feeding difficulties and phobias.

The depressive position, defence mechanisms, and ego-development

So far I have pointed out that an infant's expressions of love, interest, pleasure, etc., among other purposes serve the need for reassurance through his mother's love. Furthermore, that they express reparation, and thus are also means of overcoming grief. Freud's observations of the eighteen-month-old boy with his cotton reel pointed in this direction. By means of this play the child was overcoming not only his feelings of loss, but, as I see it, also his grief.[36]

As Susan Isaacs pointed out in her paper on Phantasy, [see p. 307] there are various typical forms of play similar to the one of the cotton-reel game. For instance, it is a general observation that children, sometimes even before the second half of the first year, enjoy throwing things out of the pram again and again and again, and expect them back. I observed a variation of this play in an infant of ten months who had recently begun to crawl. He was indefatigable in throwing a toy away from himself and then getting hold of it by crawling towards it. I was told that he had started this play about two months earlier when he made his first attempts to move himself forward.

Already in the fifth or sixth month many infants respond with pleasure to 'peep-bo'; and I have seen infants playing this actively by pulling the blanket over the head and off again as early as seven months. I observed an infant with whom the mother made a bedtime ritual of this game, thus leaving the child to go to sleep in a happy mood, which suggests that the repetition of such experiences is an important factor in helping the child to overcome his feelings of loss and grief. Another typical play which I found to be a great help and comfort to young children is to part from the child at bedtime saying 'bye-bye' and waving, leaving the room slowly, as it were disappearing gradually. I was able to observe repeatedly the effect of such experiences on the infant referred to above in daytime as well. Sometimes when the mother was about to leave the room, a fleeting expression of sadness came into the child's eyes, or she seemed near crying. But when the mother waved to her and said 'bye-bye', she appeared comforted and went on with her play activities. I saw her at the age between ten and eleven months practising again and again the gesture of waving, and it was clear that the practice itself, even before she could actually achieve the gesture, had become a source of interest and comfort to her. 'Bye-bye' was also one of her first words.

The emotional experiences of losing the loved object and regaining it are an essential part of early mental life. The various methods the ego applies at different stages in dealing with feelings of loss are, therefore, criteria by which we could measure the development of the ego. Hallucination, which primarily serves wish-fulfilment, is bound up with a sense of omnipotence and is either the basis of phantasy life or already part of it.

The bridge between the infant's sense of omnipotence and his adjustment to reality is the mother's breast which sometimes returns apparently at his wish, and thus confirms his belief in omnipotence. At other times frustration forces him to submit this feeling, and his associated phantasies, to the testing of reality and thus weakens his sense of omnipotence. When an infant is able to feel that his mother will return, because his experiences of regaining the loved object have proved this to him, he has already made fundamental steps in the progressive testing of external reality, and thus in the growth of the ego; he is also beginning to overcome his depressive position. But while this adaptation to reality goes on, the infant has not by any means yet overcome his feeling of omnipotence and his belief in the magic gesture. In fact, to some extent, the actual experience of the loved person's return, while helping the infant to test reality, also substantiates his feelings of omnipotence. But the very fact that repeated experiences of frustration force the infant to subject this belief to the testing by external reality leads to its progressive devaluation.

In normal circumstances the infant's growing capacity to perceive the external world and to understand it increases his confidence in it, and his experience of the external reality becomes the most important means of overcoming his phantastic fears and his depressive feelings. For instance, the infant whose mother had introduced the 'peep-bo' game, and a little later the waving and saying 'bye-bye' at bed time, showed a further important step in her methods of dealing with her feelings of loss and depression at eleven months. She thoroughly enjoyed crawling up and down a passage for hours on end and was quite contented by herself, but from time to time she crawled into the room where her mother was (the door had been left open), had a look at her mother or attempted to converse with her, and returned to the passage.

When an infant is able first to sit up and then to stand in his cot, he can look at his mother and father whenever he likes, and this in some sense brings him nearer to them. This is still more the case when he is able to crawl and walk. The great psychological importance for the infant of standing, crawling, and walking has been described by a few analytic writers.[37] My point here is that these achievements are the means of regaining his lost objects as well as finding new objects in their stead, and thus help the infant to overcome the depressive position. To put it from another angle, the ego's striving to overcome the depressive position furthers intellectual interests and activities of all kinds.

To return to the infant who with his first attempts to move forward took to throwing a toy away from himself and tried to get it back without help. We can draw the inference that the meaning of this absorbing game, when he was able to crawl as well as at the earlier stage, was to regain his lost objects by his own efforts. It is interesting to watch the progress in the sense of reality[38] as expressed in the stages of this play. At first the infant threw the toy out of the pram and omnipotently expected it to come back. A little later he expected his mother to bring it back to him. This already implied great progress in his relation to reality. When he attempted to fetch the toy by moving towards it, he had achieved a greater power to test reality and actively influence, modify, and control it. At the same time, since he was able to move[39] towards his loved object (for which the toy stood), his hope to retain and secure it had increased. Thus he could gain greater reassurance as well as pleasure and a satisfaction of his interests. This is also an instance of the way in which the ego's struggle to overcome the depressive position gives added impetus to mental as well as physical development, for there is little doubt that the infant's desire to crawl was stimulated by his interest in this particular game. In the same way speech development, beginning with the imitation of sounds, is one of those great achievements which bring the child (physically and mentally) nearer to the people he loves and also enables him to find new objects. In all these achievements the infant's attempts to modify and control his objects – his internal and external world – play an important part. The co-ordination of functions and of movements is bound up with a defence mechanism which I take to be one of the fundamental processes in early development, namely the manic defence. This defence is closely linked with the depressive position and implies a control over the internal world. There is a constant interplay between the testing of external reality and the attempts to modify it, control it, and come to terms with it on the one hand, and the relation to the inner world on the other. These two orientations, inwards and outwards, are gradually brought into harmony with each other; and the extent to which this is achieved is a measure of normal development.

Every step in ego development which enables the child to communicate with, perceive, and understand the external world, helps him to gain greater security about his external objects; this again assists him in overcoming his fear of losing his good internal objects. If a satisfactory balance between these interacting processes is achieved, the child is well on the way to overcome his depressive feelings.

Symbol formation

Frustration, as we know, plays a vital part in early mental life. One of the earliest methods of dealing with frustration – if not the earliest – is bound up with narcissistic states. Hallucination, a narcissistic phenomenon *par excellence*, implies the withdrawal from the external world. Our contention (cf. Dr Heimann's paper on Introjection and Projection) is that this process becomes possible by the introjection of the lost object and by a withdrawal into an internal situation which, as I see it, is an essential part of the infant's phantasy life.

Frustration, however, is also a vital factor for adaptation to reality, and for sublimation. For concurrently with narcissistic phenomena – the early ego develops methods of strengthening its relation to the external world, that is to say, by the growing adaptation to reality and by sublimation – and coping in this way with feelings of loss.

I shall here only briefly introduce the important part symbol formation plays in all these processes, as an essential means of extending love and interest from the primary objects to new objects and further sources of gratification.[40] We can observe in the infant that together with the interest first in his mother's breast and face the interest in other objects, his rattle and various toys, develops and that he loves them. In my view these toys symbolically come to stand first for his mother's breast; and this view is substantiated by the fact that the interest in his mother's body precedes the discoveries made of his own body. Very soon, however, the toys also come to stand symbolically for parts of his own body. From at least the third month onwards the infant plays with his limbs and toes, revealing an obvious interest and pleasure in his body. At five or six months he begins various experimentative forms of play with objects which at first symbolically stand for parts of his body but gradually acquire an interest in themselves. At this period the growing interest in the external world can be easily observed.

As I pointed out in one of my earliest papers,[41] I consider symbol formation which is bound up with unconscious phantasy life as one of the fundamental methods by which the growing relation to external objects is achieved and as a basic factor for all sublimations, since it is by way of symbolic equation that various activities and interests become the subject of libidinal phantasies. In a later paper,[42] I expanded my views on the fundamental role of symbol formation for early development. One of my conclusions was that by symbol formation not only are love and interest extended to new objects, but also that at the same time anxieties are deflected and distributed by this process. In the present paper I want to develop this train of thought still further. By transferring love, interest, and anxieties to new objects, the ego is also able to deflect feelings of loss and mourning away from the primary object. This substitution of other, more numerous, and therefore replaceable objects for the first and main object whose loss is feared and mourned is linked with a number of processes, such as the distribution of feelings among more objects as the diminution of feelings through the repetition of the experience of losing and regarding the object. In this way, which amounts also to a testing of phantastic fears by external reality, feelings of mourning are experienced on a minor scale, as well as gradually overcome. This contention is illustrated, I think, by the cotton-reel play in Freud's observations and the various forms of infants' play which I described above.

Frustration in relation to the first object is, as we know, a driving force for the building up of phantasies. Through the new gratifications which symbol formation and phantasy life provide, they in turn become the means of diminishing these frustrations. Thus grievance, hatred, and ultimately guilt are lessened. All this has a bearing on fixations. For the weakening – and to some extent even preventing – of the concentration of greed on the one primary object (food, mother) materially lessens aggression and hatred, and thus guilt. This is one of the prime factors which enable the libido to flow freely towards new objects and gratifications. In all these ways symbol formation and phantasy life (and thus sublimations) are the precondition for the overcoming of the depressive position and are used by the ego in coping with anxiety, guilt, and sorrow.

Growing adaptation and integration

One of the early defence methods of the mind in overcoming the depressive position is the turning away from the loved object.[43] This, however, can only be successful if the infant does not turn away from his primary objects with such strong resentment, grievance, and anxiety that the relation to new objects is impeded at its source. For these emotions – if they are too strong – are carried over into the new relation and tend to undermine it. Moreover, if grievance and hatred are the predominant driving forces for leaving the primary object, new sources of gratification cannot be sufficiently accepted, because the guilt towards the primary object acts as a barrier. A relative balance even at this early stage between love and hatred seems essential for the development of the infant's relation to his mother, since it enables him increasingly to divorce her as a source of food from her other functions and qualities. He can only make these essential steps towards sublimating his oral desires if his ambivalence, and thus his anxieties, are not too great. The success of these complex processes depends on a relative optimum in the constellation of the interacting internal and external factors. All this is bound up with his capacity to establish securely the relation to his internal as well as to his external objects. When in his narcissistic states the infant hallucinates the lost gratification he reinforces, owing to the loss of the external object, the introjection of the breast as well as re-experiences the happy feeding situation. When this happens, the good breast is, in his phantasy, kept alive as an internal object, and thus a foundation is laid for internal relations which again fundamentally influence the relation to external objects. For the infant returns to the external object, when it again reappears and gratifies him, with some of the love and hope experienced in connection with the internalized breast. The existence of a phantasy life is a precondition for such processes. This point has been elaborated by Dr Heimann in her paper on 'Introjection and Projection', and this is why I am here referring to it only summarily.

There is thus a constant interaction between the early development of relations to the internal and external world. This complex interplay includes the foundations of the infant's object relations as well as of his sublimations. All these processes, however, presuppose not only a complexity of emotions and a rich phantasy life, but also methods of the ego in dealing with them. In examining the problem whether the infant's mind is capable of some degree of integration, not only of perception and reality testing but also of his emotions, I am touching on Freud's concept of the primary process and the way Miss Freud applies it to the emotional life of the infant. Here we have an essential source of difference of opinion between Miss Freud and myself regarding the emotional life of the infant and, I think, one of the essential reasons for evaluating observed facts differently. Freud says:

> When I termed one of the psychic processes in the psychic apparatus the primary process, I did so not only in consideration of its status and function, but was also able to take account of the temporal relationship actually involved. So far as we know, a psychic apparatus possessing only the primary process does not exist, and is to that extent a theoretical fiction; but this at least is a fact: that the primary processes are present in the apparatus from the beginning, while the secondary processes only take shape gradually during the course of life, inhibiting and overlaying the primary, whilst gaining complete control over them perhaps only in the prime of life.
>
> [Freud, S. 1900:555; SE 5:603][44]

Miss Freud, however, assumes that the primary process governs the emotional life of the young child to at least one year of life. I may quote again some of the statements she made in the course of these discussions. She speaks of 'the kind of uncorrelated mental life to which dream-function regresses' (discussion of January 27th, 1943). [See p. 331.] Yet she states: 'Correlation or synthesis of perception and reality testing is achieved in degrees from birth onwards' and:

'even though correlation of perception grows continually, wishes and impulses continue to be governed by the primary process with its characteristic lack of unification'. Speaking of children even in the second year of life, she says: 'If children in the second year are not checked by fear of outside prohibition, their contrasting wishes and emotions can still flow freely. It is usual that conflicting inner urges succeed in finding successive expression without the one necessarily influencing the other.' Then again: 'The child between one and two actually possesses a wide range of libidinal and aggressive relations to objects. But the conflicting acts and emotions which arise on the basis of these relations can still coexist in his mind and in his behaviour without adding to or detracting from each other.' (Discussion of April 7th, 1943) [See p. 422.]

As the passage from *The Interpretation of Dreams* quoted above clearly shows, Miss Freud's hypothesis that the primary process operates over the whole field of the infant's emotional life does not agree with Freud's view. Moreover, Miss Freud's hypothesis clashes with the picture of the infant's mental life as it has been presented to us by a number of analytic and non-analytic observers. Conflicting acts and emotions arise no doubt strongly in a child of one or two, but this does not justify the conclusion that there is no interaction and integration going on at the same time. In fact conflicting impulses, phantasies, and emotions arise in the unconscious mind at any age, and yet no one would doubt that in the older child and in the adult a capacity for interaction and integration of impulses and emotions coexist with conflict.

Intellectual and emotional development

There is another consideration which seems to me pertinent here. Miss Freud's hypothesis implies an arbitrary division between the intellectual and emotional development in young children. This is scientifically untenable and in contradiction to all the observable facts and to the understanding of the data which analysis has given us. It also suggests too sharp a division between the ego and the id, and disregards the fact that the ego is actually but a differentiated part of the id.

A short digression with reference to technique seems to be in place here. I think that this particular difference of views regarding the emotional life of young children is one of the sources of differences in technique. Some of the main principles of Miss Freud's technique [Freud, A. 1927] appear to be based on this sharp division between

785

the intellect and the emotions (and fundamentally also between the conscious and unconscious). Miss Freud does not seem to think that young children could or should be analysed; her technique for the analysis of children in any case applies only to children from the latency period onwards. In fact, young children of say two or three, or even four years of age, can only be analysed if we understand that the intellect and the conscious mind are perpetually being influenced by emotions and phantasies and by the anxieties they produce, and if we keep in mind that the analysis of a young child's phantasies is the best key to the analysis of his mind as a whole. Furthermore, if we do not appreciate fully the interaction of the emotional and intellectual factors in infancy and in young children, the approach even to the older child's and the adult patient's mind remains too intellectual and superficial. As a result not only is the analysis of the emotions and of the unconscious bound to suffer, but also of the conscious mind and thus of the whole personality.

The capacity for integration of emotions as well of perception and reality testing does not come about suddenly. It has a history of development which takes us back to the first interactions of the emotions of love and hate and of external and internal situations in young infants. Earlier in this paper I suggested that feeding difficulties in infants arise from the inhibition of greed; this presupposes a very early modification of instincts. I have formerly [Klein 1932:212] drawn attention to the fact that the cannibalistic impulses, whose powerful and lasting impact on the unconscious mind is well known to us, do not find any commensurate expression in the infant's behaviour – which I take as another proof for modification of instincts. More proofs could be brought forward if space allowed. Here I can only refer to one of the instances by which I illustrated in this paper some aspects of the child's early emotional life. In the apparently simple case of an infant who experienced anxiety because his mother was absent, and even after he had calmed down did not enjoy the next feed, in my view a number of complex processes were involved. We can plausibly explain the infant's refusal of food on the lines that he has integrated an external and internal experience (the fact of the mother's absence and his fear that she is destroyed) and later applied this to another situation – the feeding situation. What goes on in his mind is that either the food turns bad because the mother is harmed or destroyed, or that he cannot take food because it is his very sucking and eating which destroys her. This would prove not only an interaction between emotions but also a capacity to take in a total situation and to apply it, even some time later, to another situation.

786

To return for a moment to my concept of the depressive position; in my paper 'A Contribution to the Psycho-Genesis of Manic Depressive States' [Klein 1935] I differentiated between paranoid anxieties and depressive anxieties. In the case I just interpreted, the infant's feelings that the food has turned bad, i.e. poisoned, arises from fear of retaliation by his mother (or breast) for his cannibalistic and aggressive impulses; that is to say, paranoid anxiety. The feeling that the mother is destroyed and will never return is a depressive anxiety.

The unintelligible infant

The signs of emotional integration are very subtle. This fact helps to make the infant as a whole somewhat enigmatic. A closer observation, however, of the whole context of the infant's behaviour, bringing together the various details observed, yields abundant evidence of the early steps towards emotional integration, and of the constant and intimate interplay between perception and feeling.[45] For instance every understanding paediatrician knows that the mother's attitude and her state of mind are of great importance not only on the flow of milk but on the way in which the child will take his food and thrive on it. These facts point to the existence in the infant of an unconscious knowledge and recognition of reality, far beyond his intellectual development. The valuable studies of the feeding response in the first few days made by Merrell Middlemore [Middlemore 1941] record the influence of emotional factors even from the beginning of life.

We can, however, detect such unconscious knowledge in the young infant not only as regards the mother, but even in his relation to strangers. A long and intense scrutiny very often precedes an infant's decision – how else is one to describe this process? – as to whether the stranger is acceptable as a friendly object or is to be rejected. Observation has shown me that this discrimination is very often well founded, since people who are accepted by an infant often really are kind and fond of children. This exquisite mental response which, as we know, is the basis of every psychological understanding presupposes not only a wealth of emotions in the infant but also some capacity to integrate them. I would add that his intellectual capacities, too, are greater than is commonly assumed.

In interpreting these attitudes, responses, and processes in the child, we must be guided by evanescent signs which are often difficult to define: for instance, the swift change of expression on his face, particularly the fleeting shades of expression in his eyes which light up or grow dull. The manifestations of his emotional capacities and processes greatly differ, as we have seen, from those of a later age. Though the infant's impulses and feelings are becoming integrated to some extent, they can only very partially be correlated with his activities. To transform the correlation of impulses into actions presupposes a knowledge of the external world as well as a correlation of all his functions, which young children only gradually come to possess. This is a point which, I think, is particularly misleading in considering the infant's emotions. These facts, taken together with the intensity of his desires and the depth and strength of his feelings, suggests that the infant's mental world and all his relationships to it, including his feelings of love, are bound to be very different from those of later phases of development.

Conclusion

Many of the facts I have presented in this paper have been recognized by a number of observers and therefore, in the long run, all of us should be able to check them. Closer scrutiny, more attention to details and, most of all, the correlation of observations together with some degree of inference drawn from our knowledge of the unconscious of somewhat older children should enable us to clarify our minds on the emotional life of infants.

This method of interpretation is fully in keeping with the principles on which psychoanalysis was developed. The observation of children between three and five years yielded entirely new results when Freud discovered the Oedipus complex in adults, and every further discovery about the earlier stages of development, as seen through the adult, opened up fresh fields of observation of children. Similarly, the conclusions I came to in my analyses of young children between two and three years enriched and widened the observation of the emotional life of infants.

In concluding his exposition of the hypothesis regarding object relations at the early stages of libidinal development, Abraham said: 'Now that we have become alive to certain occurrences relating to infantile development, there will not be wanting confirmatory evidence obtained from the direct observation of the child.' [Abraham 1924:488–9] If the hypothesis of the infantile depressive position is considered against the background of the whole of the emotional life of the infant, a number of observable facts find an interpretation which links them with well established theory.

Notes

1 '. . . the unmatched prototype of later sexual satisfaction'. [SE 16:314]
2 'I was further made aware of a defect in the account I have given in the text, which, in the interests of lucidity, describes the conceptual distinction between the two phases of auto-erotism and object-love as though it were also a separation in time.' [SE 7:194]
3 (Original footnote) Abraham also stressed that 'the stages placed on the same horizontal level in each column do not necessarily coincide in time' (p. 496).
4 (Original footnote) which I have expanded in Chapters XI and XII of *The Psychoanalysis of Children* (1932).
5 (Original footnote) In some of my papers I have described the importance of the masturbation phantasies, which are closely linked with infantile sexual theories, for the development of sublimation and neurosis. See my paper on 'Infant Analysis' (first published in 1923) in *IJPA*, vol. VII, 1926.
6   In regard to anxious expectation, clinical experience revealed that it has a regular connection with the libidinal economics of sexual life. The commonest cause of anxiety neurosis is unconsummated excitation. Libidinal excitation is aroused but not satisfied, not employed; apprehensiveness then appears instead of this libido, that has been diverted from its employment. I even thought I was justified in saying that this unsatisfied libido was directly changed into anxiety. This view found support in some quite regularly occurring phobias of small children. Many of these phobias are very puzzling to us, but others, such as the fear of being alone and the fear of strangers, can be explained with certainty. Loneliness as well as a strange face arouses the child's longing for his familiar mother; he is unable to control this libidinal excitation, he cannot hold it in suspense, but changes it into anxiety. This infantile anxiety must therefore be regarded not as the realistic but as of the neurotic kind. Infantile phobias and the expectation of anxiety in anxiety neurosis offer us two examples of one way in which neurotic anxiety originates: by direct transformation of libido.   [SE 22:82–3]
7 'Only a few of the manifestations of anxiety in childhood are comprehensible to us, and we must confine our attention to them. They occur, for instance, when a child is alone, or in the dark, or when it finds itself with an unknown person instead of one to whom it is used – such as its mother. These three instances can be reduced to a single condition – namely, that of missing someone who is loved and longed for.' [SE 20:136]

789

8 'Its place is taken in their sex by a fear of loss of love, which is evidently a later prolongation of the infant's anxiety if it finds its mother absent. You will realize how a real situation of danger is indicated by this anxiety. If a mother is absent or has withdrawn her love from her child, it is no longer sure of the satisfaction of its needs and is perhaps exposed to the most distressing feelings of tension.' [SE 22:87]

9 This quote from Freud (1933a) is the same as that quoted on p. 148 in SE 20.

10 (Original footnote) Here and there, of course, there are references to these findings, and in particular I wish to mention Ernest Jones's Introduction to Abraham's *Selected Papers*, in which he fully appreciates the importance of these discoveries.

11 (Original footnote) 'At any rate I can say that I have never attempted to produce a complete and a well-rounded-off theory, but that on the contrary I have myself drawn attention to faults and shortcomings in my own suggestions' (loc. cit., p. 498).

12 (Original footnote) See my paper on 'Early Stages of the Oedipus Complex' (*IJPA*, vol. IX, 1928).

13 (Original footnote) The view expressed in my paper referred to above that guilt connects with the dread of the superego is in keeping with Freud's view that guilt is always bound up with the superego, though in my view this applies to a much earlier stage. Furthermore, my hypothesis expressed in the same paper, that the severity of the superego to some extent results from the child's aggression which is projected on to the superego, has been accepted by Freud (cf. *Civilization and its Discontents*, p. 116).

14 (Original footnote) 'The Importance of Symbol Formation in the Development of the Ego' (*IJPA*, vol. XI, Part 1, 1930). At the same Congress Ernest Jones read his paper 'Fear, Guilt and Hate' (*IJPA*, vol. X, 1929) in which he made an important study of the interdependence of fear, guilt and hate, and showed conclusively that it is only in their interaction that each of these emotions can be understood.

15 (Original footnote) The proposal to which Freud refers is on p. 118, and I shall quote it now: 'We cannot disregard the conclusion that man's sense of guilt has its origin in the Oedipus complex and was acquired when the father was killed by the association of the brothers. At that time the aggression was not suppressed but carried out, and it is this same act of aggression whose suppression in the child we regard as the source of feelings of guilt.' Again, speaking of the conflict of ambivalence, he says: 'it must express itself in the Oedipus complex, cause the development of conscience and create the first feelings of guilt'. (loc. cit., p. 121)

(Editor's note) 'We cannot get away from the assumption that man's sense of guilt springs from the Oedipus conflict and was acquired at the killing of the father by the brothers banded together. On that occasion an act of aggression was not suppressed but carried out; but it was the same act of aggression whose suppression in the child is supposed to be the source of his sense of guilt . . . the conflict is bound to express itself in the Oedipus complex, to establish the conscience and create the first sense of guilt'. [SE 21:132]

16 This is, I think, the place at which to put forward for serious consideration a view which I have earlier recommended for provisional acceptance. . . . For how are we to account, on dynamic and economic grounds, for an increase in the sense of guilt appearing in place of an unfulfilled erotic demand? This only seems possible in a roundabout way – if we suppose, that is, that the prevention of erotic satisfaction calls up a piece of aggressiveness against the person who has interfered with the satisfaction, and that this aggressiveness has itself to be suppressed and made over to the superego. I am convinced that many processes will admit of a simpler and clearer exposition if the findings of psychoanalysis with regard to the derivation of the sense of guilt are restricted to the aggressive instincts.   [SE 21:138–9]

17 (Original footnote) Yet in the same book there are passages which point to the fact that conflict exists in the early stages of life. On p. 121 Freud says that 'guilt is the expression of the conflict of ambivalence, the eternal struggle between Eros and the destructive or death instinct'. And a little later: 'an intensification of the sense of guilt – resulting from the innate conflict of ambivalence, from the eternal struggle between the love and the death trends – will be inextricably bound up with it, until perhaps the sense of guilt may swell to a magnitude that individuals can hardly support' (pp. 121–2). 'Innate conflict of ambivalence', 'eternal struggle between the love and the death trends' – do they not imply a long history of intense conflict preceding the climax of the Oedipus complex?

(Editor's note) '. . . for the sense of guilt is an expression of the conflict due to ambivalence, of the eternal struggle between Eros and the instinct of destruction or death . . . as a result of the inborn conflict from ambivalence, and of the eternal struggle between the trends of love and death there is inextricably bound up with it an increase in the sense of guilt which will perhaps reach heights which the individual finds hard to tolerate'. [SE 21:131–2]

18 But there is one topic which I cannot pass over so easily – not, however, because I understand particularly much about it or have contributed very much to it. Quite the contrary; I have scarcely concerned myself with it at all. . . .

When in the treatment of an adult neurotic we followed up the determinants of his symptoms, we were regularly led back to his early childhood. A knowledge of the later aetiological factors was not sufficient either for understanding the case or for producing a therapeutic effect. We were therefore compelled to make ourselves acquainted with the psychical peculiarities of childhood; we learnt a quantity of things which could not have been learnt except through analysis, and we were able to put right many opinions that were generally held about childhood.   [SE 22:146–7]

19 (Original footnote) I am giving here a rough translation of a footnote which appeared in the latest German edition of *Three Contributions* (Gesammelte Schriften, vol. V, p. 68). As far as I know, there is no English translation with the original.

The above conclusions on infantile sexuality, to which I came in the year 1905, were justified by the results of the psychoanalysis of adults. Direct observation of children could not be fully used at that time, and had only yielded some isolated hints and a few valuable confirmations. Since then, the analysis of a few cases of nervous disease dating from early childhood has given us a direct insight into infantile psycho-sexuality. I can point out with satisfaction that direct observation has fully confirmed the conclusion of psychoanalysis and thus testifies to the reliability of this latter method of research. 'The Analysis of the Phobia of a Five Year Old Boy' (Vol. VIII in the Collected Works) has, moreover, taught us several new facts which our psychoanalytic knowledge had not led us to expect; e.g. that sexual symbolism – the representation of sexual interests through non-sexual objects and relations – dates back to the first years of the child's use of speech. Moreover, my attention was drawn to a defect in the above exposition where, for the sake of clarity, I described the conceptual division between the phase of auto-erotism and the phase of object-love as a division in time as well. The analyses quoted above (as well as reports by Bell, cf. above) teach us that children of three to five years are capable of a well-marked choice of object, and that this choice is accompanied by strong affects.

(Editor's note) (Footnote added by Freud in 1910) [SE 7:193–4]

When the account which I have given above of infantile sexuality was first published in 1905, it was founded for the most part on the results of psychoanalytic research upon adults. At that time it was impossible to make full use of direct observations on children; only isolated hints and some valuable pieces of confirmation came from that source. Since then it has become possible to gain direct insight into infantile psycho-sexuality by the analysis of some cases of neurotic illness during the early years of childhood. It is gratifying to be able to report that direct observation has fully confirmed the conclusions arrived at by psychoanalysis – which is incidentally good evidence of the trustworthiness of that method of research. In addition to this, the 'Analysis of a Phobia of a Five Year Old Boy' [Freud, S. 1909b] has taught us much that is new for which we have not been prepared by psychoanalysis: for instance, the fact that sexual symbolism, the representation of what is sexual by non-sexual objects and relations – extends back into the first years of possession of the power of speech. I was further made aware of a defect in the account I have given in the text, which, in the interests of lucidity described the conceptual distinction between the two phases of auto-erotism and object-love as though it were also a separation in time. But the analyses that I have mentioned, as well as the findings of Bell [Bell 1902:330] quoted above, show that children between the ages of three and five are capable of very clear object choice, accompanied by strong affects.

[SE 7:193–4]

20 (Original footnote) Freud says in *Civilization and its Discontents* (pp. 127–8): 'we ought not to speak of conscience before a superego is demonstrable; as to consciousness of guilt; we must admit that it comes into being before the superego, therefore before conscience. At that time it is the direct expression of the dread of external authority, the recognition of the tension between the ego and this latter; it is the direct derivative of the conflict between the need for parental love and the urgency towards instinctual gratification, and it is the thwarting of this urgency that provokes the tendency to aggression.'
(Editor's note)

We ought not to speak of a conscience until the superego is demonstrably present. As to a sense of guilt, we must admit that it is in existence before the superego, and therefore before conscience, too. At that time it is the immediate expression of fear of the external authority, a recognition of the tension between the ego and that authority, it is the direct derivative of the conflict between the need of the authority's love and the urge towards instinctual satisfaction, whose inhibition produces the inclination to aggression.

21 The same sentence as in the text above.
22 '. . . exposed to the most distressing feelings of tension'. [SE 22:87]
23 'It cannot as yet distinguish between temporary absence and permanent loss. As soon as it loses sight of its mother it behaves as if it were never going to see her again; and repeated consoling experiences to the contrary are necessary before it learns that her disappearance is usually followed by her re-appearance.' [SE 22:169]

24 (Original footnote) This is not the place to discuss our views on regression, which has been done by Susan Isaacs and Paula Heimann in the preceding paper.

25 (Original footnote) This passage can also be adduced in support of my view, stated in an earlier section of this paper, that Freud's concept of primary narcissism was a limiting concept and did not apply to a definite circumscribed period in the infant's life. For in this passage Freud appears to assume that an object relation to the mother exists from birth onwards.

(Editor's note) 'There is much more continuity between intra–uterine life and earliest infancy than the impressive caesura of the act of birth would have us believe. What happens is that the child's biological situation as a foetus is replaced for it by a psychological object relation to its mother. But we must not forget that during its intra–uterine life the mother was not an object for the foetus, and at that time there were no objects at all.' [SE 20:138]

26 (Original footnote) Imre Hermann came to the conclusion that certain features in the relation of a young infant to his mother which express the desire for physical closeness are derived from the loss of the intra–uterine state. Among other manifestations he mentions grasping and clutching and various forms of holding on to the mother's body, and even some elements in the sucking process. In his view these express the urge to gain compensation for the lost physical closeness with the mother. He also interprets in this sense the general tendency to hold on to something, to hang on to something in a moment of danger. All these activities, in Hermann's view, which are directed towards the mother are expressions of a very early object relation. (cf. 'Zum Triebleben der Primaten', *Imago*, vol. XIX, 1933. Also: 'Sich-Anklammern – Auf-Suche-Gehen', *Int. Ztschr. f. Psa*, vol. XXII, 1936).

27 In his paper 'The Problem of Melancholia' (*International Journal of Psycho-Analysis*, vol. IX, 1928) Sando Rado considers that the roots of melancholia can be found in the hunger situation of the suckling baby. Nevertheless Rado does not apply this conclusion to the actual emotional life of the infant; he refers only to aetiology. He says (loc. cit.): 'The deepest fixation-point in the depressive disposition is to be found in the situation of threatened loss of love (Freud), more especially in the hunger situation of the suckling baby.' Referring to Freud's statement that in mania the ego is once more merged with the superego in unity, Rado infers that 'this process is the faithful intra-psychic repetition of the experience of that fusing with the mother that takes place during drinking at her breast'.

28 'You should bear in mind that the dreams which we produce at night have, on the one hand, the greatest external similarity and internal

kinship that are creations of insanity, and are, on the other hand, compatible with complete health in waking life.' [SE 11:33]

29 (Original footnote) See particularly the list of diagnoses of patients in my book, *The Psychoanalysis of Children* (p. 381).

30 (Original footnote) For instance, Mrs Hoffer, in her contribution to the discussion on Phantasy (April 7th, 1943) says: 'But there is nothing to lead us to call this initial stage of mental development phantasy. In the second half of the first year the baby begins to behave humanly' (my italics). Such an attitude, which appears to lack in the most elementary understanding of the young infant, would close the door on further research about a period of life which, according to Freud's discoveries, is fundamental for all later development.

31 It is a remarkable fact that a child even with an age difference of only eleven months, is not too young to take notice of what is happening. But what the child grudges the unwanted intruder and rival is not only the suckling but all the other signs of maternal care. It feels that it is being destroyed, despoiled, prejudiced in its rights; it casts jealous hatred on the new baby and develops a grievance against the faithless mother which often finds expression in a disagreeable change in its behaviour. It becomes 'naughty', perhaps irritable and disobedient and goes back on the advances which it has made on controlling its excretions. All of this has been very long familiar and is accepted as self-evident; but we rarely form a correct idea of the strength of these jealous impulses, of the tenacity with which they persist and of the magnitude of their influence on later development.   [SE 22:123]

32 'Many of these phobias are very puzzling to us, but others such as the fear of being alone and the fear of strangers, can be explained with certainty.' [SE 22:83]

33 (Original footnote) I think it was Ferenczi who introduced the terms 'good mother' and 'bad mother'.

34 (Original footnote) In her *Social Development in Young Children* (1933) Susan Isaacs gave instances of feeding difficulties and discussed them in connection with the persecutory and depressive anxieties arising from oral sadism. There are also some interesting observations and conclusions in Dr D. W. Winnicott's book, *Disorders of Childhood* (1931).

35 'The fear of being poisoned is also probably connected with the withdrawal of the breast.' [SE 22:122]

36 (Original footnote) In his paper 'The Observations of Infants in a Set Situation' (*IJPA*, vol. XXII, 1941) Dr Winnicott discusses Freud's example (on the basis of his own more detailed studies).

37 (Original footnote) Amongst recent papers see 'On Motoring and Walking' by Dr Melitta Schmideberg (*IJPA*, vol. XVIII, 1937).

38 (Original footnote) Ferenczi's paper on the 'Stages of Development in

the Sense of Reality' contained some fundamental conclusions on this subject. Had space allowed, I should have liked to work out in detail the connections between some of the views he put forward about the infant's sense of reality with our present knowledge.

39 (Original footnote) The situation of the helpless infant who is overwhelmed by the anxiety of losing his external and internal objects and yet is unable to move towards them contributes, in my experience, to those particular anxiety dreams in which the dreamer feels immobilized.

40 (Original footnote) Ferenczi holds that identification, the forerunner of symbolism, arises out of the baby's endeavour to rediscover in every object his own organs and their functioning. In Ernest Jones's view (cf. 'The Theory of Symbolism') the pleasure principle makes it possible for two quite different things to be equated because of a similarity marked by pleasure or interest.

41 (Original footnote) 'Infant Analysis' (first published in 1923), also in *IJPA*, vol VII, 1926.

42 (Original footnote) 'The Importance of Symbol Formation in the Development of the Ego', *IJPA*, vol. XI, 1930.

43 (Original footnote) Bernfeld too speaks of the 'turning away from the mother' as occurring when the child 'overcomes its anxiety of walking without protection, of walking alone' and 'voluntarily goes away from the mother' (loc. cit., p. 255).

44 When I described one of the psychical processes occurring in the mental apparatus as the 'primary' one, what I had in mind was not merely considerations of relative importance and efficiency; I intended also to choose a name that would give an indication of its chronological priority. It is true that, so far as we know, no psychical apparatus exists which possesses a primary process only and that such an apparatus is to that extent a theoretical fiction. But this much is a fact: the primary processes are present in the mental apparatus from the first, while it is only during the course of life that secondary processes unfold and come to inhabit and overlay the primary ones; it may even be that their complete domination is not attained until the prime of life. [SE 5:603]

45 (Original footnote) Dr Brierley, in her contribution to the paper on Phantasy (March 17th, 1943) in discussing the relation between memory-traces and internalized objects, implied, as I understand it, that the connection between experience, phantasies, and impulses, and also between the conscious and unconscious, is indissoluble. She said, for instance, speaking of memory-traces: 'What is revived is not the sensory image alone but the image along with its related affects and impulses.' She then discussed Freud's contribution to what she calls the 'dynamism

of mental life'. She referred to his view that 'the unit of experience is not an isolated element, a separate impulse, feeling or image, but always a definite relationship of impulse and feeling to presentation' and drew the conclusion that 'revival of an image involves some revival of the impulses and feelings originally related to it'.

5
Ninth
Discussion of Scientific Differences

Minutes of Scientific Discussion Meeting
held on March 1st, 1944

Dr Payne was in the Chair and 18 Members and Associates were present (Miss Sharpe, Dr Franklin, Dr Winnicott, Miss Evans, Mrs Milner, Major Bowlby, Mrs Riviere, Dr Heimann, Dr K. Stephen, Major A. Stephen, Dr Herford, Major Rickman, Dr Taylor, Mr Money-Kyrle, Mrs Klein, Dr Usher, Miss Schwarz, Dr Wilson). Six Candidate-guests were present, one guest was present by invitation.

The Chairman announced that the minutes of the last meeting were not yet ready and asked the meeting whether Members wished the whole of the free discussion to be circulated, or papers only and a summary of the free discussion. It was decided to circulate a summary of the free discussion.

Commentary given by Mrs M. Klein
preliminary to discussion of her paper
'The Emotional Life of the Infant'

In this brief summary I should like to refer back to the main aims of my paper in the 'Emotional Life of the Infant'; I attempted to place my concept of the depressive position into a wider perspective, correlating it in more detail with well-established theory on the one hand, and on the other hand with the part it plays in the whole of the emotional development during the first year.

798

I attempted to show the danger of applying the limiting concept of primary narcissism too literally, that is to say to a definite stage occupying a definite period of time. The infant's attitude to his mother, from at least the second month onwards, and the close understanding and contact between mother and child in my view constitute a strong and emotional object relation. I also pointed out that this fact is actually widely acknowledged by a number of analytic and non-analytic observers.

Following Abraham's suggestion that at 'the level of partial cannibalism the individual shows the first signs of having some care for his object', I drew the conclusion that according to classical theory love exists at a stage when its manifestations differ greatly from those we connect with 'love in a stricter sense'. Thus I was brought to the following question: does love exist in the infant prior to the emergence of the genital libido? As Abraham's hypothesis suggests, and as observation definitely proves, love does exist in the young infant. This led me to re-examine my hypothesis that genital trends exist in the first year of life. After quoting various authors to substantiate my argument about the first manifestations of object love, I suggested that though the earliest relation is always one to part-objects, yet we may assume that the mother as a whole object, however vague in outline, exists from the beginning in the infant's mind. Here I find myself in line with the concept of a figure on the field developed by Gestalt psychology.

A discussion on the origins of anxiety and guilt would presuppose a clear demarcation between anxiety and guilt. But in the present state of our theory this demarcation is still incomplete. Freud approached this problem from two main angles. On the one hand he leaves no doubt that anxiety and guilt are closely connected with each other, and an important reference to their genetic relation is contained in the following passage: 'Here perhaps is the place to remark that at bottom the sense of guilt is nothing but a topographical variety of anxiety and that in its later phases it coincides completely with the dread of the superego.' [Freud, S. 1930:125; SE 21:135][1] On the other hand Freud definitely distinguishes between anxiety and guilt, and even between manifestations of guilt which precede the superego and those which are bound up with its emergence. In discussing the development of the sense of guilt, Freud says: 'We call this state of mind a "bad conscience"; but actually it does not deserve this name, for at this stage the sense of guilt is obviously only the dread of losing love, "social" anxiety. In a little child it can never be anything else, but in many adults too it has only changed in so far as the larger human community takes the place of the father or of both parents. . . . A great change takes place as soon as the authority has been internalized by the development of a superego. The manifestations of conscience are then raised to a new level; to be accurate, one should not call them conscience and sense of guilt before this.' [Freud, S. 1930:107–8; SE 21:124–5][2]

The last part of this passage illustrates Freud's view that guilt presupposes the existence of the superego. I have, however, quoted Freud as saying (footnote 23 of my paper): 'As to the consciousness of guilt, we must admit that it comes into being before the superego, therefore before conscience.' I should have added that, though Freud uses the term 'guilt' occasionally for manifestations preceding the superego, he has been careful to qualify such use – as can be seen in the statement I quoted a little earlier: 'A great change takes place as soon as the authority has been internalized by the development of a superego. The manifestations of conscience are then raised to a new level: to be accurate, one should not call them conscience and sense of guilt before this.' Thus, in Freud's view, it is only when the superego is developed that we are justified in speaking of 'guilt'.

The lack of clear demarcation between anxiety and guilt in our theory was bound to hamper my exposition in the section on the origins of anxiety and guilt. I deliberately refrained from tackling this great problem in the present paper (though I have to some extent touched upon it in former contributions, and hope to be able to do so more fully in the future). Nor did I attempt in the present paper to elaborate on the connection between anxiety arising from inner sources and objective anxiety – another problem which is far from being solved in our theory. As regards the inner sources of anxiety and guilt, I restated my hypothesis that they arise from the aggressive impulses, and substantiated this by Abraham's conclusion that anxiety and guilt are connected with the cannibalistic desires. I quoted one passage in which Freud clearly expresses the opinion that guilt arises from the aggressive instincts, and shall repeat it now: 'I am convinced that very many processes will admit of much simpler and clearer explanation if we restrict the findings of psychoanalysis in respects of the origin of the sense of guilt to the aggressive instincts.' [Freud, S. 1930:131; SE 21:138][3] Nevertheless Freud did not revise, as far as young children are concerned (and in some other cases of anxiety as well) his early hypothesis that anxiety originates from the transformation of unsatisfied libido.

The hypothesis that from the beginning the infant feels love towards an object leads to a different valuation of the impact of all his emotions while he experiences them. In this connection I attempted to throw some light on the interplay of external experience on the one hand and withdrawal into an internal situation on the other hand. The basis for these processes is the infant's relation to the mother's breast, his introjection of it during periods both of gratification and of frustration. I suggested that when the infant perceives and introjects the mother as a whole person, the elements of love, hate, anxiety, sense of loss and guilt come together in his mind and this constitutes the depressive position. Nevertheless, in my view the seeds of depressive feelings are there from the beginning of life, since the experience of birth gives rise to a sense of loss. I dealt in greater detail with evidence of grief and sense of loss in infants, and the part which the fear of destroying and thus losing the loved object plays in the development of these emotions. The infant fears that his greed may cause the destruction of his loved object. Since he feels, particularly when he is frustrated and his hatred wells up, that his greed is uncontrollable, his anxieties lest his loved object be destroyed centre on his greed. These anxieties, according to my hypothesis, are at the root of melancholia. At this point I made a brief digression to show the links between infantile phantasies and anxieties on the one hand, and the phantasies and defence mechanisms in neurotic and psychotic persons on the other.

After a brief discussion of the most fruitful approach to the understanding of the infant's emotional life, I dealt with some of the early phobias, particularly with night terrors and feeding difficulties. To understand fully the child's anxiety when the mother whom he is calling does not come to him, we have to allow for his aggressive impulses and phantasies and the part they play in the development of persecutory fears and feelings of guilt. In dealing with the various forms of feeding difficulties, I made weaning my starting point, and attempted to place it in the perspective of the infant's attitude to his food and to his mother during the whole of the suckling period. Under normal circumstances, satisfactory everyday experiences help the infant to build up trust in good objects and goodness within and without. And this contributes to the child's ability to divorce increasingly his relation to food from his relation to his mother, and to learn to love her as a person.

I devoted a section to the infant's attempts to gain reassurance through his mother's love, and described the many ways in which he tries to give pleasure, partly in order to make reparation which is a fundamental means of gaining reassurance against anxiety and guilt. The smile, the clapping of hands, the attempts to feed the mother – all the little tricks and achievements come into the picture. At the same time I tried to show how the infant uses various play activities as a help in overcoming his feelings of loss and grief.

I suggested that the various methods the ego applies at different stages in dealing with feelings of loss can be used as criteria by which to measure the development of the ego. Here we must give full weight to the different stages of adaptation to reality. With every new achievement the infant becomes more able to regain his lost object and to find new objects in their stead, and thus to overcome the depressive position. I also showed that these endeavours to overcome his feelings of loss and grief, and thus his depressive position, are a great stimulus for ego development.

Frustration, which stimulates narcissistic withdrawal, is also, as we know, a fundamental factor in adaptation to reality. In narcissistic withdrawal the infant reinforces, owing to the loss of the external object, the introjection of the breast and his relation to the inner object. In his adaptation to reality, which is supported by symbol formation, the frustrations suffered in connection with the primary object lead him to finding substitutes and new gratifications, which implies a growing relation to external objects as well as integration of internal relationships. I tried to show how both in narcissistic withdrawal and in adaptation to reality phantasy life is an essential factor. For hallucination, the precondition for narcissistic withdrawal is in my view the beginning of phantasy life. On the other hand, symbol formation – which provides the means of transferring love and interest to new objects and activities – is also bound up with phantasy life. These two orientations, inwards and outwards, are gradually brought into harmony with each other, and the extent to which this is achieved is a measure of normal development.

I referred to the constant interaction of the emotional and intellectual factors in infants and young children, and pointed out that the capacity for integration of emotions as well as of perception and reality testing is there from the beginning. Early feeding difficulties, which in my view are due to the inhibition of greed, I adduced as an evidence for the modification of instincts. I also pointed out that the cannibalistic impulses, whose powerful and lasting impact on the unconscious mind is a well-established fact, do not find any commensurate expression in the infant's behaviour, and this I took as another proof for the modification of instincts.

In interpreting the attitudes, responses, and processes in the infant, we must be guided by evanescent signs which are often difficult to define. But many of the facts which I have presented in this paper have been recognized by a number of observers and therefore, in the long run, all of us should be able to check them. Closer scrutiny, more attention to details and, most of all, the correlation of observations together with some degree of inference drawn from our knowledge of the unconscious of somewhat older children should enable us to clarify our minds on the emotional life of the infant.

Finally I should like once more to restate the essential contention of my paper. The emotional experiences of losing the loved object and regaining it are a vital part of early mental life. The depressive position has thus to be considered as the basis for depressive feelings and depressive disturbances in later life. But since the striving to regain and to preserve the loved objects, together with the hope of regaining them, is vital in the development of all sublimations – the depressive position is also the basis for the development of a rich and full personality.

Discussion (papers)

DR PAYNE: One of the main impressions which I received from reading Mrs Klein's paper was that her observations on the emotional life of the infant contained evidence on almost every page of the primary importance of frustration of libidinal wishes in the causation of the emotional manifestations described as the depressive position. Even when confronted with the part played by cannibalistic impulses we must recognize the fact that these depend on archaic sexual as well as on destructive impulses, and always play a temporary part in the primitive psyche. We must remind ourselves from time to time that the psyche has been evolved just as the body has, and that there are vestigial remnants to be discovered in both.

The whole emotional situation of depression revolves round the loss of a loved object. There seems to me to be plenty of evidence not confined to the work of psychoanalysts, to show that object relationship is slowly developed from the time of birth when the infant has to become aware of something outside itself by the experience of having the breast withdrawn. While this is true it is also true that it is easy to under-estimate the differences between primitive object relations and fully developed object relation. One of the drawbacks of our nomenclature is that we use the same terms for the immature as for the fully developed. Sometimes it seems to me that it is like calling a male foetus a man. The stress is laid on what is common to both and not on differences.

Of course there are advantages as well as disadvantages. If we observe the unhappy emotional state of the infant in the first year of life we are struck by its helplessness.

The psychical helplessness is that of the weak, immature ego that is completely dependent on the mother, and yet not part of her but separate.

The primary emotional reaction to helplessness is fear. Fear of unsatisfied needs and desires and all that implies.

The depressive position as described by Mrs Klein seems to me to be linked with the condition of helplessness. While recognizing the presence of fear and anxiety she stresses the part played by guilt. I should like to remind you of Dr Jones's article on Guilt, Hate and Fear, printed in a back number of the Journal. In it he shows how complex and intermingled the emotions of guilt and anxiety are and how easy it is to go astray in describing them because of the fact of the different layers of the mind. We have to recognize that unless we adopt the idea which has been put forward by various people that guilt reactions can occur as a result of inherited psychical values we must be prepared to trace the differentiation of guilt from primitive fear and anxiety in relation to superego development. Jones has said that guilt can be regarded as a topographical form of fear. The problem takes us to the formation of the superego, and the relation of the early pre-genital introjected imagos of the parents to those which are formed after the Oedipus complex is resolved. Here again it seems to me that we meet the same kind of problem, we come upon similarities and vast differences and the mental structures are all called superegos. The unintegrated and possibly fluctuating character of the primitive introjections, some depending on positive and some on negative impulses, creates a situation which cannot be defined with the precision and clarity of that belonging to the post-Oedipus period when the superego as described by Freud is formed.

We might make a comparison here between the relation of the component sexual impulses to genital primacy and the relation to pre-genital parental introjections to the organized superego belonging to the post-Oedipus phase.

I can summarize briefly the few points I have put forward.

1 The depressive position as described by Mrs Klein in my opinion depends primarily on libidinal frustration.
2 That more work is needed to be done on the character of the emotions developed in these primitive emotional states before they are labelled with certainty.
3 That differences are often masked by the use of identical terms.

MISS SHARPE (Paper 'Some Comments on Mrs Klein's theory of a "Depressive Position"')

I assume hopefully a possibility of discussing Mrs Klein's theory, of being critical in the constructive meaning of that word, of accepting some things without its being interpreted that one has swallowed Mrs Klein and her work whole, of rejecting, doubting, or suspending opinion without the assumption that one rejects everything or has no opinions at all. As long as I am not required, nor are students required to accept a closed system of the Alpha and Omega of human development, no matter by whom formulated, I remain in this Society. 'Should we not relate our tendency to fission to the immaturity and present limitation of our psychological reality sense? May we not hope it will tend to disappear as we become increasingly capable of maintaining a strictly scientific approach to the study of our mental life?' So said Dr Brierley in her last paper.

I find her remarks in strict accord with Freud's own statement that every analyst's achievements are conditioned by his own resistances and complexes. We shall avoid making godheads if we believe that and look to the pooling of contributions from every independent worker as the method of gathering the most comprehensive knowledge on our problems.

'If we say we have no sin (i.e. no resistances and no complexes) we deceive ourselves and there is no truth in us', no matter how much analysis has been undertaken. If analysis has ended in that last revelation of psychological realism there is a chance of possessing a scientific attitude.

If I do not quote Mrs Klein, if I have misunderstood her, she at least will believe that I grapple with clinical data to find its significance, to compare and to contrast it with her own. I do not grapple with Mrs Klein.

I will now present some of my reflections, only some, expressed through and by clinical work, about Mrs Klein's 'depressive position'.

The 'status quo' is a frequent phrase heard today. The full phrase is 'status quo ante'. How many people still hope that the end of the war may mean a restoration of the pre-war conditions for which they are most homesick, although progressive minds on every hand warn us that restoration of old conditions could only lead to renewed disaster. It was Emerson who drew attention to the amount of energy required to deal with mass inertia before mankind could be persuaded to move 'even into a cleaner sty'. Reluctance to change. A patient says, 'Something is different in this room today. I don't like it. You have a new dress on, I don't like it.' There is a new chair in the consulting room and a patient dreams of twin beds, and the associations lead to the new bed in her nursery for her new baby sister. It is Friday and one male patient tells me that he could hardly walk to the consulting room, he was so tired. He curses me for making him introspective when he ought to be interesting himself in all the external world – that is he feels he can't walk when the weekend confronts him and curses me about introspection when he has the weekend to devote to external interests. Another male patient on Friday shows me an interesting book entitled *Children on All Fours* showing pictures of children exploring their environments on all fours – agile and clever – but they haven't left mother earth yet, they aren't letting go with hands. 'I feel I've got one leg over the stile', says a woman patient, 'but I've not dared yet to get the other over.' 'I'm sick of living in other people's houses', says another patient, a middle-aged woman, 'but suppose I leave Barbara's and try living in a place of my own? Her house is very warm and her Nannie looks after me, and I might be ill, so I don't know what to do.' And I say 'What would Barbara do if you did?' 'Selfish beast, she has all she wants, clothes and money and men when she likes. I may have to go when her daughter comes home, she'll have my room then.'

'And now', says another woman patient, 'I've got what I've wanted, independent work and an office all to myself, and now I don't like it, I'm as lonely as hell, and I miss the company I was with before.'

'Sometimes', says the one with tired feet, 'I feel I've got to a place in my analysis where a new road is opening up before my very eyes. I know it's there but I'm too tired, too frightened, I'll keep the roads I know, and tramp round the same old circles again. I'd rather put up with the ills I know than meet others that might be worse. I'm used to these, damned uncomfortable they may be, but at any rate I'm used to them!' So says every hysteric, obsessional and all of us in the secret places of the heart. 'I can't push these slipper buttons through the holes, they hurt my fingers', says a child to her mother – 'you do it.' 'I can't get any thoughts, it's so difficult', says the grown-up woman in analysis, 'can't you help me?' She had enema administrations by her mother for long periods in her childhood.

Put briefly, all I have said illustrates 'status quo', resistance to change, even to a cleaner sty.

'Tired feet' says, 'I feel awful, haven't shaved, have a dirty shirt on, I feel it's so insulting to you.' But what he is doing is that he is getting his own back on me. He has not recovered from the shock, from the insult of his dirt being considered 'dirtiness'. There was a problem of hot water supply for daily baths between two women I know. One said she didn't find a hot bath really necessary as often as every day, whereupon the other wickedly replied, knowing the prudery of the other, 'Saints can go dirty, but sinners like me must wash'. We know saints often lived in filth. Melancholics hate moving, and won't move physically if they are melancholic enough, and they won't wash either. But if it's just depression the 'status quo' is in the mind. 'If I can't change my mind, at least I can change my clothes and move the furniture around', says another patient.

A girl aged eleven when told by her mother that she would soon have a new baby brother or sister, responded by sitting down on her mother's knees and saying, 'but I can still sit on your lap, can't I?' She is a woman of 50 now. Illness of one kind or another has meant bed, nurses, doctors for most of her life. The 'status quo' has been maintained whatever else has been sacrificed for it. Freud says, 'Most people are only half born'. Christ said, 'Except a man can be born again.'[4] 'Can a man enter a second time into his mother's womb and be born?' asked the man with a literal mind. 'Except a man be born of water and of the spirit he cannot enter into the Kingdom of God' was the reply.

I said in former contributions, 'I see Mrs Klein's "depressive position", i.e. the weaning, as the last of the external physical birth throes of separation. I should add walking independently is the ultimate one to complete the physical series of separation – the literal separation.' I also said that our task as psychoanalysts was to help achieve a psychical re-birth. I would agree with Freud that the most many can possibly achieve is a partial re-birth, perhaps the most any can hope to achieve?

A fit of the blues, the Monday morning feeling, are normal manifestations of recurrent and passing phases of depression. Mourning for a loved one lost is normal, prolonged mourning in depression is abnormal, genuine melancholia is the extremity of depression. Now since I believe with Mrs Klein that in the first year or 18 months we shall find precursors of all subsequent development I agree that in the orientations made to first losses we find such precursors. The birth trauma is the first massive loss, the first physical separation, the cessation of being fed by the mother, the first physical loss experienced externally. That the child should miss the breasts is surely natural and normal mourning, as natural as in later life mourning for a lost love, and this surely is a universal experience. It is the quantitative factor that is not universal, not the qualitative. This quantitative factor decides whether the outcome will result in fresh cathexes on to the outer world in a reasonable period of time or whether a nucleus of subsequent depression or melancholia is established. But the factor to which I would draw Mrs Klein's attention and which I feel she would agree with is this, that in normal mourning in later years, the real object is mourned over for a due course of time in which the cathexes attached to the lost object are slowly withdrawn and re-invested. Loss is worked over and through. If a state of melancholy ensues then we gather that the psychical state is due to something in addition to the loss of the actual object. Believing with Mrs Klein that the phenomenon in later life is the phenomenon of early life writ larger and much more complicatedly, I suggest that where the natural early mourning for the lost breasts makes virtually a forerunner of depression that it is not the breasts as such that are grieved over, just as in melancholia it is not the actual person who is lost that is the cause of the static grief. That is, I suggest, it is not the loss of the breasts as such, in themselves, that produces, when it is produced, a depressive position. In melancholia, in deep depression, there is both bodily and mentally a refusal to move, in depression the spirit stagnates in the doldrums. It is the maintenance of a psychological 'status quo'.

Now I only attempt in this communication to give what I think are a few of many factors that can increase the natural grief of an actual loss which is *normal*, to the intensity of a depression which is *abnormal*, only to suggest why I think it is not the loss of the breasts as such nor the loss of the actual mother as such. The mother remains there uneaten. First of all I think of it as a *loss of a complete situation*, and I would remind Mrs Klein of factors she never omits in her clinical material but which she does not relate and link up indispensably with what may cause the offset of later depression. I think I may possibly out-Klein Mrs Klein in my respect for the accurate perceptions of the growing infant, awareness of the mother's responses, an awareness of whether he is wanted and loved, an awareness of the mother's haste and anxiety or placidity and patience, and his first pattern of behaviour responses are inextricably bound up and fused with the mother's own 'I in her and she in me' pattern that is basic. But given that basis, the feeding period is not a 'closed season' between mother and babe in a world free from external stimuli. Parents have intercourse, another child may be born within twelve months. A woman of 40 I am analysing had a sister born within her first year. Her awareness of what was happening, that father gave mother something to make her big, and the big thing inside was the baby who appeared later, her awareness that father's penis was the means of putting some magical thing in mother, are in the third year of analysis coming to light in the most incontrovertible and astonishing manner. How she behaved during the last stage of her mother's pregnancy is reproduced in symbolic behaviour today. That at the age of one year she overcame her fury with the new sister and with her father and her mother for producing it by an assumption in her mind that the child was *her* present from father is crystal clear, as clear as the repression that overcame all her accurate perceptions and all her early understanding of facts – at one year of age. Two and a half years of analysis, and I am very little less holy and sacrosanct than at the start, the perfect and ideal mother, sometimes called the 'good' mother, who gave her the breasts. She refuses to assimilate but very slowly any interpretation from dreams and behaviour, that lead the way to linking me with that sexual mother who bore a child, i.e. the 'bad' mother. I am good, i.e. asexual, I and she live in that original world of a dualism which virtually means we are really bodily and psychically that 'status quo ante'.

Edward Glover has said 'the term narcissism has almost outworn its usefulness.' For me it is slowly becoming not a term, intellectually apprehended, but a living understanding of a state and of experience. Perhaps one has got born a little more if one begins to feel what narcissism involves and what the enmeshment really means.

To return to the 'status quo' which is really narcissism, and to the 'situation' that can cause the nucleus of depression, factors I suggest Mrs Klein has omitted in her theory of her depressive position, but never in her data.

There are two immortal stories, immortal because they are symbolic of the experience of Every Man and Every Woman. 'Every' with the capital E. The one is the story of the Garden of Eden and the other the story of Lucifer falling out of the rank of the angels from heaven. You will remember that angels are angels, neither men nor women. There is neither marriage nor giving in marriage in heaven. They are depicted in white robes and possessing wings. And in the Garden of Eden, Adam and Eve were also like the angels, they walked naked and did not know they were naked, which amounts to the same thing. Their expulsion from Eden, a depressed picture if ever there was one, synchronized with the discovery of the difference between the male and female genitals. 'Knowledge', says Dr Brierley in her recent paper, 'knowledge is the way of detachment.' In this oldest story in the world and the youngest, it is knowledge of the difference of the genitals that causes the expulsion from that garden of innocence (for which substitute ignorance), and the way back was barred by a flaming sword. Sight aroused desire, and 'desire' – *libidinal* desire for the other sex – is unerringly portrayed in eating the apple. That particular eating is not hunger for food, but for love. How else can the beginnings of libidinal trends be felt by a child in its first year but through the primacy of oral libido? And the story of Lucifer I will give you in the words of a patient. He had been complaining bitterly about a feeling of inadequacy, humiliation, futility. He felt like a weakly, drivelling, drooling infant. (Let me in passing say he is twenty years of age, has had intercourse with experienced older women, has deflowered virgins and made women pregnant.) No words were adequate for the contempt he heaped upon himself, for his feelings of utter humiliation. Suddenly a muscle of his leg twitched involuntarily, it kept on twitching. 'Damn this leg' and he banged it. He said 'What's happening, is some gremlin attacking the works? You know the airmen talk of gremlins when something gets into the works of an airplane and prevents it working?' 'This is a gremlin, an imp interfering with my leg.' I said, 'How did it get there, do you think – are you thinking of a real imp inside?' 'Don't be silly, of course not – it's a way of talking.' Then suddenly, 'I'll tell you, I've thought of something.' Then out of the mouth of this babe and suckling, who has not read Freud because he wishes to know the truth out of himself, came this: 'You remember Lucifer, who was with the angels? Got jealous of God's power and flung himself out of Heaven? That's the gremlin, the little devil.' 'Yes', I said, 'but what's he in your leg for?' With the tired patience the child so often exhibits to the stupid grown-up he went on: 'Heaven and angels mean the concord of the mind, and so you eject from your mind, repress it, you'd say, the disturbing feeling, thrust it out of your mind, it's the gremlin in my leg.' I asked myself, what did he repress? and when? He has of course told me; as a drooling infant he became aware of his inadequacy when he saw his father's penis, God's power. Then he became aware he was small and inadequate in comparison with him. Father was realized as a rival, even while he himself was suckled by his mother. He tells us what he did in an unsupportable situation, he banished, rejected, repressed, the accurate perception, and the emotional upheaval, in order to maintain the status quo, the heaven of concord, the garden of Eden, ignorance. Knowledge meant detachment from his father and his mother. Said his mother to me, concerning his sexual adventures. 'It's all so easy for him, they all fall for him at once. If he could fall in love with a young woman who'd make it hard for him to win her, or refuse him and break his heart, I feel he would grow up.' To which I replied, 'The trouble is that the baby's narcissistic heart is already broken, the blow to his pride came too soon and too suddenly.'

I remember saying to him once, 'This seems to tell us that the cry is always "Let me get back to mother's breasts".' He considered a moment and said, 'It's more than that. It's the whole set-up, not her breasts only. It's before the world was decomposed – while it was a unity; father and mother and me alike together. You know how on the stage you sometimes start with what you think is a set solid scene and then comes a moment when a bit of the background is moved, it isn't permanent after all, then another bit changes and then another, and finally it's a totally different set-up from what it was at the beginning. I think it's like that, not mother's breasts only but the whole set-up that went with them.'

'Before the world was decomposed – not mother's breasts only, but the whole set-up.'

The oral aggression in this patient is predominant. To devour for him certainly has the significance of non-separation from his object and anxiety at the mother's disappearance is inseparable from his jealousy that that if she is not with him she is with someone else, and put quite simply on an initial pattern of experience a breast is the place which predicates a baby and if one is not the baby in possession then it means that another will be – it's the only explanation when the weaning starts – even if the rival does not appear at once, it will do – one day. I do not believe that guilt arises through anger and aggression caused by actual frustration, i.e., real hunger. We are justified in our anger, for the self-preservative instincts have their own imperative right. We feel guilty when greed is not for those things we feel we are justified in desiring to get and hold. Jealousy, malice, and all uncharitableness are the accompaniment of desperate greed for a whole love situation, not for food from the breasts as such. They become the symbol of that undecomposed world which was once the baby's before knowledge entered to start him on the path of detachment – knowledge that there were others; knowledge that father and mother had a relationship he could not share, knowledge of genitals, one immensely bigger than his that made father able to possess his mother. And if such stimuli come early to a child and come often we do not wonder that the child can do little about an unbearable heightening of inner tension and that his phantasies are of oral devouring and that from that tension he seeks relief in hallucination or builds up a retreat in himself, a return to the mother image before sin entered in – the ideal imago. 'I feel in a vacuum', says my patient, 'I have withdrawn myself to a place free from stimuli, nothing can reach me, from without or from within.'

After a shock, a massive disturbance of equilibrium, physical or psychical, time is required to reach a re-settling, a fresh adjustment, a new equilibrium. That time is occupied by a working over repetitively with ever lessening affect the traumatic experience. So in some way I believe the trauma of birth must need a time appropriate

811

for a given constitution both physical and psychical to reach its own first initial readjustment. Where frequent early changes of environment occur, failure to establish good feeding situations and changes of people, the excessive stimuli are too great for mastery by an infant, but above all where prematurely jealousy over and above that which is normal is provoked, such as early and frequent disturbance by the parental intercourse, by sight of their genitals, over-excitation of any kind, we have stimulation that a child finds unbearable and unmanageable. He can do nothing about it. Then he withdraws. 'Nothing can reach me from without or from within.' As I see it, ego development in the early stages is interfered with, impeded, and delayed.

I wonder very much if a definitely depressive person has ever accomplished the early normal mourning for the 'breasts', i.e. in my interpretation the first total situation before reality knowledge, that mother and father were different beings, and the first shock to narcissism was felt? Freud says, 'A perception which is made to disappear by motor activity is recognized as external, as reality: where such activity makes no difference, the perception originates within the subject's own body – it is not real.' That is the 'depression' arises out of a denial of reality – a denial of 'loss' and the hallucination of the original 'status quo', the retention of the mother and father, as undifferentiated figures and identified with the self in the primal narcissism of the garden of Eden. 'Heaven lies about us in our infancy, in trailing clouds of glory do we come from God who is our home.' From God, or from the Madonna, it is all one, never born of the two humans through intercourse. Beneath the self-reproaches and the misery of the depressive one finds a different story, of fury and the unmitigated smart of early narcissism too soon torn and challenged.

'Wrong?' says my depressive patient. 'It's difficult to feel one is really in the wrong. I see I have offended somebody, I'm sorry, but I don't feel I am wrong. I feel as I should if I went to a foreign country, ignorant of their usages. I break one of their laws and they are angry, but I didn't do it intentionally – not in order to do a wrong thing. So I feel when one is an infant, one wants and grabs and tries to get what one wants, not on purpose to do wrong, but to get what one wants.'

Depression, status quo, narcissism, beyond ideas of good and evil, idealization – of the parental figures and of the self. Dr Brierley speaking of psychological needs in her plea for psychological realism says that probably a degree of idealization is inevitable for everyone. Freud says most people are only half born.

Fury was aroused when Copernicus demonstrated that the earth went round the sun and not vice versa. You remember his fate dictated by enraged narcissism? Even so is the fury of the young child when he realizes that it is he that must do the going round, instead of the world going round him. So Darwin drew contumely on himself when he dared to demonstrate the ascent of man instead of his fall from a grander order of beings. And I still believe that had Freud made his first exposition on life and death instincts and aggression apart from its association with sexuality he would have raised no storm comparable to that which greeted his announcements concerning infantile sexuality and the universal sexual problems underlying all mental illness.

To summarize: Within the first year I find evidence from clinical data of the following:

Accurate *perceptions* of reality that include the differences between the parents' genitals, awareness of what is going on between the parents, awareness when the mother becomes pregnant, the precursors of the Oedipus complex, repression of accurate perceptions, and so the precursors of superego formation. Phantasy formations are inseparable both from inner urges, and the reality impacts. So far I confirm Mrs Klein's data.

The relentless impact of reality assails the infant from birth onwards. The loss of the breasts may or may not be a depressive position in development, quantitative factors decide. But I do not think the mother's breasts as such are the loss, they are the symbol of a lost situation. The growing awareness of rivals, the discovery of the father–mother relationship, their sexual differences, the new child or expected new child are the causes for any establishment of a nucleus of depression. The child makes a slow painful descent from the omnipotence of godhead to his own small weak stature and helplessness concerning his massive emotions. In depression is a refusal to face the painful reality. Below depression lies outraged omnipotence and the frustration of the first love-greed. A sense of sin and guilt is associated with aggression, when that aggression is aroused not because of real physical needs but when the hunger is for love, thus involving hatred and aggression towards all rivals, actual or potential.

DR M. BRIERLEY *(read by Dr Payne in Dr Brierley's absence):* There are only a very few things we can take for granted about human infancy. Among these, I think, we may safely assert:

(a) That the infant is a distinctively human being from the time of its conception. To say that a baby is becoming human presumably means that it has reached a stage of development at which the adult observer begins to see recognizable likeness to himself, a fore-shadowing in the baby of the 'adult to be'.

(b) That the infant is a psychophysical organism at birth, if not for some time prior to birth. Many of its initial responses to external stimuli may be reflex, i.e. inherited reaction patterns activated by appropriate trigger stimuli. Evidence is not lacking that even such automatic reactions may be psycho-physiological rather than purely physiological responses. We used to be taught in hospital that the first cry was a reflex response to the stimulus of cold air on the skin. My observations on infants have been very few but I heard the first cries of the babies I delivered during my midwifery training. These cries conveyed to me something that I can only call feeling. This feeling was as far from uniform or stereotyped as the cries themselves. The type of response was stereotyped but the cry was individual. As I remember them, the cries ranged from subdued wails to quite lusty protests, with corresponding variation in the feeling conveyed. They were all unpleasant feeling, but the kind of unpleasantness varied both in quality and in quantity. Since then I have been convinced that the new-born baby is a psycho-physiological being, however immature or larval its psychic life may be.

A current reaction is always the resultant of an immediate stimulus acting on the organism as modified by past experience. The time-sequence of experience is, therefore, decisive in the sense that what happens first modifies what happens later. Although the events of the classical Oedipus stage determine subsequent normality or neurosis, the happenings at the Oedipus stage itself are, to a great extent, determined by preceding events. Hence, we can only hope to establish the average course of normal development and its more typical variations by observing all the stages of infantile developments in progress and comparing those stages with the results of analyses of older children and adults.

All knowledge of psychology, adult or infantile, is the result of inference. All observation involves interpretation. Hypotheses about infantile development differ from hypotheses about later development chiefly in being more difficult to test and more open to errors of interpretation. In the matter of evidence we can ultimately depend only on the results of our own experience. For instance, Mrs Klein can and does give us illustrations of the kind of clinical material on which she bases her views. In my opinion we cannot form any adequate judgement on such excerpts from the total of Mrs Klein's evidence. The most practical way is to compare the offered illustrations with any counterparts we may come across ourselves and then try to estimate how far Mrs Klein's views apply to them. In analysis, comparison with first-hand data is the only satisfactory way of assessing the validity of another person's observations and interpretations.

Turning now to the 'depressive position' itself I see nothing improbable in the suggestion that infants pass through earlier phases of development just as typical as the classical Oedipus stage. Indeed, we all recognize this in so far as we endorse the conception of libidinal primacies. Critics object for various reasons to Mrs Klein's expansion of a libidinal primacy into a developmental position of the whole psyche. The time for thinking of development in terms of libido alone is long past. Mrs Klein's attempt at expansion is, therefore, an effort in a very necessary direction. The problem is, how valid and how complete is her account of a 'depressive position'?

For the moment I will leave on one side the economic problems involved and keep strictly to the dynamic aspects. To me, it is a well-established clinical fact that pathological depression involves the reactivation of oral conflicts. Even a transitory depression in a mild anxiety hysteria will yield a crop of oral phantasies and evidence of cannibalistic anxiety. I do not think the form in which such material comes to light in the adult is usually the same as the primary form; usually the original drives and anxieties, the primary impulses and feelings, are revived in more modern dress. But if cannibalistic anxiety can be revived it must, presumably, have existed in the infantile period. My own difficulty is that depression in the adult involves so much more than purely oral revival. For instance, where separation anxiety is hyperacute in the adult, the physical presence of the mother substitute is not only reassurance that she has not been devoured or destroyed in a number of other ways but it is the only positive assurance that she is not in bed with father or wasting her substance on other people. Evacuation anxieties often seem to be as strong as biting ones. Hence, the doubt arises as to whether even in the infant a 'depressive position' should be posited, which is of purely oral aetiology. That a depressive state can originate during or after weaning which may amount to a true infantile psychosis and be the forerunner of serious trouble later is not in question. My own data suggest that this can and does happen. Leaving aside vexed problems of ego-precocity, etc., what is in question for me is whether the 'depressive position' as described by Mrs Klein is not too limited and narrow a concept as regards dynamics alone. I will not discuss this further because Miss Sharpe's remarkably interesting clinical material has direct bearing on this problem.

The problems of the 'death instinct' raised by Miss Sharpe's observations on the 'status quo' are in urgent need of fuller discussion but I cannot attempt to deal with them here. I would, however, like to say a few words about affects. Love seems a sophisticated word to attribute to an infant because we ordinarily think of love as a sentiment, a stable emotional attitude such as adults develop towards their nearest arnd dearest, rather than as a simple feeling. If we use the term 'love' in the same wide sense as we use the term 'libido', and define it as the feeling characteristic of libido, there is no objection to our use of it in relation to infants. If we do this we must, however, keep clear in our minds the difference between a primary simple affect and the complicated emotional attitudes of later life.

The same argument applies to the use of the word 'grief'. The new-born infant who wailed dismally seemed to feel some primary affect of distress which may well be the fundamental feeling in adult grief and, certainly, would have to be classed as a 'depressive feeling'. Such affects, however, are not characteristic of weaning experiences alone, they are characteristic of all situations of change for the worse. The degree to which they are activated by weaning will presumably be influenced by numerous and variable, qualitative and quantitative, internal and external factors. This is one of the reasons why I personally find it easier to think of development as a progressive series of psychobiological adaptations to changing life-situations rather than in terms of intrapsychic positions. I fully agree with Miss Sharpe that oral libido must be distinguished from hunger appetite. The simultaneous satisfaction of suckling-love and appetite facilitate the interplay between libido and hunger with which we are familiar in symptom-formation and in feeding disturbances such as those cited by Mrs Klein.

We shall never reach any satisfactory conclusion about infantile object relationship unless we remember, as Mrs Klein herself says [p. 755], 'We cannot, of course, apply adult standards to the object relations of the infant, and it is clear that we must expect different object relations in infants at, say, two months, six months, twelve months, and so on.' It does not seem to me that Mrs Klein herself distinguishes clearly enough between the relationship which she observes to exist between the infant and its mother and the infant's own subjective appreciation of this relationship. We agree that mental objects are founded on sensations. We probably also agree that sensations have a quality of 'thingness' about them which Freud attributed to primary projection. It apparently requires a synthesis of sensations, effected possibly by successive experience of differing simultaneous sensations to produce the unitary 'thinghood' which is a mental object. In other words, the first sensory mental object is an integration of the different sensations evoked by the external object which provides the stimuli. Suckling offers the infant a number of simultaneous and rapidly succeeding sensations. The infant will not see the breast in three dimensions until binocular vision is established, but concomitant sensations of touch, scent, and temperature would be enough to permit the early synthesis of a unitary something-suckable. This sensory 'something-suckable' could only later become an object of cognition.

In my recent paper I was concerned, for special reasons, to differentiate between identification *with* and object-relationship *to* objects but, in an earlier discussion, I suggested that every sensation experienced by the infant might be described as an object-rudiment. Bearing in mind always the vast difference between a purely sensory object and the later developed object of cognition it seems to me highly probable that sensory syntheses do occur early if, indeed, some are not already present at birth.

Our ignorance of psychological heredity impedes us here. We simply do not know how much psychic organization is inherited. Freud thought that primal scene phantasies were probably inherited because he could find no other satisfactory explanation for them. It is equally reasonable to suppose that some primitive reactions to the mother are inherited or, at least, that the tendency to develop some kinds of reaction to her is inborn. The words in which Mrs Klein phrases her assumptions sound as if they implied a degree of cognitive discrimination, as distinct from feeling and sensory awareness in the infant, which the condition of its nervous system alone would preclude. I say advisedly sound because I am far from certain that more is involved than a choice of words. I refer, in particular, to the passage on [p. 757]: 'One may assume that from the beginning the mother exists as a whole object in the child's mind, but in vague outlines as it were, and that this picture becomes gradually filled in as perception develops.' We can have no exact knowledge of what the infant may sense or feel in the last stages before birth. Possibly, we indulge in retrospective idealization in supposing that intra-uterine existence is uninterrupted paradise. There is, however, a good deal of internal evidence that its feelings, if any, are of the type described by Freud's correspondent as 'oceanic', undifferentiated awareness of continuity of being, 'primary identification'. Via the rude disturbance of birth, varying presumably in pain and anxiety values, this stage of boundless oceanic being is suddenly changed to a totally different, invariably unpleasant, state of being.

What the infant misses is a state of being and it finds voice to lament or to protest against a change of being for the worse. New sensations and, with luck, new pleasures in suckling, help to acclimatize the infant to its new conditions. The primary consolation at first may well be re-establishment, through the various ministrations of the mother, of the original oceanic feeling. Before the mother herself acquires definite outline she is more likely to be felt as a vague presence connected with the first discriminated sensory object. This presence can have no outline in the sense of visual shape nor can it take on what we should recognize as the likeness of a human being until the infant establishes binocular vision. According to Ida Mann, modulation of the optic nerves is complete by the tenth week but I have not been able to verify a precise date for the establishment of binocular vision. Speaking from memory I believe it takes place during the third month.

Apropos of footnote 45, [pp. 796–7] I should say that impulses are operative in all experience irrespective of whether any given experience is concerned with environmental reality or is a phantasy. I would also say that unconscious mental activity is an invariable concomitant of conscious mental activity, whereas conscious mental activity does not invariably accompany unconscious mentation. Freud said that psychic processes normally follow a definite course from stimulus to innervation (in chapter 'Dream Activities', *Interpretation of Dreams*). Still more succinctly, 'The reflex act remains the model for every psychic activity'. [Freud, S. 1900:426; SE 5:538][5] I should have made it plainer that Freud should not be saddled with my inference that the theoretical unit of psychic life is therefore *a complete reaction* however strictly in accord with his views I think this inference is. If the functional unit of mental process is a complete reaction the unit of experience, a subjective 'meaning', is a relation between impulse, feeling, and presentation. The relation between these three is variable and each element is capable of modification, as, for instance, when sensory synthesis results in mental objectification. But the structure of the psyche is built up by the organization of reactions, mental or psychic processes. I think that many of our present difficulties in regard to early ego and object development will disappear as we become more skilful in correlating our observations and interpretations of infantile behaviour with the theory of development expressed in terms of progressive organization.

DR P. HEIMANN: It is only a small point to which I wish to say a few words. Our views on mental development are largely based on the concept of the mobility of the libido, and since we have recognized the significance of the aggressive impulses, our views are also based on the concept of the mobility of energy of these destructive impulses. Change of object and aim, which underlie mental progress, the advance from one object to another, the widening of the field of interests, symbol formation, sublimation, denial, isolation, etc., are made possible by the fact that the instinctual cathexis of one object can be moved on to another, that instinctual energy can be spent in various ways. Thus an important aspect of analytic investigations concerns the cathexis of objects with libido and aggressive impulses, and the manifold conditions arising from the changes in cathexis.

To apply this to the problem of introjection:

We hold that introjection and projection are amongst the earliest and most important mental processes. From the beginning of life introjection takes place and results in the establishment of objects inside the mind. These objects exist in the form of 'good' or 'bad' objects according to their predominant cathexis with libido or destructive impulses respectively, and contribute largely to the feeling of well-being or discomfort, to a happy, contented mood or a discontented, restless mood (which moreover is determined by the actual experiences in relation to external objects).

To consider the libido: a certain amount of libido must be constantly invested in these internal objects whilst another amount is free and available for the cathexis of external objects as they enter into the child's field of perception. This free libido is turned outwards waiting for suitable objects. In terms of emotions this would correspond to 'longing' for the object. The infant who desires the breast, has this free amount of libido and wishes to cathect the breast with it. We know that the infant cannot bear suspense, that waiting is an attitude or a capacity acquired slowly in the process of development. Frustration results when the libido, kept ready for the cathexis of the desired object, does not meet this object. At this point the external world is devoid of 'good' objects, that is of objects suitable to be cathected with libido. One important defence is the turning away from the frustrating world (which lacks 'good' objects and abounds in 'bad' ones) and the shifting of the libido on to the previously introjected object(s) which is (are) all the time cathected with a certain amount of libido. When this defence is successful, the introjected objects bulk larger, as it were, and fill the child's horizon, they assume an increased significance, and yield satisfaction strong enough to overcome the actual frustration experienced in the outside world. In other words: the hallucinatory gratification is established. Auto-erotism dominates over the frustration from the outside world. Thus, in my view when, at times of frustration, 'introjection is reinforced', as Mrs Klein says, [p. 765] the introjected object receives an additional amount of libido, that namely which could not be used for the cathexis of an external object.

In my paper on Introjection and Projection I touched on this problem when I described that in auto-erotism the infant turns to the object which he has taken into himself, when turning away from the external object. I did not enter there into the question of the persistent cathexis with libido or the internal object and the changes in libido economy.

On this view more problems come into our field. Symbol formation and sublimation depend on a shifting of the libido from the original object on to others. One might say that the shifting of libido – at times of frustration – on to the introjected object contains one root to both, symbol formation and sublimation. Instead of succumbing to frustration and proceeding to destructive behaviour a substitute object is cathected with libido and satisfaction is obtained with the symbol of the desired object and by means of aim-inhibited libido. But the substitute object is a phantasized one and the change of aim, instead of real sucking at the breast sucking in phantasy or sucking at a symbolic breast, does not lead to an alteration in the real world; the process is a hallucinatory one, and dissatisfaction is finally acknowledged and an essential character of true sublimation, as we know it from later phases of development is lacking.

It seems to me, however, worth while to recognize the elements of sublimation in the turning to the phantasied internal breast, because this may be a pattern which, when repeated in later life, would have a bearing on the failure of sublimation.

These considerations may afford a useful approach to the problem of sublimation in narcissistic people.

Free discussion

DR WINNICOTT did not think that a baby's first cries could be called sad, or that the word 'depressive' could be used as Dr Brierley had said. He did not think that Dr Payne's description of the baby as helpless was useful although he knew what she meant. He thought that there was only a baby–mother relationship as was contained in Dr Middlemore's title of her book *The Nursing Couple*.

DR PAYNE said that Dr Brierley described the cries of a new-born baby as varying from subdued wails to lusty protests. She did not say that they were evidence of depression but showed feeling of an individual quality.

DR TAYLOR thought that the crying of babies showed depression in the second month.

DR WILSON, referring to Miss Sharpe's contribution in which she suggested that it was not the actual frustration at the breast which produced the main effect, thought that when there was no outlet for oral aggression, mourning reactions might be set up. He quoted case material illustrating the effect of losing two uncles who were the only people who had permitted the patient an outlet for his aggression. Unconscious material showed them to be identified with two good breasts.

MRS KLEIN agreed with Dr Brierley that the first cries of babies were individual, and that this view was in keeping with Dr Middlemore's observations. She thought Dr Wilson's suggestion that the capacity to give way to aggression influences the development of depression was interesting.

DR K. STEPHEN thought that the depression was connected with an inability to love as well as with the loss of a loved object.

DR HEIMANN asked whether Miss Sharpe had data connected with weaning being associated with the birth of a new baby. She was interested in the idea that the loss of the breast psychically is due to the supposed arrival of another baby, and that the father may be identified with the baby. Guilt feelings were related to greed.

MISS SHARPE said greed of love.

DR HEIMANN went on to say that she did not agree with Dr Winnicott that there was only an infant–mother relationship. The infant was an individual from birth.

DR WINNICOTT said that he recognized fully that the infant was a personality from birth. He had wanted to draw attention to the dependence of the infant in contrast to the adult.

Notes

1 'Here perhaps we may be glad to have it pointed out that the sense of guilt is at bottom nothing else but a topographical variety of anxiety; in its later phases it coincides completely with fear of the superego.' [SE 21:135]
2 'This state of mind is called a "bad conscience"; actually it does not deserve this name, for at this stage the sense of guilt is clearly only a fear of loss of love, "social" anxiety. In small children it can never be anything else, but in many adults, too, it has only changed to the extent that the place of the father or the two parents is taken by the larger human community. . . . A great change takes place only when the authority is internalized throughout the establishment of a superego. The phenomena

of conscience then reach a higher stage. Actually it is not until now that we should speak of conscience or a sense of guilt.' [SE 21:125]

3 'I am convinced that many processes will admit of a simpler and clearer exposition if the findings of psychoanalysis with regard to the derivation of the sense of guilt are restricted to the aggressive instincts.' [SE 21:138]

4 Sharpe is probably referring to Freud's statement in the *Introductory Lectures* [SE 15:88] which actually is rather different: 'The world it seems does not possess even those of us who are adults completely, but only up to two thirds; one third of us is still quite unborn.'

5 'Reflex processes remain the model of every psychical function.' [SE 5:538]

6

Tenth
Discussion of Scientific Differences

Minutes of Scientific Discussion Meeting
held on May 3rd, 1944

Dr Payne was in the Chair and 23 Members and Associates were present (Miss Sharpe, Mrs Klein, Dr Winnicott, Mrs Isaacs, Drs Usher, Wilson, Franklin, Bowlby, A. & K. Stephen, Thorner, Heimann, Taylor, Macdonald, Gillespie, Herford, Mrs Riviere, Ries, Miss Sheehan-Dare, Mrs Milner, Miss Evans, Mr Money-Kyrle). Five Candidate guests were present (Drs Little, H. Rosenfeld, Bonnard Pratt and Mr Gomperts), one guest was present (Mrs L. Brook).

The minutes of the last meeting were read, passed and signed.

The Chairman announced that the question of time of meetings had been raised again. Major Thorner urged that meetings should begin at 7 p.m. as otherwise he would not be able to attend them and be back in time at his military quarters. Upon votes being taken it appeared that the large majority of Members present preferred 8 p.m. and that only one of the Members present was unable to manage this time. As, however, a majority of Members could also come at 7.30, it was decided to fix the time for meetings at 7.30 p.m.

The Chairman communicated the programme for the three Scientific Meetings to be held before the summer holidays.

The Chairman also announced that only written papers or contributions to the discussion at this meeting will be circulated in the minutes but not contributions to a free discussion.

MRS M. KLEIN (replying formally to the previous discussion on her paper 'The Emotional Life of the Infant'):
Before beginning my reply to the discussion of my paper on 'The Emotional Life and Ego Development of the Infant', I should like to state once again what I consider to be the keynote of all satisfactory scientific discussion: namely the patient and laborious process of pooling our clinical experiences and comparing notes. For this is the only way in which we are able to test new hypotheses and widen our theoretical knowledge. Every step we are thus taking nearer to the truth is a gain for all of us in our work. This can never be done by wholesale acceptance – or, to use Miss Sharpe's words, 'swallowing as a whole' – of this or that theoretical hypothesis. But the more we can corroborate any aspect of the problems under discussion by our own material, the nearer we shall come to the full truth about the processes of the mind.

On the other hand, in the course of pooling and testing we must be able to arrive at new generalizations from the accumulated experiences gained in our work; for without that our theoretical knowledge cannot increase. We are all agreed that any addition to our clinical insight is bound to influence our theoretical views. It is our duty, as Dr Brierley reminded us in her last paper published in the Journal, constantly to correlate the increase in practical knowledge with our theoretical knowledge. Therefore, while we must be cautious and sceptical about new generalizations, we defeat our own ends if we are too timid in drawing the theoretical conclusions which present themselves from our clinical experience.

These are the two points of view from which I wish to approach this discussion. I was very much interested to see that our clinical experiences have led us to similar conclusions on some essential points. I am particularly referring to Miss Sharpe's illuminating material which threw light on various aspects that I could not deal with as fully as I should have wished.

Terms applied to earlier and later phases (in answer to Dr Payne):

Dr Payne, though she does not question the fact that the young infant from the beginning of life has some form of object relation, reminds us of the necessity to keep in mind the great differences between this early relation and later relations. [See p. 803] It is true that it is essential to keep in mind such differences as well as similarities between various stages; this is even the basis for understanding a child at any age. We must never lose sight of the development as a whole, and this implies a constant comparison of any given mental picture with earlier and later stages, while at the same time we keep in mind the individual features in each particular child; and the same applies to adult patients.

As regards terminology, Dr Payne remarks that differences are often masked by the use of identical terms. Here she raises a question repeatedly discussed in psychoanalytic literature, namely whether the same terms should be used in describing early and later aspects of development. This problem can only be solved on the ground of whether, in considering a particular manifestation of emotional life, it is more important to do justice to the continuity of development and the genetic relation between early and later stages, or to lay emphasis on the differences which characterize earlier and later manifestations.

The stress on continuity underlies, for instance, the use of the terms 'ego', 'object relations', and 'object love' in describing the young infant's development. Freud created a very important precedent for this particular choice of terms. When he discovered infantile sexuality and termed it 'sexuality' in spite of the great differences between its manifestations in children and in adults, and even between the child's sexuality at different ages, he did so with the express purpose of throwing into full relief the continuity in sexual development. He thus widened the concept of sexuality, as Dr Jones pointed out in his contribution to Susan Isaacs' paper on Phantasy.

When I put forward my findings about the early stages of the Oedipus complex and the superego, some analysts – particularly Fenichal – suggested calling these stages 'precursors' of the Oedipus complex and of the superego. In my book, *The Psychoanalysis of Children*, I explained in detail why I did not agree with this point of view; and I have not altered my opinion since. For the early stages of the Oedipus complex and of the superego can *only* be fully understood if we see them in perspective with the later ones, and vice versa. It therefore seems to me essential not to distinguish them too artificially by giving them different terms.

In my experience, shared by a number of colleagues, the superego is built up from the earliest stages of life. As I have pointed out on many occasions, the harshness of the superego as we encounter it in the melancholic – and to a much lesser degree also in the normal person – can only be accounted for through the fact that the predominantly pre-genital introjected figures are at the bottom of it. We can only appreciate the structure of the superego as we see it in the child of five or six, or in the adult, if we pay full attention to the ways in which it has been developed. And because this development is a continuous process, and there is no point at which we could say 'here the classical superego begins', we should not bring in an artificial distinction by speaking of 'precursors' and of the 'actual' superego.

On the other hand there must be, in my view, essential features in common to justify the use of the same terms for early and later phases. Where these essential features are not present in the earlier stages, I think we should not use the same terms. It is true, we are bound to assume an inherited capacity for all phenomena of development. Yet – though I assume genital trends from the beginning – I should not believe it right to speak of an Oedipus situation in the first few months of life because one of the essential features of the Oedipus situation is the relation to two persons and jealousy of one in relation to the other. This constellation of factors does not exist, in my view, at the beginning of life, but can be found in the middle months of the first year. When I suggested applying the term 'guilt' only to the stages following the introjection of the object as a whole, I was guided by the same principle, namely that only where we find essential features in common are we justified in using identical terms.

Anxiety, guilt, and grief (*in answer to Dr Payne*):

Here I come to a problem which was raised by Dr Payne from another angle, and that is the demarcation between anxiety and guilt. I was aware that I had not dealt with this demarcation in my paper, and this was the reason why I raised this point in my summary. I agree with Dr Payne that this is a topic which needs further elucidation. A fruitful approach to this obscure problem has been made by Ernest Jones in his paper 'Fear, Guilt and Hate'. (Jones 1929) He connects the interaction between hate, anxiety, and guilt with the stratification of the mind and also lays emphasis on the ways in which these emotional attitudes are affected by the defence against the primary traumatic situation of 'aphanisis'. He says that 'what the infant finds so intolerable in the primal "traumatic" situation, the danger against which it feels so helpless, is the loss of control in respect of libidinal excitation, its incapacity to relieve it and enjoy the relief of it' (loc. cit., p. 394).

Ernest Jones connects the evolution of guilt with the sadistic pre-genital stages of superego development and states that guilt is 'always and inevitably associated with the hate impulse'. He distinguishes, however, two phases in the development of guilt and suggests for the first stage (which I take to coincide with early infancy) the term 'pre-nefarious' stage of guilt.

In my paper 'A Contribution to the Psychogenesis of Manic-Depressive States' (Klein 1935) I considered the connection between anxiety and guilt, and came to the following conclusions: though from the beginning the relation to the internal and external 'good' and 'bad' breast is of fundamental importance, in the early stages anxiety relates mainly to the preservation of the ego. With the progressive integration of the ego and the introjection of and fuller identification with the object as a whole, new features are added to this anxiety for the ego; the unconscious concern lest the loved object be destroyed, a sense of responsibility for preserving it from the aggressive impulses directed against it, and sadness relating to expectation of its impending loss. Thus, with the introjection of the object as a whole, certain elements come together in the mind; and new defences also come into play, notably the drive for reparation. It is this blend of wishes, anxieties, and defences which I think differentiates guilt from the primary anxiety predominantly relating to the ego. The essentials of the depressive position can be found in the struggle between love and hatred in relation to the object as a whole, together with the complex feelings described by me as guilt.

I am open to the argument that guilt is there from the beginning, and that the particular constellation of feelings I described is only a further stage in the evolution of feelings of guilt. Indeed, my experience led me to conclude that early feeding difficulties are derived from the inhibition of greed, and this inhibition I found related to the infant's anxiety lest the breast be destroyed by his cannibalistic impulses. I was thus led to assume capacity of the ego from the beginning to mobilize one part of his impulses against the other, a capacity which could only be inherited. In this way the id would undergo a division which I think is the first step in the formation of instinctual inhibitions and of the superego. The introjected object soon becomes the vehicle of defence against the destructive impulses. [Klein 1932: 183–4]

In spite of all these arguments in favour of assuming guilt as an inherited capacity from the beginning, I find it helpful to keep to my hypothesis that guilt and grief arise with the introjection of the object as a whole. It is implicit in my definition of guilt and of the depressive position that the sense of loss which derives from the separation from the mother at birth does not yet constitute grief. It is only when guilt, essentially referring to the aggression against the loved object, comes into play that I am inclined to think of the depressive position.

Libidinal frustration and aggression (in answer to Dr Payne):

Dr Payne holds that the depressive position depends primarily on libidinal frustration, while according to my hypothesis it is predominantly the aggressive impulses which give rise to anxiety and guilt. We must, however, remember that in fact the two instincts are always fused. Even in states in which the aggressive impulse has the upper hand in the fusion, the libido is always at work as well. In my experience, anxiety arises because the ego senses his destructive impulses as a danger to itself as well as to its external and internal objects. This hypothesis does not, however, imply that the importance of frustrated libido is underrated.

I have tried in my former writings to describe the part frustrated libido plays in the circle of mental processes which is initiated by anxiety aroused by the aggressive impulses. When in the interplay of the two instincts the aggressive impulses predominate, libido is 'dammed up'; when aggression diminishes, the other side of the scales goes up, and libido becomes free to move. In the fusion of the two instincts, it is aggression which prevents the free movement of the libido. But libidinal frustration constantly reinforces the aggressive impulses.

In considering this problem, we must keep in mind that the destructive impulses give rise to anxiety and guilt because they are primarily directed against the love object. We can never discuss anxiety and guilt without keeping in mind the interaction and the polarity between libido and aggression.

Dr Payne states that anxiety is the primary emotional reaction to the infant's helplessness and complete dependence on his mother. There is no disagreement between Dr Payne and myself as to the importance of the infant's biological and psychological helplessness and dependence. Here are two passages from my paper: 'As we know, the child's actual needs for attention and help dominate his life.' And: 'If we fully appreciate the imperative need of the infant for his mother who alone can provide the gratification he craves for, we are bound to acknowledge that the emotion of loss he experiences has immediate and profound effects on his mental life.' [See pp. 763–4.]

The physical and psychological dependence on the mother is one of the preconditions for the infant's intense feeling of loss when he misses her, and it is the corresponding intensity of the feelings of frustration which stir and reinforce the aggressive impulses.

In psychoanalytic theory libido has received much more attention than the aggressive impulses. As Dr Heimann put it in her paper on

'Introjection and Projection': 'Analytic theory has treated the two instincts in an unequal manner: the libido is the first-born and privileged child, the destructive instinct is the latecomer, the stepchild. Libido was recognized as such from the first; the other instinct, its adversary, went under various disguises and had several names before its true identity was established.'

When Abraham found the connection between the cannibalistic impulses and anxiety and guilt, a turning point in our theory was reached. For at this juncture a fuller appreciation of the importance of the aggressive impulses for the aetiology of psychosis became possible. Until that time very little clinical work with melancholics had been attempted.

In 'The Development of the Libido' [Abraham 1924:433–4] Abraham introduces his own findings by referring to his and Freud's former work on melancholia. He says,

> In his paper, 'Mourning and Melancholia', [Freud, S. 1917d] Freud described in general outlines the psychosexual processes that take place in the melancholic. He was able to obtain an intuitive idea of them from the occasional treatment of depressive patients; but not very much clinical material has been published up till now in the literature of psychoanalysis in support of this theory. The material which I shall bring forward in this connection is, however, intended not merely to illustrate that theory but to prepare the way for a systematic inquiry into the pathological processes of melancholia and into the phenomena of mourning. As we shall see, the psychology of melancholia and of mourning are not as yet sufficiently understood.

In this book Abraham substantiates his conclusions, which threw new light on the connection between melancholia and normal mourning, by extracts from two case histories. These were actually the first two cases of manic-depressives which had undergone a thorough analysis – a new venture in the development of psychoanalysis. Great therapeutic possibilities were opened up at this juncture. Through an understanding of the connection between anxiety and guilt and the aggressive impulses, early phantasy life became accessible and the analysis of quite young children became possible. The therapeutic and theoretical results obtained in the last twenty years in this field have already proved that Abraham's prophecy, expressed in 1925, that the future of psychoanalysis lies with the analysis of children is coming true. Furthermore, in the course of this work and through the understanding of early psychotic anxieties and mechanisms, it has become possible to analyse patients with psychotic features, borderline cases, and even psychotics; and this has led to a much greater understanding of the neurotic and of the normal individual. Thus we have immeasurably widened the scope of our therapeutic work. Though there are many points on which we still need to clear our minds, and on which full agreement has not yet been reached, the hypothesis that aggressive impulses are the prime causative factor for anxiety and guilt has already proved its intrinsic value for psychoanalytic theory and practice. In this connection some misunderstanding seems to have arisen over my concept of the depressive position. It has sometimes been presented as an entirely new departure in my work; but this is not true. The understanding of early introjection processes, together with the recognition that aggressive impulses from various sources directed against the loved object give rise to anxiety and guilt, and form the core of the deepest conflicts in the child, was the basis from which my concept of the depressive position derived. Thus this hypothesis was no new departure, but the logical outcome from my former work – a further contribution to the endeavour of psychoanalysis to fill in the picture of early mental life.

All clinical problems must inevitably be reflected in our technique. Accumulated experience has shown that the therapeutic value of our interpretations is greatly increased if we give full weight to the part aggressive impulses and aggressive phantasies play in the causation of anxiety and guilt. Interpretations which predominantly stress frustrated libido are not effective in themselves. On the other hand, if in our interpretations we consistently link frustration with the aggressive impulses and the anxiety stirred by these impulses, anxiety will be relieved, and aggressive impulses lose in strength. Moreover we can see – and here the analysis of young children has been particularly instructive – that, whether the anxieties stirred by the aggressive impulses in turn increase these impulses, or whether anxiety leads to excessive repression of aggression, the effect will always be that the capacity for love suffers in consequence. The vicissitudes of the libido are fully comprehensible only in relation to the early anxieties with which they are intimately bound up. For the anxieties stirred by the destructive impulses constantly influence the libido, at times inhibiting, at times increasing the libidinal desires. Every step in diminishing aggressive impulses by interpretation leads to freeing libido and increases the capacity for love. If we interpret the various emotions which accompany frustrated libido from the earliest relation to the breast onwards, we are doing more than interpreting frustrated libido – we are actually doing justice to the interplay between the instincts. For libidinal frustration is from the beginning linked up with envy and jealousy, with resentment, feelings of grievance and revenge; and all these emotions are closely bound up with aggressive impulses and the anxiety about their consequences. It is for this reason that we have, in my view, in theory and in practice to acknowledge the aggressive impulses as the prime causative factor for anxiety and guilt. This approach, far from being incompatible with the full analysis of the libido, is in my experience a pre-condition for it.

Factors entering into depression (in answer to Dr Brierley):

Dr Brierley concludes from her experience with adult patients that depression involves more than purely oral revival, and therefore she suggests that anal factors and anxieties from various sources are likely to play an important part in the infantile depressive position as well. [See p. 815.] For these reasons she expresses doubts whether the infantile depressive position as described by me is not too limited and narrow a concept. This question is simple to answer, for I have never suggested that the cannibalistic impulses are the only factor in causing the depressive position, though in my paper on 'The Emotional Life of the Infant' I particularly stressed them as the original, the primary causative factor. At the same time, I referred back to my two papers ('A Contribution to the Psychogenesis of Manic-Depressive States' [Klein 1935] and 'Mourning and its Relation to Manic-Depressive States' [Klein 1940]) which contain the theoretical basis for my whole concept of the depressive position, and I made a point of these references, because I was aware that in the present paper I should be unable to do more than to select a few aspects of the infant's emotional life. In my 'Contribution to the Psychogenesis of Manic-Depressive States' I introduced my hypothesis of the depressive position and pointed out that this position arises during the phase of maximal sadism which sets in during the first few months of life.[1] I have described this phase in detail in my book, *The Psychoanalysis of Children*, [Klein 1932:186] and in other writings, and I have shown that it arises through a confluence of libidinal and aggressive impulses from all sources and gives rise to these manifold phantasies, anxieties, and defences which in my view characterize infantile emotional life. Indeed, my hypothesis, restated in the present paper, that the libidinal phases overlap in the first year of life, and my repeated reference to aggressive impulses in general, rather than to cannibalistic ones, implies that many more factors besides oral libido and anxieties contribute to the depressive position.

My view, held for many years, that the early stages of the Oedipus conflict can be found in the second half of the first year presupposes that complex emotions derived from libidinal and aggressive desires and anxieties of all kinds contribute to the depressive position.

In my paper 'The Early Stages of the Oedipus Conflict', [Klein 1928] I came to the conclusion that oral frustration experienced in relation to the mother leads to the search for other gratifications as well as for new objects. The infant who desires the mother's breast and cannot get it feels that this unique substance is withheld from him and that somebody else receives it. Envy, jealousy, and competitive feelings are thus some of the driving forces for the turning away from the primary object. Another contributing factor is the desire to preserve the loved object; and the search for new sources of gratification, which leads to finding substitutes, also plays an important part in the turning away from the first loved object. Anal and genital libido are reinforced by oral frustration. Thus the ground is prepared for the early stages of the Oedipus conflict. The implication is that libidinal and aggressive impulses from *all* sources are at work in the infant, and that complex emotions, anxieties, and defences influence his relations during the first year of life.

I come now to another of Dr Brierley's queries. In my paper, when describing the earliest object relations, I said that the mother exists from the beginning 'as a whole object in the child's mind, but in vague outlines as it were, and that this picture becomes gradually filled in as perception develops'. By this I did not mean to imply that in the first two or three months of life the infant has the perceptual capacity to see the whole object, but I agree with Dr Brierley that my description was inaccurate, and the wording of a 'vague presence' which she suggests depicts more adequately the early relation to the mother.

Adaptation to external reality and intrapsychic positions
(in answer to Dr Brierley):

Dr Brierley states: 'I personally find it easier to think of development as a progressive series of psychobiological adaptations to changing life-situations rather than in terms of intrapsychic positions.' [See p. 816.] To this I would reply that the antithesis which seems implied in this remark is rather misleading. We cannot think of development in terms only of intrapsychic positions or in terms only of a series of psychobiological adaptations to changing life situations, because they are inextricably bound up with each other. Or, to put it

832

differently: object relations exist from the beginning, and it is for this reason that the impact of the infant's emotions is so very great and that the depressive position is inevitably bound up with the relation to the primary object and with external situations. Susan Isaacs, in her paper on 'Phantasy', made it clear that phantasy life is from the outset inextricably linked with the experience of external reality. I wish to quote in this connection one passage from my paper on 'The Emotional Life of the Infant': 'There is a constant interplay between the testing of external reality and the attempts to modify it, control it, and come to terms with it on the one hand, and the relation to the inner world on the other. These two orientations, inwards and outwards, are gradually brought into harmony with each other; and the extent to which this is achieved is a measure of normal development.' [See p. 781.]

For purposes of exposition, I have at times isolated one aspect of mental life from the intrapsychic point of view; when drawing conclusions, however, I usually attempted to correlate it with the external factors which, in conjunction with the internal ones, make up a total situation. This point of view underlies my work as a whole. As soon as we think in terms of development – and how else can we understand any aspect of the child's mind at any state? – we are already considering intrapsychic happenings in the light of adaptation to changing life conditions. I said in my paper, 'Every step in ego development which enables the child to communicate with, perceive, and undersand the external world, helps him to gain greater security about his external objects; this again assists him in overcoming his fear of losing his good internal objects. If a satisfactory balance between these interacting processes is achieved, the child is well on the way to overcome his depressive feelings.' [See p. 781.] The set of emotions, anxieties and defences which I singled out under the term 'depressive position' can only be understood as part of 'a series of psychobiological adaptations to changing life-situations', to use Dr Brierley's words.

Furthermore, Dr Brierley suggests that depressive feelings 'are not characteristic of weaning experiences alone, they are characteristic of all situations of change for the worse'. If we wish to understand the importance of the depressive position in later situations, we have first to understand it in its initial setting. I do not believe, however, that the initial setting is the weaning experience. In my view the emotional experiences of losing the loved object and regaining it are an essential part of early mental life. The first loss is the separation from the mother at birth, but it is in relation to the mother's breast, to losing it (and the mother) again and again that depressive feelings develop throughout the suckling period. The core of the depressive position can be found in the infant's relation to the mother as an object as a whole (three to five months) – in the fear of losing her through his cannibalistic and aggressive impulses, and in the ensuing guilt. At weaning time a climax is reached, but its effect on the infant depends cn the ways in which he has dealt throughout the suckling period with the recurrent situation of 'change for the worse', namely the loss of the mother's breast (and the mother as a whole person).

I think it has something to do with the term 'depressive position' that it is liable to be thought of as static rather than dynamic and developmental. I am aware that this term has certain disadvantages, but the same applies to the terms 'stage', 'phase', and even 'situation'. I wish however to take every opportunity to make it clear that the depressive position is meant to describe not a static constellation of factors but an intrinsic feature of the growth of the child's emotional life, which is from the beginning constantly influenced by the impact of external reality.

The concept of love in the infant (in answer to Dr Brierley):

Dr Brierley suggests that 'if we use the term "love" in the same wide sense as we use the term "libido", and define it as the feeling characteristic of libido', there is no objection to the use of it in regard to infants. She adds: 'We must, however, keep clear in our minds the difference between a primary simple affect and the complicated emotional attitudes of later life.' Though I agree with her that we always have to keep in mind such difference, I do not agree that the infant's love feelings for his mother are a 'primary simple affect', and therefore I do not agree with Dr Brierley's definition of love in the infant as 'a feeling characteristic of libido'. [See p. 816.]

It is one of the essential points in my concept of the depressive position that love in the infant of say three to five months is already an extremely complicated emotion and that this to some extent applies even to the younger infant. Speaking of love in the infant, I said in my paper: 'The strength of these emotions and their immediate effect can only be understood in relation to an object. If we fully appreciate the imperative need of the infant for his mother who alone can provide the gratification he craves for, we are bound to acknowledge that the emotion of loss he experiences has immediate and profound effects on his mental life.' With the introjection of the objects as a whole – and this is one of the corner stones of my concept – anxieties from various sources, sense of guilt, fear of loss, etc., enter into the infant's relation to his mother. It is thus precisely because a number of features which characterize love in its later stages are already present in the infant's emotional life that I deliberately used the term 'love' in the sense we apply it to later stages, and not in the wide meaning of a 'feeling characteristic of libido'.

Hunger, aggression and guilt (in answer to Miss Sharpe):

In my reply to Miss Sharpe I first wish to clarify an important theoretical point. She puts it to me that it is not the loss of the breast as such nor the loss of the actual mother as such which produces depression. She also says that she does not believe 'that guilt arises through anger and aggression caused by actual frustration, i.e. real hunger. We are justified in our anger, for the self instincts have their own imperative right. We feel guilty when greed is not for those things we feel we are justified in desiring to get and hold.'

Here Miss Sharpe draws a distinction between justifiable hunger which does not cause guilt – even though it may be greedy and arouse anger – and greed which is not justifiable because it oversteps the demands of the self-preservative instinct. This distinction does not, in my experience, correspond to the processes of the early mind. [See p. 811.] As we know, Freud found that the instinct of self-preservation (ego instinct) is from the beginning associated with the sexual instinct. In his paper 'On Narcissism' (1914) he says: 'The first auto-erotic gratifications are experienced in connection with vital functions in the service of self-preservation. The sexual instincts are at the outset supported upon the ego-instincts; only later do they become independent of these.' [Freud, S. 1914:44; SE 14:87][2] Furthermore in *Instincts and Their Vicissitudes* [Freud, S. 1915] he says, when speaking of the sexual instincts: 'At their first appearance they support themselves upon the instincts of self-preservation, from which they only gradually detach themselves.' [Freud, S. 1915a:69; SE 14:126][3]

As development progresses, hunger becomes partially divorced from sexual desires. The infant's relation to food and the relation to the mother, which are inderdependent at the beginning of life, become to some extent divorced as development goes on.

On the one hand, the infant cannot distinguish between more hunger and sexual desires because greed has in it elements of both. On the other hand, Miss Sharpe's view also implies a degree of intellectual discrimination in the infant which goes far beyond his

835

capacities. His mother may be, and probably is in most cases, delighted with his lusty and greedy sucking; and yet the infant is apt to feel guilty because of his greed. A hungry infant cannot ascertain the limit to which his aggression is justified and beyond which it becomes murderous and destructive. Whenever we find in our patients such distinctions, we are confronted much more with the conscious adult mind than with the infant's mental processes. It is inherent in the nature of the infant's emotions – and a fundamental factor in the development of infantile neuroses – that they are very powerful and immediate, and therefore not commensurate with the actual situation which arouses them. Moreover, in the early mind desires and phantasies are felt to be omnipotent.

The fact that cannibalistic impulses exist in every infant, whether or not he is satisfied in his feeding situation, is established beyond doubt. Moreover, as Freud puts it, there is the 'innate conflict of ambivalence', 'the eternal struggle between Eros and the destructive or death instinct'. Even when the feeding situation is satisfactory, hunger and the craving for libidinal gratification stir and reinforce the destructive impulses. I fully agree with Miss Sharpe that we have to take into account the whole setting in which the infant lives, with all the manifold stimuli which he experiences. Furthermore, the quantitative factor is, as we know, of the greatest importance; and this refers both to the strength of the infant's emotions and anxieties, and to the experiences which external reality forces on him. My contention, however, which I now wish to restate is that – even under favourable circumstances – cannibalistic impulses and aggressive impulses from all sources though varying in strength arise in the infant and lead correspondingly to guilt and depressive feelings. It is the problem of guilt which, I think, is the crux of the matter and is the essence of this particular issue. However much external factors and the setting in which the infant grows up may contribute to his feelings of dissatisfaction and grievance, the feeling of guilt stirred by his fear of loss of his loved object derives primarily from his cannibalistic and aggressive impulses.

Status quo ante (in answer to Miss Sharpe):

This leads me to Miss Sharpe's apposite description of the 'status quo ante' in depressive people. [See pp. 805–6.] I have no doubt that Miss Sharpe agrees with me that this status quo, the world before it was 'decomposed' – in her patient's words – is bound up with an idealization of early situations, which implies an idealization of the loved objects as well as of one's relation to those objects. There are various external reasons why these situations may have fallen short of the infant's wishes, and thus the drive to idealize became increased. But this drive is an intrinsic part of normal development. There is an internal factor which is largely responsible for this necessity to idealize and thus to keep to the status quo; and that is the hatred, aggression, and guilt experienced in relation to loved objects. It is true that the early setting in which our patients lived may have been particularly apt to arouse dissatisfaction, to stir jealousy, and to produce excessive tension. Nevertheless the anxiety and guilt which the patient experiences relate to his hatred which in his mind injured or destroyed the people he loved and caused his world to decompose. The status quo ante in my experience always implies the ideal situation in which *aggression did not enter* into the patient's relationships to his loved objects. In this ideal situation no frustration existed; thus no grievance and no aggression arose. The train of unconscious thought underlying this idealization can be briefly put like this: I was not frustrated then – I did not hate then because I was not frustrated – I only loved – everything was perfect. Thus an important element – and from the therapeutic point of view I think the most important one – of the idealization process is the denial of the inherent aggression which is felt as 'original sin'.

The overriding longing for the status quo implies a fundamental failure in development, namely an incapacity in the young child to detach himself sufficiently from his primary objects and to find substitutes and substitute gratifications. But this capacity derives largely from excessive anxiety and guilt in connection with the aggressive impulses.

Narcissism (in answer Miss Sharpe):

The close connection between the status quo and narcissism, on which Miss Sharpe observes, goes back to the separation from the mother at birth. In this connection she quotes Freud as having said: 'Most people are only half born.' As Dr Brierley suggests, even 'in supposing that intra-uterine existence is uninterrupted paradise' a certain amount of 'retrospective idealization' may have gone on. So far, however, this is beyond the scope of our investigation. But we know more about the blissful situation of feeding at the breast, 'the unattainable prototype of every later sexual satisfaction', which is revived and reproduced in hallucination. The infant hallucinates because the loss of this gratification is so painful for him that when he is deprived of it he must recreate this gratification in his mind. In this situation we can see the prototype of the status quo.

In various passages in 'Negation' and in *Instincts and Their Vicissitudes*, Freud makes it clear that the infant introjects all that is pleasant and rejects everything unpleasant or painful.[4] This rejection of unpleasant and painful stimuli and the exclusive acceptance and clinging to the object and situations which provide pleasure, gratification, and relief of tension is the basis for narcissistic withdrawal; and I see in it also the basis for idealization. For in hallucination, a narcissistic phenomenon *par excellence*, the gratifying situation is recreated with great intensity, the frustration is denied, and with it the whole circle of aggression and anxiety to which frustration gives rise. Thus we can see in hallucination the beginnings of idealization, and we see it play a part already in the earliest relation to the mother's breast.

However, the infant's desire to reject unpleasantness, and exclusively to accept what is pleasant, can only be fulfilled in hallucination. The impact of reality forces frustration on him again and again. For various reasons the infant is at the beginning not yet capable of bringing together the two main aspects of his relation to his mother, and he uses the separation of the good object, the good breast, from the bad object, the bad breast, of love from hatred, as a fundamental way of coping with frustration. When he introjects the object as a whole, he is no longer able to keep good and bad so strongly apart from each other; at this stage ambivalence sets in and the ground is prepared for the complex feelings and anxieties which constitute the depressive position.

To return to my main argument; even in the earliest situation, the *revulsion against the destructive feelings* which are stirred by frustration contributes to narcissistic withdrawal, and thus to the earliest form of idealization and of status quo feelings. Whenever in my patients I found the desire to return to the prototype of the status quo situation, i.e. the loving and gratified relation to the mother's breast, we came to see that this was essentially a desire to recreate a situation in which no aggression against the loved object was aroused – ultimately to deny the painful fact that ambivalence and aggression are inherent.

'The complete situation' (in answer to Miss Sharpe):

I am now turning to Miss Sharpe's argument that it is never 'the loss of the breasts as such nor the loss of the actual mother as such' which is the cause for depression, but a complete situation. Miss Sharpe suggests that in my theory of the depressive position – though not in my clinical data – I have not given sufficient weight to the fact that frustration is imposed on the child by the people around him, and that here the father soon enters into the picture. In my view, however, there is a stage covering the first three or four months, in which the relation to the mother's breast dominates the whole emotional life of the infant. This is the first complete situation in the infant's life, and it is the basis for all his future relationships. The first and fundamental experiences of happiness and love, of frustration and hatred derive from this complete situation in relation to the mother's breast and to the mother. From this total situation other total situations derive which are linked up with people other than the mother, in the first place with the father. The father normally becomes an important person for the infant from about the fourth month onwards. Thus the infant goes through a series of total situations in the first year of life. A glance at the main points in my paper reveals that I have dealt with the elements which go to make up these total situations: the libidinal and aggressive relation to an object from the beginning; the interplay between the relation to the actual mother (breast) and the internal object, with the manifold stimuli provided by external situations and reflecting on internal ones; early object love; the modification of instincts as expressed in feeding difficulties; the feeling of loss, partly in connection with the aggressive impulses, partly with the actual helplessness of the infant and his dependence on his loved objects; guilt and depressive feelings (the depressive position) which are the result of these complex situations and of the relation to the internal and external objects.

Miss Sharpe describes 'the accurate perceptions of the growing infant, awareness of the mother's responses, an awareness of whether he is wanted and loved, an awareness of the mother's haste and anxiety or placidity and patience', and she states that 'his first pattern of behaviour responses are inextricably bound up and fused with the mother's own'. [See p. 808.] I fully subscribe to this picture of the infant's capacity to perceive of the external world and to respond to it. Indeed, my view that the early stages of the Oedipus conflict, which involve the relation to the father, can be found in the middle period of the first year of life, implies that there is a complex awareness of, and emotional relation to, the people who provide the setting in which the infant lives.

I shall only mention one instance, based on direct observation of a little girl. From the age of about four months onwards the relation to her brother, several years her elder, began to play a prominent part in her life. This relation, as could easily be seen, differed in many aspects from the equally close and loving relation to the mother. She admired everything her brother said and did, and persistently wooed him. Even though her brother, who was fond of her, did not always respond to her approaches, she would not be put off but used all her little tricks to ingratiate herself with him, to win his attention and love – displaying thus a fundamentally feminine attitude towards the male. At that time the father was absent, and it was not until she was ten months old that she saw him more often and developed from that time onwards a very close and loving relation to him. Though she still remained very much attached to her mother, the relation to the father showed many different features, which in some essentials paralleled the relation to the brother, i.e. admiration, devotion, and wooing. Though she still remained fond of her brother, the father became the favourite. It was significant that early on in her second year she often called her brother 'Daddy'. The delight in seeing her father, the rapture when she heard his steps or his voice, the ways in which she mentioned him again and again in his absence, and many other expressions of her feelings towards him could only be described as being in love. The mother clearly recognized that the little girl was in some ways much more fond of her father than of her. This seems to me an instance where the early Oedipus situation was displayed on to a substitute, and then re-transferred as it were to the original object.

It was to throw into relief the extent to which infants perceive, respond to and are influenced by external circumstances, that I quoted in full in my paper Freud's illuminating description of the eleven-month-old child who felt robbed and dethroned by the arrival of a new baby. I also specifically referred to Dr Middlemore's observations which proved the effect of external factors even in the first few days of life.

To return to Miss Sharpe's point that it is not merely the loss of the breast, and not even the loss of the actual mother as such, which causes depression; there is one fundamental element in the 'complete situation' which I wish to re-emphasize: the feared loss of the *introjected loved object* is foremost among the anxieties which constitute the depressive position. Miss Sharpe herself has in a former contribution to these discussions (January 27th, 1943) [see p. 338] referred to this aspect of the depressive position, to the infant's belief that he possesses the 'real tangible breast', that 'the actual breast is inside'. The particular stress on the *internal* situation which my hypothesis of the depressive position implies is in keeping with the concept of melancholia and normal mourning, as developed by Freud and Abraham. The loss of the loved mourned object drives the mourner to reinstate the lost loved object in the ego. In normal mourning in later years *not only the cathexes attached to the lost object are withdrawn and reinvested, as Miss Sharpe reminds us, but during this process the lost object is established within.* As I pointed out in my paper on 'Mourning and its Relation to Manic-Depressive States' [Klein 1940] the mourner 'not only takes into himself (re-incorporates) the person whom he has just lost, but also reinstates his internalized good objects (ultimately his loved parents) who became part of his inner world from the earliest stages of his development onwards. These too are felt to have gone under, to be destroyed, whenever the loss of a loved person is experienced.' And:

> The pain experienced in the slow process of testing reality in the work of mourning thus seems to be partly due to the necessity not only to renew the links to the external world and thus continuously to re-experience the loss, but at the same time and by means of this to rebuild with anguish the inner world, which is felt to be in danger of deteriorating and collapsing. Just as the young child passing through the depressive position is struggling, in his unconscious mind with the task of establishing and integrating his inner world, so the mourner goes through the pain of re-establishing and re-integrating it.

One of the fundamental differences between normal mourning and melancholia is, according to Abraham, that in normal mourning the individual succeeds in establishing the lost loved person in his ego, whereas in melancholia this process is not successful. Abraham also described some of the fundamental factors upon which that success or failure depends. In my paper on 'Mourning and its Relation to Manic-Depressive States', I made a further step in the same direction. To quote this paper again:

> My experience leads me to conclude that, while it is true that the characteristic feature of normal mourning is the individual's setting up the lost loved object inside himself, he is not doing so for the first time but, through the work of mourning is reinstating that object as well as all his loved internal objects which he feels he has lost. He is therefore recovering what he had already attained in childhood.
>
> [Klein 1940]

One fundamental factor in determining whether or not at a later period the loss of a loved object (through death or other causes) will lead to melancholia or will be normally overcome is, in my experience, the extent to which in the first year of life the loved introjected objects have been securely established within the ego. This achievement presupposes a satisfactory relation to the primary external objects, which furthermore enables the ego to find substitutes for the primary objects and new sources of gratification.

The vicissitudes of internal relationships (in answer to Dr Heimann):

Dr Heimann points out that 'an important aspect of analytic investigations concerns the cathexis of objects with libido and aggressive impulses, and the manifold conditions arising from changes in cathexis'. [See p. 819.]

Here she touches on what could be called the vicissitudes of the relationships with inner objects. As it was first introduced, the concept of introjection in melancholia and in normal development was primarily concerned with the process of establishing an external object within the ego. It is, however, essential not to think of introjection as a process done, as it were, once and for all, but of a fluid relationship with internal objects, constantly influenced by the relations to external objects and governed by the emotions and impulses depending on whether frustration or gratification are prevalent at the time. The vicissitudes of internal relationships, which begin with the earliest introjection processes, are a still largely unexhausted field of exploration, and I think the future will show that further knowledge in this field will give us a greater understanding not only of the aetiology of mental disturbances, but also of the ways in which these internal relationships influence and mould the normal personality.

Final remarks

In this reply only certain points from the contributions have been dealt with. I was guided in this selection by the wish to elaborate on those points which seemed to need most clarification and therefore seemed to be most productive for the discussion. This is also the reason why I have not gone into detail on those points raised in the discussion which seemed to coincide completely with my own views.

I still feel, however, that some problems would have deserved more exhaustive treatment, and I hope that further discussion will be forthcoming on them in the future.

I wish to thank all contributors for their stimulating and helpful comments.

The Chairman thanked Mrs Klein and opened the free discussion in which the following Members took part: Drs Wilson, K. Stephen, Isaacs, Winnicott, Heimann, A. Stephen, Bowlby, Macdonald, Mrs Riviere, and Mrs Klein.

Notes

1 All those papers are also to be found in vol. 1 of the recent collection of Melanie Klein's work, *Love, Guilt and Reparation and Other Works 1921–45*, Hogarth Press and The Institute of Psycho-Analysis, 1981.

2 'The first auto-erotic sexual satisfactions are experienced in connection with vital functions which serve the purpose of self-preservation.' [SE 14:87]

3 'At their first appearance they are attached to the instincts of self-preservation, from which they only gradually become separated.' [SE 14:126]

4 (Original footnote) Freud said in 'Negation' (*IJPA*, vol. VI, p. 368): 'Originally the property to be decided about might be either good or bad, useful or harmful. Expressed in the language of the oldest, that is, of the oral instinctual impulses, the alternative runs thus: "I should like to eat that, or I should like to spit it out", or, carried stage further: "I should like to take this into me and keep that out of me".' [Freud, S. 1925:368; SE 19:236–7]

   (Editor's note) 'The attribute to be decided about may originally have been good or bad, useful or harmful. Expressed in the language of the oldest – the oral – instinctual impulses, the judgement is: "I should like to eat this", or "I should like to spit it out"; and, put more generally: "I should like to take this into myself and to keep that out".'

Reorganization
after the Controversies

Editorial comments (1)

PEARL KING

The events described in Section 5 overlapped in time with some of those reported in Section 4. The Sixth Extraordinary Business meeting reported in Chapter 1 was held on 2 February 1944, two weeks before the Eighth Discussion of Scientific Controversies on 16 February 1944. It was called to discuss the proposals of the Medical Committee, 'that a course of instruction in the principles of psychoanalysis suitable for those engaged in the study of psychological medicine should be arranged as part of the Institute's regular programme of work', and that a special committee be set up to arrange this course. Membership of the Lecture Committee was a much sought-after position. It was one of the first committees in the Society to be subject to election and to a limitation in the tenure of office. (Giving public lectures was thought to give access to potential patients.)

Shortly before the meeting took place, Sylvia Payne received Edward Glover's resignation from the Society and Institute. The greater part of this meeting was therefore diverted from its original agenda, to deal with the Council's proposals for filling the offices left vacant by the resignation of Glover, his letters of resignation, and the Members' discussion on how to respond to them. It was agreed that copies of his resignation letters be sent to all Members of the Society so that they could discuss at the next meeting how the Society should respond to them.

But Glover had caused much resentment to certain Members of the Society by publicly attacking the work of Army psychiatrists[1] in broadcasts during December 1943 and January 1944 and in a weekly journal called *Cavalcade*. Four of them[2] had already decided to call for

847

an Extraordinary Business Meeting to discuss their complaints against Glover, when news of his resignation was received. The proceedings of this meeting were then complicated because these four Members tried to explain to their colleagues why they did not want to try to persuade Glover to reconsider his decision to resign.

Chapter 2 contains the minutes of the Extraordinary Business Meeting called by these four Members on 23 February 1944, to discuss a resolution dissociating the British Psycho-Analytical Society from the views expressed by Edward Glover on Army psychiatrists and selective testing,[3] as he was at the time of making these attacks the Scientific Secretary of the Society. They particularly regretted his having made public allegations on the radio and in the popular press without his having first made a thorough investigation and conveyed his considered opinions to his professional colleagues. The four Members also proposed that copies of this resolution should be sent to Brigadier J. R. Rees, Consulting Psychiatrist to the Army, and also to the appropriate psychological and medical associations.

The Eighth Extraordinary Business Meeting, the minutes of which are reported in Chapter 3, was called to receive and discuss the final report of the Training Committee and to consider Glover's reaction to the resolution passed at the previous meeting.

The next two chapters are concerned with the reorganization of the Society, the changes in the rules and the election of the new officers and Council of the Society and the Training Committee, under the new constitution. These committees did not include Anna Freud or any of her colleagues, as they had withdrawn from active participation in the Society's activities.

The steps taken by Sylvia Payne to draw Anna Freud back into the training activities of the Society are briefly described in Chapter 6. It also includes a short outline of the subsequent history of the British Psycho-Analytical Society, in order to complete the background within which the controversies contained in the book took place. Chapter 7 contains 'Editorial comments' and 'Conclusions' by Riccardo Steiner and by Pearl King, in which they each attempt to reflect on the events described in the book, the repercussions of these events and the effectiveness of their attempted solutions on the future organization and creativity of psychoanalysts and of the British Psycho-Analytical Society.

Notes

1 Glover particularly resented the Army psychiatrists, who were also Members of the Society, as they had led the attack on the holding of multiple offices in the Society and Institute, and they were the architects of the Medical Committee, whose election had swung the balance of power in the Society away from Glover to Sylvia Payne.
2 The four Members were Major John Bowlby, Dr William Gillespie, Major John Rickman, and Major Adrian Stephen.
3 In my paper on 'Activities of British Psychoanalysts during the Second World War and the Influence of their Inter-disciplinary Collaboration on the Development of Psychoanalysis in Great Britain' [King 1989a:20–6] I have described some of the work of the Army psychiatrists, especially those who worked with psychoanalysts.

1

The Sixth
Extraordinary Business Meeting

**An Extraordinary Business Meeting
was held on Wednesday, February 2nd, 1944,
at 96 Gloucester Place, London W.1.**

Dr Payne was in the Chair and 23 Members were present (Payne, Friedlander, Low, Franklin, Ruben, Sharpe, Lantos, M. Schmideberg, Isaacs, Klein, Rickman, Matthew, Wilson, Scott, Gillespie, Bowlby, Winnicott, Herford, Karin Stephen, Adrian Stephen, Heimann, Riviere, Macdonald).

DR PAYNE: Before proceeding to the business on the Agenda I have to inform the meeting that Dr Glover has resigned his membership of the Society and Institute.[1] On hearing of Dr Glover's resignation Dr Jones, the President and Chairman, asked me to deputize for him at this meeting which he could not attend.

Before reading you Dr Glover's statement I want to speak of the changes which must necessarily take place in the administration. In the second year of the war administrative authority was delegated by the Council, sanctioned by the Annual Meeting, to an Emergency War Committee consisting of Dr Glover and myself. It is obvious that the Emergency War Committee no longer exists and that authority now reverts to the Council.

At a meeting of the Council held this morning, at which the following Members were present – Dr Brierley, Miss Sharpe, Dr Payne, Dr Rickman, by invitation Dr Friedlander (Acting Treasurer), Mr Strachey (Editor of the Journal) – it was resolved that the following members of the Council shall fill vacant offices or act for officers on war service until such a time that new elections can be held:

1 That in the absence of the President Dr Jones, Dr Payne shall deputize for him.
2 That Dr Brierley shall act as Scientific Secretary in place of Dr Glover.
3 That authority shall be asked to co-opt a Business Secretary if necessary.
4 That Dr Friedlander shall continue to act as Treasurer.

It was resolved that the following resolutions shall be put to this meeting:

1 That Dr Glover's resignation be recorded in the minutes.
2 That the functions undertaken by the Emergency War Committee revert to the Council.
3 That the recommendations of the Council for interim management of the Society be accepted.

DR PAYNE read the letter of resignation Dr Glover had sent to her:

18 Wimpole Street,
W.1.
24 January, 1944

Dear Dr Payne
It is now almost 2 years since I first contemplated severing my connection with the British Psycho-Analytical Society. For many years – in fact from 1933 – I had formed the impression that sooner or later the scientific divergencies in the Society and particularly in the Training Committee would become more and more acute. But I did not think of resigning until after the Blitz, when an originally scientific discussion on 'The relations of the P.A. Society to the Public' became politically organised. This political development coincided with the return to participation in Society affairs of some members who for one reason or another had been absent for some time previously. It then became clear to me that the Society could no longer claim the status of a scientific society; also that it was unlikely to remain a purely Freudian society. In fact it had been less and less Freudian since 1933–34 when Mrs Klein first adumbrated theories belonging to what I have called elsewhere her 'second phase'.

The subsequent course of events is familiar to you: (a) the organisation of the 'Controversial series of Discussions' intended to examine the doctrines held and taught by Mrs Klein and her adherents, (b) the appointment of a Committee to examine the Society's system of electing office bearers, (c) the mandate to the Training Committee to report on the effect of current controversies on the training situation. All these activities were sufficiently far advanced by the end of 1943 to permit of an accurate estimate of future tendencies and developments in the Society; and, as you know, following the Annual Meeting of 1943[2] I decided to resign my office and membership, and was induced to postpone the decision only on urgent representations from certain members of the Society. I said then however that I would not delay longer than Christmas 1943.

The present situation as I read it is as follows: The Controversial Series of Discussions will end in smoke. Indeed it is already pointless to continue them. The Klein group will continue to maintain that their views are either strictly Freudian or legitimate, not to say valuable extensions of Freud's work. The 'old middle group' will hedge but end by saying there is no ground for a split. The unattached members will be puzzled but not see any necessity for a split. Only the Viennese Freudians and a few isolated members will continue to maintain that the Klein views are non-analytical; and these will be out-voted by a combination of the Klein group with whatever younger groups are interested less in the present controversies than in the future administration of the Society, so the outcome is a foregone conclusion.

But quite apart from these political orientations, there is, in my view, no scientific justification for continuing the series. The new Kleinian metapsychology that has already been presented to us is not only fundamentally opposed to Freudian metapsychology but can be adduced in substantiation of any possible clinical theory that the supporters may choose to bring forward.

My reading of the situation is confirmed by the activities of the 'Constitutional Committee' and of the Training Committee. The former will produce a majority report in which the importance of scientific divergencies will be discounted and the troubles of the Society attributed to its mode of electing office bearers.

The Training Committee will produce either an unrealistic 'head in the clouds' document suggesting that there is no real dilemma before the Society or a majority report suggesting that the trouble can be eliminated by a change of spirit in the members electing the Committee. It is, in my view, unlikely that the Training Committee will report to the Society the salient facts, viz. that the Committee has been for a long time at a practical deadlock and that for the past year it has sanctioned in effect the existence, as it were under one umbrella, of at least two entirely different systems of training. It will certainly not recommend either the resignation from the training staff of any existing members, or the abolition for an indefinite period of the Training Analyst system thereby leaving training analysis to be conducted by any qualified member of the Society.

In addition to these three main reasons for my resignation, it is my impression, from a study of recent events, that the Society is about to develop new orientations in the near future. E.g. (a) it is likely to make a closer move towards general psychiatry on the lines already observed in America, (b) it is likely to spend a good deal of energies on the technique of static rather than of dynamic psychology.

So, take it all over, I see no point in delaying my resignation longer. Indeed if I delayed until the Annual Meeting, it might be more likely to encourage others to follow my example. These are matters which everyone should decide for himself or herself. Personally I think it is desirable that a new Freudian society should sooner or later be formed: indeed I think it is very likely that one will be formed. But not all members are in such an independent position as myself and I do not wish to bias them in any way. Indeed I'm not at all sure that I could shoulder the burden of developing a new society.

Anyhow I wish my resignation to take effect from the 25th January, i.e. the day after the meeting of the Training Committee called to consider its draft report to the Society. In this way the comments on the Draft which I have sent by separate post will still be in order as part of the Training Committee deliberations, and therefore can be minuted as such. Any practical points arising in the process of handing over will I think be easy to deal with.

Yours sincerely, Edward Glover

DR PAYNE: When I received the letter I did not understand that Dr Glover wished me to read it to the Society but thought it was a personal letter. I wrote to him immediately for a statement which I could read to the Society. In my letter I expressed my great disappointment that the dissensions should have led him to make this decision. I also expressed personally my appreciation of the work which he had done for psychoanalysis and pointed out that we had always worked together in co-operation until these acute troubles in the Society arose. Then our aims became opposed to each other, as he worked for a split, and I worked for a compromise. Dr Glover has written another letter in reply to my request for a statement in which he refers to the point raised in my letter, in which I stated that he in my opinion worked for a split. Although these comments of mine were private and personal he asks me to read his reply. I do so therefore at his request.

This is Dr. Glover's reply to my request for a statement:

1st Feb. 1944   18 Wimpole St. W.1.
Dear Dr Payne,
Your letter of 25th Jan. asks me to send you a 'statement' regarding my resignation from the P.-A. Society for presentation to the Business Meeting on Feb. 2nd. I believe that my letter of resignation already provides you with such a statement: and I would suggest that you read it together with this present reply to a particular point raised in your letter of acknowledgement. I think also it would be proper to circulate my original contribution to the discussion in the Training Committee, together with my 'Comments on the Training Committee's Draft Report to the Society', which Draft Report finally decided my resignation. I would remind you of course that ever since the discussion on the relations of the Society to the public developed a political complexion, there has been a plethora of 'statements' from all sides, and that in the Constitutional Committee, in the Training Committee and in the Controversial Discussions I have made my position quite clear. These views are on record in the various minutes.

To come back to your letter: you say in that we worked in co-operation until the troubles in the Society became acute, and that thereafter our aims became opposed to each other, in that I 'worked for a split' and you 'worked for compromise'. On the second part of this statement it is naturally not my concern to make any personal comment. I will content myself with saying that scientific compromise must be distinguished from administrative conciliation: also that compromise on matters of principle often ends by accelerating the cleavage it is intended to prevent – as indeed has been the result in this instance. On the other hand your suggestion that I 'worked for a split' (although limited as to its time reference) might easily give rise to a false impression. I should like therefore to state categorically that I have never worked for a split, have never asked anyone to split, have refused to split when urged to do so and have consistently refused to be a party to movements behind the scenes such as have frequently occurred in the Society since 1928. I have now simply exercised the privilege of withdrawing from the Society (a) because its general tendency and training has become unscientific and (b) because it is becoming

854

less and less Freudian and has therefore lapsed from its original aims.

It is of course true that I have criticised the Klein deviation with increasing vigour and plainness ever since 1934 when the Klein party adopted the theory of a 'central depressive position' (together with all that this theory connotes). But this criticism, so far from constituting 'working for a split', is a legitimate exercise of scientific criticism. When, shortly after the publication of Rank's 'Das Trauma der Geburt', the late James Glover and myself prepared a comprehensive adverse criticism of his Birth Theory of Neurosogenesis – no one suggested that we were working for a split, although in fact he attacked the Birth Theory at a time when many analysts had swallowed it whole. Incidentally it may make the present issue more plain if I point out that Mrs Klein's latest theories, although differing in content from those of Rank, constitute a deviation from psychoanalysis of the same order. The implications are identical and the theories are unsound for precisely the same reasons as were those of Rank. The resemblance between the two deviations is indeed remarkable.

May I further point out that during what I have called the 'first phase' of Mrs Klein's theorising (i.e. prior to 1934) I went out of my way to find a common basis for some of her views and classical Freudian teaching. Anyone who attended Psycho-Analytical Congresses was perfectly aware that even her early views were not accepted by any branch of the Psycho-Analytical Association except the British Society and, for that matter, not even by the whole of the British Society. At the Oxford Congress[3] I devoted a paper to this task of compromise and was roundly taxed with the fact by many of our then European colleagues. But already during that 'first phase' I was profoundly disturbed by two manifestations that developed in the Society (a) the blanketing of scientific discussion in the Society, where acceptance or non-acceptance of Mrs. Klein's views became a sort of religious 'test'. (b) the policy of the Training Committee.

May I therefore end this letter with some further comment on the training situation as it has developed from 1928 to the present day. I have always held that the power to influence the future of psychoanalysis lies, not in the scientific discussions of the Society, but in the policy of the Training Committee. The operation of training transferences and counter-transferences is the decisive factor. When differences of opinion become acute, these transferences automatically lower the level of training from a scientific to a quasi-religious plane. Unfortunately this fact was never openly admitted in the Training Committee. Instead, lipservice to the myth of the 'trained (and therefore unbiased) analyst' developed to a degree that was, in my opinion, little short of conscious hypocrisy. The result of this policy could not be indefinitely delayed: already before the War, the Committee was driven to consider the possibility of having two distinct systems of training, and during the war period has openly countenanced two distinct and opposed systems. Candidates who wish a Kleinian training are given Kleinian analysts and controls. Candidates preferring a purely Freudian training are given Freudian analysts and controls. Those who have no particular preference are given potluck. Yet their future views and professional careers will be finally determined by this haphazard allocation. Even so, until the last few years I held out in the Training Committee against a split. But I see now that the position is an impossible one not only for candidates but for psychoanalysis.

And so when it became clear from its Draft Report that the Committee was still prepared to pretend that this real problem is 'an unreal dilemma', I could only conclude that there was no prospect of scientific progress in the Society itself. For if the training is unscientific, what hope is there of establishing scientific standards amongst members whose entry to the Society depends on their conforming to the regulations of the Training Committee? Better by far to scrap the whole system and start again.

Yours sincerely, Edward Glover

P.S.: Since writing this I hear that Miss Freud has resigned from the Training Committee. I need hardly say that although her decision was taken independently of any action of mine, I am not at all surprised: The phantastic stress laid by Mr Strachey's Draft Report on the alleged capacity of training analysts to promote objectivity in their candidates is in such glaring contradiction to the facts of the present situation: As I said in my 'Comment': if this were really the case candidates would already be more advanced than their training analysts and so be in a position to analyse their training analysts with some benefit to the latter.

DR PAYNE: In the first place I would like to put the 3 proposals of the Board connected with changes of administration to the Society.

MISS LOW: Are these two letters to be circulated to the Members of the Society?

DR PAYNE: This question must be put to the Society for decision. The 3 proposals are:

1 That Dr Glover's resignation be recorded in the Minutes.
2 That the functions undertaken by the Emergency War Committee revert to the Council.
3 That the recommendation of the Council for interim management of the Society be accepted.

Has anybody anything to say?

DR RICKMAN: Would you read the detailed recommendations of the Board?

DR PAYNE: repeats the suggestions with regard to office bearers.

DR M. SCHMIDEBERG: Could you tell us more why Miss Freud has resigned?

DR PAYNE: Perhaps we had better first discuss the Council proposals.

DR SCOTT: I vote that these 3 proposals be accepted.

DR MACDONALD: I wish to second this.

Vote being taken it was voted by a majority of Members to accept the proposals.

MISS LOW: In Dr Glover's statement the point Dr Schmideberg mentioned was involved, namely why Miss Freud resigned.

DR PAYNE: The Training Committee has not had an opportunity yet to consider this point. The draft report which Mr Strachey had submitted has not been considered by the Training Committee, since Mr Strachey withdrew it and asked for the discussion to be postponed when the resignation of Dr Glover was received.

DR M. SCHMIDEBERG: So I understand that the Training Committee will consider the matter first and then report to a meeting of Members.

MISS LOW: Will these two letters be circulated or will they be discussed?

DR FRANKLIN: Is this not a matter for Dr Glover to decide?

MISS LOW: In so vital a matter which is going to alter, in my mind at least, the whole constitution of the Society every Member should have a chance to know why Dr Glover resigned and every Associate too. Not all Members could come to the meeting tonight and would therefore not know about Dr Glover's resignation at all. I think it would be highly unsuitable not to give them notice.

DR WINNICOTT: I want to second this. It seems to me quite logical to let Members know exactly what Dr Glover said.

DR SCOTT: I would suggest to have these letters circulated together with the minutes of this meeting.

DR WILSON: I want to second this proposal. Many Members do not know the truth about the thing. There are all sorts of rumours and doubts – even obsessional doubts – going on among Members. I would suggest that it should be circulated in as little a sadistic way as possible and together with the minutes of this meeting.

DR PAYNE: Does Miss Low accept this amendment?

MISS LOW assented.

The proposal to circulate Dr Glover's letters together with the minutes of the meeting to Members and Associates was unanimously accepted.

DR M. SCHMIDEBERG: Would not someone make a statement on the situation created through Dr Glover's resignation.

MISS LOW: Is it proposed to make any formal recognition of Dr Glover's work?

DR PAYNE: It is for Members to propose it.

MISS LOW: I propose it.

DR FRANKLIN: I second it.

DR PAYNE: Would Miss Low suggest the form this statement should take?

MISS LOW: I will draw it up.

DR FRIEDLANDER: I would like to hear more about Miss Freud's resignation as the two resignations are probably connected.

DR PAYNE: The matter is not clear and I can't say anything before we have had a Training Committee. After the Training Committee has drawn up a report I will let the Society know.

DR A. STEPHEN: Did Miss Freud give any reasons for her resignation?

DR PAYNE: She gave reasons in connection with Strachey's report. I cannot tell you unless I tell the Society about the report.

DR M. SCHMIDEBERG: It is therefore to be assumed that Dr Glover and Miss Anna Freud resigned in connection with this report.

DR PAYNE: We cannot discuss this without having first a Training Committee.

MISS LOW: Freud's daughter has had to resign. Surely we must have some discussion on it. We must have a report what will be the situation after these two resignations.

DR FRANKLIN: Is Miss Freud likely to make a statement for the Society?

DR PAYNE: I don't know. If we have a discussion in the Training Committee, I will ask her for a statement.

DR M. SCHMIDEBERG: Could we leave this open for the present and discuss Dr Glover's resignation?

DR MATTHEW: We heard of Dr Glover's letters for the first time now and want to think the matter over. Some people seem to know more about it than I do, as I only came back to London recently, and I want to know more before I can speak.

MISS LOW: Would this not be a reason to circulate the two letters as soon as possible? Can we have a meeting to discuss the matter when the letters have been circulated?

DR PAYNE: This will have to be put to the meeting.

MISS LOW: I propose that when the two letters have been circulated we have a meeting to discuss the situation.

DR A. STEPHEN: I thought that Dr Glover's resignation had already been accepted and there was occasion then for anybody to speak to it.

MISS LOW: We want to find out what Members think about it and we have not accepted it.

DR A. STEPHEN: I asked Dr Payne whether Dr Glover's resignation had already been accepted and you (Dr Payne) said: Yes.

MISS LOW: Of course one has to accept, because one cannot force anybody.

DR A. STEPHEN: It is common to ask people in such a case to stay.

MISS LOW: That is exactly why we want a discussion.

DR FRANKLIN: I did not understand that in recording that we received the resignation we were voting to accept it.

DR HERFORD: I want to second Miss Low's proposal 'that we circulate the two letters to every Member and Associate Member, give them a fortnight to consider the matter further and then have another meeting to see whether we want to make any suggestion to Dr Glover, and record our views'.

MRS RIVIERE: I propose to discuss the matter now and then circulate the letters. Then Members who want another meeting could propose it.

DR FRANKLIN: We are very few Members here at the meeting. If Dr Glover's resignation had been on the Agenda there might have been more Members here tonight. I am for Miss Low's proposal.

DR PAYNE: I think the Viennese Members did know but they are not here. Miss Low makes the proposal that there should be another meeting after the papers have been circulated, which Dr Franklin seconds. Mrs Riviere has proposed an amendment.

DR HERFORD: I would like to know that the fact that you put Dr Glover's resignation in the minutes does not mean that we do not want to ask him to reconsider his decision.

MISS LOW: My proposal came before Mrs Riviere's amendment. I think my proposal comes first.

A vote being taken on Miss Low's proposal a majority voted against it.

DR M. SCHMIDEBERG: We have still not discussed the issue as far as the Society is concerned. We can leave out the questions concerning the Training Committee and discuss the situation of the Society.

DR FRANKLIN: Should we not vote for Mrs Riviere's amendment now?

DR PAYNE: That is not necessary as Miss Low's proposal has been defeated.

DR BOWLBY: Would not Miss Low state the situation for us?

MISS LOW: I will. Those who have known Dr Glover must know what a loss his resignation means to the Society internally and in its external relations. When Miss Sharpe read Dr Brierley's paper last time it seemed that many agreed with her that we should have more contacts with the scientific world. Dr Glover's resignation will make that expansion impossible because there are so many people in the medical and educational world who regard Dr Glover as the person to contact. He represents in this country psychoanalysis, Freudian psychoanalysis. From that point of view I regard his resignation as highly important to the Society.

Then there is the internal repercussion. I daresay nobody has a greater knowledge, wider experience than Dr Glover, and with his intellectual powers in this small society his resignation is a fact that will fundamentally affect the whole level of the Scientific Discussions. I have expressed myself many times that Dr Glover's point of view is Freudian, the views of many other Members are not.

From the internal and external point of view Dr Glover's resignation is absolutely fatal to the Society. I am afraid no recommendations nor requests of ours will induce Dr Glover to reconsider his decision, but if any of us who have any recognition for what Dr Glover has done for psychoanalysis will at least make the request to express this recognition by requesting him to reconsider his resignation.

DR BOWLBY: I feel that Miss Low's views meet with some dissent from some of us. It happens that I have in my hands a statement signed by four Members, concerned with the external relations of the Society as they have been influenced by Dr Glover. Miss Low states that Dr Glover has been regarded the exponent of Freudian psychoanalysis to the external world. I don't wish to discuss the question of whether Dr Glover is a valuable person in psychoanalysis or not, but I do not think he is *the* valuable person. *(Miss Low*: I said one of the most valuable persons.)

As representative of the Society in the external world he has done harm as well as good. Quite recently Dr Glover has made a broadcast and given an interview to the weekly periodical *Cavalcade* which have met with a great deal of resentment from medical and psychological colleagues. He attacked the Army psychiatrists. [King 1989] I am one myself and it may be thought there is some personal background to my point of view. This is not true. People who are not in the Army have commented on these two publications. It happens that before Dr Glover's resignation was known 4 of us had met to consider requesting the Secretary of the Society that a Special Meeting be called to consider two resolutions (proposed by *myself* and seconded by *Dr Gillespie*).

1 The British Psycho-Analytical Society wishes to dissociate itself from the views on Army psychiatrists and selective testing expressed during Dec. 1943 and Jan. 1944 in broadcasts and in the weekly journal *Cavalcade* by Dr Edward Glover, at that time the Society's Scientific Secretary. The Society particularly regrets his having made public allegations on the radio and in the popular press without his having first made a thorough investigation and conveyed his considered opinions to his professional colleagues.

2 That the Secretary be instructed to send a copy of the above resolution to Brigadier J.R. Rees, Consulting Psychiatrist to the Army, the Secretaries of the British Psychological Society and the British Medical Association and the Editor of the *British Medical Journal*.

In making this request we wish to place on record the fact that we had already met to consider the first draft of these resolutions when we heard of Dr Glover's resignation. We agreed that, since Dr Glover was an officer of the Society of many years' standing at the time of their publication, his subsequent resignation was irrelevant to the issue and that the resolutions should be proceeded with.

This request is signed by Dr Rickman and Dr Adrian Stephen besides ourselves. The reason why we met was because these publications of Dr Glover had met with great disapproval both on the part of medical and psychological colleagues. I have not heard the broadcast myself and not read the interview. But they were sent to a colleague of mine who approached me.

DR FRIEDLANDER: Would Dr Bowlby read the passages which he thinks important?

DR BOWLBY (reads): From the broadcast made on November 18, 1943,

'TOWARDS AN ADULT SOCIETY', EDWARD GLOVER ON THE ROLE OF
THE PSYCHOLOGIST IN WAR AND PEACE:

And talking of the future, there is one war-time expansion of
psychology that calls for the most careful scrutiny. Already before
the War surface psychologists had carried out extensive experiments in measuring vocational capacity both in the school and in
the factory. But during this war selection tests have been more
widely applied. For instance they have become all the rage in the
fighting services of most combatant countries. What is more,
army psychiatrists developed selection tests of their own. For
example, they have made use of the fact that persons who suffer
from excessive abnormal self-love, however normal they may
look, are likely to go to pieces in situations of danger or in jobs
calling for responsibility. Using a number of special tests by which
this condition can be detected, psychiatrists have been able to pick
and choose from amongst cadets in training. Now such selection
methods obviously serve the urgent needs of a war-machine. But
their wholesale application to peace-time conditions, particularly
in the industrial field, would of course become intolerable. It
would bring to a head the ever-present conflict between the
interests of the state and the liberties of the individual. In any case
civilization is not a rigid structure: it calls for new capacities to
meet new needs. Had our forefathers in the Stone Age instituted
mass selection tests, we might still be living in caves and scraping
hides with oyster shells. Anyhow it is to be hoped that among the
multitude of post-war planners there will be a healthy sprinkling
of democratic-minded people, ready to remind both state departments and psychological experts that service to the state should be
measured by service to the individual.

I expect nobody would think of taking exception to that. But the
interviews published by *Cavalcade*, which Dr Glover endorsed
because he circulated it, reads under the heading 'Psychology' –

'THE PARENTS PART IN PEACE' (APPEARED 1 JAN. 1944):

Few laymen have the opportunity to study adequately the
psychological aspects of world conflict, of human development or
retrogression. Stimulation was given to popular interest in the
subject when Edward Glover, a Wimpole Street practitioner,
broadcast recently on 'Psychology in Wartime'.

After a résumé of the article in the *Listener* the article continues:

> Dr Glover was invited by *Cavalcade* to amplify his views on the psychological approach to the problems of war and peace.

Following are *Cavalcade*'s questions and Dr Glover's replies:

> 6 Do you consider that an increase in surface psychology (i.e. Selection by vocational tests) is likely to be a feature of postwar industry as the result of the present experiments by Army psychiatrists? Is this a trend likely to affect adversely the rights of the individual?

> My answer to both parts of the question is yes, because not only will it suit employers and the State to aim at 100 per cent efficiency in their workers, but Army psychiatrists have developed swelled heads over the use of selection tests and are, therefore, likely to push these methods before the authorities in peace-time.

> This move will no doubt be justified on the plea that it is also good for the individual. It is, of course, good for disordered individuals to have a suitable occupation and if normal people want guidance they should have it, provided it is really good.

DIFFERENCE

> But there is a vast difference between therapeutic (or preventative) selection of abnormal persons and selection of normal individuals at the behest of the Ministries or employers' federations. A partial safeguard would be to submit all Army psychiatrists to a course of 'rehabilitation' (as it is called when applied by them to others) in order that they may regain a proper perspective regarding the rights of civilians. Without adequate safeguards the system may have the seeds of Nazism in it – whatever the experts say.

(DR BOWLBY CONT.) The point is, what is complained about is that Dr Glover has made his views known in the widest possible way on the radio and in a weekly of no great reputation and responsibility and has done it without further enquiry or investigation of the activities and principles in the Selection Board of the Army. There are documents written by myself and colleagues at the training centre which give the lie to attempts to accuse Army psychiatrists of working against the principles of psychoanalysis. Dr Glover has not been polite enough to indicate either to his fellow Members in this Society or to other individuals that he held these views, instead he proceeds to blacken their names and make wild allegations on the wireless and in the press. *It is the method and not the matter* which has caused criticism in medical circles. I call attention to that. Dr Glover's behaviour in this matter is naturally commented on. People ask, are we to take it that these views are common in the Analytical Society?

I feel further that so long as an officer in the Society does incur criticism of very serious kind (also in regard to the rules of the BMA on 'advertising'), one of the senior officers of the Society, the public relations of the Society are not improved.

DR M. SCHMIDEBERG: I don't know how far the Society is interested in selection tests. I think I would regard that as a minor issue but still hold it is a major issue that Dr Glover has resigned. Some Members are certainly pleased about it, but that does not make it less important. I am quite sure it is a beginning of further developments. If people don't want to speak about it there is no more to be said about it.

DR FRIEDLANDER: I am interested in selection tests and know something about them though not of Army selection tests. If Dr Glover is of the opinion that a very wide use of selection tests as they have been developed so far would be of disadvantage, the question is in how far is this opinion in accord with or differing from the principles of psychoanalysis. Perhaps Dr Glover is rightly of the opinion that although selection tests may be of some use, one nevertheless will overlook certain aspects of the personality which so far cannot be grasped by tests, although they may be valuable in wartime. If Dr Glover utters such an opinion we have to see whether he is against psychoanalysis by doing so.

If the coming together of psychoanalysis with psychiatry would consist in psychoanalysis being absolutely quiet because Army psychiatry at present is important, this would not serve psychoanalysis.

I can see the point in Dr Bowlby's criticism that Dr Glover has not made his publications in official scientific journals. But if we take the question of selection tests, I think that from the psychoanalytic point of view we have a lot to say against it and we should. Even if it would prevent our coming together with psychiatry. In the end I am sure it would help towards the coming together if we can hold our views. So I cannot see why the fact that psychiatry is furious about it should be made an issue. We could make the matter a subject of discussion in our Society.

DR A. STEPHEN: This is the important point. Dr Glover may object to those tests, but he ought before he does to find out what goes on in these tests, whether they are not quite compatible with psychoanalysis. As far as I know they are in no way in conflict with psychoanalysis.

DR FRIEDLANDER: He does not object to these tests in the Army, but to their wholesale application in peacetime.

DR MATTHEW: But who says that they are going to be used?

DR FRIEDLANDER: This was the question put to him by the reporter of *Cavalcade* and Dr Glover answered it.

DR A. STEPHEN: But the point is that Dr Glover does not know anything about it.

MRS RIVIERE: What is the good of Dr. Glover saying psychiatrists are swelled heads, what good can this do to the Society?

DR FRIEDLANDER: I agree, but I want to raise another point: what about Dr Winnicott's letter to the *British Medical Journal* about shock therapy? What good does that do to the Society?

DR PAYNE: That was in a medical journal, this is the place where such questions should be discussed in the first place. The Society gets condemned for doing an unprofessional thing through Dr Glover broadcasting criticisms before he discussed them in medical circles.

MISS LOW: The 'radio doctor' has just been publicly declared to be the Secretary of the BMA.

DR SCOTT: After his death.

MISS LOW: You are mistaken entirely, he broadcast only this morning.

DR SCOTT: My mistake.

DR PAYNE: I understand from Dr Bowlby he is sending in a request for a meeting to discuss this point. Therefore Miss Low's suggestion –

MISS LOW (interrupting): Dr Bowlby made out that the BPA Society wants to dissociate itself from Dr Glover's broadcast.

DR M. SCHMIDEBERG: I would like to know whether the Society wishes to discuss the consequences of Dr Glover's resignation for the Society.

DR MATTHEW: Before the war, when the EMS was set up I have not seen any report about that from Dr Glover although there were controversies going on. I did not have the impression that this was good for the public relations of our Society.

DR K. STEPHEN: If we are going to see whether Dr Glover's services to the Society were greater than his detrimental activities, it will be a very acrimonious affair and I am very much against such a thing.

DR WINNICOTT: I do think that even if we grant that Dr Glover has committed an indiscretion by having an interview with the lay press, still I think this is a red herring and would very much prefer to have left it to future years to decide whether his contributions were of importance to the Society. We cannot decide it at the moment. Dr Glover has resigned, comments have been made, others will be made. In my opinion this is, although serious, a red herring.

DR WILSON: In the process where one's head has suddenly been cut off, it is no good speculating whether this head has been good or bad. One has to accept it as an inevitable loss, express regret and not become acrimonious about it. It would be more helpful.

DR PAYNE: We better have the minutes of the last meeting and pass on to the Agenda.

The minutes of the last meeting were then read by Dr Kate Friedlander and signed.

3 DR PAYNE introduced item 2 on the Agenda, the motion received from the Medical Committee, viz.

that in view of misapprehensions of Members the report of the Medical Committee and the appointment of the Lecture Committee be reconsidered; the two proposals in the report of the Medical Committee to which the misapprehension refers are:

(i) That a course of instruction in the principles of psychoanalysis suitable for those professionally engaged in the study of psychological medicine should be arranged as part of the Institute's regular programme of work.

(ii) That the Board should be asked to appoint a Special Committee to arrange for this course, its members to be recommended by the Members of the Institute. It is suggested that it will be advisable for the Membership of this Committee to overlap with that of the present Committee/the Medical Committee/in order that the two may act in the closest co-operation.

DR ADRIAN STEPHEN gave comments to the report of the Medical Committee, saying:

They felt that just as during the last war there was a considerable expansion of interest in psychological medicine, it has been in the present war, both among the medical profession and lay people. Those people who take professional interest will either want to become psychoanalysts[4] or to know what psychoanalysis has to say upon their subject. The Medical Committee felt it was desirable that this Society should undertake part of the training of anybody who wants to take training in psychological medicine, over and above those who want to become psychoanalysts. We should not only instruct these people, but I think it would improve our relations with the psychiatric world as a whole if we were more in contact with psychiatrists as a whole and learned more about the psychiatric point of view. I personally had advantage from it. I think it is anyhow our duty to enable professional psychiatrists to become more familiar with psychoanalytic outlook and doctrine. There is no way an intention to interfere in any part with the working of the regular Training Committee.

If some Members felt that the last meeting was rushed through, all of us felt that it was only fair and proper that the Society should get a full chance of discussing and criticizing the proposal.

DR SCOTT: I should like to know whether this is to be teaching just to doctors. If so, why could not the Medical Committee deal with it itself?

DR PAYNE: The Medical Committee has not got the power to do so. The point that was most under misapprehension is the relation with the Lecture Committee. It was not so much the question of training but that we should have another Public Lecture Committee apart from the old one. The point now is how far this particular activity should be part of the activities of the old Public Lecture Committee, which is elected by the Board. Two of its members retire yearly in rotation and cannot be re-elected for two years.

DR ADRIAN STEPHEN: The committee in question can only be appointed by the Board. We tried to get round the letter of the law by asking Members to propose names.

DR ISAACS: It is a matter for Dr Payne to say whether the Public Lecture Committee is competent to deal with this special matter.

DR MACDONALD: I as Secretary of the old Public Lecture Committee agree with Dr A. Stephen. The audiences of our lectures were made up mainly by medical people. But we had to cater for the man in the street as well on subjects like music, the bringing up of children, painting, etc. Many of those audiences were psychologically trained people.

I think there is a great responsibility resting upon any one dealing with the next generation, like child welfare workers, and the importance of guidance is so great from the point of view of children being really democratic, that the matter cannot be dealt with lightheartedly. A special Training Committee is not the right body either. Perhaps another Medical Committee should be appointed. I agree with Dr Payne that this would grant further points of contact. I think that neither the Training Committee nor the old Public Lecture Committee are quite the right bodies to deal with the matter.

DR ISAACS: Did not the Public Lecture Committee arrange lectures for doctors?

DR PAYNE: But not for psychiatrists. This should be specially organized. I cannot see why the Public Lecture Committee could not deal with it if it were newly appointed.

DR ADRIAN STEPHEN: It is a matter for the Society to decide whether to have one or two committees.

DR BOWLBY: I am in favour of one committee. I feel it would be more profitable for the Society to arrange more professional lectures.

MRS RIVIERE: I am in favour of the Medical Committee to organize the lectures. This seems so far the only point the Medical Committee had in mind.

DR ADRIAN STEPHEN: I would remind you of the letter to the Interdepartmental Committee which was drawn up by the Medical Committee. I think this was perhaps even a more important step. There should be a committee to run these lectures.

DR PAYNE: The terms of reference for the Medical Committee is to consider the external relations of the Society. They proposed that two members of the Medical Committee should be included in the Lecture Committee. The same it was thought would apply to the Child Welfare Committee.

DR SCOTT: It seems that the Medical Committee is passing the buck to another committee. (Then Dr Scott elaborates on details of organization.)

DR BOWLBY: I think the Medical Committee felt it was desirable that this Institute and Society should run a course on psychoanalysis. (*To Dr Scott*) On the one hand this Institute will continue these lectures to psychiatrists. This does not exclude that individual Members will give lectures in other teaching institutions.

DR PAYNE: The central problem is: does the meeting wish to accept the report of the Medical Committee and its proposals, put by Dr Adrian Stephen and seconded by Dr Bowlby? (see(i))

On voting the proposal was accepted by a majority of Members.

DR PAYNE: Now to the second point: Does anyone propose that we revive the Public Lecture Committee or that we appoint a special committee for this purpose?

DR ISAACS: I propose the revival of the Public Lecture Committee and that the special committee should be a sub-committee to it.

DR WILSON: I second it.

DR PAYNE: Dr Isaacs, do you mean that certain members of the Medical Committee should be included in the Public Lecture Committee?

DR ISAACS: Yes, to recommend a syllabus.

DR ADRIAN STEPHEN: We should have a rule that there should be for instance 7 members on the Public Lecture Committee.

DR PAYNE: Before the war the Public Lecture Committee

consisted of 6 or 7 members. Perhaps it is now a question of the proportion of medical Members to lay Members in this committee. The proposal made by Dr Isaacs and seconded by Dr Wilson would then be

'that it should be recommended to the Board that the Public Lecture Committee should be re-established in relation of at least 4 medical and 3 lay Members'.

On voting this proposal was accepted by a majority of Members

Considering the time, it was decided to leave the rest of the Agenda (items 3, 4, and 5) to a next Business Meeting.

Members shouted their thanks to Dr Payne when the meeting ended.

Notes

1 Glover's resignation was first announced at the Training Committee, on 24 January 1944 (Section 3, Chapter 10).
2 At the AGM in 1943, in the election of members for the Medical Committee, Sylvia Payne received the most votes and Glover the least, according to an informant. This meant that if he had to stand against her in an election for the President of the Society, she would probably be elected.
3 Glover referred to the 11th International Psychoanalytical Congress, held at Oxford from 27 to 31 July 1929, with Max Eitingon as President. Glover read a paper entitled 'Grades of Ego-Differentiation'.
4 This theme is explored further in a paper by Pearl King on 'Activities of British Psychoanalysts during the Second World War and the Influence of their Inter-disciplinary Collaboration in the Development of Psychoanalysis in Great Britain' (King 1989a).

2

The Seventh
Extraordinary Business Meeting

**An Extraordinary Business Meeting
convened by the Council at the request of four Members:
Major Bowlby, Dr Gillespie, Major Rickman,
and Major Adrian Stephen,
was held on Wednesday, February 23rd, 1944,
at 8.15 p.m., at 96 Gloucester Place, London, W.1.**

Dr Payne was in the Chair and 19 Members were present: Dr Lantos, Dr Franklin, Dr Friedlander, Miss Low, Dr W. Hoffer, Mrs H. Hoffer, Mrs Ruben, Dr Wilson, Miss Sharpe, Mrs Klein, Dr Winnicott, Major A. Stephen, Mrs Riviere, Dr Gillespie, Dr Herford, Dr Heimann, Major Bowlby, Dr Karin Stephen.

DR PAYNE opened the meeting stating that before going into the Agenda she wanted to make a statement with regard to the procedure involved in the calling of this Extraordinary Business Meeting, because misunderstandings had arisen as to its correctness. She had received 3 letters reproaching her for not giving longer notice. The meeting was convened under Rule 14 of the statues of the Society, which says that 'Extraordinary meetings, which may be attended by Hon. Members and Members, may be convened at any time by the Council within seven days after the receipt by the Hon. Secretary of a written request signed by at least 4 Members stating the special business for which the meething is required'.

MISS LOW said that Rule 24 stated that notices should be sent out 7 clear days before meetings.

DR PAYNE pointed out that Rule 14 applied to the calling of an

Extraordinary Meeting only and the rules could only be taken logically in this way. She went on to say that owing to certain Members' lack of attention to the rules and consequent suspicion of the procedure employed irregularities had arisen. Counter-proposals instead of being sent to the Business Secretary for circulation had been sent out privately to selected Members.

MISS LOW asked if there was anything in the rules to forbid sending counter-resolutions.

DR PAYNE replied that all resolutions to be put to the meeting must be circulated by the Hon. Secretary unless they are presented as amendments at the meeting.

DR FRIEDLANDER said that the shortness of time and the weekend prevented her approaching the Business Secretary.

DR PAYNE read an extract from a letter of Dr Fairbairn on the subject:

> I am led to understand from a circular letter which I have received from Dr Kate Friedlander that two Counter-Resolutions have been proposed by Lt Col Carroll and seconded by Dr Marjorie Franklin. Whilst I approve of the *second* of these Resolutions, I do not desire to record my vote upon it, since I have received no official intimation regarding the Counter-Resolutions from you as Hon. Business Secretary. In this connection I desire to record the opinion that the practice whereby individual Members of the Society address circular letters to other Members regarding the business of the Society is an encroachment upon the functions of the Business Secretary and, if continued, is calculated to exercise a disruptive influence upon the life of the Society. It is a practice which has sprung up recently, and which appears to be growing; and in my opinion it is opportune for the desirability or undesirability of the practice to receive the formal considerations of the Society.

After further discussion, in which Miss Sharpe, Dr Friedlander, Dr Franklin, and Miss Low took part, Dr Payne ruled that the Counter-proposals could be introduced as amendments to Dr Bowlby's and Dr Gillespie's proposals.

It was decided to take the minutes as read as the main part of them had been circulated.

Major Bowlby was asked to present his proposals.

MAJOR BOWLBY said that he wished to amend the form of his resolutions.

MISS LOW asked if it was in order for the proposers to make an amendment before other amendments were proposed.

THE CHAIRMAN asked Major Bowlby to present the original proposals first, viz:

1 The British Psycho-Analytical Society wishes to dissociate itself from the views on Army psychiatrists and selective testing expressed during December 1943 and January 1944 in broadcasts and in the weekly journal *Cavalcade* by Dr Edward Glover, at that time the Society's Scientific Secretary. The Society particularly regrets his having made public allegations on the radio and in the popular press without his having first made a thorough investigation and conveyed his considered opinions to his professional colleagues.

2 That the Secretary be instructed to send a copy of the above resolution to Brigadier J. R. Rees, Consulting Psychiatrist to the Army, the Secretaries of the British Psychological Society and the British Medical Association and the Editor of the *British Medical Journal*.

MAJOR BOWLBY said he realized he was asking the Society to take a serious step. It was justified because of the need to develop and improve the external relations of the Society and the furtherance of psychoanalysis. The resolutions had been drafted before Dr Glover's resignation and he regretted that he was not here to reply. Further, although he himself as an Army psychiatrist was personally implicated, the opinion of non-military Members coincided with his own. He went on to say that although Dr Glover did not claim to speak as a psychoanalyst his position as a senior officer of long standing in the Society made it inevitable that his views should be taken as representing those of the Society.

He put forward 4 reasons why the Society should dissociate itself from Dr Glover in these matters.

1 The form of the criticisms of Army psychiatrists. He accused them of swelled heads and advised rehabilitation.

2 He made serious allegations against those responsible for selective testing. He asserted that selective testing in civil life would 'affect adversely the rights of the individual', and that those proposing it are undemocratically minded and have not 'a proper perspective regarding the rights of civilians'. In a country which is fighting for the principles of democracy such allegations against professional colleagues are serious.

3 His allegations were made without proper investigations.

4 He ran the risk of professional censure by using his own name in connection with the broadcast and in the article.

Major Bowlby stated that the relations of the Society to other

872

psychological and medical bodies had never been particularly good, and the recent action of a senior officer of this Society could only do them further damage. He asked the Society to pass the two resolutions in order to restore the Society's reputation for scientific integrity and professional good manners.

DR GILLESPIE said he wished to second the resolution. He said that Dr Glover's comments on Army psychiatry were largely concerned with questions of democracy and individual freedom. He did not think that Dr Glover had promoted democratic methods in the Society. In the past decisions were taken without the Society being consulted. Dr Glover's resignation had not made the resolutions unnecessary, as it would take time for it to be known. Army psychiatry was a successful organization and had proved its value. The alternative was arbitrary posting. In civil life the same principles would apply and the individual would be more likely to get what he wants than before. Of course the method could be exploited in an authoritarian regime.

It might be urged that the principles of free speech entitled Dr Glover to express what views he pleased. While he held high office this was not so any more than it was in the case of a Cabinet Minister. He submitted that the principles of free speech applied only to the private individual.

The second resolution was required to protect the relations to the Society with other members of the profession specializing in psychological medicine and in particular the Army psychiatrists.

He considered that Dr Glover's criticisms and the form in which they were made affected people's views on psychoanalysis rather than the individual analyst. They widened the rift, already wide, between psychoanalysis and psychiatry. He thought the matter concerned not only the Army psychiatrists but all Members who did not wish to regard fellow doctors in the speciality of psychological medicine as natural enemies.

DR FRIEDLANDER said that the resolutions could only stand if Major Bowlby's statements were correct, and that Dr Glover should be asked to make a statement.

1 In the first place with the exception of Dr Gillespie and the Army psychiatrists the Society was not in a position to decide the importance of Army selective testing.
2 Dr Glover should be asked if he had informed himself of the work of Army psychiatry, etc. through other channels. He did raise the question before Dr Rees and Dr R. D. Gillespie at the Psychological Committee of the BMA.

3 Before broadcasting for the first time he was in contact with the Ethical Committee of the BMA who advised him that he could speak in his own name.

MISS LOW said Dr Glover did not speak as psychoanalyst and therefore the Society was not involved.

DR WILSON deplored that Dr Glover should have 'got up against' psychiatrists in this way. He suggested that Dr Glover should be asked to publish a statement to the effect that he was speaking personally and not for the Society.

DR FRIEDLANDER proposed that Dr Wilson's proposal should be put to the vote.

DR PAYNE said that the amendments must be put before the meeting before a vote was taken.

Further discussion took place with regard to the form of Dr Glover's remarks in which Dr Stephen, Dr Friedlander, and Miss Low took part.

MAJOR A. STEPHEN emphasized the point made by Dr Gillespie that (a) Dr Glover as a senior officer of the Society could not express opinions on controversial subjects in public without involving the Society, (b) that it was the 'mud-slinging' which he objected to.

MISS SHARPE spoke of a custom which was present in the past in the Society of consulting with the Council before taking part in public discussions of importance.

THE CHAIRMAN said that the amendments received should now be put before the Society.

DR FRANKLIN proposed to amend Dr Bowlby's and Dr Gillespie's resolutions as follows:

To omit everything after the word 'wishes' in the first resolution and to substitute 'to re-affirm the right of individual members of the Society
(a) to freedom of public expression of their opinions,
(b) to take part in public discussion so long as they do not claim to speak for the Society as a whole,
and that it follows from this that it is not within the functions of this Society officially to defend or to attack the activities of Army psychiatrists or other non-analytical groups or individuals.'

She said she spoke not in defence of Dr Glover but in defence of personal liberties. She thought Members had a right to speak in public on general topics if they did not touch on psychoanalytical matters. She thought Dr Bowlby's resolution suggested that the Society should assume an ethical censorship on opinions and manners.

874

DR FRIEDLANDER said that Lt. Col. Carroll seconded Dr Franklin's resolution and read his letter:

I have been away almost continuously during the past week and have been too occupied with my duties to give much time to anything else. Your letter reached me tonight with the official notice of the meeting and I write with slight hope of the letter reaching you in time.

Similar difficulties may affect other country Members and I feel it is unfortunate that this meeting was called at such short notice, since it makes participation difficult and at best unduly hurried. The subject-matter of the Bowlby–Gillespie resolutions surprises me since I do not see why such a strong expression of opinion is called for.

Unless there is evidence that the Psycho-Analytical Society is adversely affected I do not see the need for any resolutions at all. If on the other hand the meeting feels that the Society is, or is likely to be, adversely affected, then surely a simple statement that Dr Glover spoke in a private capacity is all that is indicated.

I do not know how many members are in possession of the facts. I am not in possession of many, but those I have do not suggest that Dr Glover implicated the Society in any way – even if he did, disclaimer not censure is the correct procedure.

Either way the Society would want to know what its views on Army Psychiatry were and this would be difficult for it since its members cannot have much knowledge of the subject apart from the Army members, who are not free to discuss such a topic outside the Service.

Perhaps I should say at this point that I have never discussed Army Psychiatry with anyone outside official circles and that, in particular, I have never discussed it with Dr Glover.

As the resolutions stand and in view of the proposed distribution of them I feel the Society would need to take legal advice before acting on resolution 2.

I wish therefore to record my vote against both of the Bowlby–Gillespie resolutions and will you kindly convey this to the appropriate officers of the Society since I have no time to write another letter.

With regard to the counter-resolutions, the first has some snags [Dr Franklin interrupted here saying that Dr Carroll's numbering of the counter-resolutions referred to the original order and that in the present form of an amendment 'the first' referred to the second part of the amendment and vice versa.] the first has some snags in that the Society might, on occasion, wish to express its views on all sorts of apparently non-analytic topics. However I am willing for it to go forward in my name as seconder so that the topic may be ventilated and some idea obtained of the Society's attitude as a group to such problems in public relations. I see no reason why the Society should tie itself, but the Bowlby–Gillespie resolutions suggest a lack of clarity about what is, or is not, proper comment and this counter-resolution (unfortunate term) may help to clear the air.

The second of the resolutions [now the first part of the amendment] I heartily support. Heaven forbid that any scientific society starts a censorship – even if its members are wrong scientifically in what they say. On the first resolution I cannot vote since I will not be aware of the form it will take after discussion and amendment.

On the second my vote is emphatically for the resolution [now first part of amendment].

This is a hurried note and I feel strongly about such a matter having to be so dealt with by any member. I would like to make it clear that my views in this letter are based on a matter of principle and are not based in any way on Dr Glover's views with which I am not sufficiently familiar to express any comment. Please read this letter, if you think fit, at the meeting.

THE CHAIRMAN said she would read other amendments received.
1 DR BRIERLEY held the view that the so-called counter-resolutions were additional rather than counter-proposals. The Society was not concerned with attacks or counter-attacks. It had only to decide whether it was in its public interest that views recently expressed by Dr Glover should be credited to it or whether it should make public the simple fact that they represent Dr Glover's individual opinion.
2 MR FLUGEL wrote to say that he thought Dr Glover was speaking in a private capacity and although he did not agree with his views he could not vote for interference with the expression of private opinions of members on a matter beyond the Society's purview. If the counter-resolutions were rejected he put forward the amendment:

'That the second sentence of Resolution 1 be deleted and the following substituted: "The views expressed by Dr Glover on these occasions do not represent any expressed or implied attitude of the Society as a whole, nor do they necessarily correspond to the view of other individual members".'

876

3 MAJOR THORNER'S amendment was as follows:

'The British Psycho-Analytical Society wishes it to be known that the views on Army Psychiatrists and selective testing expressed during December 1943 and January 1944 in broadcasts and in the weekly journal *Cavalcade* by Dr Glover, at that time the Society's Scientific Secretary, were not authorized by this Society.'

4 MAJOR SCOTT wrote saying that he considered that only the method of presenting views which Dr Glover employed should be criticized.

5 MAJOR BOWLBY said he wished to substitute the following amendment for his and Dr Gillespie's first resolution:

'The British Psycho-Analytical Society has had its attention drawn to certain criticisms of and allegations against Army psychiatrists and selective testing made by Dr Edward Glover in broadcasts and in the popular weekly *Cavalcade* during November 1943 and January 1944. As Dr Glover was at that time and had for many years been its Scientific Secretary, the Society wishes to make it clear that these remarks are to be taken purely as the expression of Dr Glover's private opinion.'

He said that Resolution 1 had been amended to meet certain objections to the words 'dissociate' and 'disagree'. With reference to Dr Friedlander's comments on the question as to whether Dr Glover had investigated the work of War Office Selection Boards he was in a position to state that Dr Glover had not visited any of the Boards or approached any of the Army psychiatrists working on these Boards for purposes of investigating their methods as many other psychiatrists have done. Major Bowlby knew that Dr Glover had expressed similar opinions at the British Medical Association's Psychological Committee last summer and for that reason he had used the phrase 'considered opinion' in the original resolution.

THE CHAIRMAN said that as Major Bowlby and Dr Gillespie had withdrawn their original proposals and substituted an amendment there were 2 groups of amendments and 1 new proposal:

1 Dr Franklin's and Lt. Col. Carroll's.
2 Major Bowlby's and Dr Gillespie's which had much in common with those received from Mr Flugel and Dr Thorner.
3 Dr Wilson's new proposal that Dr Glover should be asked to state that he was speaking as a private individual.

The discussion was re-opened.

DR FRANKLIN raised the question of whether Dr Glover was actually responsible for the published interview in *Cavalcade.*

MAJOR BOWLBY replied that he must be as he had himself forwarded a copy of the article to a colleague.

DR GILLESPIE quoted from a recent article of Dr Glover's in *Horizon.*

DR FRIEDLANDER pressed that Dr Glover should be asked for a statement.

MRS RIVIERE emphasized the fact that the point at issue was whether the Society would be affected by his actions.

DR LANTOS thought that the accuracy of Major Bowlby's four reasons should be investigated by approaching Dr Glover.

DR WILSON repeated his suggestion that Dr Glover should be asked to say that he was speaking for himself only.

DR LANTOS seconded this.

MISS LOW stated that Dr Glover spoke his personal views in his broadcast and interview and did not necessarily represent the views of the Society. She regarded Dr Wilson's suggestion as an interference with individual freedom of speech. The British Psycho-Analytical Society had no jurisdiction over the private activities of its Members.

THE CHAIRMAN pointed out that final votes could not be taken on Major Bowlby's resolutions because they had been amended since circulation; nor on Dr Franklin's as they had been amended and had not been circulated to the whole Society at the beginning. It would be possible to take the vote of the meeting on Dr Wilson's proposal as it did not commit the Society to outside action.

DR FRIEDLANDER thought it would be best to ask Dr Glover if he was prepared in the medical press to dissociate his views from those of the Society.

The following *Resolution, proposed by Dr Wilson, seconded by Dr Friedlander* was put to the meeting:

'That Dr Glover should be asked to send a statement to the Medical Press (either the *BMJ* or the *Lancet*) to the effect "that the views expressed by Dr Glover in his broadcast published in the *Listener* on November 18, 1943, and in an interview published in *Cavalcade* on January 1, 1944, on Army Psychiatrists and Selection Boards were personal and did not represent any expressed or implied attitude of the British Psycho-Analytical Society as a whole".'

The resolution was carried with one dissent (Miss Low).

878

3

The Eighth
Extraordinary Business Meeting

Minutes of Extraordinary Business Meeting
held on March 8th, 1944, at 7 p.m.[1]

Dr Payne was in the Chair and 21 Members were present (Brierley, Winnicott, M. Schmideberg, Balint, Lantos, Friedlander, Low, Wilson, Sharpe, Herford, K. Stephen, A. Stephen, Riviere, Heimann, Thorner, Sheehan-Dare, Isaacs, Klein, Bowlby, Strachey, W. Hoffer)

DR BRIERLEY, continued by the Chairman, read an abstract of the minutes of the last Extraordinary Business Meeting.

MISS LOW raised a protest against the minutes and said that she had raised objections at once against Dr Wilson's proposal to ask Dr Glover for a statement and that she had voted against it. 'I said it is completely illegitimate to make such a request. We have no jurisdiction about asking an individual Member to make such a statement.'

DR PAYNE: I did not hear your objections. You cannot have voted against as no votes were taken, nor is it stated in the minutes that votes were taken on this point. The minutes say that the proposal was carried without dissent. It is possible that I and the stenographer did not hear that you objected, as the siren went and there were many people speaking at one time. But everybody spoke in favour. However, I am quite willing to amend the minutes if necessary and to insert your objection.

The minutes were passed with the addition of Miss Low's dissent.

2 The Chairman introduced the Resolution submitted by the Council:

'The Institute of Psycho-Analysis and the British Psycho-Analytical Society wish to put on record their appreciation of Dr Edward Glover's past services to the science of psychoanalysis and to the psychoanalytic movement.'

She said: 'I think members of the Council and Board know best how much work Dr Glover has put in in every respect. I am quite sure that everybody does appreciate all he has done for the Institute, and the Society and . . .'

MISS SHARPE: I will be very pleased to second this proposal for we do sincerely wish to thank Dr Glover for all the positive contributions he made to the science of psychoanalysis in the past, for all his services to the Society and the Institute, for his steadfastness during the blitz and for all the help he has given to individual Members. And we wish him well in the course he has chosen.

DR M. SCHMIDEBERG: I cannot help but have the impression that this is completely insincere after what has passed at the last meeting.

DR BRIERLEY: It is sincere.

DR BALINT: I should like to add to this resolution that we deeply regret that Dr Glover has found it necessary to leave the Society and we hope in the future he will find means and ways to join the Society again.

DR HERFORD: I would like to second this.

CHAIRMAN: We have here two motions, the one submitted by the Council and Dr Balint's addition.

DR WILSON: I should be in favour to add that we regret that Dr Glover could find no other way of dealing with the situation than resignation.

DR WINNICOTT: A question of order: As the Council made the recommendation and asked us to vote on it, is it possible for us to suggest another recommendation?

CHAIRMAN AND DR BRIERLEY explain that the Council wanted to put the resolution to the meeting and Members can of course make suggestions.

DR A. STEPHEN: I think Dr Balint's addition rather carries matters a bit too far. Every one of us, I think, is quite willing to pass a formal motion of regret under these rather unfortunate circumstances, but I think if we go so far as to say that we want Dr Glover to join again this means endorsing too much his recent activities.

DR M. SCHMIDEBERG: This proves that the whole thing is insincere.

A vote being taken on the resolution submitted by the Council this was carried by a majority (one dissenting vote).

On voting on Dr Balint's addition this was rejected against one positive vote.

MISS LOW: I understand Dr Payne has received a reply from Dr Glover.

CHAIRMAN: Yes, and I will read it at the end when the Agenda of the meeting is done.

Discussion of the
final report of the Training Committee[2]

3 MR STRACHEY: *First*, a purely personal point. I was not here at the meeting before last but gather from the minutes that the draft report of the Training Committee has been associated particularly with my name. That is a misunderstanding. It is true I was asked to draft the report and I did the wording, but the content represents the opinions of the Training Committee as far as possible. In fact the report was drafted and re-drafted three or four times and as it stands now it represents the views of those who signed it and in some parts also the views of those who did not sign it.

DR M. SCHMIDEBERG: Who is that?

DR PAYNE: Dr Glover and Miss Freud.

DR M. SCHMIDEBERG: But surely then they would not have resigned.

MR STRACHEY: I made a fair attempt of dealing with the difficult question of relating theory and practice of training. The report is not attempting to deal with the differences and disputes in the Society which I hope are now finished, but tries to prevent such disputes coming up later. All our experience shows that there are splitting tendencies not only in our Society but also in others, for instance in the USA. If we could avoid this happening again it would be a great advantage. There are always personal emotional factors involved with which we cannot deal. But we can try to revise the machinery of training and devise a machinery which will as far as possible prevent these splits. The report puts the stress in training on the technique of the training analyst rather than on the theoretical views he holds. It is possible to disagree with an analyst's theoretical views and at the same time this analyst can be a competent analyst. If this is generally adopted we can hope to be able to prevent splits.

I move that the recommendations of the Training Committee be adopted by the Society.

MISS LOW: We have not heard minority reports.

CHAIRMAN: Will you please wait?

DR BRIERLEY: (paper) In seconding this report, I would like to begin by thanking Mr Strachey for all the skill and care he exercised in its compilation and to comment, very briefly, on four points.

First, in regard to the statement on p. [670] that the Training Committee is charged 'with planning and supervising the education of future practitioners (and to a less extent of future research workers) in psychoanalysis'. I personally regard it as desirable that all future practitioners should be educated to take part at least in individual testing both of observational data and of theory. Verification is a communal responsibility in which all Members should be encouraged to share whether or not they are attached to other aspects of research.

Second, in regard to the proposal on p. [676] to appoint a particular analyst *ad hoc* for each particular Candidate. I think this proposal well worth trying out but there are a number of arguments against it, which will, I believe, be brought forward in this discussion and should be duly considered.

Third, in regard to the further proposal on p. [676] re case seminars. This proposal is very important and I recommend it strongly because it seems to me to offer the most likely means of coming to really informed conclusions about the validity of current techniques.

Fourth, in regard to Section VII, p. [677]. This section should not be read solely in the light of our present difficulties and should not be taken to mean that the residual members of the present Training Committee consider themselves 'undesirable either individually or collectively'. In my opinion, this section aims at establishing a principle which can serve as a basis for a smooth-working long-term policy. It is prophylactic in that it tends to provide against the election at any time of Members whose opinions, etc., might be likely to prevent the Committee from working as a harmonious whole and to provide for the election of Members who can work together as a team for training purposes, whatever their other differences.

I fully endorse the recommendations made in Section VIII and second their adoption [p. 678].

THE CHAIRMAN threw the report open to discussion.

DR M. SCHMIDEBERG: Has Miss Freud made a statement?

CHAIRMAN: Miss Freud has been asked whether she would like to make a statement and replied she did not want to.

MISS LOW: Has Dr Glover made a statement?

CHAIRMAN: He made a commentary to the draft report which has nothing to do with the present final report. But rather than have the Society think that we want to keep something from them, I would read his commentary.

MR STRACHEY: Dr Glover's remarks were on the first draft report and have nothing to do with the final report.

CHAIRMAN: I think the recommendations in both draft and final report are the same.

MR STRACHEY: No, I should not think that. Dr Glover's remarks do not refer to the present report.

DR BRIERLEY: If Dr Glover and Miss Freud had not resigned there would be a proper minority report. Dr Glover and Miss Freud gave no opportunity to the Training Committee at all to hear their criticism.

DR M. SCHMIDEBERG: There must have been a reason for it.

DR BALINT: I must support Mr Strachey and Dr Brierley. In point of fact Dr Glover's opposition is irrelevant as he is not any more a Member, but as we are all interested in what he says we would like to hear it.

DR LANTOS: As Mr Strachey hinted that even if the Members who did not sign the report are not in controversy with it, we ought to hear Dr. Glover's comments. Otherwise I should ask Mr Strachey on which facts he based his statement.

MR STRACHEY: All I said was there were things in the report with which they would agree.

CHAIRMAN: As this is something not according to custom I put it to the meeting whether you want me to read Dr Glover's comments.

MRS ISAACS: I don't think we should spend our time discussing past history when there are matters of importance to settle, as the contents of the training report.

MISS LOW: There could be nothing more urgent than to learn and discuss why two valuable members of the Training Committee have been forced to resign. It is ludicrous to bring forward points of order to prevent it.

CHAIRMAN: The actual reasons for their resignation are in the report: that they were not in agreement.

On votes being taken, the majority was in favour of Dr Glover's comments being read.

THE CHAIRMAN then read Dr Glover's comments on the first draft [see pp. 661–4].

CHAIRMAN: Dr Glover in this upheld one aspect of the report: that the members of the Training Committee should be elected for general qualities of character rather than for particular views they hold. One word about his contention that training has broken down. Having been Training Secretary since the outbreak of the war, I can say this has not been the case. The only difficulty that has arisen is that some members did not wish their Candidates to attend seminars held by other members. The older members of the TC had no objection and no apprehensions about anxiety being aroused in Candidates by different techniques. It is not our experience that Candidates are badly influenced by it.

MRS RIVIERE: I gather that this view was taken by Dr Glover and Miss Freud, but not by others.

DR M. SCHMIDEBERG: The importance of Dr Glover and Miss Freud was that they were the only real Freudian members in the Training Committee. Their resignation means an important development in this Society, the split that was expected for a long time has taken place. The fact that we are still in the Society does not make a difference. They are no longer on the Training Committee and it is not difficult to guess that they will not much longer be in the Society.

DR KARIN STEPHEN: I don't think we agree that they were the only Freudians.

DR FRIEDLANDER: It is a fact though that Candidates have been asked for some years whether they want to go to Freudian or Kleinian analysts.

DR PAYNE: I will explain the custom. If a Candidate is introduced by a training analyst, he or she goes to him or to somebody whom he recommends. It is a reasonable thing for a Candidate who has a preference to have the right for it to be regarded. Candidates have not been asked whether they want to go to Freudian or Kleinian analysts.

DR THORNER: Whatever Dr Glover's views may have been is not important now as he is no longer a Member. It is different with Miss Freud. She has been elected to act as an officer of the Society on the TC. She has chosen to resign. I understand the TC has asked her for a statement and that she has refused. I would suggest the Society should not be satisfied with this. An officer cannot withdraw from office without making a statement. I suggest that the Society should ask her for a statement.

DR PAYNE: It hasn't ever been a custom in the Society to resign

884

without a statement. But I don't think we have a right to force Miss Freud.

DR THORNER: Could we put it on record that Miss Freud refuses to give one?

DR FRIEDLANDER: Surely she has given her view in the TC. Therefore she does not consider it necessary to make a statement now.

DR PAYNE: She did not discuss the Training Report in the Committee.

DR BALINT: I would suggest not to discuss matters personally.

DR THORNER: This is not a personal matter, it is a duty of an officer.

DR PAYNE: I will put the Training Report to the meeting.

DR BALINT: In my view the main issue is that the Committee's recommendations are not far-reaching enough. We have a very old training system. The only difference the report suggests is to exclude a few analysts from training, all analysts that are exposed as partisans should not be training analysts. If we go back to see how this system has developed, we get some idea how the situation came to this impasse. The system came about as a mechanism of defence, so to speak, against the unhealed wounds caused by Jung, Adler, and Stekel leaving the Society. To avoid personal ambitions and the acting out of unsolved Oedipus situations against a father figure. The present system achieved this aim as long as we had Professor Freud as father imago, now he is dead there are splits again, and not only here, we have only to look to the USA, there are as many systems as societies and even more.

Here we have something working as long as we have common ideas. As soon, however, as there is no longer a patriarchal organization but an organization of equal brothers and sisters with equal rights that their views should be accepted as debatable, the whole system breaks down and must because it is not meant to stand up to that. I suggest to return the report to the Training Committee and to regard the situation in this light. Until now we mainly relied on the individual analyst. The training analyst was practically uncontrolled and had an almost autocratic power. Instead of trusting to the single member, we must devise a system now, and of this not one word is in the Training Report.

MRS ISAACS: In the Training Report emphasis is laid on discussions between training analysts on technique. Other methods too could be devised making exchange of technique possible. This would be a very important step in that direction.

DR M. SCHMIDEBERG: Such discussions were started some years

ago and were never continued because of the amount of aggression that was about.

DR PAYNE: The reason for discontinuing them was that there was so much work to be done that there was no time for discussions. This was most regrettable.

DR HEIMANN: Could Dr Balint make some practical suggestions?

DR BALINT: I would if I had time. Only to give some hints. The Training Committees all over the world are stale bodies, their members do not change. The Committee should resign after a year and should not be re-elected for two or more years. Also I was surprised that in England Candidates are allotted to a training analyst by the committee. (Dr Payne explained that this is only done when a Candidate has no particular wish.) I know this is not quite so in practice, but it is true in theory. In Budapest a Candidate was given a list from which to choose the analyst. The whole attitude here is to keep the Candidates so to speak artificially in puberty. They must be given much more freedom and maturity. It is an unbearable state of affairs that a Candidate should not be able to come to the TC at any time he wants and be allowed to state his case. Again I don't know exactly how the Training Committee of this Society works. It was surprising me that control analysts are allotted. (Dr Payne: Candidates can choose their control analyst.)

MRS KLEIN: This has been so for some years but before that time they were allotted control analysts.

(No notes taken whilst serving tea.)

MISS LOW: I find it remarkable that according to the training report 'a good technique, that is a good handling of transference and counter-transference' was the criterion of a good analyst and not a thorough knowledge of Freudian analysis.

DR BALINT: I would recommend that the report should be accepted as an interim solution but should be reconsidered by the Training Committee and that a system and not the individual analyst should be made responsible because we have no common superego any more and our loyalties are divided.

MRS ISAACS: Dr Balint would certainly not include all this in his resolution?

DR BALINT: Perhaps it is a bit too vague. I would recommend that the whole training no more should be based on the individual training analysts but on a new system.

DR BOWLBY: The report is called an interim report, this seems to me a very objective statement. . . . I was inclined to ask for another report on this topic. Would it not be a good thing for this report to be published in the Journal? It is an excellent statement of what the Society aims at and might go a long way towards attracting Candidates. I don't know whether there is any reason why it should not be published.

MR STRACHEY: I am very grateful to Dr Balint for his suggestion. But there is a certain amount of difficulty about the Society appointing training analysts. A rather clear distinction is made in the report between training analysts and Training Committee. They need not coincide at all. I think that there is a practical reason for it. It would be very much easier for a small committee to select who is suitable than for the whole Society because it has greater opportunities than the whole of the Members of the Society of judging what psychoanalysts' gifts are. I am in favour of the suggestion that the Training Committee should be re-elected every year.

DR WILSON: If the Training Committee were re-elected every year, would it not be easier to leave the choice of training analysts to the Committee and not to the Society?

DR PAYNE: I am putting the report to the meeting and also Dr Balint's resolution to be put on record for future consideration. The question is now, what should we call the report? 'Interim' report has been suggested.

Another suggestion, to call it 'Preliminary Report', was made.

DR BALINT: It does not matter what we call it. This is just words. The main thing is that the system should not be patched up but that another system should be devised.

MRS ISAACS: I would only go so far as to say that this should be considered.

On voting, the (Preliminary) Report was carried.

(It was then considered to record Dr Balint's suggestion that the whole training system should be reconsidered by the Training Committee. Dr Balint was asked to make practical suggestions.)

DR BALINT: I don't think this is in the authority of this meeting. I propose the following resolution:

That the Training Committee should consider a new system of training.

This proposal, being seconded by Miss Low, was carried.

THE CHAIRMAN then threw open to discussion the report of the Committee elected to investigate questions of tenure of office and the holding of multiple positions.

She read the report which had been previously circulated to

Members and added: This is of course only in the form of a minority report as the Committee could not agree upon questions.

DR BALINT: I only want to take this as a proof of my contention that we have passed the age of having a President for a long period. We want new methods. As long as Professor Freud was alive there was no question of changing the President.

MISS LOW: Dr Balint is under a misapprehension. Freud was never President of this Society.

DR ADRIAN STEPHEN: I was one of the two Members who advocated the first lot of suggestions included in the report. The reasons why I supported these suggestions were, partly because I was dissatisfied with the condition of affairs in the Society.

During the past years the Society had in many ways been misgoverned. We have suffered. More than two years ago I brought up before the Society what I considered unfortunate incidents. One difficulty of criticizing the government of the Society and a reason why we should have continual change of officers is that it is so difficult for the ordinary Member who sees what he considers bad management of the Society, to put his finger on what is just it. Therefore I think it useful for the purpose of providing critics to have circulation of offices among Members. We cannot get information diffused unless tenure of offices is diffused.

Secondly, I think that people who have been holding office get into a kind of paternal relation to the Society. I think that is one of the things that leads to a split in the Society. You cannot freely discuss doctrines if one or two people are in a patriarchal position. For scientific reasons too therefore frequent change of offices is an advantage.

Thirdly, there is the question of economic dependence. I think this is quite important, especially those who are just beginning practice, and especially those without medical degrees find it difficult. One or two figureheads in the Society get advertised, whether they want it or not, as the representatives of the Society. Miss Low in one of the previous meetings pointed out that Dr Glover stood for the Society. I think this was so to a large extent, people did apply to Dr Glover and it meant that he had a very large distribution of cases. It meant that Members were not free to discuss in the Society without risking to lose the patronage of the person who distributes cases.

I should like to meet one or two objections. It may be said that any change of the kind proposed will be an infringement of democratic principles: why should we not elect any Member we like at any time? The argument can be used of course against any rule whatever. No rule without infringement of liberty. This rule means that we recognize that psychoanalysts are very like other human beings and once they elected one set of people into office they get reluctant to change. I believe this is about the only scientific society in this country in which there is not some rule made that officers should change periodically. It is rather arbitrary to decide how long any particular people shall be able to hold any particular office. The suggestion we made is just a shot at a number of years. We wanted to avoid that there should be a sort of landslide every year and we are in favour of continuity of government. Thus the suggestions are a compromise between the principles of change of officers and of continuity of policy. It was also discussed in the Committee whether we should include suggestions about the Training Committee.

(CHAIRMAN: It is included.) I thought we had decided it should not be included.

DR M. SCHMIDEBERG: How would Dr Adrian Stephen suggest to stop that some analysts have a better reputation than others?

DR A. STEPHEN: I don't propose to.

DR K. STEPHEN: But we don't want them to have artificial reputations by holding office.

MISS LOW: I am much in agreement with most of what Dr Adrian Stephen said except this question about the Scientific Secretary and the Treasurer who hold different positions from other officers. I do not want them to be obliged to stay, but to have a chance to do so. Therefore I said 'they might be re-elected'. So much of the whole work of the Society is scientific work and rests on the Scientific Secretary. There again there is a loophole, as the person has to go up for re-election. Similarly this holds good for the Treasurer who, I think, wants two years to get into his job properly.

DR K. STEPHEN: Miss Low's proposal would spoil the whole reorganization. Unless we have some such rule about the President (?) we get again into a state of not being able to get them out.

DR A. STEPHEN: There would again be the danger of a split in the Society if we tried to get them out.

The Chairman asked then to put forward resolutions which should be put on the Agenda for the Annual Meeting.

DR BALINT: I want to move first to ask whether the Members present are in favour of limiting the period of tenure of office to two years. This is a question of principle which must be decided first.

This proposal was seconded and carried unanimously.

DR WINNICOTT: Could we ask the Committee to work out a proposal for the Annual Meeting?

THE CHAIRMAN pointed out that, as can be seen from the report, the Committee arrived at a deadlock.

DR BALINT: I move that the Council should be authorized to make recommendations to be circulated within two months and that Members should be asked to make suggestions on that basis.

This proposal being seconded was carried unanimously.

5 THE CHAIRMAN then read to the meeting the letter she had received from Dr Glover in reply to the request sent to him to make a statement in the medical press.
(Letter read in full)

> 18, Wimpole Street, London, W.1.
> 8 March 1944

Dear Dr. Payne –
In your letter of Feb 28th, you make a brief but somewhat unusual request. This is embodied in a resolution of the Psycho-Analytical Society inviting me to send a statement to the *BMJ* (or the *Lancet*) to the effect that my recently published contributions to the *Listener* and in *Cavalcade* were personal and did not represent any expressed or implied attitude of the Society as a whole. And I gathered from the resolution that the Psycho-Analytical Society as a whole is concerned at the effects my comments on possible post-war applications of selection tests, might have on the relations of the Society to Army Psychiatrists or to the subscribers of the *BMJ* (or *Lancet*) or to both.

I gather this from the following facts, (a) that Army Psychiatrists are specifically mentioned in the resolution; (b) that in the article in question I had drawn attention to (among other things) possible abuses of selection techniques if applied wholesale to the normal population after the war; and (c) that if the Psycho-Analytical Society were not concerned at the possible effects of my comments, it would not have been at pains to pass this unusual resolution. I am compelled to draw these deductions since, apart from transmitting the resolution and adding the solitary comment that it was passed without dissension, you gave not the slightest hint of what is behind this peculiar policy. You send me no minutes of the proceedings leading up to the passing of this resolution – not even an outline of the discussion – not even a word to indicate the evidence on the strength of which I presume the Society decided to ask me to co-operate in the task of alleviating its concern.

Moreover it is not clear whether the Society would like me to publish *only* the disclaimer as outlined in the resolution or whether it expects me to add my reasons for making such a statement, not to mention the Society's reasons for asking me to make it. If only a bare and unsupported statement were sent in, clearly the reader of the *BMJ* (or *Lancet*) would be a little mystified to know why I sought the hospitality of the medical press to clarify the domestic politics of the Psycho-Analytical Society. My own reasons I am of course capable of giving but, as I am in the dark about the Society's reasons, I might inadvertently do these less (or more) than justice, and so unwittingly mislead the readers of the *BMJ* (or *Lancet*). Furthermore it is not clear why two only of the various articles that I have published on this subject are singled out for the purposes of a disclaimer; or whether, once the precedent was established, I would be expected to preface future articles with a similar disclaimer. Further I do not know whether the policy implied in the resolution is purely personal to me or whether similar resolutions will apply to articles published by present or other past members of the Society.

I hope you will not think that I am just poking fun at your resolution. My aim is to point out that I cannot arrive at any decision until these confusions are cleared up. I cannot however refrain from saying that resolutions should not be formulated without due consideration of the implications, and that I can scarcely be expected to co-operate with the Society in its present endeavour unless the Society is prepared to give me its reasons for the request. I am sure that on sober reflection members will admit that as the situation now stands I should be quite within my rights if I replied to the above effect, adding perhaps that I am not now interested in the politics of the Society, either internal or external, and that your present method of approaching me is not calculated to awaken any such interest.

But instead of adopting this course, I propose to take the opportunity, so openly offered to me, of reviewing the situation as it appears to me. I assume, of course, that you will read this letter verbatim at the forthcoming meeting. Now the first and most obvious question is this: Why the sudden and apparently tender solicitude for Army psychiatry? Obviously selection tests cannot be the issue. It is over ten years now since I first published criticisms of selection tests; and although I have continued to do so from time to time, not a single member of the Society has batted an eyelid until now! Nor can it be that the Society has suddenly discovered the fact that I am in the habit of expressing my personal views whenever I think fit. For over 20 years I have followed the

practice of publishing in *non-analytical periodicals* or in books my
views on subjects of general interest, and it has always been open
to individual members of the Society or anyone else who disagree
with them, to follow the courageous usages of public *controversy*,
with due regard of course to professional limitations and to the
laws of libel. This was the procedure adopted by Dr Rickman and
Mrs Riviere when on the publication of my book *The Dangers of
Being Human* they wrote jointly to the *New Statesman* indicating
among other things that they who were also psychoanalysts
disagreed with some of my views. This although a trifle gratuitous
was strictly legitimate procedure as was the publication of the
reply in which I exploded their arguments. And, for the matter of
that, nobody that I knew of took exception to Mrs Riviere and
Mrs Klein publishing (*and in an official psychoanalytical series*) their
view on 'Love, Hate and Reparation', views which many
members regarded as anti-analytical and as prejudicial to the
scientific standing of the Society. Certainly no one invited these
two members to write to the *Spectator* stating that their own views
were their own and not the views of all the Society. Such a letter
would have put the Editor of the official series of the Psycho-
Analytical Epitomes in a distinctly awkward position. So far as I
know (and I can speak with certainty of the last twenty years) this
is the first time the Society has even considered acting as shock
troops to defend non-analytical organizations that are in no
particular danger. Surely then the implications are obvious. Either
the Society is a little apprehensive about its own position in the
post-war world, or the matter is a purely personal one.

As to the personal aspects of the situation I must frankly own
that I am not much interested in these. If a small group of
members who are also Army psychiatrists feel just a little piqued, I
am sorry but I think they will get over it. Indeed I would suggest
that they could accelerate their recovery by studying the full text
of the articles in question. They would then find, no doubt to their
astonishment, that it is abundantly clear that I am speaking for
myself, in short that they had discovered a mare's nest. In fact it is
much clearer that I am speaking for myself than that for instance
Dr Winnicott was speaking for himself when he recently delivered
for himself in public of his remarkable but somewhat confused
views on birching children.

As to possible apprehensions for the future, I am aware of
course that you yourself hold this view of the reactions of some
members and that you have openly expressed this view in the
Society. But I have never agreed either with your view or with

the necessity for apprehension. In my opinion the only reason the Society has for being apprehensive about the future is that it is now in effect committed to the Klein deviation from Freudian psychoanalysis. So long as the Society was a Freudian Society it had no cause to worry about Beveridge or the State Mental Services,[3] still less to worry about Army psychiatry. After the war Army psychiatrists will retire once more into the obscurity from which they have temporarily emerged. Ex-Army members will undoubtedly get Beveridge jobs if they want them. And the rest of the Society will continue to enjoy whatever success they have built up through their own individual efforts. Indeed if any members of the Society are under the illusion that their interests will be safeguarded by kowtowing to the psychiatric group I would earnestly counsel them to think again and think quickly.

This brings me to my last consideration. A few members have been persuaded that if my personal opinions are identified with those of the Society they will prejudice the relations between the Society and the rest of the profession. As to the first point I would be flattered to think that my views carried so much weight. But if they carry so much weight, the fact that they are my personal opinions will be equally clear. If, on the other hand, it is held that my personal influence is unimportant (and this I can well imagine is the hope of those who fathered the present fictitious crisis about Army psychiatry), why go to the trouble of asking me to send statements to the medical press?

As for alienating the rest of the profession, this is in my view a needless apprehension. In the first place psychiatrists are never alienated by psychoanalysts: they regard psychoanalysts as aliens. In any case analysts will not secure the respect of psychiatrists by pretending to be good little boys. They may secure it provided they produce some sound analytic work – a prospect which in the present state of the Society can be ruled out. As a matter of interest, psychiatrists are much more likely to be annoyed by such egregious documents as that distributed by the recently appointed Medical Committee on the subject of psychiatric training. As for the rest of the profession, so far from increasing the gulf between them and psychoanalysts, my recent comments have already done something to develop in influential medical circles a new respect for psychoanalytical commonsense. It would indeed appear that the real objection of the small Army group in the Society is that these comments were incontestably true. And I cannot help thinking that in its older and more robust days the Society would never have allowed itself to be dragged by a small minority of members into the present ludicrous and somewhat humiliating situation. You will, I hope, forgive me if I speak plainly but the resolution that you have transmitted to me seems conclusive proof that the Society is divided into a number of emotionally toned groups, each one prepared to exploit for its own purposes the emotional uncertainties of the others.

Anyhow, that is the situation as I see it and unless I have good evidence to the contrary, it is the view that will govern my reactions to your request for co-operation. In short if the Society will explain its policy to me and give me good reasons for co-operating, I will consider its request seriously. After all there are many ways in which I could alleviate its misgivings apart from sending a rather silly and pointless statement to the medical press. I could, for example, offer the *BMJ* (or *Lancet*) a considered article on the disadvantages of and possible abuses in applying selection tests wholesale to the whole population after the war, illustrating the thesis as before by reference to the ideologies of some Army psychiatrists. Or, even a happier thought, I could offer these journals an analytical article entitled, shall we say, 'Recent Developments in Psychoanalysis, with Special Reference to Deviations from Freudian Theory'. The more I think of it, the more attractive these ideas appear. The Society would surely be convinced of the independence of my position and I, for my part, would welcome the opportunity to publicize my views.

But I would like to make it perfectly plain that whatever goodwill I might entertain towards such a project would not be due to any concern of mine for the self-induced difficulties of the Society as a whole. As an independent Freudian I am under no obligation whatsoever to a Society from which I have resigned because I no longer regard it as a Freudian Society. My goodwill would in fact be a measure of my esteem for those colleagues who now constitute the Freudian minority of it.

Yours sincerely,
Edward Glover

DR BALINT: I am afraid that this letter and that we had to listen to it, is the first sign that Dr Glover's resignation has left a wound which is aching both sides.

CHAIRMAN: It is very difficult to make any particular suggestion now but it seems to me that it is important not to continue any conflicts more than we can help. Here is the opportunity to leave this matter altogether. We all recognize all Dr Glover has done for psychoanalysis, we also know the whole situation connected with

894

the crisis and Dr Glover's resignation. I think the Society should concentrate on its activities and leave the personal things.

DR K. STEPHEN: I think now that Dr Glover has resigned he would be less identified with the Society.

DR BOWLBY: My own feeling about it is that the whole thing is stale. It has been dragged out over several weeks. The fact of Dr Glover's resignation is known, the damage done will be healed and I think it would be a waste of time if we continued.

DR M. SCHMIDEBERG: Members should not feel that such statements as are now made are made out of consideration for Dr Glover. Secondly, the resolution proposed by Drs Franklin and Carroll still stands even if Dr Bowlby withdraws his. I want the liberty to give lectures to the public.

DR A. STEPHEN: Dr Schmideberg does not realize –

CHAIRMAN: These resolutions can be put forward some other time and need not be connected with this situation.

DR M. SCHMIDEBERG: They still stand unless they are withdrawn.

CHAIRMAN: They were replaced by Dr Wilson's resolution. Would Dr Bowlby's proposal mean that Dr Glover should be notified that –

DR BALINT (interrupting): Does it mean that Dr Bowlby wants to drop his resolution?

DR BOWLBY: Yes.

DR BALINT: Then I want to support this.

It was unanimously agreed to drop the matter.

Notes

1 These minutes were called 'rough', but as they seemed to the editors quite coherent, they are included in this form rather than as reported speech.
2 For the Training Committee report, see Section 3, Chapter 11.
3 Glover is referring to the National Health Service (NHS), the implications of which were discussed at the meeting to elect the Medical Committee on 21 July 1943.

The Business Meeting
to change the rules

**[Extracts from] An Ordinary Business Meeting
was held on Monday, June 26th, 1944, at 8 p.m.,
at 96 Gloucester Place, London, W.1.**

Dr Payne was in the Chair. Members present: Dr Bowlby, Mrs Isaacs, Miss Sheehan-Dare, Dr Winnicott, Miss Low, Dr Karin Stephen, Dr Adrian Stephen, Dr Gillespie.

The minutes of the last meeting were read and passed.

THE CHAIRMAN consulted the Members present with regard to their wishes as to whether a report on the series of Scientific Discussions should be presented to the Society or not. She reported that Dr Brierley held the opinion that the Society should express its opinion whether it would like a report drawn up on scientific lines and whether it would like a meeting to discuss such a report.

THE CHAIRMAN said that she did not think that the present meeting could make a decision, as there were so few Members present but that Members might be asked to express their views. After some discussion it appeared that the majority considered that it would be better to let individual Members put forward papers expressing individual views rather than formulate conclusions at the present time. The Chairman said that views of other Members could be ascertained in the future.

THE CHAIRMAN then put to the meeting the amendments and additions to the rules governing the Society as proposed by the Council and set out in the Agenda circulated before the meeting.

(a) That Rule 3 shall be amended to read as follows:

'The officers of the Society shall be six in number and shall consist of a President, Scientific Secretary, Training Secretary, Business Secretary, Assistant Business Secretary, Librarian, all of whom shall be elected by secret ballot annually at the Annual Meeting.'

This was passed without dissension.

(b) That Rule 5 shall be amended to read as follows:

'The management of the Society shall be in the hands of a Council consisting of the President, Scientific Secretary, Training Secretary, Business Secretary, Editor of the Journal, and the Director of the Clinic, who shall be members *ex officio*, and three other Members who shall be elected by ballot yearly at the Annual Meeting.'

DR BOWLBY asked if there was any rule preventing the Director of the Clinic and the Editor of the Journal holding another office at the same time.

DR PAYNE said that there was no such rule.

DR BOWLBY said he would like to specify this point in the rules.

DR KARIN STEPHEN said she was not sure that the Director of the Clinic should have another office at the same time as it was full-time work.

THE CHAIRMAN pointed out that the office of Director of the Clinic entailed less work than any other office, as the number of patients to be dealt with were strictly limited and consultations were held only once a week. She pointed out that according to the rules of the Society the management was in the hands of specified officers and the Council and it would be quite impossible for one person to hold more than one of the executive offices excepting under war conditions for any length of time. The rule with regard to the re-election of all officers annually was a safeguard.

Upon the vote being taken the proposed Rule 5 was carried unanimously.

(c) That the following 5 new rules shall be added and numbered 6, 7, 8, 9, 10 respectively, and the old rules formally numbered 6, 7, 8, 9, etc. shall be now numbered 11, 12, etc. in sequence.
New rules (Length of office to be reckoned from the elections held at the Annual Meeting.)

6 'No member who has served as President, Scientific Secretary, Training Secretary or Business Secretary, for three consecutive years shall be elected to the same office until two further years have elapsed.'

This was passed without dissension.

7 'One member of the Council who is not an *ex officio* member, shall be ineligible for re-election for two years. This member shall be the one who has been on the Council for the longest consecutive period, and if two or more members fulfil this condition the one to be debarred from re-election shall be selected by lot.'

This was passed unanimously.

8 'The Director of the Clinic shall be elected by the Council to hold office for five years and the Assistant Director for three years.'

MISS LOW said she did not think the Director of the Clinic should be elected by the Council but by the whole Society and the holding of the office should not be limited to five years.

DR PAYNE pointed out that it was easier for the Council composed of chosen representatives of the Society than for Members in a general meeting to judge the suitability and qualification of a person for clinical posts.

MISS LOW replied that if they were Members they were just as qualified as the Council to judge this.

DR ADRIAN STEPHEN pointed out that one must have a lot of psychiatric experience for the job.

DR GILLESPIE asked whether leaving the election to the Council implied a change.

DR PAYNE said that it had always been done, and added that she was not sure that it is not the medical Members of the Council only who can elect the Director of the Clinic. In the case of appointing the staff of a hospital the Medical Committee selects and recommends and the Lay Committee confirms.

Upon a vote being taken, the new Rule 8 was carried with one adverse vote.

9 'The Training Committee shall consist of 7 members including the Training Secretary, all of whom shall be elected annually by ballot at the Annual Meeting.'

DR BOWLBY said that he thought the relation of the Training Committee and Council was rather ambiguous. The Training Committee was probably conducting the most important part of the Society's work and it was difficult for the Council to be responsible for the Society when another committee which had no relationship to the Council was running the training.

DR PAYNE explained that the Training Secretary was on the Council and the Chairman was on both Council and Training Committee.

MRS ISAACS enquired what was the relationship of the Training Committee to the International Psychoanalytical Association.

DR PAYNE said there was a relationship only on certain broad principles.

DR KARIN STEPHEN enquired about the procedure of interviewing applicants for training and whether there was other work the Training Committee did.

DR PAYNE explained the procedure of interviewing Candidates and shortly enumerated other work, e.g. drawing up proposals, the curriculum, programmes for lectures and seminars, recording reports on the progress of each Candidate. The progress reported by training and control analysts is discussed by the Training Committee and it is decided what new things the Candidates are to do, and finally qualification for therapeutic work is decided.

DR KARIN STEPHEN enquired how training analysts were chosen.

DR PAYNE replied that they were chosen by the Training Committee. In the new report it was suggested that Candidates should be allotted training analysts.

DR KARIN STEPHEN asked how the panel was chosen.

DR PAYNE replied that they were chosen on the grounds of experience, clinical papers, etc.

DR KARIN STEPHEN said that some Members have not the knack of writing good clinical papers but might have great experience and knowledge.

MRS ISAACS said if they could not write papers they would not be good teachers.

DR KARIN STEPHEN proposed to try and work out a scheme of getting to know better the qualities of analysts.

DR PAYNE said that the Training Committee had thought of schemes, e.g. postgraduate discussions.

DR KARIN STEPHEN suggested postgraduate controls analogous to postgraduate analyses should be held.

DR BOWLBY suggested that seminars should be held by aspirants. Dr Bowlby said further that the Training Committee had adopted certain policies. Supposing the Council adopted other policies, what would happen?

DR PAYNE said the Council would bring the matter before the Society after discussion.

MISS SHEEHAN-DARE said that nominations for the Training Committee were passed by the Council first.

DR PAYNE added that they were passed by the Council after being put forward by Members.

DR KARIN STEPHEN said she wished that we could have an open debate on questions of training.

DR BOWLBY said this might perhaps be done next year.

Upon votes being taken, the new Rule 9 was carried.

10 'One of the members of the Training Committee who retire yearly shall not seek re-election for two years, but this rule shall be subject to the following provisos:

(i) The member who is debarred from seeking re-election under this rule shall be the one who has been in office for the longest consecutive period and if there are two or more members who fulfil this condition he shall be chosen from among these by lot.

(ii) Nothing in this rule shall prevent any member offering himself for re-election if he has not been in office for three consecutive years.

(iii) Nothing in this rule shall prevent any member seeking election or re-election as Training Secretary and in the event of any member being elected or re-elected Training Secretary who but for this proviso would have been ineligible the member to be debarred from re-election shall be chosen from among the other members in the manner described in proviso (i).'

Rule 10 including the 3 provisos was carried.

(It has been agreed that votes should be taken by show of hands owing to the small number of Members present.)

DR BOWLBY raised the question of publishing the names of the new Council in the medical press, e.g. the *Lancet* and the *BMJ*. It was decided that this should be considered after the Annual Meeting.

DR KARIN STEPHEN enquired where to bring up training questions. She was advised to take them up with the Training Secretary.

DR BOWLBY said that policy meetings would have to be held by the new Council.

DR PAYNE said that Council meetings had been held every three months in peacetime.

The meeting was closed at 9.45 p.m.

(signed) S. M. Payne

5

The AGM
and election of new officers

**[Extracts from] The Postponed Annual Meeting
of the British Psycho-Analytical Society
was held at the home of the Society,
96 Gloucester Place, London, W.1.,
at 8 p.m., on Wednesday, October 4th, 1944**

Dr Payne was in the Chair. Members present: Dr Payne, Dr A. Stephen, Dr Usher, Miss Low, Miss Sheehan-Dare, Dr Winnicott, Mrs Klein, Miss Sharpe, Mrs Milner, Dr Wilson, Dr Gillespie, Mrs Isaacs, Dr Bowlby, Mrs Riviere, Dr Rickman, Dr Heimann.

THE CHAIRMAN announced that letters of apology for absence had been received from Drs Jones, Brierley, who sent her good wishes to the meeting, and Dr Franklin.
1 THE CHAIRMAN asked Dr Usher to read a summary of the minutes of the last Business Meeting, as the full minutes were very long. The summary of decisions was read and, as nobody asked for full minutes, they were passed and signed.
MISS LOW asked permission to make a statement. She said that she had been asked by several Members and an Associate Member to bring forward the subject of a letter written by the Scientific Secretary to an Associate Member. It was dated Sept. 18th and contained the following passage:

'I think we have really now an opportunity of turning over a new leaf but we can only do it if we prevent the Society falling into the

901

hands of any "party", whether they are called "Kleinians" or "Freudians".'

Commenting on it, Miss Low said that it was difficult to know what the writer meant. She asked how, since the Society is a Freudian Society, there could be a Freudian *party* within it. She certainly thought there should be no Kleinian party in a Freudian Society. She said that the matter at issue was whether those who believed the Society should occupy itself with Freudian science should remain in it, or whether the others who wanted something different from Freudian theory and practice had a right to be in a Society which was a constituent branch of the International Psychoanalytical Association. The remedy lay in insisting that membership should consist solely of genuine supporters of Freudian theory. She asked that a meeting be called to discuss the issue.

DR A. STEPHEN explained that he had not meant that the Society should not be a Freudian Society. He had meant that he did not want it to get into the hands of any party.

THE CHAIRMAN said that in her view nothing in Dr Stephen's letter necessitated a special meeting and that nothing would be gained by having one.

2 Reports were presented by:

(a) Dr Brierley (read in absence by Dr A. Stephen) being the report of the Acting Scientific Secretary.
(b) Dr Payne, Dr Brierley, Mr Strachey (read by Dr A. Stephen), report on the Special Scientific Discussions.
(c) The Training Secretary (Dr A. Stephen taking the Chair meanwhile).
(d) The Business Secretary.

All reports were passed by the meeting.

4 The Chairman reported that owing to the danger situation caused by flying bombs in July it had been decided to hold the elections by post. The results which had already been circulated were as follows:

(i) Dr Jones who retired from his post as President was elected Honorary President.
(ii) The *Officers and Council* were elected as follows:

Dr Payne	President
Dr Adrian Stephen	Scientific Secretary
Dr John Bowlby	Training Secretary
Dr Ruth Usher	Business Secretary

3 members of the Council were elected by ballot:

Dr Michael Balint, Dr John Rickman, Dr D. W. Winnicott

Dr W. H. Gillespie   Director of the Clinic, and
Mr James Strachey   Editor of the Journal,
were appointed by the Council.
(iii) *Training Committee*
Elected: Dr Payne (Chairman), Dr Bowlby (Secretary), Dr M. Balint, Mrs Isaacs, Mrs Klein, Dr Scott, Mr James Strachey.

5 All Associate Members were re-elected except Dr Max Schur (USA) who had not paid his annual subscription for many years.
6 The following Associate Members, nominated by the Council for election to membership, were elected by post: .
Dr D. N. Hardcastle   Mrs M. Milner   Dr R. D. Usher

8 THE CHAIRMAN reported on Dr Jones' retirement from the office of President (report enclosed). A discussion took place on the suggestions put forward by the Council to honour Dr Jones on the occasion of his retirement.

(a) By founding of an Ernest Jones Research Fellowship from the money bequeathed by the late Mrs Fulford.

(b) To present Dr Jones with a portrait.
Other suggestions included (i) the foundation of an Annual Lecture, entitled the Ernest Jones Lecture, accompanied by an honorarium for the lecturer (proposed by Major Bowlby). (ii) A Symposium on the early development of woman introduced by Jones' paper on women's psychology (proposed by Mrs Klein). It was decided to ask Major Stephen to make enquiries about the price of a portrait to be painted by a good artist.

Some further discussion took place on the way in which the Fulford legacy should be spent. The Chairman reported that the Council would submit definite proposals when there had been time to consider the matter in detail.

Members taking part in the discussion were: Drs Bowlby, Winnicott, Rickman, Heimann, Mrs Riviere, Dr Payne, Mrs Klein, Mrs Isaacs, Dr Gillespie, Dr A. Stephen, Miss Sheehan-Dare.

Report on Special Scientific Discussions
October 1942 – May 1944 (read by Dr Adrian Stephen)

Excluding the preliminary discussion in October 1942, ten Special Meetings were held on four papers (circulated and taken as read). Mrs

Isaacs, Dr Heimann, and Mrs Klein each gave one paper; Mrs Isaacs and Dr Heimann one joint paper. Nineteen other Members read or sent in contributions to the discussions which were circulated:

Drs Balint (1 contribution), Brierley (5), Mrs Burlingham (1), Drs Fairburn (1), Foulkes (2), Miss Freud (2), Drs Friedlander (5), Glover (6), Hoffer (1), Mrs Hoffer (3), Drs Jones (1), Lantos (2), Miss Low (1), Drs Payne (4), Schmideberg (2), Scott (1), Miss Sharpe (4), Drs A. Stephen (3), K. Stephen (1). In addition, the following Members took part in short periods of spontaneous discussion: Dr Bowlby (2), Miss Evans (1), Drs Franklin (1), Gillespie (1), Macdonald (1), Mr Money-Kyrle (1), Mrs Riviere (2), Drs Taylor (1), Usher (1), Wilson (2), Winnicott (3).

The programme was as follows:

PAPER I, MRS ISAACS. 'THE NATURE AND FUNCTION OF PHANTASY'

Discussion 1 Jan. 27th, 1943. Opened by Mrs Isaacs and continued by Drs Jones, Glover, Miss Anna Freud, Drs Brierley, Payne, Mrs Burlingham, Miss Sharpe, Dr Schmideberg, Mrs Hoffer, Drs Friedlander, Balint, Lantos, Scott.

Discussion 2 Feb. 17th, 1943. Contributions by Drs Fairbairn, Adrian Stephen, Foulkes, Karin Stephen. First reply by Mrs Isaacs. Further discussion requested.

Discussion 3 March 17th, 1943. Dr Heimann, Miss Low, Drs Schmideberg, Glover, Brierley, Miss Sharpe, Drs Friedlander and Lantos.

Discussion 4 April 7th, 1943. Miss Anna Freud, Mrs Hoffer, Drs Adrian Stephen, Foulkes, Glover.

Discussion 5 May 19th, 1943. Mrs Isaacs' second reply. Contribution by Dr Brierley. Discussion closed after minuting a caveat by Miss Freud that 'not answering now does neither mean that we are satisfied with the answers she has given nor that we now agree with the views she has expressed'.

PAPER II, DR HEIMANN. 'SOME ASPECTS OF THE ROLE OF INTROJECTION AND PROJECTION IN EARLY DEVELOPMENT'

Discussion 6 Oct. 20th, 1943. Opened by Dr Heimann and continued by Drs Brierley, Friedlander, Payne, Mrs Hoffer, Mrs Isaacs and Dr Glover.

Discussion 7 November 17th, 1943. Contribution from Miss Sharpe,

Dr Heimann's reply. Spontaneous discussion by Drs Glover and Friedlander.

PAPER III, DR HEIMANN AND MRS ISAACS. 'REGRESSION'

The first set of contributions to the discussion of this paper were circulated and not read at a meeting. They were made by Drs Glover, Hoffer, Friedlander.

Discussion 8 February 16th, 1944. Reply by Dr Heimann, Mrs Isaacs being absent owing to illness. Contribution by Dr Payne. Free discussion by Dr Winnicott, Mrs Klein, Mrs Riviere, Drs Payne, Bowlby, A. Stephen, Mr Money-Kyrle, Miss Evans, Drs Usher and Gillespie.

PAPER IV, MRS KLEIN. 'THE EMOTIONAL LIFE AND EGO–DEVELOPMENT OF THE INFANT WITH SPECIAL REFERENCE TO THE DEPRESSIVE POSITION'

Discussion 9 March 1st, 1944. Opened by Mrs Klein and continued by Dr Payne, Miss Sharpe, Drs Brierley and Heimann.

Free discussion: Drs Winnicott, Payne, Taylor, Wilson, K. Stephen, Mrs Klein and Miss Sharpe.

Discussion 10 May 3rd, 1944. Reply by Mrs Klein.

Free discussion: Drs Wilson, K. Stephen, Winnicott, Heimann, A. Stephen, Bowlby, Macdonald, Mrs Isaacs, Mrs Riviere and Mrs Klein.

Chairman Discussions 1–7: Dr Glover
Discussions 8–10: Dr Payne

After Dr Glover's resignation Dr Payne further consented to act as Chairman of the Organizing Committee and to present it at meetings.

The series should have been completed by a second paper by Mrs Klein for discussions this summer but various circumstances made postponement necessary. The Committee now recommend that the Special Series be regarded as ended but that Mrs Klein be asked to give her second paper at the first Ordinary Meeting in October.[1]

Note

1 This fifth paper, the last paper planned for the Scientific Controversies, on 'The Oedipus Complex in the Light of Early Anxieties' by Melanie Klein, was read in two parts but not until March 7th and 21st 1945. No Viennese appear to have attended these meetings.

6

Anna Freud and the development of the British Psycho-Analytical Society

Reorganization of training arrangements

In July 1944, when Sylvia Payne became President, a new Training Committee was elected which did not include Miss Freud. Training, therefore, continued as before. But most people were unhappy with the situation. In 1945, Sylvia Payne and Anna Freud started a dialogue to explore the conditions under which Miss Freud and her colleagues could take part in training, even if it meant running two parallel courses of training in the Society.

It should be noted however, that while there was disagreement concerning what should be included in the syllabus, who should teach it, and what clinical approach should be passed on to the students, there was general agreement concerning training requirements, the frequency and length of the training and supervised analyses, and the organization of training along the lines recommended by Eitingon in 1925.

In June 1946 the Society agreed in principle to the introduction of two parallel courses to be referred to as *Course A*, which would continue to be organized as formerly, teachers being drawn from all groups, and *Course B*, which would teach technique along the lines supported by Miss Freud and her colleagues. An Ad Hoc Committee on training was set up (consisting of Sylvia Payne (Chairman), John Bowlby (Secretary), Anna Freud, Willi Hoffer, Melanie Klein, Susan Isaacs, Adrian Stephen, and John Rickman) to work on the details, and in November 1946 the following arrangements were agreed:

1 There should be *one Training Committee* responsible for all

    matters regarding the selection, training, and qualification of students.

2 Students could opt to take *Course A* or *Course B*, the latter being run according to the wishes of Miss Freud's Group.

3 Lectures and seminars other than those on *technique* would be common to all students.

4 Students would attend clinical and technical seminars taken by analysts from their own course. They could attend *as guests* those taken by members of the other course.

5 In the third year *all students* would attend *clinical seminars* run by teachers from Course A *and* Course B.

6 The first Supervisor must be chosen from the Student's own group, the second Supervisor of Candidates in analysis with a Kleinian or a member of the 'B' group, should be selected from those who were independent of both, that is, from a non-Kleinian member of Course A – the Middle group. (This requirement for the second Supervisor was dropped during the 1950s.)

This last requirement eventually divided the Society into three groups for administrative as well as for training purposes.

The 'Gentleman's Agreement'

Alongside this arrangement for the training was an unwritten 'gentlemen's agreement' that there should be representatives of all three 'groups' on the main committees of the Society, i.e., the Council, the Training Committee, and other policy-making bodies. This agreement still holds in the British Society, and I think it is one reason why they have been able to work together, for no one group could be eliminated by another group. More than anyone Sylvia Payne was responsible for the fact that the British Society had maintained its unity despite its diversity.

For many years this agreement was supported and the main offices of the Society held by members of the Middle group or independents, who did not owe allegiance to any one individual. Sylvia Payne was followed in the office of President by a number of analysts who were not committed to either of the opposing wings of the Society, and who came from the Middle group or Independents. In 1959 there was a significant break with this tradition in that the Presidency was placed in the hands of Willi Hoffer, a leading member of the Viennese group, and in 1962 Wilfred Bion was elected President, notwithstanding his relationship to the Klein section of the Society. Since then the Presidency has rotated among representatives of the three groups.

Growth of the British Psycho-Analytical Society

Sylvia Payne's successor as President was John Rickman. In the post-war years the Society undertook a great deal of training and so expanded rapidly. The premises at 96 Gloucester Place became totally inadequate, and under Rickman's leadership negotiations began to purchase the lease of Mansfield House, 63 New Cavendish Street, which is a beautiful building, listed by the government as a 'protected building'.

While the compromise over training arrangements was satisfactory in that there would not be two Psycho-Analytical Societies in London, in conflict or competition with each other, it was painful for those Members and students who became involved in the inter-group tensions and the consequent 'acting out' of the more 'insecure' Members and students (King 1989b).

The London Clinic of Psycho-Analysis
and the National Health Service

But concern with the validity of Klein's work was only one pre-occupation of the Members. It had become clear that a National Health Service (NHS) would be introduced after the war, and there was concern, among other issues, lest the Clinic would be taken over by it, and the Society would lose control over the selection of cases used for training their Candidates. In the event, the Ministry of Health 'disclaimed' the Clinic, but it was agreed that a number of NHS patients would be treated in the Clinic, and the Clinic would be paid for this service. This arrangement still continues.

As time went on, many of the psychoanalysts who were trained by the Society took full or part-time jobs in the NHS, so that the Society was making an important contribution to the training of NHS psychotherapy consultants. A recent survey showed that 61 per cent of the Members working in this country were working in the NHS. In 1981 the Joint Committee on Higher Psychiatric Training set up a Commission which validated the training as an approved contribution to the training of Senior Registrars in the NHS.

Developments in the field of training

During the 1950s, theoretical positions in the Society became even more polarized, and students and some Members became increasingly intolerant of the divisions in the Society. The Society had continued to operate the agreement on training whereby it offered Candidates a choice of Course A or Course B.

But in 1961, after the death of Melanie Klein, it was decided to set up a second 'Ad Hoc Committee on Training' along the lines of the 1946 Committee with representatives of the three groups, to consider if there should continue to be two courses. It consisted of William Gillespie (Chairman), Fanny Wride (Secretary), Anna Freud, Willi Hoffer, Hanna Segal, Herbert Rosenfeld, John Sutherland, and Donald Winnicott. This Committee recommended that there should be one common course which would concentrate on Freud's contributions for the first two years and deal with later developments only in the third year. A Curriculum Committee was appointed to implement this, and, with the help of Working Parties, drawn from members of the three groups, the new combined curriculum was introduced for the first-year Candidates in 1967.

Meanwhile, there was increasing agreement on the need for a new administrative structure for the training organization which would enable the heavy burden of training activities to be spread among more analysts. In 1972 an Education Committee was appointed (instead of being elected at an AGM of the Society) with Adam Limentani as Chairman and composed of the Chairmen of Executive Committees concerned with various aspects of training. This structure permitted both delegation and co-ordination of training activities.

Following wide discussions with members of all groups, and with the Candidates, who resented the chronological restriction of the 1967 course, a new form of curriculum was introduced in 1973, which offered a broad programme of teaching events. Candidates chose which courses they wished to attend in any year, in consultation with their progress advisers, each one thus having his own individual programme appropriate to his needs. This new policy has given more freedom to Candidates and also to teaching staff, to whom responsibility for designing their Courses was delegated. Over the last 10 years, there have been an average of 80 Candidates a year taking part in training. Among these have been Candidates from many parts of the world who have returned to their own countries and joined local Societies.

909

In the early days of the Society, Associate Members had to be re-elected every year, and they remained Associate Members until they read a paper to the Society to become a Full Member. Since 1975, they have had the option of taking a two-year Membership Course or reading a paper to the Society or to a 'Membership Panel' consisting of 12 voting Members, if they wished to become a Full Member.

Since its inauguration in 1919, the British Society has grown slowly, but steadily, and now has 421 Members and Associate Members, 99 of whom live abroad. However, it has not proved possible to develop a viable centre of training outside London, hence the slow growth of the membership and the concentration of psychoanalysts around London.

The British Society
and the International Psychoanalytical Association

Members of the British Society have played an important role in the International Psychoanalytical Association. Ernest Jones was its President from 1920 to 1924. He was later re-elected to this office in 1932 and was still President when the Second World War began in 1939. He therefore continued to conduct the affairs of the International Association throughout the war with assistance first of Glover and then of Anna Freud as Honorary Secretary.

In 1949 Jones resigned as President of the International Association and was made Honorary President for life. The Presidency then went to the United States for the first time and remained there for eight years.

In 1957 the British Society was once again honoured with the Presidency, with the election of William Gillespie, who held office for four years, with the assistance of Pearl King as Honorary Secretary of the Association. Over the years, many Members have taken part in international committees and assisted in the development of psychoanalysis in other countries by sponsoring their study groups or by helping in the training of their students, and they have acted as host to four international psychoanalytical congresses.

In 1981 Adam Limentani, another Member of our Society, was elected President of the International Psychoanalytical Association and he held the office for four years with Moses Laufer as Honorary Secretary. In 1989, a fourth Member of the Society, Professor Joseph Sandler, was elected President of the International Psychoanalytical Association.

Relations with European colleagues

In 1965 it was decided to form a European Psychoanalytical Federation. Since then, this organization has been very active, promoting exchanges of clinical experiences and ideas between Members of the European Psychoanalytical Societies, through Conferences and Seminars. Joseph Sandler and Anne-Marie Sandler are both past Presidents of the Federation, and did much to assist its development.

The expansion of publishing activities

Publishing has continued to be an important part of the activities of the Institute of Psycho-Analysis. Jones resigned as Editor of the International Psycho-Analytical Library series (published jointly with the Hogarth Press) on the appearance of its 50th volume. Recently the Institute has launched 'The New Library of Psychoanalysis' in co-operation with Routledge, aimed at a wider audience, and a number of books have already been published.

So great was the pressure for publication space that in 1974 a new Journal was launched entitled *The International Review of Psycho-Analysis*, on the initiative of Joseph Sandler when he was Editor of *The International Journal of Psycho-Analysis*.

Probably the most important and valuable of the Institute's publishing activities following the Second World War was that of sponsoring the translation of Freud's complete psychological works into English and their publication in 24 volumes as the 'Standard Edition'. This task was started explicitly as a Memorial to Professor Sigmund Freud, and James Strachey carried the main responsibility for this great achievement, with the help of Anna Freud.

Scientific life of the Society

Scientific meetings have always been held twice a month on Wednesdays, when clinical papers or papers on applied psychoanalysis were read and discussed. In 1965, it was decided to start a Scientific Bulletin, for circulation to Members and Candidates, which would contain papers to be read at Scientific Meetings, in the hope that more people would participate in the discussions. But as time went on, papers on applied subjects were seldom accepted, so in

1968, a special section was set up which became known as 'the Applied Section'. Through this Section and courses of public lectures, links have been made with colleagues from other professional disciplines. Recently, a new category of membership, Honorary Affiliates, has been introduced to honour outstanding colleagues from other disciplines. In 1981 the Erich Simenauer Foundation was set up, through the generosity of the late Professor Simenauer, who was an Honorary Member of the Society, to support and encourage psychoanalytic research work.

The Archives of the British Psycho-Analytical Society

When Ernest Jones died, many of his letters and papers were presented to the Society by his widow, Mrs Kathleen Jones. After she died, all remaining letters were presented to the Society by his son, Mervin Jones. These gifts are particularly important as they cover his work for the International Society as well as for the Society. This material, together with the Archives and Records of the Society and bequests from other analysts, have laid the basis of an extensive collection of archives. When Pearl King was appointed as Honorary Archivist, a complete re-organization of the Archives was started, so that eventually each item will be indexed on a computer database. When this is complete it will be an important centre for the study of the history of psychoanalysis.

Presidents of the British Psycho-Analytical Society

1913–1944	Dr Ernest Jones
1944–1947	Dr Sylvia M. Payne
1947–1950	Dr John Rickman
1950–1953	Dr William H. Gillespie
1953–1954	Dr W. Clifford M. Scott
1954–1956	Dr Sylvia M. Payne
1956–1959	Dr Donald W. Winnicott
1959–1962	Dr Willi Hoffer
1962–1965	Dr Wilfred R. Bion
1965–1968	Dr Donald W. Winnicott
1968–1970	Dr Michael Balint
1970–1972	Dr William H. Gillespie
1972–1974	Dr Wallace G. Joffe
1974–1977	Dr Adam Limentani

1977–1980	Dr Hanna M. Segal
1980–1981	Dr John Klauber
1981–1982	Dr Hanna M. Segal
1982–1984	Miss Pearl H. M. King
1984–1987	Mr Moses Laufer
1987–1990	Dr Eric Brenman
1990–	

Editorial comments (2)

RICCARDO STEINER

The way in which the Scientific Discussions were resolved and the administrative and educational problems settled down did not follow the prognostications of Edward Glover. He of all the participants to the debate seemed to be out of touch with the historical reality and the institutional status of the British Psycho-Analytical Society and of its future likely developments. His forecasts were apocalyptic and ferociously one-sided. Klein and her followers were not expelled, but Strachey's wish for an open forum did not materialize either. The Society re-organized itself into three different groups even at a scientific level after a while (King 1981).

It was of course not an easy solution and compromises have their negative aspects too. At one moment Sylvia Payne, who had been elected President of the Society, worried about the tensions, and wrote to Ernest Jones on 1 August 1945:

> I think that Anna Freud has several very weak character traits & I am sure that she will not hesitate to try & get what she wants without considering the opinions of those who differ from her. I fancy that her father was the only person who could prevent this, and as she must have taken over Freud's determination to keep psychoanalysis isolated and to allow no-one in who has character traits of omnipotence, I cannot see any hope of compromising in any way. Unfortunately, we have the same omnipotence in Melanie and this is really why her work has made so much trouble; it is her personality.[1]

And Glover in one of his letters concerning his resignation wrote to Payne on 24 January 1944:

914

I have now simply exercised the privilege of withdrawing from the Society (a) because its general tendency and training has become unscientific and (b) because it is becoming less and less Freudian and has therefore lapsed from its original aims. [According to Glover] there was no prospect of scientific progress in the Society itself. For if the training is unscientific, what hope is there of establishing scientific standards amongst members whose entry to the Society depends on their conforming to the regulations of the Training Committee. Better by far to scrap the whole system and start again.[2]

Anna Freud was also pessimistic at that moment, as is shown in a letter to Ernest Kris dated 12 December 1945:

I also do not believe that it is possible at present to establish a new Institute, or central place, which can be a stronghold of teaching in the (old) sense. . . . I suppose training has to be dispersed again as it used to be in the beginnings. People have to go here and there, to find the analysis they want, to pick out the lecturers who have something to offer . . . my own work still goes back to the times when defused training was done, and I know all the disadvantages of it. But if I had to choose between organised distortions of analysis and unorganised ones, I prefer the latter. There is a good hope that a better situation will emerge again, if a sufficient number of good people are on the job.

Here, Anna Freud is referring to the specific situation of the British Society immediately after the conclusion of the 'Controversial Discussions'.

I know that the Kleinians are hopeless. My proposal to the Society here was not based on the idea that it might be possible to co-operate with them, but on the fact that there is still a fairly strong 'middle group' whose co-operation it is a pity to lose for ever. My sole aim was to provide for just enough independence to enable our small group to do some intensive but 'diffuse' training for a few individuals who might be worthwhile, while avoiding all the fuss and upheaval of forming a new Society, which is desired by some people but which to me at the present seems completely out of place. I do not want to form a new Society at just the moment when I have lost faith in the function of societies.[3]

Whereas Klein in a letter to her friends dated 25 January 1944 written immediately after Glover's resignation from the Society could write:

As far as I am concerned [Glover's resignation] finishes now a feud which has lasted for nine years and since I have had so much patience in the interest of the work of the Society and the future of Psychoanalysis, I think we shall now have to keep for the future to a very careful policy. . . . As far as the Society is concerned . . . it will be in a state of turmoil for some time to come. I shall probably be accused by some people that I drove Glover out. Another thing is that in their need to prove that this Society is the real Psychoanalytic body, there will be a great tendency in a number of people, well-meaning people, to prove constantly that they are only Freudian and Freudian only. . . . This implies that the suspicions and the objections against my work will in the near future probably be even stronger, though they might have a less unpleasant and hostile character than they had in recent years. I think we shall just need a good deal of tact, patience and wisdom to cope with this situation. We must, of course, avoid giving any ground to feel that we are triumphing and I feel that I can now keep on for a time bearing the situation in which my work is at the same time being appreciated and depreciated, sometimes in one breath by the same people. This constant insistence on whether it completely conforms with Freud will go on for some time. But my impression is that in time it will lessen, and I myself find it much easier to cope with this situation than with Glover in the chair. I do not know what Anna Freud is going to do. . . . But without Glover she is a much less dangerous and troublesome opponent, and I think all we have to do is what we have done so far, that is to go on writing good papers and letting the Society judge for themselves who has more to give to them, we or she.[4]

At a scientific level the compromise which was achieved in its more positive aspects was based on a minimal code of reciprocal respect, in spite of the sharp divisions between the various groups. There is no doubt that especially during the first years after the Scientific Discussions, things were not easy, in part because of the still open wounds of disagreements and the presence of the main protagonists of the debate and their personal grievances and recriminations, although gradually the relationship between Anna Freud and Melanie Klein improved later on. Yet, paradoxically, in spite of the difficulties, the scientific life of the Society was characterized by an explosion of creativity in all sorts of directions. One has only to remember the work of Melanie Klein and her post-war pupils W. R. Bion, H. A. Rosenfeld, and H. Segal, on psychosis; and the contributions of M. Balint, J. Bowlby, and, above all, D. H. Winnicott, especially during the fifties and the sixties. As for those who later on rightly stressed the dangers inherent in the institutionalization of psychoanalysis beside Anna Freud, one has to remember that W. R. Bion (Bion 1970), for instance, could not have developed his ideas outside the organization of the British Psycho-Analytical Society, which followed those discussions. Especially when the narcissism of the small differences does not interfere too much, the existence of different groups can lead to a very lively comparison of ideas and viewpoints even today. There is no doubt, however, that the necessity of safeguarding one's own identity or one's own survival in the psychoanalytic community, which expressed itself in this sort of compromise, brought with it the danger of a political militarization of differences, a political and not scientific use of the various groups, a paradoxical and artificial institutionalization of splits, sometimes inside the same group, which could be harmful to the creative development of psychoanalysis.

The vicissitudes which followed the Scientific Discussions and the institutional and administrative and scientific compromise also have to be understood in a broader context. Beside the internal story of psychoanalysis and of its schools, beside the disappearance of the great historical leaders and the inevitable moments of stagnation and viscosity created by the established paradigms, which characterize every field of human research after the great creative moments and the productive discontinuity that great novelties and discoveries create, one also has to consider the professionalization of psychoanalysis, even in Great Britain. Once limited to a small group of pioneers and a characteristic group *in statu nascendi*, psychoanalysis is now an institution which has to face the problems related to its own growth and development and is confronted with the specific demands of the psychic discomfort of a post-industrial society, in a difficult political and social situation.

How seriously the discussions narrated here weighed on the subsequent history of the Society should be left to the reader to decide. With all their limitations those documents witness a unique moment in the history of the psychoanalytic movement which cannot be left out of consideration when one thinks of the way psychoanalysis developed within and outside England during the second half of this century. Progress even in our field depends on the 'immer wieder', the 'endless' comparison between the past and the present, and the present of our researches, and on the courage and honesty in accepting the dialogue with those who disagree but also are able to listen, in an attempt to clarify divergence and if necessary to modify one's own viewpoint.

917

Another important factor which has to be considered and which constitutes one, if not the main, characteristic of psychoanalytic enquiry is that the object of psychoanalytic research, the unconscious and its manifestation, inevitably affects to some degree the researcher himself in spite of one, or even more than one, personal analysis. Psychoanalysts are always participant observers. Each new discovery in our field is also based on a creative capacity of making sense of personal difficulties, anxieties, or defences. Pioneers, creative personalities, or groups in our field are constantly faced with the label not only of being dissidents or breaking conventional or established certainties, but very often of being 'mad' or 'ill' themselves, and therefore being a potential danger to patients, to Candidates, and to the development of psychoanalysis. This is an extremely delicate issue which undermines scientific discussions in our field and can affect the creative life and the development of our discipline. It contributes enormously to the militarization and polarization of differences between groups and between members of groups themselves which can lead to an endless paranoid 'ping-pong' of accusations. Groups, even when composed of psychoanalysts, have inevitably unconscious, unresolved components, as Freud (Freud, S. 1921), Rickman (1951), Bion (1961), and others (Jaques 1953; Menzies 1959), have described. Sometimes even psychoanalytic groups are defending themselves from primitive anxieties using primitive mechanisms of defence based on excessive idealization and denigration (King 1978, Steiner 1985). These issues cannot be ignored unless one believes one has been able to exorcise the unconscious in oneself and among the members of one's group once and for all. As the various aspects of the discussion reported in this book demonstrate, it is only by keeping an open mind towards oneself and one's own colleagues that those problems can at least be brought into the open constructively.

As those discussions themselves are able to show, only the passing of time and the gradual consensus of a broader community of researchers can decide on the validity of a new hypothesis or discovery in our field. This is an extremely uncertain but challenging area of observations, where the researcher is exposed to a very high level of anxieties and at the same time is required to control them even at an institutional level and to understand their nature, a task which is still far from being completed and exhausted (Steiner 1985).

For many, those documents and everything they also witness about the human anxieties of the protagonists and the way they managed to deal with them without irreparable harm, are already buried in the past or simply a matter of the past. For others, they are

918

a moment in the past of our history which is still alive and an example which does not cease to make us think.

Notes

1 See Sylvia Payne to Ernest Jones, 1 August 1945, Archives of the British Psycho-Analytical Society.
2 Letter of Edward Glover to Sylvia Payne, dated 24 January 1944, Archives of the British Psycho-Analytical Society.
3 Letter of A. Freud to E. Kris, dated 12 December 1945, in A. Young Bruehl, *Anna Freud*, quoted, p. 374.
4 Letter of Melanie Klein to her friends, dated 25 January 1944.

Conclusions

PEARL KING

To conclude my editorial task, I would now like to comment on the outcome of the Freud–Klein controversies in relation to the organizational anxieties and 'solutions', on the one hand, and the scientific or 'doctrinal' disagreements, on the other. As the reader will have realized, the problems connected with both of them looked at times like opposite sides of the same penny.

Today, with hindsight, it is possible for us to see the scientific issues concerned with possible developments in metapsychology and technique, detached from the emotional and interpersonal undercurrents present at that time, and to discuss them freely. But to many of the participants in the controversies included in this book, the possibility of an honest and open discussion of these issues was more problematical. The factors precluding some Members from putting their points of view or speaking frankly were movingly described in some of the contributions to do with changing the rules relating to the tenure of office in the Society and Institute. It was felt that those who held office had power in the Society and were in a position to promote or impede the professional progress of Members. They were often the source of patients, making Members unwilling to oppose their point of view for fear of losing future referrals of patients. While some Members felt like this, how could the Society have a frank and open discussion of scientific divergences?

This problem was described by Karin Stephen during the Fifth Business Meeting on 10 June 1942 (Section 1, Chapter 6).

While the present arrangements exist, there will always be Members who will be seriously handicapped in putting forward

920

their views both on scientific questions and on the conduct of the Society, and there will always be quarrelling and ill-feeling. It may be argued that Members ought not to allow themselves to be intimidated by their officers, even as things are, and ought not to need external changes to fortify their courage. Possibly so: but it is not easy, and we have not succeeded in doing it heretofore and now we are in a bad way, and why, after all, should we continue to put ourselves in a position which has proved too difficult for us when there is such an easy and obvious way out? We are perfectly well able to improve the whole position and introduce a new atmosphere which we shall find it much easier to cope with, if we want to do this, simply by changing the machinery of our elections so that, instead of having permanent officials re-elected to office year after year, we can split up power among a succession of different officials who, during their limited term of office, would hold themselves responsible to the rest of the Members and would not be in a position to exert undue influence over them, even if they should wish to do so.

Then, at least, we really should be in a position to attack our scientific differences with some hope of success. Such a proposal is, after all, nothing very revolutionary or unheard of. On the contrary we are, I believe, almost unique among scientific bodies in being without these democratic safeguards. If there are good reasons why, in our special case, such safeguards are undesirable, let us hear them: if there are no such reasons then surely we had better make the change.

Anna Freud replied to this that psychoanalysts were in a different position from other scientific bodies, because they were doing their own training, and if they had no training institute attached to the Society, she thought that it would be very much easier (King 1989b). Susan Isaacs in supporting the need for a change in the rules made the point 'that if one has not a rule limiting tenure of office then every election becomes an immensely personal matter and transference comes in'.

In mentioning 'transference', Susan Isaacs had brought in one of the more covert factors that were influencing the situation, in addition to the overt issues referred to above, and which arose from the nature of their work as psychoanalysts. Apart from some of the senior analysts, who were analysed on the Continent, in Berlin, Vienna, or Budapest (Sharpe, Section 3, Chapter 7), most Members of the Society would have been analysed by Members of the Society, active also in the affairs of the Society. Unresolved transferences and counter-transferences were therefore likely to influence the response of Members (in addition to the simple factor of loyalty to a colleague who had been of help as an analyst or supervisor), and make it difficult for a Member to speak frankly or to oppose them.

As a result of their training, psychoanalysts are able to know or to surmise, with some degree of accuracy, much about one another. Such insights are generally unverbalized, as most psychoanalysts are very careful not to make 'interpretations' in social situations outside a professional setting. Such 'insights', however, may sometimes be passed on to other colleagues with either benevolent concern or with malevolent innuendoes, often implying a negative judgement of their competence as psychoanalysts (Steiner, Section 5, Editorial comments). Such comments can do much to undermine the morale of a psychoanalytic Society.

When Melitta Schmideberg tried to describe and to give details of this behaviour in a spectacular broadside of accusations against the Kleinians (Section 1, Chapter 3), she was severely denounced by Ernest Jones, Sylvia Payne, and even by Ella Sharpe, who later acknowledged that she was one of the recipients of such innuendoes (Section 1, Chapter 4). It was unfortunate that Melitta Schmideberg's attempt to bring these more covert concerns into the open for discussion was so exaggerated and hostile that it was not possible to differentiate real causes for concern from mischief-making. In her correspondence with her colleagues, Klein was obviously hurt by her daughter's attacks on her and her work, but she herself seldom responded to her criticisms. Her accusations against the Kleinians were reinforced by Edward Glover, whom the Kleinians felt more able to confront, and who was a greater source of danger to Melanie Klein, openly wanting Klein and her close associates to be excluded from training activities, having accused her of trying to 'capture' the Society through participation in the training and by attracting as many Candidates as possible to Kleinian training analysts. Later he acknowledged that some of his facts were incorrect (Section 1, Chapter 7).

Following the Extraordinary Business Meeting on 13 May 1942, when it was obvious that these accusations and counter-accusations did not create a suitable climate for the exploration of scientific differences, Marjorie Brierley (Section 1, Chapter 5) wrote to Melanie Klein on 21 May 1942 to tell her that she was writing to Jones to suggest that the Society accept a temporary armistice. Accordingly, at the next meeting, on 10 June 1942, following discussion between four senior Members, Marjorie Brierley, Sylvia Payne, Ella Sharpe, and Barbara Low, Jones agreed that Marjorie

Brierley should put forward an 'armistice resolution', 'That the Society require all Members to refrain from personal attack or innuendo in discussion, but also, strongly affirm the right of all Members to complete freedom of speech within the limits of common courtesy'. This was seconded by Sylvia Payne and passed without opposition. Following the acceptance of this resolution, Brierley said: 'In our conduct of business under truce conditions, we would appeal to all Members (including ourselves) to aim, not merely at an armed truce but a real lowering of tension, a generous peace without reprisals. (General expressions of approval)' (Section 1, Chapter 6).

It was within these guidelines for the conduct of professional debate in the Society that the Members proceeded to discuss the papers presenting Klein's contributions to psychoanalysis. In spite of the lowering of tension it should be remembered that behind the discussion of Scientific differences there was still a struggle to determine who would hold 'power' in the Society, for if it was generally accepted that Klein's contributions were incompatible with those of Freud, this would put power in the hands of Glover and his associates, to exclude Klein and her colleagues from participation in training activities. These controversies, however, challenged people like Ernest Jones, Sylvia Payne, Ella Sharpe, Marjorie Brierley, and James Strachey to spell out their understanding of what constituted the fundamental tenets of psychoanalysis.

In 1948, Ernest Jones wrote, in his introduction to Melanie Klein's (1948) *Contributions to Psycho-Analysis – 1921–1945* as follows:

When, more than twenty years ago, I invited Melanie Klein first to give a course of lectures and subsequently to settle in London I knew that I was securing an extremely valuable recruit to the British Psycho-Analytical Society. But I had no perception at that time of what commotion that simple act would result in. Until then, and for a while afterwards, our Society was a model of co-operative harmony. For a time Mrs Klein was given an attentive hearing and aroused great interest. Soon – perhaps, I like to think, aided a little by my influence which was manifestly exerted in her favour – she began to win adherents and devoted followers. Before long, however, cries began to be raised that in the views she rather vehemently presented she was 'going too far', which I think simply meant she was going too fast. Not that it was easy at first to detect anything radically new in these views or methods of work. The trouble was that she was pursuing them with a novel rigour and consistent recklessness that evoked in some Members of the Society at first uneasiness and gradually an intense opposition. Other Members who championed her work with a certain degree of fanaticism found this opposition hard to bear, and in the course of time two extreme groups developed who between them vociferously, and therefore, *easily restricted the quieter scientific endeavours of cooler Members.* [My italics]

The division in the British Society will, presently, I doubt not, be produced in all other psychoanalytical societies, and in the absence of colleagues with first-hand experience of Mrs Klein's work she must expect adverse critics to be in the majority. In England itself the storm was heightened by the advent of our Viennese colleagues whose life in their homeland had become literally impossible. *They added to the other criticisms the opinion that Mrs Klein's conclusions not only diverged from but were incompatible with Freud's.* [My italics] This I find myself a grossly exaggerated statement. Not that it should be in any event a decisive consideration, if experience showed that her conclusions were nearer the truth.

[Jones 1948:9]

However, Ernest Jones himself did not always agree with Freud and his experience in the International, as well as during these scientific controversies in the British Society, taught him that the unity and close identity of the theoretical conclusions, technique, and practice of the early analysts was no longer possible, if psychoanalysis was to remain a science and not to degenerate into a theology. In his 'Valedictory Address' Jones wrote that the alternative to this was 'to distinguish between what constitutes the essential characteristics of psychoanalysis and what are superimposed and more varying features'. He quotes Freud's own definition (Freud, S. 1923a; SE 18:253) (which Strachey also refers to in his Discussion Memorandum on training, Section 3, Chapter 2): 'Psychoanalysis is simply the study of mental processes of which we are unaware, of what · for the sake of brevity we call the unconscious. The psychoanalytic method of carrying out this study is that characterized by the free association technique of analysing the observable phenomena of transference and resistance. As Freud himself said, anyone following this path is practising psycho-analysis' (Jones 1946).

In his attitude to the Freud–Klein controversies, Jones was essentially influenced by the British empirical tradition, which he shared with many of the indigenous early Members of the Society, who had grown up in the intellectual climate that fostered 'gentlemen scholars'. He expressed this tradition in his opening remarks when chairing the Symposium on 'The Relation of Psycho-analytic Theory to Psycho-analytic Technique' at the Salzburg Congress in 1924. 'In all these fundamental matters, therefore, both of theory and practice, my plea would be essentially for moderation and balance, rejecting nothing that experience has shown to be useful, while ever expectant of further increases in our knowledge and power' (Jones 1925). In chairing the Business Meetings reported in Section 1, Jones certainly adopted this approach, coming down on neither side of the argument, thus often evoking resentment from both, while being also protective of 'the scientific endeavours of the cooler Members'.

As Ernest Jones described above, the direction of the criticisms of Melanie Klein's contributions changed, following the advent of the Viennese, from their being considered as divergences from 'Freudian' or 'classical' psychoanalysis, to the accusation that Kleinian formulations were not compatible with those of Freud. The Kleinians were thus put in the position of having to prove not only that the work of Melanie Klein had grown out of Freud's work, but that it was also the result of taking into account recent researches in child development, on which topic Susan Isaacs was an acknowledged authority in the University of London. It should be noted, however, that the question of the compatibility or incompatibility of Klein's contributions to psychoanalysis with those of Freud had not been an issue as far as most Members of the British Society were concerned, but when confronted with the need to decide on this question, those who discussed it reached back to simple definitions of psychoanalysis as the base-line from which to evaluate new contributions and concepts.

It was left to Marjorie Brierley, one of the 'cooler Members', to attempt to spearhead a more scientific evaluation of Klein's contributions. In the paper entitled 'Internal Objects and Theory' which she read to the Society on 18 February 1942 (the week before the first Extraordinary Business Meeting, and which was referred to several times during the discussions), she wrote:

> The assessment of Melanie Klein's view is only a special instance of the more general problem, the attitude of any psychoanalysts towards any changes in theory, other than the numerous modifications effected by Freud himself. Most scientific societies would welcome deep and far-reaching differences of opinion amongst their members, because the occurrence of such differences is regarded as a sign of vitality and growth, indeed, uniformity

of opinion and progress in science rarely coincide. . . . Scientific truth can never be absolute, because hypotheses are formulated in the light of contemporary knowledge. In consequence, as know- ledge grows, older hypotheses become inadequate, and have to be revised, expanded or reformulated to contain new facts. Freud did this himself, time after time, and if psychoanalysis is to continue to develop as a living science this process of recasting hypotheses and expanding theory must also continue.

[Brierley 1942 and 1949a:88]

Where differences appear we need to decide whether these differences are of the nature of contradictions or expansions of pre-existing theory, and whether the differences in detail, amount to cleavage in basic principles. Any decision arrived at should be based on careful consideration and re-consideration of evi- dence. . . . Freud himself seemed always to be conscious of the uncharted ocean of ignorance surrounding the solid ground of knowledge that he established. But it would be a poor geographer who, in his delight at mapping fresh territory, threw away all his other maps. The new map only develops its full value when it is drawn to the same scale and fitted into its right context. Melanie Klein found a way through the 'dim and misty' regions of the infant mind by pursuing a thread of object relationships. . . . One way of stating the problem before us is to ask the question: Is a theory of mental development in terms of infantile object relationships compatible with theory in terms of instinct vicissi- tudes? . . . The affirmative answer derives from the consideration of the nature of instinct. By Freud's own most recent definition in the *New Introductory Lectures* [1933d:125; SE 22:96]: 'An instinct may be described as having a source, an object and an aim'.

[Brierley 1942:110–11]

Sylvia Payne also leant heavily on Freud, and like Jones and other members of the British Society, she felt the need to spell out her definition of psychoanalysis, as the psychoanalytical base-line from which to judge innovations and assess new insights arising from Melanie Klein's work. In her first statement at the beginning of the discussion of these controversies, which was read to the Society by Ella Sharpe on 25 February 1942, she said:

The basic conceptions of psychoanalysis were laid down by Professor Freud, and this Society and Institute were founded on them. It might be said why should we limit our basic principles to those laid down by Freud. My answer to this is that we have in the

926

past done so publicly and voluntarily, both by adherence to the International Psychoanalytical Association and by acclaiming our intention to the Committee set up by the British Medical Association,[1] who passed the resolution that only those analysts adhering to the conceptions of Freud had the right to call themselves psycho-analysts.[2]

The basic conceptions of psycho-analysis are: (1) The concept of a dynamic psychology, (2) The existence of the Unconscious, (3) The theory of instincts and of repression, (4) Infantile sexuality, (5) The dynamics of the transference. In my view all work which really recognizes and is built upon these conceptions has a right to be called psychoanalysis.

If we accept the concept of a dynamic psychology we cannot claim to explain the problems of all types of mental conflict by the insight into any one particular phase of psychological development. If this is true, which I believe it is, I cannot see why people with a true scientific outlook should not work in the same society on different aspects of mental functioning. Some relating to the most primitive phases of mental development, and others on more differentiated parts of the mind, conscious, and unconscious. We know so little at present about the nature of cure. We are not able to sort out cases properly, and send the right case to the right person. We ought to be able to do so as everyone does not require the same approach to regain mental health.

She continued:

There are of course many controversial ideas which should be openly discussed without personal animosity. If no one is ever willing to cede an idea or modify a point of view I cannot see anything for the future but a blind striving for leadership. [She went on to suggest] that we make a scientific effort to find out *first how much there is in common rather than search for differences.* [My italics] This investigation should include a discussion on technique, [Payne, Section 3, Chapter 8] with special reference to the possibility in certain circumstances of direct interpretation, whether of unconscious phantasy or transference, taking over the character of a suggestion rather than of an analytical communication. [Payne, Section 1, Chapter 2: p. 54]

Jones picked up Payne's suggestion of considering in discussion how much *common ground* there was between the different points of view, rather than concentrating on differences, as several resolutions had centred on this. From all the resolutions submitted for discussion, there were two main themes related to each other. One theme was the primary importance of sorting out scientific differences, while other Members thought that alteration of rules should first take place in order to facilitate the discussion of scientific issues. Jones asked the opinion of the Society as to whether they preferred to discuss the change of rules first, or whether first of all to discuss the scientific issue. In the event it took five Extraordinary Business Meetings and an AGM before these two issues could be sorted out and separate settings devised in which to discuss them.

At the end of the ten Special Scientific Meetings arranged to discuss their scientific differences, I think that it would be true to say that there was more 'common ground' than had at first been expected. The systematic presentation of Melanie Klein's contributions and the careful discussion of counter-arguments had done much to enable some Members of the British Society to understand more clearly, if not always to agree with, her approach to and conceptualization of the early development of the infant and the repercussions of this for the later intrapsychic and interpersonal development of the adult. Following the withdrawal of Glover, the Schmidebergs, Anna Freud, and her Viennese colleagues from an active participation in the Society's meetings, there seems to have been general acceptance that Klein's contributions were a valid approach to psychoanalysis, if different in many respects from that of the Viennese, focusing as she did more on object relations than on the vicissitudes of the instincts.

There was also a general acceptance of Freud's description of psychoanalysis as a base line from which new developments have grown and will continue to evolve and of the need to treat psychoanalysis as a developing science which would grow and expand as new insights were presented, for, as Brierley had said, 'if psychoanalysis is to continue to develop as a living science this process of recasting hypotheses and expanding theory must also continue' (Brierley 1942:88). The alternative was the danger that it could degenerate into a theology.

When Glover, the Schmidebergs, Anna Freud, and her Viennese colleagues withdrew from participation in the Second Series of Discussions of Scientific Differences, it was clear that 'power' had passed to the pre-war members of the Society, augmented by the active participation of William Gillespie, John Bowlby, and Adrian Stephen, with Sylvia Payne, as Jones's deputy, until she became President following the retirement of Ernest Jones and the change of rules in June 1944. A brief survey of subsequent events is included in

Chapter 6 of Section 5, which is entitled 'Anna Freud and the Development of the British Psycho-Analytical Society'.

Following the withdrawal of Glover and the Schmidebergs, a kind of peace reigned in Society meetings and the new officers got down to re-organizing the training of Candidates. But Sylvia Payne was unhappy that Anna Freud had withdrawn from the Society's activities and was not on the Training Committee. Anna Freud had rejected the possibility of starting another psychoanalytical society as out of the question, but there was no official training for her Candidates. The steps taken by Sylvia Payne, Anna Freud, and the Institute to set up conditions under which Anna Freud and her colleagues could continue training along the lines acceptable to the Viennese training analysts were outlined in Section 5, Chapter 6 (p. 906).

While this compromise over training issues ensured that there would be at least some Candidates trained according to the requirements of the Viennese, on its own it did not deal with the problem of maintaining some balance of power in the Society, so that no one group could ever seek to dominate the Society again. It was therefore informally agreed that there would be equal representation of the three groups on the main committees of the Society and in its main activities. This undertaking was referred to as the 'Gentlemen's Agreement'. Even when there were elections, each group would put up their appropriate allotment of nominations to keep their side of the bargain. From the point of view of Melanie Klein, this arrangement ensured that no other group in the Society would be able to interfere with her right to continue to make her own contributions to psychoanalysis.

This arrangement still operates in the British Society. In evaluating this compromise, it is important to remember that the groups were organized around three differing approaches to psychoanalysis. The Kleinians were organized around Melanie Klein's contributions to theory and technique, the Viennese or 'B' group, as it was called, around the approach to psychoanalysis and technique supported by Anna Freud and her colleagues, while the 'Middle' group (later referred to as 'Independents') carried on the tradition and technique of the indigenous Members of the British Society, represented by Brierley, Payne, Sharpe, and Jones, while maintaining their right to learn from all reasonable sources of knowledge.

I discussed the implications of this arrangement in a paper entitled 'Identity Crises: Splits or Compromise – Adaptive or Maladaptive' (King 1978). The British Society agreed to compromise and adapt its procedures, and in doing so, it maintained a social structure within which its Members could grow and develop without indulging in fratricide. Now, over 40 years later, this 'unofficial' arrangement is still in force. However, it is important to be aware lest what was once a facilitating structure was in danger of becoming a restricting one, inhibiting the development of those individuals who still felt required to approximate their approach to psychoanalysis and to technique, to one of the three groups, if they wished to participate in training or other Society activities. Any Member who felt that his work and his understanding of psychoanalysis was different from one of the three approved approaches could well feel that he or she had no place in the Society. On the other hand, is this a small price to pay for avoiding the upheavals that took place during the discussion of the Freud–Klein controversies? In spite of these restrictions, the British Society still offers its Members the opportunity to choose from a wide range of approaches to psychoanalysis compared with what is offered in many Societies and Institutes in the International Psychoanalytical Association.

In conclusion, I would suggest that the problems faced by the British Society are by no means unique, and I suspect that they have been the experience of most psychoanalytic groups at some period. What may be unusual is the way the problems were worked on and contained within one Psycho-Analytical Society, and then finally integrated within a new type of organization that gave space and time for each point of view to be expressed, and for the results to be watched and assessed by others. What was the 'British Society's experience' while it was happening, can now be seen as 'the British experiment' (King 1981).

One reason why the outcome of these events has been in many ways successful, and the British Society has managed to work together as one institution, is in some measure due to the personal characteristics and devotion of some of the key people in the early years of the drama; in particular, Ernest Jones, Sylvia Payne, Ella Sharpe, Barbara Low, Anna Freud, Willi Hoffer, Melanie Klein, John Rickman, Marjorie Brierley, James Strachey, John Bowlby, and William Gillespie. But it must be remembered that for such a compromise to continue to work there must be at least some key individuals in each group who, while perhaps disagreeing theoretically, are prepared to work together to help maintain the institution and to promote psychoanalysis in their locality.

I would like to conclude by quoting the final paragraph of Jones's Valedictory Address to the Society, with which I agree. He wrote: 'It may seem to some of you that the tenor of my remarks may in places have been over liberal in tendency, lacking in sufficient dogmatism or possibly even conviction. My sense of conviction however lies deeper. It is attached to the ultimate belief in the power of truth, and it is this that enables me to advocate with some confidence a great tolerance towards diversities or even divergences than is sometimes exhibited' (Jones 1946).

Notes

1 In 1927–8.
2 In Section 1, Chapter 1 (pp. 12–13) there is brief summary of the negotiations with the British Medical Association Committee on Psychoanalysis.

Appendix
Statement to Training Committee
Wednesday, 9 February, 1944

MELANIE KLEIN[1]

I wish to make a statement to the Training Committee, as part of the discussion of Mr Strachey's Draft Report. If the Report is adopted by the Training Committee as it stands, I shall also wish to submit a minority report to the Society on the lines of this statement. I have discussed this statement with Dr Rickman and am speaking in his name as well as mine.

I would like to approach Mr Strachey's report from two different angles: the validity of a number of his conclusions and the question of policy.

I consider the idea that an analyst who has rendered 'eminent services to the science of psycho-analysis' (see p. 5 of the Report) may yet not be 'best fitted' to carry out training analyses to be a contradiction in terms. No one could render eminent services to the *science* of psychoanalysis who was not a good, and a very good, analyst. The notion that any one of us might present such a combination of abilities and faults that he was (a) a good analyst for non-candidates – which is a prerequisite for (b), and (b) able to render 'eminent services to the *science* of Psycho-analysis', which can only be of (a), and *yet* be so liable to emotional bias as to be unfitted to analyse candidates – this seems a fallacy.

I would agree that an analyst might render useful, even eminent services of another sort to Psychoanalysis – administration, public representation, public influence, even lecturing, etc. – and yet be an indifferent analyst for any sort of patient. But that is not rendering services to the *science* by furthering knowledge.

Analytic research is carried on in the daily work of analysis, not in a separate department. No analyst can possibly add to our store of theoretical knowledge unless he is at one and the same time both sensitive and dispassionate – in other words aware of his patient's Ucs, and not dominated by his own. There is no other basis on which psychoanalytic theory can be advanced. It is quite possible to be a good analyst and not contribute anything to theory – either through lack of interest or through lack of the capacity to formulate what has been understood and used in practice. But the converse can never be true, that an analyst who contributes something new and valuable to the development of our science is yet so liable to

932

emotional bias, so narcissistic that he could not be trusted to analyse a candidate by the same proper and unbiased procedure that he applies to his ordinary patients.

I fully agree with, and have always advocated, the generally accepted view which Mr Strachey too endorses, that the aim of a training analysis is exactly the same as that of any other analysis. We know that the *needs* of every candidate in his analysis are exactly the same as those of other analysands and that the problem of being of use to him in his emotional life is often greater than in the case of patients who come with openly admitted and serious symptoms. At any time, quite apart from our present difficulties, transferences and counter-transferences are more complicated to deal with in the case of candidates – not because there is any inherent difference in the analysis, but because, at any rate after a certain stage in the analysis, there is far more actual personal contact and an external relationship of a kind which may readily arouse acute emotional conflict. This is to some extent present from the moment a candidate is accepted for training. Therefore we are surely all agreed that only by analysis proper, without using any other influences, can our candidates be satisfactorily analysed.

But the idea that the special problem presented by the analysis of candidates is less acute in the case of analysts who do *not* make any particular eminent contributions to the advancement of theory again seems unwarranted. Relative disinterestedness of thought (and it is *always* relative, in patients and analysts alike, no matter to what 'group' they belong) should be one of the valuable by-products of *any* analysis. If we are able to help our training analysands to greater emotional freedom and stability, they will also obtain greater objectivity in their thinking, whether or not they concern themselves directly with analytic theory. Orthodoxy on the part of the analyst, however, together with over-cautiousness, can easily lead to the candidate being inhibited in his own desire to play a part in theoretical discussions. Similarly, the counter-transference might lead the training analyst to be reluctant to come to definite conclusions about new theories still under debate, or still more, to make original contributions of his own.

Mr Strachey, in implying that candidates may be influenced to accept theoretical views from training analysts who have evolved new hypotheses, does not seem to allow for the fact that in such cases the candidates arrive at their convictions through the very experiences of their own analysis. To give you an instance of what I mean: as well as myself, Rado, Helene Deutsch, Edward Glover, James Glover and Mrs Strachey were also in analysis with Abraham. It is surely no coincidence that all those people have shown a greater understanding of the oral factors than many other colleagues. I maintain, however, that Abraham has never attempted in his analysis to influence me in this direction, and I therefore take it that he has not done so with his other analysands. Let us assume that Abraham had gone further, had he lived, in his understanding of the early phases of development. Who would doubt that he would have made use of these discoveries in the analysis of his analysands, and that whoever among them had sufficient gifts to think along theoretical lines would of course have been an exponent of such views. Would Mr Strachey, who himself is so deeply interested in the development of theory and so convinced of the value of the freedom of analytic thought, suggest that people should not be considered suitable as teachers because they have the capacity to make the best use of their own analysis in the analysis of their students?

I make these comments in order to show that the problem is more complex and difficult than Mr Strachey seems to have realized. To my mind it is so real and so difficult that there is no simple solution such as Mr Strachey suggests. To cut the Gordian knot in his way might merely mean that we should have the task of gathering all the cut ends together again, and perhaps find them in a worse tangle than ever, through our attempt to evade difficult issues inherent in the situation.

The idea that analysts who have made new contributions should thereby be excluded from training work thus seems to me most unsound. Analysts who put forward new theories – *or reject* new theories – *on other than strictly scientific grounds* should certainly be excluded from training work. But then they are not likely to have contributed 'eminent services' to our science. It is not by their theories that they should be judged, but strictly by their emotional attitude to (a) their own and other people's theories, and (b) their colleagues. Those who cannot submit their view, whether new or old, to free and co-operative discussion, are not likely to be good analysts for any sort of analysand. The same applies to those who cannot or will not participate in free and co-operative discussion about *other* people's theories.

We must all and each of us stand or fall by our *personal* attitude to these matters. And this must be considered in each case on its own merits. The fact that a member takes an active part in discussion, even an eager and enthusiastic part, is far from being a sign of bias. It is the *type of argument* which is used that matters, the personal reaction to criticism, the degree of objectivity. I fully agree with what Mr Strachey says about the unsuitability of those who are extreme or rigid in their attitudes on theoretical issues – and turn them into personal ones. Strict objectivity, as we would all agree, is not identical with the illusory notion of neutrality which leads to a timid withdrawal from committing oneself either way; nor is it identical with an unyielding reliance on well-established theory. We cannot avoid judging our fellow analysts according to the type of argument they use. We have the right, and even the duty, to do so in deciding whom to elect on the Training Committee and whom to appoint as training analyst.

Nor should any training analyst be judged by the particular *theories* – whether these are the same as or different from his own – which his analysands adhere to, but only by the personal qualities and attitudes, and first and foremost by the analytic capacities, of his analysands. In all these judgements we ought not to set up an absolute and unreal standard of perfection, and to deny the fact that we *all have feelings* on these things. The idea that any person or any group (whether right, left or middle) is, or can be, completely free from bias and partisanship is false and unrealistic. These matters are relative and must be judged relatively.

Moreover, we should not forget that transferences and counter-transferences are a part of normal life, that they occur wherever people are engaged in working together, and particularly that the relationship between teacher and pupils is essentially bound up with transferences. They are not therefore to be condemned out of hand as a reproach to all concerned, as for instance Dr Glover and, in a different way, Dr Brierley, seem to assume. Transferences and defences against them play a part in all productive work.

I agree with Mr Strachey that the present theoretical controversies are not in themselves likely to be unique. New theories of any importance and magnitude are liable always to be hotly and eagerly debated and – whenever they have been accepted by a proportion of members but not by others – will raise the practical problems of training in a somewhat acute form. And I agree that new theories which are in fact well-founded will slowly and quietly permeate the general body of psychoanalytic thought, and become part of the established body of doctrine which is taught as a matter of course.

I do *not* agree that this stage of debate and enquiry into new theories need always be as difficult and embittered as the present one. We all know that there are very special reasons why the discussions and considerations of new theories during the last ten years have become so personal and so embittered. A combination of accidental and extraneous circumstances has led to acute personal tensions arising from several different sources. These have proved very difficult to deal with, and have coloured and distorted the strictly theoretical issue in a way which one cannot but hope will *not* happen in future developments of psychoanalytic theory.

For these reasons, it may be possible that measures are required in the present situation that would not be necessary as a general policy of training. I am quite prepared to consider this possibility. But before going on to this, I wish to add two further points which would apply to the more normal situation.

I should have thought it was a good thing that different theoretical views were represented on the Training Committee – *provided only* that the people representing them were good analysts and had the requisite personal qualities, as already discussed. If those holding newer theories, or theories not yet universally accepted, are in the minority on the TC (as they are now) there is no practical danger of their being able – even assuming the unlikely case that they wanted to do so – to outvote the other members of the Committee.

Training analysts, no less than members of the TC, should be chosen for their proven ability as analysts and their capacity to co-operate, quite irrespective of their theories. Control analysts should be chosen also for their ability as analysts, plus their ability as teachers. Not all good training analysts would make good control analysts. I agree with what Mr Strachey says about the qualities required, but do not agree with his overemphasis on the *theories* that they hold.

To sum up this part of my comments: if the principles of Mr Strachey's report are accepted, many analysts may refrain from putting forward new views, for fear of being labelled 'controversial' and thereby debarred from any part in training. The growth of scientific knowledge would thus be impeded. To penalize originality seems to me extraordinarily dangerous, because science *proceeds* by differences of opinion and discussion, by theoretical enterprises and daring, and by the correction of mistakes. If we are reluctant to be labelled 'controversial', there will be no advance of knowledge.

I come now to some points which touch upon more personal issues. Here I shall deal also with some of Dr Brierley's conclusions in her contribution on Technique, since these are closely relevant. I shall speak frankly and openly, since I believe that is what we particularly need at this juncture. But I shall only be able to state my views without discussing them fully. I shall ask the Committee for another meeting at which we can exchange our views more adequately.

I referred above to the unusual concatenation of accidental and extraneous circumstances which during the last ten years have brought into the discussion of theoretical problems an element of intense personal feeling which does not properly

935

belong to them. I am forced to touch upon this, since it is a major source of the difficulties of the immediate situation with which Mr Strachey's Draft Report attempts to deal. It will be understood that it was not always easy for me to maintain a completely cool and impersonal attitude in all these discussions in the Society in which such a strongly personal element was introduced. I do not claim that I have always done so completely; yet many members, including some of those in this room, have privately expressed to me their appreciation of the degree to which I did succeed in maintaining a scientific attitude under strong human provocation to do otherwise, and the patience and forbearance that I endeavoured to show. It was not until the practical questions of *policy* were raised by various other members in the autumn of 1941 – questions of rules and administration, etc. – that I, along with many others who objected to certain aspects of the administration of the Society, took an active part in 'controversy' as such, and voiced my serious criticisms of the way things were done; but even then, on objective grounds. You will remember the intense and wholesale condemnation by some members of everything that was done by me or by those who had expressed agreement with my theoretical views. The various papers read by us on the problems raised are documentary evidence of our attempt to remain objective. In spite of the mistakes that have been made by us from time to time, I wonder whether any impartial observer from outside the Society would consider that both 'parties' to the present 'controversies' had been *equally* embittered, personal and biased.

To return to the scientific issue, which is far more important; it is true that some of my pupils and some of my analysands have shown and do show considerable enthusiasm for what they believe they have learned in working with me. Such enthusiasm is natural enough, if people feel they have gained valuable theoretical insight or a useful instrument for better work with their patients. It is an everyday phenomenon in scientific work of all kinds, whatever the subject of study. Without such enthusiasm about psychoanalytic theories when these were first taught, people would not have troubled to establish clinics and systems of training etc. What is much more important than whether or not people are enthusiastic about the theories they hold, however, is whether they are *willing to discuss them* with critics.

Now it is unfortunately true that the theories I myself have contributed, and my own work, were not – to begin with – adequately discussed by my colleagues. In the earlier years after I came to England, for various reasons into which I cannot enter, my work was not sufficiently criticized. I would like to mention though that Miss Sharpe put forward some of her criticisms even at that time, and did so throughout in an objective manner. This general lack of criticism was certainly not beneficial, either to my work or to the training of candidates. From that date, however, as you all know, what had been white became black, and criticism of a bitter, personal and wholesale kind was voiced against me on every possible occasion by some influential members. This again was unfavourable to *real discussion* of my contributions. And it led me, in my desire to avoid arousing this personal element in the Society, to refrain from reading papers and making further contributions. In fact, I did not read any papers between 1934 and 1939. I am not sure now that this patience was altogether laudable or useful. I know of several members who were so distressed by the situation in the Society that they, too, did not contribute during these years. But my hope was that the situation would wear itself out, or that the members as a whole would find some way of dealing more effectively with it.

Meanwhile, I and others did whatever we could to ensure that impersonal scientific discussion should go on. In our private discussions quite severe criticisms of one another's views were freely voiced; but we also made it plain to our Viennese colleagues from the time they came to London that we were willing and anxious to join with them in free discussion at any time. Mrs Riviere and Mrs Isaacs carried on such discussions with a number of English, and later German and Viennese members. From the time I returned to London in 1941, I myself urged upon Miss Freud the value of private discussions about differences in theory. After repeated suggestions, I was able to convince Miss Freud of the wisdom of such a course. We agreed upon the members who should be invited to join in, and it was arranged that we should meet at Miss Freud's house on a given date. But then Miss Freud suddenly changed her mind and withdrew from this plan for private discussions altogether.

It was the considered opinion of many of us – myself and Mrs Isaacs for example and, I believe, Dr Brierley – that the present series of 'discussions on controversial topics' would have been far more fruitful if they had been held in private among a few members, because the prevailing atmosphere in the Society made detailed, patient and impartial discussion infinitely more difficult. But I understand that Miss Freud and a few other members would not agree to this, obviously for reasons of policy.

Now I wish to touch on some of Dr Brierley's points. In her contribution on Technique she not only takes the enthusiasm of my pupils to be adverse to my analytic work – a point I have already dealt with – but she also expresses doubts as to whether or not my technique leads my analysands to treat my work as an 'idealized object'. She quite rightly reminds us of the importance of a fact to which I myself have devoted much attention and dealt with in detail in my book and in other places, that is, the various methods by which ambivalence – instead of being reduced – can be dealt with in unsatisfactory ways, particularly by first splitting the object and then over-idealizing the good object. Now her query is whether my work does not leave my trainees with an over-idealized mother, and consequently with a bad father-figure. I cannot see what grounds Dr Brierley has for these suggestions. That in their theoretical views my pupils recognize the important part played by the mother in the early days of life does not offer proof of Dr Brierley's implications. Freud himself attached even greater importance than I do to the mother's role, and less to the father's role, in the early mental life of the woman. That my friends have in recent years been less ready than they might otherwise have been to voice their criticisms of me and of my theories *in public*, in the Society, in view of the personal hostility shown to me by various people, is natural and understandable. But more than this cannot be maintained. The work of Freud, Abraham, Ernest Jones and many other 'father figures' is fully acknowledged and made use of by me and my pupils. I can claim that no one has done more to confirm, apply and develop Freud's work than I and some of my colleagues have done. It would be very difficult to bring forward evidence that I, or those who have accepted my theories, undervalue or belittle Freud's work.

937

It is true that Dr Brierley, in putting forward these rather grave doubts, emphasizes that she does not intend to prejudice the issue, but will only make up her mind on the evidence I shall provide in the near future. However, the way in which she puts forward these doubts seems to prejudice the issue. The reasons she gives for her doubts do not seem to me adequate, particularly as she herself admits that she has no firsthand knowledge of my technique. However, the *only* ground on which psychoanalytic technique can be adequately estimated is by a firsthand acquaintance with it, either in the control of a case or in private discussions on technique and cases. If members of this Committee would care to be present at the seminars I am holding, they would not only have the true means of forming their own opinions upon my technique, but they would also be convinced that my students are expected and do in fact voice their doubts and criticism quite freely – in great contrast to the way in which, as I am informed, Miss Freud conducts her seminars. My students are never expected to take my statements simply on trust, without adequate evidence, and they feel free to question the evidence at any given moment.

This leads me to a suggestion regarding our work on the TC. It should be one of the tasks of the TC in the near future to institute regular and frequent discussions on technique, among a selected group or groups of training analysts, for true exchange of experience. I regard this as one of the few ways in which we can really hope to 'settle' our controversies and to advance our science.

A wider problem arises here: what are the criteria by which we judge the success or failure of the analyses of our candidates? Over-enthusiasm and the idealization of the mother-figure have been suggested as possible signs of failure of my analyses of candidates. As I made clear, I do not agree that these suggestions have any foundation: that if the holding of particular theories were a way of estimating the value of a training analyst's work, we could not stop there. If we are to try and compare the value of our respective techniques by judging the effects on our analysands, there are many more vital points to be considered. We might look at the analysands of *every* training analyst with such criteria in mind as the degree of neurosis resolved, the alterations in their character and their private relationships as a result of their analysis (as well as the fruitfulness of their clinical work as shown by their patients). Such are some of the criteria we apply to our non-training patients, and they should apply also to candidates. These factors are far more significant than the theories that they happen to hold. Such an investigation would be very difficult and complicated. But if we do not want to enter into such an enquiry and apply such criteria in order to arrive at conclusions about the usefulness of our respective techniques and the soundness of our theories, then the only alternative is what I hold to be the *proper* procedure for the training analysts, namely, to discuss our technique with each other.

Psychoanalysts more than other people should be able to dispense with slogans. I claim that the 'over-enthusiasm', 'fanaticism' etc. of the analysts who work with my theories have become mere slogans and are in fact greatly exaggerated.

In any case, those candidates, postgraduates, and others who have taken up my theories 'with enthusiasm' and definite acceptance are but a small proportion of the colleagues who have come to me for analysis and teaching. I would moreover suggest that we should make a deliberate policy of sending candidates for control work to training analysts of differing theoretical opinions. For instance, I should wish my candidates to go to Miss Sharpe, Dr Brierley, Dr Payne or Mr Strachey. And I should welcome their candidates to work with me in a similar way. This would also be a way of learning something of each other's technique.

On all of these grounds, I now wish to submit a plan to the members of this Committee to reconsider Mr Strachey's Draft Report. It may be that in the present circumstances this Draft Report would have to be made known to the Society. But I should like to urge that this necessity does not debar the TC either from revising it or from presenting a second Draft Report as the result of tonight's discussion. We must remember that Mr Strachey's Draft Report – whatever its effect on Miss Freud – has never been discussed within the TC and therefore remains a mere draft. As I see it, we have not committed ourselves to this Draft Report until we have discussed and decided upon it.

All depends on the degree to which the TC feels itself bound to adhere to these formulations. I have here and now put forward various considerations which I feel have been overlooked in drawing up the Report and which I feel might form the basis of a new policy on which our training work could be reorganized. In the long run I fully believe that this policy would lead eventually to good co-operation; further, it is not really evident that even in the short term and at the present moment such a plan would rouse much opposition. Emotions *have* run high recently, but the last business meeting seemed to show a promise of a fairly rapid subsidence of such upheavals and a comparatively quick return to more normal conditions. In point of fact, when one considers actual individuals, it appears that with *very few* exceptions the great majority will find little difficulty in accepting the guidance of the TC in these matters.

It will be clear from what I have said that I believe it to be important for the work of the Society that I should remain on the Training Committee. But I wish now to state in the plainest words that I fully appreciate the present necessity that I and all those who support my views should remain in the background for the present and not take too prominent a part in discussion nor read papers unless especially invited to make contributions. Nor do we think it advisable that we should accept any office in the Society at present. We are fully prepared to abandon any future papers in the present scientific discussions, if that is considered advisable. These considerations should, I think, serve to reassure the Committee that little occasion need now arise for any further crises in the Society.

In any case, I hope that you will all feel that you can rely on me to co-operate with you in the common aim of easing difficulties and paving the way to productive work in the Society.

Note

1 See Note 4, p. 668.

References

Abraham, K. (1924) 'A Short Study of the Development of the Libido Viewed in the Light of Mental Disorders', in *Selected Papers on Psycho-Analysis*, London: Hogarth Press and Institute of Psycho-Analysis, IPAL, vol. 13, 1957.

—— (1957) *Selected Papers of Karl Abraham*, International Psychoanalytical Library No. 13, London: Hogarth Press and Institute of Psycho-Analysis, 1957.

Balint, M. (1937) 'Fruhe Entwicklungsstadien des Ichs Primäre Objektliebe', *Imago*, XXIII. Published as 'Early Developmental Stages in the Ego. Primary Object-Love', *International Journal of Psycho-Analysis*, 30: 265–73, 1949.

Bernfeld, S. (1929) *The Psychology of the Infant*, London: Routledge & Kegan Paul.

Bion, W.R. (1961) *Experiences in Groups*, London: Tavistock Publications.

—— (1970) *Attention and Interpretation*, London: Tavistock Publications.

Bleuler, E. (1921) *Die Naturgeschichte der Seele und ihres Bewusstwerdens*, Berljn: Springer.

BMA Report (1928) This extensive report is in the Archives of the British Psycho-Analytical Society.

Boehm, F. (1926) 'Homosexualität und Odipuskomplex', *Internationale Zeitschrift für Psychoanalyse*, 12: 66–79.

Breuer, J. and Freud, S. (1895) 'Studies in Hysteria', SE 2, London: Hogarth Press, 1955.

Brierley, M. (1932) 'Some Problems of Integration in Women', *International Journal of Psycho-Analaysis*, 13: 433–48.

—— (1937) 'Affects in Theory and Practice', *International Journal of Psycho-Analysis*, 18: 256–68.

—— (1939) 'A Prefatory Note on "Internalized Objects" and Depression', *International Journal of Psycho-Analysis*, 20: 241–5.

—— (1942) 'Internal Objects and Theory', *International Journal of Psycho-Analysis*, 23: 107–12.

—— (1943) 'Theory, Practice and Public Relations', *International Journal of Psycho-Analysis*, 24: 119–50.

—— (1949a) 'Problems connected with the Work of Melanie Klein', in *Trends in Psychoanalysis*, pp. 57–89, London: Hogarth Press and Institute of Psycho-Analysis, 1951.

—— (1949b) 'Introduction', in *Trends in Psycho-Analysis*, pp. 13–22, London: Hogarth Press and Institute of Psycho-Analysis, 1951.

Bühler, C. (1930) *The First Year of Life*, London: Kegan Paul.

Darwin, C. (1872) *The Expression of Emotions in Man and Animals*, London: Watts, 1934.

Eitingon, M. (1925) 'Report of meeting of Branch Societies at the Bad Homburg Congress', *International Journal of Psycho-Analysis*, 7: 130–4.

—— (1928) 'Report of the International Training Commission', *International Journal of Psycho-Analysis*, 9: 135–41.

Evans, M.G. (1942) 'The Analysis of a Child's Drawings', read to a Scientific Meeting on 21 January.

Federn, P. (1927) 'Narzissmus im Ich-Gefühle', *Internationale Zeitschrift für Psychoanalyse*, 13: 420–38.

—— (1929) 'Das Ich als Subjekt und Objekt in Narzissmus', *Internationale Zeitschrift für Psychoanalyse*, 15: 393–425.

Ferenczi, S. (1913) 'Stages in the Development of the Sense of Reality', in *First Contributions to Psychoanalysis*, London: Hogarth Press and Institute of Psycho-Analysis, 1952.

Foulkes (Fouchs), S.H. (1937) 'On Introjection', *International Journal of Psycho-Analysis*, 18: 269–93.

Freud, A. (1927) *Introduction to the Technique of the Analysis of Children*, London: Imago, 1946.

—— (1936) *The Ego and the Mechanisms of Defence*, London: Hogarth Press and Institute of Psycho-Analysis, 1937.

—— (1979) 'Personal Memories of Ernest Jones', *International Journal of Psycho-Analysis*, 60: 285–7.

—— and Burlingham, D. (1942) 'Young Children in Wartime', in *Infants Without Families and Reports on the Hampstead Nurseries 1939–45*, London: Hogarth Press and Institute of Psycho-Analysis, 1973.

Freud, S. (1895) *Studies in Hysteria*, SE 2, London: Hogarth Press and Institute of Psycho-Analysis, 1955.

—— (1900) *The Interpretation of Dreams*, London: G. Allen and Unwin, 1932; SE 4/5, London: Hogarth Press and Institute of Psycho-Analysis, 1953.

—— (1905) *Three Contributions to the Theory of Sex*, New York: Nervous and Mental Disease Publishing Co., 1930; and *Three Essays on the Theory of Sexuality*, SE 7: 125, London: Hogarth Press and Institute of Psycho-Analysis, 1953.

—— (1908) 'The Poet and Day Dreaming', *Collected Papers*, vol. IV, London: Hogarth Press and Institute of Psycho-Analysis, 1925; 'Creative Writers and Day Dreaming', SE 9: 143, London: Hogarth Press and Institute of Psycho-Analysis, 1959.

—— (1909) 'Analysis of a Phobia of a Five-Year-Old Boy', SE 10: 1–147, London: Hogarth Press and Institute of Psycho-Analysis, 1955.

—— (1910) 'The Origin and Development of Psychoanalysis', *American Journal of Psychology*, 1910; 'Five Lectures on Psychoanalysis', SE 11: 3, London: Hogarth Press and Institute of Psycho-Analysis, 1957.

—— (1911a) 'Formulations Regarding the Two Principles of Mental Functioning', *Collected Papers*, vol. IV, London: Hogarth Press and Institute of Psycho-Analysis, 1925; SE 12: 3, London: Hogarth Press and Institute of Psycho-Analysis, 1958.

—— (1911b) 'Psycho-analytical notes on an Autobiographical Account of a Case of Paranoia', *Collected Papers*, vol. II, London: Hogarth Press and Institute of Psycho-Analysis, 1925; SE 12: 3, London: Hogarth Press and Institute of Psycho-Analysis, 1958.

—— (1911c) 'Types of Neurotic Nosogenesis', *Collected Papers*, vol. II, London: Hogarth Press and Institute of Psycho-Analysis, 1925; 'Types of Onset of Neurosis', SE 12: 229, London: Hogarth Press and Institute of Psycho-Analysis, 1958.

—— (1912) 'Recommendations to Physicians Practising Psychoanalysis', *Collected Papers*, vol. II: 323, London: Hogarth Press and Institute of Psycho-Analysis, 1925; SE 12: 111, London: Hogarth Press and Institute of Psycho-Analysis, 1958.

—— (1913) *Totem and Taboo*, London: Routledge, 1919; SE 13, London: Hogarth Press and Institute of Psycho-Analysis, 1955.

—— (1914a) 'On Narcissism: an Introduction', *Collected Papers*, vol. IV, London: Hogarth Press and Institute of Psycho-Analysis, 1925; SE 14: 69, London: Hogarth Press and Institute of Psycho-Analysis, 1957.

—— (1914b) 'On the History of the Psycho-Analytic Movement', *Collected Papers*, vol. I, London: Hogarth Press and Institute of Psycho-Analysis, 1924; SE 14: 7–66.

—— (1915a) 'Instincts and Their Vicissitudes', *Collected Papers*, vol. IV, London: Hogarth Press and Institute of Psycho-Analysis, 1925; SE 14: 111, London: Hogarth Press and Institute of Psycho-Analysis, 1957.

—— (1915b) 'The Unconscious', *Collected Papers*, vol. IV, London: Hogarth Press and Institute of Psycho-Analysis, 1925; SE 14: 161, London: Hogarth Press and Institute of Psycho-Analysis, 1957.

—— (1916/17) *Introductory Lectures on Psycho-Analysis*, London: G. Allen & Unwin, 1929; SE 15/16, London: Hogarth Press and Institute of Psycho-Analysis, 1963.

—— (1917a) 'The Sexual Life of Man', in *Introductory Lectures on Psycho-Analysis*, G. Allen & Unwin, 1929; and 'The Sexual Life of Human Beings', SE 16: 303, London: Hogarth Press and Institute of Psycho-Analysis, 1963.

—— (1917b) 'The Neuroses: Symptom Formation', in *Introductory Lectures on Psycho-Analysis*, London: G. Allen & Unwin, 1929; 'General Theory of the Neuroses', in *Introductory Lectures on Psycho-Analysis*, SE 16: 243, London: Hogarth Press and Institute of Psycho-Analysis, 1963.

—— (1917c) 'A Metapsychological Supplement to the Theory of Dreams', *Collected Papers*, vol. IV, London: Hogarth Press and Institute of Psycho-Analysis, 1925; SE 14: 219, London: Hogarth Press and Institute of Psycho-Analysis, 1957.

—— (1917d) 'Mourning and Melancholia', *Collected Papers*, vol. IV: 152–70; SE 14: 237–58, London: Hogarth Press and Institute of Psycho-Analysis, 1957.

—— (1919) 'Turning in the Ways of Psycho-Analytic Therapy', *Collected Papers*, vol. II, London: Hogarth Press and Institute of Psycho-Analysis, 1924; 'Lines of Advance in Psycho-Analytic Therapy', SE 17: 159, London: Hogarth Press and Institute of Psycho-Analysis, 1955.

—— (1920a) *Beyond the Pleasure Principle*, Vienna and London: The International Psychoanalytical Press, 1922; SE 18: 3–64, London: Hogarth Press and Institute of Psycho-Analysis, 1955.

—— (1920b) 'Jenseits und Lustprinzips', *Gesammelte Werke* 13: 3–69.

—— (1921) 'Group Psychology and the Analysis of the Ego', SE 18: 65–144, London: Hogarth Press and Institute of Psycho-Analysis, 1955.

—— (1923a) 'Two Encyclopaedia Articles', *International Journal of Psycho-Analysis*, 23, 1942; SE 18: 235–55, London: Hogarth Press and Institute of Psycho-Analysis, 1955.

—— (1923b) *The Ego and the Id*, London: Hogarth Press and Institute of Psycho-Analysis, 1926; SE 19: 3, London: Hogarth Press and Institute of Psycho-Analysis, 1961.

—— (1925a) 'On Negation', *International Journal of Psycho-Analysis*, 6; SE 19: 235, London: Hogarth Press and Institute of Psycho-Analysis, 1961.

—— (1925b) 'An Autobiographical Study', London: Hogarth Press and Institute of Psycho-Analysis, 1946; SE 20: 1–70, London: Hogarth Press and Institute of Psycho-Analysis, 1959.

—— (1926) *Inhibitions, Symptoms and Anxiety*, London: Hogarth Press and Institute of Psycho-Analysis, 1936; SE 20: 77–172, London: Hogarth Press and Institute of Psycho-Analysis, 1959.

—— (1930) *Civilization and its Discontents*, London: Hogarth Press and

Institute of Psycho-Analysis, 1930; SE 21: 59–146, London: Hogarth Press and Institute of Psycho-Analysis, 1961.

—— (1931) 'Female Sexuality', *International Journal of Psycho-Analysis*, 13, 1932; SE 21: 223–46, London: Hogarth Press and Institute of Psycho-Analysis, 1961.

—— (1933a) *New Introductory Lectures on Psycho-Analysis*, London: Hogarth Press and Institute of Psycho-Analysis, 1933; SE 22:3, London: Hogarth Press and Institute of Psycho-Analysis, 1964.

—— (1933b) 'Anatomy of the Mental Personality', *New Introductory Lectures on Psycho-Analysis*, London: Hogarth Press and Institute of Psycho-Analysis, 1933; 'The Dissection of the Psychical Personality', SE 22: 57, London: Hogarth Press and Institute of Psycho-Analysis, 1964.

—— (1933c) 'The Psychology of Women', *New Introductory Lectures on Psycho-Analysis*, London: Hogarth Press and Institute of Psycho-Analysis 1933; 'Femininity', SE 22: 112, London: Hogarth Press and Institute of Psycho-Analysis, 1964.

—— (1933d) 'Anxiety and Instinctual Life', *New Introductory Lectures on Psycho-Analysis*, London: Hogarth Press and Institute of Psycho-Analysis, 1933; SE 22: 81, London: Hogarth Press and Institute of Psycho-Analysis, 1964.

—— (1937) 'Analysis Terminable and Interminable', *International Journal of Psycho-Analysis*, 18; SE 23: 209–54, London: Hogarth Press and Institute of Psycho-Analysis, 1964.

—— (1940) 'The Outline of Psycho-Analysis', *International Journal of Psycho-Analysis*, 21; SE 23: 141–208, London: Hogarth Press and Institute of Psycho-Analysis, 1964.

Glover, E. (1927) 'Symposium on Child Analysis', *International Journal of Psycho-Analysis*, 8: 385–7.

—— (1931) 'The Therapeutic Effect of Inexact Interpretation', *International Journal of Psycho-Analysis*, 12: 397–411.

—— (1932a) 'A Psychoanalytical Approach to the Classification of Mental Disorders', *Journal of Mental Science*, 78: 819–42.

—— (1932b) 'On the Aetiology of Drug Addiction', *International Journal of Psycho-Analysis*, 13: 298–328.

—— (1933a) 'The Relation of Perversion–Formation of the Development of Reality-Sense', *International Journal of Psycho-Analysis*, 14: 486–503.

—— (1933b) Review of 'The Psycho-Analysis of Children' by M. Klein, *International Journal of Psycho-Analysis*, 14: 119–29.

—— (1937) 'Symposium on the Theory of the Therapeutic Results of Psycho-Analysis', *International Journal of Psycho-Analysis*, 18: 125–32.

—— (1938a) 'A Note on Idealization', *International Journal of Psycho-Analysis*, 19: 91–6.

—— (1938b) Review of 'Inhibitions, Symptoms and Anxiety', *International Journal of Psycho-Analysis*, 19: 109–14.

—— (1942) 'Intuition and Interpretation', read at a Scientific Meeting in February.

Grosskurth, P. (1986) *Melanie Klein – Her World and her Work*, London: Hodder & Stoughton.

Hayman, A. (1986) 'On Marjorie Brierley', *International Review of Psycho-Analysis*, 13: 383–92.

—— (1989) 'What do we mean by "Phantasy"?' *International Journal of Psycho-Analysis*, 70: 105–14.

Hazlitt, V.H. (1933) *The Psychology of Infancy*, London: Methuen.

Heimann, P. (1942) 'A Contribution to the Problem of Sublimation and its Relation to Processes of Internalization', *International Journal of Psycho-Analysis*, 23: 8–17.

—— (1943) 'Certain Functions of Introjection and Projection in Early Infancy', in J. Riviere (ed.), *Developments in Psycho-Analysis*, London: Hogarth Press and Institute of Psycho-Analysis, 1952, pp. 122–68.

—— and Isaacs, S. (1943) 'Regression', in J. Riviere (ed.), *Developments in Psycho-Analysis*, London: Hogarth Press and Institute of Psycho-Analysis, 1952, pp. 169–97.

Hermann, I. (1933) 'Zum Triebleben der Primaten', *Imago*, 19: 113–25.

—— (1936) 'Sich-Anklammern, Auf-Suche-Gehen', *Internationale Zeitschrift für Psychoanalyse*, 22: 349–70.

Hoffman, E.P. (1935) 'Projektion und Ich-Entwicklung', *Internationale Zeitschrift für Psychoanalyse*, 21: 342–73.

Isaacs, S. (1933) *Social Development in Young Children*, London: Routledge.

—— (1938) 'An Acute Psychotic Anxiety Occurring in a Boy of Four Years', *International Journal of Psycho-Analysis*, 24: 13–32.

—— (1940) 'Temper Tantrums in Early Childhood in Relation to Internal Objects', *International Journal of Psycho-Analysis*, 21: 280–93.

—— (1943) 'The Nature and Function of Phantasy', in J. Riviere (ed.), *Developments in Psycho-Analysis*, London: Hogarth Press and Institute of Psycho-Analysis, 1952, pp. 67–121.

—— (1948) *Childhood and After*, London: Routledge & Kegan Paul.

Isakower, O. (1936) 'Beitrag zur Pathopsychologie der Einschlaphänomene', *Internationale Zeitschrift für Psychoanalyse*, 22: 466–77.

Jaques, E. (1953) 'The Social System as a Defence against Persecutory and Depressive Anxieties', in *New Directions in Psychoanalysis*, M. Klein, P. Heimann, and R.E. Money-Kyrle (eds), London: Tavistock Publications, 1955.

James, W. (1910) *The Principles of Psychology*, London: Macmillan.

Jones, E. (1912) *Papers on Psycho-Analysis*, 1st edition, London: Baillière, Tindall, & Cox.

—— (1916) 'The Theory of Symbolism', *Papers on Psycho-Analysis*, 5th edition, London: Baillière, Tindall, & Cox.

—— (1923) 'Rationalisation in Everyday Life', in *Papers on Psycho-Analysis*, 3rd edition, London: Baillière, Tindall, & Cox.

—— (1925) 'Introduction to the Congress Symposium on "The Relation of Psycho-analytic Theory to Psycho-analytic Technique"', *International Journal of Psycho-Analysis*, 6: 1–4.

—— (1926) 'Introductory Memoir' in Introduction to Abraham's *Selected Papers*, pp. 9–41, London: Hogarth Press and Institute of Psycho-Analysis, 1957.

—— (1927) 'The Early Development of Female Sexuality', *Papers on Psycho-Analysis*, 5th edition, pp. 438–51, London: Baillière, Tindall, & Cox; *International Journal of Psycho-Analysis*, 8: 459–72.

—— (1929) 'Fear, Guilt and Hate', *International Journal of Psycho-Analysis*, 10: 383–97; *Papers on Psycho-Analysis*, 5th edition, London: Baillière, Tindall, & Cox.

—— (1933) 'The Phallic Phase', in *Papers on Psycho-Analysis*, 5th edition, pp. 452–84, London: Baillière, Tindall, & Cox, 1948.

—— (1935) 'Early Female Sexuality', in *Papers on Psycho-Analysis*, Editions 4 & 5, London: Baillière, Tindall, & Cox, and *International Journal of Psycho-Analysis*, 16: 263–73.

—— (1936) 'The Future of Psycho-analysis', *International Journal of Psycho-Analysis*, 17: 269–77.

—— (1945) 'Reminiscent Notes on the Early History of Psychoanalysis in English-speaking Countries', *International Journal of Psycho-Analysis*, 26: 8–10.

—— (1946) 'A Valedictory Address', *International Journal of Psycho-Analysis*, 27: 7–12.

—— (1948) 'Introduction', in *Contributions to Psychoanalysis 1921–1945*, M. Klein, London: Hogarth Press and Institute of Psycho-Analysis.

King, P.H.M. (1978) 'Identity Crises: Splits and Compromise – Adaptive or Maladaptive', in *The Identity of a Psychoanalyst*, pp. 181–94, E.D. Joseph and D. Widlöcher (eds), IPA Monograph No. 2, New York: International Universities Press, 1983.

—— (1979) 'The Contributions of Ernest Jones to the British Psychoanalytical Society', *International Journal of Psycho-Analysis*, 60: 280–84.

—— (1981) 'The Education of a Psychoanalyst: the British Experience', in *La Formation du psychanalyste*, 1982, in IPA Monograph No. 3: 93–107.

—— (1983) 'The Life and Work of Melanie Klein in the British Psycho-Analytical Society', *International Journal of Psycho-Analysis*, 64: 251–60.

—— (1987) 'Early Divergences between the Psychoanalytic Societies in London and Vienna', in *Freud in Exile – Psychoanalysis and its Vicissitudes*, pp. 124–33, E. Timms and N. Segal (eds), Yale University Press, 1988.

—— (1989a) 'Activities of British Psychoanalysts during the Second World War and the Influence of their Interdisciplinary Collaboration on the Development of Psychoanalysis in Great Britain', *International Review of Psycho-Analysis*, 16: 15–33.

—— (1989b) 'On Being a Psychoanalyst: Integrity and Vulnerability in Psychoanalytic Organisations', in *The Psychoanalytic Core: Essays in Honour of Leo Rangell, M.D.*, E. Weinshel and H.P. Blum (eds), New York: International Universities Press.

Klein, M. (1921) 'The Development of a Child', *International Journal of Psycho-Analysis*, 4: 419–74, in *The Writings of Melanie Klein*, London: Hogarth Press, 1981, I: 1–53.

—— (1923) 'Early Analysis', *Imago*, 9: 222–59; *The Writings of Melanie Klein*, vol. I: 77–105, London: Hogarth Press, 1981.

—— (1926) 'Notes of the Psycho-analysis of a Child Aged Five Years', Unpublished paper, abstract in Minutes of the British Psycho-Analytical Society, 1926.

—— (1927a) 'The Importance of Words in Early Analyses', Unpublished paper, abstract in Minutes of the British Psycho-Analytical Society, 1927.

—— (1927b) 'The Psychological Principles of Infant Analysis', *International Journal of Psycho-Analysis*, 8: 25–37; in *The Writings of Melanie Klein*, London: Hogarth Press, 1981, vol. I: 128–38.

—— (1928) 'Early Stages of the Oedipus Conflict', *International Journal of Psycho-Analysis*, 9: 67–180; in *The Writings of Melanie Klein*, London: Hogarth Press, 1981, vol. I: 186–98.

—— (1929) 'Infantile Anxiety-Situations Reflected in a Work of Art and in the Creative Impulse', *International Journal of Psycho-Analysis*, 10: 436–43, and in *The Writings of Melanie Klein*, vol. I, London: Hogarth Press and Institute of Psycho-Analysis, 1975.

—— (1930) 'The Importance of Symbol-Formation in the Development of the Ego', *International Journal of Psycho-Analysis*, 11: 24–39; in *The Writings of Melanie Klein*, London: Hogarth Press, 1981, vol. I: 219–32.

—— (1931) 'A Contribution to the Theory of Intellectual Inhibitions', *International Journal of Psycho-Analysis*, 12: 206–18; in *The Writings of Melanie Klein*, vol. II, London: Hogarth Press, 1980.

—— (1932) *The Psychoanalysis of Children*, The International Psycho-Analytical Library, No. 22, London: Hogarth Press and Institute of Psycho-Analysis; *The Writings of Melanie Klein*, vol. II, London: Hogarth Press, 1980.

—— (1935) 'A Contribution to the Psychogenesis of Manic-Depressive States', *International Journal of Psycho-Analysis*, 16: 145–74; in *The Writings of Melanie Klein*, London: Hogarth Press, 1981, vol. I: 262–89.

—— (1936) 'Weaning', in *On the Bringing Up of Children*, J. Rickman (ed.),

London: Kegan Paul, pp. 31–56; in *The Writings of Melanie Klein*, London: Hogarth Press, 1981, vol. I: 290–305.

—— (1937) 'Love, Guilt and Reparation', in *Love, Hate and Reparation*, J. Rickman (ed.), Psycho-analytical Epitomes, No. 2, London: Hogarth Press, pp. 37–119; in *The Writings of Melanie Klein*, London: Hogarth Press, 1981, vol. I: 306–43.

—— (1940) 'Mourning and its Relation to Manic-depressive States', *International Journal of Psycho-Analysis*, 21: 125–53; in *The Writings of Melanie Klein*, vol. I: 344–69, London: Hogarth Press, 1981.

—— (1944) 'The Emotional Life and Ego-Development of the Infant with Special Reference to the Depressive Position' (original version in this book, Section 4, Chapter 4; amended version in *Developments in Psycho-Analysis*, J. Riviere (ed.), London: Hogarth Press, 1952, pp. 198–236); in *The Writings of Melanie Klein*, London: Hogarth Press, 1980, vol. III: 61–93.

—— (1945) 'The Oedipus Complex in the Light of Early Anxieties', *International Journal of Psycho-Analysis*, 26: 11–33; in *The Writings of Melanie Klein*, London: Hogarth Press, 1981, vol. I: 370–419.

—— , Riviere, J., Searl, M.N., Sharpe, E.F., Glover, E., and Jones, E. (1927) 'Symposium on child analysis', *International Journal of Psycho-Analysis*, 8: 339–91; in *The Writings of Melanie Klein*, London: Hogarth Press, 1981, vol. I: 139–69.

Leupold-Löwenthal, L. (1980) 'The minutes of the Vienna Psycho-Analytic Society', *Sigmund Freud House Bulletin*, vol. 4(2): 23–41.

Lewis, M.H. (1936) *Infant Speech*, London: Kegan Paul & Co.

Low, B. (1941) 'The Psycho-Analytic Society and the Public', Unpublished paper, Minutes of British Psycho-Analytical Society, Nov. to Dec. 1941.

Meisel, P. and Kendrick, W. (eds) (1986) *Bloomsbury/Freud – the Letters of James and Alix Strachey 1924–1925*, London: Chatto & Windus.

Menzies Lyth, I. (1959) 'The Functioning of Social Systems as a Defence against Anxiety – a Report on a Study of the Nursing Service of a General Hospital', *Human Relations*, 13: 95–121.

Middlemore, M. (1941) *The Nursing Couple*, London: Hamish Hamilton Medical Books.

Müller-Braunschweig, C. (1936) 'Die erste Objektbesetzung des Mädchens in ihrer Bedeutung für Penisneid und Weiblichkeit', *Internationale Zeitschrift für Psychoanalyse*, 22: 137–76.

Payne, S.M.P. (1942) Minutes of the Annual General Meeting, Archives of the British Psycho-Analytical Society.

Rado, S. (1928) 'The Problem of Melancholia', *International Journal of Psycho-Analysis*, 9: 420–38.

Rank, O. (1934) *The Trauma of Birth and its Implications for Psychoanalytic Therapy*, London: Hogarth Press and Institute of Psycho-Analysis.

Rickman, J. (ed.) (1936) *On the Bringing Up of Children*, London: Routledge & Kegan Paul.

—— (1937) 'On "Unbearable" Ideas and Impulses', *American Journal of Psychology*, 50: 248–53; in *Selected Contributions to Psycho-Analysis*, London: Hogarth Press, 1957, pp. 52–8.

—— (1951) 'Reflections on the Function and Organisation of a Psycho-analytical Society', in *Selected Contributions to Psycho-Analysis*, London: Hogarth Press and Institute of Psycho-Analysis, 1957.

Riviere, J. (1936) 'The Genesis of Psychical Conflict in Earliest Infancy', *International Journal of Psycho-Analysis*, 17: 395–422.

—— (1937) 'Hate, Greed and Aggression', in *Love, Hate and Reparation*, J. Rickman (ed.), Psycho-analytical Epitomes, No. 2, London: Hogarth Press, pp. 3–53.

Roheim, G. (1940) 'The Garden of Eden or the Psychology of Mankind', *Psychoanalytic Review*, 27: 1–26 and 177–99.

Rosenfeld, H.A. (1987) *Impasse and Interpretation*, London: Tavistock Publications.

Rotter-Kertesz, L. (1934) 'Zur Psychologie der Weiblichen Sexualität', *Internationale Zeitschrift für Psychoanalyse*, 20: 367–74.

—— (1936) 'Der Tiefenpsychologische Hintergrund der Inzestuosen Fixierung', *Internationale Zeitschrift für Psychoanalyse*, 22: 333–48.

Schilder, P. (1920) 'Über Gedankenentwicklung', *Zeitschrift für der Ger. Neurol. und Psychiatrie*, 59: 250–63.

—— (1935) *The Image and Appearance of the Human Body*, London: Kegan Paul.

Schmideberg, M. (1934) 'The Play-Analysis of a Three-Year-Old Girl', *International Journal of Psycho-Analysis*, 15: 245–64.

—— (1937) 'On Motoring and Walking', *International Journal of Psycho-Analysis*, 18: 42–53.

—— (1941) 'Introjected Objects: a Terminological Issue or a Clinical Problem', Paper read to the Society on 3 Dec. 1941.

Searl, M.N. (1933) 'The Psychology of Screaming', *International Journal of Psycho-Analysis*, 14: 193–205.

Segal, H. (1973) *Introduction to the Work of Melanie Klein*, London: Hogarth Press and Institute of Psycho-Analysis.

—— (1979) *Klein*, F. Kermode (ed.), London: Fontana.

Sharpe, E.F. (1930) 'On Certain Aspects of Sublimation and Delusion', *International Journal of Psycho-Analysis*, 11: 12–23.

—— (1934) '"The Tragedy of King Lear" by J.S. Branson', *International Journal of Psycho-Analysis*, 15: 478–80.

—— (1935) 'Similar and Divergent Unconscious Determinants Underlying the Sublimations of Pure Art and Pure Science', *International Journal of Psycho-Analysis*, 16: 186–202; in *Collected Papers on Psycho-Analysis*, pp. 137–54, London: Hogarth Press, 1950.

—— (1940) 'Psycho-physical Problems Revealed in Language: an Examination of Metaphor', *International Journal of Psycho-Analysis*, 21: 201–13.

Shirley, M.M. (1933) *The First Two Years*, Minneapolis: University of Minnesota Press.

Spearman, C. (1923) *The Nature of Intelligence and the Principle of Cognition*, London: Macmillan.

Steiner, R. (1985) 'Some Thoughts about Tradition and Change Arising from an Examination of the British Psycho-Analytical Society's Controversial Discussions (1943–1944)', *International Review of Psycho-Analysis*, 12: 27–71.

—— (1988) ' "C'est une nouvelle forme de diaspora . . ." La politique de l'émigration des psychanalystes d'après la correspondance d'Ernest Jones avec Anna Freud', *Revue Internationale d'Histoire de la Psychoanalyse*, 1: 263–321.

—— (1989) 'It's a new kind of diaspora . . .', *International Review of Psycho-Analysis*, 16: 263–321.

Stevens, R. (1966) *Medical Practice in Modern England: the Impact of Specialist and State Medicine*, New Haven: Yale University Press.

Stout, G.F. (1927) *The Groundwork of Psychology*, London: W.B. Clive.

Strachey, J. (1934) 'The Nature of the Therapeutic Action of Psycho-analysis', *International Journal of Psycho-Analysis*, 15: 127–86.

Tausk, V. (1919) 'On the Origin of the "Influencing Machine" in Schizophrenia', *Psychoanal. Quarterly*, 2: 519–56, 1933.

Wälder, R. (1937) 'The Problem of the Genesis of Psychical Conflict in Earliest Infancy', *International Journal of Psycho-Analysis*, 18: 456–73.

Ward, J. (1933) *Psychological Principles*, Cambridge University Press.

Winnicott, D.W. (1931) *Clinical Notes on Disorders of Childhood*, London: Heinemann.

—— (1935) 'The Manic Defence', in *Through Paediatrics to Psycho-Analysis*, London: Hogarth Press, 1975, pp. 129–44.

—— (1941) 'The Observation of Infants in a Set Situation', *International Journal of Psycho-Analysis*, 22: 239–49.

Yorke, S.C.B. (1971) 'Some Suggestions for a Critique of Kleinian Psychology', *Psychoanalytic Study of the Child*, 26: 129–55.

Young-Bruehl, E. (1988) *Anna Freud*, London: Macmillan.

Name index*

★ **Please note:** For substantial individual contributions see the following entries in the Subject index: Extraordinary Business Meetings; Medical and Child Welfare Committee; Scientific Discussions; Training Committee.

Subject index

'active therapy' 630
affection, earliest signs of 304
aggression 232, 283, 288, 471, 512–13;
  and anxiety 277, 456, 693, 759, 830–1;
  of early phantasies 244, 293, 347, 424,
  442–3, 747, 772, 813; and ego
  development 443, 523; and fixation
  719; S. Freud on 793n; and guilt 830–1;
  and hunger tension 290; and
  impotence/frigidity 707; inborn 302;
  Klein on 747, 828–31; libidinization
  of, in play 304, 306, 312, 691; and
  libido 700, 717–18, 741; and
  narcissism 518–19, 521; and neurosis
  causation 727; oral 719, 728, 821; and
  psychosis 829; and regression 697, 717,
  720, 726–7, 746; superego 293, 790n;
  towards the breast 290; towards self
  293; *see also* destructive impulses,
  hostility
anal aspect of development: Abraham on
  740; destructive instincts and 699; and
  fixation 695; and infant projection 694;
  see also anal phase, anal-sadistic
  impulses
anal phase: and anal-sadistic impulses
  510; and projection 515
anal-sadistic impulses: early 691;
  prohibition of 510
analogies 579–81: misuse of by Kleinians
  537, 558–9, 587–8
anxiety: and aggression 277, 456, 693,
759, 830–1; birth 404; and cannibalistic
phantasies 695, 759, 815; child 273,
310, 456; depressive 21, 767; and
destructive impulses 693, 760;
distinguished from guilt 799–800,
804, 826–7; dreams and object loss
796n; early 300, 303, 350, 380, 464,
524–5, 691, 747; and ego preservation
827; and fixation/regression 700–1,
703; S. Freud on 91, 281, 404, 700–1,
758, 763, 799; of incorporated objects
290; infant, at loss of mother 279–80,
767, 771–2; inner vs. objective 800;
and introjection/projection 524; Klein
on 637–8, 692, 724, 826; and libidinal
development 692, 695, 830;
libidinization of, in play 304, 306, 312;
and oral fixation 695; origins of 758–
64; paranoid 760; phantasy as defence
against 277–8; sadistic impulses and
early 760; *see also* guilt
Armistice proposal 164–5, 173–5 *passim*
186, 195–6, 922–3
Army psychiatry, Glover's criticism of
847–9, 860–6, 872–8, 890–5
auto-erotism 349, 351; A. Freud on 244,
418, 420; S. Freud on 278–9, 516–19;
hallucinatory gratification 519; inner
breast and 520, 522; and instinctual
inhibitions 755; and internal objects
460; Klein vs. S. Freud on 520–1, 545;
and libido 518–19, 521, 554, 756;

instincts (*cont*.):

aggression, death instinct, destructive impulses, instinctual urge, life instinct, libido

instinctual urge 277, 318n, 320n, 705–6: and ego 345; influence of 296; and introjection/projection 515; as phantasy 278, 326, 409; prohibition of 510; unconscious 330; *see also* instincts

Institute of Psycho-Analysis 12: Extended AGM (1943) 495–500; founding of 11; Glover's resignation from 665, 847–60, 869n; Lecture Committee of 564–7; link with medical profession 482–3; pressure for democracy within 31–2, 36n; publishing activities of 911; relation with the Society 30, 191n; responsibilities of 30, 70, 105; *see also* British Psycho-Analytical Society; Training Committee; Medical and Child Welfare Committee

Institute for the Scientific Treatment of Delinquency (ISTD) xiii, xx, 92

intelligence: and child development 785–7; and primary process 412

internal relationships: vicissitudes of 842; *see also* introjection, object (various sub-entries)

International Journal of Psycho-Analysis xviii, xxi, 17, 20; founding of 11

International Psychoanalytical Association xiii, 11–16 *passim*, and the British Society 910

International Review of Psycho-Analysis 911

International Training Commission 16, 144, 166n

interpretation: in analysis 619–21 *passim*, 649–51; Kleinian vs. Freudian 720

introjection 151, 274, 282, 289, 326, 502–30, 545, 546, 554–5, 558–9, 583, 631–2, 696; ambiguous use of 392; anxiety and 524; of the baby 243; as basis of object relationships 425; and body-ego 547; compared with regression 522; confused with identification 546–7, 549, 582; confused with phantasy 425; defined 503, 535; distinguished from incorporation 536, 583, 588; disturbances/failure of 523; and early oral-sadistic impulses 23; eating as 547;

and ego formation 518; of father's penis 526; S. Freud on 278–9, 467, 472, 517, 582; of the ('good') breast 278, 338, 524, 765, 783–4; and hallucination 520; of an image 555, 556; as image formation 536–7; as incorporation 275; and instinctual urge 515, 542; and Kleinian theory 425, 507–8, 711; and life instinct 510–11, 542; and loss of object 509; of melancholia 506–7; as memory-traces 711; of the mother 295, 392, 765; of objects (into ego) 279, 337, 339, 506–7, 509, 760, 767, 819, 827, 834–5, 842; and oral phase 515; oral-sadistic 251; perception as 535, 556; through phantasy 555; primary 243, 279; retarded development and 523–4; role in further development 526–7; and superego formation 508–9; of the Trinity 339

introspection 426

jealousy, and oral envy 526

Kleinians: alleged victimization at hands of 93–8 *passim*; ambiguity/vagueness of 98; criticism of attacks on 109–10, 112–19; critique of technique of argumentation 558–61; critique of term 440, 446–8; Klein's dislike of term 248; 'Kleinian group' 25, 901–2; preparation for Scientific Meetings 245–8; proselytizing of 34; use of analogies 537, 558–9; *see also* Klein, Melanie

libidinal development 343–6 *passim*, 471, 626, 687–8, 696: anxiety and 692–3, 695; and early phantasies 695; and destructive impulses 776; feelings and 692; Klein on 346, 379–80, 442–3, 448, 724, 776; overlap of phases in 736, 831; *see also* libidinal impulses, libidinization, libido

libidinal impulses: vs. aggressive impulses 741; in the baby 254, 283, 288, 443; earliest 297; A. Freud on 244–5; S. Freud on 277, 297, 344, 452; frustration of 803; repression of 345; *see also* libidinal development, libidinization, libido

phantasy around 277, 289–90; as object to infant 434, 435, 757; *see also* breast

mourning 151; analysis as 338; deflection of from primary object 782; and depressive position 767, 807–8; for lost loved object 841; and manic depression 25; melancholia and 829, 841; normal, for breasts 812; and oral aggression 821

narcissism 809, 837–8; and aggression 518–19; vs. auto-erotism 518–19; defensive 254; and ego-formation 521; S. Freud on 518, 578–9, 753–4, 794n; and infant ego 279; infantile 419, 759; Klein vs. S. Freud on 520–1, 545; 'libidinal' 253, 516, 518, 756; object relationships and 541; and oral-biting stage 519; primary 244, 253, 461–2, 707–8, 753–4, 757, 794n; and regression 708; secondary 253; sleep as 521, 540–1, 578–9, 587; states of 334; theory of 518; and unconscious phantasy 521

National Health Service, and British psychoanalysis 908

neurosis 354, 511, 630; aetiology of 346; early symptoms of 464, 523; S. Freud on 346, 511, 688, 722, 733–4, 740; infantile 771–2, 836; Klein's theory of 630, 723–4, 727, 729; masturbation phantasies and 789n; menopausal 729; normality and 740–1, 768; obsessional, and regression 345, 688–9; psycho- 568; role of aggression in 727; theory of 541, 576

night terror, in infants 771

object 276, 293, 513–27; absent 286; breast as 243, 303, 516, 553, 784; child experience of 275; and ego 290; external 243, 254, 283, 516, 517, 521, 547–8, 556, 696–7, 772, 783–4, 819–20; external, and libido 516, 518, 521; first seen 303; first sensory mental 817; father's penis as 526; 'good' and 'bad' 243, 254, 338, 340, 520, 523, 524, 571, 626–7, 693, 696–7, 772, 819, 838; of hallucination 278, 338, 339, 519–20; idealized 625–7 *passim*; incorporated 339–40; incorporated, and anxiety

290, 524–5; internal 21, 25, 243, 251, 253, 254, 276, 338, 359–60, 364–5, 390, 458, 516–24 *passim*, 631–2, 695–7 *passim*, 772, 781–4 *passim*, 819–20, 842; internal, and interpretation 621; internal, and libido 518; internalized, equated with image 535, 572; internalized, and memory images 400–3, 796n; introjection of (into ego) 279, 337, 339, 414n, 506–7, 583, 760, 819, 834, 838, 842; and introjection/ projection 515; Klein on early relation to 515–16; mother as, to infant 434, 435, 509; mother's body as 243; loss of loved 803, 827, 832–3, 840–1; love, early 755–7; oral-sadistic introjection of 251; part and whole 21, 273, 463, 519–22 *passim*, 525, 626, 757; prohibitions from introjected 510; symbolic function of external 283; *see also* introjection, object relationships, projection

object relationships 21, 300–4, 460, 547; beginnings of and phantasies 418–21; breast as core of 517; breast as first 545; compatibility with instinct theory 212, 214; earlier vs. later phases of 462–3; early 434–6 *passim*, 460, 516, 737, 753–7 *passim*, 788, 794n, 803, 816; S. Freud on 516, 553–4, 744, 794n; and genital impulses 756; genital sense of 334; vs. instinct vicissitudes 926, 928; introjection as basis of all 425, 517; Klein on early 753–5, 832; to mother 407; in narcissistic phase 541; in primary oral phase 744–5; primitive, and phantasy 334; *see also* introjection, object

Oedipus complex 335–6, 339, 347, 370, 392, 404, 432–3, 448–50, 458–9, 721–2; in analysis 621, 637; and destructive impulses 742; emergence of 254, 424; S. Freud on 433, 721, 742, 790n, 791n; and genesis of superego 22, 526; and instinct conflict 791n; Klein on 526, 721, 737, 825–6, 832; and superego 339, 526; *see also* castration complex

omnipotence 278, 779–80, 836; destructive wishes and 295; feelings of 524; vs. frustration 779–80; and hallucination 779; and mother's breast

966